THE ENCYCLOPEDIA OF WORLD SOCCER

THE ENCYCLOPEDIA
OF WORLD
SOCCER

BY RICHARD HENSHAW

FOREWORD BY SIR STANLEY ROUS,
HONORARY PRESIDENT, FIFA

New Republic Books
Washington, D.C.

Published in 1979
by New Republic Books
1220 19th St., N.W.
Washington, D.C. 20036

The publisher wishes to acknowledge these copyright holders for permission to use the following photographs: Tye, drawing on p. 34; Wide World photos, pp. 83, 198, 302, 350, 570, 744, 746, 773; Schirner, pp. 94 (top), 97; Horst Muller, pp. 94 (bottom), 565; Herbert Mehrens, pp. 137, 311; Syndication International, pp. 152, 169, 474; Publifoto, pp. 177, 470, 593; Sven Simon, pp. 263, 484, 566; Otto Metelmann, pp. 305, 608; Rota, p. 406; *Illustrated London News*, p. 553; Popperfoto, p. 644 (top); Werek, p. 644 (bottom); Reuter, p. 674; Sovfoto, p. 814.

Every attempt has been made to contact the copyright holders of the uncredited photographs. If anyone has information concerning copyright, please contact the publisher or author.

Library of Congress Cataloging in Publication Data

Henshaw, Richard, 1945-
   The encyclopedia of world soccer.

   1. Soccer—Dictionaries.   I. Title.
GV943.H367   796.33'4'03   78-26570
ISBN 0-915220-34-2

Printed in the United States of America

To my
mother and father

and

to my sister
Kathleen

Preface

Organizing vast amounts of information into an accessible format is at once the pleasure and the curse of encyclopedists. Association football is a subject of enormous complexity, because, in addition to being a game, it is linked so closely with the cultural and political lives of people everywhere. From the beginning, my central purpose has been to present the game in all its facets, and to show how and why it is loved in all four corners of the world. Rather than edit a collection of articles by others, an unsatisfying experience at best, I have chosen to compile and write the work entirely myself. This has been done over a period of seven years, the last four full-time, and, while I hasten to add that it has been a labor of love, it has in all probability fallen short of its ultimate goal. I hope, nonetheless, that readers will find it useful.

My most satisfying task is now before me: to express my deeply felt thanks to all those who have helped to make the book possible, though it is I alone who must accept responsibility for any errors or inaccuracies.

On a general note, I would mention historians F. P. Magoun, C. W. Alcock, Morris Marples, Dr. Percy M. Young, Maurice Golesworthy, and Gordon Jeffrey, whose work I have drawn upon with trust and admiration. Sir Stanley Rous, protector of the game and the author of its Laws, and his one-time collaborator, Donald Ford, have deepened my understanding of the Laws and their development.

I owe my greatest debt of gratitude to Raphael Sagalyn, whose important role in all aspects of this project is unchallenged. Martin Peretz and Joan Tapper had faith in me, and above all patience, throughout an arduous process. Their guidance and support leaves me deeply in their debt. Fran Moshos spent endless hours pouring through the manuscript with insight and skill, and I am grateful to Cindy Mynhier and the many members of the New Republic Books staff who labored so diligently.

The officials of several governing bodies graciously offered their expertise and encouragement. Of these I must call attention to René Courte, Senior Assistant Secretary of FIFA; Mourad Fahmy, General Secretary of the African Football Confederation; Dato' Teoh Chye Hin, General Secretary of the Asian Football Confederation; and General Secretary Hans Bangerter and his staff of the Union of European Football Associations. In addition, the following national associations were especially responsive to my inquiries: Union Royale Belge des Sociétés de Football-Association, Canadian Soccer Association, Fédération Française de Football, Deutscher Fussball-Bund, Knattspyrnusamband Islands, Federazione Italiana Giuoco Calcio, New Zealand Football Association, Association Suisse de Football, and United States Soccer Federation.

Several Washington embassies deserve special mention for their kind attention: Argentina, Austria, Bahrain, Bangladesh, China Republic, China People's Republic, Costa Rica, Cyprus, Denmark, Ecuador, Egypt, Greece, India, Iran, Israel, Japan, Mexico, Netherlands, Saudi Arabia, and Tunisia.

I am grateful to the staffs of the North American Soccer League, Cosmopolitan Soccer League, Cosmos, Ajax Amsterdam, and Boston Public Library, and to Robert Schaaf, Head of the Union Catalog and International Organizations Reference Section of the Library of Congress, and Dwight Beers, of the African Section of the Library of Congress.

The list of United States full internationals that appears in the text is largely based on a study by Colin Jose, my Canadian colleague, and the Hungarian proverb contained in the "Introduction" is extracted from an article by the British writer Leslie Vernon. I am indebted also to Karl-Heinz Heimann, Karl-Heinz Jens, and Hildebrand Kelber of *Kicker Sportmagazin* for their help in locating stills.

This volume might not have seen the light of day were it not for the devoted support of my friends and family, especially that of Joseph Ritchie and Bruce Stokes. Of the many others whose tireless support are deeply appreciated, I am particularly indebted to A. W. Robb, C. W. Reamer, Veronica Elliott, and Stella Santos dos Santos, who, if my memory serves me well, suggested the idea for this book in the first place.

Above all, the support of Barbara Najar was central to the project from its early days. It is unlikely that I am even aware of the extent of her sacrifices. Perhaps this acknowledgment will account for them too.

R.H.

June 1979
Washington, D.C.

Foreword

by Sir Stanley Rous, C.B.E.,
Honorary President, F.I.F.A.

This is one of the most comprehensive volumes on world soccer so far produced anywhere in the world. It is strikingly evident that only after much study and research has the work been published. It is historical and covers every aspect of the game from its early beginning to the present day. As a reference book on the laws of the game, clubs, competitions, national football associations, famous players, administrators, and referees it is a tome of information.

This book will stimulate the interest which is currently increasing in soccer in the United States. As the youth of the country become more enthusiastic for the game they will quite naturally seek information about how it is played, how administered, and controlled. Interest in those who have played it at club and international levels will also be aroused, and this encyclopedia will supply all the answers.

I know from my experience as an international referee, as Secretary of a national football association (The English F.A.), and as President of F.I.F.A. how helpful an encyclopedia such as this will be to those who seek details of football administration in the countries they visit. To retired officials it will bring back happy memories.

I hope this book will have a worldwide circulation. It should find a place on the desk or bookshelf of every administrator in the game, especially in North America. Writers about soccer and journalists will find it authoritative and helpful in their efforts to write descriptively and accurately for the education of their readers.

By producing this encyclopedia Mr. Henshaw has done a service to the game, and I hope it will be much in demand as it deserves to be.

Introduction

Soccer—no other sport has so captured the world's attention. It is the preeminent game in over 175 countries and dependencies, and its popularity continues to grow. Almost 20 million players around the world are registered with official governing bodies, and over 275,000 clubs participate in authorized leagues and tournaments. A billion people on six continents watched the most recent World Championship on television. In some parts of the world, soccer's popularity is matched by other games of long standing—field hockey in India and Pakistan, cricket in the British Caribbean, baseball in the Spanish Caribbean, and other types of football in Australia and New Zealand; but now soccer is firmly established in these areas as well. In the United States and Canada, its status is rising year by year, and by the mid-1980s it will surely take its place among North America's leading sporting institutions.

The legendary popularity of soccer grew in part from the game's potency as a social force, especially in Europe and Latin America. In the past, most Americans and Canadians viewed soccer as a kind of peasant foreign intrigue, calling to mind the image of a South American mob sacking the archrival's local consulate after a match. But Americans and Canadians have gained increased exposure to the game—especially since the arrival of Pelé in the United States in 1975—and this image has subsided, though, in fact, it contains an element of truth. *Fútbol* hysteria is better understood with an historical perspective of the passionate rituals attendant to the game.

The birthplace of soccer as we know it was the England of the late industrial revolution. Though the game had earlier been developed and codified by upper-class students and university graduates, its evolution into a popular sport was the work of laborers, coal miners, and textile workers in the English North and Midlands. By 1888, when the first league was formed, working- and middle-class values had replaced those of the gentlemanly sportsmen who had governed English soccer since the founding of The Football Association in 1863. The deposed Victorian gentlemen, finding their amateur ideals brushed aside by the adoption of professionalism, turned to rugby and other more acceptable pastimes. The game now lay open to a vast and impoverished population.

The growth of soccer coincided with Britain's zenith as a colonial power. Since it required little more than a ball or round object to kick, the game was easily exported to the far reaches of the empire and other ports of call by sailors, engineers, technicians, and missionaries, and by 1880 soccer had been introduced in Europe, North America, South America, Africa, Asia and Australia. It was first played exclusively by the British, but gradually, as the British and indigenous populations interacted, it was adopted by local residents as well. Wherever the presence of the British—and later the French, Spanish, and Portuguese—was strong and the local population poor and in need of inexpensive recreation, soccer gained a foothold.

The birth of soccer in Czarist Russia typically illustrates the exportation of English football to the four corners of the globe. In 1887, a British cotton mill opened outside Moscow at the invitation of the Russian government. Unskilled jobs at the factory were doled out to local laborers, but the directors remained entirely British. To while away management's tedious leisure hours, the directors imported a soccer ball from England, and a handful of teams were organized. When the workers expressed an interest in learning the English game, another ball was ordered from London, and before long the Russians were also playing in the mire near the factory gates, using a pair of fence posts for a goal. Barred from playing on management teams, the workers eventually formed their own teams. The pattern was repeated at other factories under British ownership, and a league of factory teams was introduced. The team representing the cotton mill, Morozov, went on to become the best in the league, winning a large following. Thirty years later, under the new Soviet government, it was adopted as the official club of the electrical workers' union under a new name, Dinamo Moscow, and is now the most famous club in Russian soccer.

This pattern—the key to understanding the game's unique position in the world of sports—was followed until the post-World War II era. Factory workers and miners from Sweden to Bolivia were drawn to the same qualities that had earlier attracted British workers in Lancashire and Lanarkshire: simplicity, low cost, and the possibility for self-expression. Smoky centers of European commerce and industry became the first hotbeds of soccer activity. Their clubs dominated early league and cup competitions, and to this day are among the most hallowed in the game. The magic of their names ultimately surpassed anything known in the American experience, though perhaps the old Brooklyn Dodgers-New York Yankees rivalry comes close. The likes of Blackburn Rovers, Glasgow Celtic, Rapid Vienna, FTC Budapest, Slavia Prague, Genoa FC, Athletic Bilbao and Union St. Gilloise were—and still are—major cultural institutions and the focus of an urban life style whose horizons seldom went beyond city limits. Except in Britain, memberships were sold to the general public, teams in a dozen or more sports were added to club activities (with soccer always at the center), and everywhere loyal fans were turned into devoted participants in the competitive process.

Between 1888 (the founding of The Football League in England) and 1933 (when professionalism was sanctioned in Brazil), the game rose in stature from a simple diversion to mass ritual. Crowds of 100,000 or more attended weekend matches in London as early as 1901. Partisanship and club loyalties became a serious matter, and provided rallying points around which ordinary people planned much of their leisure time. In some cases, loyalties were divided along ethnic or religious lines, and bitter rivalries of long standing were born. The most notorious of these rivalries over the years have been Scotland's Celtic (Roman Catholic) vs. Rangers (Protestant), Spain's Real Madrid (Castilian) vs. Barcelona (Catalan), and Peru's Alianza Lima (black and mestizo) vs. Universitario Lima (Creole), and other cross-cultural rivalries have flourished in Yugoslavia, Czechoslovakia, Belgium, Argentina, Brazil, and several countries in Africa.

In South America, where the industrial revolution of the nineteenth century made little impact, the familiar pattern of growth was intensified by an unabashed Latin style. The entire region, except those countries that were culturally influenced by the United States, latched onto the new game like a magnet. Argentina, in fact, was the first country other than Great Britain to introduce a league. Buenos Aires and Montevideo became the soccer capitals of the Western Hemisphere, and remained so until Brazil came to prominence in the 1930s. In Brazil, the game permeated every fabric of society. Clubs were founded in the most obscure corner of the Amazon basin as early as 1919, and a new word was added to the Brazilian dialect: *futebolístico* ("supreme football," or that of Friedenreich and Pelé). In the World Championship of 1938, it became evident that Brazil would someday hold a special place in world soccer—and indeed it has. The mystical quality of Brazil's style, its depth of talent, the honorable status of the game at the very center of Brazilian culture, and the unparalleled success of its national teams in the World Championship have all contributed to the Brazilian legend. Brazilian sociologist Gilberto Freyse has explained it in classical terms: "It can well be said that a peculiarly Brazilian style of playing has evolved, which displays the talents of a colorful population. It is not responsible to the formalism of Apollo but is open to the movement of Dionysus."

In Africa, public interest in soccer intensified after World War II, and several world class African stars have already played for major clubs in Europe. Large and fanatical crowds have been filling stadiums in Egypt, Tunisia, Algeria, and Morocco for decades, and Sudan, Ethiopia, Guinea, Ivory Coast, Ghana, Nigeria, Cameroon, Congo, and Zaire have emerged as Africa's great powers. In Asia, this intensity can also be seen in Singapore, Hong Kong and Malaysia, and to a certain degree in Thailand, South Korea, Indonesia, and India. Soccer has even grown by leaps and bounds—quite literally—on the islands of Oceania, the game's newest horizon.

What then of soccer in the United States and Canada? According to the present structure of FIFA, the world governing body, the game in North America is administered within a sprawling cluster of nations that includes Central America and the Caribbean (known collectively as CONCACAF). For decades, the runaway powerhouse of this region has been Mexico, with flashes of success achieved by Costa Rica, Cuba, and Haiti. All questions about gradual shifts of power in CONCACAF have been overshadowed in recent years by the shock waves rippling from the North American Soccer League (NASL), as dozens of world famous stars have been lured away from Europe and South America by vast sums of American money. This trend, in addition to a series of controversial rule changes adopted in the NASL, has put the United States and Canada on the soccer map. The entrance of American capital into the world soccer market and the potential leverage that may be gained from its economic power—both in the transfer market and in pressuring FIFA to make controversial changes in the laws of the game—is viewed abroad as a possible threat to the game's stability. Meanwhile, success on the international playing field continues to elude the United States and Canada, where officials point optimistically to the burgeoning youth soccer movement. In spite of the upward trend, the best analysis would indicate that American and Canadian national teams now rank about 40th or 50th in the world.

International controversies—economic, legal, and political—have been part of the world soccer scene for decades. Soccer first became a scapegoat for international diplomacy during the Balkan Wars of the pre-World War I era, when the frightened Ottoman rulers of Turkey suppressed teams of Greek and Bulgarian students on the grounds that student gatherings might develop into organized revolutionary activity. Countless other examples of political encroachment have followed. In 1920, the four British football associations responded to anti-German sentiment at home and withdrew from FIFA over Germany's continued membership, and they were not persuaded to come back until four years later. The USSR's 30-year political and cultural isolation from the rest of the world following the October Revolution was ultimately broken by the reaffiliation of its soccer federation with FIFA in 1946; this in turn led to the Soviets' rejoining of the Olympic movement and an eventual opening up of cultural links with the West.

Since World War II, soccer has become a major conduit for militant or benevolent political expression in new ways: the murder in 1955 of a Communist battalion by rival

Karen insurgents in Burma on the pretext of a soccer game; the refusal in 1957 by Egypt, Sudan, and Ethiopia to allow South African participation in the new African Football Confederation as a protest against the latter's racial policies; the so-called "Fútbol War" in 1969 between El Salvador and Guatemala, which was sparked (though not caused) by soccer matches between the two national teams; the famous cease fire during the Biafran civil war so that Pelé could visit both sides of the front; the rise of soccer in the oil-rich Persian Gulf states during the 1970s as a means of gaining further international recognition and prestige; the perennial FIFA and Asian Football Confederation membership battles involving the two Chinas and Israel; the assassination by guerrillas in 1976 of the president of the Argentine World Cup Organizing Committee; and, the most common example of all, refusals to engage political enemies on the playing field.

Soccer has also been a vehicle for reconciliation between nations, and its pervasive influence the world over has sometimes achieved rare moments of unity. International cooperation and excitement often reach their highest level with the unfolding of traditional competitions. The greatest of these, the World Championship, or World Cup, is staged every four years midway between Olympiads, and draws together the community of nations in a common goal unlike any other event.

The insatiable desire of soccer players everywhere to compete on an international scale has produced a host of quaint, if not curious, competitions. One, the Seven Seas Football Series, is a "world football championship at sea," contested by teams representing ocean-going vessels from over 60 nations. In one recent edition, 975 ships took part, and every continent was represented. The scheduling of these games demands extraordinary planning on a global scale, but incredibly, the series is completed each year. Norwegian teams have recently dominated the competition, and the Norwegian Football Association has expressed the hope that "the victories will set an example for Norwegian football ashore."

The cultural and political significance of a sport so widely accepted is a subject of endless fascination, and, indeed, the game's statistics are staggering. It is clear that soccer is an important social force and diplomatic tool, and it has unified groups of people or nations as an embodiment of collective pride, but these considerations mask others that are equally intriguing. To the individual, there is a more intimate response to the game—an aesthetic, or intuitive urge rather than the learned response of a citizen, comrade, or fan—and this aspect of soccer's popularity brings us to the delicate question of sport and art and the inseparability of the two. From ancient times to the present, men and women have relied on sports, no less than the arts, to release their creative energy. The presence of studio arts, music, architecture—and ball games—in all advanced cultures has affirmed people's essential desire for creative expression.

The fine distinctions that separate art from sport have become clearer since the earliest known football game, *tsu chu*, was played in ancient China. The creative act of playing skillfully with a ball was viewed by the Chinese as little more than artistic expression—an outpouring of joy on the occasion of the emperor's birthday. Ball juggling exercises in ancient Egypt, perhaps the earliest forerunner of modern football games, were indistinguishable from sculpture and painting as artistic expressions of their day.

In our own time, soccer encompasses such a broad range of characteristics— strength and delicacy, power and subtlety, speed and caution—that it sometimes appears to bridge the gap we have fashioned between art and sport over the centuries. Vladimir Beara, Yugoslavia's great goalkeeper during the 1950s, was a ballet master at the Belgrade Opera, and Bela Guttmann, the famous manager of Honvéd and Benfica, had been a dancing master until he turned to soccer. And who would deny that Brazil's Garrincha, the "Little Bird," resembled a *sambador* as he dribbled down the right wing?

To watch one's favorite team dominate the opposition or win an important game is a familiar source of satisfaction, but the private pleasure—the aesthetic response—in watching an accomplished ball artist dazzle our senses in a fleeting image is an uncommon experience. Appreciating the versatility displayed in a great game or by an individual player with complete skills, such as Alfredo Di Stefano, is much like listening to a symphony by one of the nineteenth-century masters. There are movements of depth, lyricism, dance, and quickness in either case. As the Hungarian soccer proverb says: "A team must contain people who can carry a piano, and others who can play it." Soccer is unique in having a form, rhythm, and harmony of such scope.

List of Abbreviations

AA	Associação Atlética	C	Club; Clube
A.A.	Athletic Association	CA	Club Atlético; Club Athlet-
AAAF	Asociación Amateurs Argen-		ique; Clube Atlético
	tina de Football	CAF	Confédération Africaine de
AAF	Asociación Argentina de		Football; Československá
	Football		Asociace Footballova
AAFA	American Amateur	C.A.R.A.	Club Athlétique Renaissance
	Football Associationn		Aiglons
AC	Associazione Calcio; Atlético	CBD	Confederação Brasileira de
	Clube; Atlético Club		Desportos
A.C.	Athletic Club	CCCF	Confederación Centro-
ACAF	All-China Athletic Federation		americana y del Caribe de
AEK	Athlitiki Enosis Konstan-		Fútbol
	tinoupoleos	C de R	Clube de Regatas
AFA	Amateur Football Associa	CF	Club de Football; Club de
	tion; American Football		Fútbol
	Association; Asociación del	CFI	Comité Français Interfédéral
	Fútbol Argentino; Asoci-	CFS	Československý Fotbalový
	ación de Football de		Svaz
	Aficianados	Chi	Chile
AFC	Asian Football Confederation	CNAAF	China National Amateur
A.F.C.	Amateur Football Club;		Athletic Federation
	Association Football Club	Col	Columbia
AIFF	All India Football Federation	CONCACAF	Confederación Norte-
AIK	Allmänna Idrottsklubben		Centroamericana y del
AK	Athletik Klub		Caribe de Fútbol
Arg	Argentina	CONMEBOL	Confederación Sudamericana
ARSC	Association Royale Sportive		de Fútbol
	Congolaise	CS	Cercle Sportive
AS	Association Sportive;	CSA	Canadian Soccer Association
	Associazione Sportiva	Cze	Czechoslovakia
ASA	Australian Soccer Association		
ASF	Association Suisse de Foot-	DBU	Dansk Boldspil-Union
	ball; Australian Soccer	DDR	Deutsche Demokratisch
	Federation		Republik
ASL	American Soccer League	Den	Denmark
AUF	Asociación Uruguaya de Fút-	Dep	Deportivo
	bol; Asociación Uruguaya	DFB	Deutscher Fussball-Bund
	de Football	DFV	Deutscher Fussball-Verband
Aus	Austria		der DDR
		DPR	Democratic People's Republic
B	Boldklub; Boldklubben	DR	Democratic Republic
Bel	Belgium		
BFA	Bohemian Football Asso-	EC	Esporte Clube
	ciation	Ecu	Ecuador
BK	Boldklub; Bolkdklubben	Eng	England
BNSF	Bulgarska Nationalna Sport-	EPO	Elliniki Podosfairiki
	na Federatia		Omospondia
Bol	Bolivia		
Bra	Brazil	F	Fútbol; Futebol
BSC	Ball-Spiel-Club	F.A.	Football Association; The
BTC	Budapesti Torna Club		Football Association (Lon-
Bul	Bulgaria		don)

FAI	Football Association of Ireland	HJK	Helsingin Jalkapalloklubi
FASA	Football Association of South Africa	Hond	Honduras
		Hun/Hung	Hungary
FAW	Football Association of Wales	HVV	Haagse Voetbal Vereningen
FBF	Federación Boliviana de Fútbol	IFA	Irish Football Association
		IFAB	International Football Association Board
FBS	Federação Brasileira de Sports	IFK	Idrottsföreningen Kamraterna
FC	Fútbol Club; Futebol Clube; Fussball Club	IOC	International Olympic Committee
F.C.	Football Club		
FCAF	Fédération Cycliste et Athlétique Française	ISL	International Soccer League
		It/Ita	Italy
FEF	Real Federación Española de Fútbol		
FEZAFA	Fédération Zaïroise de Football-Association	JK	Jalkapalloklubi
FF	Fotbollförening	KBV	Koninklijke Belgische Voetbalbond
F.F.	Football Federation		
FFC	Federación de Football de Chile	KC	Kalara Club
		KNVB	Koninklijke Nederlandsche Voetbalbond
FFF	Fédération Française de Football	KSI	Knattspyrnusamband Islands
FFSL	Football Federation of Sri Lanka	LAF	Liga Argentina de Football
FGSPF	Fédération Gymnique et Sportive des Patronages de France	LMEA	Liga Metropolitana de Esportes Atléticos
		LMF	Liga Metropolitana de Foot-Ball
FIFA	Fédération Internationale de Football Association	LPF	Liga Paraguaya de Fútbol
FIGC	Federazione Italiana Giuoco Calcio	Lux	Luxembourg
FK	Fussball Klub; Football Klub	Mex	Mexico
FMFA	Federación Mexicana de Fútbol Asociación	MG	Minas Gerais
		MLS	Magyar Labdarugók Szövetsége
FPF	Federação Portuguesa de Futebol; Federación Peruana de Fútbol	MSV	Meidericher Spielverein
		MTK	Magyar Testgyklorlok Köre
FR	Federal Republic		
Fra	France	NAC	North American Football Confederation
FRF	Federatia Româna de Fotbal	NASL	North American Soccer League
FRMF	Fédération Royale Marocaine de Football		
FSJ	Fudbalski Savez Jugoslavije	Net	Netherlands
FTC	Ferencvárosi Torna Club	NFF	Norges Fotballforbund
FUFA	Federation of Uganda Football Associations	NoI	Northern Ireland
		NPSL	National Professional Soccer League
FVF	Fédération Voltaïque de Football		
		ODCC	Organización Deportiva Centroamericana y del Caribe
GAFA	German-American Football Association	OFB	Österreichischer Fussball-Bund
GFA	Ghana Football Association	OFC	Oceania Football Confederation
GFR	German Federal Republic		
Gre	Greece	OFV	Österreichischer Fussball-Verband
Guat	Guatemala		

OGC	Olympique Gymnaste Club	SS	Societá Sportiva
OSC	Olympique Sporting Club	SV	Sportverein
		SVB	Surinaamse Voetbal Bond
PAOK	Panellinikos Athlitikos Omi-los Konstantinoupoleos	Swe	Sweden
Par	Paraguay	Swi	Switzerland
Per	Peru	TC	Torna Club
Pol	Poland	TFF	Türkiye Futbol Federasyonu
PR	People's Republic	TSV	Turn-und-Sportverein
PS	Palloseura	Tur	Turkey
PSSI	Persatuan Sepakbola Seluruh Indonesia	TuS	Turn-und-Spielvereinigung
PSV	Philips Sportverein	U	Universitaria; Universitario; Universidad
PZPN	Polski Zwiazek Pilki Noznej		
		UC	Unione Calcio
QFA	Qatar Football Association	UDA	Ustredni Dum Armady
Q.P.R.	Queen's Park Rangers	UEFA	Union of European Football Associations
RC	Racing Club	URBSFA	Union Royale Belge des Sociétés de Football-Association
Rep	Republic		
RG	Rio Grande do Sul		
RJ	Rio de Janeiro	Uru	Uruguay
RSC	Royal Sporting Club	US	Union Sportive; Unione Sportiva
Rum	Rumania		
		USA	United States of America; United Soccer Association
SAFA	South African Football Association	USFA	United States Football Association
SASF	South African Soccer Federation	USFSA	Union des Sociétés Fran-çaises des Sports Athléti-ques
S.C.	Soccer Club; Sports Club		
Sco	Scotland		
SE	Sociedade Esportiva; Sport Egyesület	USSF	United States Soccer Federation
SFA	Scottish Football Association; Schweizerische Football Association; Sudan Foot-ball Association	USSFA	United States Soccer Football Association
		USSR	Union of Soviet Socialist Republics
SFF	Svenska Fotbollförbundet		
SFV	Schweizerischer Fussball-Verband	Ven	Venezuela
		VfB	Verein für Bewegungsspiele
SG	Sport-Gemeinde	VfL	Verein für Leibesübungen
SK	Sport Klub; Sportovního Klubu	VM	Vörös Meteor
SL	Sport Lisboa	WAC	Wiener Athletic Club
SM	Société Municipale	WAFU	West African Football Union
SO	Sportivnoye Obscchestvo	Wal	Wales
Sov	Soviet Union	WSV	Wiener Sportvereinigung
SP	São Paulo		
Spa	Spain	Yug	Yugoslavia
SpVgg	Spielvereinigung		

KEY

A uniform set of technical abbreviations are used throughout this book. The most common are those found at the top of tournament standings:

P W D L F A P

These refer to: games played, won, drawn, lost, goals for, goals against, points.

The same data are sometimes referred to in the text, as, for example, in the following format: 44-6-8-30-47-135-20. American readers should take note of the "won-drawn-lost" columns, since many will be accustomed to the "lost" column preceding the "drawn" column. In this volume, the internationally accepted order (won-drawn-lost) has been adopted to avoid confusion with existing written records and official publications.

Other statistical abbreviations used in this book:

apps	appearances	o.g.	own goal
att.	attendance	pen	penalty kick
D-W	draw-win (NASL)	s.	substitute
FrP	French points		

Ademir (1924-   )

(Full name: Ademir Marques de Meneses.) The complete center forward, Ademir emerged as a world famous star in the 1950 World Cup and led Brazil's astounding forward line, one of the greatest ever seen in the game, with the gifted Jair at inside left and Zizinho at inside right. Ademir was a perfectly balanced player, who shot with either foot effectively, dribbled in mazes around his defenders, and had blinding speed. He was also among the most versatile of players, and, while his worldwide fame was derived from those amazing performances at center forward, he was equally well known in Brazil as an outside left. He began his career with Esporte Recife, and at age 19 was chosen for the Pernambuco selection to play in the Brazilian championship for state teams. Rio's Vasco da Gama signed him in 1944, and the following year he and Jair helped Vasco to a memorable Rio league title. In 1946, he moved to Fluminense, guiding his new club to its own championship, but in 1947 he returned to Vasco and became synonymous with that club's domination of the Rio soccer until the early 1950s. Vasco and Ademir won further league titles in 1947, 1949, 1950, and 1952. In the 1950 World Cup, he led all scorers, and in his 37 international appearances for Brazil he converted 32 times, many of them now legendary. He finally retired from Vasco in 1956, and went into broadcasting. Ademir's father was the incomparable Domingos da Guia, defender *extraordinaire* for Brazil in the 1930s.

Aden   See: **Yemen, People's Democratic Republic**

advantage clause

A discretionary decision of the referee, whereby he may refrain from stopping play for an infringement if the offending team would be given an advantage, e.g., when a foul is committed against a team mounting an apparent attack. Application of the advantage clause is irreversable.

Afars and Issas, French Territory of   See: **Djibouti**

Afghanistan

Football Association of Afghanistan
Riasat—The National Olympic Federation
Kabul

Founded: 1922
FIFA: 1948

Affiliated clubs: *30;* registered players: *3,300 (300 non-amateur);* national stadium: *National Stadium, Kabul (25,000);* largest stadium: *National Stadium;* colors: *white jerseys, white shorts;* season: *April to October;* honors: *none.*

While the level of play in Afghanistan is not advanced, an organizing body was founded as early as 1922 as an adjunct of the amateur sports committee that was to become the National Olympic Federation in 1933. An actual football association was created in the early 1950s. To date, the Football Association of Afghanistan remains an affiliate of the Olympic committee, the controlling body of all sports in the country. A league, centered in Kabul, was inaugurated during the 1930s and now numbers 30 participants.

It is uncertain when an Afghan selection first engaged in international competition, but the earliest official recording of a full international was a 6-0 loss to Luxembourg during the 1948 Olympic Games in London. This match is the only occasion on which Afghanistan played in a competition of intercontinental caliber. In 1951, however, it became one of only six nations to participate in the first Asian Games soccer tournament in New Delhi, and this was to be its finest showing ever. After losing a semi-final match to India, 3-0, the Afghan team advanced as far as the third place match against Japan but fell short of winning a bronze medal by a score of 2-0. In the 25 years since, Afghanistan has not fared as well in the Asian Games, and it has not played in the final rounds of any Asian Cup competition. Nor have Afghan clubs participated in the final rounds of the Asian Champions' Team Cup, though the number of registered players has increased seven times since World War II, and it is one of the few Asian countries with any players of non-amateur status. There is little doubt that the interest displayed by Afghans since British soldiers and residents introduced the game during the aftermath of World War I has resulted in a high degree of organization and enthusiasm, especially among the important ethnic groups, Pushtun and Tajik.

Africa   See: **African Football Confederation**

African Cup of Champion Clubs

Coupe d'Afrique des Clubs Champions.

The African club championship was introduced in 1964, by which time the success of the African Nations' Cup was assured and the number of new members in the African Football Confederation (CAF) was growing rapidly. The domestic champions of each member nation of the CAF are invited annually to play for the Kwame Nkrumah Trophy, named for the former President of Ghana. All rounds, including the final, are played on a home and away knock out basis.

The series has been dominated almost entirely by clubs from the sub-Saharan regions of the continent, though Arab North African clubs appeared to be coming into their own by the mid-1970s. Two clubs, Zaire's Englebert Lumbumbashi (later renamed Tout-Puissant Mazembe) and Guinea's Hafia de Conakry, have won the title twice. Englebert was also a losing finalist twice and established a dynasty of sorts during the late 1960s. Ghana's Kotoko Kumasi, on the other hand, has won a single championship, and it has managed to reach the final five times in a 12-year period. Two countries have produced more than one winner: Zaire (Englebert and Vita Kinshasa) and Cameroon (Oryx de Douala and Canon de Yaoundé. Egypt's Ismaili, Ivory Coast's ASEC Abidjan, and Nigeria's Rangers Club also rank high on the list of all-time successful clubs.

The series is usually played between February and December. In 1977, 26 countries took part in the competition, the newest being Mauritania. Of the 36 members of the CAF, only Mauritius and Morocco (the latter a continental power to be reckoned with), have not yet participated, and the competitions have never included all 34 others at the same time. One newly independent state, Guinea-Bissau, entered champion teams in 1976 and 1977 without having acquired full membership in the CAF. Expelled FIFA member South Africa and suspended FIFA member Rhodesia have never been seriously considered as participants, and Chad did not participate before its expulsion from FIFA in 1971.

Winners

1964	Oryx de Douala (Cameroon)	1971	Canon de Yaoundé (Cameroon)
1965	no competition	1972	Hafia de Conakry (Guinea)
1966	Stade d'Abidjan (Ivory Coast)	1973	Vita F.C. (Zaire)
1967	Englebert Lumbumbashi (Congo-Kinshasa)	1974	C.A.R.A. (Congo)
1968	Englebert Lumbumbashi (Congo-Kinshasa)	1975	Hafia de Conakry (Guinea)
		1976	Mouloudia Chalia (Algeria)
1969	Al-Ismaili Club (Egypt)	1977	Hafia de Conakry (Guinea)
1970	Kotoko Kumasi (Ghana)	1978	Canon de Yaoundé (Cameroon)

Results

1964-70 (details unavailable)

1971

Subgroup

*Esperance (Tunisia)—National Benghazi (Libya)	0-0, 1-0
*Mareikh (Sudan)—Tele D'Asmara (Ethiopia)	2-1, 0-1
*Livori Public (Somalia)—Young Africans (Tanzania)	0-0, 0-1
*M.M.M.M. (Madagascar)—Maseru Club (Lesotho)	3-2, 2-1
*Abaluhya Club (Kenya)—Great Olympics (Ghana)	0-0, 1-3
*Stade Bamako (Mali)—Jaraafs (Senegal)	4-0, 0-3
*Secteur VI Niamey (Niger)—Rangers Club (Nigeria)	1-1, 0-1
*Club V (Congo)—Association Amicale (Dahomey)	2-0, 1-0
*Canon (Cameroon)—AS Solidarité Libreville (Gabon)	7-3, 2-1

First Round

Group A

Esperance (Tunisia)—Ismaili Club (Egypt) (not played; Ismaili advanced)	———
*Mareikh—Kotoko (Ghana)	2-1, 4-6

Group B

*Young Africans—Coffee Club (Uganda) (not played; Coffee Club advanced) *M.M.M.M.—Great Olympics	——— 2-1, 0-7

Group C

*Stade Bamako—ASEC Abidjan (Ivory Coast)	2-2, 1-2
*Rangers Club—Kalum Star (Guinea)	2-1, 3-3

Group D

*Club V—Dynamic (Togo)	1-2, 0-2
*Canon—Vita F.C. (Zaire)	7-4, 0-2

Quarter-Finals

*Ismaili Club—Kotoko	1-1, 0-3
*Coffee Club—Great Olympics	0-0, 0-2
*ASEC Abidjan—Rangers Club	2-0, 1-0

*Dynamic—Canon	1-2, 3-4
*Kotoko—Great Olympics	1-0, 1-1

Semi-Finals
*ASEC Abidjan—Canon	2-1, 1-4

Final
*Kotoko—Canon	3-0, 0-2, 0-1
(replay in Yaoundé)	

*home team in first leg

1972

Subgroup
Ahly Club Tripoli (Libya)—Sudan Champion	———
(Sudanese club withdrew)	
*Saint George (Ethiopia)—Livori Publici Club (Somalia)	3-1, 1-1
*Heart of Oaks (Ghana)—Kenya champion	———
(Kenyan club withdrew)	
*A.S. Saint Michel (Madagascar)—Young Africans (Tanzania)	2-0, 0-1
*Lesotho Filding Majantja (Lesotho)—Kabwe Warriors (Zambia)	2-2, 0-9
*Hafia de Conakry (Guinea)—Force Armées Nigeriennes (Niger)	4-1, 1-1
*Asfav (Upper Volta)—Djoliba (Mali)	1-3, 0-1
*Forces Armées (Senegal)—A.S. de Cotonou (Dahomey)	3-0, 3-2
*T.P. Mazembe (Zaire)—A.S. Police (Gabon)	2-0, 1-1
*Aigle de Kongsamba (Cameroon)—Olympic Real (Central Africa)	3-1, 0-1

First Round
*Ismaili Club (Egypt)—Ahly Club Tripoli	0-1, 3-4
*Simba Club (Uganda)—Saint George	4-0, 1-1
*W.N.D.C. (Nigeria)—Heart of Oaks	1-0, 0-3
*Kabwe Warriors—A.S. Saint Michel	2-1, 3-0
*Canon (Cameroon)—Hafia de Conakry	3-2, 1-4
*Forces Armées—Djoliba	2-0, 0-2
(Forces Armées declined penalty contest and forfeited)	
*Africa-Sports Abidjan (Ivory Coast)—T.P. Mazembe	1-2, 2-0
*Dynamic (Togo)—Aigle de Kongsamba	1-1, 3-4

Quarter-Finals
*Ahly Club Tripoli—Simba Club	1-1, 0-3
*Heart of Oaks—Kabwe Warriors	7-2, 2-1
*Hafia de Conakry—Djoliba	3-0, 1-2
*T.P. Mazembe—Aigle de Kongsamba	4-1, 2-1

Semi-Finals
*Heart of Oaks—Simba Club	1-1, 0-1
*T.P. Mazembe—Hafia de Conakry	3-2, 0-2
(second leg not completed; T.P. Mazembe forfeited)	

Final
*Simba Club—Hafia de Conakry   2-3, 2-4

*home team in first leg

1973

Subgroup
*Horsed (Somalia)—Ismaili Club (Egypt)   3-1, 0-4
*Breweries (Kenya)—Asmara (Ethiopia)   —, 6-5
  (first leg drawn: results not available)
*Young Africans (Tanzania)—Mareikh (Sudan)   1-2, 1-1
*Fortior (Madagascar)—PMU (Lesotho)   5-1, 1-2
*Forces Armées (Senegal)—Modèle Lomé (Togo)   2-2, 2-4
*Mighty Jet (Nigeria)—Jeanne d'Arc (Upper Volta)   2-1, 6-8
*ASEC Abidjan (Ivory Coast)—Barolle (Liberia)   2-1, 3-1
*Renaissance (Congo)—Dynamic (Burundi)   1-0, 2-2

First Round
*Ismaili Club—Ahly Club Tripoli (Libya)   4-1, 1-0
 Simba Club (Uganda)—Breweries   1-3, 2-1
*Mareikh—Kotoko (Ghana)   1-1, 0-3
*Kabwe Warriors (Zambia)—Fortior   4-0, 3-0
*Stade Bamako (Mali)—Modèle Lomee   2-1, 0-0
 Vita F.C. (Zaire)—Mighty Jet   ———
  (qualifier Jeanne d'Arc withdrew; substitute Mighty Jet
   withdrew; Vita F.C. advanced)
*Hafia de Conakry (Guinea)—ASEC Abidjan   2-1, 3-2
*Léopard (Cameroon)—Renaissance   2-0, 0-1

Quarter-Finals
*Breweries—Ismaili Club   0-0, 2-1
*Kabwe Warrior—Kotoko   2-1, 0-2
*Stade Bamako—Vita F.C.   0-3, 1-4
*Hafia de Conakry—Léopard   2-4, 3-2

Semi-Finals
*Kotoko—Breweries   2-1, 2-0
*Vita F.C.—Léopard   3-0, 1-3

Final
*Kotoko—Vita F.C.   4-2, 0-3

1974

Subgroup
*Ahly Club Tripoli (Libya)—Hilal (Sudan)   2-2, 0-3

Horsed (Somalia)—Asmara (Ethiopia) ————
(Horsed withdrew)
*Real de Bangui (Central Africa)—Simba Club (Uganda) 4-0, 0-1
*Antalaha (Madagascar)—Sahbia Army (Zambia) 1-2, 2-4
*Linare (Lesotho)—Simba Sports (Tanzania) 1-3, 1-2
*Modèle Lomé (Togo)—Portnovo (Dahomey) 3-0, 0-1
*Barolle (Liberia)—ASEC Abidjan (Ivory Coast) 0-0, 0-2
*Port Authority (Sierra Leone)—Jeanne d'Arc (Senegal) 3-2, 1-3
*Bendel Insurance (Nigeria)—Secteur 7 (Niger) 7-0, 0-1
*C.A.R.A. (Congo)—Zalang Omnisport (Gabon) 3-1, 4-0

First Round
*Mehalla (Egypt)—Hilal 4-1, 1-4
 (Mehalla won on penalty kicks)
*Abalulya (Kenya)—Asmara 2-0, 0-1
*Heart of Oaks (Ghana)—Real de Bangui 6-1, 3-3
*Sahbia Army—Simba Sports 1-2, 0-1
*ASEC Abidjan—Modèle Lomé 3-0, —
 (Modèle Lomé forfeited)
 Jeanne d'Arc—Hafia de Conakry (Guinea) ————
 (Hafia withdrew)
*Djoliba (Mali)—Bendel Insurance 2-0, 0-1
*C.A.R.A.—Vita F.C. (Zaire) 4-0, 0-3

Quarter-Finals
*Mehalla—Abalulya 3-0, 1-1
*Heart of Oaks—Simba Sports 1-2, 0-0
*ASEC Abidjan—Jeanne d'Arc 2-1, 0-1
*Djoliba—C.A.R.A. 0-0, 0-3

Semi-Finals
*Simba Sports—Mehalla 1-0, 0-1
 (Mehalla won on penalty kicks)
*C.A.R.A.—Jeanne d'Arc 2-0, 4-1

Final
*C.A.R.A.—Mehalla 4-2, 2-1

*home team in first leg

1975

Subgroup
*Express (Uganda)—Horsed (Somalia) 1-0, 0-0
*Fatima (Central Africa)—Mareikh (Sudan) 3-0, 0-2
 (Fatima forfeited second leg after leaving the field at the half)
*Embassoira (Ethiopia)—Inter Football (Burundi) 1-1, 0-2
 Tuleare (Madagascar)—Green Buffaloes (Zambia) ————
 (Tuleare withdrew)

Bata Bullets (Malawi)—Matlama F.C. (Lesotho) ————
(Matlama suspended)
*Great Olympics (Ghana)—Rangers Club (Nigeria) 0-2, 1-2
*Olympic Niamey (Niger)—ASEC Abidjan (Ivory Coast) 0-2, 1-4
*Djoliba (Mali)—Mighty Black Pool (Sierra Leone) 2-0, 1-0
*Bame (Liberia)—Lomé I (Togo) 0-1, —
(Lomé I won second leg: result not available)
Hafia de Conakry (Guinea)—Real de Banjul (The Gambia) ————
(Real de Banjul withdrew)
*Vita F.C. (Zaire)—Petro Sport (Gabon) 4-0, 1-1
*Silures (Upper Volta)—Étoile Sportive (Dahomey) 3-2, 2-0

First Round
*Express—Mehalla (Egypt) 1-1, 0-1
*Inter Football—Mareikh 0-0, 2-4
*Bata Bullets—Green Buffaloes 0-2, 2-3
*Rangers Club—Young Africans (Tanzania) 0-0, 1-1
(Rangers advanced)
*ASEC Abidjan—Forces Armés (Senegal) 1-1, 1-1
(ASEC won on penalty kicks)
*Djoliba—Lomé I 1-1, 2-3
Djoliba walked off the field; Lomé I declared winner)
*Vita F.C.—Hafia de Conakry 2-0, 0-3
*C.A.R.A. (Congo)—Silures 4-0, 5-4

Quarter-Finals
*Mehalla—Mareikh 2-1, 0-0
*Green Buffaloes—Rangers Club 2-2, 1-2
*ASEC Abidjan—Lomé I 1-0, 1-3
*C.A.R.A.—Hafia de Conakry 2-0, 0-2
(Hafia won on penalty kicks)

Semi-Finals
*Mehalla—Rangers Club —, 0-3
(results of first leg not available)
*Hafia de Conakry—Lomé I 1-0, 1-1

Final
*Hafia de Conakry—Rangers Club 1-0, 2-1

*home team in first leg

1976

Subgroup
*Ahly Beghazi (Libya)—Mouloudia Chalia (Algeria) 3-2, 1-3
*Luo Union F.C. (Kenya)—Saint George (Ethiopia) 3-1, 2-0
*Corps Enseignant (Madagascar)—Mseto Sports (Tanzania) 4-2, 1-4

*Express (Uganda)—Caiman Club (Cameroon)	1-0, 0-1
(Express advanced)	
*Jaraafs (Senegal)—Balantas Mansâo (Guinea-Bissaü)	6-1, 4-1
*Real de Banjul (The Gambia)—Djoliba (Mali)	0-2, 0-2
Silures (Upper Volta)—Forces Armées (Niger)	———
(Silures withdrew)	
Kotoko (Ghana)—Okoume de Libreville (Gabon)	———
(Okoume withdrew)	
*Renaissance Aiglons (Congo)—Cercle Sportif "Imana" (Zaire)	4-0, 0-2

First Round

*Mouloudia Chalia—National Sporting Club (Egypt)	3-0, 0-1
Mareikh (Sudan)—Lou Union F.C.	———
(Mareikh withdrew)	
*Mseto Sports—Green Buffaloes (Zambia)	0-1, 2-3
*Rangers Club (Nigeria)—Express	0-0, 2-2
*Omnisport Lomé I (Togo)—Jaraafs	1-1, 0-1
*Djoliba—Hafia de Conakry (Guinea)	2-1, 0-2
*ASEC Abidjan (Ivory Coast)—Silures	2-0, 2-0
*Kotoko—Renaissance Aiglons	1-0, 1-2

Quarter-Finals

*Mouloudia Chalia—Luo Union F.C.	6-3, 1-0
*Green Buffaloes—Rangers Club	3-1, 0-3
*Jaraafs—Hafia de Conakry	2-2, 0-4
*Kotoko—ASEC Abidjan	2-1, 0-1

Semi-Finals

*Rangers Club—Mouloudia Chalia	2-0, 0-3
*ASEC Abidjan—Hafia de Conakry	3-0, 0-5

Final

*Hafia de Conakry—Mouloudia Chalia	3-0, 0-3
(Mouloudia Chalia won on penalty kicks)	

African Cup of Nations

Coupe d'Afrique des nations.

Introduced in 1957, the biannual African Nations' Cup is the world's third oldest continental championship for national teams. It has been dominated primarily by Egypt, Sudan, Ghana, and Zaire, but in recent years it has become apparent that no single nation can claim absolute preeminence. Ethiopia, Ivory Coast, and the Congo have been strong secondary powers, while Nigeria, Cameroon, and Guinea, whose leading clubs have been prominent in international club competition, have not yet approached the front rank in Nations' Cup competition.

The stature of this series among African national associations, players, and spectators is very high. With the lone exception of 1976, when the African Football Confederation (CAF) experimented with an anticlimactic league format, all editions have been played according to the same elimination procedures that are found in the World Cup and European

Football Championship, i.e., qualification rounds followed by elimination rounds, semifinals, and a final. In case of a draw during qualification or elimination rounds, the away-goals rule applies; if there is still a draw, penalty kicks are taken. A three-time winner retains permanent possession of the trophy. The host country and holders automatically qualify for the final rounds.

1957. With only four countries participating, Khartoum was chosen as the site of the first cup and the first CAF Congress in 1957. Egypt was still in the throes of war, while Ethiopia had no suitable stadiums, and South Africa was barred from entering because it intended to field a team without blacks. The Sudan Football Association rose to the occasion, and the tournament was carried off successfully. A new stadium for 30,000 spectators was built, and Egypt and Ethiopia were enthusiastically invited to celebrate Sudan's independence, barely one-year-old. Egypt, which for over 30 years had been Africa's most advanced soccer nation, won both its matches and was declared the first winner of the cup. The respected leader of the Egyptian team was 21-year-old right half Rifàat Al-Fanaguili, who would later be offered hefty signing-on fees by Barcelona and A.C. Milan. But the undisputed hero was Egyptian inside right Ad-Diba, who scored five of Egypt's six goals, including all four against Ethiopia. Fanaguili's home club throughout his career was Al-Ahly of Cairo; Ad-Diba played for Union Alexandria.

1959. The second competition took place in Cairo at the giant stadium of Al-Ahly, but again only three countries were entered, as most of sub-Saharan and French North Africa had yet to achieve independence, and South Africa was out of favor even more than it had been before. The growing power of Nasser's new United Arab Republic as a political force buried Ethiopia's chances of staging the second tournament, though no one could claim to be more responsible or eager to contribute to the growth of African soccer than the Ethiopian Football Federation. Unlike the first cup, each of the participants played the others once, and the winner was decided strictly on a point system. Egypt again emerged victorious with two wins, though among the leading players of 1957, only Fanaguili had returned. Egypt's inside forward Gohri was high scorer with a hat trick against Ethiopia, but the major attraction was Egyptian idol Salah Selim, the center forward

of both Egypt and Al-Ahly, whose total number of international appearances was said to reach over 100 before he joined Sturm Graz of Austria in 1962. New CAF members Ghana, Nigeria, and Uganda declined to participate while the South African question was still under review.

1962. The widespread political upheavals caused by independence of former colonies in the early 1960s forced a delay of the third Nations' Cup until January 1962. Ethiopia was selected as the host country, and the proud Ethiopian Football Federation unveiled its remodeled Haile-Selassie Stadium, which had originally been constructed in 1955. Sudan, still affected by the military coup of 1958, declined to participate, but Uganda and Tunisia entered for the first time. The final saw the host team upset Egypt by 4-2 in extra time. It was one of the most exciting finals in the history of the cup. With the Emperor himself in the stands, Ethiopia put so much pressure on Egypt's defense during the overtime period that 11 defensive players could often be seen hovering in front of Egypt's goal. Ethiopia's captain, Luciano Vassalo, was the hero of the tournament, but the greatest credit should have gone to Tunisia, most of whose team arrived in Addis Ababa suffering from malaria after a tour of Nigeria. Ethiopia surfaced from the 1962 Nations' Cup as the most complete and best prepared national team in Africa, and the recently independent black African states, in the form of Uganda, began slowly to enter the mainstream of African soccer.

1963. In an effort to maintain its original biennial schedule, the CAF scheduled the fourth edition of the cup for November 1963. Ghana was chosen as the host country, and for the first time the opening round was held in two cities (Accra and Kumasi). The competition was dominated by the zealous spirit of Ghana's national team, the Black Stars, which emerged as the finest group of players yet seen in Africa. Their fiery center forward, Wilberforce Mfum, whom African journalists likened to Scottish idol Denis Law, led the Black Stars to victory in the final over Sudan. Nigeria was the only new entry, other than Ghana, but Nigeria also conceded the worst record in the competition. Egypt was still led by the invincible Fanaguili, and narrowly missed advancing to the final on goal average. It was generally agreed that the level of play as a whole was higher than in any previous edition of the cup.

1965. The fifth Nations' Cup in Tunis marked the real beginning of sub-Saharan participation in the competition. Egypt refused to enter, having broken off relations with Tunisia, and at the last minute Sudan followed suit. Senegal, Ivory Coast, and Congo-Léopoldville entered for the first time, and the CAF grouped three of the black African teams together in the opening round. Despite a nearly complete change in their lineup, the Black Stars of Ghana were touted as not-so-strong favorites, with host team Tunisia given a strong chance. Senegal, relatively unknown in most parts of the continent, was the surprise of the tournament. Excluded from the final by the slimmest of goal averages, they drew with Tunisia, and crushed Ethiopia before losing their confidence in a third place defeat at the hands of Ivory Coast. In the final, Ghana won its second trophy in succession by defeating Tunisia in extra time. The hero was outside left Frank Odoi, who slipped the ball into the net from a Kofi Paré corner kick for the winning goal.

1968. The 1967 Nations' Cup was delayed until January 1968. The host was again Ethiopia, but the opening rounds were played in Eritrea's largest city, Asmara, as well as in Addis Ababa. The two new entrants were Algeria, perennially under the shadow of Egypt, Tunisia, and Morocco in North African soccer, and Congo-Brazzaville. With the defensive tactics of Europe otherwise infiltrating the African game, Senegal and Ethiopia shined brightly as attractive, attacking teams, and astute observers were saddened when these two were not able to face each other during the course of the competition. In the end, it was the most defensive-minded of the participants, Congo-Kinshasa (later Zaire), who won the cup with a team selected almost entirely from Englebert Lumbumbashi, the African club champions. The victory was achieved with a 1-0 win over Ghana. In the third place game, the spectacular Ivory Coast avenged their earlier loss to Ethiopia. Congo-Brazzaville and Uganda were the weakest teams on the field, and Algeria appeared to be noticeably affected by the high altitude of Ethiopia's capital city.

1970. The competition returned to the Sudan. Two locations were chosen to host the opening round: Khartoum, the grand capital, and Wad Medani, a cotton producing center and football hotbed located 100 miles up the Blue Nile from Khartoum. There were two new participants, Guinea and Cameroon, two countries destined to play a major role in the development of African soccer during the 1970s. Despite identical point totals among three members of the Khartoum group in the opening round, it was the Wad Medani group that provided the most hotly disputed contests. The Ivory Coast, led by midfield strategist "Docteur" Ernest Kallet, enhanced its reputation as perhaps the most exciting national team in Africa, but a difficult loss to Ghana in the semi-finals put the trophy out of their reach, and they lost again to the skilled Egyptians in the third place game. For the fourth consecutive time, Ghana reached the final, but the Sudanese, after so many years at the forefront of Nations' Cup competition, finally achieved victory by one goal in a lackluster game between two veteran sides. When a second Sudanese goal was disallowed by the Ethiopian referee, spectators and Ghanaian players clashed and the police were called in. The Black Stars left the field before the presentation of the trophy, and they were expelled from the country that same night.

1972. The eighth edition of the cup is fondly remembered for its abundance of great international stars. There was Cameroon's Tokoto, Mali's Salif Keita, and the Congo's M'Pelé, as well as the Moroccan national idol, Ahmed Faras; all excelled for their respective teams. Emergent soccer power Cameroon, whose champion club, Canon de Yaoundé, had won the African club championship the year before, was the host country. The chosen sites, two omnisport stadiums in Yaoundé and Douala, were the largest and most modern in central Africa. Morocco, Africa's representative in the 1970 World Cup, Mali, Togo, and Kenya reached the final rounds for the first time, though only Mali achieved success.

In one of Africa's most bitter rivalries, the Congo was shut out by Zaire after numerous clashes both on and off the field, but in the semi-finals Mali slipped by Zaire on an overtime goal by striker Fantamady Keita, and the possibility of a second meeting between the Congo and Zaire in the final was lost. In the other semi-final, perhaps the most tense of the competition, Cameroon lost to the Congo's Red Devils by 1-0, and a pall fell over the host country. Mali, Africa's first great Cinderella team, was its own victim in the final against the Congo. Three quick Congolese goals after the half put the game away, and Brazzaville became the capital of African soccer for the first time. It was also the first and only time that all four semi-finalists were countries from south of the Sahara.

1974. The competition returned to Cairo where the highly-touted Leopards of Zaire would seek to unseat their Congolese rivals. There were two new finalists: Zambia, an emerging power from southern Africa, and little Mauritius, otherwise known as the Islanders, which escaped from qualification rounds to enter the final pack of eight. Egypt, the host country, was still feeling the effects of the Yom Kippur War five months earlier and two weeks before the opening ceremonies, 49 spectators had been trampled to death in a tragic stampede at Zamalek Stadium in Cairo. The tension this accident caused lingered with both fans and officials. As a result, Egyptian authorities publicly discouraged fans from attending Nations' Cup games.

Zaire, which had already qualified for Africa's berth in the 1974 World Cup by defeating Zambia twice, now faced Zambia again in the Nations' Cup final. The magnificent Nasser Stadium provided a fair setting, but the gloom of recent events still pervaded the atmosphere. In the final, the score stood at 1-1 at the end of regulation time. Three minutes before the end of extra time Zaire's Ndaye scored his second goal to put his team ahead; but, in the 120th minute, Zaire's goalkeeper was accidentally screened from a strong cross by Zambian left wing Sinyangwe, and the ball hit the net to tie the score

and force a replay. Two days later, Zaire and Zambia squared off again, but this time Zambia's defense was less solid, Zaire's attack more vigorous, and Ndaye's two goals brought the trophy once again to Zaire.

1976. The trophy returned to North Africa, and Ethiopia played host for a record third time. The chosen venues were Addis Ababa and a new location, Dire Dawe, since the 1967 site of Asmara was now embroiled in the Eritrean civil war. Twenty-four nations, another record, attempted to qualify for the final rounds. Frightened by the potential violence of the Egyptian political situation in 1974, the CAF decided to structure the finals on a league basis, eliminating the need for semi-finals and a final. The results at the box office were a disaster, and unfortunately, Ethiopia itself did not qualify for the final loop. There were no new countries in the final rounds, and Guinea and Morocco won their opening groups, followed by Egypt and Nigeria. In the final round robin, Morocco and Guinea drew in the last game of the competition to give Morocco the edge on points and its first Nations' Cup. Morocco's deserving victory was sadly marred by the anticlimactic format in which it was won, and the CAF announced immediately that in the 1978 Nations' Cup in Ghana and the 1980 edition in Senegal, the old knockout format would be revived.

Winners

1957	Egypt	1965	Ghana	1974	Zaire
1959	Egypt	1968	Congo-Kinshasa	1976	Morocco
1962	Ethiopia	1970	Sudan	1978	Ghana
1963	Ghana	1972	Congo		

Cumulative Ranking (1957-76)*
(number of editions in parentheses)

		P	W	D	L	F	A	P
1	Egypt (7)	25	15	4	6	59	34	34
2	Ghana (4)	16	10	4	2	35	18	24
3	Zaire (6)	24	9	5	10	40	43	23
4	Sudan (6)	17	6	5	6	24	22	16
5	Ivory Coast (4)	16	7	2	8	27	24	15
6	Ethiopia (7)	21	7	1	13	28	50	15
7	Guinea (3)	12	4	6	2	19	18	14
8	Morocco (2)	9	4	5	0	14	9	13
9	Congo (3)	13	5	2	6	18	25	12

10	Cameroon (2)	8	5	1	2	17	11	11
11	Zambia (1)	6	3	1	2	9	9	7
12	Nigeria (2)	8	3	1	4	14	18	7
13	Senegal (2)	6	2	2	2	10	7	6
14	Tunisia (3)	7	2	2	3	14	12	6
15	Mali (1)	5	1	3	1	11	11	5
16	Algeria (1)	3	1	0	2	5	6	2
17	Kenya (1)	3	0	2	1	3	4	2
18	Togo (1)	3	0	2	1	4	6	2
19	Uganda (4)	11	0	1	10	8	24	1
20	Mauritius (1)	3	0	0	3	2	8	0

*The following have not reached the final rounds or have never entered the competition: Benin, Burundi, Gabon, Gambia, Lesotho, Liberia, Libya, Madagascar, Malawi, Mauritania, Niger, Sierra Leone, Somalia, Tanzania, and Upper Volta.

Results

1957 (in Sudan)

Egypt (Raafat pen, Ad-Diba)	2	Sudan (Manzul)	1
Egypt (Ad-Diba 4) (both games played in Khartoum)	4	Ethiopia	0

1959 (in Egypt)

Egypt (Gohri 3, Cherbini)	4	Ethiopia	0
Sudan (Drissa)	1	Ethiopia	0
Egypt (Issam 2) (all games played in Cairo)	2	Sudan (Manzul)	1

1962 (in Ethiopia)

First Round
  Ethiopia—Tunisia   4-2
  Egypt-Uganda   2-1

Third Place Game
  Tunisia—Uganda   3-0

Final (in Addis-Ababa)
  Ethiopia   4   Egypt   2
  (Girma, Menguistou 2, Italo)   (Abdelfattah Badawi 2)
              —after extra time—

1963 (in Ghana)

Accra Group

Ghana—Tunisia		1-1
Ghana—Ethiopia		2-0
Ethiopia—Tunisia		4-2

	P	W	D	L	F	A	P
Ghana	2	1	1	0	3	1	3
Ethiopia	2	1	0	1	4	4	2
Tunisia	2	0	1	1	3	5	1

Kumasi Group

Egypt—Nigeria	6-3
Egypt—Sudan	2-2
Sudan—Nigeria	4-0

	P	W	D	L	F	A	P
Sudan	2	1	1	0	6	2	3
Egypt	2	1	1	0	8	5	3
Nigeria	2	0	0	2	3	10	0

Third Place Game

Egypt—Ethiopia	3-0

Final (in Accra)

Ghana	3	Sudan	0

(Aggrey-Fynn pen, Mfum 2)

1965 (in Tunisia)

Group A

Tunisia—Ethiopia	4-0
Senegal—Tunisia	0-0
Senegal—Ethiopia	5-1

	P	W	D	L	F	A	P
Tunisia	2	1	1	0	4	0	3
Senegal	2	1	1	0	5	1	3
Ethiopia	2	0	0	2	1	9	0

Group B

Ghana—Congo-Léopoldville	5-2
Ivory Coast—Congo-Léopoldville	3-0
Ghana—Ivory Coast	4-1

	P	W	D	L	F	A	P
Ghana	2	2	0	0	9	3	4
Ivory Coast	2	1	0	1	4	4	2
Congo-Léopold.	2	0	0	2	2	8	0

Third Place Game
Ivory Coast—Senegal   1-0

Final (in Tunis)
Ghana   3   Tunisia   2
(Odoi 2, Kofi)   (Chaibi, Chetali)
—after extra time—

1968 (in Ethiopia)

Addis-Ababa Group
Ethiopia—Uganda   2-1
Ivory Coast—Algeria   3-0
Ethiopia—Ivory Coast   1-0
Algeria—Uganda   4-0
Ivory Coast—Uganda   2-1
Ethiopia—Algeria   3-1

	P	W	D	L	F	A	P
Ethiopia	3	3	0	0	6	2	6
Ivory Coast	3	2	0	1	5	2	4
Algeria	3	1	0	2	5	6	2
Uganda	3	0	0	3	2	8	0

Asmara Group
Ghana—Senegal   2-2
Congo-Kinshasa—Congo-Brazzaville   3-0
Senegal—Congo-Brazzaville   2-1
Ghana—Congo-Kinshasa   2-1
Congo-Kinshasa—Senegal   2-1
Ghana—Congo-Brazzaville   3-1

	P	W	D	L	F	A	P
Ghana	3	2	1	0	7	4	5
Congo-Kinshasa	3	2	0	1	6	3	4
Senegal	3	1	1	1	5	5	3
Congo-Brazzaville	3	0	0	3	2	8	0

Semi-Finals
Congo-Kinshasa—Ethiopia   3-2
(after extra time)
Ghana—Ivory Coast   4-3
(after extra time)

Third Place Game
Ivory Coast—Ethiopia   1-0

Final (in Addis-Ababa)
Congo-Kinshasa   1   Ghana   0
(Kalala)

1970 (in Sudan)

Khartoum Group
Cameroon—Ivory Coast   3-2
Sudan—Ethiopia   3-0
Cameroon—Ethiopia   3-2
Ivory Coast—Sudan   1-0
Ivory Coast—Ethiopia   6-1
Sudan—Cameroon   2-1

	P	W	D	L	F	A	P
Ivory Coast	3	2	0	1	9	4	4
Sudan	3	2	0	1	5	2	4
Cameroon	3	2	0	1	7	6	4
Ethiopia	3	0	0	3	3	12	0

Wad Medani Group
Ghana—Congo-Kinshasa   2-0
Egypt—Guinea   4-1
Congo-Kinshasa—Guinea   2-2
Egypt—Ghana   1-1
Guinea—Ghana   1-1
Egypt—Congo-Kinshasa   1-0

	P	W	D	L	F	A	P
Egypt	3	2	1	0	6	2	5
Ghana	3	1	2	0	4	2	4
Guinea	3	0	2	1	4	7	2
Congo-Kinshasa	3	0	1	2	2	5	1

Semi-Finals
Ghana—Ivory Coast   2-1
(after extra time)
Sudan—Egypt   2-1
(after extra time)

Third Place Game
Egypt—Ivory Coast   3-1

Final (in Khartoum)
Sudan   1   Ghana   0
(El-Issed)

1972 (in Cameroon)

Yaoundé Group

Cameroon—Kenya	2-1
Mali—Togo	3-3
Mali—Kenya	1-1
Cameroon—Togo	2-0
Togo—Kenya	1-1
Cameroon—Mali	1-1

	P	W	D	L	F	A	P
Cameroon	3	2	1	0	5	2	5
Mali	3	0	3	0	5	5	3
Togo	3	0	2	1	4	6	2
Kenya	3	0	2	1	3	4	2

Douala Group

Congo—Morocco	1-1
Zaire—Sudan	1-1
Morocco—Sudan	1-1
Zaire—Congo	2-0
Morocco—Zaire	1-1
Congo—Sudan	4-2

	P	W	D	L	F	A	P
Zaire	3	1	2	0	4	2	4
Congo	3	1	1	1	5	5	3
Morocco	3	0	3	0	3	3	3
Sudan	3	0	2	1	4	6	2

Semi-Finals

Congo—Cameroon	1-0
Mali—Zaire	4-3
(after extra time)	

Third Place Game

Cameroon—Zaire	5-2

Final (in Yaoundé)

Congo	3	Mali	2
(M'Bono 2, M'Pelé)		(Moussa Diakhité, Moussa Traoré)	

1974 (in Egypt)

Group A

Egypt—Uganda	2-1
Zambia—Ivory Coast	1-0
Egypt—Zambia	3-1

Ivory Coast—Uganda							2-2
Zambia—Uganda							1-0
Egypt—Ivory Coast							2-0

	P	W	D	L	F	A	P
Egypt	3	3	0	0	7	2	6
Zambia	3	2	0	1	3	3	4
Uganda	3	0	1	2	3	5	1
Ivory Coast	3	0	1	2	2	5	1

Group B

Zaire—Guinea	2-1
Congo—Mauritius	2-0
Congo—Zaire	2-1
Guinea—Mauritius	2-1
Guinea—Congo	1-1
Zaire—Mauritius	4-1

	P	W	D	L	F	A	P
Congo	3	2	1	0	5	2	5
Zaire	3	2	0	1	7	4	4
Guinea	3	1	1	1	4	4	3
Mauritius	3	0	0	3	2	8	0

Semi-Finals

Zaire—Egypt	3-2
Zambia—Congo	4-2
(after extra time)	

Third Place Game

Egypt—Congo	4-0

Final (in Cairo)

Zaire	2	Zambia	2
(Ndaye 2)		(Kaushi, Sinyangwe)	

-after extra time-

(replay in Cairo)

Zaire	2	Zambia	0
(Ndaye 2)			

1976 (in Ethiopia; league format)

Addis Ababa Group

Ethiopia—Uganda	2-0
Egypt—Guinea	1-1
Uganda—Egypt	1-2
Ethiopia—Guinea	1-2
Guinea—Uganda	2-1
Ethiopia—Egypt	1-1

	P	W	D	L	F	A	P
Guinea	3	2	1	0	5	3	5
Egypt	3	1	2	0	4	3	4
Ethiopia	3	1	1	1	4	3	3
Uganda	3	0	0	3	2	6	0

Dire Dawe Group

Zaire—Nigeria	2-4
Sudan—Morocco	2-2
Nigeria—Sudan	1-0
Zaire—Morocco	0-1
Morocco—Nigeria	3-1
Zaire—Sudan	1-1

	P	W	D	L	F	A	P
Morocco	3	2	1	0	6	3	5
Nigeria	3	2	0	1	6	3	4
Sudan	3	0	2	1	3	4	1
Zaire	3	0	1	2	3	6	1

Finals (in Addis Ababa)

Guinea—Nigeria	1-1
Morocco—Egypt	2-1
Morocco—Nigeria	2-1
Egypt—Guinea	2-4
Egypt—Nigeria	2-3
Morocco—Guinea	1-1

Final Standings

	P	W	D	L	F	A	P
Morocco	3	2	1	0	5	3	5
Guinea	3	1	2	0	6	4	4
Nigeria	3	1	1	1	5	5	3
Egypt	3	0	0	3	5	9	0

1978 (in Ghana)

Group A (in Accra)

Ghana—Zambia	2-1
Nigeria—Upper Volta	4-2
Upper Volta—Zambia	0-2
Ghana—Nigeria	1-1
Ghana—Upper Volta	3-0
Zambia—Nigeria	0-0

	P	W	D	L	F	A	P
Ghana	3	2	1	0	6	2	5
Nigeria	3	1	2	0	5	3	4
Zambia	3	1	1	1	3	2	3
Upper Volta	3	0	0	3	2	9	0

Group B (in Kumasi)

Tunisia—Morocco	1-1
Uganda—Congo	3-1
Tunisia—Uganda	3-1
Morocco—Congo	1-0
Uganda—Morocco	3-0
Tunisia—Congo	0-0

	P	W	D	L	F	A	P
Uganda	3	2	0	1	7	4	4
Tunisia	3	1	2	0	4	2	4
Morocco	3	1	1	1	2	4	3
Congo	3	0	1	2	1	4	1

Semi-Finals

Ghana—Tunisia	1-0
Uganda—Nigeria	2-1

Third Place Game

Nigeria—Tunisia	1-1

(game abandoned: Tunisia walked off the field; Nigeria declared winner)

Final

Ghana	2	Uganda	0

African Cup Winners' Cup

Coupe d'Afrique des Vainqueurs de Coupe

Introduced in 1975, the African Cup Winners' Cup, the only such competition outside Europe, is open to all winners of domestic cup competitions in member nations of the African Football Confederation (CAF). Cup competitions, which are played in addition to annual league competitions, have a widespread tradition in Africa, and all 36 members of the CAF sponsor them on the domestic level. Financial hardships, however, have so far limited the number of countries taking part in the African Cup Winners' Cup to 22. Algeria, Burundi, Congo, Ghana, Lesotho, Mali, Mauritania, Mauritius, Morocco, Sierra Leone, Somalia, Sudan, and Tunisia have not yet entered. All rounds, including the final, are played on a home and away knockout basis.

Winners

1975 Tonnerre de Yaoundé (Cameroon)
1976 Stars Club (Nigeria)

1977 Rangers Enugu (Nigeria)
1978 Horoya Conakry (Guinea)

Results

1975

First Round
(Bye: Fortior-Madagascar)

*Union Recreation (Egypt)—Saint George (Ethiopia)	2-0, 0-0
*Mighty Jet (Nigeria)—Tonnerre (Cameroon)	2-2, 0-0
(Tonnerre won by toss of the coin after extra time)	
*Mulfulira (Zambia)—Jeshi (Tanzania)	3-0, 2-1
*Postelsport (Dahomey)—Tempete (Central Africa)	1-0, 0-3
*Wallidan (The Gambia)—Jeanne D'Arc (Senegal)	0-0, 0-2
*Omnisport (Togo)—Sahel (Niger)	1-0, 2-2
*Stella Club (Ivory Coast)—Barolle (Liberia)	1-0, 1-0

Quarter-Finals

*Union Recreation—Tonnerre	4-0, 0-3
Fortior—Mufulira	— — —
(Fortior withdrew)	
*Jeanne D'Arc—Tempete	1-1, 3-1
*Omnisport—Stella Club	0-1, 0-4

Semi-Finals

*Tonnerre—Mulfulira	1-0, 2-2
*Jeanne D'Arc—Stella Club	2-2, 1-2

Final

*Stella Club—Tonnerre	1-0, 1-4

*home team in first leg

1976

Subgroup

*Liberté F.C. (Niger)—Ahly Tripoli (Libya)	0-5, 1-4
*Batta Bullets (Malawi)—Fortior Cote Ouest (Madagascar)	2-4, 4-0
*Gambia Port Authority (Gambia)—Kadiogo (Upper Volta)	1-4, 1-2
*Canon (Cameroon)—Petro Sport (Gabon)	3-0, 3-1

First Round

*Zamalek (Egypt)—Ahly Tripoli	3-0, 1-2
*Metchal (Ethiopia)—Youth League F.C. (Tanzania)	5-2, 1-2
*Stars Club (Nigeria)—Breweries (Kenya)	3-0, 2-0
*Batta Bullets—Rokana United F.C. (Zambia)	1-0, 0-4
*Kadiogo—Kaleum Star (Guinea)	1-0, 0-7

*District Sportif "Lama-Kara" (Togo)—Tonnerre (Cameroon)	1-2, 0-3
*Union Sportive Coréenne (Senegal)—Stella Club (Ivory Coast)	1-0, 6-2
*Canon—Vita Club (Zaire)	2-1, 0-1

Quarter-Finals

*Metchal—Zamalek	2-0, 1-6
*Stars Club—Rokana United F.C.	3-2, 1-1
*Tonnerre—Kaleum Star	0-0, 2-1
*Vita Club—Union Sportive Coréenne	2-0, 3-3

Semi-Finals

*Zamalek—Stars Club	2-0, 0-2
(Stars Club won on penalty kicks)	
*Vita Club—Tonnerre	1-1, 1-3

Final

*Stars Club—Tonnerre	4-1, 1-0

*home team in first leg

African Football Confederation

Address: *5 Shareh Gabalaya, Guezira, Cairo, Egypt.* **Members:** *Algeria, Benin, Burundi, Cameroon, Central Africa, Congo, Egypt Arab Republic, Ethiopia, Gabon, Gambia, Ghana, Guinea, Ivory Coast, Kenya, Lesotho, Liberia, Libya, Madagascar, Malawi, Mali, Mauritania, Mauritius, Morocco, Niger, Nigeria, Senegal, Sierra Leone, Somalia, Sudan, Tanzania, Togo, Tunisia, Uganda, Upper Volta, Zaire, Zambia.* **Affiliated clubs:** *8,056;* **registered players:** *361,695.*

Founded in 1956 after the Egyptian delegate to the FIFA Congress in Lisbon proposed the formation of an African confederation. The four existing African members of FIFA—Egypt, Sudan, Ethiopia, and South Africa—were charter members. In 1957, when Egypt, Sudan, and Ethiopia organized the first African Cup of Nations in Khartoum, the all-white South African delegation was barred, and the South African association was subsequently expelled from the new confederation. The African Football Confederation/Confédération Africaine de Football (CAF) was officially established in Khartoum during the 1957 Nation's Cup. It was the first major international organization of any kind formed by independent African states. The founding of the Organization of African Unity at Addis Ababa in 1963 was to

some extent an outgrowth of the momentum created by the fourth CAF Congress, which was held in the Ethiopian capital at the same time. Twenty-four countries were affiliated by the early 1960s. It now has the largest membership of any continental confederation (36), and many new members are due in the near future: Seychelles, Djibouti, Angola, Mozambique, Guinea-Bissau, São Tomé and Principe, and Cape Verdes. Botswana's and Swaziland's memberships are imminnent. Chad (a former member of FIFA until it was expelled from the world body for not paying dues), Rwanda, and Equitorial Guinea, however, are not expected to seek affiliation until well into the 1980s. South Africa's ostracization has remained constant, but Rhodesia's exclusion will be subject to the transition to majority rule.

The CAF is responsible for the African Cup

of Nations, African Champions' Cup, African Cup Winners' Cup, African Junior Tournament, and the soccer competition of the African Games. A peculiarity of African soccer is the presence of several unofficial regional confederations, which the CAF has encouraged to aid developing soccer countries.

These organizations include the West African Football Union (1975), East African Football Confederation (1965), East and Central African Football Confederation, and the older North African Magreb Football Confederation.

African Footballer of the Year

"Le Ballon d'Or d'Afrique," like its European counterpart, is an award sponsored by the French weekly *France Football* (African Edition). It is presented annually to the best African player of the year by a vote of *France Football's* African correspondents.

Winners

1970	Salif Keita (Mali)		1975	Ahmed Faras (Morocco)
1971	Ibrahim Sunday (Ghana)		1976	Roger Milla (Cameroon)
1972	Cherif Souleymane (Guinea)		1977	Dhiab Tarek (Morocco)
1973	Bwanga Tshimen (Zaire)		1978	Abdoul Razak (Ghana)
1974	Paul Moukila (Congo)			

African Games, Football Tournament of the

Tournoi Football des Jeux Africains.

The African Games, all amateur and based on the Olympic model, are an outgrowth of the Friendship Games, which were introduced in 1960 for all French-speaking nations of the world. The three editions of the Friendship Games were all held in Africa (Tananarive in 1960, Abidjan in 1961, and Dakar in 1963), and were eventually reconstituted as the African Games in 1965. Its soccer tournament has sometimes conflicted with the more important African Nations' Cup, but it has remained significant in many countries.

Winners

1965 (in Brazzaville) Congo-Brazzaville
1973 (in Lagos) Nigeria
1976 (in Algiers)

Ajax, Amsterdamsche Football Club

Location: *Amsterdam, Holland;* stadium: *Ajax Stadion (29,500);* colors: *white jerseys with broad red stripe, white shorts;* honors: *Intercontinental Cup (1972), Super Cup (1972, 1973), European Cup (1971, 1972, 1973), Dutch champion (1918, 1919, 1931, 1932, 1934, 1937, 1939, 1947, 1957, 1960, 1966, 1967, 1968, 1970, 1972, 1973, 1977), Dutch cup winner (1917, 1943, 1961, 1967, 1970, 1971, 1972).*

Founded 1900, Ajax remained a minor Amsterdam club until World War I. It became affiliated with the Dutch national association in 1902, and entered the league in Division III shortly thereafter. Elected to Division I in 1910, Ajax was relegated and floundered in Division II from 1914-17, but won the Dutch Cup in its first year back in the front rank, and one year later captured its first Dutch championship. Ajax's first highly successful period encompassed the 1930s, when five league titles were won in nine years, and the Ajax Stadion was built (1935). In later years, Ajax played its big games in the much larger Olympisch Stadion (capacity: 67,000).

Ajax's rise to prominence began in earnest after the introduction of semiprofessionalism in Holland around 1954. In 1956-57, the club advanced to the quarter-finals of the European Cup, experiencing its first taste of international success, but lost that round to Vasas Budapest. A non-descript Ajax team won the Dutch championship in 1960 after a play-off with Feyenoord, and the possibility of greatness did not really emerge until the signing of Johan Cruyff in 1965. Cruyff's unique skills at center forward combined masterfully with those of left winger Piet Keizer, and the team that won successive Dutch championships from 1966-68 was perhaps the best ever seen in Holland up to that time.

In 1969, Ajax moved brilliantly to the final of the European Cup after brushing aside Benfica in the semi-finals, and showed flair and sophistication in losing to a defensive AC Milan in that final. After reaching the semi-finals of the Fairs Cup in 1970, a truly magnificent Ajax team coached by the Dutch disciplinarian Rinus Michels advanced to the final of the European Cup again, eliminating Nendori Tirana, FC Basel, Celtic, and Atlético Madrid on the way, and won its first international trophy after a lackluster final against Panathinaïkos. Neither of Ajax's two goals in the final were particularly well taken, but few doubted that the Ajax of Cruyff and Keizer was one of the best clubs in Europe.

Michels suddenly left for Barcelona after the 1971 triumph, and his place was taken by the more relaxed Stefan Kovacs, a Rumanian who brought Ajax to its peak with a stunning second consecutive European Cup win. Under Kovacs, gifted players such as Cruyff, Keizer, and the booming attacking midfielder Johan Neeskens were given free rein to improvise, using an offensively-oriented *catenaccio* with an attacking sweeper as a basic approach. In the 1971-72 European Cup, Ajax eliminated Dynamo Dresden, Olympique Marseille, Arsenal, and Benfica to gain the final against Internazionale of Milan. Kovacs' tactical approach, which he called "total football," captured the imagination of European soccer, and Ajax appeared to reach the pinnacle of sophistication in its 2-0 defeat of Inter in the 1972 final. Both goals were scored by the incomparable Cruyff. The following season, Ajax became the first club since Real Madrid in the late 1950s to win three European Cups in succession, winning the 1972-73 final over Italy's Juventus, 1-0, in a solid though never brilliant performance led by the new right wing Johnny Rep. In the quarter and semi-finals, Ajax had beaten two of the strongest teams in Europe, Bayern München and Real Madrid.

In the 1973 off-season, Cruyff left to join Michels at Barcelona, and Ajax began to decline, despite the continued presence of Neeskens, Rep, and midfielder (later sweeper) Arie Haan. While in the previous season Ajax broke goalscoring records in winning its record sixteenth Dutch championship, it failed to win at all in 1974, and after the departure of Kovacs to France the team became more defensive and less successful. During its heyday, however, Ajax fed many players to the great Dutch national team of the 1970s and inspired the adoption of "total football" throughout northern and western Europe. In hindsight, Ajax now appears to have been the impetus for Europe to remove itself from the dark ages of Italian-styled *catenaccio* and enter the present era of more fluid, attacking styles.

Albania

Fédération Albanaise de Football
Rruga Kongresi I Permetit Nr. 41
Tirana

Founded: 1932
FIFA: 1932
UEFA: 1954

Affiliated clubs: *33;* **registered players:** *4,070:* **national stadium:** *Qemal Stafa, Tirana (24,000);* **largest stadium:** *Qemal Stafa;* **colors:** *red jerseys, black shorts;* **season:** *September to June;* **honors:** *Balkan Cup (1946).*

The very fact of Albania's participation in European soccer, sporadic though it has been, is the most intriguing aspect of the Albanian game. In recent years, soccer has provided most of the fleeting glimpses that western countries have had of this barricaded Balkan state. It is without doubt the odd man out in Europe, but certain periods in the growth of Albanian soccer have revealed a serious national interest in the sport.

Soccer was introduced in Albania at the turn of the century by a variety of foreign residents, but Albanians themselves played the game very little before World War I. As in other parts of the Ottoman Empire, their Turkish rulers discouraged it for political reasons, and it was left to foreign residents in Tirana to form the first league around 1909. Albanians did not participate in the league, nor were they members of its affiliated clubs. With the demise of Ottoman rule in 1912, the new principality was ravaged by war and anarchy, and again the game was not able to gain a foothold.

At the close of World War I, however, occupation forces, especially the British, revived interest, and Albanians quickly took to soccer and other sports as they shook off the legacy of Turkish domination. During the 1920s the game spread rapidly. With the accession to power of King Zog in the coup of 1928, organized sport became a facet of government policy, and the Djelmenija Shqiptare (Albanian Football Section) was founded in 1932, two years after the formation of an umbrella body Federata Sportive Shqiptare. The local leagues that had sprung up during the 1920s were structured into a national league, and a leading club, SC Tirana, emerged to dominate the next decade. Plans were made to enter the qualifying rounds of the 1938 World Cup, and for a while it seemed Albanian soccer was on the verge of entering the mainstream of Europe. Administrative difficulties, however, beset the league after 1936, and all hope of progress was ended by the Italian occupation in 1939. Until the end of World War II the game stagnated in a state of disarray with Albania yet to make its international debut.

The People's Democracy, established in 1946, immediately set out to put the game on a firm footing, and had as its motivating force a new community of neighbors in the Balkan region. As host of the 1946 Balkan Cup, the Albanian national team finished on top of the standings, despite a 3-2 loss to Yugoslavia, with wins over Bulgaria (3-1) and Rumania (1-0). This was Albania's first foray into international competition, and it remains to date its only high placing in an international tournament. Between 1947 and 1953, Albania regularly played against all the nations of Eastern Europe other than the USSR, gaining victories over Rumania, Bulgaria, Poland, and Czechoslovakia twice, while drawing five and losing nine during the same period. The relative progress of Albania's development, however, was put into perspective in 1950 when mighty Hungary won by 12-0 in Budapest on 5 goals from Puskas, and lowly Rumania crushed Albania 6-0 in Bucharest two weeks later. There must have been some consolation in its two wins over the powerful Czechs in 1952, but by the mid-1950s, Albania had begun its long, self-conscious exile.

On the field, a pattern of defensive play had already become characteristic of the Albanians (against the Czechs for example), and the few existing western accounts of domestic competition points to this as well. In 22 internationals before 1954, Albania scored only 21 goals. Indeed, this characteristic has remained, as only 19 Albanian goals have resulted in the 27 internationals *since* 1954. The most prolific Albanian international of all time, Panajotis Panou, has scored only 11 times in his record number of 40 international appearances.

From 1954 to the early 1960s, Albania remained almost totally isolated from international competition, although there was one game with the German Democratic Republic in 1958 at Tirana (1-1), and a selection from the People's Republic of China visited Tirana as early as 1961. In 1965, it made its first attempt to qualify for the World Cup, but its hard, defensive tactics were badly received, and in 1967 Albania's application for the next World Cup qualifying round was filed too late. A surprising breakthrough, however, occurred in 1962 when the national association entered its champion club, Partizan Tirana, in the European Cup, and its national team in the European Nations' Cup. Partizan lost in the first round to IFK Norrköping of Sweden, and western observers who traveled to Tirana for Partizan's home leg complained of rough tactics on the field and hostile crowd behavior. Albanian champion clubs went on to enter three successive European Cup competitions.

In the Nations' Cup of 1962-64, first round opponent Greece refused to play them, and in the second round Denmark won by 4-1 on aggregate. Its 4-0 loss in Copenhagen was the first Albanian international ever played in Western Europe. In the next Nations' Cup (1966-68), then renamed the European Football Championship, Albania entered for a second time, grouped with Germany FR and Yugoslavia. It managed to draw 0-0 in its home leg against the West Germans, its most surprising result ever, but finished at the bottom of its group. In the 1970-72 edition of the European Football Championship, it was grouped with Germany FR, Poland, and Turkey, but again finished last. Once more, the national association pulled back, and in 1974 Albania was the only member-nation of UEFA that did not enter the European Football Championship. In 1975, the national team made its first known visit to Africa and lost by 4-2 to Algeria in Algiers. In 1976, Albania participated in the revitalized Balkan Cup, and placed third in a field of five with a draw against powerful Yugoslavia and a sound defeat of Bulgaria. Albania's cumulative international record (1946-76) now stands at 50-11-9-30-40-109-31, eight of its victories occurring before 1954.

The structure of the national league's first division is similar to that of Switzerland and several countries in South America. The championship has two phases. In the first, all 12 clubs meet each other on a home and away basis until a total of 22 matches have been played by each club. The top six clubs of the first phase form Group A of the second phase to determine the national champion, all clubs meeting once again on a home and away basis. The bottom six clubs from the first phase form a Group B and play each other on a home and away basis, and the bottom club in Group B is relegated from the first division. In both groups, points from the first phase are accumulated with points from the second phase to determine the final standings.

The first division currently includes four clubs from the capital city of Tirana (Dinamo, Partizan, 17. Nendori, and Shkendija); one each from Shkoder in the north (Vllaznia); Durres on the Adriatic coast (Lokomotiva); Gjirokaster (Luftetari), Korce (Skenderbeu), and Vlore (Flamurtari), all in the south; Kavaje (Besa) and Lushnje (Traktori), in the central lowlands; and Elbasan (Labinoti), in the central highlands. By far the most successful postwar clubs have been Dinamo, the team of the Ministry of Internal Affairs (police, security, etc.), and Partizan, the army team. The leading prewar club, SC Tirana, was disbanded in the mid-1940s. A cup competition for all affiliated clubs of the upper and lower divisions was introduced in 1968. The national association is under the tutelage of the Committee for Culture and Physical Sport (Komitetit Kultures Fizike Sporteve te Republikes Popullore te Shqiperise).

Champions

1930	SC Tirana	1942	no competition	1954	Partizan Tirana
1931	SC Tirana	1943	no competition	1955	Dinamo Tirana
1932	SC Tirana	1944	no competition	1956	Dinamo Tirana
1933	Scanderbeu Korca	1945	Vllaznia	1957	Partizan Tirana
1934	SC Tirana	1946	Vllaznia	1958	Partizan Tirana
1935	no competition	1947	Partizan Tirana	1959	Partizan Tirana
1936	SC Tirana	1948	Partizan Tirana	1960	Dinamo Tirana
1937	no competition	1949	Partizan Tirana	1961	Partizan Tirana
1938	no competition	1950	Dinamo Tirana	1962	no competition
1939	no competition	1951	Dinamo Tirana	1963	Dinamo Tirana
1940	no competition	1952	Dinamo Tirana	1964	Partizan Tirana
1941	no competition	1953	Dinamo Tirana	1965	17. Nendori Tirana

1966 17. Nendori Tirana	1970 17. Nendori Tirana	1974 Vllaznia
1967 Dinamo Tirana	1971 Partizan Tirana	1975 Dinamo Tirana
1968 17. Nendori Tirana	1972 Vllaznia	1976 Dinamo Tirana
1969 17. Nendori Tirana	1973 Dinamo Tirana	1977 Dinamo Tirana

Cup Winners

1948 Partizan Tirana	1958 Partizan Tirana	1968 17. Nendori Tirana
1949 Partizan Tirana	1959 no competition	1969 17. Nendori Tirana
1950 Dinamo Tirana	1960 Dinamo Tirana	1970 17. Nendori Tirana
1951 Dinamo Tirana	1961 Partizan Tirana	1971 Partizan Tirana
1952 Dinamo Tirana	1962 no competition	1972 FC Besa
1953 Dinamo Tirana	1963 17. Nendori Tirana	1973 Dinamo Tirana
1954 Dinamo Tirana	1964 Partizan Tirana	1974 Dinamo Tirana
1955 no competition	1965 Dinamo Tirana	1975 Dinamo Tirana
1956 no competition	1966 Dinamo Tirana	1976 17. Nendori Tirana
1957 Partizan Tirana	1967 Dinamo Tirana	1977 17. Nendori Tirana

Alcock, Charles William   (1842-1907)

The outstanding figure to emerge from the earliest years of modern soccer, who influenced nearly every aspect of the game. Immediately upon his graduation from the Harrow School in 1859, he and other Old Harrovians (Harrow graduates), including his brother, J.F. Alcock, founded the Forest Football Club, the first organization devoted exclusively to playing the "dribbling game" (the precursor of soccer as we know it). C. W. Alcock became Forest's chief spokesman and guiding force. He was one of the founding members of The Football Association in 1863, and helped to draft the first Laws of the Game. When Forest was disbanded in 1864, Alcock reorganized his club as Wanderers F.C., serving as its captain and spokesman. He was elected to the Executive Committee of The Football Association in 1866, and four years later became its honorary secreaty.

As captain of Wanderers, the greatest club of its day, Alcock became the prime mover of soccer's first tactical plan: the adoption of dribbling as the most effective way to advance the ball. He expounded widely and passionately on the virtues of dribbling, and argued that it alone represented pure soccer, as distinct from the rugby or "handling" game developed at the same time. This position held sway for over 10 years, and the dribbling Wanderers dominated English soccer until Scottish passing techniques took over in the late 1870s. Alcock himself took the field on the forward line as often as he could, and played for England once in 1875.

By 1870, Alcock had become the game's most important historian and commentator. His famous *Football Annual* was first published in 1869, and he continued to write important books and articles on soccer until his death. As honorary secretary of The Football Association, he was the chief instigator of The Football Association Challenge Cup (F.A. Cup), which was launched in 1871 and was the world's first organized competition. He also initiated the first internationals between England and Scotland in 1870—hence his designation as "the father of international football"—and he was England's first unofficial captain as well. In the early 1880s, he was instrumental in drafting the earliest legislation on professionalism, which he himself supported. In 1887 Alcock became secretary of The Football Association, a post he held until 1895, when he settled into the largely honorary position of F.A. vice president. He was also an avid devotee of cricket, as were many of the early soccer personalities, and served as secretary of the prominent Surrey County Cricket Club from 1872-1907.

Algeria

Fédération Algérienne de Football
4, rue Emir Abdeldrim El Khattabi
Alger

Founded: 1962
FIFA: 1963
CAF: 1964

Affiliated clubs: *723;* **registered players:** *39,033;* **national stadium:** *Stade Olympique d'Alger, Chéraga (80,000);* **largest stadium:** *Stade Olympique d'Alger;* **colors:** *green jerseys, white shorts;* **season:** *September to June;* **honors:** *Mouloudia, African Cup of Champion Clubs (1976).*

Among the Arab nations of North Africa, Algeria has been only modestly successful in the face of more stringent opposition from Egypt, Sudan, and even Tunisia and Morocco, but the game has been well established since World War I.

French colonists and workers introduced the game in Algiers and Oran at least as far back as the 1890s. As was the custom in colonial Africa, regional football associations were formed in the key population areas. They remained in existence until a national association could be formed at the time of independence. Each Algerian association was affiliated with the Fédération Française de Football. The Ligue d'Alger was founded in 1918, and a championship of the Algiers district was introduced in 1920. The early years were dominated by FC Blidéen, which won the first four titles in succession, but in time other important clubs emerged: AS Boufarikoise, Gallia Sports, Racing Universitaire, AS Ste-Eugene, and Olympique d'Hussein-Dey. By the late 1940s, there were four divisions in the Algiers league, and at its height 125 clubs were affiliated.

The Ligue Oranaise de Football Association was founded at Oran in the western part of present-day Algeria in 1920, and its championship was introduced the same year. The first champion was A.S.M.O., but the league was eventually dominated by S.C.B.A. during the 1920s, C.D.J. in the 1930s, and U.S.M.O. in the 1940s. As in Algiers, a championship was held every year until independence, with the exception of 1939.

The game in the eastern part of present-day Algeria was centered in Constantine. The Ligue Constantinoise de Football Association was founded in 1922, and a championship began the same year. The first successful club to emerge was US Constantinoise, but during the 1930s, JS Guelmoise was the only club to win three titles in succession. After that there were few perennial winners. The league was suspended from 1940-44 as the war in North Africa raged nearby. Eventually over 120 clubs became affiliated with the Constantine league.

In addition to these local competitions, an annual series of Inter-League matches developed between Constantine and Tunis (1931), Algiers and Tunis (1932), and Constantine and Algiers (1949). During the late 1930s and '40s, Algiers participated in the Constantine-Tunis series, and in its own series with Tunis it was victorious on all but a few occasions. These precursors to international competition are the only measures available by which the relative level of play among the regional selections of French North Africa can be determined. On the club level, however, one can turn to the North African Championship, which dates from 1919, and the North African Cup, which dates from 1930. Both competitions were played by clubs from Algeria, Tunisia, and Morocco, and were won primarily by teams from Algiers, Oran, and Constantine.

The national Fédération Algérienne de Football was founded in 1962, the year of Algeria's independence, and joined FIFA and the African Football Confederation almost immediately. The association is also a member of the North African Magreb Confederation. Algeria's inclusion in the mainstream of African soccer, however, was slow in coming. It has advanced only once to the final rounds of the African Nation's Cup—in 1968 at Addis Ababa—and was disappointed to place third in its group of four. Despite Algeria's 4-0 trouncing of Uganda, the elegant Ivory Coast eleven outwitted the Algerian defense and won decisively, 3-0. Four days later a 3-1 loss to Ethiopia before a clamorous partisan crowd was blemished by rough tactics and two ejections, and Algeria was eliminated.

Algeria's first real international breakthrough was on the club level. In 1976, Mouloudia Chalia, the first Algerian club to enter either of the African club cups, won the African Champions' Cup by defeating the defending champions, Hafia of Guinea. After splitting home and away legs, 0-3 and 3-0, the winner was decided on penalty kicks. Among Mouloudia's difficult opposition in the earlier rounds was the famous Nigerian club Rangers,

runner-up to Hafia the previous year.,

Shortly after independence an Algerian national league was established. The First Division of 14 members now includes clubs from Algiers, Oran, Constantine, Sétif, Batna, Guelma, and the Algiers suburb El Harrach. The Oran derby, M.C. vs. R.C.G., attracts 30,000 spectators twice each year, and the great Olympic Stadium in Algiers is generally thought to be the best facility in Africa.

Alpine Cup

Coupe des Alpes—Coppa delle Alpi.

A summer (i.e., off-season) tournament for clubs of the Alpine region, it was introduced in 1960 as the Coppa Alpi Italo-Svizzera, and Italy and Switzerland were the only participants. France and West Germany entered clubs in succeeding years, but the four together have never competed in the same year. The format has varied enormously; at present, it is played on a home and away basis with the winners of two groups meeting in a final.

In 1960 and 1961, when only Italian and Swiss clubs were entered, the country whose teams had accumulated the most points was

awarded the cup. From 1963 on, the trophy was given to a winning club. French clubs entered for the first time in 1963, but only Italy and Switzerland returned in 1964. The tournament was suspended altogether in 1965. Italy and Switzerland reactivated the series in 1966, and West German clubs were entered from 1967 to 1969. Only Italy and Switzerland participated again in 1970 and 1971. In 1972, the Italians withdrew once again, never to return, and the French stepped in. The trophy has remained solely in the hands of the Swiss and French ever since.

Winners

1960	Italy		1970	FC Basel (Swi)
1961	Italy		1971	Lazio (Ita)
1962	Genoa (Ita)		1972	Nimes (Fra)
1963	Juventus (Ita)		1973	Servette (Swi)
1964	Genoa (Ita)		1974	Young Boys Berne (Swi)
1965	no competition		1975	Servette (Swi)
1966	Napoli (Ita)		1976	Servette (Swi)
1967	Eintracht Frankfurt (GFR)		1977	Stade de Reims (Fra)
1968	Schalke 04 (GFR)		1978	Servette (Swi)
1969	FC Basel (Swi)			

amateur

Ninety-seven percent of all the world's adult registered players are officially amateur in status, and two-thirds of FIFA's national membership remains exclusively amateur. The definition of an amateur, however, has been stretched considerably since the days when it simply meant "one who receives no

compensation for playing." The present defintion, according to FIFA regulations, is as follows:

Players who have been refunded their actual expenses for travel, necessary maintenance and hotel charges and who, in special cases, have been specifically authorized by their national association to receive expenses for equipment, physical preparation and insurance against accidents during play and whilst travelling [or those] who receive an allowance for wages lost [providing] such allowance . . . be an equitable proportion of the actual wages of the player which have been lost . . . are considered to be amateur players.

Players who receive no compensation whatsoever are still amateur (though FIFA neglects to mention this), as are all players whose compensation is less than that which is outlined in the definition.

The FIFA members that remain officially and exclusively amateur are: Algeria, Benin, Burundi, Cameroon, Congo, Egypt, Ethiopia, Gabon, Gambia, Ghana, Guinea, Ivory Coast, Kenya, Lesotho, Liberia, Libya, Madagascar, Mali, Mauritania, Mauritius, Morocco, Niger, Nigeria, Senegal, Sierra Leone, Sudan, Tanzania, Togo, Tunisia, Uganda, Upper Volta, Zaire, Antigua, Bahamas, Barbados, Bermuda, Cuba, Dominican Republic, Guyana, Haiti, Jamaica, Netherlands Antilles, Nicaragua, Panama, Puerto Rico, Surinam, Trinidad, Afghanistan, Bahrain, Brunei, Burma, China National, India, Indonesia, Iran, Iraq, Israel, Japan, Jordan, Khmer, Korea DPR, Korea Republic, Kuwait, Laos, Lebanon, Malaysia, Nepal, Pakistan, Philippines, Qatar, Saudi Arabia, Singapore, Sri Lanka, Syria, Thailand, United Arab Emirates, Vietnam DR, Yemen PDR, Albania, Bulgaria, Cyprus, Czechoslovakia, Finland, German DR, Hungary, Luxembourg, Norway, Poland, Rumania, USSR, Fiji, and Papua-New Guinea.

Few controversial issues have dogged soccer authorities so mercilessly as that of amateurism. From the 1870s, when the question of professionals was first raised, until the 1920s, when professionalism began to spread in Europe, the issue was primarily confined to Great Britain, especially England and Scotland. In Victorian England, the amateur ideal was an important element of the sporting gentlemen's mystique, and men from the leisurely classes who had given birth to modern soccer jealously guarded the ideal. In 1885, professionalism was finally sanctioned by The Football Association in London, and the game slowly but steadily became dominated by the working classes whose only hope of full participation in the game depended on professional status. The ama-

teurs, for the most part upper-class public school graduates and middle-class professionals, retreated into collective self-preservation. Still under The Football Association banner, some amateur clubs organized the F.A. Amateur Cup in 1893-94, the first exclusively amateur competition in a professional environment.

In 1907, The Football Association ordered all county associations (still bastions of the amateur ideal) to admit professional clubs, but the Surrey and Middlesex associations refused and led a movement to sever amateur soccer interests in England from The Football Association. Thus the Amateur Football Association was formed. This was the world's first all-amateur body, but its split with the F.A. lasted only until 1914, when it agreed to come under the F.A.'s aegis. As an entity, the Amateur Football Association remained intact, changing its name in 1934 to the Amateur Football Alliance, but in 1974 the F.A. Amateur Cup was discontinued when the F.A. decided not to differentiate between amateur and professional status in the future, citing the impossibility of distinguishing one from the other.

After World War I, the question arose on an international scale as professional clubs emerged in the republics of Western and Central Europe. Attention was focused on the Olympics, where the Victorian ideal was further represented by French as well as British administrators. The central issue now was that of "broken-time payments" (compensation for time lost from work). FIFA coerced the International Olympic Committee into accepting players who had received broken-time payments in the 1924 games, and Great Britain and Denmark boycotted the proceedings in protest. In 1928, when FIFA persisted, the four British football associations withdrew from FIFA altogether and did not rejoin until 1946. FIFA prevailed, and IOC resistance to broken-time payments for Olympic athletes slowly subsided over the years.

After World War II, the issue still centered on the Olympics, but the geographical focus switched to Eastern Europe, where professionalism was not officially recognized by doctrinaire regimes. The fact remained, however, that top Eastern European players were "state-sponsored," and devoted as much time to the game as did professionals in other countries. Furthermore, several Eastern-bloc states fielded virtually the same national teams for both Olympic and World Cup competition, and since 1952 the Olympic gold medal in soccer has been won each time by an East European entrant. The world, especially Western Europe, protested and a solution to the problem has not yet been found. One step in that direction was taken in 1978, however, when FIFA announced that in the future a player could not participate in both the Olympic Games and World Cup during the course of his career.

América, Copa   See: **Sudamericana, Copa**

Anderlechtois, Royal Sporting Club

Location: *Brussels, Belgium;* stadium: *Parc Astrid (38,000);* colors: *mauve jerseys, white shorts;* honors: *Super Cup (1976, 1978), European Cup Winners' Cup (1976, 1978), Belgian champion (1947, 1949, 1950, 1951, 1954, 1955, 1956, 1959, 1962, 1964, 1965, 1966, 1967, 1968, 1972, 1974), Belgian cup winner (1965, 1972, 1973, 1975, 1976).*

Founded 1908 as Sporting Club in the western Brussels suburb of Anderlecht, the club did not enter the Belgian league until 1919 with a two year stint in the second division. It won its first promotion in 1921, and after floundering in the second and third divisions in the early 1930s, gained promotion to the first division again in 1935, and has stayed there ever since. The title "Royal" was acquired in 1933. Just as Union Saint-Gilloise dominated Belgian soccer until World War II, RSC Anderlecht has reigned over the Belgian game since the war. All the greatest Belgian players of the postwar era have been on its rosters, and it has long surpassed Union Saint-Gilloise in winning a record number of Belgian championships.

Anderlecht became an important Belgian club under English coach Bill Gormlie, who guided it from 1949-59. He also coached the Belgian national team from 1949-52, and started his tenure at Anderlecht by winning three successive league titles. Despite its growing power in Belgium, the club failed to do well in European competition during the 1950s, and in 1956 lost to Manchester United in the European Cup preliminary round by a score of 10-0. The spearhead of Gormlie's Anderlecht squad was center forward Jef Mermans, the greatest Belgian player since the pre-World War I era. In 1960, Gormlie was succeeded by Frenchman Pierre Sinibaldi, formerly of Reims, who built up another generation of players—Anderlecht had a policy of harnessing local talent until the rise of professionalism in the 1970s—around goalscorer Paul van Himst and inside forward and midfielder Josef Jurion. This team won another championship in 1962 and five in a row from 1964-68, but made little impact in the European Cup. In 1969-70, Anderlecht reached the final of the Fairs Cup, having eliminated Newcastle United and Inter Milan, and lost to Arsenal in the final by an aggregate of 4-3.

In 1971, Sparta Rotterdam coach George Kessler became the manager, and after a shaky start he led the club to a league-cup double in his first year. The home-grown feel of the team began to change under Kessler, and top foreign players soon emerged in the lineup, none greater than the Dutch left winger Rob Rensenbrink. Anderlecht established itself as the best cup fighters in the country with four Belgian cup wins from 1972-76, and behind the genius of Rensenbrink won its first European trophy in 1975-76, the European Cup Winners' Cup, with a convincing win in the final over England's West Ham United. In 1976-77, Anderlecht reached the Cup Winners' Cup final again, losing this time to Hamburger SV, but the following year it won the trophy again with a second round win over Hamburger SV and an overpowering defeat of FK Austria in the final. Sadly, Anderlecht's first great European triumph came in 1976 one year after Paul van Himst, the idol of Belgian soccer, retired.

Andorra

There are two clubs in the Principality of Andorra, CF Andorra and FC Pena Blaugrana, both of which are affiliated to the Federación Catalana, Provincia de Lérida, Spain. CF Andorra competes in the first category of the Federación Catalana. The principality does not support a national association and is therefore not separately affiliated to either UEFA or FIFA.

Andrade, José Leandro   (1901-1957)

The famous right half of Uruguay during its golden era of the 1920s, who had the ball juggling skills of the greatest center forwards. He was an idol with his fellow countrymen, and commanded universal respect among both South American and European players. Andrade started with Bella Vista, the small Montevideo club, but soon moved to mighty Nacional, and when the 1924 Olympic Games opened in Paris, he was already a star with his national team. He was instrumental in Uruguay's winning of the gold medal, and in 1925, he was one of the standouts in the Nacional team that toured Europe so successfully, having played a major role in his club's three Uruguayan championships in succession from 1922-24. With his great teammate and captain, José Nasazzi, he inspired the legendary goalscoring forwards of both club and country for many years. Andrade starred in Uruguay's South American Championship triumphs of 1923, 1924, and 1926, and Uruguay's second gold medal win at the 1928 Olympic Games. After retiring from the national team he was recalled for the first World Cup in 1930, and he dazzled his opponents again, renewing his international stardom with his agility and keen sense of positioning. He finally retired from the game in 1933, but his nephew, Victor Rodriguez Andrade, carried on the famous name as a star for Uruguay in the 1950 World Cup.

Anglo-Italian Cup

Torneo Anglo-Italiano.
An occasional home and away series between invited clubs of The Football League in England and the Lega Nazionale Professionisti in Italy. In 1975 and 1976, the participants were respective F.A. Cup winners in both countries.

Winners

1970	Swindon Town	1974	no competition
1971	Blackpool	1975	Fiorentina
1972	Roma	1976	Napoli
1973	Newcastle United		

Anglo-Italian League Cup Winners' Cup

Coppa di Lega Italo-Inglese.
A suspended home and away series between the winners of The Football League Cup in England and the Coppa Italia, instigated by the

English league primarily as compensation for third division Swindon Town being ineligible for the Fairs Cup.

Winners

1969   Swindon Town
1970   Bologna
1971   Tottenham Hotspur

Anglo-Scottish Cup

Known for many years as the Texaco Cup, this series was originally open to invited first division members of the English, Scottish, and Northern Irish leagues that placed well in the previous season, but failed to qualify for the major European competitions. In recent years, however, only members of The Football League and the Scottish Football League have participated, and the series was given its present name. It remains the only competition in which English and Scottish clubs compete on a regular basis. The final rounds are preceded by a qualification round under a league system of up to 16 clubs from either country. The final rounds are played on a home and away basis (excepting the 1974 final). Each winner has been English, and since 1973, all finalists have been English. Heart of Midlothian and Airdrie, both Scottish clubs, gained the finals in 1971 and 1972.

Winners

1971   Wolverhampton Wanderers
1972   Derby County
1973   Ipswich Town
1974   Newcastle United

1975   Newcastle United
1976   Middlesbrough
1977   Nottingham Forest

Angola

Angola has not been active in international competition, but a league flourished under Portuguese colonization for many years. The Liga de Football de Luanda was founded in 1922, and in 1931 changed its name to the Associação de Futebol de Luanda. It became affliated with Portugal in 1932, a relationship that lasted until civil war intensified in 1974. While not yet a member of FIFA or the African Football Confederation, Angola's entrance into the African ranks is forthcoming. The most established clubs are Sporting Clube, Futebol Clube, Club Atlético, Clube Ferroviário, and Sport Luanda e Benfica, all of Luanda.

Antigua

Antigua Football Association
P.O. Box 773
St. John's

Founded: 1967
FIFA: 1970

Affiliated clubs: 42; **registered players:** *644;* **national stadium:** *Antigua Recreation Ground, St. John's (30,000);* **largest stadium:** *Antigua Recreation Ground;* **colors:** *gold jerseys, black shorts;* **season:** *August to December;* **honors:** *none.*

Little is recorded of the game in Antigua, a self-governing British possession in the Leeward Islands of the British West Indies. The Antigua Amateur Football Association became affiliated with The Football Association in London before World War II, and in 1967 sought and gained permission from FIFA to reconstitute its national association as an independent body. In 1972, Antigua attempted to qualify for the World Cup in West Germany, but unfortunately compiled the worst record of any entrant in the CONCACAF region. In four matches against Trinidad and Surinam, it was winless and managed to score only three goals against the oppositions' 22, including an 11-1 thrashing by Trinidad. Antigua did not attempt to qualify for the 1978 World Cup, and there is no record of its having participated in any regional competitions of CONCACAF, either at national or club level. The island's population numbers a mere 70,000, many of whom play cricket.

The Antigua Football Association sponsors a national championship and a national cup competition. There are 26 senior clubs, six of which participate in the first division.

appeal

The modern Laws of the Game severely restrict players from approaching the referee and claiming that a foul be recognized or a decision changed. Before 1896, the year referees were given the power to penalize players, a foul was called and a punishment issued only if one of the offended team appealed to the referee to do so; the referee ignored the foul if no appeal was made. From 1896, a player's right to appeal was still guaranteed, but the former significance of the appeal was lost. Gradually, appeals began to take the form of protests against referees' decisions, creating an increasing number of ugly scenes on the field. In 1924, this situation finally prompted the International Football Association Board to rule that informal inquiries of a referee's decision were allowed, but a player's inherent right to appeal no longer existed and dissent in any form would be regarded as an infringement of the Laws. In 1935, this concept was incorporated directly into the Laws, and is now found in the form of Law XII's dissent clause.

aqsaqtuk

An indigenous football game of the Eskimos in Canada and Alaska, which closely resembles soccer. The exact date of origin is unknown, but aqsaqtuk has been played for at least a few hundred years. Contested on snow or ice by two large teams of varying numbers, the object of the game is to keep the ball away from one's own goal. The size of the two goals vary and are usually spotted many hundreds of yards apart. One Alaskan legend recounts a game played between two villages with goals ten miles from one another. A basically defensive posture seems a necessity over such a large expanse.

Balls are stuffed with moss, grass, or caribou hair. Some smaller balls are filled with sand. Men and women play together, and teams are sometimes divided between married and single people. At other times, sides are arbitrarily chosen, and games may be played between two villages or groups of villages.

Aqsaqtuk, the Eskimo football game, as depicted by Baffin Island artist Tye.

Arab Football Confederation

See: **Union of Arab Football Associations**

Arabian Gulf Football Tournament

The major regional tournament for national teams of the Arabian (Persian) Gulf countries. It has acquired a new significance since the mid-1970s, when many of the oil-producing states of the region stepped up their efforts to develop competitive teams and enter the mainstream of international competition. Kuwait, however, has emerged the undisputed leader. Iran, a non-Arab country, has not participated. The series is played on a league basis in a host country.

Final Standings

1970 (in Bahrain) 1. Kuwait 2. Bahrain 3. Saudi Arabia 4. Qatar
1972 (in Riyadh) 1. Kuwait 2. Saudi Arabia 3. Bahrain 4. Qatar 5. United Arab Emirates
1974 (Details incomplete)
1976 (in Doha) 1. Kuwait 2. Iraq 3. Qatar 4. Saudi Arabia 5. Bahrain 6. Oman 7. United Arab Emirates

Argentina

Asociación del Fútbol Argentino
Viamonte 1366/76
1053 Buenos Aires

Founded: 1893
FIFA: 1912
CONMEBOL: 1916

Affiliated clubs: 2,647; **registered players:** 224,166 (2,064 professional, 52,450 non-amateur); **national stadium:** none; **largest stadium:** Estadio River Plate, Buenos Aires (100,000); **colors:** sky blue and white striped jerseys, black shorts; **season:** March to December; **honors:** World Cup winner (1978), runner-up (1930), Olympic runner-up (1928), South American Championship winner (1921, 1925, 1927, 1929, 1937, 1941, 1945, 1946, 1947, 1955, 1957, 1959), runner-up (1916, 1917, 1920, 1923, 1924, 1926, 1935, 1942, 1959, 1967), Independiente, Intercontinental Cup (1973), Copa Libertadores (1964, 1965, 1972, 1973, 1974, 1975), Copa Interamericana (1972, 1974, 1976), Estudiantes, Intercontinental Cup (1968), Copa Libertadores (1968, 1969, 1970), Copa Interamericana (1968), Rácing Club, Intercontinental Cup (1967), Copa Libertadores (1967), Boca Júniors, Intercontinental Cup (1977), Copa Libertadores (1977, 1978).

Argentina is the birthplace of soccer in South America, and for 50 years has been one of the world's leading soccer powers. South America's first club, first league competition, and first national governing body were all Argentine. The first international matches played in South America, both at the club and national levels, involved Argentine teams. Argentina, in fact, was the first independent nation outside Europe to fully develop the game. With its long and proud soccer playing heritage, it has consistently produced superbly skilled players since the 1910s, and though many of these have been lost to wealthy clubs abroad, a flood of excellent players has always seemed to take their place.

The national teams of Argentina have dominated South American competition since the beginning, even at the expense of mighty Brazil (one-fourth of all Brazil's losses have been to Argentina), and Argentine clubs have stood out decisively in the Copa Libertadores. Yet, Argentina repeatedly failed to live up to its potential and win the highest honors in world competition until it finally captured the World Cup in 1978 before its own fans in Buenos Aires. Between its amateur golden era during the 1920s and that emotionally charged triumph, Argentina was an utter disappointment, and its international reputation for intimidating behavior on the field overshadowed the genuine skill of so many of its players.

Soccer was first played in Argentina (and

South America for that matter) along the Rio de la Plata by British sailors and maritime workers in the early 1860s. In 1867, the Buenos Aires Football Club, the first of its kind in Latin America, was founded by members of the five-year-old Buenos Aires Cricket Club, most of whom were British railroad workers. Some difficulties arose in securing permission from Cricket Club authorities to organize the team, and further permission had to be granted (again with difficulty) to play on club grounds, but the aspiring footballers prevailed, and members organized games among themselves, one side wearing red caps, the other side white.

By 1880, an active league of British teams was under way in Buenos Aires, and among the active participants was Buenos Aires F.C. Alexander Hutton, the director of the English High School, took an interest in the league, and helped form teams among other British groups and organizations in the area. British railroad workers, who also played a leading role in spreading the game, founded Quilmes F.C. in the Buenos Aires suburb of the same name in 1887 and Rosario Central F.C. in the big Rio Parana city of Rosario in 1889. These two are now the oldest clubs in Argentina.

The cultural homogeneity of Argentine life during this period helped to speed up the assimilation of soccer into the activities of working class people, nearly all of whom had European backgrounds. This was in marked contrast to Brazil's multiracial society, in which Afro-Brazilians confronted racial impediments on the playing field until the 1920s. In Argentina, soccer was relatively free to make its way through all strata of a racially unified society. This process was well under way by the 1880s, despite the domination of organized competition by the British, and accounts for Argentina's early rise to the top of South American soccer. The situation in Uruguay was quite similar.

The presence of the British with their administrative and organizational knowhow was also central to Argentina's rapid development on the playing fields. (The overall British presence in Argentina during the nineteenth century was more pervasive than in any other noncolonized country in the world.) In 1891, Alexander Hutton founded the Argentine Association Football League, an expanded official version of his Buenos Aires league, but it failed and a championship was not completed. In 1893, the league was reconstituted as the Argentine Football Association under Hutton, and a championship was introduced simultaneously. This was to be the forerunner of Argentina's present first division, the Campeonato Metropolitano, and the first official league competition in South America. It was dominated for 20 years by British Clubs: Lomas Academicals won the first six titles in a row and Alumni F.C., the team of former English High School players and the most popular club of its day, won nine titles beginning in 1901.

Dozens of important clubs were founded in the 1890s and immediately after 1900, including Buenos Aires' "big five": C.A. Ríver Plate (1901), Rácing Club (1903), C. A. Boca Júniors (19050, C. A. Independiente (1905), and C.A. San Lorenzo. Ríver Plate and Independiente were formed by British players, and Rácing Club was founded by French residents and *porteños* (Argentine-born but of European extraction). Boca Júniors was founded in the main by Italians, and its formation stands out as an important harbinger in the history of Argentine soccer. After the turn of the century, British players and officials in the front ranks were gradually replaced by Euopean immigrants who poured into Argentina by the millions. The Italians became especially prominent, and it was largely through the Italian community that Argentine soccer advanced so rapidly between 1900 and 1930.

In 1902, the English baron Sir Thomas Lipton donated a trophy to the Argentine Football Association, and this prompted the introduction in 1905 of the Lipton Cup (Argentina vs. Uruguay), the first regularlq scheduled international competition outside the British Isles. The first match in Buenos Aires—resulting in a scoreless draw—was also the international debut of both countries and the beginning of international competition in South America. In 1906, Argentina and Uruguay started a second international series, the Newton Cup, and for almost 25 years these two competitions were played on an annual basis. A third and fourth trophies were added in 1908 (Trophy of the Argentine Ministry of Education) and 1911 (Trophy of the Uruguayan Ministry of Education), but these ceased to exist in 1919 and 1923, respectively. Between 1905 and 1910, Argentina and Uruguay competed 16 times, Argentina winning nine and losing three.

In 1910, Argentina found its second international opponent, Chile, when the Argentine F.A. organized a three-way unofficial South American Championship in Buenos Aires. Argentina was the nominal winner after defeating Uruguay and Chile by an aggregate of 8-1. For the next six years, Argentina's schedule was prolific, but it was again limited to Uruguay. Between 1910 and he first South American Championship in 1916, the two countries played one another 21 times, and the results were an even nine games won for either side, a marked improvement for Uruguay. In 1912, the governing body cast off its anglicized name and became known as the Asociación Argentina de Football (AAF); earlier in the year it had become the first South American association to join FIFA. In the first of many organizational upheavals, an outlaw league was formed in 1912 in the aftermath of the AAF's reformation, but this lasted only three seasons.

A more serious rift occurred in 1919, when a group of important clubs broke away from the AAF to form the Association Amateurs de Football and the great debate over professionalism was launched. Within months, the two associations were reunited as Asociación Amateurs Argentina de Football (AAAF), which remained the recognized governing body, but a second league continued to thrive until 1926. An uneasy peace remained until 1931. In that year, professionalism was adopted with the formation of a new outlaw league, the Liga Argentina de Football (LAF); the amateur

Asociación Argentina de Football, meanwhile, continued to operate for four years. In 1934, the Consejo Nacional del Football Argentino was formed as an interim body, and in the early months of that year the AAF transferred its rights of international recognition to the new Consejo Nacional, with the blessing of the LAF. Before the end of the year, the AAF agreed to merge with the LAF under the name Asociación del Football Argentino (AFA), and the Consejo Nacional quickly lost its rights to the AFA, where it has remained ever since.

In 1916, Argentina invited the governing bodies of Brazil, Uruguay, and Chile to participate in the first annual South American Championship in Buenos Aires, during which the four announced the formation of the Confederación Sudamericana de Football (CONMEBOL), the world's first continental confederation. In the first, second, and fourth editions of the South American Championship, Argentina placed second to up-and-coming Uruguay, and in the third edition placed a distant third. In the 1921 edition at Buenos Aires, Argentina finally won the title and did so with an undefeated record against Brazil, Uruguay, and Paraguay. This was its first major international honor. The South American Championship has remained Argentina's premier success story through the decades. In 27 editions (out of a possible 30) since 1916, Argentina has won 12 times (a record). Seven of these came during the 20-year stretch between 1927 and 1947, during which some of Argentina's greatest teams and players were seen.

The great romantic period in Argentine soccer began before World War I with the fall of the British clubs and the rise of Italian and other European influences. Rácing, known affectionately as "the academy," was the greatest club of this era. Indeed, no club has ever dominated the Argentine game as did Rácing with its seven consecutive championships between 1913 and 1919, followed by two more in the early 1920s. But its reign was broken up by the chaos that occurred in Argentina's multiple league structure after 1919, and it was not able to gain championship form again until the late 1940s. During the 1920s, when two leagues were in competition, the other four big Buenos Aires clubs came to the forefront, though none dominated either league consistently, except perhaps for Boca Júniors, which won the regular league's title five times. Honors in the outlaw league were shared by Rácing, Independiente, Ríver Plate,

and San Lorenzo. In 1925, Boca became the first Argentine club to make a tour of Europe, its degree of success was reflected in the results: 15 won, one drawn, and three lost.

After the introduction of professionalism in 1931, Buenos Aires' greatest rivalry began to take shape in Boca vs. Ríver. For the next 35 years, the two Buenos Aires giants dominated the Campeonato Metropolitano with occasional breakthroughs by Rácing, Independiente, and San Lorenzo. Though both clubs fielded many great teams during these years, perhaps the most invincible of them all was Ríver's 1941-47 side, which included one of the great forward lines in the history of the game: Muñoz, Moreno, Pedernera, Labruna, and Loustau or Deambrosi.

Argentina burst onto the world scene in 1928 at the Olympic Games (the world's premier international competition at that time) on the heels of Boca's triumphant European tour of 1925 and the national side's excellent record against the 1924 gold medalists, Uruguay. Its European debut in Amsterdam was an 11-2 drubbing of the USA, and after easy wins over Belgium and Egypt, the stage was set for the first all-South American Olympic final against Uruguay. The Dutch spectators were treated to tantalizing displays of skill by both teams, and after a 1-1 draw a replay was forced, won finally by Uruguay's greater spirit and desire to win. After Argentina's first exposure in Europe, however, a pattern emerged that was to haunt the future of its game: the poaching of Argentine players by wealthy European clubs, especially those of Italy and Spain. The first to go was Independiente's star outside left Raimondo Orsi, lured to Juventus after the Amsterdam Olympics, and after much protest from Argentine officials. By 1934, Orsi, Luisito Monti, and others were playing for Italy in the World Cup on the basis of their Italian parentage, and Argentina's international hopes would never be the same.

In the first World Cup at Montevideo in 1930, Argentina entered as cofavorites with mighty Uruguay, and Argentine center forward Guillermo Stabile was the high scorer in the tournament. Argentina eliminated France, Mexico, and Chile in three poorly played and badly officiated first round matches, and had only to breeze past the USA to gain the final against Uruguay. The Uruguayans' superiority was more clearly pronounced than in 1928, and, in front of thousands of Argentine fans who had crossed the Rio de la Plata, they came back from a halftime deficit to win by 4-2. Argentina's frustration after two second place finishes in world competition—and to archrival Uruguay at that—was unleashed in public displays of anger, and in Buenos Aires the Uruguayan consulate was sacked by rioters.

In the 1934 World Cup, Argentina was eliminated after only one game (to Sweden) and a long transatlantic ocean voyage. Piqued by FIFA's rejection of its bid to host the next World Cup, the AFA declined to enter the 1938 edition altogether. When FIFA passed over them again in 1950 in favor of Brazil, the AFA again declined to participate, and it was not until the 1958 edition in Sweden that Argentina consented to enter, only to be eliminated in the first round by Germany FR, Czechoslovakia, and Northern Ireland. In the intervening years, it gained some sustenance by dominating the South American Championship between 1937 and 1957. Five titles during this period were won without losing a game, and in three of those won by others, Argentina did not even participate. Drawing heavily on Boca and Ríver players, Argentina remained the lord and master of South American soccer during a time when Uruguay won its second World Championship and Brazil was rising rapidly to world prominence.

The litany of disappointing World Cup results continued to mount. In the familiar setting of Chile, Argentina once again failed to advance beyond the first round in 1962 (England and Hungary qualified from its group), and from the 1966 World Cup in England it departed under a hail of criticism after a series of ugly scenes that were eventually to become closely identified with Argentine soccer. Throughout the first round in England, the team engaged in deliberate fouls and merciless taunting of opposing players, so much so that it was assumed by others to be part of a concerted tactic to brutalize the enemy. Having reached the quarter-finals, Argentina met England at Wembley, and when captain Antonio Rattin was ordered off, he refused to go. It took ten minutes to clear him off the pitch, and at the end of the game (which England finally won 1-0) the Argentine reserves besieged the referee and drew the protective intervention of the police. Argentina's antics in England illuminated the traditional rivalry between Europe and South America; in fact, it signaled the beginning of a particularly belligerent era in the transoceanic rivalry. In the coming years, Argentina would be feared and ostracized in Europe, and a vicious war of words would detract attention from its otherwise high standard of play.

The battleground was now moved to the Intercontinental Cup, where Rácing Club, Estudiantes, and Independiente successively mauled their European opponents from 1967-74. The outcry was particularly vocal against Rácing Club in 1967, Estudiantes in all three of its forays, and Independiente in 1972. Several European Cup winners refused to participate in the competition when it was learned that their opponents would be from Argentina. At home, Argentine fans and players were bitter about the clamor, some no doubt recalling FIFA's repeated snubs over World Cup issues. Tension did not begin to diffuse until FIFA awarded the 1978 World Cup to Argentina after a demonstration of support by Brazilian FIFA President João Havelange.

Meanwhile, the national team failed to qualify for the 1970 World Cup in Mexico, and in 1974 in West Germany, it placed last in its first round group. Argentina's success in the South American Championship, however, was repeated in no uncertain terms in the Copa Libertadores, the South American club championship. Indeed, Argentina's success in that competition has been phenomenal. After some years of grass roots indifference and official concern over financial losses, Boca Júniors became the first Argentine club to take the tournament seriously, and in 1963 it advanced to the final, losing to Santos. In the next 15 years, Argentine clubs won the Copa Libertadores 12 times, including six by Independiente and three by Estudiantes; Rácing and Boca were also winners. The successes of these clubs have been due to a combination of factors, including a high level of skill. But they have also resulted from severe tactics and familiar patterns of virulent behavior. That these characteristics are not confined to international opposition is perhaps demonstrated by the extraordinary number of expulsions seen during the 1977 season of the Campeonato Metropolitano: 186! In addition, the rise of Argentine clubs in the Copa Libertadores has coincided with the decline of the Uruguayan giants Peñarol and Nacional, and the continued disinterest of Brazilian clubs in competing for South American honors.

The Argentine first division, the Campeonato Metropolitano, is a Buenos Aires-based league, and until the late 1970s it was the largest in the world. In 1977 it was reduced from 23 to 22 clubs, in 1978 from 22 to 20, and a further reduction to 20 clubs is scheduled. Aside from Buenos Aires, it draws its members from the port city of La Plata and the historic Rio Paraná cities of Rosario and Santa Fe. The second and third divisions (Primera "A" and Primera "B") are all professional and semiprofessional, and include many clubs from the Federal District and Buenos Aires Province. All three divisions are served by an automatic promotion and relegation system.

In 1967, the AFA introduced a national championship, in which the leading clubs of the lower divisions were invited to join the dozen best clubs of the Campeonato Metropolitano in a combination league system and knockout tournament. This has become an intensely attractive competition, and carries added weight because it also determines Argentina's two entrants in the Copa Libertadores. It has so far afforded one non-Buenos Aires club, the venerable Rosario Central, to gain national honors, but it too has been dominated by the big teams from the Federal District. Sponsored by a large tobacco company, it is played out during the second half of the season after the results of the various leagues are known.

Campeonato Nacional Winners

1967	Independiente	1973	Rosario Central
1968	Velez Sarsfield	1974	San Lorenzo
1969	Boca Júniors	1975	Ríver Plate
1970	Boca Júniors	1976	Boca Júniors
1971	Rosario Central	1977	Independiente
1972	San Lorenzo	1978	Independiente

Champions

1893	Lomas	1914	Rácing Club
1894	Lomas		Porteño
1895	Lomas	1915	Rácing Club
1896	Lomas	1916	Rácing Club
1897	Lomas	1917	Rácing Club
1898	Lomas	1918	Rácing Club
1899	Belgrano	1919	Boca Júniors
1900	English High School		Rácing Club (AAAF)
1901	Alumni	1920	Boca Júniors
1902	Alumni		Ríver Plate (AAAF)
1903	Alumni	1921	Huracán
1904	Belgrano		Rácing Club (AAAF)
1905	Alumni	1922	Huracán
1906	Alumni		Independiente (AAAF)
1907	Alumni	1923	Boca Júniors
1908	Belgrano		San Lorenzo (AAAF)
1909	Alumni	1924	Boca Júniors
1910	Alumni		San Lorenzo (AAAF)
1911	Alumni	1925	Huracán
1912	Quilmes		Rácing Club (AAAF)
	Porteño	1926	Boca Júniors
1913	Rácing Club		Independiente (AAAF)
	Estudiantes de La Plata	1927	San Lorenzo

1928	Huracán	1951	Rácing Club
1929	Gimnasia y Esgrimá La Plata	1952	Ríver Plate
1930	Boca Júniors	1953	Ríver Plate
1931	Boca Júniors (LAF)	1954	Boca Júniors
	Estudiantil Porteño (AAF)	1955	Ríver Plate
1932	Ríver Plate (LAF)	1956	Ríver Plate
	Sportivo Barracas (AAF)	1957	Ríver Plate
1933	San Lorenzo (LAF)	1958	Rácing Club
	Dock Sud (AAF)	1959	San Lorenzo
1934	Boca Júniors (LAF)	1960	Independiente
	Estudiantil Porteño (AAF)	1961	Rácing Club
1935	Boca Júniors	1962	Boca Júniors
1936	River Plate	1963	Independiente
1937	River Plate	1964	Boca Júniors
1938	Independiente	1965	Boca Júniors
1939	Independiente	1966	Rácing Club
1940	Boca Júniors	1967	Estudiantes de La Plata
1941	Ríver Plate	1968	San Lorenzo
1942	Ríver Plate	1969	Charcarita Juniors
1943	Boca Júniors	1970	Independiente
1944	Boca Júniors	1971	Independiente
1945	Ríver Plate	1972	San Lorenzo
1946	San Lorenzo	1973	Huracán
1947	Ríver Plate	1974	Newell's Old Boys
1948	Independiente	1975	Ríver Plate
1949	Rácing Club	1976	Boca Júniors
1950	Rácing Club	1977	Ríver Plate

Arsenal Football Club

Location: *London, England;* stadium: *Arsenal Stadium (60,000);* colors: *red jerseys with white sleeves, white shorts;* honors: *Fairs Cup winner (1970), English champion (1931, 1933, 1934, 1935, 1938, 1948, 1953, 1971), English cup winner (1930, 1936, 1950, 1971).*

Founded 1886 as Dial Square by munitions employees of the Royal Arsenal installation in Woolwich, South London. It changed its name almost immediately to Royal Arsenal F.C., and in 1891 became the second club in southern England and the first in London to adopt professionalism. In 1893, as Woolwich Arsenal, it was elected to the Second Division, gaining promotion in 1904 and suffering its first and only relegation in 1913. It was also in 1913 that a London Member of Parliament, Henry Norris, invested in the club, putting it on a sound financial footing and underwriting its move to the present location at Highbury,

North London. Once at Highbury, it adopted the name Arsenal F.C., and fared only modestly in the two remaining seasons before the outbreak of World War I. When The Football League was revived in 1919, Norris persuaded league officials to admit Arsenal to the first division and it has not been relegated since. Arsenal's longevity in the first division is an English record.

Herbert Chapman, one of the outstanding managers in the history of the game, took over at Highbury in 1925 after great success at Huddersfield, and brought Arsenal to the pinnacle of world fame. Chapman was a tactical innovator and a showman, declaring upon his arrival that he was determined to make Arsenal the greatest team in the world; in the end, he succeeded in doing just that. In response to the offside law of 1925, Chapman developed the revolutionary "third back game" and a "W-M" formation to assure its proper execution. With uncanny ability, he sought and found just the right players to fit his scheme, and as a result Arsenal dominated English soccer between 1930 and 1938, and developed a distinctive aura of inviolability.

In nine years, Arsenal won five championships and two cups, and exported (by word of mouth) the W-M to the far corners of the earth, until by the end of the decade it was the standard tactical system for modern teams everywhere. Arsenal and Chapman became household words and the club's leading players became the most famous in Britain: mastermind inside forward Alex James, inside forward David Jack, center forward Ted Drake, left winger Cliff Bastin, left back Eddie Hapgood, and others. Though the W-M became known for its defensive capabilities, the Arsenal of Herbert Chapman was also a goalscoring machine. It won the league title in 1931 with 127 goals (and a league record of 66 points), in 1933 with 118, and in 1935 with 115. When Chapman tragically died after a short illness in 1935, the strength of the team he had built continued unabated with an additional F.A. Cup in 1936 and a league championship in 1938 dedicated to his memory. The Arsenal golden era was brought to an end with the outbreak of war during the 1939-40 season; otherwise it might have continued well into the 1940s.

After World War II, with only a handful of prewar players remaining, Chapman's trainer Tom Whittaker succeeded in guiding the club to championships in 1948 and 1953, as well as an F.A. Cup win in 1950, but the foundation was less solid than it had been before. A 17-year period followed in which players and managers alike were unable of living up to the superhuman reputation of "the Gunners'" past, and the club languished uneventfully in the first division, outshined by the growing prestige of its North London archrival Tottenham Hotspur. Under Bertie Mee in the late 1960s, it moved up to the first division ladder, and in the Fairs Cup of 1969-70, gained its first and only European title to date by eliminating Ajax in the semi-finals and defeating RSC Anderlecht in the final. The following year, Mee led his young team to its historic double—a league championship and F.A. Cup win in the same season—and the future looked bright once again for the big London club. But in the 1970s, it slid down in the first division, Mee left the organization in an uncertain state, and it was only in 1978 that Arsenal placed well enough to gain a berth in the UEFA Cup again.

Artigas Cup

Copa General Artigas.

A series played irregularly between the national teams of Uruguay and Paraguay, often counting double as part of a second competition, such as the Atlantic Cup. The trophy may only be awarded after home and away legs have been played. It is named for the patriot who gained Uruguayan independence from Brazil and Argentina in the early nineteenth century but was later forced to flee to Paraguay.

Asia   See: **Asian Football Confederation**

Asian Champion Teams' Cup

The club championship of the Asian Football Confederation, which was open to national title-holders of each member-nation. Introduced in 1967, the cup was discontinued after the fourth edition in 1971, owing to the financial difficulties of long-distance travel and persistent organizational impediments caused by Arab entrants refusing to compete against Israel, the most successful country in the competition. Like the Asian Cup, it was held in two phases: a preliminary round in which participants were divided into zoned groups, and a final round for winners and runners-up of each preliminary group. The final round was played over a period of two weeks in a designated city.

Israeli clubs dominated the four tournaments. Maccabi Tel-Aviv won twice, and Hapoel Tel-Aviv won once and placed second once, losing to the Iranian club Taj Tehran. Maccabi's second win resulted when Police Club Baghdad refused to take the field in the final.

Champion clubs of the Far East have participated vigorously; Malaysian entrants Selangor (Kuala Lumpur) and Perak (Ipoh) were state selections, as were India's entrants, Mysore, West Bengal, and Punjab. Israeli, Malaysian, and Thai participants advanced to the final rounds in all four tournaments. South Korean, Indian, and Iranian participants advanced three times. One club, Bangkok Bank (Thailand), advanced to the final rounds three times, a record. Two South Korean clubs, Yangzee and ROK Army, have been losing finalists.

The most successful club in the competition was Maccabi Tel-Aviv (12-10-2-0-27-6-22). The least successful club was Manila Lions Athletic Fraternity (4-0-0-4-1-20-0). Maccabi's 27 goals is a record, and Maccabi shares the record for the most number of games played (12) with Bangkok Bank.

A fifth tournament scheduled for Tehran in 1972 proceeded through preliminary rounds, but the final round was cancelled when participants from Kuwait and Lebanon withdrew for political reasons, and Hong Kong's entry withdrew over finances. The champions of Israel, Iran, South Korea, and Thailand remained.

Winners

1967   Hapoel Tel-Aviv
1968   Maccabi Tel-Aviv
1970   Taj Club
1971   Maccabi Tel-Aviv

Results

1967

*F.A. of Selangor (Malaysia)—Vietnam Customs (Vietnam Rep)	0-0, 2-1
*South China A.A. (Hong Kong)—Bangkok Bank (Thailand)	1-0, 0-2
*F.A. of Selangor—Bangkok Bank	1-0, 0-0
*Tungsten Mining (Korea Rep)—F.A. of Selangor	0-0, 0-1

Final (in Bangkok)
Hapoel Tel-Aviv (Israel)—F.A. of Selangor   2-1

*home team in first leg

1968 (January 1969 in Bangkok)

Group A

Vietnam Police (Vietnam Rep)—Bangkok Bank (Thailand)	1-1
Mysore State Team (India)—Yangzee Football Team (Korea Rep)	0-5
Manila Lions Athl. Frat. (Philippines)—Vietnam Police	0-7
Mysore State Team—Bangkok Bank	1-1
Yangzee Football Team—Manila Lions Athl. Frat.	7-0
Vietnam Police—Mysore State Team	1-2

Yangzee Football Team—Bangkok Bank	1-0
Manila Lions Athl. Frat.—Mysore State Team	1-2
Vietnam Police—Yangzee Football Team	1-4
Manila Lions Athl. Frat.—Bangkok Bank	0-4

	P	W	D	L	F	A	P
Yangzee	4	4	0	0	17	1	8
Mysore State Team	4	2	1	1	5	8	5
Bangkok Bank	4	1	2	1	6	3	4
Vietnam Police	4	1	1	2	10	7	3
Manila Lions	4	0	0	4	1	20	0

Group B

Toyo Kogyo (Japan)—Maccabi Tel-Aviv (Israel)	2-3
Perak A.F.A. (Malaysia)—Kowloon Motor Bus S.C. (Hong Kong)	6-2
Teheran Club (Iran)—Toyo Kogyo	0-1
Perak A.F.A.—Teheran Club	2-4
Maccabi Tel-Aviv—Kowloon Motor Bus S.C.	5-0
Toyo Kogyo—Kowloon Motor Bus S.C.	1-0
Maccabi Tel-Aviv—Perak A.F.A.	1-1
Kowloon Motor Bus S.C.—Teheran Club	0-4
Perak A.F.A.—Toyo Kogyo	0-2
Maccabi Tel-Aviv—Teheran Club	0-0

	P	W	D	L	F	A	P
Maccabi Tel-Aviv	4	2	2	0	9	3	6
Toyo Kogyo	4	3	0	1	6	3	6
Teheran Club	4	2	1	1	8	3	5
Perak A.F.A.	4	1	2	1	9	9	3
Kowloon Motor Bus	4	0	0	4	2	16	0

Semi-Finals

| Togyo Kogyo—Yangzee Football Team | 0-2 |
| Maccabi Tel-Aviv—Mysore State Team | 6-1 |

Third Place Game

| Toyo Kogyo—Mysore State Team | 2-0 |

Final

| Maccabi Tel-Aviv—Yangzee Football Team | 1-0 |

1970 (in Tehran)

Group A

Taj Club (Iran)—Club Homenetmen (Lebanon)	3-0
Club Homenetmen—F.A. of Selangor (Malaysia)	4-2
Taj Club—F.A. of Selangor	3-0

	P	W	D	L	F	A	P
Taj Club	2	2	0	0	6	4	4
Club Homenetmen	2	1	0	1	4	5	2
F.A. of Selangor	2	0	0	2	2	7	0

Group B

West Bengal (India)—P.S.M.S. (Indonesia)	0-1
Hapoel Tel-Aviv (Israel)—Police (Thailand)	5-0
Police—P.S.M.S.	0-4
Hapoel Tel-Aviv—West Bengal	3-1
Police—West Bengal	1-2
Hapoel Tel-Aviv—P.S.M.S.	3-1

	P	W	D	L	F	A	P
Hapoel Tel-Aviv	3	3	0	0	11	2	6
P.S.M.S.	3	2	0	1	6	3	4
West Bengal	3	1	0	2	3	5	2
Police	3	0	0	3	1	11	0

Semi-Finals

Taj Club—P.S.M.S.	2-0
Hapoel Tel-Aviv—Club Homenetmen	—
(Homenetmen withdrew)	

Third Place Game

Club Homenetmen—Hapoel Tel-Aviv	1-0

Final

Taj Club—Hapoel Tel-Aviv	2-1

1971 (in Bangkok)

Group A
ROK Army Football Team (Korea Rep)
Taj Club (Iran)
Al-Arabi S.C. (Kuwait)
Perak A.F.A. (Malaysia)

Group B
Punjab F.A. (India)
Police Club (Iraq)
Maccabi Tel-Aviv (Israel)
Bangkok Bank (Thailand)

(some members of Group A played some members of Group B)

Bangkok Bank—ROK Army	1-2
Police Club—Taj Club	3-2
Punjab F.A.—Al-Arabi S.C.	1-8

Maccabi Tel-Aviv—Perak A.F.A.	1-0
Al-Arabi S.C.—Perak A.F.A.	3-0
ROK Army—Taj Club	1-2
Bangkok Bank—Punjab F.A.	2-0
Maccabi Tel-Aviv—Police Club	—
(Police Club forfeited)	
ROK Army—Perak A.F.A.	3-0
Taj Club—Al-Arabi S.C.	0-0
Punjab F.A.—Macabbi Tel-Aviv	1-4
Police Club—Bangkok Bank	2-0
Taj Club—Perak A.F.A.	3-0
Al-Arabi S.C.—ROK Army	0-1
Police Club—Punjab F.A.	6-1
Maccabi Tel-Aviv—Bangkok Bank	4-1

Semi-Finals

Police Club—Taj Club	2-0
Maccabi Tel-Aviv—ROK Army	2-0

Third Place Game

Taj Club—ROK Army	3-2

Final

Maccabi Tel-Aviv—Police Club	—
(Police Club forfeited)	

Asian Football Confederation

Address: *No. 88, Jalan Sultan Idris Shah (Jalan Brewster), P.O. Box 285, Ipoh, Malaysia.* **Members:** *Afghanistan, Bahrain, Bangladesh, Brunei, Burma, China People's Republic, Hong Kong, India, Indonesia, Iran, Iraq, Japan, Jordan, Khmer, Korea Republic, Kuwait, Laos, Lebanon, Malaysia, Nepal, Pakistan, Philippines, Qatar, Saudi Arabia, Singapore, Sri Lanka, Syria, Thailand, United Arab Emirates, Yemen PDR.* **Affiliated clubs:** *25,026;* **registered players:** *565,682 (both figures include China National, Israel, Korea DPR, and Vietnam but exclude Bangladesh and China People's Republic).*

Founded in 1954 by Hong Kong, India, Indonesia, Japan, Korea Republic, Malaysia, Philippines, Singapore, and Vietnam Republic. China National was admitted in 1955, Israel in 1956, other East and South Asian countries subsequently, and finally the Middle East states during the 1960s and '70s. The first headquarters were located in Hong Kong before moving to their present location in Ipoh, Malaysia.

The AFC was founded and administered by East and Southeast Asians until the 1970s, when an Arab and socialist bloc emerged to gain a foothold, led ironically by Iran and Hong Kong. In 1975, the AFC Congress voted to expel China National and Israel, and Asian soccer was thrown into a momentous crisis. This effectively politicized the organization in a way seldom seen since the highly charged atmosphere of FIFA in post-World War I

Europe. FIFA directed the AFC to reinstate the expelled members, but in late 1977 the world body backed away from its position and suggested various compromises, fearful of losing its Asian membership entirely. The AFC rebuffed the FIFA proposals, and stood its ground. The events came to a boiling point in December 1977 when AFC president, Tengku Abdul Rahman, the former Prime Minister of Malaysia, resigned, bringing to an end the era of moderate leadership. It remained for FIFA to take up the Asian challenge and decide whether or not to assert its authority at the 1978 FIFA Congress.

Meanwhile, the AFC has been responsible for the Asian Cup, the soccer competition of the Asian Games, the Asian Champion Teams' Cup (now in hiatus), the Asian Youth Tournament, an Asian Women's Football Championship (the world's first), and other ambitious programs.

Asian Games, Football Tournament of the

The first international soccer competition for all of Asia, this series is also the showcase of the Asian Games as a whole. Open only to amateur players, the games are held every four years in a host country, midway between each Olympiad. Surprisingly, the soccer tournament has retained much of its significance even today, drawing increasingly greater participation in recent years, despite the introduction of an Asian Cup in 1956. The political embroilments of the Asian region, however, have interfered with the last two editions, and promise to do so in the future. In 1970 and 1974, Arab countries declined to play Israel, resulting in significant defaults, and China National was kept out of the 1974 edition, as China PR made its Asian debut in Taiwan's place.

The first tournament in 1951 included India, Indonesia, Afghanistan, Japan, Iran, and Burma. Prior to the advance of Iran as Asia's leading power in the 1970s, the series was dominated decisively by East and South Asian countries. The Arab states did not enter the competition until 1970. Regional qualification tournaments became an important element in 1970 and 1974. India's successes in the early years have given way to poor showings of late, and South Korea's consistency throughout the series took its first downward turn in the latest edition. Israel, historically one of the strongest soccer nations in Asia, has suffered repeatedly from political interference, and in many instances has not even entered the tournament.

Winners

1951	(in New Delhi)	India
1954	(in Manila)	China National
1958	(in Tokyo)	China National
1962	(in Jakarta)	India
1966	(in Bangkok)	Burma

1970	(in Bangkok)	Burma and Korea Republic*
1974	(in Tehran)	Iran
1978		Korea DPR and Korea Republic*

*final ended in a draw

Asian Cup

The regional competition for national teams of Asia and held every Olympiad year since 1956, two years after the founding of its organizing body, the Asian Football Confederation. It is played in two phases: a preliminary round in which participating countries are divided into zoned groups (presently four), and a final round contested among the winners and runners-up of each preliminary group. The final round is played over a period of days in a designated city. The first four final rounds (1956, 1960, 1964, and 1968) were played under a league system. Participants of the fifth and sixth competitions (1972 and 1976) were divided into two groups with the winners and runners-up advancing to a semi-final and final.

Early editions of the Asian Cup were dominated by nations of the Far East, but since the early 1970s, when many Arab countries initiated stepped-up soccer programs, a large number of participants from the Middle East have gone through the final round. The most successful entries from the Middle East, however, have been non-Arab states, Israel and Iran. In addition, the Indian subcontinent has not figured prominently in the tournament, nor have the Communist-bloc countries of the Far East. As in the case of the Asian Champions' Cup, political considerations have strongly influenced the outcome of the competition. In the Middle East, much of the reason for reluctant Arab participation has been the presence of Israel, finalist in the first four tournaments. In the Far East, the China question prevented the People's Republic of China from participating until the most recent edition, when member-states of the Confederation chose to replace the Republic of China with China PR. FIFA did not block China PR's participation, and China PR promptly went through to the semi-finals of the 1976 edition and placed third.

South Korea has gone through to the final round five times, Israel four times, Iran and Hong Kong three times. While South Korea has won the competition twice, Iran has emerged victorious in each of the last three editions. Israel has won the cup once, and has been runner-up twice. Kuwait, South Vietnam, Iraq, and China Republic have each been finalists twice.

Winners

1956	**Korea Rep**
1960	**Korea Rep**
1964	**Israel**
1968	**Iran**
1972	**Iran**
1976	**Iran**

Cumulative Ranking (1956-76)*
(number of editions in parentheses)

		P	W	D	L	F	A	P
1	Iran (3)	12	12	0	0	34	6	24
2	Israel (4)	13	9	2	3	31	16	19
3	Korea Rep (4)	13	8	1	4	27	17	17
4	Kuwait (2)	6	4	0	2	8	8	8
5	Burma (1)	4	2	1	1	5	4	5
6	India (1)	3	2	0	1	5	3	4
7	China Rep (2)	7	1	2	4	5	12	4
8	Thailand (1)	4	1	1	2	6	7	3
9	China PR (1)**	4	1	1	2	2	4	3
10	Iraq (2)	6	1	1	4	4	10	3
11	Hong Kong (3)	10	0	3	7	9	23	3
12	Khmer (1)	4	1	0	3	8	8	2
13	Malaysia (1)	2	0	1	1	1	3	1
14	Vietnam Rep (2)	6	0	1	5	8	21	1
15	Yemen PDR (1)	2	0	0	2	0	9	0

*The following have not reached the final rounds or have never entered the competition: Afghanistan, Bahrain, Bangladesh, Brunei, Indonesia, Japan, Jordan, Laos, Lebanon, Nepal, Pakistan, Philippines, Qatar, Saudi Arabia, Singapore, Sri Lanka, Syria, and United Arab Emirates. Korea DPR and Vietnam DPR are FIFA members but not affiliated to the AFC.
**affiliated to the AFC but not a member of FIFA.

Results

1956

Finals (in Hong Kong)

Korea Rep—Israel	2-1
Korea Rep—Hong Kong	2-2
Korea Rep—Vietnam Rep	5-3
Israel—Hong Kong	3-2
Israel—Vietnam Rep	2-1
Hong Kong—Vietnam Rep	2-2

	P	W	D	L	F	A	P
Korea Rep	3	2	1	0	9	6	5
Israel	3	2	0	1	6	5	4
Hong Kong	3	0	2	1	6	7	2
Vietnam Rep	3	0	1	2	6	9	1

1960

Finals (in Seoul)

Korea Rep—Vietnam Rep	5-1
China Rep—Vietnam Rep	2-0
Israel—Korea Rep	0-3
Israel—Vietnam Rep	5-1
China Rep—Korea Rep	0-1
China Rep—Israel	0-1

	P	W	D	L	F	A	P
Korea Rep	3	3	0	0	9	1	6
Israel	3	2	0	1	6	4	4
China Rep	3	1	0	2	2	2	2
Vietnam Rep	3	0	0	3	2	12	0

1964

Finals (in Tel-Aviv)

Israel—Hong Kong	1-0
India—Korea Rep	2-0
Israel—India	2-0
Korea Rep—Hong Kong	1-0
India—Hong Kong	3-1
Israel—Korea Rep	2-1

	P	W	D	L	F	A	P
Israel	3	3	0	0	5	1	6
India	3	2	0	1	5	3	4
Korea Rep	3	1	0	2	2	4	2
Hong Kong	3	0	0	3	1	5	0

1968

Finals (in Tehran)

Hong Kong—Iran	0-2
China Rep—Burma	1-1
Israel—Hong Kong	6-1
Iran—China Rep	4-0
Israel—Burma	0-1
China Rep—Hong Kong	1-1
Iran—Burma	3-1
China Rep—Israel	1-4
Hong Kong—Burma	0-2
Iran—Israel	2-1

	P	W	D	L	F	A	P
Iran	4	4	0	0	11	2	8
Burma	4	2	1	1	5	4	5
Israel	4	2	0	2	11	5	4
China Rep	4	0	2	2	3	10	2
Hong Kong	4	0	1	3	2	11	1

1972

Final Rounds (in Bangkok)
Israel withdrew

Group A

Iran—Iraq	3-0
Iraq—Thailand	1-1
Thailand—Iran	2-3

	P	W	D	L	F	A	P
Iran	2	2	0	0	6	2	4
Thailand	2	0	1	1	3	4	1
Iraq	2	0	1	1	1	4	1

Group B

Khmer—Korea Rep	1-4
Korea Rep—Kuwait	1-2
Khmer—Kuwait	4-0

	P	W	D	L	F	A	P
Korea Rep	2	1	0	1	5	3	2
Khmer	2	1	0	1	5	4	2
Kuwait	2	1	0	1	2	5	2

Semi-Finals
Iran—Khmer   2-1
Korea Rep—Thailand   1-1
(Korea won on penalty kicks)

Third Place Game
Khmer—Thailand   2-2
(Thailand won on penalty kicks)

Final
Iran—Korea Rep   2-1

1976

Final Rounds (in Iran)
Korea DPR, Saudi Arabia, and Thailand withdrew; Iran qualified as holder

Group A (in Tabriz)
Kuwait—Malayasia   2-0
China PR—Malaysia   1-1
China PR—Kuwait   1-0

	P	W	D	L	F	A	P
Kuwait	2	2	0	0	3	0	4
China PR	2	0	1	1	1	2	1
Malaysia	2	0	1	1	1	3	1

Group B (in Tehran)
Iran—Iraq   2-0
Iraq—Yemen PDR   1-0
Iran—Yemen PDR   8-0

	P	W	D	L	F	A	P
Iran	2	2	0	0	10	0	4
Iraq	2	1	0	1	1	2	2
Yemen PDR	2	0	0	2	0	9	0

Semi-Finals (in Tehran)
Kuwait—Iraq   3-2
(after extra time)
Iran—China PR   2-0
(after extra time)

Third Place Game (in Tehran)
China PR—Iraq   1-0

Final (in Tehran)
Iran—Kuwait   1-0

---

assist

In the North American Soccer League, a player whose pass to a teammate has immediately preceded his teammate's scoring a goal, or who has in some other way assisted directly in his teammate's scoring a goal, is credited with an assist. According to NASL goalscoring tabulations, which are based on a point system, a player who makes an assist is awarded one point. Assist points are added to the two points awarded for each goal scored to arrive at an individual player's total. The concept of an "assist" is borrowed from statistical procedures in professional basketball and ice hockey, and is not sanctioned by the International Football Association Board, nor is it found in senior competition outside the United States and Canada.

---

association football

The traditional term, now more literary than colloquial, for the game of soccer. It is commonly understood in the United Kingdom, Eire, and the British Commonwealth, but has increasingly fallen out of general usage in recent decades, except in formal designations, e.g., Fédération Internationale de Football Association (FIFA), which translates as International Federation of Association Football. Originating in the 1860s, the game administered by The Football *Association* in London came to be known as *association* football, as distinct from the game based on handling codes, which came to be known as *rugby* football. The term "soccer" is derived from the second syllable of the word "association."

The only non-British country to acquire the term on a widespread basis has been France.

---

association rules

A term used primarily in reference to soccer during the first few decades after 1863—the date of the founding of The Football *Association* in London—to distinguish it from rugby, or handling, codes.

Aston Villa Football Club

Location: *Birmingham, England:* stadium: *Villa Park (53,000);* colors: *claret jerseys with light blue sleeves and collar, white shorts;* honors: *English champion (1894, 1896, 1897, 1899, 1900, 1910), English cup winner (1887, 1895, 1897, 1905, 1913, 1920, 1957), English league cup winner (1961, 1975, 1977).*

Founded 1874 by young members of the Villa Cross Wesleyan Chapel in the North Birmingham suburb of Aston. Aided by two Scottish immigrants who had played for Queen's Park Glasgow, the founding members were cricket players looking for a winter game to occupy themselves. They were also faithful Methodist church members, and their crosstown rivalry with Small Health Alliance (founded 1875 by members of an Anglican church and later renamed Birmingham City) became one of the country's first interdenominational rivalries.

Aston Villa, one of England's best supported clubs, has won more major domestic honors than any other club in The Football League—13 in all. Its phenomenal success between 1887 and 1913 brought it to the front ranks of the English game, and introduced a tradition of club loyalty that is still felt today. Since World War I, the club's honors have been few and far between, but the name of Aston Villa remains one of the most respected in England, and Villa's attendance figures are still among the top five in the country. In the early 1970s, Villa ended a brief stay in the Third Division by breaking divisional point and attendance records.

Its first major honor was an F.A. Cup victory in 1887 against its second crosstown rival, West Bromwich Albion. In 1888, Villa became one of the original 12 members of The Football League, gaining second place in its first season, though a distant 11 points behind undefeated Preston North End. After mixed results for four years, it won the title itself in 1894, and entered its golden era as the first club to dominate the league. Four more championships followed before the turn of the century, and it won two additional F.A. Cups during the same period.

In 1897, it won the league-cup double with an 11 point margin in the league and a famous 3-2 win over Everton in the cup final. Today Villa remains one of only four English clubs to win the double. Before the outbreak of World War I, it captured another league championship and cup victory, and was runner-up in the league five times.

The backbone of this great team included attacking center half James Cowan, fullback Howard Spencer, left half Jimmy Crabtree, and after 1904, goalscoring center forward Harold Hampton. The effort was directed by the club secretary, George Ramsay, a Scot who was actually the manager as well, and he remained in this post from 1884-1926. Villa never won another league championship after 1910, though it won the F.A. Cup again in 1920 and 1957, the latter against a 10-player Manchester United side. But in 1930-31 the club broke the First Division scoring record with 128 goals (the record still stands), only to finish second behind Arsenal.

There were brief sojourns in the Second Division during the late 1930s and late 1950s, and in 1967 Villa began an eight-year slump in the Second and Third Divisions, its worst period ever. Between 1972 and 1975, the club moved rapidly back to the First Division, resolved to keep its rightful place in the top flight. Villa's inconsistencies during the 1960s and 70s have been punctuated by victories in the newly established Football League Cup, England's second cup competition, and its three wins in this series is a record.

Athletic Club de Bilbao

Location: *Bilbao, Spain;* stadium: *Estadio San Mamés (41,400);* colors: *red and white striped jerseys, black shorts;* honors: *Spanish champion (1930, 1931, 1934, 1936, 1943, 1956), Spanish cup winner (1902, 1903, 1904, 1910, 1911, 1914, 1915, 1916, 1921, 1923, 1930, 1931, 1932, 1933, 1943, 1944, 1945, 1950, 1955, 1956, 1958, 1969, 1973).*

Founded in 1898 as Athletic Club by Manuel Smith and other Basque alumni of schools in England, who returned to Bilbao having learned the English game. Smith's descendants are still associated with the club today. Many of the earliest members were miners.

The earliest games were played against other teams from Vizcaya province, including those of local British residents. Athletic's primary adversary in 1901 was Bilbao Football Club (founded 1900), and in 1902, when the city of Bilbao was invited to participate in a cup tournament in Madrid to celebrate the coronation of Alfonso XIII. The two rivals joined forces under the name Bizcaya (not Vizcaya) and defeated all opposition (Barcelona, Español, and Madrid F.C.). The prestige of the Basque capital as a stronghold of Spanish soccer was established with that victory. Later in 1902, Athletic absorbed Bilbao F.C., and Athletic's hegemony in the Basque region was solidified.

Athletic Bilbao is the oldest league club in Spain, and has won a record 23 Spanish cups since the first in 1902. It is Spain's greatest cup fighter, owing much of its cup tradition to its distinctly British origin. Located in one of the most anglicized cities in Europe, the club has played under at least seven British managers through the years. The greatest source of its success, however, is the pride in knowing that it represents so much in the patriotic Basque movement. Clearly remaining unidentified with the violent elements of the Basque separatist struggle, Athletic Bilbao has nonetheless been the single most important Basque rallying point. The management still maintains a strict policy of signing only Basque players, and though they are unable to make purchases of leading players in Spain or abroad, Athletic has maintained its popularity as every Spaniard's second favorite club.

In the years before the Spanish league was introduced, Athletic was the dominant club in the country. Winning 10 editions of the King's Cup, it was already an inspiration to other clubs. (In 1903, Atlético Madrid was formed by a group of dissidents from another club, and the young players adopted Athletic's name and colors in tribute.) After a brief merger with Union Vizcaino in 1907, the club moved from its location in central Bilbao to the Neguri Jolaseta on the edge of town, but its new start was hampered by disorganization in the league (1910-13). As this rancorous period in Spanish soccer drew to a close, Athletic built the first Estadio San Mamés (nicknamed *la catedral*), giving renewed life to the club and resulting in three consecutive cup victories and many exciting wins over the big clubs of Madrid and Barcelona. Athletic emerged from the pre-World War I era with eight cup wins and the outstanding record in Spanish soccer.

After World War I, it was no less successful. Athletic, in fact, has won Spanish cups in each decade since the turn of the century, perhaps its only weak link being the 1960s. It has also seen considerable success in the Spanish league. Its six championships since introduction of the league in 1928 is the fourth highest total among Spanish clubs, and it has never been relegated.

Athletic first entered European club competition in the 1956-57 European Cup, finally going out to Manchester United after eliminating Porto and Honvéd. Its away leg with the Hungarian champions Honvéd— staged by special arrangement with the Belgian F.A. at Anderlecht—was played on the very day Soviet tanks rolled into Budapest to put down the 1956 uprising, and was to be the last game ever played by the famous Puskás-Kocsis team. In 1977, Athletic achieved its best results in Europe by losing the final of the UEFA Cup to Juventus on away goals, bringing to an end yet another spirited assault on the big-money clubs of international competition. It is fitting that only one club, AC Milan, has ever won a game at San Mamés in European competition. Athletic's greatest star has probably been its current goalkeeper, José Angel Iribar, who has kept the nets for both his club and Spain since the early 1960s, and has often been ranked as Spain's greatest keeper since Zamora.

Atlantic Cup

Copa del Atlantico.

The most significant of the many South American regional competitions between countries, in that three of its four participants are Brazil, Argentina, and Uruguay. Paraguay, a middle-level power, is the fourth.

Launched in 1956, the Atlantic Cup was supposed to have been held once every other year, but second and third competitions were not held until 1960 and 1976, thus diminishing its potential stature in the face of older and traditionally intense tournaments, i.e., Lipton Cup, Roca Cup, and Rio Branco Cup. It remains the only regional competition played by South America's three great footballing powers.

Winners

1956   Brazil
1960   Brazil
1976   Brazil

Results

1956

Brazil—Uruguay	2-0
Uruguay—Argentina	1-2
Argentina—Brazil	0-0

	P	W	D	L	F	A	P
Brazil	2	1	1	0	2	0	3
Argentina	2	1	1	0	2	1	3
Uruguay	2	0	0	2	1	4	0

1960

Paraguay—Brazil	1-2
Uruguay—Brazil	1-0
Argentina—Paraguay	1-0
Brazil—Argentina	5-1
Uruguay—Paraguay	2-0
Argentina—Uruguay	4-1

	P	W	D	L	F	A	P
Brazil	3	2	0	1	7	3	4
Argentina	3	2	0	1	6	5	4
Uruguay	3	2	0	1	3	5	4

1976 (home and away basis; French point system)

Uruguay—Brazil	1-2
Paraguay—Argentina	2-3
Argentina—Brazil	1-2
Uruguay—Paraguay	2-2
Paraguay—Brazil	1-1
Argentina—Uruguay	4-1
Argentina—Paraguay	2-2
Brazil—Uruguay	2-1
Paraguay—Uruguay	1-0
Brazil—Argentina	2-0
Uruguay—Argentina	0-3
Brazil—Paraguay	3-1

	P	W	D	L	F	A	P	FrP
Brazil	6	5	1	0	12	5	11	2
Argentina	6	3	1	2	13	9	7	2
Paraguay	6	1	3	2	9	11	5	—
Uruguay	6	0	1	5	5	14	1	—

Atlético de Madrid, Club

Location: *Madrid, Spain;* stadium: *Estadio Vicente Calderon (70,000);* colors: *red and white striped jerseys, blue shorts;* honors: *Intercontinental Cup (1974), European Cup Winners' Cup (1962), Spanish champion (1940, 1941, 1950, 1951, 1966, 1970, 1973, 1977), Spanish cup winner (1960, 1961, 1965, 1972, 1976).*

Founded 1903 as Athletic Club de Madrid by dissident members of Madrid F.C. (later Real Madrid) who gained permission from Athletic Bilbao, the greatest club of the day, to adopt its name and colors (the color of Atlético's shorts has since been changed from black to blue). In 1966, it moved from the Estadio Metropolitano near the university to its present quarters, the former Estadio Manzanares, in the Arganzuela section, located on the Manzanares River next to the municipal gas and electric works.

Atlético has become one of the Spain's most famous and successful clubs, largely as an effort to emulate its legenday crosstown rival Real Madrid. But its rise to the front ranks came late, and not without considerable help from political forces during the Spanish Civil War. Always the second or third Madrid club in Spanish cup and league competition, it slipped into the second division in 1930 without having a single honor to its name. Atlético gained promotion again in 1934, and after two seasons with poor results, the Civil War halted league activity and saved the club from almost certain relegation. The Comandante of the Air Force, Don Luis Navarro, worked a merger between Atlético and Club Aviación, the Air Force team whose league fortunes were rising rapidly, and until 1947 the revitalized club was known as Atlético Aviación. In 1939, the legendary Ricardo Zamora, the greates name in Spanish soccer, became manager of the club, and in the first two seasons of post-civil war competition, took it to its first two championships.

Atlético's first chance in European club competition occurred in 1958-59, when it qualified as runner-up to the European champion Real, and after eliminating Drumcondra, CDNA Sofia, and Schalke 04, met none other than archrivals Real in the semifinals. In one of the most thrilling European Cup rounds of all time, the Madrid giants were elvel on points and goals after home and away legs, and in the replay at Zaragoza, Real emerged the winner by one goal. In 1961-62, Atlético was the first Spanish club to enter the European Cup Winners' Cup, and advanced convincingly to the final, where it unseated holders Fiorentina in a replay at Stuttgart after a scoreless draw. With this win, it became the third Spanish club to win one of the big European titles, and finally joined the world-famous Real and Barcelona in the international limelight. Atlético won three editions of the Spanish Cup during the early 1960s/its first ever—benefiting, as did many clubs in Spain at the time, from a productive and competitive spirit around the league.

As the holder, Atlético reached the final of the 1962-63 European Cup Winners' Cup, but Tottenham Hotspur rolled over the club 5-1. Not discouraged, it bounced back to another cup win at home in 1965 and a championship in 1966. There were many fine attackers on these teams, most notably Joaquim Peiro, who would have gained great fame had he not moved to Torino after his triumphs for Spain in the 1962 World Cup, and best of all, the Brazilian Vavá, who played for Atlético for two brief years after the 1958 World Cup. Atlético's reputation for producing skillful teams—albeit not on the level of a Real or Barcelona—was swept aside in the early 1970s under Austrian manager Max Merkl, who brought the club to a Spanish Cup in 1972 and a championship in 1973 with a strong disciplinarian approach. Atlético soon developed a reputation for rough play at the expense of skills. This, however, was well suited to the challenge of Independiente in the

Intercontinental Cup of 1974 (European Cup winner Bayern München refused to play the South American champions and as the European Cup finalist, it won the two-leg series, ironically with a goal from its new Argentine star Rubén Ayala.

attendances

The range of attendances for international matches is illustrated by the qualification rounds of the 1970 World Cup, in which the highest was 183,341 (Maracanã Stadium, Rio de Janeiro, for Brazil vs. Paraguay in 1969), and the lowest was 500 (Municipal Stadium, Kansas City, Missouri, for USA vs. Bermuda in 1968).

World attendance record: 199,850 (Brazil vs. Uruguay in World Cup final round, July 16, 1950, Maracanã Stadium, Rio de Janeiro).

European attendance record: 149,547 (Scotland vs. England in Home International Championship, April 17, 1937, Hampden Park, Glasgow).

World club attendance record: 177,656 (Flamengo vs. Fluminense in Rio de Janeiro league match, August 1963, Maracanã Stadium, Rio de Janeiro).

European club attendance record: 146,433 (Celtic vs. Aberdeen in Scottish Cup final, April 24, 1937, Hampden Park, Glasgow).

North American attendance record: 77,691 (Cosmos vs. Fort Lauderdale in NASL divisional championship play-off, August 14, 1977, Giants Stadium, Meadowlands, New Jersey).

The unofficial African attendance record of 100,000 has been achieved more than once at both the Nasser Stadium, Cairo, and the Stade Ahmadou-Ahidjo, Yaoundé.

The earliest attendance of 100,000 was achieved at the English F.A. Cup final of 1901 at the Crystal Palace ground, London, Tottenham Hotspur vs. Sheffield United. The actual figure was 110,820.

Australia

Australian Soccer Federation
36-38 Clarence Street
1st Floor
Sydney, N.S.W. 2000

Founded: 1961
FIFA: 1963

Affiliated clubs: *1,100;* **registered players:** *165,000 (5,000 non-amateur);* **national stadium:** *Olympic Park, Melbourne (48,500);* **largest stadium:** *Olympic Park;* **colors:** *amber jerseys with green trim, white shorts;* **season:** *March to October;* **honors:** *none.*

Soccer in Australia has suffered mightily from intense competition with three other types of football—Rugby Union, Rugby League, and Australian Rules—all of which have a stronger tradition than soccer in many parts of the country. To make matters more difficult, all four seasons run simultaneously during the winter months. A second major obstacle has been Australia's geographical location. With 10,500 miles between Melbourne and London, and 8,200 miles between Melbourne and Rio

de Janeiro, much of the world's best soccer has been out of reach. Geographical dilemmas have extended even to its own region, as the Australian Soccer Federation has sought to establish ties with Asia at the expense of its own Oceania Football Confederation. Australia's attempted defection has caused insoluble problems for Oceania, and it has become unwittingly entangled in the bitter political disputes in Asia over China and Israel. In spite of all this, Australia emerged as a regional power beyond the confines of Australasia when it qualified to represent Asia and Oceania at the World Cup in 1974.

Soccer was brought to australia by British coal miners as early as 1870. By 1881, there were at least five clubs in New South Wales, and the first association, the New South Wales Football Association, was founded in 1882. The first organized competition was the Rainsford Trophy, a knockout tournament introduced in 1885 and first won by Granville FC of Sydney. Though some interest in the game was kindled in certain parts of New South Wales, it took an immediate back seat to Rugby League in Queensland, to Australian Rules in South Australia, Victoria, Tasmania, and Western Australia, and to Rugby Union almost everywhere.

In 1904, a New South Wales selection visited New Zealand and met eight teams over a one-month period, including a New Zealand representative side, winning five games, drawing two, and losing two. The New South Wales-New Zealand scores were 1-0 and 3-3. The visit was returned one year later by a New Zealand selection, which played eleven games, including three against a New South Wales representative side. Australian teams in this series won three, drew two, and lost six. The New South Wales-New Zealand results this time were 4-6, 2-0, and 1-1.

An Australian Soccer Association (ASA), operating almost exclusively in New South Wales, was finally established in 1921, and became affiliated with The Football Association in London. A year later, the first officially sanctioned national team was put on the field, though the ASA's non-independent status precluded its team's recognition as a full international side. In 1925, an amateur team representing the London F.A. toured Australia and defeated selections from Brisbane, Sydney, Maitland, and Melbourne in succession.

Other than the numerous homogeneous ethnic communities in Sydney, interest in soccer grew most rapidly around the coalfields of New South Wales, with Newcastle emerging as the focal point between 1900 and 1920. The ASA, in fact, was based in Newcastle rather than Sydney. Eventually, hotly contested rivalries grew between Cessnock and West Wallsend near Newcastle, and between Balmain, Fernleigh, Gladesville, and Metters in Sydney. The ASA formed a limited company in 1945, but in 1957 the New South Wales Federation of Soccer Clubs was founded, and within a few years had ousted the old

association from its official position. This led to the formation of the Australian Soccer Federation (ASF) in 1961, which in turn was recognized by FIFA two years later. The time had come for Australia to enter the international arena outside the British Commonwealth. An attractive inducement to expand its interests now existed in the 1966 World Cup, scheduled to be held in England. FIFA alloted one berth to Asia-Oceania, which was sought by only two countries, North Korea and Australia. The Koreans won both qualifying matches in Phnom Penh (6-1 and 3-1).

Australia's second organizational effort during the 1960s was to help create a confederation for the South Pacific region. In 1966, FIFA authorized the formation of the Oceania Football Confederation (OFC). Australia was its chief instigator and ultimately its most important component, though there were only four charter and two provisional members. Increasingly, however, the ASF sought to establish ties with East and Southeast Asian countries in an effort to improve their level of opposition in international competition. In 1967, the "Socceroos" experienced their first significant breakthrough in completing an undefeated 10-match Asian tour, culminating with the winning of the (South) Vietnam Independence Day tournament. By 1970, the ASF had begun to turn its back on the OFC, and this put the confederation in serious jeopardy. The last straw occurred in 1971, when the ASF withdrew from the first Oceania Cup because the host nation, New Caledonia, failed to guarantee air fares. A short while later, Australia withdrew from the OFC altogether, and announced its intention to seek affiliation with the Asian Football Confederation.

FIFA, fearing the collapse of the OFC, objected, and new snags were confronted when the Asian Football Confederation voted to expel Taiwan and Israel. The Australia question was relegated to a back seat while FIFA and the Asian body endeavored to resolve the serious problem of what to do with Israel and the two Chinas. Australia's best hope for entry into the Asian confederation subsequently came about when Taiwan offered to trade places, and join the OFC, but by 1978 the matter was still not settled and the ASF remained unaffiliated.

Meanwhile, on the playing field, the "Socceroos" continued to improve. In 1970, it missed qualification for the World Cup in Mexico by an own goal against Israel in Tel Aviv. Four years later, it advanced to the World Cup finals for the first time after eliminating New Zealand, Iraq, Indonesia, Iran, and South Korea in the Asia-Oceania group. In West Germany, its presence marked a new high point in the history of Australian soccer. Instructed in no uncertain terms to play defensively against its stiff opposition, the Australian's managed to lose to West Germany and East Germany by only 3-0 and 2-0 respectively, and in its best showing, gained a scoreless draw with a Chilean team in poor form. At home, its participation in the World Championship gave the domestic game renewed impetus.

In 1977, the five regional leagues at home, New South Wales, Victoria, South Australia, Queensland, and Western Australia, gave way to the creation of Australia's first national league. Sponsored by the giant Dutch consortium, Philips Industries, the new loop was named the Philips Soccer League. It started with 14 clubs, all but three having strong ethnic backgrounds: Eastern Suburbs (formerly Hakoah Sydney), Marconi Sydney, St. George Sydney (formerly St. George-Budapest), Sydney Olympic (formerly Pan Hellenic), Western Suburbs Sydney, Fitzroy United (formerly Alexander Melbourne), Footscray Melbourne (formerly J.U.S.T.), Mooroolbark Melbourne, South Melbourne (formerly Hellas), Adelaide City (formerly Juventus Adelaide), West Adelaide (formerly Adelaide Hellas), Brisbane City (formerly Brisbane Azzuri), Brisbane Lions (formerly Hollandia), and Canberra City (newly formed). The regional leagues, now without their top teams, continue to exist, and it is planned that after three years they will serve as regional sections of a second division, and will be subject to promotions and relegations. A national cup competition, called the Philips Cup, was also introduced in 1977; it is contested by provincial selections rather than by clubs.

With its international affiliation in limbo, and while awaiting the success or failure of the experimental national league, soccer in Australia is now passing through an unprecedented period of transition. International results since 1974 have been mixed. The Aussies' superior height and strength have afforded them good results with most of their East Asian opposition (including China PR), but the Middle East countries have often proved to be more advanced in skills and technique. In qualification rounds for the 1978 World Cup, Australia was eliminated by Iran, Kuwait and South Korea. The main thrust of Australian soccer for some time to nome will be to shake off its provincial character, and gain as much experience as possible against the leading teams of Europe and South America. Australia's only full-level internationals against European opposition have been with Greece, yielding quite favorable results (won two, drawn one, and lost one).

Austria

Österreichischer Fussball-Bund
Mariahilferstrasse 99
Postfach 161
A-1061 Wien

Founded: 1904
FIFA: 1905
UEFA: 1954

Affiliated clubs: *1,918;* **registered players:** *267,000 (274 non-amateur);* **national stadium:** *Wienerstadion Prater, Vienna (73,243);* **largest stadium:** *Wienerstadion Prater;* **colors:** *white jerseys, black shorts;* **season:** *August to December, February to June;* **honors:** *World Cup third place (1954), Olympic Games runner-up (1936), International Cup (1932), FK Austria, Mitropa Cup (1933, 1936), Rapid Vienna, Mitropa Cup (1930), First Vienna, Mitropa Cup (1931).*

Austria was one of the great powers in world soccer until its downfall in international competition during the 1960s. But the legacy of two golden eras lives on. Vienna, the capital of Austria-Hungary, became one of Europe's early soccer hotbeds before and after the turn of the century, and in 1902 Austria was the winner of the first officially recognized international played by two non-British countries. Its opponent on that day was its historic archrival Hungary, which has met Austria in 125 full internationals in the ensuing 76 years. Together, Austria and Hungary rose to prominence over the decades and have thrived in a friendly competitive spirit. (On the field, Hungary has dominated by a 2-1 margin.) In the early 1930s, Austria's national team was probably the best in Europe, and achieved lasting fame for its "Danubian style" of play that was based on short passing in the classic Scottish mode. A second great era occurred when a new generation of superbly skilled players won third place in the 1954 World Cup. Austria's success during these two periods yielded such an excellent winning percentage in international competition that the national team still has a favorable overall record, even today after 20 years of poor results.

Vienna was a bastion of British culture and technology during the Victorian era, and soccer was the most popular recreational pastime imported by British residents. Austrians took to the game with ease and enthusiasm. Soccer was first played in Vienna and Graz in the 1880s, and its gradual adoption followed the usual pattern of British domination for several years until Austrian players gained experience. In Austria-Hungary as a whole, teams were organized earlier in Bohemia than in Austria proper, but the first two Austrian clubs were founded as early as 1894 by British workers and businessmen. They were First Vienna Football Club, still known today as First Vienna, and Vienna Cricket and Football Club, which was commonly known as Cricketer and ultimately became FK Austria in 1925. The first meeting of these two famous clubs in 1894 was the first official match ever played on Austrian soil.

Graz soon receded into a secondary role as a soccer center, and Vienna's natural leadership came to the fore. A handful of Viennese clubs, as well as some in Graz and Innsbruck, appeared after 1894, and in 1897 the first competition, a knockout tournament called Der Challenge-Cup, was introduced. This was the first of three successive Austrian cup competitions, and it was open only to Viennese clubs. The first winner was Cricketer, and it was dominated until 1904 by Cricketer, First Vienna, and Wiener Athletic Club (WAC). Some Budapest clubs were

eventually allowed to participate, and Ferencváros Budapest won the title once before the cup's folding in 1911. Sportklub Rapid, which eventually became the most successful of all Austrian clubs, was founded in 1898 as I. Wiener Arbeiter-Fussballklub (First Vienna Workers' F.C.), and Vienna's great triumvirate clubs—Cricketer, First Vienna, and Rapid—was born.

In 1896, England (Amateur) played against a Vienna selection, and in 1899, an unofficial international was played between representative teams from Vienna and Prague. Six players in the latter Viennese team were from Cricketer, three were from First Vienna, and two from WAC. Southhampton became the first professional English club to visit Austria in 1900, and defeated a Vienna selection, 6-0. These matches increased interest in international competition, and English clubs on several levels toured Austria after the turn of the century. In 1902, full international teams from Austria and Hungary met in their historic match in Vienna, and Austria was an easy 5-0 winner on a hat trick by WAC's Jan Studnicka. The strong British influence that had been present since the beginning and the wealth of highly motivated players in anglophile Vienna laid the foundation for Austria's pioneer role in European soccer—a reputation shared with Bohemia and Hungary. In 1904, the forerunner of the present governing body, the Wiener Sportvereinigung (WSV), or Vienna Sports Union, was founded, and it joined already established associations in Bohemia and Hungary in putting Central European soccer on a firm footing. In 1905, the WSV's soccer section, known as the Österreichischer Fussball-Verband (ÖFV) became one of the first associations to join FIFA after the seven charter-members had founded the federation one year earlier.

Austria's first 10 internationals—and 19 of its first 24—were played against Hungary. In the first 10 (1902-08), Austria emerged with five victories and four defeats. In 1908, England visited Austria-Hungary on its first European tour and met Austria twice in three days, winning 6-1 and 11-1. This was followed by an 8-1 loss to England in 1909, bringing Austria's aggregate goal difference for the three matches to 3-25. These results were less successful than either Hungary's or Bohemia's on the 1908-09 English tours, but Austria was still considered one of the big three European powers (with Bohemia and Hungary) and had already gained more experience than any other non-Central European country on the continent.

The two greatest personalities in Austrian soccer emerged during this period. Hugo Meisl, the "father of Austrian soccer," was one of the founders of Wiener Amateure-Sportverein (Amateure) in 1911, which was an outgrowth of Cricketer and would later become FK Austria. Already a force in the OFV, Meisl became an international referee in 1907, and in 1912 he brought the English coach Jimmy Hogan, the second legendary figure in the Austrian game, to work with Amateure. Hogan coached the Austrian national team briefly before the 1912 Olympics in Stockholm, and with Meisl's blessing introduced the fluid and effective Scottish short passing game to Austrian players. In so doing, Hogan created a tactical revolution that was to bring fame and glory to Austrian soccer for 45 years. The fruits of his teachings, however, were not immediately seen, and Austria bowed out of the 1912 Olympics in the second round after a surprising loss to Holland. In the Olympic consolation tournament of 1912, Austria lost to Hungary, but defeated Norway and Italy and with its earlier first round thrashing of Germany went home with three wins and two defeats. This was Austria's official debut in international competition. After the 1912 Olympics, Austria defeated Italy twice again and lost three times to Hungary before World War I intervened.

The Austrian national league was introduced in 1911-12, but it was limited to Viennese clubs and took the name Wiener Liga (Vienna League). (Provincial clubs were finally accepted in 1949-50.) It was in this league that Rapid Vienna started to make its mark on Austrian soccer by winning eight of the first 12 championships, including the first two in 1912 and 1913. Amazingly, the Wiener Liga was uninterrupted during World War I, and when the new Austrian republic was born in 1918, a new cup competition—the Vienna Cup—was introduced, the old Challenge Cup having folded in 1911. Like the Challenge Cup and Wiener Liga, the new Vienna Cup was open only to Viennese clubs. Rapid won the first two Vienna Cups in 1919 and 1920 to tighten its hold on the Austrian game, but during the 1920s and '30s SK Admira (later Admira-Energie-Wacker) came to the fore with seven championships, and First Vienna and Amateure reemerged to take a pair of league titles apiece. Rapid, FK Austria, and

First Vienna each won the coveted Mitropa Cup and Austria's first international honors in the early 1930s. In 1925, Hakoah Vienna became the first and only Jewish-based club to win a first division championship in European soccer.

The impact of Meisl and Hogan became fully evident in the years following World War I. While Hogan took coaching jobs in Hungary, Germany, North Africa, and Switzerland, Meisl guided Austrian soccer as the secretary of the OFV and manager of the national team, in addition to having close ties with SK Admira. Under his tutelage, both Austria and Admira played the slow and attractive short passing game, and, while Admira became the greatest club of its day, Austria began to achieve excellent international results on a relatively consistent basis in 1924. Hungary and Czechoslovakia continued to be Austria's most difficult opponents throughout this period, and accounted for nine of its 13 losses between 1924-30. Against these 13 losses, however, were 30 victories and nine draws. In 1927-29, Austria placed second to Italy—an emerging power—in the first International Cup (later to be renamed the Dr. Gero Cup after the postwar president of the Austrian association). In 1931, Meisl's famous *Wunderteam* was born when Scotland went down to a 5-0 defeat in Vienna. It was an historic performance, and in this and the 26 matches that followed (1931-34) Austria lost only twice (to England and Czechoslovakia), accumulating a goal difference of 97-39.

There were 6-0 and 5-0 wins over Germany, an 8-2 defeat of Hungary, an 8-1 victory over Switzerland, 6-1 wins over Belgium and Bulgaria, and Austria won its first honor at full international level by capturing the International Cup of 1931-32. In 1932, Jimmy Hogan returned to Vienna and took over the national team from Meisl, infusing yet more of the philosophy that had carried Austrian soccer so far. Meisl remained the father figure of the team and its guiding light, but Hogan gave it polish and was an important factor behind Austria's extraordinary success after 1931. The *Wunderteam* was based on Admira, FK Austria, and First Vienna players, and a typical lineup consisted of the following: Hiden; Schramseis, Blum; Braun, Smistik, Nausch; Zischek, Gschweidl, Sindelar, Schall, Vogl. Rudi Hiden of WAC and Racing Club de Paris was one of Europe's best goalkeepers. Center forward Matthias Sindelar of FK Austria, nicknamed "the man made of paper," because he was truly paper-thin and weaved on the pitch like a piece of paper flowing in the wind, was perhaps the greatest Austrian player of all time. Josef Bican of Rapid and Admira, who played inside right or center forward after 1933, was Sindelar's equal in skill and undoubtedly his country's most gifted goalscorer in history. The *Wunderteam's* downfall came sadly with a 1-0 semifinal loss to Italy in the 1934 World Cup in Milan. Meisl had warned of his team's age and tiredness and of the decided advantage afforded to Italy by passionate home crowds cheering from the stands, and he was right. The end of an era was sealed when Germany won the third place game over a disconsolate Austria by 3-2.

Between 1934 and 1937, the glories of the now disbanded *Wunderteam* faded rapidly. Austria was unable to defeat Hungary in eight attempts, and other results were spotty at best. It managed to salvage a second place finish in the 1933-35 International Cup, but tragedy lay ahead as 1937 approached. In this bleak year, Hugo Meisl died, the national team seemed headed for a poor finish in the 1936-38 International Cup, and Austria barely qualified for the 1938 World Cup with a 2-1 win over lowly Latvia in Vienna. Hitler's occupation of Austria in March 1938 ended the International Cup before it could be completed, and, sadly, it also prevented Austria from entering the 1938 World Cup.

In 1937, the ÖFV was replaced in FIFA by the Allgemeiner Österreichischer Fussball-Bund, whose name was later shortened to the present Österreichischer Fussball-Bund (ÖFB). During the German occupation, four Austrian clubs participated in the German league, and Rapid Vienna actually won the German cup in 1938 and the German championship in 1941. Austrian champions during the war—Rapid and First Vienna—were in fact winners of the Austrian regional league under German auspices. When international competition was resumed after the war, semiprofessionalism (recognized in the early 1920s) was not reintroduced, and this enabled the full national team to enter the 1948 Olympics in London. Its hopes were dashed in the first round by a defeat to Sweden, the eventual winner, but the seeds of another great era in Austrian soccer were sown.

Though results in the 1948-53 International Cup were disappointing, a winning team was assembled by 1950, and in May of that year Austria conquered mighty Hungary in what was to be the Magyars' last defeat in four years.

This 5-3 victory launched Austria upward again, and was followed by lopsided wins over Yugoslavia, Denmark, Scotland, Belgium, the Republic of Ireland, and a rare 2-2 draw in England. Finally, Austria qualified for the 1954 World Cup final rounds with a 9-1 thrashing of Portugal. The backbone of this extraordinary new Austrian team was attacking center half Ernst Ocwirk of FK Austria, who orchestrated another version of the old "Danubian style." Despite their long-standing success, the tactics taught long ago to Austrian players by Jimmy Hogan were finally abandoned before the 1954 World Cup. Ocwirk became an orthodox wing half and with outstanding Rapid Vienna players such as Gerd Hanappi at right back and Ernst Happel in the role of stopper center half, the Austrians took third place in the 1954 World Cup, their highest honor ever. After a certain amount of luck in not having to play against Uruguay in its first round group, Austria uncharacteristically kicked long balls past Switzerland to win one of the highest scoring World Cup matches of all time (7-5). In the semi-final, however, Germany scored six robust goals (two from corner kicks, two from crosses, and two from penalties), and Austria, returning to a more familiar and delicate approach, could only answer with one. In the third place game, Ocwirk performed with precision, and downtrodden Uruguay was defeated 3-1.

This was Austria's last hurrah to date in international competition. Though it qualified for the 1958 World Cup (for the last time until 1978), Austria's fortunes came to an end with the decline of the Ocwirk ensemble. Meanwhile, the Austrians have participated in each edition of the European Football Championship from the beginning, but have not advanced beyond the first or second round. Semiprofessionalism was reintroduced in the 1950s, but this advance has been overshadowed by the rise of provincial clubs and a decline of the game in Vienna, as a revitalized and sophisticated Viennese popoulation has turned to more urbane pastimes. The 1970s have been totally dominated by Tirol-Swarowski-Innsbruck (formerly Wacker Innsbruck), which thus far has won five championships and four cups in nine years. Austria's qualification for the 1978 World Cup was impressive (six games without a defeat), but its long range effect on the Austrian game remains questionable. Linzer ASK was the first provincial club to win the first division title in 1965, and by this time the best Austrian players were beginning to seek higher financial rewards in Germany, Belgium, Holland, and Spain. Full-time professionalism has still not been introduced even among the wealthier clubs.

In 1949-50, the year after three provincial clubs were admitted to the new Division A for the first time, a Division B was added to the league, and 10 years later Division B was expanded into three sections (East, Central, and West). In 1965-66, Division A became known as the Nationaliga. A smaller 10-team "super league" was introduced in 1974-75 in an effort to increase spectator interest, but the experiment has not been successful. In the meantime, Austrian clubs have failed to achieve international honors in the various European club championships, though Rapid Vienna, winner of a record 25 Austrian championships, advanced to the semifinal of the 1960-61 European Cup, and FK Austria reached the final of the 1977-78 European Cup Winners' Cup. This has hardly been compensation for the many decades of entertaining soccer provided by Austrian teams in the past.

Champions

1912	Rapid Vienna	1935	Rapid Vienna	1958	Wiener Sport-Klub
1913	Rapid Vienna	1936	SK Admira	1959	Weiner Sport-Klub
1914	WAF	1937	SK Admira	1960	Rapid Vienna
1915	WAC	1938	Rapid Vienna	1961	FK Austria
1916	Rapid Vienna	1939	SK Admira	1962	FK Austria
1917	Rapid Vienna	1940	Rapid Vienna	1963	FK Austria
1918	Floridsdorfer AC	1941	Rapid Vienna	1964	Rapid Vienna
1919	Rapid Vienna	1942	First Vienna	1965	Linzer ASK
1920	Rapid Vienna	1943	First Vienna	1966	Admira-Energie
1921	Rapid Vienna	1944	First Vienna	1967	Rapid Vienna
1922	Weiner Sport-Klub	1945	not completed	1968	Rapid Vienna
1923	Rapid Vienna	1946	Rapid Vienna	1969	FK Austria
1924	Amateure	1947	Wacker Vienna	1970	FK Austria
1925	Hakoah Vienna	1948	Rapid Vienna	1971	Wacker Innsbruck
1926	FK Austria	1949	FK Austria	1972	Tirol-Swarowski-Innsbruck
1927	SK Admira	1950	FK Austria	1973	Tirol-Swarowski-Innsbruck
1928	SK Admira	1951	Rapid Vienna	1974	VÖEST Linz
1929	Rapid Vienna	1952	Rapid Vienna	1975	Tirol-Swarowski-Innsbruck
1930	Rapid Vienna	1953	FK Austria	1976	FK Austria/WAC
1931	First Vienna	1954	Rapid Vienna	1977	Tirol-Swarowski-Innsbruck
1932	SK Admira	1955	FK Austria	1978	FK Austria/WAC
1933	First Vienna	1956	Rapid Vienna		
1934	SK Admira	1957	Rapid Vienna		

Challenge Cup Winners

1897	Cricketer	1905	Sportclub
1898	Cricketer	1906	no competition
1899	First Vienna	1907	no competition
1900	First Vienna	1908	no competition
1901	WAC	1909	Ferencváros Budapest
1902	Cricketer	1910	no competition
1903	WAC	1911	Sportclub
1904	WAC		

Vienna Cup Winners

1919	Rapid Vienna	1930	First Vienna	1941	no competition
1920	Rapid Vienna	1931	WAC	1942	no competition
1921	Amateure	1932	SK Admira	1943	no competition
1922	WAF	1933	FK Austria	1944	no competition
1923	Sportclub	1934	SK Admira	1945	no competition
1924	Amateure	1935	FK Austria	1946	Rapid Vienna
1925	FK Austria	1936	FK Austria	1947	Wacker Vienna
1926	FK Austria	1937	First Vienna	1948	FK Austria
1927	Rapid Vienna	1938	WAC	1949	FK Austria
1928	SK Admira	1939	no competition		
1929	First Vienna	1940	no competition		

Austrian Cup Winners

1948	FK Austria	1959	Wiener Sport-Klub	1970	Wacker Innsbruck
1949	FK Austria	1960	FK Austria	1971	FK Austria
1950	no competition	1961	Rapid Vienna	1972	Rapid Vienna
1951	no competition	1962	FK Austria	1973	Tirol-Swarowski-Innsbruck
1952	no competition	1963	FK Austria	1974	FK Austria
1953	no competition	1964	SK Admira	1975	Tirol-Swarowski-Innsbruck
1954	no competition	1965	Linzer ASK	1976	Rapid Vienna
1955	no competition	1966	Admira-Energie	1977	FK Austria/WAC
1956	no competition	1967	FK Austria	1978	Tirol-Swarowski-Innsbruck
1957	no competition	1968	Rapid Vienna		
1958	no competition	1969	Rapid Vienna		

Austria/Wiener Athletic Club-Elementar, Fussball Klub

Location: *Vienna, Austria;* stadium: *Wienerstadion Prater (73,243);* colors: *violet jerseys, white shorts;* honors: *Mitropa Cup (1933, 1936), Austrian champion (1924, 1926, 1949, 1950, 1953, 1955, 1961, 1962, 1963, 1969, 1970, 1976, 1978), Austrian cup winner (1948, 1949, 1960, 1962, 1963, 1967, 1971, 1974, 1977).*

Founded 1911 as Wiener Amateure-Sportverein and known for many years as Amateure, the club's present name was adopted in 1926. Amateure was an outgrowth of the Vienna Cricket and Football Club, which was founded by British residents in Vienna in 1894, and with First Vienna was one of the first clubs in Austria. Cricketer, as the Vienna Cricket and Football Club was commonly called, participated in the very first game ever played on Austrian soil in the year of its formation. It was the first winner of old Challenge Cup, the country's first cup competition, and won this trophy in 1897, 1898,

and 1902. Under the name Amateure, FK Austria won the Vienna Cup in 1921 and 1924, and as FK Austria won again in 1925, 1926, 1933, 1935, 1936, 1948, and 1949. (The Austrian national cup—won by FK Austria nine times—was officially introduced in 1949 and overlapped the Vienna Cup by two years.) In 1973, FK Austria absorbed Wiener Athletic Club (WAC) and a smaller Vienna club called Elementar to form the present amalgamation. WAC had won the Austrian championship in 1915, the Challenge Cup in 1901, 1903, and 1904, and the Vienna Cup in 1931 and 1938. Elementar had never won an Austrian title.

In 1949 and 1950, FK Austria won league titles with possibly the best team in its history, including captain and wing half Ernst Ocwirk, who led Austria to its grand comeback in the early 1950s, and went on to win many more honors throughout the decade. While the Austrian game floundered in the 1960s, FK Austria enjoyed several years of domestic success, mainly under manager Karl Schlechta, and in 1969 and 1970 it won further championships under manager Ocwirk. It failed to make any headway in European club championships until 1978, when it suddenly broke through to the final of the European Cup Winners' Cup and lost decisively to RSC Anderlecht.

FK Austria has been the major rival of Rapid Vienna for many decades, stemming from the early days of the Austrian league. But its first string of successes began with the Vienna Cup during the 1920s, when it won and lost the final four times each, and in the 1930s, when it won three more cups. Its attractive style during these glorious years— and one that had much influence on the great Austrian *wunderteam* that dominated European soccer during the early 1930s—was based on the Scottish short passing game, which English coach Jimmy Hogan had taught to Amateure players in 1912-13, changing forever the way Austrians played the game. The FK Austria of the 1930s was led by center forward Matthias Sindelar, the greatest Austrian player of all time, whose thin, bony frame seemed to work wonders in the act of ball juggling.

away   See: **home and away**

away-goals rule

A tie-breaking calibration, which is used in certain competitions to determine the relative standing of two teams finishing equal on points in a league table or after home and away legs. There are two variations. A winner may result from: 1) scoring a superior number of goals in away legs; or 2) accumulating a superior number of total "goals for" after doubling the number of goals scored in away legs.

B

back door

The area adjacent to the goalpost on the opposite side of the goalmouth from which a cross or corner kick is being taken. A ball well placed at the "back door" is often disadvantageous to the goalkeeper.

back-heel

A kick taken with the heel of the foot in order to move the ball to the rear of the kicker.

back pass

A pass directed away from the opponent's goal.

Bahamas

Bahamas Football Association
P.O. Box 3919
Nassau, N.P.

Founded: 1967
FIFA: 1968

Affiliated clubs: *27;* registered players: *476;* national stadium: *none;* largest stadiums: *Clifford Park (5,000), Queen Elizabeth Sports Centre (5,000);* colors: *royal blue jerseys, white shorts;* season: *October to May;* honors: *none*

The Bahamas is one of the least active FIFA members in international competition, probably since the 200,000 people over its 700 islands are more preoccupied with cricket than soccer. Among British colonies in the Caribbean region, Bahamas soccer was one of the last to get off the ground, and the Bahamas F.A. was not formed until 1967. Some interest has now been expressed in future Olympic tournaments, but as yet no attempt has been made to qualify for the World Cup. Since the association lacks membership in CONCACAF, regional championships on both club and national level are out of reach. In domestic competition, fifteen clubs play on the senior level with a total of 260 players between them. There is a national league and a national cup competition, but the small number of clubs precludes the possibility of upper and lower divisions. Recently a fair number of good Bahaman players have come to play in the United States.

Bahrain

Bahrain Football Association
P.O. Box 5464
Manama

Founded: 1951
FIFA: 1966
AFC: 1970

Affiliated clubs: *36;* **registered players:** *2,714;* **national stadium:** *Isa Town Stadium, Isa Town (16,000);* **largest stadium:** *Isa Town Stadium;* **colors:** *white jerseys, red shorts;* **season:** *October to June;* **honors:** *none.*

Bahrain is one of the Persian (Arabian) Gulf states whose rapid economic rise has prompted a concerted effort to advance the level of native soccer. Like neighboring rivals Qatar and United Arab Emirates, it is trying to achieve regional success by the early 1980s by importing the best coaches money can buy. Some progress can be seen, though the gulf states as a group have a difficult obstacle to overcome in Kuwait, the major power of the region.

Soccer arrived on Bahrain Island after World War II with the influx of British workers who were brought in to develop the fledgling petroleum industry. The Bahrain Football Association, founded in 1951 as the Football Association of Bahrain, was the first national association established in the Trucial States region, and the first in the immediate area to join FIFA and the Union of Arab Football Associations. Some indication of its early standing in Asian competition was a 10-1 thrashing by Iraq in the Arab Cup of 1966. In 1970, Bahrain played host to the first Arabian Gulf Tournament, the most important competition in the region, and placed well by finishing second to Kuwait and ahead of Saudi Arabia and Qatar. Bahrain defeated Qatar, drew with Saudi Arabia, and lost to Kuwait. In the tournaments of 1972, 1974, and 1976, however, its standing as an equal with other small gulf states became a pattern, as Kuwait continued to dominate the competition.

Bahrain has yet to advance to the final stages of the Asian Cup, and hasn't participated extensively in either the Asian Games or in Olympic qualification rounds. In an attempt to qualify for the 1970 World Cup, Bahrain placed a poor second in its group to runaway winner Kuwait and ahead of Qatar. A comparison of international results with other nations of the Arabian Peninsula reveals that little divides the quality of play among Bahrain, Saudi Arabia, Qatar, and United Arab Emirates, while Oman, Yemen PDR, and North Yemen lag far behind.

The Bahrain first division is composed of six clubs; 30 additional clubs take part in senior competition, which includes both a national championship and annual cup competition. The Asian Champions' Cup ceased operation before Bahrain had a chance to prove itself in international club competition, though the BFA joined the Asian Football Confederation in 1970. The future of soccer in oil-rich Bahrain now rests in the hands of FIFA instructors whose problems start with constructing a grass field to play on.

Balkan Cup

A regional competition for nations of the Balkan peninsula held irregularly since 1929. Like the Scandinavian Championship, the Balkan Cup has not garnered much attention outside the region, but some interesting results have emerged, particularly Albania's only international honor to date, its winning of the seventh Balkan Cup in 1946. The original participants in the competition were Rumania, Yugoslavia, Greece, and Bulgaria. Yugoslavia dropped out of the sixth cup in 1936, and Greece was replaced by Albania in 1946, the seventh cup. Turkey participated in the eighth cup in 1975, as well as Greece, while Albania once again declined to participate. In 1976, for the first time, all five Balkan states participated in the same tournament. With the exception of the 1975 edition, each competition has been held under a league system, the country accumulating the highest number of points declared the winner.

In 1947, the Balkan Cup was extended to include Czechoslovakia, Hungary, and Poland, and went by the name Balkan-Central European Cup. An actual tournament was not held; rather, the results of scheduled international matches between participating countries doubled as cup results. The winner was Hungary and the runner-up Yugoslavia. The Balkan Cup itself did not resurface until 1975.

An attempt is now under way to revive the tournament on an annual basis, but its existence is so tenuous that home and away legs, a feature of the first edition, have not yet been reintroduced. The tradition of holding the competition in one or another capital city over a span of days continues. The biggest wins and losses in the tournament have been Rumania's 8-1 trouncing of Greece at Bucharest in 1930, and Rumania's 8-0 win over Bulgaria in 1933, also at Bucharest. The seventh Balkan Cup, held in Tirana, represents the only example of Albania's hosting of a soccer competition.

Since the cup was suspended for nearly 30 years of the postwar period, the overwhelming strength of Yugoslavia, the region's unrivaled power, is not reflected in the standings. On the other hand, Bulgaria's three wins and Rumania's two represent these countries' major international achievements to date, although Bulgaria has won a silver and bronze medal in Olympic competition.

Winners

1931	Rumania		1936	Rumania
1932	Bulgaria		1946	Albania
1933	Rumania		1975	Bulgaria
1934	Yugoslavia		1976	Yugoslavia
1935	Bulgaria			

Cumulative Ranking (1931-76)
(number of editions in parentheses)

	P	W	D	L	F	A	P
Rumania (9)	28	15	4	9	73	50	34
Yugoslavia (8)	26	15	2	9	62	46	32
Bulgaria (9)	29	13	4	12	59	68	30
Greece (8)	24	5	3	16	45	72	13
Albania (2)	6	3	1	2	12	10	7
Turkey (1)	2	0	0	2	1	6	0

Standings

1929-31

	P	W	D	L	F	A	P
Rumania	6	5	0	1	26	13	10
Yugoslavia	6	3	0	3	12	9	6
Greece	6	2	0	4	13	20	4
Bulgaria	6	2	0	4	10	19	4

1932 (in Belgrade)

	P	W	D	L	F	A	P
Bulgaria	3	3	0	0	7	2	6
Yugoslavia	3	2	0	1	12	5	4
Rumania	3	1	0	2	4	5	2
Greece	3	0	0	3	1	12	0

1933 (in Bucharest)

	P	W	D	L	F	A	P
Rumania	3	3	0	0	13	0	6
Yugoslavia	3	2	0	1	9	8	4

	P	W	D	L	F	A	P
Bulgaria	3	1	0	2	2	11	2
Greece	3	0	0	3	3	8	0

1934-35 (in Athens)

	P	W	D	L	F	A	P
Yugoslavia	3	3	0	0	10	4	6
Rumania	3	1	1	1	5	8	3
Bulgaria	3	1	0	2	7	8	2
Greece	3	0	1	2	4	6	1

1935 (in Sofia)

	P	W	D	L	F	A	P
Bulgaria	3	2	1	0	12	5	5
Greece	3	1	1	1	10	8	3
Rumania	3	1	1	1	4	6	3
Yugoslavia	3	0	1	2	4	11	1

1936 (in Bucharest)

	P	W	D	L	F	A	P
Rumania	2	2	0	0	9	3	4
Bulgaria	2	1	0	1	6	8	2
Greece	2	0	0	2	6	10	0

1946 (in Tirana)

	P	W	D	L	F	A	P
Albania	3	2	0	1	6	4	4
Yugoslavia	3	2	0	1	6	5	4
Rumania	3	1	1	1	4	4	3
Bulgaria	3	0	1	2	4	7	1

1975
Group A

	P	W	D	L	F	A	P
Bulgaria	2	2	0	0	7	2	4
Rumania	2	1	0	1	5	5	2
Turkey	2	0	0	2	1	6	0

Group B

	P	W	D	L	F	A	P
Yugoslavia	1	1	0	0	5	3	2
Greece	1	0	0	1	3	5	0

Third Place Game
Greece—Rumania   3-2

Final
Bulgaria—Yugoslavia   0-0
(Bulgaria won on penalty kicks)

1976

	P	W	D	L	F	A	P
Yugoslavia	3	2	1	0	4	1	5
Greece	2	1	1	0	2	1	3
Albania	3	1	1	1	6	6	3
Bulgaria	3	0	2	1	4	6	2
Rumania	2	0	1	1	2	3	1

Baltic Cup

During their 20-year long period of independence between the world wars, the Baltic states formed their own national associations, and engaged in international competition. Between them they played other European opponents a total of 89 times, but most of their concentration was placed on the Baltic Cup, an annual tournament introduced in 1928. Estonia and Latvia fared better in Europe than the more insular Lithuania, and achieved a margin of superiority in this series as well. The competition ended, as did national bodies that participated in it, when these short-lived republics were absorbed into the USSR in 1940.

Winners

1928 Latvia	1934 no competition
1929 Estonia	1935 Lithuania
1930 Lithuania	1936 Latvia
1931 Estonia	1937 Latvia
1932 Latvia	1938 Estonia
1933 invalidated	

banana kick

A kick that "bends" or curves, as in a free kick around a wall of players. Its curvature is created by striking the ball with the side of the foot to give it a fast spin. In Brazil it's called *fôlha sêca*, or "dry leaf."

Bangladesh

Bangladesh Football Federation
Stadium
Dacca 2

Founded: 1974
FIFA: 1974

National stadium: *Dacca Stadium, Dacca (23,000);* largest stadium: *Dacca Stadium;* colors: *orange jerseys, white shorts (further information unavailable).*

The Bangladesh Football Federation is the world's newest independent national association, and in 1974 it joined Liechtenstein in becoming the latest member of FIFA. The game, however, had been well established for many decades, when the area was known as East Pakistan. With the formation of the Pakistan Football Federation in 1948, a regional association for East Pakistan was formed to administer one of Pakistan's four provincial championships, the Dacca League, traditionally held between March and November. The South Asian custom of barefooted play was officially banned in the early 1950s, and at the same time the official duration of league matches was increased from 70 minutes to the standard 90. Prior to independence in 1972, the Dacca regional selection was an important participant in the national championship of Pakistan.

Today, despite strong interest in field hockey throughout South Asia, soccer is unquestionably the national sport of Bangla-desh, and since 1974 efforts have been made to enter the Asian mainstream. In 1976, Bangladesh participated in the twentieth Merdeka Football Tournament in Malaysia, Southeast Asia's biggest competition, and the national team also entered the Asian Nations' Cup of 1976. Grouped with Afghanistan, India, Iraq, Jordan, Qatar, and Saudia Arabia, Bangladesh placed poorly, but its participation was hailed as an advancement in itself. One of the first demonstrative signs of political reconciliation with Pakistan following the civil war was Bangladesh's inclusion in the Quaid-I-Azam Football Cup in 1976 at Karachi.

Banks, Gordon, O.B.E. (1937-   )

The finest English goalkeeper of all time and an inspiration to a whole generation of European keepers. His level-headedness and ceaseless drive to improve on past performance earned him immense popularity among players and fans alike. Banks had natural acrobatic abilities from the beginning, and he became an exceptionally astute student of the geometry of goalkeeping, as evidenced by the brinkmanship he displayed in the penalty area so consistently throughout his career.

Signed by third division Chesterfield at age 18, he was snapped up immediately after military duty in 1959 by first division Leicester City (the second of his three unfashionable club affiliations). Three years after his international debut in 1963, he excelled for England in its World Cup triumph, and drew world acclaim. Widely thought to be the best keeper in the world—"as safe as the Banks of England"—he was transferred to Stoke City in 1967 when understudy Peter Shilton, himself an England keeper in later years, appeared a better long range investment. In 1970, Banks was awarded an O.B.E., and at the World Cup in Mexico topped all goalkeeping performances in recent memory with saves that left Pelé and others shaking their heads in disbelief. He reached his peak in 1972 when he led Stoke to a League Cup victory at Wembley, the first title in the club's history, and Banks led the celebration. Seven months later, in a sudden turn of fate, he was the victim of a tragic car accident in which he lost the use of one eye. An attempted comeback following his long recuperation was unsatisfactory, and he turned to coaching (England Under-23 and youth teams), working diligently to regain his form in the meantime. After insurance companies failed to back his contract with the Scottish club Morton, he was finally given his chance for a comeback by the Fort Lauderdale Strikers in 1977, where he has remained as an assistant coach, as wise and experienced as ever.

Barbados

Barbados Football Association
c/o M/S Da Costa & Musson Ltd.
Broad Street
Bridgetown

Founded: 1910
FIFA: 1968
CONCACAF: 1968

Affiliated clubs: *43;* **registered players:** *950;* **national stadium:** *Barbados National Stadium, St. Michael (12,000);* **stadium of equal size:** *Kensington Oval, Bridgetown*

(12,000); **colors:** *royal blue and gold jerseys, gold shorts;* **season:** *February to May;* honors: *none.*

Barbados has only recently entered international competition on a regular basis, but soccer has been established there for many decades. At first, the game in Barbados was closely linked with cricket, as was the custom in small British colonies, and the formation of the Barbados Amateur Football Society in 1910 occurred about the same time Jamaica and Trinidad started their associations. Indeed, these three got a head start on all the Caribbean colonies. Throughout the colonial period the Barbados Association was affiliated with The Football Association in London. Though full independence from Britain was achieved by 1961, the Barbados Amateur F.A. did not join FIFA until 1968; unlike the Bahamas and Antigua, however, Barbados did join ranks with CONCACAF and intends to participate actively in future regional competitons.

With such a small number of players at its disposal, Barbados rarely has the opportunity to engage in international friendlies; many of its results are in connection with Olympic and World Cup qualifying rounds. In both cases, Barbados has faced elimination in the first round. In 1975 its run for the Olympics was stopped by neighboring Trinidad in a play-off match after both home and away legs were drawn. In the first qualification round for the 1978 World Cup, Trinidad again eliminated Barbados in a play-off match after home and away legs were split.

In 1972, the government of Barbados proclaimed a "National Football Development Year" in an official effort to foster new enthusiasm for the game and to encourage youth participation. Forty-eight senior teams take part in a national league with a First Division of eight clubs. There is also an annual cup competition. With over 250,000 people lodged in a mere 166 square miles of land, there is no need for regional leagues, and a system of upper and lower divisions in the national league exists instead. There are two major playing fields, but soccer must share a portion of the spotlight with the venerable cricket.

Barcelona, Fútbol Club

Location: *Barcelona, Spain;* **stadium:** *Estadio Nou Camp (90,138);* **colors:** *red and blue striped jerseys, blue shorts;* **honors:** *Fairs Cup (1958, 1960, 1966), Latin Cup (1949, 1953), Spanish champion (1929, 1945, 1948, 1949, 1952, 1953, 1959, 1960, 1974), Spanish cup winner (1910 unofficial, 1912, 1913 unofficial, 1920, 1922, 1925, 1926, 1928, 1942, 1951, 1952, 1953, 1957, 1959, 1963, 1968, 1971).*

Founded 1899 as Foot-ball Club Barcelona by the naturalized Swiss Hans Gamper (also known as Don Juan Gamper), who introduced soccer to the Catalan capital. After playing its first matches against teams of British sailors, it soon found other Spanish opponents, notably Barcelona rivals Espanol, and in 1902 it was one of four clubs to participate in the first Spanish Cup, an invitation-only series to celebrate the coronation of Alfonso XIII. Eight years later the club won its first cup, Athletic Bilbao and Madrid F.C. (later Real Madrid) having already won several apiece. By this time, Barcelona had become embroiled in regional organizational squabbles that lasted for four seasons, and two of its cup victories during this time were actually recorded as unofficial. The strength of the club, however, was unquestioned, and by World War I it was one of Spain's major clubs. During the 1920s, it experienced the first of many successful periods, dominating Spanish soccer with five cup wins, and, after becoming the first Spanish club to turn professional, the first league championship in 1929. Today it is one of the few Spanish clubs that has never been relegated.

Barca has been one of the great clubs of Europe since the late 1940s, and the consistency of its postwar success has led to an explosive archrivalry with Real Madrid, much to the chagrin of the other Madrid club, Atlético. Its first world famous team was that of 1947-53, when it won four league championships and three Spanish cups, punctuated by two victories in the Latin Cup, then Europe's premier international club competition. Its Latin Cup trophies were won with victories over Stade de Reims, Sporting Lisbon, Juventus, and OGC Nice. The kingpins of this great team, especially during the early 1950s, were goalkeeper Antonio Ramallets and Hungarian international star Ladislav Kubala, both of whom made the transition to Barca's second great era in the late 1950s.

Though Barcelona thoroughly dominated Spanish soccer in the immediate postwar era, it was unlucky to have its spotlight taken away by the surging Real Madrid, which by 1954 was in the process of putting together the greatest club side in history. Real's accomplishments of the late 1950s have tended to obscure Barcelona's of the same period, for this was quite possibly the finest Barcelona team ever seen. Few other clubs could challenge its claim to being Europe's second best—after Real Madrid. Barca was led through part of this golden era by the naturalized French manager Helenio Herrera, who benefited greatly from the growing international player market.

By the start of the first Inter-Cities Fairs Cup in 1955-58, Barca had already signed Luis Suarez, who with Francisco Gento ranks as the greatest Spanish-born forward of all time. The club later signed Hungarian stars Sandor Kocsis and Zoltan Czibor, and won the first two editions of the Fairs Cup. In 1960-61, it became the first club to eliminate Real from the European Cup, losing ultimately to Benfica

in the final on an own goal by Ramallets. Barca's extraordinary forward line in this series included Kubala, Kocsis, Evaristo, Suárez, and Czibor. The victory over Real was especially sweet because of Barca's elimination at the hands of Real the year before, after which Herrera was systematically fired. The effort to emulate Real since the late 1950s has earned Barcelona a particularly coarse reputation in its hiring and firing of managers. At one point, there were 11 managers in 10 years.

Additional championships and Spanish cups were won throughout the 1960s, though Barcelona was thwarted each time in the international arena, much the same as Italy's Juventus. It did win a record third Fairs Cup in 1966—defeating other Spanish clubs in two of the later rounds—yet, no European Cup or European Cup Winners' Cup honors. In Barcelona, despite the best overall international club record in Europe, failure or success was, and still is, measured by one yardstick: Real Madrid. With seemingly unlimited wealth, Barca eventually built one of Europe's greatest sporting complexes, and improved existing facilities with religious zeal. (Its old Estadio Las Corts, which it had occupied since 1922, was abandoned for the grand new Estadio Nou Camp in 1957, and in 1966 the Nou Camp was enlarged and remodeled into one of the most beautiful grounds in Europe.) The hirings and firings continued, and finally in 1973, Barca secured the services of Ajax Amsterdam manager Rinus Michels, and Europe's greatest star of the 1970s, the Ajax striker Johan Cruyff. Cruyff led Barcelona to one championship in 1974, but by 1978 he too had tired of the pressure and announced his departure.

Bayern München, Fussball-Club

Location: *Munich, West Germany;* stadium: *Olympiastadion (75,600);* colors: *red jerseys with white trim, red shorts;* honors: *Intercontinental Cup (1976), Super Cup (1974), European Cup (1974, 1975, 1976), European Cup Winners' Cup (1967), German champion (1932), West German champion (1969, 1972, 1973, 1974), West German cup winner (1957, 1966, 1967, 1969, 1971).*

Founded 1900. Under the German system of regional leagues that was in operation until 1963, Bayern München (Bavarian Munich) played in the Southern Regional League

(Suddeutschland Regionalliga), winning regional championships in 1926 and 1928 and one isolated national championship in 1932, but it failed to gain any other national honors until its West German cup victory of 1957. Its mediocre record was overshadowed for many decades by the other big Munich club, TSV 1860 München, and when the Bundesliga (Federal League) was formed in 1963 it was TSV 1860 that was chosen to participate rather than Bayern. In 1965, Bayern won the Süddeutschland championship once again, and gained promotion to the Bundesliga in 1965-66.

Already in its lineup were midfield genius Franz Beckenbauer and the burly goalscoring center forward Gerd Müller. They led Bayern to a third place finish in the Bundesliga in its first season in the upper ranks and a convincing West German cup victory the same year. Subsequently, the name of Bayern München became so closely linked with the growth of West German soccer and the extraordinary success of the national team that the two squads appeared at times indistinguishable. In 1966, goalkeeper Sepp Maier joined the team, and Bayern grew stronger each year. Its first foray into a European club championship, the European Cup Winners' Cup (1967), resulted in triumph with a 1-0 win over Glasgow Rangers in the final. In this year also, Bayern won its second West German cup in succession, and in 1969 won its first league-cup double, finishing with a stunning eight-point margin in the league. The following year it was disappointed in its first European Cup competition after a first round loss to St. Étienne of France.

Bayern won another West German cup in 1970-71, and in 1971-72 reached new heights with a brilliantly mounted league championship. West Germany's winning of the European Football Championship in 1972 with a host of Bayern stars, including Beckenbauer, Müller, and Maier, and the redoubtable midfielders Paul Breitner and Uli Hoeness, gave Bayern the confidence it had been looking for. It won another West German championship in 1973 with sophistication and aplomb—inspired by Beckenbauer—and reminiscent of the fluid style employed by three-time European Cup winner Ajax Amsterdam. In the 1973-74 European Cup, Bayern eliminated Atvidaberg, Dynamo Dresden, CSKA Sofia, and Újpest Dózsa to gain the final, and there played Atlético Madrid to a 1-1 draw, forcing a play-off. In the play-off, a new level of goalscoring efficiency

was reached and Atlético was buried, 4-0. Bayern's high standard continued unabated in international competition for three years, despite the loss of successive league honors to archrival Borussia Mönchengladbach.

Bayern became an invincible force in European competition, and rightfully so; at least five of its players were stars of the West German national team that won the World Cup in 1974. Meanwhile, Bayern's second European Cup victory in 1975 was attained with early round wins over FC Magdeburg, Ararat Erevan, and St. Étienne, but its 2-0 win over Leeds United in the Parisian final was tarnished by clashes between Leeds fans and the French police. Bayern's victory meant automatic qualification for the next European Cup in 1975-76, and, as expected, this too was won by a seemingly unstoppable Bayern goalscoring machine. Bayern's passage to this final was not especially difficult—its opponents were Jeunesse Esch, Malmö FF, Benfica, and Real Madrid—but in St. Étienne the Germans not only had an old rival to displace but an elegant French team fully capable of defeating the veteran Bayern stars. In the end, only one goal was scored on a misty Scottish night in Glasgow and it went to Bayern's midfielder Franz Roth. Bayern had now duplicated the European Cup treble of Ajax in the early 1970s, and, in addition, had provided the foundation for a world championship winning national team. Beckenbauer was widely regarded as the world's most complete player, Müller the finest center forward in Europe, and Maier the safest goalkeeper since England's Gordon Banks.

It came as a shock when Bayern lost to Dinamo Kiev in the quarter-finals of the 1976-77 European Cup, and ended an era in European soccer that was highlighted by Bayern's superb craftsmanship as a team and the immense popularity of its individual stars. In 1977, Bayern lost Hoeness (later to be general manager), and Beckenbauer was lured to the Cosmos to play with Pelé. The first season without Beckenbauer was a disaster, and Bayern fought to the final week to stay out of relegation trouble. Between November 1976 and April 1978, Bayern failed to win a single away game in the Bundesliga. Yet, despite Müller's move to Ft. Lauderdale in 1979, Bayern still attracted attention by producing new players of international caliber.

Beckenbauer, Franz   (1945-   )

The elegant, commanding, and flawless attacking sweeper of Bayern München and West Germany. In the late 1960s and early '70s, Beckenbauer did more than any player in the world to revolutionize the tactics of the game. From his early role as a midfielder, he moved into the sweeper position, traditionally a defensive plug as part of the negative approach in Italy's *catenaccio*, and deployed himself in front of as well as behind his defensive backs to make frequent runs toward the opponent's goal. Sometimes he took the ball to the front of the attack himself and let loose a seering shot, but more often he utilized his pinpoint accuracy to distribute to an attacking teammate. His passes, casual in appearance and made to either side or up the middle, always hit their mark. Above all Beckenbauer has consistently revealed a complete confidence in himself. In addition to his technical perfections, he is an intuitive and astute reader of the game, and this combination of attributes has led to his natural role as undisputed team leader. Hence, his nickname, "Kaiser Franz."

As a boy, Beckenbauer played for München 1906, and in 1958, at the age of 13, he was signed by Bayern's youth team. He made three appearances for West Germany "Junior," two for the "B" squad, and entered Bayern's first team in 1964 at left wing. In 1965, he made his full international debut for West Germany against Sweden, and was soon playing in the midfield for both club and country. One year later, at age 20, he was elected West German Footballer of the Year for the first time. In the 1966 World Cup, he became firmly established as one of Europe's best midfielders. He rapidly assumed a leadership role at Bayern, and led his club to successive German cups and a European Cup Winners' Cup victory in 1967.

In the late 1960s, he evolved his new role as attacking sweeper, and the fortunes of Bayern and West Germany grew under his guidance. He was a sensation at the 1970 World Cup, and in 1972 he led the finest German team ever seen to a stunning European Football Championship win over the USSR. He was European Footballer of the Year in 1972, an award that was repeated in 1976, and entered the 1974 World Cup widely regarded as the most complete player in the world. As captain of the World Cup-winning West German team of 1974, he rode a wave of success. His club Bayern went on to win three European Cups in succession under his tutelage, and his name became synonymous with fluid, attacking soccer, indeed, with the whole tactical approach known as "total football."

Having finally come to a parting of the ways with Bayern's management, he moved to the Cosmos in 1977 for a reported $2.5 million (seven million marks), and was dropped (reluctantly) from the national team following a 1977 friendly with France. He made 396 appearances for Bayern, scoring 43 goals, and ended his international career with 103 caps, a German record. Elected West German Footballer of the Year four times, he was, and still is, the highest paid and one of the most popular players his country has ever produced. In 1977, he made 16 appearances for the Cosmos and scored four goals, and the following year he was moved to a central midfield role for the New York club—still the most important player on the field.

Belgium

Union Royale Belge des Sociétés de
   Football-Association/Koninklijke
   Belgische Voetbalbond
Rue Guimard, 14
1040 Bruxelles

Founded: 1895
FIFA: 1904
UEFA: 1954

Affiliated clubs: *3,071;* registered players: *197,065 (83 professional, 1,225 non-amatuer);* national stadium: *Stade du Centenaire, Brussels (70,000);* largest stadium: *Stade du Centenaire;* colors: *white with tricolor trimmed jerseys, white shorts,* season:

August to May; **honors:** *Olympic Games winner (1920), RSC Anderlecht, Super Cup (1976, 1978), European Cup Winners' Cup (1976, 1978).*

Cycling is the traditional national sport of Belgium, but soccer is the most popular. Belgium's proximity to England meant that it was destined to become one of Europe's first soccer playing countries and one of the first to establish a governing body and a league. Belgium was also one of the founding members of FIFA, and has remained active in international administration through the years. On the other hand, its relatively small population and the old conflicts between Flemings (Dutch) in the north and Walloons (French) in the south have reduced Belgium's real impact in international competition. Its low profile has only recently become more visible with the success of its greatest club, RSC Anderlecht, in European championships and the boost given to its domestic game by the official recognition of professionalism.

Various hybrid forms of football—some resembling soccer and others rugby—appeared in Belgium around 1860. Football was included in the athletic programs of English schools in Brussels, Jenkins College, Harlock College, Xavierian College in Brussels, and St. Andries in Bruges. British workers and residents in the port city of Antwerp and in the industrial city of Liège preferred the round ball game as early as 1860-65. At Melle near Ghent, students at the local Josephite college ' took to the game enthusiastically in 1865. Belgian students finally began to play in significant numbers by learning from British teachers in the schools.

Soccer surpassed rugby in the race for supremacy during the formative years between 1865-90. The first club, Cercle des Régates de Bruxelles, was founded in Brussels in 1878, and two years later Sporting de Bruxelles and Antwerp Harriers appeared. All three of these early clubs were founded by Belgians who had learned the game either in Britain or from British residents in Belgium. In 1881, organized soccer spread to Ghent with the founding of the Ghent Athletic Association's soccer section. (Under the name AA Gent, or FC Ghent, this remains the oldest Belgian club still in existence.) A similar team sponsored by Brussels' Athletic and Running Club was formed in 1883. Antwerp FC was founded in 1890, and Racing de Bruxelles, Antwerp Lyon's Club, FC Brugge, and Léopold Club were founded in 1891. Antwerp, FC

Brugge, and Léopold Club were founded in 1891. Antwerp, FC Brugge, and Racing de Bruxelles (as part of RWD Molenbeek) are also extant today.

In 1895, under the leadership of Louis De Schrijver, 10 clubs banded together and formed a governing body called the Union Belge des Sociétés de Sports Athlétiques (UBSSA) to administer track and field and soccer competitions. The Belgian championship was introduced during the calender year 1896, lasting several weeks, and the first winner was FC Liège from the big industrial city of the same name on the Meuse River. The league trophy was donated by King Léopold II. Racing Club Brussels won its first championship in 1897 and with Liège dominated the first eight league seasons. Racing won four in succession from 1900-03. In 1904, a new era began when Union St-Gilloise from the south Brussels suburb of St. Gilles won its first of seven titles over a 10-year period. After a slow start in attracting new members, the number of affiliated clubs listed with the UBSSA jumped to 97 by 1910.

At the beginning, most internationals were played at the club level, though some British amateur selections visited Belgium just before the turn of the century. Racing Club Brussels became the first Belgian team to go abroad in 1900 with a visit to Hastings, England. On May 1, 1904, Belgium and France met in their first full international at Uccle, just south of Brussels—the game ended in a 3-3 draw—and officials of the two governing bodies decided that an international federation should be formed to oversee such contests in the future. The Belgian and French associations contacted those of Denmark, Holland, Spain, Sweden, and Switzerland, and at their behest convened the charter meeting of FIFA in Paris three weeks later. Belgium's L. Mühlinghaus became the first secretary.

Belgium's first 12 internationals were all played against France or Holland. Results were mixed; the first Belgium-Holland match in 1905 ended with a 4-1 Dutch win, but in the second meeting with France in 1905 Belgium won 7-0. In 1908, Sweden became Belgium's first opponent other than France or Holland, and Germany, Switzerland, and Italy joined the list of opponents before World War I. Despite a favorable record during the prewar period (won 19, drew 3, lost 17), Belgium did not participate in either the 1908 or 1912 Olympic soccer tournaments. In 1912, the present governing body for soccer was formed under the name Union Belge des Sociétés de Football-Association by separating the soccer section from the UBSSA. (King Albert I bestowed the title of "Royal" on the union in 1920. Its current name—Dutch as well as French—dates from that time, and in deference to the sensitive issue of ethnic equality, it became known by the abbreviation URBSFA/KBV.) The Coupe de Belgique (Belgian Cup) was introduced in 1911-12, and Racing Club Brussels won the first edition by defeating Racing Ghent in the final. In the meantime, Division II had been added to the league in 1909. (Division III came along in 1923 and Division IV in 1926.) Belgium's greatest player during the prewar period was the center forward Six, who sometimes played inside right for the national team and was often called the most skillful forward outside Great Britain.

In 1920, Belgium's great port city in the north, Antwerp, was the site of the sixth Olympic Games, and it was here on its own turf that Belgium entered its first official competition and gained its first and only international honor. As host Belgium had a bye to the second round, where it easily defeated fledgling Spain (itself the conqueror of experienced Denmark), and in the semifinal achieved its biggest win over Holland since 1906 with a 3-0 shutout. The 1920 final, refereed by the Englishman J. Lewis, was a hard-hitting affair between Belgium and Czechoslovakia. When Lewis finally sent off a Czech player with Belgium leading 2-0, the entire Czech team walked off the field in protest. The score was allowed to stand, and Belgium won the gold medal.

The momentum that might have materialized from Belgium's Olympic victory never occurred. Sweden buried the Belgian XI in the first round of the 1924 Olympics, 8-1, and Argentina did the same in the second round of the 1928 edition by a score of 6-3. Belgium played in its first full internationals against England during the 1920s—eight in all—and lost all but one, a draw in 1923. The growth of soccer in Scandinavia, Central Europe, and South America left Belgium far behind, and the national team emerged from the 1920s having lost twice as many games as it won. At home the league remained vibrant and growing, Antwerp's second club

Beerschot taking many of the honors, but the Belgian cup did not start up again until 1926 and then only for one year. This was followed by a 25-year-long hiatus in cup competition. In the 1930s, meanwhile, Brussels and Antwerp clubs continued to dominate the league.

Through its close association with France, the major instigator of the World Cup, Belgium felt duty bound in 1930 to enter the first World Championship in Uruguay. While three-fourths of Europe boycotted the tournament to protest its distant location from Europe, Belgium sailed to Montevideo to lend its support. Other than receiving FIFA's thanks, however, this long journey resulted in little more than depressing losses to Paraguay and the USA. Belgium was quickly eliminated. Losses to the big European powers continued to pile up during the 1930s. The low point was reached in 1934 when Belgium failed to win a single game, though it qualified for the 1934 World Cup after narrowly eliminating Eire. Having lost its main scoring threat, Stanley van den Eynde, through injury in Dublin, Belgium was lucky to start its first round match against Germany with two goals, but the second half belonged entirely to the Germans and Belgium lost 5-2. In 1938, Belgium eliminated Holland and Luxembourg to gain the final rounds of the World Cup, but its form were so inconsistent that the old rival France, formerly one of Belgium's easiest opponents, won convincingly in first round, and the Belgians were out. The Belgian league and all international competitions were suspended in the spring of 1940, but an official wartime league was reintroduced in 1941-42.

Perhaps the brightest spot in Belgian soccer history was the postwar period between 1948-54. This was the era of Anderlecht's goalscoring center forward Josef ("Jef") Mermans, Beerschot's center forward Henri ("Rik") Coppens, FC Liège's inside left Leopold ("Pol") Anoul, and the FC Liège stopper Louis Carré. This gifted group was brought together by national team manager Bill Gormlie, an Englishman hired by the URBSFA/KBV in 1946 to direct all nationwide soccer activities. Gormlie made the best of a potentially mediocre situation, and in 1948-49 his team played nine consecutive games without a defeat. To solve the Mermans-Coppens center forward conflict, Gormlie usually placed Coppens on the left wing so both could play together. Belgium's victories during this period included important wins over Sweden and Yugoslavia (away) and Italy and Wales at home. Success continued with its qualifying for the 1954 World Cup in Switzerland at the expense of Sweden and Finland. A final gallant effort by this fine team was seen in the famous 4-4 draw with England in Basle after the English had been ahead by 3-1. Belgium equalized before the end of regulation time, and in extra time it was lucky to equalize again on an own goal. This was Belgium's last hurrah in international competition for several years, as it lost to Italy 4-1 in the next match, and for the fourth time in as many attempts bowed out of the World Cup in an early round.

Semi-professionalism had appeared in the 1950s in big clubs such as Royal Sporting Club Anderlecht and Royal Standard Club, Liège, but official sanctioning of full-time professionalism was not forthcoming. Immediately after World War II, Anderlecht and Standard began their strong hold on league and cup honors. Between them they consistently managed to attract many of Belgium's finest players, and Anderlecht especially enjoyed several successive runs of league titles. Anderlecht's rise to the top was achieved under the tutelage of Bill Gormlie, who took over the club in 1949 after leaving his national post; he stayed with Anderlecht for 10 years. Standard's rise started in the late 1950s under the leadership of Paul Henrard, the former chairman of the huge steel factory that sits next to the stadium.

In the early 1960s, Anderlecht became internationally famous with the rise of its two greatest stars, Paul van Himst and the bespectacled "Jef" Jurion at inside left and right, respectively, and in 1962 the Anderlechtois eliminated Real Madrid from the European Cup in the first round and reached the quarter-finals. Standard Liège, in the meantime, advanced to the semifinals of the European Cup in 1961-62 under Hungarian coach Geza Kalocsai. The national team qualified for the World Cup a fifth time in 1970, boldly eliminating Yugoslavia and Spain in the process. This appeared to be the finest Belgian team since 1949, but after an easy win over war-torn El Salvador, Belgium was thwarted by the technically polished Soviets and Mexico, the home team, both of whom won handily. It was later understood that this fine Belgian team was drained by internal disputes over shoe sponsorships, and its morale was broken as a result. Whatever the cause, the team's potential vanished in a series of deplorable performances.

As the nagging question of professionalism continued to smolder and Paul van Himst went on to become the most famous Belgian player of all time, Anderlecht and Standard Liège furthered their reputations in the 1970s. Anderlecht began to import top players from Holland and Sweden, and in 1976 its ceaseless knocking at the gates of international success finally reaped a big reward. This was Anderlecht's first winning of the European Cup Winners' Cup behind the extraordinary artistry of Dutch left winger Robby Rensenbrink and the subsequent upset of Bayern München in the unofficial Super Cup some months later. After reaching the final of the Cup Winners' Cup again in 1977 and losing to Hamburg, the Rensenbrink-led club repeated its win in 1978 over FK Austria.

In recent years, FC Brugge as become the third important club in Belgium, threatening to win international honors, and the floodgates of professionalism have broken open for the big clubs that can afford it. The big three clubs and a few others are making Belgium a lucrative magnet for Dutch as well as Belgian players, and the recent successes of Belgian clubs in international competition are the first products of that transformation. The national team, other than winning third place in the 1970-72 European Football Championship, continued to do poorly until the professional boom of the mid-1970s and then began to show considerable signs of progress. Belgium's elimination of Scotland, Portugal, and Italy in the 1970-72 European Championship might eventually be regarded as the first signs of a Belgian revival.

Champions

1896	FC Liège	1901	Racing Club Brussels	1906	Union St. Gilloise
1897	Racing Club Brussels	1902	Racing Club Brussels	1907	Union St. Gilloise
1898	FC Liège	1903	Racing Club Brussels	1908	Racing Club Brussels
1899	FC Liège	1904	Union St. Gilloise	1909	Union St. Gilloise
1900	Racing Club Brussels	1905	Union St. Gilloise	1910	Union St. Gilloise

1911 CS Brugge	1934 Union St. Gilloise	1957 Antwerp
1912 Daring Brussels	1935 Union St. Gilloise	1958 Standard Liège
1913 Union St. Gilloise	1936 Daring Brussels	1959 RSC Anderlecht
1914 Daring Brussels	1937 Daring Brussels	1960 Lierse SK
1915 no competition	1938 Beerschot	1961 Standard Liège
1916 no competition	1939 Beerschot	1962 RSC Anderlecht
1917 no competition	1940 no competition	1963 Standard Liège
1918 no competition	1941 no competition	1964 RSC Anderlecht
1919 no competition	1942 Lierse SK	1965 RSC Anderlecht
1920 FC Brugge	1943 Malines	1966 RSC Anderlecht
1921 Daring Brussels	1944 Antwerp	1967 RSC Anderlecht
1922 Beerschot	1945 no competition	1968 RSC Anderlecht
1923 Union St. Gilloise	1946 Malines	1969 Standard Liège
1924 Beerschot	1947 RSC Anderlecht	1970 Standard Liège
1925 Beerschot	1948 Malines	1971 Standard Liège
1926 Beerschot	1949 RSC Anderlecht	1972 RSC Anderlecht
1927 CS Brugge	1950 RSC Anderlecht	1973 FC Brugge
1928 Beerschot	1951 RSC Anderlecht	1974 RSC Anderlecht
1929 Antwerp	1952 FC Liège	1975 RWD Molenbeek
1930 CS Brugge	1953 FC Liège	1976 FC Brugge
1931 Antwerp	1954 RSC Anderlecht	1977 FC Brugge
1932 Lierse SK	1955 RSC Anderlecht	1978 FC Brugge
1933 Union St. Gilloise	1956 RSC Anderlecht	

Cup Winners

1912 Racing Club Brussels	1959 no competition	1970 FC Brugge
1913 Union St. Gilloise	1960 no competition	1971 Beerschot
1914 Union St. Gilloise	1961 no competition	1972 RSC Anderlecht
1915-26 no competition	1962 no competition	1973 RSC Anderlecht
1927 CS Brugge	1963 no competition	1974 SV Waregem
1928-53 no competition	1964 AA Gent	1975 RSC Anderlecht
1954 Standard Liège	1965 RSC Anderlecht	1976 RSC Anderlecht
1955 Antwerp	1966 Standard Liège	1977 FC Brugge
1956 Racing de Tournai	1967 Standard Liège	1978 SK Beveren
1957 no competition	1968 FC Brugge	
1958 no competition	1969 Lierse SK	

Benfica, Sport Lisboa e

Location: *Lisbon, Portugal;* stadium: *Estádio da Luz (70,000);* colors: *red jerseys with white trim, white shorts;* honors: *European Cup (1961, 1962), Latin Cup (1950), Portuguese champion (1936, 1937, 1938, 1942, 1943, 1945, 1950, 1955, 1957, 1960, 1961, 1963, 1964, 1965, 1967, 1968, 1969, 1971, 1972, 1973, 1975, 1976, 1977), Portuguese cup winner (1930, 1931, 1935, 1940, 1943, 1944, 1949, 1951, 1952, 1953, 1955, 1957, 1959, 1962, 1964, 1969, 1970, 1972).*

Founded 1904 as Benfica Football Club by a young Lisboan named Cosmé Damião in the Benfica section of northwest Lisbon. Damião, who had learned the game from British residents, became its first president, secretary, treasurer, and center forward, and initiated the club's policy of admitting only players from Portugal and its colonies. In 1907, Benfica absorbed two smaller Lisbon clubs, and took its present name. After playing for 30 years in local leagues, Benfica became a charter-member of the Portuguese first division in 1934-35, and has never been relegated. Its success was immediate, and it won a hat trick of national championships from 1936-38. This, in addition to its three Portuguese cup wins from 1930-35, gave Benfica a total of six national trophies during the 1930s; one of Benfica's main strengths has been its ability to win several league and cup titles in every decade that has followed.

There were three league and four cup titles during the 1940s, and in 1950 Benfica won its first big international trophy in the Latin Cup, an important forerunner of the European Cup, with defeats of Italy's Lazio and the French club Girondins de Bordeaux. From the early 1950s, Benfica won either a league or cup title in almost every season. In 1954, it moved into the new "Stadium of Light," and acquired its first great stars of the golden age to come: Mozambiquan goalkeeper Alberto da Costa Pereira, and inside left and left half Mario Coluna, who later became the team's midfield general. In 1959, after several more championships, Bela Guttmann took over as manager and turned Benfica into one of the best teams in the world, with the aid of new signings Simoes on the left wing and Jose Augusto on the right.

After winning another league title in 1960, Benfica entered the European Cup for a second time in 1960-61, eliminating Scotland's Heart of Midlothian in the first round and Újpest Dózsa, Aarhus, and Rapid Vienna in subsequent rounds. A 4-1 goal aggregate over Rapid in the semi-finalu put Benfica in the final against mighty Barcelona, conqueror of five-time winner Real Madrid, and with a bit of luck the Portuguese won its first European club championship: with the score tied at two each, the superb Spanish goalkeeper Ramallets let in an own goal to give the Portuguese a 3-2 victory.

In the summer of 1961, Guttmann flew to Mozambique to sign the young Eusebio, and the new star made his debut for Benfica at the Tournoi de Paris some weeks later, scoring a hat trick against Santos. In the years that followed the Mozambiquan striker became the most exciting goalscorer in Europe. He led Benfica to another European Cup triumph in 1961-62 with wins over FK Austria, FC Nürnberg, Tottenham Hotspur, and, in the final, Real Madrid. The final was a goalscoring bonanza with Eusebio converting twice and the final score ending in Benfica's favor at 5-3—a classic European club championship. This was Benfica at its peak, and there was little surprise when the great Lisbon club advanced to the final again the following year, despite the departure of Bela Guttmann. Unfortunately, the wide open style of Benfica was shattered in the 1962-63 final by AC Milan's *catenaccio* and the famous Italian club won 2-1. Benfica again made the final of the European Cup in 1964-65, disposing of Real Madrid along the way, and for a second time ran into the Italian *catenaccio*, this time in the presence of AC Milan's crosstown rival Inter Milan. Playing at its own stadium, Inter held Benfica scoreless after the Portuguese champions had showed such promise in earlier rounds. Benfica's legendary goalscoring abilities were quieted once again by a defensive Italian team.

Many more Portuguese championships and cup victories were to come, and in 1967-68, Benfica reached the final of the European Cup for the fifth time, losing to Manchester United in London on a night that was destined to go United's way. After a 1-1 score at the end of regulation time, United won 4-1 in an emotional game that British fans will never forget.

Eusebio remained faithfully with Benfica until in 1975, leading his club to many more Portuguese league and cup titles during the late 1960s and early 1970s, though no further European championships could be won. Benfica is the runaway Portuguese record holder for most championships and cup victories with 23 and 18, respectively. It is extraordinary that throughout Benfica's years of international success, the club was rarely able to hold onto a manager for more than three years at a time, and during the early 1960s managers were hired and fired annually. An inspirational revival of the old Benifica spirit occurred from 1971-73, when Jose Augusto, Benfica's great captain and right winger of the 1960s, took over as manager.

Benin

Fédération Dahoméenne de Football
B.B. no. 965
Cotonou

Founded: 1968
FIFA: 1969
CAF: 1969

Affiliated clubs: *31;* **registered players:** *5,165;* **national stadium:** *René Pleven, Cotonou (8,000);* **largest stadium:** *Charles de Gaulle, Porto-Novo (15,000);* **colors:** *green jerseys, yellow shorts;* **season:** *November to June; honors:* **none.**

The Republic of Benin, formerly Dahomey, has been one of the least successful participants among active African nations, especially when measured by the level of play in other countries of French West Africa. The Fédération Dahoméenne de Football was not founded until eight years after independence, though a league had been established for some years. In addition to a Dahoman national championship, the FDF has recently launched a national cup competition, which, despite Benin's weak showing in international competition, demonstrates an active domestic organization. Benin is also a member of FIFA and the African Football Confederation, as well as the regional West African Football Union.

Partially because of political instability the

national team has never qualified for final rounds of the African Nation's Cup. The Dahoman champion clubs, however, have entered many editions of the African Cup of Club Champions. Some recent entrants were: Association Amicale (1971), AS de Cotonou (1972), Portnovo (1974), and Étoile Sportive (1975). All were eliminated in either the preliminary or first round. There were no entrants in 1973 or 1976. The best Dahoman club showing to date was by Postelsport, which was defeated by Tempete of Central Africa in the first African Cup of Cup Winners (1975) after winning the home leg, 1-0. Not one of the Champions' Cup participants has won a game in recent years. Nearly all top clubs come from the two capital cities, Contonou and Porto-Novo.

Bermuda

Bermuda Football Association
P.O. Box 745
Hamilton 5

Founded: 1928
FIFA: 1962
CONCACAF: 1966

Affiliated clubs: *33;* **registered players:** *1,257;* **national stadium:** *The National Stadium, Prospect-Devonshire, (10,000);* **largest stadium:** *The National Stadium;* **colors:** *royal blue jerseys, white shorts;* **season:** *October to April; honors:* **none.**

Bermuda, a cricket-loving British dependency in the Western Atlantic, has maintained separate affiliation with FIFA since a large measure of self-government was achieved in the early 1960s. Before 1962 the Bermuda Football Association was affiliated with The Football Association in London. Despite its closeness to the North American mainland, Bermuda's historical and cultural connections

with other British colonies of the Caribbean have resulted in administrative links with that section of CONCACAF rather than the USA, Canada, and Mexico. Like the small island nations of the Caribbean, Bermuda has struggled against difficult odds to achieve a semblance of success in regional international competition. Even Jamaica and Trinidad, which themselves compare unfavorably against the relative strength of Central America, Haiti, and Mexico, are clearly superior in their quality of play than the minnows Bermuda, Bahamas, Barbados, and Antigua.

With a shortage of funds and many of its better players in the USA, Bermuda has not been consistently active in either Olympic or World Cup qualification rounds. In friendlies, however, Bermuda has made a few note-worthy achievements: in 1975, for example, it defeated Surinam 2-1 in Hamilton, and one of its most frequent opponents has been the USA. It has played the USA at full inter-national level four times, winning one and losing three. In 1975, it narrowly edged the USA Olympic team at home, 3-2, but lost the return match some weeks later.

As a member of CONCACAF, Bermuda has occasionally entered its champion club in the CONCACAF Champions' Cup. In 1969, Somerset Cricket defeated Violette Athletic, one of Haiti's strongest clubs, by an aggregate of 6-1, and advanced to the semi-finals where Saprissa of Costa Rica trounced the Ber-mudians by an aggregate of 7-0. The national league in Bermuda includes a First Division of 10 clubs and a total of 22 additional clubs participating in lower divisions. There is also an annual cup competition. The leading teams are generally associated with the many cricket clubs or general sports clubs on Bermuda, Somerset, St. George, or St. David Islands.

Bernardo O'Higgins Cup

Copa Bernardo O'Higgins.

An irregular home and away series between the national teams of Brazil and Chile. It is named for the father of Chilean independence, who was Chilean-Irish. The trophy has not been awarded since the mid-1960s, when crowded international schedules began to cause difficulties in planning two-leg com-petitions.

Winners

1955	Brazil
1957	Chile
1959	Brazil
1961	Brazil
1966	shared

Best, George (1946-   )

This Irish phenomenon from the slums of Belfast captured the imagination of the soccer world and the press for 10 turbulent years during his stay with Manchester United, but ultimately he buckled under the intense pressure of publicity and lost his form before receding into the lower echelons. Best's mastery of ball control skills was complete, and he was equally brilliant with either foot or his head, gaining lasting fame as a dazzling and theatrical dribbler. A child prodigy, Best was discovered and signed by a Manchester United scout at age 15 in 1961, and two years later made his debut for United at right wing. He won his first cap for Northern Ireland against Wales at age 17, and scored three goals in his first seven internationals. In over 350 appearances for United, he scored 135 goals.

Playing on the same team as Bobby Charlton and Denis Law, heroes of England and Scotland, respectively, Best won the English Footballer of the Year award in 1967 and 1968, and joined Law and Charlton in becoming European Footballer of the Year (1968) after starring in United's win in the European Cup. All his peak years were spent as a central striker, but he was also a schemer and often came dribbling out of the midfield to place a dangerous ball or take a shot. Out-spoken in his disdain for tactics, Best brought the art of improvisation to the level of absurdist theater. He once taunted a Chelsea defender by taking off his red jersey, and, with his foot on the ball, held it in front of his opponent like a bullfighter. Best has sat on the ball in an F.A. Cup final, scored a goal from a headstand with a volley, dribbled the ball down half the length of the field with his thighs, and on numerous occasions trapped the ball with his backside. His playboy image off the field became equally notorious, and eventually he transcended the world of professional soccer as a symbol in Britain for the new breed of athlete-superstar.

In 1972, exhausted by the demands he placed on himself, Best walked away from United and all the commotion, returned briefly in 1973, resigned again in January 1974, and while still registered with United played two games on loan for Dunstable in the Southern League. He secured his release from United in 1975, and played with game-to-game contracts for Cork Celtic in the Republic of Ireland and lowly Stockport County before going to Spain later in the year. After a fleeting stay at La Coruña, he signed with the Los Angeles Aztecs in December 1975, and returned to the Aztecs for two subsequent summer seasons. A one-year stint at second division Fulham in 1976-77 resulted in an unresolved contract dispute and a worldwide FIFA ban, despite his signing with the Ft. Lauderdale Strikers the following season. With 31 international appearances behind him before his first retirement in 1972, Danny Blanchflower gave Best another chance with Northern Ireland in 1976 and 1977, and he added three more caps to his total. But, like his club-level performances after leaving United, he showed only glimpses of his earlier genius.

Bican, Josef   (1913-   )

Born of Czech parents in Vienna, "Pepi" Bican played for the national teams of both Czechoslovakia and Austria, and was probably the most accomplished goalscorer ever to play for either country. He was a crowd-pleasing ball artist who scored and created goals with equal agility, though his preference was always to keep the ball on the ground rather than volley or head it. His shooting and passing skills were based on accuracy, and were invariably linked to uncanny ball juggling movements that frustrated his defenders and brought his fans to their feet.

In 1923, two years after his father had died of an injury received while playing for Hertha Vienna, Bican was signed by the same club, though he was only 10 at the time. It was not merely a sentimental gesture, because his skills were already apparent. Rapid Vienna, one of Austria's greatest clubs, secured his transfer while he was still in his mid-teens, and he was soon selected to play on Austria's great national team under Hugo Meisl. At age 21, he was one of the few bright stars in the sagging Austrian team at the 1934 World Cup, and after playing at Admira Vienna, he moved to Slavia Prague in 1937. Having played for Austria 19 times before his move to Prague, Czechoslovakia was delighted to include him on its national team from 1937 until the outbreak of war, and there he scored 17 goals in 14 international appearances. At Slavia, he became a great favorite and led the Czech league in goalscoring eight consecutive times, twice scoring over 50 goals in one season.

In 1948, at age 35, he was still Czechoslovakia's leading scorer, but he lost his first team place with Slavia and moved to Vitkovice ZKG. Slavia replaced him with a younger prospect which proved to be a mistake because the great Prague club slipped in league standings, while Bican continued to lead the league in scoring and took his adopted club to new heights. He retired in 1952, and became coach of Hradec Kralove in Czechoslovakia for one year. In 1953, he took the coaching post at Slavia, and after a short time moved to Pilzen, then to Belgium's Tongeren, which he led from the fourth division to the second division in three seasons.

bicycle kick   Also known as "overhead volley."

An overhead kick with a scissors movement of the legs. Perhaps the most exciting of all individual skills, it was made famous in Europe during the 1940s by Carlo Parola, the great center halfback of Juventus and Italy. In South America, the bicycle kick was perfected by Leônidas, the incomparable "Rubber Man" of Brazil during the 1930s. In Spanish, the kick is known popularly as *chilena*, in French *retourne*, in Portuguese *bicicleta*.

See also: **overhead kick** and **scissors kick**

Uwe Seeler's version of the bicycle kick; Hamburger SV vs. Burnley in a European Cup quarter-final match in Hamburg, 1961. At right is Burnley's center half Adamson.

Black Sea Cup

A regional competition between selected clubs from the major cities on the Black Sea: Istanbul, Turkey; Odessa, USSR; Varna, Bulgaria; and Constanta, Rumania. The participants in the first edition (1970) were: Farul Constanta, Fenerbahçe, Istanbul, Tcherno-More Varna, and Tchernomoretz Odessa.

Blanchflower, Robert "Danny"   (1926-   )

A world-class right halfback from Northern Ireland whose tactical brilliance was a highlight of British soccer for over a decade. As captain of Tottenham Hotspur·between 1959-64, he was the brains behind the most sophisticated team in postwar Britain—a team that also won the first English league and cup double in this century (1960-61). In addition to his extraordinary skills, Blanchflower's open rebellion against the traditional British emphasis on physical conditioning at the expense of ball control skills and his inspiring leadership abilities, especially in directing tactical maneuvers on the field, catapulted him into national prominence. Similar characteristics were seen in his captaincy of Northern Ireland, a team he led through its greatest era in the late 1950s when it qualified for the World Cup and advanced to the second round over Czechoslovakia and Argentina.

Originally signed by Glentoran of Belfast in 1945, Blanchflower moved to Barnsley of the English second division in 1949, and from there went on to the venerable Aston Villa. But he was a thorn in the side of Villa's team management, and in 1954, after three years, found more amenable surroundings at Tottenham. He made his international debut against Scotland in 1949 and, making 56 appearances, continued to play for his national team until 1963. In 1964, after well over 600 club appearances and two Footballer of the Year awards (1958 and 1961), he was advised by his Spurs manager, Bill Nicholson, that he was about to be dropped from the first team, and he retired. Having already found a new outlet for his outspoken ideas in journalism, Blanchflower pursued his new career with vigor and characteristic self-confidence until he accepted the post of Northern Ireland manager in 1976. His brother, Jackie, was a star with Manchester United and Northern Ireland during the 1950s.

blind side

The side of a player or group of players that is away from the ball or the play.

block tackle   See: front block tackle

Bloomer, Stephen   (1874-1938)

The greatest goalscoring legend of the pre-World War I era, whose record-breaking statistics in English annals have stood the test of time. An inside right throughout his 22-year career, Bloomer was an instinctive shooter, less skilled with the ball than some, but awesome in his ability to fire at the net without hesitation from any position. He was even criticized at times for not being a team player. Bloomer's official total of 352 league goals (1892-1914) was actually somewhat higher, since his club records before 1900 are unreliable. This total was surpassed by only one English player before World War II (Dixie Dean), and remains the fourth highest among English players to this day. His record of 28 goals for England in 23 appearances was not broken until 1956. Bloomer's name is synonymous with that of Derby County, an established though less-than-glamorous club he helped to keep in the first division between 1892-1906. Immediately after his move to Middlesbrough in 1906, Derby was relegated, and one year after his return in 1910, it regained a place in the first division. He stayed with his beloved Derby until 1914, and set out to coach in Germany just before the outbreak of World War I. Interned there as a civilian prisoner of war between 1914-18, he organized a league in the internment camp, and after the war coached in Rotterdam (1919), Canada (1922), Derby (1922-24), and finally, Spain (1924), before returning to Derby's ground crew. Suffering from bronchial disorders, he was cared for by a grateful club until his death 14 years later.

Boca Júniors, Club Atlético

Location: *Buenos Aires, Argentina;* stadium: *Estadio Bonbonera (80,000);* colors: *dark blue jerseys with broad yellow hoop, dark blue shorts;* honors: *Intercontinental Cup (1977), Copa Libertadores (1977, 1978), Campeonato Nacional winner (1969, 1970, 1976), Argentine league champion (1919 AAF, 1920 AAF, 1923 AAF, 1924 AAF, 1926 AAF, 1930, 1931 LAF, 1934 LAF, 1935, 1940, 1943, 1944, 1954, 1962, 1964, 1965, 1976).*

Founded 1905 by an Irishman, Patrick MacCarthy, and Italian immigrants in the predominantly Italian barrio of central Buenos Aires called Boca. Its formation was an important step in the transition from the British domination of Argentine soccer to the Italian influence that would eventually become the backbone of its game. Boca was the first great Italian-based club, joining the First Division in the midst of the league's first organizational conflicts in 1913. When the breakaway league was formed in 1919, Boca stayed with the "regular" league (Asociación Argentina de Football) and won five of its championships in eight years. In 1925, it became the first Argentine club to make a tour of Europe, and was astonishingly successful with 15 wins and only three losses. After World War II, Boca was taken over Argentine millionaire Alberto Armando.

Boca is Argentina's most popular and successful club. It has won a record 17 First Division titles, and the Campeonato Nacional three times, more than any other club. Its twice-yearly league matches (plus more in the Campeonato Nacional) with archrival Ríver Plate are the highlights of the Argentine season, and over the years have resulted in a remarkably even record, Boca winning a total of 42 and losing 40 in 110 outings since professionalism was adopted in 1931. But Boca's stadium, the "Chocolate Box," has been the scene of many bloody struggles as well, as no club in the top flight of Argentine soccer has escaped the stadium's highly charged atmosphere.

Boca entered its golden era just before the formation of the professional league in 1931, winning the last amateur championship in 1930, the first professional championship in 1931, another in 1934, and the first league title of the reunited First Division in 1935—a total of four championships in six years. Boca's greatest team of all time was that of 1934-35, which bridged the gap between the Liga Argentina de Football and the Asociación del Football Argentino. In 1934, it scored 101 goals in 39 games, and the next year lost only three games in 34 outings, scoring 100 goals and allowing only 29! Boca's great stars of this period were goalscoring aces Francisco Varallo and Cherro Roberto, halfback Juan Evaristo, and in 1935 the Brazilian center half Domingos da Guia. In the summer of 1931, its greatest star of all, Luisito Monti of 1930 World Cup fame, left for Juventus in Italy and he was the first of many such heartbreaking departures for Boca fans.

Another fine series of championships were won in the early 1940s, but despite the presence of goalscoring forward Jaime Sarlanga, the legendary Ríver Plate team of this era drew more attention—and deservedly so. Another great Boca team was built during the early 1960s, initially under Brazil's 1958 World Cup manager Vicente Feola, but actually winning its three championships under José D'Amico and the former Ríver Plate idol Adolfo Pedernera. This side included the Argentina as well as Boca captain, Antonio Rattin, the attacking center half of 1966 World Cup notoriety; Antonio Roma, the greatest goalkeeper in Argentina since Tesoriero; and the blonde left back, Silvio Marzolini. In 1963, D'Amico's Boca became the first Argentine club to show a serious interest in the Copa Libertadores, and it changed many minds elsewhere in Argentina by advancing to the final against mighty Santos, losing by an aggregate of 5-3 but reaping financial rewards as a result.

In 1969, Alfredo Di Stefano took over the club for one season, and caused a furor by releasing Rattin from the team; all was forgiven, however, when he guided the club to its first Campeonato Nacional win, losing only one game in 17. Though Di Stefano left Boca after only one season, the club won a second consecutive Campeonato in 1970 with Roma and Marzolini still in the lineup. In 1976, it won its first double—a first division (Campeonato Metropolitano) title and a Campeonato Nacional trophy in the same year, and also became the first club to win the Campeonato Nacional three times. After many years of Argentine domination of the Copa Libertadores by other clubs, Boca finally won its first South American club championship in 1977, but only after a violent ride to the final. In the semi-finals, three Boca players were sent off in their home leg against Paraguay's Libertad, and a variety of off-the-field acts of sabotage caused a bitter and rancorous series with Deportivo Cali of Colombia. In the final, Boca won the trophy from Cruzeiro on penalty kicks after a scoreless rain-soaked replay. In 1978, it won its second consecutive Libertadores title with a breathtaking 4-0 win over Deportivo Cali in the final.

Bogado Cup

Copa Coronel Bogado.

One of two series played between the national teams of Argentina and Paraguay (the other is the older Rosa Chevallier Boutell Cup). The 1976 edition doubled as part of the revived Atlantic Cup. Since it is decided under a point system rather than by goal aggregate, a penalty decision is forced when home and away legs are split, as occurred in 1977.

Winners

1976 Argentina
1977 Paraguay

Bohemia   See: **Czechoslovakia**

Bolivarian Games

The Juegos Bolivaranos were organized on the Olympic model in 1938 by countries that were liberated from Spain by Simon Bolivar: Bolivia, Colombia, Ecuador, Panama, Peru, and Venezuela. Among the 15 events is a soccer tournament, which has faded in importance since the widespread introduction of professionalism in South America during the 1950s. Eight editions have been held: 1938, 1947, 1950, 1961, 1965, 1970, 1973, and 1977. Peru, the first winner, has dominated the competition; Panama did not field a team until 1950.

Bolivia

Federación Boliviana de Fútbol
Av. 16 de Julio No. 5053
P.O. Box 484
Cochabamba

Founded: 1925
FIFA: 1926
CONMEBOL: 1926

Affiliated clubs: 305; **registered players:** *11,789 (895 non-amateur);* **national stadium:** *Hernando Siles, La Paz (60,000);* **largest stadium:** *Hernando Siles;* **colors:** *green jerseys with white trim, white shorts;* **season:** *April to December;* **honors:** *South American Championship winner (1963).*

Bolivia is one of the weakest soccer nations in South America, ranking just above Ecuador and Venezuela on its record, though the game has been pursued throughout the country with vigor and keen interest since the turn of the century. For decades, foreign players have winced at the thought of having to play in Bolivia, where the altitude of La Paz, the capital city and location of most leading clubs, is 12,000 feet. The national team has won the South American Championship only once—in 1963 when the competition was held in La Paz—and has never been a runner-up. None of Bolivia's champion clubs has a winning record in the Copa Libertadores, but the relatively even standard of play among top Bolivian clubs is illustrated by the fact that Bolivia has sent more representatives to the South American club championship than any other country.

Soccer was brought to Bolivia via Chile in the 1890s. Leoncio Zuaznabar is credited for having introduced the game, uniforms and all, to Oruro, an important railway and mining center. In 1896, Zuaznabar founded the first Bolivian club, Oruro Royal Club, and became its first captain and treasurer. The game spread to La Paz, Sucre, Cochabamba, and other important mining districts, and in 1908, The Strongest, which remains today the senior club of La Paz, was founded in the two-mile high capital. The Stormers, the first important club in Sucre, was formed in 1914; Highlands Players in Potosi and Racing in Cochabamba were founded in 1922.

The mid-1920s was a watershed in Bolivian soccer. The Fédéracion Boliviana de Fut-bol was founded at Cochabamba in 1925, and remains the national governing body. One year later, the Torneo Nacional was introduced as a knockout tournament for regional selections, and the only truly nationwide competition until 1978. The year 1926 also marked Bolivia's official entrance into international competition. The newly formed national team competed in the South American Championship in Santiago, and lost all four matches to Argentina, Uruguay, Paraguay, and Chile. It was an inauspicious start, and Bolivia returned the following year

only to suffer the same fate. Bolivian officials reacted strongly to a second humiliation, and kept Bolivian teams out of the competition until 1945.

In 1930, the national stadium was built in the center of La Paz and named for the President of Bolivia, Hernando Siles. In the same year, Bolivia entered the first World Cup in Uruguay. Grouped with Yugoslavia, Bolivia's first European opponent, and Brazil, the Bolivians suffered 4-0 losses to both. Bolivia's only subsequent appearance in World Cup final rounds occurred in 1950, when Uruguay, its only first round group opponent, delivered an 8-0 thrashing. Bolivia's first relative success in the South American Championship was achieved in 1949 with a fourth place finish in a field of eight.

The domestic organization, meanwhile, was bewildered by extraordinary logistical problems caused by alpine terrain and primitive transportation. The La Paz league, formed in 1914, emerged as a kind of national championship, and was officially designated as Bolivia's first division. It was dominated until the mid-1930s by The Strongest. Bolivar Independiente Unificada was founded in 1927, and La Paz's greatest rivalry (Bolivar vs. The Strongest) was born. Professionalism was introduced in the La Paz league in 1950 (the name of the league was changed to the Campeonato Professional de Fútbol) and in some of the leading provincial clubs in 1954. With the advance of professionalism, new clubs, such as Jorge Wilsterman and Deportivo Municipal, arose to challenge the supremacy of The Strongest and Bolivar. A handful of professional clubs from outlying areas were invited to join the La Paz league.

Many of the amateur regional clubs were and still are affiliated with mines, some composed entirely of miners, perhaps the best known among them being Racing de Llallagua. By the early 1950s, the number of clubs in Bolivia was so great that three divisions were formed: the Campeonato Professional or "Primera A" (La Paz League), the "Primera B" (with La Paz and regional sections), and regional third divisions.

Bolivia continued without a truly national league until 1977, a second watershed year for the Bolivian game. Having won its regional World Cup qualification group from Uruguay and Venzuela, Bolivia then faced Hungary for the odd berth in the 1978 World Cup final rounds. The unprecedented journey to Budapest resulted in a despairing 6-0 defeat, and in the thin air of La Paz one month later, the well-prepared Hungarians managed to win by one goal. The ensuing disappointment was compounded when the leading clubs of La Paz broke away from the Primera A to form their own first division. The mounting frustration of provincial clubs left out of the top level competition forced the national association to act decisively, and for the first time a Major League of 16 clubs, including teams from all the major population centers, was formed. It was hoped that the new league would eventually lead to a general increase in the level of play, and ultimately, for Bolivia, entrance into the mainstream of international competition.

Champions

1914	The Strongest	1936	Ayacucho	1958	Jorge Wilsterman
1915	Colegio Militar	1937	The Strongest	1959	Jorge Wilsterman
1916	The Strongest	1938	The Strongest	1960	Deportivo Municipal
1917	The Strongest	1939	Bolivar	1961	Deportivo Municipal
1918	no competition	1940	Bolivar	1962	Deportivo Municipal
1919	no competition	1941	Bolivar	1963	The Strongest
1920	The Strongest	1942	Bolivar	1964	The Strongest
1921	no competition	1943	The Strongest	1965	Deportivo Municipal
1922	no competition	1944	Ferroviario	1966	Jorge Wilsterman
1923	Universitario	1945	The Strongest	1967	Jorge Wilsterman
1924	The Strongest	1946	no competition	1968	Bolivar
1925	no competition	1947	Litoral	1969	Universitario
1926	Universitario	1948	Litoral	1970	Chaco Petrolero
1927	Nimbles Sport	1949	Litoral	1971	Oriente Petrolero
1928	Deportivo Militar	1950	Bolivar	1972	Jorge Wilsternan
1929	The Strongest	1951	Always Ready	1973	Jorge Wilsterman
1930	The Strongest	1952	The Strongest	1974	Oriente Petroler
1931	Nimbles Rail	1953	Bolivar	1975	The Strongest
1932	The Strongest	1954	Litoral	1976	Bolivar
1933	no competition	1955	San José	1977	The Strongest
1934	no competition	1956	Bolivar		
1935	The Strongest	1957	Always Ready		

Botafogo de Futebol e Regatas

Location: *Rio de Janeiro, Brazil;* stadium: *Estádio General Severiano (23,000);* colors: *black and white striped jerseys, black shorts:* honors: *Rio-São Paulo Tournament (1962, 1964 shared, 1966 shared), Rio de Janeiro champion (1907 shared, 1910, 1930, 1932, 1933 AMEA, 1934 AMEA, 1935 AMEA, 1948, 1957, 1961, 1962, 1967, 1968).*

Founded 1904 as Botafogo Futebol Clube in what was then the southern Rio suburb of Botafogo—now a section of Rio itself adjacent to Copacabana—by teenage students at the

Colégio Alfredo Gomes. The club moved from ground to ground in Botafogo, but eventually settled in its present location directly under the Sugar Loaf. Botafogo plays its big games at the giant Estádio Maracanã.

Of the six clubs that founded the Rio league in 1905, Botafogo is one of the two still in existence (Fluminense is the other). Next to Fluminense, it was the leading club in Rio competition until the emergence of Flamengo in 1912. It shared the championship with Flu in 1907, and captured its first title outright in 1910 winning 18 games on 66 goals and allowing only 9. Inside right Abelardo Delamare, Botafogo's first great star, scored 22 goals that season. In 1906, Rio de Janeiro was represented by Botafogo (average age in the mid-teens) in an early Rio vs. São Paulo confrontation, and the Botafogo teens won 2-1. After winning the last amateur Rio league in 1932, Botafogo joined the professional league the following year and won three consecutive titles. Its reluctance to adopt professionalism was partially the result of long and fruitful association with wealthy and powerful Rio interests. Though its following was smaller than that of Flamengo or Fluminense, its resources were greater, and its new stadium, when that came to be built in the 1920s, was appropriately designed in the colonial manner. Largely through that influence, Botafogo has supplied a dispropor-tionately large number of players to the national team (23), especially before World War II. In 1942, it merged with the Clube de Regatas Botafogo (Botafogo Sailing Club), and adopted its present name.

While Botafogo has won fewer league titles over the years than Flamengo, Fluminense, and Vasco da Gama—the other big three of Rio—it has consistently been in the running for honors, and has had its share of truly great players. Its greatest team was that of the late 1950s and early 1960s. Garrincha, Nilton Santos, and Didi, each a sublime practitioner of his craft, took Botafogo to a memorable league championship in 1957 and, after Didi's return from a one-year stint with Real Madrid, two more in 1961 and 1962. Ultimately, this marvelously gifted team won the 1962 Rio-São Paulo Tournament as well. Brazil's 1962 World Cup-winning team included five Botafogo stars: Garrincha, Nilton Santos, Didi, Zagalo, and Amarildo. Nilton Santos and Didi retired shortly thereafter, and Garrincha, hobbled by injuries, finally moved on in 1966, breaking up Botafogo's superb lineup.

Two further Rio-São Paulo Tournaments were won with shared trophies, and in the late 1960s the club hit its stride again under manager Mario Zagalo. This time a team full of stars won two consecutive championships led by Botafogo's own Jairzinho and the gifted Gerson.

Botswana

The game was being organized during the late 1960s and early '70s, though Botswana has not yet become a member of FIFA. The former Bechuanaland Football Association applied for membership with FIFA in 1966, but later withdrew its application. Some members of the African Football Confederation have ostracized Botswana because it did not openly oppose South Africa's racial policies in sport during the early 1960s.

box

The penalty area.

Bozsik, Jószef (1925-1978)

The finest attacking wing half in Europe during the 1950s, and the playmaker of mighty Honvéd and Hungary during their golden eras. He was the greatest halfback Hungary has ever produced, and became a model for hundreds of others in Europe after the glorious international successes of his national team. Bozsik was an immaculate passer at both long and short distances, and delighted in anticipating the moves of his forward line, which happened to include the incomparable Puskás, his best friend since childhood, Kocsis, Hidegkuti, and Czibor, among others.

He and Puskás played sandlot ball together in their native Kispest, a suburb of Budapest long known as Hungary's major spawning ground for great players, and while in their mid-teens both joined Kispest SE, which in 1948 became Honvéd. Bozsik made his international debut for Hungary in 1947 against Bulgaria, and for the next nine years won a host of domestic and international honors. As midfield general he played on five Hungarian championship teams with Honvéd and the legendary Hungarian national team that won the 1952 Olympic gold medal. In 1953 he took the British by storm with his breathtaking performance in Hungary's 6-3 defeat of England, in which he scored a scintillating goal from 30 yards. His only major embarrassment occurred in the semifinals of the 1954 World Cup—in the so-called "Battle of Berne"—when he and Brazil's Nilton Santos were sent off for fighting.

After the Hungarian uprising in 1956, he returned to Budapest with the touring Honvéd team rather than join Puskás and others in the West, and was elected to the national House of Deputies. Always a family man and loyal member of the Honvéd organization, he stayed with his fallen club until his retirement in 1962. He was selected to play for Hungary in the 1958 World Cup—at center forward and inside forward—and returned to the national team before the 1962 World Cup to help his country qualify, though he did not play in the 1962 finals. In his farewell match in 1962 against Uruguay, he gained his 100th cap, and celebrated the occasion by scoring his eleventh international goal, a testament to his tendencies as an attacking halfback. Having turned down dozens of huge offers to coach clubs and national teams in the West, he managed Honvéd briefly in 1966-67, and took over the national team for a short spell in the early 1970s, but heart trouble forced him to retire. He retreated to his family clothing store in Budapest, which he and his family had opened together in 1962, and finally succumbed to his heart ailment at age 53.

Brazil

Confederação Brasileira de Desportos
Rua de Alfandega 70
P.O. 1078
Rio de Janeiro

Founded: 1914
FIFA: 1917
CONMEBOL: 1916

Affiliated clubs: *5,024;* **registered players:** *82,400 (7,300 professional);* **national stadium:** *Estádio Mário Filho, o Maracanã, Rio de Janeiro (220,000);* **largest stadium:** *Estádio Mário Filho;* **colors:** *yellow jerseys with green trim, blue shorts;* **season:** *January to June, August to December;* **honors:** *World Cup winner (1958, 1962, 1970), runner-up (1950), third place (1938, 1978), South American Championship winner (1919, 1922, 1949), runner-up (1921, 1925, 1937, 1945, 1946, 1953, 1956, 1957, 1959), Atlantic Cup (1956, 1960, 1976), Santos, Intercontinental Cup (1962, 1963), Copa Libertadores (1962, 1963), Cruzeiro, Copa Libertadores (1976).*

It is perhaps extraordinary that in a world where more than 125 sovereign nations claim soccer as their national sport, there is one that stands out as the standard bearer of the game. For 20 years, this has been Brazil's distinction. A vast and sprawling, multiracial country comprising half of South America's land mass and population, it is at once the world's greatest and most complex soccer power. Brazil's standing in the world soccer community is the result of a unique combination of factors: first, an endless reservoir of talented and creative players; second, the unequaled stature of the game in the country's national life, even by Latin America standards; and third, the support and administration of Brazilian soccer by a bewildering, yet effective, organizational structure, whose arms have penetrated the farthest reaches of Rondônia and Amazonas, as any low-lying flight over the rain forests will reveal.

Still, it is astonishing that after 90 years there is no national league, and it was only in 1967 that a knockout tournament of sorts was established to determine a truly national champion. Until then, the state leagues and wealthy clubs of Rio de Janeiro and São Paulo monopolized Brazilian soccer in all respects, and the winner of their inter-city competition was crowned the Brazilian champion. As an indirect result of Brazil's present boom economy, along with the introduction of the National Championship in 1967, the power bases of Brazilian soccer have spread to include Belo Horizonte, as well as Pôrto Alegre. In the near future, clubs from the states of Paraná, Santa Catarina, Bahia, and Pernambuco will surely challenge the current big four. The stage is already set for this ongoing Brazilian spectacle: major population centers boast seven of the world's 10 largest stadiums, each with a capacity of 110,000 spectators or more.

In international competition, Brazil is the only country in the world to qualify for all 11 World Championships, and the only country to win the world's highest prize three times, taking permanent possession of the Jules Rimet trophy in 1970. Brazil has also placed second, third, and fourth in World Cup competition, and leads all participants in total points accumulated.

Ironically, Brazil's international standing in the South American Championship and the Copa Libertadores is a distint third to that of Argentina and Uruguay, caused by some important historical differences: the game itself was introduced in Brazil three decades later than in either Argentina or Uruguay, and the working classes of Brazil, especially blacks and mestizos, were excluded from top flight competition until the 1920s, when racial barriers finally broke down. (The racially homogeneous populations of Argentina and Uruguay, on the other hand, were participating as early as 1880.) The ultimate turning point in Brazil's development came with the 1938 World Cup in France, when the acrobatic center forward Leônidas, instructor to the world on performing the bicycle kick, dazzled European audiences and led Brazil to a third place finish.

Soccer was introduced in Brazil by Charles Miller (b. 1875), the Brazilian-born son of English parents who is said to have returned home from school in Southampton in 1894 with two soccer balls in his luggage. Miller immediately began to organize teams among fellow British residents at the São Paulo Railway Company, where he was employed, the English Gas Company, and the London Bank. He eventually persuaded the São Paulo Athletic Club, of which he was a member, to play soccer as well as cricket. These teams, as well as others in São Paulo and Rio de Janeiro before the turn of the century, were almost entirely comprised of British residents. The first team of native Brazilians was that of Mackenzie College, São Paulo (founded 1898), which continued to be a force in the São Paulo league until World War I.

British residents in Rio de Janeiro, then Brazil's largest and most important city, were not far behind Miller in their determination to introduce soccer to the capital city. In 1895, the Clube de Regatas do Flamengo (Flamengo Sailing Club) formed a team, and encouraged other sporting and athletic clubs in the city to do the same. Today, CR Flamengo is the oldest and most popular club in Brazil. In 1902, British residents in Rio founded the Fluminense Foot-Ball Club, the second oldest Brazilian club in existence today. The first match between teams from Rio and São Paulo took place in 1901, when the São Paulo Scratch Team and the Rio Team fought to a 1-1 draw.

In 1901, the first regional league was founded, the Campeonato Paulista de Futebol (São Paulo), by five clubs: São Paulo A.C., CA Paulistano, EC Germânia, A.A. Mackenzie, and EC Internacional, all of which are now extinct as independent clubs or have been absorbed into other clubs. São Paulo A.C., won the first three *paulista* championships, but British clubs receded from the front ranks before the end of the first decade, and CA Paulistano emerged as the most successful São Paulo club by 1920. The eventual giants of *paulista* competition, Corinthians and SE Palmeiras (originally Palestra Italia), were not founded until 1910 and 1914, respectively. Their domination of the São Paulo leagues lasted from 1920 until the emergence of Santos in 1955.

In Rio, Brazil's second league was founded in 1905, the Liga Metropolitana de Foot-Ball do Rio de Janeiro, by six clubs: Fluminense F.C., América F.C., Bangu AC, Botafogo F.C., Sporte Clube Petropolis, and Foot-Ball and Athletic. América and Petropolis dropped out before the start of the first season (1906), while Paissandu AC and Rio Cricket and Athletic Club took their place. The first champion was Fluminense, which dominated Rio (*carioca*) soccer during the first five seasons along with Botafogo. In 1907, the Liga Metropolitana de Foot-Ball was dissolved and replaced by the Liga Metropolitana de Esportes Athléticos (LMEA). Flamengo did not join the *carioca* league until 1912, but rose to the top rapidly once it did. South America's greatest archrivalry, Flamengo vs. Fluminense (or *Fla-Flu*), was launched that same year and Flamengo won its first championship in 1914. The *carioca* league was dominated decisively by Flamengo and Fluminense from 1914 to 1921.

Brazil's first unofficial international was played in 1906 at São Paulo between a *paulista* selection of British-born players and a team representing the Cape Colony and Natal of British South Africa. The visitors won 6-0. In 1908, a visiting representative team from Argentina played and won two matches each against selections from Rio and São Paulo, and in 1910, the legendary English amateur team Corinthian F.C. stopped in São Paulo on their tour of North and South America and defeated AA das Palmeiras (not to be confused with the more famous SE Palmeiras), Paulistano, and São Paulo A.C. by an aggregate of 15-2. In 1911, an Uruguayan representative team visited São Paulo and drew with Paulistano and São Paulo A.C., 3-3 and 2-2, respectively, and lost to EC Americano by 3-0. These were Brazil's first successful international results.

For the first 20 years, the administration of Brazil's game was carried on separately by the Rio and São Paulo leagues, but an umbrella governing body for all sports in Brazil, the Federação Brasileira de Sports (FBS), was created in 1914. The Federação immediately gained international recognition from several world bodies, though FIFA was not among them. A rival administrative organization, the Comitê Olimpico Nacional, was also formed in 1914. When the Comitê managed to win its own measure of international recognition, an intense struggle between the two groups ensued, and in 1916, the two merged under the banner of the FBS. The new governing body was provisionally admitted to FIFA one year later, gaining full membership in 1923. Its name was eventually changed to the Confederação Brasileira de Desportos (CBD). The CBD is today the administrative body for all sports in Brazil, with soccer its primary concern and main source of revenues.

Two months after the founding of the FBS in 1914, the first representative team of Brazil was assembled at Fluminense's ground in Rio to meet the visiting Exeter City F.C. of England's Southern League. The victorious Brazilian team (2-0) was composed of three players who were destined to become the first immortals of Brazilian soccer: goalkeeper Marcos de Mendonça, center half Rubens Salles, and center forward Artur Friedenreich, who lost two teeth in a collision with an Exeter fullback. Brazil's first unofficial an international involving national teams occurred in Buenos Aires two months after the Exeter City match—against Argentina. Brazil won 1-0 on a goal by Ruben Salles. This was the first edition of the Roca Cup, an occasional series between the two countries and the first of many ongoing competitions between Brazil and various South American countries. In 1916, Brazil entered the first edition of the South American Championship in Buenos Aires, but failed to win any matches against Argentina, Uruguay, and Chile. Brazilian teams participated in the next six South American Championships, winning two and finishing second, third, and last in the others. This series, in addition to the Roca Cup, represented Brazil's first forays into full international competition.

During the 1910s, soccer spread to the furthest reaches of Brazil. The first club in Amazonas state was founded at Manaus in 1912 (Club de Manaus) by the British administrators and technicians who operated the world's largest rubber plantations. The last soccer frontier was conquered in 1919, when a club was formed at Rio Branco in Acre state, the most remote region in northwestern Brazil. Five important provincial leagues were founded by 1915. In fact, the second oldest league in Brazil was not the Rio league but the Campeonato Baiano (Bahia), founded in 1905. The others were Campeonato Gaucho (Rio Grande do Sul), 1910; Campeonato Mineiro (Minas Gerais), 1914; Campeonato Pernambucano (Pernambuco), 1915; and Campeonato Paranaense (Paraná), 1915.

In São Paulo, the authority of the Liga Paulista was challenged in 1914 by the Associação Paulista de Esportes Atléticos (APEA), an umbrella organization that went on to embrace the cause of professionalism in São Paulo when that issue became prominent in the early 1930s. In Rio, a confusing battle for authority resulted from administrative rivalries of the 1920s. By the time professionalism became a key concern, two distinct Rio leagues were in competition: the Associação Metropolitana de Esportes Atléticos (amateur), and the Liga Carioca de Futebol (professional). Professionalism in Brazil was finally introduced in 1933 by Santos FC and São Paulo FC, but the amateur leagues lingered through 1936, after which the Rio and São Paulo leagues were once again unified within their respective regions. They reemerged in 1937 as the Federação Paulista de Futebol and the Liga de Football do Rio de Janeiro. None of the other major state leagues experienced such upheavals.

The first inter-league competition, the Taça Correio da Manhã, was introduced in 1913 by the Rio newspaper of the same name for state selections from Rio and São Paulo only. This was superceded in 1923 by the introduction of the Campeonato Brasileiro de Seleçoes (Brazilian Championship of State Teams), which became the first important national competition (discontinued 1963). Not surprisingly, it was won only once in its 40-year history by a team other than Rio or São Paulo—Bahia in 1934.

By World War I, the game in Brazil had moved away from the influence of the class-conscious British and with the influx of workers from Italy, Spain, and Portugal found a new and vital acceptance among all strata of society—with one major exception. Clubs throughout the country refused to sign black players or those of mixed black and white or black and Indian parentage. The first widely known *mestiço* to break the race barrier was Artur Friedenreich, who started with Germânia FC of São Paulo in 1909. Friedenreich's incomparable artistry on the field and his tawny appearance made him the first idol of impoverished Brazilians and led directly to the eventual entry of blacks into senior-level competition. The first black player to gain a regular place on a major team was Manteiga of América F.C. (RJ), but his signing caused many América players to leave the club.

The most important breakthrough occurred in 1923, when the second division Rio club Vasco da Gama, which had adopted a non-discriminatory policy in the late 1910's, gained promotion to the *carioca* first division and won the championship that same year. More than half of Vasco's first string team was nonwhite, an unprecedented occurrence in the upper reaches of Brazilian soccer and one that prompted the established clubs of Rio to break away temporarily and form their own league in 1924 (the AMEA). By 1930, the barriers had further broken down, and black and *mestiço*

heroes such as Fausto, the *Maravilha Negra* (Black Wonder) became almost commonplace. Brazilian historians do not hesitate to point out that Brazil's earliest challenge to Argentina's and Uruguay's domination of South American soccer coincided with the opening of Brazilian soccer to all segments of the population.

The jurisdictional controversies of the mid-1920s also led to Brazil's temporary withdrawal from official international competition. In the six South American Championships held between 1924 and 1935, Brazil participated only once, and while Uruguay and Argentina were blazing their way to international glory in the Olympic Games, the CBD showed little interest in what was then the only worldwide competition available.

The first World Championship in 1930, however, was an opportunity not to be missed, especially since it was being held in neighboring Uruguay. A disorganized if gifted Brazilian team, lacking European tactical knowhow and the international experience of Argentina and Uruguay, was grouped in the first round with Bolivia and Yugoslavia. The surprising Yugoslavs, Brazil's first full international European opponents, proceeded to win 2-1, but lowly Bolivia was clearly outclassed (4-0) by a goalscoring efficiency that was already becoming characteristic of Brazilian teams. Three of Brazil's five goals in the competition were scored by the captain, Neto. Eliminated and disappointed, the team came home and played a friendly with the USA in Rio, winning by 4-3.

In spite of the destructive power struggle at home between rival national governing bodies from 1930 to 1936 (the CBD favored amateurism and the new Federaçao Brasileira de Futebol, founded in 1930, supported professionalism), Brazil was one of two South American nations to make the long voyage to the 1934 World Cup in Italy. Under the knockout format of the early World Championships, Brazil was eliminated after only one match (a loss to Spain) before stepping onto an Italian liner once again to sail for Rio. The loss to Spain was a nervous contest, in which Brazil's star inside forward Waldemar de Brito (discoverer of Pelé) missed a penalty. Genoese spectators were generally deprived of seeing a Brazilian XI on form.

European audiences were by now aware of Brazil's ability to produce players of dazzling skill, proven by the first and second World Cups. But this reputation had existed as early as 1925, when the São Paulo club A.C.

Brazilian rituals. (Top) After defeating Sweden in the final of the 1958 World Cup in Stockholm, Gilmar, Zagalo, and Garrincha lead Brazilian players and officials around the stadium—carrying a Swedish flag—to pay tribute to their host nation and losing opponent. (Bottom) Wilson Piazza (l) and Gerson (r) fall to their knees in prayer and thanksgiving at Mexico City's Aztec Stadium after winning the 1970 World Cup final.

Paulistano made a spellbinding tour of Europe with Friedenreich at center forward. The legacy of this famous club found its national counterpart in Brazil's World Cup squad of 1938. Indeed, it was at this juncture that Brazil made its debut as a potential world power, and in coming to France, became the only South American country to participate in all three prewar World Cup competitions.

With the breathtaking Leônidas at the center of the attack, the Brazilians slipped by Poland in the first round by six goals to five in extra time on a rain soaked pitch. Leônidas and Poland's Willimowski scored four goals apiece. In the second round, the Brazilians' redoubtable spirit was unleashed against Czechoslovakia in the first of Brazil's many violent matches in World Cup competition. The first game against Czechoslovakia, which ended in a draw after extra time (and subsequently known as the "Battle of Bordeaux") featured three ejections as well as broken limbs for two of Czechoslovakia's greatest stars, Plánička and Nejedly. The replay, in which there were 15 new players on the field, was won uneventfully by Brazil. Overconfident and lacking two of its most important players, Leônidas and Tim, Brazil fell to the eventual winner of the tournament, Italy, in the semi-finals. In the third place match, Leônidas increased his scoring total to eight (best in the competition), and Brazil defeated the gentlemanly Swedes 4-2. It was now abundantly clear, as Brazil entered the war years with its first World Cup honor, that reaching the world summit would depend primarily on its ability to coordinate a plethora of dazzling ball artists into a cohesive tactical unit. This was not to be accomplished until 1958.

In the meantime, Brazil failed to enter any South American Championship during the 1930s, establishing a pattern of disinterest that has lasted to the present time. There were some victories in regional competitions during the 1920s and '30s (one Roca Cup and two Rio Branco Cups), but the CBD already appeared to be putting all its energies into World Cup efforts at the expense of other international competition, a characteristic that became a tradition in the postwar era.

During the period between the wars, the Rio and São Paulo leagues remained unchallenged in their seats of power, and other state leagues began to complain of discrimination. In São Paulo, three clubs emerged after World War I as the dominant powers: Paulistano during the 1920s until its demise in 1929, Corinthians, and Palestra Itália (later to be renamed Palmeiras).

In Rio, the honors were shared. Vasco da Gama, after its groundbreaking success of 1923, repeated its triumph the following year and achieved a total of five championships before World War II. Vasco also made a successful tour of seven cities in Portugal and Spain in 1931. Flamengo's five titles between the wars were the only equal of Vasco's record, and the remainder of *carioca* league honors were shared among Botafogo, Fluminense, América, and two small Rio clubs, Bangu and São Cristovão. In other state leagues, many famous clubs became firmly established powers during this period: Grêmio and EC Internacional (Rio Grande do Sul), Atlético Mineiro (Minas Gerais), EC Bahia (Bahia), EC do Recife (Pernambuco), and Cortiba FC (Parana.) Fame and glory came to Santos FC, São Paulo F.C. (São Paulo), and Cruzeiro (Minas Gerais) during and after World War II.

Before the war, Brazil had already produced at least a dozen players of indisputable world class rank. After the war that list grew, and in recognition of Brazil potential, FIFA chose it to play host to the 1950 World Cup. Under the sponsorship of the Rio de Janeiro government, the gigantic Maracanã Stadium, easily the world's largest with a capacity for 200,000 spectators (later increased to 220,000), was built as the showpiece of the fourth World Championship and as a testament to the future of Brazilian soccer. The interior of the stadium was barely finished in time for the opening game, and the area around it resembled a battlefield of mud and construction material for the duration of the competition. But the stadium's staggering dimensions and futuristic appearance contributed much to Brazil's stature in the world sporting community.

The Brazilian team, more aware than before of its need to coalesce raw talent into winning form, entered the competition firmly set on winning the trophy. Nothing less would do, and the pundits in Europe as well as in South America declared the Brazilians a strong favorite. In the first round they were grouped with Mexico, Switzerland, and Yugoslavia. Skillful attacking combinations proved too strenuous for Yugoslavia and Mexico—the former among the most talented teams in Europe—but in Switzerland, Brazil confronted Karl Rappan's effective *verrou* formation, the tight defensive system that anticipated the era of *catenaccio* and the home team stumbled to a 2-2 draw.

However, Brazil's ultimate goal looked attainable in the second round (played under a controversial league system), as manager Flavio Costa set free his extraordinary new front three, Zizinho, Ademir, and Jair. The Brazilian's buried Sweden and Spain by an aggregate of 13-2, and awaited the final match against talented Uruguay sitting on top of the table with a one point lead. Uruguay, however, which had drawn with Spain and edged by Sweden uncomfortably, rose to the occasion as it always had against its northern archrival. Brazilian overconfidence once again contributed to a losing result, and little Uruguay won its second World Championship in one of the most exciting international contests ever played. A world record 199,850 spectators watched Brazil attack unmercifully in the first half, but the Brazilian defense was caught off guard by an unexpected Uruguayan onslaught after the interval. The final score was 2-1 in favor of Uruguay. The host country, which had virtually ground to a halt during the tournament, was stunned. It was some weeks before fans could turn their attention once again to the perennial rivalries of domestic competition.

In the three World Championships before the war, Rio clubs had supplied 74 players to the national side while only five had come from the great clubs of São Paulo. In 1950, this trend reversed itself to some extent and began to edge toward a balance, though as late as 1974 the numbers still reflected an imbalance in favor of Rio. In the 1954 World Cup, *paulista* players were dominant for the first time, and the seeds of Brazil's later glory were sown. Brazil's two backs in 1954 were Djalma Santos and Nilton Santos, probably the greatest backfield in the history of the game and holders of their position on the national team for three successive World Cups. At inside right, Fluminense's Didi (later of Botafogo) drew worldwide attention to his rare combination of leadership abilities and skillful playmaking.

The 1954 World Cup, however, was another dark chapter in sequel to the 1938 "Battle of Bordeaux." In Switzerland, it was the notorious "Battle of Berne," and the opponent was another Central European team, the incomparable Hungary. It is clear from hindsight that this quarter final match might have erupted into a pitched battle: Hungary was undefeated in four years, and determined

to crown its recordbreaking achievement with a World Championship: Brazil felt it had been denied the World Cup its last two times out; the defeats of 1938 and 1950 still hovered like a cloud, and Brazil was determined to vindicate its claim. Billed appropriately as a contest between the two best teams in the competition, the 4-2 result in favor of Hungary was not a fair test of relative worth, and brawls in the locker room after the game were among the ugliest ever associated with a major international competition. In the end, the Brazilians, in the end, were eliminated and bitter.

Fortunately, the fanciful memories of international fans continued to be focused on images of the giant Maracanã and the skills of players like Friedenreich, Fausto, Leônidas, Zizinho, Ademir, Jair, Djalma Santos, Nilton Santos, and Didi rather than on rough play on the field, but knowledgable observers continued to hold that without a cohesive tactical approach Brazil would not achieve its ultimate goal.

In domestic competition, the Rio-São Paulo rivalry finally crystallized in an official competition, the Torneio Rio-São Paulo, introduced in 1950 though unofficial editions had been held in 1933 and 1940. Its proper name was the Torneio Roberto Gomes Pedrosa, and it was played annually between the leading clubs of either league until 1967, when the competition was expanded and transformed into a national championship. The first six editions were won by São Paulo clubs (Corinthians won three of these and Portuguêsa two).

In São Paulo, the 1940s had seen the rise to prominence of São Paulo FC, the winner of five *paulista* titles between 1934 and 1949, and Palmeiras continued its historical role as one of the standard-bearers of the league. In Rio, the war years were dominated by Flamengo and Fluminense, but the five-year period leading up to the 1950 World Cup clearly belonged to Vasco da Gama, a club that supplied eight of Brazil's 17 players in 1950. In the Minas Gerais league, Cruzeiro won its first series of championships, though Atlético Mineiro continued to dominate, and in Rio Grande do Sul, Internacional took over leadership in the *gaucho* league from Grêmio.

In the early 1950s, Flamengo and Corinthians excelled in their respective leagues, but in 1955 a new phenomenon appeared in the *paulista* club Santos FC (from the coastal city of the same name). The spark that ignited Santos' fire was a 15-year-old boy wonder named Pelé. The "Black Pearl" transformed an already excellent side into an astonishing goalscoring machine. With one previous São Paulo championship to its credit (1935), Santos won the title in 1955 and 1956 and nine additional years in the period after that, and with Pelé at inside left became the most famous club in the world, eclipsing even Arsenal and Real Madrid in the minds and hearts of fans around the world.

At the same time Santos was on the rise, a tactical breakthrough transformed for the national team. Manager Vincente Feola decided to drop the traditional third back game in favor of the little-known 4-2-4 system, introduced in 1953 by Paraguay's manager Fleitas Solich in the South American Championship. At the 1958 World Cup in Sweden, Brazil brought the new system into full bloom. The forward line, which under the 4-2-4 was freed from a defensive role altogether, featured an array of sublimely skilled players: Garrincha, Vavá, Pelé, and Zagalo. This awesome group, in addition to midfielder Didi, won the 1958 World Cup for Brazil.

Everything finally seemed to come together for Brazil at the sixth World Championship. Pelé and Garrincha, both in the flower of their youth, were the two most gifted ball artists of the postwar era; the unique Didi was at the height of his form; Vavá ranked close to Pelé as an intuitive goalscorer, though their styles were completely different; Zagalo's ceaseless stamina absorbed the whole left side of the field like a sponge; Zito was appropriately versatile at right half; Djalma Santos and Nilton Santos continued to justify their deserved international reputations; and Gilmar was and remains the finest goalkeeper Brazil has ever produced. To these attributes were added the facts that the 4-2-4 suited Brazil's talent admirably, and that Sweden proved to be an agreeable locale. The entire team and coaching staff entered the competition with what can only be described as a joyous spirit and eager desire to win.

After eliminating England, Austria, and the USSR in the first round, Brazil defeated the strong Welsh team in the quarter-finals and France, perhaps the second most exciting team in the tournament, in the semi-finals.

Brazil's scintillating lineup for the 1958 World Cup final, a squad of "pure footballers" whose unique combination of individual and collective genius dominated world soccer for 12 years: (standing, left to right) Djalma Santos, Zito, Bellini, Nilton Santos, Orlando, Gilmar; (seated) Garrincha, Didi, Pelé, Vavá, Zagalo, masseur.

Game after game, Brazil staged dazzling displays of wide open yet modern soccer, especially against the USSR and France, and Pelé and Vavá scored one memorable goal after another. In the final against Sweden, the front four and Didi beat their defenders and dominated the game. Pelé and Vavá scored a pair each, Zagalo scored once, and the final result was 5-2. Brazil was finally the World Champion, and the wealthy clubs of Europe came rushing to its doorstep, contracts in hand.

It was not just another World Cup victory; Brazil's win was celebrated on an international scale. The balance of world power in the soccer community started to shift, though the domestic leagues in many European countries were still stronger than their South American counterparts. Fans everywhere declared that Brazil's was the brand of soccer they most wanted to see. And in the record books, Brazil had now accumulated a third, second, and first place finish in four successive World Cups.

Brazil's postwar record in the South American Championship was mediocre, as always. Its only victory until 1975 was in 1949, when Brazil was the host country. There were periodic wins in the smaller regional contests, but nothing was won during the 1950s and early 1960s to amplify the exalted position that Brazil held after winning the World Cup. Brazil's World Cup form deserted it only a few months after Stockholm. In 1959, it suffered lopsided losses to Uruguay and Argentina in the South American Championship, and lost to Costa Rica by 3-0 in 1960. Argentina defeated Brazil four times in a row between December 1959 and May 1960. In 1961, it regained its seriousness of purpose as well as its stars who had signed on with European clubs after 1958, and went undefeated in 22 matches over a period of two years. This period included the 1962 World Cup in Chile.

In Chile, Brazil won its second World Championship, but the exuberant atmosphere of Sweden was absent. In the more familiar surroundings of South America, the Brazilian approach was less intense though every bit as skillful. A 4-3-3 replaced the 4-2-4, and Feola was forced to step down prior to the competition due to illness. In the opening round against Czechoslovakia, Pelé was injured and sadly rendered unable to play for the remainder of the series. Vavá, Didi, Zagalo, Zito, Nilton Santos, Djalma Santos, and Gilmar were all present again, the two

Santoses for the third World Cup in succession, but Brazil's heroes were Garrincha, scorer of two goals each against England and Chile, and Pelé's replacement Amarildo, who almost single-handedly beat Spain in the opening round and equalized in the final against Czechoslovakia. The final was won 3-1 with an on-and-off performance, and the Jules Rimet Cup was again enveloped by the musical sounds of *samba*.

In 1963, the national team slumped once again. Brazil did not participate in the South American Championship again until 1975, but everyone was anxious to hold friendlies with the *bi-campeão do mundo*, and there were still the regular bilateral series played against neighboring South American countries. In 1963, Brazil lost eight matches, one-third of its total number of losses between 1958 and 1970, and while results improved before the 1966 World Cup in England, Brazil entered the eighth World Championship as one of three or four possible winners rather than as a clear favorite.

Pelé, injured Garrincha, and the aging Djalma Santos and Zito returned, as did Bellini and Orlando from 1958. Feola was back at the helm, and there were gifted newcomers in Gerson and Tostão, but in the first round it became apparent that less talented players—and that meant nearly everyone else in the competition—were intent on hacking the redoubtable Brazilian strikers to the turf. Pelé especially was victimized so consistently by fearful defenders that his saga became little more than a tragedy. Finally, against Portugal, he was hacked out of the tournament and bitterly promised never to return to World Cup competition. Brazil's hopes suffered with each hack and trip, and after first round losses to Hungary and Portugal, it was eliminated.

Meanwhile, on the club level, Brazil entered international competition with timidity and suspicion. In 1959, the CBD introduced the Taça Brasil (Brazil Cup), which was contested between winners of the major state championships to determine Brazil's entrants in the new Copa Libertadores. The Taça Brasil came close to superceding the Torneio Rio-Sao Paulo as the major club competition in the country, but in 1968 it was discontinued. The first winner was Salvador's leading club EC Bahia, which was promptly knocked out of the first Copa Libertadores (1960) in the quarterfinals. Palmeiras advanced to the final the following year, but Santos was the first and only Brazilian club for many years to enter the South American club championship with genuine enthusiasm. Pelé's club, indeed, won the competition in 1962 and 1963 (a Brazilian club—Cruzeiro—did not win again until 1976), and proceeded also to win the Intercontinental Cup twice in a row, defeating Benfica Lisbon and AC Milan. In addition to its successful world and European tours, it was the Intercontinental Cup which spread Santos's fame abroad. The accolades heaped on Santos, as well as the World Cup victories of 1958 and 1962, contributed to the near-mythical quality of Brazil's reputation in international soccer.

In the meantime, the Taça Brasil was won five years in a row by Santos (1961-65). The Rio-São Paulo tournament during this period was dominated by no one in particular, except perhaps by Santos, and the Rio league was reconquered by the venerable Botafogo, a club that had been supported historically by wealthy Rio interests. Botafogo's link with the elite and powerful of Rio de Janeiro is reflected in its having supplied a highly disporportionate number of players to Brazil's World Cup squads over the years. The Botafogo of the early 1960s featured Didi, Nilton Santos, and Garrincha, though not all at the same time.

The 1960s also saw the beginning of a boom in the construction of giant stadiums up and down the country that was still in full swing in the late 1970s. Stadiums with capacities for over 100,000 spectators were built in São Paulo, Belo Horizonte, Curtiba, Pôrto Alegre, Belém, Fortaleza, Salvador, and Maceio. Individually or collectively, these huge futuristic edifices remain unrivaled anywhere in the world.

The national team, revitalized by Pelé's newly found enthusiasm and a fresh crop of supremely talented players, returned to winning form by 1968. Between the summer of 1968 and the 1970 World Cup, Brazil won 21 matches and lost only three. In the midst of this was the national jubilation over Pelé's one-thousandth goal, scored for Santos in a 1969 league match, and the promise that he would be available for Mexico after all.

The festive atmosphere of Mexico's soccer-crazed cities was well suited to a Brazilian comeback (the altitudes and heat were not), but England, Italy, and West Germany were serious threats to Brazil's chances. The threat was compounded by discord at home in the form of a controversial managerial change in

1969, when Botafogo's outspoken messiah of the early 1960s, João Saldanha, was called in by the CBD, though this proved to be short lived. Three months before the World Cup began, former international hero Mario Zagalo replaced Saldanha, the latter rumored to be dropping Pelé. Zagalo, who was well liked and respected by all concerned, turned out to be the necessary stablizer.

The World Cup of 1970 was a brilliant high point in soccer history. This was due to the manner in which Brazil won its third World Championship. For 15 years, the game was dominated by the negative tactics of *catenaccio,* with brief respites provided by Brazil and Portugal. Zagalo's open and exciting team showed the world once again how the game might be played. With Pelé and the splendid Tostao in the middle of the attack, the right and left flanks were occupied by Jairzinho and Rivelino, respectively, both players of world class stature. Out of the midfield came the orchestrator Gerson, and from even further back came the elegant, attacking right fullback Carlos Alberto, the new captain. The striking potential of these six alone was among the greatest the game has ever seen. Czechoslovakia, England, Rumania, Peru, and Uruguay all succumbed in due course, and in the final against Italy, Brazil painted a canvas of footballing delights. Though Italy played superbly in the adversary role and even managed to score a goal, Pelé, Gerson, Jairzinho, and Carlos Alberto each hit the back of the net, leaving no doubt that Brazil was back on top. Its third World Cup win earned Brazil the right to retain permanent possession of the Jules Rimet Trophy, and today the little gold statue stands on proud display at the headquarters of the CBD in Rio.

Brazil's domination of world soccer was thus extended from the 1950s to the early 1970s. Unfortunately, Brazil was not to repeat its accomplishment in 1974. In West Germany, the always seething violence underneath Brazil's emotional artistry surfaced yet again, and the national side was lucky to place fourth after defensive and temperamental displays against Yugoslavia, Scotland, Holland, and Argentina. Brazil's plight was sealed with an embarrassing 3-0 win over lowly Zaire, and it was only in its loss to Poland in the third place match that a semblance of order was reintroduced for the sake of posterity.

In 1975, Brazil was eliminated from the

revitalized South American Championship by Peru, and the Brazilian game sank to an all-time low. The rebuilding process did not begin in earnest until 1977, when the national team manager, Claudio Coutinho, set out to introduce elements of European teamwork. In Brazil's eleventh attempt to gain World Cup honors in 1978, Coutinho's idea backfired. Individual skills were apparent, as always, but apart from a splendid 3-0 defeat of Peru, the Brazilian team was disorganized and ineffective. It finally settled for an uneasy third place, despite the fact that it finished as the only unbeaten team in the competition.

In the late 1960s, the structure of Brazil's domestic game was altered considerably. The Taça Brasil lingered on through the 1968 season, but in 1967 the CBD finally decided to expand the role of the Torneio Roberto Gomes Pedrosa (Torneio Rio-São Paulo). State leagues other than Rio and São Paulo argued that their standards of play were now approaching that of the big two. They pointed out, for example, that in the Taça Brasil CE, Bahia had not only won the competition once, but had also been the losing finalist twice. Furthermore, Fortaleza, from Ceara in the far northeast, had been runners-up twice, Cruzeiro had won the competition in 1966, upsetting the mighty Santos during their peak years, and in 1967 Nautico Recife had advanced to the final as well.

In 1967, the Torneio Pedrosa dropped the reference to "Rio-São Paulo" in its name, and three other state leagues were added to the competition. The first edition of the expanded Torneio Pedrosa included five clubs each from Rio and São Paulo, two each from Minas Gerais and Rio Grande do Sul, and one from Parana. In subsequent years, the number of invited leagues and clubs grew, and in 1971 the series became known officially as the Campeonato Nacional. Like the Torneio Rio-São Paulo before it, the National Championship occupied the second half of each season, following a summer break at the close of the state championships. In 1969, after two overlapping years, the Taça Brasil became redundant and was discontinued. From 1969, the Torneio Pedrosa—and later the Campeonato Nacional—was alone in providing Brazil with a national champion and runner-up, as well as with two entrants for the Copa Libertadores, and slowly but surely, the CBD began to open up the new competition to leagues and clubs from the interior.

The growth of the National Championship is reflected in the following list of participating state leagues and clubs: 1967 (5 leagues, 15 clubs); 1968 (7, 17); 1969 (7, 17); 1970 (7, 17); 1971 (8, 20); 1972 (13, 26); 1973 (20, 40); 1974 (20, 40); 1975 (21, 42); 1976 (21, 54); 1977 (21, 62); 1978 (22 leagues). By 1978, only the state of Acre in the western Amazon basin was not represented, and the number of clubs that were judged fit for national competition had increased four times. The vast majority of clubs in Brazil, including some first division clubs in Rio, São Paulo, and other major cities, however, remain excluded.

The format for the Campeonato Nacional is as follows (using figures for the 1977 edition): The competition is in three phases. In the first phase, the 62 participating clubs are divided into six groups of 10 and 11 clubs each. The four highest placed clubs from each group automatically qualify for phase two. These 24 clubs are grouped in four sections of six clubs each. The 38 clubs that did not automatically qualify for phase two are grouped into six groups of five and six clubs each to form a consolation section that runs parallel to phase two. From phase two, the top three clubs from each group qualify for the third and final phase. From the consolation section, only the winner of each group qualifies for the final phase. In the first round of the final phase, 18 clubs (12 from the second phase and six from the consolation section) participate. They are divided into two groups of nine clubs each. The winner and runners-up of either group qualify for the second round of the final phase. The winner of one first round group plays the runner-up of the other first round group. The winners of these two matches play each other for the Copa Brasil. (From 1967 to 1970, the championship trophy was the Taça de Prata.)

The National Championship has started to achieve what it set out to do. Provincial clubs have won the competition three times (Atlético Mineiro in 1971 and Internacional Pôrto Alegre in 1975 and 1976), and in 1975 the two finalists were both from provincial leagues (Internacional and Cruzeiro). São Paulo's Palmeiras, meanwhile, has excelled in winning four National Championships (1967, 1969, 1972, 1973).

In the Liga Paulista, the big five clubs down through the decades have been (in descending order of points accumulated): Palmeiras, Santos, São Paulo, Corinthians, and Portuguesa. In the Liga Carioca, the big five are (in order): Fluminense, Flamengo, Vasco da Gama, Botafogo, and América. Cruzeiro's winning of the 1976 Copa Libertadores, however, was the clearest signal yet that the hegemony of these giant sporting establishments is open to challenge. Cruzeiro, Atlético Mineiro, and Internacional have reached the front ranks of Brazilian soccer, and in future years other provincial clubs are likely to have a heavy impact on the National Championship.

Soccer is the outstanding passion of the Brazilian people. The depth of their *religião Brasileira* (a term used frequently by Brazilians themselves) may be felt not only on the terraces of giant stadiums, but up and down the beaches and in the unlikeliest of the wet jungles. The famous government sponsored amateur league matches take place on the beach in most coastal states and perennially attract thousands of spectators and as many barefooted players. In the interior, visitors are startled to discover, an occasional soccer pitch holed out of rain forests, to which local Indian tribes gravitate both as observers and participants.

For the rest of world, however, Brazilian soccer will continue to be associated with the yellow, green, and blue uniform of the national team. Brazil's record of 13 consecutive victories in World Cup play (1958-66) will not be broken soon. In all the years, Brazil has lost only 20 percent of its full internationals (one-fourth of these to Argentina), and, as of 1978, the national team had not lost a single match in the Maracanã since 1957. The CBD's confidence in native-born players is indicated by the present regulation that each club is allowed no more than one foreign player in a starting lineup. It is not a coincidence, the CBD points out, that three of the world's five highest goalscorers of all time (Friedenreich, Pelé, and Flavio) are Brazilian.

See also: **Maracanã; Estádio Mário Filho, o**

Torneio Rio-São Paulo Winners

1933	Palestra Itália (unofficial)	1958	Vasco da Gama
1940	Flamengo/Fluminense (unofficial)	1959	Santos
1950	Corinthians	1960	Fluminense
1951	SE Palmeiras	1961	Flamengo
1952	Portuguesa	1962	Botafogo
1953	Corinthians	1963	Santos
1954	Corinthians	1964	Santos/Botafogo (draw)
1955	Portuguesa	1965	SE Palmeiras
1956	no competition	1966	Corinthians/Santos/Vasco da Gama/Botafogo (draw)
1957	Fluminense		

Campeonato Nacional Winners

1967	SE Palmeiras	1973	S.E. Palmeiras
1968	Santos	1974	Vasco da Gama
1969	SE Palmeiras	1975	Internacional
1970	Fluminense	1976	Internacional
1971	Atlético Mineiro	1977	São Paulo FC
1972	SE Palmeiras	1978	Guarani

São Paulo Champions

1902	São Paulo A.C.		1937	Corinthians
1903	São Paulo A.C.		1938	Corinthians
1904	São Paulo A.C.		1939	Corinthians
1905	Paulistano		1940	Palestra Itália
1906	Germania		1941	Corinthians
1907	Internacional (SP)		1942	SE Palmeiras
1908	Paulistano		1943	São Paulo FC
1909	AA das Palmeiras		1944	SE Palmeiras
1910	AA das Palmeiras		1945	São Paulo FC
1911	São Paulo A.C.		1946	São Paulo FC
1912	Americano		1947	SE Palmeiras
1913	Americano		1948	São Paulo FC
1914	Corinthians (LPF)		1949	São Paulo FC
	São Bento (APEA)		1950	SE Palmeiras
1915	Germânia (LPF)		1951	Corinthians
	AA das Palmeiras (APEA)		1952	Corinthians
1916	Corinthians (LPF)		1953	São Paulo FC
	Paulistano (APEA)		1954	Corinthians
1917	Paulistano		1955	Santos
1918	Paulistano		1956	Santos
1919	Paulistano		1957	São Paulo FC
1920	Palestra Itália		1958	Santos
1921	Paulistano		1959	SE Palmeiras
1922	Corinthians		1960	Santos
1923	Corinthians		1961	Santos
1924	Corinthians		1962	Santos
1925	São Bento		1963	SE Palmeiras
1926	Palestra Itália (APEA)		1964	Santos
	Paulistano (LAF)		1965	Santos
1927	Palestra Itália (APEA)		1966	SE Palmeiras
	Paulistano (LEF)		1967	Santos
1928	Corinthians (APEA)		1968	Santos
	Internacional (SP) (LAF)		1969	Santos
1929	Corinthians (APEA)		1970	São Paulo FC
	Paulistano (LAF)		1971	São Paulo FC
1930	Corinthians		1972	SE Palmeiras
1931	São Paulo FC		1973	Santos/Portuguesa (draw)
1932	Palestra Itália		1974	SE Palmeiras
1933	Palestra Itália		1975	São Paulo FC
1934	Palestra Itália		1976	SE Palmeiras
1935	Portuguêsa (APEA)		1977	Corinthians
	Santos (LPF)			
1936	Portuguêsa (APEA)			
	Palestra Itália (LPF)			

Rio de Janeiro Champions

1906	Fluminense	1940	Fluminense
1907	Fluminense/Botafogo (draw)	1941	Fluminense
1908	Fluminense	1942	Flamengo
1909	Fluminense	1943	Flamengo
1910	Botafogo	1944	Flamengo
1911	Fluminense	1945	Vasco da Gama
1912	Paissandu	1946	Fluminense
1913	América	1947	Vasco da Gama
1914	Flamengo	1948	Botafogo
1915	Flamengo	1949	Vasco da Gama
1916	América	1950	Vasco da Gama
1917	Fluminense	1951	Fluminense
1918	Fluminense	1952	Vasco da Gama
1919	Fluminense	1953	Flamengo
1920	Flamengo	1954	Flamengo
1921	Flamengo	1955	Flamengo
1922	América	1956	Vasco da Gama
1923	Vasco da Gama	1957	Botafogo
1924	Vasco da Gama (LMDT)	1958	Vasco da Gama
	Fluminense (AMEA)	1959	Fluminense
1925	Flamengo	1960	América
1926	São Cristovão	1961	Botafogo
1927	Flamengo	1962	Botafogo
1928	América	1963	Flamengo
1929	Vasco da Gama	1964	Fluminense
1930	Botafogo	1965	Flamengo
1931	América	1966	Bangu
1932	Botafogo	1967	Botafogo
1933	Bangu (LCF)	1968	Botafogo
	Botafogo (AMEA)	1969	Fluminense
1934	Vasco da Gama (LCF)	1970	Vasco da Gama
	Botafogo (AMEA)	1971	Fluminense
1935	América (LCF)	1972	Flamengo
	Botafogo (FMD)	1973	Fluminense
1936	Fluminense (LCF)	1974	Flamengo
	Vasco da Gama (FMD)	1975	Fluminense
1937	Fluminense	1976	Fluminense
1938	Fluminense	1977	Vasco da Gama
1939	Flamengo	1978	Flamengo

Rio Grande do Sul Champions

1911	Grêmio	1945	Internacional
1912	Grêmio	1946	Grêmio
1913	Grêmio/Internacional (draw)	1947	Internacional
1914	Grêmio/Internacional (draw)	1948	Internacional
1915	Grêmio/Internacional (draw)	1949	Grêmio
1916	Internacional	1950	Internacional
1917	Internacional	1951	Internacional
1918	Cruzeiro (RG)	1952	Internacional
1919	Grêmio	1953	Internacional
1920	Grêmio/Internacional (draw)	1954	Renner
1921	Grêmio	1955	Internacional
1922	Internacional	1956	Grêmio
1923	Grêmio	1957	Grêmio
1924	not completed	1958	Grêmio
1925	Grêmio	1959	Grêmio
1926	Grêmio	1960	Grêmio
1927	Internacional	1961	Internacional
1928	Americano (RG)	1962	Grêmio
1929	Cruzeiro (RG)	1963	Grêmio
1930	Grémio	1964	Grêmio
1931	Grêmio	1965	Grêmio
1932	Grêmio	1966	Grêmio
1933	Grêmio	1967	Grêmio
1934	Internacional	1968	Grêmio
1935	Grêmio	1969	Internacional
1936	Internacional	1970	Internacional
1937	Grèmio	1971	Internacional
1938	Grêmio	1972	Internacional
1939	Grêmio	1973	Internacional
1940	Internacional	1974	Internacional
1941	Internacional	1975	Internacional
1942	Internacional	1976	Internacional
1943	Internacional	1977	Grêmio
1944	Internacional	1978	Internacional

Minas Gerais Champions

1914	Atlético Mineiro	1920	América (MG)
1915	América (MG)	1921	América (MG)
1916	América (MG)	1922	América (MG)
1917	América (MG)	1923	América (MG)
1918	América (MG)	1924	América (MG)
1919	América (MG)	1925	Atlético Mineiro

1926	Atlético Mineiro	1952	Atlético Mineiro
1927	América (MG)	1953	Atlético Mineiro
1928	Palestra Itália (MG)	1954	Atlético Mineiro
1929	Palestra Itália (MG)	1955	Atlético Mineiro
1930	Palestra Itália (MG)	1956	Atlético Mineiro
1931	Atlético Mineiro	1957	América (MG)
1932	Atlético Mineiro	1958	Atlético Mineiro
1933	Vila Nova	1959	Cruzeiro
1934	Vila Nova	1960	Cruzeiro
1935	Vila Nova	1961	Cruzeiro
1936	Atlético Mineiro	1962	Atlético Mineiro
1937	Siderurgica	1963	Atlético Mineiro
1938	Atlético Mineiro	1964	Siderurgica
1939	Atlético Mineiro	1965	Cruzeiro
1940	Cruzeiro	1966	Cruzeiro
1941	Atlético Mineiro	1967	Cruzeiro
1942	Atlético Mineiro	1968	Cruzeiro
1943	Cruzeiro	1969	Cruzeiro
1944	Cruzeiro	1970	Atlético Mineiro
1945	Cruzeiro	1971	Vila Nova
1946	Atlético Mineiro	1972	Cruzeiro
1947	Atlético Mineiro	1973	Cruzeiro
1948	América (MG)	1974	Cruzeiro
1949	Atlético Mineiro	1975	Cruzeiro
1950	Atlético Mineiro	1976	Atlético Mineiro
1951	Vila Nova	1977	Cruzeiro

British International Championship

See: **Home International Championship**

broadcasting

The first radio broadcast of a soccer game was of a first division match between Arsenal and Sheffield United on January 22, 1927, from Highbury, London.

The first television transmission was an extract of the 1937 F.A. Cup Final between Preston North End and Sunderland from Wembley Stadium, London.

To date, some national leagues, including those of Great Britain, do not permit complete, live coverage of league or cup matches, since league administrators fear that a loss of box office receipts would result. The British Broadcasting Corporation, for example, can only transmit edited 57-minute versions of a given match at some time after the match is completed. In contrast, in the United States, the leagues have vigorously sought to gain air time in an effort to gather revenues from lucrative contracts. Latin American leagues have vacillated despite the central position radio and television broadcasts have played in the lives of supporters.

Brunei

Brunei Amateur Football Association
P.O. Box 2010
Bandar Seri Begawan

Founded: 1959
FIFA: 1969
AFC: 1970

Affiliated clubs: *22;* registered players: *83;* national stadium: *none;* largest stadium: *?;* colors: *gold jerseys, black shorts;* season: *September to March;* honors: *none.*

The rise of soccer in Brunei, a sultanate sandwiched between the Malaysian states of Sarawak and Sabah on the island of Borneo, is attributable to the strong British influence in its colonial background. It was the influx of workers to develop the petroleum industry after the discovery of onshore oil in 1929 and the start of offshore drilling in the 1950s that introduced the game. The Brunei State Amateur Football Association was founded in 1959, the year of the first national constitution, and affiliation with FIFA was sought in anticipation of full self-government in 1971. Soccer is now played by Malay as well as Chinese natives, most of whom are not officially registered with the national association, but a major impediment has been the social restrictions of Islam, the major religion. One of the priority tasks that lies ahead is to construct a suitable stadium for major competitions.

Much of Brunei's international experience involves teams from neighboring Malaysia. But in 1975, Brunei entered the Sixth Asian Nations' Cup. In its opening qualification round at Hong Kong, it was grouped with Singapore, Japan, North Korea, People's Republic of China (unlawfully admitted to the Asian Football Confederation prior to the tournament), and Hong Kong. Brunei placed last in the group, suffering severe defeats at the hands of Singapore (6-0), China PR (10-1), and Hong Kong (3-0). Otherwise, little has been seen of Brunei in either the Asian Games or the important regional tournaments of Malaysia, South Vietnam, Thailand, or Indonesia. Only 12 teams take part in the national championship—the number of players is unknown—and the F.A. also sponsors regional cup competitions. Brunei's great trump card for the future is its extreme wealth derived from oil exports. That, combined with FIFA's coaching program for the developing countries, could eventually lead to Brunei teams flung far and wide in Asian competition and ultimately an attempt to qualify for the Olympic Games or World Cup.

Bulgaria

Bulgarska Futbal Federatia
Vassil Levski Stadium
Boul, Tolbuhin, 18
Sofia

Founded: 1923
FIFA: 1924
UEFA: 1954

Affiliated clubs: *2,307;* registered players: *109,772;* national stadium: *Vassil Levski Stadium, Sofia (60,000);* largest stadium: *Vassil Levski Stadium;* colors: *white jerseys, green shorts;* season: *August to December, March to June;* honors: *Olympic Games runner-up (1968), third place (1956), Balkan Cup (1932, 1935, 1975).*

Since its entry into the international mainstream at the 1956 Olympics, Bulgaria's record among European countries is exceeded only by six of Europe's major powers—USSR,

Germany FR, Yugoslavia, Hungary, Italy, and Czechoslovakia—yet it has virtually no major honors. Bulgaria qualified for four successive World Cups between 1962 and 1974, and failed to move beyond the first round in any of them. In the European Football Championship, it has participated in every edition, but has advanced to the second round only once. In the Olympic Games, which since World War II have actually been little more than a showcase for Eastern European teams, Bulgaria has achieved a degree of success, but its overall Olympic record is inferior to those of five other Eastern European states. At the club level, its disappointments have been no less consistent on the international cup circuit.

While it is true Bulgarian soccer made important advances during the 1920s and again during the first decade after World War II, it continues to suffer from the legacy left by defensive tactics introduced after the war by Russian coaches. In addition, it stands as the clearest example in Eastern Europe of the impediments to natural growth that result when state interference becomes heavy-handed and counterproductive. CSKA Sofia, the army club, was so pampered after its formation in 1948 that the rest of the clubs suffered, and it was only in the mid-1970s, despite a general crisis of confidence in the domestic game, that the venerable Levski-Spartak, the country's most popular club, showed signs of leading Bulgaria out of its frustrations.

Soccer was introduced to Bulgaria in 1894, when Georges de Regibus, one of a dozen Swiss athletic instructors hired by the newly independent Kingdom of Bulgaria to establish a sports program, taught the game as a warm-up exercise to youth organizations in Varna. The "English game" did not take root, however, and Bulgarian soccer actually received its first impetus from Bulgarian students at universities in Constantinople, Turkey, who in 1909 formed Football Club 13, named for its 13 members. At the end of the academic year, the students returned to Sofia, and the club was relocated in the capital. Shortly thereafter, Sportist Varna was founded, and by 1910 Football Club 13 was joined by Slavia Sofia and Levski Sofia, which remain the oldest clubs in Bulgaria. An unofficial championship was held in Sofia in 1913, won by Slavia over F.C. 13, but before World War I Bulgarian soccer continued to be held back by the political turbulence of the period and the state's

inability to organize and administer sports programs.

The first era of concentrated growth occurred immediately after World War I. The Bulgarska Nationalna Sportna Federatia (BNSF) was founded in 1923, admitted to FIFA six months later, and in 1924 the first national championship was introduced. Owing to logistical difficulties, it was left incompleted in its first year, but was reintroduced in 1925 as a series of regional leagues in Sofia, Plovdiv, Varna, Burgas, and other major centers, whose winners then competed in a knockout competition to determine the national champion. This format was followed until 1937, when a true national league was established. The new league was made up of 10 clubs, and continued without serious interruption until the change of government in 1944. The first 20 years of the league were dominated by the popular Slavia Sofia and Levski. Sofia, Varna, and Plovdiv emerged as the nation's major soccer hotbeds.

Only weeks after the founding of the BNSF, Bulgaria made its international debut in Vienna against Austria, one of Europe's most advanced teams, losing by a predictable 6-0. Within a year, Bulgaria entered the Olympic Games in Paris, but again it lost, this time to the Irish Free State by 1-0. It lost its first seven games, and did not win until its 15th game, which took place in 1930 against Rumania in the first Balkan Cup. Other than Austria and the Irish Free State, all of Bulgaria's internationals between 1924 and 1932 (28 in all) were played against neighboring Balkan countries including Turkey. In 1933, the team travelled to Madrid to face Zamora and his strong Spanish side, and lost by the biggest margin in its history, 13-0.

Lacking any experience against the strong national teams of Central and Western Europe, Bulgaria bravely entered the World Championships of 1934 and 1938, and achieved its first honors in winning two editions of the prewar Balkan Cup. In the 1932 Balkan Cup at Belgrade, it was undefeated against Yugoslavia, Rumania, and Greece, though it scored only seven goals in three matches, and in the 1935 edition in its own capital of Sofia, Bulgaria won again with an undefeated record against the same opposition. In its 1934 World Cup qualifying round, however, the team stood little chance against Austria and Hungary, losing three games by an aggregate of 14-3. Four years later,

Bulgaria's only opposition in the qualifying round was Czechoslovakia, which had been the losing finalist in 1934, and here the Bulgarians achieved their finest pre-war result, a 1-1 draw in Sofia. In the away leg, however, the Czechs returned to form with a 6-0 win over a disappointed Bulgarian team that had also lost to France by 6-1 the previous month. The national side's leading player during this period was Levski inside-forward Asen Peschev, who appeared in three-fourths of Bulgaria's 53 prewar internationals and scored 11 goals.

With the birth of the socialist state in 1944, Bulgaria entered a splendid period of growth in all sports, and soccer was one of the primary beneficiaries. The championships of 1945-48 temporarily reverted to a knockout format, but the league revived in 1948 with a national first division. In 1946, the regional cup competitions gave way to the national cup—its trophy donated by the Soviet Army—and both the league and the cup were dominated during the immediate postwar years by Levski, which had put together quite the most outstanding team ever seen in Bulgaria. It won the double in 1946, 1947, 1949, and 1950, but its potential was soon to be thwarted by the formation of CDNA Sofia, the Central Army club, in 1948. The reconstituted Supreme Committee for Physical Culture and Sports threw all its weight behind the new showcase club, and while this was to be a pattern among Warsaw Pact states, the case of CDNA (later named CSKA) was special. Funds and personnel were channeled to the army club, and in its first 15 years it won the league title 12 times, including 1948, its first year in existence, and nine in a row between 1954 and 1962. Levski continued as the most popular club, winning a well-deserved share of honors (six league and eight cup titles between 1953 and 1977), and in 1969 it was ordered to merge with Spartak Sofia as Levski-Spartak.

After the war, Bulgaria continued its uninterrupted participation in the Balkan Cup, but in 1946 fared poorly against Albania, Rumania, and Yugoslavia. The postwar national teams, which until 1955 played only against Eastern European opposition, were largely unsuccessful even against the weak Albanians, Rumanians, and Poles. Having skipped over the 1948 Olympics in London, as did all of Eastern Europe except Yugoslavia, Bulgaria entered the 1952 games in Helsinki and proved the cumbersome Soviet squad a worthy match in losing after extra time. Its first encouragement in international competition came at the poorly attended 1956 Olympics in Melbourne. After racing past the Great Britain amateurs by 6-1, it faced the USSR once again, and this time lost by an identical result to its win four years earlier. In the third place game, Bulgaria blanked India by a respectable 3-0, and gained a bronze medal, its first major international honor.

Bulgaria's winning the bronze did not represent the birth of a major international power—the presence in Australia of only one genuine world class team (Yugoslavia) relegated the competition to obscurity—but in 1962, after failing in two previous tries, Bulgaria qualified for the World Cup in Chile by eliminating France and Finland. At Rancagua, it lost to Argentina and was smothered by the resurgent Hungarians, finishing at the bottom of its group after a debilitating 0-0 draw with England. Though the 1962 World Cup was only its second competitive foray outside Europe, Bulgaria had previously traveled overseas in 1955 to Egypt and Lebanon (losing and winning respectively) and in 1958 to Brazil, where it lost twice in a World Cup warm-up series for the soon-to-be crowned world champions.

The 1956 Olympic Games and the 1962 World Cup was spanned by the career of Bulgaria's first international star, the inside left Ivan Kolev, on whose shoulders fell the distinction of attracting some international attention to the Bulgarian game. The early 1960s saw the emergence of several important Bulgarian players. The most gifted, and probably the greatest Bulgarian player of all time, was Georgi Asparoukhov, the goalscoring center forward for Levski, whose injuries sadly kept him at half pace in the 1966 and 1970 World Cup finals. Had Asparoukhov been in form, it is difficult to imagine Bulgaria suffering two winless World Cup final rounds in a row. Tragically, in 1971, Bulgarian soccer was dealt a severe blow when Asparoukhov was killed in a car accident. His death signaled a frustrating decline in the Bulgarian game. Four years earlier, his mantle had been taken over by CSKA stars Petar Jekov and Dimiter Yakimov, who helped Bulgaria to a silver medal at the 1968 Olympics in Mexico. But in the final of the 1968 games, Bulgaria's physical tendencies were once again predominant, and it had three players sent off in a 4-1 loss to Hungary. In the 1974 World Cup finals, Bulgaria again failed to win a match, and after four tries remained the only country to have played in more than one edition of the final rounds without a victory.

On the international club circuit, Bulgarian teams have failed consistently to achieve the big victories. CSKA Sofia has participated in the European Cup 14 times, more than any club in Europe except for Real Madrid and Benfica, but its highest advance has been to the semi-finals in 1966-67. Both CSKA in the European Cup and Levski-Spartak in the European Cup Winners' Cup have overall winning records, yet their reputation is one of faltering at the finishing line. The results of Bulgarian clubs in the Fairs/UEFA Cup has been much the same story, despite isolated triumphs.

The turn upward in Bulgarian soccer that was experienced after CSKA's hegemony was broken in 1963, resulted in the production of more talented players than had ever been seen before, and Bulgaria's displays in international competition were attractive. It was significant that during this same period—1963-69—six different clubs won the league championship, and Slavia Sofia reemerged as multiple cup winners. In the early 1970s, when CSKA again dominated domestic competition, Bulgarian soccer receded into another crisis. Levski-Spartak's 19-3 aggregate burial of Reipas Lahti of Finland in the 1976-77 European Cup Winners' Cup, as well as its encouraging form in domestic competition since 1976, bodes well for a resurgence of Bulgarian soccer via the venerable Sofia club.

Champions

1925	Vladislav Varna	1943	Slavia Sofia	1961	CDNA Sofia
1926	Vladislav Varna	1944	no competition	1962	CDNA Sofia
1927	no competition	1945	Lokomotiv Sofia	1963	Spartak Plovdiv
1928	Slavia Sofia	1946	Levski Sofia	1964	Lokomotiv Sofia
1929	Botev Plovdiv	1947	Levski Sofia	1965	Levski Sofia
1930	Slavia Sofia	1948	CDNA Sofia	1966	CSKA Sofia
1931	AS 23 Sofia	1949	Levski Sofia	1967	Trakia Plovdiv
1932	Sokol Varna	1950	Levski Sofia	1968	Levski Sofia
1933	Levski Sofia	1951	CDNA Sofia	1969	CSKA Sofia
1934	Vladislav Varna	1952	CDNA Sofia	1970	Levski-Spartak
1935	SC Sofia	1953	Levski Sofia	1971	CSKA Sofia
1936	Slavia Sofia	1954	CDNA Sofia	1972	CSKA Sofia
1937	Levski Sofia	1955	CDNA Sofia	1973	CSKA Sofia
1938	Tichka Varna	1956	CDNA Sofia	1974	Levski-Spartak
1939	Slavia Sofia	1957	CDNA Sofia	1975	CSKA Sofia
1940	ZSK Sofia	1958	CDNA Sofia	1976	CSKA Sofia
1941	Slavia Sofia	1959	CDNA Sofia	1977	Levski-Spartak
1942	Levski Sofia	1960	CDNA Sofia	1978	Lokomotiv Sofia

Cup Winners

1946	Levski Sofia	1950	Levski Sofia	1954	CDNA Sofia
1947	Levski Sofia	1951	CDNA Sofia	1955	CDNA Sofia
1948	Lokomotiv Sofia	1952	Slavia Sofia	1956	Levski Sofia
1949	Levski Sofia	1953	Lokomotiv Sofia	1957	Levski Sofia

1958	Spartak Plovdiv	1966	Slavia Sofia	1974	CSKA Sofia
1959	Levski Sofia	1967	Levski Sofia	1975	Slavia Sofia
1960	CDNA Sofia	1968	Spartak Sofia	1976	Levski-Spartak
1961	CDNA Sofia	1969	CSKA Sofia	1977	Levski-Spartak
1962	Botev Plovdiv	1970	Levski-Spartak	1978	Marek Stanke
1963	Slavia Sofia	1971	Levski-Spartak		Dimitrov
1964	Slavia Sofia	1972	CSKA Sofia		
1965	CSKA Sofia	1973	CSKA Sofia		

Burma

Burma Football Federation
Victoria Avenue
Kandawgalay Post Office
Rangoon

Founded: 1947
FIFA: 1947
AFC: 1958

Affiliated clubs: *550;* **registered players:** *14,000;* **national stadium:** *Aungsan Memorial Stadium, Rangoon (45,000);* **largest stadium:** *Aungsan Memorial Stadium;* **colors:** *red jerseys, white shorts;* **season:** *May to February;* **honors:** *Asian Cup runner-up (1968).*

Burma is a middle-level Asian soccer power, which has accumulated many honors in the minor regional tournaments of Southeast Asia, but has made few inroads outside its own area. Soccer is unquestionably the national sport (though it has serious competition from field hockey) and enjoys a constant rate of growth in remote as well as populated sections of the country. It is one of only two East Asian countries to place highly in the Asian Cup, taking second place to Iran in 1968, and winning the Asian Games soccer tournament in 1966, followed four years later by a shared win with South Korea.

The popularity of soccer in Burma is attributable to the country's strong colonial links with Great Britain. Soldiers and residents in British outposts and major population centers played the game throughout the period when Burma was a province of India (1885-1942). The major turning point was World War II, which brought a huge influx of British military personnel and cultural staples, such as soccer and cricket. By the time the Burma Football Federation was founded in 1947, shortly before independence, there was a thriving league of first and second divisions and two annual cup competitions. The leading clubs of this early period were Irrawaddy Flotilla Co., which won the inaugural first division title in 1947; Customs Club, which won the first league cup in 1948; Burma Police S.C., the first winner of a second major knockout competition in 1948; Friends Union Club; Burma Army Sports Club; Fifth Advance Base W/Shop; and the Asiatic Sports Club. The military and civil service orientation of the first major clubs was eventually supplemented by corporate sponsored teams in the 1950s and '60s. Rangoon has always been the major center of activity, but many clubs have been formed over the years in trading centers along the Irrawaddy, in Mandalay, and in Taung-gyi in Shan State.

Burma was one of six participants in the first soccer tournaments of the Asian Games (1951), losing its only match to Iran in the first round. Its inclusion in this series at such an early stage indicates the relatively advanced state of organization in Burmese soccer. In 1952, Burma played host to the International Quadrangular Tournament, finishing ahead of Ceylon but behind India and Pakistan. Its most consistent international successes have been seen in the various regional tournaments of Southeast Asia. Burma has won no less than five soccer tournaments of the Southeast Asian Peninsula (SEAP) Games, including four in succession between 1967 and 1973. It has won the highly-touted Merdeka Football Tournament of Malaysia three times (1964, 1967, and 1971), the second shared with South Korea; the Djakarta Anniversary Tournament four times (1971, 1973, 1974, and 1975); and the South Korean President's Cup three times in succession (1971-73), the second outright.

Burma's two highest achievements in international competition are winning the Asian Games tournament in 1966 with a 1-0 final victory over continental power Iran, and its second place finish in the 1968 Asian Cup, the most important competition in Asia. The latter included a win over Israel, which for years has shared domination of Asian soccer with Iran. Perhaps a greater source of pride to Burmese players and officials, however, was their qualification for the 1972 Olympic tournament in Munich, in which the team lost narrowly to the USSR and Mexico, and defeated Sudan in its first round group. Burma's two 1-0 losses, especially to the state sponsored Soviet team, are rightfully considered upsets, and mark Burma's only senior-level participation in a worldwide competition. It is somewhat surprising, then, that Burma has not yet attempted to qualify for the World Cup. If political stability can be maintained, Burma will continue to rise in the ranks of Asian soccer and will no doubt challenge the tentative supremacy of Hong Kong, Singapore, and the two Koreas in East Asia.

Burundi

Confédération des Sports (CSB)	Founded: 1948
B.P. 1810	FIFA: 1972
Bujumbura	CAF: 1972

Affiliated clubs: *132;* registered players: *3,930;* national stadium: *Fédération de Football du Burundi Stadium (6,000);* largest stadium: *FFB Stadium;* colors: *red jerseys, white shorts;* season: *?;* honors: *none.*

Burundi, which ranks with its neighbor Rwanda as the world's poorest nation, has enthusiastically adopted soccer as the national sport. It is uncertain whether the game was introduced to the territory of Ruanda-Urundi by Germans, who took control of the area in the late nineteenth century, or by Belgians, who leased the colony during World War I. In any case, the country's concerted effort to organize the domestic game and actively seek international arenas is a testament to the people's enthusiasm for soccer and signifies a triumph of will over extraordinary odds. The years of continuous civil unrest following independence from Belgium in 1962 impeded the growth of the game, but in 1972 sports officials closed ranks and sought membership in FIFA and the African Football Confedera-

tion. Actual control of soccer in Burundi is in the hands of the Fédération de Football du Burundi (FFB), an adjunct of the Confédération des Sports, which was founded with Belgian initiative immediately after World War II.

Twenty-six teams participate in league competition. The national championship is contested by eight provincial clubs and 10 clubs from Bujumbura, the capital. There is no annual cup competition as yet. One of Burundi's leading clubs, Inter Football, entered the African Champions' Cup in 1975, and eliminated Embassoira of Ethiopia in the first round, winning the home leg 2-0 after drawing 1-1 away. In the next round, Inter itself was eliminated by Mareikh of the Sudan after losing both legs by an aggregate score of

6-0. This remains the only instance of a Burundi club entering African competition. Though Burundi has not yet attempted to qualify for the World Cup, an unsuccessful bid has been made for each African Nations' Cup since 1972. Its most recent elimination was in the preliminary round of 1975 to Egypt, one of Africa's perennial powers, by an aggregate score of 5-0. Burundi warmed up for that confrontation by defeating Somalia 2-0 in a friendly at Mogadiscio.

Burundi's potential as a regional power is minimal. Yet, it has proven convincingly that rank poverty and the simplest game are often good bedfellows. Neighboring Rwanda is culturally more diverse and unstable than Burundi, and soccer's lack of success there is in marked contrast to the organizational abilities demonstrated by Burundi's CSB.

C

Cambodia   See: **Khmer**

Cambridge University Rules

Of all the English schools and universities associated with the birth of modern soccer, Cambridge University holds the most important place. The football rules formulated at Cambridge in 1848 more closely resembled and anticipated the first Laws of the Game (1863) than any set of rules before them, and the revised Cambridge codes that were written during the 15 years after 1848 proved to be the model on which the Laws themselves were based.

Cambridge players appear to have had a greater liking for the dribbling game (as distinct from the handling game) than those of Oxford, but this was perhaps a matter of chance. As it happened, most of the students who drafted the first Cambridge rules in 1848 were graduates of public schools where the dribbling game was dominant, and their rules reflected this fact. The text of the 1848 rules has not survived, but a derivative code drawn up between 1854 and 1858 by the University Foot Ball Club has been preserved and must have been quite similar to the original 1848 issue. They were called the "Laws of the University Foot Ball Club":

1. This Club shall be called the University Football Club.
2. At the commencement of play, the ball shall be kicked off from the middle of the ground; after every goal there shall be a kickoff in the same way or manner.
3. After a goal, the losing side shall kick off; the sides changing goals unless a previous arrangement be made to the contrary.
4. The ball is out when it has passed the line of the flag-posts on either side of the ground, in which case it shall be thrown in straight.
5. The ball is "behind" when it has passed the goal on either side of it.
6. When the ball is behind, it shall be brought forward at the place where it left the ground not more than ten paces, and kicked off.
7. Goal is when the ball is kicked through the flag-posts and under the string.
8. When a player catches the ball directly from the foot, he may kick it as he can without running with it. In no other case may the ball be touched with the hands, except to stop it.
9. If the ball has passed a player and has come from the direction of his own goal, he may not touch it till the other side have kicked it, unless there are more than three of the other side before him. No player is allowed to loiter between the ball and the adversaries' goals.
10. In no case is holding a player, pushing with the hands, or tripping up allowed. Any player may prevent another from getting to the ball by any means consistent with this rule.
11. Every match shall be decided by a majority of goals.

Although many details are left to doubt, these rules clearly anticipate modern soccer rather than rugby. For example, the offside rule (no. 9) more closely resembles the modern concept of offside than does the offside rule in the original Laws of the Game. Points are won only by scoring between the flagposts and beneath a connecting horizontal string (no. 6). The mention of string (no. 7) is unique during this period, and predates its incorporation into the Laws of the Game by almost 20 years. No other method of scoring, such as the "tries" of rugby-oriented games, is mentioned (no. 7). Handling the ball is strictly limited to the fair catch (no. 8), a universal characteristic of football games before 1866. Unlike contemporary handling codes, holding, tripping, and the more severe act of "hacking," are forbidden. All these characteristics combine to form a game whose appearance would not be unfamiliar to modern soccer fans.

The origins of these rules are found in the idiosyncratic house codes of Harrow and Shrewsbury Schools and, to a lesser extent of Eton College, Winchester School, and Rugby School, but they coalesced unmistakably at Cambridge. When the revised Cambridge rules of 1863 were drawn up, the influence of dribbling schools like Harrow, Shrewsbury, and Westminster was even more keenly felt.

The text of the Cambridge University Rules of 1863, which appeared only weeks before the original Laws of the Game and influenced them immeasurably, is as follows:

1. The length of the ground shall not be more than 150 yards, and the breadth not more than 100 yards.
   The ground shall be marked out by posts, and two posts shall be placed on each side-line at distances of 25 yards from each goal-line.
2. The goals shall consist of two upright poles at a distance of 15 feet from each other.
3. The choice of goals and kick-off shall be determined by tossing and the ball shall be kicked off from the middle of the ground.
4. In a match when half the time agreed upon has elapsed, the sides shall change goals when the ball is next out of play. After such change or a goal obtained, the kick-off shall be from the middle of the ground in the same direction as before.
   The time during which the game shall last and the numbers on each side are to be settled by the heads of the sides.
5. When a player has kicked the ball, any one of the same side who is nearer to the opponents' goal-line is out of play and may not touch the ball himself nor in any way whatsoever prevent any other player from doing so.
6. When the ball goes out of the ground by crossing the side-lines, it is out of play and shall be kicked straight into the ground from the point where it is first stopped.
7. When a player has kicked the ball beyond the opponents' goal-line, whoever first touches the ball when it is on the ground with his hand, may have a free kick bringing the ball straight out from the goal-line.
8. No player may touch the ball behind his opponents' goal-line, who is behind it when the ball is kicked there.
9. If the ball is touched down behind the goal-line and beyond the line of the side-posts, the free kick shall be from the 25-yards post.
10. When a player has a free kick, no one of his own side may be between him and his opponents' goal-line, and no one of the opposite side may stand within 15 yards of him.
11. A free kick may be taken in any manner the player may choose.
12. A goal is obtained when the ball goes out of the ground by passing between the poles or in such a manner that it would have passed between them had they been of sufficient height.
13. The ball, when in play, may be stopped by any part of the body, but may not be held or hit by the hands, arms or shoulders.
14. All charging is fair, but holding, pushing with the hands, tripping up and shinning are forbidden.

The offside rule (no. 5), the appearance of the goal (no. 2), and the method of scoring (no. 12) in these rules were less similar to modern soccer than their counterparts in the Cambridge rules of 1854-58, but handling and hacking were expressly ruled out (nos. 13 & 14), and the spirit and sophistication of the revised Cambridge code ended one era and prefaced another.

See also: **Harrow Game, Rules of the** and **Laws of the Game**

Cameroon

Fédération Camérounaise de Football	Founded: 1960
B.P. 1116	FIFA: 1962
Yaoundé	CAF: 1963

Affiliated clubs: *200;* **registered players:** *796;* **national stadium:** *Stade Ahmadou Ahidjo, Yaoundé (50,000);* **largest stadium:** *Stade Ahmadou Ahidjo;* **colors:** *green jerseys, red shorts;* **season:** *October to August;* **honors:** *Canon de Yaoundé, African*

Cup of Champions (1971, 1978), Oryx de Douala, African Cup of Champions (1964), Canon de Yaoundé, Tonnerre KC, African Cup Winners' Cup (1975).

Cameroon (or Cameroun) is the home of two great African clubs, Canon de Yaoundé and Tonnerre Kalara Club Yaoundé, and the location of two of the most modern stadium facilities in sub-Saharan Africa: the national stadium in Yaoundé, the capital, and the Stade Réunification in Douala. It is a rising influence in African soccer in many respects, and now ranks among the top ten African countries in international standings.

The game was introduced to Cameroon by German colonists in Buea before World War I, but the French did more to popularize it during their League of Nations mandate between the wars. The biggest surge of interest was seen after World War II, when an organizational structure of sorts rose from the chaos of French Equatorial African soccer. This was the only area in French Africa that was not governed by one of the primary colonial soccer administrations linked to the French Football Federation, thus relegating it to relative obscurity until independence in 1960. French Cameroon had not even been governed politically as part of Equatorial Africa or West Africa, and building a soccer administration was further complicated by the longstanding partition of West (British) and East (French) Cameroon.

Great encouragement was given to *Camerounais* soccer when Oryx de Douala plunged unmericifully through the inaugural African Champions' Cup in 1964, and brought home the first African club trophy. Cameroon clubs were to figure prominently in African club championships for years to come. Only the continental powers Zaire, Ghana, and Guinea have fared better in this arena. In 1971, Canon de Yaoundé won the African Champions' Cup after hard fought battles with ASEC Abidjan (Ivory Coast), and Kotoko Kumasi (Ghana) in the final—both leading African clubs. The final was forced into a replay, which fortunately for Canon was held in Yaoundé. Léopard Club advanced to the semi-finals of the Champions' Cup in 1973, but this has been the last hurrah for Cameroon clubs in this competition to date, and, in fact, Cameroon champions did not even participate in 1974 and 1975. In the first two editions of the African Cup Winners' Cup, however, Tonnerre KC of Yaoundé advanced to the final both times, and in the first year defeated the mighty Stella of Ivory Coast to complete a unique record in African competition: Cameroon clubs have won the first editions of both major African club championships.

On the national level, Cameroon has been less successful. The national side has qualified for the final stages of the African Nation's Cup only twice. In 1970, it was extremely unlucky not to advance beyond the first round, as it finished equal on points with Ivory Coast and Sudan but failed to achieve the necessary goal difference. Two years later, however, when the competition was held in Cameroon, it won its first round group handsomely, but lost to archrival Congo in the semi-final by 1-0 in what has become the most memorable match ever seen in this tropical country. A spirited 5-2 thrashing of Zaire in the third place game provided a modicum of revenge, but the streets of Yaoundé remained in a virtual state of siege for days following. Rumania once visited Yaoundé but managed to gain only a 1-1 draw.

The Premier Division of the Cameroon league now comprises 19 clubs, including five from Douala and three from Yaoundé. The second division of 16 clubs also takes five from Douala, and the third division, the Poule de l'Ouest, whose name indicates the lower stature of West Cameroon clubs, is made up of 16 teams. There is also a national cup competition.

Canada

Canadian Soccer Association
333 River Road
Ottawa
Ontario KIL 8B9

Founded: 1912
FIFA: 1912-26
1948
CONCACAF: ?

Affiliated clubs: *1,000;* registered players: *90,872 (36 professional, 336 non-amateur);* national stadium: *none;* largest stadium: *Stade Olympique, Montreal (72,000);* colors: *red jerseys, red shorts;* season: *April to August;* honors: *none.*

Soccer in Canada was rejected in the early stages of its development for the more idiosyncratic Canadian rugby football (now akin to American football) and other than a period of moderate growth in the 1920s, soccer did not show signs of taking root again until the formation of the North American Soccer League in 1968. Meanwhile, lacrosse and ice hockey remain the national team sports, the former by tradition, the latter in practice. Aside from the popularity of Canadian football, the major obstacle to the growth of soccer has been, of course, the great distance between population centers of the Pacific and Atlantic regions, and this has been reflected in the administrative antagonism exhibited between British Columbia and the eastern provinces. As in the United States, the immigrant communities have provided the base for most soccer activity on the professional or semiprofessional level.

It is likely that the first football played in Canada was the Eskimo game *aqsaqtuk,* which bears a remarkable resemblance to soccer but is unrelated to the direct lineage of the modern game. *Aqsaqtuk* was and still is played on ice sheets from Baffin Island to Alaska.

In the mid-nineteenth century, English football in its various forms was played by British regiments stationed in Ontario and Quebec. The earliest reference to the dribbling game dates from 1859, but football games are known to have been played as early as 1846. Although the earlier date is generally associated with handling codes, it is nearly impossible to determine which loosely adopted set of rules was prevalent before the 1860s. The first club to play by association rules was the Montreal Football Club, founded in 1868. Montreal's most frequent opponent during the first years was an officers' team from Her Majesty's Regiment in Montreal. In 1873, the Canadian Football Association was established, and Montreal F.C. put up a challenge cup to introduce Canada's first organized competition.

The losing battle with rugby began in 1874, when McGill University in Montreal formed a rugby team. It was McGill that introduced the rugby game to Harvard in the same year, leading to the birth and ultimate domination of gridiron football in the United States. Association rules were played at Queen's

University, Kingston, Ontario, in the early 1870s. Queen's played two games in Toronto in 1874 against local teams and lost both. Upper Canada College played under association rules until 1876, but subsequently switched to rugby. Both types of football were reserved exclusively for students and graduates of boarding schools during the 1870s and '80s.

Western Ontario became Canada's first soccer hotbed in the 1880s. There were teams in Galt, London, Strathroy, Clinton, Berlin, and Aylmer, and the first floodlit game in Canada took place in 1885 before 1500 people at Toronto's Jarvis Street grounds. It was also in 1885 that a team representing Canada made its international debut against the USA in Newark (winning 1-0), though some Canadians have suggested that the first match actually took place in Galt earlier in the year. A Galt contest (won by Canada 2-0) was possibly part of a three-game series known to have been played between the two countries in 1886. In 1887, there was another three-game series played in Newark. The six games played in 1886 and 1887 were split evenly between the two teams: 2 won, 2 drawn, 2 lost. Canada's early interest in international competition not only helped launch North American soccer on an international course, but in 1888 a Canadian team visited Scotland, and was treated with notable hospitality. On a second tour in 1891, Canada played against representative (though less than full international) teams from England, Scotland, Wales, and Ireland. These Canadian tours were the first ever made of the British Isles by a non-British team.

Meanwhile, the game had spread westward from Ontario. Teams sprang up in Manitoba, British Columbia, and Northwest Territories, despite the increased popularity of rugby. Rivalries took shape between teams of local townspeople and mounted police or military garrisons. In Northwest Territories, the first tournament played under association rules was in 1891 between a mounted police club and local teams in honor of Queen Victoria's 72nd birthday. In British Columbia, association rules found a place in costal regions, while rugby was established further inland. By the 1890s, however, Canadian football began to dominate, and soccer and rugby purists gradually receded from the limelight, though crowds of 5000 still turned out to watch important soccer matches in Ottawa, Toronto, and Montreal until the turn of the century. Its popularity at the school and university level continued unabated into the 20th Century.

Canada's first and only international honor was won at the 1904 Olympic Games in St. Louis, but, unfortunately, the tournament was only an exhibition series and never entered the record books. Ontario's Galt F.C., representing Canada, defeated a team called USA I (actually Christian Brothers College, St. Louis) by 7-0 and USA II (St. Rose, St. Louis) by 4-0. No other teams were entered, and Canada was declared the winner. Another major event in Canada was the 1911 tour of Corinthians F.C., the great amateur team from England. Corinthians, which also traveled across the United States at this time, played throughout Canada, defeating nearly all its opponents but making a deep impression on Dominion fans and players.

The Dominion of Canada Football Association (DFA as it was known) was founded in 1912 in Toronto, and held its first meeting in Winnipeg the same year. The DFA was the first truly national governing body, and became the precursor of the Football Association of Canada and eventually the present Canadian Soccer Association. Representatives from Quebec, Ontario, Manitoba, Saskatchewan, and Alberta were charter members. A national cup competition was established in 1912 for champion teams from each province, and a trophy was given by the Duke of Connaught. Norwood Wanderers won the first and second Connaught Cup in 1913 and 1914, but almost immediately the leading clubs of Manitoba, Alberta, and especially British Columbia challenged Ontario's and Quebec's supremacy. Four of the first ten winners were from western provinces. The Connaught Cup, later to become the Dominion Challenge Cup (now the Challenge Cup), has remained the only authentic national championship down through the decades. The first edition was played entirely in Winnipeg, but all subsequent competitions have been held on a home and away knockout basis.

From the beginning, the DFA was beset by problems concerning professionalism and provincial antagonism. In British Columbia, where soccer had become particularly strong, many clubs had broken away from the provincial British Columbia Football Association to form a professional league. During the

first year of the DFA's existence, rival associations were set up in Vancouver: the British Columbia Provincial F.A., which affiliated with the DFA, and the British Columbia F.A., which joined the Amateur Athletic Union of Canada. The Connaught Cup, meanwhile, was declared the official trophy of the DFA, replacing the old People's Shield, which for some years had been the only national cup competition in the dominion. The People's Shield was sponsored by the old Canadian Football Association, but after 1912 it faded into oblivion.

In the 1920s, there was a soccer revival caused by vast numbers of European immigrants who had arrived after World War I. Numerous British teams visited Canada, and Canadian teams toured Australia and New Zealand. While Canadian teams at home won a portion of these international friendlies, the relative lack of interest shown by Canadian fans was not enough to make the tours financially viable. Canadian tours abroad, on the other hand, were more successful. On the 1929 tour of New Zealand, the Canadian national team won 20 matches while losing and drawing only one each. In domestic competition between the wars, important rivalries between new immigrant communities took their place beside English, Scottish, Welsh, and Irish rivalries.

After World War II, the game at club level was played almost exclusively by immigrants, and was seen less and less outside the major urban areas of Ontario, Quebec, and British Columbia. The postwar era also saw the rise of British Columbian teams dominant as the force in interprovincial competition. Between 1946 and 1977, clubs from the Vancouver area won the Dominion Challenge Cup 19 times. Even Toronto has been unable to break the hegemony of clubs such as New Westminster Royals (whose eight victories is a Canadian record) and immigrant based teams from Vancouver and Victoria.

In international competition, Canada has suffered from a lack of funds and the difficulty of molding a cohesive national unit of players who must travel thousands of miles to prepare for a match. Canada's most frequent opponent has been the USA, and to its delight Canadian teams have won more games in this series than they have lost. Of their 13 full internationals against the USA, the Canadians have won six and lost five while compiling a deficit goal difference of 25 to 27. They eliminated the USA from both the 1974 and 1978 World

Cup qualification rounds (Canada's first World Cup forays), and in the latter stunned the optimistic American team with a 3-0 shutout in neutral Haiti. Encounters with Mexico—the second North American group rival—have met with less success, and among other CONCACAF opponents in recent years, Canada has defeated Haiti, Surinam, and Guatemala once each.

After its anomalous victory in 1904 at St. Louis, Canada did not attempt to qualify for the Olympic tournament until 1968. Its first participation in the final rounds was as the host country in 1976, when it lost to the USSR's full international team by only 2-1 and North Korea by a more decisive 3-1 in the first round. Elsewhere, Canadian teams have found attentive European opponents in Poland and East Germany, losing three matches to the former by an aggregate 14-2, and two matches to the East Germans by an aggregate of 9-1, all at full level. There have been no full internationals played against British countries.

After 60 years of scattered semi-professionalism, Canada's first professional league, the Eastern Canada Professional Soccer League (ECPSL), was founded in 1961. With clubs from Toronto, Montreal, and Hamilton, the ECPSL lasted five seasons and folded. When the National Professional Soccer League (NPSL) and the United Soccer Association opened for business in the United States in 1967, Canada was represented by three clubs. In the United Soccer Association, Hibernian F.C. of Edinburgh, Scotland, played under a Toronto banner with moderate success and compiled a winning record. In the NPSL, Toronto was represented by the Falcons, who went on to play for one season in the North American Soccer League in 1969. The Vancouver Royals also played in the NPSL, and in 1968 merged with the United Soccer Association's San Francisco Gales to enter the North American Soccer League (one season only) under the stewardship of Ferenc Puskás. A Montreal franchise, Olympique de Montreal, participated in the North American Soccer League for three seasons (1971-73). In 1971, the newly formed Toronto Metros joined the NASL, merging with a local ethnic power, Toronto Croatia, in 1975. In 1976, Toronto Metros-Croatia won the NASL championship with the Portuguese idol Eusebio playing under a one-year contract, and the following year reemerged without either Eusebio or Croatia in their fold. Vancouver, meanwhile, received a new NASL franchise—the Whitecaps—in 1974. Around two dozen Canadian players are now listed in NASL rosters.

See also: **aqsaqtuk**

Champions

1913	Norwood Wanderers	1930	New Westminster Royals
1914	Norwood Wanderers	1931	New Westminster Royals
1915	Winnipeg Scots	1932	Toronto Scots
1916	no competition	1933	Toronto Scots
1917	no competition	1934	Verduns Montreal
1918	no competition	1935	Aldreds Montreal
1919	Grand Trunk, Quebec	1936	New Westminster, Royals
1920	Westinghouse, Ontario	1937	Johnston Nationals
1921	Toronto Scots	1938	North Shore Vancouver
1922	Hillhurst Calgary	1939	Radials Vancouver
1923	Nanaimo, British Columbia	1940	no competition
1924	Weston University Winnipeg	1941	no competition
1925	Toronto Ulsters	1942	no competition
1926	Weston University Winnipeg	1943	no competition
1927	Nanaimo, British Columbia	1944	no competition
1928	New Westminster Royals	1945	no competition
1929	C.N.R. Montreal	1946	Toronto Ulsters

1947	St. Andrews Vancouver	1963	no competition

1947 St. Andrews Vancouver
1948 Carsteel Montreal
1949 North Shore Vancouver
1950 Vancouver City
1951 Ulster United Toronto
1952 Steelco Montreal
1953 New Westminster Royals
1954 Scottish Winnipeg
1955 New Westminster Royals
1956 Halecos Vancouver
1957 Ukrainia S.C. Montreal
1958 New Westminster Royals
1959 Alouetts Montreal
1960 New Westminster Royals
1961 Concordia Montreal
1962 Scottish Winnipeg

1963 no competition
1964 Columbus Vancouver
1965 Firefighters Vancouver
1966 Firefighters Vancouver
1967 Toronto
1968 Toronto Royals
1969 Columbus Vancouver
1970 Manitoba Selects
1971 Eintracht Vancouver
1972 New Westminster Blues
1973 Firefighters Vancouver
1974 Calgary Springer Kickers
1975 London Boxing Club Victoria
1976 Victoria West S.C.
1977 Columbus Vancouver
1978 Columbus Vancouver

Carlos Dittborn Cup

Copa Carlos Dittborn.
An irregular series between the national teams of Argentina and Chile, played on a home and away basis.

Winners

1965 Argentina
1968 Argentina
1971 Argentina
1972 Argentina
1974 Argentina
1976 Argentina

carry

The goalkeeper's holding of the ball in his hands as a result of a save or interception, usually in preparation for a punt or throw. Carrying is unlawful outside the goalkeeper's own penalty area. Since a 1967 ruling, the goalkeeper has been required to give up possession of the ball after four paces (usually by bouncing the ball on the ground). Previously, he was required only to release the ball from his hands (with a slight toss in the air) at least once every four paces, and before 1931 once every two paces.

See also: **hands**

caution   Also known as "booking"

A referee's official warning to a player who has committed certain serious offenses.

To administer a caution the referee must stop play and show the offending player a yellow card. The player is cautioned verbally, and his name is noted in what has become known as "the book." All cautions must be reported by the referee to the committee under whose aegis the match is being played.

The Laws of the Game require that a player be cautioned for the following: 1) entering or leaving the field of play unlawfully; 2) persistently infringing the Laws; 3) dissent from a referee's decision; 4) ungentlemanly conduct.

The yellow card policy was officially introduced by FIFA at the Olympic Games of 1968.

See also: **send off**

Celtic Football Club

Location: *Glasgow, Scotland;* stadium: *Celtic Park (80,000);* colors: *green and white hooped jerseys, white shorts;* honors: *European Cup (1967), Scottish champion (1893, 1894, 1896, 1898, 1905, 1906, 1907, 1908, 1909, 1910, 1914, 1915, 1916, 1917, 1919, 1922, 1926, 1936, 1938, 1954, 1966, 1967, 1968, 1969, 1970, 1971, 1972, 1973, 1974, 1977), Scottish Cup winner (1892, 1899, 1900, 1904, 1907, 1908, 1911, 1912, 1914, 1923, 1925, 1927, 1931, 1933, 1937, 1951, 1954, 1965, 1967, 1969, 1971, 1972, 1974, 1975, 1977), Scottish league cup winner (1957, 1958, 1966, 1967, 1968, 1969, 1970, 1975).*

Founded 1888 by Irish Roman Catholics in the East End of Glasgow to help finance soup kitchens for the neighborhood's poor. Some of the more experienced players in this group had already played for Renton, Dumbarton, and Hibernian. The members' humanitarian ideals were quite genuine, but within a few short years they found their popularity and revenues rising so rapidly that before they knew it the club was a big business. By the end of its first decade, Celtic owned the finest stadium in Europe, and was the wealthiest club in Britain with an annual income of over £15,000. Celtic became a founding member of the Scottish Football League, placing third in the first season, and the year before, it was the losing finalist in its first attempt to capture the Scottish cup. Its archrivalry with the Protestant-based Rangers F.C. commenced almost immediately; in 1893 the first Celtic vs. Rangers cup final took place before 30,000 spectators and was won by Rangers. Celtic's first cup victory occurred in 1892, and its first league championship was won the year of the first Celtic-Rangers cup final.

Celtic has won 30 Scottish league championships (Rangers have won 37) and 25 Scottish cups (a record), and has never been relegated from the Scottish First (later Premier) Division. The overwhelming prominence of Celtic and Rangers in Scottish soccer has led to a belief that the big Glasgow clubs face token opposition in their domestic schedule, diminishing their international importance. But Celtic successfully belied this old charge in 1967, when it won the European Cup in its first attempt with a much praised 2-1 win over Inter Milan at Lisbon, and in so doing became the first club to win the European Cup with players from just one country in its lineup. In that same year, it won the treble at home, and scored a record 111 goals in first division competition. Three years later Celtic advanced to the finals of the European Cup again, but it was less successful against Holland's Feyenoord. Celtic was by now in the midst of its greatest era, winning nine consecutive league championships (a world record) between 1966 and 1974, including five doubles and two trebles. The heroes of this extraordinary side were the solid center half and captain Billy McNeill and the dynamic little winger Jimmy Johnstone.

Celtic fans were keen to point out, however, that at least two other Celtic teams in the past must rank with this record-breaking team. The first was that of 1905-10, which won five consecutive titles and back-to-back doubles in 1907 and 1908, losing only 23 games of a possible 192 and winning 305 points of a maximum 384. The two great goalscorers of this period were "Napoleon" Jimmy McMenemy, who described his shooting as passing "the ball inside the post," and "Iron Man" Jimmy Quinn, whose shot was thought to be the hardest ever seen in Scotland. This team was tactically innovative, and may also be noted for switching from vertical green and white striped jerseys to the present hooped variety in 1906. The second legendary Celtic team was that of the late 1930s, which won successive league and cup honors. This Celtic team was the winning side in the 1937 cup final vs. Aberdeen at Hampden Park, which set a European club attendance record that still stands today (146,433).

In its 90-year history, Celtic has had only four managers: Bill Maley, who was with the club for 50 years from its inception, overseeing its operations from an office at Celtic Park and building the great pre-World War I and interwar teams; Jimmy McStay; Jimmy McGrory (1946-65), who, as a player, set a Scottish league record for scoring 397 goals in 378 appearances for Celtic; and Jock Stein, who took over in 1965 and led the club to world glory, becoming the most successful manager in the history of British soccer. Stein's is a living legend and one that continues to this day. Each of the four was a former Celtic player.

Celtic is perhaps most famous for two qualities: one, its consistent reputation for producing attacking teams that have seldom if ever been prone to defensive tactics; and two, its Roman Catholic background. The foundation for its rivalry with Rangers—the most intense in all of Europe—is, indeed, religious animosity, a rarity in modern European soccer. Celtic's support among the legions of Irish Roman Catholics in Glasgow is complete, and it was only well into this century that non-Roman Catholic players were allowed on its rosters. The "Auld Firm," as the rivalry is known, has bred considerable violence over the years, perhaps the most significant being the 1909 cup final, when a drawn replay caused serious rioting and the trophy was withheld altogether.

center back

A primarily defensive position at the rear of a formation. It differs from that of center halfback because it is always deep-lying and may be one of two such positions on a team.

center forward   Also known as "No. 9."

The player positioned in the middle of the foward line, whose function is primarily to score goals. This has been the glamor spot on the field since the early days of the game, though some modern formations have supplanted the center forward position with central strikers or inside forwards. The oddest function of a center forward may be found in the archaic "echelon formation," in which the center forward is positioned at the point of a "V" setup, with both insides and wingers playing closer to the goal.

center halfback   Also known as "No. 5" and "the pivot."

The middle position among halfbacks or on the midfield line. The center halfback is the most varied of all traditional positions on the field. Its function is pivotal, in that it can be both offensive and defensive, and sometimes encompasses most of the playing area.

Successful center halfbacks tend to possess unusual reserves of stamina, distribute with precision, and tackle with authority. Most formations have now dispensed with the traditional center half in favor of a deep-lying center back or midfield lines of two or four players.

Central Africa

Fédération Centraficaine de Football
B.P. 344
Bangui

Founded: 1937
FIFA: 1963
CAF: 1965

Affiliated clubs: *256;* **registered players:** *7,200 (1,500 non-amateur);* **national stadium:** *Barthélemy Boganda, Bangui (35,000);* **largest stadium:** *Barthélemy Boganda;* **colors:** *grey-blue jerseys, white shorts;* **season:** *October to July;* **honors:** *none.*

While the domestic game in Central Africa is widespread and active, the country's international reputation is similar to that of its foreign policy—unpredictable. It has been characterized by numerous withdrawals from competitions, with the result that soccer in the Central African Empire is virtually an unknown quantity. In the preliminary round of the 1976 African Nation's Cup, Central Africa withdrew from playing Nigeria at the last moment. In an early qualification round for the 1978 World Cup, it withdrew from a scheduled series with Zaire. In 1975, its champion club Fatima entered the African Champions' Cup, won its first match against Mareikh of Sudan, 3-0, and in the return leg left the field at halftime, giving up a probable advance to the next round. Meanwhile, it has not yet qualified for the final rounds of the African Nations' Cup, the continent's major competition, nor has it advanced in Olympic qualification tournaments.

At home, there are over 250 senior clubs participating in the league. The First Division of the national championship is composed of 12 clubs, and it is supported by a group of regional leagues. There are also national and regional cup competitions. Central Africa is one of only four countries on the continent to employ non-amateur players, though there is little chance of full professionalism being adopted in the near future. About one-third of all senior level players are non-amateur. In the 1974 African Champions' Cup, Real de Bangui advanced beyond the preliminary round by upsetting Simba of Uganda; in the following round, however, the vastly superior Heart of Oaks (Ghana) turned away Real's bid by scoring 9 goals in two games. Tempete, Central Africa's third major club, entered the first African Cup Winners' Cup in 1975 and eliminated Postelsport of Benin before succumbing to Jeanne D'Arc of Senegal in the quarter-finals. Thus far, this has been the extent of Central African participation in African club competitions.

The game was introduced in the Ubangi-Chari Territory of French Equatorial Africa after World War I by French colonists and missionaries along the settlements of the Ubangi River. Bangui, Fort de Possel, and Fort Crampel (up-country) were probably the first locations to have organized competitions. The original sports federation of 1937 was established primarily for Europeans, but there were also provisions for "barefooted" leagues, as was the custom in French-speaking colonial Africa.

Central African Games, Football Tournament of the

Tournoi de Football des Jeux Centrafricains.
   The first edition of the Central African Games was scheduled to take place in 1976 at Libreville, Gabon, with a soccer competition

between national teams as a focal point of the festival. The announced participants were: Cameroon, Congo, Gabon, Central Africa, Chad, and Zaire. The trophy is descended from that of the old Central African Cup, which ceased to exist in 1972 and was itself the descendant of an earlier trophy representing the soccer tournament of the defunct Tropical Games.

Central America

See: **Confederación Norte-Centroamericana y del Caribe de Fútbol (CONCACAF)**

Central American and Caribbean Games, Football Tournament of the

Torneo Fútbol de los Juegos Deportivos Centroamericanos y del Caribe.

The Central American and Caribbean Games were first held in 1930 at Havana, and were among the first regional offspring of the Olympic movement. The parent body of the games, the Organización Deportiva Centroamericana y del Caribe (ODCC), founded at the 1924 Olympics, administered the soccer tournament with the rest of the events of the first two editions in 1930 and 1935, but in 1938 the Central American and Caribbean Football Confederation (CCCF) was founded, and at the third edition (1938) the CCCF took over the direct administration of the soccer competition. The games as a whole were, of course, open only to amateurs, but the soccer tournament remained the only one of its kind in the area until 1941, when the CCCF organized the Central American and Caribbean Championship (Championship of the CCCF), forerunner of the present-day Championship of CONCACAF.

With the introduction of the Central American and Caribbean Championship, the importance of the soccer tournament of the Central American and Caribbean Games declined. Only the first three winners of the latter series should be considered regional champions: Cuba (1930), and Mexico (1935 and 1938). The games were resumed in 1946, and have been held every four years since. The twelfth edition took place at Medellin in 1978. Current participants in the games are: Bahamas, Barbados, Belize, Bermuda, Colombia, Costa Rica, Cuba, Dominican Republic, El Salvador, Guatemala, Guyana, Haiti, Mexico, Netherlands Antilles, Nicaragua, Panama, Puerto Rico, Surinam, Trinidad & Tobago, and Venezuela.

Winners

1973 (in Guatemala City) Panama
1977 (in San Salvador) —

Central American Games, Football Tournament of the

Torneo Fútbol de los Juegos Deportivos Centroamericanos.

The quadrennial Central American Games, administered by the Organización Deportiva Centroamericana (founded in 1972 in Guatemala City), are open to the six countries and territories of Central America: Belize, Costa Rica, El Salvador, Guatemala, Honduras, and Panama. The games are an all-amateur competition (15 sports) based on the Olympic model with a vigorously contested soccer tournament.

Ceylon

See: **Sri Lanka**

Chaco Cup

Copa del Chaco.

An irregular series between the national teams of Bolivia and Paraguay. It is named for the sprawling region of forested plains that were in dispute by the two countries until 1938, when they mutually agreed upon a border.

Chad

The former French Equitorial African colony of Chad was a member of FIFA from 1962-71, but was expelled for repeated non-payment of dues. Several countries are suspended from FIFA each year for late payments, but Chad's financial predicament prompted the world body to take its permanent action when the delays persisted. Chad is the only country ever to have suffered this fate. Its 13-year-long civil war has further aggravated the plight of the Fédération Tchadienne de Football, whose headquarters are located in Ndjamena (formerly Fort Lamy). Chadian teams were rarely seen in international competition during the nine years of affiliation. National colors: yellow jerseys and blue shorts.

charge

Running into or leaning on an opponent with the full weight of one's body. Intentional, violent charges, other than a shoulder charge, are unlawful and draw the penalty of a direct free kick.

See also: **shoulder charge**

Charles, William John (1931-   )

The unique career of John Charles, the greatest Welsh player since Billy Meredith, peaked in the unlikely milieu of Italy.

Charles, with his muscular six-foot two-inch frame, was an uncommon center forward whose skills with the ball belied his size. He was revered as much for his temperament as for his gifts as a player, and he also possessed the priceless ability to play well at all positions on the field. He was signed by second division Leeds United at age 16 while working on the grounds staff of Swansea, his home-town club, and started by playing at center half. In 1950, he became the youngest Welsh international in history and three years later won a regular place in the Wales lineup after his Leeds manager switched him to center forward. His rare combination of assets drew the attention of Juventus in Italy, and a British record fee of £ 65,000 (150 million lira) was paid for his transfer. In his five seasons with Juventus (1957-62), he was a key element in the winning of three Italian championships and two Italian league cups, and without a trace of the adversities that hampered other British players in Italy, he endeared himself to his multitude of Turin fans. Juventus placed the highest value of any player in the world on him, and the Italian press called him the most valuable commodity a club of that era could have.

Homesickness prompted a three-month return to Leeds in 1962, but, having regretted leaving Italy, he sought and secured a transfer to AS Roma. After nine months, he returned to Wales and Cardiff City, where he remained until 1966. Well into his decline, he moved to non-league Hereford United, and eventually became player-manager before taking on a similar post with the non-league Welsh club Merthyr Tydfil for one season in 1972. He continued to run a sports shop in Cardiff, and occasionally managed Wales's Under-23 team, but managerial posts were mysteriously not forthcoming. The Football League of England has sometimes called upon him for temporary services, but most of his recent years have been spent by operating a pub in Leeds. John Charles, the "gentle giant," scored over 260 goals in his career, and made 543 league appearances. His 15 goals for Wales were scored in 38 games, a total that would have been much higher if Italy had not captured his imagination so early.

Charlton, Robert, O.B.E. (1937-   )

The premier English forward of the postwar era and the most admired player in England since Sir Stanley Matthews. He was equally respected by foreign observers, who saw him as a ball artist with panache and elusive skills in the Latin style, though in fact he was the son of a Northumberland miner. His left foot produced a powerful and accurate shot, as well as hairsplitting passes and pinpoint flicks, and he was equally adept at all positions on the forward line except right wing. Charlton scored 198 goals in 606 appearances with Manchester United, whose youth team he joined at age 15, starting at inside left in 1956 but achieving his greatest fame at center forward. Between 1958-70, he appeared for England 106 times, a world record until it was broken by Bobby Moore in the early 1970s, and he scored 49 goals, another English record that is unlikely to be broken for many years to come.

Bobby Charlton was truly the archetype of a national idol. A prodigy when he was signed by England's most famous club, he survived the 1958 Munich air disaster, and together with his famous manager, Matt Busby, represented the transition between the two phenomenal teams that United produced before and after that shattering tragedy. He was a model of decorum and sportsmanship, and rarely, if ever, fouled an opposing player. Teamed with his famous brother (the England and Leeds United center half Jackie), he was the spearhead of England's World Cup triumph of 1966, and in that same year was chosen both European and English Footballer of the Year. Two years later, he and Busby, whose relationship with him had grown into one of great intimacy and affection, remembered with bitter tears the nightmare of 1958, as United won the European Cup after a 10-year climb back to the top of international club competition. Charlton was awarded an O.B.E. in 1969, and after his retirement in 1973, played briefly in the League of Ireland, and managed Preston North End without success (1975-76).

Chile

Federación de Football de Chile
Calle Erasmo Escala No. 1872
Casilla No. 3733
Santiago de Chile

Founded: 1895
FIFA: 1912
CONMEBOL: 1916

Affiliated clubs: *4,350;* registered players: *282,696 (850 professional, 66 non-amateur);* national stadium: *Estadio Nácional de Chile, Santiago (77,127);* largest stadium: *Estadio Nacional de Chile;* colors: *red jerseys, blue shorts;* season: *April to December;* honors: *World Cup third place (1962), South American Championship runner-up (1955).*

Soccer has a long and distinguished history in Chile. Like its more famous soccer-playing neighbors to the east, Argentina and Uruguay, Chile was introduced to the game as early as the mid-nineteenth century, and its pioneers were able to organize clubs and competitions earlier than in many European countries. Chile has been a leader in promoting soccer throughout South America, and its continental rank as a power to be reckoned with hovers around fourth or fifth place behind the mighty Argentina, Brazil and Uruguay (possibly Peru as well), though its teams have never won a major international competition. Many Chilean players down through the years have been actively pursued by wealthy foreign clubs.

Football and cricket were played at British schools in the port city of Valparaíso during the 1850s, though what form of football was played then is uncertain. Chileans watched students and teachers play on the grounds of Mackay and Sutherland School and other British establishments, and the locals' fascination with the *juego de los gringos* grew in the years ahead. By the 1880s, a recognizable form of soccer was played by the British in both Valparaíso and Santiago. In 1889, the first club in Chile, Valparaíso Football Club, was founded by David Scott, but expansion was halted temporarily during the political upheavals of 1891. In 1892, other British-based clubs were formed to take up the challenge posed by the already famous Valparaíso F.C.: Mackay and Sutherland, English Stocking, Hall School, and Rogers F.C. (founded by a firm importing tea by that name). Few of these clubs included any Chileans until 1893 when Mackay and Sutherland met the all-British Valparaíso F.C. in a showdown at the Parque Cousino (now the Parque O'Higgins) with a mixed Chilean-British lineup: Tapia; Bourdon, Urra; Gallardo, Yeoman, Velasco; Pérez, Nuñez, Gemmell, Cerrutti, Page. Valparaíso won 2-1.

Two inter-city matches between Valparaíso and Santiago representative teams were played in 1893 at the Parque Counsino, Valparaíso, and at the Sporting Club in the nearby city of Viña del Mar (site of some 1962 World Cup matches); Valparaíso won these games 7-2 and 5-0, but this time both sides featured Chilean players. Late in 1893, the first international involving Chile was played at the Sporting Club between Valparaíso and an Argentine selection with a 1-1 result. Both teams were made up entirely of British players. In 1895, a group of nine clubs from Valparaíso, Santiago, Viña del Mar, and Concepcion met to form the Football Association of Chile, forerunner of the present governing body, and organize a formal competition. The nine clubs were: Valparaíso F.C., Mackay and Sutherland, Cable West World, Liga de Fútbol de Valparaíso, Inglaterra, Escocia, Santiago, Viña del Mar, and Cerro Concepción. Several other clubs joined the competition almost immediately, chief among them Victoria Rangers, Valparaíso's strongest rival, Valparaíso Wanderers, and Santiago Wanderers.

After 1895, soccer gained a stronger foothold in Santiago under the stewardship of Juan Ramsay, the "father of Santiago soccer," and the first truly Chilean club in the capital, Santiago Rangers, was founded in 1896. By 1897, the game had spread north to Coquimbo and Antofagasta, and the following year Iquique Wanderers F.C. was founded in the city of that name, Chile's northernmost population center. Regional associations were formed beginning with the Asociación Provincial de Coquimbo in 1898, followed by the Liga de Iquique in 1902, Asociación Santiago in 1903, Asociación Concepción in 1906, and Asociación Talca in 1907. In 1912, the old Football Association of Chile was reorganized as the Asociación de Fútbol de Chile (AFC). For five years the AFC struggled with the Federación Sportiva Nacional over the question of jurisdiction, but in 1917 the latter gave up all claims of control.

With British influence on the wane, the AFC became the second South American governing body (after Argentina) to join FIFA in 1912. In 1910, the Copa Arturo Allessandri, a popular cup competition named for Chile's president, was introduced for representative teams of each regional association. This remained the premier Chilean tournament until the founding of the national league in 1933. Also in 1910, Chile made its international debut in Buenos Aires in a tournament with Argentina and Uruguay to commemorate Argentina's centennial. The Chilean team played three games, losing to Argentina 3-1 and 5-1 and losing to Uruguay 3-0. Chile's next international appearance was in the first South American Championship in 1916 at Buenos Aires, where it met Argentina and Uruguay again and for the first time Brazil. The Chileans gained a 1-1 draw with Brazil but lost again to Argentina,

6-1, and Uruguay, 4-0, to settle for last place in the standings. Chile and the "big three" were the only participants in the first four editions of the South American Championship, but Chile placed last on each occasion and failed to win a single game.

The clubs that were to figure prominently in Chilean soccer were all founded between 1900 and 1925. Magallanes (Magellan) appeared in 1904. Unión Deportiva Española was founded in 1921, an outgrowth of a cyclists' club called Ibérico Ciclista that was founded in 1900 by Spanish immigrants. Audax Italiano was originally an Italian-based cyclists' club named Club Ciclista Italiano, founded in 1910. Bádminton F.C., later Ferrobádminton, was formed in 1912, Green Cross F.C. in 1916, and the most important of all Chilean clubs, Club de Deportes Colo Colo, was organized in 1925 by dissident members of Magallanes. All of these famous clubs are located in Santiago.

After passing over the 1921 South American Championship, Chile reentered in 1922, again placing last without a win, and Chilean officials became embroiled in several controversies involving the host city, Rio de Janeiro, and other teams in the tournament. Chile was suspended from FIFA on account of this scandal, and, embarassed by the crisis, the AFC underwent complete reevaluation and ultimately reorganization. The governing body was relocated from Valparaíso to Santiago, and adopted new name, Federación de Football de Chile (FFC). FIFA reinstated Chile in 1926. On the playing field, Chile did not win an international contest until 1926, when the South American Championship was finally held in Santiago itself. Paraguay and Bolivia went down to defeat, 5-1 and 7-1 respectively, and Chile placed third in a field of five.

The growing problem of professionalism caused further tensions in Chilean soccer during the late 1920s and early 1930s, and the national teams stayed out of the South American Championship until 1935. In 1928, the FFC organized an Olympic team to accompany the Chilean contingent to the Amsterdam games. This journey of 7,500 sea miles resulted in Chile's European debut and its first ever contest with a European opponent—a 4-2 loss to Portugal in the preliminary round—but it also meant quick elimination under the Olympic knockout format and a premature end to an arduous voyage.

For several decades, domestic competition in Chile centered on the regional leagues, each of which was affiliated with a regional association, which in turn was affiliated with the FFC. The Santiago league, called the Liga Metropolitana, became the most important of these regional leagues after World War I. The birth of Santiago's Colo Colo in 1925, marked a watershed in Chilean soccer history. The new club, under captain and founder David Arellano, became a huge hit with the public, because its style was flashy and outgoing, and Arellano developed a sense of urgency and comradeship that Santiago fans appreciated. The rise of Colo Colo and the new enthusiasm for the game that it generated led directly to the growth of professionalism and the founding of the first national—and professional—league in 1933. The founding members were: Colo Colo, Audax Italiano, Bádminton, Green Cross, Morning Star, Magallanes, Santiago National, and Unión Española, all from Santiago. Ironically Magallanes, from which Colo Colo had sprung eight years earlier, won the first three titles in succession. Other clubs gained a share of the trophies, but eventually Colo Colo went on to gain a record number of championships. A second division and automatic promotion and relegation were instituted in 1943.

Meanwhile, Chile had participated in the first World Cup in 1930, held in Montevideo, Uruguay and had acquitted itself well with a strong win over Mexico and a 1-0 shutout of France. Argentina, on the other hand, whom Chile has not managed to defeat in nine attempts, won an easy victory, 3-1, on the goalscoring might of Guillermo Stabile. In 1934 and 1938, Chile decided not to make the long trip to Italy and France, and until the 1950 World Cup Chile's international schedule was restricted to the South American Championship. Chile continued to place poorly in this competition until it finally achieved third place in a field of seven when the tournament was staged in Santiago in 1945. After further middle-of-the-table results, Chile finally finished as runner-up in the 1955 edition, again at Santiago, just two points behind Argentina. It has not bettered this mark in the seven editions that have been held since.

Chile was not one of the glamorous South American teams in the 1950 World Cup—Brazil and Uruguay were unequaled in that respect—but its showing drew some praise.

After losing to England and Spain by identical scores of 2-0, it defeated the surprising Americans, conquerors of England, by five goals to two with a hat trick by Cremaschi. The star of this Chilean team was the Anglo-Chilean center forward George (Jorge) Robledo, formerly of Newcastle United and soon to be with Colo Colo. Chile now played with the classic English "W-M" system that had been brought to the country in 1941 by Hungarian coach Ferenc (Francisco) Plattko. Having introduced sophisticated teamwork and tactical systems into Chilean soccer when he took over Colo Colo, Plattko remains the most respected soccer figure in the country's history. His influence also solidified still further the importance of Colo Colo.

Eliminated from the 1954 and 1958 World Cups, Chile was awarded the next edition in 1962 simply "because we have nothing else" as FFC chairman Carlos Dittborn put it. Ultimately, the 1962 World Cup served to draw world attention to the terrible devastation caused by the 1961 earthquake; to Chileans it brought much pride and great excitement. As host, Chile automatically qualified for the final rounds, and Chilean soccer finally arrived in the international spotlight. Splendid new stadiums were built in Santiago, the Estadio Nacional, and Viña del Mar, the resort town near Valparaíso, and matches were also played in a copper mining company's stadium in Rancagua, and at Arica, Dittborn's home town, near the Peruvian border.

Chile's 1962 team was managed by Fernando Riera, a former player in France, and it played under a 4-2-4 system that was sparked by Universidad de Chile's left winger Leonel Sánchez. In preparation for the competition, Chile had lost to the USSR and played Hungary twice, winning by a huge score and then drawing. In the first round proper, Chile showed its worth by coming from behind to defeat Switzerland 3-1, but the second game against Italy was a brawl. It had been exacerbated by the Chilean and Italian press, which had made certain charges about drugs in Italian soccer, and living conditions in Chile, respectively, and before the game was over there were two ejections and an injured referee. Sánchez broke Humbert Maschio's nose with an internationally televised punch, and goals by Ramirez and Toro gave the home team a 2-0 upset victory. Its third game of the round was against West Germany, and here Chile was no match for European tactical sophistication; the Germans won 2-0. West Germany and, to everyone's surprise, Chile went on the quarter-finals.

In Arica, Chile upset the USSR by 2-1 on goals by Sánchez and Rojaz, causing excited Chilean fans to erupt in festive celebration. Astonishingly, this put Chile into the semi-finals with Brazil, Yugoslavia, and Czechoslovakia. Chile's unlucky draw for the round was Brazil. This game was the biggest event in Chilean sports history, as evidenced by public demonstrations of euphoria, but the Brazilians were in an entirely different class on the field, and the home team never had a chance. Garrincha and Vavá both scored a pair of goals for Brazil, and one of Chile's two goals was scored from a penalty, leaving the final result, 4-2, slightly misleading as to the winner's massive superiority. The Chileans, however, still had a chance to win a medal with the third place game, and their determination showed in a 1-0 defeat of Yugoslavia on a goal scored in the last minute by Rojas. Chile's third place finish in the 1962 World Cup was by far its highest accomplishment in international competition.

The Chilean league in the 1960s was dominated by Universidad de Chile, an important Santiago club that had entered the league in 1938 and had never been relegated. The "U" of 1961-65 was thought to be the finest Chilean team since Colo Colo's of the early 1940s under Plattko. While Chilean champion clubs and runners-up have participated in the Copa Libertadores regularly since the first edition in 1960, they did not achieve any measure of success until Universidad Católica reached the semi-finals in 1969 with stiff opposition. Universidad de Chile repeated this feat in 1970. The only Chilean club to advance to the final of the Copa Libertadores has been Colo Colo in 1973, when it scored 26 goals in 10 games over first and second round opposition. The final against Argentina's Independiente was forced to a replay before Colo Colo lost.

The idea for the Copa Libertadores, in fact, had originated with Colo Colo, which had assumed the responsibility for organizing a South American club championship in 1948 called the Campeonato Sudamericano de Campeones. After this competition failed to become an annual event, 12 years intervened before the present series could get under way.

Since the great era of the "U," five different clubs have won the championship, including Viña del Mar's quaintly named Everton, and Huachipato from the coastal city of Talcahuano. Huachipato is the first club from outside the Santiago-Valpairaíso region to win the league title. The greatest Chilean player of the 1970s, and perhaps of all time, is the majestic sweeper Elias Figueroa, who was the Latin American Footballer of the Year three times in a row while playing for Internacional Pôrto Alegre in Brazil. In 1977, he returned home to elevate Santiago's Arab-based club Palestino to new league heights.

The political upheavals of the post-Allende era worked ironically in Chile's favor as far as international soccer was concerned. After Chile won its South American qualification group for the 1974 World Cup, it was scheduled to meet the USSR, winner of the odd group in Europe, to decide a berth in the final rounds. The Soviets, however, refused to play Chile in Santiago's national stadium, because the stadium had been used to hold political prisoners after the Pinochet coup d'etat. On that basis, Chile received free passage to the finals in West Germany by forfeit. In West Germany, Chile's defensive tactics produced two draws with East Germany and Australia, and a 1-0 loss to eventual world champions West Germany. In qualification rounds for the 1978 finals, Chile was eliminated by Peru.

Champions

1933 Magallanes	1949 Universidad Católica	1965 Universidad de Chile
1934 Magallanes	1950 Everton	1966 Universidad Católica
1935 Magallanes	1951 Union Española	1967 Universidad de Chile
1936 Audax Italiano	1952 Everton	1968 Santiago Wanderers
1937 Colo Colo	1953 Colo Colo	1969 Universidad de Chile
1938 Magallanes	1954 Universidad Católica	1970 Colo Colo
1939 Colo Colo	1955 Palestino	1971 Universidad San Felipe
1940 Universidad de Chile	1956 Colo Colo	1972 Colo Colo
1941 Colo Colo	1957 Audax Italiano	1973 Union Española
1942 Santiago Morning	1958 Santiago Wanderers	1974 Huachipato
1943 Union Española	1959 Universidad de Chile	1975 Union Española
1944 Colo Colo	1960 Colo Colo	1976 Everton
1945 Green Cross	1961 Universidad Católica	1977 Union Española
1946 Audax Italiano	1962 Universidad de Chile	1978 Palestino
1947 Colo Colo	1963 Colo Colo	
1948 Audax Italiano	1964 Universidad de Chile	

China, National

Republic of China Football Association
50A Lung-Chiang St.
Taipei, Taiwan

Founded: 1936
FIFA: 1954

Affiliated clubs: *24;* registered players: *4,600;* national stadium: *Taipei Stadium, Taipei (22,000);* largest stadium: *Taipei Stadium;* colors: *blue jerseys, white shorts;* season: *January to December;* honors: *none.*

The soccer section of the old China National Amateur Athletic Federation, founded in Nanking in 1936, was reestablished in Taipei. in the early 1950s as the China National Football Association. Despite the objection of China PR, the Taiwan governing body was admitted to FIFA in 1954, and for four years coexisted in the world organization with the People's Republic. It joined the Asian Football Conferation in 1955. When China PR withdrew from FIFA in 1958, China National happily stayed on, and proceeded to establish itself in the international soccer community. Taiwan's international participation, while occasionally thwarted by political snags, continued until the mid-1970s, when its official status was put in serious jeopardy.

With strong competition from baseball and basketball, soccer in the Republic of China has lagged behind that of many Far East nations. A small number of regional and continental honors were won during the 1950s and '60s, but since the late 1960s, the Republic of China has not been an influential factor in Asian competition. After its admission to FIFA in 1954, there were two consecutive victories in the Football Tournament of the Asian Games (1954 and 1958), South Korea being the losing finalist on both occasions. At the important Merdeka Football Tournament of Malaysia, Taiwan won an outright victory in 1963, again over South Korea, and in 1965 it shared the trophy, yet again with South Korea. It has advanced to the final rounds of the Asian Cup, the continent's most important competition, twice (1960 and 1968). Its participation in the highly competitive final rounds in 1968 remains the highest accomplishment of a Nationalist Chinese team to date. In 1960, it was one of two Asian countries to qualify for the final rounds of the Olympic tournament in Rome. Grouped with the amateur teams of Italy, Brazil, and Great Britain, it lost to all three, accumulating a 3-12 goal difference.

In 1976, the Asian Football Confederation expelled China National and admitted the People's Republic, setting off a chain of reactions and counterreactions that threatened to split the world soccer community. China National, seeking nations willing to compete on the field, looked to Oceania for opponents and increased its international fixture list with numerous island republics and territories. This new association with Oceania resulted in Taiwan's grouping with Australia and New Zealand in the qualification rounds for the 1978 World Cup, which resulted in four consecutive losses and a dismal goal difference of 1-17.

In domestic competition, the Republic of China Football Association (present name adopted in the early 1970s) sponsors a senior level league of 24 clubs. There is a national cup competition and lower divisions include numerous regional leagues. The relative strength of Nationalist Chinese clubs has been untested because they never participated in the Asian Champion Teams' Cup during that competition's five-year existence. Before the revolution of 1949, the island of Taiwan was little more than a recreational backwater in Chinese sports.

See also: **China, People's Republic**

China, People's Republic

[The Republic of China (Taiwan) from 1954 to the present is treated under its own heading above.]

China has two separate histories of football. One is the story of *tsu chu,* the ancient Chinese ritual that is widely thought to be the world's first football game. The second is that of modern soccer, entering China just as it did other countries of the Far East—via European colonists.

Scholars have concluded that the first recording of *tsu chu* was made during the reign of Emperor Huang-Ti around 2500 B.C.

Tsu chu was mentioned frequently as a celebration of the emperor's birthday during the Han Dynasty (206 B.C.-202 A.D.), and has a unique fascination for soccer historians because of its emphasis on dribbling and other elements of modern soccer. There are ample records to suggest that some forms of football continued to be played throughout succeeding dynasties of the first and second millennia A.D., though the details of its evolution are exceedingly complex. Italian explorers in the Middle Ages were reported to have returned with knowledge of some form of Chinese football (ca. 1300).

The exact date and location of the modern game's importation to China are nebulous, but it is likely that the British introduced it in their treaty ports (Shanghai, Ningpo, Amoy, Hong Kong, and Canton) during the 1860s. By the turn of the century, substantial numbers of Chinese were playing, and some Chinese teams had been formed.

The revolution of 1912 prompted the creation of a national team and the semblance of administrative organization, despite the political chaos of the period. In February 1913, a Chinese team of students traveled to Manila to play the Philippines in the first Football Tournament of the Far East Games, and lost 2-1. This was the earliest officially recognized international on the continent of Asia, and it launched the oldest soccer rivalry East of Suez, Australasia included. China engaged the Philippines a total of 12 times between 1913 and 1934, all in the Far East Games winning 10, losing two, and accumulating a 63-24 goal difference. These victories also resulted in nine consecutive gold medals in the Far East Games from 1915-34. The first recorded international on Chinese soil was against the Philippines in the 1915 edition at Shanghai, won by the home side 1-0.

China's second and only other consistent opponent before World War II was Japan, again in the Far East Games, the first in 1917, resulting in an 8-0 win for China. China met Japan seven times in the Far East Games from 1918-34, winning six and drawing one with a 31-9 goal difference. At the 1934 edition in Manila, China defeated a national team representing the Dutch East Indies, but this remained the only match ever played between the two. China made its intercontinental debut at the 1936 Olympic Games in Berlin, losing its only match of the tournament to Great Britain's amateur team after a 9,000-mile voyage by sea. This was China's last international foray until 1948, when it lost to Turkey, 4-0, at the Olympic Games in London after another 9,000-mile trip.

In 1924, the China National Amateur Athletic Federation (CNAAF) was founded in Nanking as an attempt to create an umbrella body for all organized sports. It became affiliated with FIFA in 1931, and five years later a more autonomous soccer association was established (now claimed by the Nationalist Chinese to be the forerunner of their governing body) to supervise the direct administration of the game from the CNAAF's soccer section.

By the immediate postwar period, there were over 20 stadiums in China capable of holding large soccer crowds (almost 300,000 seats in all). The main centers of activity until general reorganization in the 1950s were: Peking, Shanghai, Tientsin, Canton, Mukden, Hankow, Wuchang, Chungking, and Sian. Domestic competitions were plentiful, and more than 1,000 clubs and 20,000 players were affiliated with the federation.

A few weeks after the founding of the People's Republic of China in October 1949, a new umbrella governing body was formed in Peking, the All-China Athletic Federation (ACAF). The administration of soccer in the People's Republic was immediately put under the collective aegis of the ACAF, where it remains to this day. Branch offices were established in 98 localities throughout the country, with 29 provincial offices uniting regional interests. Two playing seasons were scheduled (March-June and September-December). A national championship for regional and nationwide teams was introduced in 1951, won by the Northeast China Team and the People's Liberation Army Team in the first and second editions, respectively.

After the revolution, FIFA continued to recognize the mainland governing body as a matter of course, since the geographical area it represented was the same as pre-1949 China. China's isolation, however, precluded any significant international contact on the playing field except with North Korea and the Soviet Union. It remained a member *de jure* of FIFA until 1958, when the ACAF withdrew of its own volition in protest over FIFA admitting China National four years earlier.

Despite the FIFA rule which prohibits members from engaging in international competition with nonmembers, permission has often been sought and gained to play Chinese teams in a variety of circumstances. A Chinese selection played in Tirana as early as 1961, and Albanian teams visited China on more than one occasion in succeeding years. In the aftermath of "ping-pong diplomacy" during the early 1970s, Chinese participation in international competition increased dramatically. The number of countries or territories visited or hosted by Chinese soccer teams during 1971-77 eventually rose to over 50.

In 1971, the Peking Football Team (founded 1964) toured Tanzania and won all but one match against leading clubs of Tanganyika and Zanzibar, and in 1975, it made an extensive tour of Tanzania, Mauritius, Mozambique, and Madagascar. Chinese teams have also visited select nations of West Africa. Cordial relations on the soccer field with Oceania and Australasia during this period have been a hallmark of China's increasing international participation. A 1975 tour of Australia, New Zealand, and Fiji produced mixed results, including numerous losses to the national teams, regional selections, and clubs of Australia and New Zealand, and in 1976 the Australian national team won two unofficial internationals in China.

Other than Albania, the first European team to tour China was the Yugoslav national amateur team in 1975. The Yugoslavs won all three matches against selections from Shanghai (1-0), Canton (1-0), and Northwest China (2-0). The first Chinese foray into the Western Hemisphere occurred in 1977 in the United States. A Chinese national selection drew once with the USA (1-1) and lost twice (1-0 and 2-1). Against club opponents on the same tour, China fared slightly better (1-1 vs. Cosmos and a 2-1 win vs. Tampa Bay). By 1980, Chinese teams will have played their first matches in Western Europe, probably against West German and British Amateur teams.

Meanwhile, China's unofficial status in the world soccer community has been an anathema. FIFA's position on the China question has remained simple and unchanged: The world body seeks the membership of all sovereign nations regardless of political ideology, provided the basic human rights of athletes as described in the charter are maintained by the national governing body. Ironically, it is FIFA's steadfastly apolitical stance that has prevented China from being admitted. FIFA has repeatedly declared that it strongly desires China PR's membership. Though it has often applied for membership the stumbling block has always been that China PR would only accept if China National were expelled at the same time. FIFA's policy, as opposed to its private wishes, precludes the expulsion of one member at the expense of another. (FIFA expelled Germany and Japan on political grounds in 1946, but since that exception the world body has rescinded the membership of only two countries: South Africa for its violation of human rights provisions in the FIFA charter and Chad for repeated nonpayment of dues and levies.)

The majority of FIFA's membership agrees with the official position, and it is understood that members would not vote to keep China PR out of the world body if the Chinese would abandon their condition. The fact is, however, that a growing number of members are in favor of China's PR's membership at any cost. In 1976, the matter was thrown into a tailspin that threatened the overall authority of FIFA and the future of Asian soccer when the Asian Football Confederation (AFC) admitted China PR at the expense of Taiwan. The move was avowedly political in motivation (fostered by Middle Eastern and Communist-bloc states), and Israel was also expelled. After much silence and wonderment, FIFA suggested a plan to reverse the expulsions, whereby Israel would join the floundering Oceania Football Confederation in return for the reinstatement of China National in the AFC. FIFA warned that the Asian body itself risked expulsion if this proposal was not agreed upon. In 1978, the AFC rejected the plan out of hand and forced FIFA to consider the possibility of excluding two-thirds of humankind from the official world soccer community.

China PR's membership in the AFC enabled the national team to enter and ultimately qualify for the final rounds of the 1976 Asian Cup, marking China PR's first participation in an officially sponsored international competition. The results were encouraging. It was one of nine countries to advance to the quarter-finals in Iran, and there drew with Malaysia before losing to Kuwait. In the third place game, China PR defeated Iraq to gain its first international honor.

The All-China Athletic Federation remains steadfast in its unique conditions for membership in FIFA and points to growing public opinion in its favor and a similar precedent recently established in the sport of badminton, when the Asian governing body pulled out the world body rather than compromise political viewpoints.

See also: **tsu chu**

chip

A delicately lofted kick that is usually placed over the head of a nearby defender. A chip is shorter than a standard lofted kick, and is considerably longer than an arcing flick. It may be either a pass or shot on goal.

clearance

A kick, throw, or punch by a goalkeeper or a defending player, which moves the ball out of his own penalty area or away from his own goal.

Colo Colo, Club de Deportes

Location: *Santiago, Chile;* stadium: *Estadio Colo Colo (10,000),* colors: *white jerseys, black shorts;* honors: *Chilean champion (1937, 1939, 1941, 1944, 1947, 1953, 1956, 1960, 1963, 1970, 1972).*

Founded 1925 as Colo Colo Foot Ball Club by five disgruntled players from Magallanes F.C. who objected to the election of a new captain. Their choice for the honor was David Arellano, who, along with his brother, was among the founding members of Colo Colo. ("Colo colo" is a Chilean expression meaning wildcat.) The new club immediately joined the Liga Metropolitana (Santiago), and in 1927 became the first Chilean club to compete against teams from other countries, specifically Ecuador, Cuba, and Mexico. Arellano, player-coach and president of the club, organized a tour of Spain and Portugal late in 1927, and this set the stage for Chile's entry into the 1928 Olympic Games in Amsterdam—not just the soccer team but the entire contingent. These activities endeared Colo Colo to the Chilean public, and two years after its formation, the club became the most popular in the country.

Colo Colo was a founding member of the professional league in 1933, and, under the guidance of Arellano, became a pioneer of creative ideas not only in Chilean soccer but in South America as a whole. In 1941, Hungarian coach Ferenc Plattko was hired, and he introduced the W-M formation to the club, eventually revolutionizing Chilean soccer. Plattko's 1941 team is still remembered as the greatest ever seen in Chile. In another stroke of genius, the Colo management suggested and organized the first South American club championship in 1948—named the Campeonato Sudamericano de Campeones—and the champion clubs of Brazil, Argentina, Uruguay, Bolivia, Ecuador, Peru, and Chile (represented by Colo) participated. Brazil's Vasco da Gama won the trophy. Although this tournament failed to develop into an annual affair, it is duly regarded as the forerunner of the Copa Libertadores.

On the playing field, Colo holds the Chilean record for most national championships (11), and has the best overall record of any Chilean club in the Copa Libertadores. In 1973, Colo advanced to the final of the Copa Libertadores, losing to Independiente, 1-1, 0-0, and 1-2. Its cumulative record in the Chilean league, as of 1977, was considerably better than any of its closest rivals: 1145-603-272-270-2695-1489-1478. The famous Colo Colo mystique, so prevalent among Chilean fans, is derived from the club's initial image as a group of visionary martyrs—Magallanes was an important club at the time of the breakaway—and the unique personality of David Arellano, who remains the undisputed hero of Chilean soccer.

Most of Colo's games are played in the Estadio Nacional de Chile (77,127).

Colombia

Federación Colómbiana de Fútbol
Carrérá 5a. No. 16-73, 6/Piso
Apartado Aéreo No. 17.602
Bogotá, D.E.

Founded: 1924
FIFA: 1931
CONMEBOL: 1940

Affiliated clubs: *3,685;* **registered players:** *74,172 (420 professional, 252 non-amateur);* **national stadium:** *Estadio distrital nemesio camacho "El Campin," Bogotá (57,000);* **largest stadium:** *Pascual Guerrero, Cali (61,000);* **colors:** *orange jerseys with yellow, blue, and red stripes, cream shorts;* **season:** *February to December;* **honors:** *South American Championship runner-up (1975).*

Only Ecuador and Venezuela have amassed a poorer international record than Colombia among the ten members of the South American confederation, but none of the ten has experienced the same feuding and chaos that Colombian soccer authorities have suffered in trying to organize its domestic game. Colombia has been in conflict with FIFA repeatedly over the past 30 years, but its good standing was restored when Colombia was chosen to host the 1986 World Cup, a challenge of immense proportions for a country which, as of 1978, had no stadiums to satisfy FIFA's World Cup specifications. On the playing field, Colombia began to show signs of emerging from the lower ranks of South American soccer with its fine run for the 1975 South American Championship, but to most people Colombian soccer is synonymous with Millonarios, the famous club from Bogotá that attracted some of the world's greatest players briefly in the early 1950s.

Soccer in Colombia was first established in the Caribbean port city of Barranquilla, where the influence of British and other European commerce was strongly felt after the turn of the century. The influx of European military and commercial visitors during World War II accelerated growth, and in the early 1920s Colombian soccer enjoyed its first great expansion. In 1924, the Liga de Football del Atlántico (LFA), forerunner of the present governing body, was founded in Barranquilla, and it was admitted to FIFA in 1931. The LFA, which was really a regional association restricted to the Atlántico Department (Barranquilla and environs) was reorganized in 1936 under the name Asociación Colombiana de Fútbol (ACF). Regional leagues were introduced in major population centers, notably Bogotá, Medellín, Cali, Bucumaranga,

Manizales, Cúcuta, Pasto, and Quibdó, and clubs became affiliated directly to the local associations that administered their leagues. Clubs did not affiliate directly with the national association until after World War II. The only national championship before World War II was an annual tournament for representative teams of each regional association.

The ACF looked to the Caribbean and Central America rather than South America when it sought regional international affiliation in the 1930s. In 1938, it became a charter member of the Confederación Centroamericano y del Caribe de Fútbol (CCCF), and participated in the soccer tournament of the third Central American and Caribbean Games that took place in Panama immediately after the CCCF had been founded. This was Colombia's debut in international competition, and it produced mixed results in a relatively weak field. In its first match, Colombia lost to Mexico 3-1 but subsequently bounced back with a 4-0 win over Panama. This was followed by a 3-1 loss to Costa Rica, a 3-2 defeat of El Salvador, and, finally, an upsetting 2-1 loss to Venezuela. Colombia settled for third place behind Mexico and Costa Rica with only a fractional lead on El Salvador based on goal average. Later in 1938, Barranquilla played host to the first edition of the Bolivarian Games, a multi-sport competition based on the Olympic model, which included a soccer tournament. The Colombian team lost to Peru, Bolivia, and Ecuador, but managed to defeat Venezuela and hold on to a fourth place finish. This represented Colombia's first foray into South American soccer, though the Bolivarian Games tournament was considerably less important than other South American competitions.

In 1940, the ACF also joined CONMEBOL, the South American Football Confederation, but continued its affiliation with the CCCF at the same time. Colombia is the only country in the world that has been a member of two regional confederations simultaneously. Its first participation in the South American Championship came with the eighteenth edition in 1945, and it finished a distant fifth in a field of eight. Its only victory in six games was over Ecuador (3-1), while losses to Brazil, Uruguay, Argentina, and Chile were substantial—3-0, 7-0, 9-1, and 2-0, respectively. Colombia returned to the Central American and Caribbean Games in 1946, the fourth edition and the first held in Barranquilla. There were seven entrants, and Colombia came out on top with six consecutive victories over Curaçao, Venezuela, Guatemala, Puerto Rico, Costa Rica, and Panama. This was the first and last time Colombia won an international competition, but it counted for very little because the main tournament for Central American and Carribbean countries was by now the Championship of the CCCF, in which Colombia never participated. After 1946, Colombia's official affiliation remained with South America. In 1947, it played again in the South American Championship, and failed to win a single game in seven. Its goal difference of 2-19 was the worst in the tournament, and it tied for last place with Bolivia. Colombia finished in last place again in the 1949 edition.

In 1948, professionalism was recognized (15 years later than in most South American countries), and a national league was finally introduced. The focus of Colombian soccer switched from Barranquilla to Bogotá, and the big Bogotá clubs, Millonarios and Independiente Santa Fe, came to the fore. The latter won the first league title in 1948, but in 1949 Millonarios secured the services of Alfredo Di Stefano from Ríver Plate in Buenos Aires and became the strongest team ever seen in Colombia. The two-year-old Millonarios, which seemed to have a millionaire's bank account, won its first championship in 1949, and in 1950 it and several other clubs broke away from the ACF to form a renegade league, resulting in Colombia's suspension from FIFA. Millonarios signed Ríver Plate's great center forward Adolfo Pedernera, as well as Nestor Rossi, and with Di Stefano and Pedernera spearheading the attack, easily won three more league titles in succession. Dozens of leading foreign players were lured to the renegade league, many of them from Argen-

tina and several from Great Britain. Since the renegade clubs were now outside the jurisdiction of FIFA, they were not obligated to pay transfer fees, and Colombian soccer received the wrath of soccer officials all over Europe and South America. In 1953, most of the foreign players left in frustration; Pedernera stayed on as player-coach of Millonarios and later the Colombian national team, and order was finally restored with the reinstatement of the ACF in FIFA in 1956.

Colombia returned to the South American Championship in 1957, winning two games and losing four, and participated again in 1963. In 1965, the newly formed Federación del Fútbol Colombiana challenged the ACF's authority, and FIFA was sought to mediate the controversy. In an unprecedented move, FIFA took over direct control of the administration of Colombian soccer in 1966 with an interim organization called the Comité Provisional Colombiano de la FIFA, and the matter was not settled until the formation of the present governing body, the Federación Colombiana de Fútbol, in 1971.

Colombian clubs have participated in the Copa Libertadores since the first edition in 1960, but they have never reached the final. National amateur teams, however, have appeared in the 1968 and 1972 Olympic Games. Colombia eventually became a regular entrant in World Cup qualifying rounds, but the only time it has ever advanced to the final rounds was in 1962, when it eliminated Peru in the process. This was another strong period for Millonarios, and its players figured prominently in the 1962 World Cup squad. The Colombians lost narrowly to Uruguay, 2-1, in the first round, and nearly caused one of the greatest upsets in recent years by holding the USSR to a 4-4 draw—this after losing early in the game 3-0 and 4-1. But the highly skilled team of Yugoslavia proved far too advanced in technique and stamina, and Colombia crashed in its third and final game, 5-0. The subsequent rise of Deportivo Cali in the national league was the impetus for much improvement in Colombia's international results after 1969. In the 1975 South American Championship, the national team swept all four games in the first round against Paraguay and Ecuador, and stunned a weakened Uruguay in the semi-finals by winning 3-1 on aggregate. In the final against Peru, Colombia won first the leg 1-0 in Bogotá, but in the second leg in Lima had the wind taken out of its sails with an own goal. A second Peruvian goal assured Peru a win and play-off in neutral Caracas. Colombia failed to rally to the occasion, and lost the play-off 1-0, taking second place. It was, nevertheless, Colombia's finest showing ever in international competition.

The first division of the national league now has 14 clubs, and the season is divided into three phases. In the *apertura*, or first phase, all 14 clubs compete on a home and away basis.

The top seven go on to Group A of the *finalizacion*, or second phase, and the bottom seven play in Group B of the *finalizacion*, each club playing on a home and away basis within its group and accumulating points from the first and second phases. The top clubs of the *finalizacion* (based on points) enter a third round to determine the national champion and runner-up, and these two clubs represent Colombia in the Copa Libertadores.

Champions

1948	Independiente Santa Fe
1949	Millonarios
1950	Deportes Caldas
1951	Millonarios
1952	Millonarios
1953	Millonarios
1954	Nacional
1955	Independiente Medellín
1956	Atlético Quindio
1957	Independiente Medellín
1958	Independiente Santa Fe
1959	Millonarios
1960	Independiente Santa Fe
1961	Millonarios
1962	Millonarios
1963	Millonarios
1964	Millonarios
1965	Deportivo Cali
1966	Independiente Santa Fe
1967	Deportivo Cali
1968	Union Magdalena
1969	Deportivo Cali
1970	Deportivo Cali
1971	Independiente Santa Fe
1972	Millonarios
1973	Nacional
1974	Deportivo Cali
1975	Independiente Santa Fe
1976	Nacional
1977	Júnior Barranquilla
1978	Millonarios

Combi, Giampiero (1902-1956)

Generally regarded as Italy's greatest goalkeeper, and one of the three or four finest anywhere between the world wars. More than any other player, Combi represented the transition from Italy's building years during the 1920s and its golden era of the World Cup triumphs in 1934 and 1938. His entire career was spent with Juventus, whom he inspired to championships in 1926 and 1931-34, playing behind some of the greatest backfields of his day. His international career, however, was tenuous at first. He made his debut for Italy in 1924 against Hungary, but after seven goals were scored against him, he was not selected again until the following year, and not regularly until the 1928 Olympic Games in Amsterdam. As the automatic choice in goal from 1928 on, he accumulated enough caps to captain the 1934 World Cup team (by Italian tradition that role automatically goes to the player with the most international appearances), and retired from active play altogether immediately afterwards. His 47 international appearances was a record for an Italian goalkeeper until it was broken in the 1970s by Dino Zoff, who is sometimes mentioned as Combi's equal.

commemorative games

Sponsored by FIFA, continental confederations, national associations, or clubs, commemorative games have been played since the late 1930s to celebrate anniversaries, retirements of great players, or other important events. They are played by at least one international all-star team and the region, country, or club associated with the honored occasion, offering the rare chance to see many of the world's greatest players on the field at one time. For some observers it is that fanciful moment when one's impossible combination of players actually take form, if only fleetingly.

The details of each official commemorative game (1937-1975) are listed below. Testimonials between clubs are not included.

Commemorative games: holding to tradition, England's captain, Billy Wright (l), presents pregame souvenir pennant to Austrian immortal Ernst Ocwirk (r), captain of the Rest of Europe; England vs. Rest of Europe, Wembley Stadium, London, 1953. Welsh referee M. B. Griffith looks on.

CENTRAL EUROPE—WESTERN EUROPE: 3-1
(Celebration of Olympics Day)

20 June 1937, Olympisch Stadion, Amsterdam. Attendance: 60,000.

CENTRAL EUROPE: Olivieri (Italy); Sesta (Austria), Schmaus (Austria); Serantoni (Italy), Andreolo (Italy), Lázár (Hungary); Sas (Hungary), Meazza (Italy), Piola (Italy), Sárosi (Hungary), Nejedly (Czechoslovakia). *Substitution:* Rava (Italy) for Schmaus.

WESTERN EUROPE: Jakob (Germany); Paverick (Belgium), Caldenhove (Netherlands); Kitzinger (Germany), Goldbrunner (Germany), Delfour (France); Lehner (Germany), Braine (Belgium), Bakhuys (Netherlands), Smit (Netherlands), Van den Eynde (Belgium). *Substitution:* Joakin (Belgium) for Paverick.

Goals: 17' and 48' Sas (C.E.), 75' Nejedlý (C.E.), 87' Bakhuys (W.E.)

ENGLAND—REST OF EUROPE: 3-0
(Seventy-fifth Anniversary of The Football Association)

26 October 1938, Arsenal Stadium, London. Attendance: 45,000.

ENGLAND: Woodley (Chelsea); Sproston (Tottenham), Hapgood (Arsenal) cap; Willingham (Huddersfield), Cullis (Wolverhampton), Copping (Arsenal); Matthews (Stoke), Hall (Tottenham), Lawton (Everton), Goulden (West Ham), Boyes (Everton). *Selector:* Whittaker.

REST OF EUROPE: Olivieri (Italy); Foni (Italy), Rava (Italy); Kupfer (Germany), Andreolo

(Italy), Kitzinger (Germany); Aston (France), Braine (Belgium) cap, Piola (Italy), Zsengeller (Hungary), Brustad (Norway). *Selector:* Pozzo (Italy).

Goals: 20' Hall, 29' Lawton, 73' Goulden

GREAT BRITAIN—REST OF EUROPE: 6-1
(Celebration of the addition of Great Britain to FIFA)

10 May 1947, Hampden Park, Glasgow. Attendance: 130,000.

GREAT BRITAIN: Swift (England); Hardwick (England), Hughes (Wales); Macaulay (Scotland), Vernon (Northern Ireland), Burgess (Wales); Matthews (England), Lawton (England), Steel (Scotland), Liddell (Scotland). *Selector:* Winterbottom (England).

REST OF EUROPE: Da Rui (France); Peterson (Denmark), Steffen (Switzerland); Carey (Eire), Parola (Italy), Ludl (Czechoslovakia); Lembrechts (Belgium), Gren (Sweden), Nordahl (Sweden), Wilkes (Netherlands), Praest (Denmark). *Selector:* Rappan (Austria).

Goals: 22' Mannion (G.B.), 24' Nordahl (R.E.), 33' Mannion (G.B.) pen, 35' Steel (G.B.), 37' Lawton (G.B.), 74' Parola-Da Rui (R.E.) own goal, 82' Lawton (G.B.)

WALES—REST OF THE UNITED KINGDOM: 3-2
(Seventy-fifth Anniversary of the Football Association of Wales)

5 December 1951, Ninian Park, Cardiff. Attendance: 26,454.

WALES: Shortt (Plymouth); Barnes (Arsenal), Sherwood (Cardiff); Paul (Manchester C.), Daniel (Arsenal), Burgess (Tottenham); Foulkes (Newcastle), Morris (Burnley), Ford (Sunderland), Allchurch (Swansea), Clarke (Manchester C.).

REST OF THE UNITED KINGDOM: Cowan (Morton & Scotland); G. Young (Rangers & Scotland), McMichael (Newcastle & Northern Ireland); Docherty (Preston & Scotland), Vernon (West Bromwich & Northern Ireland), Wright (Wolverhampton & England); G. Smith (Hibernian & Scotland), Fleming (East Fife & Scotland), Lofthouse (Bolton & England), Baily (Tottenham & England), Medley (Tottenham & England).

Goals: 15' Allchurch (W.), 23' Ford (W.), 62' Allchurch (W.), 64' Fleming (R.U.K.), 83' Medley (R.U.K.)

ENGLAND—REST OF EUROPE: 4-4
(Ninetieth Anniversary of The Football Association)

21 October 1953, Wembley Stadium, London. Attendance: 100,000.

ENGLAND: Merrick (Birmingham); Ramsey (Tottenham), Eckersley (Blackburn); Wright (Wolverhampton), Ufton (Charlton), Dickinson (Portsmouth); Matthews (Blackpool), Mortensen (Blackpool), Lofthouse (Bolton), Quixall (Sheffield Wednesday), Mullen (Wolverhampton). *Selector:* Winterbottom.

REST OF EUROPE: Zeman (Austria); Navarro (Spain), Hanappi (Austria); Cajkovski (Yugoslavia), Posipal (Germany FR), Ocwirk (Austria); Boniperti (Italy), Kubala (Spain), Nordahl (Sweden), Vukas (Yugoslavia), Zebec (Yugoslavia). *Substitution:* Beara (Yugoslavia) for Zeman. *Manager:* Lotsy (Netherlands).

Goals: 5' Kubala (R.E.) pen, 7' Mortensen (E.), 14' & 36' Boniperti (R.E.), 42' & 48' Mullen (E.), 63' Kubala (R.E.), 90' Ramsey (E.) pen.

REST OF EUROPE—GREAT BRITAIN: 4-1
(Seventy-fifth Anniversary of the Irish Football Association)

13 August 1955, Windsor Park, Belfast. Attendance: 35,000.

GREAT BRITAIN: Kelsey (Wales); Sillet (England), McDonald (Scotland); Blanchflower (Northern Ireland), Charles (Wales), Peacock (Northern Ireland); Matthews (England), R. Johnstone (Scotland), Bentley (England), McIlroy (Northern Ireland), Liddell (Scotland). *Selector*: Winterbottom.

REST OF EUROPE: Buffon (Italy); Gustavsson (Sweden), Van Brandt (Belgium); Ocwirk (Austria), Jonquet (France), Boskov (Yugoslavia); Sörensen (Denmark), Vukas (Yugoslavia), Kopa (France), Travaços (Portugal), Vincent (France). *Selector:* **Crahay (Belgium).**

Goals: 25' Johnstone (G.B.), 27' Vincent (R.E.), 77', 87', & 88' pen Vukas (R.E.)

ENGLAND—REST OF THE WORLD: 2-1
(Centenary of The Football Association)

23 October 1963, Wembley Stadium London. Attendance: 100,000.

ENGLAND: Banks (Leicester); Armfield (Blackpool), Wilson (Huddersfield); Milne (Liverpool), Norman (Tottenham), Moore (West Ham); Paine (Southampton), Greaves (Tottenham), R. Smith (Tottenham), Eastham (Arsenal), R. Charlton (Manchester U). *Selector:* Ramsey.

REST OF THE WORLD: *First half*—Yashin (USSR); D. Santos (Brazil), Schnellinger (Germany FR); Pluskal (Czechoslovakia), Popluhár (Czechoslovakia), Masopust (Czechoslovakia); Kopa (France), Law (Scotland), Di Stefano (Spain), Eusebio (Portugal), Gento (Spain). *Second half*—Soskić (Yugoslavia); Eizaguirre (Chile), Schnellinger; Pluskal, Popluhár, Baxter (Scotland); Kopa, Law, Di Stefano, Puskás (Spain), Gento. *Substitution:* Seeler (Germany FR) for Kopa. *Selector:* Reira (Chile)

Goals: 66' Paine (E.), 82' Law (R.W.), 97' Greaves (E.)

REST OF EUROPE—SCANDINAVIA: 4-2
(Sixtieth Anniversary of the Dansk Boldspil-Union)

20 May 1964, Idraetspark, Copenhagen. Attendance: 45,000.

SCANDINAVIA: S. Andersen (Norway); J. Hansen (Denmark), Rosander (Sweden); B. Hansen (Denmark), A. Johansson (Sweden), Heinonen (Finland); R. Jensen (Norway), Öberg (Sweden), Madsen (Denmark), Bild (Sweden), Peltonen (Finland). *Substitution:* J. Petersen (Denmark) for Peltonen.

REST OF EUROPE: Yashin (USSR); Bomba (Czechoslovakia), Wilson (England); Voronin (USSR), Popluhár (Czechoslovakia), Baxter (Scotland); José Augusto (Portugal), Greaves (England), van Himst (Belgium), Law (Scotland), R. Charlton (England). *Substitutions:*

Tilkowski (Germany FR) for Yashin, Hamilton (Scotland) for Bomba, Eusebio (Portugal) for van Himst.

Goals: 4' & 41' Greaves (R.E.), 49' Law (R.E.), 51' Peltonen (S.), 56' Eusebio (R.E.), 75' Bild (S.)

REST OF EUROPE—YUGOSLAVIA: 7-2
(Testimonial to the victims of the Skopje earthquake)

23 September 1964, Yugoslav National Army Stadium, Belgrade. Attendance: 20,000

YUGOSLAVIA: Soskić; Belin, Jusufi; Melić; Cop, Vasović; Samardzić, Zambata, Galić, Kostić, Skoblar. *Substitutions:* Skorić for Soskić, Cebinac for Samardzić. *Selector:* Lovrić.
REST OF EUROPE: Yashin (USSR); Lala (Czechoslovakia), Schnellinger (Germany FR); Voronin (USSR), Meszoly (Hungary), Pluskal (Czechoslovakia); José Augusto (Portugal), Masopust (Czechoslovakia), Seeler (Germany FR), Eusebio (Portugal), Simoes (Portugal). *Substitution:* Sándor (Hungary) for Simoes. *Selector:* Schön (Germany FR).

Goals: 22' Seeler (R.E.), 24' Eusebio (R.E.) pen, 31' Kostić (Y.), 44', 52' & 56' pen Eusebio (R.E.), 62' Galić (Y.), 68' Seeler (R.E.), 72' José Augusto (R.E.)

REST OF EUROPE—GREAT BRITAIN: 6-4
(In honor of Sir Stanley Matthews)

28 April 1965, Victoria Ground, Stoke-on-Trent. Attendance: 20,000.

GREAT BRITAIN: Waiters (England); Cohen (England), Thomson (England); Haynes (England), Flowers (England), Baxter (Scotland); Matthews (England), Greaves (England), Gilzean (Scotland), B. Douglas (England), C. Jones (Wales). *Substitution:* Ritchie (England) for Gilzean.
REST OF EUROPE: Yashin (USSR); Johannsen (Denmark), Schnellinger (Germany FR); Pluskal (Czechoslovakia), Popluhár (Czechoslovakia), Masopust (Czechoslovakia); Henderson (Scotland), Kubala (Spain), Di Stefano (Spain), Puskás (Spain), Vandeboer (Belgium). *Substitution:* Sörensen (Denmark) for Di Stefano.

Goals: 4' Vandeboer (R.E.), 7' Puskás (R.E.), 12' Douglas (G.B.), 24' Puskás (R.E.), 34' Greaves (G.B.), 43' Masopust (R.E.), 66' Kubala (R.E.), 75' Ritchie (G.B.), 81' Douglas (G.B.), 89' Henderson (R.E.)

INTERNATIONAL SELECTION—SPAIN: 3-0
(In honor of Ricardo Zamora)

27 September 1967, Estadio Bernabéu, Madrid. Attendance: 35,000.

SPAIN: Iribar; Sanchís, De Felipe; Reija, Glaría, Gallego; Ufarte, Grosso, Marcelino, Adelardo, José Maria. *Substitutions:* Bueno for De Felipe, Sadurni for Iribar, Eladio for Sanchís. *Selector:* Balmamya.
INTERNATIONAL SELECTION: Sarti (Italy); Burgnich (Italy), Schnellinger (Germany FR); Cooke (England), Ure (Scotland), Coluña (Portugal); Hamrin (Sweden), Rivera (Italy), Mazzola (Italy), Eusebio (Portugal), Corso (Italy). *Substitutions:* Benitez (Uruguay) for

Coluña, Waldo (Brazil) for Hamrin, Goywaert (Belgium) for Eusebio. *Manager:* Herrera (Argentina)

Goals: 23' Mazzola, 30' Eusebio, 88' Goywaert

BRAZIL—REST OF THE WORLD: 2-1
(Celebration of the Tenth Anniversary of Brazil's first World Cup victory)

6 November 1968, Estádio Maracanã, Rio de Janeiro. Attendance: 93,000.

BRAZIL: Picasso; Carlos Alberto, Everaldo; Natal, Jurandir, Dias; Jairzinho, Gerson, Pelé, Rivelino, Paulo Cesar. *Substitutions:* Moreira for Carlos Alberto, Paulo Borges for Natal, Tostão for Jairzinho. *Selector:* Moreira (Brazil).

REST OF THE WORLD: *First half*—Yashin (USSR); Novák (Czechoslovakia), Marzolini (Argentina); Beckenbauer (Germany FR), Schulz (Germany FR), Shesternev (USSR); Amancio (Spain), Szücs (Hungary), Albert (Hungary), Overath (Germany FR), Džajić (Yugoslavia). *Second half*—Mazurkiewicz (Uruguay); Novák, Perfumo (Argentina); Beckenbauer, Schulz, Shesternev; Metreveli (USSR), Szücs, Rocha (Uruguay), Overath, Farkás (Hungary). *Selector:* Cramer (Germany FR).

Goals: 20' Rivelino (B.), 33' Albert (R.W.), 89' Tostão (B.)

REST OF THE UNITED KINGDOM—WALES: 1-0
(Celebration of the investiture of Prince Charles)

21 July 1969, Ninian Park, Cardiff. Attendance: 13,605.

WALES: Sprake (Leeds); Rodrigues (Leicester), R. Thomas (Swindon); Hennessey (Nottingham F), England (Tottenham), Moore (Charlton); B. Jones (Cardiff), C. Jones (Fulham), Davies (Southampton), Toshack (Cardiff), Rees (Nottingham F). *Substitution:* Reece (Sheffield U) for Rees. *Selector:* Bowen.

REST OF THE UNITED KINGDOM: Jennings (Tottenham & Northern Ireland); Gemmell (Celtic & Scotland), Cooper (Leeds & England); Bremner (Leeds & Scotland); J. Charlton (Leeds & England), Mullery (Tottenham & England); Best (Manchester U & Northern Ireland), Lee (Manchester C & England), Dougan (Wolverhampton & Northern Ireland), R. Charlton (Manchester U & England), Hughes (Celtic & Scotland). *Substitutions:* Newton (Blackburn & England) for Cooper, Henderson (Rangers & Scotland) for Lee. *Selector:* Ramsey (England).

Goals: 34' Lee

BENFICA—EUROPEAN SELECTION: 3-2
(In honor of Mario Coluña)

8 December 1970, Estádio Nacional, Lisbon. Attendance: 46,387.

BENFICA: Henrique; Toni, Adolfo; Vitor Martina, Humberto Coelho, Zeca; Coluña, Jaime Graça, Artur Jorge, Eusebio, Simoes. *Substitutions:* Fonseca for Henrique, Nene for Vitor Martina, Matihe for Coluña.

EUROPEAN SELECTION: Iribar (Spain); Suárez (Spain), Gemmell (Scotland); Pirri (Spain), Gallego (Spain), Moore (England); Cruyff (Netherlands), Seeler (Germany FR), Hurst

(England), Osgood (England), Džajić (Yugoslavia). *Substitutions:* Andersson (Denmark) for Cruyff, Hunt (England) for Pirri, Bento (Portugal) for Iribar, Garate (Spain) for Hurst, Rodilla (Spain) for Džajić.

Goals: 32' Eusebio (B.), 44' Simoes (B.), 47' Seeler (E.), 57' Garate (E.), 76) A Jorge (B.)

BOCA JÚNIORS—REST OF SOUTH AMERICA: 1-1
(In honor of Antonio Rattin)

10 December 1970, Estadio La Bombonera, Buenos Aires. Attendance: unknown.

BOCA JÚNIORS: Roma; Suñé, Marzolini; Rattin cap, Rogel, Meléndez; Ponce, Medina, Novello, Curioni, Villagra. *Substitutions:* Ovide for Suñé, Savoy for Novello, La Rosa for Curioni, Peña for Villagra.
REST OF SOUTH AMERICA: Mazurkiewicz (Uruguay); Forlan (Uruguay), Perfumo (Argentina); Mifflin (Peru), Ancheta (Uruguay), Matosas (Uruguay) cap; Prieto (Chile), Rocha (Uruguay), Artime (Argentina), Bernao (Argentina), Mas (Argentina). *Substitution:* Manga (Brazil) for Mazurkiewicz.

Goals: 47' Artime (R.S.A.), 77' La Rosa pen

MOSCOW SELECTION—REST OF THE WORLD: 2-2
(In honor of Lev Yashin)

27 May 1971, Lenin Stadium Moscow. Attendance: 90,000.

MOSCOW SELECTION: Yashin; Chatov, Zukov; Sabo, Zikov, Sumin; Pusac, Khmelnitzki, Malafeev, Khurts, Sakarov. *Substitutions:* Metreveli for Khmelnitzki, Koslov for Malafeev, Pilgul for Yashin.
REST OF THE WORLD: *First half*—Mazurkiewicz (Uruguay); Djorkaeff (France), Facchetti (Italy); Schulz (Germany FR), Mészöly (Hungary), Peña (Mexico); Dumitrache (Rumania), Bonev (Bulgaria), Müller (Germany FR), R. Charlton (England), Džajić (Yugoslavia). *Second half*—Viktor (Czechoslovakia); Kuna (Czechoslovakia), Facchetti; Schulz, Mészöly, Anczok (Poland); Dumitrache, Lubanski (Poland), Müller, R. Charlton, Jekov (Bulgaria).

Goals: 7' Khmelnitzki (M.), 10' Sabo (M.), 52' Mészöly (R.W.), 78' Jekov (R.W.)

EUROPEAN SELECTION—HAMBURGER SV: 7-3
(In honor of Uwe Seeler)

1 May 1972, Volksparkstadion, Hamburg. Attendance: 62,000.

HAMBURGER SV: Özcan; Sandmann, Ripp; Hellfritz, Schulz, Nogly; Björnmose, Zaczyk, Seeler, Hönig, Volkert. *Substitutions:* Kargus for Özcan, Memering for Sandmann, Winkler for Björnmose, Lübeke for Winkler, Dringelstein for Zaczyk, Dörfel for Volkert. *Manager:* Ochs.
EUROPEAN SELECTION: *First half*—Banks (England); Gemmell (Scotland), Schnellinger (Germany FR), Beckenbauer (Germany FR.), Moore (England), R. Charlton (England); Bene (Hungary), Rivera (Italy), Müller (Germany FR), Hurst (England), Best (Northern Ireland). *Second half*—Maier (Germany FR); Gemmell, Höttges (Germany FR); Mészöly (Hungary),

Moore, R. Charlton; Bene, Rivera, Eusebio (Portugal), Best, Džajić (Yugoslavia). *Manager:* Rocco (Italy).

Goals: 15' Hurst (E.), 37' Bene (E.), 40' Beckenbauer (E.), 41' Seeler (H.) pen, 43' Müller (E.), 45' Zaczyk (H.), 55' Mészöly (E.), 71' Best (E.), 79' Eusebio (E.), 84' Seeler (H.)

RED STAR BELGRADE—WORLD SELECTION: 2-2
(Tenth Anniversary of SPORT, the Yugoslav daily)

9 June 1972, Crvena Zvezda Stadium, Belgrade. Attendance: 50,000.

RED STAR BELGRADE: Dujković; Krivokuca, Stepanović; Pavlović, Dojcinovski, Jerković; Petković, Acimović, Koskić, Sekularac, Džajić. *Substitution:* Lazareivić for Koskić.

WORLD SELECTION: Marić (Yugoslavia); Suurbier (Netherlands), Carlos Alberto (Brazil); Mészöly (Hungary), Holcer (Yugoslavia), Dumitru (Rumania); Albert (Hungary), Mühren (Netherlands), Netzer (Germany FR), Skoblar (Yugoslavia), Cruyff (Netherlands).

Goals: 18' Cruyff (W.), 30' Petković (R.S.), 42' Netzer (W.), 69' Acimović (R.S.); Red Star won on penalty kicks (7-6)

SOUTH AMERICA—EUROPE: 2-0
(Benefit for homeless children around the world)

3 October 1972, Basle, Switzerland. Attendance: 20,000.

EUROPE: *First half*—Viktor (Czechoslovakia); Hilario (Portugal), Facchetti (Italy) cap; Salvadore (Italy), Schnellinger (Germany FR), Hasil (Austria); Cruyff (Netherlands), van Hanegem (Netherlands), Lubanski (Poland), Haller (Germany FR), Džajić (Yugoslavia). *Second half*—Marić (Yugoslavia); Hilario, Facchetti; Juliano (Italy), Anquilletti (Italy), Salvadore; Amancio (Spain), Velazquez (Spain), Lubanski, Albert (Hungary), Bene (Hungary). *Substitution:* Džajić for Lubanski in 2nd half. *Selector:* Herrera (France).

SOUTH AMERICA: *First Half*—Santoro (Argentina); Wolff (Argentina), Pavoni (Uruguay); Chumpitaz (Peru), Bargas (Argentina), Montero-Castillo (Uruguay); Brindisi (Argentina), Ayala (Argentina), Sotil (Peru), Cubillas (Peru), Alonso (Argentina). *Second half*—Manga (Brazil); Wolff, Pavoni; Chumpitaz, Heredia (Argentina), Montero Castillo; (Maneiro (Uruguay), Baylon (Peru), Sotil, Cubillas, Alonso. *Substitution:* Uriarte (Paraguay) for Alonso. *Selector:* Sivori (Argentina).

Goals: 34' Cubillas, 64' Maniero

NEW ECM—OLD ECM: 2-0
(Celebration of the admission of Great Britain, Eire, and Denmark to the European Common Market)

3 January 1973, London, England. Attendance: 36,500.

NEW ECM: Jennings (Northern Ireland); Storey (England), Hughes (England); Bell (England), Hunter (Northern Ireland), Moore (England); Lorimer (Scotland), Giles (Eire), Stein (Scotland), R. Charlton (England), Jensen (Denmark). *Substitutions:* Ball (England) for Jensen, Olsen (Denmark) for Bell. *Selector:* Ramsey (England).

OLD ECM: Piot (Belgium); Tresor (France), Vogts (Germany FR); Neeskens (Netherlands),

Blankenburg (Germany FR), Beckenbauer (Germany FR); Grabowski (Germany FR), van Hanegem (Netherlands), Müller (Germany FR), Netzer (Germany FR), Bereta (France). *Substitutions:* Zoff (Italy) for Piot, Suurbier (Netherlands) for Tresor, Krol (Netherlands) for Beckenbauer, Pilot (Luxembourg) for van Hanegem. *Selector:* Schön (Germany FR).

Goals: 47' Jensen, 69' Stein

REST OF THE WORLD—HAMBURGER SV: 5-2
(In honor of Willi Schulz)

25 April 1973, Volksparkstadion, Hamburg. Attendance: 35,000.

HAMBURGER SV: Özcan; Kaltz, Hidien; Nogly, Schulz, Björnmose; Heese, Memering, Zaczyk, Hönig, Volkert. *Substitutions:* Sandmann for Nogly, Winkler for Memering.
REST OF THE WORLD: Maier (Germany FR); Carlos Alberto (Brazil), McKinnon (Scotland); Beckenbauer (Germany FR), Seeler (Germany FR), Moore (England); Albert (Hungary), Law (Scotland), R. Charlton (England), Müller (Germany FR), Skoblar (Yugoslavia). *Substitutions:* Bernard (Germany FR) for Maier, Höttges (Germany FR) for Mc Kinnon, Grabowski (Germany FR) for Albert, Macari (Scotland) for Charlton, Gordon (England) for Skoblar.

Goals: 33' Zaczyk (H.), 38' Heese (H.), 53' Macari (R.W.), 55' Beckenbauer (R.W.), 56' Seeler (R.W.), 74' Macari (R.W.), 86' Müller (R.W.)

BENFICA—REST OF THE WORLD: 2-2
(In honor of Eusebio)

25 September 1973, Estádio da Luz, Lisbon. Attendance: 40,000.

BENFICA: José Henrique; Artur, Barros; Rui Rodriguez, Messias, Bastos Lopes; Nene, Victor Martins, Jordão, Eusebio, Simoes. *Substitutions:* Bento for José Henrique, Humberto Coelho for Bastos Lopes, Toni for Victor Martins, Artur Jorge for Jordão, Nelinho for Eusebio.
REST OF THE WORLD: Banks (England); Blankenburg (Germany FR), Hilario (Portugal); R. Charlton (England), J. Charlton (England), Badeco (Brazil); Best (Northern Ireland), Paulo Cesar (Brazil), Keita (Mali), Netzer (Germany FR), Keizer (Netherlands).*Substitutions:* Iribar (Spain) for Banks, Gento (Spain) for Hilario, Seeler (Germany FR) for R. Charlton, Dirceu Lopes (Brazil) for Best, Hilario for Keizer, Garcia Ramon (Spain) for Iribar. *Selector:* Muñoz (Spain).

Goals: 3' Nene (B.), 43' Keita (R.W.), 52' Nene (B.), 63' Seeler (R.W.)

SOUTH AMERICA—EUROPE: 4-4
(Benefit for FIFA Beneficiary Fund for World Poverty)

31 October 1973, Estadio Nou Camp, Barcelona. Attendance: 30,000.

EUROPE: *First half*—Viktor (Czechoslovakia); Sol (Spain), Facchetti (Italy); Asensi (Spain), Krivokuca (Yugoslavia), Pavlović (Yugoslavia); Bene (Hungary), Keita (Mali), Cruyff (Netherlands) cap, Eusebio (Portugal), Jara (Austria). *Second half*—Iribar (Spain); Sol, Facchetti cap; Pirri (Spain), Krivokuca, Pavlović; Nene (Portugal), Asensi, Edström

(Sweden), Odermatt (Switzerland), Jara. *Substitutions:* Kapsis (Greece) for Krivokuca, Dimitru (Greece) for Pavlović. *Selector:* Kubala (Spain).

SOUTH AMERICA: *First half*—Santoro (Argentina); Wolff (Argentina), Marco Antonio (Brazil); Esparrago (Uruguay), Luis Pereira (Brazil), Chumpitaz (Peru) cap; Sotil (Peru), Brindisi (Argentina), Cubillas (Peru), Rivelino (Brazil), Paulo Cesar (Brazil). *Second half*— Carnevali (Argentina); Arrua (Paraguay), Marco Antonio; Esparrago, Luis Pereira, Chumpitaz cap; Caszely (Chile), Brindisi, Sotil, Rivelino, Cubillas. *Substitutions:* Lasso (Ecuador) for Brindisi, Morena (Uruguay) for Lasso, Borja (Mexico) for Sotil, Ortiz (Colombia) for Cubillas. *Selector:* Sivori (Argentina).

Goals: 14' Sotil (S.A.), 15' Eusebio (E.), 23' Keita (E.), 27' Cubillas (S.A.), 52' Asensi (E.), 58' Jara (E.), 63' Brindisi (S.A.), 80' Chumpitaz (S.A.) pen; South America won on penalty kicks (7-6)

BRAZIL—INTERNATIONAL SELECTION: 2-1
(In honor of Garrincha)

19 December 1973, Estádio Maracanã, Rio de Janeiro. Attendance: 131,555.

BRAZIL: Felix; Carlos Alberto, Everaldo; Clodoaldo, Brito, Piazza; Garrincha, Rivelino, Jairzinho, Pelé, Paulo Cesar. *Substitutions:* Leão for Felix, Ze Maria for Carlos Alberto, Luis Pereira for Brito, Zequinha for Garrincha, Ademir for Pelé.

INTERNATIONAL SELECTION: Andrada (Argentina); Forlan (Uruguay), Brunel (Uruguay); Dreyer (Argentina), Alex (Germany FR), Reyes (Paraguay); Houseman (Argentina), Brindisi (Argentina), Doval (Argentina), Rocha (Uruguay), Onishenko (USSR). *Substitutions:* Babington (Argentina) for Houseman, Lovchev (USSR) for Onishenko.

Goals: 18' Brindisi (I.), 36' Pelé (B.), 66' Luis Pereira (B.)

RSC ANDERLECHT—REST OF THE WORLD: 8-3
(In honor of Paul van Himst)

26 March 1975, Parc Astrid, Brussels. Attendance: 35,000.

RSC ANDERLECHT: Ruiter; van Binst, Broos; van den Daele, Thissen, van der Elst; Andersen, Coeck, Ladinszki, van Himst cap, Rensenbrink. *Substitutions:* Dockx for van den Daele, Verheyen for Coeck, Nicolaes for Ladinszki. *Manager:* Braems.

REST OF THE WORLD: *First half*—Tomaszewski (Poland); Rijsbergen (Netherlands), van Hanegem (Netherlands); Viera (Uruguay), Katalinski (Yugoslavia), Heredia (Argentina); Amancio (Spain), Eusebio (Portugal), Altafini (Italy), Pelé (Brazil), Cruyff (Netherlands) cap. *Second half*—Piot (Belgium); Rijsbergen, Delikaris (Greece); Babington (Argentina), Katalinski, Heredia; Jairzinho (Brazil), Rivera (Italy), Sotil (Peru), van Hanegem, Paulo Cesar (Brazil). *Selector:* Michels (Netherlands).

Goals: 3' van Himst (A.) pen, 17' Ladinszki (A.), 30' van der Elst (A.), 31' Altafini (R.W.), 36' Ladinszki (A.), 40' Altafini (R.W.), 48' Andersen (A.), 57' Verheyen (A.), 61' & 70' Nicolaes (A.), 76' Paulo Cesar (R.W.)

CONCACAF See: **Confederación Norte-Centroamericana y del Caribe de Fútbol (CONCACAF)**

CONCACAF, Championship of

Campeonato Norte-Centroamericano y del Caribe de Fútbol Mayor.

The regional competition for national teams of CONCACAF member-states. It is not to be confused with the soccer tournament of the Central American and Caribbean Games, which is open only to amateur players and excludes the countries of North America. While the Championship of CONCACAF has only been in existence since 1963, its precursor, the Campeonato Centroamericano y del Caribe was launched in 1941. Costa Rica has dominated the series with 9 wins in 16 tournaments, but Costa Rica's accomplishments are necessarily tempered by the vastly differing makeup of the competition from year to year.

The tournament was introduced in 1941 as the championship of the Confederación Centroamericano y del Caribe de Fútbol (CCCF), an organization formed in 1938 to administer the soccer tournament of the Central American and Caribbean Games. Its purpose was to provide a competition that would be under the complete supervision of the new CCCF and one that would be open to all players regardless of their amateur or professional status, thus allowing the best national teams of each country to participate. In fact, professionalism had not yet become a prominent factor in the region.

Its first four editions attracted only four to six countries each; Costa Rica and El Salvador sent teams to all four; Guatemala, Panama, and Nicaragua participated in three. Occasional participants were Curaçao and Honduras. The series continued to be unrepresentative of the region throughout the 1950s, as the old Central American and Caribbean confederation gradually faded from existence. The competition was given new impetus in 1963 when the new confederation of the region, CONCACAF, adopted its sponsorship, but again the lack of financial resources and organizational sophistication of most Caribbean countries, in addition to an absence of interest by the United States and Canada, resulted in small tournaments (six entrants in both 1967 and 1969).

In 1972-73 and 1976-77, the series was incorporated into qualification rounds for the World Cup, and a larger representation emerged from the scattered island nations and North American monoliths that provide the bulk of CONCACAF's membership. Even then only 11 states entered in 1972-73 and only 16 in 1976-77. Nevertheless, qualification for the World Cup was clearly a greater incentive than the championship of CONCACAF.

The major embarrassment of the early CCCF championships was Nicaragua, which failed to win a game in its first three tournaments. Its 10-1 trouncing by El Salvador remained a record until Trinidad buried Antigua by 11-1 in 1972, though Antigua's loss would surely have been equalled after 1972 if other tiny countries of the Caribbean had displayed the same boldness in entering the competition. At the other end of the table, Costa Rica's success is noteworthy for its consistency. Never have more than two tournaments gone by without Costa Rica winning the championship.

The countries that participated in either the CCCF Championship or CONCACAF Championship before 1973 were: Costa Rica, Curaçao (Netherlands Antilles), El Salvador, Guatemala, Haiti, Honduras, Mexico, Nicaragua, Panama, and Trinidad. In 1972-73 and 1976-77, the following were added: Antigua, Barbados, Canada, Cuba, Dominican Republic, Guyana, Jamaica, Puerto Rico, Surinam, and the USA.

See also: **North American Football Confederation, Championship of the**

Winners

(Championship of CCCF)

1941	Costa Rica		1953	Costa Rica
1943	El Salvador		1955	Costa Rica
1946	Costa Rica		1957	Haiti
1948	Costa Rica		1960	Costa Rica
1951	Panama		1961	Costa Rica

(Championship of CONCACAF)

1963	Costa Rica		1969	Costa Rica
1965	Mexico		1973	Haiti
1967	Guatemala		1977	Mexico

CONCACAF Club Champions, Championship of

Campeonato Norte-Centroamericano y del Caribe de Fútbol Mayor de Campeones.

The most erratic of all regional club championships (except for the Asian Champions' Cup, suspended for the past several years). The annual CONCACAF club championship is modeled loosely on the Copa Libertadores, and is open to all champions and runners-up of the CONCACAF membership. Mexican clubs have won seven of the 13 competitions.

The generally accepted format is to divide the participants into three first round groups. The top clubs from each group advance to a semi-final round, which comprises two groups of three clubs each. The winners of these two groups play each other for the championship. All rounds are played on a home and away basis.

Unfortunately, the greatest number of CONCACAF countries to enter the tournament is 11 (in 1975 and 1976), just over half the total membership. This lack of representation—caused by low funds, fear of financial loss, and schedule conflicts due to seasonal variations of domestic league competitions—has rendered the competition just short of meaningless. Since the formation of the North American Soccer League in 1967, only two NASL champions have entered the tournament (Rochester Lancers, representing the USA, in 1971, and Toronto Metros-Croatia, representing Canada, in 1976). German-American League members and other semiprofessional clubs have otherwise filled American and Canadian openings. The number of participating clubs has grown gradually from 10 in 1969 to 20 in 1976, but during the same period of time the number of countries represented has grown only marginally, from nine to 11.

The participants in 1976 were: AS Italia and Toronto Metros-Croatia (Canada), Aguila and Alianza (El Salvador), Aurora and Comunicaciones (Guatemala), Thomas United and Christianburg (Guyana), España and Olympia (Honduras), Olympia and Diriangen (Nicaragua), Toluca and León (Mexico), Jong Colombia and SU Brion Trappers (Netherlands Antilles), Robin Hood and Vorwaarts (Surinam), Malvers and Palo Seco (Trinidad & Tobago), and Inter-Giuliana (USA). Bermuda, Costa Rica, and Haiti have also participated in past editions.

Since 1968, the champion has gone on to play in the Copa Interamericana against the winner of the Copa Libertadores, the South American champion emerging victorious each time.

Winners

1963	Guadalajara (Mexico)		1966	Racing (Haiti)
1964	Guadalajara		1967	Alianza (El Salvador)
1965	Guadalajara		1968	Toluca (Mexico)

1969   Cruz Azul (Mexico)
1970   final round canceled; Cruz Azul, Saprissa (Costa Rica), and Transvaal (Surinam) shared trophy
1971   Cruz Azul
1972   Olympia (Honduras)
1973   Transvaal
1974   Deportivo Municipal (Guatemala)
1975   Atlético Español (Mexico)
[1976   results unavailable]
1977   América (Mexico)
1978   Comunicaciones (Guatemala)

Confederación Norte-Centroamericana y del Caribe de Fútbol (CONCACAF)

Address: *Calle Mariscal Cruz, 9-56, Zona 4, Apartado Postal 86-A, Guatemala, C.A., Guatemala.* **Members:** *Barbados, Bermuda, Canada, Costa Rica, Cuba, Dominican Republic, Guatemala, Guyana, Haiti, Honduras, Jamaica, Mexico, Netherlands Antilles, Nicaragua, Panama, Puerto Rico, El Salvador, Surinam, Trinidad and Tobago, and the USA. Antigua and the Bahamas are FIFA members but not affiliated with CONCACAF.* **Affiliated clubs:** *6,294;* **registered players:** *1,594,507 (both figures include Antigua and the Bahamas, but exclude Panama).*

Known commonly by its abbreviated name, CONCACAF is the regional governing body whose jurisdiciton includes North America, Central America, and the Caribbean. It has also attracted the membership of Surinam and Guyana, whose cultural links are with the Caribbean region rather than South America. CONCACAF will eventually absorb French Guiana when that colony seeks international affiliation in the future. It is directly responsible to FIFA, the world governing body.

The confederation as it is today was formed in 1961, but for many years prior to that the geographical areas under its domain were administered by a confusing web of organizations. Its basic pattern of reorganization has reflected a shift of allegiance from the Olympic movement to FIFA—typical among regional confederations as the sophistication of their game grows—and a greater need to break away from the administration of less popular sports. The complex geopolitical makeup of the region has also contributed to endless overlappings of administrative responsibility.

In 1924, during the seventh Olympic Games, Olympic participants from the region conferred in Paris and formed the Congreso Deportivo Centroamericano, later renamed the Organización Deportiva Centroamericano y del Caribe (ODCC), and resolved to organize amateur games based on the Olympic model. The first edition of the new sports festival was held in 1930 at Havana, Cuba, and included soccer among a dozen other events. The Juegos Deportivos Centroamericanos y del Caribe (Central American and Caribbean Games), as the games were called, were open to all members of the ODCC. A second edition was held in 1935, but it was not until the third games in 1938 at Panama City that a separate governing body for soccer was formed—the Confederación Centroamericano y del Caribe de Fútbol (CCCF).

Although the soccer tournament of the Central American and Caribbean Games continued to be administered by the CCCF under the tutelage of the ODCC (much like FIFA administers the soccer tournament of the Olympic Games), the CCCF launched its own international competition for national teams in 1941, the Championship of the CCCF. Unlike the amateur games based on the Olympic model, the Championship of the CCCF would be open to the best team each member state could field, regardless of its amateur or professional standing. Eligibility requirements did not become a major factor, however, until professionalism surfaced in a half dozen nations of the region after World War II. The championship of the CCCF was held almost every other year from 1941 to 1961, and, with only a handful of countries supporting professionalism in its upper ranks, most entrants sent the same team to both regional competitions.

The original membership of the Confederación Centroamericano y del Caribe in 1938 included: Colombia, Costa Rica, El Salvador, Curaçao (Curaçao would later become part of the Netherlands Antilles), Dominican Republic, Guatemala, Haiti, Honduras, Jamaica, Nicaragua, Panama, Puerto Rico, and Venezuela. Colombia and Venezuela subsequently switched their affiliation to CONMEBOL, the South American Confederation.

Mexico consented to join the United States and Cuba in forming a North American Football Confederation (NAFC) in 1939; a championship for national teams was held in 1947 and 1949. Mexico and Cuba's allegiances, however, were to their Spanish speaking neighbors, and by the 1950s the United States was out in the cold. The NAFC faded slowly from view, and, at the same time, the CCCF practically ground to a halt. Finally, in 1961,

FIFA threw its full support behind a merger of North America with Central America and the Caribbean, and CONCACAF was organized in its present form. Its charter members were: Cuba, Guatemala, Honduras, Mexico, and Netherlands Antilles. Fourteen additional members were acquired before the end of the decade.

The former Championship of the CCCF became the biennial Championship of CONCACAF in 1963, and was extended to include the national teams of Mexico, Canada, and the United States, though the latter two showed little interest. In addition, a Championship of CONCACAF Club Champions was established in 1963, held annually ever since. CONCACAF also oversees the regional qualification rounds for the World Cup and Olympic Games. The soccer tournament of the Central American and Caribbean Games is held every four years under the separate aegis of the governing body for amateur sports in the region, with direct supervision by CONCACAF.

In late 1977, Caribbean members announced the formation of a Caribbean Football Federation, which they hoped would lead eventually to CONCACAF splitting into two FIFA-sanctioned confederations.

Confederación Panamericana de Football

The Pan American Football Confederation was a short-lived umbrella organization that sought to unite soccer interests throughout the Western Hemisphere and organize a championship of all the Americas. It was founded at Barranquilla, Colombia, in 1946 by the membership of the South American, Central American and Caribbean, and North American football confederations. The charter members were: Cuba, Mexico, USA, Costa Rica, Curaçao, Dominican Republic, Guatemala, Honduras, Panama, El Salvador, Venezuela, Argentina, Bolivia, Chile, Columbia, Ecuador, Paraguay, Peru, and Uruguay. Haiti, Nicaragua, Surinam, and Brazil joined subsequently. Its headquarters was variously located in Santiago, Chile, and Mexico City.

In 1952, it managed to organize the first Pan American Championship (not to be confused with the amateur soccer tournament of the Pan American Games) in Santiago, Chile. Six countries were invited: the current South American champion (Brazil), the current Central American and Caribbean

champion (Panama), the host country, and three random members (Uruguay, Peru, and Mexico). Brazil emerged on top of the table with four wins and a scoreless draw with Peru. Runner-up Chile won four of its matches and lost decisively to Brazil. Uruguay and Peru held their own with six and five points respectively, while Mexico managed only to defeat hapless Panama, which went without a point in five attempts. Panama's goal difference was five goals for and 28 against. Several members of Uruguay's world champion team were not given permission by their clubs to play, and the Brazilian CBD, in a manner characteristic of its involvement in the South American Championship, also failed to rally home support—all of which served to dampen Brazil's 4-2 win over World Cup rival Uruguay.

The possibility of further hemispheric championships died with the demise of the Pan American Football Confederation in the mid-1950s.

Confederación Sudamericana de Fútbol (CONMEBOL)

Address: *Estadio Nacional, Puerta No. 4, Calle José Diaz, Lima, Peru.* **Members:** *Argentina, Bolivia, Brazil, Chile, Colombia, Ecuador, Paraguay, Peru, Uruguay, Venezuela.* **Affiliated clubs:** *24,651;* **registered players:** *1,053,553.*

Founded in 1916 by Argentina, Uruguay, Brazil, and Chile in Buenos Aires on the occasion of the first South American Championship. Paraguay joined in 1917, Peru in 1924, Bolivia in 1925, Ecuador in 1927, Colombia (formerly affiliated with the Central American Confederation) in 1940, and Venezuela in 1952. Guyana and Surinam are affiliated with CONCACAF, and French Guiana remains attached to the Fédération Française de Football.

CONMEBOL is the oldest continental confederation in the world and the brainchild of Uruguayan Hector R. Gomez, who urged its formation as early as 1912. When Argentina decided to organize the first South American Championship to commemorate its centenary, Gomez seized the opportunity and convened the first convention. The history of CONMEBOL has been tranquil and uneventful—at least by comparison with the other regional confederations—though it is less active than many others in organizing international competitions below the level of the South American Championship and the Copa Libertadores de América.

Congo

Fédération Congolaise de Football
B.P. 4041
Brazzaville

Founded: 1962
FIFA: 1963
CAF: 1966

Affiliated clubs: *141;* **registered players:** *4,230;* **national stadium:** *Stade de la Révolution, Brazzaville (50,000);* **largest stadium:** *Stade de la Révolution;* **colors:** *red jerseys, red shorts;* **season:** *February to October;* **honors:** *African Nations' Cup winner (1972), C.A.R.A., African Cup of Champions (1974).*

One of Africa's leading soccer nations, the Congo (formerly Congo-Brazzaville) has achieved success on both the national and club levels entirely out of proportion to its tiny population.

Soccer in French Congo gained its first foothold in Brazzaville and, as elsewhere in colonial Africa, was first played by resident colonists. As a result of Brazzaville's location directly across the Stanley Pool from Léopoldville, the capital of the Belgian Congo (now Zaire), Belgians as well as French influenced the local game. When the Fédération de Football Association du Pool was founded in 1924 at Léopoldville, clubs from Brazzaville were invited to join the new league. The affiliation was retained until independence. As a result, the leading Brazzaville club, Cercle Athlétique Brazzavillois, won the Pool championship in 1931, 1937, 1941, 1945, and 1949, as well as the Cup de Léopoldville in 1937.

Other important Brazzaville clubs were founded in the early days of the Pool league, among them Poto-Poto (1930), the forerunner of C.A.R.A., which is now one of Africa's greatest clubs.

The Fédération Congolaise de Football was founded two years after independence, and joined FIFA the following year and the African Football Confederation in 1966. The Congo's strong, historical interest in soccer was revitalized after the coup of 1963. Then, prophetically, a national selection won the soccer tournament of the 1965 African Games. Since the 1960s, the Congolese game has developed rapidly. After losing all three matches in the final rounds of the 1968 African Nations' Cup to Congo-Kinshasa, Senegal, and Ghana, and failing to qualify for the 1970 edition, a strong Congolese national side prevailed against Africa's best teams and won the eighth Nations' Cup in 1972. The Red

Devils' route to the top was difficult: in the first round it placed second to Zaire but above Morocco and Sudan, each a continental power, and managed to defeat the hosts, Cameroon, in a semi-final. In the final, it met Mali with its international class striker Salif Keita, and from a goal by the great attacking midfielder, M'Pelé, completed a second upset in three days by winning 3-2. M'Pelé has since become a star with the French club Paris St-Germain. It was a stunning run for the African championship, one that would not soon be forgotten. In 1974, the Congo placed fourth after winning a first round group that included eventual winner Zaire.

On the club level, meanwhile, one club was emerging as the dominant force at home. C.A.R.A., or Club Athlétique Renaissance Aiglons, had been saved from extinction in 1952, and in subsequent years adopted a policy of recruiting young players from what is known in central Africa as *mwanafoot,* the "football of the roads and rough ground". C.A.R.A. won the national championship five times in succession and the Brazzaville championship eight times in succession during the late 1960s and early 1970s. In 1974, it won the African Cup of Club Champions after defeating the Egyptian champions Mehalla in both home and away legs of the final. In 1975, it lost to Hafia of Guinea on penalty kicks in the quarter finals and in 1976, its withdrawal after gaining the quarter finals cast some doubt on its future in international competition. Congolese clubs have not participated in the African Cup Winners' Cup.

CONMEBOL   See: **Confederación Sudamericana de Fútbol**

Corinthians Football Club

Location: *London, England;* **stadium:** *Kennington Oval, various grounds at Leyton, Crystal Palace;* **colors:** *white shirts, blue shorts.*

Founded 1882 by N. Lane "Pa" Jackson, Honorary Assistance Secretary of The Football Association. Troubled that England had won only twice in 12 contests against Scotland since the series began in 1872, Jackson set out to organize a group of experienced English players who, if given the opportunity to play together on a regular basis, might provide a base for the England XI and build a challenge to Scotland's dominance. From a tactical viewpoint, Jackson noted that Scotland's success was built on its adoption of the highly effective "passing game" of Queen's Park Glasgow, which had proved superior time and again to England's more antiquated "dribbling game." The Corinthians sought to perfect this style from the outset.

Jackson's selection of players was made entirely from Oxford and Cambridge University students and graduates, whose soccer playing days had begun in the public schools that had given birth to the game in the first place. The Corinthians, therefore, immediately gained an advantage with the vast experience of its players. As a collection of "gentlemen" players, the club was all-amateur, and even declined to participate in any organized competitions, including the F.A. Cup and The Football League. Its schedule was made up entirely of friendlies.

Corinthians F.C. became a living legend from the start, and in no uncertain terms achieved everything it set out to do. Between 1883 and 1904, its golden era, it was the finest amateur club in Britain and perhaps the finest club on any level. Its success made it very popular, and invitations to play were plentiful and widespread. The club became famous as the embodiment of the amateur ideal in the the new age of professionalism, and its sportsmanship was unquestioned. Corinthian players seldom fouled, and when a penalty kick was taken against them, the goalkeeper routinely stood aside to let the shot pass uncontested.

In 1884, its second year in existence, the Corinthians crushed F.A. Cup holders Blackburn Rovers by 8-1, and in 1889, romped over Preston North End, the recent winners of the league and cup double, by an astonishing 5-0.

In 1900, it defeated Aston Villa, five-time league champions, and in 1904, brushed aside Bury, the F.A. Cup holders, by 10-3. Corinthian players found their way into the England side almost immediately. In 1886, with nine Corinthians in the squad, England defeated Scotland 5-0, and eight years later, an England side composed entirely of Corinthians defeated Wales 5-1.

It greatest contribution, however, was to popularize the "passing game" throughout England, leading ultimately to its spread overseas. The Corinthians became world famous with international tours, and many nations can point to such visits as turning points in the development of their game. Among the most important of these were visits to North America in 1906 and 1911, and one to Brazil in 1910.

In all, Corinthians F.C. supplied a total of 83 players to England teams between 1883 and the 1920s, a record for all English clubs. G.O. Smith (20 international appearances) was the greatest center forward of his day; he played for the Corinthians from 1892-1903. William Cobbold (9 international appearances), "the Prince of Dribblers," preceded Smith as perhaps the most clever forward of the 1880s. Edward Bambridge (18) was widely thought to be the finest outside left of the 1880s. These and other names of Corinthian players are among the most romantic in England's long soccer tradition, held aloft by their unique role in the transition between the nineteenth century "gentlemen's" game and the professional era.

In 1922, the Corinthians finally consented to participate in the F.A. Cup, and in that decade still managed to supply eight players at various times to the full England side. In 1939, it merged with another South London amateur club, Casuals F.C., to form the Corinthian-Casuals F.C., and is now ensconced at the Sandy Lane grounds, Mitcham, South London, competing in the all-amateur Isthmian League.

The Corinthians' lineup of 1901. Since the 1880s, this team of gentlemen-amateurs had been the finest in England. Its brightest star, G. O. Smith, was the premier center forward of the Victorian era. (Back row, left to right) C. Wreford Brown, B. Middleditch, A. T. B. Dunn, C. B. Fry, W. J. Oakley, C. F. Ryder, B. O. Corbett, H. Vickers; (middle row) R. E. Foster, G. O. Smith, M. H. Stanbrough; (front) G. E. Wilkinson.

Corinthians Paulista, Esporte Clube

Location: *São Paulo, Brazil;* stadium: *Parque São Jorge;* colors: *white jerseys, black shorts;* honors: *Rio-São Paulo Tournament (1950, 1953, 1954, 1966 shared), São Paulo champion (1914 LPF, 1916 LPF, 1922, 1924, 1928 APEA, 1929 APEA, 1930, 1937, 1938, 1939, 1941, 1951, 1952, 1954, 1977).*

Founded 1910 by five young Brazilians of Portuguese descent—a house painter and four São Paulo Railroad employees—in the Bom Retiro barrio of São Paulo after the Brazilian tour of the famous English amateur club Corinthians F.C. In the fall of 1910, Corinthians Paulista met its first opposition, Uniáo and Atlética Lapa, and in 1913 joined the "regular" São Paulo league (Liga Paulista de Football), winning its first championship one year later.

Corinthians, sometimes called by its Portuguese name *Coríntians,* is São Paulo's wealthiest and most popular club, and after Flamengo probably the most widely supported club in Brazil. It has won 16 São Paulo championships—two less than record holder Palmeiras—and four Rio-São Paulo Tournaments, a record, though its cumulative standing in *paulista* competition (1913-77) is fourth. Its golden era was the period between the world wars, when it walked off with nine titles, many of them won in the breakaway Associação Paulista de Esportes Athléticos (APEA) during the 1920s. Corinthians' great rival stemming from this era is Palestra Itália (now Palmeiras), which shared its domination of the *paulista* leagues for many years.

In the immediate postwar period, Corinthians enjoyed another highly successful run, winning three *paulista* titles during the early 1950s, and, at the same time, winning three of the earliest editions of the Rio-São Paulo Tournament, including the first official edition in 1950. Corinthians thus became Brazil's first national champion, a unique honor that the club has long cherished. Its goalscoring star during these years was center forward Baltasar, who appeared sporadically for Brazil in the 1950 World Cup. In 1951 the club signed goalkeeper Gilmar from the little Santos club of Jabaquara, but despite his leadership—he was undoubtedly the finest keeper Brazil has ever produced—Corinthians embarked on a long and desolate period with no honors, save a four-way tie for the lead in the 1966 Rio-São Paulo Tournament.

In the 1960s, after Gilmar had left for Santos FC, Corinthians made its greatest discovery of all in the brilliant winger Rivelino, who was later to become a hero of the 1970 World Cup and captain of Brazil in 1974. It was he who led his famous club to the final of the Campeonato Nacional in 1976, an event that caused such an outburst of celebration in São Paulo that the city was virtually under siege for a week. Rivelino abruptly left the following year for Fluminense, but in 1977 Corinthians succeeded in winning its first *paulista* championship in 23 years. Today, most of its big matches are played in the mammoth Estádio Morumbi (150,000), the official home grounds of São Paulo FC.

corner kick

A direct free kick taken from within a corner area. It is awarded to an attacking team when the ball passes over the goal line of the defending team, other than into the goal, having last been played by one of the defending team. The kick is taken from that corner nearest to where the ball crossed over the goal line. Opposing players must be 10 yards from the ball when the kick is taken. A player who receives the ball direct from a corner kick cannot be offside.

Corner kicks were introduced in England by The Football Association in 1872. The 10-yard rule was added in 1914. Until 1924, corner kicks were "indirect."

Cosmos

Location: *New York, New York;* stadium: *Giants Stadium, The Meadowlands, East Rutherford, New Jersey;* colors: *green jerseys with white trim, white shorts;* honors: *North American Soccer League champion (1972, 1977, 1978).*

Founded in 1971 as New York Cosmos by record industry tycoons Nesuhi and Ahmet Ertegun (Warner, Elektra/Asylum, & Atlantic labels, all subsidiaries of the vast Warner Communications entertainment empire). The Ertegun brothers, Turkish-American soccer aficionados, immediately hired Englishman Clive Toye, the former London *Daily Express* soccer correspondent and at that time Director of Administration and Information for the North American Soccer League (NASL), as president of the club. Toye was given the upper hand in building the club over the next five years, but he was finally ousted in 1977. The Erteguns, in the meantime, have remained the chief officers and Cosmos' conduit to extensive financial resources in the Warner conglomerate. The club changed its name to Cosmos after the 1976 season.

Cosmos' unique success story in American soccer has been the direct result of superior wealth and the knowledgeable enterprise of Clive Toye, one of the few NASL club presidents with a mastery of international diplomacy in the world soccer community. As one of three NASL expansion clubs in 1971, the New York Cosmos gained a play-off berth in the eight-member league, and the following season won the championship behind the goalscoring of Bermudan striker Randy Horton, the only Cosmos player of even moderate fame before 1975. They reached the play-offs again in 1973, but compiled the NASL's worst record in 1974, when the league was expanded to 15 clubs.

Midway through the 1975 season, with his club struggling in the league once again, Toye managed to sign none other than Pelé to a $2^1/_2$-year contract—after three years of negotiations—and instantly the New York Cosmos and American soccer were thrust into the limelight of world attention. Appearances by Toye's club and its star attraction became a major media event everywhere, but the mediocre quality of the team as a whole did not provide the necessary framework—even with the presence of Pelé—to produce a winning side. The tide began to turn in 1976 with the signing of Giorgio Chinaglia, the Italian international striker from Lazio, and the attacking midfield-striker combination of Pelé and Chinaglia was potent enough to carry the club almost single-handedly to a divisional championship that same year. Toye's heterogeneous assemblage of foreign stars, however, continued to lack cohesion and consistency.

The 1977 season looked more promising, though Pelé was tiring under the burden of his task. The press, meanwhile, speculated wildly on who would be the next international stars to find their way onto Cosmos' payroll. At the end of the 1976-77 European season, Franz Beckenbauer—perhaps the world's most admired active player next to Pelé, and captain of the world champion West Germans—joined the club, and this addition finally laid the groundwork for a good team. Beckenbauer, still in peak form, started as a sweeper, as was his custom, but the eventual importation of Carlos Alberto, captain of the Brazilian world champion winning team of 1970, eventually pushed Beckenbauer into a schemer role in the midfield as Eddie Firmani took over the coaching role from Gordon Bradley. Pelé, Beckenbauer, Carlos Alberto, and Chinaglia forged their way to an easy NASL championship in 1977, and Pelé retired for the second time with a farewell friendly against Santos. Speculation over Cosmos' potential against the great clubs of Europe and South America mounted as Red Star Belgrade's Vladislav Bogicevic and Manchester City's Dennis Tueart were signed in 1978 and another NASL title was won without serious opposition. Holland's Wim Rijsbergen and Johan Neeskens and Brazil's Francisco Marinho came on board in 1979. Sadly, the ultimate quality of this astounding collection of stars was unlikely to be ascertained—much like Colombia's Millonarios in the early 1950s—because Cosmos has had little opportunity to compete against other top level clubs.

Costa Rica

Federación Costarricense de Fútbol
Calle 42
Apartado postal No. 670
San José

Founded: 1921
FIFA: 1921
CONCACAF: 1962

Affiliated clubs: *431;* **registered players:** *12,429 (504 non-amateur);* **national stadium:** *Estadio Nacional de Costa Rica, San José (30,000);* **largest stadium:** *Estadio Saprissa (40,000);* **colors:** *red jerseys, blue shorts;* **season:** *March to october;* **honors:** *Central American and Caribbean Championship (1941, 1946, 1948, 1953, 1955, 1960), Championship of CONCACAF (1961, 1963, 1969), Saprissa, Championship of CONCACAF Club Champions (1970 shared).*

For 30 years, Costa Rica was the runaway powerhouse of Central America, but curiously it was never able to capitalize on its apparent strength and carry that momentum into major international competitions. As the nine-time champion of either the Central American and Caribbean region or CONCACAF (Central America, the Caribbean, and North America), Costa Rica remains five titles ahead of its closest challenger, Mexico. Yet Mexico has consistently represented the region in the World Cup and Olympic Games, and several weaker Central American states have also qualified for the Olympics. Costa Rica's regional success is due in no small part to its political stability, which in turn has enabled clubs and leagues to flourish in a calm atmosphere, and to Mexico's absence in most of its winning competitions.

The Costa Rican governing body has gone through several name changes and reorganizations. It was founded in 1921 as the Liga Nacional de Football, the British influence evident at this early date, and in 1927 it was incorporated into an umbrella sports union called the Federación Deportiva de Costa Rica. It reemerged in 1940, shortly after the Central American and Caribbean Football Confederation was founded, as the Federación Nacional de Fútbol. The present name was adopted around 1961. Costa Rica was a participant in the first regional soccer championships—the tournament of the Central American and Caribbean Games—in 1930 at Havana, and it placed second, defeating Guatemala in its international debut (8-1). Costa Rica also buried Honduras in that series 8-0, and El Salvador 9-2, but it lost to eventual winner, Cuba, by 2-1. In the 1935 games, it took second place again, defeating Guatemala, El Salvador, Cuba, and Honduras, but losing to the winner, Mexico. Costa Rica placed second yet again in the third edition in 1938, bowing only to Mexico in the standings.

Its remarkable winning streak began with the first Championship of the Central American and Caribbean Confederation in 1941, and went on to include the third, fourth, sixth, seventh, ninth, and tenth editions, none of which included Mexico in the field of competititors, and the first and fourth editions of the CONCACAF Championship, which succeeded the earlier series. Much of Costa Rica's opposition in these tournaments came from the five other republics of Central America, and occasionally from Curaçao, Colombia, Venezuela, and Puerto Rico. In the odd 1946 edition of the old championship, held in San José, the entire tournament consisted of Costa Rica playing each of its five opponents once—and winning each time; none of the other teams played one another. In the 1948 tournament, the situation was similar, except that each team played Costa Rica twice—and played no one else. Costa Rica's 1963 and 1969 CONCACAF Championship wins are more significant, because they included genuine regional powers, such as Mexico and Haiti. In its first 40 years in regional competition, Costa Rica won 34, drew 1, and lost 11, beating its long-standing rival El Salvador 10 times.

The Costa Rican league was highly structured by the late 1940s. The league included three divisions and was played in conjunction with a cup competition—called the Great Britain Cup—which is no longer in existence. The present first division consists of eight clubs, several of them from San José, and a total of 360 clubs compete in a system of national and regional leagues. The major clubs are in San José, Alajuela, Heredia, and Cartago, all of which are located within 20 miles of each other. Costa Rica's greatest club is Deportivo Saprissa, which was the losing finalist in the 1978 CONCACAF club championship; Saprissa was also a co-winner of that competition in 1970.

Croatia

Croatian nationals organized a quasi-official national team for a brief two-year period under the German occupation around 1942. The significance of its international results are negligible, since it was impossible to put together a truly representative "national team" during years of such stress, and wartime internationals in Europe are not part of the official record. Croatia played six matches against national teams from the Axis Powers or occupied states: a 4-0 loss in Genoa to the full international team of Italy; three losses to Germany by an aggregate score 2-12; a 6-0 loss to Bulgaria; and a 2-2 draw with Rumania.

cross   Also known as "center."

A pass to the center of the field from either the left or right flank.

crossbar

The horizontal beam that joins the goalposts. The lower edge of the crossbar must be eight feet (2.4 meters) from the ground, and its width and depth cannot exceed five inches (12 cm).

Crossbars were specifically forbidden in the first Laws of The Football Association in 1863. In subsequent years, a tape connecting the posts became prevalent throughout England, especially on public school grounds, but eventually the tapes gave way to crossbars. The Sheffield Association required crossbars by the early 1870s. In 1875, The Football Association changed its rules to permit their use and in 1882, five years after the two associations merged, crossbars became obligatory for F. A. members.

Cruyff, Johan (1947-   )

The most exciting player in Europe during the 1970s, Cruyff's most important asset is his ability to excel at any function on the field. Easily the greatest Dutch player of all time, he was the driving force behind Holland's rise to the top of world soccer after 1970. Cruyff led his original club, Ajax Amsterdam, to three successive European Cup triumphs and his national team to a worldwide reputation as the leading exponent of "total football," though he and Holland failed the ultimate test in the 1974 World Cup final. On the field, he is at once an awesome striker and orchestrator *par excellence,* pushing his forward line while drawing the defense out to help the attack. His skills are complete, but he has been most effective as an attacking midfielder or deep-lying forward.

Cruyff joined Ajax in his native Amsterdam at the age of 10. Seven years later he was a starting player, and at age 18 he made his international debut for Holland against Hungary, scoring a goal from the midfield. Though he twice led the Dutch league in scoring (1967 and 1972), he has set up many more goals than he has converted, and his unique skills led Ajax to the Dutch championship six times. Awarded the Dutch Footballer of the Year award in 1968 and 1969, he was voted European Footballer of the Year a record three

Holland's Johan Cruyff—a player who invariably dominates the ebb and flow of a game—in action for Ajax Amsterdam; 1972.

times (1971, 1973, and 1974), the last coming after his controversial transfer to Barcelona in 1973 for $1.53 million. Despite his rather frail appearance, he has been prone to temperamental antics that have sometimes resulted in ejection, and he has run into disciplinary problems with the Dutch and Spanish associations, as well as his own clubs. In Spain, he was given the nickname *El Flaco* ("The Thin Man"). Shortly before the 1978 World Cup, Cruyff retired from the Dutch national team, and in the 1978 close-season, he left Barcelona having scored 42 goals in his four seasons there. Less than one year later he came out of retirement to play for his long-time friend and former coach, Rinus Michels, with the Los Angeles Aztecs.

Cruzeiro Esporte Clube

Location: *Belo Horizonte, Brazil;* stadium: *Estádio Magalhaes Pinto-Mineirão (110,000);* colors: *blue jerseys, white shorts;* honors: *Copa Libertadores (1976), Minas Gerais champion (1928, 1929, 1930, 1940, 1943, 1944, 1945, 1959, 1960, 1961, 1965, 1966, 1967, 1968, 1969, 1972, 1973, 1974, 1975, 1977.)*

Founded 1921 as Societá Sportiva Palestra Itália by Italian immigrants in Belo Horizonte, one of the major cities in Minas Gerais state north of Rio. The name was taken from the already established Italian-based club of the same name in São Paulo. Palestra Itália entered the second division of the Minas Gerais state championship immediately after its founding, and during the course of its first season, met its great archrival, Atlético Mineiro, for the first time, winning 2-0. In 1925, it was promoted to the first division, and the following year, the Italian "Societá Sportiva" was changed to the Portuguese "Sociedade Esportiva." Anti-Italian sentiment

in 1941 forced the management to drop the original name altogether, and, after naming the club "Ipiranga" for a brief few days, the name Cruzeiro (after the *Cruzeiro do Sul,* or, Southern Cross) was finally chosen.

The Minas Gerais league, Brazil's third most important after Rio de Janeiro and São Paulo, was dominated until the 1930s by América and Atlético, but Palestra won three titles in succession from 1928-30 and made a second breakthrough in the early 1940s. Facing the possibility of relegation in the early 1960s, it was saved from obscurity by a new president, Félicio Brándi, who injected new enthusiasm and money into the club, and in

1973 he purchased the incomparable Tostão from América. Cruzeiro began a phenomenal run of league titles in 1965, and, with Tostão at the fore, defeated Santos in 1966 to win the Brazil Cup. The era of Cruzeiro began in earnest, and the building of the great Mineiro stadium gave the club all it needed to become one of the most powerful in all Brazil.

Despite the loss of Tostão to Vasco da Gama in 1972, Cruzeiro's strength proved to be resilient, and Mineiro titles continued to come in rapid succession. In 1975, the world class winger Jairzinho was signed, and Cruzeiro reached the semi-finals of the Copa Libertadores. The following year, Cruzeiro became the first Brazilian club since Santos to win the Libertadores, defeating Argentina's Ríver Plate in the final, and did so without losing a match. Its record in this series was staggering: 11-10-1-0-42-13-21. Cruzeiro's South American triumph firmly launched provincial soccer in Brazil, and helped to set in motion a whole rethinking of the format of Brazilian competition. In 1977, Cruzeiro reached the final of the Copa Libertadores again, without Jairzinho, but lost to Argentina's Boca Júniors. Cruzeiro's ambitious management announced its intention to join the Rio league in an effort to find stiffer opposition, but in 1978, rather than abandon Minas Gerais completely, it rescued the floundering Rio club São Cristovão from extinction and sent its "B" team to compete under São Cristovão's name.

Crvena Zvezda, Fudbal Klub

Location: *Belgrade, Yugoslavia;* stadium: *Stadion Crvena Zvezda (95,000);* colors: *red and white striped jerseys, white shorts;* honors: *Yugoslav champion (1951, 1953, 1956, 1957, 1959, 1960, 1964, 1968, 1969, 1970, 1973, 1977), Yugoslav cup winner (1948, 1949, 1950, 1958, 1959, 1964, 1968, 1970, 1971).*

Founded 1945 by Yugoslav students in Belgrade only six months after the city's liberation from occupation forces. It was established as the successor to Jugoslavija Belgrade, a popular prewar club that won two Yugoslav championships in 1924-25, and is associated with Belgrade University. Red Star Belgrade is the most popular and successful of all Yugoslav clubs despite its young age. It holds the record for most championships and cups won, and is the proud resident of one of Europe's largest and finest stadiums, nicknamed the "Marakana," which can hold over 100,000 people and features a hotel on the premises.

Red Star's consistency in league and cup competitions has been achieved with many of Yugoslavia's greatest stars. In the 1950s, goalkeeper Vladimir Beara was a spectacular player with both Red Star and the national team; inside right Rajko Mitic was captain of both club and country; and, during the last part of the decade the club was led to several titles by the incomparable Dragoslav Sekularac, perhaps the most gifted player Yugoslavia has ever produced. Bora Kostic on the left wing was another important star of the 1950s with the national team as well as Red Star. In the 1960s, left winger Dragan Džajić became the most popular player in Yugoslav history, and achieved international fame as Europe's finest exponent of a fading art—that of orthodox winger. Red Star has won four league-cup doubles, another Yugoslav record, all between 1959-70. Its first participation in the European Cup (1956-57) resulted in a fine run to the semi-finals, when it bowed out to Italy's Fiorentina by a single goal. In 1957-58, it was narrowly eliminated by Mancester United just hours before United's plane crashed at Munich airport on its return to England from Belgrade. Red Star was not seen in the semi-finals of the European Cup again until 1971, and did not advance that far in the European Cup Winners' Cup until 1974-75. Its manager for several years until the mid-1970s was the resourceful Miljan Miljanic, who studied with Manchester United during his early years and helped to westernize the Red Star organization.

Cuba

Asociación de Fútbol de Cuba
Hotel Habana Libre, L y 23, Vedado
Habana

Founded: 1924
FIFA: 1932
CONCACAF: 1961

Affiliated clubs: *70;* **registered players:** *12,900;* **national stadium:** *Juan Abrantes de la Universidad de Occidente, Havana (18,000);* **largest stadium:** *Estadio Latino-Americano, Havana (55,000);* **colors:** *white jerseys with red trim, dark blue shorts;* **season:** *July to November;* **honors:** *Central American and Caribbean Championship (1930), North American Championship (1947).*

Cuba's traditional love of baseball has subsided in recent years with the elevation of soccer and boxing as the nation's first and second most popular spectator sports. This has been the result of an official government campaign since the revolution of 1959, but soccer has always been very popular on the island; during the 1930s and '40s Cuba was an important regional soccer power. For several years, Cuba shared domination of the area with Mexico, and it was an early organizer of important competitions.

The first Cuban association, the Asociación de Football de la Republica de Cuba, was founded in 1924 and became affiliated with FIFA in 1932. The national championship was launched in 1929, and was first won by Real Iberia Football Club. The league has had a continuous existence ever since. In the 1930s, the dominant club was Deportivo Centro Gallego, which won six league titles from 1931-40. Other winners before World War II were Club Deportivo Español (Santiago de Cuba) and Club Juventud Asturiana (Havana). After the war, Deportivo Puentes Grandes and Deportivo Almedia, as well as Centro Gallego and Juventud Asturiana, won top honors in the amateur national league. In 1949, a professional league with five clubs was introduced; the first winner was Puentes Grandes. Semiprofessionalism had existed sporadically in the 1930s, but the fully professional league of 1949-59 was a complete departure. Ninety amateur clubs remained in the other Cuban competitions, and they continued to be well supported despite the presence of the new league.

Cuba made its international debut in 1930 when it was host to the first Central American and Caribbean Games in Havana. The Cuban team finished the tournament undefeated with wins over Jamaica (in its first inter-national), 3-1, Honduras (twice), Costa Rica, and El Salvador. In 1934, Cuba tried to qualify for the World Cup, but was eliminated by Mexico in three consecutive losses after earlier defeating Haiti twice. Cuba also participated in the second edition of the regional games at San Salvador, but lost three games out of five. In 1938, it qualified for the final rounds of the World Cup in France when Colombia, Costa Rica, Mexico, Surinam, and El Salvador all withdrew from the qualifying round. In France, Cuba had its first encounter with a European team, and drew with Rumania, 3-3, forcing a replay which it won 2-1. Facing Sweden in the second round, Cuba succumbed to a goalscoring bonanza by the Swedish forward Gustav Wetterström, and lost 8-0, ending its first and only World Cup experience.

Rather than join the new Central American and Caribbean Football Confederation, Cuba became one of three members in the new North American Football Confederation (NAFC) that was founded in 1939—the other members were the United States and Mexico—and in 1947, it staged the first Championship of the NAFC in Havana. Cuba lost to Mexico, 3-1, and defeated the USA, 5-2, to take second place. In the second edition in 1949, Cuba placed third, winning only once in four games. It lost to Mexico twice and to the USA, 5-2, and defeated the USA, 6-2. In 1949, Cuba was eliminated from the World Cup qualifying rounds by the USA (1-1 and 2-5). Cuban teams were relatively inactive in international competition during the 1950s while regional governing bodies were in a state of confusion, but they returned in the 1960s and have since entered all World Cup qualifying tournaments.

Under the aegis of INDER, the national institute for Cuban sports, the Asociación de

Fútbol de Cuba has committed itself to establishing Cuba once again as a soccer force in the Caribbean. The national league is now composed of 12 clubs, including the most recent champions of each provincial league (Havana, Oriente, Pinar del Rio, Las Villas, Matanzas, and Camaguey), in addition to an all-star team from each provincial league with players selected from among the clubs that did not win their respective titles. The national league is divided into two sections. The top teams from both sections engage in a play-off to determine the national champion. Havana clubs have dominated the national championship under this format.

Cuba's international opponents in recent years have sometimes reflected the country's directions in international relations. In 1977, for example, Cuba defeated Mozambique "A" in Maputo by the score of 2-0. The first contact between post-1959 Cuba and an American professional team in any sport was Cuba vs. Chicago Sting in March 1978 at the Estadio Marrero in Havana. Cuba won 2-0 (attendance: 15,000).

Cubillas, Teofilo (1949-   )

The explosive Peruvian star, equally potent as an attacking midfielder or striker, whose combination of delicate skills and scintillating shots on goal is one of the wonders of South American soccer. He is without question the most stunning player Peru has ever produced, and in the mid-1970s he ranked at or near the top of great South American stars. Cubillas made his first team debut for Alianza Lima in 1968 at age 18, and one year later he was picked to play for Peru in the World Cup qualifying round. At the 1970 World Cup, he burst onto the world scene with five goals in four games, and contributed much to Peru's fluid attack and unexpected success.

After the World Cup of 1970, he received offers from several dozen clubs in Europe and South America, but the Peruvian government blocked his transfer until 1973, when he joined Switzerland's FC Basel. This association was short-lived, however, and he moved to FC Porto in Portugal, remaining there for four years and delighting Portuguese fans. While at Porto he adopted an attacking midfield role, which he used very effectively with his powerful shot. Urged home to help Peru qualify for the 1978 World Cup, he returned to Alianza in 1977, helping his famous old club win a first division title and scoring 22 goals in 35 games, and produced one of the few genuine world-class performances in the final rounds in Argentina. Having completed his international commitment to Peru's 1978 World Cup venture, he accepted a lucrative offer from the Ft. Lauderdale Strikers in 1979. In 1972, he was elected Latin American Footballer of the Year.

cup competition

A knockout tournament or series, in which the winning side is the only team to remain undefeated, as distinct from a league competition, in which the winning side is the team that has accumulated the most points and stands at the top of a table. In most countries cup competition allows clubs on all levels to play one another, regardless of divisional standing in the league. A lower division club has the opportunity to knock out a first division club, and it is this possibility that gives a cup competition its dramatic appeal. Cup competitions are played throughout the course of the soccer season on alternating dates with the league schedule.

Cup competitions are relatively uncommon in most team sports, except in play-off series, but their tradition in soccer is almost as old as the modern game itself. This was the original form of competition devised by English organizers after the founding of The Football Association in 1863. The first cup competition, The Football Association Challenge Cup (F.A., Cup), was launched in 1871, 17 years before the first English league. As the game spread across Europe in the last decades of the nineteenth century, the knockout format was adopted more readily than league competition, though it gave way gradually to the rising popularity of leagues by World War I. Its prestige in the British Isles, however, has always remained high. In England, the F.A. Cup often draws more enthusiastic support than the First Division of the Football League. In Wales, where a national league does not exist, the Welsh Cup takes on a significance all its own. Central European countries, on the other hand, have seldom given their national cups more than secondary notice, even though the Union of European Football Associations introduced an international competition for all national cup winners, the European Cup Winners' Cup, in 1960. Competition in this tournament rekindled interest in cup competititons in other parts of Europe.

Cup competitions have also been organized in many nations of Africa, and a small number of Asian states have introduced their versions of national cups. In 1975, the African Football Confederation launched the annual African Cup Winners' Cup along the same lines as its European counterpart. In Latin America, national cup competitions as adjuncts to league competitions are unknown, though some levels of league play are conducted on a knockout basis.

Curaçao   See: **Netherlands Antilles**

Cyprus

Cyprus Football Association
Stasinos Street 1, Engomi 114
P.O. Box 1471
Nicosia

Founded: 1934
FIFA: 1948
UEFA: 1962

Affiliated clubs: *42;* **registered players:** *11,850;* **national stadium:** *G.S.P. Nicosia (12,000);* **largest stadium:** *G.S.P.;* **colors:** *blue jerseys, white shorts;* **season:** *October to June;* **honors:** *none.*

One element of Cypriot soccer that is a constant source of encouragement is the Cypriots' devotion to the game. Soccer is the major cultural pastime on the island, and will continue to be so no matter what the outcome of political events. Cypriot clubs are strongly supported, and international matches at both club and national levels are eagerly anticipated. In international competition, Cyprus is at the bottom of the list of European countries, and it is no wonder: unlike Malta, Luxembourg, and Iceland, Cyprus is ethnically divided into two camps—Greek and Turkish—and has not known political stability for decades. The Cypriot game is controlled and dominated by Greeks and Greek-based clubs, a situation that has not changed since the political upheavals of 1974-76.

Soccer was played in Cyprus as early as the 1870s by British soldiers and sailors, but it got its real impetus from the infusion of British troops during World War I. British residents helped to set up the Cyprus Football Association in 1934, and an official Cypriot league and cup competition were introduced in 1934-35. Trust Athletic Club of Nicosia won the double that first season, and proceeded to dominate the cup for several years while relinquishing control of the league title to Apoel Football Club of Nicosia, the island's first power. Trust's soccer section sadly folded before the outbreak of World War II, but the club is still a great name in Cyrpus and sponsors teams in other competitive sports. The popular Limassol club Athletiki Enosis Lemesou (AEL), or Athletic Association of Limassol, won it first Cyprus Cup in 1939 and its first league championship in 1941. This broke Nicosia's unchallenged hold on Cypriot competitions.

After World War II, bouyed yet further by the swarm of foreign troops on the island, Cypriot soccer made important organizational inroads. In 1948, the Cyprus F.A. became affiliated with The Football Association in London, and only three months later secured permission from the English to seek separate membership in FIFA. This was granted without hesitation, and Cyprus entered the mainstream of international soccer, though political independence was still 12 years away. Cyprus's first international took place in 1949 in Tel Aviv against Israel's "B" team and was lost 3-1. Only 11 Cypriot clubs existed at that time; today there are 42. In 1945, EPA F.C. became the first Larnaca club to win either the championship or the cup, and in 1950 Famagusta's major club, Anorthosis F.C., won its first title. Omonia F.C. and Olympiakos F.C., both of Nicosia, came to the fore during the 1960s. Only one champion or cup winner in Cypriot soccer history has been a Turkish-based club. This was the Chetin Kaya Turkish Sports Club of Nicosia, which won a championship in 1950 and a pair of cup competitions in 1952 and 1954. All of the remaining Cypriot champions and cup winners have been Greek.

Since 1949, Cyprus has played on 53 full internationals, winning only five and losing a staggering 46. Its aggregate goal difference of 26-186 is the worst in European soccer. Egypt and Libya account for two of the five victories (3-2 and 2-0, respectively). In the 1966-68 European Football Championship, Cyprus defeated Switzerland on a typically sandy Cypriot field—the score was 2-1—and in 1975, Cyprus defeated Greece in a friendly at Limassol, 2-1, in a match designed to boost Greek Cypriots' morale after the devastation of the Turkish invasion. Cyprus's biggest triumph, however, was a 1-0 shutout of Northern Ireland at Nicosia in a 1973 World Cup qualifying match. The Cypriot goal was scored by center forward Antoniou in the second half. Cyprus has also played to a draw with Greece and Israel. The rest of Cyprus's international opposition has been composed of European countries—15 in all.

In 1962, two years after political independence, Cyprus joined UEFA, and it began to participate in the European Football Championship in 1966-68. Cyprus has placed last in its first round group in each of its three attempts to qualify for the final rounds European championship. The same has held true for Cypriot bids in World Cup qualification rounds, and, though Cyprus is still entirely amateur, little interest has been taken in Olympic competitions. Cypriot clubs have participated in all three European club championships. In the European Cup, Omonia advanced to the second round once in 1972-73 after defeating the Republic of Ireland's Waterford, but in the next round it crashed by an aggregate of 13-0 to Bayern München. In the 1963 European Cup Winners' Cup, Apoel Nicosia recorded the biggest win by a Cypriot club in international competition with a 6-0 thrashing of Norway's Gjøvik Lyn in Nicosia. In the next round, Apoel suffered a 16-1 loss to Sporting Lisbon, which still stands as the highest score in a European Cup Winners' Cup match. In the Fairs/UEFA Cup, Cypriot clubs have no wins whatsoever to their credit.

After the occupation of northeastern Cyprus by Turkey in 1974, an insurgent Turkish Cyprus Football Organization was formed which attempted to obtain official recognition from FIFA. The Greek-based Cyprus F.A. strenuously objected; FIFA concurred and tried to encourage the Turkish organization to affiliate with the Cyprus F.A. Although the Turkish clubs in Cyprus severed relations with the Cyprus F.A. and joined the new Turkish organization, there are so few Turkish clubs on the island that the defections have generally made little impact on Cypriot soccer. Two Greek clubs that have been affected by the partition are Anorthosis and Nea Salamis, which have moved from their home in Famagusta (now behind Turkish lines) to Greek-held Larnaca a few miles down the coast. All the major clubs in Nicosia are still active and thriving in remaining Greek sections of that city. The Cypriot first division now has 16 clubs with a second division to support it (founded 1936-37), and since 1975 there have been no Cypriot clubs competing in the national league of Greece, as had been the custom before. The geographical breakdown of first division clubs (in most years) is: Nicosia (5 clubs), Limassol (4), Larnaca (3), Famagusta (2), and other towns (2). Traditionally, the best Cypriot players are snatched away at a tender age by big clubs in Greece.

Champions

1935	Trust Nicosia	1938	Apoel Nicosia
1936	Apoel Nicosia	1939	Apoel Nicosia
1937	Apoel Nicosia	1940	Apoel Nicosia

1941	AEL Limassol	1960	Anorthosis Famagusta
1942	no competition	1961	Omonia Nicosia
1943	no competition	1962	Anorthosis Famagusta
1944	no competition	1963	Anorthosis Famagusta
1945	EPA Larnaca	1964	no competition
1946	EPA Larnaca	1965	Apoel Nicosia
1947	Apoel Nicosia	1966	Omonia Nicosia
1948	Apoel Nicosia	1967	Olympiakos Nicosia
1949	Apoel Nicosia	1968	AEL Limassol
1950	Anorthosis Famagusta	1969	Olympiakos Nicosia
1951	Chetin Kaya TSC Nicosia	1970	EPA Larnaca
1952	Apoel Nicosia	1971	Olympiakos Nicosia
1953	AEL Limassol	1972	Omonia Nicosia
1954	Pezoporikos Larnaca	1973	Apoel Nicosia
1955	AEL Limassol	1974	Omonia Nicosia
1956	AEL Limassol	1975	Omonia Nicosia
1957	Anorthosis Famagusta	1976	Omonia Nicosia
1958	Anorthosis Famagusta	1977	Omonia Nicosia
1959	no competition	1978	Omonia Nicosia

Cup Winners

1935	Trust Nicosia	1957	no competition
1936	Trust Nicosia	1958	no competition
1937	Apoel Nicosia	1959	no competition
1938	Trust Nicosia	1960	no competition
1939	AEL Limassol	1961	no competition
1940	AEL Limassol	1962	Anorthosis Famagusta
1941	Apoel Nicosia	1963	Apoel Nicosia
1942	no competition	1964	no competition
1943	no competition	1965	Omonia Nicosia
1944	no competition	1966	Apollon Limassol
1945	EPA Larnaca	1967	Apollon Limassol
1946	EPA Larnaca	1968	Apoel Nicosia
1947	Apoel Nicosia	1969	Apoel Nicosia
1948	AEL Limassol	1970	Pezoporikos Larnaca
1949	Anorthosis Famagusta	1971	Anorthosis Famagusta
1950	EPA Larnaca	1972	Omonia Nicosia
1951	Apoel Nicosia	1973	Apoel Nicosia
1952	Chetin Kaya TSC Nicosia	1974	Omonia Nicosia
1953	EPA Larnaca	1975	Anorthosis Famagusta
1954	Chetin Kaya TSC Nicosia	1976	Apoel Nicosia
1955	EPA Larnaca	1977	Olympiakos Nicosia
1956	no competition	1978	Apoel Nicosia

Czechoslovakia

Československý Fotbalový Svaz   Founded: 1901
Na Poříčí 12   FIFA: 1906
Praha 1   UEFA: 1954

Affiliated clubs: *6,776;* **registered players:** *348,000;* **national stadium:** *Strahov, Prague (60,000);* **largest stadium:** *Zbrojovka, Brno (70,000);* **colors:** *red jerseys, white shorts;* **season:** *August to November, March to June;* **honors:** *World Cup runner-up (1934, 1962), Olympic Games runner-up (1920, 1964), European Football Championship winner (1976), Dr. Gëro Cup (1960), Slovan Bratislava, European Cup Winners' Cup (1969), Sparta Prague, Mitropa Cup (1927, 1935), Slavia Prague, Mitropa Cup (1938).*

Czechoslovakia has been a mainstay of European soccer since the turn of the century, and it represents one-third of the great triumvirate of Central European powers that also includes Austria and Hungary. The Czechs have been remarkable in achieving success consistently over the decades, usually peaking at 15-year intervals, and they have many important honors to prove it. Like the Austrians and Hungarians, they were exposed early to the Scottish short passing game, and became masterful practitioners of its derivative, the so-called "Danubian style." Soccer in Bohemia and Moravia have historically been more advanced than the game in Slovakia, but this has changed since the 1960s, when clubs from Bratislava and Trnava began to dominate the league and cup. Prague, however, is still the traditional center of Czech soccer. Slavia and Sparta, the legendary crosstown archrivals from the capital city, have lost their former importance—especially Slavia—but at one time they not only had an iron grip on the Czech league but were unquestionably among the finest clubs in Europe.

Of the three great capital cities of the Austro-Hungarian empire, Prague was the first to produce really competitive teams. Soccer was first played in the Bohemian capital during the 1880s, and the first important club was founded in 1892. This was the soccer section of the famous Sport Klub Slavia, which was originally formed in 1882 as a cyclist and gymnastic club. In 1893, Athletic Club Kral (later AC Sparta) was founded, and the greatest archrivalry in Central Europe was born. The unofficial debut of competitive soccer in Bohemia, however, did not involve either Slavia or Sparta. In December 1893, the

soccer section of Ruderklub Regatta, a sailing club, lost to Viktoria Berlin, 7-0, in Prague. This was the first soccer game played under regular conditions in Austria-Hungary. Representative matches were played between Prague and Vienna routinely after 1896, and internationals between Prague and Berlin selections became common from 1899. England (Amateur) first visited Prague in 1896, and a representative team of the English F.A. defeated a Prague selection, 8-0, in 1899.

The Bohemian Football Association (BFA), whose jurisdiction included Bohemia and Moravia (Slovakia was not then part of Austria-Hungary), was founded in 1901. The BFA became a pioneer in organizing Central European soccer. It joined FIFA in 1906 and in that same year was one of six continental associations that formulated the revised laws of the game with the International Football Association Board, a revision that has remained very influential in twentieth-century soccer. Between 1903-08, Bohemia played in seven full internationals, six against Hungary, and won two and lost four with a goal difference of 15-24. Its only victory was achieved against Hungary in 1907 in Prague (5-3). In 1908, England defeated Bohemia 4-0, in Prague. Bohemia also entered the 1908 Olympic Games, the world's first officially recognized international soccer competition, but withdrew before its opening round match with France "A." The social and political turmoil that was starting to brew in the empire took its toll, and Bohemia never competed in international competition after 1908.

Bohemia's poor results against other national teams were in marked contrast to the success of Bohemian clubs. During the first decade of this century, Slavia and Sparta were probably the strongest clubs on the continent. Slavia especially, with its exciting inside left Jan Košek, put other clubs to shame between 1903-08: 8-2 and 11-0 over First Vienna, 12-2 over FC Nürnberg, 10-1 over Union Berlin, 13-0 over Bayern München, 14-0 over Sturm Graz, and 12-0 over Budapest Torna Club.

The first official Czech league, which was restricted to Bohemian clubs, was finally introduced in 1912. Sparta and Slavia won the first two championships, respectively, and the league was promptly suspended for five years with the outbreak of war in 1914. The birth of the Czechoslovak republic in 1918 signaled a major reorganization, and Slovakian soccer was included for the first time. The league was reintroduced in 1918-19, and the unbroken hegemony of Slavia and Sparta continued. With the exception of Viktoria Zizkov's championship in 1928, the two Prague giants went on to win every league title from 1919-48, a period of 30 years. Sparta won all but one championship from 1919-27 and Slavia won seven of nine between 1929-37.

Though the official Czech governing body had not yet been formed, Czechoslovakia entered the 1920 Olympic Games in Antwerp, but unfortunately its international debut was seriously marred. Czechoslovakia's strength on the playing field was unquestioned as it rolled to sweeping victories over Yugoslavia (7-0), Norway (4-0), and France (4-1) to reach the final against Belgium. As the heavy favorite, Czechoslovakia found itself down by 2-0 in a violent final. After strong objections to Belgium's second goal and the explusion of one of its own players, the Czech team walked off the field, handing the gold medal over to Belgium by forfeit. Olympic authorities ruled that Czechoslovakia was ineligible for a medal of any kind, and a special game was scheduled between Spain and Holland for the silver and bronze.

In 1922, the Československá Asociace Footballova (CAF), Czecholovakia's first governing body, was founded and the CAF was officially admitted to FIFA in place of the BFA in 1923. (The CAF became the Českosloven-ská Obec Sokolska in 1949, and was an adjunct of the State Committee for Physical Culture until an independent body was created in 1968 under the present name.) The CAF sanctioned professionalism almost immediately, and the quality of soccer in Czechoslovakia continued to grow. Czechoslovakia's strength, proven in the 1920 Olympic Games, was primarily the result of welding its many talented players with the "Danubian style" that swept over Central Europe before World War I. In Czechoslovakia, this elegant blend of short passing and slow buildups was imported and taught widely by Scottish coach John Dick, a former Woolwich Arsenal player, and was first demonstrated in all its glory in 1906 by Celtic Glasgow on a visit to Prague.

Another major disappointment in Olympic competition occurred in 1924 when unherald-ed Switzerland eliminated the Czechs in the first round, but in general Czechoslovakia continued to maintain its reputation as one of the most advanced countries in Europe throughout the 1920s. In 1924, Yugoslavia, Poland, Austria, and Hungary were defeated in successive games, and during one stretch of 12 games from 1926-28 not a loss was incurred. While Italy, Austria, and Hungary had the best of Czechoslovakia in the first three editions of the International Cup (1927-35), the Czechs' overall win-draw-loss percentage was very high. Meanwhile, profes-sionalism became so widespread that the CAF declined even to enter a team in the 1928 Olympics, so aside from the Inter-national Cup, the Czechs waited a full ten years to compete in their next major international tournament. The wait, as it turned out, was vindicated.

In the 1934 World Cup, Czechoslovakia emerged as one of Europe's three strongest teams. Its gifted duo of Slavia's Antonin Puc on the wing and Sparta's Oldrich Nejedly at inside was probably the finest left side pair in Europe, and Slavia's František Plánička, the captain, ranked with Spain's Zamora as the safest goalkeeper anywhere. Plánička, indeed, had already become—and still is—the greatest sports idol in his country's history. Playing its "Danubian" game in the World Cup, the Czechs slipped by Rumania and Switzerland, and outwitted cumbersome Germany in the semifinals with relative ease. Nejedly had scored four of Czechoslovakia's eight goals in these three games, but his finishing power was not enough to raise his team above the role of underdog in the final against Italy. In Rome, the Italians had the home advantage and manager Vittorio Pozzo instilled high motiva-tion in his team, yet Italy still managed to achieve only a 1-1 draw at the end of regulation time. Italy's goal was a fluke scored by Raimondo Orsi from an impossible angle, which Plánička has always maintained was his fault. In extra time, Italy's goal by Schiavio proved to be the difference, and Czechoslovakia lost the World Cup final by 2-1.

This may have been the best team Czechoslovakia has ever produced, but four years later in the World Cup, events were to take a different course. Czechoslovakia had cause for concern when it dropped five matches in 1937, two in Prague itself and one each to England and Scotland away from home. In retrospect, the wisdom of taking on such powerful opponents on home ground just before the World Cup was questionable, but there was little doubt that these matches provided combative readiness for what lay ahead.

In the first round of the 1938 World Cup, Czechoslovakia and Holland played to a scoreless draw at regulation time, but the Czechs scored three goals after the restart. In the second round, Plánička's team engaged Brazil at Bordeaux in what became known as "the Battle of Bordeaux," surely one of the most vicious international matches on record. Nejedly, the sublime scoring artist, had his leg broken, Plánička's right arm was also broken, and the stomach of right half Kostalek was badly injured, not to mention several minor injuries to Brazilian players, and at the end of extra time the score remained 1-1. Czechoslovakia's goal came on a penalty by Nejedly, whose leg miraculously held together. The replay, in which the Czechs fielded six new players and Brazil nine, was won by Brazil 2-1 in a plodding anticlimax. The burden of responsibility for "the Battle of Bordeaux" was placed on Brazil, but it was Czechoslovakia who suffered for it with elimination from the tournament and physical decimation. Czechoslovakia played only three more internationsl before the German takeover of Sudetenland in 1938 initiated a seven-year-long hiatus.

During World War II, the Prague-based Czech league continued to operate with Slavia and Sparta's complete domination of league titles, and six Sudentenland clubs competed in the German league. Slovakia, which had been granted political semi-autonomy by the Nazis, organized its own quasi-official national team in 1939, and in the following six years played several internationals. Slovakia lost to Bulgaria 4-1; won, drew, and lost once each to Rumania; and played against Germany five times, losing four, winning one, and accumulating an aggregate goal difference of 1-13.

It took many years for the game in Czechoslovakia to get itself back on its feet after World War II, and the 15-year period from 1945-60 was—relatively speaking—its worst ever. There were especially bleak runs of six straight losses in 1947-48 and similar results in 1952 and 1956 (on a South American tour), and countries that Czechoslovakia had routinely defeated before the war now gave the postwar Czechs serious trouble. Gone were the prewar players trained in the "Danubian style"—Josef Bican and the rest played their last internationals in the late 1940s—and much of Czechoslovakia's international exposure during the Stalinist years was limited to Eastern Europe. None of the Stalinist states, including Czechoslovakia, entered the 1950 World Cup. Occasional signs of encouragement appeared—such as a second place finish in the 1948-53 International Cup and qualification for the 1954 World Cup at the expense of Bulgaria and Rumania—but Austria and of course Hungary were far superior during the 1940s and most of the 1950s. In the 1954 World Cup itself, Czechoslovakia lost to Uruguay 2-0 and Austria 5-0 in the first round.

The reorganization of Czech soccer after the Communist takeover in 1948 spelled the end of Sparta's and Slavia's domination of the league. Even their venerable names were changed for a while to drive the point home further. As in other countries of the Warsaw Pact, an elite army club was founded in Prague called ATK (later to be renamed UDA and still later Dukla), and considerable resources and money were channeled into the club. The army club was given first choice of the best players, and by 1953 it had already won its first championship after only five years in existence. Before the era of Dukla began, however, the province of Slovakia, now a fully recognized part of the Czech soccer scene, produced is first champion, NV Bratislava winner of three league titles from 1949-51. Dukla won championships in 1956 and 1958, and after 1960 won with consistency for several years. In 1960-61, Czechoslovakia's first cup competition was introduced in response to the creation of the European Cup Winners' Cup. Its first winner was Dukla, which won three more cups during the 1960s, but the club that developed the biggest reputation for gallantry in the cup was Slovan (formerly NV) Bratislava. In the meantime, Sparta managed to win a handful of championships and cups, but Slavia, while remaining for the most part in the first division, was out of the running for domestic honors after its last hurrah in 1947.

A comeback for the national team was seen with the winning of the 1955-60 Dr. Gëro Cup (formerly International Cup). Czechoslovakia lost only one in 10 matches during this prolonged series, and that loss was to the still magnificent Magyars back in 1955. In the 1958 World Cup, the Czechs were barely eliminated in the first round after a special play-off with Northern Ireland. Another good Czech team was in the making. Its backbone was in the midfield and defense and featured Dukla's right back Ladislav Novák, captain of club and country; Dukla's attacking left half Josef Masopust, Czechoslovakia's only European Footballer of the Year (1962); and Slovan's stopper Jan Popluhár. Novák's team qualified for the 1962 World Cup in Chile by eliminating Scotland (after a play-off in Brussels) and the Republic of Ireland in qualification rounds, and entered the final rounds with one of the world's most solid defenses. Its style was by now completely transformed from the delicate "Danubian style" to a robust and physical approach, but individually Czech players retained their reputation for good technique. The Czechs' effectiveness in the 1962 World Cup was seen in their first round win over Spain. In other first round matches it was in the Czechoslovakia-Brazil game that Pelé left the competition with a torn thigh muscle—perhaps the most celebrated injury of all time—and Mexico's 3-1 defeat of Czechoslovakia after being down 1-0 in the first minute was probably Mexico's greatest performance ever.

In the 1962 quarter-finals, the Czechs met Hungary for the first time since 1955 and with a characteristic lack of striking power won in spite of Hungary's domination of the game. A tight defense and mistakes by Yugoslavia in the semi-finals put Czechoslovakia through to the final and a rematch of the 1938 "Battle of Bordeaux" against Brazil. The Czechs were decided underdogs, as they had been in most of their previous matches, but, whereas goalkeeper Schroiff had played beyond his capabilities in earlier rounds, he fell apart against Brazil. Czechoslovakia scored first through Masopust, but Amarildo and Zito took advantage of defensive mistakes, scoring brilliantly for Brazil. Brazil's third goal was kicked in by Vavá after Schroiff dropped the ball at his feet. For the second time, Czechoslovakia had gained and lost the World

Cup final, but this time it was to an obviously superior team and it was lost without the flair of prewar stars such as Puc and Nejedly.

In the European Football Championship (formerly the European Nations' Cup), Czechoslovakia dutifully participated in the first edition with its eastern bloc neighbors, and finally bowed out in the semi-finals against the USSR. In the next three editions, however, Czechoslovakia failed to reach the second round. Finally, in 1974-76, the Czechs struck gold and won their greatest victory in history by nosing out West Germany on penalty kicks in the European Football Championship final. The retirement of Masopust, Popluhár, and the other stars of Czechoslovakia's defensive era turned out to be a blessing in disguise. The new Czechoslovakia was entertaining and attractive in its attack, and it boasted a world class goalkeeper, Dukla's Ivo Viktor. Czechoslovakia eliminated England, Portugal, and the USSR to reach the semi-finals, and there won international accolades by defeating the slumping Dutch, 3-1. The final was the most talked-about international in years, because both the world champion West Germans and the Czechs played elegantly and aggressively. In the end, Viktor and consistent penalty kicking won the day and the trophy. It is unfortunate that Czechoslovakia has not been able to build a new golden era on this much praised victory and the 24 consecutive games it played between 1974-76 without a loss, but it failed to qualify for either the 1974 or 1978 World Cups, and after 1976, with the untimely retirement of several European Championship stars, Czechoslovakia receded into the second ranks once again.

At home, the capital city of Prague lost much of its former glory after the 1950s. In 1969, Slovan Bratislava (from Slovakia) became the first Czech club to win a European competition with its fine victory in the European Cup Winners' Cup, and this only eight years after a domestic cup competition was introduced. Slovan's opponent in the final was Barcelona, the runaway favorite. When Slovan won the trophy only a few short months after the Soviet invasion of Czechoslovakia, there was a great outpouring of sentiment and joy, not only in Slovakia but throughout Western Europe as well. After 1967, Slovakian clubs—Slovan Bratislava and Spartak Trnava—won the league title eight times in succession, and the increasingly popular national cup has been won by Slovan and Spartak a total of eight times since 1961.

The first division has in recent years included as many Slovakian clubs as Bohemian (Moravia is perennially a distant third), resulting in the shift of power from Prague to Bratislava (Slovan and Internacional), Trnava (Spartak), and Košice (Lokomotiv and VSS).

Champions

1912	Sparta Prague	1935	Slavia Prague	1958	Dukla Prague
1913	Slavia Prague	1936	Sparta Prague	1959	Inter Bratislava
1914	no competition	1937	Slavia Prague	1960	Spartak Hradec Králové
1915	no competition	1938	Sparta Prague	1961	Dukla Prague
1916	no competition	1939	Sparta Prague	1962	Dukla Prague
1917	no competition	1940	Slavia Prague	1963	Dukla Prague
1918	no competition	1941	Slavia Prague	1964	Dukla Prague
1919	Sparta Prague	1942	Slavia Prague	1965	Sparta Prague
1920	Sparta Prague	1943	Slavia Prague	1966	Dukla Prague
1921	Sparta Prague	1944	Slavia Prague	1967	Sparta Prague
1922	Sparta Prague	1945	no competition	1968	Spartak Trnava
1923	Sparta Prague	1946	Sparta Prauge	1969	Spartak Trnava
1924	Slavia Prague	1947	Slavia Prague	1970	Slovan Bratislava
1925	Sparta Prague	1948	Sparta Prague	1971	Spartak Trnava
1926	Sparta Prague	1949	NV Bratislava	1972	Spartak Trnava
1927	Sparta Prague	1950	NV Bratislava	1973	Spartak Trnava
1928	Viktoria Zizkov	1951	NV Bratislava	1974	Slovan Bratislava
1929	Slavia Prague	1952	Sparta Prague	1975	Slovan Bratislava
1930	Slavia Prague	1953	UDA Prague	1976	Banik Ostrava
1931	Slavia Prague	1954	Sparta Prague	1977	Dukla Prague
1932	Sparta Prague	1955	Slovan Bratislava	1978	Zbrojovka Brno
1933	Slavia Prague	1956	UDA Prague		
1934	Slavia Prague	1957	(unofficial 3-way tie)		

Cup Winners

1961	Dukla Prague	1967	Spartak Trnava	1973	Banik Ostrava
1962	Slovan Bratislava	1968	Slovan Bratislava	1974	Slovan Bratislava
1963	Slovan Bratislava	1969	Dukla Prague	1975	Spartak Trnava
1964	Sparta Prague	1970	TJ Gottwaldov	1976	Sparta Prague
1965	Dukla Prague	1971	Spartak Trnava	1977	Lokomotiv Košice
1966	Dukla Prague	1972	Sparta Prague	1978	Banik Ostrava

D

Dahomey   See: **Benin**

dangerous ball

A ball that has been put in such a position that an attacking player or team may gain a definite advantage by playing it or a ball put up for grabs that appears to give a player or team a scoring opportunity.

dead ball

A ball that is stationary or one that has passed over either the goal line or touch line, and is out of play.

Dean, William "Dixie"   (1907-   )

England's greatest goalscoring center forward, whose record-breaking feats have stood the test of time. Dean was a classic English center forward—strong, aggressive, and, above all, powerful in the air—who scored not so much with nimbleness of feet as with determination and a sense of authority. I 1927-28, he scored 60 goals in league competition for Everton, an English record that still stands today and is not far off from the world record for 42 games in top-level competition. This total, in fact, was achieved in only 39 games due to injury. Dean's English record of 379 league goals has been surpassed only once in subsequent years (by A.G. Rowley mainly in the lower divisions). His total of 349 goals for one club, however, remains unbeaten. In international competition, he scored an incredible 18 goals in 16 appearances for England, including 12 in his first five games, all five played before the age of 21. His 37 career hat tricks are also an English record. Each of these figures would be even higher were it not for his endless battle with injuries. A marked player from his earliest days, his life once hung in the balance after an abdominal injury, and in 1925 he broke his skull in an automobile accident. In the end, he scored more goals with his head than any player in English soccer history.

It is often pointed out that Dean established these records during the enviable period of time when the new offside rule of 1925 threw

Dixie Dean, the greatest English goalscorer of all time, displays his famous leaping header for Everton against Arsenal. Everton vs. Arsenal was England's foremost archrivalry during the 1920s and '30s.

defensive formations into chaos. Indeed, his feats were a primary motivation for Arsenal's development of the W-M system, whose revolutionary "stopper" position eventually halted the rising fortunes of center forwards. Dean, however, was not thwarted by the new W-M, and he soon acquired highly successful skills in marking the ball with his head, setting up his advancing inside forwards, and creating a constant threat to the opposition. Such confrontations were the mainstay of the great Arsenal-Everton rivalry that dominated The Football League for many years.

At age 16, Dean was signed by Tranmere Rovers, across the river from Liverpool, and two years later, in 1925, he moved to Everton, where he achieved lasting fame and popularity. His appearances for England were made from 1927-33, and would have been doubled or tripled had it not been for his injuries. He also lost as many as 100 league appearances through injury. In 1937-38, Everton replaced him with Tommy Lawton, and he moved on to Notts County for one season. In 1939, he went to the Republic of Ireland, where he appeared with Sligo Rovers for half a season, and with Hurst briefly before retiring at the outbreak of the war. He eventually opened a pub in Chester—called "The Dublin Packet"—and when that failed in 1962, along with his health, the Everton management found him a job in Liverpool as a porter. He retired for good in 1972, and in 1976, it was reported that his right leg was amputated in a Liverpool hospital.

deep-lying

The positioning of a player behind his normal area of play or to the rear of his team's formation, e.g., a deep-lying center forward or a deep-lying halfback.

Denmark

Dansk Boldspil-Union
P.H. Lings Alle 4
2100-Copenhagen

Founded: 1889
FIFA: 1904
UEFA: 1954

Affiliated clubs: *1,390;* **registered players:** *208,000;* **national stadium:** *Københavns Idraetspark, Copenhagen (50,000);* **largest stadium:** *Københavns Idraetspark;* **colors:** *red jerseys, white shorts;* **season:** *April to November;* **honors:** *Olympic Games runner-up (1908, 1912, 1960), third place (1948), Scandinavian Championship (1929).*

Little Denmark was a giant in European soccer for many years before the outbreak of World War I, and since that time has fared disproportionately well in international competition against the rising tide of professionalism and nonprofessional state sponsorship in Eastern Europe. It was one of the first countries to learn the game from British travelers, and historically and by temperament has maintained a strong link with the British style of play. Denmark has been one of the last Western European nations to relinquish its amateur status, having done so in 1978, and this has been both its legacy and an impediment to winning higher honors.

Soccer was played in Denmark by British residents in Copehagen and Odense as early as the 1860s. The oldest club, KB (Københavns Boldklub), was founded in 1876 and is still the most famous and successful club in the history of the Danish game. Most clubs that formed during these and subsequent years had both soccer and cricket teams, and some clubs turned to soccer from other sports, such as cricket and gymnastics. In 1889, the Dansk Boldspil-Union (DBU) was founded with a membership of 21 clubs from Copenhagen and five from other regions. Most of Denmark's leading clubs were started between 1893 and 1910 with the common practice of including their year of formation in the name, e.g., Boldklub 93, Boldklub 03, and Boldklub 09.

Although the first official international match on the European continent was Austria vs. Hungary in 1902, a Danish selection is known to have traveled to Athens in 1896 to play a team representing Greece in an exhibition game at the first modern Olympics. The Danes won by an unknown score, and with this match helped to initiate international competition outside the British Isles. Their association with the Olympic Games was to be long and extraordinarily successful. In 1906, a Danish selection won the soccer competition of the unofficial Intermediate Olympic Games in Athens. Denmark's first FIFA-recognized internationals were played at the 1908 Olympics in London, where a full international team defeated the so-called France "A" and France "B" teams 17-1 and 9-0, respectively. This 17-1 score is still a record for any international match. In the 1908 final, Denmark lost to Britain, 2-0, but in so doing, established itself as a frontrunner among soccer nations. Its second place finish was repeated in 1912 at Stockholm when again it lost to Great Britain in the final, this time by 4-2. Despite the fact that Britain did not field its best team in either of these Olympic tournaments, Denmark's 7-0 defeat of Norway and 4-1 defeat of Holland at Stockholm indicated the relatively high level of play in Denmark during this period. It was, in fact, Denmark's greatest era.

Excellent British coaching over the preceding decades had helped to produce an inordinate number of knowledgable players and sophisticated teams. In addition, many Danish players were brought to England to play in the Football League, none more famous than Nils Middleboe, who played for Chelsea from 1913 to 1921 and became its captain. The Middleboe family made a great impact on Danish soccer during its golden era and beyond. Kristian Middleboe, who along with Nils was active in the administration of Danish soccer from the mid-1910's, was Secretary of the DBU for many years during the 1930s and '40s.

After the Olympic Games of 1912, Denmark began its long association with other Scandinavian countries. All but a small handful of its internationals before 1920 were against Sweden and Norway, including 8-0 and 10-0 defeats of Sweden and 8-1, 8-0, and 12-0 wins over Norway. Denmark's clear superiority over other Scandinavian nations

from 1912-30 helped to shape the appearance of its excellent overall international record, and subsequent domination of Finland and Iceland has further enhanced that record. Half of Denmark's 156 international wins have been against Norway, Finland, or Iceland. Other than Sweden, which emerged as the leading Scandinavian power after World War II, Danish teams have maintained their superiority over Scandinavian opponents to this day. The cumulative records to date against Norway (1912-76) are 68-42-9-17-193-87-93; Finland (1925-76), 44-28-6-10-133-51-62; and Iceland (1946-76), 12-10-2-0-51-12-22. It is surprising then to realize that of the three editions of the Scandinavian Championship completed before World War II (1929, 1932, and 1936), Denmark won only the first in 1929. But the Danish team fielded during the 1930s was not up to the usual Danish standard, and in fact, this was probably Denmark's weakest period ever in international competition, coinciding with the rise of Sweden to the mainstream of European soccer: Denmark's record against Sweden is divided neatly into two parts. Its pre-World War II record against Sweden (1913-39) was 30-17-3-10-74-76-37, while its postwar record (1946-75) has been 46-8-11-27-64-109-27.

Although Denmark had been one of the founding members of FIFA in 1904, its continental opponents between the wars were restricted to Germany, Poland, and the Benelux. Denmark did not qualify for the final rounds of the Olympics between 1920 and 1948. At the 1948 games, however, it defied the pundits again by defeating Egypt and the Olympic teams of Italy and Great Britain to gain third place. At the Rome games in 1960, Denmark achieved its most impressive success ever by reaching the final against Yugoslavia after defeating the full international teams of Poland (2-1) and Hungary (2-0). Its appearance in the final and eventual 3-1 loss to the talented Yugoslavs was a moral victory and one of the great moments in Danish sports history. Having qualified for the final rounds of the Olympic Games at Munich in 1972 the Danish team advanced to the semi-final group of eight, which was dominated by four Eastern European powers, and in the major upset of the tournament, managed a 1-1 draw with Poland, the eventual gold medal winner. Denmark's international reputation as spirited amateurs with an old-fashioned will to succeed has been assured for all time with these three postwar Olympic showings.

The World Cup, on the other hand, has eluded Denmark, and Danish teams have failed to qualify on each occasion. This may change in years to come. In 1976, the DBU reversed its previous policy and for the first time allowed Danish professionals under contract to foreign clubs to be selected for the national team. This helped to solve a major problem that has existed for Danish national managers since Juventus attracted Denmark's Olympic forward line of 1948 to Turin (Karl Aage, John Hansen, and Carl Praest), and Danish clubs were first depleted of all their best talent. The DBU's acceptance of professionalism in 1978 was an inevitable outgrowth of this decision.

At the domestic level, Danish clubs have not done well in any of the European competitions, but the DBU's organization of league play has been strong since the turn of the century. In 1903, the four major clubs of Copenhagen (KB, Boldklub 93, Frem, and Akademisk Boldklub) formed a loosely knit group called Staevnet to field a Copenhagen selection and schedule intercity matches.

Staevnet was active into the 1960s when it was still sponsoring Copenhagen's representative team in the Fairs Cup. The first real Danish league, centered in Copenhagen, got under way in 1913. A national league was founded in 1929 with two divisions. A third division was added in 1936. Since the league's founding, KB and Boldklub 03 are the only clubs that have never been relegated. Although clubs from Copenhagen and Odense have historically dominated the Danish game, regional powers from smaller towns, most notably Esbjerg and Aarhus GF, have come into their own at various times. The Danish Cup was launched in 1940 with KB defeating Akademisk (AB) in the final 2-0, but the next cup competition was not held until 1954-55. The success of non-Copenhagen clubs has been a chief characteristic of cup competition.

Meanwhile, Denmark remains one of Europe's best examples of the traditional amateur spirit and northern Europe's greatest exporter of good players.

Champions

1913	Kjøbenhavns Boldklub	1937	Akademisk
1914	Kjøbenhavns Boldklub	1938	Boldklub 03
1915	no competition	1939	Boldklub 93
1916	Boldklub 93	1940	Kjøbenhavns Boldklub
1917	Kjøbenhavns Boldklub	1941	Frem
1918	Kjøbenhavns Boldklub	1942	Boldklub 93
1919	Akademisk	1943	Akademisk
1920	Boldklub 03	1944	Frem
1921	Akademisk	1945	Akademisk
1922	Kjøbenhavns Boldklub	1946	Boldklub 93
1923	Frem	1947	Akademisk
1924	Boldklub 03	1948	Kjøbenhavns Boldklub
1925	Kjøbenhavns Boldklub	1949	Kjøbenhavns Boldklub
1926	Boldklub 03	1950	Kjøbenhavns Boldklub
1927	Boldklub 93	1951	Akademisk
1928	no competition	1952	Akademisk
1929	Boldklub 93	1953	Kjøbenhavns Boldklub
1930	Boldklub 93	1954	Köge BK
1931	Frem	1955	Aarhus GF
1932	Kjøbenhavns Boldklub	1956	Aarhus GF
1933	Frem	1957	Aarhus GF
1934	Boldklub 93	1958	Vejle BK
1935	Boldklub 93	1959	Boldklub 09 Odense
1936	Frem	1960	Aarhus GF

1961	Esbjerg		1970	Boldklub 03
1962	Esbjerg		1971	Vejle BK
1963	Esbjerg		1972	Vejle BK
1964	Boldklub 09 Odense		1973	Hvidovre Copenhagen
1965	Esbjerg		1974	Kjøbenhavns Boldklub
1966	Hvidovre Copenhagen		1975	Köge BK
1967	Akademisk		1976	Boldklub 03
1968	Kjøbenhavns Boldklub		1977	Boldklub 09 Odense
1969	Boldklub 03		1978	Vejle BK

Cup Winners

1940	Kjøbenhavns Boldklub		1967	Randers Freja
1955	Aarhus GF		1968	Randers Freja
1956	Frem		1969	Boldklub 85 Aalborg
1957	Aarhus GF		1970	Boldklub 85 Aalborg
1958	Vejle BK		1971	Boldklub 09 Odense
1959	Vejle BK		1972	Vejle BK
1960	Aarhus GF		1973	Randers Freja
1961	Aarhus GF		1974	Vanlose IF
1962	Boldklub 09 Odense		1975	Vejle BK
1963	Boldklub 13 Odense		1976	Esbjerg
1964	Esbjerg		1977	Vejle BK
1965	Aarhus GF		1978	Frem
1966	Boldklub 85 Aalborg			

---

derby

A British term to indicate the games played by two local rivals. The Manchester derby, for example, refers to those matches played each year between Manchester United and Manchester City.

See also: **rivalries**

De Vecchi, Renzo (1894-1967)

Italy's first great idol of the amateur era and the greatest name in Italian soccer before the golden era of the 1930s. De Vecchi was a left back of great skill, whose level of expertise compared favorably with his counterparts in the more developed European soccer countries of that period. Though he antedated Italy's rise to the front ranks of international competition, his following was so loyal that he became known as *il figlio di dio* ("The Son of God"). He was signed by Milan while still in his early teens, and in 1910, at age 16, made his international debut as a substitute against Hungary. His place in Italy's first team was established against Hungary the following year—Italy's third international— and he went on to make a record 43 appearances before his retirement in 1925, 26 of these (1920-25) as captain. In 1913, Genoa, the dominant Italian club around the turn of the century, enticed him from Milan, and he soon inspired Genoa to a highly successful comeback with national championships in 1915, 1923, and 1924. He was the first non-Scandinavian player to participate in three Olympic competitions (1912, 1920, and 1924), and in his last international in 1925, he led the *azzurri* to their greatest win ever, a 7-0 trouncing of France in Turin.

Didi (1928-   )

(Full name: Valdir Pereira.) The master of the midfield strategy, who probably knew more about his role as an orchestrator and linkman than any South American player before or since. Didi was also world famous as a dead ball artist, especially for his astonishing *fôlha sêca* ("dry leaf"), or banana kick. It was in his former capacity, however, that he achieved lasting fame. Indeed, it was Didi who led the Brazilian team to its stunning World Cup triumph in 1958, a tribute eagerly acknowledged by the players and press alike, and he emerged from this campaign with the tag "world's greatest player." By 1958 he was a skilled veteran, having begun his career 12 years before with Americano of Campos. In 1949, he joined the small Rio club Madureira, and one year later the mighty Fluminense signed him as a deep-lying inside forward. There he developed his skills to the fullest, and in 1950 he entered the record books as part of a Rio selection by scoring the first goal ever converted in the new Maracanã Stadium.

In 1952 he made his international debut for Brazil against Mexico, and eventually accumulated a total of 73 appearances. He played in the 1954 World Cup in Switzerland, and in 1956 moved to Botafogo where he was to play out his career, except for one brief interlude. After his extraordinary impact on the 1958 World Cup, he was signed by Real Madrid, but his star billing raised the ire of Alfredo Di Stefano, who in his own eyes was the world's greatest player. Di Stefano made Didi's life in Madrid uncomfortable and Real loaned him to Valencia. Disappointed, Didi asked to be returned to Botafogo in 1960, and he led his old club to two Rio titles in 1961 and 1962 before retiring.

Didi embarked on a second highly successful career as a coach, first with Sporting Cristal in Lima, Peru, and in 1970 with the talented Peruvian national team that performed so well in the World Cup of that year. In 1971, he took over the helm at Ríver Plate, which, ironically, was Di Stefano's old club, and eventually he coached in Turkey and Brazil.

Dinamo (Moscow), Sportivnoye Obshchestvo

Location: *Moscow, USSR;* **stadium:** *Dinamo Stadium (54,000);* **colors:** *white jerseys, blue shorts with white trim;* **honors:** *Soviet champion (1936 Spring, 1937, 1940, 1945, 1949, 1954, 1955, 1957, 1959, 1963, 1976 Spring), Soviet cup winner (1937, 1953, 1954, 1967, 1970, 1977).*

Founded 1923 as the club of the Soviet Electrical Trades Union. Dinamo Moscow, reorganized in that year, was an outgrowth of the oldest club in Russia, Morozovtsi, founded in 1887. It was originally formed at the Morozov Cotton Mills in Orekhovo Zuyevo, an industrial town about 50 miles east of Moscow, by Clement and Harry Charnock, the British owners of the mill, for their Russian workers. Morozovtsi was the most successful club in the Moscow area when factory leagues sprang up during the 1890s and after the turn of the century when it joined the new Moscow league. In 1906, it was renamed Orekhovo Klub Sport (OKS) and relocated to Moscow. Its name was changed again to Morozovtsi and after the October Revolution it fell under the sponsorship of the Electrical Trades Union. In 1923, already one of the most popular clubs in Moscow, it officially merged with the union and was given its present name. During its early years as a factory team, the Charnock brothers chose the colors of their beloved Blackburn Rovers, blue and white, and the colors have stuck with the club ever since. In more recent years, Dinamo has been linked to the Interior Department and the Soviet secret police, the KGB.

Of Moscow's four great clubs—Dinamo, Torpedo, CSKA, and Spartak—Dinamo is the most famous abroad, and holds the Soviet record for championships. Spartak, however, has the better record in cup victories. From the beginning, Dinamo was groomed to be a flagship of Soviet soccer. When the national league was introduced in 1936, Dinamo was the first winner. Before World War II, it shared honors with Spartak, and immediately after the war it shared them with CSKA. In the 1950s, perhaps its greatest era, the main rival was again Spartak. In 1945, the Soviet Football Federation chose Dinamo to make a goodwill tour of Great Britain and Sweden. In the 1945 season, the club had just won the league with 40 points from 22 games, losing only once, and scored 73 goals to the 13 of its opponents. Dinamo's tour caused a sensation in Britain, drawing curious crowds and splashy headlines, and it was a huge success. Playing in a physically demanding style yet with excellent teamwork, Dinamo drew with Chelsea 3-3, defeated third division Cardiff City 10-0, drew with Glasgow Rangers 2-2, and defeated Arsenal 4-3. Then it defeated Sweden's Norrköping 5-0 before returning home. This, it was generally agreed, was the best foreign club seen in Britain up to that time, and it reintroduced Soviet soccer to the West for the first time since Dinamo's tour of France and Czechoslovakia in the late 1930s. After the 1945 tour, Dinamo and Soviet soccer as a whole disappeared from international sight until 1952. The stars of this postwar Dinamo team were goalscoring center forward Konstantin Beskov, "the bombadier," goalkeeper Alexei "Tiger" Komich, and

Mikhail Semichastny, center half and captain of the club for 14 years. Komich was the first in a long line of outstanding goalkeepers with Dinamo, and it was he who discovered the incomparable Lev Yashin in 1949 playing for Dinamo's ice hockey team.

Yashin joined the team in 1951 and took over the goalkeeper's role from Komich in 1953, just in time to help the club win the Soviet cup, a league-cup double in 1954, and another championship in 1955. Yashin's development into the world's greatest goalkeeper did much to spread the prestige of Dinamo, and on the field contributed significantly to Dinamo's success. In the 1960s, Dinamo was not the powerful force it had been in the 1940s and '50s, but with its new right winger Igor Chislenko and Yashin still in goal, it won another league title in 1963 and a cup in 1967. Dinamo was not exposed to the rigors of European competition, however, until the European Cup Winners' Cup of 1971-72, and it was immediately successful. It eliminated Greece's Olympiakos in the first round, Turkey's Eskisehirspor in the second round, Red Star Belgrade in the quarter-finals, Dynamo East Berlin in the semifinals (on penalty kicks), and reached the final against Glasgow Rangers, only to be beaten 3-2. Dinamo appealed this result to UEFA after Rangers' fans rioted and taunted the Soviet players, but, while the Scottish club received a short ban from European competition, the result was allowed to stand. Dinamo's appearance in this final, a significant milestone in Soviet soccer, was sadly marred by these events. Ironically, this milestone occurred in the season following Yashin's retirement from active play, but appropriately the new coach of Dinamo that year was and continues to be the master himself.

direct free kick

A free kick from which a goal may be scored. It is awarded to the offended side for the following serious infringements: kicking, tripping or throwing, jumping, charging violently, charging from behind other than when obstructed, striking, holding, and pushing. Handling violations also call for a direct free kick.

See also: **free kick**

---

disallow

A ruling by the referee that nullifies an action on the field. A goal may be disallowed when a player on the attacking side commits an infringement before the ball crosses the goal line.

---

disasters and tragedies

April 5, 1902: The West Stand at Ibrox Park, Glasgow, collapsed during an international between England and Scotland. Twenty-five spectators were killed and 517 injured. The game was resumed after 30 minutes and resulted in a 1-1 draw. It was subsequently nullified and stricken from official records.

March 9, 1946: Prior to the start of an English F.A. Cup tie between Bolton Wanderers and Stoke City at Burden Park, Bolton, a containing wall fell open in one section of the stands and the spectators were crushed together. Pandemonium broke out, and hundreds of people were pushed and trampled. Thirty-three died, and over 400 were injured.

May 4, 1949: Torino, the Italian champion, was returning home after a game in Lisbon when its plane crashed into the Superga Basilica near Turin. The entire team, including reserves, the manager, trainer, and coach were killed. Within a matter of days, the team would have realized its fifth consecutive Italian championship. A total of 28 people perished.

June 1950: Eight Uruguayans were reported to have died of heart attacks as a result of Uruguay's World Cup victory.

March 22, 1955: Details have remained sketchy, but during the long postwar civil disturbances in Burma, a Karen batallion in Lower Burma invited a group of rival communist insurgents for a friendly game of soccer. When the latter arrived at the designated venue, the Karen hosts murdered the entire visiting team. Number of dead unknown.

November 6, 1955: At the Stadio San Paolo, Naples, the Roman referee who awarded an equalizing penalty to visitors Bologna was attacked by Napoli fans. The referee was near death when police opened fire with carbines and tear gas. Though the riot worsened, the referee's life was saved. There were 152 casualties, including over 50 police and *carabinieri*.

February 6, 1958: A plane carrying English champion Manchester United home from a European Cup leg in Belgrade crashed at Munich Airport, killing eight players, the club coach, trainer, secretary, and eight journalists. United had just drawn with Red Star Belgrade, 3-3, and advanced to the semi-finals of the competition.

June 30, 1958: Five Brazilians were killed in shootings related to celebrations for Brazil's World Cup victory. Another Brazilian died of a heart attack listening to a radio broadcast of the final.

April 3, 1961: A plane carrying the First Division Chilean team Green Cross to Santiago from a game in Osorno crashed into the side of Las Lastimas mountain. The entire team and all passengers aboard were killed.

September 21, 1962: In Libreville, Gabon, a game between the national sides of Congo-Brazzaville and Gabon was interrupted when a landslide hit the stadium. Nine spectators died and 30 were injured.

May 24, 1964: The worst disaster in the history of recorded sport occured in Lima, Peru, when a riot broke out at the National Stadium during an Olympic qualifying match with Argentina.

With two minutes left in the game, Argentina led 1-0. The Uruguayan referee Pazos disallowed a Peruvian goal. Two Peruvian fans ran onto the field and attacked Pazos, who suspended the game. When hundreds more stormed the field, the security force of 40 strong fired tear gas and some shots into the crowd. Fleeing the police, spectators rushed to the north exit, but they found the gates locked. Because of the stampede, deaths and injuries mounted rapidly. The crowds were finally able to knock down a fence, and

(Top) May 4, 1949: The horrifying remains of the Torino air disaster at Superga that killed the entire Turin team only weeks before it was to win its fifth consecutive Italian championship. (Bottom) Torino at the height of its glory in 1947. (Back row, left to right) Rigamonti, Castigliano, Mazzola, Menti II, Loik, Ferraris II, Bacigalupo; (front row) Grezar, Gabetto, Maroso, Ballarin I. All 11 were Italian internationals; only Ferraris II, dropped from the team in 1948, was not present on the ill-fated flight.

the 45,000 spectators began to pour into the streets. Outside, three buildings and a dozen cars were set on fire by rioters and youth gangs, which had joined the melee. Rioters then marched on the Municipal Palace and the National Palace. At the end of the bleak afternoon, 318 people, including many children, were dead, and over 500 injured.

On May 25, the following day, a national state of emergency was declared, and search and seizure rights were lifted. Students at the university clashed with police, and called for the resignation of the Interior Minister Juan Languasco in protest of police action at the stadium. Rioters attempted to break into the

offices of the Peruvian Sports Federation, and demonstrations near the home of the police commander in charge of stadium security were dispersed by police. On May 26, there were mass funerals for 285 of the dead at Lima's central public cemetery.

June 23, 1968: At River Plate's Estadio Monumental in Buenos Aires, site of the 1978 World Cup final, archrivals River and Boca Juniors had just completed an intense match in their run for the National Championship, and the spectators moved toward the exits. Jubilant fans threw burning paper from an upper tier, causing thousands to flee. Pressing crowds confronted closed gates and began to stampede. Seventy-four died and over 150 were injured.

September 26, 1969: Returning home to La Paz from an out-of-town game, the plane carrying Bolivia's most popular team, The Strongest, crashed in the Andes some 72 miles from the capital. The entire team of 19 players and all club officials were killed.

December 31, 1970: The lower division amateur club Air Liquide of Algeria perished in a plane crash while en route to Spain to play a friendly which had been arranged by club officials as a gesture of gratitude to the players for their loyalty and service to the club.

January 2, 1971: Toward the end of an encounter between Scottish Titans Celtic and Rangers in Glasgow, the crush of spectators leaving Ibrox Park became panic-stricken when a group of Rangers fans attempted to return upon hearing that Rangers had scored an equalizer. A steel barrier collapsed causing 66 deaths and upward of 140 injuries.

September 17, 1971: During a lower division match between Turkish clubs Kayseri and Siwas, a platform collapsed. Forty people were killed and 600 injured.

February 1972: In Cordoba, Argentina, the players of Sportivo Rural assaulted a linesman named Alfredo Basso and kicked him to death.

February 17, 1974: In Cairo, the crowds attempting to enter an important local match broke down barriers, and 49 people were trampled to death. This caused the Egyptian F.A. to publicly discourage fans from attending final round matches of the African Nations' Cup scheduled to begin a few days later in Cairo and Mehalla.

August 19, 1976: Left-wing guerrillas assassinated Retired General Omar Actis, President of the Argentine World Cup Organizing Committee, sending ripples of fear over the fate of the 1978 games. Responsibility for the World Championship was taken over directly by the new military junta of Argentina.

See also: **Fútbol War**

October 31, 1976: When the Gambian referee awarded a penalty kick to Cameroon during a World Cup qualifying match with the Congo in Yaoundé, the Congolese goalkeeper attacked him in a rage. A melee broke out, and the President of Cameroon, who had been watching the game on television, sent in paratroopers by helicopter to quash the riot. Two *camerounais* bystanders died. The Congo subsequently accused Cameroon of staging the affair, pointing to the latter's swift military reaction.

December 6, 1976: In Port-au-Prince, Cuba equalized in a World Cup qualifying match with Haiti, and a Haitian fan set off a firecracker. Assuming they heard gunfire, spectators behind one of the goals panicked and knocked down a soldier whose machine gun went off, killing a small boy and a girl in the crowd. As the panic heightened, two more people were trampled to death, and one man died jumping over a wall. The soldier made his way out of the stadium and committed suicide. Toll: six dead.

June 1977: Fifteen deaths occured in Sao Paulo, Brazil, as a result of "celebrations" (eight crimes, five traffic accidents, two heart attacks) after Corinthians Paulista won the Sao Paulo league title, their first in 23 years.

October 1977: In the Colombian second division, Santa Rosa de Cabal left winger Libardo Zuniga was assigned to replace his team's injured goalkeeper for the remaining minutes of an important league contest with a local rival. Zuniga astonished everyone by making one spectacular save after another, but late in the game an opposing striker became so angry with Zuniga's success that he ran up to him and kicked him in the groin with full force. Zuniga died immediately, and the striker was arrested and charged with murder.

June 1978: Several suicides in Argentina and Brazil, deaths by heart attack in Argentina, Brazil, and Mexico, and a murder in France were reported to be the result of fans watching the 1978 World Cup on television.

Di Stefano Lauthe, Alfredo (1926-   )

Next to Pelé, the name most often mentioned as the greatest player of all time. Di Stefano's ability to perform all tasks on the field exceedingly well elevated him above the stature of other great players. His ball control and shooting skills were peerless in themselves, but aside from this he invariably determined the style and pace of the game, and organized and supported the defense as well as the attack. He was powerfully built, showed endless stamina, stayed at peak condition throughout his career, and rarely, if ever, was caught motionless on the field. As a manager in later years, he attempted to adopt the demands he had earlier placed on himself as a player, but his uncompromising approach was often poorly received and he moved from one coaching job to another.

Born of Italian parents in Argentina, he joined Ríver Plate in 1942 and won a place on its first team two years later. After a one-year loan to Huracán in 1945 (scoring 50 goals in 66 games), he returned to Ríver Plate, and in 1947, replacing the legendary Adolfo Pedernera at center forward, topped the Argentine goalscoring list, and made the first of seven appearances for Argentina. In 1949, he joined the mass movement of South American players to the breakaway Colombian league, and until 1953 was the hero of Millonarios de Bogota, guiding it to two championships during his five-year tenure and collecting four caps from Colombia along the way. In 292 appearances for Millonarios, he scored 259 goals. Santiago Bernabéu, the owner and sage of Real Madrid, got wind of his exploits and signed him in 1953, transforming European soccer with one stroke of the pen. "The Blond Arrow of River Plate" remained with Real until 1964, and achieved everything that could possibly be asked of a player. As a deep-lying center forward and orchestrator for the greatest club-level team ever seen, he scored 405 goals in 624 appearances, raising his cumulative goalscoring figure to over 800 (fourth highest ranking in history), and played on a record six European Cup winning teams. He was European Footballer of the Year twice (1957 and 1959) and led the Spanish league in scoring in 1954 (29), 1956 (24), 1957 (31), 1958 (19), and 1959 (23). Perhaps his most unique accomplishment was scoring 49 goals in European Cup competition alone. He became a naturalized Spaniard and made 31 international appearances for Spain, scoring 23 goals, and finally rounded out his career with a two-year stint at Español (1964-66), scoring 19 goals in 81 games as he approached his fortieth year. As other world class players came and left Real over the years, Di Stefano remained the guiding light and dominant personality, a situation that proved too much for the likes of Didi and Raymond Kopa. His most successful partnerships were with the gifted left wing Francisco Gento and Hungary's immortal inside left Ferenc Puskás, both of whom would have dominated any other team in the world were it not for Di Stefano's presence.

"Di Stef" became manager of Elche for one season (1967-68), and then returned to Argentina to serve as Technical Advisor to Boca Júniors for one year, guiding them to the National Championship as manager in 1970. He did the same for Spain's Valencia in 1971, but his managerial posts in subsequent years (Sporting Lisbon, Castellon, etc.) have not been as successful.

---

distribute

After having gained possession, the act of passing or throwing the ball in an effort to initiate or continue an attacking action. The term is commonly applied to goalkeepers, who "distribute" the ball to a teammate after making a save, or to halfbacks, who may be described as having well developed "distribution" skills.

Djakarta Anniversary Tournament

One of the major competitions for national teams of Southeast Asia. Held each year in the Indonesian capital, it was introduced in 1970 and enjoys the active support of the Indonesian government. The participants have included: Australia, Burma, Indonesia, Korea Republic, Malaysia, and Thailand. Two editions (1973 and '74) were played on a league basis, the rest as a knockout tournament.

Winners

1970	Malaysia		1974	Burma
1971	Burma		1975	Burma
1972	Indonesia		1976	Korea Republic
1973	Burma			

Djibouti

Formerly French Somaliland, then the French Territory of Afars and Issas until its independence in 1977, Djibouti, the last surviving colony in Africa, has a long and active soccer history. The Ligue de Football de la Côte Français des Somalis, with headquarters in the city of Djibouti, became affiliated with the French Football Federation in 1947. Eight clubs and 250 players were registered with the league at that time, and the number has since increased.

In 1948, a Djibouti selection engaged Ethiopia for the first of six internationals over a period of eight years. This was the first international foray by either side. Djibouti lost all six encounters, the first by 5-0. Financial problems may impede official entry into the African soccer community, but independence surely will speed up the process.

Dr. Gëro Cup

Also known as "International Cup," "Nations' Cup," and "Europe Cup.".

Dr. Gëro-Pokal—Coppa D. Gëro/Coppa Internazionale.

The first major European competition between nations outside the United Kingdom, though the less important Scandinavian Championship had been introduced three years earlier. This was, in effect, the Central European championship, involving four of the continent's front ranks power and eventually a fifth. The participants were Austria, Czechoslovakia, Hungary, Italy, and Switzerland. Yugoslavia subsequently entered in the final postwar edition.

Known first as the International Cup, then variously as the Nations' Cup and the Europe Cup, it was organized in 1927 by Hugo Meisl, the guiding force behind Austria's golden era of the 1920s and '30s and the founder of the club counterpart to this series, the Mitropa Cup. There were six editions held between 1927-60. The four prewar competitions spanned a period of two or three years each, but after the war, crowded international schedules stretched the remaining two editions into six-year marathons. All were played on a home and away basis under a league system. The fourth edition (1936-37) was left incomplete after German troops occupied Austria and Sudetenland.

Against a background of postwar political divisions, the fifth edition was not completed until 1953, by which time the Hungarian national team had established its hegemony over all Europe. The series was resumed in 1955, despite further political obstacles, with powerful Yugoslavia added to the list of entrants, and a new name for the competition was adopted in honor of Dr. Josef Gëro, the recently deceased President of the Osterreichischer Fussball-Bund. The final match was not played until January 1960. The Dr. Gëro Cup is noteworthy for its accurate reflection of the relative balances of power on the playing field that existed during the respective editions, and it is interesting also that Austria, Czechoslovakia, Hungary, and Italy each gained about 50 points from the six competitions, most at the expense of little Switzerland, which finished last on each occasion.

Winners

1927-29	Italy
1931-32	Austria
1933-35	Italy
1936-37	not completed
1948-53	Hungary
1955-60	Czechoslovakia

Results
(home legs listed first)

1937-29

Austria—Czechoslovakia	0-1, 0-2
Czechoslovakia—Hungary	1-1, 0-2
Hungary—Italy	0-5, 3-4
Italy—Switzerland	3-2, 3-2
Austria—Hungary	5-1, 3-5
Czechoslovakia—Italy	2-2, 2-4
Hungary—Switzerland	3-1, 5-4
Italy—Austria	0-1, 0-3
Switzerland—Austria	1-3, 0-2
Czechoslovakia—Switzerland	5-0, 4-1

	P	W	D	L	F	A	P
Italy	8	5	1	2	21	15	11
Austria	8	5	0	3	17	10	10
Czechoslovakia	8	4	2	2	17	10	10
Hungary	8	4	1	3	20	23	9
Switzerland	8	0	0	8	11	28	0

1931-32

Austria—Czechoslovakia	2-1, 1-1
Czechoslovakia—Hungary	3-3, 1-2
Hungary—Italy	1-1, 2-3
Italy—Switzerland	3-0, 1-1
Austria—Hungary	0-0, 2-2
Czechoslovakia—Italy	2-1, 2-2
Hungary—Switzerland	6-2, 1-3
Italy—Austria	2-1, 1-2
Switzerland—Austria	1-8, 1-3
Czechoslovakia—Switzerland	7-3, 1-5

	P	W	D	L	F	A	P
Austria	8	4	3	1	19	9	11
Italy	8	3	3	2	14	11	9
Hungary	8	2	4	2	17	15	8
Czechoslovakia	8	2	3	3	18	19	7
Switzerland	8	2	1	5	16	30	5

1933-35

Austria—Czechoslovakia	2-2, 0-0
Czechoslovakia—Hungary	2-2, 0-1
Hungary—Italy	0-1, 2-2
Italy—Switzerland	5-2, 3-0
Austria—Hungary	4-4, 1-3
Czechoslovakia—Italy	2-1, 0-2
Hungary—Switzerland	3-0, 2-6
Italy—Austria	2-4, 2-0
Switzerland—Austria	2-3, 0-3
Czechoslovakia—Switzerland	3-1, 2-2

	P	W	D	L	F	A	P
Italy	8	5	1	2	18	10	11
Austria	8	3	3	2	17	15	9
Hungary	8	3	3	2	17	16	9
Czechoslovakia	8	2	4	2	11	11	8
Switzerland	8	1	1	6	13	24	3

1936-37

Austria—Czechoslovakia	1-1, 1-2
Czechoslovakia—Hungary	5-2, 3-8
Hungary—Italy	—, 0-2
Italy—Switzerland	4-2, 2-2
Austria—Hungary	1-2, 3-5
Czechoslovakia—Italy	0-1, —
Hungary—Switzerland	2-0, 5-1
Italy—Austria	— —
Switzerland—Austria	1-3. 3-4
Czechoslovakia—Switzerland	5-3, 0-4

1948-53

Austria—Czechoslovakia	3-1, 1-3
Czechoslovakia—Hungary	5-2, 1-2

Hungary—Italy				3-0, 3-0
Italy—Switzerland				2-0, 1-1
Austria—Hungary				3-2, 1-6
Czechoslovakia—Italy				2-0, 0-3
Hungary—Switzerland				7-4, 4-2
Italy—Austria				3-1, 0-1
Switzerland—Austria				1-2, 3-3
Czechoslovakia—Switzerland				5-0, 1-1

	P	W	D	L	F	A	P
Hungary	8	5	1	2	27	17	11
Czechoslovakia	8	4	1	3	18	12	9
Austria	8	4	1	3	15	19	9
Italy	8	3	2	3	10	9	8
Switzerland	8	0	3	5	12	25	3

1955-60

Austria—Czechoslovakia		2-2, 2-3
Czechoslovakia—Hungary		1-3, 4-2
Hungary—Italy		2-0, 1-1
Italy—Switzerland		3-0, 1-1
Switzerland—Yugoslavia		1-5, 0-0
Yugoslavia—Austria		1-1, 1-2
Austria—Hungary		2-2, 1-6
Czechoslovakia—Italy		2-1, 1-1
Hungary—Switzerland		8-0, 5-4
Italy—Yugoslavia		0-4, 1-6
Austria—Italy		3-2, 1-2
Switzerland—Austria		2-3, 0-4
Yugoslavia—Czechoslovakia		1-2, 0-1
Czechoslovakia—Switzerland		3-2, 6-1
Hungary—Yugoslavia		2-2, 3-1

	P	W	D	L	F	A	P
Czechoslovakia	10	7	2	1	25	15	16
Hungary	10	6	3	1	34	16	15
Austria	10	4	3	3	21	21	11
Yugoslavia	10	3	3	4	21	13	9
Italy	10	2	3	5	12	21	7
Switzerland	10	0	2	8	11	38	2

Domingos da Guia (1912-)

(Full name: Domingos Antônio da Guia.) A classic center back, probably the most accomplished ever produced in Brazil, whose particular expertise was marking the man with the ball—a pure defender. Djalma and Nilton Santos must have learned much from this extraordinary player, whose career was long and complex. One of his lasting contributions to Brazilian soccer was his role as the vanguard of Brazilian professionalism, which resulted from his highly competitive nature and frequent moves from one club to another to secure better contracts.

Born in the Rio suburb of Bangu, he started his career with Bangu AC in 1929, and two years later he moved to Rio's Vasco da Gama, one of the great clubs of the day, and this led to his first international appearance against Uruguay in 1932. This performance in Montevideo in turn led to his transfer to Nacional Montevideo one year later, where he acquired the nickname *El divino mestre* ("The Divine Master"), referring to his defensive abilities. In a financially motivated series of transfers he rejoined Vasco for one season, played for Boca Juniors in Buenos Aires for one year, and signed with Rio's Flamengo in 1935. He was the mainstay of Flamengo's four Rio championships from 1939-44, and he starred for Brazil in the 1938 World Cup, though his histrionic duel with Italy's Silvio Piola ultimately led to Brazil's downfall in the semifinals. In 1944 he moved to Corinthians Paulista for a spell, and spent his last years of active play with his original club, Bangu. Two years after his 1948 retirement, his son, Ademir, electrified the world with his performances in the fourth World Cup.

Dominican Republic

Federación Dominicana de Fútbol
Apartado de Correos No. 1953
Santo Domingo

Founded: 1953
FIFA: 1958
CONCACAF: 1964

Affiliated clubs: *72;* **registered players:** *5,531;* **national stadium:** *Estadio Olimpico-Juan Pablo Duarte, Santo Domingo (22,000);* **largest stadium:** *Estadio Olimpico;* **colors:** *navy blue jerseys, white shorts;* **seasons:** *March to September;* **honors:** *none.*

The Dominican Republic, an independent baseball-mad nation under various foreign influences, including American, since the early nineteenth century, has been, historically, the least active Spanish-speaking state in the Central America-Caribbean region, and has fallen behind the level of play in former British and Dutch colonies of the Caribbean too. Participation in CONCACAF tournaments is rare, and it was not until the qualification rounds of the 1978 edition that the Dominican Republic tried its luck in the World Cup, losing to Haiti in the first round by 3-0 in both home and away legs. Although the Federación Dominicana de Fútbol was not founded until 1953, the now defunct Central American and Caribbean Confederation accepted "Santo Domingo's" membership after World War II; as it happened, Santo Domingo never participated in the confederations' tournaments.

Twelve senior clubs participate in the Dominican first division. Most of the major clubs hail from Santo Domingo and Santiago, but San Pedro de Marcoris, La Vega, Moca, Salcedo, and San Cristobal are also centers of much soccer activity. There is an annual cup competition, but no regional leagues.

double

In most countries, the winning of the first division championship and the national cup competition in the same year. The term may also be used to indicate the winning of any two major competitions in the same year. A "treble" is the winning of three such honors.

dribble

The act of moving the ball protectively and skillfully with one's feet, usually to advance the ball up or down the field or to avoid being tackled.

The art of dribbling has flourished and withered at different times throughout the history of the game. Its classical era was surely the 1870s, when English clubs, led by Wanderers F.C. and its influential captain, C.W. Alcock, put their emphasis staunchly on attack and fielded a seven-man forward line. Dribbling had been primarily a product of the English public schools, from which most of the contemporary players of the day came. Holding onto the ball for as long as possible was encouraged and became a measure of one's skill as a player. Little attempt was made at passing. With only three defenders in Alcock's basic formation, an enterprising foward could often be seen dribbling the ball with cunning down the length of the field to openly challenge a sparse defense. Among the greatest dribblers were the legendary Robert Vidal, of Westminister and Oxford, and William Kenyon-Slaney, of Eton and Household Brigade. Inevitably, the preoccupations of dribbling gave way to the virtues of the short pass, which was to become a mainstay of all tactical innovations to come. The prime movers away from the dribbling game were Queen's Park Glasgow, Royal Engineers, and Sheffield, and by the mid-1870s nearly all the important teams had followed their lead.

Since then there have been many skillful dribblers from all parts of the world, but with the adoption of more and more defensive tactics, there are probably fewer now than ever before. The 1930s, '40s, and '50s are seen by many observers as a second high plateau in the history of dribbling, as exemplified by the legendary Sir Stanley Matthews. But the dribbling game of halcyon days will never be duplicated. Its closest equivalent was seen in the freewheeling play of Brazil between the mid-1930s and mid-1950s, prior to its adoption of modern tactical innovations, and only in South America has a consistent reverence for the art of dribbling been maintained.

See also: **offside**

drop ball   Also known as "bouncing."

The referee's placing of the ball back in play after he has stopped the game without penalizing one side or the other. The referee drops the ball on the ground between two players, one representative from either side, who are positioned face-to-face at a designated spot on the field. The ball must bounce on the ground at least once before being played.

The Laws of the Game require a drop ball for specific infringements: a substitute entering the field before securing permission from the referee; intentional tripping or striking another player while both players are outside the touch line or goal line; during a friendly, when the crossbar is broken or displaced causing the game to be temporarily suspended; an offense committed before a previously dropped ball has touched the ground; interference of a shot on goal by an outside agent, other than at a penalty kick; and, restarting the game after temporary suspension for any reason not mentioned in the Laws.

Dynamo Moscow   See: **Dinamo (Moscow), Sportivnoye Obshchestvo**

Džajić, Dragan (1946-)

Yugoslavia's outstanding orthodox left winger, perhaps the world's best following the retirement of Francisco Gento. He made a record number of appearances for Yugoslavia (over 80), and found unending popularity with his fans. Among all the great players Yugoslavia has produced, he ranks with Sekularac as the greatest. Džajić made his debut for Red Star Belgrade in 1961, and was Yugoslav Footballer of the Year in 1963, 1966, 1968, 1969, 1970, and 1972. In 1965, at age 18, he took over the left wing spot for Yugoslavia, and eventually came to personify that now out-of-favor role, not only in Yugoslavia but throughout Europe. His 25 international goals indicate a keen sense for scoring—he led the Yugoslav league in goals three times—and also his ability to create goals for others. In 1975, he secured permission from Red Star for a transfer to the West after 554 club appearances and 284 goals. The unlikely Corsican club Bastia attracted his attention, and he spent two seasons there helping to bring Corsican soccer into the French mainstream. He returned to Red Star for one season and finally retired in 1978, the greatest soccer hero in Yugoslav history. Nicknamed "Magic Dragan," he was a superb dribbler, a master technician, and ultimately helped to revitalize the left wing position in an era of three and four player front lines.

East African Challenge Cup

An irregular series between the national teams of Ethiopia, Kenya, Sudan, and Tanzania. Uganda and Somalia have participated on occasion. It was introduced in 1966 as the Friendship Cup Competition of East Africa, and is organized by the East African Football Confederation, an unofficial body whose function is to promote soccer in the region.

East and Central African Challenge Cup

A biannual series between the national teams of Kenya, Malawi, Tanzania, Uganda, Zaire, and Zambia. Zanzibar has sometimes entered its own national team, depending on the state of its fluctuating autonomy with Tanzania, and Somalia has also entered irregularly. It is organized by the unofficial East and Central African Football Federation. Zaire, Kenya, and Zambia have dominated the competition.

East and Central African Club Cup

An annual competition for the leading clubs of Kenya, Malawi, Somalia, Tanzania, Uganda, Zambia, and (irregularly) Zanzibar. It was introduced in 1974 by the unofficial East and Central African Football Federation, whose biggest member, Zaire, has not yet participated. Simba Club (Tanzania), Young Africans (Tanzania), and Luo Union (Kenya) won the first three editions.

The East and Central African Football Federation

A loose federation of countries—Kenya, Tanzania, Zanzibar, Uganda, Somalia, Zambia, and Malawi—not officially sanctioned by FIFA, but encouraged by the African Football Confederation, much like its West African counterpart. The Federation organizes the biannual East and Central African Challenge Cup between national sides and the annual East and Central African Club Cup.

East Germany   See: German Democratic Republic

Ecuador

Asociación Ecuatoriana de Fútbol
Calle Chimborazo 206, 2° Piso, Of. 4
Casilla 7447
Guayaquil

Founded: 1925
FIFA: 1926
CONMEBOL: 1930

Affiliated clubs: *170;* registered players: *5,750 (250 professional, 1,500 non-amateur);* national stadium: *Estadio Modelo Guayaquil (48,772);* largest stadium: *Estadio Modelo Guayaquil;* colors: *yellow jerseys with blue fringe, blue shorts;* season: *May to December;* honors: *none.*

This small Andean republic—with South America's highest population density—has struggled long and hard to make a dent in international competition, but, with the exception of fledgling Venezuela, it remains the least successful country in the South American group. The chief interest of Ecuadorean soccer is the intense rivalry between the two great cities of the country, Guayaquil, the commercial and industrial center, and Quito, the capital. These two very different cities provide the backdrop for a classic confrontation of lifestyles, and it is on the soccer field that this cultural clash is acted out. If national championships were used as a measuring stick, Quito would now have a slight edge.

Soccer was introduced in Ecuador via the port city of Guayaquil after the turn of the century, and some form of organized competition emerged before World War I. The country's exposure to foreign players during that war increased local interest considerably, and in 1922 a league was organized in Guayaquil. This ran for seven seasons before it was discontinued, and featured several sporting clubs with an international membership. Rácing Club won the first and third editions, and Club Sport General Cordova won a total of three titles between 1925-28. The other winners were Club Sport Oriente and Sporting Packard.

An umbrella sports association, the Federación Deportiva Guayaquil, was founded in 1925 to control soccer as well as all other sports, and it was admitted to FIFA in 1926. Its name was changed to the Federación Deportiva Nacional del Ecuador several years later when Quito and other cities began to participate actively in organized competitions. Local associations were formed in major towns, and a national soccer championship was introduced for representative teams of each locale. A national team was organized in 1938 to join other Ecuadorean athletes taking part in the first Bolivarian Games at Barranquilla, Colombia. It was here that Ecuador made its international debut against Peru, losing 9-1, and in five games won only once—over Colombia 2-1—capturing third place in a field of five.

The next year Ecuador entered the South American Championship for the first time, and for four consecutive editions of this competition (1939-45) Ecuador compiled the following record: 20-0-1-19-17-87-1. Its one draw was with Bolivia in 1945. In 1947, the South American Championship was held in Guayaquil, and Ecuador rallied to the occasion by placing sixth in a field of eight teams,

though once again it failed to win a game. Three draws in 1947 saved the team from a last place tie with Bolivia and Colombia. In 1949, the national team finally won its first South American Championship match—over Colombia 4-1—but it did not win another until the 1959 edition that was held in Guayaquil. It won a third match in 1963, and that has been the total of Ecuadorean victories in South American Championship competition.

A separate governing body for soccer, the present Asociación Ecuatoriana de Fútbol, was created in 1957, and a national championship was introduced with no restrictions on professionalism. A two-year hiatus in league competition followed in 1958-59, but in the 20 years since then it has flourished, and a second division has been added. For many decades, the playing season in mountainous regions ran from November to July and in the lowlands from May to December, but the national league eventually unified the schedule to conform to the summer season prevalent throughout South America.

Ecuador has never qualified for the final rounds of the World Cup or Olympic Games, and Ecuadorean clubs have not achieved anything of note in the Copa Libertadores. Many of the best players find their way to Brazil, Uruguay, and Argentina, making it difficult for Ecuadorean clubs to do well in international competition. The Campeonato Ecuatoriano, as the first division is called, includes 15 clubs. Aside from Guayaquil and Quito, the leading clubs hail from Portoviejo, Manta, Ambato, and Cuenca. The biggest rivalry in Quito is between Nacional and Liga Deportiva Universitaria; in Guayaquil it is between Emelec and Barcelona. Other strong clubs from the capital are Aucas and Deportivo Quito. Emelec, the team of the state electrical company, is the only club of any wealth.

The first division season is divided into three phases. All clubs compete in the *apertura*, or first phase, on a home and away basis. The top finishers from the *apertura* make up Division A of the *finalizacion*, or second phase, and the bottom clubs from the *apertura* go into Division B of the *finalizacion*. Points are accumulated through both phases, and the top two clubs of Division A enter the Copa Libertadores. The winner of Division A is the national champion, and the bottom clubs from Division B are relegated.

Champions

1957	Emelec	1968	Deportivo Quito
1958	no competition	1969	Liga Deportiva Universitaria
1959	no competition	1970	Barcelona
1960	Emelec	1971	Barcelona
1961	Everest	1972	Emelec
1962	Everest	1973	Liga Deportiva Universitaria
1963	Barcelona	1974	Nacional
1964	Deportivo Quito	1975	Liga Deportiva Universitaria
1965	Emelec	1976	Nacional
1966	Barcelona	1977	Nacional
1967	Nacional		

Egypt, Arab Republic

All Ettihad el Masri li Korat el Kadam
(Egyptian Football Association)
5, Shareh Gabalaya, Guezira
Al Borg Post Office
Cairo

Founded: 1921
FIFA: 1923
CAF: 1956

Affiliated clubs: *168;* registered players: *8,000;* national stadium: *Nasser Stadium, Cairo (100,000);* largest stadium: *Nasser Stadium;* colors: *red jerseys, white shorts;* season: *September to June;* honors: *African Nations' Cup winner (1957, 1959), runner-up (1962), Ismaili, African Cup of Champion Clubs (1969).*

Egypt was the undisputed leader of soccer in the Arab world and Africa for more than 40 years, but of late it has been strongly challenged by Morocco and Tunisia on the one hand and several black African states on the other. On the African continent, Egypt has had more experience in organized competition and administration than any other country. It has been the home of the African Football Confederation for over 20 years, and the confederation is still influenced by Egyptian personnel despite the rapid growth of the game south of the Sahara. Although soccer first reached Africa via the South African colonies, and Ghana was the pioneer among black African states, soccer flourished in Egypt as nowhere else on the continent. Egypt was the only African country to be represented in major international tournaments before World War II, and as early as the 1920s three European countries—Hungary, Holland, and Portugal—fell to Egyptian teams on European soil. Cairo's Nasser Stadium, where crowds of 80-100,000 fans are

routine for big games, was the first facility in Africa to hold 100,000 people. The Egyptian game, generally regarded as the most advanced in Africa, features a more sophisticated style and technique than elsewhere on the continent, and at its best sometimes resembles the deliberate short passing game of northern Europe.

Soccer was played in Egypt for the first time by the British around 1895, some 30 years after its introduction to South Africa and about 15 years after it was played by colonists on the Gold Coast. The earliest clubs were formed in Cairo in 1903 by British players, and a handful of Egyptian clubs, such as the famous Al-Ahly, emerged before World War I. The first major competition, the Sultan's Cup, named for Sultan (later to be King) Fouad, was introduced in 1916 for clubs of the Cairo and Alexandria districts. It was contested annually under a knockout format until 1938, and during the First World War was won by military teams exclusively—G.H.Q. Signals of Ismailia, M.G. Corps Base Depot of Cairo, Infantry Base

Depot of Kantara, and 2nd Bn Sherwood Foresters of Alexandria. During World War I, the enormous influx of British military and government personnel heightened soccer activity, and organizational efforts were seen on every level of the game. Without the benefit of a properly authorized national association, an Egyptian national team entered the 1920 Olympics in Antwerp, losing to Italy's full international team in the first round by a mere 2-1, an astonishing entry into world competition.

The Egyptian Football Association (EFA) was founded in Cairo in 1921 under the patronage of the king, and was admitted to FIFA in 1923, the first member of the world body from the African-Asian bloc. A second cup competition, Farouk's Cup, named for the then Crown Prince Farouk, was introduced in 1921-22 for clubs and was contested separately from the Sultan's Cup. With the growing popularity of both these competitions, the great clubs of early Egyptian soccer emerged. Between the world wars, Cairo International Sporting Club won Farouk's Cup five times, including the first edition in 1922, and the Sultan's Cup twice. National Sporting Club, Cairo, won Farouk's Cup and the Sultan's Cup eight times each. Other multiple winners were Arsenal S.C., Union Recreation Club Alexandria, Egyptian Olympic Club Alexandria, and Egyptian Athletic Club Port Said. In 1925-26, the EFA launched an annual competition called King Fouad's Cup, for representative teams of each district association. With two exceptions, Canal District in 1936 and 1938, this trophy was shared by Cairo and Alexandria continuously.

In 1924, Egypt entered the Olympic Games again, and in the first round upset Hungary 3-0 in one of the great upsets in Olympic history. Egyptian glory was short-lived, however, and in the second round the stronger and more cohesive Swedish team knocked Egypt out of the tournament with a 5-0 thrashing. Egypt returned in 1928 with more surprises for the confident Europeans, defeating Turkey in the first round 7-1, and Portugal in the second round 2-1. This brought Egypt's record against European opposition from 1920-28 to four wins and one defeat. In the 1928 semi-finals, mighty Argentina buried Egypt 6-0, to put it all in perspective, and in the third place game a vastly improved Italy dealt demoralized Egypt its worst defeat ever in international competition, 11-3. Egypt went on to enter Olympic qualification rounds a total of 10

times through 1976 (the third highest number of any country in the world), and participated in the final rounds eight times (second only to France). It qualified in 1936, 1948, 1952, 1960, and 1964, failing to win any medals by achieving one or two more fine victories such as those over Chile in 1952 and South Korea and Ghana in 1964. Egypt's 5-1 defeat in Ghana in 1964 earned a spot in the semi-finals for the first time since 1928—in the company of three full national teams from Eastern Europe—and an eventual fourth place finish, its highest in world competition.

Egypt made its first and only appearance in the final rounds of the World Cup in 1934 having eliminated Palestine—in that protectorate's first internationals—in the qualification round. Hungary avenged its 1924 Olympic loss by defeating Egypt 4-2 in the first round, a win made all the more satisfying since Egypt had also held the frustrated Magyars to a scoreless draw in Cairo in 1932. In addition to its Olympic and World Cup games during the 1920s and '30s, Egypt bravely took on several other European opponents in friendlies, usually just before and after Olympic tournaments. These included a 2-1 win over Holland in Rotterdam (1928), a 3-1 loss to Austria in Vienna (1924), a 1-1 draw with Luxembourg in Esch (1928), and a 5-0 loss to Sweden in Stockholm (1924).

Farouk's Cup and King Fouad's Cup were still played during World War II, but their names were changed to the Cup of Egypt and Districts Cup in 1950-51, and the cups were upstaged in 1948-49 with the introduction of the national league. National S.C. Cairo won the first two league titles, but many of the old prewar names began to fade. Two of the greatest clubs in Egyptian soccer then emerged: Ismailia S.C., from the town of the same name near the Suez Canal, and Al-Zamalek, which was founded in 1928 in Cairo and became the great crosstown rival of the venerable Al-Ahly. In 1949, Egypt participated in the Friendship Cup with national teams of Turkey, Greece, and Italy ("B"), and in 1950-53 and 1953-57 Egypt competed unsuccessfully for the Mediterranean Cup, successor to the Friendship Cup. Egypt also became a regular participant in the soccer tournament of the all-amateur Mediterranean Games, held every four years from 1951, and in 1955 walked away with the trophy, its first outright victory in international competition.

In 1956, Egypt was one of the three founding members of the African Football

Confederation (CAF) in Khartoum, and, after 35 years as the most successful representative of the non-Western world in international competition, Egyptian soccer changed its focus radically. In 1957, the CAF introduced the African Nations' Cup, and this was to be Egypt's great international showcase in the years to come. Its record in this series has been far and away the best in Africa, with continued success from the beginning. Egypt won the first two editions in 1957 and 1959, placed second in the third edition in 1962, third in the fourth edition in 1963, and would surely have done well throughout the 1960s had not the national team been almost dormant from 1965-69 due to Arab-Israeli conflicts. Despite the disorganization of this troublesome period, the national teams managed to qualify for the 1970 African Nations' Cup, and gained another third place finish in a powerful field. In 1974, when the final rounds were held in Egypt for the second time, Egypt again placed third, and two years later placed fourth.

The national league was suspended from 1965-72, but its popularity continued to grow by leaps and bounds in the years that followed. Other than Al-Ahly and Al-Zamalek, the most successful club in Egyptian soccer in recent years has been Al-Mehalla, from the new texile manufacturing city of the same name 100 miles north of Cairo. Al-Mehalla represents new organizational developments in Egyptian soccer, not only because it has created a trend in industrial sponsorship of clubs, but in its modern techniques on the field. Al-Ahly, under the management of Hungarian great Nandor Hidegkuti, has also been influential in bringing European techniques to the Egyptian league. Al-Ahly's winning of the national championships of 1975 and 1976 was carried out with exceptional flair. Indeed, the most popular player in Egyptian soccer today is Ahly's dynamic striker Abdul Azeez Abdul Shafie, better known as "Zeezoo."

In African competition, Egyptian clubs have been dominated by the great clubs of Ghana, Zaire, Guinea, and Cameroon, but in 1969 Al-Ismailia won the Africa Champions' Cup, and Al-Mehalla and Al-Zamalek have reached the semi-finals of the Champions' Cup and the African Cup Winners' Cup.

The Egyptian league is divided into two divisions with a "Super League" (first division) of 15 clubs. in 1975-76, the EFA experimented with a first division of two groups with 12 clubs each, but the 15-club system was reestablished after only one season.

Egypt's desire to keep in contact with European opposition has diminished since it joined forces with other African states. Since World War II, the national team has played Austria nine times (half of these at less than "A" level), winning four and losing four; Yugoslavia five times, the first in 1952, losing three and drawing two; Czechoslovakia once, a loss in 1957; Bulgaria four times, winning once and losing twice; Rumania once, a loss; Denmark once, a loss; France twice, a loss and a draw; and Greece eight times with three wins and three losses. Most of these matches were in connection with the Olympic Games.

Eire   See: Ireland, Republic of

El Salvador

Federación Salvadoreña de Fútbol
Colonia La Esperanza, pasaje 1, casa 130
Apartado Postal 1029
San Salvador

Founded: 1935
FIFA: 1938
CONCACAF: 1962

Affiliated clubs: *592;* registered players: *12,806 (175 professional, 1,344 non-amateur);* national stadium: *Estadio Nacional de Flor Blanca, San Salvador (30,000);* largest stadium: *Estadio Nacional de Flor Blanca;* colors: *white jerseys with blue trim, white shorts;* season: *January to November;* honors: *Central American and Caribbean Championship (1943), Alianza, Championship of CONCACAF Club Champions (1967).*

Tiny, populous El Salvador has broken through to the front ranks of Central American soccer on three occasions but over the long run has been forced to take a secondary position to Costa Rica, the major Central American power, and to Mexico and the Caribbean states in regional competition. Its notoriety, however, is dominated by the tragic "Fútbol War" it waged with neighboring Honduras in 1969, and it is unlikely that that indelible legacy will be worn down for many years to come. The notoriety of that war has led to a reputation of "banana republic" fanaticism on the playing field, though Honduras must share this burden as well. Actually, the reputation is unfair; peculiar sociopolitical circumstances rather than Salvadoran and Honduran chauvinism in the stands led to the outburst.

The game began to establish itself in San Salvador sometime after World War I. The Federación Salvadoreña de Fútbol was founded in 1935, and became affiliated with FIFA three years later. Following World War II, the association's name was changed to Federación Nacional de Football de El Salvador, and eventually it was reconstituted as the present FSF. The governing body has always maintained membership in whatever regional confederation existed at the time: the Confederación Panamericana de Football, the Confederación Centroamericana y del Caribe de Fútbol, and CONCACAF. Shortly after the founding of the association, a national league consisting of two divisions was formed, and a national cup competition was introduced in 1950. A third division and various regional leagues were organized subsequently. El Salvador is the only country in Central America and the only CONCACAF member outside North America to support full professionalism. It also boasts the largest number of non-amateurs of any CONCACAF member. The leading clubs in recent years have been Alianza, Aguila, Universidad, Atlante, FAS, and A. Marte, with San Slavador's Alianza the first and only Salvadoran club to gain a regional title by winning the Championship of CONCACAF Club Champions in 1967. Aguila and Alianza have represented El Salvador in this competition most frequently, though their placement in the standings has been erratic.

Like many Central American and Caribbean states, El Salvador's international debut was made at the first Championship of the Central American and Caribbean Confederation at Havana in 1930, where its first opponent was Guatemala. The Salvadoran team won by 8-2, but lost its four remaining games in the tournament and finished fourth in a field of six. To their credit, Salvadorans have competed in each regional championship since, emerging victorious in 1943, the year San Salvador itself was the host city. In fact, its championship in 1943 was a clear victory; the Salvadorans battered Nicaragua twice by an aggregate of 18 goals to two, and managed to defeat powerful Costa Rica—El Salvador's most consistent and most difficult opponent over the years—for the first time in its history. Between 1930-38, Salvadoran teams lost to Costa Rica by 9-2, 5-0, 6-1, and 7-0. Nicaragua, Guatemala, and Panama, on the other hand, have been relatively easy prey, while Honduras has been roughly El Salvador's equal.

The relative level of the Central American game has been sorely exposed against vastly superior Mexico, except in the bizarre case of the 1970 World Cup at Mexico City. By eliminating Honduras, whose government was then in a state of war with El Salvador, the Salvadoran national team went through to the final rounds, occupying the lone Central American berth in the competition. Mexico qualified automatically as host country. Belgium and the USSR quickly disposed of El Salvador, 3-0 and 2-0 respectively, but the third opponent in its first round group was Mexico. In this match, El Salvador became the victim of one of the most flagrant errors ever committed by a referee in World Cup competition. Late in the first half, the Egyptian referee, Hussain Kandil, awarded El Salvador a free kick. The kick, however, was taken by the Mexican Perez and went to his left wing Padilla, who crossed the ball to Mexican right wing Valdivia. In an instant, Valdivia had scored. Kandil allowed the goal to stand. Emotional appeals and cries of despair from Salvadoran players were to no avail, and a thoroughly demoralized El Salvador went down to a 4-0 defeat. Coming as it did after its bitter qualifying round victory over Honduras, Kandil's injustice was little short of tragic.

See also: **Fútbol War**

England

The Football Association
16 Lancaster Gate
London, W2 3LW

Founded: 1863
FIFA: 1905-20
1924-28
1946
UEFA: 1954

Afflilated clubs: *36,904;* **registered players:** *1,108,000 (8,000 professional);* national stadium: *Empire Stadium, Wembley (100,000);* **largest stadium:** *Empire Stadium;* colors: *white jerseys with red and blue trim, royal blue shorts with red and white trim;* season: *August to June;* honors: *World Cup winner (1966), Home International Championship (1886 shared, 1888, 1890 shared, 1891, 1892, 1893, 1898, 1899, 1901, 1903 shared, 1904, 1905, 1906 shared, 1908 shared, 1909, 1911, 1912 shared, 1913, 1927 shared, 1930, 1931 shared, 1932, 1935 shared, 1938, 1939 shared, 1947, 1948, 1950, 1952 shared, 1953 shared, 1954, 1955, 1956 shared, 1957, 1958 shared, 1959 shared, 1960 shared, 1961, 1964 shared, 1965, 1966, 1968, 1969, 1970, 1971, 1972 shared, 1973, 1974 shared, 1975), Liverpool, European Cup (1977, 1978), UEFA Cup (1973, 1976), Manchester United, European Cup (1968), Tottenham Hotspur, European Cup Winners' Cup (1963), UEFA Cup (1972), West Ham United, European Cup Winners' Cup (1965), Manchester City, European Cup Winners' Cup (1970), Chelsea, European Cup Winners' Cup (1971), Leeds United, Fairs Cup (1968, 1971), Newcastle United, Fairs Cup (1969), Arsenal, Fairs Cup (1970).*

England is the birthplace of soccer and the source of all modern football games. Soccer, rugby, American football, Canadian football, Gaelic football, and Australian Rules were all derived from the rough and tumble English football of centuries past. Originally played in country lanes and village streets, the various forms of football were adopted in the nineteenth century and given shape and discipline by schoolboys and university men of the upper classes who developed the rules and customs of the modern game, as well as most of its terminology. The expansion of the British Empire and dissemination of British learning and technology eventually served as a vehicle for exporting the game to all parts of the globe. As a result, the growth of soccer in almost any country one can name is attributable to English residents or someone who learned the game from English players.

England also exported soccer to the other countries of the United Kingdom—Scotland, Wales, and Ireland—which in turn did much to spread the game to all parts of the world. The unique political structure of the United Kingdom, with its separate national identities, gave rise to autonomous governing bodies for control of the game in their respective countries. While the Home countries' economic dependence on England has tended to homogenize the British game in many respects, their separation on an organizational basis is solidified by tradition. The world governing body—FIFA—has continued to respect this tradition, in deference to the unique position of Great Britain as the birthplace of the modern game.

On the playing field, England has watched with mixed emotion as the major soccer countries of the world have emulated and surpassed its own level of expertise, beginning, in fact, with Scotland in the 1870s. From the middle of the nineteenth century until the 1920s, there was little doubt that the finest soccer in the world was being played in the British Isles, but the rise of Uruguay, Austria, Italy, Hungary, Brazil, and West Germany, in succession, put an end to England's presumption of superiority. Nevertheless, few would argue that the qualitative depth of England's league can be rivaled even to this day, and English teams have certainly won their share of international honors.

The history of football in England from the Roman conquest to the industrial revolution is virtually synonymous with the direct lineage of modern soccer as a whole. Other areas of the ancient Roman Empire, such as France, Italy, and Dalmatia, also fostered games that were descended from Roman football, but in the end, these remained mere tangents on the genealogical tree. Still further removed from modern football games are the various indigenous forms that have existed for centuries in many parts of the world. Their resemblance to soccer or rugby is purely coincidental, though of considerable interest. [For a discussion of football from ancient times to 1863 see: *origins of the game.*]

Modern football, before it diverged into two separate but related games—rugby football and association football (soccer)—took shape in the English public schools (private schools to North Americans), and eventually made its way to the universities, particularly Cambridge. Between 1820-63, dozens of schools played according to idiosyncratic rules that were largely dependent on shapes and sizes of existing playing areas. Among those most closely associated with the dribbling codes (thus influencing association football more than rugby football) were Harrow, Eton, Charterhouse, Westminster, Aldenham, Shrewsbury, and Uppingham. All but the last two were located in or near London. In 1846, Old Salopians (Shrewsbury graduates) and Old Etonians started the first Cambridge University team with rules closely resembling the dribbling code.

The first football clubs, Sheffield and Hallam, were founded in Sheffield, Yorkshire, in 1857, but each developed its own set of rules and wavered in its allegiance to the dribbling code. The first club to devote itself exclusively to the dribbling game was the Forest Football Club, founded in 1859 at Snaresbrook in Epping Forest, about two miles from the present location of Orient F.C. in East London. The other pioneer dribbling clubs were: Crystal Palace, South London (1861), which bears no relation to the modern club of the same name; Notts County, Nottingham (1862), which played by rules closely resembling those of Sheffield; Barnes, Southwest London (1863), which had a strong interest in rowing; Civil Service London, (1863); and Stoke City, Stafford (1863), which was started by Old Carthusians (Charterhouse). Notts County and Stoke City are today leading members of The Football League, and, thus the oldest extant soccer clubs in the world.

With the formation of these clubs, followed by a host of others in 1863, the need to codify the many rules and regulations emerging from each campus and from diverse regions of the country became all too apparent. Two factors led to an effort to standardize the laws of the game: first, the growing use of railroads enabled teams from separate locations to compete against one another more frequently; second, the increasing polarization of schools and clubs into camps that favored either a code allowing the use of hands and hacking (the handling game), or a code prohibiting these practices and emphasizing footwork (the dribbling game), became a nuisance.

On October 26, 1863, the representatives of 14 London clubs and schools met at the Freemasons' Tavern near Lincoln Inn Fields, London, to establish The Football Association (F.A.) and propose a uniform set of rules. Weeks of discussion ensued over which code to adopt, but the supporters of a dribbling code based on the Harrow-Cambridge model were predominant, and on December 8, the first Football Association Laws, based on the Cambridge University Rules of 1863, were officially adopted. The three handling code-oriented (or rugby) members—Blackheath F.C., Blackheath School, and Perceval House of Blackheath—resigned. The remaining charter members were: Forest FC., "No Name" Kilburn, War Office F.C., Crusaders F.C., Crystal Palace F.C., Kensington School, and Surbiton F.C. Conspicuous in their absence were the major public schools, Cambridge University, and outlying clubs such as Sheffield, Notts County, and Stoke.

The Football Association, the world's first governing body for soccer, did not develop into a truly national association until the 1870s, because ten years were spent unifying England according to mutually acceptable rules. The most important agreement was between the F.A. and the Sheffield F.A. in 1867. Meanwhile, innovations that were to mold the character of the sport appeared in rapid succession: tapes were first stretched across the goalmouth in 1865; the goal kick was introduced in 1869; the corner kick appeared in 1872, and in that same year the official size of the ball was fixed; umpires were employed for the first time in 1874; crossbars replaced tapes in 1876; the first electric lights and whistles appeared in 1878; and shinguards were sanctioned in 1880.

In 1871, The Football Association Challenge Cup (F.A. Cup) was introduced as the world's first organized competition. There were 15 entrants: Barnes, Civil Service, Crystal Palace, Clapham Rovers, Donnington School (Spalding), Hampstead Heathens, Harrow Chequers, Hitchin, Maidenhead, Marlow, Queen's Park (Glasgow), Reigate Priory, Royal Engineers, Upton Park, and Wanderers. (Only Queen's Park Glasgow is still in existence today.) All but Donnington and Queen's Park were from London or other parts of southeastern England, and eventually Donnington, Harrow Chequers, and Reigate withdrew. The first trophy was won in 1872 by Wanderers F.C. (formerly Forest F.C.), a club of public school graduates that went on to become the first dominant team in English soccer, winning five F.A. Cups between 1872-78.

The 1870s was the era of the "gentlemen's" game, in which most of the leading teams were either named for or consisted of public school and university graduates (Oxford University, Old Etonians, Old Carthusians, and Wanderers). Geographically, their base of operation was London or the home counties surrounding the capital. In the 1880s, however, enormous changes occurred that forever altered the appearance of the game. In the North and Midlands, clubs sprang up in vast numbers, most of them connected in some way or another with parishes, churches, or chapels. Nearly all were characterized by a working class membership, and it was this new social base that provided the impetus for an unparalleled rise in the popularity of soccer in England. By 1879, most of the participants in the F.A. Cup were located in the industrial regions, and officials soon introduced a series of regional elimination tournaments to accommodate them.

With the F.A. Cup of 1882-83, a non-London-based club won the cup for the first time, and the trophy was not to return to the capital city for another 20 years. Blackburn Rovers became the first important club from the industrial North, winning five cups during the 1880s. The southern clubs of upper- and upper-middle-class composition fell by the wayside and eventually receded into amateur competition as the rising tide of professionalism swept the country.

International competition, meanwhile, was introduced in 1870 when representative teams from England and Scotland met in London and played to a 1-1 draw. In 1872, the first official international between England and Scotland took place in Glasgow, ending in a goalless draw. This archrivalry, the world's oldest, has since continued on an annual basis. After the formation of the Scottish F.A. (1873), the Welsh F.A. (1876), and the Irish F.A. (1880), England initiated the formation of an International Football Association Board in 1882 to regulate differences among the four governing bodies and organize an international championship. The introduction of the Home International Championship followed in 1883 between England, Scotland, Wales, and Ireland.

The meteoric rise of worker-based clubs in the North and Midlands during the 1880s resulted in the formation of The Football League in 1888. The 12 original members were (in the order they finished the first season): Preston North End, Aston Villa, Wolverhampton Wanderers, Blackburn Rovers, Bolton Wanderers, West Bromwich Albion, Accrington Stanley, Everton, Burnley, Derby County, Notts County, and Stoke City. Accrington is the only one of these no longer in existence (it folded in 1962); the rest are still important members of The Football League. All 12 clubs hailed from Lancashire County or the Midlands, and all emerged from the great debate over professionalism during the 1880s as fully professional clubs. The number of clubs clamoring to gain membership in the league grew steadily, and in 1892 a second division was added (the third and fourth divisions were added in 1920 and 1958, respectively). The first southern member of the league was Royal Arsenal F.C. (later to become the famous Arsenal F.C.), elected in 1893.

Preston North End, which won the first league championship without conceding a defeat, also won the F.A. Cup of 1888-89 and the first double. "Proud Preston" must receive credit for launching competitive soccer on its course; in addition to its extraordinary feats of 1888-89, it was the first club to turn professional in 1882, signaling once and for all the demise of the great amateur clubs of the South. The outstanding exception to the trend toward professionalism was Corinthians F.C., founded in 1882 by university graduates, which successfully challenged the best professional teams throughout the 1880s and '90s, though it never attempted to join The Football League. Even Blackburn Rovers succumbed to Corinthians by eight goals to one in 1884, and for much of the 1880s and '90s the English national team was composed mainly of Corinthian players. It was the amateurs' last hurrah.

After Preston, the first dominant clubs of

The Football League were Aston Villa and Sunderland. Villa won five championships between 1894-1900, including its famous double in 1897. In 1895, the F.A. Cup Final, that most venerable of English soccer institutions, found its first permanent home at Crystal Palace, South London. At the 1901 final, an attendance figure above 100,000 was reached for the first time when the London club Tottenham Hotspur drew with Sheffield United to force a replay. Soccer as a spectator sport for everybody had arrived. After the turn of the century, Newcastle United achieved fame and fortune with the winning of three championships and appearances in five F.A. Cup finals. Northern and Midlands clubs continued to dominate both league and cup, and the first London-based league champion did not emerge until 1930 (Arsenal).

As the rules and customs of modern soccer developed during the last four decades of the nineteenth century, the English game was exported to all corners of the world. The first tour of an English team abroad was that of Oxford University to Germany in 1875. Association rules were introduced to southern Africa in 1865, Argentina in 1867, Australia in 1870, West Africa around 1880, Russia in 1887, Singapore in 1892, and throughout Europe during the 1870s and '80s. Association rules reached the United States in 1867, though a club playing under similar rules, Oneida F.C. of Boston, was formed as early as 1862. The first representative team from abroad to visit England was a Canadian selection in 1891. An unofficial English team toured Germany in 1896, and three years later the first official representative team of the F.A. visited Germany and won all four matches.

When FIFA was founded in 1904 (at the urging of France and Belgium), the F.A. rebuffed an invitation to join, dismissing the notion of an international governing body as an unattainable dream. Actually the F.A. was fearful that the new organization would tamper with the authority of its own International Football Association Board, but when it became apparent that the seven charter members of FIFA were serious in their intent, and at the same time respectful of British authority on matters relating to rules and regulations, there was a change of heart. In 1905, the F.A. became affiliated with FIFA, and in 1906, D.B. Woodfall of the F.A. Council was elected President of the world body. The International Football Association Board was acknowledged as the sole authority over the Laws of the Game, and in 1913, FIFA was given two seats on the board. In 1920, England, as well as the other British associations, withdrew from FIFA, declaring that they would not intermingle with their former enemies of the Great War. They rejoined in 1924, but four years later all four withdrew again over FIFA's sanctioning of part-time wages for amateur players at the 1928 Olympic Games. All the British associations were reaffiliated in 1946.

England's first official international against a non-British team was with Austria in 1908, won in Vienna 6-1 and followed within a week by a second win over Austria (11-1), and defeats of Hungary (7-0), and Bohemia (4-0). Prior to World War I, there were only three additional full internationals with non-British teams (against Austria and Hungary), all victorious. Belgium became the first European country to play on English soil at full international level in 1923. Amateur teams representing Great Britain won the soccer tournaments of the 1908 and 1912 Olympic Games, but this was of little consequence in a country now almost entirely professional in its upper ranks.

Between 1919-29, only 18 of England's 50 full-level internationals were played against continental opponents. Its first loss to a foreign team was to Spain in 1929 at Madrid (4-3), but Belgium, France, Sweden, and Luxembourg all fell to England's superiority during the 1920s. In the next decade, England lost seven of its 27 matches with European teams (all away), and its claim to inviolability on the playing field was suspect for the first time. Without membership in FIFA, however, England could not participate in the three World Cups of this period, depriving everyone of a chance to know its true strength. England itself was confident that it remained the unrivaled power in its own game, though its strength, as measured against Uruguay, Argentina, and Brazil, for example, was wholly untested.

On the domestic front, the dominant clubs between the wars were Huddersfield, which had risen from relative obscurity in the 1920s to league champions three times in succession, and Arsenal. Under Herbert Chapman, who had previously taken Huddersfield to its glory, Arsenal won five championships and two F.A. Cups between 1930-38, and with Chapman's revolutionary third-back game, the W-M formation, its fame spread around the world.

The influence of this all-conquering team on soccer worldwide was pervasive, and from a tactical standpoint, helped England retain its position of international leadership. Chapman, meanwhile, wrote a chapter in English soccer annals by creating the only two teams ever to have won a hat trick of league championships. His reputation as the greatest manager in England's history was challenged only once in later years—by Sir Matt Busby of Manchester United fame.

England's prophetic losses to seven continental teams during the 1930s were tempered by a hiatus of international competition during the war years, but the realities of the new balance of power on the playing field began to settle in by 1950. England entered the World Cup for the first time in Brazil, and after defeating Chile, its first South American opponent in international competition, England received the greatest shock in its 80-year soccer history—a 1-0 defeat by the United States. To make matters worse, it failed to recover from the trauma, and was eliminated after losing to Spain three days later. The nightmare, however, did not end there. Later that year, Yugoslavia became the first non-British country to gain a draw at Wembley, and in 1951, France and Austria managed to attain the same result. In 1953, undefeated Hungary, already touted as the greatest team ever seen, buried the English by 6-3, and became the first foreign country to defeat England at home. The decisiveness of Hungary's victory was sobering. In Budapest seven months later, Hungary crushed England by 7-1, and sealed the end of an era.

Having been toppled from its international throne—apocryphal as that seat might have been—England struggled through the remainder of the 1950s. Its World Cup results in 1954 and 1958 were a disappointment. In 1954, Uruguay defeated England in the quarter-finals for the second time in two years, displaying superior ball control skills, and in 1958, three draws against Brazil, the USSR, and Austria, followed by a loss to the Russians, further eroded morale. In 1959, England made a disastrous tour of South America, in which it lost to Brazil, Peru, and Mexico by an aggregate score of 2-8, and on its return home, lost at Wembley to Sweden.

The state of England's domestic game, however, was healthy and vibrant. This was an era of exciting, attacking teams in league and cup competition. It was the era of "Busby's Babes," the Manchester United team said to be the finest in England and one destined to challenge Real Madrid's supremacy in Europe. The tragic airplane disaster at Munich in 1958 that killed most of the team brought the nation to a grinding halt. This was also the era of Wolverhampton Wanderers, winner of three championships during the 1950s, led by English captain Billy Wright; and of Newcastle United, whose spearhead was the redoubtable Jackie Milburn. Stanley Matthews, the world's most famous player, continued to dazzle fans with his genius after more than 25 years in senior-level competition, and the other heroes of this golden era, Finney, Mortensen, Lofthouse, Dickinson, and Mannion, left an unforgettable legacy in the hearts and minds of English fans.

In the national team, spirits were revived under the tutelage of manager Alf Ramsey and captain Bobby Moore in the mid-1960s, aided no doubt by the prospect of staging the 1966 World Cup in England itself. With the exception of Moore, Gordon Banks, and Bobby Charlton, there were few in the lineup who could claim world class status, but with the best coordinated backfield in international competition and a confidence of purpose, England entered the eighth World Championship with a reasonable chance of toppling mighty Brazil and surpassing Hungary and Portugal, the other favorites in the competition. England's major stumbling blocks proved to be Argentina and Portugal, but it advanced to the final and won the World Cup with that most controversial of goals—off the right foot of Geoff Hurst. The World Championship had at last been won by the pretender to the throne, albeit on a rain-soaked day with a shot that many believed did not cross the line.

The winning of the World Cup sparked a revival of domestic interest in the game. Manchester United, now rebuilt by Matt Busby into a glorious array of world class talent, became the first English club to win the European Cup in 1968. Though London teams Tottenham Hotspur and West Ham United had earlier won the European Cup Winners' Cup in 1963 and 1965, respectively, the major trophy in European club competition had previously been unattainable. In addition, United's championship team included no less than three recipients of the European Footballer of the Year award—more than any other European club since the prize has been awarded. Coupled with a considerable holdover of sentiment from the Munich air

England's national team in preparation for the 1966 World Cup at Roehampton. Its triumph in the final against West Germany was the most controversial game in history. (Back row, left to right) asst. Sheperdson, asst. Cocker, Hunt, Flowers, Bonetti, Springett, Banks, Moore, Greaves, manager Ramsey; (middle row) Armfield, Callaghan, G. Byrne, Eastham, Hurst, J. Charlton, Stiles; (front row) Hunter, Cohen, Payne, Wilson, B. Charlton, Peters, Connelly.

disaster, these factors resulted in an unprecedented following for the new Manchester United.

Liverpool and Leeds United emerged as two new powers in the 1960s, later dominating the 1970s as well, while Tottenham and Arsenal enjoyed doubles in 1961 and 1971, respectively. Before Liverpool advanced to win the European Cup in 1977, English clubs were conspicuously absent from the final rounds of the two big European club championships (despite the fact that Chelsea and Manchester City had won the European Cup Winners' Cup). The depth of English league soccer, however, was demonstrated by the six English clubs that won the Fairs/UEFA Cup between 1968-76 (four successive years during one stretch): Leeds, Newcastle, Arsenal, Wolverhampton, Tottenham and Liverpool (twice).

Since 1966, English soccer has suffered an unprecedented crisis of confidence, owing much to its inability to compete with more advanced styles of play on the continent. Its club successes in recent years have been due to an occasional coalescence of traditional English characteristics on the playing field:

superb conditioning and speed, decisive tackling, strength, excellence in the air, and consistent goalkeeping. Yet the attractive ball control skills that were prevalent in England during the 1930s and '50s now appear to be lost to the majority of English players, and tactical advances, such as those under the heading of "total football," have not yet crossed the English Channel. Today there are only 13 countries left that have failed to defeat a once proud England (besides those countries England has yet to meet): Bulgaria, Chile, Colombia, Cyprus, Denmark, Ecuador, Finland, German DR, Greece, Luxembourg, Malta, Norway, and Rumania. Having failed to advance to the final stages of the 1974 and 1978 World Cups (as well as to the 1974-76 European Football Championship), England has not qualified for the World Championship since 1962, except as hosts or current title holders.

The vast majority of England's international meetings over the decades have been in connection with the Home Internationals. England's consistent superiority over Wales and Ireland (including Northern Ireland) in this series helps to account for its very high overall success rate in cumulative won-lost tabulations. Ireland did not defeat England at all until 1913, and Wales not until 1920. England and Scotland, on the other hand, have amassed near equal records, with Scotland holding a slight lead on points, and England on goal difference.

See also: **origins of the game; history of the game; Cambridge University Rules; Sheffield Rules; Harrow Game, Rules of the;** and **Home International Championship.**

Champions

1889	Preston North End	1923	Liverpool
1890	Preston North End	1924	Huddersfield
1891	Everton	1925	Huddersfield
1892	Sunderland	1926	Huddersfield
1893	Sunderland	1927	Newcastle United
1894	Aston Villa	1928	Everton
1895	Sunderland	1929	Sheffield Wednesday
1896	Aston Villa	1930	Sheffield Wednesday
1897	Aston Villa	1931	Arsenal
1898	Sheffield United	1932	Everton
1899	Aston Villa	1933	Arsenal
1900	Aston Villa	1934	Arsenal
1901	Liverpool	1935	Arsenal
1902	Sunderland	1936	Sunderland
1903	Sheffield Wednesday	1937	Manchester City
1904	Sheffield Wednesday	1938	Arsenal
1905	Newcastle United	1939	Everton
1906	Liverpool	1940	no competition
1907	Newcastle United	1941	no competition
1908	Manchester United	1942	no competition
1909	Newcastle United	1943	no competition
1910	Aston Villa	1944	no competition
1911	Manchester United	1945	no competition
1912	Blackburn Rovers	1946	no competition
1913	Sunderland	1947	Liverpool
1914	Blackburn Rovers	1948	Arsenal
1915	Everton	1949	Portsmouth
1916	no competition	1950	Portsmouth
1917	no competition	1951	Tottenham Hotspur
1918	no competition	1952	Manchester United
1919	no competition	1953	Arsenal
1920	West Bromwich Albion	1954	Wolverhampton Wanderers
1921	Burnley	1955	Chelsea
1922	Liverpool	1956	Manchester United

1957 Manchester United	1968 Manchester City
1958 Wolverhampton Wanderers	1969 Leeds United
1959 Wolverhampton Wanderers	1970 Everton
1960 Burnley	1971 Arsenal
1961 Tottenham Hotspur	1972 Derby County
1962 Ipswich Town	1973 Liverpool
1963 Everton	1974 Leeds United
1964 Liverpool	1975 Derby County
1965 Manchester United	1976 Liverpool
1966 Liverpool	1977 Liverpool
1967 Manchester United	1978 Nottingham Forest

Cup Winners

1872 Wanderers	1906 Everton
1873 Wanderers	1907 Sheffield Wednesday
1874 Oxford University	1908 Wolverhampton Wanderers
1875 Royal Engineers	1909 Manchester United
1876 Wanderers	1910 Newcastle United
1877 Wanderers	1911 Bradford City
1878 Wanderers	1912 Barnsley
1879 Old Etonians	1913 Aston Villa
1880 Clapham Rovers	1914 Burnley
1881 Old Carthusians	1915 Sheffield United
1882 Old Etonians	1916 no competition
1883 Blackburn Olympic	1917 no competition
1884 Blackburn Rovers	1918 no competition
1885 Blackburn Rovers	1919 no competition
1886 Blackburn Rovers	1920 Aston Villa
1887 Aston Villa	1921 Tottenham Hotspur
1888 West Bromwich Albion	1922 Huddersfield
1889 Preston North End	1923 Bolton Wanderers
1890 Blackburn Rovers	1924 Newcastle United
1891 Blackburn Rovers	1925 Sheffield United
1892 West Bromwich Albion	1926 Bolton Wanderers
1893 Wolverhampton Wanderers	1927 Cardiff City
1894 Notts County	1928 Blackburn Rovers
1895 Aston Villa	1929 Bolton Wanderers
1896 Sheffield Wednesday	1930 Arsenal
1897 Aston Villa	1931 West Bromwich Albion
1898 Nottingham Forest	1932 Newcastle United
1899 Sheffield United	1933 Everton
1900 Bury	1934 Manchester City
1901 Tottenham Hotspur	1935 Sheffield Wednesday
1902 Sheffield United	1936 Arsenal
1903 Bury	1937 Sunderland
1904 Manchester City	1938 Preston North End
1905 Aston Villa	1939 Portsmouth

1940	no competition	1960	Wolverhampton Wanderers
1941	no competition	1961	Tottenham Hotspur
1942	no competition	1962	Tottenham Hotspur
1943	no competition	1963	Manchester United
1944	no competition	1964	West Ham United
1945	no competition	1965	Liverpool
1946	Derby County	1966	Everton
1947	Charlton Athletic	1967	Tottenham Hotspur
1948	Manchester United	1968	West Bromwich Albion
1949	Wolverhampton Wanderers	1969	Manchester City
1950	Arsenal	1970	Chelsea
1951	Newcastle United	1971	Arsenal
1952	Newcastle United	1972	Leeds United
1953	Blackpool	1973	Sunderland
1954	West Bromwich Albion	1974	Liverpool
1955	Newcastle United	1975	West Ham United
1956	Manchester City	1976	Southampton
1957	Aston Villa	1977	Manchester United
1958	Bolton Wanderers	1978	Ipswich Town
1959	Nottingham Forest		

Estonia

One of the expressions of self-assertion made by the Baltic states during their 20-year period of independence between the world wars was to engage other countries in the world game. The most prolific of the three states was Estonia, which had 44 encounters against European teams other than those from Latvia and Lithuania. Estonia's record was less than successful: 44-6-8-30-47-135-20. Twenty-one of these were played against Finland and an additional 12 against Sweden. Against Finland there were five victories and six draws, but against Sweden the Estonians were winless and only managed to draw once.

Estonia was the only Baltic nation to have a winning record against an opponent in Europe, its one encounter with Rumania, a 2-1 win in 1937 at Tallinn. Its solitary meetings with Turkey, France, and the Republic of Ireland were all lost, as were three matches with Germany by an aggregate score of 1-11. Estonia managed to draw once with Poland, but lost three other games against Polish teams. Its biggest win occurred at home in 1930 over Finland (4-0), and it was Finland that dealt Estonia its severest blow, a 10-2 loss at Helsinki in 1922. Its European debut having been made in 1920 in the Finnish capital, Estonia ventured into Europe three years before either Latvia or Lithuania, and in late 1939 it was still attempting to gain a foothold against Finnish supremacy, only a few short months before the Baltic states were absorbed into the USSR.

Estudiantes de La Plata

Location: *La Plata, Argentina;* stadium: *Paseo del Bosque;* colors: *red and white striped jerseys, black shorts;* honors: *Intercontinental Cup (1968), Copa Libertadores (1968, 1969, 1970), Copa Interamericana (1968), Argentine league champion (1913 shared, 1967).*

Founded 1905 at La Plata, the coastal city of Buenos Aires Province and located 30 miles from the Federal District (city of Buenos Aires), by members of Gimnasia y Esgrimá de La Plata. The gymnasts and fencers of the parent club had refused to allow them to play soccer within the structure of their organization. Many of the original members were *estudiantes* at the University of La Plata. The club joined the first division in 1912. It was the first and only club from outside Buenos Aires to win an Argentine championship (ironically with the lone exception of Gimnasia y Esgrimá de La Plata in 1929), until Rosario Central in 1971. Having won only two league championships in all that time, it has failed to make any lasting impression on domestic competition.

One of these first division victories, however, opened a Pandora's Box. In 1967, under coach Osvaldo Zubeldía, Estudiantes won the Campeonato Metropolitano (First Division) and placed second in the first—and somewhat disorganized—edition of the Campeonato Nacional, earning the club a berth in the 1968 Copa Libertadores. Zubeldía, who took pride in developing players from relative obscurity, achieved an uncanny momentum based on determination and a great deal of rough play, and in its first attempt, the club won the coveted Libertadores. On the basis of this victory, the road was now open to face Manchester United in the Intercontinental Cup.

This transoceanic showcase exposed Estudiantes to the scrutiny of European public opinion for the first time, and Europe objected strongly to what it saw. Though Argentina's Rácing Club had been guilty of violent behavior and unsportsmanlike conduct in the world club championship the year before, the Estudiantes brand of conduct was worse still. In Estudiantes' home leg, Manchester United was effectively nudged out of the game by unfair refereeing, despite ceaseless Estudiantes fouls, and in Manchester the Argentines managed to draw and win the competition on goal aggregate. Vehement protests from Europe followed, but the series was, after all, unofficial.

With the aid of automatic entry and byes to the semi-final round, Estudiantes proceeded to win two additional South American club championships in 1969 and 1970 without having to win another domestic title to qualify, and again the same pattern emerged. Kicking, pushing, spitting, and taunting were all part of game plan, and it worked. In the 1969 Intercontinental Cup, AC Milan won convincingly at San Siro, and in Argentina the Italian team saved its goal aggregate with a 2-1 loss, but only after some noses were broken and Milan's Pierino Prati was kicked in the back while being attended for another injury. The crisis boiled over when Argentine President General Onganía urged the Argentine F.A. to impose penalties on some Estudiantes players after seeing the Milan game on television. In the 1970 edition, Estudiantes lost to the Dutch club Feyenoord after more of the same, and the next year, having been defeated in the final of the Copa Libertadores by Nacional, the dread era of Estudiantes ended.

In subsequent years, it faded back into mediocrity, and home support, which had swelled in the space of three years, receded to its former place. In Europe, as well as the rest of South America, there was scarcely a club anywhere that had suffered a worse reputation than Estudiantes de La Plata.

Ethiopia

Yeitiopia Football Federechin
Addis Ababa Stadium
C.P. 1080
Addis Ababa

Founded: 1943
FIFA: 1953
CAF: 1957

Affiliated clubs: *160;* **registered players:** *13,425;* **national stadium:** *Addis Ababa Stadium (30,000);* **largest stadium:** *Addis Ababa Stadium;* **colors:** *green jerseys with yellow trim, yellow shorts;* **season:** *September to June;* **honors:** *African Nations' Cup winner (1962).*

Ethiopia was one of the early pillars of organized soccer in Africa. Before the rise of sub-Saharan soccer-playing countries in the mid-1960s, no country on the continent was more respected for its contribution to the game's growth, and there were few who were able to match wits with the skill and determination of Ethiopian players. The level of play in Ethiopia, however, did not stay ahead of its new rivals in the South, and, while Ethiopian national teams have retained a high overall ranking, they are no longer the major force they once were. The political turmoil and famine of the 1970s have wreaked havoc on the game, casting serious doubts on its immediate future. Ethiopia's role as a leader in African soccer, however, is still reflected in the confidence shown in the African Football Confederation's president, an Ethiopian named Yidnekatchew Tessema.

Soccer was introduced to Ethiopia in Addis Ababa around 1924 by Italians and other immigrants, including, Greeks, Armenians, and Indians. The Italians were especially active in Eritrea as well as the capital, and they formed several teams and organized *ad hoc* tournaments. Schools such as Jan Hoy Meda began to play the game, and school teams surfaced by the early 1930s. Despite soccer's growth, the first important Ethiopian players were better known as stars of track and field, Ethiopia's traditional national sport. Perhaps the most famous of these was Ato Bekele Mamuye, whose lethal shot on goal became the subject of many tales and legends. Most of the early clubs, however, were restricted to Italian, Greek, or Armenian players, and Ethiopians themselves were left out of the mainstream of their country's soccer growth until the liberation of 1941. The first important Ethiopian-based club was Saint George Sports Association, founded in 1935 in the Arada section of Addis Ababa. During the Italian occupation (1936-41), a strict policy of segregating Ethiopian players from Italians and other ethnic groups was maintained by the "Sports Office for the Indigenous." Interracial matches were not allowed, and Ethiopians could not even play on fields reserved for immigrants.

In 1941, interracial matches were resumed—cautiously—and the Sports Office of Ethiopia was founded in Addis Ababa. Ethiopian soccer received its first real impetus from the 1942 victory of Saint George over the Italian-club Fortitudo, and this famous game became a rallying point for nationalistic pride. A second important Ethiopian-based club emerged at this time, Kaeye Baher, but the ethnic clubs of Addis Ababa remained the strongest competitors.

Finally, in 1943 the Yeitiopia Football Federechin was founded in Addis Ababa by a group of nine prominent clubs, none of which was Italian: Army, Saint George, Body Guard, Kaeye Baher, Mesfin Harar, Cadet School, and Public Health (all Ethiopian); Ararat (Armenian); and Olympiakos (Greek). A league based in Addis Ababa (the Ethiopian Cup) was introduced simultaneously, and a second division was added in 1948. Ethiopia's first unofficial international was played in 1948 in Addis Ababa against a representative team from Djibouti, capital of neighboring French Somaliland, resulting on a 5-0 win. Ethiopia met Djibouti selections on six occasions between 1948-56, winning each time but failing to gain real international experience. In the Ethiopian Cup, Metchal-Army (a club formed with the merger of Metchal S.C. and Army S.C.) became the first team to dominate the league with several championships during the early 1950s. In 1955, the Coronation Cup was introduced, but it was not contested again until 1960, when it permanently replaced the Ethiopian Cup as the national championship.

Ethiopia's first full international was a 4-1 loss to Egypt in 1956 at Addis Ababa. This was also the year in which Ethiopia joined forces with Egypt and Sudan (and abortively with South Africa) to establish the African Football Confederation. In 1957, the three founding members met in Khartoum to play out the first African Nations' Cup. Egypt defeated both Ethiopia (4-0) and Sudan to win the first trophy. In 1959, Ethiopia paid its first visit to Europe, and lost to the USSR in Moscow, 12-3. In the second African Nations' Cup (1959), Ethiopia, Egypt, and Sudan were again the only participants, and Ethiopia lost to Egypt 4-0 and to Sudan 1-0 for another third place finish.

In the third edition in 1962, the slightly expanded competition was held in Ethiopia—the Haile Selassie Stadium in Addis Ababa was then one of the finest grounds in Africa—and the home team defeated Tunisia and, in the final, Egypt, to win its first and only international trophy. The final was witnessed by Emperor Haile Selassie himself and went into an exciting overtime, during which the Ethiopian team bombarded Egypt's goal with countless shots and finally won, 4-2. Ironically, the captain and guiding spirit of this team was Luciano Vassalo, the son of Italian immigrants. In the 1963 African Nations' Cup, Ethiopia lost the third place game to its old rival Egypt, and after a dismal showing in the

1965 edition, once again lost in a third place game in the 1968 competition, this time to Ivory Coast. Ethiopia was not to figure prominently in the African Nations' Cup again, even in 1976 when it was held in Ethiopia. By this time, internal strife had taken its toll on the Ethiopian game and little was expected.

In the national championship, two more dynasties were created by Cotton S.C. during the early 1960s and by Saint George during the latter half of the 1960s. Ethiopian clubs have benefited greatly from their exposure to a stream of European clubs that have made their way to Addis Ababa and Asmara. Over 200 internationals have been played between European clubs and Ethiopian teams. In 1963, the national team made an extensive tour of Europe—mainly Eastern Europe—and came away with one win and one draw in 11 games. A 4-0 loss to France "B" in Paris in 1962 was especially helpful in determining the progress of Ethiopia's game up to that time. In relative terms, international results show that Ethiopian soccer has declined since then. Of Ethiopia's leading stars, Cotton S.C.'s Luciano Vassalo made almost 100 international appearances from 1959-69, scoring 40 goals, and Saint George's Mengistou Worku scored a record 60 goals for Ethiopia in his 90-odd appearances from 1959-69. With Eritrea's virtual cessation of cultural activities during the civil war in the 1970s, Ethiopia lost its second most important center of soccer activity.

Europe   See: **Union of European Football Associations**

European Champion Clubs' Cup

Coupe des Clubs Champions Européens—Pokal der Europäischen Meistervereine.

Known popularly as the European Cup, this is the premier international club competition in Europe. It is played annually, and is open to all European league champions and the previous year's winner. The country of the current holder is entitled to enter a second club if it wishes, usually its new champion or the runner-up if the champion remains the same, and this has been done on all but five occasions. The European Cup winner also competes against the reigning South American club champion for the Intercontinental Cup and the reigning European Cup Winners' Cup victor for the "Super Cup," but both of these competitions are unofficial.

With the wealth of great teams Europe has produced, it is perhaps surprising that only ten clubs have won this coveted prize in 23 years. Real Madrid's unparalleled accomplishment in winning a total of six, including the first five in succession, appears unapproachable in soccer annals. Ajax Amsterdam and Bayern München have both won three in a row, adding a touch of immortality to their illustrious names, and the two Milan giants, Internazionale and AC Milan, as well as Liverpool and Lisbon's Benfica, have each won two. The other winners have been Celtic Glasgow, Manchester United, and Feyenoord Rotterdam, and Liverpool, while the great clubs of Eastern Europe have yet to reach this pantheonic list.

All rounds except the final are played on a home and away knockout basis with the winners determined by goal aggregate. Away goals count double if goal aggregates are even, and in the event of even away goals the winner is decided on penalty kicks at the end of the second leg. The final is played at a predetermined venue.

The idea of bringing together European national champions in an international club competition had existed for many years prior to the introduction of the European Cup in 1955. Two important regional tournaments for champion clubs had nurtured the concept in previous years: the Mitropa Cup, introduced in 1927 for champion clubs of Central Europe, and the Latin Cup, which ran from 1949-57, for champion clubs of the western Mediterranean region. In addition, there had been the tepid experience from 1951-53 of the International Cup played between some of the leading champion clubs of Europe and South America. By the mid-1950s one school of thought adhered to the idea of a European Super League, whose members would include all the leading clubs of Europe. (This ideal still exists in the hearts and minds of a small minority today.) To others, a knockout competition appeared to be more practical.

The formation of the Union of European Football Associations (UEFA) in 1954 prompted one enthusiastic proponent to take action. In the spring of 1955, Gabriel Hanot, the soccer editor of the French sports daily *L'Equipe*, invited representatives of 18 clubs to meet in Paris, though not all were reigning champions. Fifteen clubs accepted; Scotland's Hibernian sent a letter of support, and Spartak Prague and Dinamo Moscow declined because of domestic business and weather conditions. *L'Equipe*, which had tried and failed to interest UEFA in sponsoring the concept of a European championship, convened the meeting on its own behalf. A short debate ensued, and all agreed to hold an inaugural competition the following season. FIFA immediately announced its official authorization, and UEFA dulq offered to sponsor and administer the new event. To guarantee the support of both governing bodies, each club had to secure permission from its national association to enter the tournament.

1955-56. There were 16 participants in the first edition. England's Football League blocked Chelsea's entrance on grounds that it would interfere with domestic schedules, and its place was taken by Gwardia Warsaw. Of the original 18 invitees, only Czechoslovakia and the USSR declined. Holland's PSV Eindhoven and Denmark's AGF Aarhus had replaced Holland Sport and KB Copenhagen, respectively, since the spring meeting in Paris. This was the only edition of the European Cup in which some entrants (about half) were not reigning champions; some national associations chose to send other leading clubs instead. Of the seven participants that were reigning champions (Real Madrid, AC Milan, Rot-Weiss Essen, Djurgaarden Stockholm, RSC Anderlecht, Stade de Reims, and AGF Aarhus), three were eliminated in the first round. The presence of FC Saarbrücken was made possible by the Saar's political autonomy during this period and the official recognition of its governing body as a separate entity, though FC Saarbrücken and other non-amateur clubs from the Saar actually played in the Southwest section of the West German league.

The looming greatness of Real Madrid was made evident throughout the competition by its superlative play on the field, led by Alfredo Di Stefano, the greatest player of his genera-

tion. Decisive home victories over Partizan Belgrade and the mighty AC Milan were preceded by twin shutouts of Servette Geneva, placing it in the final at Paris. France's own Stade de Reims, spearheaded by Raymond Kopa, was less trouble-free in the early rounds than Real, but its gaining the final against the Spaniards was both appropriate and deserving. In the final, Reims led by 2-0 and 3-2 before succumbing to goals by Real's Rial and Marquitos. The tournament appeared to be well and truly launched, but even the exciting win by the Spanish champions could hardly have foretold the consistency of events over the next four years.

1956-57. The first edition of the European Cup had been an unqualified success, and in the second edition six new countries were allowed to enter, including England, adventuresome little Luxembourg, and Turkey (which was not to become a member of UEFA for another eight years). A preliminary round was introduced, and weather conditions started to play an important part in the competition. Real Madrid, now further bolstered by the presence of Kopa, its most formidable opponent the year before, entered as the runaway favorite, especially since the final was scheduled to be held in its own stadium. Manchester United, Real's primary challenger, buried RSC Anderlecht by 10-0 in the preliminary round, and in the second round was unlucky to lose at Athletic Bilbao in a blizzard before winning nicely at home to achieve the necessary goal aggregate. Real and United, the two best club-level teams in Europe, faced each other in the semi-finals (the Madrid leg drew a Spanish record attendance of 134,000 that still stands today), but Real's scoring talent proved unbeatable, even in Manchester. Fiorentina, the defense-minded club from Florence, met Real in the final, but stood little chance against the incomparable Kopa-Di Stefano-Gento front line. Real won with a shutout, and logged its second consecutive European club championship.

1957-58. Real Madrid and Manchester United were again favorites in the third edition. Despite internal disorders on the managerial level, Real forged through the first three rounds with lopsided home-leg shutouts over Antwerp, Seville, and Vasas Budapest, eventually reaching the final again. Real's fame had spread so widely that when the team traveled to Budapest after winning decisively in Madrid, an astonishing 118,000 Hungarian fans turned out to see the club. Manchester

United, however, was struck by an earth-shattering tragedy. On its return home from a drawn second round match at Red Star Belgrade, its airplane crashed on takeoff in Munich, killing eight first team players and forcing the retirement of two more through serious injury. A courageous team of reserves and new signings miraculously won the home leg of the next round against high-scoring AC Milan, but in Italy the new Manchester United buckled under the strain of its terrible burden and was eliminated. AC Milan's win put it in the final against Real Madrid. The awesome forward line of Real was now backed by the great Uruguayan center half Santamaria, but for the first time in a final, Real met its match. Two goals by both teams in rapid succession forced an extra time period, but the clever Gento won the trophy for the cup holders with a typically opportunistic goal from the wing. Real Madrid's third successive European Cup win was less sweet than the previous two, because Milan was a serious challenger and the Munich tragedy hung like a cloud over the proceedings, but there appeared to be no end in sight of Real's domination of European soccer.

1958-59. There were now 28 participants. Manchester United was invited to enter as England's second representative (in addition to current champions Wolverhampton), but United withdrew before the preliminary round in order to minimize its scheduling difficulties in building a new team. Real Madrid's major challengers were thought to be talent-heavy Juventus of Italy and Wolverhampton, but neither advanced beyond the first round. Genuine giant-killers emerged in the form of Austria's Wiener SK and Switzerland's Young Boys Berne, the latter upsetting MTK Budapest with a 6-2 goal aggregate and defeating Stade de Reims in one leg of the semi-finals. Reims had returned to form with only Robert Jonquet remaining from its past list of great stars, but this was sufficient to gain a berth in the final against Real Madrid. Both Reims' and Real's paths to the final were rocky. In the semi-finals, Real was forced to a replay against its crosstown rival Atlético Madrid in one of the most thrilling Spanish derbies of all time. Real's newest team member, the immortal Ferenc Puskás, missed the final through injury, but his absence made little difference in the outcome. Reims had little chance against the unrestrained scoring power of a team that by this time had become a living legend in the world of soccer. The final score of 2-0 barely reflected Real's complete superiority. The meeting of Real and Reims carried with it an emotional twist, since Real's Raymond Kopa had to play against his former teammates. He rejoined Reims a few weeks after the final.

1959-60. The extraordinary odyssey of Di Stefano, Gento, and Real Madrid, rather than showing signs of diminishing, was to come to a glorious climax in this fifth year of the European Champion Clubs' Cup. It is argued by many that the 1959-60 series was the most memorable ever. Real, on the road to a fifth consecutive final, breezed through the first two rounds, and in the semi-finals found itself up against archrival Barcelona, which the previous year had completed a spectacular Spanish double. Barcelona's lineup featured a list of soccer greats that rivaled even that of Real: Ladislav Kubala, Luis Suárez, Antonio Ramallets, and Puskás' former Hungarian teammate, the "Golden Head," Sandor Kocsis. The Barcelona challenge to Real's hegemony was taken most seriously because Barca had easily defeated three fine clubs in earlq rounds: CDNA Sofia, AC Milan, and Wolverhampton. Unfortunately, Barcelona's most valuable player, Kubala, was lost to the games against Real due to his dispute with manager Helenio Herrera. Di Stefano and Puskás dominated play on the field, and Real won both legs by a 3-1 score. West German champion Eintracht Frankfurt, meanwhile, prepared for its entry into the final by decimating Glasgow Rangers by an aggregate score of 12-4.

The final, at Hampden Park, Glasgow, before 135,000 spectators, pitted Real Madrid, buoyed by its wins over Barcelona, against a game Eintracht Frankfurt. Eintracht scored the first goal through Kress in the eighteenth minute. Di Stefano equalized and scored a second with finesse, but Eintracht remained very much in the game. Before the half, Puskás scored his first goal from an impossible canon-like shot at a 10-degree angle next to Eintracht's goal line. In the second half, Di Stefano, Puskás, and Gento achieved miracle after miracle, as Puskás drove home a penalty and a few minutes later completed a hat trick. At 5-1 Real refused to lay down and defend its goal and Puskás scored his fourth goal on a dazzling pivot kick in the box. Eintracht had somehow not lost its composure throughout Real's barrage of goals, and Stein scored a brace late in the second half. Di Stefano's third goal came between Stein's two, and the final score was Real Madrid's by 7-3. This legendary game—surely one of the most spectacular of all time—achieved the ideal of matching the finest team ever assembled with a good team in its own right that was prepared to fight it out all the way. In the years to come, the Real-Eintracht final became exemplary of excitement and excellence in international club competition.

1960-61. After capturing the creative imagination of the soccer world and winning five European club championships in succession, Real Madrid's prestige suffered little when it was eliminated in the first round of the sixth edition, though in a sardonic twist, its conqueror was Barcelona. This was Barcelona's make-or-break European Cup run, at least as far as the management was concerned, and the trophy appeared to be free for the taking. Only Hamburg, led by the formidable Uwe Seeler, offered significant resistance, forcing a semi-final play-off in Brussels. But Barcelona's potpourri of international superstars prevailed against German durability and Barca advanced to the final. Benfica, the revitalized Portuguese champions under Hungarian manager Bela Guttmann, emerged from the first rounds as an unlikely yet attractive challenger. Even the stalwart defense of Rapid Vienna could not contain Benfica's goalscoring power in the semi-finals, and the Portuguese team, resplendent with skillful players from the African colonies, gained the final in faint hope that its rear guard could withstand Barcelona's world class forward line (Kubala, Kocsis, Evaristo, Suárez, and Czibor). In the end, a telling 2-2 draw was broken with an own goal by Barcelona's outstanding goalkeeper Ramallets, and Benfica Lisbon become the first non-*Madrileño* club to win the European Cup.

1961-62. Benfica was now poised to come into its own as the preeminent club in Europe. Its extraordinary new teenage star from Mozambique, Eusebio, had already made his European and South American debuts in no uncertain terms, and now it appeared that Benfica's attempt to recapture the cup was closely linked to his presence on the field. In the second round against FC Nürnberg, the Portuguese club lost with Eusebio out of the lineup. In the return leg at Lisbon, a 3-1 deficit was turned into a 7-3 advantage with Eusebio providing the spark at all levels of play. After keen resistance from England's Tottenham Hotspur in the semi-finals, Benfica deservedly moved into the final. Its path to a second cup victory, however, was called into question by

the return of Real Madrid, whose impressive comeback was itself nearly halted by Juventus in the second round, both teams losing at home. (This was Real's first home loss in European Cup competition.) In the exciting final at Amsterdam, a hat trick by Puskás was equalized by one goal each from Benfica's Aguas, Cavem, and Coluña, and in the second half Eusebio won the day with two heroic goals, one each from the penalty spot and a free kick. The victory over mighty Real Madrid was Benfica's greatest achievement among many during the golden era of Portuguese soccer.

1962-63. Though Benfica was as talented as any team in Europe at this time, the departure of Bela Guttmann dealt a serious blow to its attempt to take over the mantle of Real Madrid. There were additional problems for Benfica with the injuries of several starting players, and at home it relinquished the league championship to archrival Sporting Lisbon. Nevertheless, successive wins over Norrköping, Dukla Prague, and Feyenoord put it through to the final in London. AC Milan, meanwhile, possessing sufficient goalscoring power to make up for its emphasis on defense, ripped through the early rounds with a goal difference of 31-5 and many spectacular displays by Altafini and the young Rivera, though Ipswich Town and Dundee FC had won their home legs. Dundee was responsible for one of the best series of upsets in European Cup competition thus far, winning decisively over FC Köln (including an 8-0 trouncing in Scotland), Sporting Lisbon, and RSC Anderlecht. Feyenoord, the fourth semi-finalist, was steady enough to withstand play-offs in both early rounds. In the final, there was an authentic hero in Milan's Brazilian center forward Altafini, who scored both goals against Benfica. Eusebio tallied for his side, but the Italian counterattack, which by now had become an Italian trademark, was allowed to dominate the flow of the game at least once too often, and the European Cup left the Iberian Peninsula for the first time since the competition began.

1963-64. The ninth edition saw the return of the trophy to the same city as the year before but on the merits of a different club. AC Milan's archrival, Internazionale, determined to wrestle the international prize from its neighbor, had developed a more taut, more efficient brand of *catenaccio*. Manager Herrera had brought the gifted Luis Suárez with him from Barcelona, and in Facchetti and

Mazzola, young players of great ability, Inter Milan seemed to have the right mixture of youth and experience. Inter's progression through the early rounds was not so much convincing as it was indicative of its defensive style: all games were low scoring in both home and away legs, and there had not been a single loss. Real Madrid's aging team of living legends appeared on the horizon once again, achieving massive shutouts over Glasgow Rangers and FC Zürich on the way to the final, and upsetting the holders, AC Milan, in the meantime. But the impenetrable defense of Inter in Vienna stopped Di Stefano and Puskás, the former at the end of his incomparable playing career, and established once and for all the beginning of a new era of garrisoned soccer. Italy became the first country to have two clubs win the European club championship.

1964-65. For the first time in the 11-year history of the competition, egregious mistakes by a referee caused serious repercussions in the outcome of the tournament. Liverpool won handsomely at home in the semi-finals against holder Inter Milan, but two unlawful goals by the Italians were allowed to stand in the return leg at San Siro, resulting ultimately in the elimination of Liverpool and Inter's advancement to the final for a second time. Benfica, achieving its fourth final in five years, was on form throughout the early rounds, especially in routing the still excellent Real Madrid by 5-1. In six matches, the Portuguese champions scored 27 goals, but in the final against Inter, the Italian garrison stifled its attack, and the hostile atmosphere of Inter's own home ground helped demoralize the talented Benfica side still further. A shoddy goal by Inter's Jair won the cup, and Benfica went home to the safety of Lisbon.

1965-66. Real mardid was appropriately returned to the European Cup summit by eliminating two-time winner Inter Milan in the semi-finals, its ironic victory achieved by defending a draw at San Siro. Puskás, after scoring five goals against Feyenoord in the first round, was retired before the latter rounds, but the rebuilt side had a new leader in Amancio, and the timeless speed and agility of Gento was still on hand. Real's opponent in the final was Partizan Belgrade, the first club from Eastern Europe to reach the last round. Partizan's main obstacle had been another returnee, Manchester United, dazzling throughout the early rounds with its huge collection of international stars (Best,

Charlton, and Law each won the European Footballer of the Year award by the end of the decade). But the English champions faltered in Belgrade in the semi-finals, and Partizan was fortunate to qualify for the final at Brussels. Partizan went ahead by a goal, but the youthful and proud Real team scored twice on determination and brought a sixth European Cup victory back home to Spain. The continent's most coveted club-level prize had still not left the Latin countries of Southern Europe.

1966-67. In the twelfth edition, Inter Milan's locked-tight defense and the hegemony of Latin teams was finally broken by the champion club of Scotland—Celtic Glasgow—not that Celtic had shown any earlier indication of its potential. Its luck in the draw produced a series of relatively weak opponents in the early rounds, though the Scottish team was forced into defensive postures consistently, and Yugoslavia's Vojvodina Novi Sad and Czechoslovakia's Dukla Prague had given Celtic a genuine fright. Meanwhile, Inter characteristically squeaked past three Eastern European teams and Real Madrid in early rounds, and advanced to the final. Celtic emerged in the final as an attacking side, and superb goals by Gemmell and Chalmers shocked the Italians into submission. The Scots maintained complete control throughout, and the Portuguese spectators on hand expressed the jubilant appreciation of a public accustomed to Celtic's type of attractive playmaking. This edition of the European Cup was also noteworthy for the prominent role played by Eastern European clubs and the first appearance of a Soviet team, Torpedo Moscow. Ajax Amsterdam's impressive showing against Liverpool in the first round stood out as a prophetic indication of events to come.

1967-68. The high emotion of the 1968 final was unsurpassed in the history of the competition. Ten years earlier, Manchester United had been sure finalists against Real Madrid when its team was decimated by the Munich air disaster. There had been two European Cup attempts in the meantime, both ending commendably in the semi-final round, and now United was to gain the final at last. Its compromising form in early rounds was a cause for concern, but in the second leg of the semi-finals against Real Madrid, the Spaniards having lost by one goal at Manchester, United rose to the occasion magnificently and equalized after being down by two. The all-important third goal was scored by Bill Foulkes, who with Bobby Charlton and manager Matt Busby were the only surviving members of the 1958 team. United's opponent in the final was four-time finalist Benfica—still dangerous with Eusebio, Coluña, and Simoes—but the venue was London and the stage was set for a possible melodrama of the highest order. A 1-1 score at the end of regulation time was more than some observers could bear. George Best broke the deadlock in extra time, and his tally was added to by Charlton and Kidd. The final score was 4-1, and England erupted in an outpouring of emotional release equal to that of the 1966 World Cup victory two years earlier. Matt Busby was knighted by the Queen, and the already lofty stature of Manchester United became a new chapter of English folklore.

1968-69. Manchester United, however, could not hold to form the following year, and in the semi-finals of the fourteenth edition it was eliminated by AC Milan. A new European force was emerging to replace the Italian-dominated era of droll tactics. The most exciting performances in the 1968-69 competition were displayed by Holland's rising club Ajax Amsterdam, led by its breathtaking center forward Johan Cruyff. Ajax's 3-0 win over Benfica in the quarter-final replay at Paris was a tour de force, yet in the end it appeared that its time had not yet arrived. The eventual winner of the cup, AC Milan, had done well to knock out United and Celtic, but its strength was suspect after mediocre displays against Swedish champions Malmö in the first round, and the sheer luck of not having to face anybody in the second round. In the final, Ajax was contained well enough to allow Rivera control of the tempo of the game and the setting up of a hat trick by left wing Prati. A penalty conversion by Yugoslav defender Vasović was all that Ajax could muster, and a relatively uninteresting edition of the European Cup was again won by AC Milan.

1969-70. For the first time, all 33 member associations of UEFA were represented in the European Cup. In the recent past, there had been scant participation by the champion clubs of the USSR (conflict with winter, i.e., regular season, fixtures), Iceland (financial restrictions due to long-distance travel), and Albania (political isolation); but for three seasons in a row (from 1969-70 to 1971-72) there was full representation. (Since 1972,

only Albania has failed to participate.)

The promise of Ajax Amsterdam was held in abeyance for one year while the unlikeliest of situations occurred: the rising prominence of Dutch archrival Feyenoord Rotterdam. The rise of Dutch soccer, it seemed, was not limited to one club. Feyenoord benefited from some relatively easy draws, entering the 1970 final with a 22-2 goal difference in eight matches, though the statistics failed to point out serious problems the Dutch team encountered against AC Milan, East Berlin's ASK Vorwärts, and Legia Warsaw. Celtic, Feyenoord's opponent in the final, was more decisive in elimination rounds, although its second round result against Benfica was decided by a toss of the coin. Feyenoord was not a practitioner of the more fluid attacking style of Ajax, but its *catenaccio*-based system was resilient enough to stop Celtic in the final, and an overtime goal by Swedish center forward Kindvall won Holland's first European club championship. The event, however, was somewhat compromised by everyone's lingering anticipation of the more exciting Ajax Amsterdam and the new darling of European soccer, Johan Cruyff.

1970-71. The Ajax era now began in earnest. Its opponent in the final, Panathinaïkos Athens, under the leadership of manager Ferenc Puskás, was the biggest surprise since Dundee's triumphs of 1962-63. The Greek champion had won the quarter-final and semi-final rounds on the away-goals rule, but its accomplishment was sweetened by the knowledge that both opponents, Everton and Red Star Belgrade, were seasoned international competitors and favorites to win. In the semi-finals, the talented Greek club was impressive in coming back from an away loss to Red Star to equalize goals. Ajax, meanwhile, moved in and out of defensive postures, especially against quarter-final opponents Celtic, and in the semi-finals was forced to escape from a near disaster against Atlético Madrid to gain the final. In the final, Ajax scored one goal near the beginning and one near the end of the game, and spent much of the second half defending its lead. Haan's goal in the 87th minute showed that Ajax was capable of scoring many more, if only its strategy had permitted an all-out attack. Ajax's potential had not yet been realized, but with so much evident brilliance on display, it went into the next edition of the cup as a runaway favorite.

1971-72. The presence of Inter Milan in the 1972 final against Ajax underscored the negative expression inherent in *catenaccio*. It was now clear that the freedom of movement and intelligent tactical basis being offered by Dutch and West German clubs would somehow have to triumph over the drab style of the successful Italians if the game in general were to thrive once again. Ajax's entertaining display of skills in the final and throughout the competition did much to further this cause. In spite of Inter's tactics, the Italian club advanced to the final, though by an unfortunate series of events. A replay was ordered after its 7-1 second round loss to Borussia Mönchengladbach of West Germany when Inter's Bonensegna was knocked unconscious by a bottle thrown from the German crowd. After winning the regularly scheduled second leg in Milan, Inter forced a scoreless draw in the replay in Berlin and moved on to the next round. In the semi-finals, Inter and Celtic battled to two scoreless draws, and Inter finally won on penalty kicks. Cruyff scored both Ajax goals in the final, Inter's fourth in nine years, and Ajax assured itself of an epoch-making hold on European club soccer.

1972-73. The exciting Dutch club was further enhanced by a new right winger, Johnny Rep, who brought the team to its peak level of quality. Ajax's road to the final was strewn with formidable opponents. In the quarter-finals, it met West German champion Bayern München, whose stars formed the backbone of the astonishing West German national team that had just won the European Football Championship. This quarter-final draw was by consensus the coming together of the world's two best clubs. In the Amsterdam leg, however, West German international goalkeeper Sepp Maier faltered and allowed four Dutch goals, demoralizing the Bayern players beyond repair. In the return leg, there was little chance for even Gerd Müller and Franz Beckenbauer to surmount the obstacles presented by Ajax, and the Dutch went through to face Real Madrid in the semi-finals. The Spanish champions—no match for the evenly spread talent of Ajax—went down by a 3-0 goal aggregate. Meanwhile, the great Italian club Juventus reached the final after disposing of English champion Derby County, though few could have known that in the years to come, the matches played between these two clubs would come under suspicion for charges of bribery and under-the-table dealings. (It has been asserted that the culprits were Juventus and the referee.) In the huge Red Star Stadium in Belgrade, Ajax played

below form, but Juve could not overcome a 1-0 deficit after a goal by Rep. Ajax became the first club since Real Madrid to win three European Cup competitions in succession, and in so doing brought to Holland a fourth such trophy in as many years.

1973-74. The West German *Wunderteam* Bayern München could no longer be contained within its national boundaries. Despite an inauspicious start in the first round against Sweden's Atvidaberg and consistent resistance all along the road to the final, Bayern's technical brilliance was the major feature of the 1973-74 edition. Ajax, now minus Cruyff, was eliminated in the second round by CSKA Sofia, the perennial champions of Bulgaria. Atlético Madrid, which had finally outdistanced its crosstown rival in Spanish league competition, stumbled over Turkey's Galatasaray in the first round, then managed the unusual feat of winning only the away legs in the next two rounds. In the Glasgow leg of the semi-finals against Celtic, Atlético's growing reputation for brutal conduct on the field came to fruition, as three of its players were ejected in a scoreless draw and Celtic appealed to UEFA for a disqualification ruling. The appeal was turned down, and Atlético boorishly won its home leg and advanced to the final. Bayern's successes against CSKA Sofia and Újpest Dózsa in the later rounds were ironically the result of goals scored by new teammate Torstensson from Atvidaberg, who had played so impressively for the Swedish club in the first round earlier in the season. The final in Brussels ended in a 1-1 draw after two scoreless halves, and a replay was forced. The second time around Bayern played up to its extraordinary capabilities, and two goals each from Hoeness and Müller won a deserving European club championship for Bayern and set the stage for West Germany's World Cup victory some weeks later.

1974-75. Bayern entered the twentieth edition of the European Cup sitting on the crest of a West German wave. The momentum created by Bayern's success this coupled with West Germany's World Championship victory by a team based on Bayern players, caused euphoric expectations. In the second round, Bayern met East Germany's FC Magdeburg, and both managements agreed that the results of this round would count double as the 1974 edition of the European "Super Cup," Magdeburg having won the European Cup Winners' Cup in 1974. Both legs were handily won by Bayern. In the distant Armenian capital of Erevan, Bayern held Ararat to a one goal victory in the second leg of the semi-finals to save an aggregate goal advantage, then advanced to its second final by withstanding a strong challenge by the up-and-coming French champion, St. Étienne. Its opponents in the final, Leeds United, surmounted stiff opposition from Újpest Dózsa, RSC Anderlecht, and, in the semi-finals, a frustrated Barcelona led by Johan Cruyff. Leed's holding of Barcelona to a draw in Spain was one of the finest achievements by an English club in Europe for many years. In the final at Paris, Roth and Müller scored a goal apiece to retain the cup for Bayern, but Leeds' admirable challenge was marred by a shocking outburst of violent behavior by Leeds fans. The Parc des Princes was literally torn to shreds, and the Yorkshire club's disappointment in losing was compounded by an embarrassing reprimand and suspension from UEFA.

1975-76. The general malaise that many formerly great clubs of Europe were now experiencing helped to magnify the exalted position in which Bayern now found itself. The club not only appeared unbeatable, but the fame and glory of its extraordinary players reached dizzying heights. Beckenbauer, Maier, and Müller were now thought to be the world's best in their respective positions, and they developed an increasing reputation as "specialists" in winning international honors (having failed twice in a row to win the league championship at home). Bayern's vast experience in Europe carried it through once again to the final in 1976 when it faced the captivating St. Étienne, currently at the forefront of a French revival on both club and national levels. St. Étienne had moved confidently past Glasgow Rangers and co-favorite Dinamo Kiev before eliminating PSV Eindhoven to gain the final. At the giant Hampden

Park Stadium in Glasgow, there was little doubt that both teams performed well, though St. Étienne emerged with the lion's share of the praise. But a goal by Bayern's Roth made the difference and French hopes for a new golden era à la Reims were temporarily shelved. Ultimately, it was Bayern's last hurrah, as front office shenanigans threw the weary German heroes into a tailspin.

1976-77. Bayern was eliminated in 1977 by Dinamo Kiev in the quarter-finals, Franz Beckenbauer departed for the United States, and one of the greatest club-level teams of the decade disappeared from international view. Borussia Mönchengladbach, West German league winner three years in succession, was waiting in the wings. Its attractive, fluid style, similar to that of Bayern, made it an instant favorite to retain the cup for West Germany. Among its impressive wins was the semi-final elimination of the same Dinamo Kiev that had earlier knocked out Bayern. With experienced defender Berti Vogts in command, Borussia entered the final in Rome as a slight favorite. But Liverpool—always a difficult opponent for Borussia in European competition—was achieving phenomenal success both home and abroad, sparked by the speedy artistry of Kevin Keegan. Liverpool's path to the final had been deceptively easy with only St. Étienne putting up a serious challenge in the quarter-finals. In Rome, Liverpool emerged with a remarkably fluid style not unfamiliar to the West Germans. The difference, however, was its added ability to challenge the opposition in any part of the field (a trademark of English league competition). Despite the brilliance of the Danish international Simonsen, Vogts and his team were outplayed, and the European Cup returned to England for the first time since 1968. Liverpool's 3-1 win was convincing, and helped to lift England out of its international doldrums.

Winners

1955-56	Real Madrid	1963-64	Inter Milan	1971-72	Ajax Amsterdam
1956-57	Real Madrid	1964-65	Inter Milan	1972-73	Ajax Amsterdam
1957-58	Real Madrid	1965-66	Real Madrid	1973-74	Bayern München
1958-59	Real Madrid	1966-67	Celtic	1974-75	Bayern München
1959-60	Real Madrid	1967-68	Manchester United	1975-76	Bayern München
1960-61	Benfica	1968-69	AC Milan	1976-77	Liverpool
1961-62	Benfica	1969-70	Feyenoord	1977-78	Liverpool
1962-63	AC Milan	1970-71	Ajax Amsterdam		

Cumulative Ranking of the Top 75 Clubs (1956-77)
(number of editions in parentheses)

			P	W	D	L	F	A	P
1	Real Madrid (18)	(Spa)	115	68	17	30	293	134	153
2	Benfica (15)	(Por)	86	43	19	24	189	103	105
3	Celtic (9)	(Sco)	54	30	11	13	105	47	71
4	Ajax (9)	(Net)	51	31	9	11	91	46	71
5	Manchester United (5)	(Eng)	41	26	7	8	100	45	59
6	AC Milan (7)	(Ita)	44	26	5	13	116	59	57
7	Bayern München (6)	(GFR)	40	25	7	8	93	37	57
8	Inter Milan (5)	(Ita)	41	23	10	8	64	30	56
9	CSKA Sofia (14)	(Bul)	52	22	9	21	83	80	53
10	Feyenoord (7)	(Net)	37	20	9	8	89	39	49
11	Dukla Prague (7)	(Cze)	37	19	8	10	67	49	46
12	Red Star Belgrade (9)	(Yug)	39	19	6	14	85	60	44
13	St. Étienne (9)	(Fra)	39	19	6	14	49	41	44
14	Atlético Madrid (4)	(Spa)	33	18	6	9	56	31	42
15	Standard Liège (6)	(Bel)	32	20	1	11	55	33	41
16	Újpest Dózsa (7)	(Hun)	34	16	7	11	60	50	39
17	Juventus (7)	(Ita)	35	16	7	12	43	40	39
18	Rangers (8)	(Sco)	37	18	3	16	66	72	39
19	RSC Anderlecht (11)	(Bel)	44	16	6	22	84	89	38
20	Dinamo Kiev (5)	(Sov)	28	16	5	7	41	22	37
21	Górnik Zabrze (8)	(Pol)	31	17	3	11	52	45	37
22	Barcelona (3)	(Spa)	26	15	6	5	60	25	36
23	Liverpool (4)	(Eng)	27	15	5	7	55	27	35
24	Rapid Vienna (7)	(Aus)	33	15	4	14	53	49	34
24	Spartak Trnava (5)	(Cze)	24	13	7	4	44	20	33
26	Stade de Reims (4)	(Fra)	24	14	3	7	63	30	31
27	Vasas Budapest (5)	(Hun)	25	12	5	8	61	30	29
28	Borussia M'gladbach (4)	(GFR)	24	10	8	5	52	22	28
29	Dinamo Bucharest (8)	(Rum)	28	12	4	12	50	52	28
30	PSV Eindhoven (4)	(Net)	20	11	4	5	43	20	26
31	Legia Warsaw (4)	(Pol)	18	11	2	5	29	16	24
32	Leeds United (2)	(Eng)	17	11	1	5	42	13	23
33	Partizan Belgrade (6)	(Yug)	27	10	3	14	47	47	23
34	Galatasaray (7)	(Tur)	25	8	6	11	29	39	22
35	FC Zürich (6)	(Swi)	25	10	2	13	33	46	22
36	Panathinaïkos (8)	(Gre)	27	6	8	13	34	39	20
37	Borussia Dortmund (3)	(GFR)	18	8	3	7	44	31	19
38	Vorwärts Frankfurt/Oder (6)	(DDR)	22	9	1	12	35	33	19
39	Hajduk Split (3)	(Yug)	12	8	2	2	32	13	18
40	Ferencváros (4)	(Hun)	16	8	2	6	36	28	18
41	OGC Nice (2)	(Fra)	14	8	2	4	30	24	18
42	Sparta Prague (2)	(Cze)	12	7	3	2	23	17	17

43	Young Boys Berne (4)	(Swi)	15	6	5	4	27	26	17
44	Sporting Lisbon (7)	(Por)	20	7	2	11	35	42	16
45	Austria/WAC (6)	(Aus)	19	7	2	10	24	34	16
46	Fenerbahçe (8)	(Tur)	23	6	3	14	20	46	15
47	Derby County (2)	(Eng)	12	6	2	4	18	12	14
48	Wismut Aue (3)	(DDR)	16	5	4	7	26	23	14
49	FC Basel (5)	(Swi)	16	6	2	8	35	34	14
50	FC Brugge (2)	(Bel)	10	5	3	2	23	12	13
51	Slovan Bratislava (4)	(Cze)	12	6	1	5	17	19	13
52	Aarhus GF (4)	(Den)	14	5	3	6	18	22	13
53	Malmö FF (7)	(Swe)	16	6	1	9	18	34	13
54	Jeunesse Esch (11)	(Lux)	25	5	3	17	23	58	13
55	Wiener SK (2)	(Aus)	12	4	4	4	21	18	12
56	Ruch Chorzów (2)	(Pol)	10	5	2	3	17	15	12
57	FC Nürnberg (2)	(GFR)	8	5	1	2	16	14	11
58	FC Köln (2)	(GFR)	9	3	5	1	12	12	11
59	Ararat Erevan (1)	(Sov)	6	5	0	1	14	5	10
60	Eintracht Frankfurt (1)	(GFR)	7	4	2	1	23	15	10
61	Dundee F.C. (1)	(Sco)	8	5	0	3	20	14	10
62	Carl Zeiss Jena (2)	(DDR)	8	5	0	3	12	11	10
63	Linfield (7)	(NoI)	17	3	4	10	25	48	10
64	DWS Amsterdam (1)	(Net)	6	4	1	1	13	4	9
65	Tottenham Hotspur (1)	(Eng)	8	4	1	3	21	13	9
66	MTK/VM (2)	(Hun)	8	4	1	3	24	18	9
67	Everton (2)	(Eng)	8	2	5	1	12	6	9
68	Athletic Bilbao (1)	(Spa)	6	4	1	1	16	14	9
69	Vasas ETO Györ (1)	(Hun)	8	4	1	3	16	15	9
70	Vojvodina Novi Sad (1)	(Yug)	7	4	1	2	8	7	9
71	AEK Athens (3)	(Gre)	10	3	3	4	16	20	9
72	IFK Norrköping (4)	(Swe)	12	2	5	5	14	20	9
73	IFK Göteborg (4)	(Swe)	14	4	1	9	24	36	9
74	Arsenal (1)	(Eng)	6	4	0	2	13	4	8
75	Schalke 04 (1)	(GFR)	7	3	2	2	13	13	8

Scoring Leaders

1955-56	Milutinovic (Partizan Belgrade) 7
1956-57	Viollet (Manchester United) 9
1957-58	Di Stefano (Real Madrid) 10
1958-59	Fontaine (Stade de Reims) 10
1959-60	Puskás (Real Madrid) 13
1960-61	Aguas (Benfica) 10
1961-62	Di Stefano (Real Madrid) 8
1962-63	Altafini (AC Milan) 14
1963-64	S. Mazzola (Inter Milan) 8
1964-65	Torres (Benfica) 10
1965-66	Eusebio (Benfica) 7
1966-67	van Himst (RSC Anderlecht) 6
1967-68	Eusebio (Benfica) 6
1968-69	Law (Manchester United) 9
1969-70	Jones (Leeds United) 8
1970-71	Antoniadis (Panathinaïkos) 10
1971-72	Cruyff (Ajax), Takac (Standard Liège), & Macari (Celtic) 5

1972-73	Müller (Bayern München) 11	
1973-74	Müller (Bayern München) 8	
1974-75	Almquist (Atvidaberg), Makarov (Ararat), & Müller (Bayern München) 5	
1975-76	Santillana (Real Madrid) &	

Heynckes (Borussia Mönchengladbach) 6

1976-77 Müller (Bayern München) & Cucinotta (FC Zürich) 5

1977-78 Simonsen (Borussia Mönchengladbach) 5

Miscellaneous Records and Statistics

Most editions participated in: 18, by Real Madrid.

Most games played: 115, by Real Madrid.

Most wins: 68, by Real Madrid.

Most losses: 30, by Real Madrid.

Most goals for: 293, by Real Madrid.

Most goals against: 134, by Real Madrid.

Record home victory: Dinamo Bucharest 11, Crusaders 0, 1973-74.

Record away victory: Valkeakosken Haka 1, RSC Anderlecht 10, 1966-67.

Record victory in a final: Bayern München 4, Atlético Madrid 0, 1973-74; Real Madrid 7, Eintracht Frankfurt 3, 1959-60.

Highest aggregate score in a match: 14 (Feyenoord 12, KR Reykjavik 2, 1969-70).

Highest aggregate score in a final: 10 (Real Madrid 7, Eintracht Frankfurt 3, 1959-60).

Best goal aggregate in a round: 18-0 (Benfica defeated Stade Dudelange by 8-0 and 10-0, 1965-66).

Leading cumulative goalscorer: Alfredo Di Stefano, 49 goals in 58 matches (1955-64).

Highest number of individual goals in one edition: 14, by Altafini (AC Milan), 1962-63.

Highest number of individual goals in a final: 4, by Puskás (Real Madrid), 1959-60.

Hat tricks scored in the final: by Di Stefano (Real Madrid), 1959-60; Puskás (Real Madrid), 1961-62; and Prati (AC Milan), 1968-69.

Record attendance: 135,826 (Celtic vs. Leeds United, Hampden Park, Glasgow, 1969-70).

Record attendance for a final: 127,621 (Real Madrid vs. Eintracht Frankfurt, Hampden Park, Glasgow, 1959-60).

Results

1955-56

First Round

Real Madrid—*Servette	2-0, 5-0
Partizan Belgrade—*Sporting Lisbon	3-3, 5-2
*AC Milan—FC Saarbrücken	3-4, 4-1
*Rapid Vienna—PSV Eindhoven	6-1, 0-1
Hibernian—*Rot-Weiss Essen	4-0, 1-1
*Djurgaarden—Gwardia Warsaw	0-0, 4-1
*Vörös Lobogo—RSC Anderlecht	6-3, 4-1
Stade de Reims—*Aarhus GF	2-0, 2-2

Second Round
*Real Madrid—Partizan Belgrade	4-0, 0-3
AC Milan—*Rapid Vienna	1-1, 7-2
*Hibernian—Djurgaarden	3-1, 1-0
*Stade de Reims—Vörös Lobogo	4-2, 4-4

Semi-Finals
*Real Madrid—AC Milan	4-2, 1-2
*Stade de Reims—Hibernian	2-0, 1-0

Final (in Paris; att. 38,000)

Real Madrid	4	Stade de Reims	3
(Di Stefano, Rial 2, Marquitos)		(Leblond, Templin, Hidalgo)	

*home team in first leg

1956-57

Preliminary Round
OGC Nice—*Aarhus GF	1-1, 5-1
Athletic Bilbao—*FC Porto	2-1, 3-2
*Borussia Dortmund—Spora Luxembourg	4-3, 1-2, 7-0
(play-off in Dortmund)	
Manchester United—*RSC Anderlecht	2-0, 10-0
*Dinamo Bucharest—Galatasaray	3-1, 1-2
*Slovan Bratislava—Legia Warsaw	4-0, 0-2

First Round
*Real Madrid—Rapid Vienna	4-2, 1-3, 2-0
(play-off in Madrid)	
OGC Nice—*Rangers	1-2, 2-1, 3-1
(play-off in Paris)	
*Athletic Bilbao—Honvéd	3-2, 3-3
(second leg in Brussels)	
*Manchester United—Borussia Dortmund	3-2, 0-0
Red Star Belgrade—*Rapid JC Haarlem	4-3, 2-0
*CDNA Sofia—Dinamo Bucharest	8-1, 2-3
Grasshoppers—*Slovan Bratislava	0-1, 2-0
*Fiorentina—IFK Norrköping	1-1, 1-0
(second leg in Rome)	

Second Round
*Real Madrid—OGC Nice	3-0, 3-2
Manchester United—*Athletic Bilbao	3-5, 3-0
*Red Star Belgrade—CDNA Sofia	3-1, 1-2
*Fiorentina—Grasshoppers	3-1, 2-2

Semi-Finals
*Real Madrid—Manchester United   3-1, 2-2
Fiorentina—*Red Star Belgrade   1-0, 0-0

Final (in Madrid; att. 124,000)

Real Madrid	2	Fiorentina	0

(Di Stefano pen, Gento)

*home team in first leg

1957-58

Preliminary Round

*Seville—Benfica	3-1, 0-0
*Aarhus GF—Glenavon	0-0, 3-0
Wismut Karl-Marx-Stadt—*Gwardia Warsaw	1-3, 3-1, 1-1
(play-off in Berlin; Wismut won by toss of the coin)	
Vasas Budapest—*CDNA Sofia	1-2, 6-1
Manchester United—*Shamrock Rovers	6-0, 3-2
Red Star Belgrade—*Stade Dudelange	5-0, 9-1
*Rangers—St. Étienne	3-1, 1-2
*AC Milan—Rapid Vienna	4-1, 2-5, 4-2
(play-off in Zurich)	

First Round

*Seville—Aarhus GF	4-0, 0-2
Ajax—*Wismut Karl-Marx-Stadt	3-1, 1-0
*Manchester United—Dukla Prague	3-0, 0-1
Red Star Belgrade—*IFK Norrköping	2-2, 2-1
*Borussia Dortmund—CCA Bucharest	4-2, 1-3, 3-1
(play-off in Bologna)	
AC Milan—*Rangers	4-1, 2-0
Real Madrid—*Antwerp	2-1, 6-0

Second Round

*Real Madrid—Seville	8-0, 2-2
Vasas Budapest—*Ajax	2-2, 4-0
*Manchester United—Red Star Belgrade	2-1, 3-3
AC Milan—*Borussia Dortmund	1-1, 4-1

Semi-Finals

*Real Madrid—Vasas Budapest	4-0, 0-2
AC Milan—*Manchester United	1-2, 4-0

Final (in Brussels; att. 67,000)

Real Madrid	3	AC Milan	2

(Di Stefano, Rial, Gento)   (Schiaffino, Grillo)

-after extra time; 2-2 at regulation time-

*home team in first leg

1958-59
(Bye: Real Madrid, CDNA Sofia, Wolverhampton Wanderers, Palloseura Helsinki)

Preliminary Round
Wiener SK—*Juventus	1-3, 7-0
Dukla Prague—*Dinamo Zagreb	2-2, 2-1
Schalke 04—*KB Copenhagen	0-3, 5-2, 3-1
(play-off in Enschede)	
*Atlético Madrid—Drumcondra	8-0, 5-1
MTK Budapest—*Polonia Bytom	3-0, 3-0
*Wismut Karl-Marx-Stadt—Petrolul Ploesti	4-2, 0-2, 5-0
(play-off in Kiev)	
*IFK Göteborg—Jeunesse Esch	2-1, 0-1, 5-1
(play-off in Gothenburg)	
Sporting Lisbon—*DOS Utrecht	4-3, 2-1
*Standard Liège—Heart of Midlothian	5-1, 1-2
Stade de Reims—*Ards	4-1, 6-2
Besiktas Istanbul won by default: Olympiakos withdrew	
Young Boys Berne won by default: Manchester United withdrew	

First Round
*Real Madrid—Besiktas Istanbul	2-0, 1-1
*Wiener SK—Dukla Prague	3-1, 0-1
Schalke 04—*Wolverhampton Wanderers	2-2, 2-1
*Atlético Madrid—CDNA Sofia	2-1, 0-1, 3-1
(play-off in Geneva won after extra time)	
Young Boys Berne—*MTK Budapest	2-1, 4-1
*Wismut Karl-Marx-Stadt—IFK Göteborg	3-0, 2-2
Standard Liège—*Sporting Lisbon	3-2, 3-0
*Stade de Reims—Palloseura Helsinki	4-0, 3-0

Second Round
Real Madrid—*Wiener SK	0-0, 7-1
*Atlético Madrid—Schalke 04	3-0, 1-1
*Young Boys Berne—Wismut Karl-Marx-Stadt	2-2, 0-0, 2-1
(play-off in Amsterdam)	
Stade de Reims—*Standard Liège	0-2, 3-0

Semi-Finals
*Real Madrid—Atlético Madrid	2-1, 0-1, 2-1
(play-off in Zaragoza)	
Stade de Reims—*Young Boys Berne	0-1, 3-0

Final (in Stuttgart; att. 80,000)
Real Madrid	2	Stade de Reims	0
(Mateos, Di Stefano)			

*home team in first leg

1959-60
(Bye: Sparta Rotterdam, Red Star Belgrade, Young Boys Berne, BK 09 Odense)

Preliminary Round

*Jeunesse Esch—LKS Lódź	6-0, 1-2
*OGC Nice—Shamrock Rovers	3-2, 1-1
*Fenerbahçe—Csepel Budapest	1-1, 3-2
*Barcelona—CDNA Sofia	2-2, 6-2
*AC Milan—Olympiakos	2-2, 3-1
Wolverhampton Wanderers—*ASK Vorwärts Berlin	1-2, 2-0
IFK Göteborg—*Linfield	1-2, 6-1
*Red Star Bratislava—FC Porto	2-1, 2-0
*Rangers—RSC Anderlecht	5-2, 2-0
Wiener SK—*Petrolul Ploesti	0-0, 2-1
Eintracht Frankfurt won by default: Palloseura Helsinki withdrew	

First Round

*Real Madrid—Jeunesse Esch	7-0, 5-2
OGC Nice—*Fenerbahçe	1-2, 2-1, 5-1
(play-off in Geneva)	
Barcelona—*AC Milan	2-0, 5-1
Wolverhampton Wanderers—*Red Star Belgrade	1-1, 3-0
*Sparta Rotterdam—IFK Göteborg	3-1, 1-3, 3-1
(play-off in Bremen)	
*Rangers—Red Star Bratislava	4-3, 1-1
Wiener SK—*BK 09 Odense	3-0, 2-2
Eintracht Frankfurt—*Young Boys Berne	4-1, 1-1

Second Round

Real Madrid—*OGC Nice	2-3, 4-0
*Barcelona—Wolverhampton Wanderers	4-0, 5-2
Rangers—*Sparta Rotterdam	3-2, 0-1, 3-2
(play-off in London)	
*Eintracht Frankfurt—Wiener SK	2-1, 1-1

Semi-Finals

*Real Madrid—Barcelona	3-1, 3-1
*Eintracht Frankfurt—Rangers	6-1, 6-3

Final (in Glasgow; att. 127,621)

Real Madrid (Di Stefano 3, Puskás 4)	7	Eintracht Frankfurt (Kress, Stein 2)	3

*home team in first leg

1960-61

(Bye: Panathinaïkos, Burnley, Hamburger SV, Real Madrid)

Preliminary Round

Benfica—*Heart of Midlothian	2-1, 3-0
Újpest Dózsa—*Red Star Belgrade	2-1, 3-0
*Aarhus GF—Legia Warsaw	3-0, 0-1
*Fredrikstad—Ajax	4-3, 0-0
*Rapid Vienna—Besiktas Istanbul	4-0, 0-1
Malmö FF—*IFK Helsinki	3-1, 2-1
CDNA Sofia—*Juventus	0-2, 4-1
*Stade de Reims—Jeunesse Esch	6-1, 5-0
Young Boys Berne—*Limerick	5-0, 4-2
Spartak Kralove—*CCA Bucharest	3-0, —
(CCA withdrew after first leg)	
*Barcelona—Lierse SK	2-0, 3-0
Wismut Karl-Marx-Stadt won by default: Glenavon withdrew	

First Round

*Benfica—Újpest Dózsa	6-2, 1-2
*Aarhus GF—Fredrikstad	3-0, 1-0
*Rapid Vienna—Wismut Karl-Marx-Stadt	3-1, 0-2, 1-0
(play-off in Basle)	
*Malmö FF—CDNA Sofia	1-0, 1-1
*Burnley—Stade de Reims	2-0, 2-3
Hamburger SV—*Young Boys Berne	5-0, 3-3
*Spartak Kralove—Panathinaïkos	1-0, 0-0
Barcelona—*Real Madrid	2-2, 2-1

Second Round

*Benfica—Aarhus GF	3-1, 4-1
*Rapid Vienna—Malmö FF	2-0, 2-0
Hamburger SV—*Burnley	1-3, 4-1
*Barcelona—Spartak Kralove	4-0, 1-1

Semi-Finals
*Benfica—Rapid Vienna   3-0, 1-1
*Barcelona—Hamburger SV   1-0, 1-2, 1-0
(play-off in Brussels)

Final (in Berne; att. 28,000)

Benfica	3	Barcelona	2
(Aguas, Coluña, Ramallets o.g.)		(Kocsis, Czibor)	

*home team in first leg

1961-62

(Bye: Benfica, Fenerbahçe, Valkeakosken Haka)

Preliminary Round

FK Austria—*CCA Bucharest	0-0, 2-0
*FC Nürnberg—Drumcondra	5-0, 4-1
Servette—*Hibernians Valetta	5-0, 2-1
Dukla Prague—*CDNA Sofia	4-4, 2-1
Feyenoord—*IFK Göteborg	3-0, 8-2
Tottenham Hotspur—*Górnik Zabrze	2-4, 8-1
Standard Liège—*Fredrikstad	2-1, 2-0
*ASK Vorwärts Berlin—Linfield	3-0, —
(Linfield withdrew after first leg)	
Rangers—*AS Monaco	3-2, 3-2
Partizan Belgrade—*Sporting Lisbon	1-1, 2-0
Juventus—*Panathinaïkos	2-1, 1-1
BK 13 Odense—*Spora Luxembourg	6-0, 9-2
Real Madrid—*Vasas Budapest	2-0, 3-1

First Round

Benfica—*FK Austria	1-1, 5-1
FC Nürnberg—*Fenerbahçe	2-1, 1-0
Dukla Prague—*Servette	3-4, 2-0
Tottenham Hotspur—*Feyenoord	3-1, 1-1
*Standard Liège—Valkeakosken Haka	5-1, 2-0
Rangers—*ASK Vorwärts Berlin	2-1, 4-1
Juventus—*Partizan Belgrade	2-1, 5-0
Real Madrid—*BK 13 Odense	3-0, 9-0

Second Round

Benfica—*FC Nürnberg	1-3, 6-0
Tottenham Hotspur—*Dukla Prague	0-1, 4-1
*Standard Liège—Rangers	4-1, 0-2
Real Madrid—*Juventus	1-0, 0-1, 3-1
(play-off in Paris)	

Semi-Finals
*Benfica—Tottenham Hotspur	3-1, 1-2
*Real Madrid—Standard Liège	4-0, 2-0

Final (in Amsterdam; att. 65,000)

Benfica	5	Real Madrid	3
(Eusebio 2 (1 pen)		(Puskás 3)	
Aguas, Cavem, Coluña)			

*home team in first leg

1962-63
(Bye: Stade de Reims, Benfica)

Preliminary Round
*AC Milan—Union Sportif Luxembourg	8-0, 6-0
Ipswich Town—*Floriana Valetta	4-1, 10-0
Galatasaray—*Dinamo Bucharest	1-1, 3-0
*Polonia Bytom—Panathinaïkos	2-1, 4-1
*Dundee—FC Köln	8-1, 0-4
Sporting Lisbon—*Shelbourne	2-0, 5-1
RSC Anderlecht—*Real Madrid	3-3, 1-0
*CDNA Sofia—Partizan Belgrade	2-1, 4-1
Feyenoord—*Servette	3-1, 1-3, 3-1
(play-off in Dusseldorf)	
Vasas Budapest—*Fredrikstad	4-1, 7-0
*FK Austria—IFK Helsinki	5-3, 2-0
BK Esbjerg—*Linfield	2-1, 0-0
Dukla Prague—*ASK Vorwärts Berlin	3-0, 1-0
*IFK Norrköping—Partizan Tirana	2-0, 1-1

First Round
*AC Milan—Ipswich Town	3-0, 1-2
*Galatasaray—Polonia Bytom	4-1, 0-1
Dundee—*Sporting Lisbon	0-1, 4-1
RSC Anderlecht—*CDNA Sofia	2-2, 2-0
*Feyenoord—Vasas Budapest	1-1, 2-2, 1-0
(play-off in Anvers)	
Stade de Reims—FK Austria	2-3, 5-0
Dukla Prague—*BK Esbjerg	0-0, 5-0
Benfica—*IFK Norrköping	1-1, 5-1

Second Round
AC Milan—*Galatasaray	3-1, 5-0
Dundee—*RSC Anderlecht	4-1, 2-1
Feyenoord—*Stade de Reims	1-0, 1-1
*Benfica—Dukla Prague	2-1, 0-0

Semi-Finals
*AC Milan—Dundee	5-1, 0-1
Benfica—*Feyenoord	0-0, 3-1

Final (in London; att. 45,000)

AC Milan	2	Benfica	1
(Altafini 2)		(Eusebio)	

*home team in first leg

1963-64
(Bye: AC Milan)

Preliminary Round
Inter—*Everton	0-0, 1-0
*AS Monaco—AEK Athens	7-2, 1-1
Jeunesse Esch—*Valkeakosken Haka	1-4, 4-0
*Partizan Belgrade—Anorthosis Famagusta	3-0, 3-1
Benfica—*Distillery	3-3, 5-0
Borussia Dortmund—*Lyn Oslo	4-2, 3-1
*Górnik Zabrze—FK Austria	1-0, 0-1, 2-1
(play-off in Vienna)	
*Dukla Prague—Valetta FC	6-0, 2-0
*FC Zürich—Dundalk	3-0, 1-2
*Galatasaray—Ferencváros	4-0, 0-2
Spartak Plovdiv—*Partizan Tirana	0-1, 3-1
PSV Eindhoven—*BK Esbjerg	4-3, 7-1
IFK Norrköping—*Standard Liège	0-1, 2-0
*Dinamo Bucharest—Motor Jena	2-0, 1-0
Real Madrid—*Rangers	1-0, 6-0

First Round
*Inter—AS Monaco	1-0, 3-1
Partizan Belgrade—*Jeunesse Esch	1-2, 6-2
Borussia Dortmund—*Benfica	1-2, 5-0
Dukla Prague—*Górnik Zabrze	0-2, 4-1
*FC Zürich—Galatasaray	2-0, 0-2, 2-2
(play-off in Rome; Zürich won by toss of the coin)	
PSV Eindhoven—*Spartak Plovdiv	1-0, 0-0
AC Milan—*IFK Norrköping	1-1, 5-2
Real Madrid—*Dinamo Bucharest	3-1, 5-3

Second Round
Inter—*Partizan Belgrade	2-0, 2-1
Borussia Dortmund—*Dukla Prague	4-0, 1-3
FC Zürich—*PSV Eindhoven	0-1, 3-1
*Real Madrid—AC Milan	4-1, 0-2

Semi-Finals
    Inter—*Borussia Dortmund   2-2, 2-0
    Real Madrid—*FC Zürich   2-1, 6-0

Final (in Vienna; att. 74,000)

Inter	3	Real Madrid	1
(Mazzola 2, Milani)		(Felo)	

*home team in first leg

1964-65
(Bye: Inter)

Preliminary Round
  Dinamo Bucharest—*Sliema Wanderers   2-0, 5-0
*Rangers—Red Star Belgrade   3-1, 2-4, 3-1
  (play-off in London)
*Rapid Vienna—Shamrock Rovers   3-0, 2-0
  Liverpool—*KR Reykjavik   5-0, 6-1
*RSC Anderlecht—Bologna   1-0, 1-2, 0-0
  (play-off in Barcelona; Anderlecht won by toss of the coin)
  Panathinaïkos—*Glentoran   2-2, 3-2
  FC Köln—*Partizan Tirana   0-0, 2-0
*DWS Amsterdam—Fenerbahçe   3-1, 1-0
  Lyn Oslo—*Lahden Reipas   1-2, 3-0
  Vasas Györ—*Chemie Leipzig   2-0, 4-2
*Lokomotiv Sofia—Malmö FF   8-3, 0-2
*Real Madrid—BK 09 Odense   4-0, 5-2
*Dukla Prague—Górnik Zabrze   4-1, 0-3, 0-0
  (play-off in Duisburg; Dukla won by toss of the coin)
  La Chaux de Fonds—*St. Étienne   2-2, 2-1
  Benfica—*Aris Bonnevoie   5-1, 5-1

First Round
*Inter—Dinamo Bucharest   6-0, 1-0
*Rangers—Rapid Vienna   1-0, 2-0
*Liverpool—RSC Anderlecht   3-0, 1-0
  FC Köln—*Panathinaïkos   1-1, 2-1
*DWS Amsterdam—Lyn Oslo   5-0, 3-1
*Vasas Györ—Lokomotiv Sofia   5-3, 3-4
*Real Madrid—Dukla Prague   4-0, 2-2
  Benfica—*La Chaux de Fonds   1-1, 5-0

Second Round
*Inter—Rangers   3-1, 0-1
  Liverpool—*FC Köln   0-0, 0-0, 2-2
  (play-off in Rotterdam; Liverpool won by toss of the coin)

Vasas Györ—*DWS Amsterdam	1-1, 1-0
*Benfica—Real Madrid	5-1, 1-2

Semi-Finals

Inter—*Liverpool	1-3, 3-0
Benfica—*Vasas Györ	1-0, 4-0

Final (in Milan; att. 80,000)

Inter	1	Benfica	0
(Jair)			

*home team in first leg

1965-66
(Bye: Inter)

Preliminary Round

Real Madrid—*Feyenoord	1-2, 5-0
Kilmarnock—*17. Nendori Tirana	0-0, 1-0
RSC Anderlecht—*Fenerbahçe	0-0, 5-1
Derry City—*Lyn Oslo	3-5, 5-1
*Dinamo Bucharest—BK 09 Odense	4-0, 3-2
Ferencváros—*IB Keflavik	4-1, 9-1
*Panathinaïkos—Sliema Wanderers	4-1, 0-1
Manchester United—*HIK Helsinki	3-2, 6-0
ASK Vorwärts Berlin—*Drumcondra	0-1, 3-0
Benfica—*Stade Dudelange	8-0, 10-0
Levski Sofia—*Djurgaarden	1-2, 6-0
Sparta Prague—*Lausanne	0-0, 4-0
Górnik Zabrze—*Linz ASK	3-1, 2-1
Werder Bremen—*Apoel Nicosia	5-0, 5-0
*Partizan Belgrade—FC Nantes	2-0, 2-2

First Round

Real Madrid—*Kilmarnock	2-2, 5-1
*RSC Anderlecht—Derry City	9-0, —
(Derry conceded second leg: field ruled unsuitable)	
Inter—*Dinamo Bucharest	1-2, 2-0
*Ferencváros—Panathinaïkos	0-0, 3-1
Manchester United—*ASK Vorwärts Berlin	2-0, 3-1
Benfica—*Levski Sofia	2-2, 3-2
*Sparta Prague—Górnik Zabrze	3-0, 2-1
*Partizan Belgrade—Werder Bremen	3-0, 0-1

Second Round
Real Madrid—*RSC Anderlecht	0-1, 4-2
*Inter—Ferencváros	4-0, 1-1
*Manchester United—Benfica	3-2, 5-1
Partizan Belgrade—*Sparta Prague	1-4, 5-0

Semi-Finals
*Real Madrid—Inter	1-0, 1-1
*Partizan Belgrade—Manchester United	0, 0-1

Final (in Brussels; att. 55,000)

Real Madrid	2	Partizan Belgrade	1
(Amancio, Serena)		(Vasovic)	

*home team in first leg

1966-67
(Bye: Real Madrid)

Extra Preliminary Round
CSKA Sofia—*Sliema Wanderers	2-1, 4-0
*ASK Vorwärts Berlin—Waterford	6-0, 6-1

Preliminary Round
*Celtic—FC Zürich	2-0, 3-0
FC Nantes—*KR Reykjavik	3-2, 5-2
Vojvodina Novi Sad—*Admira Vienna	1-0, 0-0
Atlético Madrid—*Malmö FF	2-0, 3-1
*Ajax—Besiktas Istanbul	2-0, 2-1
*Liverpool—Petrolul Ploesti	2-0, 1-3, 2-0
(play-off in Brussels)	
RSC Anderlecht—*Valkeakosken Haka	10-1, 2-0
*Górnik Zabrze—ASK Vorwärts Berlin	2-1, 1-2, 3-1
(play-off in Budapest)	
*CSKA Sofia—Olympiakos	3-1, 0-1
Dukla Prague—*BK Esbjerg	2-0, 4-0
Linfield—*Aris Bonnevoie	3-3, 6-1
*1860 München—Omonia Nicosia	8-0, 2-1
*Vasas Budapest—Sporting Lisbon	5-0, 2-0
*Inter—Torpedo Moscow	1-0, 0-0
Valerengen won by default: 17. Nendori Tirana withdrew	

First Round
Celtic—*FC Nantes	3-1, 3-1
*Vojvodina Novi Sad—Atlético Madrid	3-1, 0-2, 3-2
(play-off in Madrid)	

*Ajax—Liverpool	5-1, 2-2
*Dukla Prague—RSC Anderlecht	4-1, 2-1
*CSKA Sofia—Górnik Zabrze	4-0, 0-3
Linfield—Valerengen	4-1, 1-1
Real Madrid—*1860 München	0-1, 3-1
*Inter—Vasas Budapest	2-1, 2-0

Second Round
Celtic—*Vojvodina Novi Sad	0-1, 2-0
Dukla Prague—*Ajax	1-1, 2-1
CSKA Sofia—*Linfield	2-2, 1-0
*Inter—Real Madrid	1-0, 2-0

Semi-Finals
Celtic—*Dukla Prague	3-1, 0-0
*Inter—CSKA Sofia	1-1, 1-1, 1-0
(play-off in Bologna)	

Final (in Lisbon; att. 56,000)

Celtic	2	Inter	1
(Gemmell, Chalmers)		(Mazzola pen)	

*home team in first leg

1967-68

First Round
Benfica—*Glentoran	1-1, 0-0
(Benfica won on away-goals rule)	
Rapid Vienna—*Besiktas Istanbul	1-0, 3-0
Dinamo Kiev—*Celtic	2-1, 1-1
Juventus—*Olympiakos	0-0, 2-0
Vasas Budapest—*Dundalk	1-0, 8-1
*Manchester United—Hibernians Valetta	4-0, 0-0
*St. Étienne—Kuopion Palloseura	2-0, 3-0
RSC Anderlecht—*Wismut Karl-Marx-Stadt	3-1, 2-1
Hvidovre Copenhagen—*FC Basel	2-1, 3-3
Sparta Prague—*Skeid Oslo	1-0, 1-1
Sarajevo—*Olympiakos Nicosia	2-2, 3-1
Real Madrid—*Ajax	1-1, 2-1
*Valur Reykjavik—Jeunesse Esch	1-1, 3-3
(Valur won on away-goals rule)	
*Górnik Zabrze—Djurgaarden	3-0, 1-0
Rapid Bucharest—*Trakia Plovdiv	0-2, 3-0
Eintracht Braunschweig won by default: Dinamo Tirana withdrew	

Second Round

*Manchester United—Sarajevo	0-0, 2-1
Real Madrid—Hvidovre Copenhagen	2-2, 4-1
Eintracht Braunschweig—*Rapid Vienna	0-1, 2-0
*Benfica—St. Étienne	2-0, 0-1
*Vasas Budapest—Valur Reykjavik	6-0, 5-1
Górnik Zabrze—*Dinamo Kiev	2-1, 1-1
*Juventus—Rapid Bucharest	1-0, 0-0
*Sparta Prague—RSC Anderlecht	3-2, 3-3

Quarter-Finals

Juventus—*Eintracht Braunschweig	2-3, 1-0, 1-0
(play-off in Berne)	
*Manchester United—Górnik Zabrze	2-0, 0-1
*Real Madrid—Sparta Prague	3-0, 1-2
Benfica—*Vasas Budapest	0-0, 3-0

Semi-Finals

*Manchester United—Real Madrid	1-0, 3-3
*Benfica—Juventus	2-0, 1-0

Final (in London; att. 100,000)

Manchester United	4	Benfica	1
(Charlton 2, Best, Kidd)		(Graca)	

—after extra time: 1-1 at regulation time—

*home team in first leg

1968-69

First Round

Celtic—*St. Étienne	0-2, 4-0
Manchester United—*Waterford	3-1, 7-1
Fenerbahçe—*Manchester City	0-0, 2-1
*RSC Anderlecht—Glentoran	3-0, 2-2
*AEK Athens—Jeunesse Esch	3-0, 2-3
Ajax—*FC Nürnberg	1-1, 4-0
*AC Milan—Malmö FF	1-2, 4-1
Spartak Trnava—*Steaua Bucharest	1-3, 4-0
Akademisk Copenhagen—*FC Zürich	3-1, 1-2
Rapid Vienna—*Rosenborg Trondheim	3-1, 3-3
Lahden Reipas—*Floriana Valetta	1-1, 2-0
*Real Madrid—AEL Limassol	6-0, 6-0
Benfica—*Valur Reykjavik	0-0, 8-1
Red Star Belgrade won by default: Carl Zeiss Jena withdrew	

Second Round
(Bye: AC Milan, Benfica)
*Manchester United—RSC Anderlecht	3-0, 1-3
*Celtic—Red Star Belgrade	5-1, 1-1
*Rapid Vienna—Real Madrid	1-0, 1-2
(Rapid won on away-goals rule)	
Spartak Trnava—*Lahden Reipas	9-1, 7-1
*AEK Athens—Akademisk Copenhagen	0-0, 2-0
*Ajax—Fenerbahçe	2-0, 2-0

Quarter-Finals
Ajax—*Benfica	1-3, 3-1, 3-0
(play-off in Paris)	
*AC Milan—Celtic	0-0, 1-0
*Manchester United—Rapid Vienna	3-0, 0-0
*Spartak Trnava—AEK Athens	2-1, 1-1

Semi-Finals
*AC Milan—Manchester United	2-1, 0-0
*Ajax—Spartak Trnava	3-0, 0-2

Final (in Madrid; att. 50,000)

AC Milan	4	Ajax	1
(Prati 3, Sormani)		(Vasovic pen)	

*home team in first leg

1969-70

Preliminary Round
KB Copenhagen—*Turun PS Turku	1-0, 4-0

First Round
*AC Milan—Avenir Beggen	5-0, 3-0
*Leeds United—Lyn Oslo	10-0, 6-0
*Red Star Belgrade—Linfield	8-0, 4-2
Celtic—*FC Basel	0-0, 2-0
Spartak Trnava—*Hibernians Valetta	2-2, 4-0
*Galatasaray—Waterford	2-0, 3-2
Ferencváros—*CSKA Sofia	1-2, 4-1
Legia Warsaw—*UT Arad	2-1, 8-0
*ASK Vorwärts Verlin—Panathinaïkos	2-0, 1-1
St.Étienne—*Bayern München	0-2, 3-0
*Standard Liège—17. Nendori Tirana	3-0, 1-1
*Feyenoord—KR Reykjavik	12-2, 4-0
(second leg in Rotterdam)	
Dinamo Kiev—*FK Austria	2-1, 3-1

*Fiorentina—Öster Växjö	1-0, 2-1
*Benfica—KB Copenhagen	2-0, 3-2
*Real Madrid—Olympiakos Nicosia	8-0, 6-1
(second leg in Madrid)	

Second Round

*Leeds United—Ferencváros	3-0, 3-0
*Celtic—Benfica	3-0, 0-3
(Celtic won by toss of the coin)	
Fiorentina—*Dinamo Kiev	2-1, 0-0
*Feyenoord—AC Milan	0-1, 2-0
Galatasaray—*Spartak Trnava	0-1, 2-0
(Galatasaray won by toss of the coin)	
*Legia Warsaw—St. Étienne	2-1, 1-0
*ASK Vorwärts Berlin—Red Star Belgrade	2-1, 2-3
(ASK Vorwärts won on away-goals rule)	
*Standard Liège—Real Madrid	1-0, 3-2

Quarter-Finals

Leeds United—*Standard Liège	1-0, 1-0
*Celtic—Fiorentina	3-0, 0-1
Legia Warsaw—*Galatasaray	1-1, 2-0
Feyenoord—*ASK Vorwärts Berlin	0-1, 2-0

Semi-Finals

Celtic—*Leeds United	1-0, 2-1
Feyenoord—*Legia Warsaw	0-0, 2-0

Final (in Milan; att. 50,000)

Feyenoord	2	Celtic		1
(Israel, Kindvall)		(Gemmell)		

—after extra time: 1-1 at regulation time—

1970-71

Preliminary Round

FK Austria—*Levski-Spartak	1-3, 3-0

First Round

*Everton—IB Keflavik	6-2, 3-0
*Celtic—Kokolan PV	9-0, 5-0
Waterford—*Glentoran	3-1, 1-0
*Cagliari—St. Étienne	3-0, 0-1
*Slovan Bratislava—BK 03 Copenhagen	2-1, 2-2
Ajax—*17. Nendori Tirana	2-2, 2-0
Legia Warsaw—*IFK Göteborg	4-0, 2-1
Red Star Belgrade—*Újpest Dózsa	0-2, 4-0

Standard Liège—*Rosenborg Trondheim	2-0, 5-0
*Borussia Mönchengladbach—EPA Larnaca	6-0, 10-0
FC Basel—*Spartak Moscow	2-3, 2-1
(Basel won on away-goals rule)	
UT Arad—*Feyenoord	1-1, 0-0
(UT won on away-goals rule)	
*Atlético Madrid—FK Austria	2-0, 2-1
Panathinaïkos—*Jeunesse Esch	2-1, 5-0
Carl Zeiss Jena—*Fenerbahçe	4-0, 1-0
*Sporting Lisbon—Floriana Valetta	5-0, 4-0

Second Round

Everton—*Borussia Mönchengladbach	1-1, 1-1
(Everton won on penalty kicks)	
Celtic—*Waterford	7-0, 3-2
*Red Star Belgrade—UT Arad	3-0, 3-1
*Carl Zeiss Jena—Sporting Lisbon	2-1, 2-1
*Panathinaïkos—Slovan Bratislava	3-0, 1-2
Legia Warsaw—*Standard Liège	0-1, 2-0
Atlético Madrid—*Cagliari	1-2, 3-0
*Ajax—FC Basel	3-0, 2-1

Quarter-Finals

Panathinaïkos—*Everton	1-1, 0-0
(Panathinaïkos won on away-goals rule)	
*Ajax—Celtic	3-0, 0-1
*Atlético Madrid—Legia Warsaw	1-0, 1-2
(Atlético won on away goals rule)	
Red Star Belgrade—*Carl Zeiss Jena	2-3, 4-0

Semi-Finals

Panathinaïkos—*Red Star Belgrade	1-4, 3-0
(Panathinaïkos won on away-goals rule)	
Ajax—*Atlético Madrid	0-1, 3-0

Final (in London; att. 90,000)

Ajax	2	Panathinaïkos	0
(van Dijk, Haan)			

*home team in first leg

1971-72

Preliminary Round

*Valencia—Union Sportif Luxembourg	3-1, 1-0

First Round

*Inter—AEK Athens	4-1, 2-3
Arsenal—*Stromsgodset Drammen	3-1, 4-0
Benfica—*Wacker Innsbruck	4-0, 3-1
Celtic—*BK 03 Copenhagen	1-2, 3-0
CSKA Moscow—*Galatasaray	1-1, 3-0
*Ajax—Dynamo Dresden	2-0, 0-0
*Olympique Marseille—Górnik Zabrze	2-1, 1-1
Grasshoppers—*Lahden Reipas	1-1, 8-0
*Valencia—Hajduk Split	0-0, 1-1
(Valencia won on away-goals rule)	
*Standard Liège—Linfield	2-0, 3-2
*Újpest Dózsa—Malmö FF	4-0, 0-1
Borussia Mönchengladbach—*Cork Hibernian	5-0, 2-1
*Feyenoord—Olympiakos Nicosia	8-0, 9-0
*CSKA Sofia—Partizan Tirana	3-0, 1-0
Sliema Wanderers—*Akranes	4-0, 0-0
*Dinamo Bucharest—Spartak Trnava	0-0, 2-2
(Dinamo won on away-goals rule)	

Second Round

Ajax—*Olympique Marseille	2-1, 4-1
Arsenal—*Grasshoppers	2-0, 3-0
*Benfica—CSKA Sofia	2-1, 0-0
Feyenoord—*Dinamo Bucharest	3-0, 2-0
Inter—*Borussia Mönchengladbach	1-7, 4-2, 0-0
(first leg ordered replayed due to spectator violence; second leg played before replayed first leg)	
*Celtic—Sliema Wanderers	5-0, 2-1
Standard Liège—*CSKA Moscow	0-1, 2-0
Újpest Dózsa—*Valencia	1-0, 2-1

Quarter-Finals

*Ajax—Arsenal	2-1, 1-0
Benfica—*Feyenoord	0-1, 5-1
*Inter—Standard Liège	1-0, 1-2
(Inter won on away-goals rule)	
Celtic—*Újpest Dózsa	2-1, 1-1

Semi-Finals

*Ajax—Benfica	1-0, 0-0
*Inter—Celtic	0-0, 0-0
(Inter won on penalty kicks)	

Final (in Rotterdam; att. 67,000)

Ajax	2	Inter	0
(Cruyff 2)			

*home team in first leg

1972-73
(Bye: Ajax, Spartak Trnava)

First Round

*CSKA Sofia—Panathinaïkos	2-1, 2-0
*Galatasaray—Bayern München	1-1, 0-6
*Waterford—Omonia Nicosia	2-1, 0-2
*T-S Innsbruck—Dinamo Kiev	0-1, 0-2
*Sliema Wanderers—Górnik Zabrze	0-5, 0-5
*Aris Bonnevoie—Arges Pitesti	0-2, 0-4
*Real Madrid—IB Keflavik	3-0, 1-0
*RSC Anderlecht—Vejle BK	4-2, 3-0
*Derby County—Zeljeznicar	2-0, 2-1
*Malmö FF—Benfica	1-0, 1-4
*Celtic—Trondheim Rosenborg	2-1, 3-1
*Újpest Dózsa—FC Basel	2-0, 2-3
*FC Magdeburg—Turun PS Turku	6-0, 3-1
*Olympique Marseille—Juventus	1-0, 0-3

Second Round

Ajax—*CSKA Sofia	3-1, 3-0
*Bayern München—Omonia Nicosia	9-0, 4-0
*Dinamo Kiev—Górnik Zabrze	2-0, 1-2
*Arges Pitesti—Real Madrid	2-1, 1-3
*Spartak Trnava—RSC Anderlecht	1-0, 1-0
*Derby County—Benfica	3-0, 0-0
*Celtic—Újpest Dózsa	2-1, 0-3
*Juventus—FC Magdeburg	1-0, 1-0

Quarter-Finals

*Ajax—Bayern München	4-0, 1-2
*Dinamo Kiev—Real Madrid	0-0, 0-3
*Spartak Trnava—Derby County	1-0, 0-2
*Juventus—Újpest Dózsa	0-0, 2-2

Semi-Finals

*Ajax—Real Madrid	2-0, 1-0
*Juventus—Derby County	3-1, 0-0

The lack of widespread enthusiasm for the series in its early years was caused by the low esteem of national cup competitions in certain countries, particularly Eastern and Central Europe. Ultimately, however, the very existence of the new competition generated a greater interest in domestic knockout tournaments than ever before. UEFA took control of the competiton in 1961, and the number of participants more than doubled in one year. Close to full European representation was achieved by 1966.

1960-61. In the first edition, only 10 countries entered teams. Of the three favored to win (Rangers, Wolverhampton, and Fiorentina), Rangers was the most impressive in defeating Borussia Mönchengladbach with an 11-0 aggregate of goals. Wolverhampton itself fell prey to the Scottish side in Glasgow, and was unable to recoup when its all-British semi-final moved to England. In the final, played in two legs, the strong and resourceful Rangers could not break down Fiorentina's massive *catenaccio*-style defense, and the Florentines' counterattack, led by the gifted Swede Hamrin, won the first cup for Italy. Scottish clubs were not yet ready to master the Italian garrisons, as Celtic succeeded in doing to win the European Champions' Cup of 1966-67.

1961-62. The number of participants jumped to 23, and UEFA decided to hold a one-leg final at a predetermined venue. The competition was replete with small and unfashionable clubs (La Chaux de Fonds, Sedan-Torcy, Floriana Valetta, Leixoes Porto, Alliance Dudelange, and many others), but the final in Glasgow was eventually played by Atlético Madrid, seasoned by its battles with Real Madrid and Barcelona at home, and the holder Fiorentina. The result was a drab 1-1 draw, and in the replay in Stuttgart, the Spanish team found its way to three unanswered goals.

1962-63 Atlético Madrid advanced to the final a second time, but nonleague Bangor City of Wales forced the big Italian club Napoli to a third match in the preliminary round, resulting in the highlight of the competition. Sixty-five hundred disbelieving Welsh fans had watched the old Caernarvon club win the first leg, but Napoli made up the deficit in Naples and won the replay by only the odd goal in three. In the final at Rotterdam, English hero Tottenham Hotspur buried Atlético by a four goal margin on two goals each from Dyson and Greaves.

1963-64. The fourth edition had 29 participants, and Tottenham was eliminated in the first round by league rival Manchester United. Sporting Lisbon, which had set the series record with a 16-1 thrashing of Apoel Nicosia in the first round, eliminated Manchester United and Olympique Lyon to reach the final. MTK Budapest slipped past each of its four early opponents by one goal and emerged from a heroic semi-final with Celtic to meet Sporting in the final at Brussels before an astonishingly small crowd of 3,000 spectators. An unfortunate own goal by MTK's left back Dansky lost the title for the Hungarians, as Sporting came back in the replay to win with a "Sunday shot" from the corner.

1964-65. In contrast to the dismal aura of the 1964 final, the fifth edition ended with a European Cup Winners' Cup record attendance of 98,000 at Wembley, prompted by the presence of London's own West Ham. The English cup holder, making its European debut, was little fancied to achieve such heights, but the team had certainly earned the right to face TSV München 1860 with its commendable performance in Spain against Real Zaragoza in the semi-finals. The West German club, having suffered through three semi-final matches against Italy's Torino, was dominated in the final by high spirits, and two goals from right winger Sealey.

1965-66. It was an English-West German final for the second year in a row. Borussia Dortmund, one of the first clubs to benefit from the reorganization of West German soccer in the early 1960s, had to eliminate Atlético Madrid and holder West Ham to gain the final in Glasgow. Three of the four berths in the semi-final were taken up by British teams. In Scotland, the anticipation of a Celtic vs. West Ham final swelled to inaudible proportions, but the Scottish fans ultimately settled for Liverpool vs. Borussia Dortmund. In left wing Lothar Emmerich, however, Borussia had the record goalscorer in the history of the competition. The final ended anticlimactically with a win by Borussia on an own goal by Liverpool's Ron Yeats in extra time.

1966-67. The seventh edition was significant for the successful entry into European competition of Bayern München, the club that later played such a prominent part in West Germany's domination of the 1970s. The final in Nuremburg was a West German-British affair for the third time in succession, and Bayern won in extra time after two scoreless halves in which Rangers was outplayed almost from start to finish. Both clubs faltered on the way to Nüremburg, Bayern barely eliminating Shamrock Rovers, the darlings of Eire, and Rangers having to dispose of holder Borussia Dortmund. This edition also established the common pattern for full representation of all UEFA members (except Albania).

1967-68. The return of an Italian cup holder to the final was overshadowed by second division Cardiff City, the perennial Welsh Cup winner, which advanced to the semi-finals in the company of three European giants. In the quarter-finals, Cardiff won at home over Torpedo Moscow, the big Soviet auto workers' club. The Russian leg was moved to the ancient Asian city of Tashkent because of icy fields in the capital, but Cardiff held Torpedo to a one goal victory, forcing a replay in West Germany. Cardiff's astounding win in Augsburg was one of the sensations of European international competition in the late 1960s. In the final, Hamburg, which eliminated Cardiff in the semi-finals, met AC Milan at Rotterdam and succumbed to the lethal combination of Rivera on the front line and German international Schnellinger (only recently signed from AS Roma), in the backfield. Two goals by Hamrin, a Swede, won the game for AC Milan.

1968-69. Another British giant-killing act surfaced when Scotland's Dunfermline Athletic reached the semi-finals after knocking out West Bromwich in the previous round. Eight months after the Soviet invasion of Czechoslovakia, Eastern Europe produced its first winner of the series, Slovan Bratislava, the popular club from Slovakia. Ironically, Slovan was the only entrant from the Soviet bloc. Barcelona, meanwhile, whose lineup had been completely transformed since the early 1960s, advanced to the final in the hope of winning another European prize. Despite the sentimental favoritism directed to Slovan, it was Barcelona that appeared to be the easy winner. Perhaps it was overconfidence—a trademark of Barcelona teams—or the unexpected early Czech goal, but Slovan was victorious by the odd goal in five, and Czechoslovakia welcomed a brief respite in its turbulent national life.

1969-70. Górnik Zabrze, one of the popular Silesian clubs behind Poland's rise to the front ranks of European soccer, forged its way to the final by defeating consistently stiff opposition in the early rounds (Rangers, Levski Sofia, and AS Roma). Górnik's attack was spearheaded by the redoubtable Wlozmierz Lubanski—the leading goalscorer in two successive editions of the series—backed by a stalwart defense. Manchester City, Górnik's opponent in the final, had advanced by turning around a one goal deficit in the semi-finals with a huge victory at home over West Germany's Schalke 04. The poorly attended final at Vienna was won by Manchester City from the spot by penalty specialist Francis Lee, but Górnik's impressive presence helped to underscore the growth of Polish soccer.

1970-71. For the first time in the history of the competition, all 33 members of UEFA participated in the cup. Real Madrid, the lord and master of European club championships, celebrated its debut in the series by advancing to the final with the aging yet brilliant Gento still in the lineup. The previous year's final between Manchester City and Górnik Zabrze was replayed in the quarter-finals with City winning again. The two English entrants, as luck would have it, met in the semi-finals, thereby precluding an all-English final, and Chelsea gained that final on an own goal in the Manchester leg. The final at Athens was drawn 1-1, though Real looked like the better team, and in the replay Chelsea attacked with uncharacteristic finesse to become the third club from London to win the European Cup Winners' Cup.

1971-72. Glasgow Rangers, in its fifth bid for the trophy, finally won the title after eliminating the mighty Bayern München in the semi-finals by a two-goal margin. In a fitting tribute to itself as the most famous Soviet Club of the postwar era, Dinamo Moscow became the first from the USSR to reach the final of a European club competition. In Barcelona, Rangers nearly let a 3-0 lead slip away, but managed to hold on and win its first European honor in a dozen attempts. Sadly, the victory was seriously marred by rioting Rangers fans unable to control their passionate support for a team that had for so many years played second fiddle to archrival Celtic. They clashed with Spanish police, and suffered countless injuries and arrests. Dinamo's protest to UEFA resulted in a two-year suspension for Rangers (later reduced to one year), but the Scots were allowed to keep the trophy.

1972-73. AC Milan, two-time winner of the European Champions' Cup, became the first club to win a second European Cup Winners' Cup. On its way to the final, Milan met and defeated three clubs from Eastern Europe:

Legia Warsaw, Spartak Moscow, and Sparta Prague, winning each round by one goal. Italian soccer, as characterized by AC Milan, had by now abandoned whatever attacking skills were attached to *catenaccio*, and was reduced to little more than rough play by skillful athletes. The final in Salonika against luckless Leeds United was another example. Leeds was loath to equalize Chiarugi's lone Milan goal against the hacking and furious defense of its opponents, a situation that was made still worse by the absence of Schnellinger and Prati from the Italians' roster.

1973-74. Once again a final involving an Eastern European club was miserably attended because supporters, in this case East Germans, were not allowed to travel. The East German cup holder FC Magdeburg was undoubtedly the most accomplished club yet seen from that country. Its deliberate style combined with attacking flair was akin to the "total football" of the West Germans and Dutch, as the East German national team was to substantiate in the 1974 World Cup. Its opponent in the final was none other than AC Milan, unchanged and diametrically opposed to Magdeburg in personality and strategy. In the early rounds, however, Milan's results were better than the year before, and the final was a difficult one to forecast. As it happened, the tiny Rotterdam crowd saw an own goal by Lanzi early in the game give Magdeburg an unexpected lift, and a second goal later in the game gave East Germany its first major European title.

1974-75. The fifteenth edition featured the series' first all-Eastern European final. Ferencváros, the traditional hub of Hungarian soccer, escaped from an away-goals win over Liverpool in the second round and a difficult win over Red Star Belgrade in the semi-finals to earn a berth in the final at Basel. The Hungarians were given little chance, however, against the great Ukrainian club Dinamo Kiev, whose free-flowing left wing Oleg Blokhin was now touted as the best new player in Europe since Johan Cruyff. Dinamo's advance to the final had been relatively

painless, but a semi-final away loss to PSV Eindhoven pointed to its weaknesses in defense. In the final, the orchestral concert of Blokhin and striker Onishenko performed with precision, and Dınamo won the Soviet Union's first European club championship. Its 3-0 win was decisive, attractive, and encouraging for the growth of fluid and thoughtful tactics in an age of defense-minded teams.

1975-76. The gradual rise of Belgian soccer during the mid-1970s was best exemplified in the Royal Sporting Club from the Brussels suburb of Anderlecht, whose second run for the European Cup Winners' Cup ended in an impressive victory. Opposition in the early rounds was minimal, with the exception of Rapid Bucharest, which was always difficult at home. Anderlecht's opponent in the final was the surprisingly resilient West Ham United, the winner in 1965. West Ham, a curious, free-flowing English club, had advanced to the last round after losing the away legs of both the quarter and semi-finals, but it was given little chance against RSC Anderlecht. The Belgian cup holders, led by Dutch star Robby Rensenbrink, scored four goals before a hometown crowd, and won its first big European championship, though West Ham was credited with a fine performance and a pair of goals.

1976-77. There was little surprise when Anderlecht advanced to the final a second time in 1977. Its opposition in the quarter-finals was Southampton of the English Second Division, which nearly pulled the upset of the tournament after earlier eliminating the big French club Olympique Marseille. Atlético Madrid, revitalized and searching for another international honor, was picked to meet Anderlecht in the final, but Hamburg was skillful and tenacious, and came back from a 3-1 deficit to win the semi-finals against Atlético by two goals on aggregate. The venerable north German club, frustrated by the strength of its domestic opposition in the Bundesliga, found comfort in directing all energies to the European competition, upsetting Anderlecht in the final without conceding a goal.

Winners

1960-61	Fiorentina	1964-65	West Ham United
1961-62	Atlético Madrid	1965-66	Borussia Dortmund
1962-63	Tottenham Hotspur	1966-67	Bayern München
1963-64	Sporting Lisbon	1967-68	AC Milan

1968-69	Slovan Bratislava	1973-74	FC Magdeburg
1969-70	Manchester City	1974-75	Dinamo Kiev
1970-71	Chelsea	1975-76	RSC Anderlecht
1971-72	Rangers	1976-77	Hamburger SV
1972-73	AC Milan	1977-78	RSC Anderlecht

Cumulative Ranking of the Top 50 Clubs (1960-77)
(number of editions in parentheses)

		P	W	D	L	F	A	P
1	Atlético Madrid (6) (Spa)	39	23	8	8	74	37	54
2	Rangers (6) (Sco)	38	19	7	12	68	46	45
3	AC Milan (3) (Ita)	28	16	10	2	45	17	42
4	Cardiff City (10) (Wal)	30	15	11	13	58	43	41
5	Hamburger SV (3) (GFR)	26	16	6	4	58	30	38
6	Bayern München (3) (GFR)	25	13	9	3	44	21	35
7	Sporting Lisbon (5) (Por)	28	14	7	7	64	35	35
8	Celtic (3) (Sco)	22	15	3	4	47	13	33
9	West Ham United (3) (Eng)	24	12	6	6	46	33	30
10	FC Magdeburg (4) (DDR)	22	10	9	3	33	16	29
11	Fiorentina (4) (Ita)	20	14	1	5	44	20	29
12	PSV Eindhoven (3) (Net)	20	13	2	5	45	16	28
13	Steaua Bucharest (7) (Rum)	24	11	6	7	23	27	28
14	RSC Anderlecht (3) (Bel)	20	13	1	6	39	18	27
15	Slovan Bratislava (4) (Cze)	21	12	3	6	35	21	27
16	Dinamo Kiev (2) (Sov)	15	12	1	2	34	11	25
17	Manchester City (2) (Eng)	18	11	2	5	32	13	24
18	Standard Liège (4) (Bel)	23	10	4	9	37	30	24
19	Olympique Lyon (4) (Fra)	22	9	5	8	31	28	23
20	Chelsea (2) (Eng)	14	9	4	1	39	7	22
21	Górnik Zabrze (2) (Pol)	17	9	4	4	39	21	22
22	Torino (3) (Ita)	19	9	4	6	28	17	22
23	Rapid Vienna (6) (Aug)	24	6	10	8	32	36	22
24	MTK/VM (3) (Hung)	19	8	5	6	27	21	21
25	Real Madrid (2) (Spa)	16	8	4	4	28	10	20
26	Tottenham Hotspur (3) (Eng)	13	10	0	3	37	20	20
27	Liverpool (3) (Eng)	17	8	4	5	29	12	20
28	Barcelona (3) (Spa)	16	8	4	4	36	22	20
29	Schalke 04 (2) (GFR)	14	9	2	3	21	14	20
30	Levski-Spartak (4) (Bul)	16	8	3	5	43	22	19
31	Olympiakos (6) (Gre)	19	8	3	8	24	13	19
32	Ferencváros (3) (Hun)	15	7	4	4	28	20	18
33	Eintracht Frankfurt (2) (GFR)	12	8	1	3	28	15	17
34	Újpest Dózsa (2) (Hun)	13	7	3	3	33	17	17
35	Real Zaragoza (2) (Spa)	14	7	3	4	26	16	17
36	Dunfermline (2) (Sco)	14	7	2	5	34	14	16

37	Borussia Dortmund (2) (GFR)	11	7	2	2	28	11	16
38	Carl Zeiss Jena (3) (DDR)	16	5	6	5	30	20	16
39	Legia Warsaw (4) (Pol)	15	6	4	5	23	17	16
40	FC Den Haag (3) (Net)	12	7	1	4	21	14	15
41	Red Star Belgrade (2) (Yug)	14	6	3	5	31	18	15
42	Slavia Sofia (5) (Bul)	19	6	3	10	22	21	15
43	TSV München 1860 (1) (GFR)	10	6	2	2	21	6	14
44	Leeds United (1) (Eng)	9	5	3	1	13	3	13
45	Sparta Prague (2) (Cze)	12	6	0	6	30	13	12
46	Benfica (2) (Por)	10	4	4	2	21	8	12
47	Wrexham (2) (Wal)	10	4	4	2	13	10	12
48	Borussia M'bach (2) (GFR)	10	6	0	4	29	17	12
49	Vasas ETO Györ (2) (Hun)	10	5	2	3	21	11	12
50	FC Zürich (3) (Swi)	12	4	4	4	24	16	12

Scoring Leaders

1965-66	Emmerich (Borussia Dortmund) 14
1966-67	Müller (Bayern München) 9
1967-68	Seeler (Hamburger SV) 6
1968-69	Rühl (FC Köln) 6
1969-70	Lubanski (Górnik Zabrze) 8
1970-71	Lubanski (Górnik Zabrze) 8
1971-72	Osgood (Chelsea) 8
1972-73	Chiarugi (AC Milan) 7
1973-74	Heynckes (Borussia Mönchengladbach) 10
1974-75	Onishenko (Dinamo Kiev) 7
1975-76	Rensenbrink (RSC Anderlecht) 8
1976-77	Milanov (Levski-Spartak) 13

Miscellaneous Records and Statistics

Most editions participated in: 10, by Cardiff City.

Most games played: 39, by Cardiff City and Atlético Madrid.

Most wins: 23, by Atlético Madrid.

Most losses: 13, by Cardiff City.

Most goals for: 74, by Atlético Madrid.

Most goals against: 46, by Rangers.

Record home victory: Sporting Lisbon 16, Apoel Nicosia 1, 1963-64.

Record away victory: Lahden Reipas 2, Honvéd 10, 1965-66; Jeunesse Hautcharage 0, Chelsea 8, 1971-72.

Record victory in a final: Tottenham Hotspur 5, Atlético Madrid 1, 1962-63.

Highest aggregate score in a match: 17 (Sporting Lisbon 16, Apoel Nicosia 1, 1963-64).

Highest aggregate score in a final: 6 (Tottenham Hotspur 5, Atlético Madrid 1, 1962-63; RSC Anderlecht 4, West Ham United 2, 1975-76).

Best goal aggregate in a round: 21-0 (Chelsea defeated Jeunesse Hautcharage by 8-0 and 13-0, 1971-72).

Highest number of individual goals in a final: 2, by Greaves and Dyson (Tottenham Hotspur), 1962-63; Sealey (West Ham United), 1964-65; Hamrin (AC Milan), 1967-68; Johnston (Rangers), 1971-72; Onishenko (Dinamo Kiev), 1974-75; Rensenbrink and Van der Elst (RSC Anderlecht), 1975-76.

Record attendance: 97,974 (West Ham United vs. München 1860, Empire Stadium, Wembley, 1964-65).

Results

1960-61

Qualifying Round

Red Star Brno—*ASK Vorwärts Berlin	1-2, 2-0
*Rangers—Ferencváros	4-2, 1-2

Quarter-Finals

Fiorentina—*Lucerne	3-0, 6-2
Dinamo Zagreb—*Red Star Brno	0-0, 2-0
Wolverhampton Wanderers—*FK Austria	0-2, 5-0
Rangers—*Borussia Mönchengladbach	3-0, 8-0

Semi-Finals

*Fiorentina—Dinamo Zagreb	3-0, 1-2
*Rangers—Wolverhampton Wanderers	2-0, 1-1

Final

(first leg in Glasgow)

Fiorentina	2	Rangers	0
(Milan 2)			

(second leg in Florence)

Fiorentina	2	Rangers	1
(Milan, Hamrin)		(Scott)	

*home team in first leg

1961-62

Atlético Madrid—*Sedan-Torcy	3-2, 4-1
Leicester City—*Glenavon	4-1, 3-1
Motor Jena—*Swansea Town	2-2, 5-1
(first leg in Linz)	
Leixoes Porto—*La Chaux de Fonds	2-6, 5-0
Újpest Dózsa—*Floriana Valetta	5-2, 10-2
*Dunfermline—St. Patrick's Athletic	4-1, 4-0
*Rapid Vienna—Spartak Varna	0-0, 5-2

First Round

Atlético Madrid—*Leicester City	1-1, 2-0
*Werder Bremen—Aarhus GF	2-0, 3-2
*Motor Jena—Alliance Dudelange	7-0, 2-2
(second leg in Erfurt)	
*Leixoes Porto—SK Progressul	1-1, 1-0
Újpest Dózsa—*Ajax	1-2, 3-1

*Dunfermline—Vardar Skopje	5-0, 0-2
Dynamo Zilina—*Olympiakos	3-2, 1-0
*Fiorentina—Rapid Vienna	3-1, 6-2

Quarter-Finals

Atlético Madrid—*Werder Bremen	1-1, 3-1
*Motor Jena—Leixoes Porto	1-1, 3-1
(second leg in Gera)	
*Újpest Dózsa—Dunfermline	4-3, 1-0
Fiorentina—*Dynamo Zilina	2-3, 2-0

Semi-Finals

Atlético Madrid—*Motor Jena	1-0, 4-0
(second leg in Malmö)	
*Fiorentina—Újpest Dózsa	2-0, 1-0

Final (in Glasgow; att. 29,066)

Atlético Madrid	1	Fiorentina	1
(Peiro)		(Hamrin)	

(replay in Stuttgart; att. 38,120)

Atlético Madrid	3	Fiorentina	0
(Jones, Mendonca, Peiró)			

*home team in first leg

1962-63

Preliminary Round

*Rangers—Seville	4-0, 0-2
*Lausanne—Sparta Rotterdam	3-0, 2-4
*OFK Belgrade—Cemie Halle	2-0, 3-3
*Újpest Dózsa—Zaglebie Sosnowiec	0-0, 5-0
Napoli—*Bangor City	0-2, 3-1, 2-1
(play-off in London)	
*St. Étienne—Vitoria Setubal	1-1, 3-1
BK 09 Odense—*Alliance Dudelange	1-1, 8-1
Botev Plovdiv—*Steaua Bucharest	2-3, 5-1

First Round

*Tottenham Hotspur—Rangers	5-2, 3-2
Slovan Bratislava—*Lausanne	1-1, 1-0
*OFK Belgrade—Portadown	5-1, 2-3
Napoli—*Újpest Dózsa	1-1, 1-1, 3-1
(play-off in Lausanne)	
FC Nürnberg—*St. Étienne	0-0, 3-0
BK 09 Odense—*Sturm Graz	1-1, 5-3

Botev Plovdiv—*Shamrock Rovers	4-0, 1-0
*Atlético Madrid—Hibernians Valetta	4-0, 1-0

Quarter-Finals

Tottenham Hotspur—*Slovan Bratislava	0-2, 6-0
*OFK Belgrade—Napoli	2-0, 1-3, 3-1
(play-off at Marseille)	
FC Nürnberg—*BK 09 Odense	1-0, 6-0
Atlético Madrid—*Botev Plovdiv	1-1, 4-0

Semi-Finals

Tottenham Hotspur—*OFK Belgrade	2-1, 3-1
Atlético Madrid—*FC Nürnberg	1-2, 2-0

Final (in Rotterdam; att. 49,143)

Tottenham Hotspur	5	Atlético Madrid	1
(Greaves 2, White, Dyson 2)		(Collar pen)	

*home team in first leg

1963-64

Preliminary Round

Sporting Lisbon—*Atalanta	0-2, 3-1, 3-1
(play-off won in Madrid after extra time)	
*Apoel Nicosia—Gjøvik Lyn	6-0, 0-1
Manchester United—*Willem II Tiburg	1-1, 6-1
*Olympique Lyon—BK 09 Odense	3-1, 3-1
*Olympiakos—Zaglebie Sosnowiec	2-1, 0-1, 2-0
(play-off in Vienna)	
*Hamburger SV—US Luxembourg	4-0, 3-2
Barcelona—*Shelborne	2-0, 3-1
Celtic—*FC Basel	5-1, 5-0
Dinamo Zagreb—*Linz ASK	0-1, 1-0, 1-1
(play-off in Linz; Dinamo won by toss of the coin)	
Slovan Bratislava—*Palloseura Helsinki	4-1, 8-1
Borough United—*Sliema Wanderers	0-0, 2-0
*Fenerbahçe—Petrolul Ploesti	4-1, 0-1
*MTK Budapest—Slavia Sofia	1-0, 1-1

First Round

*Sporting Lisbon—Apoel Nicosia	16-1, 2-0
(second leg in Lisbon)	
Manchester United—*Tottenham Hotspur	0-2, 4-1
*Olympique Lyon—Olympiakos	4-1, 1-2
Hamburger SV—*Barcelona	4-4, 0-0, 3-2
(play-off in Lausanne)	

*Celtic—Dinamo Zagreb	3-0, 1-2
Slovan Bratislava—*Borough United	1-0, 3-0
*Fenerbahçe—Linfield	4-1, 0-2
MTK Budapest—*Motor Zwickau	0-1, 2-0

Quarter-Finals

Sporting Lisbon—*Manchester United	1-4, 5-0
Olympique Lyon—*Hamburger SV	1-1, 2-0
*Celtic—Slovan Bratislava	1-0, 1-0
*MTK Budapest—Fenerbahçe	2-0, 1-3, 1-0
(play-off in Rome)	

Semi-Finals

Sporting Lisbon—*Olympique Lyon	0-0, 1-1, 1-0
(play-off in Madrid)	
MTK Budapest—*Celtic	0-3, 4-0

Final (in Brussels; att. 3,208)

Sporting Lisbon	3	MTK Budapest	3
(Figueiredo 2, Dansky o.g.)		(Sandor 2, Kuti)	

(replay in Antwerp; att. 19,924)

Sporting Lisbon	1	MTK Budapest	0
(Morais)			

*home team in first leg

1964-65

Preliminary Round

West Ham United—*AA Gent	1-0, 1-1
*Sparta Prague—Anorthosis Famagusta	10-0, 6-0
(second leg in Polzno)	
*Slavia Sofia—Cork Celtic	2-0, 0-1
*Lausanne—Honvéd	2-0, 1-1
Real Zaragoza—*Valetta FC	3-0, 3-1
Cardiff City—*BK Esbjerg	0-0, 1-0
Valkeakosken Haka—*Skeid Oslo	0-1, 2-0
*Torino—Fortuna Geleen	3-1, 2-2
*Steaua Bucharest—Derry City	3-0, 2-0
Dinamo Zagreb—*AEK Athens	0-2, 3-0
Legia Warsaw—*Admira Vienna	3-1, 1-0
Galatasaray—*Magdeburg Aufbau	1-1, 1-1, 1-1
(play-off in Vienna; Galatasaray won by toss of the coin)	
*FC Porto—Olympique Lyon	3-0, 1-0
TSV München 1860—*US Luxembourg	4-0, 6-0

First Round
*West Ham United—Sparta Prague	2-0, 1-2
Lausanne—*Slavia Sofia	0-1, 2-1, 3-2
(play-off in Rome)	
Real Zaragoza—*Dundee	2-2, 2-1
Cardiff City—*Sporting Lisbon	2-1, 0-0
Torino—*Valkeakosken Haka	1-0, 5-0
Dinamo Zagreb—*Steaua Bucharest	3-1, 2-0
*Legia Warsaw—Galatasaray	2-1, 0-1, 1-0
(play-off in Bucharest)	
TSV München 1860—*FC Porto	1-0, 1-1

Quarter-Finals
West Ham United—*Lausanne	2-1, 4-3
*Real Zaragoza—Cardiff City	2-2, 1-0
*Torino—Dinamo Zagreb	1-1, 2-1
TSV München 1860—*Legia Warsaw	4-0, 0-0

Semi-Finals
*West Ham United—Real Zaragoza	2-1, 1-1
TSV München 1860—*Torino	0-2, 3-1, 2-0
(play-off in Zurich)	

Final (in London; att. 97,974)

West Ham United	2	TSV München 1860	0
(Sealey 2)			

*home team in first leg

1965-66

First Round
Borussia Dortmund—*Floriana Valetta	5-1, 8-0
CSKA Sofia—*Limerick	2-1, 2-0
Stiinta Cluj—*Wiener Neustadt	1-0, 2-0
*Atlético Madrid—Dinamo Zagreb	4-0, 1-0
Olympiakos—*Omonia Nicosia	1-0, 1-1
*Magdeburg Aufbau—Spora Luxembourg	1-0, 2-0
*Sion—Galatasaray	5-1, 1-2
Celtic—*Go Ahead Deventer	6-0, 1-0
*Aarhus GF—Vitoria Setubal	2-1, 2-1
Dinamo Kiev—*Coleraine	6-1, 4-0
Rosenborg Trondheim—*KR Reykjavik	3-1, 3-1
Honvéd—*Lahden Reipas	10-2, 6-0
*Dukla Prague—Stade Rennes	2-0, 0-0
Standard Liège—*Cardiff City	2-1, 1-0
Liverpool—*Juventus	0-1, 2-0

Second Round

*Borussia Dortmund—CSKA Sofia	3-0, 2-4
Atlético Madrid—*Stiinta Cluj	2-0, 4-0
*West Ham United—Olympiakos	4-0, 2-2
*Magdeburg Aufbau—Sion	8-1, 2-2
Celtic—*Aarhus GF	1-0, 2-0
Dinamo Kiev—*Rosenborg Trondheim	4-1, 2-0
Honvéd—*Dukla Prague	3-2, 1-2
(Honvéd won on away-goals rule)	
*Liverpool—Standard Liège	3-1, 2-1

Quarter-Finals

Borussia Dortmund—*Atlético Madrid	1-1, 1-0
*West Ham United—Magdeburg Aufbau	1-0, 1-1
*Celtic—Dinamo Kiev	3-0, 1-1
Liverpool—*Honvéd	0-0, 2-0

Semi-Finals

Borussia Dortmund—*West Ham United	2-1, 3-1
Liverpool—*Celtic	0-1, 2-0

Final (in Glasgow; att. 41,657)

Borussia Dortmund	2	Liverpool	1
(Held, Yeats o.g.)		(Hunt)	

- after extra time -

*home team in first leg

1966-67

Preliminary Round

Standard Liège—*Valur Reykjavik	1-1, 8-1

First Round

Bayern München—*Tatran Presov	1-1, 3-2
*Shamrock Rovers—Spora Luxembourg	4-1, 4-1
Spartak Moscow—*OFK Belgrade	3-1, 3-0
*Rapid Vienna—Galatasaray	4-0, 5-3
*Standard Liège—Apollon Limassol	5-1, 1-0
(second leg in Namur)	
*Chemie Leipzig—Legia Warsaw	3-0, 2-2
Vasas Györ—*Fiorentina	0-1, 4-2
Sporting Braga—*AEK Athens	1-0, 3-2
*Racing Club Strasbourg—Steaua Bucharest	1-0, 1-1
Slavia Sofia—*Swansea Town	1-1, 4-0
*Servette—IF Finströms Kamreterna	1-1, 2-1
Sparta Rotterdam—*Floriana Valetta	1-1, 6-0

Real Zaragoza—*Skeid Oslo	2-3, 3-1
Everton—*BK 85 Aalborg	0-0, 2-1
Rangers—Glentoran	1-1, 4-0

Second Round

Bayern München—*Shamrock Rovers	1-1, 3-2
Rapid Vienna—*Spartak Moscow	1-1, 1-0
Standard Liège—*Chemie Leipzig	1-2, 1-0
(Standard won on away-goals rule)	
*Vasas Györ—Sporting Braga	3-0, 0-2
Slavia Sofia—*Racing Club Strasbourg	0-1, 2-0
*Servette—Sparta Rotterdam	2-0, 0-1
*Real Zaragoza—Everton	2-0, 0-1
*Rangers—Borussia Dortmund	2-1, 0-0

Quarter Finals

Bayern München—*Rapid Vienna	0-1, 2-0
(Bayern won after extra time)	
Standard Liège—*Vasas Györ	1-2, 2-0
Slavia Sofia—*Servette	0-1, 3-0
*Rangers—Real Zaragoza	2-0, 0-2
(Rangers won by toss of the coin)	

Semi-Finals

*Bayern Müchen—Standard Liège	2-0, 3-1
Rangers—*Slavia Sofia	1-0, 1-0

Final (in Nuremburg; att. 69,480)

Bayern München	1	Rangers	0
(Roth)			

- after extra time -

*home team in first leg

1967-68

First Round

Steaua Bucharest—*FK Austria	2-0, 2-1
*Hamburger SV—Randers Freja	5-3, 2-0
*AC Milan—Levski Sofia	5-1, 1-1
Tottenham Hotspur—*Hajduk Split	2-0, 4-3
Cardiff City—*Shamrock Rovers	1-1, 2-0
Spartak Trnava—*Lausanne	2-3, 2-0
*Aberdeen—KR Reykjavik	10-0, 4-1
*Valencia—Crusaders	4-0, 4-2
*Torpedo Moscow—Motor Zwickau	0-0, 1-0
Standard Liège—*Altay Izmir	3-2, 0-0

Olympique Lyon—*Aris Bonnevoie	3-0, 2-1
Vitoria Setubal—*Fredrikstad	5-1, 2-1
*Vasas Györ—Apollon Limassol	5-0, 4-0
*Bayern München—Panathinaïkos	5-0, 2-1
Wisla Kraców—*HJK Helsinki	4-1, 4-0
NAC Breda—*Floriana Valetta	2-1, 1-0

Second Round

*Bayern München—Vitoria Setubal	6-2, 1-1
Hamburger SV—*Wisla Kraców	1-0, 4-0
Cardiff City—*NAC Breda	1-1, 4-1
AC Milan—*Vasas Györ	2-2, 1-1
(Milan won on away-goals rule)	
*Olympique Lyon—Tottenham Hotspur	1-0, 3-4
(Olympique won on away-goals rule)	
*Standard Liège—Aberdeen	3-0, 0-2
*Torpedo Moscow—Spartak Trnava	3-1, 3-1
*Valencia—Steaua Bucharest	3-0, 0-1

Quarter-Finals

*Hamburger SV—Olympique Lyon	2-0, 0-2, 2-0
(play-off in Hamburg)	
AC Milan—*Standard Liège	1-1, 1-1, 2-0
(play-off in Milan)	
*Cardiff City—Torpedo Moscow	1-0, 0-1, 1-0
(play-off in Augsburg)	
Bayern München—*Valencia	1-1, 1-0

Semi-Finals

*Hamburger SV—Cardiff City	1-1, 3-2
*AC Milan—Bayern München	2-0, 0-0

Final (in Rotterdam; att. 53,276)

AC Milan	2	Hamburger SV	0
(Hamrin 2)			

*home team in first leg

1968-69

First Round

West Bromwich Albion—*FC Brugge	1-3, 2-0
(West Bromwich won on away-goals rule)	
*Dunfermline—Apoel Nicosia	10-1, 2-0
IFK Norrköping—*Crusaders	2-2, 4-1
FC Porto—*Cardiff City	2-2, 2-1
FC Köln—*Girondins	1-2, 3-0

*Slovan Bratislava—Bor	3-0, 0-2
Torino—*Partizan Tirana	0-1, 3-1
Sliema Wanderers—*US Rumelange	1-2, 1-0
(Wanderers won on away-goals rule)	
Lyn Oslo—*Altay Izmir	1-3, 4-1
*Randers Freja—Shamrock Rovers	1-0, 2-1
Barcelona—*FC Lugano	1-0, 3-0
*Olympiakos—Fram Reykjavik	2-0, 2-0
ADO Den Haag—*AK Grazer	4-1, 2-0
Dinamo Bucharest won by default: Vasas Györ withdrew	

Second Round

West Bromwich Albion—*Dinamo Bucharest	1-1, 4-0
*Dunfermline—Olympiakos Piraeus	4-0, 0-3
*Lyn Oslo—IFK Norrköping	2-0, 2-3
Slovan Bratislava—*FC Porto	0-1, 4-0
*Randers Freja—Shamrock Rovers	6-0, 2-0
FC Köln—ADO Den Haag	1-0, 3-0
Torino	bye
Barcelona	bye

Quarter-Finals

*Barcelona—Lyn Oslo	3-2, 2-2
*FC Köln—Randers Freja	2-1, 3-0
Slovan Bratislava—*Torino	1-0, 2-1
*Dunfermline—West Bromwich Albion	0-0, 1-0

Semi-Finals

Slovan Bratislava—*Dunfermline	1-1, 1-0
Barcelona—*FC Köln	2-2, 4-1

Final (in Basel; att. 19,478)

Slovan Bratislava	3	Barcelona	2
(Cvetler, Hrivnak, J. Capkovic)		(Zaldua, Rexach)	

*home team in first leg

1969-70

Preliminary Round

*Rapid Vienna—Torpedo Moscow	0-0, 1-1
(Rapid won on away-goals rule)	

First Round

Manchester City—*Athletic Bilbao	3-3, 3-0
AS Roma—*Ards	0-0, 3-1
*Rangers—Steaua Bucharest	2-0, 0-0

Cardiff City—*Mjøndalen JF	7-1, 5-1
Schalke 04—*Shamrock Rovers	1-2, 3-0
*Magdeburg Aufbau—MTK Budapest	1-0, 1-1
Olympique Marseille—*Dukla Prague	0-1, 2-0
PSV Eindhoven—*Rapid Vienna	2-1, 4-2
St. Gallen—*Frem Copenhagen	1-2, 1-0
*IFK Norrköping—Sliema Wanderers	5-1, 0-1
*Dinamo Zagreb—Slovan Bratislava	3-0, 0-0
*Lierse SK—Apoel Nicosia	10-0, 1-0
Górnik Zabrze—*Olympiakos	2-2, 5-0
*Goeztepe Izmir—US Luxembourg	3-0, 3-2
Levski Sofia—*IB Vestmannaey	4-0, 4-0
*Academica Coimbra—Kuopion Palloseura	0-0, 1-0

Second Round

Manchester City—*Lierse SK	3-0, 5-0
*Górnik Zabrze—Rangers	3-1, 3-1
*Goeztepe Izmir—Cardiff City	3-0, 0-1
*AS Roma—PSV Eindhoven	1-0, 0-1
(Roma won by toss of the coin)	
Schalke 04—*IFK Norrköping	0-0, 1-0
*Levski Sofia—St. Gallen	4-0, 0-0
Academica Coimbra—*Magdeburg Aufbau	0-1, 2-0
Dinamo Zagreb—*Olympique Marseille	1-1, 2-0

Quarter-Finals

Manchester City—*Academica Coimbra	0-0, 1-0
*AS Roma—Goeztepe Izmir	2-0, 0-0
Górnik Zabrze—*Levski Sofia	2-3, 2-1
(Górnik won on away-goals rule)	
Schalke 04—*Dinamo Zagreb	3-1, 1-0

Semi-Finals

Manchester City—*Schalke 04	0-1, 5-1
Górnik Zabrze—*AS Roma	1-1, 2-2, 1-1
(replay in Strasbourg; Górnik won by toss of the coin)	

Final (in Vienna; att. 7,968)

Manchester City	2	Górnik Zabrze	1
(Young, Lee pen)		(Oslizlo)	

*home team in first leg

1970-71

Preliminary Round

TJ Gottwaldov—*Bohemians	2-1, 2-2
Partizan Tirana—*Atvidaberg	1-1, 2-0

First Round

Honvéd—*Aberdeen	1-3, 3-1
(Honvéd won on penalty kicks)	
*Cardiff City—Pezoporikos Larnaca	8-0, 0-0
Chelsea—*Aris Salonika	1-1, 5-1
*Manchester City—Linfield	1-0, 1-2
(Manchester City won on away-goals rule)	
Real Madrid—*Hibernians Valetta	0-0, 5-0
PSV Eindhoven—*TJ Gottwaldov	1-2, 1-0
(Eindhoven won on away-goals rule)	
Benfica—*Olympija Ljubljana	1-1, 8-1
FC Nantes—*Stromsgodset Drammen	5-0, 2-3
*Wacker Innsbruck—Partizan Tirana	3-2, 2-1
*CSKA Sofia—Valkeakosken Haka	9-0, 2-1
*ASK Vorwärts Berlin—Bologna	0-0, 1-1
(Vorwärts won on away-goals rule)	
FC Brugge—*Offenbach Kickers	1-2, 2-0
*Goeztepe Izmir—US Luxembourg	5-0, 0-1
Górnik Zabrze—*BK 85 Aalborg	1-0, 8-1
FC Zürich—*Akureyi	7-1, 7-0
*Steaua Bucharest—Karpaty Lvov	1-0, 1-0

Second Round

Chelsea—*CSKA Sofia	1-0, 1-0
Manchester City—*Honvéd	1-0, 2-0
Górnik Zabrze—*Goeztepe Izmir	1-0, 3-0
*PSV Eindhoven—Steaua Bucharest	4-0, 3-0
ASK Vorwärts Berlin—*Benfica	0-2, 2-0
(Vorwärts won on penalty kicks)	
*FC Brugge—FC Zürich	2-0, 2-3
*Cardiff City—FC Nantes	5-1, 2-1
*Real Madrid—Wacker Innsbruck	0-1, 2-0

Quarter-Finals

Real Madrid—*Cardiff City	0-1, 2-0
Chelsea—*FC Brugge	0-2, 4-0
*Manchester City—Górnik Zabrze	0-2, 2-0, 3-1
(play-off in Copenhagen)	
PSV Eindhoven—ASK Vorwärts Berlin	2-0, 0-1

Semi-Finals

*Chelsea—Manchester City	1-0, 1-0
Real Madrid—*PSV Eindhoven	0-0, 2-1

Final (in Athens; att. 42,000)

Chelsea	1	Real Madrid	1
(Osgood)		(Zoco)	

(replay in Athens; att. 24,000)

Chelsea	2	Real Madrid	1
(Dempsey, Osgood)		(Fleitas)	

*home team in first leg

1971-72

Preliminary Round
FK Austria—*BK 09 Odense	2-4, 2-0
(FK Austria won on away-goals rule)	

First Round
Atvidaberg—*Zaglebie Sosnowiec	4-3, 1-1
FK Austria—*Dinamo Tirana	1-1, 1-0
Barcelona—*Distillery	3-1, 3-0
Bayern München—*Skoda Pilzen	1-0, 6-1
*Dynamo Berlin—Cardiff City	1-1, 1-1
(Dynamo won on penalty kicks)	
Chelsea—*Jeunesse Hautcharage	8-0, 13-0
Dinamo Moscow—*Olympiakos	2-0, 1-2
Eskisehirspor—*Mikkelin Palloilijat	0-0, 4-0
*Beerschot—Anorthosis Famagusta	7-0, 1-0
Liverpool—*Servette	1-2, 2-0
*Sporting Lisbon—Lyn Oslo	4-0, 3-0
Rangers—*Stade Rennes	1-1, 1-0
Red Star Belgrade—*Komlo Banyasi	7-2, 1-2
Sparta Rotterdam—*Levski-Spartak	1-1, 2-0
Steaua Bucharest—Hibernians Valetta	0-0, 1-0
Torino—*Limerick	1-0, 4-0

Second Round
*Torino—FK Austria	1-0, 0-0
Bayern München—*Liverpool	0-0, 3-1
*Atvidaberg—Chelsea	0-0, 1-1
(Atvidaberg won on away-goals rule)	
Dinamo Moscow—*Eskisehirspor	1-0, 1-0
Red Star Belgrade—*Sparta Rotterdam	1-1, 2-1
*Rangers—Sporting Lisbon	3-2, 3-4
(Rangers won on away-goals rule)	
Dynamo Berlin—*Beerschot	3-1, 3-1
Steaua Bucharest—*Barcelona	1-0, 2-1

Quarter-Finals
Bayern München—*Steaua Bucharest	1-1, 0-0
(Bayern won on away-goals rule)	
Dynamo Berlin—*Atvidaberg	2-0, 2-2

Dinamo Moscow—*Red Star Belgrade			2-1, 1-1
Rangers—*Torino			1-1, 1-0

Semi-Finals

Dinamo Moscow—*Dynamo Berlin			1-1, 1-1
(Dinamo Moscow won on penalty kicks)			
Rangers—*Bayern München			1-1, 2-0

Final (in Barcelona; att. 24,701)

Rangers	3	**Dinamo Moscow**	2
(Stein, Johnston 2)		(Eshtrekhov, Mahovikov)	

*home team in first leg

1972-73

First Round

AC Milan—*Red Boys Differdange	4-1, 3-0
Legia Warsaw—*Vikingur	2-0, 9-0
*Spartak Moscow—FC Den Haag	1-0, 0-0
Atlético Madrid—*Bastia	0-0, 2-1
Sparta Prague—*Standard Liège	0-1, 4-2
Ferencváros—*Floriana Valetta	0-1, 6-0
*Schalke 04—Slavia Sofia	2-1, 3-1
Cork Hibernian—*Pezoporikos Larnaca	2-1, 4-1
Besa—*Fremad Amager	1-1, 0-0
(Besa won on away-goals rule)	
Hibernian—*Sporting Lisbon	1-2, 6-1
Wrexham—*FC Zürich	1-1, 2-1
*Hajduk Split—Fredrikstad	1-0, 1-0
*Rapid Vienna—PAOK Salonika	0-0, 2-2
(Rapid won on away-goals rule)	
*Rapid Bucharest—Landskrona	3-0, 0-1
Carl Zeiss Jena—Mikkelin Palloilijat	6-1, 2-3
Leeds United—*Ankaragücü	1-1, 1-0

Second Round

AC Milan—*Legia Warsaw	1-1, 2-1
(AC Milan won after extra time in the second leg)	
Spartak Moscow—*Atlético Madrid	4-3, 1-2
(Spartak won on away-goals rule)	
Sparta Prague—*Ferencváros	0-2, 4-1
Schalke 04—*Cork Hibernian	0-0, 3-0
*Hibernian—Besa	7-1, 1-1
Hajduk Split—*Wrexham	1-3, 2-0
(Hajduk won on away-goals rule)	
Rapid Bucharest—*Rapid Vienna	1-1, 3-1
Leeds United—*Carl Zeiss Jena	0-0, 2-0

Quarter-Finals

AC Milan—*Spartak Moscow	1-0, 1-1
Sparta Prague—*Schalke 04	1-2, 3-0
Hajduk Split—*Hibernian	2-4, 3-0
*Leeds United—Rapid Bucharest	5-0, 3-1

Semi-Finals

*AC Milan—Sparta Prague	1-0, 1-0
*Leeds United—Hajduk Split	1-0, 0-0

Final (in Salonika, att. 45,000)

AC Milan	1	Leeds United	0
(Chiarugi)			

*home team in first leg

1973-74

First Round

*NAC Breda—FC Magdeburg	0-0, 0-2
*AC Milan—Dinamo Zagreb	3-1, 1-0
*Randers Freja—Rapid Vienna	0-0, 1-2
*IB Vestmannaey—Borussia Mönchengladbach	0-7, 1-9
*RSC Anderlecht—FC Zürich	3-2, 0-1
*Beroe St. Zagora—Fola Esch	7-0, 4-1
*Banik Ostrava—Cork Hibernians	1-0, 2-1
*Legia Warsaw—PAOK Salonika	1-1, 0-1
*Vasas Budapest—Sunderland	0-2, 0-1
*Ankaragücü—Rangers	0-2, 0-4
*Torpedo Moscow—Athletic Bilbao	0-0, 0-2
*Gzira United—SK Brann	0-2, 0-7
*Chimia Ramnicu Vilcea—Glentoran	2-2, 0-2
*Pezoporikos Larnaca—Malmö FF	0-0, 0-11
*Lahden Reipas—Olympique Lyon	0-0, 0-2
*Cardiff City—Sporting Lisbon	0-0, 1-2

Second Round

*Banik Ostrava—FC Magdeburg	2-0, 0-3
*AC Milan—Rapid Vienna	0-0, 2-0
*Sunderland—Sporting Lisbon	2-1, 0-2
*FC Zürich—Malmö FF	0-0, 1-1
(Zürich won on away-goals rule)	
*Beroe St. Zagora—Athletic Bilbao	3-0, 0-1
*Olympique Lyon—PAOK Salonika	3-3, 0-4
*Borussia Mönchengladbach—Rangers	3-0, 2-3
*SK Brann—Glentoran	1-1, 1-3

Quarter-Finals

*FC Magdeburg—Beroe St. Zagora	2-0, 1-1
*AC Milan—PAOK Salonika	3-0, 2-2
*Sporting Lisbon—FC Zürich	3-0, 1-1
*Glentoran—Borussia Mönchengladbach	0-2, 0-5

Semi-Finals

*Sporting Lisbon—FC Magdeburg	1-1, 1-2
*AC Milan—Borussia Mönchengladbach	2-0, 0-1

Final (in Rotterdam; att. 4,641)

FC Magdeburg	2	AC Milan	0
(Lanzi o.g., Seguin)			

*home team in first leg

-3

1974-75

2

First Round

*Dinamo Kiev—CSKA Sofia	1-0
*Ferencváros—Cardiff City	2-(
*Liverpool—Strömsgodset	11-(
*Eintracht Frankfurt—AS Monaco	3-(
*Slavia Prague—Carl Zeiss Jena	1-(
(Carl Zeiss Jena won on penalty kicks)	
*PSV Eindhoven—Ards	10-0, 4-
*Gwardia Warsaw—Bologna	2-1, 1-2
(Gwardia won on penalty kicks)	
*PAOK Salonika—Red Star Belgrade	1-0, 0-2
*Sliema Wanderers—Lahden Reipas	2-0, 1-4
*Benfica—Vanlose IF	4-0, 4-1
*Malmö FF—FC Sion	1-0, 0-1
(Malmö won on penalty kicks)	
*Fram Reykjavik—Real Madrid	0-2, 0-6
*SV Waregem—Austria/WAC	2-1, 1-4
*Bursapor—Finn Harps	4-2, 0-0
*Dundee United—Jiul Petrosani	3-0, 0-2
Avenir won by default: Paralimni withdrew	

Second Round

*Eintracht Frankfurt—Dinamo Kiev	2-3, 1-2
*Liverpool—Ferencváros	1-1, 0-0
(Ferencváros won on away-goals rule)	
*Dundee United—Bursapor	0-0, 0-2
*Avenir—Red Star Belgrade	1-6, (-1
*Carl Zeiss Jena—Benfica	1-1, 0-2
(Benfica won on away-goals rule)	
	, 7-1
*Gwardia Warsaw—PSV Eindhoven	1-4, 0-2

Second Round

*Hamburger SV—Heart of Midlothian	4-2, 4-1
*Dinamo Tiflis—MTK/VM	1-4, 0-1
*RSC Anderlecht—Galatasaray	5-1, 5-1
*Boavista—Levski-Spartak	3-1, 0-2
(Levski-Spartak won on away-goals rule)	
*Atlético Madrid—Hajduk Split	1-0, 2-1
*Carrick Rangers—Southampton	2-5, 1-4
*Slask Wroclaw—Bohemians	3-0, 1-0
*Apoel Nicosia—Napoli	1-1, 0-2

Quarter-Finals

*MTK/VM—Hamburger SV	1-1, 1-4
*RSC Anderlecht—Southampton	2-0, 1-2
*Levski-Spartak—Atlético Madrid	2-1, 0-2
*Slask Wroclaw—Napoli	0-0, 0-2

Semi-Finals

*Atlético Madrid—Hamburger SV	3-1, 0-3
*Napoli—RSC Anderlecht	1-0, 0-2

Final (in Amsterdam; att. 65,000)

Hamburger SV	2	RSC Anderlecht	0
(Volkert pen, Magath)			

*home team in first leg

1977-78

Preliminary Round

*Rangers—Young Boys Berne	1-0, 2-2

First Round

*Lokomotiv Sofia—RSC Anderlecht	1-6, 0-2
*Rangers—FC Twente	0-0, 0-3
*FC Köln—Porto	2-2, 0-1
*Betis—AC Milan	2-0, 1-2
*Olympiakos Nicosia—Uni. Craiova	1-6, 2-0
*Besiktas—Diósgyör	2-0, 0-5
*SK Brann—IA Akranes	1-0, 4-0
*Progress Niederkorn—Vejle BK	0-1, 0-9
*Dundalk—Hajduk Split	1-0, 0-4
*Hamburger SV—Lahden Reipas	8-1, 5-2
*Coleraine—Lokomotiv Leipzig	1-4, 2-2
*St. Étienne—Manchester United	1-1, 2-0
*PAOK Salonika—Zaglebie Sosnowiec	2-0, 2-0

*Valetta FC—Dinamo Moscow	0-2, 0-5
*Lokomotive Kosice—Öster Växjö	0-0, 2-2
(Lokomotive won on away-goals rule)	
*Cardiff City—FK Austria/WAC	0-0, 0-1

Second Round
*Hamburger SV—RSC Anderlecht	1-2, 1-1
*FC Twente—SK Brann	2-0, 2-1
*Dinamo Moscow—Uni. Craiova	2-0, 0-2
(Dinamo won on penalty kicks)	
*Vejle BK—PAOK Salonika	3-0, 1-2
*Lokomotiv Leipzig—Betis	4-0, 2-5
*Diósgyör—Hajduk Split	2-1, 1-2
(Hajduk won on penalty kicks)	
*FK Austria/WAC—Lokomotive Kosice	0-0, 1-1
(Austria/WAC won on away-goals rule)	

Quarter-Finals
*Porto—RSC Anderlecht	1-0, 0-3
*Vejle BK—FC Twente	0-3, 0-4
*Betis—Dinamo Moscow	0-0, 0-3
*FK Austria/WAC—Hajduk Split	1-1, 1-1
(Austria/WAC won on penalty kicks)	

Semi-Finals
*FC Twente—RSC Anderlecht	0-1, 0-2
*Dinamo Moscow—FK Austria/WAC	2-1, 1-2
(Austria/WAC won on penalty kicks)	

Final (in Paris; att. 48, 679)

RSC Anderlecht	4	FK Austria/WAC	0
(Rensenbrink 2, Van Binst 2)			

European Football Championship

Championnat d'Europe de Football—Fussball-Europameisterschaft.

The European championship for national teams, introduced in 1958 as the European Nations' Cup. Held quadrennially during the two-year period between World Cups, this competition is open to all members of the Union of European Football Associations (UEFA). Its trophy is the Henri Delaunay Cup, named for the former General Secretary of UEFA and the Fédération Française de Football, who conceived the idea for the series but unfortunately did not live long enough to see its realization.

The first two editions were played on a home and away, knockout basis with semi-finals and the final staged in a single country. In the third, fourth, and fifth editions, following a sharp increase in the number of participants, the countries were divided into eight first round groups that competed individually on a league basis with eight teams advancing to quarter-final and semi-final elimination rounds. The semi-finals and the final were held in a host country. In 1978-80, the quarter-finals will be held in conjunction with the semi-finals and the final in a host country (Italy), and the host country will receive a bye to the quarter-finals. The 31 participants in the first round have been divided into seven groups of four, five or six teams each.

1958-60. The initial impact of this series was somewhat less than its currently high prestige would indicate. Only 17 countries participated in the first edition, including all of Eastern Europe except Albania. (This helps to account for Eastern Europe's apparent domination of the cumulative ranking table.) Belgium, England, Finland, Germany FR, Iceland, Northern Ireland, Italy, Luxembourg, Netherlands, Scotland, Sweden, Switzerland, and Wales declined to enter, while Cyprus and Malta had not yet joined UEFA.

The well-motivated Warsaw Pact countries dominated the first competition with the USSR, Yugoslavia, and Czechoslovakia, advancing to the semi-finals along with France. Yugoslavia had been putting a succession of

dazzling teams on the field since the early 1950s, and the Soviets were making a concerted effort to enter the upper echelons of world soccer at about the same time the Nations' Cup came into existence. The only two countries that were likely to give them serious trouble were France, which lost a high scoring semi-final to Yugoslavia in Paris, and Spain, whose talented exploits were not given proper exposure after its refusal to meet the USSR in the quarter-finals. Spain's withdrawal and subsequent default was one of Europe's few overtly political gestures on the playing field in the postwar era.

1962-64. In the second edition, only Germany FR, England, and Scotland failed to enter. Cyprus did not join UEFA soon enough in 1962 to qualify, and West Germany's continued self-exile was linked to East-West political hostilities. But England and Scotland had only their elitism to blame. Spain, blessed

The West German national team that won the 1972 European Football Championship, perhaps the best national team to emerge anywhere in the world during the 1970s, shown here at a 1973 friendly against the USSR in Moscow. (Left to right) Beckenbauer, Maier, Schwarzenbeck, Heynckes, Netzer, Wimmer, Müller, Höttges, E. Kremers, Breitner, Hoeness.

with a new generation of talented players, played host to the final rounds, and defeated, of all countries the USSR in the final. It was significant, however, that with 29 countries participating, the USSR reached its second consecutive final. With so many great Western European powers competing, it was little Denmark that advanced to the semi-finals in one of its periodic displays of courage and drive, though Denmark was fortunate in having to eliminate the likes of Malta, Albania, and Luxembourg in the first three rounds. This edition of the Nations' Cup also marked Albania's first foray into official international competition since the Balkan Cup of 1946.

1966-68. The series was by now an unqualified success for UEFA organizers, and in 1966-68 only Iceland, bedeviled by its Arctic location, failed to enter. The present format of first round groupings took shape, and for the first time England and Scotland joined the competition after UEFA suggested that the Home International Championship serve as their qualification round. West Germany, playing in its first European championship, was eliminated in the first round after suffering a goalless draw in Albania that remains to date the biggest upset in the history of the competition. Yugoslavia advanced to the final for the second time, but Italy's stiff *catenaccio* strangled Yugoslavia's attack so well that Italy's sparse goals were enough to achieve victory before a home crowd. England, the world champion, placed third, and the USSR gained semi-final status for the third time in a row.

1970-72. The fourth European championship, whose final rounds were held in Belgium, exposed once and for all the advanced state of West German soccer, and signified the transfer of world domination from Rio de Janeiro to Frankfurt-am-Main. The Germans walked over Poland, Turkey, Albania, England, and Belgium, and in the final subjugated the hapless Russians in a stunning display of skill and technique. Russia's laudable achievement in reaching the final for the third time in four attempts was relegated to a footnote. In other developments, Iceland was the only UEFA member absent, and the great Dutch team, spurred by Ajax's enormous success in European club competition, was disappointed to face elimination at the hands of Yugoslavia and rapidly improving East Germany. The 1970-72 edition also announced England's decline as a major international power, as demonstrated by its surprising draw at home to Switzerland and decisive home defeat to West Germany.

1974-76. In the fifth edition, Yugoslavia and the USSR continued to excel in opening round competition, but in later rounds Czechoslovakia came to the fore and matched co-finalists West Germany in precision and attractive playmaking. The final could have gone either way, but in the end Czechoslovakia won the penalty kick contest and drew under its wing a new international following. Unfortunately, the Czechs' glory quickly abated with the team's demise in 1977. During Czechoslovakia's day in the sun, however, England, Portugal, Russia, and Holland each succumbed in European champsionship competition. Meanwhile, Albania relapsed into self-exile, and prevented 100 percent UEFA participation yet again. Yugoslavia, the host country in later rounds, reached the semifinals for the third time, but continued to disappoint its fans with uneven play. Wales and Belgium used this edition as a springboard for reviving their game, as both entered a new era of international success, while England, by virtue of its results against Czechoslavikia, Portugal, and Cyprus, faced an unprecedented crisis of confidence and leadership.

The draw for the 1978-80 edition of the European Football Championship was as follows: **Group 1**: England, Northern Ireland, Ireland Republic, Bulgaria, Denmark; **Group 2**: Belgium, Norway, Austria, Scotland, Portugal; **Group 3**: Yugoslavia, Rumania, Spain, Cyprus; **Group 4**: Netherlands, Iceland, Poland, Germany DR, Switzerland; **Group 5**: Czechoslovakia, Luxembourg, Sweden, France; **Group 6**: USSR, Finland, Hungary, Greece; **Group 7**: Germany FR, Wales, Turkey, Malta. Bye: Italy.

Winners

1958-60	USSR
1962-64	Spain
1966-68	Italy
1970-72	Germany FR
1974-76	Czechoslovakia

Cumulative Ranking (1958-76)*
(number of editions in parentheses)

		P	W	D	L	F	A	P
1	USSR (5)	39	24	6	9	67	34	54
2	Yugoslavia (5)	37	19	9	9	63	40	47
3	Spain (5)	33	17	9	7	59	25	43
4	Hungary (5)	35	18	7	10	69	42	43
5	Czechoslovakia (5)	31	18	6	7	61	30	42
6	Italy (4)	29	16	9	4	48	19	41
7	Germany FR (3)	24	14	8	2	50	15	36
8	England (4)	26	15	6	5	50	22	36
9	France (5)	31	13	8	10	65	47	34
10	Bulgaria (5)	27	13	6	8	44	30	32
11	Netherlands (4)	26	13	4	9	60	36	30
12	Belgium (4)	26	12	5	9	39	30	29
13	Rumania (5)	27	10	8	9	51	41	28
14	Portugal (5)	25	11	6	8	32	32	28
15	Austria (5)	24	10	5	9	45	27	25
16	German DR (5)	24	9	7	8	38	35	25
17	Sweden (4)	24	9	6	9	26	33	24
18	Poland (5)	22	8	5	9	34	31	21
19	Scotland (3)	18	8	5	5	22	21	21
20	Wales (4)	22	8	5	9	29	30	21
21	Ireland Republic (5)	26	8	5	13	30	46	21
22	Northern Ireland (4)	22	8	4	10	25	21	20
23	Switzerland (4)	20	7	4	9	36	32	18
24	Greece (4)	21	5	7	9	25	34	17
25	Turkey (5)	22	6	5	11	15	41	17
26	Denmark (5)	29	6	5	18	33	62	17
27	Albania (3)	13	3	2	8	6	25	8
28	Norway (5)	22	2	3	17	22	56	7
29	Luxembourg (4)	23	1	5	17	17	77	7
30	Iceland (2)	8	1	3	4	6	13	5
31	Finland (3)	18	0	4	14	9	41	4
32	Malta (3)	14	1	1	12	6	45	3
33	Cyprus (3)	18	1	0	17	5	67	2

*Liechtenstein has not participated.

Results

1958-60

Preliminary Round

Czechoslovakia—*Ireland Rep   0-2, 4-0

First Round

*France—Greece	7-1, 1-1	*Rumania—Turkey	3-0, 0-2
*USSR—Hungary	3-1, 1-0	Austria—*Norway	1-0, 5-2

*Yugoslavia—Bulgaria	2-0, 1-1
*Portugal—Germany DR	2-0, 3-2
Czechoslovakia—*Denmark	2-2, 5-1
Spain—*Poland	4-2, 3-0

Quarter-Finals

Yugoslavia—*Portugal	1-2, 5-1
*France—Austria	5-2, 4-2
Czechoslovakia—*Rumania	2-0, 3-0
USSR won by default: Spain withdrew	

Semi-Finals (in France)

Yugoslavia	5	France	4
USSR	3	Czechoslovakia	0

Final (in Paris; att. 17,966)

USSR	2	Yugoslavia	1
(Metreveli, Ponedelnik)		(Netto, o.g.)	
	(after extra time)		

*home team in first leg

1962-64

First Round

		Second Round	
*Spain—Rumania	6-0, 1-3		
Northern Ireland—*Poland	2-0, 2-0	*Spain—Northern Ireland	1-1, 1-0
*Denmark—Malta	6-1, 3-1	*Denmark—Albania	4-0, 0-1
*German DR—Czechoslovakia	2-1, 1-1	Ireland Rep—*Austria	0-0, 3-2
*Hungary—Wales	3-1, 1-1	Hungary—*Germany DR	2-1, 3-3
*Italy—Turkey	6-0, 1-0	USSR—Italy	2-0, 1-1
*Netherlands—Switzerland	3-1, 1-1	Luxembourg—*Netherlands	1-1, 2-1
Sweden—*Norway	2-0, 1-1	Sweden—*Yugoslavia	0-0, 3-2
*Ireland Rep—Iceland	4-2, 1-1	France—*Bulgaria	0-1, 3-1
*Yugoslavia—Belgium	3-2, 1-0		
*Bulgaria—Portugal	3-1, 1-3, 1-0		
(play-off in Bulgaria)		*Quarter-Finals*	
France—*England	1-1, 5-2	Denmark—*Luxembourg	3-3, 2-2, 1-0
Albania won be default: Greece withdrew		(play-off in Denmark)	
Luxembourg	bye	*Spain—Ireland Rep	5-1, 2-0
USSR	bye	Hungary—*France	3-2, 2-1
Austria	bye	USSR—*Sweden	1-1, 3-1

Semi-Finals (in Spain)

USSR	3	Denmark	0
Spain	2	Hungary	1

Third Place Game

Hungary	3	Denmark	0

Final (in Madrid; att. 120,000)

Spain (Pereda, Marcelino)	2	USSR (Khusainov)	1

*home team in first leg

1966-68

Group 1

Spain—*Ireland Rep	0-0, 2-0
*Ireland Rep—Turkey	2-1, 1-2
Spain—*Turkey	0-0, 2-0
Czechoslovakia—*Ireland Rep	2-0, 1-2
*Czechoslovakia—Turkey	3-0, 0-0
Spain—*Czechoslovakia	0-1, 2-1

	P	W	D	L	F	A	P
Spain	6	3	2	1	6	2	8
Czechoslovakia	6	3	1	2	8	4	7
Ireland Rep	6	2	1	3	5	8	5
Turkey	6	1	2	3	3	8	4

Group 2

*Bulgaria—Norway	4-2, 0-0
*Portugal—Sweden	1-2, 1-1
Portugal—*Norway	2-1, 2-1
Bulgaria—*Sweden	2-0, 3-0
Sweden—*Norway	1-3, 5-2
*Bulgaria—Portugal	1-0, 0-0

	P	W	D	L	F	A	P
Bulgaria	6	4	2	0	10	2	10
Portugal	6	2	2	2	6	6	6
Sweden	6	2	1	3	9	12	5
Norway	6	1	1	4	9	14	3

Group 3

Austria—*Finland	0-0, 2-1
*Greece—Finland	2-1, 1-1
*USSR—Austria	4-3, 0-1
*USSR—Greece	4-0, 1-0
*USSR—Finland	2-0, 5-2
*Greece—Austria	4-1, 1-1
(second leg stopped after 84 minutes)	

	P	W	D	L	F	A	P
USSR	6	5	0	1	16	6	10
Greece	6	2	2	2	8	9	6
Austria	6	2	2	2	8	10	6
Finland	6	0	2	4	5	12	2

Group 4

*Germany FR—Albania	6-0, 0-0
*Yugoslavia—Germany FR	1-0, 1-3
Yugoslavia—*Albania	2-0, 4-0

	P	W	D	L	F	A	P
Yugoslavia	4	3	0	1	8	3	6
Germany FR	4	2	1	1	9	2	5
Albania	4	0	1	3	0	12	1

Group 5

Hungary—*Netherlands	2-2, 2-1
*Hungary—Denmark	6-0, 2-0
*Netherlands—Denmark	2-0, 2-3
*German DR—Netherlands	4-3, 0-1
German DR—*Denmark	1-1, 3-2
*Hungary—German DR	3-1, 0-1

	P	W	D	L	F	A	P
Hungary	6	4	1	1	15	5	9
German DR	6	3	1	2	10	10	7
Netherlands	6	2	1	3	11	11	5
Denmark	6	1	1	4	6	16	3

Group 6

*Rumania—Switzerland	4-2, 1-7
*Italy—Rumania	3-1, 1-0
Rumania—*Cyprus	5-1, 7-0
Italy—*Cyprus	2-0, 5-0
*Switzerland—Cyprus	5-0, 1-2
Italy—*Switzerland	2-2, 4-0

	P	W	D	L	F	A	P
Italy	6	5	1	0	17	3	11
Rumania	6	3	0	3	18	14	6
Switzerland	6	2	1	3	17	13	5
Cyprus	6	1	0	5	3	25	2

Group 7

*Poland—Luxembourg	4-0, 0-0
*France—Poland	2-1, 4-1

France—*Belgium 1-2, 1-1
France—*Luxembourg 3-0, 3-1
Belgium—*Luxembourg 5-0, 3-0
Belguim—*Poland 1-3, 2-4

	P	W	D	L	F	A	P
France	6	4	1	1	14	6	9
Belgium	6	3	1	2	14	9	7
Poland	6	3	1	2	13	9	7
Luxembourg	6	0	1	5	1	18	1

Group 8
Scotland—*Wales 1-1, 3-2
England—*Northern Ireland 2-0, 2-0
*Scotland—Northern Ireland 2-1, 0-1
*England—Wales 5-1, 3-0
Wales—*Northern Ireland 0-0, 2-0
*England—Scotland 2-3, 1-1
(all matches in this group also credited to Home International Championship for year in which match was played)

	P	W	D	L	F	A	P
England	6	4	1	1	15	5	9
Scotland	6	3	2	1	10	8	8
Wales	6	1	2	3	6	12	4
Northern Ireland	6	1	1	4	2	8	3

Quarter-Finals
*England—Spain 1-0, 2-1
Yugoslavia—*France 1-1, 5-1
Italy—*Bulgaria 2-3, 2-0
USSR—*Hungary 0-2, 3-0

Semi-Finals (in Italy)

Yugoslavia	1	England	0
Italy	0	USSR	0

(Italy won by toss of the coin after extra time)

Third Place Game

England	2	USSR	0

Final (in Rome; att. 75,000)

Italy	1	Yugoslavia	1
(Domenghini)		(Džajić)	

269

(replay in Rome; att. 60,000)

| Italy | 2 | Yugoslavia | 0 |

(Riva, Anastasi)

*home team in first leg

1970-72

Group 1

*Czechoslovakia—Finland	1-1, 4-0
*Rumania—Finland	3-0, 4-0
Rumania—*Wales	1-1, 2-0
Czechoslovakia—*Wales	3-1, 1-0
Rumania—*Czechoslovakia	0-1, 2-1
Wales—*Finland	1-0, 3-0

	P	W	D	L	F	A	P
Rumania	6	4	1	1	12	2	9
Czechoslovakia	6	4	1	1	11	4	9
Wales	6	2	1	3	6	7	5
Finland	6	0	1	5	1	16	1

Group 2

Hungary—*Norway	3-1, 4-0
*France—Norway	3-1, 3-1
*Bulgaria—Norway	1-1, 4-1
*Hungary—France	1-1, 2-0
Hungary—*Bulgaria	0-3, 2-0
Bulgaria—*France	1-2, 2-1

	P	W	D	L	F	A	P
Hungary	6	4	1	1	12	5	9
Bulgaria	6	3	1	2	11	7	7
France	6	3	1	2	10	8	7
Norway	6	0	1	5	5	18	1

Group 3

Greece—*Malta	1-1, 2-0
Switzerland—*Greece	1-0, 1-0
Switzerland—*Malta	2-1, 5-0
England—*Malta	1-0, 5-0
*England—Greece	3-0, 2-0
England—*Switzerland	3-2, 1-1

	P	W	D	L	F	A	P
England	6	5	1	0	15	3	11
Switzerland	6	4	1	1	12	5	9
Greece	6	1	1	4	3	8	3
Malta	6	0	1	5	2	16	1

Group 4

*Spain—Northern Ireland	3-0, 1-1
USSR—*Cyprus	3-1, 6-1
Northern Ireland—*Cyprus	3-0, 5-0
Spain—*Cyprus	2-0, 7-0
*USSR—Spain	2-1, 0-0
*USSR—Northern Ireland	1-0, 1-1

	P	W	D	L	F	A	P
USSR	6	4	2	0	13	4	10
Spain	6	3	2	1	14	3	8
Northern Ireland	6	2	2	2	10	6	6
Cyprus	6	0	0	6	2	26	0

Group 5

Portugal—*Denmark	1-0, 5-0
*Scotland—Denmark	1-0, 0-1
*Belgium—Denmark	2-0, 2-1
*Belgium—Scotland	3-0, 0-1
*Belgium—Portugal	3-0, 1-1
*Portugal—Scotland	2-0, 1-2

	P	W	D	L	F	A	P
Belgium	6	4	1	1	11	3	9
Portugal	6	3	1	2	10	6	7
Scotland	6	3	0	3	4	7	6
Denmark	6	1	0	5	2	11	2

Group 6

Sweden—*Ireland Rep	1-1, 1-0
Italy—*Austria	2-1, 2-2
*Italy—Ireland Rep	3-0, 2-1
Austria—*Sweden	0-1, 1-0
Austria—*Ireland Rep	4-1, 6-0
Italy—*Sweden	0-0, 3-0

	P	W	D	L	F	A	P
Italy	6	4	2	0	12	4	10
Austria	6	3	1	2	14	6	7
Sweden	6	2	2	2	3	5	6
Ireland Rep	6	0	1	5	3	17	1

Group 7

Yugoslavia—*Netherlands							1-1, 2-0
Yugoslavia—*Luxembourg							2-0, 0-0
Netherlands—*German DR							0-1, 3-2
German DR—*Luxembourg							5-0, 2-1
*Netherlands—Luxembourg							6-0, 8-1
Yugoslavia—*German DR							2-1, 0-0

	P	W	D	L	F	A	P
Yugoslavia	6	3	3	0	7	2	9
Netherlands	6	3	1	2	18	6	7
German DR	6	3	1	2	11	6	7
Luxembourg	6	0	1	5	1	23	1

Group 8

*Poland—Albania	3-0, 1-1
*Germany FR—Turkey	1-1, 3-0
*Turkey—Albania	2-1, 0-3
Germany FR—*Albania	1-0, 2-0
*Poland—Turkey	5-1, 0-1
Germany FR—*Poland	3-1, 0-0

	P	W	D	L	F	A	P
Germany FR	6	4	2	0	10	2	10
Poland	6	2	2	2	10	6	6
Turkey	6	2	1	3	5	13	5
Albania	6	1	1	4	5	9	3

Quarter-Finals

Germany FR—*England	3-1, 0-0
Belgium—*Italy	0-0, 2-1
USSR—*Yugoslavia	0-0, 3-0
*Hungary—Rumania	1-1, 2-2, 2-1
(play-off in Yugoslavia)	

Semi-Finals (in Belgium)

USSR	1	Hungary	0
Germany FR	2	Belgium	1

Third Place Game

Belgium	2	Hungary	1

Final (in Brussels; att. 43,437)

Germany FR	3	USSR	0
(Müller 2, Wimmer)			

*home team in first leg

1974-76

Group 1
Czechoslovakia—England	2-1, 0-3
Czechoslovakia—Portugal	5-0, 1-1
Czechoslovakia—Cyprus	4-0, 3-0
England—Portugal	0-0, 1-1
England—Cyprus	5-0, 1-0
Portugal—Cyprus	1-0, 2-0

	P	W	D	L	F	A	P
Czechoslovakia	6	4	1	1	15	5	9
England	6	3	2	1	11	3	8
Portugal	6	2	3	1	5	7	7
Cyprus	6	0	0	6	0	16	0

Group 2
Wales—Hungary	2-0, 2-1
Wales—Austria	1-0, 1-2
Wales—Luxembourg	5-0, 3-1
Hungary—Austria	2-1, 0-0
Hungary—Luxembourg	8-1, 4-2
Austria—Luxembourg	6-2, 2-1

	P	W	D	L	F	A	P
Wales	6	5	0	1	14	4	10
Hungary	6	3	1	2	15	8	7
Austria	6	3	1	2	11	7	7
Luxembourg	6	0	0	6	7	28	0

Group 3
Yugoslavia—Northern Ireland	1-0, 0-1
Yugoslavia—Sweden	3-0, 2-1
Yugoslavia—Norway	3-1, 3-1
Northern Ireland—Sweden	1-2, 2-0
Northern Ireland—Norway	3-0, 1-2
Sweden—Norway	3-1, 2-0

	P	W	D	L	F	A	P
Yugoslavia	6	5	0	1	12	4	10
Northern Ireland	6	3	0	3	8	5	6
Sweden	6	3	0	3	8	9	6
Norway	6	1	0	5	5	15	2

Group 4
Spain—Rumania	1-1, 2-2
Spain—Scotland	1-1, 2-1

Spain—Denmark							2-0, 2-1
Rumania—Scotland							1-1, 1-1
Rumania—Denmark							6-1, 0-0
Scotland—Denmark							3-1, 1-0

	P	W	D	L	F	A	P
Spain	6	3	3	0	10	6	9
Rumania	6	1	5	0	11	6	7
Scotland	6	2	3	1	8	6	7
Denmark	6	0	1	5	3	14	1

Group 5

Netherlands—Poland							3-0, 1-4
Netherlands—Italy							3-1, 0-1
Netherlands—Finland							4-1, 3-1
Poland—Italy							0-0, 0-0
Poland—Finland							3-0, 2-1
Italy—Finland							0-0, 1-0

	P	W	D	L	F	A	P
Netherlands	6	4	0	2	14	8	8
Poland	6	3	2	1	9	5	8
Italy	6	2	3	1	3	3	7
Finland	6	0	1	5	3	12	1

Group 6

USSR—Ireland Rep							2-1, 0-3
USSR—Turkey							3-0, 0-1
USSR—Switzerland							4-1, 1-0
Ireland Rep—Turkey							4-0, 1-1
Ireland Rep—Switzerland							2-1, 0-1
Turkey—Switzerland							2-1, 1-1

	P	W	D	L	F	A	P
USSR	6	4	0	2	10	6	8
Ireland Rep	6	3	1	2	11	5	7
Turkey	6	2	2	2	5	10	6
Switzerland	6	1	1	4	5	10	3

Group 7

Belgium—German DR							1-2, 0-0
Belgium—France							2-1, 0-0
Belgium—Iceland							2-0, 1-0
German DR—France							2-1, 2-2
German DR—Iceland							1-1, 1-2
France—Iceland							3-0, 0-0

2. Rob Rensenbrink (Anderlecht)

3. Ivo Viktor (Dukla Prague)

1977 1. Allan Simonsen (Borussia Mönchengladbach)

2. Kevin Keegan (Liverpool)

3. Michel Platini (Nancy)

1978 1. Kevin Keegan (Hamburger)

2. Hans Krankl (Rapid Vienna)

3. Rob Rensenbrink (Anderlecht)

Eusebio (1942-   )

(Full name: Eusebio da Silva Ferreira.) The Mozambiquan shooter *extraordinario* who led Benfica and Portugal to the heights of world soccer and became the most lethal goalscorer in Europe during the 1960s. His rare combination of lightening speed and ability to pivot and dribble through a phalanx of defenders made him one of the most explosive and entertaining players of the postwar era. He was the high scorer in the 1966 World Cup with nine goals, and the leading scorer in Portugal for nine seasons between 1964-73; he twice scored the most goals of any European player in one season (1968 and 1973), made a record 77 international appearances for Portugal, and was voted European Footballer of the Year in 1965. His 42 league goals in 1967-68 were scored in 26 matches. In the 1966 World Cup, with Portugal losing to North Korea by 3-0, he scored four goals in succession and set up a fifth to take Portugal to an astounding 5-3 victory.

A child prodigy in the African shantytown section of Lourenço Marques, the capital of Portuguese Mozambique, he was signed at age 15 by the leading local club, Sporting Clube de Lourenço Marques, and before his eighteenth birthday he had scored 55 league goals. In 1960, he was discovered by the Brazilian manager José Bauer, who suggested to Benfica's Bela Guttmann that the big Lisbon club might do well to exploit this unknown genius. His arrival in Portugal in 1960 was enshrouded in secrecy and intrigue until his proper release and signing could be secured, and his first appearance for Benfica was made in the 1961 Tournoi de Paris, during which he and Pelé alternately outdazzled each other in a series of unforgettable displays. Three months later he made his international debut for Portugal while still aged 19. The following season he was the spearhead in Benfica's second European Cup win in a row. All told he led his club to 10 Portuguese championships and five cup victories in 14 seasons. Serious knee operations in 1967 and 1969 initiated his slow decline, but it was not until 1974 that he showed serious signs of weakening. After faithfully serving Benfica for the whole of his European career, he signed with the American Soccer League's Rhode Island Oceaners for one season in 1975, transferred to the North American Soccer League's Boston Minutemen for the remainder of the 1975 season, and in 1976 captained Toronto Metros-Croatia to its surprise NASL championship. In 1976-77, he played with SC Beira-Mar of Portugal, and after appearing with Las Vegas Quicksilvers in 1977 he continued to play in Mexico and the American Soccer League.

Everton Football Club

Location: *Liverpool, England;* stadium: *Goodison Park (58,000);* colors: *royal blue jerseys with white trim, white shorts;* honors: *English champion (1891, 1915, 1928, 1932, 1939, 1963, 1970), English cup winner (1906, 1933, 1966).*

Founded 1878 as the Sunday School team of St. Domingo Congregational Church in the Everton section of Liverpool. It adopted the Everton name in 1879, and played for six years in the expansive Stanley Park, which separates the Anfield Road grounds from Goodison

Park. In 1884, the club moved to Anfield Road. When the owner raised the rent in 1892, it moved to Goodison Park, leaving behind a group of disgruntled players to form Liverpool F.C. at Anfield.

Everton holds the English record for the most years spent in the first division, and it has accumulated more first division points than any other club in the league. Its greatest era was that of the 1930s, when it won a pair of championships and an F.A. Cup, led by its immortal center forward Dixie Dean and another great center forward, Tommy Lawton, who replaced Dean in 1938. The club's primary achievement in English soccer has been consistency and the ability to spread its numerous honors over many decades. Everton's only period of real mediocrity was the immediate postwar era, in which it had a three year stint in the Second Division (1951-54). No other club in England can approach its record for having spent only four seasons out of the First Division since the founding of the Football League in 1888.

Everton was a founding member of that league when it began operation, and it waited only three seasons for its first championship. Subsequently, the "Toffeemen" won major honors in each succeeding decade until the 1940s. During the 1890s, it was the losing finalist in the F.A. Cup twice, and in the first decade of the twentieth century, it placed second in the league three times. Between 1927 and 1932, Everton experienced an eye-popping series of ups and downs that captured the imagination of the country and made it the glamour club of northern England. In 1927-28, it won the first division with Dixie Dean scoring his legendary 60 goals in one season (a league record which still stands); one year later it finished fifth from the bottom, and the year after that Everton ended the season dead last and was relegated. In its first year in the Second Division, it won the divisional title by a seven point margin, gaining promotion after only one year, and its first year back in the First Division (1931-32), it raced to the top of the standings and won another league championship. This was followed in 1933 by a second F.A. Cup victory at Wembley with a big 3-0 win over Manchester City.

Everton's archrivalry with Liverpool is the most intense in all of England, exacerbated as it is by the promixity of Goodison Park and Anfield Road. During the years between the wars, Everton reigned supreme, but Liverpool's extraordinary successes of the 1960s and '70s have put the "Reds" first among Liverpudlian fans. This is not to suggest that Everton's loyal support has been eroded. The city of Liverpool has, in fact, been the home of two top teams during the 1960s and '70s, as Everton collected two league championships and a cup win between 1963 and 1970. The great difference between these two clubs has been Everton's mediocre record in the elite European club championships.

F

Facchetti, Giacinto (1942-   )

The nonpareil of European attacking fullbacks, Facchetti is one of the unique players in the history of the game. Standing over six-feet two-inches tall and weighing 185 pounds, he developed a keen smell for the goal while playing center forward as a boy. Throughout his professional career, he was never content with being a mere overlapping back—a role that alone would have made him an international star by virtue of his commanding presence—but his deft ball control skills and exceptionally powerful right foot shot often led him into face-to-face challenges with opposing goalkeepers. In his 18 years with Inter Milan, he scored nearly 60 goals, all coming forward from the left back or sweeper position. In international competition he scored three goals for Italy. Moreover, these tallies were often in open field situations, and in 1965, his goal against Liverpool in the European Cup semifinals was the winner that eventually led Inter to its second consecutive European club championship.

He first appeared as a center forward for his fourth division home town club, Trevigliese, while still in his mid-teens, and in 1960 was transferred to nearby Inter Milan, where he was converted into a left back. He remained at Inter for the duration of his career, and gained a first team place in 1962-63, scoring four goals in 31 appearances that season. His hard tackling, gazelle-like control of the air, and accurate reading of attacks, in addition to his striking instincts, soon brought him national fame, and in 1963 he made his international debut against Turkey in Istanbul. Under manager Helenio Herrera, he and Inter won three Italian championships, two European Cups, and two Intercontinental Cups between 1963-66. Immediately following Italy's depressing showing at the 1966 World Cup, he gained the captaincy of the national team, and in the years ahead he became one of the most recognizable figures in international competition. Having long since surpassed the Italian record for most international appearances, he reached the 90 mark in 1977, and captained the team 65 times (another Italian record). In the same year, Facchetti and Gianni Rivera broke Boniperti's record (444) for most appearances with a single club in domestic competition. Injuries slowed him down in 1977-78, and he was forced to bow out of international competition before the 1978 World Cup, retiring from active play altogether at the end of that season.

Faeroe Islands

The semiautonomous Faeroe Islands, a Danish possession located midway between Iceland and Norway, were exposed to soccer in the early years of this century as Danish settlements took root. The Danes and other north Europeans on the islands have a local governing body that is affiliated with the Dansk Boldspil-Union, and since 1959 have been engaging in friendly internationals with various national teams of Iceland. Faeroese selections have played Iceland "A" four times, twice at home, and Iceland "B" five times, three of these at home, losing all seven by an aggregate score of 4-30. There is also an organized domestic competition, and one or two Danish teams have been known to make the cold journey north.

fair catch

The fair catch was an integral part of the various football games during the early and mid-nineteenth century, and even found its way into the original Laws of the Game in 1863. It was mentioned in the Harrow Rules (no. 5), Cambridge Rules of 1854-58 (no. 8), and the Laws of the Game (nos. 8 & 13). After its removal from the Laws of the Game in

1866, it continued to find expression in one form or another within the structure of Rugby Union and Rugby League.

Defined in its original form, a fair catch is made when a player catches the ball directly from the kick or "knock-on" of an opposing player, before the ball has touched either the ground or a teammate of the catcher. In most codes, fair catches could not be made from a kick or throw-in from beyond the touch or goal lines. In games where the dribbling code prevailed over the handling code, a free kick or pass was substituted for running with the ball from a fair catch.

Fairs Cup   See: UEFA Cup

Far East Games, Football Tournament of the

The Far East Games, also known as the Far Eastern Championship Games and the Far Eastern Olympic Games, was the world's first regional competition based on the Olympic model. This soccer tournament was the first of its kind outside Great Britain. Played under the sponsorship of the Far Eastern Athletic Association, there were 10 editions staged between 1913-34. The host cities were Manila (1913, 1919, 1925, and 1934); Shanghai (1915, 1921, and 1927); Tokyo (1917 and 1930); and Osaka (1923). Although as many as six countries participated in the games as a whole, only China and the Philippines took part in each soccer tournament, while Japan played in all but the first two and the fourth. These three were joined by the Dutch East Indies in 1934. The first edition in 1913 was organized by the Philippine Amateur Athletic Federation, the only such governing body in the region at the time. The Philippines won the first soccer tournament, and the remaining nine were won by China.

With the exception of the China-Philippines rivalry, which extended to a total of 12 matches during this period, the Far East Games tournament provided the only opportunity for international contests in the region before World War II. An important trademark of these competitions was their orientation toward university and school-level players. In the case of China, most team members came from South China, where many of the first and foremost Chinese school teams were located.

China's complete domination of this series is further reflected by its individual results against Japan and the Philippines. Against Japan, for example, China was undefeated in seven games, compiling a goal difference of 31-9. Its total record against the Philippines, furthermore, was 10 won and two lost, one of the losses occurring during their mutual international debut at the Manila games of 1913. The Philippines, meanwhile, finished second almost consistently after 1913, and in the 1934 edition, when there were four participants, it finished third. The second place finisher in 1934 was the Dutch East Indies (the present Indonesia), which earned its place by defeating Japan 7-1. Japan, more often than not, finished in last place, and accumulated the worst record of the three major participants.

In 1934, the political disruptions that had caused a two-year postponement of the tenth edition, finally preempted this extraordinary and little-known experiment in international athletic cooperation, never to be reintroduced.

Winners

1913	Philippines	1923	China
1915	China	1925	China
1917	China	1927	China
1919	China	1930	China
1921	China	1934	China

far post

The area adjacent to the goalpost that is farther away from the ball at a given time, especially when an attack on the goal is being made. On a corner kick, for example, the far post is on the opposite side of the goalmouth from the active corner.

Fausto (1905-1939)

(Full name: Fausto dos Santos.) This world-class center half was one of the first Brazilian players to enjoy an international reputation, largely through his superb performance in the 1930 World Cup. He began his career in 1926 as an amateur with his hometown club, Bangu AC, in the Rio suburb of that name, and two years later, having achieved much respect as an inside forward, he moved to Vasco da Gama as a center half. His highly intelligent tactics as a linkman and his superb ball control were the main factor in Vasco's winning the 1929 Rio league championship, and that same year he made his international debut for Brazil in a friendly with Yugoslavia. In the 1930 World Cup, he combined masterfully with inside forward Preguinho, and soon acquired the nickname *Maravilha Negra* ("Black Wonder"). On Vasco's 1931 tour of Europe, he captured the attention of Barcelona, and returned to play for the giant Catalan club until 1933, when his health began to decline and he was transferred to Young Fellows Berne. In 1934, he returned to Vasco, helping his old club to win another Rio title, but he was left out of the 1934 World Cup squad because of his professional status (a controversial issue in Brazil at the time). In 1936, he moved to Flamengo, where his poor health continued to plague him, and one of his numerous bouts with influenza prevented him from playing in the 1938 World Cup. In 1939, he became tubercular, and was finally admitted to a sanitorium in Minas Gerais, where he died at age 34. Fausto's career was as melodramatic as was his personality, but he added a new dimension to the position of center half in Brazilian soccer, and will always be remembered for his technical perfection.

Fédération Internationale de Football Association (FIFA)

Address: *FIFA House, Hitzigweg 11, CH-8032 Zurich, Switzerland.*

The controlling body of world soccer has 140 member-nations, two less than its peak in 1974-75, due to the expulsion of South Africa for violating antidiscrimination statutes and to the withdrawal of Vietnam Republic after that country ceased to exist. Chad was expelled in 1972 when it repeatedly failed to meet its financial obligations, but South Africa and Chad have been the only expulsions in recent years. (Germany was expelled for four years after World War II.) One other country, Rhodesia, has been under suspension since 1970.

Membership in FIFA is restricted solely to national associations—one per country—and the associations must represent either a sovereign nation, e.g., India; a dominion, e.g., Canada; or protectorate, e.g., Brunei. Governing bodies that are affiliated with national associations as a result of colonization (e.g., French Polynesia with the Fédération Française de Football) are ineligible for membership. In some cases, a colonial association may seek affiliation with FIFA, but only with the consent of the national association of the country to whom the applicant is responsible, e.g., the British Crown Colony of Hong Kong to England. By special arrangement, England, Scotland,

Wales, and Northern Ireland have maintained separate membership in FIFA in deference to their unique role in the development of the game and especially in light of their historical control of the International Football Association Board. The separate membership of one is contingent upon the continued recognition of the autonomy of the other three.

FIFA is responsible for regulating the Laws of the Game worldwide (via the International Football Association Board), organizing and administering international competitions under its jurisdiction (FIFA World Cup, Olympic Games tournament, and World Youth Tournament), regulating the international movement of players in order to protect clubs from "poaching," and, by means of a vast network of standing committees, FIFA administers standards for referees, coordinates developments in sports medicine, settles disputes over questions involving amateurism and professionalism, aids in the development of soccer in underdeveloped countries, provides information for the press and other interested parties, disciplines persons or countries in violation of the statutes and regulations, and manages the finances that make all this activity possible. Every other year a Congress is held in a designated city, at which time members may bring up grievances of various kinds or suggestions for change. Alterations in the statutes, new members, suspensions, and expulsions must be agreed upon by a three-fourths vote of the delegates present. Proposals for any change in the Laws must come before the International Board.

FIFA has weathered a turbulent century of political and social upheaval, emerging thus far as a stable and respected overseer of the world's most popular sport. At times the adversities have been extraordinary, but in the end it has been the organization's steadfastly democratic and nonpolitical profile that has proved to be the safety valve. FIFA has grown from an international organization of old-world western European countries into a world colossus. Two-thirds of its present membership is comprised of developing nations in Africa, Asia, Latin America, and the Caribbean. Despite two world wars and a variety of political encroachments in past decades, FIFA is at this moment meeting its most serious challenge: the threat of administrative anarchy in the Asian Football Confederation over issues relating to China and Israel.

Spurred by the success of the revived Olympic movement just before the turn of the century, the idea for an international governing body was urged by soccer officials of France and Belgium, and with the help of C.A.W. Hirschman, a Dutch banker, and Robert Guérin, one of the founders of the French F.A., the organization came to fruition. On May 21, 1904, representatives of France, Belgium, Holland, Denmark, Sweden, Switzerland, and Spain convened in Paris and founded FIFA. The new organization's most nagging problem—one that caused the most consistent frustration over the decades—was the rebuff it received from the British associations. England, the birthplace of soccer, refused to participate, and the other three British associations (Scotland, Wales, and Ireland), not yet recognized as autonomous entities by the Europeans, languished under England's thumb. Sir Frederick Wall, Secretary of The Football Association in London, responded to the charter-members' invitation to join by sending a terse letter of acknowledgement, and the matter was summarily closed.

Britain's involvement in the fledgling organization was important to the young soccer playing countries of western Europe, because the British had already benefited from 40 years' experience in soccer administration, and the International Football Association Board, whose members were England, Scotland, Wales, and Ireland, had been the acknowledged lawmaking body of the game since the 1880s. England, on the other hand, was threatened by the challenge to the International Board that FIFA seemed to represent. In 1905, FIFA assured the British associations that the International Board would continue to be the sole lawmaking body of the game, and England consented to join. In 1906, an Englishman became the second President of FIFA, and all parties seemed satisfied. The other three British associations joined in 1910, and in 1913, the British allowed two FIFA representatives to join the International Board.

In 1920, however, the four British associations resigned over the continued membership of Germany and the Central Powers, and eliminated FIFA's two seats on the International Board. This matter was resolved (largely through the leadership of Norway and Denmark) when the British rejoined in 1924, reinstating FIFA's two seats on the International Board. In 1928, the

British resigned again when FIFA urged the International Olympic Committee to allow players at the 1928 Amsterdam Games to accept compensatory living expenses (broken-time payments). The British were so affronted by FIFA's position that they stayed out of the world body for 22 years, depriving themselves of the opportunity to participate in the new World Cup until after World War II. Meanwhile, FIFA got along well enough without British knowhow, and in fact, maintained contact with British officials during this period. The President of FIFA throughout most of these controversies was the admirable Jules Rimet of France, instigator of the World Cup and occupant of the head office in Zurich from 1921-54.

The flare-up over the Central Powers after World War I was an overtly political matter, but it was initiated by individual members, not by FIFA as a body; it was settled democratically and by resignations. FIFA's political neutrality has more than once put the organization in the position of seeming to lean in one ideological direction or another, but closer examination of the circumstances usually revealed that the official FIFA policy was merely to maintain the integrity of its statutes. There has been no better example of this than the China question. FIFA Congresses have repeatedly failed to achieve a three-fourths majority when the motion to unseat Taiwan in favor of China PR has been called to a vote. FIFA officially supports this view, but not because it is against China PR gaining membership. On the contrary, FIFA has often stated that it strongly desires Peking's membership, but Peking's condition for joining—the expulsion of Taiwan—violates the nonpolitical spirit of FIFA policy. FIFA, therefore, could not be a party to such a political trade-off. FIFA wants both Chinas in its membership, unless, of course, Taiwan withdraws voluntarily.

In 1953, FIFA authorized the formation of continental confederations to help in the coordination of international activities and to assist in regulating international matters on a regional basis. Europe and Asia established confederations in 1954, Africa in 1956, North and Central America in 1961, and Oceania in 1966. The South American confederation, which had been in existence since 1916, also became an affiliate of FIFA. The following is a simplified organizational chart of world soccer, showing FIFA's position in the overall scheme.

World Soccer Hierarchy

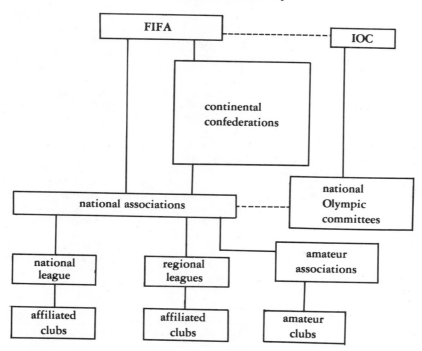

Growth of FIFA Membership

1907	(7)	1946	(57)
1910	(18)	1948	(67)
1914	(24)	1954	(85)
1923	(31)	1962	(102)
1924	(46)	1966	(130)
1938	(51)	1977	(140)

FIFA Presidents

1904-06	Robert Guérin (France)	1956-61	Arthur Drewry (England)
1906-18	D.B. Woodfall (England)	1961-74	Sir Stanley Rous (England)
1921-54	Jules Rimet (France)	1974-	João Havelange (Brazil)
1954-55	Rodolphe Seeldrayers (Belgium)		

Ferencvárosi Torna Club

Location: *Budapest, Hungary;* stadium: *Ferencvárosi Torna Club-Stadion (80,000);* colors: *green and white striped jerseys, white shorts;* honors: *Fairs Cup (1965), Mitropa Cup (1928, 1937), Hungarian champion (1903, 1905, 1906, 1907, 1909, 1910, 1911, 1912, 1913, 1926, 1927, 1928, 1932, 1934, 1938, 1940, 1941, 1949, 1963, 1964, 1967, 1968, 1976), Hungarian cup winner (1913, 1922, 1927, 1928, 1933, 1935, 1942, 1943, 1944, 1956, 1957, 1958, 1972, 1974, 1976, 1978), Viennese cup winner (1909).*

Founded 1899 in Budapest on the Pest side of the Danube. It was known popularly as FTC until 1926, Ferencváros Futball Club from 1926-37, and Ferencvárosi Torna Club again until the late 1940s. The name translates as "City of Francis Gymnastics Club," referring to Emperor Franz Josef I of Austria-Hungary. This imperial tribute was embarassing to the post-World War II government, and the club went through several name changes at that time, including Kinizsi (after a hero of the Turko-Hungarian War). It was incorporated into the army club, Honvéd for a few years and finally reemerged once again as Ferencvárosi Torna Club in the 1950s. It has always been the most popular club in Hungary, and it has also been the most successful. Other than those bleak years immediately after World War II, when Ferencváros lost its identity and all the greatest Hungarian stars were being channeled into Honvéd, this was the home of many gifted players. The "Fradi's" big games are played in the giant Nép Stadion, the national stadium of Hungary.

FTC was one of the important athletic clubs in Budapest around the turn of the century, and its fledgling soccer team won its first championship in 1903, the third year of the Hungarian league. At the beginning, FTC was overshadowed by Budapesti Torna Club (BTC), but by the 1910s it had already won eight championships, a Viennese cup, and one Hungarian cup, largely due to the goalscoring prowess of Imre Schlosser, Hungary's first great player. During this period, MTK became Ferencváros's great crosstown rival, and from 1913-26 the balance of power swung in MTK's favor, though FTC managed to win a cup in 1922.

In the late 1920s, Ferencváros entered another highly successful period that lasted until World War II. Its great star during these years was record goalscorer Dr. György Sárosi, perhaps the Fradi's most popular player of all time and a major force behind Hungary's rise to international prominence in the 1930s. In 1928, Ferencváros defeated Rapid Vienna in the final of the coveted Mitropa Cup, the Central European club championship, and won again in 1937 with a win over Lazio. It was also a losing finalist in this competition three times during the 1930s, bowing out to Sparta Prague in 1935, Slavia Prague in 1938, and Budapest's own Újpest Dózsa in 1939. In

1931-32, Ferencváros won the Hungarian championship without losing a single point.

During the great era of Honvéd after World War II, Ferencváros won only one league title (1949), and did not become a major force in the league again until the 1960s, when it once again produced Hungary's biggest star of the day, center forward Florian Albert. In 1964-65, Albert led Ferencváros through six rounds of the Fairs Cup and a 1-0 victory over Juventus in the final to capture Hungary's first European club championship. In 1967-68, the Fradi advanced to the final of the Fairs Cup again, losing to Leeds United by a single goal,

and in 1974-75, they entered the European Cup Winners' Cup and eliminated Cardiff City, Liverpool (on the away-goals rule), Malmö FF, and Red Star Belgrade to gain the final against Russia's stunning Dinamo Kiev. In that final, Dinamo's one-two combination of Onishenko and Blokhin ran circles around a declining Ferencváros team, and scored three unanswered goals. With its unrivaled popularity among Hungarian fans, however, a revitalized team was sure to emerge, and in 1976 the famous green and white uniforms of Ferencváros won another league-cup double.

Ferreyra, Bernabé (1909-1972)

A pivotal figure in Argentine soccer, Ferreyra became the greatest box office draw of his era and was instrumental in leading Argentina into professionalism. He was a goalscoring center forward with breathtaking skills, and acquired such a reputation that for some time a Buenos Aires newspaper presented gold medals to goalkeepers he failed to score against. As a youth player, he joined lowly Rufino, but at age 22 moved to Tigre, a middle-level Buenos Aires club, where he remained for one year. In 1932, Ríver Plate paid a record transfer fee for his services, and he immediately became the darling of Argentine crowds—perhaps the first true idol of Argentine soccer other than Tesoriero. Fans

gave him the nickname *el Dynamitero*, in recognition of his unstoppable, cannon-like shot on goal. In his second season with Ríver Plate, he scored 43 goals, averaging at least one in every game and setting an Argentine record that was not beaten for many decades. His popularity prompted Ríver and other clubs to form the breakaway professional league, because all that was needed to become a financial success was Ferreyra on one of the league rosters. He led Ríver to the top of Argentine soccer, and remained with his club until his retirement in 1939, scoring 204 goals in 195 appearances. Internal politics in the Argentine association, however, limited his international appearances to four.

Feyenoord, Sportclub

Location: *Rotterdam, Holland;* **stadium:** *Feyenoord Stadion (66,000);* **colors:** *red and white halved jerseys, black shorts;* **honors:** *Intercontinental Cup (1970), European Cup (1970), UEFA Cup (1974), Dutch champion (1924, 1928, 1936, 1938, 1940, 1961, 1962, 1965, 1969, 1971, 1974), Dutch cup winner (1930, 1935, 1965, 1969).*

Founded 1908 as Stadionclub Feyenoord in the great Dutch port city of Rotterdam and financed by mining millionaire C.R.J. Kieboom. For almost 20 years, Feyenoord played in the shadow of Rotterdam's first great club, Sparta. It joined the Dutch football association in 1912, gained promotion to the second division in 1916 and the first division in 1921. Three years later, just as the club's greatest player of all time, Puck van Heel, started to make his mark, Feyenoord won its first Dutch championship. Van Heel, a quiet and methodical left half, led the club to two more titles in 1928 and 1936, and a pair of cup victories in 1930 and 1935 before retiring shortly after the 1938 World Cup. With his record 64 international appearances for Holland, he was the greatest Dutch star until Johan Cruyff. The team van Heel helped to build continued to challenge the emerging power in Dutch soccer, Ajax Amsterdam, after his departure, and it won two more championships before the outbreak of war. Meanwhile, Feyenoord had built the first great stadium in Holland in the mid-1930s.

After the war, Feyenoord disappeared from the front ranks of Dutch soccer for several years, but in 1954 it signed its best player since van Heel, left winger Coen Moulijn, and his popularity led the club management to search for other high quality players in the late 1950s. In 1959 Feyehoord obtained goalkeeper Eddie Pieters-Graafland and right half Reiner Kreyermaat, and a championship team emerged in 1960-61, its first in 21 years; unfortunately, nothing came of it in European Cup competition the following year. After another championship in 1962, however, Feyenoord reached the semifinals of the European Cup, bowing out to the unstoppable Portuguese team Benfica. A league-cup double followed in 1965 but Feyenoord was again stopped cold in the European Cup.

In the late 1960s, Austrian manager Ernst Happel took over the club, and he employed a flexible *catenaccio* with Rinus Israel in the sweeper role and a powerful inside forward, Wim van Hanegem, to support the marvelous Swedish center forward Ove Kindvall. In 1969, this talented team won another league-cup double, while at the same time its more exciting cross-country rival Ajax advanced to the final of the European Cup. The differing styles of the two teams—both effective in their own way—drew international attention to Dutch soccer. As it happened, Feyenoord got the jump on Ajax by winning the 1970 European Cup with a convincing march to the final. Feyenoord swept past KR Reykjavik, AC Milan, ASK Vorwärts, and Legia Warsaw in early rounds, and in the final completely dominated the much-favored Glasgow Celtic 2-1, though the game went into overtime. Pieters-Graafland continued to play in goal and Moulijn was still on the left wing, but success really was due to the efforts of Kindvall and Israel, who scored the two goals against Celtic. After the European Cup, Feyenoord managed to cope with Argentina's brutal Estudiantes in the Intercontinental Cup, and with that win the big Rotterdam club reached the pinnacle of world soccer.

The reign was to be short-lived. Ajax's more exciting and fluid brand of *catenaccio* proved to be the wave of the future, and Feyenoord was eclipsed by the Amsterdamers' three scintillating European Cup victories in as many years. After another league title in 1971, Kindvall left for his native Sweden, and Feyenoord faltered. Van Hanegem led the club to a UEFA Cup victory in 1973-74, with a convincing win in the final over Tottenham Hotspur, and an eleventh league title in the same year, but thereafter Feyenoord settled for second and third place in the league and several UEFA Cup appearances, none yielding any real successes. Feyenoord has amassed an impressive overall European record, most of it in the UEFA Cup (it has never appeared in the European Cup Winners' Cup), a record that would have gained more international attention had it not been for the parallel rise of Ajax.

field of play

The size, markings, and characteristics of the playing field are carefully supervised by the International Football Asssociation Board. The evolution of the present field of play, however, was in the making for many decades, as shown by the following chronology of major changes and developments:

1863   a)maximum length of 200 yards and maximum width of 100 yards specified.
b)corner flags required.
c)goals defined as two upright posts eight yards apart without any tape or crossbar between them.

1865   tapes stretched between either goal post eight feet above the ground.

1875   minimum length of 100 yards and minimum width of 50 yards specified.

1883   a)crossbars replace tapes.
b)touch lines added to all sides of the field.

1891   a)center spot added.
b)center circle added.
c)semi-circular lines six yards from either goal post added to designate the goal area.

d)12-yard line at either end of the field marked off to designate the penalty area.

e)a theoretical 18-yard line sanctioned to indicate the position of a penalty kick.

f)goal nets sanctioned.

1894 maximum width of goal posts and crossbars fixed at five inches.

1896 minimum height of corner flags fixed at five feet.

1897 dimensions of the field of play altered: for domestic competition, a maximum length of 130 yards, a minimum length of 100 yeards a maximum width of 100 yards, and a minimum width of 50 yards; for international competition, a maximum length of 120 yards, a minimum length of 110 yards, a maximum width of 80 yards, and a minimum width of 70 yards.

1901 a broken line 18 yards from the goal line added to determine the position of penalty kicks.

1902 a)halfway line added.
b)present rectangular goal area and penalty area introduced.
c)penalty mark added 12 yards from the goal line.

1937 penalty arc added.

1939 maximum width of touch line and goal line fixed at five inches.

1966 minimum width and depth of crossbar and goal post fixed at four inches.

The International Board has been reluctant to act on the composition of playing surfaces, but with sophisticated technologies emerging and expanded international competition in differing climates, this is becoming an increasingly important factor in modern soccer. Grass surfaces abound in most parts of the world, but in Iceland all playing surfaces are gravel. In Malta, Cyprus, and many countries of North Africa and the Middle East, most pitches are composed of dirt or sand.

The advance of artificial surfaces in North America has presented a new set of problems, particularly in regard to their punishing effect on players' legs. The first soccer match ever played on an artificial surface was an exhibiton match between Real Madrid and West Ham United at the Astrodome, Houston, Texas, in 1966. The surface was Monsanto's Astro-Turf. The first World Cup qualification match to be played on artificial surface was Syria vs. Iraq in 1976 at the Malaz Ground, Riyadh, Saudi Arabia, and it was followed some weeks later by a second match between the same teams. The first European club to announce that it would install an artificial surface was Arsenal F.C. of London, with a completion date set at 1980.

FIFA   See: Fédération Internationale de Football Association

---

Fiji

Fiji Football Association
Mr. Younas M. Haniff
National Secretary
H.M. Customs
Suva

Founded: 1936
FIFA: 1963
OFC: 1963

Affiliated clubs: *18;* **registered players:** *15,000;* **national stadium:** *none;* **largest stadium:** *Burkhurst Park, Suva (20,000);* **colors:** *white jerseys, black shorts;* **season:** *March to September;* **honors:** *none.*

Among the dozens of small island nations and protectorates in Oceania, Fiji is the only full-fledged member of FIFA and the Oceania Football Confederation (OFC). The game was brought to the Fiji Islands by British colonists, and by the early 1950s Fiji selections had become active in international competition. Though the Fiji Football Association was founded in 1936, it was not affiliated with The Football Association in London. Competitive links were established early with New Zealand and other British colonies in the area, and from the early 1960s Fiji became active in all regional competitions in Oceania.

In 1951, New Zealand defeated a Suva all-star team 6-1 and won over a full international Fiji team 6-4 in a friendly series at Suva. One year later, New Zealand defeated Fiji 9-0 in a friendly at Lautoka; this remains New Zealand's biggest win and Fiji's worst loss to date. Fiji has been an active participant in all the area's regional tournaments. Its best result is the winning of the third South Pacific Games soccer tournament in 1969. In seven matches Fiji won four and lost two against opposition from Papua-New Guinea, French Polynesia, New Caledonia, Tahiti, New Hebrides, and the British Solomons. In 1975, Fiji placed fourth in a field of seven at the fifth South Pacific Games.

Its most disappointing result was a last place finish in the first Oceania Cup (1973), the region's most important tournament. Fiji was winless against all four opponents—New Zealand, Tahiti, New Caledonia, and New Hebrides—three of whom were not even members of FIFA or the OFC. Later Fiji was designated as host of the second Oceania Cup in 1977.

The leading club in Fiji is Western Star F.C. of Suva, which in 1972 made an extensive tour of New Zealand and lost most of its matches against Northern League First Division sides. The Fiji league includes a total of 16 clubs, of which eight are in the first division. There is a national championship and an annual cup competition, and there are regional leagues on the outlying islands. A truly national league was scheduled to start in 1977. Fiji remains one of only three full members of the Oceania Football Confederation and has not yet attempted to qualify for Olympic or World Cup competition.

Finland

Suomen Palloliitto-Finlands Bollförbund
Stadion
00250 Helsinki 25

Founded: 1907
FIFA: 1908
UEFA: 1954

Affiliated clubs: *750;* **registered players:** *35,500;* **national stadium:** *Olympiastadion, Helsinki (50,000);* **largest stadium:** *Olympiastadion;* **colors:** *white jerseys, blue shorts;* **season:** *April to October;* **honors:** *Scandinavian Championship (1963).*

The weakest of all Scandinavian countries except Iceland, Finland has nevertheless remained a cut above the level of play at the bottom of the European heap, i.e., Cyprus and Malta. Finnish soccer is dominated by the question of amateurism, but like many of the so-called amateur countries, players in the higher echelons of the Finnish league receive bonuses and ad hoc payments. Full-fledged professionalism is unlikely to surface, however, in a country where a small population is strewn over such a sparse landscape. On the playing field, Finnish teams have consistently failed to show winning form, other than the Olympic Games of 1912 and the Scandinavian Championship of 1960-63.

English businessmen and workers brought soccer to Helsinki around 1890, but the game was slow to emerge. Its stature as a national pastime is still below that of track and field and any number of winter sports, though it has probably become the leading team sport. The SPB-FBF was founded in 1907, and one year later a league was introduced that centered in Helsinki and Turku. The formation of a national team was accomplished in 1911 when Finland played host to a visiting Swedish selection and lost 5-2. Its first and perhaps most laudable victory occurred the following year at the 1912 Olympic Games in Stockholm with a 3-2 win over Italy, not yet the international power of later years, and a solemn 2-1 defeat of Czarist Russia the next day. In the next two rounds of the 1912 games, however, the future of Finnish soccer was determined with a 4-0 defeat at the hands of an amateur British side and a 9-0 trouncing by Holland, yet another minor continental team at the time.

Finland has a poor record against all

European opposition other than Iceland. The only major deviation occurred during the 1920s and '30s against the impermanent Baltic states, Estonia, Latvia, and Lithuania. Between 1921-39, Finland's cumulative record on Baltic playing fields was: 35-19-7-9-88-46-45. Its 19 victories account for almost one third of all Finland's wins to date in international competition, though its record against the Netherlands is nearly level in 13 matches from 1912-76. Nevertheless, the Finns have lost to Sweden 50 of 65 matches; Norway, 34 of 51; Denmark, 28 of 44; Austria, 5 of 6; England, 9 of 10; West Germany (and prewar Germany), 10 of 15; Hungary, 6 of 7; Italy, 4 of 5; Poland, 13 of 16; and the USSR, 6 of 8 matches played. Finland's only international against a South American team resulted in a 7-3 loss to Peru at the Olympic Games of 1936 in Berlin, the second games in which Finland participated. Its biggest loss was 13-0 to Germany in 1940. As host to the 1952 Olympic Games, a bye to the second round did not help in its 4-3 elimination to the amateur Austrian team, but Finland's exposure to postwar Hungary and other first rate teams was a big boost to Finnish experience. Not surprisingly, the World Cup and European Championship finals have remained out of reach.

On the club level the cities of Helsinki and Turku dominated league play until the 1940s, as to a great extent they still do, but after World War II the top clubs from Vaasa, Kotka, Kuopio, and Lahti began to receive their share of the honors. 25 championships between 1908-39 were won by Helsinki clubs, mainly IFK, (Idrottsföreningen Kamraterna), JK (Jalkapalloklubi), and PS (Palloseura), but after the war 22 championships went to cities other than Helsinki, inlcuding Turku and those named above. The degree to which amateurism is a central factor in the domestic game is indicated by the fact that no club has been allowed to dominate the league significantly since the war. The highest placement to date by a Finnish club in the three European club competitions has been the second round. The First Division is comprised of 12 clubs, of which the bottom two are relegated each year to the Second Division. A national cup competition was introduced in 1955.

Champions

1908 Unitas Helsinki	1931 IFK Helsinki	1954 Pentterit Helsinki
1909 PUS Helsinki	1932 PS Helsinki	1955 IFK Helsinki
1910 Abo IFK	1933 IFK Helsinki	1956 PS Kuopio
1911 JK Helsinki	1934 PS Helsinki	1957 PS Helsinki
1912 JK Helsinki	1935 PS Helsinki	1958 PS Kuopio
1913 KJF Turku	1936 JK Helsinki	1959 IFK Helsinki
1914 no competition	1937 IFK Helsinki	1960 Valkeakosken Haka
1915 KJF Helsinki	1938 JK Helsinki	1961 IFK Helsinki
1916 KJF Helsinki	1939 Turun PS Turku	1962 Valkeakosken Haka
1917 JK Helsinki	1940 Sudet Helsinki	1963 Reipas Lahti
1918 JK Helsinki	1941 Turun PS Turku	1964 HJK Helsinki
1919 JK Helsinki	1942 HT Helsinki	1965 Valkeakosken Haka
1920 Abo IFK	1943 no competition	1966 PS Kuopio
1921 PS Helsinki	1944 IFK Vaasa	1967 Reipas Lahti
1922 PS Helsinki	1945 Turun PS Turku	1968 Turun PS Turku
1923 JK Helsinki	1946 IFK Vaasa	1969 Kokolan PV
1924 Abo IFK	1947 IFK Helsinki	1970 Reipas Lahti
1925 JK Helsinki	1948 PS Vaasa	1971 Turun PS Turku
1926 PS Helsinki	1949 Turun PS Turku	1972 Turun PS Turku
1927 PS Helsinki	1950 Ilves-Kissat	1973 HJK Helsinki
1928 Turun PS Turku	1951 Kotkan TP	1974 PS Kuopio
1929 PS Helsinki	1952 Kotkan TP	1975 Turun PS Turku
1930 IFK Helsinki	1953 IFK Vaasa	1976 PS Kuopio

1977 Valkeakosken Haka
1978 HJK Helsinki

Cup Winners

1955 Valkeakosken Haka	1963 Valkeakosken Haka	1971 Millelin Palloilijat
1956 Pallo-Peikot	1964 Reipas Lahti	1972 Reipas Lahti
1957 IF Drott	1965 Abo IFK	1973 Reipas Lahti
1958 Kotkan TP	1966 HJK Helsinki	1974 Reipas Lahti
1959 Valkeakosken Haka	1967 Kitkan TP	1975 Reipas Lahti
1960 Valkeakosken Haka	1968 PS Kuopio	1976 Reipas Lahti
1961 Kotkan TP	1969 Valkeakosken Haka	1977 Valkeakosken Haka
1962 PS Helsinki	1970 Mikkelin Palloilijat	1978 Reipas Lahti

Finney, Thomas, O.B.E. (1922-   )

Inevitably compared to his contemporary at outside right, Stanley Matthews, Finney was perhaps the most complete No. 7 in English soccer history. He was a master ball artist, and, unlike Matthews, he was equally adept with either foot and could finish with great authority on a consistent basis. He scored a record 30 goals for England in 76 appearances. The most troubling controversy in the postwar English game was whom to select on the right wing—Matthews or Finney—and it was often settled by playing both, Finney on the left, and Matthews on the right. Ultimately, Finney played 40 times for England on the right, and 33 on the left. His 12-year international career began in 1947, one month after he joined the first team of Preston North End. Preston was the only club Finney ever played for; he signed with them as an amateur in 1937, and, despite turning professional in 1940, his official debut was put off until 1946 because of the war. In 1960, at age 38, he was prematurely forced to retire from Preston with a sustained groin injury while still the top scorer for his club. For 23 years, he almost single-handedly kept Preston in the top flight of league competition, but failed to gain a single league or cup honor. Finney's name became so synonymous with his home town club that he eventually became its president after his retirement, a post that he still holds today while running his lucrative plumbing business. In September 1963, he came out of retirement to play one European Cup match for Belfast's Distillery against Benfica.

Finney started as an inside forward, but when playing for military teams during World War II he found that his natural position was on the right wing, where his left foot bias was allowed to operate freely. While the Matthews-Finney controversy raged among the fans and commentators during the late 1940s, the two wingers became close friends and the rivalry remained beneath them personally. Except for those times when Finney played opposite Matthews, the selection usually went to the player who was in better form. Though he eventually compiled more caps than Matthews—a tribute to his extraordinary gifts—he would have earned even more had he not suffered repeatedly from injuries. In the end, however, his proudest accomplishment was in owning nearly every Preston appearance and scoring record, and returning to his fans their unceasing devotion throughout his career.

Flamengo, Clube de Regatas do

Location: *Rio de Janeiro, Brazil;* stadium: *Estádio da Gavea;* colors: *red and black hooped jerseys, white shorts;* honors: *Rio-São Paulo Tournament (1940 shared-*

unofficial, 1961), Rio de Janeiro champion (1914, 1915, 1920, 1921, 1925, 1927, 1939, 1942, 1943, 1944, 1953, 1954, 1955, 1963, 1965, 1972, 1974, 1978).

Founded 1895 as a sailing club, Flamengo has the largest following in Brazil, and is the oldest Brazilian club still in existence. Its name holds a near-mystical quality among the *torcedoros,* or unabiding fans of Rio de Janeiro, and while Brazilian soccer in general has been famous the world over for its exciting, attacking style of play, Flamengo has been largely responsible for this tradition. Its little Estadio da Gavea has long been the club's training ground, while the big matches are all played at Maracanã, the world's largest stadium.

Despite Flamengo's early founding date, a soccer team was not organized until 1911 (by disgruntled Fluminense players), and it did not participate in the Rio league (Liga Metropolitana de Esportes Atléticos) until 1912, along with newcomers Bangu, Sao Cristovao, and Mangueira. In its very first league match, Flamengo defeated Mangueira 16-2. The great archrivalry with Fluminense got under way later in the season, and Flamengo lost the first encounter 3-2. By 1913, this sparkling club had already gathered Rio's second biggest following after Fluminense, and in 1914 it won its first Rio title. In 1915, it repeated this honor without losing a game,

and third and fourth championships were won in 1920 and 1921. In 1925 and 1927, Flamengo triumphed again with its greatest star of the pre-professional era, center forward Araken Patuska, who scored goal after goal. Another high point was reached in the late 1930s, when the brilliant Domingos da Guia and breathtaking Leônidas were setting Brazilian soccer on fire, and the club's consistency was demonstrated by winning three more titles during the 1940s. In the early 1950s, Flamengo reached new heights with three successive Rio championships, led by its famous lineup known as the *rolo compressor* ("steam roller"). The vanguard of this extraordinary team was center forward Indio.

Still regarded as "the peoples' club," Flamengo has recently been less successful than many of the other great Rio clubs, but it has carried on its tradition of winning important titles in each decade. In 1961, Flamengo won the coveted Rio-São Paulo Tournament, and it won two more league championships in 1963 and 1965. Its three league victories in the 1970s were followed by the acquisition of its greatest star since Leônidas, the new national idol, Zico.

flick

A very light kick made with a quick, snappy motion, usually in the form of a short pass.

floodlit soccer

The first match played under lights took place at Bramall Lane, Sheffield, England, on October 14, 1878, and was played between two representative teams of the Sheffield Football Association. Four lights, each projecting the equivalent of 8,000 candles, were mounted on 30-foot high poles, one at each corner of the field. The power was supplied by a pair of Siemens dynamo engines situated separately

behind either goal. The novelty of a match under lights proved to be a great attraction, and nearly 20,000 people crowded into the grounds, far surpassing the record attendance figures of the period. The Football Association, however, did not sanction floodlit games until 1887, and their use did not become widespread in England or elsewhere until the late 1920s.

Fluminense Futebol Clube

Location: *Rio de Janeiro, Brazil;* stadium: *Estádio Alvaro Chaves;* colors: *red, green and white striped jerseys, white shorts;* honors: *Rio-São Paulo Tournament (1940 shared unofficial 1957, 1960), National Championship (1970), Rio de Janeiro champion (1906, 1907 shared, 1908, 1909, 1911, 1917, 1918, 1919, 1924 AMEA, 1936 LCF, 1937, 1938, 1940, 1941, 1946, 1951, 1959, 1964, 1969, 1971, 1973, 1975, 1976).*

Founded 1902 as Fluminense Foot-Ball Club in Rio de Janeiro (though its unofficial formation had occurred one year earlier), this famous club became the great pioneer of organized soccer in Brazil. Its chief founder was an Englishman, Oscar Cox, and many of its early players were British residents. Fluminense was the prime mover in establishing the Rio league (Liga Metropolitana) in 1905; it helped to organize the first Brazilian national team and governing body, and in 1932 became the first club to openly adopt professionalism and push for a fully professional league. As a founding member of the Rio league, it won the first four *carioca* championships (1906-09), and dominated the league until 1920, winning more often than not by astonishing goal differences. Its first meeting with Flamengo in 1912 initiated South America's greatest archrivalry, the "Fla-Flu," which culminated with a world record attendance figure of 177,656 in 1963. Flu is generally acknowledged as the wealthiest club in Brazil. The term "Fluminense" refers to the residents of Rio de Janeiro State.

Until the construction of Vasco da Gama's huge stadium in 1926, Fluminense's ground at Alvaro Chaves was the site of most Brazilian internationals. By 1930, Flu was publishing its own weekly newspaper, and had already won eight Rio championships. In the mid to late-1930s, it boasted the greatest Brazilian forward line to date, with Romeu at inside right, Tim at inside left, and Carreio on the left wing, and from 1936-41 it won five Rio championships. Its wealth and well-heeled connections resulted in the nickname *Po de Arroz* ("Face Powder").

In 1951, Flu won both the Rio league title and the Rio Cup (over several leading clubs of Europe and South America) with the great Didi at inside forward. The club's success was intermittent after this until 1964, when it signed the elegant back and later captain of Brazil, Carlos Alberto, who was the guiding light of Flu's many important triumphs from 1969-76. Fluminense returned to a dominant position in Rio soccer during this period, winning four league titles in six years and the national championship in 1970. Its most recent star has been the transplanted Rivelino, whose midfield orchestration combined masterfully with Carlos Alberto's role as attacking sweeper until the latter's transfer to Cosmos in 1977. Flu's little Estádio Alvaro Chaves is primarily used as a training ground, while most league matches are held in the giant Maracana, the world's largest stadium.

flying kick

A kick taken by a player in mid-air.

Forest Football Club   See: Wanderers Football Club

forward

A player whose position on the field is on or near the front line of the attack. The five traditional positions on the forward line are: outside right, inside right, center forward, inside left, and outside left. One may add the less defined position of striker, though this player sometimes operates from the midfield.

France

Fédération Française de Football
60bis, Avenue d'Iéna
75783 Paris 16e

Founded: 1918
FIFA: 1904
UEFA: 1954

Affiliated clubs: *16,242;* **registered players:** *1,121,797 (419 professional, 115 non-amateur);* **national stadium:** *Parc des Princes, Paris (50,000);* **largest stadium:** *Stade Yves du Manoir, Colombes-Paris (65,000);* **colors:** *blue jerseys, white shorts;* **season:** *August to June;* **honors:** *World Cup third place (1958), Stade de Reims, Latin Cup (1953).*

The French have made enormous contributions to the world game as administrators and organizers of soccer, but they have seldom achieved the success one would expect on the playing field. Frenchmen were the principal organizers of FIFA, the World Cup, various European championships, and several other international competitions and awards, and *France Football*, the Paris weekly, has been the world's most respected soccer publication for decades. Ironically, the game in France was in organizational chaos for over forty years, and it was not until after World War II that soccer finally mounted a strong challenge to the popularity of rugby. Even today the French are proud of their heritage as the only major rugby power outside the British Commonwealth. In soccer, France had one bright period during the 1950s, when the immortal Raymond Kopa and Just Fontaine led the national team and their club, Stade de Reims, to high honors in the World and European Cups. Twenty years later, French teams again began to make their mark on international competition, employing highly attractive tactics that spoke well of the national effort to make up for lost time.

France also played a central role in the early history of football games in general. No other country outside the British Isles is so closely linked to the development of those sprawling medieval versions of football that preceded modern soccer and rugby. It is possible that at some point before or during the Middle Ages France was either the birthplace of these games or the hub for their proliferation throughout Northwestern Europe. While more substantiated and traditional theories point to England in this role, there is little doubt that France was in some way an important link in the chain. No one, including the French, doubt that soccer and rugby as we know them took shape in nineteenth-century

England after at least 700 years of continuous development—football virtually disappeared in France during the eighteenth century—but a question remains as to the role of France before and during the Middle Ages.

The football game of *la soule* in late medieval France is well documented and may have come from any one or combination of four sources: 1) The Romans were known to have played *harpastrum* and other ball games in their wanderings, and there are records of football-like exercises with a Roman character at Nîmes and Lyons in Southern France from the fifth century A.D. 2) *La soule* possibly originated in Celtic Britain with the Bretons, a Celtic people who settled in Northwestern France. The Bretons may have taught their ball game—called *la soule*—to their eventual conquerors, the Normans, whose influence over much of France was pervasive. The Normans named their ball game *la choule*, and it is significant that late medieval France also adopted the term *la soule*. 3) *La soule* may have been invented or imported by the influential Normans from Scandinavia, the ancestral home of Norman aristocracy. 4) The Normans may have discovered football being played by the conquered Anglo-Saxon and Scandinavian tribes of Britain after 1066, and imported it to France. Based on available evidence, the Roman and Celtic theories are the most creditable.

Whatever the origins of French football, various forms of *la soule* were widely played in France throughout the late medieval period. The reign of Louis VII (1137-80) is generally considered *la soule's* first era of widespread popularity. Some form of the game was played in Southern France (Languedoc) as early as 1147. Despite a century of royal bans, *la soule* grew in popularity throughout the fourteenth century, and wherever it was played crowds gathered and prizes were given to the winners. In 1396, a playing code was issued under the title *Ordinatio de Pila facienda*, and this may represent the first written rules of medieval football anywhere. Like the English and Norman games, *la soule* was often played during Shrovetide, the annual carnival season just before Lent. With lenient enforcement of the royal bans and little official opposition from the church, the game was allowed to flourish.

During the Renaissance period, French country gentlemen were not above playing an occasional game with their servants, and *la soule* was finally embraced by the monarchy in the sixteenth century. Henry II (1547-59) played regularly on the Pré-aux-Clercs, where he captained the "white" team against M. de Laval's "red" team. In the seventeenth century, *la soule* declined as a pastime for the average citizen, but it grew steadily among the aristocracy, largely as a result of the highly fashionable Florentine game *calcio* that had recently been described by French travelers in Italy. Having lost its earlier strength in Normandy and Brittany, *la soule* was finally revitalized there too, as well as in Picardy, in the early eighteenth century, and a highly structured version similar to Florentine *calcio* was played in Lyons around 1737. *La soule's* general decline, however, continued, and the French Parliament banned the game altogether in 1781. By 1810, it had all but disappeared from the provinces.

France was oblivious to the growth of organized football in England during the early and mid-nineteenth century, and by the time the French were reintroduced to the game after 1870, football had already split into two camps—soccer and rugby. Football was imported to France by British sailors who founded Le Havre Athletic Club in 1872. Paris Football Club was founded in 1879, Racing Club de France in 1882, and Stade Francais in 1883, but these clubs played rugby exclusively for many years. Rugby, in fact, became much more popular than soccer and remained so until well into the twentieth century. In 1887, Racing Club and Stade Français formed the Union des Sociétés Françaises des Sports Athlétiques (USFSA), the first governing body of French football, but the USFSA did not recognize soccer. Finally, in 1891, the first two clubs in France devoted exclusively to soccer were founded in Paris by British residents: White Rovers F.C., comprised entirely of Scots, and Gordon F.C., later renamed Standard A.C. A pivotal year for French soccer was 1892, when White Rovers defeated Standard, 10-1, at Bécon-les-Bruyères in the first soccer game between French clubs. Club Français, the first soccer club founded by Frenchmen, also appeared in 1892.

The first period of expansion occurred between 1892-94 with the founding of Le Havre's soccer section, US Lycée du Havre, and Blue Star in Normandy; Lille OSC, RC Roubaix, US Tourcoing, A.C. Cambrai, Cercle Pédestre d'Asnières, US Dunkerque, and US Saint-Omer in the industrial north; and SA Bordeaux in Guyenne. In 1893, six Parisian soccer clubs were admitted to the USFSA, and Marylebone F.C., the first English club to visit France, defeated three of the new USFSA members. A year later, the USFSA introduced the first competition, the Championnat de France, for the six Parisian clubs. The six competed over a four week period in a knockout series, and Standard won the first edition with an all British roster. After the first year, the Championnat de France was decided on points. The major issue during this period was selecting the minimum number of French nationals for each team.

In 1895, the first unofficial international involving a French team took place in Paris, when Folkestone A.C., a minor English club, defeated a Parisian selection, 3-0. The English club won 8-0 six weeks later in Folkestone. The soccer section of Racing Club de France, later to become the most famous club in the country, was started in 1896, but by 1897 there were still only 30 soccer clubs in all of France, and rugby continued to be the most popular form of football in the country. The first French-Belgian club internationals were played in 1896, and in 1899 one of the world's first international club tournaments, the Challenge International du Nord, between French and Belgian clubs, was introduced in Tourcoing on the Belgian border.

After Standard A.C. won four French titles in five years, the century ended with the first winning of the Championnat de France by a provincial club—appropriately Le Havre A.C.—and the founding of several important clubs of the future, including Olympique de Marseille and F.C. Rouen.

French officials had already become pioneers in organizing international competition before the turn of the century, but after 1900, despite the game's second-class status at home, the French continued to take the lead in bringing together the soccer-playing nations of Europe. Robert Guérin, a founder of the USFSA, was a primary instigator of FIFA, the world governing body, and with the Dutch banker C.A.W. Hirschman, Guérin did more than anyone to get the new federation off the ground. Not only was the first FIFA Congress held in Paris, but Guérin became the first president of FIFA in 1904 and helped to establish an Anglo-French hold in the FIFA leadership that lasted until 1974.

In 1905, the Fédération de Gymnastique Sportive des Patronages de France (FGSPF) entered the French soccer picture and started a second league that was dominated until its demise in 1914 by L'Étoile des Deux Lacs (Star of the Two Lakes). A year later the Fédération Cycliste et Athlétique Française (FCAF) introduced a third league, and it also folded in 1914 after SM de Puteaux and Vie au Grand Air du Médoc (Life in the Magnificent Air of Medoc) won three championships each. While both these leagues continued to operate separately—in addition to the old USFSA league—they merged as a loose affiliation in 1906 under the name Comité Français Interfédéral (CFI). In 1908, the USFSA withdrew from FIFA because FIFA refused to accept its proposal to recognize the Amateur Football Association in England. Before the end of 1908, the CFI was provisionally admitted as the official French representative in FIFA, and full membership was granted in 1910. The CFI's main interest in domestic competition was its annual Trophée de France, which was given to winners of regional championships.

Several important clubs, including CA Paris and Red Star Paris, left the USFSA in 1911, and formed yet another league, the Ligue de Football Association (LFA). This was the first governing body in France for soccer only, but it too lasted no longer than the outbreak of war in 1914. Meanwhile, the USFSA, an increasingly outmoded federation dedicated to amateur ideals, continued to ignore the CFI until it finally merged with the CFI in 1913. With the clubs of the LFA safely under the CFI's wing by 1914, the CFI's full absorption of French leagues was complete. In early 1917, the spirit of unity engendered by the war led to the introduction of a national cup competition, the Coupe Charles Simon (after the ex-president of the CFI), later renamed the Coupe de France. By 1918 the CFI finally became a truly national governing body with a new name, the Fédération Française de Football (FFF).

The first president of the FFF was Jules Rimet, who in 1921 also became the president of FIFA, a post he held for 33 years. Rimet became the prime mover in launching the World Cup during the 1920s, and for many years the World Cup trophy bore his name. Henri Delaunay, the general secretary of the NFF and the CFI before it from 1908-55, became the first general secretary of UEFA, the European governing body, in 1954. The trophy of the European Football Championship is named for Delaunay.

France's first full international took place at Brussels in 1904, a 3-3 draw with Belgium. The next two games against Belgium resulted in 7-0 and 5-0 losses, and these crushing defeats set the tone for the French national team in the years ahead. The chaos that was raging in domestic administration during the pre-World War I era, in addition to the country's relatively late start in adopting the game, took a serious toll on international results for decades. In its first seven encounters with England (1906-20), France lost every game and compiled a 3-64 goal difference. In the 1908 Olympic Games, Denmark defeated two different French national teams, 17-1 and 9-0. The former remains a record loss in the history of international competition (shared with Germany's 16-0 win over Czarist Russia in 1912). Several defeats of Switzerland, Luxembourg, Belgium, and Italy helped France's overall record before World War I, but between the two world wars, as the schedule increased and other European countries became great international powers, France's reputation on the playing field declined even further. There were severe losses in the 1920s to Italy, Holland, England, Spain, and Austria, and in 1927 Hungary won in Budapest by a staggering 13-1.

The French entered all three Olympic tournaments during the 1920s, reaching the semi-finals in 1920 but failing to advance beyond the second round in 1924 and 1928. When the first World Cup was assigned to distant Uruguay in 1930, Rimet was obliged to keep France in the competition despite the widespread boycott by European countries, because he and France had been so instrumental in organizing the series. In Montevideo, the French, respected for their role in FIFA though not on the playing field, defeated Mexico and suffered surprisingly low 1-0 shutouts to Argentina and Chile. In 1934, they were unfairly eliminated in the first round by the great Austrian team when the winning goal was scored in overtime by inside left Schall, who was clearly offside. France itself was chosen to stage the 1938 World Cup in recognition of Rimet an his tireless work on behalf of soccer. The atmosphere was in marked contrast to Mussolini's dour show in Italy four years earlier, and the biggest event was France's second round rendezvous with the world champion Italians, who were scorned by French fans. This match was played in Paris at the Colombes Stadium, the largest in the country, and it was decided in the second half by Italian center forward Piola, scorer of two goals in a 3-1 Italian win.

The Coupe de France (French Cup), which had been introduced in 1917, was the only national competition in France for a period of eight years. The cup was won by four different Parisian clubs in the first four seasons, and by 1922, there were 249 participating clubs. Red Star Paris, one of the great names in French soccer, won three in a row during the early 1920s, and in 1924 Olympique Marseille won its first of a record nine cups to launch its reputation as the country's leading cup competitor. Red Star and Olympique Marseille dominated French soccer in the 1920s, but ultimately had to share the headlines with the growing issue of professionalism and the formation of a new league competition. In 1926, the FFF launched its first national championship (amateur) with 11 clubs participating in three divisions: CA Paris, Olympique Marseille, Bastidienne, Rouen, Amiens, Messin, Valentigney, Saint-Chamond, SC Reims, Clamency, and Centre de Tours. After three years, the league broke apart through lack of interest, since many important clubs had not yet joined. The three winners of the top division were: CA Paris, Stade Français, and Olympique Marseille.

A new league, the Coupe Sochaux, was formed in 1930 at the instigation of FC Sochaux Montbéliard (Franche Comte), and was underwritten by the Peugeot automobile company. Its status with the FFF was official, but it included only eight clubs divided into two groups; Sochaux and Mulhouse were the winners in 1931 and 1932. It was superseded when the FFF finally sanctioned professionalism and in 1932 introduced a new Championnat de France, the first professional league in French soccer and still the French national league today. Twenty of the greatest clubs in France were charter members: Red Star Paris, Racing Club Paris, CA Paris, Club Français, Lille OSC, Olympique Marseille, Sète, Stade Rennais, Sochaux, Olympique Antibes, Sporting Club Nimes, Cannes, OGC Nice, SO Montpellier, Olympique Alès, Hyères, FC Mulhouse, Excelsior de Roubaix, Metz, and SC Fives. The participants were divided into two groups of 10, and the winners were Lille OSC and Antibes. The latter was disqualified from the play-off, and second place Cannes finally lost the play-off to Lille OSC for the championship. In the following year, a first division of 14 clubs and a second division of two sections—north and south—were created, and Sète, from Languedoc's port city of the same name and one of the great clubs of the 1930s, became the first champion of the multidivisional league. Sète and Sochaux won several league and cup titles during the 1930s, some by spectacular margins, as did the famous Racing Club de Paris and Olympique Marseille.

After an unofficial wartime league that lasted for six seasons—the Coupe de France was played officially throughout the war without a break—the regular league reappeared in 1945-46 with another win by Lille OSC. Lille proceeded to win three cups in a row and then achieved the extraordinary feat of placing second in the first division for four consecutive seasons (1948-51) while OGC Nice and Stade de Reims won titles and built up winning reputations. Reims' win of 1949, in fact, inaugurated an unprecedented era of success in French and European competition. After winning another championship in 1953, the famous Champagne club won the Latin Cup that same year with a magnificent 3-0 defeat of AC Milan, a club widely touted as the best on the continent. Reims' victory in this elite competition was the first and only major international honor won by a French club, initiating Reims' lasting fame as the finest team ever produced in France. With Robert Jonquet (and until 1953 Roger Marché) in the backfield and the immortal Raymond Kopa— the most talented French player of all time— on the forward line (replaced in 1956 by France's greatest goalscorer Just Fontaine), Reims gained the European Cup final twice (1956 and 1959) only to face the unbeatable Real Madrid on both occasions. Led by manager Albert Batteux, Reims brought glory to French soccer, and had it not been for the presence of Real Madrid, Reims might have been the first club in Europe to dominate the European Cup.

After early elimination by Yugoslavia in the

1954 World Cup, the Reims-based French national team entered its golden era under manager Paul Nicholas. At the 1958 World Cup in Sweden, France won its first round group despite a loss to Yugoslavia, and delighted observers with its entertaining and attacking style. A crushing win over Northern Ireland in the quarter-finals confirmed its status as a major international power, and in the semi-finals its reputation suffered little in a 5-2 loss to the scintillating Brazilian team of Pelé and Garrincha. The stalwart center half Jonquet and a forward line made up of both Kopa and Fontaine were highlights of the competition. In the third place game, it was hardly surprising when the French demoralized West Germany with a 6-3 win. Fontaine scored four goals, each assisted by Kopa—Kopa himself scoring from the penalty spot—and France won third place in the World Championship, its highest achievement to date at the national level. France's place in the sun, however, was short lived. Kopa and Fontaine began to suffer from injuries, the latter having to bow out of organized competition altogether in 1961, and Nicholas was killed in an accident in 1959.

France again took a leading role in international organization and was instrumental in setting up UEFA, the European governing body, in 1954. When UEFA introduced the European Nations' Cup in the late 1950s, the final rounds of the first edition in 1958-60 were staged in France. In a repeat of the circumstances surrounding the first World Cup in 1930, the French were nearly alone in representing Western Europe (Eastern Europe was fully represented), and this enabled France to gain the semi-finals with relative ease, where once again its old nemesis Yugoslavia kept the *tricolores* out of the final. France's 5-4 loss to the Yugoslavs was its last hurrah in international competition until the rise of a new generation of talented players during the mid-1970s. Surprisingly, the French have maintained an overall winning record in the European Football Championship with fine appearances in the first and

third editions, but no honors have resulted. In the World Cup, France advanced to the final rounds again in 1966, but was no match for England and Uruguay in the first round. The enthusiasm of the late 1950s was revived before the 1978 World Cup, and on the basis of qualification rounds and a new hope generated by Saint-Étienne's 1976 European Cup showing there were high hopes for progress in Argentina. Unfortunately, France was drawn in the toughest first round group in recent memory, and despite good play, it bowed out after being eliminated by Italy and Argentina. There is little doubt, however, that the French have entered a bright period in their soccer history in recent years, abetted by the country's strong identification with the open tactics and the attacking frame of mind associated with "total football."

In domestic competition, the legacy of Stade de Reims was assumed in the 1960s by Saint-Étienne from the industrial city of the Massif Central region. Under former Reims manager Batteux, Saint-Étienne raced to the top of the first division in 1964 and won four titles in succession from 1967-70. In 1974, it won three more in a row, and in 1976, it finally made headway in the European Cup by reaching the final. Saint-Étienne's loss to Bayern München in that final resulted from its lack of experience in big international matches rather than inferior talent.

The French league has gone through several format changes in the past 30 years with Division II spread among one, two, or three sections at various times, but professionalism is widespread throughout both first and second divisions. These are supported by huge amateur divisions with regional and local leagues, all of which are covered with great interest by the French soccer press, one of the world's most active. A peculiarity of the French championship until 1976 was the French point system, in which an additional point was awarded by a club each time it defeated an opponent by two goals or more. The universal point system was reestablished after the 1975-76 season.

Champions

1933	Lille OSC	1938	Sochaux
1934	Sète	1939	Sète
1935	Sochaux	1940	unofficial competition
1936	Racing Club de Paris	1941	unofficial competition
1937	Olympique Marseille	1942	unofficial competition

1943	unofficial competition	1961	Monaco
1944	unofficial competition	1962	Stade de Reims
1945	unofficial competition	1963	Monaco
1946	Lille OSC	1964	Saint-Étienne
1947	CO Roubaix-Tourcoing	1965	Nantes
1948	Olympique Marseille	1966	Nantes
1949	Stade de Reims	1967	Saint-Étienne
1950	Girondins Bordeaux	1968	Saint-Étienne
1951	OGC Nice	1969	Saint-Étienne
1952	OGC Nice	1970	Saint-Étienne
1953	Stade de Reims	1971	Olympique Marseille
1954	Lille OSC	1972	Olympique Marseille
1955	Stade de Reims	1973	Nantes
1956	OGC Nice	1974	Saint-Étienne
1957	Saint-Étienne	1975	Saint-Étienne
1958	Stade de Reims	1976	Saint-Étienne
1959	OGC Nice	1977	Nantes
1960	Stade de Reims	1978	Monaco

Cup Winners

1918	Olympique de Pantin Paris	1944	Lorraine selection
1919	CAS Généreaux Paris	1945	Racing Club de Paris
1920	CA Paris	1946	Lille OSC
1921	Red Star Paris	1947	Lille OSC
1922	Red Star Paris	1948	Lille OSC
1923	Red Star Paris	1949	Racing Club de Paris
1924	Olympique Marseille	1950	Stade de Reims
1925	CAS Généreaux Paris	1951	Racing Club Strasbourg
1926	Olympique Marseille	1952	OGC Nice
1927	Olympique Marseille	1953	Lille OSC
1928	Red Star Paris	1954	OGC Nice
1929	SO Montpelier	1955	Lille OSC
1930	Sète	1956	UA Sedan-Torcy
1931	Club Francais	1957	Toulouse
1932	Cannes	1958	Stade de Reims
1933	Excelsior Roubaix	1959	Le Havre AC
1934	Sète	1960	Monaco
1935	Olympique Marseille	1961	UA Sedan-Torcy
1936	Racing Club de Paris	1962	Saint-Étienne
1937	Sochaux	1963	Monaco
1938	Olympique Marseille	1964	Olympique Lyon
1939	Racing Club de Paris	1965	Stade Rennais
1940	Racing Club de Paris	1966	Racing Club Strasbourg
1941	Girondins Bordeaux	1967	Olympique Lyon
1942	Red Star Paris	1968	Saint-Étienne
1943	Olympique Marseille	1969	Olympique Marseille

1970	Saint-Étienne	1975	Saint-Étienne
1971	Stade Rennais	1976	Olympique Marseille
1972	Olympique Marseille	1977	Saint-Étienne
1973	Olympique Lyon	1978	Nancy-Lorraine
1974	Saint-Étienne		

Fraternidad Centroamericana, Torneo de la

An annual competition introduced in 1970 for the champion and runner-up clubs of Costa Rica, El Salvador, and Guatemala.

free kick

An unimpeded kick from a dead ball that is awarded to a team for certain infringements committed by the opposition. There are two classifications of free kicks: a direct free kick, from which a goal may be scored directly; and an indirect free kick, from which a goal may not be scored directly. Certain rules apply to all free kicks:

1. opposing players must be 10 yards from the ball when the kick is taken;

2. the kicker may not play the ball a second time until the ball has been touched by another player;
3. when a free kick is being taken from within the kicker's own penalty area, opposing players must be outside that penalty area, and the ball must be kicked outside the penalty area; and
4. a kicker's own goalkeeper may not receive a ball directly from a free kick in order to kick it into play.

See also: **direct free kick** and **indirect free kick.**

French Guiana

The Fédération Sportive de la Guyane Française was founded in 1934, and was affiliated directly with the French federation the same year. Its activities are primarily restricted to organizing domestic competition for the colony's mere 55,000 inhabitants. With such a small population French Guiana has been unable to produce teams of high quality, and is rarely seen in international competition other than an occasional friendly with a team from neighboring Surinam or Guyana.

French Polynesia

The governing body of the five groups of islands known as French Polynesia—the Fédération Générale des Sociétés Sportives des Établissements Français de l'Océanie—became affiliated with the French Football Federation in 1932. Its administrative offices have been located in Papeete, Tahiti, the capital of the Overseas Territory and supplier of most of French Polynesia's players. Over 3,000 players were registered with the soccer section of the FGSSEFO as early as the 1930s. Though all the islands of the territory are under the aegis of one federation, the relative importance of Tahiti as a population center has resulted in separate representative teams for Tahiti, which has moved toward autonomous representation since the late 1960s, and for French Polynesia as a whole. Meanwhile, "French Polynesia" has provisional membership in the Oceania Football Confederation (OFC) despite its territorial status. (New Caledonia, another French Overseas Territory in the Pacific, is in the same category.)

French Polynesian and Tahitian teams have been among the area's most active participants in regional competitions. During the 1960s, both teams entered tournaments side-by-side, but since the early 1970s, only one team representing French Polynesia—Tahiti—has entered the major competitions. In the soccer tournament of the third South Pacific Games in 1969, French Polynesia placed third in a field of seven after winning two of its four matches, while Tahiti played only one game and placed fifth. The highest achievement to date, however, is Tahiti's winning of the fifth South Pacific Games in

1975 at Guam. French Polynesia, by this time, was not seen in regional competition. Tahiti's biggest win in the Guam tournament was a 3-0 defeat of Fiji in the semi-finals. In the final, it took extra time to win over New Caledonia, but its victory over six other contenders was a savored achievement at home. In the first edition of the Oceania Cup (1973), the region's most important competition, Tahiti was the runner-up behind New Zealand. New Caledonia, New Hebrides, and Fiji each lost to the Tahitians and the match with New Zealand ended in a draw. In the play-off for first place, New Zealand blanked Tahiti by 2-0.

Though not yet a member of FIFA, French Polynesia, especially Tahiti, has moved itself to the front ranks of soccer in the South Pacific. Australia's withdrawal from the OFC will further strengthen the position of regional runners-up, such as Tahiti and New Zealand.

Friedenreich, Artur (1892-1969)

The first idol of Brazilian soccer, Friedenreich was a center forward of dazzling skills and untold popularity. Pelé notwithstanding, he is still considered by many to be the best player Brazil has ever produced, and he is the greatest goalscorer in world soccer history, his 1329 career goals in senior competition having officially been acknowledged by FIFA. Friedenreich was the phenomenon of his age, showing imagination, an unprecedented understanding of the game, total mastery of his skills, and an improvisational style. The legends that sprang up around him were legion. There were myths concerning his exotic name, his powerful kick, and other superhuman movements, and in 1930 the country nearly came to a standstill when it was rumored that he had been killed during the revolution of that year. In addition, he paved the way for blacks and *mesticos* to play with top flight Brazilian clubs: he himself was one of the first *mesticos* to do so.

The son of a German father and black Brazilian mother of humble origins, "Fried" started his career in 1909 with Germânia FC, the club of the German immigrant colony in his native São Paulo (it had won the São Paulo championship in 1906), but he soon moved up the coast to CA Ipiranga in Bahia (Salvador). From there he returned to São Paulo to join

Americano FC, then one of the major *paulista* clubs, and he spearheaded Americano's São Paulo championships of 1912 and 1913. His longest and most important association, however, was with CA Paulistano of São Paulo. He led this great team to championships in 1917, 1918, 1919, and 1921, and his fame spread across the ocean when he dominated Paulistano's triumphant tour of Europe in 1925, scoring bewildering goals wherever he went. Having guided Paulistano to three more championships in the late 1920s, Friedenreich remained with his favorite club until it folded in 1929, but the following year he became one of the original members of the new São Paulo FC. In 1931, after only one year in existence, São Paulo FC won the *paulista* title on the heels of his incredible goalscoring artistry. Fried closed his career in 1935 with Flamengo, the only Rio de Janeiro club he ever consented to join.

Friedenreich made 22 appearances for Brazil, a high number in that era of limited international competition, and his debut coincided with Brazil's very first international contest—against Exeter City F.C. in 1914—on a team that also featured the great Marcos de Mendonça in goal and Rubens Salles at left half. he scored a total of 10 goals for Brazil, his dazzling displays of footwork and ball control delighting foreign fans no less than at home, and in Argentina, he was dubbed *el Tigre* by appreciative crowds. His high points in international competition were Brazil's South American Championship victories of 1919 and 1922.

To this day, Friedenreich remains one of only three players anywhere to surpass the 1,000 goals mark (Pelé and Austria's Franz Binder are the others). He also held numerous Brazilian scoring records, and he led the São Paulo league in scoring nine times and the old Brazilian championship 11 times. By virtue of his great success and popularity, he was responsible not only for the admission of racially mixed players in the upper levels of Brazilian competition but also for black and *mestico* fans embracing the game as their own—changes that were to significantly alter the course of Brazilian soccer. He did more than any other individual in South American soccer to advance the arts of dribbling, passing, feints, and trick shots, and it is no wonder that when he finally retired from active play at age 43, he had been a living legend for over 20 years.

friendly

A game between two teams that is not part of an official league competition, cup competition, or tournament of any kind. A friendly may be scheduled to prepare for an official tournament or as a testimonial to an outstanding individual, or it may have charitable purposes, such as catastrophe relief or social welfare aid. A friendly may also be included as part of a specific transfer deal and may have no other motivation than to increase box office receipts.

front block tackle
Also known as "front tackle" and "block tackle."

A tackle in which the defending player meets the dribbler from the front and blocks movement of the ball by pressing it against the dribbler's foot or ankle. The tackle is completed by the ball spinning off the dribbler's foot into the defender's possession.

fullback
Also known as "back," "No. 2," and "No. 3."

A defender at the rear of a formation who rarely participates in an attack. The number of fullbacks may vary according to the formation. In the traditional 2-3-5, there are two (right and left), and in the 4-2-4, 4-3-3, and 4-4-2, there are as many as four, though some of these may be overlapping. An important modern adaptation of the fullback position is the sweeper.

See also: **overlap** and **sweeper**

Fútbol War
Also known as "Soccer War," "Football War," and "One Hundred Hour War."

The two week "Fútbol War" was fought between El Salvador and Honduras during the summer of 1969. Although it is the only full-fledged international military action linked directly with soccer, the sporting contests on the field were not *per se* the cause of the war. Rather, its origin lay in complex socio-political problems that had existed for decades.

Throughout the post-World War II period, the populous Salvadorans had sought work, and in many cases a new life, across the border

This 1969 scene occurred after the third and deciding World Cup qualifying match between El Salvador and Honduras in neutral Mexico City, which El Salvador won, 3-2. Weeks earlier, the first two legs of the same qualifying round had sparked a full-scale war (the "Fútbol War") between the two countries. In this postgame emotional letdown Honduran manager Mario Mifflin (standing at right) comforts Salvadoran back Salvador Mariona, who himself consoles his Honduran counterpart, Donaldo Rosales.

in Honduras where land was available and abundant. In 1958, a treaty between the two governments permitted the free transit of inhabitants and the migration intensified, but the growing numbers of Salvadorans in Honduras prompted fears of agitation for land reform among Honduran landowners. The government of Honduras responded with a series of new regulations that culminated in a 1968 law prohibiting Salvadorans from owning land. Adding to the strain was the Central American common market, which hurt the Honduran economy and benefited El Salvador. Furthermore, treaties written just after the turn of the century to settle old boundary disputes had never been ratified. In 1967, border troops and nearby civilians were seized by both sides, and late in the year diplomatic relations were broken off. President Lyndon Johnson visited El Salvador in 1968 and helped to restore relations temporarily.

As luck would have it, the two countries

faced each other in a World Cup qualifying round in June 1969; the winner would probably represent CONCACAF at the World Cup the following year. Honduras won the first leg at home on June 8, and El Salvador won the second leg at home on June 15, thus necessitating a third and deciding match. Both games triggered fierce rioting, especially during the return match in San Salvador, and provided the spark that ignited the fire. In Honduras, Salvadoran residents were attacked with a zeal born of years of frustration. Most of the 300,000 migrants began to flee across the border. Reprisals were made against the few Hondurans in El Salvador, and diplomatic relations were again broken off. On June 24, El Salvador declared a state of siege. Charges of human rights violations and demands for reparations were made by both sides. On June 27, the day El Salvador's national team finally defeated Honduras in neutral Mexico to qualify for the World Cup, Salvadoran settlers in Honduras were accused of having mounted a "massive agricultural invasion." El Salvador defended its nationals' humble intentions. Both parties appealed to the OAS's Inter-American Commission on Human Rights, and requested a delegation of mediators. As propaganda in the press intensified, so did the level of skirmishes along the frontier. Both sides accused the other of violating air space, and on July 3, a Honduran plane was reported to have attacked Salvadoran border troops. Mediation proposals made by the Human Rights Commission, as well as by neighboring Costa Rica, Nicaragua, and Guatemala, were approved and promptly broken. By July 11, the military conflict had clearly escalated. Three days later El Salvador's forces invaded Honduras and penetrated more than 40 miles in a single day. Honduras retaliated by bombing San Salvador and Acajutla. On July 18, after both sides suffered heavy damage and many casualties, the OAS arranged a cease-fire, though Salvadoran troops lingered in Honduras for several weeks. The death toll between the two countries was put at 2,000.

Unfortunately, the dispute, did not end with the cessation of war. In 1970, new skirmishes arose, and a demilitarized zone was agreed upon. Further conflicts flared up again in 1974 and July 1976, the latter lasting a full week. The OAS again stepped in, and in August 1976 a new agreement was reached in which a revised demilitarized zone was drawn up. Today, relations between the two states remain tense.

G

Gabon

Fédération Gabonaise de Football
Stade Révérend Père Lefèbre
B.P. 181
Libreville

Founded: 1962
FIFA: 1963
CAF: 1967

Affiliated clubs: *275;* registered players: *8,086;* national stadium: *Stade Révérend Père Lefèbre, Libreville (7,000);* largest stadium: *Stade Révérend Père Lefèbre;* colors: *blue, yellow, and green jerseys, white shorts;* season: *October to July;* honors: *none.*

The Gabon Republic, a tropical African rain forest, has one of the smallest population densities on the continent and the highest per-capita income in black Africa—two important strikes against the possibility of a thriving soccer program. The primary motivation for a growing interest in the game is the presence of many foreign oil, uranium, and manganese companies, whose workers comprise the bulk of Gabon's 8,000 players. Practically all competitive soccer activity is confined to the capital, Libreville, where the country's one modern stadium is located. There is a national league and a national cup competition, which are contested by clubs from Libreville and Port Gentil, the oil production center on the Atlantic coast. The national league is made up of 10 clubs.

Gabon has never qualified for the final stages of the African Nations' Cup, and has seen little playing time in Olympic or World Cup qualification rounds. Gabonese clubs, however, have participated in the African Champions' Cup since the late 1960s, though irregularly. Petro Sport is the leading club, but others, such as Association Sportive Police, Association Sportive Solidarité, and Zalang Omnisport, have also won championships in recent years. One oddity about Gabonese soccer is that it has produced an unusually high number of qualified referees for its small population, perhaps as the result of an influx of foreign businessmen.

Gallacher, Hugh (1903-1957)

Scotland's greatest center forward ever and one of Europe's most opportunistic goalscorers during the period between the wars. From 1921-39, Hughie Gallacher scored 387 league goals in 541 appearances, the vast majority with English clubs, and in a mere 20 international appearances tallied for 22 goals, including five in one match against Northern Ireland in 1929. His "wee" five-foot five-inch frame was massively built and gave him extraordinary balance as he weaved his way through defenders with uncanny control. Sadly, his personal life was tormented and depressing; this, in addition to his fiery temper, led to notoriety on and off the field, along with several suspensions, and cut short his number of appearances for Scotland. Throughout it all, however, he was excep-tionally hard-working and devoted to soccer, always mindful that most defenders were incapable of dispossessing him of the ball except by a brutal tackle.

While playing for his home town amateur club, Bellshill Athletic, in 1920, he was selected for Scotland's Junior team, and in that same year was signed by the Scottish second division club Queen of the South. Scottish first division Airdrieonians lured him away after one season, and he led little Airdrie to a Scottish cup in 1924, and three successive second place finishes behind Rangers in the Scottish league. His inevitable transfer to one of the well-heeled clubs of England came in 1925—to Newcastle United—and there he became an instant favorite. He was made captain of the club at age 24, and in his first year as captain (1926-27) led Newcastle to a championship. Having toiled through his bleak amateur days in Lanarkshire as a part-time coal miner and boxer, as well a footballer, he took to the life of a hero in the big city with unrivaled flair and intensity; his public image (expensive homburgs, white spats, and other natty attire, as well as a considerable nightlife) was developed during this period at Newcastle and continued until the waning years of his career. He moved to Chelsea and the bright lights of London in 1930, and played at peak or near peak form for four more years before his transfer to Derby County in 1934 signaled the start of his decline. He was transferred to third division Notts County in 1936, to first division Grimsby Town for one season in 1937, and to third division Gateshead for his final season in 1938-39. Having lost his money in a debilitating divorce case, and thereafter by reckless spending and bad luck, he spent the remainder of his days moving from one nondescript job to another. In 1957, he committed suicide in front of a passing train the day before he was to appear in court to answer charges of maltreating his daughter.

Gambia

Gambia Football Association
Box-Bar Stadium, Box-Bar Road
P.O. Box 523
Bathurst

Founded: 1952
FIFA: 1966
CAF: 1962

Affiliated clubs: *39;* registered players: *850;* national stadium: *Box-Bar Stadium, Bathurst (6,000);* largest stadium: *Box-Bar Stadium;* colors: *white jerseys with red, blue, and green stripes; white shorts;* season: *October to July;* honors: *none.*

Soccer has been slow to gain a foothold in Gambia, despite the former British presence, because much of the African population is Moslem. The relatively early founding date of the Gambia Football Association reflects the interest of British residents rather than Gambians themselves. Its early affiliation with the African Football Confederation and then with FIFA immediately after independence has been unfulfilled. Gambian clubs have never participated in the African Champions' Cup, and only one has entered the Cup Winners' Cup, Bathurst's Wallidan in 1975. Furthermore, a Gambian national team has not yet attempted to qualify for the African Nations' Cup, Olympic Games, or World Cup. There are 15 senior-level clubs in Gambia, nearly all located in Bathurst, and they play out a season that includes both a league and cup competition, the latter being of greater interest to Gambian fans. All competitive activities are confined to the Box-Bar Stadium in Bathurst.

Garrincha (1933-   )

(Full name: Manuel Francisco dos Santos.) "Garrincha" is a Portuguese expression meaning "little bird," and it was given to this astonishing Brazilian player, because the polio he had suffered from as a child made one of his legs look slightly distorted—an unlikely beginning for the player some would call the greatest dribbler the game has ever seen. Garrincha was a right wing phenomenon who glided to the heights of world soccer with Brazil in the World Cups of 1958 and 1962. His style was intoxicating and spirited, and, as a result, he acquired a host of descriptive nicknames including "the force of Nature," *o Torto* ("the deformed one"), *Mané* ("the fool"), and sometimes *Mané Garrincha*. In 51 appearances for Brazil, he was on the losing side only once.

At age 14, he joined his local club, Pau Grande, as an inside left, and in 1953 tried out for the big Rio club Botafogo, winning a place on the team from the start. The following year he was chosen to play on a Rio selection. In 1957, he made his debut for Brazil in the South American Championship, but was dropped until a World Cup qualifying match some months later, his reinstatement having been demanded by the other players. He burst onto the world scene in Brazil's third game in the 1958 World Cup against the USSR, and in the final against Sweden he set up the first two goals by dribbling around his defenders to the gasps of the Stockholm crowd. He helped Botafogo win three Rio championships from 1957-62, and in the 1962 World Cup reached his peak of dazzling artistry, scoring two goals against England in the quarter-finals and two against Chile in the semi-finals, each more incredible than the other. In 1964, doctors discovered that his knee joints were deteriorating, and this slowed him down considerably. Two years later he was transferred to Corinthians Paulista, but, despite one memorable performance against Bulgaria in the 1966 World Cup, he rarely showed his old form.

There were several short stays at Flamengo, Bangu, and Portuguêsa Santista, and, while his popularity never subsided—except when he caused a scandal by leaving his wife and eight children for a night club singer—he could not hold down a job, and he left the game. In 1972, after playing briefly in France and Italy, he attempted a comeback with Olaria, but was forced to end his career permanently only a few months later.

Brazil's Garrincha, the most breathtaking dribbler in the history of the game—and a childhood victim of polio.

Gento Lopez, Francisco (1933-   )

The speediest left winger of his time, Gento was the only player of Real Madrid's golden era who stayed with the club from its first to its most recent success. Though he was sometimes erratic in shooting, he will always be remembered for his blistering runs with the ball and the brilliant partnership he developed with Alfredo Di Stefano throughout the 11 years they played together. Gento, in fact, was Di Stefano's favorite playmaking partner, Kopa and Puskás notwithstanding, and they could sometimes be seen together on the Spanish national team as well.

"Paco" started as a boy with Nueva Montana, Astillero Santander, and Real Santander before Real Madrid signed him and Di Stefano at the same time in 1953. His 18 years with Real bridged the gap between three generations of Real teams, and his longevity helped to create a set of unique records. He was the only player to participate in all eight of Real's European Cup finals, and he stands alone by scoring in 11 consecutive European Cup competitions (1956-66). When Di Stefano retired in 1964, Gento became captain, and led Real to its sixth European title two years later. He made 43 international appearances for Spain, though unfortunately, he was not selected for Spain's 1964 European Nations' Cup winning team, which would have been his only chance to collect an honor at the national level. In his later years, he was Spain's captain. In 1971, at the age of 38, he played in the European Cup Winners' Cup final against Chelsea, completing a remarkable career that saw him win 12 league championship and six European Cup medals—probably the greatest array of individual trophies in the game's history. After his retirement, he joined the Real organization as a trainer for the club's youth teams.

German Democratic Republic

Deutscher Fussball-Verband der DDR
Storkower Strasse 118
1055 Berlin

Founded: 1948
FIFA: 1952
UEFA: 1954

Affiliated clubs: *4,880;* **registered players:** *487,570;* **national stadium:** *Zentralstadion, Leipzig (100,000);* **largest stadium:** *Zentralstadion;* **colors:** *white jerseys, blue shorts;* **season:** *August to June;* **honors:** *Olympic Games winner (1976), third place (1964, 1972), FC Magdeburg, Super Cup (1974), European Cup Winners' Cup (1974).*

Soccer in the Soviet zone of Germany was slow to develop after 1945. Without economic stability in the country, and lacking the strong foundation of so many West German clubs, DDR officials were thwarted in their attempt to enter the mainstream of European soccer until the 1950s. Just as important was the refusal of western European countries to engage in any international competition with the East Germans, other than obligatory World Cup qualifying matches in 1958, until England broke the ice in 1960. As a result, the level of domestic play advanced more rapidly than the quality of the national team, though the western European embargo had been in effect on the club level as well. Since its inclusion in European competition, however, East Germany's rise to respectability has been consistent and impressive. Magdeburg's success in 1974 and the national team's fine showings in the 1974 World Cup and 1976 Olympic Games were telling indications of the future of East German soccer.

Other than VfB Leipzig, which won the first German championship in 1903 (and two others), and Dresdner SC, which dominated German competitions during World War II, eastern Germany was far less important in its impact on the German game before 1945 than the western regions of the Ruhr and Bavaria. Thus, a long road lay ahead when in 1948 the Sektion Fussball in der DDR was founded. The Sektion immediately organized a national championship, won in 1948 by SG Planitz, and a national cup was introduced one year later. The new league was comprised of a first division of 14 clubs and a second division of two sections with 14 clubs each. In 1952, the DDR was finally admitted to FIFA, and two months later an East German national team began to haul itself out of obscurity. The first

match, against Poland in Warsaw, was won by the home team, 3-0. Poland, Rumania, and Bulgaria remained its only opponents through 1956, except on the odd occasion when Indonesia visited Karl-Marx-Stadt and was dealt a 3-1 loss. East Germany's first victory had come in 1955 against Rumania at Bucharest (3-2), and was followed by successive wins over Bulgaria and Poland. Meanwhile, the western embargo was in full force, so it was noteworthy when Wales, drawn in the same World Cup qualifying group with East Germany and Czechoslovakia, ventured to Leipzig in 1958 and became East Germany's first non-Warsaw Pact adversary. It also marked East Germany's debut in World Cup competition. East Germany won the match, 2-1, but lost in subsequent matches to Czechoslovakia twice and to Wales in the away leg at Cardiff. In a second disappointment, Portugal defeated the national team in both legs of the first round in the 1958-60 European Nations' Cup.

In 1961, the national association, now renamed Deutscher Fussball-Verband der DDR (DFV), hired Hungarian coach Karoly Soos to manage the national team. Soos's seven-year stint proved to be the turning point in East German soccer. His knowledge and experience was decisive in reversing the losing East German record, which prior to 1962 stood at: 38-10-7-21-56-72-27. During Soos's stewardship, a winning trend was established that has been maintained into the 1970s. Since 1961, East Germany's record has stood at: 108-57-28-23-210-116-142. Nevertheless, much of East Germany's opposition continued to be the other Warsaw Pact states with a sprinkling of some politically suitable African countries. The exceptions have been in World Cup, European Football Championship, and especially Olympic competiton.

The World Cup finals were not reached until 1974, and advancement in the European Football Championship has eluded East Germany on each occasion, except in the 1962-64 edition when it reached the second round by surprising Czechoslovakia (2-1 and 1-1) before elimination by Hungary. In the Olympic Games, however, the East Germans have distinguished themselves, following the now established tradition of Eastern European dominance in this competition. In 1964, they were bronze medalists, defeating Iran, Mexico and the full Yugoslav national team before succumbing to powerful Czechoslovakia in the semifinals. Disappointed at being knocked out of the 1968 Olympic qualification tournament, East Germany began its most successful era with its entry into the 1972 games at Munich. Disposing easily of Ghana and Colombia by an aggregate score of 10 to one, it found Poland, the new European powerhouse and eventual winner, an impossible obstacle in first round competition. In the semi-final round, however, it was grouped with host team West Germany, as well as Hungary and Mexico. While its match with the amateur West Germans was not taken seriously in the Bundesrepublik, the fans at home had come to realize a near-impossible dream. In the end, East Germany's 3-2 win was put in its proper perspective since the West German amateur eleven was not at all the same team that a few weeks before had won the European Football Championship. In the third place game, the East Germans battled the USSR to a draw, and the bronze medal had to be shared.

East Germany's highest achievements were to come under former Carl Zeiss Jena manager Georg Buschner, who led the national team into its first World Cup in 1974 after an easy qualifying round. It was here the ultimate consolation prize was attained. There was an easy win over Australia, followed by a disappointing draw with defensive minded Chile, and finally a meeting of the two Germanys, picked by luck (or design) to play in the same group. Both teams, sensitive to the occasion, played a close, controlled passing game, but a goal by East Germany's attacking midfielder Jurgen Sparwasser was the only score of the day, and a polite West German team, some would say deferential, took its lone upset of the competition with poise. Across the border, a nation of unparalleled sports enthusiasts was celebrating its finest hour.

In the less challenging Olympic Games of 1976, East German soccer fortunes were commensurate with its domination of the entire games. A scoreless draw with Brazil's amateurs was the only blemish in its successful run for the gold medal. Once again, the primary opposition came from Eastern European teams; the USSR fell in the semifinals, and in the final Poland's great World Cup team from 1974 succumbed by 3-1. East Germany won its first major victory in international competition, and observers could not forget the impressive growth of its game since the pre-Soos era.

During the first decade of domestic competition, a dominant club did not emerge until Karl-Marx-Stadt won three championships in a row in the late 1950s. But it became evident that the DFV favored the army team, ASK Vorwärts Berlin (since relocated as Vorwärts Frankfurt), and from 1958-69 Vorwärts won six championships. Two major reorganizations of the league were put into effect, one in 1954-55 and the other in 1960-61. Eventually, the growing number of top flight players was dispersed, and in the 1960s and '70s, FC Carl Zeiss Jena (the team of the famous optical factory), Dynamo Dresden, (the electrical workers' team), and FC Magdeburg shared most of the honors. The composition of the national team reflected these changes, and by the late 1960s few Vorwärts players were seen in international competition. Magdeburg gained East Germany's first international club honor with the winning of the European Cup Winners' Cup in 1974. Though not necessarily the best team in the competition, Magdeburg was judged a worthy victor. In the unofficial Super Cup between the winners of European Cup and European Cup Winners' Cup, Magdeburg completed an East vs. West treble and defeated the unassailable Bayern München with the Magdeburg home leg being played in neutral Rotterdam. With the number of clubs in East Germany totaling less than one-third the number in West Germany, Magdeburg's accomplishment was an understandable boost to soccer in the DDR.

The East German game has now entered the middle ranks of European soccer from a state of nonexistence only 25 years before. Since the early 1960s, East Germany's international record has been better than that of Bulgaria, Scotland, Rumania, France, Austria, Portugal, and Belgium, not to mention the smaller nations sitting permanently in the lower reaches.

Champions

1948	SG Planitz	1964	Chemie Leipzig
1949	Union Halle	1965	Vorwärts Berlin
1950	Horch Zwickau	1966	Vorwärts Berlin
1951	Chemie Leipzig	1967	Karl-Marx-Stadt
1952	Turbine Halle	1968	Carl Zeiss Jena
1953	Dynamo Dresden	1969	Vorwärts Berlin
1954	Turbine Erfurt	1970	Carl Zeiss Jena
1955	Turbine Erfurt/Karl-Marx-Stadt*	1971	Dynamo Dresden
1956	Karl-Marx-Stadt	1972	FC Magdeburg
1957	Karl-Marx-Stadt	1973	Dynamo Dresden
1958	Vorwärts Berlin	1974	FC Magdeburg
1959	Karl-Marx-Stadt	1975	FC Magdeburg
1960	Vorwärts Berlin	1976	Dynamo Dresden
1961	no competition	1977	Dynamo Dresden
1962	Vorwärts Berlin	1978	Dynamo Dresden
1963	Motor Jena		

Cup Winners

1949	Waggonbau Nord-Bressau	1964	Aufbau Magdeburg
1950	EHW Thale	1965	Aufbau Magdeburg
1951	no competition	1966	Chemie Leipzig
1952	VP Dresden	1967	Motor Zwickau
1953	no competition	1968	Union Berlin
1954	Vorwärts Berlin	1969	FC Magdeburg
1955	Karl-Marx-Stadt	1970	Vorwärts Berlin
1956	Chemie Halle-Leuna	1971	Dynamo Dresden
1957	Lokomotive Leipzig	1972	Carl Zeiss Jena
1958	Einheit Dresden	1973	FC Magdeburg
1959	Dynamo Berlin	1974	Carl Zeiss Jena
1960	Motor Jena	1975	Sachsenring Zwickau
1961	Motor Jena	1976	Lokomotive Leipzig
1962	Chemie Halle	1977	Dynamo Dresden
1963	Motor Zwickau	1978	FC Magdeburg

*Two separate competitions

Germany, Federal Republic of

Deutscher Fussball Bund
Otto-Fleck-Schneise 6
Postschliessfach 710405
6 Frankfurt (Main) — 71

Founded: 1900
FIFA: 1904-46
1950
UEFA: 1954

Affiliated clubs: *16,890;* registered players: *3,199,569 (360 professional, 1,450 non-amateur);* national stadium: *none;* largest stadium: *Olympia-Stadion, Berlin (85,000);* colors: *white jerseys, black shorts;* season: *August to June;* honors: *World*

Cup winner (1954, 1974), runner-up (1966), third place (1934, 1970), European Football Championship winner (1972), runner-up (1976), Bayern München Intercontinental Cup (1976), European Cup (1974, 1975, 1976), European Cup Winners' Cup (1967), Borussia Dortmund, European Cup Winners' Cup (1966), Hamburger SV, European Cup Winners' Cup (1977), Borussia Mönchengladbach, UEFA Cup (1975).

If England is the titular leader of European soccer, West Germany is its practicing master, having amassed an extraordinary record of success at all levels of competition. The Bundesliga, the national league that was formed only in 1963, is currently the showplace of modern soccer in Europe, and in recent years has sent more teams to the final stages of European club championships than any other league. From a global perspective, West Germany now threatens to surpass even Brazil's record at the highest reaches of organized competition, and, in so doing, has sparked a renaissance of tactical innovation on the playing field.

West Germany's growth from a moderately successful European power during the Hitler era to that of standard-bearer in the postwar years has resulted from the unification of long-range planning, exceptional coaching techniques and practices, and a fair share of highly skilled players. Since World War II, the national team has had only three managers, each the assistant to his past predecessor, and in the past 50 years there have been only four. In addition, the Deutscher Fussball-Bund (DFB) has established a national coaching school, which is widely regarded as a model of its kind, providing a level of continuity and uniformity of standards that seeps down through the domestic game. These factors, lacking a certainty of success in and of themselves, have resulted in the large number of excellent players who have turned German methods and practices into victories on the field.

The prosperity of western Germany's soccer amid the political realities of a divided country is dictated by historical precedent. Geographically, most of the first and strongest clubs in Germany hailed from the present-day Federal Republic. Soccer was introduced to Germany by British residents via the North Sea ports and Berlin in 1870. In 1875, the Oxford University XI toured Germany in the first overseas trip ever taken by a British team. Association football rules were written in German for the first time at the Gelehrten-

schule des Johanneums, Hamburg, in 1876. For many years soccer was slow in developing due to the strong objection of leaders in the *Turnvater Jahn* movement, an indigenous German effort to foster the arts of gymnastics and other sports that emphasized individual athletic accomplishments. Both English games, soccer and rugby, were called brutal and boorish by many civic leaders and educators, and the effect of this sentiment was keenly felt.

The growing popularity of the game, however, sparked the formation of football clubs as early as the 1880s. Some of the earliest clubs tended to favor the rugby game rather than soccer, e.g., Berliner FC Frankfurt, founded in Berlin in 1884, and some were or had already been established as sports clubs that were to add soccer sections in later years, e.g., TSV 1860 München and ETB Schwarz-Weiss Essen, founded in 1881. The first club that was formed principally for soccer was SC Germania Hamburg (later to become the famous Hamburger SV) in 1887. Most of the earliest clubs were established along the Elbe or Weser Rivers in the North and in Berlin, but by 1900 nearly all regions of the German Empire supported some clubs devoted to association rules.

The first clubs in each of the empire's eight soccer regions were the following (by region): Süddeutschland (Bavaria), SSV Jahn Regensburg (1889); Südwestdeutschland (Baden-Wurttemberg, Alsace-Lorraine, southern Rhineland), Karlsruher Fussball-Verein (1891); Westdeutschland (North-Rhineland, Westfalia, Hessen), Fortuna Düsseldorf (1895); Norddeutschland (Schleswig-Holstein, Lower Saxony), SC Germania Hamburg (1887); Berlin-Brandenburg-Berliner FC Germania (1888); Mitteldeutschland (Saxony, Thuringia), VfB Leipzig (1893); Südostdeutschland (Silesia), Alter Turn-Verein Liegnitz (1896); and the Baltenverband (East and West Prussia), Ball-und Eislauf-Verein Danzig (ca. 1898).

In 1890, the Bund-deutscher Fussballspieler, the first regional association, was founded in Berlin to unify soccer activities in the capital, but it was supplanted one year later by the Deutsche Fussball und Cricket Bund, also a Berlin-based organization. The regional leagues that would figure prominently in German soccer for the next 70 years began to take shape during the 1890s, and in 1896 the first intercity match was held between representative teams from Berlin and Hamburg. The Berliners won 13-0. A truly national association was not formed until 1900, when regional delegates met in Leipzig and established the Deutscher Fussball-Bund. The DFB introduced the first national championship in 1902-03, but decided to retain the various regional leagues (rather than form a nationwide league of top teams), and bring the regional champions together at the end of the season for a play-off to determine the overall German champion. This format was followed without change until 1962. In 1904, the DFB became one of the first governing bodies to join FIFA, and in 1908-09, the first cup competition was introduced—the Bundespokal—which was contested by representative teams from each league.

The hazy beginnings of German participation in international competition are indicated by some activity as early as 1896, when unofficial representative teams from Germany and England met for the first time. In 1899, a representative team of The Football Association in London toured Germany and defeated a "German" selection three times and "German-Austrian" selection once. In 1901, a German selection returned the visit and lost two games by double-figure scores to a pair of teams called "England Amateur" and "England Professional." A properly authorized national team was not organized until 1908, however, and it was only then that the first official full international was played against Switzerland in Basle, resulting in a 5-3 win by the Swiss. Later in the year, Germany lost to Austria in Vienna by 3-2.

While all these developments were taking place, opposition to the game continued to flourish at the school level, as Prussian mores and the effects of the *Turnvater Jahn* movement were slow in disappearing. In Bavaria, soccer was banned from schools altogether as late as 1913, because it was thought to interfere with studies and impede character development, but in that same year some members of the House of Hohenzollern began to actively support the game and the eventual development of German soccer faced an open future for the first time.

Before World War I, the eleven national championships were widely divided between clubs from Berlin, Leipzig, and Karlsruhe, as well as Freiburg, Kiel, and Fürth. Between the wars, however, two clubs, FC Nürnberg and Schalke 04, came to dominate and establish once and for all their fame and popularity. During the Weimar Republic, FC Nürnberg won an astounding five national titles, and during the Third Reich won another title and placed second twice. Nürnberg also won two German cups in the 1930s, and lost an additional cup final in 1940. The north Bavarian club became so popular with its attractive, fluid style, particularly during the 1920s, that it became known simply as *der Club,* and influenced German soccer for a generation.

The second team to emerge during the period between the wars was Schalke 04 from the Ruhr city of Gelsenkirchen, a region that was to take over as the soccer hotbed of the industrialized Third Reich and postwar Germany. Schalke was the major power during the Hitler era, winning six championships, placing second three times, and advancing to five cup finals, all between 1934-42. Its adoption of Arsenal's W-M formation and productive utilization of many fine stars relegated Nürnberg to second place in the Third Reich pantheon, though Nürnberg's fame and following never subsided.

During the Ostmark and German occupation of other neighboring countries between 1938-44, 18 leading clubs from the occupied regions participated in the German regional leagues. Rapid Vienna, Austria's greatest club, went so far as to win the German Cup in 1938 and a national championship in 1941. Six of these clubs were from Sudetenland, five from Poland, four from Austria, two from Alsace, and one from Luxembourg. The German national team was also open to certain players from occupied lands. The leagues were not suspended until after the 1943-44 season, and remained closed for three years. The finals of the national cup, which since 1937 had been held at the new Olympic Stadium in Berlin, drew capacity crowds of 95,000-100,000 spectators until 1943, but were themselves halted after 1944, when the attendance figure dropped to 70,000.

Most of Germany's international opposition before 1933 came from Central Europe, Scandinavia, and the Benelux. Germany entered the Olympic soccer tournaments of 1912 (in which it achieved its best result ever, a 16-0 drubbing of Czarist Russia) and 1928 (to face elimination by the sensational Uruguayans).

With numerous wins over Switzerland, Denmark, Norway, and Finland, in addition to mixed results against the stronger teams from Central Europe, Germany became a middle-level power in continental soccer.

Under Hitler, the motivation to achieve better results was heightened considerably. Using Schalke as a base for the national team, a strong challenge was made to the major powers of Europe during the 1930s beginning with the 1934 World Cup in Italy, and Germany achieved third place after losing in the semi-finals to Czechoslovakia in Rome. Political hopes on the playing field, however, were not enough to compensate for a lack of cohesion created by sectionalized league competition at home, and Germany suffered humiliating defeats in the 1936 Olympic Games in Berlin (elimination by lowly Norway) and in the 1938 World Cup in France (elimination by Switzerland). To make matters worse in this era of politicized sports, Germany's rivalry with Mussolini's Italy between the world wars resulted in one victory and five defeats. The brightest hope for German soccer to emerge in this period was the hiring of Sepp Herberger in 1936 as manager of the national team, an association

that was to pay off handsomely during the postwar era.

At the 1946 Congress in Luxembourg, FIFA delegates voted to expel the DFB from the world body, and German soccer entered a five-year period of international ostracization and domestic reorganization. An East German national association, the Sektion Fussball in der DDR, was formed in 1948, and soccer in the German Democratic Republic was launched on its own path, gaining separate membership with FIFA four years later. Meanwhile, the old DFB became dormant during the Allied occupation, and in January 1950 it was reconstituted under its original name to continue its administration of the game in West Germany. In June 1950, at the FIFA Congress in Rio de Janeiro, the DFB was readmitted to the world body. The regional leagues were revitalized, and in the 1953-54 season, the reorganization process was concluded with a domestic structure consisting of five leagues (Berlin, North, West, South, and Southwest).

Repeating its debut in 1908, West Germany reentered international competition with a friendly against Switzerland in November 1950, a 1-0 win in Stuttgart. Friendlies were

West Germany emerges as a world power. On this goal by German right wing Helmut Rahn in the final of the 1954 World Cup, the mighty Hungarian national team—undefeated in four years—went down to defeat, 3-2. (A) Hungary's Zakarias (no. 6) and Lantos (no. 3) fail to stop Rahn's shot; (B) Hungarian goalkeeper Grosics dives for the ball; (C) Grosics is beaten; (D) English referee confirms the winning goal, as Rahn and Lantos recover from their collision.

arranged with Turkey, Austria, Eire, Luxembourg, and others, and under the leadership of Sepp Herberger, it soon became apparent that the Germans had resurfaced with a strong national team. Despite some excellent results against Austria and Yugoslavia between 1951 and 1953, West Germany entered the 1954 World Cup with a slim chance of overcoming the likes of Uruguay, Brazil, England, Scotland, and mighty Hungary, not to mention Austria and Yugoslavia, but in the end the cunning of Herberger, master strategist, and extraordinary performances by captain Fritz Walter and his teammates caused one of the great upsets in World Cup history. In the final against unbeatable Hungary, two goals from Helmut Rahn were enough to defeat the overconfident Magyars and proclaim in no uncertain terms the reentry of German soccer on the world scene. The score on that rain-soaked day in Berne was 3-2, and it was all the more remarkable because at one point in the first half the Germans were down by 2-0.

In the 1958 World Cup, Germany took fourth place after conceding six goals to France in the third place game, and its performance throughout the competition was again impressive. It won its first round group over Argentina, Czechoslovakia, and Eire, and in the quarter-finals eliminated Yugoslavia. Fritz Walter, the first of West Germany's influential postwar stars, was joined by a new idol, Uwe Seeler of Hamburger SV, whose international career would eventually overlap elements of both the 1954 and 1974 World Championship teams.

In the early 1960s, the DFB set out to reorganize the domestic structure of the game again. Two important changes were advanced that were calculated by design to thrust West Germany into the front ranks of international competition. One was to sanction full-time professionalism for the first time, though semi-professionalism had surfaced in the early 1950s. The second was to realign the domestic format by creating a national league and reassigning the regional competitions to lower divisions. The Bundesliga (Federal League) was introduced in the 1963-64 season, and drew its 16 charter members from the regional leagues: from the West (5), South (5), North (3), Southwest (2), and Berlin (1). Each of the 16 clubs were top finishers in their respective leagues the year before. (In 1965-66, the number of clubs in the Bundesliga was increased to 18.)

The new second division, meanwhile, was structured into two sections, North and South, with 20 clubs in either section. Each year the two second division winners, as well as the winner of a play-off between the two runners-up, gain promotion to the Bundesliga, and the bottom three teams from the Bundesliga are relegated into vacancies in the North or South. The third division is entirely amateur and is divided into 19 regional sections. The four bottom clubs from the Second Division North and the Second Division South are relegated, and eight clubs from the regional leagues are promoted upward, four each into the North and South.

These belated changes represented little more than an emulation of existing leagues throughout Europe, but their effects were far-reaching. West German clubs began to do well in international competition for the first time. Borussia Dortmund and Bayern München won the European Cup Winners' Cup in 1966 and 1967, respectively, West Germany's first major club honors. The national team meanwhile, spurred by Uwe Seeler and the revelation of young Franz Beckenbauer, advanced to the final of the 1966 World Cup. Its performance in this event was significant, because it marked the beginning of a more delicate, fluid style of play than had previously been associated with German soccer, and it signaled the debut of tactical innovations that were to carry West Germany to the summit of world competition in the years ahead.

The 1966 World Cup final against England at Wembley was perhaps the most controversial international match ever played. In overtime with the score 2-2, England's Geoff Hurst tallied home a shot that hit the German crossbar and bounced downward to the edge of the goal line. English players insisted it was a goal; German players insisted it was not; neutral observers were unable to agree. The linesman, on appeal from the referee, awarded the goal; the Germans wilted in justifiable despondency, and Hurst put away a fourth England goal. Sportsmen to the end, the West German team, which was now led by Herberger's former assistant Helmut Schön, left the field at the end of the game certain that a second World Championship had been stolen from them, and to this day there are many who agree.

Vindication, however, was forthcoming. In succeeding years, Schön's attractive and intelligent methods were masterfully combined with the flowering of great players. Franz Beckenbauer, who innovated a fluid all-purpose role for the sweeper position, goal-keeper Sepp Maier, and goalscoring genius Gerd Müller, all of Bayern München, provided the backbone of what was to become one of the finest national teams of the 1970s. At the 1970 World Cup in Mexico, West Germany gained third place, and might just as easily have advanced to the final but for a superbly played 4-3 loss to Italy in the semi-finals. In 1972, West Germany's exciting, attacking style reached its peak in the European Football Championship, which was won with an incomparable 3-0 victory over the USSR. The Bayern threesome were joined at that time by Günter Netzer, perhaps the most elegant German midfielder of all time and orchestrator of Borussia Mönchengladbach, a club that had come to share domination of the Bundesliga with Bayern in the late 1960s. West Germany again reached the final of the European Championship in 1976, which was won by Czechoslovakia on penalty kicks.

The crowning achievement came in 1974 with the winning of the tenth World Championship. Though the 1972 European Championship team was retained nearly intact (Netzer had fallen out of favor), Holland was touted by some to win the cup, as David to West Germany's Goliath. Indeed, it was Holland and West Germany that met in the final with similar styles of play and immense reserves of talent. At 1-1 in the first half, the intuitive Gerd Müller drove home the winning goal, and West Germany's containment of Johan Cruyff for the remainder of the game sealed Holland's fate. Though its World Championship team was thought to be marginally inferior to that of 1972, there was no question that West Germany had now arrived as the pre-eminent power in world soccer. The strength of West Germany's game was borne out by the emergence of a new generation of brilliant players, taking the place of Beckenbauer, Müller, and Netzer as the 1978 World Cup approached.

At the club level, Bayern München won three European Cup titles in succession (1974-76), and Borussia Mönchengladbach, while managing to win a UEFA Cup in 1975, advanced to the final stages of all international competitions it entered. Hamburger SV, the oldest German club still in senior competition, won the European Cup Winners' Cup in 1977, and pointed out the extraordinary depth of the Bundesliga. To many observers, West German domination of the final rounds of European club competitions appeared all but certain for years to come.

Champions

1903	VfB Leipzig	1924	FC Nürnberg
1904	suspended	1925	FC Nürnberg
1905	Union 92 Berlin	1926	SpVgg. Fürth
1906	VfB Leipzig	1927	FC Nürnberg
1907	Freiburger FC	1928	Hamburger SV
1908	Viktoria 89 Berlin	1929	SpVgg. Fürth
1909	Phönix Karlsruhe	1930	Hertha BSC Berlin
1910	Karlsruhe FV	1931	Hertha BSC Berlin
1911	Viktoria 89 Berlin	1932	Bayern München
1912	Holstein Kiel	1933	Fortuna Düsseldorf
1913	VfB Leipzig	1934	Schalke 04
1914	SpVgg. Fürth	1935	Schalke 04
1915	no competition	1936	FC Nürnberg
1916	no competition	1937	Schalke 04
1917	no competition	1938	Hannover 96
1918	no competition	1939	Schalke 04
1919	no competition	1940	Schalke 04
1920	FC Nürnberg	1941	Rapid Vienna
1921	FC Nürnberg	1942	Schalke 04
1922	not awarded*	1943	Dresdner SC
1923	Hamburger SV	1944	Dresdner SC

1945	no competition	1962	FC Köln
1946	no competition	1963	Borussia Dortmund
1947	no competition	1964	FC Köln**
1948	FC Nürnberg	1965	Werder Bremen
1949	VfR Mannheim	1966	TSV München 1860
1950	VfB Stuttgart	1967	Eintracht Braunschweig
1951	FC Kaiserslautern	1968	FC Nürnberg
1952	VfB Stuttgart	1969	Bayern München
1953	FC Kaiserslautern	1970	Borussia Mönchengladbach
1954	Hannover 96	1971	Borussia Mönchengladbach
1955	Rot-Weiss Essen	1972	Bayern München
1956	Borussia Dortmund	1973	Bayern München
1957	Borussia Dortmund	1974	Bayern München
1958	Schalke 04	1975	Borussia Mönchengladbach
1959	Eintracht Frankfurt	1976	Borussia Mönchengladbach
1960	Hamburger SV	1977	Borussia Mönchengladbach
1961	FC Nürnberg	1978	FC Köln

Cup Winners

1935	FC Nürnberg	1957	Bayern München
1936	VfB Leipzig	1958	VfB Stuttgart
1937	Schalke 04	1959	Schwarz-Weiss Essen
1938	Rapid Vienna	1960	Borussia Mönchengladbach
1939	FC Nürnberg	1961	Werder Bremen
1940	Dresdner SC	1962	FC Nürnberg
1941	Dresdner SC	1963	Hamburger SV
1942	TSV München 1860	1964	TSV München 1860
1943	First Vienna	1965	Borussia Dortmund
1944	no competition	1966	Bayern München
1945	no competition	1967	Bayern München
1946	no competition	1968	FC Köln
1947	no competition	1969	Bayern München
1948	no competition	1970	Kickers Offenbach
1949	no competition	1971	Bayern München
1950	no competition	1972	Schalke 04
1951	no competition	1973	Borussia Mönchengladbach
1952	no competition	1974	Eintracht Frankfurt
1953	Rot-Weiss Essen	1975	Eintracht Frankfurt
1954	VfB Stuttgart	1976	Hamburger SV
1955	Karlsruher SC	1977	FC Köln
1956	Karlsruher SC	1978	FC Köln

*finalists Hamburger SV and FC Nürnberg
drew twice.
**first Bundesliga champion.

Ghana

Ghana Football Association
P.O. Box 1272
Accra

Founded: 1957
FIFA: 1958
CAF: 1958

Affiliated clubs: *300;* registered players: *4,000;* national stadium: *Accra Sports Stadium, Accra (30,000);* largest stadium: *Accra Sports Stadium;* colors: *yellow jerseys, yellow shorts;* season: *January to October;* honors: *African Nations' Cup winner (1963, 1965, 1978), runner-up (1968, 1970), Kotoko Kumasi, African Champions' Cup (1970).*

Ghana is the preeminent soccer power in black Africa, though not by a wide margin, and it is also the birthplace of African soccer north of the Zambezi. It was the first black African country to form a governing body, the first to join FIFA, the first to win a place in the final rounds of the Olympic Games, and the first to win the African Nations' Cup. At club level, the mighty Kotoko Kumasi has appeared in the African Champions' Cup final five times, an impressive record in this intensely fought tournament.

A Jamaican introduced soccer on the Gold Coast around 1880. This represents the earliest known date associated with soccer on the African continent with the sole exception of South Africa (ca. 1865). That a Jamaican rather than a Britisher should take credit for this astonishing historical oddity makes the event all the more intriguing, but, unfortunately, little is known of the game's development until the British established the Gold Coast Football Association in 1922. (This founding date is officially superseded by the formation of the Ghanaian association in 1957.) By this time, much of the Gold Coast's soccer activity was being carried out by British residents, though many African-based clubs were founded during the 1920s and '30s. Ghana's greatest club, Asante Kotoko Sporting Club, was founded in Kumasi in 1926 as Ashanti United. The City Championship Cup was introduced in 1922 for clubs in Accra, remaining the most important competition until the 1950s, and the Asantehene Cup was established soon thereafter for clubs in Kumasi. In 1938, the first national cup competition, the Gold Coast Football Championship, was introduced under the sponsorship of the governor. Several local championships emerged before World War II in

secondary cities such as Obuasi, Sekondi, and Tarkwa.

The Gold Coast Football Association became affiliated with FIFA in 1948, and two years later a Gold Coast national team made its unofficial international debut against Nigeria in Accra, winning 1-0. The governing body was renamed the United Gold Coast Amateur Football Association in 1952. In 1957, the year of Ghanaian independence, the Ghana Football Association was established, and a national championship was introduced under a league format. Kotoko Kumasi started its long domination over the league with a title in 1959, and this was followed by further championships in 1963, 1966, 1967, 1969, 1970, 1972, and 1975. Kotoko's captain during the early 1960s was Baba Yara, regarded by many as the greatest Ghanaian player of all time. Kotoko won the African Champions' Cup in 1970, and was the losing finalist in 1964, 1967, 1971, and 1973. Heart of Oaks S.C. has also been prominent in the African Champions' Cup.

In 1963, Ghana played host to the fourth African Nations' Cup—the first to be held in black Africa—and defeated Sudan in the final to win its first big trophy. The star of this series was Wilberforce Mfum, who in 1971 became one of the first players signed by the fledgling New York Cosmos. In 1965, Ghana reached its peak with a stunning sweep of Congo-Léopoldville, Ivory Coast, and Tunisia, to take its second consecutive Nations' Cup. Left winger Frank Odoi scored the winning goal in the 3-2 final after extra time. In the 1968 edition, Ghana reached the final for a third straight time after going undefeated in its first round group and defeating Ivory Coast in the semifinals. The final was lost to Congo-Kinshasa 1-0, but Ghana played to attack while the Congolese shut off the goalmouth in a defensive showdown. Ghana's capacity to rejuvenate itself and produce fine players seemed endless, and in 1970 it reached the Nations' Cup final yet again after placing second in its first round group. In the final against Sudan, Sudanese fans clashed with Ghanaian players on the field and the home team held on to a 1-0 lead, leaving Ghana frustrated and physically battered. In 1972, 1974, and 1976, Ghana failed to qualify for the final rounds with a new generation of players. The 1978 edition was held in Ghana, giving the "Black Stars," as the national team is called, automatic entry, and this led to an unprecedented third African Nations' Cup triumph.

Ghana has also qualified for four consecutive Olympic Games tournaments since 1964; it is the only black African country to appear in the Olympics four times. In 1964, it won its first round group over Japan, Argentina, and Italy, but lost in the quarterfinals to Egypt. In 1968 and 1972, Ghana failed to gain the second round or even win a game, and in 1976, it joined the African bloc of nations in their boycott of the entire proceedings. Ghanaian attempts to qualify for the one World Cup berth allocated to Africa since 1970 have been surprisingly unsuccessful.

goal [i]

The enclosure into which the ball must pass to score. A goal consists of two vertical goalposts joined by a horizontal crossbar. A net may be attached to the structure and the ground behind it to trap the ball, if it does not interfere with play at the goalmouth. Goalposts must be eight yards (7.32 meters) apart and equidistant from the corner flags. The lower edge of the crossbar must be eight feet (2.44 meters) from the ground. The width and depth of the goalposts and crossbar must not exceed five inches (12 cm); both must be the same width. The back edges of the goalpost, crossbar, and goal line must be on the same vertical plane.

goal [ii]

The winning of a point. In order to score, a ball must pass entirely through the imaginary vertical plane that connects the back edges of the goalposts, crossbar, and goal line.

goal aggregate

The total number of goals scored by a team in a multigame series, often used in determining the winner of a two-game round in a knockout competition.

goal average

"Goals for" divided by "goals against." As a tie-breaking calibration, it has been used traditionally to determine the relative standing of two teams that finish equal on points in a league table. The Football League of England, which adopted it as the official tie-breaking procedure with the league's formation in 1888, was one of the last major loops in the world to drop it in the 1970s in favor of the more equitable "goal difference" procedure.

goal difference

"Goals for" minus "goals against." A somewhat more equitable tie-breaking calibration than its precursor, "goal average," it has been adopted by most of the world's leading league competitions to determine the relative standing of two teams that finish equal on points in the table.

goalkeeper

Also known as "goalie," "keeper," "custodian," "between the sticks," "stiffie," "goalminder," and "netminder."

The guardian of the goal, and the only player on the field allowed to use his hands (other than for throw-ins). His primary function is to gather, punch, or deflect shots on goal. As the last line of defense, the goalkeeper's task demands a unique set of skills, which are among the game's most spectacular to observe when performed with precision.

In the early years of modern soccer, the English rule makers did not acknowledge a separate goaltending position. Revisions in the Sheffield Rules during the 1860s referred to the "goalkeeper" as that player who, for the time being, was closest to his own goal. In the new Football Association Rules of 1870, goalkeeping became a fixed position for the first time and the goalkeeper's use of hands was sanctioned in the defensive half of the field. After 1894 a goalkeeper could not be charged except when he was playing the ball or obstructing an opponent. The area in which a goalkeeper could handle the ball was reduced to his own penalty area in 1912, but he was still required to release the ball after every two steps (a flip into the air would suffice). In 1931, the number of steps was increased to four, and in 1967 he was directed to give up possession of the ball altogether after four steps (usually by bouncing the ball on the ground or by passing to a teammate). Outside his own penalty area, a goalkeeper is confined by the same rules that applied to other players.

The Laws also direct that goalkeepers wear colors to distinguish themselves from other players and the referee. This rule dates back to 1909, when it was determined that goalkeepers in The Football League of England should wear either white, scarlet, or royal blue for the benefit of the referee. In subsequent years, yellow was prescribed for international matches.

goal kick

An indirect free kick required after the ball has passed over the goal line, other than into the goal, having last been played by the attacking side. The kick is taken within that half of the goal area nearest to where the ball crossed over the goal line and must be kicked beyond the penalty area. The kicker may not touch the ball again until it has been played by another player. Opposing players must be outside the kicker's penalty area when the kick is taken. A player who receives the ball direct from a goal kick cannot be offside.

Goal kicks were introduced in England by The Football Association in 1869 to replace the kick out. As a result of the 1936 rule that prohibits a goalkeeper from gathering a goal kick with his hands, goalkeepers themselves are usually designated to take goal kicks.

goal net

Also known as "rigging" and "netting."

A net of hemp, jute, or nylon that may be attached to the goal posts, crossbar, and ground behind the goal to trap the ball. Nets are not required by the Laws, but certain restrictions are placed upon them. Nets must be rigged in such a way that they do not interfere with play at the goalmouth, and nylon netting must be as thick as that of hemp or jute.

Nets were invented in 1890 by J. A Brodie of

Liverpool and came into wide use among Football League clubs the following year. The first league-level game in which they appeared was North vs. South at Nottingham in January 1891.

goalscoring

The top goalscorers in the history of world soccer (first class, senior-level competition only) are:

Artur Friedenreich (Brazil; 1909-35*), 1329 goals.

Pelé (Brazil; 1956-77*), 1280.

Franz Binder (Austria, Germany; 1930-50*), 1006.

Alfredo Di Stefano (Argentina, Colombia, Spain; 1942-66*), 786*.

Flavio (Brazil; 1961- *), 732**.

Gerd Müller (Germany FR; 1964- *), 590**.

James McGrory (Scotland; 1922-38*), 550.

Most international career goals: 97 by Pelé.

Most goals in one international: 10 by G. Fuchs for Germany vs. Czarist Russia at Stockholm in 1912.

The most goals scored in one season is thought to be Pelé's 127 in 1959.

Most career hat tricks: 92 by Pelé.

Most career international hat tricks: Seven each by Pelé and Sandor Kocsis.

Highest score in a full international: 17-1 by Denmark vs. France "A" at 1908 Olympic Games in London (official match), and 16-0 by Germany vs. Czarist Russia at Stockholm in 1912 (unofficial match).

Highest amateur international score: 20-0 by England vs. France at Ipswich in 1910.

Highest full international score in South America: 12-0 by Argentina vs. Ecuador at Buenos Aires in the 1942 South American Championship.

The highest score in first class club competition (Europe or South America) is thought to be 36-0 by Arbroath vs. Bon Accord in the Scottish Cup first round in 1885.

*active playing years
*excludes club goals 1942-46 and South American internationals
**through 1977

See also: **North American Soccer League** and individual competitions

Great Britain   See: **England; Scotland; Wales;** and **Ireland, Northern**

Greaves, James (1940-   )

England's phenomenal goalscorer of the postwar era and a latter-day Steve Bloomer who could score from any angle without the slightest warning. His 357 league goals, the third highest total in English soccer, were all scored in the first division, and his 44 goals for England were accumulated in only 57 appearances. An intuitive inside forward, he was discovered in his native East London by Chelsea, and made his first team debut at age 17. After four seasons he had already tallied 124 times, and in 1961, AC Milan attracted him with a huge transfer fee. But he was unhappy away from home, and returned to London and Tottenham Hotspur after four months of hectic rows with the Italian press. At Spurs he continued to play at peak form for several seasons, eventually scoring 220 goals in 321 appearances before moving to West Ham in 1970.

Greaves was the leading English league scorer six times, and in his first 12 seasons in the league he led his own club in scoring as well. A natural choice for England throughout the early 1960s, he came down with hepatitis in November 1965 and failed to recover thoroughly enough to regain his peak form during the early rounds of the World Cup in 1966. This, coupled with a shin injury suffered in the early rounds of the competition itself, led Alf Ramsey to bench Greaves for the victorious final against West Germany. This bitter disappointment took the wind out of his sails for at least three seasons, and by the time he had regained his form in 1968, he and Ramsey could not agree on his role in the team. His short stint with West Ham—slightly more than one season in 1970-71—was unproductive, and he retired prematurely at age 31 to tend his burgeoning business concerns. In 1977, he surfaced to play for the North London amateur club Barnet in the Southern League. Had he continued to play in the first division, all English goalscoring records would easily have been his for the taking.

Greece

Elliniki Podosfairiki Omospondia
(Greek Football Federation)
93, Academy Street
Athinai

Founded: 1926
FIFA: 1927
UEFA: 1954

Affiliated clubs: *1,758;* **registered players:** *87,050 (1,800 non-amateur);* **national stadium:** *Karaiskaki, Athens (47,000);* **stadium of equal size;** *Kaftantzoglion, Salonica (47,000);* **colors:** *white jerseys, blue shorts;* **season:** *September to June;* **honors:** *none.*

Greek soccer has long been the victim of political and cultural hostilities, though the game has been a passion among Greeks since the turn of the century. Before World War I, Greek soccer suffered from political strife involving Turkey and Bulgaria and from upheaval caused by the Balkan Wars. The instability of domestic politics between the world wars put a newly organized Greek game on rocky footing. After World War II, when soccer in Greece had its first real chance to settle down and modernize, the ceaseless clash between Athenians and Salonicans, the two principal parties in Greek soccer, continuously got in the way of unifying national soccer interests. As a result of these many troubles, Greece has nothing to show for itself in international competition, and appears to be permanently ensconced in the bottom quarter of European soccer.

There is no evidence to suggest that the early popularity of soccer in Greece had any historical link with ancient Greek cultures. The Athenian and Spartan ball games, such as *episkyros,* were lost in history and stood almost no chance of making their way down through the centuries into the industrialized age of the nineteenth century. In Greece, as elsewhere, the introduction of soccer was left to British sailors and engineers in the 1880s and perhaps earlier. Greek residents in Piraeus, Athens, Salonica, and Smyrna (now Izmir and part of Turkey) saw the British play soccer near the docks and in city squares, and from the beginning they too took an interest in the game. An unofficial exhibition match was held in conjunction with the first modern Olympic Games in Athens in 1896 between a Danish selection and a "Greek" team that was probably made up of British players. The result of this game is unknown, but it surely accelerated Athenian curiosity. Meanwhile, Greek students who were scattered throughout the region in Constantinople and Balkan cities picked up the game and managed to play occasionally despite its suppression by Ottoman authorities. Their enthusiasm for starting teams after returning to Greece was an important shot in the arm in the early expansion of Greek soccer.

Several teams were organized in port cities around the turn of the century, and at the Intermediate Olympics of 1906 in Athens, Greek teams made their first major public appearance. In an exhibition series, a Danish selection defeated a representative team from

319

Smyrna 5-2 and one from Athens 9-0, and a team from Salonica then lost to Smyrna 3-0 and Athens 5-0. While the Smyrna selection included British and Greek athletes who engaged in other sports as well, the Salonica and Athens selections were made up entirely of soccer-playing Greeks. Support for the Salonica and Athens teams was fiercely loyal, and their match together produced many violent scenes. The archrivalry between these two bastions of Greek soccer had begun.

The first important Greek club was Panhellenic, whose English name was later changed to the Greek "Panathinaïkos" (Pan-Athenian) in 1908. Olympiakos (Olympian) was founded in Athens' port city of Piraeus in 1914. Together these two clubs have dominated Greek soccer decisively over the decades. Despite the game's domestic popularity, international matches remained an impossibility before World War I, and there are few indications that attempts were even made, save for an occasional intercity match with Tirana or Bucharest.

Greece's first genuine foray into international competition came with the 1920 Olympic Games at Antwerp. With the formation of a Greek soccer association still several years away, a Greek national team banded together and was pitted against experienced Sweden in the first round. This resulted in an overwhelming 9-0 loss, and Greece was not seen in international competition again for nine years. At home, the return of Greeks to their native land after World War I sparked the formation of many new clubs and the first significant expansion of soccer in Greece. In 1922, Greek refugees from Constantinople founded Athlitiki Enosis Konstantinoupoleos (AEK), or Athletic Union of Constantinople, in Athens (it is now the team of the Electrical Supply Co.), and in Salonica Greek refugees founded Panellinikos Athlitikos Omilos Konstantinoupoleos (PAOK), or Pan-Hellenic Athletic Club of Constantinople. AEK Athens and PAOK Salonica eventually became the third and fourth most important clubs in Greece.

The Greek republic was proclaimed in 1925, and the following year a governing body for soccer, the Elliniki Podosfairiki Omospondia (EPO), was founded in Athens. A national championship was finally introduced in 1927-28, but it was restricted to clubs from the two major cities, Athens (including Piraeus) and Salonica, until 1959, when the first real national league was launched. To the dismay

of Athenians, the first champion was Aris Salonica, but Olympiakos, Panathinaïkos, and AEK rapidly took over, and, aside from other Aris league titles in 1932 and 1946 and one to PAOK Salonica in 1976, they have won every championship since. A cup competition was launched in 1931-32, and it too was won exclusively by the "big three" of Athens and Piraeus until the 1970s, with the lone exception of a single win to Ethnikos, the second Piraeus club, in 1933. (In the 1970s, Salonican clubs have done as well as Olympiakos and Panathinaikos in cup competition.)

Greece did not easily take to the international playing fields with confidence, even after the formation of the EPO in 1926. In 1929, Greece drew 1-1 with Bulgaria in Sofia, and in 1930 entered the first Balkan Cup (1929-31). It emerged from this two-year series with its first two wins in international competition, 2-1 over Yugoslavia and a whopping 6-1 over Bulgaria, but it lost four games along the way and placed third in a field of five. Greece went on to compete in each edition of the Balkan Cup with Bulgaria, Rumania, and Yugoslavia before World War II, and until 1938 these home and away games made up almost all of its international schedule. Yet in six prewar attempts, Greece was the only one of the four Balkan participants that failed to win a trophy even once. With such limited experience in the backwaters of European soccer, it was not surprising that its attempts to qualify for the 1934 and 1938 World Cups met with resounding failure. Greece was eliminated in the 1934 qualifying rounds by Italy (4-0) and in 1938 by Hungary (11-1). Before its staggering defeat to Hungary, however, the Greeks played a home and away qualifying round with Palestine and won 3-1 and 1-0.

Middle Eastern countries were the most significant opponents in Greece's post-World War II schedule. Greece played Turkey for the first time in two friendlies in 1948. This was a matter more of necessity than of political reconciliation, because postwar Greece was in the throes of waging an anti-Communist civil war at home and lost all its traditional Balkan rivals to hostile governments. In 1949, Athens played host to the first Friendship Cup with Turkey, Egypt, and the Italian "B" team, losing all three matches and placing last. This tournament was revived on a home and away basis in 1950-53 as the Mediterranean Cup, and there Greece fared somewhat better with wins over Egypt and Turkey to capture second place. In 1951, the national team journeyed to Alexandria for the Mediterranean Games soccer competition and took the trophy by defeating Egypt and Syria, the latter by a score of 4-0. In the second Mediterranean Cup (1953-57), the original four contestants were joined by "B" teams of France and Spain, and in this edition Greece won only one match in eight (over Spain "B"), finishing in fifth place.

The last major competition Greece qualified for was the 1952 Olympic Games in Helsinki, but it lost in the first round to Denmark. It has attempted to gain the final rounds of each postwar World Cup without success, and has participated in four editions of the European Football Championship, declining to enter in 1962-64. In 1960, Greece was eliminated from the final rounds of the Olympic Games in Rome by Israel on a toss of the coin. The rise of professionalism since the 1960s has put further Olympic possibilities out of reach. Greece's overall international record (as of 1978) shows 40 wins and 75 defeats at full level, including winning percentages over Ethiopia, Cyprus, Israel, Libya, Syria, and Portugal. Signs of improvement were seen in its third place finish in the reintroduced Balkan Cup of 1975 and its second place triumph in the 1976 edition of the same series.

Under a succession of British and Western European coaches, Greek clubs have been regular participants in the European club championships. The finest hour in Greek soccer occurred in 1971 when Panathinaïkos, under the managership of Hungarian immortal Ferenc Puskás, advanced to the final of the European Cup. "Panas" eliminated Jeunesse Esch and Slovan Bratislava in early rounds, and in the quarter-finals slipped by Everton on the away-goals rule, startling the English champions. In the semifinals, Panathinaïkos again won on the away-goals rule, this time over Red Star Belgrade, and gained the final. Its opponent in the final at Wembley was Ajax Amsterdam, which played cautiously and won by a comfortable 2-0 margin. Three-hundred thousand people greeted the Athens team on its return home, and Greek soccer basked in world glory for the first time. When Ajax refused to meet Nacional Montevideo in the Intercontinental Cup, "Panas" happily substituted. The Greek heroes performed admirably in holding Nacional to a 1-1 draw in the Athens leg, and in Uruguay succumbed by 2-1, losing the "world club championship" by an aggregate of only 3-2. Greek fans have not yet recovered from their instant, if brief, stardom.

Greek soccer continues to suffer from regional rivalries, dusty playing surfaces, an absence of good Greek coaches, and the EPO's traditionally lax approach to the rules and customs of the game. Until recently, Greek clubs were awarded a point in the league standings for simply completing a match. Most of the big clubs continue to be managed by British expatriates. Polish national team trainer Kazimierz Gorski managed at Panathinaïkos in 1976-78, and raised the standard of his club's play considerably, but boons such as this are rare.

The first division now consists of 18 clubs, sometimes including one from Crete, and 10 of these are divided into two sections, whose winners are automatically promoted. One recently promoted club was Rodhos from the island of Rhodes. Professionalism exists only among the top clubs, and a few of the wealthier clubs have started to import players from countries other than Cyprus. Olympiakos Piraeus is the runaway record holder with 20 championships and 17 cup victories; Panathinaïkos is a distant second.

Champions

1928	Aris Salonica	1937	Olympiakos
1929	no competition	1938	Olympiakos
1930	Panathinaïkos	1939	AEK Athens
1931	Olympiakos	1940	AEK Athens
1932	Aris Salonica	1941	no competition
1933	Olympiakos	1942	no competition
1934	Olympiakos	1943	no competition
1935	no competition	1944	no competition
1936	Olympiakos	1945	no competition

Greece

1946	Aris Salonica	1963	AEK Athens
1947	Olympiakos	1964	Panathinaïkos
1948	Olympiakos	1965	Panathinaïkos
1949	Panathinaïkos	1966	Olympiakos
1950	no competition	1967	Olympiakos
1951	Olympiakos	1968	AEK Athens
1952	no competition	1969	Panathinaïkos
1953	Panathinaïkos	1970	Panathinaïkos
1954	Olympiakos	1971	AEK Athens
1955	Olympiakos	1972	Panathinaïkos
1956	Olympiakos	1973	Olympiakos
1957	Olympiakos	1974	Olympiakos
1958	Olympiakos	1975	Olympiakos
1959	Olympiakos	1976	PAOK Salonica
1960	Panathinaïkos	1977	Panathinaïkos
1961	Panathinaïkos	1978	AEK Athens
1962	Panathinaïkos		

Cup Winners

1932	AEK Athens	1956	AEK Athens
1933	Ethnikos	1957	Olympiakos
1934	no competition	1958	Olympiakos
1935	no competition	1959	Olympiakos
1936	no competition	1960	Olympiakos
1937	no competition	1961	Olympiakos
1938	no competition	1962	Olympiakos
1939	AEK Athens	1963	Olympiakos
1940	Panathinaïkos	1964	AEK Athens
1941	no competition	1965	Olympiakos
1942	no competition	1966	AEK Athens
1943	no competition	1967	Panathinaïkos
1944	no competition	1968	Olympiakos
1945	no competition	1969	Panathinaïkos
1946	no competition	1970	Aris Salonica
1947	Olympiakos	1971	Olympiakos
1948	Panathinaïkos	1972	PAOK Salonica
1949	AEK Athens	1973	Olympiakos
1950	AEK Athens	1974	PAOK Salonica
1951	Olympiakos	1975	Olympiakos
1952	Olympiakos	1976	Heraklis Salonica
1953	Olympiakos	1977	Panathinaïkos
1954	Olympiakos	1978	AEK Athens
1955	Panathinaïkos		

Guadeloupe

This French Overseas Department has long been a production center for fine players, many of whom migrate to France to play with major clubs. The most famous of these in recent years has been the captain of Olympique Marseille and the French national team, Marius Trésor, an elegant attacking sweeper. Guadeloupe's political status entitles it to send representative teams each year to play in the Coupe de France. There have been three official internationals involving Guadeloupe and France: in 1957, France "Amateur" defeated a Guadeloupe selection 3-1 at Basse-Terre and 4-1 at Pointe-à-Pitre, and in 1969 France "Amateur" won again at Pointe-à-Pitre, 3-1.

Guatemala

Federación Nacional de Fútbol de Guatemala C.A.
Palacio de los Deportes, 20 piso, Zona 4
Guatemala C.A.

Founded: ?
FIFA: 1933
CONCACAF: 1961

Affiliated clubs: *1,611;* registered players: *30,440 (220 non-amateur);* national stadium: *Mateo Flores, Guatemala (50,000);* largest stadium: *Mateo Flores;* colors: *white jerseys, white shorts;* season: *May to October;* honors: *Championship of CONCACAF (1967), Municipal, Championship of CONCACAF Club Champions (1974), Comunicaciones, Championship of CONCACAF Club Champions (1978).*

Internal disorder has kept Guatemala from dominating soccer in Central America, despite its large population and historical importance in the region. Above all, Guatemala has been an Olympic specialist of late, appearing twice in the final rounds and in one edition advancing to the quarter-finals after a series of scintillating upsets and narrow losses. Its leading clubs often do well in the CONCACAF club championship, and Guatemala City is the home of CONCACAF itself.

The Federación Nacional de Fútbol was founded in the 1920s (exact date uncertain), and joined FIFA in 1933, the second Central American federation to do so. Before World War II, a multidivisional league was established with the Liga Mayor (national league), consisting of a Division Mayor and a Division Primera, and the Liga Menor (regional leagues) totaling almost 100 clubs. Guatemala made its international debut in the first Central American and Caribbean Games in 1930, and played two matches in that competition, losing both, to Costa Rica 8-1 and El Salvador 8-2. In the second edition in 1935,

Guatemala played five games without a win, though it managed to hold Honduras to a scoreless draw. These were inauspicious beginnings, and Guatemala did not compete in regional competition again until the second Championship of the Central American and Caribbean Confederation in 1943. A regular participant in this series from then on, it finally achieved its first international success in the Championship of CONCACAF in 1967.

That same year, Guatemala qualified for the final rounds of the 1968 Olympic Games in Mexico City, and found itself grouped in the first round with two teams from Eastern Europe, Czechoslovakia and Bulgaria. Guatemala held Bulgaria to a respectable 2-1 win, and, after defeating Thailand convincingly, 4-1, stunned Czechoslovakia with a 1-1 draw, preventing the Czechs from moving on to their expected berth in the quarter-finals. Instead, it was Guatemala that advanced, poised to meet the excellent Hungarian team that was about to win its second consecutive gold medal. Hungary squeaked by Guatemala 1-0, a result that amounted to an upset.

Guatemala qualified for the Olympic final rounds again in 1976, and on this occasion its best result in the first round was a 1-1 draw with Mexico, though it also drew with Israel before losing to the French amateurs. The expectations that both these Olympic runs created, however, did not materialize, and Guatemala failed to mount a real challenge to Haiti and Mexico in the 1974 and 1978 World Cup qualifying rounds.

Guatemala City's most popular club, Comunicaciones, advanced to the final of the CONCACAF Champions' Cup in 1969, and after additional strong bids finally won the cup in 1978 over Costa Rica's Deportivo Saprissa. The center of Guatemalan soccer is located in the big earthquake-bound cities of the south—Guatemala City, Quezaltenango, Mazatenango, and Escuintla. The national stadium in Guatemala City, Mateo Flores, is the largest in Central America, but all of Guatemalan soccer suffered tragically in the massive earthquake of 1976.

Guinea

Fédération Guinéenne de Football
P.O. Box 262
Conakry

Founded: 1959
FIFA: 1961
CAF: 1962

Affiliated clubs: *300;* registered players: *6,711;* national stadium: *Stade du 28 Septembre, Conakry (40,000);* largest stadium: *Stade du 28 Septembre;* colors: *red and white jerseys, yellow and white shorts;* season: *October to June;* honors: *African Nations' Cup runner-up (1976), Hafia de Conakry, African Cup of Champion Clubs (1972, 1975, 1977), Horoya de Conakry, African Cup Winners' Cup (1978).*

Guinea's fierce archrivalry with neighboring Ivory Coast is the most intense in all of French-speaking West Africa and has generated a high standard of play in domestic competition. The country's relatively early date of independence helped to coalesce soccer interests, especially in the capital of Conakry, and by 1970 Guinea had emerged as a leading continental power. In the mid-1970s, the national team's forward line was thought to be the most sophisticated and effective in Africa.

Guineans learned the game from French colonists after World War I, and by the late 1940s were active in local tournaments. The Fédération Guinéenne de Football introduced a league and cup competition based in Conakry shortly after its founding in 1959. Guinean clubs became active in the African Champions' Cup in the late 1960s, when Hafia Football Club of Conakry emerged as the major force in the league. Hafia remains the runaway record holder in league championships with eight (1967-69 and 1971-75).

In 1972, Hafia eliminated two powerful African champions, Cameroon's Canon de Yaoundé and Zaire's T.P. Mazembe to reach the final of the Champions' Cup, and there defeated Uganda's Simba Club in two hard fought games to gain its first African title. In 1975, Hafia won a second time, having eliminated two more continental powers, Zaire's Vita Club and Congo's C.A.R.A. In the final, it won both legs over Nigeria's leading club, Rangers. The following year, Hafia again had to overcome a major African club, Ivory Coast's ASEC Abidjan, to gain the final against Algeria's surprising Mouloudia Chalia. After splitting the two legs of the final with Mouloudia, 0-3 and 3-0, Hafia was unlucky to lose a second trophy in as many years on penalty kicks. In 1977, however, Hafia returned and became the first club to win champions' cup three times.

Guinea's first big international success at the national level was in qualifying for the 1968 Olympics in Mexico City, but in the first round the Mexican and French amateurs defeated Guinea convincingly, and Guinea's 3-2 win over Colombia was not sufficient to prevent a last place finish in its first round group. In 1973, Guinea placed second in the soccer tournament of the African Games in Nigeria. Guinea first qualified for the final rounds of the more coveted African Nations' Cup in 1970. A loss to Egypt and draws with Congo-Kinshasa and Ghana, however, proved fatal, and it bowed out after the first round. There were similar results in 1974, but in 1976, behind the gifted inside forwards Nabylaye Papa Camara and Ibrahim "Petit" Sory Keita, Guinea went undefeated in six games and took second place to the talented Moroccans. In the first round, Ethiopia and Uganda went down to defeat, and a nervous 1-1 draw with Egypt produced the necessary point to advance to the final pool of four. This time Guinea's inside pair led their gifted team to a 4-2 defeat of Egypt and a 1-1 draw with Nigeria. In the last game of the competition,

Guinea needed to defeat Morocco for the title, but a 1-1 draw was the best it could do and Guinea settled for second place, its best result ever in a major international competition. This was the second time Morocco had ended Guinea's hopes for high international honors. In the 1974 World Cup qualifying rounds, the North Africans had eliminated Guinea 1-1 and 2-0. In the 1978 qualifying rounds, Guinea advanced through two rounds, eliminating Ghana and Togo, and in the third round met the eventual qualifier—Morocco.

Guinea-Bissau

While not yet a member of FIFA or the African Football Confederation (CAF), the former colony of Portuguese Guinea has made substantial progress in organizing its soccer activities. In 1976 its champion club Balantas

Mansôa entered the African Champions' Cup, with permission from the CAF, and lost in the first round to Jaraafs Dakar, 6-1 and 4-1. Earlier that year Guinea-Bissau had applied for provisional membership with FIFA.

Guyana

Guyana Football Association
7 Brickdam
Georgetown

Founded: 1902
FIFA: 1968
CONCACAF: 1969

Affiliated clubs: *103;* **registered players:** *1,605;* **national stadium:** *Guyana Sports Club, Georgetown (5,800);* **largest stadium:** *Georgetown Cricket Club (15,000),* **colors:** *green and yellow jerseys, black shorts;* **season:** *March to December;* **honors:** *none.*

The British Guiana Football Association, founded at Georgetown in 1902, was the first regulatory body of soccer in any of the three Guianas. It immediately established affiliation with The Football Association in London, and appeared for a time to be the focal point of soccer on the northeast coast of South America. Between the world wars, however, competition with cricket and other factors hampered its growth, and by the late 1920s the game in neighboring Dutch Guiana (Surinam) had surpassed British Guiana both in the sophistication of its administration and the level of play. While Surinam was able to join FIFA in 1929 and the Central American and Caribbean Confederation a few years later,

British Guiana lagged behind and became satisfied with official ties to London. Though the Dutch colonies of the region played one another regularly during the 1930s, and British island colonies in the Caribbean competed as early as 1934, British Guiana was not in any meaningful international competition until after World War II.

The Guyana Football Association was reconstituted two years after independence was achieved in 1966, and in 1969 Guyana joined CONCACAF. (None of the Guianas have ever been associated with the South American Confederation.) Guyana has entered CONCACAF tournaments only sporadically. Two of Georgetown's leading clubs,

Thomas United and Christianburg, recently participated in the CONCACAF Champions' Cup. Guyana's first attempt to qualify for the World Cup was met with failure in 1976 at the hands of Surinam.

About 85 teams participate in senior club competition, twenty-four of which are in the upper levels. The country is divided into six district associations which sponsor leagues and local cup competitions. There is also an interdistrict league competition that represents the national championship.

H

hack

Kicking the shin of an opponent in order to trip or otherwise impede his mobility. This practice has been prohibited by the Laws of the Game since the first Football Association rules were drawn up in 1863, although it had a place in early nineteenth century football. It is represented in the modern Laws by the phrase "kicking an opponent."

The controversy over hacking became one of the important touchstones marking the break between rugby and soccer during the 1860s. The Rugby School Rules of 1846, which were a hallmark in the development of the rugby game, allowed kicking below the knee. The Harrow School Rules of ca.1830, the Cambridge University Rules of 1848, and the Sheffield Rules of 1857, each an important step in the growth of modern soccer, specifically banned hacking of any kind. With the prohibition of hacking in The Football Association Laws of 1863, the break between soccer and rugby became clearly delineated. Hacking apologists gravitated to the rugby camp, as did defenders of the handling game, the second major controversy of the rugby-soccer split. In the late 1860s, the physical dangers of hacking became a matter of public concern throughout England. Although its use was forbidden by the soccer code, most rugby clubs continued to practice hacking. Finally, at its inaugural meeting in 1871, the new Rugby Football Union abolished hacking and tripping altogether, and the matter was laid to rest.

Haiti

Fédération Haïtienne de Football
Stade Sylvio Cator
Port-au-Prince

Founded: 1912
FIFA: 1937
CONCACAF: 1957

Affiliated clubs: *40;* **registered players:** *750;* **national stadium:** *Stade Sylvio Cator, Port-au-Prince (15,000);* **largest stadium:** *Stade Sylvio Cator;* **colors:** *black and red jerseys, black shorts;* **season:** *October to June;* **honors:** *Central American and Caribbean Championship (1957), Championship of CONCACAF (1973), Racing, Championship of CONCACAF Club Champions (1966).*

The success of Haiti, for many years one of the leading soccer-playing countries of the Caribbean, has become unsure with the advance of soccer in the new island republics. Historically, the only serious opposition in the region was Cuba, but that was before the revolution of 1959 which left Haiti holding the West Indian torch alone. Unfortunately, an embarrassing showing in the 1974 World Cup final rounds proved to be an unpleasant experience, but Haiti's relative stature in the region has been fairly consistent and not unjustified.

The Fédération Haïtienne de Football Amateur has been an autonomous body from its founding in 1912, though French influence left over from the colonial experience was considerable. Still, Haitian soccer has developed quite independently from outside domination. Haiti's first official international matches date from a seven-day World Cup qualifying tournament in Port-au-Prince in 1934 with a Cuban selection that was superior in technique and skills. The results of the three matches were 1-3, 1-1, and 0-6, and Cuba won the right to meet the USA for a place in Rome. (Indeed, Cuba maintained a higher level of play during the 1930s and eventually qualified for the 1938 World Cup in Paris four years later.) In 1938, Haiti played host to Jamaica for a series of five matches, of which Haiti won three and lost one. The results against Jamaica were inconclusive, as the scores indicate: 0-0, 5-2, 0-3, 2-0, and 2-0. Similar friendlies were organized with Panama in 1939 (won 3, lost 1) and in 1941 with an unofficial American selection (won 3, lost 1). Haiti did not enter the Championship of the Central American and Caribbean Football Confederation, however, until the 1950s, many years after it had become a member, nor was Port-au-Prince ever the host city. But since 1957, the year it won the championship, its regular participation has been assured. Haiti has played against the USA in 12 officially recognized matches between 1954-76. (won 5, lost 4).

The word "Amateur" was dropped from the name of the governing body during the 1960s, though professionalism remained illegal. The surprisingly small number of players registered with the FHF probably does not accurately reflect the actual number of players in competition, and many are known to be playing abroad, especially in the United States. Two members of the 1974 World Cup squad, for example, were Haitians registered with the semiprofessional German-American League of New York. The leading clubs in Haiti are: SC Victory, Racing, Violette, Don Bosco, Aigle Noir, and Étoile Haïtienne. In 1966, Racing Port-au-Prince was the first and only Caribbean club to win the CONCACAF Club Championship.

In 1966, Haiti staged a major regional tournament, the Coupe Dr. François Duvalier. in which Netherlands Antilles, Jamaica,

Trinidad, Surinam, Guadeloupe, and Haiti participated. Haiti was the winner while Trinidad and Surinam gained second and third place, respectively. Haiti's relatively high position among the CONCACAF membership received a serious setback in the 1967 Championship of CONCACAF at Tegucigalpa, Honduras. Haiti placed fifth in a field of six nations after losing to Guatemala, Trinidad, Mexico, and Honduras. Its only win was against lowly Nicaragua (2-1); the poor showing demonstrated once again the difficulty that the best Caribbean teams have against Central American opposition. Haiti's first foray into genuine world class competition was at the 1974 World Cup in West Germany. It gained the berth by crushing Puerto Rico and going on to defeat Netherlands Antilles, Trinidad, Honduras, and Guatemala, though it lost to Mexico, 1-0. Its record in the final rounds was only marginally better than that of Zaire, but it did manage to achieve an upset of sorts in holding mighty Italy to a 3-1 win. The great Polish side crushed them 7-0, and Argentina probably should have done better by its 4-1 victory over the Haitian amateurs. Sannon, center forward from Don Bosco, scored both Haitian goals.

halfback
Also known as "No. 4," "No. 5," and "No. 6."

In traditional tactical formations, most notably the 2-3-5, the three positions that link the defense and attack. Their functions may vary, but most commonly halfbacks—right, left, and center—drop back to defend and move up to support the attack as the situation warrants. The pivotal aspects of the position are most pronounced at center halfback. In some formations, the center halfback may be strictly a defensive player. Right and left halfbacks who confine themselves to corridors on either side of the field may be referred to as wing halfbacks and are rarely assigned to purely defensive tasks. At the same time, traditional halfbacks are almost never offensive players only. The term "halfback" has fallen out of general use in recent years with the advent of systems that use two, three, or four "midfielders," i.e., the 4-2-4, 4-3-3, and 4-4-2.

half time

A period of time between the two halves of a game. A half time interval is not specifically required by the Laws, but the players' right to have a period of rest between halves has been asserted by a decision of the International Football Association Board. The letter of the Laws, however, restricts the interval to five minutes, unless otherwise agreed upon by the referee. In fact, half time periods are customarily longer than five minutes and may vary from country to country. In Great Britain, the interval used to be called Lemon Time, a reminder of the early days of the game when it was common to suck on lemons during the break.

half volley

A kick taken the instant after the ball has bounced off the ground.

Hanappi, Gerhardt (1929-)

Hanappi must surely rank as one of the most versatile players of all time. His finest accomplishments were achieved at right half, where his talents flowered to their fullest, but he played in at least six and as many as nine different positions for Austria, an astounding feat at Austria's level of international competition. (The only positions he did not play were left wing and goalkeeper.) Hanappi signed with Wacker Vienna in 1946, and at age 17 he was instrumental in helping his club win the league title. In 1950, he was transferred to Rapid Vienna for a record fee, having made his international debut in 1948 against Sweden, and went on to inspire Rapid to six championships in 14 years. Hanappi was chosen Austrian Footballer of the Year eight times, including seven in a row from 1954-60. At one point, he made 55 consecutive international appearances, and after the great Ocwirk left the national team in 1955, Hanappi became captain.

Nicknamed "The Engineer," he was an exemplary midfield orchestrator who always found openings either for himself or a teammate. Though his natural tendency was to attack, his marking was near perfect and he fell into a defensive posture whenever needed. During the first half of his career the flowing Austrian style was particularly well suited to his own intuitive playmaking, and even after the big change in Austria's tactical approach from 1954 on, his ability to adapt was extraordinary. In his 100th international appearance for Austria (against Czechoslovakia) he performed poorly, and was jeered by the disappointed fans. When asked to return for his 101st cap, he declined, and finally retired from Rapid in 1964. The most popular Austrian player of all time, he settled comfortably into his thriving architectural practice that he had been building since the beginning of his playing career.

hands   Also known as "hand ball."

An infringement in which a player other than the goalkeeper intentionally touches the ball with a hand or any part of the arm, except when making a throw-in. The opposing side is awarded a direct free kick.

Handling of the ball has been prohibited since 1866 when the fair catch rule was deleted from the English Laws. Earlier, even after the first break had occurred between rugby and soccer over the issue of hacking, some degree of handling had been permitted. The Cambridge Rules of 1848 allowed players

to stop the ball momentarily with their hands or to catch the ball directly from an opponent's kick, (the latter known as a fair catch), and the Sheffield Rules of 1857 sanctioned similar use of the hands. Even the Laws of The Football Association, which in 1863 were the rules from which the modern game developed, provided for the fair catch and did not prohibit manual deflection of the ball. The importance of the fair catch rule change of 1866, therefore, cannot be underestimated in a determination of the birth of modern soccer.

Hardy, Samuel (1883-1966)

The first goalkeeper ever to achieve fame in his own right, and as written descriptions and

film footage show, a keeper whose anticipation would have placed him in the front ranks of any era. Hardy was one of the first students of sophisticated angles and the geometry of goalkeeping. Legend has it that his anticipation was so sharp he rarely had to dive for the ball, and he saved more penalties than any British goalkeeper in history. As a teenage amateur, he played center forward before signing with his local club, Chesterfield, in 1903. Two years later he moved to Liverpool, winning a league championship medal in 1906. In 1912, he began a glorious nine-year career with Aston Villa, the most successful club in pre-World War I England, helping "the Villans" to F.A. Cup victories in 1913 and 1920. In 1921, he moved to Nottingham Forest and remained there until the end of his career four years later. With the exception of England's tour of Austria-Hungary in 1908, and an occasional home international, he was England's regular goalkeeper from 1907-20—24 appearances in all—in addition to three of England's four wartime internationals in 1919. "Silent Sam" made nearly 600 club-level appearances, over 200 of them for Liverpool, and 160 for Aston Villa. After his retirement, he became a hotel owner in his native Derbyshire.

Harrow Game, Rules of the

The English public schools whose indigenous ball games of the early nineteenth century were the forerunners of modern soccer—Harrow, Eton, Charterhouse, Westminster, Shrewsbury, Uppingham, and others—each made a contribution to the development of the game, but among them Harrow stands out for the consistency and longevity of its influence, and because the Harrow rules more closely resemble the Laws of the Game than those of any other major school. At Harrow, the dribbling game was dominant, and running with the ball and passing by hand were banned altogether, as was hacking, another early rugby characteristic. Methods of scoring that we now associate with rugby, such as "tries" and "touchdowns," were not part of the Harrow game: the only way to score a goal was by sending the ball over the goal line and between the poles. And it is likely that Harrow was the first school to settle on 11 players to a team (as early as 1814), rather than the limitless number found in other school games.

Although football at Harrow had achieved a semblance of organization by 1815, the Rules of the Harrow Game as we now understand them probably date from the 1830s. Their influence is seen to some extent in the formulation of the Cambridge University Rules, which were also central in the drafting of the Laws of the Game, and by the presence of so many Old Harrovians among The Football Association membership in the early years. The most influential personality during the first four decades of the modern soccer era was an Old Harrovian, C.W. Alcock.

The Harrow rules were designed to accommodate the peculiarities of playing in fields that lay at the foot of a hill. Drainage was poor, and considerable movement of players, as well as an unusually large ball, were required to keep the game lively. The goals, called "bases," consisted of two 12-foot-high poles, and Harrow boys initiated another custom for important games: a school uniform that consisted of white pants and on certain occasions black gaiters.

The following text is representative of the Rules of the Harrow Game from 1830 on:

1. The choice of Bases is determined by tossing: the side that wins the toss must have the choice of Bases, the side that loses has the right to kick off.

2. The Bases must be 18 feet in width, and the distance between them not greater than 150 yards. The width of the ground must be not more than 100 yards.

3. The Ball must be kicked off from the middle of the ground, half way between the two Bases. A Base may not be obtained unless the Ball has touched one of the opposite side to the kicker previously to passing between the Base Poles.

4. When the Ball is kicked, any one on the same side as the kicker is entitled to kick

or catch it, provided that at the same time of the delivery of the kick he is not nearer the line of the opponents' Base than the kicker. If he is nearer he is "offside," and virtually out of the Game till the Ball has been touched by one of the opposite side. Nor may he interfere with anyone of the opposite side, or in any way prevent or obstruct his kicking or catching the Ball.

5-9. (These refer to peculiarities of the Harrow game that have little bearing on the Laws of the Game.)

10. The Ball, if kicked beyond the prescribed limits of the ground, must be thrown in again (at least six yards from the thrower) by one of the opposite side to the player who shall have last touched the Ball, and his throw may be made in any direction, but may not obtain a Base unless the Ball has previously touched one of the players. In making the throw, the thrower may not hold the Ball by the lace, nor may he touch the Ball after the throw, until it has been touched by one of the other players.

11. From behind his own Base a player must kick the Ball instead of throwing it, the preliminary run not being longer than three running strides from the Base Line. From behind the opponent's Base the throw must be straight in, and may be of any length. In the first case the kicker, and in the second the thrower, must not again touch the Ball until it has been touched by another player. (Neither in Rule 10 nor in this Rule does Rule 4 apply.)

12. All charging is fair, but no holding, tripping, pushing with hands, shinning, or back-shinning, either of the Ball or the players, is allowed.

13. If the Ball strike the Base Pole and go through, it shall count as a Base, but if, in the opinion of the Umpires, it shall have passed over the Pole, it shall not count as a Base.

14. If the Ball strike the Base Pole and rebound into the ground play shall continue.

15. No nails or spikes of any sort are allowed in Football Boots.

16. There must always be two Umpires in a House Match, and, if possible, in School Matches. Their decision shall be final as to matters of fact, but they are at liberty to refer any question of law to the Committee of the Philathletic Club if they feel unable to decide it at the time.

17. It shall be the duty of the Umpires in all Football Matches to take away a Base or "Yards" ["Yards" referring to Rule 6] unfairly obtained; to award them if clearly and undoubtedly obtained, or stopped by unfair means, and in House Matches to put out of the Game any player wilfully breaking any of the Football Rules.

18. If it is necessary to replay a House Match, the distance between the Base Poles shall be doubled, the sides tossing again for choice of Bases.

19. After a tie each House is at liberty to play with any alterations or substitutions in its team that it may wish.

20. On the second day of a House Match, if a draw be the result, the Umpires must compel an extra quarter-of-an-hour to be played, changing ends after seven minutes. The same to apply to Champion House Match on the first day's play if it be a draw, at the end of the hour.

*Note—the following variations of given rules were in effect ca. 1863: Rule 2) bases 12 feet in width; Rules 10 & 11) throw-in replaced by kick-in; Rule 15) nails allowed but only within an inch of the toe or half-inch of the sides of the boot.

See also: Cambridge University Rules

hat trick

The scoring of three goals in one game by the same individual, or the winning of a title three years in succession by the same team. Traditionally, a hat trick is not credited to a player unless his three goals are uninterrupted by a goal from another player of the same team. The term has its origin in cricket, where a player used to be awarded a new hat for taking three wickets with three balls.

Pelé holds both major world hat trick records: most hat tricks in career (92) and most hat tricks in international play (seven), the latter shared with Sandor Kocsis of Hungary. Neither record takes into account the tradition of successive goals.

head

To pass or shoot the ball with one's head. The art of heading has been perfected by a gallery of great players, perhaps none more so than the inside-right Sandor Kocsis of Honvéd, Barcelona, and Hungary, whose dazzling work in the air complemented the lethal left-foot shot of his teammate at inside-left, Ferenc Puskás. Kocsis' nickname was the "Golden Head."

Hidegkuti, Nandor (1922-   )

The vital element of Hungary's revolutionary "W" attack during the early 1950s, Hidegkuti was one of the only players on this national team who was not a member of Honvéd at one time or another. As Hungary's deep-lying center forward, his function was primarily to feed the ball to Puskás and Kocsis, but he himself scored 39 goals in his 68 international appearances, and he was so skilled a player that he turned his role into a multi-purpose pivot or linkman as well as center forward.

Hidegkuti learned the game in the streets of a poor section of Budapest, and in 1943 he signed with lowly Elektromos. In 1947, two years after his international debut, he moved to MTK, one of Budapest's great sporting institutions, and he soon became one of the league's leading scorers. He was not a regular choice for the national team, however, until 1952, when he participated with great success in Hungary's gold medal-winning effort in the Olympic Games. He figured prominently in Hungary's 6-3 thrashing of England in 1953 and in the 1954 World Cup, where he scored one of his most famous goals with a diving header against Uruguay. He continued to play for MTK—at inside right rather than center forward—until his retirement, and also played for Hungary in the 1958 World Cup, though with little of his old flair. His relatively late start as an international put him well into his thirties by this time, and he finally retired in 1958, with the nickname "Old Man."

He took up coaching at MTK for awhile, and went to Italy to manage Fiorentina and Mantova during the early 1960s, returning to MTK briefly before moving on restlessly to Poland and several other countries, and since 1974 he has been manager of the big Egyptian club Al-Ahly, taking them to several league titles since his arrival.

history of the game

ca 2500 BC	Chinese Emperor Huang-Ti believed to have drawn up the first rules for *tsu chu*

1700 BC- 200 AD		*tsu chu* documented in China
ca 600 BC	*a)*	documentation of a Greek football game, the forerunner of *episkyros*
	b)	the Roman game *harpastum* played
1st cent. BC		form of indigenous football believed played in Ireland
1st-5th cent. AD		the Roman handball and football games spread throughout the empire
2nd cent.		football believed played in Dalmatia, possibly Roman inspired
217		a Roman army team defeated by a select team of British, though this match is assumed to be mythical
5th cent.		Celtic peoples of Britannia and Gaul may have adopted handball-football as legacy of departed Romans
6th cent.		a pre-Columbian ball game including elements of football depicted by artists in Guatemala
7th-11th cent.		indigenous football games of Normandy, Brittany, Picardy, Cornwall, Wales, Scotland, Ireland, and English towns develop
12th cent. -ca 1830		annual Shrovetide celebrations in England include game of football, documented in 1175 by William Fitzstephen
1154-89		during reign of Henry II *ludus pilae* receives patronage from established classes in England
ca 1250		a legendary hero, St. Hugh of Lincoln, displays unprecedented ball control skills
1314		Edward II bans football
1349		Edward III bans football
1389		Richard II bans football
1423		football in Scotland supported by deposed House of Stewart
1425		players paid for the first time (4 pence) by the Prior of Bicester
1457		James II of Scotland bans football
1491		James IV of Scotland bans football
16th cent.	*a)*	interest in football throughout Britain expands rapidly
	b)	*calcio,* the Florentine game, institutionalized and played annually, in the Piazza della Novere
	c)	further denunciations by the English crown
1527		"the great foot balle" supported in Ireland by Statutes of Galway while other sports forbidden
17th cent.		the pre-Columbian ball game becomes extinct with the destruction of Mexican culture
1609		football played in the Virginia colony
ca 1620		football organized at Trinity and St. John's Colleges, Cambridge
1654		Cromwell attends a hurling match
1681		Charles II sponsors a servants' football match
1720	*a)*	a Welsh football competition between local teams described by Anna Beynon, a fan

	b)	transfer of players first documented in the poems of Irishman Matthew Concanen
ca 1750		football established in Lancashire
ca 1800		interest in the game wanes throughout Britain
1814		football organized at Harrow
1823		pupil at Rugby School breaks school rules and runs with the ball, leading to the beginning of rugby football
1827	*a)*	unsportsmanlike conduct in football at Eton is widely publicized, drawing negative reaction to the game
	b)	annual football contest at Harvard begins
1845		referees introduced at Eton
1846		Rugby School Rules drawn up establishing forerunner of modern rugby game
1848		Cambridge University Rules, precursor of The Football Association Laws of 1863, drawn up
1857		Sheffield F.C., the first football club, founded and Sheffield Rules written
1859		Forest Football Club, the first devoted exclusively to the dribbling game and forerunner of Wanderers F.C., founded in northeast London
1860		rules approximating the association game introduced in the USA
1861-67		clubs spring up throughout England but rules still vary
ca 1862		Sheffield becomes center of football activity in northern England, London in the south
1862	*a)*	rules drawn up for Old Etonians vs. Old Harrovians at Cambridge
	b)	Notts County Football Club, oldest club still in The Football League, founded in Nottingham
1863		the watershed year in soccer history:
	a)	The Football Association founded in London to promote and regulate the game in England and rules are drawn up
	b)	the Blackheath club resigns from the new organization over issues of carrying and hacking, resulting in the split between rugby and soccer
ca 1865		game introduced in Africa by Englishmen via Port Elizabeth, South Africa
1865		tapes first stretched across goalmouth width eight feet above the ground
1867	*a)*	Queen's Park Football Club, the oldest Scottish club, founded in Glasgow
	b)	Buenos Aires Football Club, the first club in South America, founded in Argentina by British railway workers
1869		goal kick introduced to replace kick out
1870	*a)*	first match between representative teams from England and Scotland
	b)	Association rules first played in Germany
	c)	game introduced in Australia by British coal miners
1871	*a)*	The Football Association Challenge Cup (F.A. Cup) launched
	b)	The Rugby Football Union founded, marking the final break between rugby and soccer

1872	*a)*	first official international between England and Scotland in Glasgow
	b)	Wanderers F.C. wins the first F.A. Cup
	c)	game introduced in France by English sailors at Le Havre
	d)	corner kick introduced
	e)	official size of ball fixed
1873	*a)*	Scottish Football Association founded
	b)	Scottish F.A. Cup launched
	c)	Wrexham Football Club, the first Welsh club, founded
1874		umpires introduced by The Football Association
1875		first club in Portugal founded in Lisbon by British residents
1876	*a)*	crossbars replace tapes across goalmouth
	b)	KB Copenhagen, the first Danish club, founded
1877		The Football Association and the Sheffield Football Association agree on rules
1878	*a)*	first game under lights played in Sheffield
	b)	whistles used by English referees
	c)	game introduced in Ireland via Belfast
1879	*a)*	Haarlem Football Club, the first Dutch club, founded
	b)	game introduced in Hungary
ca 1880		game introduced in West Africa via the Gold Coast
1880	*a)*	shinguards sanctioned by The Football Association
	b)	Irish Football Association founded
	c)	Irish Cup launched
1882	*a)*	first Uruguayan club founded at Montevideo University by a British professor
	b)	International Football Association Board established
	c)	two-handed throw-in introduced
	d)	SK Slavia, Bohemia's first club, founded
1883		Home International Championship, the world's first full international competition, begins
1884		American Football Association, first governing body in the USA, founded in Newark, N.J.
1885	*a)*	professionalism legalized in England
	b)	first North American international: USA vs. Canada in Newark
1886		caps first awarded in England for international appearances
1887	*a)*	game introduced in Russia via Orekhovo by British textile workers
	b)	Hamburger SV, the oldest German club still in league competition, founded in Hamburg
1888		The Football League, world's first national league, founded in England

1889	a)	Royal Netherlands Football Association, the oldest F.A. outside the United Kingdom, founded
	b)	Preston North End F.C. wins the first Football League championship and the F.A. Cup: the first double
	c)	Vienna Cricket and Football Club (Cricketer), the influential pioneer club of Austria, founded
	d)	a representative eleven from England tours Germany
	e)	Valparaiso Football Club, the oldest club in Chile, founded by British residents
1890	a)	game introduced in Finland by British residents
	b)	F.C. Internazionale, the first Italian club, founded in Turin
1891	a)	referees and linesmen replace umpires in The Football League
	b)	goal nets introduced in The Football League
	c)	game introduced in Greece by British sailors
1892	a)	Division II of The Football League founded
	b)	game introduced in Singapore by the British
1893	a)	Argentine Football Association, the oldest F.A. in South America, founded, and an Argentine championship, South America's first, introduced
	b)	first attempt to organize a players' union in England fails
	c)	professionalism legalized in Scotland
1894	a)	game introduced in Brazil by English ex-schoolboy Charles Miller
	b)	game introduced in Bulgaria
1895	a)	the F.A.'s of Chile, Belgium, and Switzerland founded
	b)	CR Flamengo, the oldest club in Brazil, founded in Rio de Janeiro
1896	a)	an unofficial demonstration match is played at the first modern Olympic Games in Athens
	b)	amateur internationals played between some British countries and German, Austrian, and Bohemian selections
	c)	Oruro Royal Club, the first club in Bolivia, founded
1897	a)	concept of "intentional" introduced in the Laws
	b)	Corinthians Football Club tours South America and South Africa
1898	a)	promotion and relegation system introduced in The Football League
	b)	first players' union organized successfully in England
	c)	Italian Football Association founded
	d)	Athletic Bilbao, the oldest Spanish club still in competition, founded by British engineers
1900		the F.A.'s of Germany and Uruguay founded
1901	a)	110,820 spectators watch F.A. Cup final at Crystal Palace, London
	b)	the F.A.'s of Bohemia and Hungary founded
1902	a)	first tragic crowd disaster occurs at Ibrox Park, Glasgow: 25 dead and 500 injured

	b)	in Vienna, Austria and Hungary engage in first non-British full international
	c)	a Mexican championship, the first in North America, introduced
1904	a)	FIFA founded in Paris by France, Belgium, Denmark, Netherlands, Spain, Sweden, and Switzerland
	b)	F.A.'s of Austria and Sweden founded
1905		Argentina and Uruguay engage in first South American international in Buenos Aires
1906	a)	Laws of the Game substantially rewritten
	b)	Cracovia Football Club, the oldest club in Poland, founded in Cracow
	c)	São Paulo League founded in Brazil
1908	a)	England 'A' team tours outside Home countries for the first time, to Austria, Hungary, and Bohemia
	b)	first official Olympic soccer competition
1910		a Philippine national championship, the first in Asia, introduced
1912		All-Russian Football Union founded
1913	a)	United States Soccer Football Federation founded
	b)	China and the Philippines engage in first Asian international in Manila
1914	a)	first Brazilian international, against Argentina in Buenos Aires
	b)	Brazilian Sports Federation founded
1916	a)	South American Football Confederation founded
	b)	South American Championship, the first regional competition between nations, launched
1921		Egyptian Football Association founded
1923		Wembley Stadium, London, Mecca of world soccer, opens with celebrated "White Horse Final"
1924	a)	Uruguay becomes first non-European nation to win Olympic soccer tournament
	b)	Scandinavian Championship, the first non-British European regional competition between nations, launched
1927	a)	International Cup, the first regional competition between nations on the continent of Europe, launched
	b)	Mitropa Cup, the first international club competition, launched
	c)	first radio broadcast of a soccer match: Arsenal vs. Sheffield United
1928	a)	Uruguay wins Olympic soccer tournament a second time
	b)	Home countries leave FIFA over issue of part-time payments to amateurs
1929		Balkan Cup launched
1930		Uruguay wins first World Cup, in Uruguay
1931		Argentina becomes first South American country to adopt professionalism
1932		substitution first sanctioned for consenting national teams
1933		numbers first worn by players in England
1934		Italy wins second World Cup, in Italy

1937	a)	world record 149,547 spectators watch England vs. Scotland at Hampden Park, Glasgow
	b)	first television broadcast of a soccer match: Preston North End vs. Sunderland in F.A. Cup final
	c)	official weight of the ball increased from 13-15 oz. to 14-16 oz.
1938	a)	Italy wins third World Cup, in France
	b)	Laws of the Game rewritten
1940		Central American Championship launched
1946		Home countries rejoin FIFA
1950	a)	world's largest stadium, the Maracanã, Rio de Janeiro, opened at fourth World Cup
	b)	World Cup final at Maracanã attracts 199,850 spectators, still a world record for any game
	c)	Uruguay wins fourth World Cup, in Brazil
	d)	most famous upset of all time: England loses to USA 1-0 in Belo Horizonte
1954	a)	West Germany wins fifth World Cup, in Switzerland
	b)	Union of European Football Associations and Asian Football Confederation founded
1955	a)	European Cup launched
	b)	Fairs Cup launched
1956	a)	Asian Nations' Cup launched
	b)	Stanley Matthews elected first European Footballer of the Year
1957	a)	African Football Confederation founded
	b)	African Nations' Cup launched
1958	a)	Brazil wins fifth World Cup, in Sweden
	b)	European Nations' Cup launched
1959		Alfredo Di Stefano elected European Footballer of the Year a second time
1960	a)	Copa Libertadores launched
	b)	Real Madrid wins fifth consecutive European Cup
	c)	the unofficial Intercontinental Cup launched
	d)	European Cup Winners' Cup launched
	e)	USSR wins first European Nations' Cup
1961		maximum wage abolished in England
1962		Brazil wins seventh World Cup, in Chile
1963		world club attendance record set for Flamengo-Fluminense derby at Maracanã, Rio de Janeiro: 177,656
1964	a)	African Champions' Cup launched
	b)	worst soccer disaster in history: 301 killed in riot following Peru vs. Argentina game, in Lima
	c)	Spain wins second European Nations' Cup

1965		The Football League in England sanctions use of one nominated substitute in case of injury
1966		England wins eighth World Cup, in England
1967	*a)*	use of two substitutes sanctioned by FIFA
	b)	CONCACAF Champions' Cup launched
	c)	Asian Champions' Cup launched
1968	*a)*	Italy wins third European Nations' Cup
	b)	Juventus pays first million dollar transfer fee to Varese for Pietro Anastasi
	c)	Copa Interamericana launched
1969	*a)*	El Salvador and Honduras wage the Fútbol War
	b)	Pelé scores 1000th goal
1970	*a)*	Brazil wins ninth World Cup, in Mexico, and becomes first nation to win three world titles
	b)	Estudiantes wins third Copa Libertadores in succession
1971	*a)*	Tostão elected first American (Latin American) Footballer of the Year
	b)	use of five substitutes legalized by consenting clubs
1972		West Germany wins fourth European Football Championship
1973		Ajax wins third European Cup in succession
1974	*a)*	West Germany wins tenth World Cup, in West Germany
	b)	Johan Cruyff elected European Footballer of the Year for record third time
1975	*a)*	African Cup Winners' Cup launched
	b)	Independiente wins fourth Copa Libertadores in succession and sixth altogether
	c)	Pelé signs contract for record $3.5 million with New York Cosmos
1976	*a)*	Bayern München wins third European Cup in succession
	b)	Czechoslovakia wins fifth European Football Championship
	c)	Asian Football Confederation thrown into chaos over China and Israel questions
1977		world transfer market thrown into chaos by rising American purchasing power
1978		Argentina wins eleventh World Cup, in Argentina

hold

To grip an opponent or his clothing with the hand, an infringement penalized by the awarding of a direct free kick. Holding has been prohibited since the first football rules were drawn up in England during the early decades of the nineteenth century.

Holland   See: **Netherlands**

home and away   Also known as "home and home."

A two-legged series with one match played on a given team's home ground and the second match played on the opponent's home ground.

Home International Championship

Also known as "British International Championship."

The oldest international competition in the world. The Home Internationals have been contested annually between the four countries of the United Kingdom—England, Scotland, Wales, and Northern Ireland (formerly Ireland)—since 1883-84. The format has barely changed in all that time: the four teams play each other once on a point system and in case of an equal number of points the championship is shared. As of 1979-80, the title will be determined by goal difference in case of a tie.

International competition between the Home (British) countries actually began before 1883-84. The great England-Scotland confrontation officially got under way in 1872 (unofficially in 1870). England first played Wales in 1879 and Ireland in 1882. Wales began its series with Scotland in 1876 and Ireland in 1882. The four-way championship was heralded by Scotland's first meeting with Ireland in 1884.

It has been won outright 63 times as of 1978 (England-31, Scotland-24, Wales-7, and Ireland-1). In 83 competitions, there has been only one quadruple tie (1956). England's predominance has been due largely to post-World War II results; before 1940, Scotland had the edge over England by 18-16. All the Welsh victories occurred before World War II, and Ireland won its lone title in 1914, eight years before the Irish Free State was founded.

Until 1968, Home International matches were played during the course of the regular season, but the declining importance of the series, as British national teams increased their participation in other international competition, eventually forced the planners to set aside a week at the end of the season. In Scotland, the series is still highly significant, especially the ancient rivalry with England, the "auld enemy," and in Wales and Northern Ireland the series has become an important source of revenue. Eire has not yet participated, but in the mid-1970s its repeated efforts to be included fell on increasingly sympathetic ears.

A number of peculiarities regarding the series deviate from FIFA regulations and accepted customs elsewhere. Its very existence is based on a unique autonomy allowed the Home countries in deference to the fact that the modern game was created and developed in Britain, and because FIFA has been under the influence of the British associations since 1906. Traditional rules governing the nationality of British players stated that a player must play for a country in which he was born. Players born abroad were allowed to choose the country of their father's birth. In 1971, however, the qualifications were loosened to allow all players to choose their father's country. By special arrangement with FIFA, Northern Ireland may choose players born in Eire for Home Internationals only. In addition, since 1924 the British associations have been exempt from paying a levy to FIFA on any Home International matches, though the agreement does not apply to other internationals involving British teams.

The championship was suspended during the war years from 1914-15 to 1918-19 and from 1939-40 to 1945-46. It doubled as a World Cup qualifying group in 1949-50 and 1953-54, Scotland proudly refusing to make the trip to Brazil in 1950 unless they placed first (they did not), and in 1966-67 and 1967-68 it doubled as a European Football Championship qualification group.

Final Standings

Year		P		P		P		P
1884	Scotland	6	England	4	Wales	2	Ireland	0
1885	Scotland	5	England	4	Wales	3	Ireland	0
1886	Scotland	5	England	5	Wales	2	Ireland	0
1887	Scotland	6	England	4	Ireland	2	Wales	0
1888	England	6	Scotland	4	Wales	2	Ireland	
1889	Scotland	5	England	4	Wales	3	Ireland	0
1890	Scotland	5	England	5	Wales	2	Ireland	0
1891	England	6	Scotland	4	Ireland	2	Wales	0
1892	England	6	Scotland	4	Ireland	1	Wales	1
1893	England	6	Scotland	4	Ireland	2	Wales	0
1894	Scotland	5	England	4	Wales	2	Ireland	1
1895	England	5	Scotland	3	Wales	2	Ireland	2
1896	Scotland	5	England	4	Wales	2	Ireland	1
1897	Scotland	5	England	4	Ireland	2	Wales	1
1898	England	6	Scotland	4	Ireland	2	Wales	0
1899	England	6	Scotland	4	Ireland	2	Wales	0
1900	Scotland	6	England	3	Wales	3	Ireland	0
1901	England	5	Scotland	4	Wales	3	Ireland	0
1902	Scotland	5	England	4	Ireland	2	Wales	1
1903	Scotland	4	England	4	Ireland	4	Wales	0
1904	England	5	Ireland	3	Scotland	2	Wales	2
1905	England	5	Wales	3	Ireland	2	Scotland	2
1906	England	4	Scotland	4	Wales	3	Ireland	1
1907	Wales	5	England	4	Scotland	3	Ireland	0
1908	England	5	Scotland	5	Ireland	2	Wales	0
1909	England	6	Wales	4	Scotland	2	Ireland	0
1910	Scotland	4	England	3	Ireland	3	Wales	2
1911	England	5	Scotland	4	Wales	3	Ireland	0
1912	England	5	Scotland	5	Ireland	2	Ireland	0
1913	England	4	Scotland	3	Wales	3	Ireland	2
1914	Ireland	5	Scotland	4	England	2	Wales	1
1915-20			(not played during war years)					
1920	Wales	4	Scotland	3	England	3	Ireland	2
1921	Scotland	6	Wales	3	England	3	Ireland	0
1922	Scotland	4	Wales	3	England	3	Ireland	2
1923	Scotland	5	England	4	Ireland	2	Wales	1
1924	Wales	6	Scotland	3	Ireland	2	England	1
1925	Scotland	6	England	4	Wales	1	Ireland	1
1926	Scotland	6	Ireland	3	Wales	2	England	1
1927	Scotland	4	England	4	Ireland	2	Wales	2
1928	Wales	5	Ireland	4	Scotland	3	England	0
1929	Scotland	6	England	4	Wales	1	Ireland	1
1930	England	6	Scotland	4	Ireland	2	Wales	0
1931	England	4	Scotland	4	Wales	3	Ireland	1
1932	England	6	Scotland	4	Ireland	2	Wales	0

1933	Wales	5	Scotland	4	England	3	Ireland	0
1934	Wales	5	England	4	Ireland	3	Scotland	0
1935	England	4	Scotland	4	Wales	2	Ireland	2
1936	Scotland	4	England	3	Wales	3	Ireland	2
1937	Wales	6	Scotland	4	England	2	Ireland	0
1938	England	4	Scotland	3	Ireland	3	Wales	2
1939	England	4	Scotland	4	Wales	4	Ireland	0
1940-46			(not played during war years)					
1947	England	5	Ireland	3	Scotland	2	Wales	2
1948	England	5	Wales	4	Ireland	3	Scotland	0
1949	Scotland	6	England	4	Wales	2	Ireland	0
1950	England	6	Scotland	4	Wales	1	Ireland	1
1951	Scotland	6	England	4	Wales	2	Ireland	0
1952	England	5	Wales	5	Scotland	2	Ireland	0
1953	England	4	Scotland	4	Wales	2	Ireland	2
1954	England	6	Scotland	3	Ireland	2	Wales	1
1955	England	6	Scotland	3	Wales	2	No. Ireland	1
1956	England	3	Scotland	3	Wales	3	No. Ireland	3
1957	England	5	Scotland	3	Wales	2	No. Ireland	2
1958	England	4	No. Ireland	4	Scotland	2	Wales	2
1959	England	4	No. Ireland	4	Scotland	3	Wales	1
1960	England	4	Scotland	4	Wales	4	No. Ireland	0
1961	England	6	Wales	4	Scotland	2	No. Ireland	0
1962	Scotland	6	Wales	3	England	2	No. Ireland	1
1963	Scotland	6	England	4	Wales	2	No. Ireland	0
1964	England	4	Scotland	4	No. Ireland	4	Wales	0
1965	England	5	Wales	4	Scotland	3	No. Ireland	0
1966	England	5	No. Ireland	4	Scotland	2	Wales	1
1967	Scotland	5	England	4	Wales	2	No. Ireland	1
1968	England	5	Scotland	3	Wales	2	No. Ireland	2
1969	England	6	Scotland	3	No. Ireland	2	Wales	1
1970	England	4	Scotland	4	Wales	4	No. Ireland	0
1971	England	5	Scotland	3	Wales	2	No. Ireland	2
1972	England	4	Scotland	4	No. Ireland	3	Wales	1
1973	England	6	No. Ireland	4	Scotland	2	Wales	0
1974	England	4	Scotland	4	Wales	2	No. Ireland	2
1975	England	4	Scotland	3	No. Ireland	3	Wales	2
1976	England	6	England	4	Wales	2	No. Ireland	0
1977	Scotland	5	Wales	4	England	2	No. Ireland	1
1978	England	6	Wales	3	Scotland	2	No. Ireland	1

Honduras

Federación Nacional Deportiva Extraescolar
  de Honduras
Apartado 331
Tegucigalpa, D.C.

Founded: 1935
FIFA: 1946
CONCACAF: 1961

Affiliated clubs: *365;* registered players: *10,510 (300 non-amateur);* national stadium: *Estadio Nacional, Norte e Sur (22,000);* stadium of equal size: *Francisco Morazan, San Pedro Sula (22,000);* colors: *blue jerseys, white shorts;* season: *February to October;* honors: *Olimpia, CONCACAF Club Champions' Cup (1972).*

Honduras is not the weakest soccer-playing country in Central America—that honor is shared by Nicaragua and Panama, not to mention Belize—but it is one of the few that has failed to have at least one period of encouraging international results at the national level. The future of Honduran soccer rests in its clubs because two distinct centers of soccer activity have emerged in recent years—Tegucigalpa, the capital, and San Pedro Sula, the industrial center on the other side of the country. Like Ecuador, Honduras promises to profit from this sort of cross-cultural rivalry.

The post-World War I soccer boom in Central America took place in Honduras as it did in Costa Rica, Guatemala, and El Salvador. The national association was founded as part of the Federación Nacional de Cultura Fisica y Deportes de Honduras in 1935, and joined FIFA in 1946 with over 40 clubs registered and a thousand players on the rosters. A national team played in the first Central American and Caribbean Games in 1930, winning in its international debut over Jamaica (5-4) and crashing to Cuba only two days later by a score of 7-0. In the same tournament, Honduras suffered lopsided defeats to Cuba (5-0) and Costa Rica (8-0), but recorded its second victory over hapless El Salvador (4-1). Ultimately, it placed third in a field of six. After a fifth place finish in the second edition

in 1935, Honduras did not appear in regional competition again until the third edition of the Central American and Caribbean Championship in 1946, in which it was one of five countries that played and lost to Costa Rica.

In 1951, an upheaval in Honduran sports administration circles produced a new governing body, the Directorio de la Federación Nacional Deportiva Extraescolar (Directorate of the National Federation of Extracurricular Sports). By this time, there were a pair of national championships, the Winston Churchill Cup and the Copa Comunicaciones Electricas, contested by regional and departmental champions, but there was still no national league. All of these competitions were played under a league format, and this tradition is carried on today with a national league of 89 clubs and various regional leagues that include almost 200 clubs throughout the country. Two clubs have stood out in Honduran competition—Olímpia, which brought glory to Honduras by winning the CONCACAF club championship in 1972, and Deportiva Motagua, from the Caribbean port town of the same name. Honduras has frequently participated in CONCACAF championships since the 1950s, but after placing well in the 1974 World Cup qualifying rounds it failed to enter the 1978 edition.

Hong Kong

Hong Kong Football Association
Sports Road-Happy Valley
G.P.O. Box 233
Hong Kong

Founded: 1915
FIFA: 1954
AFC: 1954

Affiliated clubs: *66;* registered players: *2,350 (70 professional, 180 non-amateur);* national stadium: *Hong Kong Government Stadium, Hong Kong (28,000);* largest stadium: *Hong Kong Government Stadium;* colors: *red jerseys, blue shorts;* season: *September to June;* honors: *none.*

Hong Kong, the first Asian country to adopt full professionalism in senior-level competition, is on the verge of becoming a major soccer power in East Asia. Hong Kong has produced highly skilled players for many

years, but in general has been unable to mold cohesive teams and sound tactics. Yet in recent World Cup qualifying rounds and other Asian tournaments, it has been a genuine threat to the more established countries of the region.

Soccer was introduced in the Hong Kong colony by British missionaries, military personnel, and technicians in the 1880s or before. The game was primarily played by the British for several decades, though some Chinese schoolboys learned it in British schools, and the British founded the Hong Kong Football Association (HKFA) in 1915. The HKFA was affiliated with The Football Association in London until 1954, when it secured permission from the English to join FIFA. Many clubs were established before and after the First World War by the British, but the Chinese did not become important participants until the 1920s.

The first recorded Hong Kong internationals were a series of three unofficial matches against the Philippines in the late 1940s. Hong Kong won all three, by 4-1 in 1948 (in Hong Kong), 5-1 in 1949 (Manila), and 5-1 in 1950 (Hong Kong). In 1953, an all-Hong Kong team lost to Indonesia at home, 4-1, and, in four matches with a representative team from South Africa, won two and lost two. The colony's fine facilities attracted the first Asian Cup in 1956, in which Hong Kong—in its official international debut—placed third in a field of four, losing to Israel and drawing with Republic of Korea and Republic of Vietnam. In 1964 and 1968, Hong Kong qualified for the final rounds of an expanded Asian Cup, but placed last on both occasions and failed to win a single game. Hong Kong has participated in three Asian Cups, and has played a total of 10 matches without a win.

There are 57 clubs in Hong Kong, 14 of which play in the first division, and all compete in an annual cup competition that attracts a wide following. The three major clubs are South China Athletic Association, Kowloon Motor Bus Sports Club, and Hong Kong Football Club.

Honvéd Sport Egyesület, Budapesti

Location: *Budapest, Hungary;* stadium: *Honvéd-Stadion (30,000);* colors: *red and white striped jerseys, white shorts;* honors: *Hungarian champion (1949-50, 1950, 1952, 1954, 1955), Hungarian cup winner (1964).*

Founded in 1948, this is the Budapest-based club of the Hungarian army (other army clubs are located elsewhere in the country). It is an outgrowth of Kispest SE from the southeastern Budapest suburb of that name, an historic spawning ground for high quality players. Honvéd is a term meaning "Hungarian soldier." Following the East European pattern, the Hungarian Ministry of Sports created Honvéd immediately after the Communist takeover to serve as a showcase for Hungarian soccer, and from the beginning every possible effort was put into making it successful. In its first few years of existence, it became, without question, one of the world's greatest teams, and generated the rise of Hungary to world preeminence as a soccer power in the early 1950s.

Honvéd entered league competition with the immortal Ferenc Puskás and Jószef Bozsik already in its lineup, at inside left and right half, respectively, and between the 1949-50 league season and the short 1950 season, of which Honvéd won, it acquired inside right Sandor Kocsis from Dorog and goalkeeper Gyula Grosics from Ferencváros. Honvéd was virtually unbeatable by 1950, though other Europeans had little chance to see it in action, given the absence of international competition at that time. Most of its players, however, were widely seen in the form of Hungary's national team, which included as many as six Honvéd members at one time during its world-record-breaking run of victories from 1950-54. Zoltan Czibor joined the team for a spell from Ferencváros, and most of the other famous names linked with the national team wore Honvéd jerseys at one time or another. In its peak year of 1952, the Honvéd lineup was as follows: Grosics; Rakoczi, Lorant, Banyai; Bozsik, Varosi; Budai II, Kocsis, Budai I, Puskás, Babolcsay.

In 1955-56, Honvéd was on its way to winning another title when the 1956 uprising broke out, and the league was suspended. As the tanks rolled into Budapest, Honvéd was in Bilbao, Spain, losing to Athletic Bilbao, 3-2, in a first round European Cup match. The return leg was held in neutral Brussels some days later, and the dampened spirits of the

Hungarian players could not be hidden as they barely held on to a 3-3 draw. This result was not enough to gain entry into the next round of the cup, and the legendary Honvéd team of the early 1950s disappeared from international competition. Puskás, Kocsis, and others fled to the West, and Honvéd was decimated by the loss. Government backing kept the club in the first division, but it never achieved anything like its former greatness, and since then has won little more than the Mitropa Cup in 1959 and one Hungarian cup in 1964.

Hungary

Magyar Labdarugok Szövetsége
(Hungarian Football Association)
Népköztársaság utja 47
1393 Budapest VI

Founded: 1901
FIFA: 1907
UEFA: 1954

Affiliated clubs: *2,915;* registered players: *157,102;* national stadium: *Népstadion, Budapest (80,000);* stadium of equal size: *Ferencvárosi T.C. Stadion, Budapest (80,000);* colors: *red jerseys, white shorts;* season: *August to November, March to June;* honors: *World Cup runner-up (1938, 1954), Olympic Games winner (1952, 1964, 1968), runner-up (1972), International Cup (1953), Ferencváros, Fairs Cup (1965), Mitropa Cup (1928, 1937), Újpest Dózsa, Mitropa Cup (1929, 1939).*

If England is traditionally the most respected country in world soccer and Brazil the most successful, then Hungary is the sentimental favorite. This exalted reputation stems from the extraordinary Hungarian national team that dominated international competition in the early 1950s—the "Magic Magyars"—without a doubt the greatest team ever assembled up to that time. This famous team has continued to be a source of pride in Hungary, but it has been a difficult image to live up to. Unfortunately, fine Hungarian teams that preceded or followed it have been overshadowed. Nor is it well known that Hungary was a genuine pioneer in European soccer and contributed enormously to the growth of the game in Central Europe, a region of considerable importance in the early years.

In company with Austria and Bohemia, Hungarian teams learned the sophisticated Scottish short passing game from British coaches and combined it with their growing high standards of skill. Unlike Austria and Czechoslovakia, however, the focus of Hungarian soccer has remained on the capital city—Budapest—throughout the post-World War II era.

Soccer is thought to have been introduced in Budapest in 1879 by an English student by the name of Ray, a few years before it arrived in Austria or Czechoslovakia. Újpest Sport Club (later Újpest Dózsa) was formed in the Budapest suburb of Ujpest in 1885. The Budapest Gymnastic and Athletic Club introduced a soccer team in 1888 under the name Magyar Testgyakorlók Köre (MTK), or "Hungarian Gymnastics Club," and other British-based clubs followed. Despite the later fame of Újpest and MTK, the first important name in Hungarian soccer was Budapesti Torna Club (BTC), or "Budapest Gymnastics Club," which arranged the first public soccer match in the country: in 1897, two teams from BTC played a game at the Millenaris grounds in Budapest before 100 spectators. The most important club in Hungarian soccer, Ferencváros Torna Club (FTC), was founded in 1899.

In 1901, the Magyar Labdarugok Szövetsége (MLS), the first and only national governing body in Hungary, was founded in Budapest by 13 clubs, and an annual championship was introduced simultaneously, the first two league titles going to BTC. The famous Southampton F. C. tour of Austria-Hungary also occurred in 1901. This was an important milestone in Central European soccer, and the English club defeated Budapest selections twice, 8-0 and 13-0. BTC's leadership role was taken over after the turn of the century by FTC, which won its first championship in 1903. Lacking the experience of Austrian players who had competed annually since 1896 with Bohemian teams, Hungary was a participant in the very first full international played outside the British Isles in 1902. This was Austria's historic 5-0 defeat of the Magyars in Vienna, and it was the beginning of the world's longest-running non-British rivalry. In 1903, Hungary played host to Bohemia and Austria in Budapest, and won its first matches (2-1 and 3-2, respectively).

The MLS joined FIFA in 1907 and entered the soccer competition of the 1908 Olympic Games, the first officially recognized international tournament, but withdrew before its opening round match with Holland because of political tensions at home. Meanwhile, several Budapest clubs had begun to participate in Vienna's Der Challenge Cup, and FTC, which was already sharing all the honors in the Hungarian league with MTK, won the Austrian trophy in 1909. England became the first full international team other than Austria and Bohemia to play Hungary in 1908; it won 7-0 in Budapest. There were several additional matches with Austria and Bohemia, and Germany visited Budapest in 1909, gaining a 3-3 draw. Subsequently, Hungary lost twice again to England, defeated Italy twice (home and away), defeated France (in Paris), and split home and away matches with Switzerland and two more with Germany before traveling to Sweden for the 1912 Olympic Games.

In Sweden, a 7-0 loss to Great Britain's amateurs put the Hungarians out of the official competition, but in the consolation tournament for disqualified teams they defeated Germany and Austria and were declared the best of that group. One week later, the Olympic team went to Moscow and trounced Czarist Russia 9-0 and 12-0. Hungary produced its first great star during this period, Imre Schlosser, a goalscoring inside left who became famous throughout Europe after his international debut in 1906 and who led FTC to seven championships between 1905-13. FTC's hold on the league was broken in 1914 by MTK, FTC's keen crosstown rival.

In 1916, English coach Jimmy Hogan arrived at MTK from an internment camp in Vienna and single-handedly changed the course of Hungarian soccer. Hogan brought with him the philosophy and tactics of the Scottish short passing game that he had earlier taught in Austria, and he transformed MTK into an all-conquering team. One of his first important acts was the discovery of György

Orth in a Budapest park in 1916, and it was Orth who led MTK to 10 successive Budapest championships through 1925 (the first four from 1916-19 did not count as official titles). Hogan's teachings spread throughout Budapest, and by the time his all too brief stay was over, a Hungarian version of the "Danubian style" emerged. It was based on skilled passing and a sophisticated sense of positioning, and contributed significantly to Hungary's development as an international power.

The rivalry with Austria continued unabated after World War I until the Olympic break of 1924 with mixed results. This combination of success and failure was typical of Hungary's overall status in international competition at that time. At the 1924 Olympics, Hungary suffered one of its worst upsets of all time: after a 5-0 defeat of Poland the Magyars were eliminated by Egypt (3-0) in the first round. Mixed results continued over the next several years, and in the first edition of International Cup (1927-29) Hungary placed fourth in a field of five. This competition was the beginning of Austria's hegemony over Central European soccer, and Italy was rapidly on the upswing; Hungary's day would come. In 1926, professionalism was sanctioned by the MLS, signaling an important change. Ferencváros, as FTC was now called, won the important Mitropa Cup in 1928 and Újpest did the same in 1929. Full-time devotion to their work enabled Hungary's wealth of talented players to polish their technique and develop their inimitable style. In the course of Hungary's 10 years of legalized professionalism (1926-35), the national cup competition, which had been running intermittently since 1909 under the name Wanderer's Cup, enjoyed almost unbroken competition, and for the first time non-Budapest clubs participated in the first division: the coveted Budapest championship was no longer one and the same as the national championship. Ferencváros, Újpest, and Hungaria (MTK's temporary new name) dominated the professional era and the prewar years that followed.

There were further mixed results in international competition, however, and in the second and third editions of the International Cup (1931-32 and 1933-35) Hungary finished in the middle of the table. In the 1934 World Cup, gained after eliminating Bulgaria with considerable ease, Hungary partially avenged its 1924 Olympic loss to Egypt by defeating the Egyptians 4-2. In the second round, Hungary faced its old rival Austria; this match was uncharacteristically turbulent, Austria's *Wunderteam* getting the upper hand over the Magyars by a score of 2-1.

Hungary's national team was by now one of the best in Europe despite its failure to beat mighty Austria. The stars were center forward Dr. György Sarosi of Ferencváros, outside left Pal Titkos of MTK, and inside left Geza Toldi of Ferencváros, the latter one of the finest tandems on the international scene. Immediately preceding the 1934 World Cup, Hungary had defeated England for the first time (in Budapest) by a score of 2-1. After mixed results in 1935 and 1936, Hungary's stature was given a new boost in 1937 with a 8-3 win over Czechoslovakia in the International Cup. Seven goals were scored by Dr. Sarosi. Hungary's 11-1 trouncing of Greece in the World Cup qualification rounds set the stage for its entry into the 1938 World Championship in France.

In the first round at Reims, Sarosi and his exceptional inside left Gyula Zsengeller scored two goals apiece in a 6-0 rout of the Dutch East Indies, and in the second round Zsengeller again scored two in a 2-0 win over Switzerland. Hungary's opponent in the semifinal was Sweden, which like Brazil was coached by a Hungarian, but the so-called "team of steel" proved to be Hungary's easiest opponent. Zsengeller converted a hat trick, and Hungary was merciful in holding the score down to 5-1. With its advance to the final of the 1938 World Cup, Hungary had deservedly reached the pinnacle of international competition. Italy, however, was a most formidable opponent and the Italian forward trio of Meazza, Piola, and Ferrari was too highly motivated to be contained by the Hungarian defense. Despite the presence of Hungary's excellent goalkeeper Antal Szabo and speedy left back Sandor Biro, both of MTK, Meazza was able to set up three goals and keep Italy in Hungary's half of the field for most of the game. The final score was 4-2, but, as in 1934 against Austria, Hungary had lost to the best team in Europe. Hungary's sinuous style in the "Danubian" tradition was firmly established, and even if the harshness of Italy's technique had won the day, Hungary's prestige as a major international power was assured. This was further reflected by the growing demand for Hungarian coaches in both Europe and South America from the 1930s on.

During World War II Ferencváros and Vasas Csepel (another Budapest club) took most of the honors in the national league, and the Hungarian cup was revitalized after a five-year absence in the late 1930s. In 1941, Szolnok became the first club from outside the Budapest area to win the cup, and Ferencvaros captured the other three wartime editions. The first division championship was also won for the first time in 1943-44 by a non-Budapest club—Nagyvarad, from the present-day Rumanian city of Oradea. This was to be one of only two league titles won by a provincial club in the history of Hungarian soccer. (Vasas Györ's in 1963 was the other.)

After World War II, all official competitions except the national league came to a halt while political matters were resolved. The cup did not resume until 1952 and then only sporadically. Meanwhile the domestic structure of the Hungarian game changed considerably after the birth of the Communist government in 1947. The most important event was the founding of the army club, Honvéd Sport Egyesület, in 1948, which absorbed the suburban club Kispest in the process. Honvéd was given priority treatment from the beginning and got first choice of the best players. In 1948-49, its first season in the first division, Honvéd won the championship. Other clubs were reorganized by the new Ministry of Sport. Újpest became Újpest Dózsa, and MTK went through several more name changes including Bastya and Vörös Lobogo.

Seething under all this reorganization was a stunning array of talent. Honvéd alone came alive with inside left Ferenc Puskás and right half József Bozsik on the roster, and in 1950 the club acquired inside right Sandor Kocsis and goalkeeper Gyula Groscis; MTK had inside right Nandor Hidegkuti and Ferencváros had ouside left Zoltan Czibor. These gifted players were eventually rated as the world's greatest at their respective positions—Hidegkuti in his adopted function as deep-lying center forward for the national team—and all but Hidegkuti eventually played for Honvéd. Gustav Sebes emerged in the late 1940s as overseer of the national team, and while the Ministry of Sport kept Hungary virtually out of postwar international competition (except for the new edition of the International Cup in 1948), Sebes was able to bring together the unique talents of his players to build a remarkable team.

Between May 1950, when it lost to Austria in Vienna, and February 1956, a loss to Turkey in Istanbul, Hungary played 48 games with only one defeat. Its full international record during this unprecedented run was: 48-40-7-1-205-57-87. Hungary managed to score at least once in every match, and averaged almost four goals per game. A stretch of 29 consecutive matches without a defeat from 1950-54 still stands as a world record. In fact, excluding the war years, Hungary was undefeated at home for 17 consecutive years from 1939-56, an all-time European record.

In the years immediately preceding this period, there were numerous lopsided victories—with scores like 9-0, 8-2, and 5-0—over Rumania, Bulgaria, Poland, Sweden, Czechoslovakia, and Austria. Shortly after the 1950 loss to Austria, Albania was buried 12-0, and Hungary began its climb to the top in earnest. Its first real showcase was the 1952 Olympic Games, whose list of entrants included full international teams from Eastern Europe and Scandinavia. After a modest 2-1 win over Rumania in the first round, Sebes' goalscoring machine buried Italy, Turkey, and Sweden, and in the final dominated the great Yugoslav team with a 2-0 win to take the gold medal. This was followed by the winning of the prolonged 1948-53 International Cup after a 3-0 romp over Italy in Rome. In November 1953, England's much-ballyhooed record of never having been beaten at home by a non-British team came to an end with a colossal 6-3 Hungarian win at Wembley. No single game in soccer history has achieved more fame and attention than this pivotal upset on England's sacred turf. It not only shocked English soccer out of its lingering complacency, but solidified Hungary's reputation as the greatest team of the era if not of all time. Hungary's lineup on that fateful day in London included: Grosics; Buzanszky, Lantos; Bozsik, Lorant, Zakarias; Budai II, Kocsis, Hidegkuti, Puskás, Czibor. To make things worse, Hungary flogged the English 7-1 in Budapest five months later.

The "Magic Magyars" entered the 1954 World Cup in Switzerland as the odds-on favorite in every bookmaking establishment from Belfast to Melbourne. Sebes had been elevated to deputy minister of sport, though he was still in charge of the national team, and Gyula Mandi took care of discipline and day-to-day training as field coach. In the first round, Hungary scored 17 goals to its opponents' three in huge wins over South Korea and cunning West Germany. In its 8-3 defeat of the Germans, however, Hungary lost Puskás, its captain and supreme player, on

a brutal tackle by Werner Liebrich. Kocsis scored seven goals between these two matches, Puskás another three, and five other players also scored.

Even without Puskás, Hungary went on to defeat Brazil in the quarter-finals and Uruguay, world champion, in the semifinals. The game with Brazil was particularly violent—known as the "Battle of Berne"—and is still a subject of great discussion. The final result, 4-2, was overshadowed by rough play, fights, and hurled missiles from the sidelines—some would say from Puskás himself—and afterward a wholesale invasion of the Hungarian locker room by Brazilian players. Bozsik, who by now had become a member of the Hungarian House of Deputies, was sent off, and players on both teams were stained with blood and caked with mud. This game was billed as the unofficial "final" between the world's two best teams, but neither would comment later on their belligerent behavior. The semifinal against Uruguay, on the other hand, was won by a similar score but the quality of play was close to perfection and the game still ranks as one of the most memorable internationals on record. Hungary was ahead by two goals until late in the second half, but Uruguay equalized on two goals by Juan Hohberg to force an overtime period. Kocsis scored twice in extra time to bring his total in the competition to 10, and Uruguay lost its first match ever in the World Cup.

Against the wishes of Sebes and Mandi, Puskás insisted on playing in the final against West Germany despite his nagging injury. This proved to be one of the key elements in Hungary's loss of the World Cup final—tragically its only defeat during that 48-game run between 1950-56. The other key element was manager Sepp Herberger's shrewd unleashing of his team's emotional energy after holding the Germans back in that deceptive first round loss. Through Puskás and Czibor, Hungary was leading 2-0 after eight minutes, but the limping Puskás and soaking rain neutralized Hungary's momentum, and the same swung Germany's way. By sheer determination, the Germans came back with three goals before the final whistle, and Hungary went down to defeat. The final score of 3-2 was indicative of the game's lasting image as a "classic" upset in World Cup history.

To prove that the World Cup result was indeed a fluke, the MLS drew up a heavy schedule for its national team in the remaining months of 1954 and throughout 1955. The upshot was another stunning series of 15 wins and three draws in only 16 months, including decisive victories over Austria, Czechoslovakia, Scotland, Italy, and Sweden. In 1956, Hungary's watershed loss to Turkey was followed by two more to Czechoslovakia and Belgium, and the entire glorious era was finally shattered in November by the Soviet invasion of Budapest. Puskás, Kocsis, and Czibor fled to the West, and international opinion turned against the remaining members of the world famous team.

The success of the "Magic Magyars" was rooted in the "Danubian style" that had grown out of Jimmy Hogan's teachings, and the level of expertise that players like Puskás, Kocsis, Hidegkuti, Bozsik, Czibor, and Budai II achieved was truly breathtaking. Yet their coalescence was actually the work of Gustav Sebes and a strict disciplinary system that may not have been possible in a different political climate. Tactical innovations to accommodate particular talents were also a key factor. The Hungarians reached their peak by playing a modified form of the 4-2-4 with a forward line that resembled a "W"—hence its designation as the "Hungarian W attack." The focal point was deep-lying center forward Hidegkuti, whose primary purpose was to feed his inside forwards in their more advanced positions. It was astonishing that these inside forwards were players of such complementary virtuosity—Puskás on the left probably had the hardest left-foot shot ever seen and Kocsis on the right possessed such command in the air that he was nicknamed the "Golden Head." Dazzling orthodox wingers, usually Lazslo Budai (Budai II) and Czibor, played the right and left, respectively, and the midfield consisted of two staggered players, Bozsik on the right side in constant support of the attack and MTK's Joszef Zakarias on the left, who dropped back into a virtual fullback position. The defense, which usually advanced into the opponent's half of the field on attacks, comprised Dorog's Jeno Buzanszky at right back and MTK's Mihaly Lantos at left back. At center back was the tough Vasas and Honvéd stopper Gyula Lorant. Grosics, a magnificent goalkeeper who inspired his defense with verbal directions, came out of the penalty area often and was sometimes referred to as a "fourth back." Their outstanding skills produced an intuitive and sophisticated style of play.

The 1956 political uprising would surely have ended Hungary's rank as an international power, but the depth of talent in the country, the players' sureness of style, and productive training techniques ensured another generation of potential excellence. Hungary qualified for the 1958 World Cup by eliminating Norway and Bulgaria, but in the final rounds a nervous and intimidated team—taunted by heckling fans and police—lost to Sweden and drew with Wales to force a replay with the latter. Wales won after center back Ferenc Sipos was sent off, and Hungary was eliminated from its first post-1956 World Cup. Bozsik, Hidegkuti, Grosics, and Budai II played in some of these matches, but they were now aging, and the goalscoring was left to Honvéd's young inside forward Lajos Tichy. Better results were seen in the 1962 World Cup, which the Hungarians reached by eliminating the Netherlands and East Germany. Tichy was now joined by Ferencváros' superb center forward Florian Albert, probably Hungary's finest player since the Puskás era, and England and Bulgaria were dutifully disposed of in the first round. In the quarter-finals, the much improved Czechs stopped the Albert-Tichy scoring machine with a 1-0 shutout, and Hungary bowed out again.

In addition to its World Cup endeavors, Hungary moved aggressively in the new European Nations' Cup and especially in Olympic tournaments. In 1962-64, Hungary placed third in the Nation's Cup after a semifinal loss to Spain (in Spain itself, the new home of Puskás and Kocsis), and in 1970-72 placed fourth. In Olympic competition, Hungary won its second and third gold medals in 1964 and 1968, and in 1972 won the silver medal. These Nations' Cup and Olympic teams were bolstered by Újpest's goalscoring forward Ferenc Bene, who led all scorers in the 1974 games at Tokyo. The prestige of these two Olympic wins was compromised because the first was actually won on an own goal by Czechoslovakia and in 1968 Hungary's opposition in all rounds but the final (Israel, Ghana, El Salvador, Guatemala, and Japan) was exceptionally weak.

The 1966 World Cup, however, enabled Hungary to stage a comeback. This team, led by Albert and Bene, had the misfortune of being in a first round group with Brazil and Portugal, the latter a sentimental favorite to challenge Brazil's hegemony. Portugal won its match after Hungarian goalkeeper Szentmihalyi was injured, but in the next game Albert

Perhaps the greatest team ever assembled: the incomparable "Magic Magyars," Hungary's national team of the early 1950s, on a Parisian stopover en route to their history-making 6-3 defeat of England in London; November 1953. (Back row, left to right) Landor, Palotas, Hidegkuti, Varhidi, Kovacs, Kocsis, Czibor, Budai II, Zakarias, Lorant; (front row) Geller II, Csordas, J. Toth, Sandor, Puskás, Grosics, Buzanszky. Missing: Bozsik.

gave one of the finest performances of the competition and led his team to a 3-1 defeat of Brazil, the latter's first World Cup loss since 1954. The game was a feast for the eyes in every way, and endeared Hungary to the hearts of international fans once again. In the quarter-finals, however, Hungary's growing nemesis, the USSR, played with power and intelligence—mainly power—and neutralized Albert to win.

Despite its 1968 Olympic gold medal, Hungary's decline began after the 1966 World Cup. With the eventual fading of Albert and Bene, Hungary's international fortunes suffered greatly, and its second place finish in the 1972 Olympics was achieved primarily because Hungary did not have to face another Eastern European opponent until the final. The post-Albert decline, unlike the short-lived shock of 1956-57, was genuine and pervasive in Hungarian soccer. Though Ferencvaros had become the first Eastern European club to win a major European championship in the 1964-

65 Fairs Cup, Hungarian clubs generally failed to do well in international competitions throughout the 1960s and 1970s. The level of play at home deteriorated substantially, and above all the grace and elegance of the old style was rarely seen. In the league, Vasas Budapest, the metalworkers' club, emerged in the 1960s and Újpest Dózsa started an amazing run of seven consecutive championships in 1969 that included four doubles.

The Hungarian first division of 18 clubs is now supported by a second division with another 18 clubs, and a third division of four regional sections with 20 clubs each. The impact of Hungary's qualification for the 1978 World Cup, its first in 12 years, was probably deleterious, given its eventual poor showing. In the meantime, Hungary is still one of the world's most successful international competitors with an overall record of 275 wins and only 130 defeats after approximately 500 matches (1902-78).

Champions

1901	BTC	1904	MTK
1902	BTC	1905	FTC
1003	FTC	1906	no champion

1907	FTC	1944	Nagyvarad/Ferencváros
1908	MTK	1945	Újpest
1909	FTC	1946	Újpest
1910	FTC	1947	Újpest
1911	FTC	1948	Vasas Csepel
1912	FTC	1949	Ferencváros
1913	FTC	1949-50	Honvéd
1914	MTK	1950	Honvéd
1915	no competition	1951	Bastya
1916	no competition	1952	Honvéd
1917	no competition	1953	Vörös Lobogo
1918	no competition	1954	Honvéd
1919	no competition	1955	Honvéd
1920	MTK	1956	discontinued
1921	MTK	1957	Vasas Budapest (shortened)
1922	MTK	1958	MTK
1923	MTK	1959	Vasas Csepel
1924	MTK	1960	Újpest Dózsa
1925	MTK	1961	Vasas Budapest
1926	FTC	1962	Vasas Budapest
1027	Ferencváros	1963	Ferencváros/Vasas Györ
1928	Ferencváros	1964	Ferencváros
1929	Hungaria	1965	Vasas Budapest
1930	Újpest	1966	Vasas Budapest
1931	Újpest	1967	Ferencváros
1932	Ferencváros	1968	Ferencváros
1933	Újpest	1969	Újpest Dózsa
1934	Ferencváros	1970	Újpest Dózsa
1935	Újpest	1971	Újpest Dózsa
1936	Hungaria	1972	Újpest Dózsa
1937	Hungaria	1973	Újpest Dózsa
1938	Ferencváros	1974	Újpest Dózsa
1939	Újpest	1974	Újpest Dózsa
1940	Ferencváros	1975	Újpest Dózsa
1941	Ferencváros	1976	Ferencváros
1942	Vasas Csepel	1977	Vasas Budapest
1943	Vasas Csepel	1978	Újpest Dózsa

Cup Winners

1910	MTK	1916	no competition	1922	FTC
1911	MTK	1917	no competition	1923	MTK
1912	MTK	1918	no competition	1924	no competition
1913	FTC	1919	no competition	1925	MTK
1914	MTK	1920	no competition	1926	Kispest
1915	no competition	1921	no competition	1927	Ferencváros

1928	Ferencváros	1945	no competition	1962	no competition
1929	no competition	1946	no competition	1963	no competition
1930	Bocskai	1947	no competition	1964	Honvéd
1931	III. Ker	1948	no competition	1965	Vasas Györ
1932	Hungaria	1949	no competition	1966	Vasas Györ
1933	Ferencváros	1950	no competition	1967	Vasas Györ
1934	Soroksar	1951	no competition	1968	MTK
1935	Ferencváros	1952	Bastya	1969	Újpest Dózsa
1936	no competition	1953	no competition	1970	Újpest Dózsa
1937	no competition	1954	no competition	1971	Újpest Dózsa
1938	no competition	1955	Vasas Budapest	1972	Ferencváros
1939	no competition	1956	Ferencváros	1973	Vasas Budapest
1940	no competition	1957	Ferencváros	1974	Ferencváros
1941	Szolnok	1958	Ferencváros	1975	Újpest Dózsa
1942	Ferencváros	1959	no competition	1976	Ferencváros
1943	Ferencváros	1960	no competition	1977	Diösgyör
1944	Ferencváros	1961	no competition	1978	Ferencváros

I

Iceland

Knattspyrnusamband Islands
(Football Association of Iceland)
P.O. Box 1011
Reykjavik

Founded: 1947
FIFA: 1929
UEFA: 1954

Affiliated clubs: *65;* **registered players:** *11,456 (one non-amateur);* **national stadium:** *Laugardalsvöllur, Reykjavik (15,000);* **largest stadium:** *Laugardalsvöllur;* **colors:** *blue jerseys, white shorts;* **season:** *May to October;* **honors:** *none.*

Tucked away on the Arctic Circle, Iceland has made the most of difficult circumstances, and may no longer be ranked with Malta and Cyprus at the bottom of the European charts. In the mid-1970s, within the space of two years, the Icelandic national team defeated East Germany, Norway, and Luxembourg, drew with France and East Germany, and lost by a respectable 1-0 to Holland, USSR, and Belgium (twice). For decades, soccer has been enthusiastically supported by Icelanders, and has served as a primary link between Iceland and its European cousins, though it is one of the smallest of all UEFA member-nations.

The oldest republic in the world began playing the game back in 1895, when a Scottish printer and bookseller named James Ferguson introduced it in Reykjavik. Little time was wasted in organizing clubs, and by 1912 an Icelandic championship was under way. International competition was still many years away, but in 1929 the Ithrottasamband Islands (Athletic Union of Iceland, founded 1912) was admitted to FIFA, and Iceland has remained a respected member of the world body ever since. The Knattspyrnusamband Islands (KSI) was formed in 1947 as an independent governing body for soccer, and immediately received FIFA's blessing. In 1954, Iceland became a charter member of UEFA, and today it remains almost entirely amateur.

In 1946, only eight months before the KSI's formation, Iceland made its international debut against Denmark in Reykjavik, losing 3-0, and two years later won for the first time in a home friendly against Finland (2-0). Since then, Iceland has played about 70 full internationals, one-third of them against Norway and Denmark, and has won a dozen times, including four against Norway. In 1953, the KSI filed an application to enter the 1954 World Cup, but unfortunately the papers were received after the deadline. Four years later, an inexperienced national team entered the World Cup qualifying rounds, and dropped two games apiece to France and Belgium by an aggregate of 6-26. Only financial difficulties, however, kept Iceland out of further World Cup qualifying rounds until 1974. Its first attempt to reach the Olympic Games was in 1959, when it achieved some decent results against Denmark and Norway in qualifying rounds.

Meanwhile, it boldly entered the 1962-64 European Nations' Cup, but was eliminated by the Republic of Ireland, gaining a draw at home. Iceland and Malta were the only two UEFA members not to participate in the 1966-68 edition, and Iceland was alone in this respect in 1970-72. But in 1974-76, the national team achieved its first genuine taste of success with the above-mentioned results against East Germany, France, and Belgium, though in group standings it still was not able to fare better than fourth place. The same fate awaited Iceland in the qualification rounds for the 1974 and 1978 World Cup. In 1974, it was grouped with Holland, Belgium, and Norway, and in 1978 with Holland, Belgium, and Northern Ireland. In friendlies over the years, Iceland has defeated the USA (3-2 in 1955), Bermuda twice, Finland, Sweden (back in 1951), and Norway. Its worst defeat was to Denmark in 1967 (14-2).

In domestic competition, the big four Reykjavik clubs—Fram, KR, Valur, and Vikingur—dominated the league consistently from 1912-51. Since the early 1950s, two provincial clubs, IA Akranes and IB Keflavik, both from towns nearby the capital, have managed to win a dozen championships between them. In the cup competition. which started in 1960, Reykjavik's strong grip has been broken occasionally by IB Akureyri, from a town of the same name in the north, and IB Vestmannaey, the main club of the volcanic Vestmannaeyjar Islands off the southern coast.

An Icelandic champion club first entered the European Cup in 1964-65. KR Reykjavik was unfortunate to meet Liverpool in the first round of that edition, but Icelandic clubs have entered the competition each year since. Valur reached the second round in 1967-68, as did IA Akranes in 1975-76. Iceland's frequency of participation in the European Cup Winners' Cup has been consistent since 1965-66, but none of the entrants has advanced beyond the first round. This has also been true of Icelandic clubs in the Fairs/UEFA Cup since 1969-70.

Climatic conditions on the island restrict the playing season to a seven-month period from May to October. With the exception of Reykjavik's big stadium, the Laugardalsvöllur, all the playing surfaces are composed of ash.

Consequently, all league and cup matches in the capital, as well as all internationals, are played on a staggered schedule in one stadium. Still, it is common for 10,000 spectators to turn out for an international, and most domestic games are viewed by 3,000-4,000 chilled customers. The league is divided into three divisions, eight clubs in the first, eight in the second, and 28 in the various regional sections of the third. The country's outstanding soccer personality is Albert Gudmundsson, who once played for Arsenal, Nice, Racing Club de Paris, and AC Milan, and whose assumption of the KSI presidency in 1968 led directly to the development of a higher international profile and a strong internal training program.

Champions

1912	KR Reykjavik	1935	Valur	1957	IA Akranes
1913	IA Fram (unofficial)	1936	Valur	1958	IA Akranes
1914	IA Fram (unofficial)	1937	Valur	1959	KR Reykjavik
1915	IA Fram	1938	Valur	1960	IA Akranes
1916	IA Fram	1939	IA Fram	1961	KR Reykjavik
1917	IA Fram	1940	Valur	1962	IA Fram
1918	IA Fram	1941	KR Reykjavik	1963	KR Reykjavik
1919	KR Reykjavik	1942	Valur	1964	IB Keflavik
1920	Vikingur	1943	Valur	1965	KR Reykjavik
1921	IA Fram	1944	Valur	1966	Valur
1922	IA Fram	1945	Valur	1967	Valur
1923	IA Fram	1946	IA Fram	1968	KR Reykajavik
1924	Vikingur	1947	IA Fram	1969	IB Keflavik
1925	IA Fram	1948	KR Reykjavik	1970	IA Akranes
1926	KR Reykjavik	1949	KR Reykjavik	1971	IB Keflavik
1927	KR Reykjavik	1950	KR Reykjavik	1972	IA Fram
1928	KR Reykjavik	1951	IA Akranes	1973	IB Keflavik
1929	KR Rekjavik	1952	KR Reykjavik	1974	IA Akranes
1930	Valur	1953	IA Akranes	1975	IA Akranes
1931	KR Reykjavik	1954	IA Akranes	1976	Valur
1932	KR Reykjavik	1955	KR Reykjavik	1977	IA Akranes
1933	Valur	1956	Valur	1978	Valur
1934	KR Reykjavik				

Cup Winners

1960	KR Reykjavik	1964	KR Reykjavik	1968	IB Vestmannaey
1961	KR Reykjavik	1965	Valur	1969	IB Akureyri
1962	KR Reykjavik	1966	KR Reykjavik	1970	IA Fram
1963	KR Reykjavik	1967	KR Reykjavik	1971	Vikingur

1972	IB Vestmannaey	1975	Valur	1977	Valur
1973	IA Fram	1976	Valur	1978	IA Akranes
1974	Valur				

Independiente, Club Atlético

Location: *Avellaneda, Argentina;* stadium: *Estadio Avellaneda (65,000);* colors: *red jerseys, red shorts;* honors: *Intercontinental Cup (1973), Copa Libertadores (1964, 1965, 1972, 1973, 1974, 1975), Copa Interamericana (1973, 1974, 1976), National Championship winner (1967, 1977, 1978), Argentine league champion (1922 AAAF, 1926 AAAF, 1938, 1939, 1948, 1960, 1963, 1970, 1971).*

Founded 1905 in the Buenos Aires suburb of Banfield by Argentine employees of a British-run store called the City of London who also played for Club Maipú Banfield. Their independence from Maipú was the source of the name for their new club. Among its early bases of operation was the industrial suburb of Avellaneda, where it finally settled down to become one of the first major clubs associated with working class interests. Independiente joined the first division in 1912, and moved to its present grounds, the first cement stadium in South America, in 1928. Its first few years were uneventful, but after joining the "outlaw" league of the early 1920s, two championships came its way and the club established itself among the "big five" of Argentine soccer.

Having joined the professional league in 1931, it entered its first era of greatness in the mid-1930s. Led by center forward Arsenio Erico, the finest player ever to have come out of Paraguay, "Inde" won back-to-back championships in 1938 and 1939. Erico scored 47 goals in the 1937 season, an Argentine record which still stands, and in the following two seasons he scored 43 and 40, respectively. This was the most attractive, and perhaps the greatest, team in Independiente's history. In the immediate postwar era, a second attack-oriented team supplied the forward line for Argentina's three consecutive South American Championships and won a first division championship in 1948.

In the 1960s, Independiente embarked on an extraordinary odyssey of domestic and international success with a tactical system rooted in the Italian *catenaccio,* the defensive-oriented formation that was to bring fame and glory to many Italian teams. In 1963, it won the first division without a defeat, led by the vicious Ruben Navarro at sweeper, and on the basis of this title won the next two editions of the Copa Libertadores (1964 and 1965). In 1964, Independiente entered the first of a record-breaking five Intercontinental Cup competitions, losing in three games to Inter Milan, the true masters of *catenaccio.* Its adopted tactical approach failed again in 1965 against Inter Milan, but in 1967, "Inde" achieved additional domestic honors by winning the first Campeonato Nacional of Argentina.

Independiente's second wave of international triumphs (1972-75) was more terrifying in its execution. All pretenses at a *catenaccio*-like system were laid to rest, and on the heels of Rácing Club's and Estudiantes' great success with violent tactics, Independiente entered its own era of brutality—then so much associated with Argentine soccer at all levels. It won four consecutive editions of the Copa Libertadores, followed by as many Intercontinental Cup competitions as the club could organize. But Rácing's and Estudiantes' reputations had preceded them, and in three of four possible transoceanic confrontations, the qualified European opponent refused to participate. In a one-match edition against Juventus (a substitute) in 1973, it finally won its first and only Intercontinental Cup in five attempts. All this had come about as a result of two first division championships in 1970 and 1971, its last domestic honors before a national championship was won again in 1977.

India

All India Football Federation
113/22, Brigade Road
Bangalore 560001

Founded: 1937
FIFA: 1948
AFC: 1954

Affiliated clubs: *1,857;* **registered players:** *40,854;* **national stadium:** *National Stadium, New Delhi (40,000);* **largest stadiums:** *Eden Garden Stadium, Calcutta (100,000), Corporation Stadium, Calicut (100,000);* **colors:** *light blue jerseys, white shorts;* **season:** *January to December;* **honors:** *Asian Cup runner-up (1964).*

The story of soccer in India is as varied as the regions within its borders. Despite the present location of the All India Football Federation in Mysore State, the Indian game is centered primarily in Calcutta, where in 1977 untold millions swarmed the streets hoping to get a glimpse of Pelé on his triumphant worldwide tour with the Cosmos. In much of the rest of the country, soccer takes a back seat to the traditional national game, field hockey. It is hardly surprising that with the pervasive British influence on the subcontinent, soccer was introduced to India at a very early date. The momentum that was generated by this longevity helped to keep Indian soccer at the forefront of the Asian game for several decades. The golden age of Indian soccer emerged during the 15-odd years following World War II. But other parts of Asia have caught up with and surpassed India's momentum since then, and there is no telling when the chaotic conditions in one of the world's most complex societies will allow it to flourish once again.

The birth of soccer in India is credited to A.G. Stack, an Englishman who was a professor at Presidency College in Calcutta. In 1883, Stack taught the game to his Indian students, who adopted it enthusiastically and passed it on to others. Within five years, many clubs had sprung up all over Calcutta, among them Shovabazar National Sport Club, Wellington Club, Canal Club, and Mohan Bagan. In 1888, the British established the Indian Football Association in Calcutta and gained direct affiliation with The Football Association in London. A knockout tournament was introduced in 1892, but it was confined to a few clubs, and in 1893, the much larger Indian Football Association Shield was launched and became the first important Indian competition. An Indian club did not wrestle the shield from British-based clubs

until 1911, when Mohan Bagan, later to become the most venerated name in Indian soccer, finally won. The first two Indian leagues of any importance were the Calcutta Football League (1898) and the Bombay Football League (1902).

The All India Football Federation (AIFF), a truly national association, was founded in 1937, and claimed an affiliated membership of 14 regional associations. In 1941, the AIFF introduced the National Football Championship (the Maharaja Santosh Trophy), contested by representative teams of each provincial association to determine the Indian champion. Its first winner was Bengal-Delhi. Before 1950, the trophy had been won at least once by Bengal-Bombay, Bengal-Mysore, and Bengal-Hyderabad.

India made its official international debut at the Olympic Games of 1948 in London, losing in the first round to France (Amateur) 2-1. This was followed by two friendlies with Wales (Amateur), lost 4-1 and drawn 0-0 in Wrexham and Swansea, respectively. In 1950, India actually qualified for the World Cup in Brazil after the withdrawal of Burma, the only other country in its qualifying group, but India too withdrew before the start of the competition, citing financial and organizational pressures. In 1951, India entered Asian competition with its winning of the first Asian Games Tournament—held in New Delhi—defeating Indonesia, Afghanistan, and Iran without conceding a goal. Qualifying again for the final rounds of the Olympic Games in 1952, India received its first serious international drubbing by Yugoslavia (10-1). The following year, it won the first International Quadrangular Tournament in Rangoon, defeating Pakistan, Ceylon, and Burma in consecutive matches.

India qualified for the Olympics again in 1956, and competing against a sparse field of

11 countries—only one of them a top flight team—it just missed collecting a bronze medal by losing to powerful Yugoslavia in the semifinals. In its final appearance in the Olympic Games in 1960, India placed last in its first round group and effectively bowed out of world competition. Its last hurrah in Asian tournament play occurred in 1964 when it took second place in the fourth Asian Cup, defeating Republic of Korea and Hong Kong and losing to the eventual winner, Israel. In A-level friendlies during its highly successful postwar era, India lost four games to the USSR by an aggregate score of 22-1.

One of India's main difficulties when it entered international competition was ad-justing to full-length games. Until the 1950s, all matches on the subcontinent lasted only 55 minutes, rather than the usual 90, to accommodate the damp and heavy heat in that part of the world. Three Indian teams—representative teams of state associations rather than actual clubs—participated in the now defunct Asian Champion Teams' Cup from 1968-71: Mysore State Team, West Bengal, and Punjab F.A. The hotly contested Calcutta League, still the nation's strongest, is dominated by East Bengal F.C., Mohammedan Sporting, and the ancient Mohan Bagan. Support for area clubs is divided strictly along religious or ethnic lines, as in the case of West Bengalis and East Bengalis.

Indirect free kick

A free kick from which a goal may not be scored. It is awarded to the offended side for the following infringements: dangerous play, charging unfairly, obstruction, charging the goalkeeper, a goalkeeper's taking more than four steps before releasing the ball from his hands, and a goalkeeper's holding up the game. In addition, an indirect free kick is awarded to an offended side when the offender is cautioned for: persistent infringements of the Laws, dissent, and ungentlemanly conduct. Finally, an indirect free kick is awarded to the opponent to restart the game after play has been stopped by the referee to send off a player, except when a separate offense requiring a more severe penalty has been committed at the same time.

Indonesia

Persatuan Sepakbola Seluruh Indonesia
(All Indonesia Football Federation)
Main Stadium Senagan, Gate VII
P.O. Box 2305
Djakarta

Founded: 1930
FIFA: 1952
AFC: 1954

Affiliated clubs: *1,900;* **registered players:** *69,000;* **national stadium:** *Senajan Stadium, Djakarta (110,000);* **largest stadium:** *Senajan Stadium;* **colors:** *red jerseys, white shorts;* **season:** *January to December;* **honors:** *none.*

In the world's largest archipelago, soccer officials have coped surprisingly well with insurmountable organizational difficulties. While only a small number of Indonesia's 130 million citizens (spread across 13,000 islands) compete in soccer leagues, the game is very popular and the government has gone to great lengths to accommodate this following. Indonesia has miraculously surfaced in the final rounds of two worldwide competitions. As Dutch East Indies, a representative team of the colonial *voetbalbond* qualified for the 1938 World Cup in France, where it was defeated in the first round. In 1956, Indonesia, a fledgling competitor on the international circuit, went through to the final rounds of the Olympic Games in Melbourne, and held mighty Russia to a scoreless draw before losing the replay 4-0. These were great moments in Indonesian soccer.

The Dutch were very handy in organizing soccer in their colonies, and in Batavia

(Djakarta) they established a governing body as early as 1930; this federation was affiliated for a short time with the KNVD in Holland. Six "county" associations were formed to organize competitions at the local level: West Java (in Bandung), Mid Java (Semarang), East Java (Surabaja), Sumatra (Medan), East (Celebes, Lesser Sunda Isles, and Moluccas), and Kalimantan Bandjarmasin (Borneo).

In 1949, the new government of Indonesia gave the governing body its present name, known under the abbreviation PSSI, and introduced a national championship in 1951. The first winner was Persibaja from the Javan city of Surabaja. Indonesia made its official international debut in the first Asian Games in 1951 at New Delhi—one of only six participants—losing to India, Afghanistan, and Iran without scoring a goal, and to Burma 4-1. Competing in Singapore on the way home, Indonesia won its first international against an unofficial Singapore selection, 4-1. In 1953, Indonesia defeated Hong Kong and the Philippines in away friendlies, 4-1 and 5-0, respectively, and in its first full international

against a European team lost to a traveling Yugoslav national team, 2-0. Indonesia's active participation in international competition during this period helped to pave the way for its fine performance in the 1956 Olympics.

Though Indonesia has been unsuccessful in qualifying for the World Cup and the Asian Cup, its prestige has been enhanced by its fine organization of the 1962 Asian Games tournament in Djakarta and especially by its own Djakarta Anniversary Tournament, launched in 1970 for national teams of Southeast Asia. Indonesia itself won the competition in 1972. It has also won Singapore's Pesta Sukan Tournament once, Malaysia's Merdeka Anniversary Tournament three times, and Thailand's King's Cup Tournament once.

Senajan Stadium in Djakarta is the largest facility in all of Asia, and the rest of the country features at least eight stadiums with capacities of 20,000 or more. Of the 270 clubs in Indonesia, 16 play in the national championship, and there are several national and regional cup competitions.

Infringement

A foul or offense against the Laws of the Game.

---

injury time

Time allowed at the end of either half to compensate for time lost because of an injury or any other stoppage. The decision to add injury time and how much to add is at the referee's discretion.

---

in play

A ball is "in play" when it has traveled the distance of its own circumference, unless: 1) the referee has not started play; 2) the ball is situated in touch or entirely across the goal line; or 3) otherwise prescribed by the Laws. An example of the third exception is the goal kick, in which the ball must travel beyond the kicker's penalty area to be "in play."

The most significant change in regulations governing "in play" is that relating to throw-ins. The original Laws of the Game (1863) stated that a ball was not "in play" from a throw-in until it touched the ground, whereas, today a ball from a throw-in needs only to cross the touch line.

Inside   Also known as "No. 8," and "No. 10."

The positions on a five-player forward line that lie between either wing and the center forward: the inside right on the right side of the line and the inside left on the left side. Inside forwards are usually at the vanguard of the attack, but they may also be deep-lying, as in the W-M system and its derivatives. A large number of the game's goalscoring masters have been inside forwards: Pelé, Puskás, Kocsis, Law, Sivori, and Košek, to name a few.

Inswinger

A pass or shot which curves toward the goal, usually in reference to a corner kick.

See also: **outswinger**

Intention

A concept in the Laws of the Game that refers to a player's deliberately taking an action. The Laws became significantly more sophisticated with the introduction of the word "intentional" to the revised Laws of 1897. It specifically referred to the handling rule, but the new term eventually clarified the rules governing most fouls and misconducts, i.e., kicking, tripping, jumping, charging, striking, holding, and pushing, and for this reason its addition holds an important place in the history of the game.

Interamericana, Copa

An annual club competition, in which the winner of the Copa Libertadores, the South American championship, meets the winner of the CONCACAF Champions' Cup, the championship of North and Central America and the Caribbean. The South American entries have won every year but one. It was not played in 1969, 1970, 1973, and 1975, because competing clubs could not agree on mutually beneficial conditions. Though games are played on a home and away basis (on a point system), sites are usually set in neutral countries to help defray travel costs. The cup is not recognized by FIFA, and is therefore unofficial.

Results

1968	Estudiantes (Arg)—Toluca (Mex)	1-2, 2-1, 3-0
1971	Nacional (Uru)—Cruz Azul (Mex)	2-1, 1-1
1972	Independiente (Arg)—Olímpia (Hond)	2-0, 2-1
1974	Independiente (Arg)—Dep. Municipal (Guat)	1-0, 0-1
	(Independiente won on penalty kicks)	
1976	Independiente (Arg)—Atlético Español (Mex)	2-2, 0-0
	(Independiente won on penalty kicks)	
1978	Boca Júniors (Arg)—América (Mex)	3-0, 0-1, 1-2

Intercept

To interrupt the course of an opponent's pass.

Intercontinental Cup

Also known as "World Club Championship,"
"European-South American Cup," and
"European-South American Friendship Cup."

Coupe Intercontinentale—Weltpokal—Campeonato Mundial dos Clubes—Copa Intercontinental—Coppa Intercontinentale/Coppa Europa-Sud America.

An annual competition played on a home and away basis between the winners of the European Champions' Cup and the Copa Libertadores, the South American club championship. It was inaugurated in 1960 by UEFA and CONMEBOL to determine a "world" club champion. Before 1969, it was played on a point basis, necessitating a play-off in case of split results, and from 1969 the winner has been decided on goal aggregate. The earlier system was replaced because play-offs were invariably held on the continent of the second leg home team in order to help curb travel costs, and in each case where a play-off determined the winner the home team had won the competition.

The Intercontinental Cup has produced nine winners from South America and eight from Europe, but the results have been vastly overshadowed through the years by an epidemic of brutal and bloody playing tactics on the field, giving rise to the series' reputation as the battleground for European-South American bitterness. In addition, the tendency of European and South American elements to regard the winner as a "world" champion has consistently been opposed by African, Asian, and CONCACAF officials, as well as by FIFA. In 1962, FIFA formally declined to sponsor the competition, stating that a contest between the champion clubs of two continents did not constitute a world club championship, but a friendly between two clubs. To signify its position, FIFA donated a trophy called the "European-South American Friendship Cup," and it is by this name that FIFA refers to the series. Although champions' cups of Europe, South America, Africa, CONCACAF, and Asia already exist, FIFA regards the idea of a true world club championship as premature.

The only bright spots in the ravaged history of the Intercontinental Cup were the first three editions. Real Madrid, the champion club of Europe five times in a row, defeated the mighty Peñarol of Uruguay in the first competition in 1960 after a memorable exhibition of five goals in the second leg at Madrid. In 1961, Peñarol reversed the figures and scored five goals in its home leg against the rising star of Benfica Lisbon, and in the play-off at Montevideo, Peñarol prevailed in spite of the debut of Benfica's new sensation Eusebio, who had been flown in from Portugal for the game. In 1962, Benfica again represented Europe, but this time its opponent was Santos of Brazil and the incomparable Pelé. After an imaginative win at home, Santos defeated Benfica in Lisbon with a dazzling display that caught the imagination of all Europe and helped to gain worldwide recognition for the club. Among Santos' five goals in Lisbon was a hat trick from Pelé, and Santos became the first and only Brazilian club to win the Intercontinental Cup.

The rumblings of serious trouble began the following year. Santos and AC Milan split the first two legs by identical scores, and a play-off was scheduled for Rio de Janeiro. Predictably, Santos emerged the winner with a home field advantage, but there were many incidents throughout the game. Two players were ejected, and the trophy was won by a controversial penalty kick.

In 1964 and 1965, the contest was played by Inter Milan and Independiente, the Buenos Aires club that was to win six South American club championships. Inter won both these editions with its patented *catenaccio* system, and despite some hard play there were no serious incidents. The 1966 edition was marked by Peñarol's inevitable rise to the summit of international club competition. On three goals by Alberto Spencer, the Uruguayan champion won both legs against a rebuilt Real Madrid side that no longer included the legendary Di Stefano and Puskás.

In 1967, the European champion, Celtic of Glasgow, defeated Argentina's Rácing Club in a deceptively trouble-free and well-played first leg at home. The return leg in Buenos Aires, however, had not yet started when spectators pelted Celtic goalkeeper Simpson with stones, forcing him to withdraw from the game before the kickoff. The match was allowed to start, and despite some rough play and Celtic indignation it was finished without further incident. Rácing won, and a play-off in Montevideo was scheduled. In the Uruguayan capital tempers were short from the outset. When Rácing's Basile spat on Celtic's Lennox, the small Scottish forward Jimmy Johnstone retaliated, and the ire of both teams was unleashed. A melee broke out on the field; three Scots and two Argentines were ejected. The Celtic management fined each of its offending players £250, and the high international reputation of British sportsmanship was dealt a major blow. Rácing, meanwhile, was handed the trophy by virtue of its 1-0 win in Montevideo, and the world press decried the dirty tactics that were rapidly becoming associated with the Argentine game.

The series was terrorized for the next three years by Argentina's Estudiantes, winner of three successive South American club championships after a single domestic title in 1967. In 1968 Manchester United was hacked to a first leg 1-0 defeat in Buenos Aires, and Stiles and Charlton were ejected for innocuous fouls. At Manchester, Best and Medina were ejected for taking punches at each other, and Estudiantes' playing tactics on the field included numerous distractions that were meant to be seen and felt by United players and not the referee. The second leg ended in a dissatisfying draw. Sir Stanley Rous, President of FIFA, sent an official letter of reprimand to Estudiantes' management.

After AC Milan's first leg home victory over Estudiantes in 1969, the Argentine players openly taunted the winning team, and "warned" it not to make the trip to Buenos Aires for the return leg. In Buenos Aires, Milan midfielder Nector Combin, an Argentine by birth, was provoked incessantly. Estudiantes back Aguirre Suárez called him a

"traitor" and in the scuffle broke his nose and knocked him unconscious. Aguirre Suárez and Estudiantes' second back Manera were ejected, and a full-scale fight ensued. Though Estudiantes nominally won the match, Milan won the competition and took the Intercontinental Cup to Italy for a third time. The incidents, however, were so shocking that three Estudiantes players were eventually jailed on orders from Argentina's President, General Onganía, and suspensions were levied against them.

Neither Aguirre Suárez nor Manera appeared for Estudiantes in the 1970 edition of the series against Feyenoord, won by the Dutch club on a victory in the home leg, but Feyenoord publically denounced Estudiantes for playing "anti-football," and European clubs were by now wary of participating in the competition at all. In 1971, European champions Ajax Amsterdam became the first to decline (causing more hurt feelings in South America), and UEFA offered the berth to losing finalist Panathinaïkos of Athens, which jumped at the chance for a brief period of world glory. Its opponent was Nacional of Uruguay, the archrival of Peñarol. It was an incident-free series, and Panathinaïkos represented Europe admirably, but in the end, Nacional's vast superiority prevailed on three goals by its opportunistic center forward Luis Artime.

The next four competitions, in which the Copa Libertadores winners Independiente of Buenos Aires represented South America on each occasion, saw the resumption of bullying tactics and European reluctance to participate. In 1972, Ajax was hesitant but agreed to play. In the first leg at Buenos Aires, Johan Cruyff, the Dutch striker who had become the new idol of European soccer, was fouled by left wing Mircoli and had to leave the game, but Ajax still managed to force a draw. In Amsterdam, however, Ajax upheld its reputation as the finest club in the world, and flowed skillfully to a 3-0 shutout and Intercontinental Cup victory. The Ajax management announced in a public statement that its club would never again play in the Argentine Republic.

To take Ajax's place in 1973, the losing European Cup finalist, Juventus of Italy, consented to play in a one-match tournament that must take place on European soil. Rome was selected as the venue, and the Argentine club won the game. It was the first victory for Independiente in four attempts, and ultimately it would be its only win among a total of six Intercontinental Cup tournaments. In 1974, Bayern München declined to participate, fearing violence and financial loss, and UEFA invited the losing finalist Atlético Madrid to take its place. Atlético consented and won the trophy in its home leg on a goal by recently acquired Argentine star Reuben Ayala. The reputation of Argentine clubs in the Intercontinental Cup was by now so solidified that European participation in the series could not be assumed. In 1975, both Bayern and losing finalist Leeds United turned down UEFA's invitation, and Independiente was left out in the cold with no competition.

Fearing financial loss, Bayern entered the 1976 edition with the greatest reluctance, though its opponent would be the skillful Brazilian club Cruzeiro, which was riding high on its newly found place among Brazil's elite. As expected, during the first leg in Munich, only 22,000 spectators turned out in the snow, but the home team won in a shutout. At Belo

Horizonte, however, spirits were high, and 114,000 watched Cruzeiro struggle to a drawn game. The trophy went to Germany for the first time. For Bayern the win was virtually an anticlimax after so many successful years at the forefront of European soccer. In Belo Horizonte, the second leg of this edition produced an all-time South American record for gate receipts (Cr $6,318,855).

It is likely that the Bayern-Cruzeiro series saved the Intercontinental Cup from extinction, though CONMEBOL is undoubtedly committed to keeping the competition alive at all costs. Its popularity with South American fans is well-established, and its financial benefits for CONMEBOL entrants are proven. In Europe, there is a natural curiosity about the results of the tournament, but club officials remain wary of participation. Indeed, Liverpool refused to play warlike Boca Júniors in 1977, and European Cup runner-up Borussia Mönchengladbach took its place.

Results

1960 (Real Madrid)
First leg, in Montevideo

Peñarol	0	Real Madrid	0

Second leg, in Madrid

Real Madrid	5	Peñarol	1
(Puskás 2, Di Stefano, Herrera, Gento)		(Borges)	

1961 (Peñarol)
First leg, in Lisbon

Benfica	1	Peñarol	0
(Coluña)			

Second leg, in Montevideo

Peñarol	5	Benfica	0
(Sasia pen, Joya 2, Spencer 2)			

play-off, in Montevideo

Peñarol	2	Benfica	1
(Sasia 2, 1 pen)		(Eusebio)	

1962 (Santos)
First leg, in Rio de Janeiro

Santos	3	Benfica	2
(Pelé 2, Coutinho)		(Santana 2)	

Second leg, in Lisbon

Benfica (Santana, Eusebio)	2	**Santos** (Pelé 3, Coutinho, Pepe)	5

1963 (Santos)
First leg, in Milan

AC Milan (Trapattoni, Amarildo 2, Mora)	4	**Santos** (Pelé 2, 1 pen)	2

Second leg, in Rio de Janeiro

Santos (Pepe 2, Mengalvio, Lima)	4	**AC Milan** (Altafini, Mora)	2

play-off, in Rio de Janeiro

Santos (Dalmo pen)	1	**AC Milan**	0

1964 (Inter Milan)
First leg, in Buenos Aires

Independiente (Rodriguez)	1	**Inter Milan**	0

Second leg, in Milan

Inter Milan (Mazzola, Corso)	2	**Independiente**	0

play-off in Madrid

Inter Milan (Corso)	1	**Independiente**	0

-after extra time-

1965 (Inter Milan)
First leg, in Milan

Inter Milan (Peiro, Mazzola 2)	3	**Independiente**	0

Second leg, in Buenos Aires

Independiente	0	**Inter Milan**	0

1966 (Peñarol)
First leg, in Madrid

Peñarol (Spencer 2)	2	**Real Madrid**	0

Second leg, in Madrid

| Real Madrid | 0 | Peñarol
(Rocha pen, Spencer) | 2 |

1967 (Rácing Club)
First leg, in Glasgow

| Celtic
(McNeill) | 0 | Rácing Club | 0 |

Second leg, in Buenos Aires

| Rácing Club
(Raffo, Cardenas) | 2 | Celtic
(Gemmell pen) | 1 |

play-off, in Montevideo

| Rácing Club
(Cardenas) | 1 | Celtic | 0 |

1968 (Estudiantes)
First leg, in Buenos Aires

| Estudiantes
(Cornigliaro) | 1 | Manchester United | 0 |

Second leg, in Manchester

| Manchester United
(Morgan) | 1 | Estudiantes
(Veron) | 1 |

1969 (AC Milan)
First leg, in Milan

| AC Milan
(Sormani 2, Combin) | 3 | Estudiantes | 0 |

Second leg, in Buenos Aires

| Estudiantes
(Aguirre Suárez, Cornigliaro) | 2 | AC Milan
(Prati) | 1 |

1970 (Feyenoord)
First leg, in Buenos Aires

| Estudiantes
(Echecopar, Veron) | 2 | Feyenoord
(Kindvall, van Hanegem) | 2 |

Second leg, in Rotterdam

| Feyenoord
(van Deale) | 1 | Estudiantes | 0 |

1971 (Nacional)
First leg, in Athens

| Panathinaïkos
(Fylakouris) | 1 | Nacional
(Artime) | 1 |

Second leg, in Montevideo

Nacional	2	**Panathinaïkos**	1
(Artime 2)		(Fylakouris)	

1972 (Ajax)
First leg, in Buenos Aires

Independiente	1	**Ajax**	1
(Sá)		(Cruyff)	

Second leg, in Amsterdam

Ajax	3	**Independiente**	0
(Rep 2, Neeskens)			

1973 (Independiente)
one match only, in Rome

Juventus	0	**Independiente**	1
		(Bochini)	

1974 (Atlético Madrid)
First leg, in Buenos Aires

Independiente	1	**Atlético Madrid**	0
(Balbuena)			

Second leg, in Madrid

Atlético Madrid	2	**Independiente**	0
(Irureta, Ayala)			

1975 (no competition)

1976 (Bayern München)
First leg, in Munich

Bayern München	2	**Cruzeiro**	0
(Müller, Kapellmann)			

Second leg, in Belo Horizonte

Cruzeiro	0	**Bayern München**	0

1977 (Boca Júniors)
First leg, in Buenos Aires

Boca Júniors	2	**Borussia Mönchengladbach**	2
(Mastrangelo, Ribolzi)		(Hannes, Bonhof)	

Second leg, in Karlsrube

Borussia Mönchengladbach	0	**Boca Júniors**	3
		(Felman, Mastrangelo, Salinas)	

Interfere

To wrongfully impede an opponent or play on the field, whether by obstruction or other means.

International [i]

A game between two teams sanctioned by the appropriate national governing bodies to represent their countries, i.e., a game between national teams. There are five official levels of international play:

1. "A" team, or full international
2. "B" team, or reserve
3. "Under 23" team (*Espoirs, Menor de 23, Unter-23*)
4. "Amateur" team (*Amateur, Aficionado, Amateur*)
5. "Youth" team, "Under 21" or "Junior" (*Junior, Juvenil, Jugend*)

In addition, some national associations are able to field national "Veteran" teams, women's teams, and various other youth-level teams. "Veteran" teams are composed of ex-members of the five categories listed above or other retired players of suitable quality, and women's teams have come about only since the late 1960s.

An "A" team is the country's best representative team. The World Cup and all regional nations' cups are contested by "A" teams. Their rosters may include either amateurs or professionals, depending on a given country's policy with regard to professionalism, but the presence of a single professional on a team precludes that team from participating in any "Amateur" competition.

A "B" team is the reserve squad of the full national team, and is usually made up of players from the same club level as "A" team members. In many countries, it has its own separate schedule of games.

A nation's "Under 23" team is made up of the best players aged 21 and 22 who have not been selected for the "A" team. An "Under 23" team maintains its own international schedule, and some regional confederations have tournaments set aside to determine international championships in this category. Many full international players graduate from "Under 23" teams.

The status of various national "Amateur" teams may vary. In countries where professionalism has been adopted, the "Amateur" team comprises non-professional players whose level of play may be lower than that of an "A," "B," or "Under 23" team. It may also have its own separate international schedule. Some countries, on the other hand, do not recognize professionalism or are simply too small to afford such costs and have been granted permission to be represented by their "A" team in either "A" team competitions or in "Amateur" competitions. In such cases, the "A" team is also the "Amateur" team. The soccer tournament of the Olympic Games is played by "Amateur" national teams, as are the various regional athletic tournaments, such as the Asian Games.

A "Youth" team is the national team for players 20 years old or less. As with the "Under 23" group, an exceptional player who is under 21 years of age may also be selected for the "A" team, in which case he is not likely to play for the lesser "Youth" team. Some regional confederations sponsor international "Youth" tournaments. Most journalistic references to this category use the term "Under 21" or "Junior," e.g., Italy "Under 21" vs. Spain "Under 21."

All internationals, whether friendlies or in conjunction with an official competition, must conform to FIFA regulations. However, responsibility for actually organizing the matches—transportation, accommodations, collection of revenue, selection of neutral referees, and other logistical concerns—rests with the host country. Making the draw, official observation of the match, and administration of any protests or punitive actions are the duties of either FIFA or the relevant confederation, whichever is sponsoring the contest.

FIFA regulations stipulate that each national association participating in a full international pay a levy to the world body, the amount of which is dependent on gate receipts. The four British associations (England, Scotland, Wales, and Northern Ireland) have been exempt from this rule since 1924, but only with regard to the Home International Championship. The regulations also require that the FIFA flag be flown at all full internationals to show that the Laws of the Game are being respected.

The first unofficial international contest between representative national teams was held at Kennington Oval, London, on March 5, 1870, between England and Scotland. The result was a 1-1 draw. The match was conceived and organized by C.W. Alcock, honorary secretary of The Football Association in London. The Scottish players were all residents of England and played for English clubs. *The Sportsman*, which led all London newspapers in its coverage of soccer at the time, published the following report on March 8, 1870:

This match, which has for some weeks past occupied the attention of the numerous sections of players who follow the guidance of the Football Association, took place at Kennington Oval on Saturday in the presence of an assemblage of spectators such as has, in point of numbers, never been equalled, the entire limit of the ground being lined by an enthusiastic array of the supporters of the two sides. . . . Both sides were well represented though the Scottish eleven were at the eleventh hour crippled by the unavoidable retirement of Lord Kilmarnock and R.N. Ferguson, both of whom were no mean members of the team. Soon after a quarter past three o'clock the English captain, having lost the toss for choice of goals and thereby placed the eleven under the great disadvantage of contending against an unusually strong wind, kicked off, the ground it may be added being rather too greasy for dribbling purposes. During the early portion of the game the Scottish team held a slight advantage, the opposition of the wind combined with the slippery state of the ground, preventing the Englishmen from making any impression on the ranks of their opponents. Gradually, however, warming to their work and becoming more accustomed to each other's game the Englishmen commenced to assail the quarters occupied by their rivals, and although, when three-quarters of an hour had elapsed, and a change of ends was necessitated, no event of moment had fallen to either side, it was apparent that the tide was steadily turning in favour of the English. At four o'clock positions were accordingly reversed, and from this time the English aided by the wind kept their opponents closely besieged, the excellent defence of Messrs W.H. Gladstone and A. Morten, the latter of whom proved a most efficient goalkeeper, alone frustrating the ceaseless attack of Baker, Crake and Vidal among the English forwards. This siege of the Scottish lines was never raised until a quarter of an hour before the time fixed for the cessation of the game when, owing to a reprehensible excess of confidence on the part of the English captain, the English goal, which had been left thoroughly unprotected, fell to a long and rather lucky kick by H.E. Crawford, this evidently unexpected success of the Scotchmen creating no little excitement among the partisans of the northern side. After the further change of ends the Englishmen awakened to the necessity of renewed exertions, played up with desperate energy, and their efforts were happily rewarded just as time was called by a most brilliant run on the part of A. Baker, who thus saved England from the odium of defeat, and left the question of the respective merits of the two countries on the football field as open a question as before the commencement of the match. The play on both sides was remarkable for the spirit and determination that actuated every member of the two sides, the Scottish eleven especially meriting the highest praise for the gallant stand they made throughout the game. . . . On the side of Scotland, W.H. Gladstone shone out conspicuously among his brethren, his kicking and backplay generally showing no lack of the skill for which he was so distinguished at Eton, and Crawford, Hamilton and Lindsay were also worthy of the highest commendation. For England, A. Baker was remarkable for the speed as well as the energy of his play, and

E. Freeth and E. Lubbock were also very effective as backs. The sides were:

England: C. W. Alcock (Old Harrovians) captain, E. E. Bowen (Wanderers), A. Baker (NNs), W.C. Butler (Barnes Club), W.P. Crake (Harrow School), E. Freeth (Civil Service), E. Lubbock (Old Etonians), A. Nash (Clapham Rovers), J.C. Smith (Crusaders), A.H. Thornton (Old Harrovians) and R.W. Vidal (Westminster School).

Scotland: J. Kirkpatrick (Civil Service) captain, H.W. Crawford (Harrow School), W.H. Gladstone M.P. (Old Etonians), G.C. Gordon (NNs), C.R.B. Hamilton (Civil Service), W.A.B. Hamilton (Old Harrovians), A.F. Kinnaird (Crusaders), W. Lindsay (Old Wykehamists), J.W. Malcolm M.P. (London Scottish Rifles), A. Morten (Crystal Palace) and K. Muir Mackenzie (Old Carthusians).

Four additional internationals were played at Kennington Oval between England and Scotland in subsequent months, but none is considered official. They were: November 19, 1870 (England 1, Scotland 0); February 28, 1871 (England 1, Scotland 1); November 18, 1871 (England 2, Scotland 1); and, February 24, 1872 (England 1, Scotland 0).

The first official full international was played between England and Scotland on November 30, 1872, at the West of Scotland Cricket Club, Partick, Scotland, and ended in a goalless draw. The teams were:

Scotland: Gardner (capt.), goal; Ker, Taylor, backs; Thomson, J. Smith, half-backs; R. Smith, Leckie, Rhind, M'Kinnon, Weir, Wotherspoon, forwards. All from Queen's Park F.C.

England: Barker (Herts. Rangers), goal; Greenhalgh (Notts), three-quarter back; Welch (Harrow Chequers), halfback; Chappel, (Oxford Univ.), fly-kick; Ottaway (Oxford Univ.), capt., Chenery (Crystal Palace and Oxford Univ.), Clegg (Sheffield), A. K. Smith (Oxford Univ.), middles; Brockbank (Oxford Univ.), right side; Maynard (1st Surrey Rifles), Morice (Barnes), left side.

(Since most players' functions in the early years of modern soccer were somewhat ill-defined, much confusion persists over the actual field positions of many participants in this match. The above designations are based primarily on the work of historian Dr. Percy M. Young.)

Important official landmarks in international competition:

First international in North America: Canada 1, USA 0; Newark, N.J.; November 28, 1885. (Official status uncertain.)

First international between European countries: Austria 5, Hungary 0; Vienna; October 12, 1902.

First international in South America: Argentina 0, Uruguay 0; Buenos Aires; August 15, 1905.

First international between any British country and a foreign country: England 6, Austria 1; Vienna; June 6, 1908.

First international in Asia: Philippines 2, China 1; Manila; February 4, 1913.

First international between a European and South American country: Uruguay 3, Switzerland 0; Paris; June 9, 1924. Olympic Games.

First international in the Middle East: Egypt 7, Palestine 1; Cairo; March 16, 1934.

See also: **amateur, non-amateur,** and **professional**

International [ii]

A player who participates in an international [i].

International appearance

A player who has participated in an official international match on any one of his national teams is said to have made an international appearance, or, been "awarded a cap." International appearances may be credited for any recognized level of play (A-level, B-level, Under-23 level, Amateur level, Youth level, etc.), depending on whether or not the relevant national governing body sponsors such a team. It is customary that players from Youth level upwards are eligible for A-level, or "full" level, teams. (George Best, for example, was selected to play for Nothern Ireland's full international team at age 17.) After reaching the age of 23, however, a player is only eligible for the A-level team, unless there are peculiar domestic regulations stating otherwise, or unless amateurism is a factor.

Until 1971, the FIFA statutes allowed players to play only for their country of birth or for countries in which they had become naturalized citizens. Since then, however, players have been authorized to play also in the country of their father's birth, as well as their own country. The choice is made by the player, though only one country at a time may be chosen. Under the naturalization rule, two players in soccer history have made international appearances for three different countries: Ladislav Kubala (Hungary, Czechoslovakia, and Spain) and Alfredo Di Stefano (Argentina, Colombia, and Spain).

The term "cap," used universally among English-speaking countries outside North America, refers to the time-honored custom of wearing caps as part of the uniform. Caps of different colors were worn to distinguish one team from another as early as 1654 in England, and continued to be seen until the 1880s. After the custom had fallen out of use, The Football Association in England began awarding caps in 1886 to each player who had made an appearance on the field for England's national team. The tradition, especially the term, remained, and the F.A. now awards caps on an annual basis: One cap per year is given to each player who has made an appearance on the field with the name of each of his opposing teams embroidered on it.

The players who have made the most full international appearances in the history of the game are (through 1978):

Björn Nordqvist (Sweden)	115
Bobby Moore (England)	108
Bobby Charlton (England)	106
Billy Wright (England)	105
Thorbjørn Svenssen (Norway)	104
Franz Beckenbauer (Germany FR)	103
Kazimierz Deyna (Poland)	103
Jószef Bozsik (Hungary)	100

Record keepers in South America, unfortunately, have continued the practice of including B-internationals and internationals against regional selections with officially-recognized full internationals, thus rendering their statistics useless. Brazil's Roberto Rivelino, for example, is claimed by South American journalists to have amassed 107 international appearances by the end of 1977, but only 90 were full caps. Pelé is often credited with 110 international appearances, but FIFA recognizes only 93. The well-publicized figures for Chile's Leonel Sánchez (104), Peru's Hector Chumpitaz (102), and Brazil's Djalma Santos (100) and Gilmar (100) are highly suspect. Elsewhere in the world, Tunisia's perennial goalkeeper Attouga is one of several African players who claim over 100 appearances (Attouga claims 175!), but FIFA regards these figures as unreliable.

Billy Wright holds the world record for most consecutive international appearances with 70 for England between 1951-59.

International Cup

Copa Internacional—Taça Internacional.

An irregular competition for invited club champions of Europe and South America. It was held only four times: three years in succession during the early 1950s and again in the early 1960s. The 1951, 1952, and 1963 editions were played in Brazil (mainly Rio), and were given the name Taça Rio (Rio Cup);

the 1953 edition was played in Montevideo, Uruguay, and given the name Copa Montevideo. Though this series is little remembered, the first three editions were significant for their bringing together leading European and South American clubs on an organized basis *en masse*, and were contested by some of the most powerful clubs of their day.

The first Taça Rio (1951) was played at Maracanã Stadium in Rio and Pacaembu Stadium in São Paulo. The participants were: Vasco de Gama (Rio champion), SE Palmeiras (São Paulo champion), Nacional (Uruguay), Juventus (Italy), Sporting Lisbon (Portugal), Red Star Belgrade (Yugoslavia), FK Austria (Austria), and OGC Nice (France). Palmeiras won the final by defeating Juventus 1-0 and settling for a 2-2 draw in the second leg.

The participants in the second Taca Rio (1952) were: Fluminense (Rio champion), Corinthians (São Paulo champion), Peñarol (Uruguay), Libertad (Paraguay), Grasshoppers (Switzerland), Sporting Lisbon, FC Saarbrücken (German FR), and FK Austria. Fluminense won the final by first defeating then drawing with Corinthians 2-0 and 2-2.

The first and only Copa Montevideo (1953), which was played on a league basis, did not attract the two primary Brazilian champions of the previous year, Vasco de Gama and Corinthians, but Botafogo and Fluminense, both of Rio, substituted. The other participants were: Nacional, Colo Colo (Chile), Presidente Hayes (Paraguay), Dinamo Zagreb (Yugoslavia), and FK Austria. Nacional won the trophy by defeating each of its opponents except Fluminense (drew 0-0).

Winners

1951   SE Palmeiras
1952   Fluminense
1953   Nacional
1963   Botafogo

International Football Association Board

The international committee that makes or approves changes in the Laws of the Game. It is composed of four representatives each from England, Scotland, Wales, and Northern Ireland, and one representative each from four other FIFA members who serve elected terms of office. All four British countries have permanent seats. The committee is responsible for drafting the Laws themselves, inquiries and clarifications relating to the Laws, instructions to governing bodies and referees, and approval of alterations in the Laws proposed by national associations for use in their own jurisdictions. The board meets every June to consider these questions, and all decisions must pass by a three-quarter majority. Each of the 20 representatives has one vote.

The greater power given to the British associations is indicative of Britain's place in the administrative history of world soccer. In 1882, more than 20 years before the birth of FIFA, The Football Association in London called for a meeting of the four British associations to draw up a uniform set of rules. At first Scotland declined to participate, favoring independence and its own idiosyncratic laws, but when England warned that international competition between the two could cease as a result, the Scots relented. The conference convened in Manchester on December 6, 1882, and a regularized code was adopted. England, Scotland, Wales, and Ireland (Irish Football Association) established the International Football Association Board to perpetuate the work they had done, and each association was given equal voting rights.

The paternalism and prestige of British soccer was such that not until 1913 did the British allow two additional FIFA members to join the board. In 1920, when the British associations withdrew from FIFA as a postwar protest against Austro-German membership, the two FIFA seats were voted off the board. With British reinstatement in FIFA four years later, FIFA's participation resumed. Since 1924, non-British membership on the board has been uninterrupted despite a second British withdrawal from FIFA between 1928-46.

International Football Cup

Coupe Internationale de Football—Internationaler Fussball-Cup—Coppa Internazionale di Calcio.

Known popularly as the Intertoto Cup, this summer tournament for clubs exists exclusively to provide a competition for betting during the European off-season. Leading clubs from 20 countries have participated in the competition since its introduction in 1961, and bettors in nearly every country in Europe, both East and West, have reaped its rewards. Legalized betting on a variety of sports, soccer chief among them, is a tradition in most parts of Europe, and in many countries bookmaking is handled by a state agency. The major exception is France, where organized pools are not allowed. In Great Britain, bookmaking is also a passion, but all the agencies are privately operated on a commercial basis. On the continent, much of the revenue gained from betting is returned to the administration of the sport at stake.

The Intertoto Cup was the creation of Karl Rappan, the famous Austrian who coached the Swiss national team to moderate success during the postwar years. With the backing of Swiss Football Association treasurer Ernst Thommen, and with the sanction of UEFA (though not its sponsorship), the tournament was established ostensibly for major clubs left out of European club championships to gain experience in international competition. The tournament's bookmaking function, however, soon predominated, and when the Fairs Cup became firmly established in the mid-1960s, Rappan's loftier ideals were superseded. From 1961-66, an actual champion was decided, with group winners coming together in knockout rounds to determine the eventual finalists. Since 1967, the group winners have stood as multiple winners of the tournament. Between 25-40 clubs enter the competition each summer.

Winners

1961 Ajax (Netherlands)
Group winners: Slovan Bratislava, Banik Ostrava, Spartak Hradec Kralove, First Vienna, Feyenoord, Ajax, Örgryte, Sparta Rotterdam.

1962 Red Star Bratislava (Czechoslovakia)
Group winners: Red Star Bratislava, Padova, Servette, Újpest Dózsa, OFK Belgrade, Rijeka, Tatabanya, Pecsi Dózsa.

1963 Slovnaft Bratislava (formerly Red Star)
Group winners: Standard Liège, Sampdoria, Modena, Rouen, Rapid Vienna, Bayern München, Örgryte, Norrköping, Slovnaft, Slovan Bratislava, Polonia Bytom, Odra Opole.

1964 Polonia Bytom (Poland)
Group winners: Hertha Berlin, DWS Amsterdam, Kaiserslautern, FC Liège, Lokomotiv Leipzig, Empor Rostock, Szombierki Bytom, Karl-Marx-Stadt, Malmö, Slovnaft, Polonia Bytom.

1965 Lokomotiv Leipzig (German DR)
Group winners: Lugano, Fortuna Geelen, Norrköping, Örgryte, Motor Jena, Empor Rostock, Lokomotiv Leipzig, Chemie Leipzig.

1966 Eintracht Frankfurt (Germany FR)
Group winners: Eintracht Frankfurt, DWS Amsterdam, Go Ahead Deventer, ADO Den Haag, Zaglebie Sosnowiecz, IFK Göteborg, Górnik Zabrze, Inter Bratislava (formerly Slovnaft), Vorwärts Berlin, Norrköping.

1967 *Group winners:* Lugano, Feyenoord, Lille, Lierse, Hannover, Zaglebie Sosnowiecz, Polonia Bytom, IFK Göteborg, Ruch Chorzów, VSS Kosice, KB Copenhagen, Fortuna Düsseldorf.

1968 *Group winners:* Karl-Marx-Stadt, Hansa Rostock, Slovan Bratislava, VSS Kosice, Lokomotive Kosice, Odra Opole, Eintracht Braunschweig, Legia Warsaw, FC Nürnberg, Ajax, Sporting Lisbon, Feyenoord, Español, ADO Den Haag.

1969 *Group winners:* Malmö, Norrköping, Szombierki, Wisla Kraków, Odra Opole, SV Fürth, ZVL Zilina, Jednota Trencin, Frem Copenhagen.

1970 *Group winners:* Slovan Bratislava, Hamburger SV, Union Teplice, Maastricht, VSS Kosice, Eintracht Braunschweig, Slavia Prague, Marseille, Östers Växjö, Wisla Kraków, Austria Salzburg, Banik Ostrava, Polonia Bytom.

1971 *Group winners:* Hertha Berlin, Stal Mielec, Servette, TZ Trinec, Atvidaberg, Eintracht Braunschweig, Austria Salzburg.

1972 *Group winners:* Eintracht Braunschweig, Hannover, Saint Étienne, VÖeEST Linz, Norrköping, AC Nitra, Slavia Prague, Slovan Bratislava.

1973 *Group winners:* Hannover, Slovan Bratislava, Hertha Berlin, Zürich, Row Rybnik, Union Teplice, Feyenoord, Wisla Kraków, AC Nitra, Östers Växjö.

1974 *Group winners:* Zürich, Hamburger SV, Malmö, Standard Liège, Slovan Bratislava, Spartak Trnava, MSV Duisburg, Banik Ostrava, VSS Kosice, CUF Barreiro.

1975 *Group winners:* SW Innsbruck, VÖeEST Linz, Eintracht Braunschweig, Zaglebie Sosnowiecz, Zbrojovka Brno, Row Rybnik, Atvidaberg, Kaiserslautern, Belenenses, Celik Zenica.

1976 *Group winners:* Hertha Berlin, Vojvodina Novi Sad, Widzew Lódź, Djurgaardens, Östers Växjö, Young Boys Berne, Union Teplice, Banik Ostrava, Zbrojovka Brno, Trnava, Inter Bratislava.

1977 *Group winners:* Vojvodina Novi Sad, MSV Duisburg, Inter Bratislava, Slavia Prague, Slavia Sofia, Frem Copenhagen, Jednota Trencin, Slovan Bratislava, Östers Växjö, Pogon Szczecin.

1978 *Group winners:* MSV Duisburg, Slavia Prague, Hertha Berlin, Eintracht Braunschweig, Malmö, Lokomotive Kosice, Tatran Presov, Maccabi Nath, AK Grazer.

International Quadrangular Tournament

A competition for national teams of the Asian subcontinent (Pakistan, India, Burma, and Ceylon), whose eventual fate is uncertain. At least two editions were played, in 1952 at Colombo and 1953 at Rangoon, with India emerging the winner on both occasions. In 1952, India defeated Burma and Ceylon and drew with Pakistan, while Pakistan defeated both Burma and Ceylon. In 1953, India defeated all three, Pakistan drew with Burma and buried Ceylon (6-0), and Burma narrowly won over Ceylon.

International Soccer League

Also known as "United States International Soccer League."

A professional league in the United States founded in 1959 by Bill Cox, a former owner of the Philadelphia Phillies baseball club. It folded in 1965 after six seasons.

In the late 1950s, observers of the game in the United States agreed that big-time professional soccer was still a few years away, despite the presence of the quasiprofessional American Soccer League and semiprofessional "ethnic" leagues. Bill Cox, on the other hand, thought there was an audience for senior level competition among certain urban populations and especially among first-generation immigrant communities. In late 1959, Cox began to promote his new loop, the International Soccer League, in which leading clubs from abroad would be imported to compete among themselves under their own names. The league was divided into two sections, Division I and Division II, and all clubs played one another on an equal basis, accumulating points under a league system. At the end of the season, the divisional winners played each other for the ISL championship. The City of New York was to be its base of operation with most games taking place at either the Polo Grounds, Randall's Island, or Roosevelt Stadium in Jersey City. In 1963, Chicago, Detroit, and Chicopee, Massachusetts, were added to the list, and in 1964, some games were played in Boston and Los Angeles.

In addition to low attendance figures, the major disappointment of the ISL was the clubs' reluctance to send their star players. There were some exceptions—Dukla Prague and Górnik Zabrze, for example—and Dukla threw so much weight behind American excursions that a special play-off, the American Challenge Cup, was set up during the last four years, in which Dukla met the current champions of the ISL in a post-season play-off.

1960: **Division I**—Bayern München (Germany FR), Burnley (England), Glenavon (Northern Ireland), Kilmarnock (Scotland), New York Americans (USA), O.G.C. Nice (France). **Division II**—Bangu (Brazil), Norrköping (Sweden), Rapid Vienna (Austria), Red Star Belgrade (Yugoslavia), Sampdoria (Italy), Sporting Club Lisbon (Portugal). **Championship**—Bangu defeated Kilmarnock, 2-0.

1961: **Division I**—Bangu (Brazil), Besiktas (Turkey), Concordia (Canada), Dinamo Bucharest (Rumania), Everton (England), Karlsruher (Germany FR), Kilmarnock (Scotland), New York Americans (USA). **Division II**—Concordia (Canada), Dukla Prague (Czechoslovakia), Español (Spain), Monaco (France), Rapid Vienna (Austria), Red Star Belgrade (Yugoslavia), Shamrock Rovers (Eire). **Championship**—Dukla Prague defeated Everton, 7-2 and 2-0, on goal aggregate.

1962: **Division I**—America RJ (Brazil), Guadalajara (Mexico), Dundee F.C. (Scotland), Hajduk Split (Yugoslavia), Palermo (Italy), Reutlingen (Germany FR). **Division II**—Belenenses (Portugal), Elfsborg (Sweden), MTK (Hungary), Panathinaïkos (Greece), Real Oviedo (Spain), Wiener A.C. (Austria). **Championship**—America defeated Belenenses, 2-1 and 1-0, on goal aggregate. **American Challenge Cup**—Dukla Prague defeated America, 1-1 and 2-1, on goal aggregate.

1963: **Division I**—Kilmarnock (Scotland), Mantova (Italy), Oro (Mexico), Preussen Münster (Germany FR), S.C. Recife (Brazil), Valenciennes (France), West Ham United (England). **Division II**—Belenenses (Portugal), Dinamo Zagreb (Yugoslavia), Górnik Zabrze (Poland), Hälsingborg (Sweden), Újpest Dózsa (Hungary), Real Valladolid (Spain), Wiener A.C. (Austria). **Championship**—West Ham defeated Górnik, 1-1 and 1-0, on goal aggregate. **American Challenge Cup**—Dukla Prague defeated West Ham, 1-0 and 1-1, on goal aggregate.

1964: **Division I**—E.C. Bahia (Brazil), Blackburn Rovers (England), Heart of Midlothian (Scotland), Lanerossi-Vicenza S.S. (Italy), SV Werder Bremen (Germany FR). **Division II**—AEK Athens (Greece), Vitoria Guimaraes (Portugal), Red Star Belgrade (Yugoslavia), Schwechater (Austria), Zaglebie Sosnowiec (Poland). **Championship**—Zaglebie defeated Werder Bremen, 4-0 and 1-0, on goal aggregate. **American Challenge Cup**—Dukla Prague defeated Zaglebie, 3-1 and 1-1, on goal aggregate.

1965: **Division I**—TSV München 1860 (Germany FR), New York Americans (USA), Portuguêsa (Brazil), Varese (Italy), West Ham United (England). **Division II**—Ferencváros (Hungary), Kilmarnock (Scotland), Polonia Bytom (Poland), West Bromwich Albion (England). **Championship**—Polonia defeated New York Americans, 3-0 and 2-1, on goal aggregate. **American Challenge Cup**—Polonia defeated Dukla Prague, 2-0 and 1-1, on goal aggregate.

Internazionale Football Club

Location: *Milan, Italy;* **stadium:** *Stadio di San Siro (83,141);* **colors:** *blue and black striped jerseys, black shorts;* **honors:** *Intercontinental Cup (1964, 1965), European Cup (1964, 1965), Italian champion (1910, 1920, 1930, 1938, 1940, 1953, 1954, 1963, 1965, 1966, 1971), Italian cup winner (1939, 1978).*

Founded 1908 as Football Club Internazionale by dissident members of AC Milan. In 1909, Internazionale entered the Italian championship in the Lombardy regional section, losing to both AC Milan and US Milanese in the only games of that season, but in 1910 it won the Italian championship in its second attempt by defeating two-time champion Pro

Vercelli in the final, 10-3. World War I interrupted the club's progress, but in 1920 Inter won the Italian title again with a much wider field of opponents than ten years before. In 1928, Inter merged with US Milanese and became Ambrosiana-Internazionale until it reverted to its original name in 1945.

When the first Italian national league was introduced in 1929-30, Ambrosiana-Inter was not only one of the original 18 members but also the first winner. Having turned professional in 1929, Ambrosiana was now the home of Italy's greatest goalscorer of the prewar years, center forward Giuseppe Meazza, whose 31 tallies in 1929-30 topped the next highest scorer in the league by 10. Ambrosiana placed second in league standings for three consecutive years from 1933-35, and in 1938 and 1940 it won the title again. In the meantime, it was the runner-up in the 1933 Mitropa Cup, losing the final to FK Austria. Inter placed second in the league again in 1941 and 1946, and continued to finish in the top three throughout the late 1940s and early '50s.

Under manager Alfredo Foni, the *nerazzuri* emerged during the early 1950s with a tactical philosophy based on defense. With central defenders lined up several deep, this team was uninspiring to watch, but it achieved great success and won back-to-back championships in 1953 and 1954, scoring a mere 113 goals in 68 games. Foni's modified Swiss Bolt system was an answer to the lethal goalscoring potential of Inter's archrival AC Milan and other Italian clubs that had several goalscoring artists on their rosters, and in retrospect it now appears to have anticipated the more severe entrenchment of Inter's defense in later years. While Inter was one of Italy's three great powers during the early 1950s, AC Milan captured international attention with its superb performances in the Latin Cup, and it was Milan and Juventus that continued to dominate the late 1950s when Inter faltered.

In 1960, the Argentine-French manager Helenio Herrera arrived at Inter from Barcelona and instituted a rigorous *catenaccio*, employing the veteran Armando Picchi as his *libero*. Herrera secured his former Barcelona star Luis Suárez for a world record fee of $420,000, assigning to him the role of midfield general—actually a deep-lying inside forward—in his new scheme, and developed two extraordinary new Italian stars, the towering left back Giacinto Facchetti and inside-right Sandro Mazzola. A new Brazilian star, Jair, on the right wing, and Mario Corso on the left wing combined with Mazzola to give

Herrera's *catenaccio* a significant counterattack, and Inter took off for the heights of European soccer.

Inter won the Italian championship in 1962-63, and the following year, while placing second in the league, won its first European Cup by neutralizing Real Madrid's scoring machine in the final, winning by a score of 3-1. In the 1964 Intercontinental Cup, Inter overpowered the tough South American champion from Argentina, Independiente, and in 1964-65, Inter's peak season, the club won another Italian championship, the European Cup, and the International Cup in rapid succession. The final of that European Cup was played in Inter's own stadium against Portugal's Benfica, with *catenaccio* rising to its zenith of efficiency. This had also been evident in Inter's defeats of Glasgow Rangers and Liverpool in earlier rounds. In 1965-66, Inter won another league title with virtually the same team, but by 1968 it had slipped to fifth place in the standings and Herrera finally left the club, tired and scarred from trying to maintain his authoritarian ways over a team of national heroes.

In the immediate years following Herrera's departure, the brilliant Mazzola developed into a schemer, causing much-publicized tensions between himself and Mario Corso. The unique Facchetti, a gentleman among Italian players, took over the sweeper position with startling results. Under manager Giovanni Invernizzi, Inter won another league title in 1971, and Inter's new scoring ace was Roberto Boninsegna, who led the league in goals for two consecutive seasons. Inter's style was still based on a plodding defense and quick counterattack, but with the presence of Facchetti the club was able to exhibit a slightly more positive image. In the 1971-72 European Cup, Inter gained the finals by eliminating Glasgow Celtic on penalty kicks in the semifinals, but in the final failed to contain the sophisticated Ajax attack. This game, in fact, marked an unofficial end to the era of *catenaccio*, as personified by Inter, and a beginning of a brighter era spawned by the rise of Ajax's "total football."

Inter declined during the mid-1970s, but in 1977-78, Facchetti's final season, a measure of success returned with its second Italian Cup win in 40 years. Meanwhile, Inter's fame and following continue unabated, as it has for almost 60 years, driven annually by the intense rivalry with AC Milan, another international giant and with whom Inter shares the magnificent Stadio di San Siro.

Intertoto Cup   See: **International Football Cup**

In touch

A ball is "in touch" when it crosses entirely over a touch line and out of bounds.

See also: **out of play**

Iran

Iranian Football Federation
269, Av. Sepahbod Zahedi
P.O. Box 11-1642
Tehran

Founded: 1922
FIFA: 1948
AFC: 1958

Affiliated clubs: *422;* registered players: *43,300;* national stadium: *Aria Mehre, Karadj Auto Band (100,000);* largest stadium: *Aria Mehre;* colors: *green jerseys, white shorts;* season: *April to February;* honors: *Asian Cup winner (1968, 1972, 1976), Taj Club, Asian Champion Teams' Cup (1970).*

Iran's solid position as the leader in Asian soccer was virtually assured for several years to come, until the recent revolution. The kingdom had been grooming itself ever since Reza Shah the Great ascended to the throne in 1925 and instituted a national sports program. The former shah's general interest in developing this sports program was translated into a personal interest in soccer by his son, the presently deposed shah, who was captain of his high school soccer team in Switzerland. The solidity of Iranian soccer before the revolution was demonstrated by a high degree of organization at both domestic and international levels. Several cities in Iran were genuine soccer hotbeds, and beginning in the 1960s, this unusual combination of official support and grass roots enthusiasm reaped one reward after another on the playing field. The future of soccer in the new Islamic republic may be another matter.

Other than the presence of European soccer-playing residents, the game gradually infiltrated the country by means of Iranian students returning home from school in Europe. The Persian Amateur Football Federation was founded as early as 1922 ("Iranian" became part of the name in the late 1940s and the present name was adopted ca. 1952), and until World War II this body functioned primarily to promote the development of soccer as part of the overall sports program. Clubs were founded in Tehran and the larger cities, and during the 1930s there were even some international friendlies with teams from the Soviet republics in the Caucasus. In 1939, the first large stadium was built for soccer and track events in Tehran—Amjadiyeh Stadium—and in 1943 the government played host to CSKA Moscow and other foreign teams in a tournament called the Shah's Cup.

In 1948, the Iranian federation was admitted to FIFA, and Iran entered international competition in earnest. Its officially recognized debut was a friendly against Turkey at Ankara in 1950, which the Iranians lost 6-1. Later in that year, Iran played Pakistan in Tehran and lost again, 5-1. In 1951, Iran was one of six countries to compete in the soccer tournament of the first Asian Games in New Delhi, and here it achieved its first victories, a 2-0 win over Burma and a 3-2 defeat of Japan (in a replay after a scoreless draw). These wins were enough to put Iran into the final against India, which it lost 1-0 to take second place. Iran continued to participate in this quadrennial event with mixed results until it finally won in 1974, the final rounds having been held in Iran. At home, there were 180 clubs registered with the federation when it joined FIFA, 12 of them in Tehran, and 2,700 registered players. Regional competitions were held in each of the ten provinces, and every year a national competition was held for the best clubs from each province. This tournament was organized by a different province each year.

Iran did not enter the Asian Cup until the fourth edition in Tehran in 1968, and in this and the next two editions it walked away the winner each time. In 1968, it went undefeated in four games with victories over Hong Kong, Republic of China, Burma, and Israel. In 1972 at Bangkok, Iran was again undefeated in four games, winning this time over Thailand and Iraq in the first round, Khmer in the semi-finals, and Republic of Korea in the final. At Tehran in 1976, the Iranians continued their winning streak with victories over Iraq and Yemen PDR in the first round, the People's Republic of China in the semi-finals (after extra time), and Kuwait in the final. In its three consecutive Asian Cup triumphs, Iran won 12 straight games and amassed a goal difference of 34-6, elevating itself to the top of the overall Asian Cup standings.

Much of Iran's growth as an international power during the 1960s and '70s was due to the steady influx of good European coaches, among them the following Iranian national team managers: Massaroche (Austria), Sotch (Hungary), Zadarvko Raykoff (Yugoslavia), Igor Netto (USSR), Danny McLenon (Scotland), and Frank O'Farrell (Eire). O'Farrell was responsible for the third Asian Cup victory and for taking Iran through to the finals of the 1978 World Cup. After the qualifying rounds for 1978 were finished, O'Farrell handed the reins over to his assistant, Heshmat Mohadjerani, the first Iranian to manage the national team. To qualify for the 1978 World Cup, Iran played 12 games without a defeat. It drew with Republic of Korea both home and away, and defeated Saudi Arabia, Syria, Kuwait, Australia, and Hong Kong twice each. In the 1974 World Cup qualifying rounds, Iran was narrowly edged out of the running by Australia after eliminating Syria, Korea PDR, and Kuwait. Iran has also qualified for the final rounds of Olympic Games in 1964, 1972 (when it defeated Brazil's amateurs in the first round), and 1976 (winning a match over Cuba's full international squad in the first round). Iran has not lost at home to another Asian team since the mid-1960s, but its record against European and South American "A" teams is sparse. Iran has played Turkey five times, mostly in the R.C.D. Pact Football Tournament, drawing three times and losing twice; it has lost to Czechoslovakia 1-0, and it fell to Eire 2-1 in 1972 at the "little World Cup" staged by Brazil.

The Iranian league has been restructured twice since the postwar period. A national league was introduced in 1962, and a semi-professional league was fashioned from that in 1973, although all Iranian players are nominally amateurs. The first division is called the Copa Takht-é-Djamchid (National Division), and consists of 16 clubs, eight of which are from Tehran. Two clubs are relegated each year, and one must be from the capital regardless of position in the standings. The second division includes 12 clubs, four of which are from Tehran. Promotion to the first division is given to the second division winner (regardless of its geographical location), and the runner-up, unless the winner is from Tehran, in which case the highest placed provincial club is promoted.

The big archrivals in Tehran in recent years were Persepolis F.C. and Taj F.C. (the army club that won the Asian Champions' Cup in 1970). Their derbies regularly filled the 100,000 capacity Aria Mehre, and international FIFA referees were imported for each of these derbies by special arrangement. In the wake of the Islamic revolution, however, the future of Taj is tenuous at best. Other major Tehran clubs are (or have been) Homa F.C., PAS, and Oghab, the air force club. Abomoslem is an important provincial club.

Iraq

Iraq Football Association
Antar Square
P.O. Box 484
Baghdad

Founded: 1948
FIFA: 1951
AFC: 1971

Affiliated clubs: *141;* registered players: *1,120;* national stadium: *Sha'ab Stadium, Baghdad (50,000);* largest stadium: *Sha'ab Stadium;* colors: *white jerseys, white shorts;* season: *October to May;* honors: *none.*

Soccer was introduced in Iraq by British soldiers and residents during the short British mandate of 1920-32, but the game really began to sprout immediately after World War II, when foreign (mainly British) workers and technicians arrived to develop the rich oil fields. The domestic side of Iraqi soccer was organized immediately. In 1948, four district associations were set up in Baghdad, Mosul, Basra, and Kirkuk, each with its own league, and a knockout competition for league winners was introduced the same year. The first winner was Royal Body Guard. The Iraq Championship was also introduced in 1948 for representative teams of each district and major sponsored teams. The first two Iraqi Champions in 1949 and 1950 were Basra Petroleum Co. and a Baghdad selection.

Though the domestic game was strong in the postwar years, imperial Iraq showed little interest in international competition. Iraq's regular participation in official tournaments was further delayed by the coup of 1958, after which many of the leading clubs ceased to exist. The reorganization process was thwarted by political upheaval, and the current face of domestic competition did not take form until after the socialist coup of 1968. By 1963, an Iraqi national side was participating in the first Arab Cup, and an indication of Iraq's progress was seen in 1966 when it won the second edition of the Arab Cup (the soccer tournament of the Pan Arab Games), held in Iraq itself. Iraq has since participated regularly in this competition.

Under the socialist regime, Iraqi soccer has taken a sharp swing upward. The national team has qualified for the final rounds of two Asian Cups. In 1972, it was eliminated from the first round after losing to Iran 3-0 and drawing with Thailand 1-1. In the 1976 Asian Cup, it achieved its biggest success to date by gaining fourth place after losing the third place game to the People's Republic of China, 1-0. In the first round, Iraq had again lost to Iran (2-0), but defeated Yemen PDR and narrowly lost to Kuwait in the semi-finals after extra time. Iraq attempted to qualify for the World Cup in 1974, when it was grouped with Australia (the eventual qualifier), Indonesia, and New Zealand. In this series, it lost only one match in six (away to Australia), and won three, including two against New Zealand; the rest were drawn. Participating for the first time in 1976 in the Arabian Gulf Tournament, Iraq drew level on points with Kuwait at the head of the standings but lost the play-off for the title.

On the club level, Baghdad's Police Club advanced to the final rounds of the 1971 Asian Champions' Cup, and might have been crowned Asian Champion had it not forfeited the final against Maccabi Tel-Aviv. Police Club had also refused to play Maccabi in the first round of that competition, and it was the difficulty created by these two walkovers that eventually led to the discontinuation of the Champions' Cup altogether. Meanwhile, domestic league and cup competitions continue to thrive with 32 clubs participating on the national level.

Ireland, Northern

Irish Football Association Ltd.
20 Windsor Avenue
Belfast BT9 6EG

Founded: 1880
FIFA: 1911-20
1924-28
1946
UEFA: 1954

Affiliated clubs: *740;* registered players: *14,800 (160 professional);* national stadium: *Windsor Park, Belfast (58,000);* largest stadium: *Windsor Park;* colors: *green jerseys with white trim, white shorts;* season: *August to May;* honors: *Home*

International Championship (1903 shared, 1914, 1956 shared, 1958 shared, 1959 shared, 1964 shared).

For almost 60 years, Irish soccer has been split into two camps: Northern Ireland (Ulster) and the Republic of Ireland. But during the four decades between the first appearance of organized soccer on Irish shores in 1878 and the birth of the Republic in 1921, there was only one Ireland and one Irish Football Association. In 1921, the Republic of Ireland formed its own governing body—the Football Association of Ireland—and set out on its own. Because the focus of Irish soccer and the original Irish Football Association had always been in Ulster, soccer in Northern Ireland suffered little when the south broke away, and, to a great extent, Northern Ireland has remained the more significant of the two Irelands in international competition to this day. The game has been so well entrenched in Ulster that it has continued to thrive at the forefront of working class life, despite bitter national divisions, civil war, and the ceaseless drain of its best players to England and Scotland.

Northern Ireland has produced several players of world class caliber, including the incomparable George Best, perhaps the greatest ball juggling artist ever to have come out of the British Isles. The Irish Football Association, as one of the four British governing bodies, sits permanently on the International Football Association Board, and has contributed significantly to the development of the Laws of the Game. The penalty kick, an important soccer institution, originated in Northern Ireland in 1890. In international competition, the Irish F.A. was the last British association to forage away from the home countries. Northern Ireland's non-British first full international did not take place until 1951, but seven years later it qualified for the World Cup and reached the quarter-finals.

Irish students were involved in medieval football games in England as early as the thirteenth century, and the Irish continued to participate in the growth of football until the modern era. [A discussion of early football in Ireland is found under *Ireland, Republic of.*] Soccer was introduced by the Scots in Belfast, where a large working class population gave it a base of operation. Rugby had already been established in Belfast in 1878, when the first game under soccer rules was played by two visiting Scottish teams. J.M. McAlery, the

"father of Irish soccer" and a keen sportsman, had watched several soccer games on a visit to Glasgow, and upon his return home contacted Glasgow's Caledonian F.C., suggesting that an exhibition match be staged in Belfast in the near future. Caledonian arranged the visit with Queen's Park Glasgow, and in October 1878, representative teams from the two Scottish clubs met at the Ulster Cricket Ground in Belfast under the sponsorship of the rugby-playing Ulster and Windsor Football Clubs. The Queen's Park team won 3-2. Ulster F.C. formed a soccer team shortly after the exhibition match and invited another Scottish club, Lenzie F.C., to play in the first match involving an Irish team.

The first Irish club devoted entirely to soccer was Cliftonville F.C., founded in 1879 by J.M. McAlery in Ballyclare, County Antrim. In its first game, Cliftonville lost to a team of rugby players, 2-1, at the Ballyclare cricket grounds. Most Irish clubs that sprang up immediately after Cliftonville contained Scottish players, and Scottish-based clubs dominated Belfast competition for almost a decade. In 1880, McAlery led the formation of the Irish Football Association (IFA) in Belfast with jurisdiction over all of Ireland. Its ties to the English, Scottish, and Welsh associations were made official, and an IFA Cup, Britain's fourth cup competition, was introduced that same year. The seven participants in the inaugural competition of 1880-81 were Alexander Limavady, Avoniel, Cliftonville, Distillery, Knock, Moyola Park, and Old Park. Moyola Park defeated Cliftonville, 1-0, in the first final. Queen's Island, which won the second edition in 1881-82, was made up almost entirely of Scottish players. Cliftonville, the parent club of the IFA, won its first trophy in 1882-83 after losing in the first two finals.

Distillery became the first really successful Belfast club with four cup wins before 1890, but two other important Belfast clubs that made their mark in years ahead were also founded during this period, Belfast Celtic (1881) and Linfield (1887). Belfast's Glentoran came along about the same time. Clubs from the present-day Republic of Ireland were rarely seen in the early competitions. In 1890-91, the Irish League was formed by Clarence, Cliftonville, Distillery, Glentoran, Linfield, Milford, Old Park, and Ulster. The winner of the first three editions, as well as the IFA Cup in the same years, was Linfield, which went on to win five doubles before 1900. Glentoran and Distillery, the other major Belfast clubs, provided the greatest challenge to Linfield in the 1890s, and Northern Ireland's greatest rivalry originated at this time: Linfield of West Belfast's Windsor Park versus Glentoran of East Belfast's Oval.

In 1882, Ireland entered international competition with a 13-0 loss to England in Belfast, and the following week in Wrexham Ireland met Wales for the first time, losing 7-1. Further crushing defeats to England and Wales followed, and in 1884, in what became the first edition of the Home International Championship, Ireland made its debut against Scotland, losing 5-0 in Belfast. More often than not, Ireland finished last in those early editions of the Home Internationals, but for the next 70 years this series provided the entire Irish international schedule. Ireland's first win in Home Internationals was a 4-1 defeat of Wales in 1887. Between 1882-1900, the Irish won a total of six games (all against Wales), drew five, and lost 41 (nine of these to Wales). Ireland's first success in the competition occurred in 1902-03, when England, Scotland, and Ireland shared the trophy. The 1900-14 period, during which time Ireland won 10 and lost 29, ended in 1913-14 with Ireland's only outright win in its history. The year before, Ireland defeated England for the first time, 2-1, in Belfast, and in its trophy winning year of 1913-14, it achieved its biggest win over England, a 3-0 shutout at Middlesbrough. Of the 16 players who made appearances for Ireland in 1913-14, only four were from Ulster clubs, (three from Linfield, one from Belfast Celtic). Two were from southern county clubs, two from Scotland, and eight from England. The exodus across the Irish Sea had already begun.

At home, Belfast clubs continued to dominate the league and cup, and Dublin clubs won the cup for the first and only times in 1906, 1908, 1911, and 1920. By 1920, Linfield had won 12 championships and 13 Cups. An unofficial Belfast League supplanted the national league during World War I, but the IFA Cup continued unabated throughout the war until, ironically, the final of 1919-20 was called off after civil disorders relating to Irish independence.

With the formation of the Dublin-based Football Association of Ireland in 1921, some Ulster clubs defected to the south. The famous meeting of the four British associations in 1923 that determined once and for all the autonomy of the Dublin association ordered the defectors to return to the fold, and from that point on all clubs located in the five counties of the north remained affiliated with the Belfast association. Domestic competitions moved forward during the violent unrest of the early 1920s, and in 1921-22 the south's Football Association of Ireland introduced its own league and cup, taking with it three major Dublin clubs—Shelbourne, Shamrock Rovers, and Bohemians—and a host of minor provincial clubs—but soccer in the new province of Northern Ireland kept its power base intact and suffered little from the disruption.

Between the world wars, Northern Ireland failed to win or share a single Home International Championship trophy, and there were only two wins over England and two over Scotland. In the league, Belfast Celtic mounted a series of championships from 1926-29 and 1936-40, and five Belfast clubs, Linfield, Glentoran, Distillery, Belfast Celtic, and Ards, dominated the IFL Cup.

The 1950s were Northern Ireland's most successful era in international competition. In 1949-50 and 1953-54, the Home Internationals doubled as qualification rounds for the World Cup, Scotland and England qualifying on both occasions, and in 1951 Northern Ireland played in its first international against a non-British team, drawing with France in Belfast, 2-2. In a return friendly in Paris one year later France won, 3-1. After 70 years, the Ulstermen had tasted their first bite of true international competition. The Republic of Ireland, by contrast, had been playing European teams since 1924—14 in all—and had won almost as many games as it had lost.

Northern Ireland shared Home International trophies in 1956, 1958 and 1959, and entered qualification rounds for the 1958 World Cup. With home defeats over Italy and Portugal, this marvelously talented team advanced to the final rounds in Sweden under the management of Peter Doherty, holding Italy to a 1-0 win in Rome and winning the return match in Belfast. Meanwhile, Portugal was disposed of by a 4-1 aggregate. In Sweden, the Irish outplayed Czechoslovakia in the first round, winning 1-0 on a goal by the Leeds United left half Wilbur Cush. A 3-1 loss to Argentina, Northern Ireland's first South American opponent, temporarily derailed the

Irish, but they reemerged with great flair against the physically strong West Germans. Only a mighty 35-yard goal by German star Uwe Seeler prevented the Irish from upsetting the World Cup holders, and the final result was a surprising 2-2. This exciting match represented the high point .in Irish soccer up to that point and enabled Northern Ireland to meet Czechoslovakia in the play-off. The charged Irish team defeated the Czechs 2-1, after extra time, on two goals by the Aston Villa left wing Peter McParland, who had also scored three of his team's four goals in earlier games. Northern Ireland advanced to the quarter-finals with this win, and found itself pitted against the French team of Kopa, Fontaine, and Jonquet, whose goalscoring might was overwhelming. The Irish lost 4-0 and bowed out of its first and, thus far, last World Cup. The backbone of the World Cup team was Tottenham Hotspur's right half Danny Blanchflower, a virtual midfield coach on the field whose knowledge of the game made him one of the most respected British players of the postwar era. Blanchflower guided his team into an effective man-to-man defense, and with a talented forward line that included McParland, Burnley's inside left Jimmy McIlroy, and Sunderland's right wing Billy Bingham, he fostered creativity in the attack. Danny Blanchflower's brother from Manchester United, Jackie, was an outstanding center half on this Ulster team.

In the years since 1958 and the Blanchflower era, Northern Ireland has participated in four editions of the European Football Championship, gaining the second round once (1962-64) and has shared the Home International trophy once. Unfortunately, the George Best era of the 1960s and early 1970s did not produce the desired international results, and Northern Ireland teams during the strife-torn years of the 1970s have been decidedly weak. In 1976, the IFA hired Danny Blanchflower to manage and improve the national team in a new bid for international glory.

At home, Linfield has continued to dominate postwar league standings and to a lesser extent the IFA Cup. Its record-breaking total has now reached 31 championships and 31 cup wins, with victories in both competitions to its credit in each and every decade since the 1890s. Glentoran has accumulated 16 league titles and nine cup victories, and Belfast Celtic, now defunct, ranks third in overall trophy standings with 14 league titles and eight cups. Distillery's success has fallen off sharply since the pre-World War I era, as has the venerable Cliftonville's, but both clubs are frequent contenders in the first division. Glenavon (Larne) and Coleraine have been important provincial clubs in post-World War II competition. (In 1977, Distillery relocated to Lambeg, Co. Antrim, at the height of civil unrest in Belfast.)

Aside from the two major competitions—the 12-member Irish League, now underwritten by and named for the Fiat automobile company, and the IFA Cup—Northern Ireland has also generated a handful of subordinate competitions that are open to leading clubs, such as the Ulster Cup (played on a league basis) and the Hennessey Gold Cup (until 1977 a knockout tournament). Winners of these trophies down through the decades have been the familiar league and cup powers. A third subordinate competition called the City Cup was introduced in 1895 and absorbed into the Hennessey Gold Cup in 1977. Due to the civil unrest in Northern Ireland, all home internationals between October 1971 and April 1975 were played either in Europe or various locations in England and Scotland.

Northern Ireland and the Republic of Ireland had never met on the playing field before they were finally drawn together in the same qualifying group for the 1978-80 European Football Championship. Their first meeting, held in Dublin in 1978, resulted in a scoreless draw. The selection of Irish players for Northern Ireland and Republic of Ireland national teams has caused much agitation since 1950, when it was finally decided that Irish players could not play for both teams at the same time. (Thirty-two had done so before 1950.) In 1954, FIFA officially changed Ulster's name from "Ireland" to "Northern Ireland," and nullified the rule that allowed Northern Ireland to choose Republic-born players for its matches with other British national teams. (Selection was always restricted to Ulster-born players for matches against anyone else.) An experimental merger was put into effect in July 1973 when an all-Ireland team, called Shamrock Rovers XI, was defeated in Dublin, 3-2, by Brazil.

Champions

1891	Linfield	1921	Glentoran	1950	Linfield
1892	Linfield	1922	Linfield	1951	Glentoran
1893	Linfield	1923	Linfield	1952	Glenavon
1894	Glentoran	1924	Queens's Island	1953	Glentoran
1895	Linfield	1925	Glentoran	1954	Linfield
1896	Distillery	1926	Belfast Celtic	1955	Linfield
1897	Glentoran	1927	Belfast Celtic	1956	Linfield
1898	Linfield	1928	Belfast Celtic	1957	Glenavon
1899	Distillery	1929	Belfast Celtic	1958	Ards
1900	Belfast Celtic	1930	Linfield	1959	Linfield
1901	Distillery	1931	Glentoran	1960	Glenavon
1902	Linfield	1932	Linfield	1961	Linfield
1903	Distillery	1933	Belfast Celtic	1962	Linfield
1904	Linfield	1934	Linfield	1963	Distillery
1905	Glentoran	1935	Linfield	1964	Glentoran
1906	Cliftonville/Distillery	1936	Belfast Celtic	1965	Derry City
1907	Linfield	1937	Belfast Celtic	1966	Linfield
1908	Linfield	1938	Belfast Celtic	1967	Glentoran
1909	Linfield	1939	Belfast Celtic	1968	Glentoran
1910	Cliftonville	1940	Belfast Celtic	1969	Linfield
1911	Linfield	1941	no competition	1970	Glentoran
1912	Glentoran	1942	no competition	1971	Linfield
1913	Glentoran	1943	no competition	1972	Glentoran
1914	Linfield	1944	no competition	1973	Crusaders
1915	Belfast Celtic	1945	no competition	1974	Coleraine
1916	no competition	1946	no competition	1975	Linfield
1917	no competition	1947	no competition	1976	Crusaders
1918	no competition	1948	Belfast Celtic	1977	Glentoran
1919	no competition	1949	Linfield	1978	Linfield
1920	Belfast Celtic				

Cup Winners

1881	Moyola Park	1894	Distillery	1907	Cliftonville
1882	Queens's Island	1895	Linfield	1908	Bohemians
1883	Cliftonville	1896	Distillery	1909	Cliftonville
1884	Distillery	1897	Cliftonville	1910	Distillery
1885	Distillery	1898	Linfield	1911	Shelbourne
1886	Distillery	1899	Linfield	1912	Linfield
1887	Ulster	1900	Cliftonville	1913	Linfield
1888	Cliftonville	1901	Cliftonville	1914	Glentoran
1889	Distillery	1902	Linfield	1915	Linfield
1890	Gordon Highlanders	1903	Distillery	1916	Linfield
1891	Linfield	1904	Linfield	1917	Glentoran
1892	Linfield	1905	Distillery	1918	Belfast Celtic
1893	Linfield	1906	Shelbourne	1919	Linfield

1920	Shelbourne	1940	Ballymena	1960	Linfield
1921	Glentoran	1941	Belfast Celtic	1961	Glenavon
1922	Linfield	1942	Linfield	1962	Linfield
1923	Linfield	1943	Belfast Celtic	1963	Linfield
1924	Queen's Island	1944	Belfast Celtic	1964	Derry City
1925	Distillery	1945	Linfield	1965	Coleraine
1926	Belfast Celtic	1946	Linfield	1966	Glentoran
1927	Ards	1947	Belfast Celtic	1967	Crusaders
1928	Willowfield	1948	Linfield	1968	Crusaders
1929	Ballymena	1949	Derry City	1969	Ards
1930	Linfield	1950	Linfield	1970	Linfield
1931	Linfield	1951	Glentoran	1971	Distillery
1932	Glentoran	1952	Ards	1972	Coleraine
1933	Glentoran	1953	Linfield	1973	Glentoran
1934	Linfield	1954	Derry City	1974	Ards
1935	Glentoran	1955	Dundela	1975	Coleraine
1936	Linfield	1956	Distillery	1976	Carrick Rangers
1937	Belfast Celtic	1957	Glenavon	1977	Coleraine
1938	Belfast Celtic	1958	Ballymena United	1978	Linfield
1939	Linfield	1959	Glenavon		

Ireland, Republic of

Cumann Peile Na h-Eireann
(Football Association of Ireland)
80, Merrion Square, South
Dublin 2

Founded: 1921
FIFA: 1923
UEFA: 1954

Affiliated clubs: *2,716;* **registered players:** *50,328 (28 professional, 300 non-amateur);* **national stadium:** *none;* **largest stadium:** *Landsdowne Road, Dublin (48,000);* **colors:** *green jerseys with white trim, white shorts;* **season:** *August to May;* **honors:** *none.*

The liabilities of international politics have remained at the center of Eire's game since the founding of the independent state in 1921. The confusion over international recognition and the question of birthrights of Eire and Ulster players have prevented the country from developing to its fullest potential, though the support and enthusiasm of Irish Republic fans have never been dampened by the political hardships to which they have become accustomed. A second important factor has been the small population of the country and the difficulties arising from a dependent economy. Nearly all of Ireland's best players have gravitated across the Irish Sea to the wealthy clubs of England and Scotland, a persistent exodus that has left the League of

Ireland in a permanent state of crisis, in regard to both finances and playing standards. Despite the problems, however, no one has ever excluded an Eire team on a given day. While not quite among the middle-level powers in Europe, Eire is not among the weakest either, ranking about level with Greece and Turkey.

The history of football games in Ireland is ancient and linked intimately with England. An indigenous football is thought to have existed as early as the first century B.C. If so, native Celtic football games were perhaps as influential to the development of medieval football in England as were the Roman games brought to the British Isles by Caesar's legions. Certainly, some form of football was being played in Ireland by the fifth century A.D., though it may have more closely resembled Irish hurling, which historically has been the national sport. The existence of hurling in Ireland during the early middle ages is not in dispute. Throughout the medieval period, some forms of football were played in Ireland, but, as in other Celtic areas, they were not as popular as they were in Anglo-Saxon Britain.

By the thirteenth century, the rough Irish students at the University of Oxford had developed a reputation for the wild and bloody manner in which they engaged in hurling and football in town streets. An unusual piece of legislation from Galway in 1527 indicated a progressive tolerance for football in Ireland when it decreed that all ball games *except* football were prohibited in public places because they interfered with the beloved archery. The Statutes of Galway are unique in early football annals, but their motivation is unknown. Perhaps it was a mere love of the game, more likely authorities had by this time given up on an attempt to eradicate such a popular exercise as "the great foote balle." Specifically included in the ban were hurling and handball:

". . .at no tyme to use ne ocupye the horlinge of the litill balle with hockie stickes or staves, nor use no hande ball to playe withoute the walles, but onely the great foote balle, on payn of the paynis above lymittid."

The growing number of written accounts of Irish culture during the Renaissance did not clarify the place of football in daily life on the island. One English observer in Ireland during the seventeenth century reported that the game was only played in Fingal near Dublin (present-day Finglas in County Dublin), and he describes the Irish players as excellent practitioners and adept at tripping and shouldering. In 1780, the Dublin poet Lysaght described a game of football that was played each evening in front of Trinity College, Dublin, but by local working men rather than university students. This observation is in tune with contemporary trends in England, which pointed to a rejection of the game by eighteenth-century upper class society.

Irish poets of the eighteenth century were included among the surge of Restoration and Georgian authors turning to football as a subject. The most famous example was Matthew Concanen's "A Match at FootBall: a Poem. In Three Cantos," published in Dublin

in 1720. In describing a game between representatives of Lusk and Swords in County Dublin, he reveals a host of interesting details of the game as played at the time. There were many similarities with rugby: handling, throwing, and a scrum of sorts. But there were two goals on either side of the pitch, much kicking, tackling, and a ball made of leather with hay stuffed inside.

From the early nineteenth century, the development of the game in Ireland closely follows the fluctuations in England and Scotland. Irish students in the public schools and universities took to the playing fields as did their English classmates. The wealthy and landed classes began once again to identify with its growth, as the various school rules were formulated and the modern game was codified by upper class sportsmen. The eventual direction of Irish soccer as a cultural institution was decided, as elsewhere in the British Isles, by the adoption of the game by the working classes during the last decades of the nineteenth century. This important development, which was caused primarily by the industrial revolution, led to Belfast, Ireland's industrial center, becoming the ultimate hotbed of soccer activity on the island. Indeed, when the Irish Football Association (then responsible for all Ireland) was founded in 1880, it was unhesitatingly located in Belfast rather than Dublin. It followed that with the exception of Shelbourne F.C., all the leading clubs of pre-independence Ireland came from the North, with its concentration of population, industry, and experienced players from England and Scotland. The first soccer club founded in present-day Eire was the Dublin Association in 1883, though some historians have placed the formation of Bohemians F.C., also of Dublin, in 1882. Dublin Association played against a team from Dublin University in the year of its birth, and competitive soccer in the South got under way. Shelbourne's Irish Cup victories in 1906, 1911, and 1920, and Bohemians' cup win in 1908 were the only honors won by southern teams under a unified Irish association. The league championship trophy never left Ulster.

The proper history of Republic of Ireland soccer begins with independence from Great Britain in 1921. Immediately after World War I, many southern clubs defected from the Irish Football Association, which was still centered in Belfast. The Irish F.A. did not sanction these defections, but there was little it could do about it. In 1921, the year of Great Britain's offer of dominion status to Ireland, the Football Association of Ireland was founded in Dublin. The defected clubs of the South joined their new governing body, and were accompanied by a number of clubs from Belfast and Derry as well, a situation that was not tolerated by the Irish F.A. in Belfast. The new F.A. of Ireland was granted membership in FIFA in 1923, and a dominion representative was delegated to The Football Association in London. Later in the year, at a meeting of the F.A. of Ireland and the four British associations, it was agreed that the new association be called the F.A. of the Irish Free State, in deference to Northern Ireland, and that the four British associations, which were not members of FIFA at the time, would recognize Dublin's legitimacy. Irish players would continue to play freely in England, and British clubs could engage in friendlies with Irish Free State clubs. The name Irish Free State was retained by both F.A. and the nation as a whole until dominion status was relinquished in 1937 and a republic was declared. Meanwhile, the League of Ireland and the Cup of Ireland were introduced in 1921-22.

The Irish Free State's international debut was made at the Olympic Games of 1924 in Paris, where it defeated Bulgaria, 1-0, and lost to the Netherlands, 2-1, after extra time. A quick friendly with little Estonia before the team left Paris resulted in a 3-1 win, and two weeks later the USA Olympic side stopped in Dublin to play in the Irish Free State's first international at home and lost to a superior Irish team, 3-1. Having declined to enter the World Cup of 1930 in Montevideo, the Irish Free State enthusiastically tried to qualify for the 1934 and 1938 world championships. It was eliminated from the final rounds in 1934 by the Netherlands, and in 1937 by Norway after an aggregate score of five to six, a narrow defeat. But Ireland's record before World War II (33-14-8-11-72-68-36) placed it well into the middle ranking of European countries. There were three wins over Belgium, three over Switzerland, and, above all, a 5-2 drubbing of Germany in 1936 at Dublin. In addition, it drew three times with Hungary, twice in Budapest.

Though the Republic of Ireland and Northern Ireland did not play each other until 1978 (in the 1978-80 European Football Championship), the ice was broken with other British associations in 1946, when England won a friendly in Dublin by 1-0 despite superior play by the Irish team. That match has long been remembered in Ireland, and England's great winger Tom Finney, who scored the goal, has long been vilified. The return friendly in Liverpool three years later resulted in England's first defeat by a foreign country on home soil. (The English, however, are prone to award this distinction to the great Hungarian team of 1953 rather than recognize the Republic of Ireland as strictly "foreign.") The score was 2-0, and the Irish team was made up entirely of players from English clubs. England figured prominently in Irish fortunes again in 1957 when Ireland was grouped with England and Denmark in World Cup qualifying rounds. While Denmark was easily disposed of, Ireland lost decisively in England. In the return match at Dublin the result was a 1-1 draw, but England did not equalize until the final seconds of the match and only after consistent domination of the game by Irish players. Elsewhere against British teams, Republic of Ireland results have been scattered and inconclusive, though Scotland has an edge after four matches. To date only 11 matches have been played between Eire and the three relenting British associations, and six have been with England.

Ireland has attempted to qualify for each World Cup since 1934 and each European Football Championship since its inception in 1958. Its failings in these competitions, unfortunately, have not been compensated by Irish Olympic results. Its only participation in the Olympic finals was in 1948 when the Dutch won a preliminary round match, 3-1. Since the introduction of Olympic qualification rounds in 1960, Ireland has not gone through to the finals. In all international competition, Ireland has winning records against Belgium, Chile, Denmark, Ecuador, Finland, Iceland, Luxembourg, Netherlands, Norway (won six, drawn 3, lost 1, its best record), Switzerland, and Turkey, but its record since World War II has been just about the reverse of the prewar figures.

Among the nagging problems that lingered for many decades after independence was the question of both Irish associations claiming the rights to field certain Irish players. The FIFA ruling on this matter for many years was that Northern Ireland could select players born in Eire for its matches with other British associations, but was restricted to Ulster-born players for matches with anyone else. The F.A. of Ireland vehemently opposed this ruling without success. In 1954, FIFA ruled on the names of the two Irelands, Republic of Ireland and Northern Ireland. In recent years, the curtain has been lifted on friendly club matches between consenting Irish Republic and Northern Irish sides.

The original membership of the League of Ireland in 1921 consisted entirely of Dublin clubs. The first outsider was Athlone Town, elected in 1922. In 1924, Fordsons became the first club from Cork, Ireland's second largest city. Cork has since supplied 10 different clubs to the league, though never more than two at one time. Professional soccer has had considerable difficulty in surviving away from the capital city. By far the most successful club has been the famous Shamrock Rovers, which has won a record 10 championships and 20 cups. Until World War II, Shamrock Rovers also provided the majority of players selected for the national side, a source that has since shifted to English and Scottish clubs. In addition to the Rovers, two other Dublin clubs have dominated the league, Bohemians and Shelbourne, but during the 1960s and early 1970s, the most successful provincial club, Waterford, won six championships in eight years. Irish Republic clubs are still looking for their first breakthrough in European club competition.

Champions

1922	St. James Gate	1941	Cork United	1960	Limerick
1923	Shamrock Rovers	1942	Cork United	1961	Drumcondra
1924	Bohemians	1943	Cork United	1962	Shelbourne
1925	Shamrock Rovers	1944	Shelbourne	1963	Dundalk
1926	Shelbourne	1945	Cork United	1964	Shamrock Rovers
1927	Shamrock Rovers	1946	Cork United	1965	Drumcondra
1928	Bohemians	1947	Shelbourne	1966	Waterford
1929	Shelbourne	1948	Drumcondra	1967	Dundalk
1930	Bohemians	1949	Drumcondra	1968	Waterford
1931	Shelbourne	1950	Cork Athletic	1969	Waterford
1932	Shamrock Rovers	1951	Cork Athletic	1970	Waterford
1933	Dundalk	1952	St. Patrick's Athletic	1971	Hibernian Cork
1934	Bohemians	1953	Shelbourne	1972	Waterford
1935	Dolphin	1954	Shamrock Rovers	1973	Waterford
1936	Bohemians	1955	St. Patrick's Athletic	1974	Cork Celtic
1937	Sligo Rovers	1956	St. Patrick's Athletic	1975	Bohemians
1938	Shamrock Rovers	1957	Shamrock Rovers	1976	Dundalk
1939	Shamrock Rovers	1958	Drumcondra	1977	Sligo Rovers
1940	St. James Gate	1959	Shamrock Rovers	1978	Bohemians

Cup Winners

1922	St. James Gate	1932	Shamrock Rovers	1942	Dundalk
1923	Alton United	1933	Shamrock Rovers	1943	Drumcondra
1924	Athlone Town	1934	Cork	1944	Shamrock Rovers
1925	Shamrock Rovers	1935	Bohemians	1945	Shamrock Rovers
1926	Fordsons	1936	Shamrock Rovers	1946	Drumcondra
1927	Drumcondra	1937	Waterford	1947	Cork United
1928	Bohemians	1938	St. James Gate	1948	Shamrock Rovers
1929	Shamrock Rovers	1939	Shelbourne	1949	Dundalk
1930	Shamrock Rovers	1940	Shamrock Rovers	1950	Transport
1931	Shamrock Rovers	1941	Cork United	1951	Cork Athletic

1952	Dundalk	1961	St. Patrick's Athletic	1970	Bohemians
1953	Cork Athletic	1962	Shamrock Rovers	1971	Limerick
1954	Drumcondra	1963	Shelbourne	1972	Hibernian Cork
1955	Shamrock Rovers	1964	Shamrock Rovers	1973	Hibernian Cork
1956	Shamrock Rovers	1965	Shamrock Rovers	1974	Finn Harps
1957	Drumcondra	1966	Shamrock Rovers	1975	Home Farm
1958	Dundalk	1967	Shamrock Rovers	1976	Bohemians
1959	St. Patrick's Athletic	1968	Shamrock Rovers	1977	Dundalk
1960	Shelbourne	1969	Shamrock Rovers	1978	Shamrock Rov.

Israel

Hitachdut Lekaduregel Beisrael
(Israel Football Association)
12 Carlibach Street
P.O.B. 20188
Tel Aviv

Founded: 1928
FIFA: 1929

Affiliated clubs: *544;* registered players: *20,000;* national stadium: *Ramat-Gan (55,000);* largest stadium: *Ramat-Gan;* colors: *blue jerseys, white shorts;* season: *September to June;* honors: *Asian Cup winner (1964), runner-up (1956, 1960), Maccabi Tel Aviv, Asian Champion Teams' Cup (1968, 1971), Hapoel Tel Aviv, Asian Champion Teams' Cup (1967).*

Israel is one of Asia's leading soccer nations. Israeli teams at both national and club levels have won several international competitions and have placed high in the standings of almost every Asian tournament they have entered. By Asian standards, Israel has had considerable experience in organizing domestic competitions, and by virtue of its links with Europe the standard of play is quite high. The history of soccer in Israel, and Palestine before it, is intimately connected with the strong British influence before independence, and had involved Jews to the exclusion of Palestinian Arabs. Islamic beliefs throughout the Arab world resisted Western cultural institutions such as soccer until well after World War II, by which time Arab participation in the development of Israeli soccer was nearly impossible.

From the beginning, Israel has been forced to seek international opposition on the playing field outside its immediate region. One exception to this, ironically, was its very first opponent in 1934—Egypt—when a Jewish-based national team played under the name of Palestine. In World Cup and Olympic qualification rounds and other official Asian tournaments—Israel has consistently entered

all of these—international administrators have had to schedule Israeli teams around potential confrontation with Arab opposition. This has caused many hardships for the Israelis, but on those occasions when such meetings could not be avoided, Israel has invariably benefited on account of Arab forfeits.

In the mid-1970s, the power base in the Asian Football Confederation changed drastically, and in 1976, in one of the most overtly political moves by an official governing body in the history of soccer, Israel was expelled from the AFC. The Arab bloc and friends of the People's Republic of China struck a deal to get the necessary votes to admit China and remove Israel. FIFA deplored this action, and set about to have Israel reinstated or find it a new home. In 1978, the European confederation turned down Israel's request for membership, citing logistical and financial difficulties, and left the Israel Football Association to seek membership with either Oceania, whose governing body is practically dormant, or Africa, which is already overworked with nearly 40 members. Its alternative was to remain unaffiliated on the regional level.

Soccer was brought to Palestine by the infusion of British military personnel during World War I. Interest in the game was compounded immediately after the war by the immigration of European Jews who had been exposed to soccer in their native countries. Clubs and local tournaments sprang up quickly during the 1920s, and the Palestine Football Association was founded in 1928 in Tel Aviv. The new association introduced the annual Palestine Challenge Cup—a knockout competition—that same year, and a national league in 1932. The early winners of the league and cup were the same clubs that still dominate the Israeli game, Hapoel Tel Aviv and Maccabi Tel Aviv. Between 1928-48, Hapoel won a total of six cups, including the first, and six championships, and Maccabi won six cups and four championships. The first league champion in 1932 was Palestine Police, a British-based club which also won a cup in 1932. Other Challenge Cup victories went to Beitar Tel Aviv (twice) and Maccabi-Avshalom Petach-Tikva. Both competitions continued unabated during World War II. The league was suspended from 1946-48 because of political upheavals, and the cup was interrupted briefly in 1948-49, immediately after the partition.

In 1934, Palestine entered World Cup qualification rounds, and made its international debut against Egypt in a home and away series to determine the Asia-Africa berth. The Egyptians won in Cairo 7-1 and in Tel Aviv 4-1. Palestine's next internationals were in qualifying rounds for the 1938 World Cup in January and February of that year against Greece, and these too were lost, 3-1 in Tel Aviv and 1-0 in Athens. In 1940, Palestine met Lebanon in a friendly in Tel Aviv and won 5-1, its first international victory. There were no more full internationals played by Palestine before 1948.

In 1948, the authority of the Palestine Football Association was passed on to the new Hitachdut Lekaduregel Beisrael (Israel Football Association). In its first international game under the name of Israel, the national team was again grouped with European opposition in qualifying rounds for the 1950 World Cup, this time with Yugoslavia, which won both legs and qualified. Israel then played home and away friendlies with Turkey, and in Tel Aviv won its first international as an independent country, 5-1. Full international opposition was exceedingly difficult to find during the 1950s, though many European clubs and representative teams visited Israel. Seeking a berth in the World Cup continued to provide Israel with its most strenuous challenge. Greece and Yugoslavia both won home and away legs in 1954 to eliminate the Israelis, and in 1958 Israel was grouped with Turkey and Indonesia after FIFA's original choices for that group (all African) refused to play them. But Turkey and Indonesia also refused to meet Israel, and it appeared that Israel would enter the final rounds of the World Cup in Sweden without having played a single game. This being unacceptable, FIFA selected Wales to play a home and away qualifying series with Israel, and Wales won both legs 2-0 to gain the berth.

Having joined the Asian Football Confederation in 1956, Israel entered the first Asian Cup that same year. There were only four participants, and Israel placed second, defeating Hong Kong and South Vietnam and losing to South Korea, the winner of the competition. All matches were played in Hong Kong. Israel also entered the second Asian Cup in 1960, held in Seoul, and placed second by defeating South Vietnam and Taiwan and again losing to South Korea. In 1964, Israel itself was the host, and the field was again limited to four. This time Israel emerged with its first international triumph, and defeated Hong Kong, India, and South Korea. The Israelis' last chance to compete in the Asian Cup came in 1968 in Tehran, when they finished a distant third in a field of five, winning over Taiwan and Hong Kong and losing to Burma and Asia's emerging power, Iran. Israel now stands with the second best overall record in Asian Cup listings, behind Iran, and this, in addition to its later successes in entering World Cup and Olympic final rounds, has made Israel one of Asia's three or four leading soccer powers.

In the 1960s and early 1970s, Israel managed to schedule several international friendlies with European national teams. The most notable were a loss to Belgium in Tel Aviv in 1965, losses to Northern Ireland and Belgium in a triangular tournament in Jaffa in 1968, and a 2-1 win over Norway in Tel Aviv in 1972. In 1971-72, Israel's "A" team lost home and away friendlies to Italy (Under-23) in Bari and Tel Aviv, 2-0 and 1-0, respectively. In 1968, the Israelis qualified for the Olympic Games in Mexico, and achieved great success in advancing to the quarter-finals at the expense of Ghana and El Salvador. The other quarter-final qualifier from this first round group was Hungary. In the quarter-finals, Israel battled Bulgaria to a 1-1 draw, and then had the misfortune of losing the coin toss for the semi-final.

Having gained valuable experience playing in Mexico's high altitudes in 1968, Israel achieved its greatest feat in 1970 when it qualified for the World Cup final rounds—to be held in Mexico. The Israelis had to eliminate South Korea and Australia to get there, but in their first round group there was a whole new set of challenges with the presence of Italy, Uruguay, and Sweden, each a great international competitor. Israel began by losing doggedly to Uruguay 2-0, a respectable outcome, but in its next match held Sweden to a 1-1 draw on a goal by inside left Mordecai Spiegler. In the third match of the first round group, the Italians tried desperately to punch their way through Israel's defense in an unattractive game, but Israel held on for an astonishing scoreless draw. It was Israel's first success against a proven world power, though in the standings it finished at the bottom of its group.

Israel also qualified for the 1976 Olympic Games in Montreal, emerging from its first round group with France, Mexico, and Guatemala to play in the quarter-finals, where it lost to Brazil's amateurs, 4-1.

Israeli clubs have been just as successful in Asian competition as the national team. In the four editions of the now defunct Asian Champion Teams' Cup (1967-71), Israeli clubs won the trophy three times, two by Maccabi Tel Aviv and one by Hapoel Tel Aviv. In the one edition where they did not win, Taj Club of Tehran defeated Hapoel in the final. The Israeli league continues to produce fine teams. It is presently divided into three divisions. The first division was reduced from 16 to 14 clubs in 1977. The leading names in the league, aside from Maccabi Tel Aviv and Hapoel Tel Aviv, are Maccabi Haifa, Hapoel Haifa, Hapoel Tetach-Tikva, Maccabi Natania, Beitar Jerusalem, Hapoel Jerusalem, Hacoach Ramat-Gan, and Hapoel Kfar-Saba.

Italian-French Friendship Cup

Coppa dell'Amicizia Italo-Francese—Coupe de l'Amitie Français-Italien.

An annual summer competition between first and second division clubs of the Italian and French leagues, discontinued after the fifth edition in 1963. Swiss clubs participated in 1962. Ten clubs from either country were usually entered. Italian clubs were paired with French clubs, and in the space of two weekends the ten groups played home and away legs. The results of these 20 matches were tabulated, and the country whose clubs accumulated the most points was declared the winner. Clubs from the same country never met each other. In the fourth and fifth editions, individual clubs were awarded the trophy.

Winners

1959 Italy
1960 Italy
1961 Italy
1962 RC Lens (France)
1963 Genoa (Italy)

Italy

Federazione Italiana Giuoco Calcio
Via Gregorio Allegri, 14
C.P. 2450
00198-Roma

Founded: 1898
FIFA: 1905
UEFA: 1954

Affiliated clubs: *16,307;* registered players: *710,040 (682 professional; 4,447 non-amateur);* national stadium: *Stadio Olimpico, Rome (90,000);* largest stadium: *Stadio Olimpico;* colors: *blue jerseys, white shorts;* season: *September to June;* honors: *World Cup winner (1934, 1938), runner-up (1970), Olympic Games winner (1936), third place (1928, 1960), European Football Championship winner (1968), International Cup (1929, 1935), Internazionale, Intercontinental Cup (1964, 1965), European Cup (1964, 1965), AC Milan, Intercontinental Cup (1969), European Cup (1963, 1969), European Cup Winners' Cup (1968, 1973), Latin Cup (1951, 1956), Fiorentina, European Cup Winners' Cup (1961), AS Roma, Fairs Cup (1961), Juventus, UEFA Cup (1977), Bologna, Mitropa Cup (1932, 1934).*

Italy's place among the elite of world soccer is assured for posterity on several counts. The Italians dominated international competition during the 1930s with two World Championships and an Olympic gold medal, and Italian clubs have been constantly at the forefront of the European game since international club competitions became popular in the 1950s. Italian soccer has been one of Europe's greatest spawning grounds for talented players, and the heavy commercialization of postwar Italian clubs led inextricably to a high concentration of international stars before the ban on foreign players was implemented in 1964. On the more dubious though no less significant side, Italian teams of the 1950s and '60s caused a revolution in the tactics of soccer with their *catenaccio* system, which more than 25 years after its introduction is still affecting the way people all over the world play the game.

Italy, the bastion of defensive soccer, has the additional distinction of having been the source for the various football games that were spread to the British Isles and France by Roman legions—games that quite possibly established some of the first links in the chain of modern football. The Roman ball games, *harpastrum* and others, owed their origin in turn to the ancient Greek ball games, but it was left to the well-traveled Romans to export football to other parts of Europe. When the Celtic tribes of Britain adopted the Roman ball games, according to one theory, in addition to having their own indigenous forms of football, the historical groundwork for the modern game was laid. If we accept the idea of a Roman-Celtic linkage, we can see that Italy's role in the history of football is unique.

As it happened, Italian life in the post-Renaissance era was not as conducive to the continual development of the game as in England, and it was in the latter that modern football was born. The Roman football tradition in Italy, however, was carried at least into the Renaissance itself, because in Florence, between the fifteenth and seventeenth centuries, we find the most glorious example of soccer ancestry before the modern era. This was the ritualized football game known as *giuoco del calcio fiorentino* (Florentine kickball). *Calcio* was a regulated game, more closely resembling rugby than soccer, which was played by the aristocracy during the Medici epoch, and it featured much running, jumping, and tackling (in the American football sense). Goals were scored by throwing the ball over a designated spot on the perimeter of the field. The "field" was actually the Piazza di Santa Croce, and games were held every night between Epiphany and Lent. Its avowed purpose was to express the aristocratic graces and celebrate the common rank of all participants, but, as in the art and literature of the period, it was also typical of the Renaissance revival of classical mores.

Ironically, its prominence in Florentine culture led visiting English aristocrats to look upon their own sprawling versions of football with more favor, and this lead ultimately to the entrance of football into the mainstream of English life. *Calcio,* however, was an aristocrat's game, meant for a certain time and place, and it did not survive into the modern era except as an annual pageant for tourists. Its only legacy is the use of the word itself in place of an Italian adaptation of the English word "football," e.g., Federazione Italiana Giuoco Calcio (Italian Kickball Game Federation).

After all was said and done, it was left to the British to import modern soccer to Italian shores, though an Italian businessman, Edoardo Bisio, is generally credited with introducing it in Turin in 1887. The game first took root in that city, spreading rapidly to Genoa and Milan, and from there to other cities in the northern provinces. The first club was Football Club Internazionale (not to be confused with Internazionale Milan), founded in Turin in 1890. F.C. Torinese was formed in Turin in 1894, and the Sezione Calcio della Societá Ginnastica di Torino followed soon after that. A fourth major Turin club, Sport Club Juventus, was formed in 1897. In 1893, the Genoa Cricket and Football Club—*il vecchio Genoa*—was established, destined to become the first great club in Italian soccer. A second Genoa club, Sezione Calcio dell'Andrea Doria, was started in 1895. In Milan, the first club was the Milan Cricket and Football Club, founded in 1899.

All but one of these pioneering clubs were to figure prominently in the development of the Italian game. In 1906, F.C. Internazionale merged with F.C. Torinese to form the venerable F.C. Torino (later Torino). In 1899, S.C. Juventus became F.C. Juventus, Italy's most popular club after the 1920s. Milan C.F.C. was eventually renamed AC Milan, and in 1908 spawned F.C Internazionale when a group of dissident Milan players broke away to form their own club. Genoa Cricket and Football Club proudly holds on to its original name to this day, as do dozens of other Italian clubs with English-sounding names. In 1946, Andrea Doria merged with another Genoese club, Sampierdarenese, to form UC Sampdoria, Genoa's archrival. Of the seven pioneering clubs, only Ginnastica Torino did not survive the first years of Italian soccer. Meanwhile, the game spread across the northern provinces from the early centers in Piemonte, Liguria, and Lombardy, and by 1898 it was being played by students in Vicenza, and in Padua by 1899. In Bergamo, Busto Arizio, Vercelli, Udine, Ascoli, and Palermo, sports clubs or gymnastic societies that in later years would become the parent bodies of important soccer clubs were founded before the turn of the century.

In 1898, the Federazione Italiana del Football was founded in Turin, and in 1905 it became one of the first associations after the charter group of seven to join FIFA. Its present name, Federazione Italiana Giuoco Calcio (FIGC), was adopted in 1909. An Italian championship was also introduced in 1898, but it was not to take on the appearance of a national league until 1929-30. For 33 years, the format of the Campeonato Prime del Girone Unico was altered and realtered under various knockout formats to accommodate the ever-growing number of clubs participating and to appease one region or another in the perennial geographic struggle for power. The FIGC itself was so entwined in these regional struggles that it shifted the location of its headquarters four times after it was founded: Milan (1905), Turin again (1911), Bologna (1926), and Rome (1929).

Genoa, led by its illustrious English goalkeeper, Dr. Spensley, won six of the first seven championships, though its opposition was indeed sparse. Only four clubs participated in 1898 and 1899—the three Turin clubs and Genoa—and only five or six until 1909. Milan became the first Lombard club to participate in 1900, and a fourth province was not represented until 1909 (the Veneto club, Venezia). In 1911, Emilia was added in the form of Bologna F.C., and in 1913, three central provinces, Tuscany, Lazio, and Campania (the Florence and Rome regions), were permitted to enter a total of 12 clubs between them. By this time, 30 clubs in all were participating, and the championship was being decided by a two-leg home and away final between the winner of the North and the winner of the Central-South. When the knockout formats were finally discontinued in 1929, 12 of Italy's 19 provinces had participated.

Other than Bologna's pair of wins in 1925 and 1929, every championship between 1898-29 was won by clubs from Piemonte, Liguria, or Lombardy. Genoa won eight (including one for the unfinished 1914-15 season), Pro Vercelli seven (one in the breakaway CCI league in 1922), Milan three, Internazionale Milan two, Juventus two, and Torino two (one revoked). The domination of Italian soccer by the big northern clubs became firmly established. At least two of them became wealthy by their intitmate connections with huge corporations: AC Milan with the Pirelli tire company (before World War I) and Juventus with the vast Fiat automobile concern (in the early 1920s). Though foreigners—especially British and Swiss—were still seen in some lineups as late as 1914, the first Italian soccer idol was a native-born player, the AC Milan and Genoa fullback Renzo De Vecchi, known as *Il figlio di dio* ("The Son of God"), who made his international debut for Italy in 1910 while only 16.

The FIGC was 12 years old before Italy finally entered international competition. In 1910, it played host to France in Milan and won 6-2. Ten days later, the Italians traveled to Budapest, and were jolted by a 6-1 loss to Hungary. Before the outbreak of World War I, Italy played in 19 full internationals, winning only six and losing nine. The sophisticated

Central European teams, Austria and Hungary, were responsible for five of these losses. Italy's biggest disappointment was a loss to lowly Finland in extra time at the 1912 Olympic Games in Stockholm, eliminating it from the competition. Switzerland and France, its most frequent opponents during the 1910-15 period, were both defeated twice in five attempts.

The manager of the 1912 Olympic team was a Piemontese named Vittorio Pozzo. Pozzo was the outstanding figure in Italian soccer history. Among other things, he was to be the guiding force behind Italy's great successes of the interwar years and a prime mover in the creation of a national league. He returned briefly as manager of Italy at the 1924 Olympics, and in 1929 he became the permanent *Commissario Tecnico* of the national team, a post he held for 20 years. His influence was seen in Italy's winning of the first International Cup in 1927-29 and the bronze medal at the Amsterdam Olympics in 1928, but the ultimate effect of his leadership was Italy's outright domination of world soccer during the 1930s. Pozzo developed a system, known as *metodo*, from similar tactics used by Manchester United, the club he had watched closely during the first decade of the century as a resident in England. The key to *metodo* was an attacking center half who distributed freely to either wing, and Pozzo's ideal center half was eventually found in

Luisito Monti, the Argentine *oriundo* (foreigner of Italian extraction), who joined the national side in 1932.

Italy's winning form commenced immediately after Pozzo took over in 1929. Between 1930 and the outbreak of war in 1940, Italy lost only seven games out of a total 67 full internationals, a mere two of these at home. Austria and Czechoslovakia accounted for two apiece, and international powers England and Spain accounted for two between them. Austria, the second great international power during the 1930s, was Italy's strongest opposition until the German occupation in 1938. Italy's tough blend of hard tackling and scintillating skills were in marked contrast to the slower, short passing "Danubian" game of Austria. This endlessly fascinating contrast, as well as the presence of Europe's two most celebrated national managers, Pozzo and his Austrian counterpart Hugo Meisl, resulted in one of the greatest ongoing rivalries in soccer history.

In 1934, with Italy itself playing host, the *azzurri* ("blues") won the World Championship before zealous home crowds whose fervor was heightened by the Fascist spirit of the day. Mussolini, a devoted *azzurri* supporter, witnessed the victorious final in the Stadio PNF (Rome) against Czechoslovakia, but the big match of the tournament was played in the semi-finals at Milan's San Siro, when an off-form Austria allowed Italy to

The Italian national team obediently gives the Fascist salute to a capacity Austrian crowd before an International Cup match, Vienna's Städtischer Stadion, 1932. The azzurri, though losers to Austria's great Wunderteam on this day, were on the verge of world domination. (Left to right) Costantino, Orsi, Selavi, Magnossi, Ferraris IV, Sansone, Meazza, Bertolini, Pitto, Rosetta, Allemandi.

advance to the final with a close 1-0 win. Italy's goal was fittingly scored by its Argentine right wing Guaita. Its earlier wins in the first round had been against the USA (7-1) and Spain, the latter a replay after a 1-1 draw the day before. In the final, Italy won by 2-1 on goals by the sublime Orsi, another *oriundo*, and Schiavio. Away from the playing field, the entire competition was dominated by Fascist salutes and martial music, celebrations, and tributes to *Il Duce*. On the field, the *azzurri* had won their first World Championship with a fair bit of muscle and Vittorio Pozzo's wholly genuine enthusiasm.

In 1938, under more tenuous conditions in France, Italy returned to the World Cup without Monti, Orsi, or the veteran goal-keeper Combi. But Giuseppe Meazza, the gifted inside right of World Cup and Highbury fame in 1934, was joined on the forward line by Silvio Piola, who was to be the hero of this World Championship and an Italian idol for years to come. In the first round, however, Italy stumbled over its 1936 Olympic nemesis Norway, and was barely able to achieve a 2-1 win in extra time on a goal by Piola. None of its later opponents—France, Brazil, and Hungary—were as troublesome as Norway, though Brazil and Hungary were astonishing-ly gifted teams. In the final against Hungary, Italy was superior in all respects. Piola and the left wing Colaussi scored a pair of goals each, Hungary managed only two, and Italy won its second World Championship. In contrast to 1934, Italy's success in France was untainted by mitigating political factors, and not only was Italy's the best team in the competition, but its style had become less physical and more attractive in appearance. This was, indeed, the finest team Italy had ever produced, and its victory represented the high point in Italian soccer.

In domestic competition, Genoa and Pro Vercelli held on to their leadership of the Italian championship after World War I with a pair of titles apiece, but in the mid-1920s, the tide turned away from them in favor of the bigger, wealthier clubs. Juventus, led by its *azzurri* captain Giampiero Combi, won a championship in 1926, three years after Fiat's Agnelli family purchased majority holdings in the club, but 1926 was only a preamble to Juve's "Great Epoch." With British coaching and half the lineup filled with foreign stars, Juve won five championships in a row between 1931-35, and began its climb to becoming the most successful of all Italian clubs. Pozzo's national team during this period

was based on Juventus players. Aside from Combi, Monti, and Orsi, Juventus had the most celebrated backfield of its time—Rosetta and Caligaris—and when this extraordinary duo fell out of favor by the mid-1930s, Juve brought in Foni and Rava to take their place, and these two became as celebrated as their famous predecessors. Both Rosetta and Caligaris in their time and Foni and Rava in theirs played for Italy under Pozzo.

Juve's hold on the new national league was broken in 1935-36 by Bologna, the first non-northern club to win the championship. Bologna won four titles between 1936-41, its greatest star being the Uruguayan *oriundo* Michael Andreolo. The third great club of the interwar era was Inter Milan, renamed Ambrosiana-Inter during the Fascist era after a merger with UC Milanese. Ambrosiana's idol from 1928-38 was the elegant Meazza. With him playing either center forward or inside right, the giant Milanese club won titles in 1930 and 1938. A national cup competition, the Coppa Italia, was started in 1922, but then as now it was not much fancied by the fans, and a second edition was not played until 1935-36. During the late 1930s, 156 clubs were participating in the cup, but from 1941 to the present, the Coppa Italia has been restricted to first and second division clubs only, and there was a hiatus altogether between 1943-58.

At Mussolini's insistence, a wartime league continued until the Fascist downfall in 1943, by which time Torino had risen to the forefront, destined to become the finest club team Italy had yet seen. Torino won the 1942-43 series, and when the league resumed in 1945-46 (a 1943-44 season was cut short by the Allied invasions) Torino emerged on top again. It won in 1947 (by 10 points) and 1948 (by an astounding 16 points and scoring 125 goals in 40 games). Among its stars was the legendary inside left Valentino Mazzola, the father of Sandro Mazzola of later Inter Milan fame, and eight members of the current national team. Four weeks before the end of the 1948-49 season, with four points clear at the top of the standings and sure of the league title for a fifth consecutive year, the airplane that was carrying the team home from a friendly in Lisbon crashed in the Turin suburb of Superga, killing all aboard, including the entire first and second team, manager, coach, and trainer. A state funeral was held, and the nation went into deep mourning. The remaining four games in its league schedule were played out by Torino's youth team against the youth teams of the opposition, and all four were won. Torino was awarded the championship on the basis of these results with a five point margin in the standings.

The Torino disaster shook Italian soccer to its foundation. The national team was decimated and, to add to the confusion, the game in Italy was in the throes of undergoing a revolutionary tactical transformation. Pozzo's *metodo* (method) had finally given way during the 1940s to his *sistema* (system)—the nomenclature here is not without significance—in which he replaced the attacking center half with a full-blown stopper. This change, made with great reluctance by Pozzo, was noteworthy because it anticipated Italy's preoccupation with defensive tactics starting in the late 1940s. *Catenaccio*, the defensively oriented system in which there were four positioned defenders as well as one mobile defender (the *libero*, or sweeper) behind them, began at Triestina in 1948 with considerable success under manager Nereo Rocco. By the early 1950s, *catenaccio* ("great chain" or "bolt") or some variation of the *verrou* system to which it is related, had spread to some clubs of the upper divisions, especially the smaller ones which found the going very difficult against the Milan and Turin giants that were importing one lethal goalscorer after another.

The immediate postwar years saw a startling increase in the number of foreign stars in Italian ranks. There had been many famous *oriundi* and other foreigners before the war, of course, but a virtual epidemic was reached following the 1948 Olympics in London, the first great postwar showcase of international stars. The first really important signing was probably that of Hungary's György Sarosi to Bologna in 1946. Juventus signed the fabulous Danish left wing pair from the London Olympics, John Hansen and Carl Praest, in 1948 and 1949, respectively. But the most important of all was the arrival of Sweden's Olympic front line heroes, Gren, Nordahl, and Liedholm, to AC Milan, the only club among the big four that had not won any championships since the pre-World War I era. *Grenoli*, as the Swedish threesome were fondly called, led Milan back into a leadership role in Italian soccer.

After Torino entered a depressing and protracted decline following the Superga air disaster, the league was dominated by Milan, Inter Milan, and Juventus, each of which took a pair of titles between 1950-55. The goalscoring bonanza reached its height between 1949-51 before defensive systems began to grow in both size and ferocity. Juventus and Milan topped 100 goals in 1949-50, and the following year they were joined in this extraordinary feat by Inter Milan. In 1952-53, however, Inter won the league championship with a total of 46 goals, and became the first of the big four clubs to adopt a rugged *catenaccio* system without supplementing it with an efficient counterattack; the result of this trend was a noticeable decline of goals scored throughout the country. AC Milan, meanwhile, entered the era of the European Cup rated as one of the best club teams in Europe, and in 1951 and 1956 won the Latin Cup with convincing wins over Atlético Madrid, Lille, Benfica, and Athletic Bilbao.

In the late 1950s, AC Milan won three Italian championships, and struggled with Stade de Reims and the invincible Real Madrid for European supremacy, making a durable impression wherever it went with Liedholm and its Uruguayan forward Juan Schiaffino. This period also saw the rise to prominence of Fiorentina, the Florentine club that became the first from Central Italy to break the hegemony of the northern big four and Bologna. Fiorentina won the championship in 1956 (employing *catenaccio* very successfully) without losing a single game until the final week of the season, and then gained second place in the league for the next four consecutive years. In 1956-57, it advanced to the final of the European Cup, but Real Madrid swept the Florentines aside with ease.

Unfortunately, the influx of foreign stars, particularly in forward positions, and the negative attitude engendered by *catenaccio* resulted in a disappointing period for the *azzurri* in international competition. Though Italy qualified for the World Championships of 1950, 1954, 1962, and 1966, it failed to advance to the second round each time. In 1958, Italy failed to qualify altogether when the Northern Ireland of Danny Blanchflower and Jimmy McIlroy won both Rome and Belfast legs in the qualifying round. These results were shocking to a country used to hovering around the top echelons of world soccer, and the FIGC finally accepted the fact that Italian players were not getting enough top flight playing time. In 1964 the floodgates were closed to foreign players completely, and it was only in 1978 that a small group of wealthy clubs began once again to pressure the Federazione to reconsider.

The ultimate degradation occurred at the 1966 World Cup in England, when the resourceful Korea DPR defeated a star-filled

Italian team in the opening round by 1-0. Embarrassed and fearful of widespread reaction at home, the team flew back to Genoa in the early hours of the morning, and were greeted by a barrage of vegetables. Many jobs were lost, and *azzurri* team members were dogged for months by derisive fans at league matches. A semblance of order was finally restored in time for the 1966-68 European Nations' Cup, but it was an uninspiring team that ultimately won that competition—in Rome—after a replay against Yugoslavia.

At the World Cup of 1970 in Mexico, a team replete with world class talent was expected to atone for the sins of 1966, and left side striker Gigi Riva was expected to do more than the others. Its droll *catenaccio* was still at the heart of the plan, but in Mazzola, Rivera, and Riva, there was thought to be enough striking power to have an effective counterattack. Concern mounted when Italy won its first round group after scoring only one goal, but it was lucky in the next round to face Mexico, the weakest of the eight quarter-finalists, and advance with ease to the next round. Its best match was the semi-final against Germany FR, which it won by 4-3 in a thrilling—though not necessarily good—end-to-end contest between strikers and defenders. In the final, Italy was given the thankless task of holding back one of the greatest goalscoring machines ever assembled, as Brazil offered Italy and the world a textbook lesson on ball control skills and intuitive playmaking. The result was a respectable 4-1 loss to Pelé & Co., and the team must have been relieved to go home with a second place medal. In 1974, Italy was once again shut out of second round World Cup competition by Argentina, its old South American adversary, and Poland, the revelation of the tournament.

Despite the pervasive influence of *catenaccio,* Italy's biggest contribution to postwar soccer has been its great success in European club competition. Inter Milan and AC Milan, brimming with talent, scaled the heights between 1963-69, first one then the other, bringing international glory to Italy's largest city. AC Milan, led by the phenomenal Gianni Rivera, won the league in 1962 and the European Cup the following year, and after its 1969 league triumph, won both the European Cup and the Intercontinental Cup. The Brazilian Jose Altafini was there to help from 1958-65, and the West German international back Karl-Heinz Schnellinger after 1965.

Milan also won the European Cup Winners' Cup convincingly in 1968 and 1973.

AC Milan's crosstown archrival Inter, always the more brash of the two clubs, opted for a more garrisoned *catenaccio* under its manager Helenio Herrera, and, in some respects, was even more successful than Milan. Inter won three league championships during the 1960s, and these were followed by two successive European Cup wins and two Intercontinental Cup wins.

Fiorentina, in the meantime, achieved victory in the first European Cup Winners' Cup against a Glasgow Rangers team not yet versed in *catenaccio*, and AS Roma, the first Roman club ever to win the league championship (1941), became the first and only Roman club to win a European honor in the fledgling Fairs Cup of 1961. The biggest domestic story of the 1960s, however, was the rise of the little Sardinian club Cagliari from rags to riches on the heels of Gigi Riva. When Riva arrived at Cagliari in 1963, it was a third division club with little hope for the bright lights of Europe. In his first year, Riva carried the club to *Serie B* (Division II), and one year later to *Serie A*. In 1969-70, it won the championship, and in the European Cup one year later, Cagliari eliminated St. Étienne of France, and was itself ousted in the second round by Atlético Madrid.

The Italian league is divided into four divisions—*Serie A* through *D. A* and *B* are national in composition and are entirely professional, the latter having been created in 1933. *Serie C* is made up of three regional sections, and *Serie D* is a huge amalgamation of nine regional sections; both *C* and *D* are semiprofessional. Promotion and relegation are possible from top to bottom. Average attendances in the *Serie A* are the highest in Europe, each club boasting exceptionally loyal followings. SSC Napoli has the highest attendance average of any club on the continent (over 70,000). The greatest sources of public interest are the two world famous archrivalries: Juventus-Torino and AC Milan-Inter Milan. Their stature ranks with the great English, Scottish, and Spanish rivalries in intensity. Other less world-renowned, though equally passionate, rivalries exist in Rome (AS Roma vs. Lazio) and Genoa (Genoa vs. Sampdoria). In each of these four cities, the two big clubs share home grounds, but unfortunately, violence in the stands has been commonplace for years.

Champions

1898	Genoa	1925	Bologna	1952	Juventus
1899	Genoa	1926	Juventus	1953	Internazionale
1900	Genoa	1927	Torino (revoked)	1954	Internazionale
1901	AC Milan	1928	Torino	1955	AC Milan
1902	Genoa	1929	Bologna	1956	Fiorentina
1903	Genoa	1930	Ambrosiana-Inter	1957	AC Milan
1904	Genoa	1931	Juventus	1958	Juventus
1905	Juventus	1932	Juventus	1959	AC Milan
1906	AC Milan	1933	Juventus	1960	Juventus
1907	AC Milan	1934	Juventus	1961	Juventus
1908	Pro Vercelli	1935	Juventus	1962	AC Milan
1909	Pro Vercelli	1936	Bologna	1963	Internazionale
1910	Internazionale	1937	Bologna	1964	Bologna
1911	Pro Vercelli	1938	Ambrosiana-Inter	1965	Internazionale
1912	Pro Vercelli	1939	Bologna	1966	Internazionale
1913	Pro Vercelli	1940	Ambrosiana-Inter	1967	Juventus
1914	Casale	1941	Bologna	1968	AC Milan
1915	Genoa	1942	AS Roma	1969	Fiorentina
1916	no competition	1943	Torino	1970	Cagliari
1917	no competition	1944	no competition	1971	Internazionale
1918	no competition	1945	no competition	1972	Juventus
1919	no competition	1946	Torino	1973	Juventus
1920	Internazionale	1947	Torino	1974	Lazio
1921	Pro Vercelli	1948	Torino	1975	Juventus
1922	Novese (FIGC)	1949	Torino	1976	Torino
	Pro Vercelli (CCI)	1950	Juventus	1977	Juventus
1923	Genoa	1951	AC Milan	1978	Juventus
1924	Genoa				

Cup Winners

1922	Vado	1937	Genoa	1952	no competition
1923	no competition	1938	Juventus	1953	no competition
1924	no competition	1939	Ambrosiana-Inter	1954	no competition
1925	no competition	1940	Fiorentina	1955	no competition
1926	no competition	1941	Venezia	1956	no competition
1927	no competition	1942	Juventus	1957	no competition
1928	no competition	1943	Torino	1958	Lazio
1929	no competition	1944	no competition	1959	Juventus
1930	no competition	1945	no competition	1960	Juventus
1931	no competition	1946	no competition	1961	Fiorentina
1932	no competition	1947	no competition	1962	Napoli
1933	no competition	1948	no competition	1963	Atalanta
1934	no competition	1949	no competition	1964	AS Roma
1935	no competition	1950	no competition	1965	Juventus
1936	Torino	1951	no competition	1966	Fiorentina

1967	AC Milan	1971	Torino	1975	Fiorentina
1968	Torino	1972	AC Milan	1976	Napoli
1969	AS Roma	1973	AC Milan	1977	AC Milan
1970	Bologna	1974	Bologna	1978	Internazionale

Ivory Coast

Fédération Ivoirienne de Football	Founded: 1960
B.P. 1807	FIFA: 1960
Abidjan	CAF: 1960

Affiliated clubs: *78;* **registered players:** *3,255;* **national stadium:** *Stade Houphouet-Boigny, Abidjan (27,456);* **largest stadium:** *Stade Houphouet-Boigny;* **colors:** *orange jerseys, white shorts;* **season:** *November to August;* **honors:** *Stade d'Abidjan, African Cup of Champion Clubs (1966).*

Ivory Coast ranks with Guinea, its bitter archrival to the west, as the leading exponent of good soccer in French-speaking West Africa. Ties with the French have always been strong and cordial in the Ivory Coast, and this fact quickened *ivoirienne* interest in the game. After World War II, there were links with the colonial soccer federation of French West Africa in Dakar, and by the 1950s, Abidjan, the capital, had become one of the most active soccer-playing cities in the region. A national championship and cup competition (Coupe Nationale) were established in the early 1960s, and the major preoccupation since then has been to break the stranglehold of *le mythe Abidjanais,* or the dominance by clubs from Abidjan of the national game. This has been a tall order because three Abidjan clubs, A.S.E.C., Stade d'Abidjan, and Stella Club, are leading international powers in African soccer.

The national team, known as *les éléphants,* became one of the first representatives of the former French colonies to qualify for the final rounds of the African Nations' Cup in 1965. It met with immediate success, defeating Congo-Léopoldville in the first round by 3-0 to gain a berth in the third place game, and there it blanked Senegal, 1-0, to win its first international honor. In the 1968 edition of the Nations' Cup, Ivory Coast qualified with the most talented lineup in the competition, and won third place again with a victory over Ethiopia that avenged an earlier loss to Ethiopia in the first round.

In the 1970 edition of the Nation's Cup, having qualified for a third time in succession, Ivory Coast finished on top of its first round group. Led by midfielder Ernest Kallet, a sophisticated orchestrator of attacks, it was again the most potent offensive team in the field, shutting out the home team Sudan and demolishing Ethiopia 6-1. In the semi-finals, however, another overtime loss to Ghana, as in the previous competition, thwarted the Ivory Coast's seemingly inevitable march to the final. In the third place game, Egypt took advantage of *les éléphants'* exhaustion following the semi-finals and won 3-1. In three consecutive African Nations' Cup tournaments, Ivory Coast had placed in the top four three times, an exceptional record. In the 1974 African Nations' Cup, however, it finished at the bottom of its first round group, having failed to win a single game against Egypt, Uganda, or Zambia. Ivory Coast also reached the third qualifying rounds for both the 1974 and 1978 World Cups.

In 1966, Stade d'Abidjan won the second edition of the African Champions' Cup with a fine win in the final over Mali's Stade Bamako. While *ivoirienne* clubs have not won that coveted title again, A.S.E.C. Abidjan was a finalist in 1971, losing to Cameroon's Canon de Yaounde, and again in 1976, losing to feared Guinean rivals Hafia F.C. Stella Club, meanwhile, was the losing finalist in the first African Cup Winners' Cup in 1975.

Other than Abidjan, Ivory Coast's secondary soccer hotbeds are Bouaké, Gagnoa, Man (in the far west), Daloa, and Abengourou. The first division of the national league is made up of 16 clubs, and it is supported by a second division and a host of regional leagues and cup competitions contested by a total of 70 clubs.

J

Jab kick   Also known as "stab kick."

A quick, sudden kick, usually short, in which the leg does not straighten to its full extent.

Jamaica

Jamaica Football Association
70 Border Avenue
Kingston 8

Founded: 1910
FIFA: 1962
CONCACAF: 1963

Affiliated clubs: *146;* **registered players:** *20,124;* **national stadium:** *National Stadium, Kingston (40,000);* **largest stadium:** *National Stadium;* **colors:** *green jerseys, black shorts;* **season:** *August to April;* **honors:** *none.*

British residents introduced the game to Jamaica during the last years of the nineteenth century, and the Jamaican Football Federation (JFF), founded in 1910, was affiliated with The Football Association in London until independence in 1962. (The "Federation" in its name was changed to "Association" in the early 1970s.)

The first recorded international by a Jamaican team was during the first Championship of the Central American and Caribbean Confederation in 1930 at Havana. Jamaica lost both its matches in the first round, by 3-1 to Cuba and 5-4 to Honduras, and was eliminated. In 1938, it played a five-match series over nine days with Haiti in Port-au-Prince, and won once (3-0), drew once (0-0), and lost three times (5-2, 2-0, and 2-0). It did not participate in further Central American and Caribbean championships until 1962, when the tournament was held in Kingston, but it did enter some editions of the Championship of CONCACAF during the 1960s without good results. Financial limitations have been an obstacle to the JFA sending its champion clubs to the CONCACAF Club Championship. As recently as 1976, the Jamaican champion was not entered. A number of good Jamaican players have sought professional careers in the United States.

James, Alexander   (1902-1953)

The outstanding character in British soccer between the wars, James was a soccer genius whose scheming for the legendary Arsenal team of the 1930s was the central factor in that club's success. As a deep-lying inside forward, it was James who often initiated counterattacks in the midfield and, through his deft and imaginative distribution of the ball, gave life to a tactical theory that eventually altered the way soccer was played everywhere for decades. Above all, he was known for the knee-length baggy shorts he wore throughout his career, prompting a continuous stream of cartoons about the short Scot who seemed to have no torso.

James started playing in his native Scotland with the amateur clubs Belshill Athletic and Ashfield before moving to Raith Rovers in 1922. By the time Preston North End had signed him three years later, he had developed into a goalscoring inside forward, and with Preston scored 53 goals in 147 appearances between 1925-29. His new assignment at Arsenal (schemer) required a complete change of roles, but since this was a condition for his signing with Arsenal in the first place, he accepted it grudgingly. Arsenal's success during James' tenure there—four league championships and two F.A. Cup wins—vindicated his personal sacrifice. Unfortunately, he was selected to play for Scotland only eight times (four of them before his move to Arsenal) during a period when the Scottish F.A. frowned on deserters to the English league. He retired from Arsenal in 1937 after 231 appearances and 26 goals, and joined a commercial bookmaking outfit, which ruled out any possiblity of coaching in the upper echelons, though he did coach briefly in Poland just before the outbreak of war. After World War II, he was hired for a spell as an assistant manager by Arsenal, and worked periodically as a journalist.

Scotland's Alex James, the most popular British player of his day, wearing his famous baggy shorts—the subject of a thousand cartoons—and Arsenal's equally famous red and white jersey.

Japan

Nippon Shukyu Kyokai
(Football Association of Japan)
1-1-1 Jinnan, Shibuya-Ku
Tokyo

Founded: 1921
FIFA: 1929-45
1950
AFC: 1954

Affiliated clubs: *16,317;* registered players: *260,000;* national stadium: *National*

Stadium of Tokyo (72,000); largest stadium: *National Stadium;* colors: *blue jerseys, white shorts;* season: *March to January;* honors: *Olympic Games third place (1968).*

Japan is not considered a major soccer power in Asia, but Japanese national teams have a long history of participating in Asian competitions. Only since the Tokyo Olympics of 1974 has the game made headway, and with an all-amateur program under the sponsorship of industrial and commercial enterprises it is unlikely that Japanese soccer will make a noticeable impact on the international scene until the 1980s. Japan's customary devotion to excellence, however, has already made its mark on the domestic game, and the seriousness of Japanese players and officials has been striking to foreign observers.

Japan is the home of the ancient football game *kemari,* which more closely resembled modern soccer than any other ancient ball game except China's *tsu chu.* It is known to have been played as early as 600 B.C. and as late as 300 A.D., but a derivative, usually called *kemari asobi* may have been played as late as the thirteenth or fifteenth centuries. The ancient version was significant in both religious and political contexts, and it featured the kicking of a ball into a "goal." After 300 B.C., the "goal" was described as a pair of five-yard high bamboo stakes. In later centuries, the ball is described as measuring 22 cm. in diameter, and 20-minute games were played on a court 14 meters wide. Proper codes of conduct in the finest samurai tradition were both expected and observed.

It is believed that modern soccer was introduced in Japan by an English teacher named Johns in 1874 at the Kogakuryo School just north of Tokyo. In a pattern not unlike that of China, the game was primarily restricted to a small number of schools until well after the turn of the century, and few Japanese were exposed to soccer unless they had connections with British-oriented learning institutions. The growth of the Olympic movement in Japan resulted in the first steps toward organize teams. A national team of college-age students was entered in the third edition of the Far East Games in 1917, held in Tokyo, and this represented Japan's international soccer debut. The only other countries in the tournament, China and the Philippines, were easy victors on this occasion, 8-0 and 15-2, respectively, indicating the oppositions greater experience. But Japan can claim to have been the third country in Asia to

become involved with international soccer competition by virtue of these matches.

In 1921, the Nippon Shukyu Kyokai (Football Association of Japan) was founded in Tokyo, and a national cup competition was instituted that same year. The association was admitted to FIFA in 1929. The formation of the Nippon Shukyu Kyokai was instigated by Japan's second participation in the Far East Game just a few weeks earlier in Shanghai. Japan's losses in this competition were less painful than they had been before (4-1 to China and 3-0 to the Philippines), and the association resolved to enter each biannual edition in the future. In 1923 and 1925, Japan again lost to China and the Philippines and for the third and fourth time finished in third place. In the 1927 edition, however, the Japanese team managed to defeat the Philippines 2-1 and was runner-up to China in the standings. In 1930, when the games were held in Tokyo once again, Japan had its most challenging run at China's perennial first place finish. The Philippines were defeated 7-2 and China was held to a 3-3 draw. When China defeated the Philippines 5-0, however, China won the trophy on goal average; Japan settled for second place again. In the 1934 edition, a fourth entrant made its appearance, the Dutch East Indies, and the newcomer dealt Japan its worst defeat in the tournament, 7-1, assuring Japan of a lowly fourth place. With the cessation of the Far East Games after the 1934 edition, Japan emerged with the worst overall record of the three major participants.

In the national championship that began in 1921, champions came from every part of Japan. The first winner was Tokyo Club, but many titles were won by university teams and clubs from other cities. Keio University Club was a four-time winner during the 1930s, and Hiroshima Club won two in a row in 1924-25. Other winners before the war were Nagoya Club, Astra Club, Kobe Club, Waseda University, Kwansai Gakuin, Tokyo Imperial University Club, and Tokyo Old Boys. Chosen Kelo Club from occupied Korea was the winner in 1935 and after World War II, Tokyo Imperial University Club dominated the competition.

Japan's greatest achievement before the war occurred at the 1936 Olympic Games in Berlin. In the first round, a national team made up almost entirely of Koreans defeated Sweden 3-

2 before a stunned European crowd. In the second round, however, the Italian amateurs out-muscled the Korean upstarts and handed them an 8-0 drubbing. Japan entered the war having won four internationals, drawn one, and lost 12. At the FIFA Congress of Luxembourg in 1946, Japan was expelled from the world body for its part in the war, though it was reinstated in 1950 at the Congress of Rio de Janeiro. Its reinstatement enabled a national team to enter the first Asian Games at New Delhi in 1951. With a bye to the second round, Japan met Iran and played to a scoreless draw, but Iran won the replay 3-2 and Japan failed to place in a field of six countries. Japan has remained very active in the Asian Games, and while it has yet to win a gold medal, even in 1958 when it was held in Tokyo itself, Japanese teams have won many more games than they have lost, especially against Far Eastern opposition. In 1953, Sweden journeyed to Japan to avenge its 1936 loss and won twice, 6-1 and 9-1. In higher competition, Japan has made a late start and has had little success. It has not yet qualified for the final rounds of the Asian Cup and in World Cup qualification rounds (1970-78) has not advanced beyond the first round.

A big turning point in Japanese soccer occurred in 1960 with the hiring of West German coach Dettmar Cramer to prepare the national team for the Tokyo Olympics in 1964. Cramer introduced sophisticated European techniques to an already enthusiastic soccer community, and brought the national team to the quarter-finals of the Olympics with a first round win over Argentina's amateurs. In its other first round match, Japan lost to the group winner, Ghana. The state-sponsored "amateurs" of Czechoslovakia knocked Japan out of the quarter-finals, but Japan's fine showing in the tournament and exposure to top flight foreign teams made a great impression on the Japanese public. In the post-Olympic fervor, Japanese soccer was reborn.

The Japanese Football League was introduced in 1965 with eight participating clubs. A second division was added in 1972 with 10 clubs, bringing the total in the league to 18, and automatic promotion and relegation followed. The Emperor's Cup, a knockout tournament, was also launched in 1972. Clubs in the national league remain all-amateur, and each is sponsored by a large industrial or commercial firm. Typically, three or four first division clubs come from Tokyo, and one club each from Hiroshima, Yokohama, Osaka, and Nagoya complete the list. Hiroshima became an important soccer center, because British rather than American troops were stationed there after the war. The first four national league championships were won by Toyo Kogyo of Hiroshima, the club of the Toyota automobile company. The other winners have been Mitsubishi F.C. Tokyo, Yanmar Diesel Osaka, and Hitachi F.C. Tokyo. Mitsubishi has toured South America, and has sent many players to Europe for training.

The Football Association of Japan rehired Dettmar Cramer for the 1968 Olympic Games in Mexico, and he led Japan to its highest achievement in international competition. In a first round group consisting of Spanish and Brazilian amateur national teams, as well as the full Nigerian national team, Japan placed second, after defeating Nigeria and drawing with Spain and Brazil. In the quarter-finals, France was eliminated 3-1, setting up a semifinal confrontation with the full international team of Hungary. Japan lost to the Hungarian gold medal winners, but in the third place game defeated Mexico's amateurs to take the bronze medal. The star of this fine Japanese team, and the leading scorer in the tournament, was Yanmar Diesel's striker Kunishige Kamamoto, Japanese Footballer of the Year in 1966, 1968, 1971, and 1974, and the first Asian Footballer of the Year in 1976. Another internationally acclaimed player is left winger Yasuhiko Okudera, who became the first Japanese to enter top level European competition when he joined West Germany's FC Köln in 1977, helping his adopted team to a national championship in his first year.

Jockey   Also known as "shepherd."

A defensive action in which an opponent is closely marked but no attempt is made to tackle him. The purpose is to deprive a player with the ball of a good play. Effective jockeying may force a player wide or into an otherwise difficult circumstance without the defender's having to commit himself.

See also: **mark**

Jordan

Jordan Football Association
P.O. Box 1054
Amman

Founded: 1949
FIFA: 1958
AFC: 1970

Affiliated clubs: *22;* registered players: *1,000;* national stadium: *Amman International Stadium, Amman (30,000);* largest stadium: *Amman International Stadium;* colors: *white jerseys, white shorts;* season: *June to December;* honors: *none.*

Even among the membership of the Union of Arab Football Associations, Jordanian soccer is considered weak and undeveloped. Each of the surrounding Arab states have considerably more experience in international competition and a more ambitious domestic program. The game was introduced by British soldiers during the Mandate and as Islamic opposition to Western sports gradually subsided it was played enthusiastically. In 1949, three years after independence, the Jordan Football Association was founded. Affiliation with FIFA was not sought for nearly 10 years, and membership in the Asian Football Conferation did not occur for another 21 years, delays that indicate the preoccupation of the JFA with domestic organization and Jordan's lack of international exposure.

Jordan has not yet advanced to the final rounds of the Asian Cup, nor have Jordanian clubs entered the Asian Champions' Cup. Furthermore, Jordan has not yet been in World Cup qualifying rounds. The JFA has entered the Football Tournament of the Union of Arab Football Associations, but without success. Otherwise, Jordan's highest level of international competition has been the annual International Military Championship for amateur armed forces teams. (In the 1975-77 edition, it was grouped in the first round with Kuwait and Belgium.)

Only 17 senior clubs compete in domestic competition, which includes a national championship and an annual cup competition named for King Hussein. The first division is composed of six clubs. Barely 500 adult players are registered in the whole country. All three major stadiums in Jordan are located within the Hussein Sports City complex in Amman.

Juventus, Football Club

Location: *Turin, Italy;* stadium: *Stadio Comunale (71,180);* colors: *black and white striped jerseys, white shorts;* honors: *UEFA Cup (1977), Italian champion (1905, 1926, 1931, 1932, 1933, 1934, 1935, 1950, 1952, 1958, 1960, 1961, 1967, 1972, 1973, 1975, 1977, 1978), Italian cup winner (1938, 1942, 1959, 1960, 1965).*

Founded 1897 as Sport Club Juventus ("youth") by high school and gymnasium students, some of them British and all under the age of 18. It was the fourth club to be formed in Turin, the birthplace of Italian soccer. In 1899, it was renamed Football Club Juventus. The club has acquired myriad nicknames, among them, "Juve," *la vecchia signora* ("the old lady"), *la fidanzata d'Italia* ("the Italian sweetheart"), and *le zebre* ("the zebras"), all household terms in Italy. In 1923, the club was purchased by the Agnelli family, owners of the giant Fiat company and overlords of Italian industry, and their money and personal supervision of Juve's affairs continue to this day. Juventus shares the Stadio Comunale with archrival Torino, which is the more popular club in and around Turin, though Juve is the most popular and influential club in Italy as a whole. This oddity is the result of a natural backlash on the part of Torinese workers, many of whom are employed by Fiat. Another reason for Juve's national popularity is that it holds the Italian record for most league titles and cup victories.

Juventus entered the Italian championship in 1900, and won its first title in 1905 after the original members of the club had matured. This victory was significant, because it unseated the mighty Genoa from its perennial domination of the Italian league. Juve also advanced to the final of the league championship, then a knock-out competition, in 1906, but it forfeited a possible second title when it refused to play AC Milan in the replay of a scoreless draw. It did not win another championship until 1926 with a 12-1 aggregate score over Alba of Rome in the two-leg final. The great star of the club during the 1920s was goalkeeper Giampiero Combi, who later became captain of Italy.

With a third championship in 1931, Juventus embarked on a run of five consecutive titles, the most successful streak of wins in Italian soccer history. This legendary group of players became the backbone of the national team that eventually dominated Europe and won two World Cups in the 1930s. In the backfield, besides Combi, were Umberto Caligaris at left back and Virginio Rosetta at right back, possibly the best fullback pair in Europe during the early 1930s. The center half was Luisito Monti, the strong Argentine-born *oriundo*, who figured prominently in Italy's 1934 World Cup victory. On the forward line were *oriundo* Raimondo Orsi, on the left wing, and Giovanni Ferrari at inside left, a lethal striking duo that sometimes combined with a third Argentine-born player Renato Cesarini at inside right. From the mid-1930s, a new backfield emerged in Pietro Rava and Alfredo Foni, and they became almost as celebrated as their predecessors. In 1932-33, Juventus won the league title by an eight-point margin over Ambrosiana-Inter, and the following year won it by scoring 88 goals in 34 games, 22 more

than its next highest challenger. By this time, nine Juventus players were starters on the national team—Combi, Rosetta, Caligaris, Monti, Bertolini, Cesarini, Borel II, Ferrari, and Orsi.

This team finally aged and slipped to several second, fifth, and eighth place finishes in the league by the late 1930s, but the legacy it had left behind was the source for many legends in subsequent years. The only decade in which Juventus did not win an Italian championship was the 1940s, but it did win an Italian cup in 1942. In the early 1950s, Torino's team having been decimated in 1949 by the Superga air disaster, Juventus emerged once again and shared domination of the Italian game with AC Milan and Internazionale. This team featured the famous Carlo Parola at center half, famous for his high kicks in the air, and forward Giampiero Boniperti, who in 1971 would become Juve's president. Championships were won in 1950 and 1952, and another bright period was seen in the late 1950s when Boniperti teamed with the Welsh idol John Charles and *oriundo* Omar Sivori. The former Hungarian idol Dr. Gyorgi Sárosi managed Juventus in its 1952 championship year, when it finished the season with a seven-point margin over AC Milan. The Charles-Sivori era yielded championships in 1958, 1960, and 1961, and an Italian cup in 1959 and the double-winning year of 1960.

In the late 1960s and early '70s, Juventus again built a strong team with goalkeeper Dino Zoff, the best Italian player in that position since Combi, and strikers Pietro Anastasi and Roberto Bettega. Libero Gaetano Scirea and forward Franco Causio added considerable depth to this talented team, and Juventus won five more league titles from 1972-78.

Juventus has consistently failed to do well in European club championships, and this has been its great downfall. This weakness has been puzzling, frustrating, and costly, and continues to compromise its image abroad. The one exception thus far has been a UEFA Cup win in 1977, when "the old lady" eliminated both Manchester City and Manchester United in early rounds before squeaking through the final against Athletic Bilbao on the away-goals rule, an anticlimactic route to winning its first European prize after almost 20 consecutive seasons in international competition.

K

Kampuchea, Democratic   See: **Khmer**

Keegan, Kevin (1951-   )

England's most consistent player of world class caliber during the 1970s, and one of Europe's most sought-after strikers. Keegan's dribbling skills have been likened to those of Stanley Matthews, and his popularity in other countries, like that of his England predecessor Bobby Charlton, is linked to his improvisational gifts in the "Latin style." He has great speed and consistently shows a phenomenally high work rate, both on and off the ball. All of these qualities are considerably heightened visually by his short stature and a stumpy pair of legs that always seem to be in perpetual motion. Signed by lowly Scunthorpe United in 1969, he was grabbed by Liverpool in 1971, and immediately became the Reds'

new hero, the "King of the Kop." His international debut for England was made in 1973 against Wales after five appearances for Alf Ramsey's Under-23 squad, and by 1979 he had accumulated over 40 caps. After 316 appearances and 74 goals for Liverpool, including inspiring performances in its UEFA Cup victory of 1976 and European Cup triumph of 1977, he moved to Hamburg for a British record transfer fee of £500,000. At Hamburger SV his skills flourished still further, and he became the most popular player in West Germany. In 1978, he was elected European Footballer of the Year after placing second in that poll the year before.

Kenya

Football Association of Kenya
P.O. Box 40234
Nairobi

Founded: ?
FIFA: 1960
CAF: ?

Affiliated clubs: *190;* **registered players:** *6,840;* **national stadium:** *City Stadium, Nairobi (18,000);* **largest stadium:** *City Stadium;* **colors:** *red, green, and white jerseys, red, green, and black shorts;* **season:** *June to March;* **honors:** *none.*

Kenya is not the African soccer power one would expect it to be. This is perhaps the one country on the continent where soccer still plays a subordinate role to track and field, the traditional of East Africa. The strong British presence in Kenya assured an early founding date for the national association (sometime during the 1920s or early 1930s), but this was mainly for the benefit of the British themselves, and the Football Association of Kenya was directly affiliated with The Football Association in London from its formation until well into the 1950s.

Kenya secured permission from London to join FIFA separately three years before independence, yet internal organization remained plodding and chaotic for 15 years. In the early 1970s, the fledgling Kenya Football

League and the Football Association of Kenya feuded over the formation of a new league, and the present national championship was not established until 1974. Kenya is also the focal point of a lasting problem in East African soccer: witchcraft. The African confederation and the F.A. of Kenya are committed to ending the use of witch doctors in "destabilizing" opposing teams, but as of 1971 one of the most successful clubs in Nairobi, Gor Mahia, was still spending the equivalent of $3000 per game on the burgeoning witch doctor industry. By the mid-1970s, the practice was thought to be on the wane, but over the years it has slowly progress considerably, both from a tactical and technical point of view.

Surprisingly, Kenya qualified for the final rounds of the African Nations' Cup in 1972, the only time a Kenyan team has participated in a major international competition at full level. Not surprisingly, it finished at the bottom of its first round group, but not until it had managed to draw with Mali, a continental power to be reckoned with, and Togo. The F.A. of Kenya is earnestly trying to improve Kenya's lot in international competition, most noticeably by its participation in three regional competitions under the sponsorship of the East and Central African Football Federation—the East African Challenge Cup and the East and Central African Challenge Cup (both for national teams) and the East and Central African Club Cup. The national team has had little success in the first two, but in 1976, one of Nairobi's big clubs, Luo Union, won the Club Cup. While soccer in East Africa is probably on a lower level than in any other region in Africa, this win was an indication of potential importance.

Kenyan clubs have been occasional participants in both major African club championships. In 1973, Breweries F.C. of Nairobi advanced to the semi-finals of the African Champions' Cup by upsetting Egypt's Al-Ismailia (0-0 and 2-1) in the previous round. Gor Mahia and Luo Union have dominated soccer in Nairobi, and they have been joined in the upper ranks by Abaluhya F.C. The top club in Mombasa is Mwenge. Aside from Nairobi and Mombasa, there are also important regional associations in Nakuru and the Lake Victoria port town of Kisumu, but with the largest stadium in a country of 13 million people seating only 18,000, Kenya is far from becoming a major soccer hotbed in Africa.

Khmer

Fédération Khmère de Football Association
C.P. 380, Complexe Sportif National
Phnom-Penh

Founded: 1933
FIFA: 1953
AFC: 1957

Affiliated clubs: *30;* registered players: *650;* national stadium: *Complexe Sportif National-C.S.N., Phnom-Penh (stadium capacity unknown);* largest stadium: *Complexe Sportif National;* colors: *blue, red, and white jerseys, white shorts;* season: *November to October;* honors: *none.*

The state of the game in Cambodia (known to FIFA as Khmer) after 1975 is completely unknown, but as of this writing membership in FIFA had not been withdrawn. Prior to 1975, the Cambodian league had 14 clubs in senior competition, six of which were in the first division. Four hundred players participated in a national championship, an annual cup competition, and regional championships. There were eight stadiums in the country with capacities of 15,000 or more, excluding the National Sports Complex in Phnom-Penh whose total capacity is officially recorded at 170,000. In addition to the capital city of Phnom-Penh, the major soccer centers of Cambodia were Battambang, Siem Reap, Kompong Chhang, Kompong Cham, Takeo, and Svay Rieng.

The Fédération Cambodgienne de Football Association was founded in 1933, 10 years after the Cochinchina Federation was formed in Saigon. In 1934, these two existing Indo-chinese associations became affiliated with the Fédération Française de Football in Paris. The Cambodian game did not advance as rapidly as did the Vietnamese, but it had already been well established for many years by the time laos formed a governing body in the early 1950s. Soccer in Cambodia was given new impetus by the presence of British and French soldiers during World War II. Most of the modern-day clubs had been formed by the late 1940s.

Cambodia's highest achievement to date in international competition was a fine run for the Asian Cup in 1972. The national team of the Khmer Republic advanced to the final rounds in Bangkok, and in its first round group defeated Kuwait (4-0) after losing to South Korea, a major continental power, to finish second in a field of three. this entitled Khmer to a spot in the semi-finals where mighty Iran won by a mere 2-1. In the third place game, Thailand won on penalty kicks, and Khmer finished fourth. the Cambodians came close to success again when Burma narrowly eliminated them in the qualification rounds of the 1968 Football Tournament of the Asian Games. In the Western Region qualification round at Rangoon, both Burma and Cambodia defeated Pakistan and India, but against each other Burma prevailed (1-0) and advanced to the final rounds. This was the first good showing by Cambodia in international competition. Cambodian clubs did not enter any editions of the Asian Champions' Cup before the tournament's demise in 1972.

On the whole, Cambodia ranks just above Laos at the bottom of the list of Southeast Asian soccer countries, and its future in international competition looks bleaker still.

kickoff

A place kick taken from the center spot at the start of a game, at the start of the second half, at the start of extra time periods, and after a goal is scored. A kickoff must be taken by one of the 22 authorized players on the field, and it must be directed into the opponent's half of the field. At the time of a kickoff all players are required to be in their own halves of the field with those of the opposing team not less than 10 yards away from the center spot. The kicker may not play the ball a second time until it has been touched by another player. A goal may be scored from a kickoff, but it is the rarest of all conversions in the game. Kickoffs have been the accepted form of starting play at least as far back as the Rules of the Harrow Game ca. 1830.

King's Cup Football Tournament

One of the annual competitions for national teams of Southeast Asia, held each year since 1968 in Bangkok, and officially sponsored by the King of Thailand. The invited partici- pants are: Burma, Indonesia, Korea Republic, Malaysia, Singapore, and Thailand. All editions have been played on a knockout basis.

Winners

1968	Indonesia	1972	Malaysia
1969	Korea Republic	1973	Korea Republic
1970	Korea Republic	1974	Korea Republic
1971	Korea Republic	1975	Korea Republic

Kocsis, Sandor (1929-)

Perhaps the greatest header of the ball in the history of the game, Kocsis was the prolific goalscoring inside right of the "Magic Magyars" in the early 1950s. He was, above all, an acrobat on the field, and for his specialty he acquired the nickname "Golden Head," but he could also perform all the other functions of a forward with alarming agility. In 1948, at age 19, he entered the first team of Ferencváros, and, after helping this great "Fradi" team win a championship, he made his first appearance for Hungary in 1949. After a one-year stint at EDOSZ, Honvéd snapped him up in 1950, and he remained there in the company with so many great Hungarian stars of the period. He was the Hungarian scoring leader in 1951 (30), 1952 (36), and 1954 (33), and during this period scored 75 goals for Hungary, including 11 in the 1954 World Cup and seven hat tricks, a world record he still shares with Pelé.

When the 1956 Hungarian uprising broke out, Honvéd was on tour, and, like Puskás and Czibor, Kocsis decided to flee to the West. For several months, he was a player-coach at Young Fellows in Switzerland. Barcelona signed him in 1957, but he was used sparingly because of a FIFA ban he received after leaving Honvéd. In 1958-59, he began a long run of high scoring seasons with Barcelona reminiscent of his great days in Budapest. Though he failed to achieve the fame and adulation of Puskás, who was now at Real Madrid, he was nonetheless an exceptionally popular player, and his contribution to Barcelona's several intense assaults on European club championships was significant. In 1964-65, he lost his place on the first team, and retired in 1966 with a festive and memorable testimonial He has since been a salesman and a coach for minor Spanish clubs, making occasional appearances for Barcelona's veteran team.

The "Golden Head," Sandor Kocsis of Hungary, heads the ball toward the goal in Hungary's stunning 6-3 defeat of England at Wembley Stadium, 1953. England's Jimmy Dickinson defends in vain.

Kopa, Raymond (1931-   )

The greatest French player of all time and one of the most versatile forwards of the postwar era. Originally an outside right, he eventually became a roaming center forward whose chief asset among many was a gift for dribbling. During his peak years in the late 1950s, he was often mentioned with Di Stefano and Puskás as one of the world's top players. Having started his career with SCO Angers, he was signed by Albert Batteux's Stade de Reims in 1951, and made his first appearance for France "B" in 1952. With Reims, he adopted the role of orchestrating center forward, and helped his club win the French championship in 1955.

In the 1955-56 European Cup, he played so superbly against Real Madrid in the final that the Spanish champions lured him away, and he proceeded to play in the next three European Cup finals for them. Unfortunately, he was coopted from his favorite position by Alfredo Di Stefano, and spent three years holding down the right wing, frustrated though brilliant as ever to watch.

In 1958, he combined with inside forward Just Fontaine to lead his country to a marvelous third place finish in the World Cup, and his spirits were rejuvenated. Elected European Footballer of the Year in 1958, he returned to Reims the following year, and took up where he left off, playing happily with the old club until 1964. His last international appearance was in 1962 against Hungary, his 45th, and he retired with 17 international goals. Subsequently, he went into business for himself in Reims, and of late has served on the board of the French football federation.

Korea, Democratic People's Republic

Football Association of the Democratic People's
   Republic of Korea
Munsin 2, Dongdaiwan District
Pyongyang

Founded: 1945
FIFA: 1958

Affiliated clubs: *45;* registered players: *?;* national stadium: *Moranbong Stadium, Pyongyang (60,000);* largest stadium: *Moranbong Stadium;* colors: *red jerseys, white shorts;* season: *March to November;* honors: *none.*

A North Korean football association was formed immediately after Soviet troops entered the region in 1945 and defection from the old Korean Football Association in Seoul was declared. Little information has surfaced about the North Korean game, but there is no doubt that the F.A. of Korea DPR has been highly active and determined. There have been many international contacts with Russian and Chinese teams, depending on the political climate at the time, but for almost three decades little attempt was made to enter the mainstream of Asian soccer, primarily because of South Korea's exceptionally active participation. In the 1950s, however, the F.A. set its sights on the World Cup, and in 1958 it was admitted to FIFA as Korea DPR.

At the time few would have guessed that by 1966 the unknown North Koreans would come close to reaching the summit of world soccer, advancing to the final rounds of the World Cup in England because Asian and African entries withdrew from qualifying rounds *en masse* to protest FIFA's awarding a solitary berth in the finals to the Asian-African bloc. North Korea's only hurdle was Australia, representing Oceania, whom it defeated soundly in neutral Phnom-Penh, 6-1 and 3-1. Rumblings of this surprisingly good team reached Europe, but when the Koreans stopped off on their way to England to receive a 7-0 thrashing by Hungary, the rumors lessened. All that anyone knew about the Koreans was that the team was comprised entirely of players picked from the highly disciplined army, and they apparently dedicated themselves exclusively to playing soccer.

In the first round at Middlesbrough, North Korea was grouped with Chile, the powerful Russians, and Italy, one of the favorites to win the cup and resplendent with world class players. Playing nervously and unable to compensate for its small size, North Korea lost to the USSR by 3-0. In its next match against Chile, however, it found its stride in the second half, and Pak Seung Zin equalized two minutes before the final whistle to give North Korea its first point in world competition. A true Cinderella story was emerging, and it became the talk of the tournament, bolstered by an exotic image perpetuated in the press.

Mighty Italy was waiting in the wings. In the greatest World Cup upset since 1950, the soldiers from Pyongyang dazzled the English crowd and forced the cumbersome Italian defense into submission. At 42 minutes, shortly after Italy lost midfielder Bulgarelli through injury, inside-left Pak Doo Ik scored against Albertosi after stealing the ball from Rivera. The 1-0 score stood at game's end, and the stunned Italians warily returned home to a hostile reception, knowing they had been outplayed. Moreover, the Koreans were through to the quarter-final round. Their team on the field vs. Italy was: Li Chan Myung; Sim Zoong Sun, Shin Yung Kyoo, Ha Jung Won, Oh Yoon Kyung, Im Seung Hwi, Pak Seung Zin, Han Bong Zin, Pak Doo Ik, Kim Bong Hwan, and Yang Sung Kook.

Its quarter-final opponent was Portugal with the incomparable Eusebio at his peak, but the North Koreans did not disappoint. At Goodison Park, Liverpool, 52,000 spectators were treated to the best game of the tournament. North Korea scored a goal at 60 seconds and two in rapid-fire succession to give them a 3-0 lead at the outset. With the crowd clearly on their side, the Koreans again played brilliantly, but on 4 goals by Eusebio, two from the penalty spot, Portugal came from behind to gain a 5-3 win. North Korea was out of the World Cup.

In 1976, North Korea advanced to the final rounds of the Asian Nations' Cup in Tehran but withdrew shortly before the competition got under way. It had been grouped with Malaysia, Kuwait, and China PR. It also withdrew from World Cup qualification rounds in 1974 (over the South Korea issue) and in 1978 (to protest having to compete against Israel). In domestic competition, 20 clubs participate in a national championship and an annual cup competition, and a growing number of youth and veteran teams have been formed. There are now nine stadiums that meet with FIFA approval.

Korea, Republic

Korea Football Association
P.O. Box 143, Kwangwhamoon
14 Namdaemoonro 1Ka, Choong-Ku
Seoul

Founded: 1928
FIFA: 1948
AFC: 1954

Affiliated clubs: 476; **registered players:** *2,047;* **national stadium:** *Seoul Municipal Stadium, Seoul (30,000);* **largest stadium:** *Seoul Municipal Stadium;* **colors:** *red jerseys, white shorts;* **season:** *March to November;* **honors:** *Asian Cup winner (1956, 1960), runner-up (1972.)*

South Korea has been one of Asia's leading soccer-playing countries since World War II, having won more tournaments—large and small—than practically anyone on the continent, but once outside its own sphere of influence South Korea has achieved very little. Though it has reached the final rounds of the World Cup once and the Olympic Games twice, its record in both these competitions is embarrassingly poor. In the World Cup, its goal difference of 0-16 is the lowest of all World Cup participants. Its achievements in Asia, however, cannot be overlooked. Only Iran and Israel have earned more honors. Since the mid-1960s, there has been a decline in international success, except in regional East and Southeast Asian competition.

Soccer found its way to the Korean peninsula long before baseball and other American sports entered the scene, European technicians and missionaries having introduced the game before the Japanese annexation in 1910. The Korean Football Association was founded in 1938 in Seoul, and stayed under the wing of the Japanese association until it finally joined FIFA in 1940 in order to play in Olympic qualifying rounds that never materialized because of the war. As "Korea," it entered the Olympic Games of 1948 as one of two Far East representatives, and defeated Mexico's amateurs, 5-3, in the first round. Sweden punished Korea with 12 unanswered goals in the second round, and this gave the Koreans their first taste of Latin American and European soccer. It was not in the strictest sense South Korea's first Olympic competition, however, because in 1936 Japan had entered the Olympics with a nearly all-Korean team, defeating the same European opponent, Sweden, by a score of 3-2. The Korean War, meanwhile, disturbed plans to increase international activity, but at home a league was introduced shortly after World War II and continued throughout the 1950-53 war. Most of the important clubs were either connected with military units or under the sponsorship of commercial enterprises such as the Korean Fertile Company. In 1952, the President's Cup competition was introduced for league clubs, but in recent years this trophy has been used for the international President's Cup tournament.

In 1953, a national team representing South Korea made its international debut with an extended tour of Hong Kong and Singapore, playing several teams in those colonies over a period of one month. In Hong Kong, the team played four matches, winning two and losing two, and in Singapore, it played nine, winning four and losing three. After eliminating Japan in the qualifying round, the South Koreans found themselves in the company of the world's best teams at the 1954 World Cup in Switzerland. Their first opponent in the opening round was none other than Hungary in what should have been the greatest mismatch in World Cup history, but Kocsis and Puskas were held to five goals, and the South Koreans lost by only 9-0. Far worse was a 7-0 loss to Turkey several days later, and the South Koreans luckily did not have to play West Germany, the other country in its group. South Korea's strength in Asia, however,

was demonstrated in no uncertain terms when it won the first two editions of the Asian Cup in 1956 and 1960 at a time when the anti-Communist states of the Far East dominated Asian soccer. At Hong Kong in 1956, South Korea topped Israel, Hong Kong, and fledgling South Vietnam in the standings, and in 1960, when the competition was held in Seoul itself, the South Koreans were undefeated against Israel, Taiwan, and South Vietnam. In 1964, South Korea qualified for the Olympic final rounds again, as did North Korea, and lost in its first round group to Brazil's amateurs, Egypt (by a resounding 10-0), and Czechoslovakia. North Korea, meanwhile, withdrew from the tournament to protest South Korea's participation. Since 1964, South Korea has not won a major tournament or qualified for worldwide competition. It has won Malaysia's Merdeka tournament at least six times and the King's Cup Tournament of Thailand six times, both records, as well as the Djakarta Anniversary tournament and its own President's Cup. In 1976-78, it returned to form and placed second to Iran in World Cup qualifying rounds.

Košek, Jan   (1884-1927)

Czechoslovakia's goalscoring genius in the period immediately following the turn of the century. He was the central figure in the legendary SK Slavia team from Prague that dominated Central European club soccer before World War I, scoring six goals in Slavia's famous 11-0 defeat of First Vienna and a hat trick in its equally fine 4-0 victory over Southampton. Košek was Central Europe's first soccer hero, and he was also famous as a sprinter—he was clocked in the 100 meter dash at 11 seconds in 1905. Košek joined Slavia from lowly Letenském in 1903,

guiding it to prominence in Austro-Hungarian competitions, and between 1906-11 he played for respresentative teams of both Poland and Bohemia. Primarily an inside left, Košek was noted for his cannon-like shot in addition to his speed, and at the peak of his fame, Slavia's archrival AC Sparta secured permission to use him intermittently, though not in Slavia-Sparta derbies. Three years after his retirement in 1911, he attempted a short comeback, but the war intervened, and he never returned to active play.

Kuwait

Kuwait Football Association
North Shuwaikh St. 71, No. 34
P.O. Box 2029
Kuwait

Founded: 1952
FIFA: 1962
AFC: 1964

Affiliated clubs: *13;* registered players: *900;* national stadium: *Shuweikh Secondary*

School Stadium, Kuwait (25,000); **largest** **stadium:** *Shuweikh Stadium;* **colors:** *blue and white jerseys, white shorts;* **season:** *October to May;* **honors:** *Asian Cup runner-up (1976).*

In the aftermath of the Middle East soccer boom of the 1970s, Kuwait has emerged as the first genuine power to be reckoned with—excluding Egypt—among the Arab countries of the region. Little was heard of Kuwaiti soccer until 1970, but the vast financial reservoir of the Kuwait Football Association (KFA) has since attracted some of the world's best coaches to establish a stable domestic program and carry the national team to international honors. By any standards, this effort has succeeded. Mario Zagalo, manager of Brazil in the 1970 and 1974 World Cups, was hired for a two-year stint beginning in 1975, and in 1978 his place was taken by Poland's 1974 World Cup manager Kazimierz Gorski. Given the unavailability of Helmut Schön and Rinus Michels, the KFA could not have done better.

Soccer was first played in Kuwait by British sailors and civil servants shortly after colonization in 1889. Islamic customs and beliefs prohibited the local inhabitants from playing the game and the British were quite happy to play it only among themselves. The discovery of oil in the 1930s brought hordes of soccer-playing British technicians, yet the game was not allowed wide access until well into the postwar era. The KFA was founded in 1952, but it did not join FIFA until after Kuwait had gained its full independence from Great Britain in 1961. In the 1960s, most of the KFA's resources were put into building a sound league structure.

Kuwait has participated in all four biannual editions of the Arabian Gulf Tournament since its inception in 1970, winning at least three and proving itself the undisputed leader of soccer on the Arabian Peninsula. In each of its three wins (1970-72-76), it finished undefeated, though in 1972 it won on goal difference from Saudi Arabia and in 1976 was level on points with Iraq and had to win the trophy by defeating the Iraqis in a play-off. Throughout this series, Kuwait had disposed easily of Bahrain, Qatar, United Arab Emirates, Oman, and to a great extent Saudi Arabia, in the race for oil-state superiority. In the qualification rounds for the 1978 World Cup, Kuwait handily won all its games against Bahrain and Qatar in the opening group, and in the deciding round defeated Hong Kong and Australia (twice). Its elimination from World Cup glory came at the hands of mighty Iran and upset-minded Korea Republic, but among the 17 Asian nations attempting to qualify for the 1978 World Cup, Kuwait finished third.

Kuwait's record against non-Arab Asian opponents has been less consistent than its regional results, but it has managed to accumulate the highest overall ranking (fourth) of any Arab state in the Asian Cup, gaining the final rounds of Asia's most important competition twice. In 1972, Kuwait was eliminated in the quarter-final round after defeating Korea Republic and losing to war-torn Khmer by 4-0. In 1976, however, Zagalo's "Kuwait National Team," as the name is emblazoned across the jerseys, blanked Malaysia and the People's Republic of China in the quarter-finals, defeated Iraq in the semis after extra time, and won a second place honor by losing to unbeatable Iran in the final. Its narrow loss to Iran—by a mere 1-0—spoke well of Zagalo's accomplishments at the national helm, but the Brazilian manager quietly complained to the Rio de Janeiro press that Kuwait players lacked the discipline and drive to really do well in international competition.

In the discontinued Asian Champions' Cup, Kuwait City's Al Arabi S.C. entered the 1971 edition, and brushed aside India's Punjab F.A. and Malaysia's Perak and nearly upset Taj Tehran before facing elimination with a 1-0 loss to South Korea's ROK Army. The withdrawal of the KFA's entrant in 1972 to protest Israel's participation in the competition helped to bring about the demise of the series altogether. In domestic competition, there are 40 senior-level clubs with a Premier Division of eight and a Second Division of six. The Premier Division clubs are: Kuwait, Al Arabi, Khitah, Al Qadisiya, Al Salimiya, Zazma, Al Shabab, and Tadhamon. In addition to league competition, possession of the Emir's Cup is vigorously contested.

L

Labruna, Angelo (1918-)

The "Stanley Matthews of Argentina," so named for his longevity, Angel Labruna played for Ríver Plate from 1939-1959, finally retiring at age 41. If one includes his 10 years as a junior player for Ríver, his total comes to 29 years. Nicknamed *El Viego* ("The Old One,") he made his last international appearance for Argentina in the 1958 World Cup, having accumulated 36 caps, an Argintine record until the mid-1970s. Labruna was an inside left who controlled the ball masterfully and shot accurately, but, aside from his endless productivity, his greatest role was in playing on the great forward line of Ríver Plate in the early 1940s, nicknamed *la maquina* ("the machine"). He was an unorthodox strategist as a forward, who was often seen dribbling across the penalty area laterally looking for an opening and only then firing at the goal. His dribbling skills were accomplished, but it was in his quickly-taken shots that he really made his mark.

Labruna is unique in Argentine soccer for having played on nine championship-winning teams, and he scored an astonishing 490 goals in over 1,000 appearances for Ríver before moving to Platense, Green Cross in Chile, and Rampla Júniors in Uruguay. His 17 goals for Argentina spanned an international career that had started in 1942 at the height of *la maquina's* fame. After his retirement, he took up coaching with Platense, Ríver Plate, Argentino Júniors, and Rosario Central, and in the late 1970s he returned to Ríver once again.

Laos

Fédération Lao de Foot-ball
c/o Dir. des Sports et de la Jeunesse
B.P. 268
Vientiane

Founded: 1951
FIFA: 1952
AFC: 1968

Affiliated clubs: *93;* **registered players:** *2,812;* **national stadium:** *Stade National Vientiane, Vientiane (5,000);* **largest stadium:** *Stade National Vientiane;* **colors:** *red jerseys, white shorts;* **season:** *October to May;* **honors:** *none.*

Laotian soccer has made little impact on the Asian game as a whole, or in its own Southeast Asian region. Its inland geographical position and small, sparse population thwarted the pervasive foreign influence of other French colonies in Indo-China, and the larger British colonies to the west, and once soccer in Laos began to be organized after World War II, the wars of the 1950s and 1960s put a damper on what progress had been made.

French colonists introduced soccer after the turn of the century in Luang Prabang and Kiang Kwang (now Xieng Khouang), which were the colonial administrative centers of the region following the French occupation in 1893. The game was very slow to establish itself. There is no record of a Laotian football association before World War II, though the governing bodies of Vietnam and Cambodia were formed by 1923 and 1933, respectively. Interest in the game was finally sparked by the considerable exposure it was given during World War II by French and British soldiers who swarmed over the area. Some teams had formed by 1949, the year of independence, and the new government eventually helped to form a national association. The Fédération Lao de Foot-ball was founded in 1951 and gained membership in FIFA less than one year later.

Five regional leagues were formed, the first and most important being the League of Vientiane in the new capital. It started with two divisions, and the first champion was Pavie-Sport in 1951-52. The second and third major leagues were situated further down the Mekong River: the League of Savannakhet, whose first champion in 1952-53 was Eleves Officiers de Dong Hene, and the League of Champassac, whose first champion in 1952-53 was the Military team of the Union Française. In addition, a national cup, the Inter-Province Cup, was launched in 1951 and played among selections representing each league. Its winner during most of the early years was the League of Vientiane. The Vientiane Cup for club sides was also introduced in 1951, and won its first year by Laotienne Artistique et Sportive. French military teams were included in these competitions during the 1950s.

There is no indication that any national team engaged in international competition before the mid-1970s, nor have Laotian clubs entered the Asian Champions' Cup. With the virtual annexation of Laos into Vietnam in 1977, Laotian soccer appeared headed for yet another upheaval.

Latin American Footballer of the Year

Though officially the "American" Footballer of the Year, the winner is actually chosen from among players in Latin America rather than the Western Hemisphere as a whole. The award is determined each year by a vote of leading soccer journalists from Central and South America, and is sponsored by the Caracas daily *El Mundo*. Players associated with clubs outside the region are eligible, providing their official home country is in Latin America.

Winners

1971   Tostão (Cruzeiro and Brazil)
1972   Teofilo Cubillas (Alianza and Peru)
1973   Pelé (Santos and Brazil)
1974   Elias Figueroa (Internacional Pôrto Alegre and Chile)
1975   Elias Figueroa (Internacional Pôrto Alegre and Chile)
1976   Elias Figueroa (Internacional Pôrto Alegre and Chile)
1977   Zico (Flamengo and Brazil)
1978   Mario Kempes (Valencia and Argentina)

Latin Cup

Coupe Latine—Coppa Latina—Copa Latin—Taça Latim.

An important forerunner of the European Cup, the Latin Cup was contested by the champion clubs of France, Italy, Spain, and Portugal over a period of nine years from 1949-57. It was significant, because many of the greatest clubs in Europe at the time hailed from these four countries, and the Latin Cup remained their only forum throughout most of its existence. It also served to announce the rise of two great powers of the era, Stade de Reims and Real Madrid, through their memorable Latin Cup victories of 1953 and 1955, respectively.

The format was more complex than any other major club competition. Though played annually, it was actually divided into two editions (1949-53 and 1953-57). Each year an individual club was declared the winner for that year. At the end of each four-year edition, however, the clubs' points were added together and the country whose clubs had accumulated the most points was declared the winner of that edition. Points were awarded on the following basis: winner (4 pts.), runner-up (3 pts.), third place (2 pts.), and fourth place (1 pt.). There were, in other words, separate results for club and country. The series was officially abolished in 1959 after a two-year hiatus caused by the introduction of the European Cup. The Latin Cup will always retain a special place in the history of European soccer for the exciting teams and great games it produced, and for its place as the link between the immediate postwar years and the great era of Real Madrid in the late 1950s.

Winners

First Edition (Spain)
1949   Barcelona (Spain)
1950   Benfica (Portugal)
1951   AC Milan (Italy)
1953   Barcelona (Spain)

Second Edition (Spain)
1953   Stade de Reims (France)
1955   Real Madrid (Spain)
1956   AC Milan (Italy)
1957   Real Madrid (Spain)

Results

FIRST EDITION

1949

Semi-Finals

Sporting Lisbon—Torino	3-1
Barcelona—Stade de Reims	5-0

Third Place Game

Torino—Stade de Reims	5-3

Final

Barcelona—Sporting Lisbon	2-1

1950

Semi-Finals

Bordeaux—Atlético Madrid	4-2
Benfica—Lazio	3-0

Third Place Game

Atlético Madrid—Lazio	3-2

Final

Benfica—Bordeaux	3-3, 2-1

1951

Semi-Finals

AC Milan—Atlético Madrid	4-1
Lille—Sporting Lisbon	1-1, 6-4

Third Place Game

Atlético Madrid—Sporting Lisbon	3-1

Final

AC Milan—Lille	5-0

1952

Semi-Finals

OGC Nice—Sporting Lisbon	4-2
Barcelona—Juventus	4-2

Third Place Game

Juventus—Sporting Lisbon	3-2

Final

Barcelona—OGC Nice	1-0

First edition standings: Spain, 12 pts.; France, 10; Italy 9; Portugal 9.

SECOND EDITION

1953

Semi-Finals

Stade de Reims—Valencia	2-1
AC Milan—Sporting Lisbon	4-2

-after extra time-

Third Place Game
  Sporting Lisbon—Valencia   4-1

Final
  Stade de Reims—AC Milan   3-0

1955

Semi-Finals
  Real Madrid—Belenenses   2-0
  Stade de Reims—AC Milan
                          -after extra time-

Third Place Game
  AC Milan—Belenenses   3-1

Final
  Real Madrid—Stade de Reims   2-0

1956

Semi-Finals
  AC Milan—Benfica   4-2
  Athletic Bilbao—OGC Nice   2-0

Third Place Game
  Benfica—OGC Nice   2-1
                          -after extra time-

Final
  AC Milan—Athletic Bilbao   2-1

1957

Semi-Finals
  Benfica—Saint Étienne   1-0
  Real Madrid—AC Milan   5-1

Third Place Game
  AC Milan—Saint Étienne   4-3

Final
  Real Madrid—Benfica   1-0

Second edition standings: Spain, 12 pts.; Italy, 11; France, 9; Portugal, 8.

Latvia

Like Estonia and Lithuania, Latvia, formed a national association and initiated an international schedule in Europe during the Baltic states' 20-year-long independence between the world wars. Latvian teams completed 35 full internationals, other than their matches with Estonia and Lithuania, between 1923-38, including 11 matches each against Finland and Sweden. Latvia's overall European record was 35-5-7-23-37-114-17, and three of its victories were against Finland. Its biggest wins occured in 1930 against Finland at Riga (3-0), and in 1926 against Sweden (4-1), also at Riga. Its worst losses were to Sweden in 1927 (12-0) and 1929 (10-0) at Stockholm and Malmo.

Latvia met Poland on seven occasions between 1931-38. Aside from one win in Riga, its record against the Poles was more successful away than at home. In three matches away, Latvia drew once with Poland and lost twice by 2-1. Perhaps its most astonishing success was a mere 2-1 loss to Austria in 1937 at Vienna in a World Cup qualifying round. In 1935 and 1937, Latvia lost to Germany by a mere 3-0 and 3-1. Among its further international accomplishments were three draws with Sweden, one of them at Stockholm in 1938.

Law, Denis (1940-)

One of Europe's most clever and exciting inside forwards of the postwar era and the finest British player in that position since his fellow Scot, Alex James, though unlike James, Law functioned as a goalscorer rather than a schemer. Law's skills were completely developed both in the air and on the ground. A measure of his magnetic qualities was his great popularity and selection as European Footballer of the Year (1964) while playing with two other immortals, Bobby Charlton and George Best, at Manchester United. He was signed at age 15 by an English club (Huddersfield) directly from his schoolplaying days in Aberdeen, and in 1959 he became the youngest Scottish international in this century. One year later, he went to Manchester City for the British record transfer fee of £ 55,000, but stayed for only one season after Italy's Torino paided £ 100,000 for him, seeking to find its own counterpart to John Charles of crosstown rival Juventus. Though acclaimed by some Italians as the most determined inside forward ever to play in the Italian league, his volatile personality clashed with the ever-present Italian press, and he returned to England the following year. His new club was Manchester United, with whom he had always hoped to play, and his fee (£ 115,000) set another British transfer record.

Matt Busby, the paragon of British managers, was sensitive to Law's needs and gave him the freedom he wanted to exploit his extraordinary talents. By the mid-1960s, however, injuries began to hamper his game, and, sadly, he was not among those who contributed to United's winning of the European Cup in 1968. After the 1969-70 season, injuries forced Busby to put Law on the transfer list, but there were no takers, and, as Law himself describes it, Pelé's performance in the 1970 World Cup performance in 1970 renewed his determination to regain his form. He was moderately successful for two seasons, but in 1973 he moved back to Manchester City on a free transfer. Law appeared a record 55 times for Scotland, the last being his World Cup debut against Zaire in 1974. After scoring over 210 league and 29 international goals, he finally left active play and embarked on a new career in sports broadcasting with the B.B.C.

Laws of the Game

The Laws of the Game, which govern all aspects of soccer the world over, are the responsibility of the International Football Association Board (IFAB), which meets every June to consider proposed changes, clarifications, and instructions to national associations and referees. The Laws have been attentively scrutinized on an ongoing basis since their original drafting in 1863, first by The Football Association in London, and by the IFAB since 1882.

The first Laws, formulated at the inaugural meetings of The Football Association from October to December 1863, were based on the Harrow School Rules and Cambridge University Rules of 1848, 1854-58, and 1863, and to a lesser extent by the Eton College Rules of 1862. They were also anticipated by the Sheffield Rules of 1857 and The Rules of The Simplest Game (Uppingham School) of 1860. Prior to 1863, there were as many differing sets of rules as there were schools, universities, and clubs. The Football Association Laws were an experiment by which teams from different locales could play under a uniform code for the first time.

The acrimonious discussion that ensued for two months while the Laws were being drawn up ultimately produced a split that led to the birth of association football (soccer), as distinct from rugby football, ending the era of razzle-dazzle English ball games known collectively as "football." The original version of the Laws of the Game contained some elements of rugby (e.g., the fair catch), but the major proposals as set forth by rugby adherents (hacking and handling) were voted down, and this led to the famous withdrawal of the Blackheath group and the eventual formation of the Rugby Union.

The Laws of the Game were drafted originally for members of the F.A. only, all of which were based in the London area. In the north, the Sheffield Rules had exited since 1857, and though they were similar in many ways to The Football Association Laws, it was not until 1877 that The Football Association and the Sheffield Association agreed on a set of rules, unifying England under the London associaiton. The various indigenous schools rules, meanwhile, continued to be used on school grounds, but as of 1863, club level and all first class soccer followed the dictates of The Football Association Laws of the Game.

The exact text of the original Laws is as follows:

1. The maximum length of the ground shall be 200 yards, the maximum breadth shall be 100 yards, the length and breadth shall be marked off with flags; and the goal shall be defined by two upright posts, 8 yards apart, without any tape or bar across them.

2. A toss for goals shall take place and the game shall be commenced by a place kick from the centre of the ground by the side losing the toss for goals; the other side shall not approach within 10 yards of the ball until it is kicked off.

3. After a goal is won, the losing side shall be entitled to kick off, and the two sides shall change goals after each goal is won.

4. A goal shall be won when the ball passes between the goal posts or over the space between the goal-posts (at whatever height), not being thrown, knocked on, or carried.

5. When the ball is in touch, the first player who touches it shall throw it from the point on the boundary line where it left the ground, in a direction at right angles with the boundary line, and the ball shall not be in play until it has touched the ground.

6. When a player has kicked the ball, any one of the same side who is nearer to the opponent's goal line is out of play, and may not touch the ball himself, nor in any way whatever prevent any other player from doing so, until he is in play; but no player is out of play when the ball is kicked off from behind the goal line.

7. In case the ball goes behind the goal line, if a player on the side to whom the goal belongs first touches the ball, one of his side shall be entitled to a free kick from the goal line at the point opposite the place where the ball shall be touched. If a player of the opposite side first touches the ball, one of his side shall be entitled to a free kick at the goal only from a point 15 yards outside the goal line, opposite the place where the ball is touched, the opposing side standing within their goal line until he has had his kick.

8. If a player makes a fair catch, he shall be entitled to a free kick, providing he claims it by making a mark with his heel at once; and in order to take such a kick he may go back as far as he pleases, and no player on the opposite side shall advance beyond his mark until he has kicked.

9. No player shall run with the ball.

10. Neither tripping nor hacking shall be allowed, and no player shall use his hands to hold or push his adversary.

11. A player shall not be allowed to throw the ball or pass it to another with his hands.

12. No player shall be allowed to take the ball from the ground with his hands under any pretext whatever while it is in play.

13. A player shall be allowed to throw the ball or pass it to another if he made a fair catch or catches the ball on the first bounce.

14. No player shall be allowed to wear projecting nails, iron plates, or gutta percha on the sole or heels of his boots.

DEFINITION OF TERMS

place kick—is a kick while it is one the ground in any position which the kicker may choose to place it.

free kick—is the privilege of kicking the ball, without obstruction in such manner as the kicker may think fit.

fair catch—is when the ball is caught, after it has touched the person of an adversary or has been kicked, knocked on, or thrown by an adversary, and before it has touched the ground or one of the side catching it; but if the ball is kicked from out of touch, or from behind the goal line, a fair catch cannot be made.

hacking—is kicking an adversary on the front of the leg, below the knee.

tripping—is throwing an adversary by the use of the legs without the hands, and without hacking or charging.

charging—is attacking an adversary with the shoulder, chest, or body, without using the hands or legs.

knocking on—is when a player strikes or propels the ball with his hands, arms or body, without kicking of throwing it.

holding—includes the obstruction of a player by the hand or any part of the arm below the elbow.

touch—is that part of the field, on either side of the ground, which is beyond the line of flags.

Laws 1-8 were virtually uncontested by the rugby adherents of the F.A., but Laws 9-12 plainly rejected the main elements of rugby (hacking and handling) and were responsible for the soccer-rugby split. Yet none of the original Laws has remained intact down to the present time. During their first few years of existence, major changes appeared in rapid succession, as befitting their experimental nature.

Comprehensive Chronology of Major Changes in the Laws
(including important decisions of the International Board)

(for changes in field markings and substitution rules see: *field of play* and *substitution*.)

1863-70   The following 1863 Laws were amended as described:

Law I (tapes added between goal posts)

Law II (change goals at halftime if game is scoreless)

Law IV (goals must be won under the tape)

Law V (player making throw-in may not play ball twice)

Law VI (player is offside when less than three opponents are between him and the opponent's goal line when the ball is played to him, if he himself is between his teammate with the ball and the opponent's goal line, replacing the old rule by which a player was offside merely by being between his teammate with the ball and the opponent's goal line when the ball was played to him)

Law VII (goal kick replaces kick out, 1869)

Law VIII (fair catch and all handling eliminated, 1866)

Law X (charging from behind forbidden)

Law XIII (fair catch and all handling eliminated, 1866)

1871-78   The following additions or changes were made:

   a) players of either side required to line up in their own half of the field before each kick off.

   b) change of goals required only at halftime.

   c) side that did not kick off at start of first half does so at start of second.

   d) player of the opposite side that last touched the ball before going into touch makes the resulting throw-in.

   e) ball from a throw-in may travel in any direction and is required to travel six yards, being in play when it crosses the touch line.

   f) corner kick introduced (1872).

   g) goalkeepers sanctioned, and goalkeeper's punching or throwing the ball, though not carrying, authorized.

   h) charging of a player who is facing his own goal authorized (1877).

   i) cleats sanctioned.

   j) free kick required as punishment for offside, handling, tripping, hacking, and charging.

   k) kick-offs, corner kicks, and all free kicks defined as "indirect."

   l) umpire's authority broadened: ball remains in play after possible offside, handling, tripping, hacking, or charging until the umpire himself, on appeal, decides the foul has occurred (1874).

1880   a) attacking player cannot be offside if ball last played by an opponent.

1881   a) referees introduced with limited authority.

   b) goal awarded against a team whose player prevents a goal from being scored by handling.

   c) corner kicks exempted from offside rule.

1882   a) 1881 handling rule rescinded.

   b) two-hand throw-in introduced.

1891   a) penalty kick introduced for tripping, holding, or handling committed within 12 yards of the offending player's own goal line.

   b) goalkeeper facing a penalty kick permitted to advance not more than six yards from his own goal.

   c) weight of ball fixed at 13-15 oz.

   d) referees brought onto the field and given authority, including timekeeping; two linesmen authorized to assist referee; umpires abolished.

   e) cleats restricted to specified studs or bars.

1892   a) penalty kicker prohibited from playing the ball twice in succession.
        b) extra time for penalty kicks authorized.

1893   player permitted to charge a goalkeeper fairly if goalkeeper is playing the ball or obstructing an opponent.

1895   a) referee's absolute authority and linesman's neutrality established.
        b) ball must pass wholly over the goal line or touch line to be out of play.
        c) standing throw-in replaces running throw-in.

1896-99 a) number of players on a team limited to eleven.
        b) length of game fixed at 90 minutes.
        c) goalkeeper restricted to handling in his own half of the field.
        d) handling added to list of infringements requiring a penalty kick.
        e) goalkeeper limited to two paces while carrying ball.

1897   concept of "intentionality" introduced in the Laws (adapted from an 1893 instruction to referees).

1903   a) direct free kick introduced for major infringements.
        b) advantage clause introduced.

1904   linesman's role as assistant to referee clarified.

1905   a) drop ball introduced.
        b) leather required for outer casing of balls.
        c) fair charging (shoulder charging) expressly authorized.
        d) goalkeeper limited to lateral movements on his goal line during penalty kick.

1907   offside law limited to opponent's half of the field.

1913   a) goalkeeper limited to handling within his own penalty area.
        b) distance of opposing players from the position of a free kick increased to 10 yards.

1914   a) 10 yard rule applied to corner kicks.
        b) striking an opponent mentioned as a major infringement.

1921   a) throw-ins exempted from offside rule.
        b) goalkeepers required to wear yellow jerseys.

1925   a) offside rule altered to require only two opponents between player and goal line.
        b) player taking throw-in required to have both feet on touch line.

1927   a) corner kick changed from indirect to direct free kick.
        b) direct free kick replaces indirect free kick as punishment for holding, hacking, charging, striking, handling, and other serious infringements.

1929   goalkeeper limited to standing still on his goal line until penalty kick is taken.

1931   a) goalkeeper permitted to take four paces while carrying.
b) unlawful throw-ins punishable by throw-in for opposing side rather than free kick.

1935   player's right to appeal rescinded; informal inquiry of a decision permitted (adapted from a 1924 decision of the IFAB).

1936   player prohibited from tapping the ball to his goalkeeper on a goal kick.

1937   a) player prohibited from tapping ball to his goalkeeper on a free kick taken inside his penalty area, i.e., the ball from a goal kick required to travel beyond the penalty area.
b) weight of ball increased to 14-16 oz.
c) goalkeeper *required* to stand on his goal line between the posts for a penalty kick, i.e., to confront his opponent.

1938   Laws of the Game completely remodeled and rewritten by Sir Stanley Rous; the only substantive changes are the addition of certain infringements punishable by an indirect free kick.

1950   referee for an international match required to be a citizen of a neutral country, unless otherwise agreed upon by both sides.

1951   a) obstruction made punishable offense by an indirect free kick.
b) authorized length of studs increased to three-quarters of an inch.

1956   a) goalkeepers in international matches required to wear jerseys that are distinct in color from those of other players, rather than yellow jerseys only.
b) referee for international match must be chosen from official list of International Referees.
c) a decision by the referee is irreversible if the game has been restarted.
d) application of the advantage clause is irreversible, even though the expected advantage does not materialize (adapted from a 1934 decision of the FIFA Referee's Committee).

See also: **field of play; substitution; International Football Association Board; Cambridge University Rules; Harrow Game, Rules of the; Sheffield Rules; offside; England**

Lawton, Thomas (1919-)

England's legendary center forward of the 1940s who succeeded Dixie Dean in that position at Everton and successfully challeng-ed Dean's reputation as the greatest center forward in his country's history. He was the most commanding header of the ball ever seen in Britain, and ranks with Sandor Kocsis as perhaps the premier header of all time. Lawton was a teenage prodigy with Burnley from 1935, and in 1937, at age 17, he joined Everton, establishing a precedent for hard bargaining with club managements. Before his career was over in 1956, he had played officially for six clubs. His first great season was in 1937-38 with Everton, and during the war he played for several clubs around the country while in uniform, reaching his peak of skill and goalscoring power. It was estimated that during the war he scored almost 300 goals in over 250 club and 22 international appearances—all unofficial—and with Stanley Matthews shone brightly as England's greatest diversion from wartime's bleakness.

In 1945, he moved to Chelsea for a two-year stint, and two years later stunned everyone by accepting an offer from third division Notts County for a record £ 20,000, helping Eng-land's oldest club to an immediate promotion. He remained with Notts County throughout his remaining peak years, moving again to second division Brentford in 1952, and finally to Arsenal in 1953, where he rounded out his career as a supplier rather than a taker of goals. In 23 peacetime internationals, he scored 22 goals, but his wartime record brought these figures to an unofficial 45 and 46, respectively. His peacetime totals at the club level were in the neighborhood of 235 goals in 390 appearances. The interruption of World War II very likely prevented Lawton from setting numerous English goalscoring records. After his retirement, he became player-manager of non-league Kettering Town, manager of Notts County (briefly and unsuccessfully), an innkeeper, Kettering Town manager again, a salesman, a coach at Notts County (1968-70), and finally retired from the game.

league competition

A series in which the winning side is the team that has accumulated the most points and stands at the top of the standings, as distinct from a cup competition, in which the winning side is the only team to remain undefeated at the end of a knockout series.

Lebanon

Fédération Libanaise de Football Association
Rue Omar Ben Khattab
B.P. 4732
Beyrouth

Founded: 1933
FIFA: 1933
AFC: 1964

Affiliated clubs: *92;* **registered players:** *2,720;* **national stadium:** *Cité Sportive-Camille Chamoun, Beirut (60,000);* **largest stadium:** *Cité Sportive-Camille Chamoun;* **colors:** *red and white jerseys, white shorts;* **season:** *October to June;* **honors:** *none.*

Lebanon was one of the first countries in the Middle East to establish an administrative body for soccer (the F.A.'s of Egypt, Israel, and Iran are older), and it was an early participant in international competition (only Egypt and Israel started earlier). Still, Lebanon has no honors to its credit, and its profile in Asian tournaments, not to mention worldwide tournaments, has remained very low. Lebanon's poor standing even among Middle East countries has been caused by the absence of a large working class population to support the game, and Lebanon's decentralized economic system and the Moslem-Christian split have been built-in obstacles to the development of a cohesive national sports program.

The heyday of Lebanese soccer was perhaps the 1930s, when the French mandate was still in full swing and French soldiers and workers in residence provided a strong impetus for Christian Lebanese to learn the game. The oldest clubs had been founded in the 1920s, and in 1933, one year after the formation of the Fédération Libanaise de Football Association, the Lebanese league was introduced. After one year, there were already two divisions in the league, with six clubs in the first division. D.P.H.B. was the first champion, but the second and third titles were won by the American College team. D.P.H.B. won two additional championships before the outbreak of World War II, and the war years were dominated by Renaissance Sportive and the famous Club Homenetmen, which won three in a row, the year it won from promotion from the second division in 1943. The Coupe du Libanon was introduced in 1937-38, and was dominated early on by Renaissance, Helmi, and Homenetmen. The country was also divided into three regional associations, Beirut, Mt. Lebanon, and North Lebanon, each of which had its own district league.

Lebanon made its international debut in 1940 at Tel-Aviv against Palestine, losing 5-1, but there have been precious few forays into international competition since then. In 1959, a Lebanese national team surfaced to participate in the Mediterranean Games, hosted by the city of Beirut, and succeeded in gaining third place behind the Italian amateurs and Turkey, but Lebanon has not participated in any subsequent editions of these games. In recent years, Hungary paid a visit to Beirut, and won 5-1 with a less-than-full international team. Otherwise, Lebanon has not entered World Cup, Olympic, or Asian Cup qualifying rounds, and its participation in the Arab Cup and Palestine Football Cup has been irregular.

In 1970, Homenetmen succeeded in taking third place at the Asian Champions' Cup after defeating Selangor of Malaysia, losing to Taj Tehran, and refusing to play a semi-final match against Hapoel Tel-Aviv. Its third place game was won by 1-0 over Indonesia's P.S.M.S. In 1972, the Lebanese F.A. withdrew from the aborted sixth edition of the Champions' Cup for political reasons (i.e., Israel's participation). In the early 1970s, league and cup competitions continued with 12 clubs making up the first division, but the civil war of 1975-77 put an end to all official soccer activities for the time being.

Leônidas (1913-)

(Full name: Leônidas da Silva.) The small, rubbery Brazilian center forward, who made the bicycle kick famous in the late 1930s. He was so agile that he could take bicycle kicks with both feet, sometimes controlling the ball with one foot and kicking it with the other. Leônidas stole the show at the 1938 World Cup, and helped Brazil to win its first big international success: third place in the world championship. In addition, his speed and exceptional ability to read the field elevated him to the top rank of all-time great center forwards. He was probably the most complete player in that position Brazil has ever had. Furthermore, he drew the world's attention to Brazil as a potential international power, and in a sense was the last bridge between the chaotic years of Brazilian amateurism and Brazil's rise to world prominence after World War II.

His nicknames were *O Diamante Negro* ("The Black Diamond") and *O Homen Borracha* ("The Rubber Man"). In his international debut for Brazil, against Uruguay in 1932 at age 18, he scored two goals. Nacional Montevideo signed him immediately thereafter, and one year later, having played a major part in Nacional's winning the Uruguayan championship in 1933, he returned to Brazil and helped Vasco da Gama win a Rio championship. He played in the 1934 World Cup, returned to spearhead Botafogo's Rio title in 1935, and finally settled at Flamengo from 1936-42, his most productive period. He rounded out his career with a long stay at São Paulo, and finally retired in 1950. Three years later he returned to São Paulo as manager, and eventually he became a radio commentator. The subject of a hundred songs, dances, poems and films since his stary-eyed days of the late 1930s and early '40s, he now operates a furniture store in São Paulo.

Lesotho

Lesotho Sports Council
P.O. Box 138
Maseru

Founded: 1932
FIFA: 1964
CAF: 1964

Affiliated clubs: *56;* **registered players:** *1,400;* **national stadium:** *Lesotho National Stadium, Maseru (10,700);* **largest stadium:** *Lesotho National Stadium;* **colors:** *blue, white, green, and red jerseys, white shorts;* **season:** *November to October;* **honors:** *none.*

Soccer in Lesotho is characterized by vigorous activity at the club level and a certain degree of exclusion by some other black African states over the question of the kingdom's close relations with South Africa. Thirty-six clubs participate in senior-level competition with about 700 players on the rosters. The upper division includes 16 of the 36 clubs, and there is a national championship and an annual cup competition, as well as regional leagues.

Most of Lesotho's international exposure has been at the club level. With the exception of 1976, the national champion has entered each of the last several editions of the African Champions' Cup: Maseru Club (1971), Lesotho Filding Majantja (1972), PMU (1973), Linare (1974), and Matlama F.C. (1975). In each case, Lesotho clubs have been eliminated in the preliminary round; Matlama was suspended in 1975 before the preliminary round began. The only victory by a Lesotho club in the Champions' Cup thus far has been PMU's 2-1 defeat of Fortior of Madagascar in

the home leg of 1973. The worst defeat was Filding Majantja's 9-0 trouncing by Kabwe Warriors, one of Zambia's leading clubs, in 1972. Lesotho has not yet participated in the African Cup Winners' Cup.

At the national level, Lesotho has failed to qualify for the final rounds of the African Nations' Cup, Africa's most popular tournament, and in many cases has not made the attempt. Its only run in World Cup qualification rounds met with disaster in 1972 when Zambia won a second leg by 6-1 in the first round.

The game arrived early in Lesotho because of geographical proximity to South Africa, the first stronghold of soccer on the continent. The Lesotho Sports Association (later Council) took over administration of the game from the old Basutoland Association when Lesotho became independent in 1966. Lesotho's primary concern in the near future will be to spread its sphere of acceptance beyond the reaches of neighboring Botswana.

Liberia

Liberia Football Association
P.O. 1066
Monrovia

Founded: ?
FIFA: 1962
CAF: ?

Largest stadium: *Antoinette Tubman Stadium, Monrovia:* **colors:** *red and white jerseys, white shorts.* (further information unavailable)

One of the countries held in low esteem among FIFA members in Africa, Liberia is perhaps the least known quantity in African competition, isolated and lacking desire to make itself known abroad. So little information is available about the domestic game that

it is difficult to approach an evaluation. Ironically, the primary reasons for Liberia's low position in African soccer is the country's unique absence of a colonial past. Much of Liberia's international relations over the decades has been with the United States, the only western power that did not export soccer to the developing countries. Liberia's relative political isolation in Africa has contributed further to its slow progress on the playing field.

The domestic game includes a national championship and a cup competition, but the number of participating clubs and players is not known. The leading club is Barolle, which has entered two editions of the African Champions' Cup (1973 and 1974) and the first African Cup Winners' Cup in 1975. In each case, Barolle was eliminated in the first round. Barolle's opposition in both its Champions' Cup runs was the mighty ASEC Abidjan of neighboring Ivory Coast. Bame, the only other Liberian club to enter the African Champions' Cup (1975), was also eliminated in the first round.

The national team of Liberia has not yet advanced to the final rounds of the African Nations' Cup, nor has it made many attempts. It has also stayed clear of World Cup qualification rounds. The Liberia Football Association, however, is a member of the West African Football Union, though how actively it will participate in this new venture remains to be seen. The Tubman Stadium in Monrovia is named for the wife of Liberia's President (1944-71), William V.S. Tubman, and a George Tubman is the current President of the Liberia F.A.

Libya, Arab Republic

Libyan Arab General Football Federation
P.O. Box 879
Tripoli

Founded: 1963
FIFA: 1963
CAF: 1965

Affiliated clubs: *69;* registered players: *2,088;* national stadium: *Tripoli Sports City Stadium, Gurgi (70,000);* largest stadium: *Tripoli Sports City Stadium;* colors: *orange and white jerseys, white shorts;* season: *September to April;* honors: *none.*

Soccer was introduced to the coastal cities of Libya by Italian soldiers and workers shortly after the occupation in 1912, but the game did not really take root among Libyans themselves until well into the post-World War II era. The Islamic states in general were late in developing national sports programs, but Libya was later than most. The Libyan General Football Federation, as it was then called, did not surface until 1963, but it wasted no time in joining FIFA and the African Football Confederation.

Libya's first participation in international competition was in the fifth Mediterranean Games in 1967, and its final standing was a dismal eighth, or last, place. Libya entered the games again in the seventh edition, which took place in 1975 at Algiers, and placed eighth a second time. In 1973, Tripoli played host to the second Palestine Football Cup. Libya has only recently attempted to qualify for the African Nations's Cup, with no success whatsoever, and it first entered World Cup qualifying rounds in 1976, only to be eliminated in the preliminary round by neighboring Algeria. Its first and only full international against a European opponent was a 4-0 loss to Greece in the 1975 Mediterranean Games.

Libyan clubs have achieved a small handful of wins in the African Champions' Cup, especially Ahly Club of Tripoli, which advanced to the quarter-finals in 1972 after upsetting Ismaili of Egypt. Ahly was eliminated in the quarter-finals by Uganda's experienced Simba Club. National Benghazi and Ahly Benghazi have also participated in the African Champions' Cup, and in 1976, Ahly Tripoli defeated Liberté FC of Niger in the African Cup Winners' Cup. The most actively supported clubs in Libya are in Tripoli, Benghazi, Darnah, Misratah, and the Saharan town of Sabhah. The first division is made up of 11 clubs, though a total of 58 compete in officially-sponsored competitions.

Libertadores de América, Copa

Taça Libertadores da America.

The Copa Libertadores (Liberators' Cup) is the club championship of South America, contested annually by two representatives each from the 10 member-nations of the South American Football Confederation, CONOEBOL. The winner moves on to play the concurrent European Champions' Cup winner in the Intercontinental Cup, though that competition has never been officially recognized by FIFA. The promise of a European-South American championship was a primary motivation for the creation of the South American competition. The series has been dominated since the mid-1960s by Argentine clubs, but Uruguay has also received a large share of the honors, as in the South American Championship for national teams, Brazil has taken a distant third place in the standings.

The idea of a South American champions' cup was suggested and organized by Colo Colo, the leading Chilean club from Santiago, as early as 1948. A competition was inaugurated the same year under the name Campeonato Sudamericano de Campeones. The participants were Vasco da Gama (Brazil), Ríver Plate (Argentina), Nacional (Uruguay), Litoral (Bolivia), Emelec (Ecuador), Municipal (Peru), and Colo Colo. The winner was Vasco da Gama of Rio, but the tournament's financial failure and other complications prevented it from ever taking root as a permanent fixture. In 1958, CONMEBOL decided to pusue a similar idea based on the apparent success of the new European Champions' Cup, and so launched the Copa de Campeones (the original name of the Copa Libertadores) in 1960.

The first two editions of the series were knockout tournaments from beginning to end, with all matches played on a home and away basis. From 1962, the first round was played on a league basis with all participants other than the holders divided into groups of two or three. The winners of each group advanced to a semi-final round from which the finalists emerged. This system continues to the present day, and all rounds, including the final, are still played on a home and away basis.

Initially, the competition was open only to national champions, though the various national championships were determined in a variety of ways. In 1965, Uruguay, assured that its two great clubs, Peñarol and Nacional, would always qualify for the competition, proposed that national runners-up should also be included. The proposal was implemented by CONMEBOL in 1966. The basic format of group winners advancing to a knockout, semi-final round remained unchanged despite a great increase in the number of participants. No longer a champions' cup, the competition was given its present name and a new trophy was awarded. It was also decided in 1966 that two clubs from the same country could not advance together to the final, and after 1967, two clubs from the same country could not advance beyond the first round.

From the outset, the Copa Libertadores was plagued by serious setbacks. First, there was the question of support and enthusiasm. Brazil, the world champion, was skeptical of the tournament from the beginning. With the exception of internationally famous Santos, there was little motivation on the club level, and Brazil's national association—the CBD—faced considerable financial losses during the early years of the competition. There were three years in which Brazilian clubs stayed out of the tournament altogether.

A year-by-year breakdown of the results illustrates Brazil's surprisingly poor showing: 1960—Bahia eliminated in quarter-finals; 1961—Palmeiras advanced to the final and lost; 1962—Santos won the tournament; 1963—Santos repeated its win; 1964—Bahia eliminated in preliminary round, Santos eliminated in semi-finals; 1965—Santos eliminated in semi-finals; 1966—Brazilian clubs did not participate; 1967—Cruzeiro eliminated in semi-finals, second club did not participate; 1968—Nautico eliminated in first round, Palmeiras advanced to the final and lost; 1969—Brazilian clubs did not participate; 1970—Brazilian clubs did not participate; 1971—Fluminense eliminated in first round, Palmeiras eliminated in semi-finals; 1972—Atletico Mineiro eliminated in first round, São Paulo eliminated in semi-finals; 1973—Palmeiras eliminated in first round, Botafogo eliminated in semi-finals; 1974—Palmeiras eliminated in first round, São Paulo advanced to the final and lost; 1975—Vasco da Gama eliminated in first round, Cruzeiro eliminated in semi-finals; 1976—Internacional eliminated in first round, Cruzeiro first Brazilian club to win the competition since 1963; 1977—Internacional eliminated in semi-finals, Cruzeiro advanced to the final and lost.

In Argentina, the national governing body, clubs, and fans alike took slowly to the new competition. Clubs feared financial losses, which, indeed, were the ironic results of all those Argentine victories until the early 1970s. The governing body became concerned about the tournament's impact on national team players and schedule conflicts. Fans were simply preoccupied with domestic competition and the international trials of the national team. In 1963, Boca Júniors, the most popular club in Argentina, broke the ice by throwing all its weight behind a fine run to the final. It was a spark that ignited the fire. Between 1964-77, Argentine clubs advanced to every Copa Libertadores final and won 11 of 14 competitions outright. Boca itself did not emerge victorious until 1977. Until recently, the most serious problem confronting Argentine entrants was financial loss. In addition to players' demands for bonus payments, some expenses resulted from extensive bribes to referees, a further smear on the reputation of the tournament.

Uruguay's problems, as always, were much simpler. Peñarol and Nacional placed first and second in the Uruguayan first division year after year and perennially represented their country in the Copa Libertadores (except in 1975, when Wanderers Montevideo went through on the tail of Peñarol, and in 1977, when Defensor qualified as first division champion). Interest in the South American club championship was always high in Uruguay, because Peñarol and Nacional supporters were used to their clubs' traditional interest in international competition. In addition, Peñarol was one of the world's best teams during the early 1960s, and it came as no surprise that it won the first two editions of the Copa Libertadores in 1960 and 1961. Either Nacional or Peñarol reached 10 finals between 1960-71, Peñarol winning three and Nacional finally taking the cup in 1971. Their absence from the final round of the competition after 1972 has coincided with the tragic demise of Uruguayan soccer in the 1970s.

South America's secondary powers—Chile, Peru, and Paraguay—have been more consistent in their enthusiasm. Each has sent at least one club to the final, but they have never produced a winning team. The consistent success of Universitario Lima in domestic competition since the early 1960s has earned the club a very high placing in the table of cumulative rankings. In 1972, Universitario finally reached the final after eight previous attempts, and was unlucky to lose to a weak Independiente of Argentina. Olímpia, one of Paraguay's two leading clubs, took advantage of a small field and advanced to the first final in 1960. Paraguay's other big club from La Paz, Cerro Porteño, has not been as lucky. The surprisingly high placing of three Paraguayan clubs in the cumulative standings is due to the small number of teams that have represented Paraguay over the 17-year history of the tournament. Two Chilean clubs, Colo Colo and Union Española, have reached the final in recent years, but there was little they could to to withstand the terrifying tactics of Independiente on either occasion.

None of the clubs from Colombia and Ecuador have achieved any success, except Ecuador's Deportivo Liga Universitaria, whose luck of the draw has figured prominently in its standing. Bolivian clubs, despite their participation in the tournament from its inception, have been consistent losers. Bolivia holds the record for the most number of entrants with 12. The weakest country in South America soccer, Venezuela, was the last to enter in 1964 and has accumulated the worst record of all.

An overriding characteristic of the Copa Liberatadores has been the prevalence of violence both on the field and in the stands. It started with the final of 1962 between Santos and Peñarol, in which the second leg lasted 3 1/2 hours after repeated stoppages. At one point, the Chilean referee, Carlos Robles, was knocked unconscious by missiles from the crowd, and some time later a linesman succumbed to an anonymous bottle. After much official wrangling, the result of the match (Peñarol by three goals to two) remained in question. In 1967, Rácing Club of Buenos Aires established the pattern of bullying tactics and delays on the field that were to become a trademark of Argentine clubs. In succeeding years, Estudiantes de la Plata solidified Argentina's reputation for fielding clubs of high skill that resorted to all kinds of tricks and rough play. Estudiantes' reputation carried over to the Intercontinental Cup in 1968, 1969, and 1970, and caused fears and apprehensions that are still felt in Europe to this day.

There is little doubt, however, that the Copa

Libertadores has replaced the Copa Sudamericana (South American Championship) as the premier competition on the continent. The eight-year hiatus of the Copa Sudamericana between 1967-75 bore witness to the ultimate success of the Copa Libertadores as a public spectacle.

Team scoring record: 46, by Cruzeiro in 1976. Most individual appearances: 77, by Nestor Gonçalves (Peñarol).

Winners

1960	Peñarol	1967	Rácing Club	1974	Independiente
1961	Peñarol	1968	Estudiantes	1975	Independiente
1962	Santos	1969	Estudiantes	1976	Cruzeiro
1963	Santos	1970	Estudiantes	1977	Boca Júniors
1964	Independiente	1971	Nacional	1978	Boca Júniors
1965	Independiente	1972	Independiente		
1966	Peñarol	1973	Independients		

Cumulative Ranking of All Clubs (1960-76)

(number of editions in parentheses)

			P	W	D	L	F	A	P
1.	Peñarol (16)	(Uru)	140	70	32	38	236	144	172
2.	Nacional (12)	(Uru)	113	54	30	29	194	112	138
3.	Universitario (11)	(Per)	91	35	24	32	123	119	94
4.	Independiente (10)	(Arg)	72	37	16	19	104	64	90
5.	River Plate (5)	(Arg)	68	35	13	20	132	80	83
6.	Olímpia (11)	(Par)	70	25	20	25	97	93	70
7.	Boca Júniors (5)	(Arg)	47	27	8	12	76	41	62
8.	Cerro Porteño (9)	(Par)	74	22	18	24	93	97	62
9.	Palmeiras (5)	(Bra)	44	28	4	12	73	43	60
10.	Guarani (6)	(Par)	59	21	17	21	78	74	59
11.	Estudiantes (5)	(Arg)	37	26	4	7	55	23	56
12.	Universidad Cat. (5)	(Chi)	52	23	10	19	91	79	56
13.	Cruzeiro (3)	(Bra)	36	25	3	7	88	44	53
14.	Colo Colo (6)	(Chi)	51	19	9	23	87	95	47
15.	Millonarios (9)	(Col)	44	15	10	19	54	55	47
16.	Emelec (6)	(Ecu)	51	17	10	24	62	81	44
17.	Dep. Cali (6)	(Col)	41	17	9	16	62	66	41
18.	Union Española (5)	(Chi)	41	15	11	15	51	54	41
19.	Barcelona (6)	(Ecu)	45	15	11	19	53	60	41
20.	Rosario Central (5)	(Arg)	30	16	7	7	44	29	39
21.	Sport. Cristal (6)	(Per)	42	12	15	15	49	60	39
22.	Rácing Club (3)	(Arg)	27	16	6	5	54	26	38
23.	Univ. de Chile (7)	(Chi)	44	15	8	21	64	70	38
24.	Dep. Italia (6)	(Ven)	44	14	9	21	44	81	37
25.	Liga Univ. (3)	(Ecu)	30	12	8	10	45	40	32
26.	Santos (4)	(Bra)	22	14	3	5	60	32	31

27.	São Paulo (2)	(Bra)	23	12	7	4	39	18	31
28.	Jorge Wilster. (7)	(Bol)	38	11	9	18	39	70	31
29.	Alianza (5)	(Per)	34	10	7	17	36	54	27
30.	Bolívar (4)	(Bol)	29	8	9	12	41	51	25
31.	Botafogo (2)	(Bra)	17	10	3	4	30	23	23
32.	Nacional (4)	(Ecu)	24	8	6	10	27	30	22
33.	Indep. Santa Fe (4)	(Col)	28	6	8	14	37	55	20
34.	San Lorenzo (2)	(Arg)	15	7	4	4	26	10	18
35.	Dep. Portuguesa (3)	(Ven)	18	5	7	6	17	24	17
36.	Nacional Med. (3)	(Col)	18	5	5	8	18	24	15
37.	Dep. Municipal (3)	(Bol)	20	6	3	11	39	49	15
38.	Dep. Galicia (7)	(Ven)	42	5	5	32	33	79	15
39.	Huracán (1)	(Arg)	11	6	2	3	19	12	14
40.	The Strongest (3)	(Bol)	16	4	4	8	18	39	12
41.	Wanderers (1)	(Chi)	12	4	3	5	20	22	11
42.	América (2)	(Ecu)	12	4	2	6	13	22	10
43.	Defensor Lima (1)	(Per)	10	4	1	5	8	12	9
44.	Dep. Indep. Med. (1)	(Col)	10	4	1	5	15	21	9
45.	Fluminense (1)	(Bra)	6	4	0	2	16	6	8
46.	Dep. Cuenca (1)	(Ecu)	6	3	2	1	9	6	8
47.	Newell's Old Boys (1)	(Arg)	7	3	2	2	9	9	8
48.	Oriente Petro. (2)	(Bol)	12	3	2	7	15	26	8
49.	Portugues (1)	(Ven)	12	3	2	7	8	23	8
50.	Valencia (3)	(Ven)	16	2	4	10	16	35	8
51.	Internacional (1)	(Bra)	6	3	1	2	10	8	7
52.	Huachipato (1)	(Chi)	6	2	2	2	10	10	6
53.	Juan Aurich (1)	(Per)	8	2	2	4	14	20	6
54.	Alf Ugarte Puno (1)	(Per)	6	1	4	1	5	8	6
55.	Dep. Quito (2)	(Ecu)	10	1	4	5	7	19	6
56.	Vasco da Gama (1)	(Bra)	6	1	3	2	7	7	2
57.	U. Magdalena (1)	(Col)	6	2	1	3	7	8	5
58.	Palestino (1)	(Chi)	6	2	1	3	5	6	5
59.	Defensor Arica (1)	(Per)	6	1	3	2	5	6	5
60.	Sport Boys (1)	(Per)	8	2	1	5	10	11	5
61.	América (1)	(Col)	10	1	3	6	12	22	5
62.	31 de Octubre (1)	(Bol)	10	2	1	7	11	28	5
63.	Chaco Petrolero (2)	(Bol)	12	2	1	9	8	22	5
64.	Nautico (1)	(Bra)	6	1	2	3	7	8	4
65.	Atlet. Mineiro (1)	(Bra)	6	0	4	2	5	6	4
66.	Union S. Felipe (1)	(Chi)	6	1	2	3	5	8	4
67.	U. Católica (1)	(Ecu)	6	1	2	3	2	5	4
68.	Atlético Junior (1)	(Col)	6	1	2	3	5	9	4
69.	U.D. Canarias (1)	(Ven)	6	1	2	3	3	7	4
70.	Dep. Lara (1)	(Ven)	10	1	2	7	5	16	4
71.	Bahia (2)	(Bra)	4	1	1	2	4	7	3
72.	Wanderers (1)	(Uru)	6	1	1	4	8	10	3
73.	Union Huaral (1)	(Per)	6	0	3	3	8	17	3
74.	Libertad (1)	(Par)	6	1	1	4	2	13	3

			P	W	D	L	F	A	P
75.	Nueve de Oct. (2)	(Ecu)	10	1	1	8	14	28	3
76.	Rangers (1)	(Chi)	10	1	1	8	11	26	3
77.	Sp. Lugueno (1)	(Par)	6	1	0	5	5	14	2
78.	Guabira (1)	(Bol)	6	1	0	5	2	15	2
79.	Always Ready (1)	(Bol)	6	0	2	4	2	17	2
80.	Universitario (2)	(Bol)	6	0	2	4	2	19	2
81.	Aurora (1)	(Bol)	4	0	1	3	2	14	1
82.	Litoral (1)	(Bol)	6	0	1	5	1	14	1
83.	Everest (1)	(Ecu)	2	0	0	2	1	14	0

Standing of Nations Table (1960-76)
(number of clubs participating in parentheses)

		P	W	D	L	F	A	P
1.	Argentina (9)	314	173	62	79	519	294	408
2.	Uruguay (3)	259	125	63	71	438	266	313
3.	Brazil (11)	176	99	31	45	339	202	229
4.	Chile (9)	228	82	47	99	344	370	211
5.	Paraguay (5)	215	70	56	79	275	291	196
6.	Peru (9)	211	67	60	84	258	307	194
7.	Ecuador (10)	196	62	46	88	233	305	170
8.	Colombia (8)	163	51	39	74	210	260	146
9.	Bolivia (12)	165	37	35	93	180	364	111
10.	Venezuela (7)	148	31	31	86	126	265	93

Scoring Leaders

1960   Spencer (Peñarol), 7

1961   Sasia, Spencer & Cubilla (Peñarol), 3

1962   Spencer (Peñarol) & Coutinho (Santos), 6

1963   Sanfilipo (Boca Júniors), 7

1964   M. Rodriguez (Independiente) & C. Mora (Cerro Porteño), 6

1965   Pelé (Santos), 7

1966   D. Onega (Ríver Plate), 18

1967   Raffo (Rácing Club), 14

1968   Rupazinho (Palmeiras), 11

1969   Isella (Univ. Católica), Iroldo (Dep. Cali), & Ferrero (Wanderers Santiago), 7

1970   Mas (Ríver Plate) & Bertochi (Liga Universitaria), 9

1971   Artime (Nacional) & Castronovo (Peñarol), 10

1972   Toninho (São Paulo), 7

1973   Caszelly (Colo Colo), 9

1974   Terto & Rocha (São Paulo), 7

1975   Morena (Peñarol) & Ramirez (Universitario), 8

1976   Jairzinho (Cruzeiro), 14

Results

1960
(Bye: Olímpia)

First Round

San Lorenzo (Arg)—EC Bahia (Bra)	3-0, 2-3
Peñarol (Uru)—Wilsterman (Bol)	7-1, 1-1
Millonarios (Col)—Universidad de Chile	6-0, 1-0

Semi-Finals

Peñarol—San Lorenzo	1-1, 0-0, 2-1
Olímpia (Par)—Millonarios	0-0, 5-1

Final

Peñarol—Olímpia	1-0, 0-0

1961

Preliminary Round

Independiente Santa Fe (Col)—Barcelona (Ecu)	2-2, 3-0

First Round

Olímpia—Colo Colo (Chi)	5-2, 2-1
Peñarol (Uru)—Universitario (Per)	5-0, 0-2
Independiente Santa Fe—Wilsterman (Bol)	1-3, 2-0
(Independiente Santa Fe won by toss of the coin)	
Palmeiras (Bra)—Independiente (Arg)	2-0, 1-0

Semi-Finals

Peñarol—Olímpia	3-1, 2-1
Palmeiras—Independiente Santa Fe	2-2, 4-1

Final

Peñarol—Palmeiras	1-0, 1-1

1962
(Bye: Peñarol)

First Round
Group 1

	P	W	D	L	F	A	P
Nacional (Uru)	4	3	1	0	9	6	7
Rácing Club (Arg)	4	1	1	2	7	8	3
Sporting Cristal (Per)	4	1	0	3	5	7	2

Group 2

	P	W	D	L	F	A	P
Santos (Bra)	4	3	1	0	20	6	7
Cerro Porteño (Par)	4	1	1	2	6	12	3
Deportívo Municipal (Per)	4	1	0	3	6	14	2

Group 3

	P	W	D	L	F	A	P
Universidad Católica (Chi)	4	2	1	1	10	9	5
Emelec (Ecu)	4	2	0	2	12	10	4
Millonarios (Col)	4	1	1	2	7	10	3

Semi-Finals

Peñarol—Nacional 1-2, 3-1, 0-0
(Peñarol won on goal aggregate)
Santos—Universidad Católica 1-1, 1-0, 8-1

Final

Santos—Peñarol 2-1, 2-3, 3-0

1963
(Bye: Santos)

First Round
Group 1

	P	W	D	L	F	A	P
Boca Júniors (Arg)	4	3	0	1	9	3	6
Olímpia (Par)	4	2	0	2	4	10	4
Universidad de Chile	4	1	0	3	7	7	2

Group 2

	P	W	D	L	F	A	P
Botafogo (Bra)	3	3	0	0	5	1	8
Alianza (Per)	4	1	1	2	2	3	3
Millonarios (Col)	3	0	1	2	0	3	1

Group 3

	P	W	D	L	F	A	P
Peñarol (Uru)	2	2	0	0	14	1	4
Everest (Per)	2	0	0	2	1	14	0

Semi-Finals

Santos—Botafogo	1-1, 4-0
Boca Júniors—Peñarol	2-1, 1-0

Final

Santos—Boca Júniors	3-2, 2-1

1964
(Bye: Santos)

First Round
Group 1

	P	W	D	L	F	A	P
Independiente (Arg)	3	2	1	0	11	3	7
Alianza (Per)	3	0	1	2	3	8	3
Millonarios (Col)	2	1	0	1	3	6	2

Group 2

	P	W	D	L	F	A	P
Nacional (Uru)	4	3	1	0	9	2	7
Cerro Porteño (Par)	3	0	2	1	4	6	2
Aurora (Bol)	3	0	1	2	2	7	1

Group 3

	P	W	D	L	F	A	P
Colo Colo (Chi)	4	3	0	1	3	6	6
Barcelona (Ecu)	4	2	0	2	9	4	4
Deportivo Italia (Ven)	4	1	0	3	1	3	2

Semi-Finals

Independiente—Santos	3-2, 2-1
Nacional—Colo Colo	4-2, 4-2

Final

Independiente—Nacional	0-0, 1-0

1965
(Bye: Independiente)

First Round
Group 1

	P	W	D	L	F	A	P
Boca Júniors (Arg)	4	4	0	0	11	3	8
The Strongest (Bol)	4	1	1	2	5	7	3
Deportivo Quito (Ecu)	4	0	1	3	3	9	1

Group 2

	P	W	D	L	F	A	P
Santos (Bra)	4	4	0	0	10	3	8
Universidad de Chile	4	1	0	3	6	9	2
Universitario (Per)	4	1	0	3	5	9	2

Group 3

	P	W	D	L	F	A	P
Peñarol (Uru)	4	3	0	1	5	2	6
(Peñarol won on goal average)							
Guarani (Par)	4	3	0	1	6	5	6
Deportivo Galicia (Ven)	4	0	0	4	2	6	0

Semi-Finals

Independiente—Boca Júniors	2-0, 0-1, 0-0
Peñarol—Santos	4-5, 3-2, 2-1

Final

Independiente—Peñarol	1-0, 1-3, 4-1

1966
(Bye: Independiente)

First Round
Group 1

	P	W	D	L	F	A	P
Ríver Plate (Arg)	10	8	1	1	23	8	17
Boca Júniors (Arg)	10	7	0	3	19	9	14
Deportivo Italia (Ven)	10	4	2	4	15	18	10
Universitario (Per)	10	3	4	3	10	14	10
Alianza (Per)	10	2	1	7	9	16	5
Lara (Ven)	10	1	2	7	5	16	4

Group 2

	P	W	D	L	F	A	P
Peñarol (Uru)	10	8	0	2	20	10	16
Nacional (Uru)	10	7	1	2	22	10	15
Municipal (Bol)	9	4	1	4	21	19	9
Wilsterman (Bol)	9	3	2	4	11	14	8
Emelec (Ecu)	9	3	0	6	11	18	6
Nueve de Octubre (Ecu)	9	1	0	8	13	27	2

Group 3

	P	W	D	L	F	A	P
Universidad Católica (Chi)	6	2	3	1	9	5	7
Guarani (Par)	6	2	2	2	9	9	6
Olímpia (Par)	6	2	2	2	7	10	6
Universidad de Chile	6	1	3	2	6	7	5

Second place play-off:

Guarani	2	Olímpia	1

Semi-Finals
Group 1

Guarani	1	Boca Júniors	3
Guarani	1	Ríver Plate	3
Boca Júniors	0	Independiente	2
Independiente	1	Ríver Plate	1
Ríver Plate	2	Boca Júniors	2
Guarani	0	Independiente	2
Ríver Plate	4	Independiente	2
Boca Júniors	1	Guarani	1
Ríver Plate	3	Guarani	1
Independiente	2	Guarani	1
Independiente	0	Boca Júniors	0
Boca Júniors	1	Ríver Plate	0

	P	W	D	L	F	A	P
Ríver Plate	6	3	2	1	13	8	8
Independiente	6	3	2	1	9	6	8
Boca Júniors	6	2	3	1	7	6	7
Guarani	6	0	1	5	5	14	1

First place play-off:

Ríver Plate	2	Independiente	1

Group 2

Universidad Católica	1	Peñarol	0
Universidad Católica	1	Nacional	0
Peñarol	3	Nacional	0
Nacional	3	Universidad Católica	2
Peñarol	2	Universidad Católica	0
Peñarol	1	Nacional	0

	P	W	D	L	F	A	P
Peñarol	4	3	0	1	6	1	6
Universidad Católica	4	2	0	2	4	5	4
Nacional	4	1	0	3	3	7	2

Final

Peñarol—Ríver Plate	2-0, 2-3, 4-2

1967
(Bye: Peñarol)

First Round
Group 1

	P	W	D	L	F	A	P
Cruzeiro (Bra)	8	7	1	0	22	6	15
Universitario (Per)	8	5	1	2	11	8	11
Sport Boys (Per)	8	2	1	5	10	11	5
Deportivo Galicia (Ven)	7	2	0	5	5	10	4
Deportivo Italia (Ven)	7	1	1	5	3	16	3

Group 2

	P	W	D	L	F	A	P
Rácing Club (Arg)	10	8	1	1	29	7	17
Ríver Plate (Arg)	10	6	3	1	29	9	15
Dep. Indep. Melellin (Col)	9	3	1	5	12	21	7
Bolivar (Bol)	9	2	3	4	10	20	7
Indep. Santa Fe (Col)	10	2	2	6	15	24	6
31 de Octubre (Bol)	8	2	0	6	10	24	4

Group 3

	P	W	D	L	F	A	P
Nacional (Uru)	12	9	1	2	34	12	19
Colo Colo (Chi)	12	7	1	4	30	28	15
Universidad Católica (Chi)	12	5	3	4	23	18	13
Guarani (Par)	12	4	2	6	18	15	10
Emelec (Ecu)	12	4	1	7	18	28	9
Barcelona (Ecu)	12	4	1	7	14	24	9
Cerro Porteño (Par)	12	4	1	7	14	26	9

Semi-Finals
Group 1

Nacional	1	Peñarol	0
Cruzeiro	2	Nacional	1
Cruzeiro	1	Peñarol	0
Peñarol	3	Cruzeiro	2
Nacional	2	Cruzeiro	0
Nacional	2	Peñarol	2

	P	W	D	L	F	A	P
Nacional	4	2	1	1	6	4	5
Cruzeiro	4	2	0	2	5	6	4
Peñarol	4	1	1	2	5	6	3

Group 2

Universitario	3	Colo Colo	0
Ríver Plate	0	Rácing Club	0
Universitario	1	Rácing Club	2
Colo Colo	1	Ríver Plate	0
Ríver Plate	0	Universitario	1
Rácing Club	1	Universitario	2
Colo Colo	0	Rácing Club	2
Rácing Club	3	Colo Colo	1
Universitario	2	Ríver Plate	2
Ríver Plate	1	Colo Colo	1
Colo Colo	0	Universitario	1
Rácing Club	3	Ríver Plate	1

	P	W	D	L	F	A	P
Rácing Club	6	4	1	1	11	5	9
Universitario	6	4	1	1	10	5	9
Ríver Plate	6	0	3	3	4	8	3
Colo Colo	6	1	1	4	3	10	3

First place play-off:

Rácing Club	2	Universitario	1

Final
Rácing Club—Nacional

0-0, 0-0, 2-1

1968
(Bye: Rácing Club)

First Round
Group 1

	P	W	D	L	F	A	P
Universitario (Per)	6	3	3	0	17	4	9
Sporting Cristal (Per)	6	3	3	0	11	5	9
Wilsterman (Bol)	5	1	1	3	4	8	3
Always Ready (Bol)	5	0	1	4	2	17	1

Group 2

	P	W	D	L	F	A	P
Estudiantes (Arg)	6	5	1	0	12	3	11
Independiente (Arg)	6	2	1	3	8	10	5
Deportivo Cali (Col)	6	2	1	3	6	10	5
Millonarios (Col)	6	1	1	4	6	9	3

Second place play-off:
Independiente   3   Deportivo Cali   2

Group 3

	P	W	D	L	F	A	P
Universidad Católica (Chi)	6	4	1	1	11	7	9
Emelec (Ecu)	6	2	3	1	5	4	7
Nacional (Ecu)	6	2	1	3	5	6	5
Universidad de Chile	6	1	1	4	6	10	3

Group 4

	P	W	D	L	F	A	P
Peñarol (Ura)	6	3	2	1	8	2	8
Guarani (Par)	6	2	3	1	8	7	7
Nacional (Uru)	6	2	2	2	9	5	6
Libertad (Par)	6	1	1	4	2	13	3

Group 5

	P	W	D	L	F	A	P
Palmeiras (Bra)	6	5	1	0	12	3	11
Deportivo Portugues (Ven)	6	2	1	3	5	11	5
Deportivo Galicia (Ven)	6	2	0	4	5	7	4
Nautico Capibaribe (Bra)	6	1	2	3	7	8	4

Second Round

Group 1

Universitario	1	Estudiantes	0
Universitario	0	Independiente	3
Estudiantes	2	Independiente	1
Estudiantes	1	Independiente	0
Estudiantes	1	Universitario	0
Independiente	3	Universitario	0

	P	W	D	L	F	A	P
Estudiantes	4	3	0	1	4	2	6
Independiente	4	2	0	2	7	3	4
Universitario	4	1	0	3	1	7	2

Group 2

Deportivo Portugues	0	Peñarol	3
Emelec	0	Sporting Cristal	2
Deportivo Portugues	1	Sporting Cristal	1
Emelec	0	Peñarol	1
Emelec	2	Deportivo Portugues	0
Sporting Cristal	0	Peñarol	0
Sporting Cristal	2	Deportivo Portugues	0
Peñarol	4	Deportivo Portugues	0
Sporting Cristal	1	Emelec	1
Peñarol	1	Sporting Cristal	1
Peñarol	1	Emelec	0

	P	W	D	L	F	A	P
Peñarol	6	4	2	0	10	1	10
Sporting Cristal	6	2	4	0	7	3	8
Emelec	5	1	1	3	3	5	3
Deportivo Portugues	5	0	1	4	1	12	1

Group 3

Universidad Católica	4	Guarani	1
Guarani	3	Universidad Católica	1
Palmeiras	4	Universidad Católica	1

Guarani				2	Palmeiras		0
Universidad Católica				0	Palmeiras		1
Palmeiras				2	Guarani		1

	P	W	D	L	F	A	P
Palmeiras	4	3	0	1	7	4	6
Guarani	4	2	0	2	7	7	4
Universidad Católica	4	1	0	3	6	9	2

Semi-Finals
Palmeiras—Peñarol   1-0, 2-1
Estudiantes—Rácing Club   0-2, 3-0, 1-1
(Estudiantes won on goal aggregate)

Final
Estudiantes—Palmeiras   2-1, 1-3, 2-0

1969
(Bye: Estudiantes)

First Round
Group 1

	P	W	D	L	F	A	P
Deportivo Cali (Col)	6	3	2	1	12	7	8
Deportivo Italia (Ven)	6	3	1	2	8	8	7
Únion Magdalena (Col)	6	2	1	3	7	8	5
Deportivo Canaries (Ven)	6	1	2	3	3	7	4

Group 2

	P	W	D	L	F	A	P
Santiago Wanderers (Chi)	6	3	0	3	13	10	6
Sporting Cristal (Per)	6	2	2	2	11	11	6
Universidad Católica (Chi)	6	3	0	3	12	13	6
Aurich de Chiclana (Per)	6	2	2	2	13	15	6

Play-offs:

Santiago Wanderers	1	Sporting Cristal	1
Universidad Católica	4	Aurich de Chiclana	1

Aurich de Chiclana	0		Santiago Wanderers				1
Sporting Cristal	1		Universidad Católica				2

	P	W	D	L	F	A	P
Universidad Católica	2	2	0	0	6	2	4
Santiago Wanderers	2	1	1	0	3	1	3
Sporting Cristal	2	0	1	1	2	3	1
Aurich de Chiclana	2	0	0	2	1	5	0

Group 3

	P	W	D	L	F	A	P
Cerro Porteño (Par)	6	4	1	1	15	5	9
Olímpia (Par)	6	3	1	2	12	7	7
Bolivar (Bol)	6	2	3	1	6	8	7
Litoral (Bol)	6	0	1	5	1	14	1

Second place play-off:

Olímpia	2	Bolivar	1

Group 4

	P	W	D	L	F	A	P
Peñarol (Uru)	6	3	3	0	16	8	9
Nacional (Uru)	6	2	4	0	10	4	8
Deportivo Quito (Ecu)	6	1	3	2	4	10	5
Barcelona (Ecu)	6	0	2	4	3	11	2

Second Round
Group 1

Deportivo	0	Cerro Porteño	0
Cerro Porteño	1	Deportivo Italia	0
Universidad Católica	1	Cerro Porteño	0
Universidad Católica	4	Deportivo Italia	0
Cerro Porteño	0	Universidad Católica	0
Deportivo Italia	3	Universidad Católica	2

	P	W	D	L	F	A	P
Universidad Católica (Chi)	4	2	1	1	7	3	5
Cerro Porteño (Par)	4	1	2	1	1	1	4
Deportivo Italia (Ven)	4	1	1	2	3	7	3

Group 2

Santiago Wanderers	1	Nacional	1

Deportivo Cali	1	Nacional	5
Deportivo Cali	5	Santiago Wanderers	1
Nacional	2	Santiago Wanderers	0
Nacional	2	Deportivo Cali	0
Santiago Wanderers	3	Deportivo Cali	3

	P	W	D	L	F	A	P
Nacional	4	3	1	0	10	2	7
Deportivo Cali	4	1	1	2	9	11	3
Santiago Wanderers	4	0	2	2	5	11	2

Group 3

| Peñarol | 1 | Olímpia | 1 |
| Olímpia | 0 | Peñarol | 1 |

	P	W	D	L	F	A	P
Peñarol	2	1	1	0	2	1	3
Olímpia	2	0	1	1	1	2	1

Semi-Finals

Nacional—Peñarol	2-0, 0-1, 0-0
(Nacional won on goal aggregate)	
Estudiantes—Universidad Católica	3-1, 3-1

Final

| Estudiantes—Nacional | 1-0, 2-0 |

1970
(Bye: Estudiantes)

First round
Group 1

	P	W	D	L	F	A	P
Boca Júniors (Arg)	6	5	1	0	14	4	11
Ríver Plate (Arg)	6	3	1	2	15	6	7
Bolivar (Bol)	6	1	2	3	7	9	4
Universitario (Bol)	6	0	2	4	2	19	2

Group 2

	P	W	D	L	F	A	P
Nacional (Uru)	6	4	2	0	13	3	10
Peñarol (Uru)	6	3	3	0	17	4	9
Valencia (Ven)	6	2	1	3	9	18	5
Deportivo Galicia (Ven)	6	0	0	6	2	16	0

Group 3

	P	W	D	L	F	A	P
Guarani (Par)	10	5	5	0	11	4	15
Universidad de Chile	10	5	3	2	19	11	13
Olímpia (Par)	10	4	4	2	19	11	12
Deportivo Cali (Col)	10	5	2	3	18	16	12
América (Col)	10	1	3	6	12	22	5
Rangers (Chi)	10	1	1	8	11	26	3

Group 4

	P	W	D	L	F	A	P
Universitario (Per)	6	4	1	1	11	4	9
Liga Dep. Universitaria (Ecu)	6	3	1	2	10	6	7
Defensores de Arica (Per)	6	1	3	2	5	6	5
América (Ecu)	6	1	1	4	4	14	3

Second Round

Group 1

Universitario	1	Boca Júniors	3
Ríver Plate	1	Boca Júniors	0
Boca Júniors	1	Universitario	0
Ríver Plate	5	Universitario	3
Universitario	1	Ríver Plate	2
Boca Júniors	1	Ríver Plate	1

	P	W	D	L	F	A	P
Ríver Plate	4	3	1	0	9	5	7
Boca Júniors	4	2	1	1	5	3	5
Universitario	4	0	0	4	5	11	0

Group 2

Liga Dep. Universitaria	1	Peñarol	3
Guarani	2	Peñarol	0
Lega Dep. Universitaria	1	Guarani	0
Peñarol	1	Guarani	0
Guarnai	1	Liga Dep. Universitaria	1
Peñarol	2	Liga Dep. Universitaria	1

	P	W	D	L	F	A	P
Peñarol	4	3	0	1	6	4	6
Guarani	4	1	1	2	3	3	3
Liga Dep. Universitaria	4	1	1	2	4	6	3

Group 3

| Universidad de Chile | 3 | Nacional | 0 |
| Nacional | 2 | Universidad de Chile | 0 |

	P	W	D	L	F	A	P
Universidad de Chile	2	1	0	1	3	2	2
Nacional	2	1	0	1	2	3	2

Play-off:

| Universidad de Chile | 2 | Nacional | 1 |

Semi-Finals

Peñarol—Universidad de Chile	0-1, 2-0, 2-2
(Peñarol won on goal aggregate)	
Estudiantes—Ríver Plate	1-0, 3-1

Final

| Estudiantes—Peñarol | 1-0, 0-0 |

1971
(Bye: Estudiantes)

First Round
Group 1

	P	W	D	L	F	A	P
Universitario (Per)	5	2	3	0	8	4	9
Rosario Central (Arg)	5	2	1	2	11	8	7
Boca Júniors (Arg)	4	1	2	1	4	5	4
Sporting Cristal (Per)	6	1	2	3	5	11	4

Group 2

	P	W	D	L	F	A	P
Nacional (Uru)	6	5	1	0	14	2	11
Peñarol (Uru)	6	3	1	2	14	6	7
Chaco Petrolero (Bol)	6	1	1	4	5	9	3
The Strongest (Bol)	6	1	1	4	5	21	3

Group 3

	P	W	D	L	F	A	P
Palmeiras (Bra)	6	5	0	1	13	5	10
Fluminense (Bra)	6	4	0	2	16	6	8
Deportivo Italia (Ven)	6	2	1	3	7	15	5
Deportivo Galaicia (Ven)	6	0	1	5	9	19	1

Group 4

	P	W	D	L	F	A	P
Union Española (Chi)	6	2	3	1	7	6	7
Colo Colo (Chi)	6	2	2	2	6	7	6
Cerro Porteño (Par)	6	1	4	1	5	5	6
Guarani (Par)	6	1	3	2	9	9	5

Group 5

	P	W	D	L	F	A	P
Barcelona (Ecu)	6	3	1	2	8	6	7
Emelec (Ecu)	6	2	3	1	6	4	7
Deportivo Cali (Col)	6	3	0	3	8	8	6
Atlético Júnior (Col)	6	1	2	3	5	9	4

Play-off:

Barcelona	3	Emelec	0

Semi-Finals
Group 1

Universitario	1	Palmeiras	2
Universitario	0	Nacional	0
Nacional	3	Universitario	0
Palmeiras	0	Nacional	3
Palmeiras	3	Universitario	0
Nacional	3	Palmeiras	1

	P	W	D	L	F	A	P
Nacional	4	3	1	0	9	1	7
Palmeiras	4	2	0	2	6	7	4
Univereitario	4	0	1	3	1	8	1

Group 2

Barcelona	0	Estudiantes	1
Barcelona	1	Union Española	0
Estudiantes	0	Barcelona	1
Union Española	3	Barcelona	1
Union Española	0	Estudiantes	1
Estudiantes	2	Union Española	1

	P	W	D	L	F	A	P
Estudiantes	4	3	0	1	4	2	6
Barcelona	4	2	0	2	3	4	4
Union Española	4	1	0	3	4	5	2

Final

Nacional—Estudiantes

0-1, 1-0, 2-0

1972
(Bye: Nacional)

First Round
Group 1

	P	W	D	L	F	A	P
Independiente (Arg)	6	4	2	0	13	5	10
Rosario Central (Arg)	6	3	2	1	8	5	8
Independiente Santa Fe (Col)	6	1	2	3	4	9	4
Nacional (Col)	6	0	2	4	3	9	2

Group 2

	P	W	D	L	F	A	P
Barcelona (Ecu)	6	3	3	0	9	3	9
América (Ecu)	6	3	1	2	9	8	7
Oriente Petrolero (Bol)	6	2	2	2	10	7	6
Deportivo Chaco (Bol)	6	1	0	5	3	13	2

Group 3

	P	W	D	L	F	A	P
São Paulo (Bra)	6	3	2	1	12	6	8
Olímpia (Par)	6	1	3	2	7	8	6
Cerro Porteño (Par)	6	2	2	2	7	11	6
Atlético Mineiro (Bra)	6	0	5	1	5	6	4

Group 4

	P	W	D	L	F	A	P
Universitario (Per)	6	3	2	1	9	6	8
Universidad de Chile	6	3	0	3	12	12	6
Alianza (Per)	6	2	2	2	10	10	6
Union San Felipe (Chi)	6	1	2	3	5	8	4

Group 5

	P	W	D	L	F	A	P
Peñarol (Uru)	4	4	0	0	12	3	8
Deportivo Italia (Ven)	4	1	1	2	4	7	3
Valencia (Ven)	4	0	1	3	3	9	1

Semi-Finals
Group 1

Universitario	2	Peñarol	3
Universitario	3	Nacional	0
Peñarol	1	Nacional	1
Nacional	3	Universitario	3
Peñarol	1	Universitario	1
Nacional	3	Peñarol	0

	P	W	D	L	F	A	P
Universitario	4	1	2	1	9	7	4
Nacional	4	1	2	1	7	7	4
Peñarol	4	1	2	1	5	7	4

(Universitario won on goal average)

Group 2

Barcelona	1	Independiente	1
Barcelona	0	São Paulo	0
Independiente	1	Barcelona	0
(Barcelona walked off)			
São Paulo	1	Barcelona	1
São Paulo	1	Independiente	0
Independiente	2	São Paulo	0

	P	W	D	L	F	A	P
Independiente	4	2	1	1	4	2	5
São Paulo	4	1	2	1	2	3	4
Barcelona	4	0	3	1	2	3	3

Final
Independiente—Universitario   0-0, 2-1

1973
(Bye: Independiente)

First Round
Group 1

	P	W	D	L	F	A	P
San Lorenzo (Arg)	6	5	0	1	15	1	10
Jorge Wilsterman (Bol)	6	3	1	2	6	8	7
Ríver Plate (Arg)	6	2	1	3	12	10	5
Oriente Petrolero (Bol)	6	1	0	5	5	19	2

Group 2

	P	W	D	L	F	A	P
Botafogo (Bra)	6	4	1	1	14	8	9
Palmeiras (Bra)	6	4	1	1	10	6	9
Nacional (Uru)	6	1	2	3	8	9	4
Peñarol (Uru)	6	0	2	4	3	12	2

Play-off:

Botafogo	2	Palmeiras	1

Group 3

	P	W	D	L	F	A	P
Colo Colo (Chi)	6	3	2	1	16	4	8
Emelec (Ecu)	6	3	1	2	6	6	7
Nacional (Ecu)	6	2	1	3	5	10	5
Union Española (Chi)	6	1	2	3	3	10	4

Group 4

	P	W	D	L	F	A	P
Millionarios (Col)	2	1	1	0	6	2	3
Deportivo Cali (Col)	2	0	1	1	2	6	1

(Venezuela's entrants withdrew)

Group 5

	P	W	D	L	F	A	P
Cerro Porteño (Par)	6	4	1	1	14	5	9
Olímpia (Par)	6	3	0	3	7	8	6
Sporting Cristal (Per)	6	2	2	2	5	9	6
Universitario (Per)	6	1	1	4	4	8	3

Semi-Finals
Group 1

Millonarios	1	Independiente	0
Millonarios	0	San Lorenzo	0

San Lorenzo	2	Millonarios	0
Independiente	2	Millonarios	0
San Lorenzo	2	Independiente	2
Independiente	1	San Lorenzo	0

	P	W	D	L	F	A	P
Independiente	4	2	1	1	5	3	5
San Lorenzo	4	1	2	1	4	3	4
Millonarios	4	1	1	2	1	4	3

Group 2

Botafogo	1	Colo Colo	2
Cerro Porteño	5	Colo Colo	1
Cerro Porteño	3	Botafogo	2
Colo Colo	4	Cerro Porteño	0
Colo Colo	3	Botafogo	3
Botafogo	2	Cerro Porteño	0

	P	W	D	L	F	A	P
Colo Colo	4	2	1	1	10	9	5
Cerro Porteño	4	2	0	2	8	9	4
Botafogo	4	1	1	2	8	8	3

Final

Independiente—Colo Colo	1-1, 0-0, 2-1

(1974-75 results unavailable)

1976
(Bye: Independiente)

First Round
Group 1

	P	W	D	L	F	A	P
Ríver Plate (Arg)	6	5	0	1	10	3	10
Estudiantes (Arg)	6	4	1	1	11	3	9
Portuguesa (Ven)	6	2	1	3	8	11	5
Dep. Galicia (Ven)	6	0	0	6	3	15	0

Group 2

	P	W	D	L	F	A	P
Liga Universitaria (Ecu)	6	3	2	1	10	5	8
Dep. Cuenca (Ecu)	6	3	2	1	9	6	8
Bolivar (Bol)	6	3	0	3	16	11	6
Guabira (Bol)	6	1	0	5	2	15	2

(Universitaria won play-off, 2-1)

Group 3

	P	W	D	L	F	A	P
Cruzeiro (Bra)	6	5	1	0	20	9	11
Internacional (Bra)	6	3	1	2	10	8	7
Olímpia (Par)	6	1	2	3	7	11	4
Sp. Lugueno (Par)	6	1	0	5	5	14	2

Group 4

	P	W	D	L	F	A	P
Alianza (Per)	6	3	2	1	8	4	8
Millonarios (Col)	6	2	2	2	8	5	6
Alf. Ugarte Puno (Per)	6	1	4	1	5	8	6
Indep. Sante Fe (Col)	6	1	2	3	7	11	4

Group 5

	P	W	D	L	F	A	P
Peñarol (Uru)	6	3	2	1	7	4	8
Union Española (Chi)	6	3	2	1	5	3	8
Palestino (Chi)	6	2	1	3	5	6	5
Nacional (Uru)	6	0	3	3	5	9	3

(Peñarol won on goal difference)

Semi-Finals
Group 1

Liga Universitaria	2	Alianza	1
Liga Universitaria	1	Cruzeiro	3
Alianza	0	Cruzeiro	3
Cruzeiro	7	Alianza	1
Cruzeiro	4	Liga Universitaria	1
Alianza	2	Liga Universitaria	0

	P	W	D	L	F	A	P
Cruzeiro	4	4	0	0	18	3	8
Liga Universitaria	4	1	0	3	4	10	2
Alianza	4	1	0	3	4	13	2

Group 2

Ríver Plate	0	Independiente	0
Independiente	1	Peñarol	0
Peñarol	1	Ríver Plate	0
Independiente	0	Ríver Plate	1
Ríver Plate	3	Peñarol	0
Peñarol	0	Independiente	1

	P	W	D	L	F	A	P
Ríver Plate	4	2	1	1	4	1	5
Independiente	4	2	1	1	2	1	5
Peñarol	4	1	0	3	1	5	2

Play-off:

Ríver Plate	1	Independiente	0

Final
Cruzeiro—Ríver Plate
(play-off in Montevideo)

4-1, 1-2, 3-2

1977
(Bye: Cruzeiro)

First Round
Group 1

	P	W	D	L	F	A	P
Boca Júniors (Arg)	6	4	2	0	5	0	10
Ríver Plate (Arg)	6	1	4	1	5	5	6
Defensor (Uru)	6	1	3	2	5	7	5
Peñarol (Uru)	6	1	1	4	7	10	3

Group 2

	P	W	D	L	F	A	P
Dep. Cali (Col)	6	4	0	2	12	5	8
Bolivar (Bol)	6	3	1	2	7	4	7
Oriente Petrolero (Bol)	6	2	1	3	5	7	5
Nacional (Col)	6	2	0	4	6	14	4

Group 3

	P	W	D	L	F	A	P
Internacional (Bra)	6	4	1	1	9	4	9
Nacional (Ecu)	6	3	1	2	6	3	7
Corinthians (Bra)	6	2	1	3	10	6	5
Dep. Cuenca (Ecu)	6	1	1	4	3	12	3

Group 4

	P	W	D	L	F	A	P
Libertad (Par)	6	4	0	2	10	5	8
Universidad de Chile	6	3	0	3	3	5	6
Everton (Chile)	6	2	1	3	7	8	5
Olímpia (Par)	6	2	1	3	4	6	5

Group 5

	P	W	D	L	F	A	P
Portuguesa (Ven)	6	4	2	0	10	2	10
Union Huaral (Per)	6	2	2	2	4	5	6
Estudiantes (Ven)	6	3	0	3	6	8	6
Sport Boys (Per)	6	0	2	4	2	7	2

Semi-Finals
Group 1

Boca Júniors	1	Libertad	0
Libertad	0	Boca Júniors	1
Dep. Cali	0	Libertad	0
Dep. Cali	1	Boca Júniors	1
Libertad	2	Dep. Cali	1
Boca Júniors	1	Dep. Cali	1

	P	W	D	L	F	A	P
Boca Júniors	4	2	2	0	4	2	6
Libertad	4	1	1	2	2	3	3
Dep. Cali	4	0	3	1	3	4	3

Group 2

Internacional	0	Cruzeiro	1
Portuguesa	3	Internacional	0
Portuguesa	0	Cruzeiro	4
Cruzeiro	0	Internacional	0
Internacional	2	Portuguesa	1
Cruzeiro	2	Portuguesa	1

	P	W	D	L	F	A	P
Cruzeiro	4	3	1	0	7	1	7
Internacional	4	1	1	2	2	5	3
Portuguesa	4	1	0	3	5	8	2

Final

Boca Júniors—Cruzeiro	1-0, 0-1, 0-0

(play-off in Montevideo; Boca won on penalty kicks)

Liechtenstein

Liechtensteiner Fussballverband
Egertastrasse 14,
Postfach 165
9490-Vaduz

Founded: 1933
FIFA: 1974
UEFA: 1974

Affiliated clubs: *7;* **registered players:** *1,103;* **national stadium:** *Landessportplatz, Vaduz (10,000);* **largest stadium:** *Landessportplatz;* **colors:** *blue jerseys, red shorts;* **season:** *July to June;* **honors:** *none.*

The Principality of Liechtenstein is the smallest and newest member of FIFA, and there are a number of unique aspects to its administrative structure and official relationship with the rest of European soccer. Six of the seven major Liechtensteiner clubs play in the Swiss League—specifically the Ostschweiz regional league of the 4th Division (ZUS)—while FC Balzers was just promoted to Division Three. All seven clubs, in addition to the 13 that are not affiliated with the Liechtensteiner Fussballverband, play in an annual cup competition introduced in 1975-76 (first winner, USV Eschen/Mauren). There is no national league, and the principality is too small to support any regional competitions. The only national team in international competition is at the Under-21 level. This precludes Liechtenstein's participation in any of the major FIFA or UEFA-sponsored tournaments. In addition, Liechtensteiner clubs do not have access to any international club competitions. These conditions are anomalous in European soccer, with the exception of Andorra and San Marino, neither of which are affiliated with UEFA or FIFA.

Surrounded by two soccer nations of long standing, Liechtenstein first brought a degree of organization to its game in the spring of 1932 when five clubs were founded: FC Vaduz, FC Balzers, FC Triesen, FC Schaan, and Kickers Mühleholz. In the fall of that year, Balzers joined the Swiss F.A. The following year, 1933, Vaduz, Triesen, and Schaan also joined the Swiss association, but Mühleholz preferred to become affiliated with Austria. Some years later Mühleholz faded and dropped from sight. After World War II, additional clubs were founded and the best of them became affiliated with Switzerland: FC Ruggell (1958), USV Eschen/Mauren (1963),

and FC Triesenberg (1972). In 1954, FC Mauren was founded and joined the Swiss F.A., but the club was dissolved six years later and eventually merged with USV Eschen.

By the early 1970s, Liechtenstein began to explore the possibility of reconstituting the national association, which had been established in 1933 only to see its influence weakened by the flight of clubs to the Swiss league. The idea of becoming separately affiliated with FIFA and UEFA was instigated by Herbert Moser in 1971, when the Liechtenstein Olympic Committee was mapping out a plan to enter the Munich Olympic Games. With the intention of concentrating solely on the formation of an Under-21 team, Moser and his colleagues gained permission from the Swiss F.A. to form a functional governing body—the Liechtensteiner Fussballverband—in 1974. Provisional membership in both FIFA and UEFA were accepted the same year.

A Liechtenstein Under-21 team surfaced almost immediately. In the opening round of the 1975 UEFA International Youth Tournament, the new team lost to Luxembourg by an aggregate score of 6-1, and to West Germany by an aggregate of 15-1—quite disappointing results. The first international foray of Liechtensteiner clubs was to a tournament of the Lake Constance region that included participants from Östschweiz (Switzerland), Vorarlberg (Austria), and the West German states of Südbaden, Würtemburg, and Bayern. The Liechtensteiner Fussballverband, meanwhile, has continued to retain its reputation as a responsible, if small, member of the European soccer community. All 351 Liechtensteiner players in senior competition have remained amateur.

Cup Winners

1976   USV Eschen/Mauren

---

linesmen   See: **referees and linesmen**

Lipton Cup

Copa Lipton.

This is the first international competition played on a regular basis anywhere outside the United Kingdom. The participants are Uruguay and Argentina, and its long and eventful history has produced some of the most famous international contests in South American soccer. Introduced in 1905, it was played almost annually until 1929, after which the controversies surrounding the growth of professionalism, interference from World Cup competition, and increasingly crowded schedules forced it into a seven-year hiatus. It was resumed on an irregular basis in 1937, but there were additional periods of dormancy, including a 12-year stretch between 1945-57, and a nine-year stretch between 1962-71. The archrivalry created by the Lipton Cup was

heightened with the introduction of the Newton Cup, also contested by Uruguay and Argentina, in 1906.

Argentina has dominated the competition with 11 wins to Uruguay's six, and the trophy has been shared nine times. The winner is decided on a one-match basis with alternating venues. There have been some exceptions to these alternations: 1915, 1927, 1942, and 1945. In 1976, the result was included as one leg of the Argentina-Uruguay series in the revived Atlantic Cup. The sheer volume of other contests between these two countries through the years has served to lessen the importance of the Lipton Cup, but its historical value remains unchallenged.

The trophy was donated in 1902 by the English tea baron, Sir Thomas Lipton.

Winners

1905	shared	1915	Argentina	1929	shared
1906	Argentina	1916	Argentina	1937	Argentina
1907	Argentina	1917	Argentina	1942	shared
1908	shared	1918	shared	1945	shared
1909	Argentina	1919	Uruguay	1957	shared
1910	Uruguay	1922	Uruguay	1962	Argentina
1911	Uruguay	1923	shared	1971	Argentina
1912	Uruguay	1927	Uruguay	1976	Argentina
1913	Argentina	1928	shared		

Lithuania

The most insular of the Baltic states, Lithuania was also the least successful in its encounters on the playing field. It formed a national association during the early 1920s after independence from Russia, but the Lithuanian game was not as active as that of Estonia or Latvia, and the level of play was somewhat lower.

Of its 10 full internationals against European opponents (Finland, Rumania, Sweden, Switzerland, and Turkey), it was victorious only once, against Finland at Kaunas in 1934 (1-0). Lithuania's overall record in Europe was 10-1-0-9-8-47-2. Nearly all of its European experience occured during the 1930s, but in

1924 it went through to the final rounds of the Olympic Games in Paris by luck of the draw. There it suffered its worst defeat when it was crushed by Switzerland, 9-0. Lithuania was defeated three times by Sweden, scoring one goal to the Swedes' 17. In 1924, it lost by 3-1 to Turkey, and in 1931 and 1937, it lost at home to Rumania. As late as June 1939, only a few weeks before the Baltic states' absorption into the USSR, the Lithuanian team was in Karlstad, Sweden, bearing the weight of a crushing 7-0 loss. From that date on, Baltic soccer was to be relegated to the Russian second division.

Liverpool Football Club

Location: *Liverpool, England;* stadium: *Anfield Road (56,318);* colors: *red jerseys with white trim, red shorts;* honors: *European Cup (1977, 1978), UEFA Cup winner (1973, 1976), English champion (1901, 1906, 1922, 1923, 1947, 1964, 1966, 1973, 1976, 1977), English cup winner (1965, 1974).*

Founded 1892 by the owner of the Anfield Road grounds and dissident Everton players. Everton, which had been using the Anfield location since 1884, moved to Goodison Park when the Anfield owner, John Houlding, raised the rent. A group of disgruntled Everton players joined forces with Houlding, and stayed on at Anfield to form Liverpool F.C. In 1893, it was elected to Division 2, and promptly won the divisional title the first year without a defeat. One year later, it was relegated to Division 2 after finishing last. One season after that, the club again won the divisional title, and remained in Division 1 until 1904, collecting its first league championship along the way in 1901. In 1905, after one year in Division 2, it won the divisional title again, and one year later became the first club to win a second division and League Championship in successive years. After that it stayed in the first division until 1954. The club was made up almost entirely of Scottish players during its first few years of existence.

After the all-conquering triumphs of the 1970s, Liverpool has become unquestionably the most successful English club of all time. The implications of this honor are staggering, given the great strength of the English league, but the record speaks for itself. Its 14 consecutive seasons in European club championships is easily an English record, and no doubt there are more records to be broken. Liverpool has benefited over the years by its location in the liveliest soccer hotbed in England; and its archrivalry with Goodison Park neighbors Everton is the most passionate in the country. Liverpool's fame is rivaled only by that of its fans, whose most vocal corps—20,000 strong—are in regular attendance at the "Kop," an end terrace at Anfield Road. The "Kop" and other elements of Liverpool's following have given to England's second most popular club (after Manchester United) the country's most loyal fans.

Liverpool had some success in the First Division during the early 1920s, winning a pair of championships in front of its Irish goalkeeper Elisha Scott, but the remainder of the interwar years were spent floundering in the middle of the first division. The postwar teams showed considerable promise in winning the championship in 1947 and nearly completing the double in 1950, but they slumped after that and in 1954 were relegated.

Huddersfield manager Bill Shankly came on in 1959, and in his third season took "the Reds" back to the first division to embark upon its most glorious era. Shankly became one of the most successful managers in English soccer history. In its second season back in the top division, Liverpool won the league title, and with Ian St. John, Ron Yeats, and Ian Callaghan in the lineup, already had the seeds of its future great teams. In 1964-65, it entered the European Cup, and advanced to the semi-finals, losing to European Champions Inter Milan on a controversial goal. This was also the year in which it won its first F.A. Cup. By this time the team included Roger Hunt, Tommy Smith, and Chris Lawler, and "Shanks'" style had emerged as an admirable though unexciting no-nonsense approach in which emphasis was placed on strength and stamina. In 1965-66, it tied Arsenal's old record for the most league championships, and made its way past Juventus, Standard Liège, Honvéd, and Celtic in the European Cup Winners' Cup, losing to Borussia Dortmund in the final.

Liverpool continued to be in the running for either a league championship or an F.A. Cup trophy in each season under Shankly's stewardship. A new crop of stars emerged to fit the Liverpool style, especially goalkeeper Ray Clemence and defender Emlyn Hughes. In the early 1970s, Shankly added touches of artistry to his durable team with forwards Steve Heighway and Kevin Keegan, perhaps the two most gifted ball artists in the league. In 1973, shortly before Shankly retired, another league title was won, tying Arsenal's new record. When Shankly's assistant Bob Paisley took over in 1974, he was able to adopt a more fluid style for his highly skilled team, and with this transformation Liverpool became not only one of Europe's most successful clubs, but one of its most attractive as well.

In 1976, it won its second UEFA Cup and a record shattering ninth league championship. This was followed in 1977 by a tenth championship, and, in the midst of England's most despairing period ever in international competition, its first European Cup victory, attained with authority over West Germany's

Borussia Mönchengladbach Rome. Liverpool was only the second English club to win this title, and in the following year it repeated its European triumph with a lackluster win over Belgium's FC Brugge in the final. Despite two European Cup victories in succession, Liverpool's complete domination of European clubs remained questionable.

lofted kick

Any long-distance kick that sails through the air high off the ground.

Luxembourg

Fédération Luxembourgeoise de Football
50, rue de Strasbourg
Luxembourg

Founded: 1908
FIFA: 1910
UEFA: 1954

Affiliated clubs: *203;* registered players: *12,047;*national stadium: *Stade Municipal de la Ville de Luxembourg, Luxembourg (15,000);* largest stadium: *Stade Municipal de la Ville de Luxembourg;* colors: *red jerseys, white shorts;* season: *August to June;* honors: *none.*

Little Luxembourg continues to move relentlessly among the titans of European soccer. The Luxembourgeoises have played in international competition since 1911, and have never softened in their devotion to the game. Yet their full international team is often paired against the "B" teams of other countries, and even then it wins less than 20 percent of its matches. With an area the size of Rhode Island and a population one-third of Rhode Island's, there is little else to do but play hard for an occasional victory or draw, and this the Luxembourgeoises are eager to do. Like other industrialized countries of Western Europe, soccer in the Grand Duchy is centered on factory life—Luxembourg's case, steel mills—and reaches high levels of emotional intensity. In addition to the capital city of Luxembourg, the game has been strongest in the industrial cities of the South—Esch-sur-Alzette, Dudelange, Differdange, and Rumelange. Over 80 percent of Luxembourg's championships have been won by clubs from these four cities.

The first clubs in Luxembourg were founded in the capital around the turn of the century, and in 1908 an umbrella governing body called the Fédération des Sociétés Luxembourgeoises de Sports Athlétiques was founded to administer soccer and other sports. This body gained admission to FIFA in 1910, and the following year Luxembourg played host to France in its first international, won by the visitors 4-1. The Luxembourg league was introduced in 1909-10, and the first and second champions, respectively, were Racing Club Luxembourg and Sporting Club Luxembourg, both from the capital. The national team journeyed to Paris in 1913, and lost to France 8-0, but in 1914, won the return in Luxembourg by the score of 5-4. This completed Luxembourg's schedule of full internationals before World War I. In the national league, Luxembourg's first dynasty was claimed by Union Sportive Hollerich-Bonnevoie (Luxembourg), which won five titles from 1912-17. Fola and Jeunesse, both from Esch, launched the industrial belt's domination of the league toward the end of World War I, and with only occasional interruptions by Spora

Luxembourg and Union Sportive Luxembourg, this hegemony has been maintained to the present day.

In 1920, Luxembourg entered the Olympic Games soccer tournament for the first time—it has tried to qualify for every edition since—and lost its only game to Holland, eventual bronze medalists, by a respectable 3-0. The necessity to play "B" teams of other countries, especially France and Belgium, and selections from Alsace, Lorraine, South Netherlands, and Rhineland became more evident between the world wars. Luxembourg played in only 13 full internationals between 1920-40, losing 12 and drawing one, the latter against Egypt in a 1928 friendly after the Amsterdam Olympics. Luxembourg was eliminated from the 1924 Olympics by Italy (2-0 and the 1928 Olympics by Belgium (5-3). Meanwhile, in 1927, England's full international team visited Esch and came away with only a 5-2 win.

After 1928 there was a six-year period of inactivity before the next full internationals, and these were World Cup qualification matches with Germany and France (lost 9-1 and 6-1 respectively). Luxembourg has attempted to qualify for each World Cup since 1934. In 1936, Luxembourg was eliminated from the Olympics in Berlin by Germany (9-0), and Holland and Belgium knocked their little neighbor out of the running for the 1938 World Cup the following year. Other than the above mentioned games against England and Egypt, there were three friendlies at full international level between the world wars—losses to Eire, Hungary, and Holland. At home, the Luxembourg Cup was introduced in 1921-22, and the Fédération Luxembourgeoise de Football separated from the old umbrella federation in 1930. The league and cup were dominated betwen the world wars by Red Boys Differdange and Spora Luxembourg. During the Nazi occupation, Stade Dudelange (founded 1913) played in the Southwest regional league of Germany for one year.

The ever-increasing gulf between Luxembourg and bigger countries grew wider after World War II, except on a few noteworthy occasions. Only weeks after the liberation from Germany, Luxembourg defeated Belgium 4-1 in its first full international victory since 1914, and a 3-2 win over Norway came on the heels of this in 1946. Enormous losses to Belgium, Holland, and Scotland followed soon thereafter, but at the Olympic Games of 1948, Luxembourg achieved its biggest full international win by shutting out

Afghanistan, 6-0, in London. Yugoslavia turned the tide five days later and Luxembourg was again out of the Olympics. A second major upset took place at the 1952 Olympics when the full international team defeated Great Britain's Olympic squad 5-3, then lost to the Brazilian amateurs by only 2-1. This was Luxembourg's last appearance in the final rounds of the Olympics, and with the improbability of its qualifying for the World Cup in the near future, quite possibly its last appearance in a worldwide competition at the "A" level.

Luxembourg has continually entered every international competition at its disposal. Perhaps its finest achievement to date was a stunning upset over Portugal in 1961 during qualifying rounds for the 1962 World Cup. This famous game—made legendary because it was Eusebio's very first international for Portugal—took place in Luxembourg, and was all the more decisive because the home team led throughout the entire game. The final score was 4-2, and a hat trick was scored by center forward Andy Schmidt, a 21-year-old locksmith. Since then Luxembourg has managed to defeat Holland twice (once in the European Nations' Cup of 1962-64), Norway a second time, Mexico, and Turkey. But its overall international record remains near the bottom of the European heap (with Cyprus and Malta). In less than 100 full internationals, Luxembourg has won only 11 and lost over 80.

Its great club of the 1960s and '70s has been Jeunesse Esch, perennial contenders in the Europeans club championships. Jeunesse is owned and operated by a large steel mill whose factory is located next door to the Emile Mayrisch Stadium. Jeunesse is typical of first division Luxembourg clubs in having to call practice sessions three times each day to accommodate workers on different shifts. All Jeunesse players work in the mill, and, like players in Luxembourg, all are amateur. The best Luxembourg players find gainful employment with professional clubs in Belgium, Holland, or France. Perhaps Luxembourg's greatest player of all time was sweeper Louis Pilot, who first played for Fola Esch before moving to Belgium to stake out a long career with Antwerp and Standard Liège. Pilot is now the national team manager.

The Luxembourg league, one of the smallest in Europe, includes a first division of 12 clubs and three lower divisions with automatic promotion and relegation. Despite Luxembourg's highly organized league and cup competitions, a telling indication of its quality of play is the fact that Luxembourg teams have been on the losing end of several European record defeats at both national and club levels.

Champions

1910	Racing Luxembourg		
1911	Sporting Luxembourg	1945	Stade Dudelange
1912	US Hollerich-Bonnevoie	1946	Stade Dudelange
1913	no competition	1947	Stade Dudelange
1914	US Hollerich-Bonnevoie	1948	Stade Dudelange
1915	US Hollerich-Bonnevoie	1949	Spora Luxembourg
1916	US Hollerich-Bonnevoie	1950	Stade Dudelange
1917	US Hollerich-Bonnevoie	1951	Jeunesse Esch
1918	Fola Esch	1952	National Schifflge
1919	Sporting Luxembourg	1953	Progres Niedercorn
1920	Fola Esch	1954	Jeunesse Esch
1921	Jeunesse Esch	1955	Stade Dudelange
1922	Fola Esch	1956	Sport Luxembourg
1923	Red Boys Differdange	1957	Stade Dudelange
1924	Fola Esch	1958	Jeunesse Esch
1925	Spora Luxembourg	1959	Jeunesse Esch
1926	Red Boys Differdange	1960	Jeunesse Esch
1927	US Luxembourg	1961	Spora Luxembourg
1928	Spora Luxembourg	1962	US Luxembourg
1929	Spora Luxembourg	1963	Jeunesse Esch
1930	Fola Esch	1964	Aris Bonnevoie
1931	Red Boys Differdange	1965	Stade Dudelange
1932	Red Boys Differdange	1966	Aris Bonnevoie
1933	Red Boys Differdange	1967	Jeunesse Esch
1934	Spora Luxembourg	1968	Jeunesse Esch
1935	Spora Luxembourg	1969	Avenir Beggen
1936	Spora Luxembourg	1970	Jeunesse Esch
1937	Jeunesse Esch	1971	US Luxembourg
1938	Spora Luxembourg	1972	Aris Bonnevoie
1939	Stade Dudelange	1973	Jeunesse Esch
1940	Stade Dudelange	1974	Jeunesse Esch
1941	no competition	1975	Jeunesse Esch
1942	no competition	1976	Jeunesse Esch
1943	no competition	1977	Jeunesse Esch
1944	no competition	1978	Progres Niedercorn

Cup Winners

1922	Racing Luxembourg	1924	Fola Esch
1923	Fola Esch	1925	Red Boys Differdange

1926	Red Boys Differdange		1953	Red Boys Differdange
1927	Red Boys Differdange		1954	Jeunesse Esch
1928	Spora Luxembourg		1955	Fola Esch
1929	Red Boys Differdange		1956	Stade Dudelange
1930	Red Boys Differdange		1957	Spora Luxembourg
1931	Red Boys Differdange		1958	Red Boys Differdange
1932	Spora Luxembourg		1959	US Luxembourg
1933	Progres Niedercorn		1960	National Schifflge
1934	Red Boys Differdange		1961	Alliance Dudelange
1935	Jeunesse Esch		1962	Alliance Dudelange
1936	Red Boys Differdange		1963	US Luxembourg
1937	Jeunesse Esch		1964	US Luxembourg
1938	Stade Dudelange		1965	Spora Luxembourg
1939	US Dudelange		1966	Spora Luxembourg
1940	Spora Luxembourg		1967	Aris Bonnevoie
1941	no competition		1968	US Remelange
1942	no competition		1969	US Luxembourg
1943	no competition		1970	US Luxembourg
1944	no competition		1971	Jeunesse Hautcharage
1945	Progres Niedercorn		1972	Red Boys Differdange
1946	Jeunesse Esch		1973	Jeunesse Esch
1947	US Luxembourg		1974	Jeunesse Esch
1948	Stade Dudelange		1975	US Rumelange
1949	Stade Dudelange		1976	Jeunesse Esch
1950	Spora Luxembourg		1977	Progres Niedercorn
1951	Sport Club Tetange		1978	Progres Niedercorn
1952	Red Boys Differdange			

M

Macao

The Portuguese introduced soccer to Asia's oldest European colony in the early decades of this century, but the cultural separation between the native Chinese and Portuguese colonists hampered growth of the sport, and dense living conditions became an increasing impediment. The Associação de Futebol de Macáu was founded in 1939 and became affiliated with the Portuguese governing body in 1950 with eight clubs registered. Most of Macao's infrequent internationals are played against teams from Hong Kong, but in 1975 the top Macao selection managed to draw 1-1 with visiting New Zealand.

Maccabiade, Football Tournament of the

The Maccabiah Games are an international sports festival for amateur Jewish athletes, which has always included a soccer competition in its program. The first games were held in Antwerp in 1930, when the soccer tournament was played by many of the well-known Jewish-based clubs of the era: Bar Kochba London, SC Maccabi Antwerp, Maccabi Paris, and Bar Kochba Hakoah Berlin. The final was won by Hakoah Berlin over Maccabi Antwerp. The second games were held in Palestine in 1935, and the pattern was set for future editions by replacing clubs with national Jewish selections. Germany, Great Britain, Lithuania, Palestine, Poland, and Rumania were represented, and the contest was won by the Rumanians.

The third games were held in Israel in 1950. A strong Israeli selection won with an undefeated record over representative teams from France, Great Britain, South Africa, and Switzerland, while France finished at the bottom of the standings without a win. Since 1950, the Maccabiah Games have convened in Israel approximately every four years, between Olympiads. Jewish selections from a variety of countries, including the United States, continue to participate, though the stature of the teams present cannot claim to equal that of the famous clubs of the 1930 games at Antwerp.

Madagascar

Fédération Malagasy de Football
26, rue du 11 Novembre
Antanimena-B.P. 1565
Tananarive

Founded: 1961
FIFA: 1964
CAF: 1963

Affiliated clubs: *528;* registered players: *11,041;* national stadium: *Stade Municipal de Mahamasina, Tananarive (13,600);* largest stadium: *Stade Municipal de Mahamasina;* colors: *red jerseys, white shorts;* season: *November to October;* honors: *none.*

This island republic has not yet emerged from the backwaters of African soccer, but it inherited a solid soccer tradition from its French colonial days. Financial and geographical considerations have impeded international competition. Yet, there is no lack of enthusiasm for the game at home, and soccer ranks as the leading sport.

The colonial governing body was founded as an outgrowth of World War II, and became affiliated with the Fédération Française de Football in 1947. At the time, almost 250 clubs and approximately 6,000 players were registered. In 1958, the year of self-proclaimed political autonomy, France "Amateur" traveled to Tananarive, and defeated a Tananarive selection 5-1 before an identical win over a West Coast of Madagascar selection at Majunga. These were the first officially recorded internationals played by Madagascan teams. In 1960, Madagascar played host to the first Friendship Games (Jeux de la Communauté), which included a triangular soccer competition between Madagascar, France "Amateur", and Cameroon, the home team finishing third after a 2-1 loss to France. The governing body was reconstituted in 1961, one year after independence, and league and cup competitions were introduced. The national cup tournament, the Coupe du Président de la République, was contested by regional selections until the mid-1970s and is now for clubs only.

The national team has not yet been able to gain the final rounds of the African Nations' Cup, but Madagascan clubs have participated actively in African club championships. The leading clubs are Tuléar Club, from the southern city of that name, and AS Saint Michel de Tana from the capital. Domestic competitions are dominated by clubs from Tananarive, Tuléar, and Majunga. Madagascan champions have entered the African Champions' Cup since the late 1960s, though they have never advanced past the first round. Their biggest win in the Champions' Cup was Saint Michel's preliminary round victory over the Tanzanian club Young Africans in 1972. Madagascan cup winners have participated in the African Cup Winners' Cup since 1976 without success.

Maier, Josef "Sepp"   (1944-   )

Widely regarded the successor to Gordon Banks as the world's greatest goalkeeper of the 1970s. After a shaky start in international competition, Maier became an important element in West Germany's rise to the top after the 1970 World Cup, and he has been an inspiration to his club, Bayern München, despite the more pervasive influence of Franz Beckenbauer. A devotee of physical fitness programs, Maier is fundamentally an acrobat—with a clowning personality—and has often remarked that were he no longer able to play soccer he would join the circus. His health and fitness have become legendary in West Germany, and as of 1978 he had competed in over 400 consecutive league matches for Bayern without missing a single game—easily a German and perhaps a world record.

Maier started with the youth team of TSV Haar, but at age 14 he was signed by Bayern and placed in its youth team with the young Beckenbauer. He made 11 West German Youth international appearances, as well as four for West Germany "Amateur," and entered Bayern's first team at age 18. His extraordinary career has included winning the World Cup, European Football Championship, European Cup (three times), European Cup Winners' Cup, Intercontinental Cup, West German league championship (four times), and the West German cup (four times). He has been voted West German Footballer of the Year three times, and in 1978 was still accumulating international appearances after the 85 mark, already the third highest number in German history.

Malagasy Republic   See: **Madagascar**

Malawi

National Football Association of Malawi
P.O. Box 865
Blantyre

Founded: 1966
FIFA: 1967
CAF: ?

Affiliated clubs: *58;* registered players: *744 (1 professional, 127 non-amateur);* national stadium: *Kamuzu Stadium, Blantyre (52,970);* largest stadium: *Kamuzu*

Stadium; colors: *red, green and black jerseys, red shorts;* season: *March to October;* honors: *none.*

This small, picturesque country—formerly Nyasaland—was introduced to soccer by British colonists, but the game was slow to spread among the African population. Ostracization from other black African states, because of the government's political ties to white Rhodesia from 1953-63, also hindered development. The Football Association of Nyasaland was established in Limbe during the colonial era, and was affiliated with The Football Association in London until self-government came about in 1964. The reconstituted Football Association of Malawi was founded under the office of the Director of Sports and Culture in Blantyre immediately after independence two years later, and it adopted its present name in the early 1970s.

Malawi did not become active in international competition until the mid-1970s, and as a result is among the most backward soccer nations in Africa. Its first attempt to qualify for the World Cup was for the 1978 edition, when it was eliminated by Zambia, and no progress had been made in the African Nations' Cup. Batta Bullets, Malawi's most important club, entered the African Champions' Cup in 1975 and the African Cup Winners' Cup in 1976, but failed to advance beyond the first round on either occasion. Another leading club is Yamaha F.C., which is underwritten by the Japanese motoring firm of the same name. There are national and regional championships and cup competitions, and the league is comprised of 30 clubs. Malawi is one of only three black African states to establish a non-amateur and professional status for its players, and it intends to move further toward professionalism in the future.

Malaysia

Football Association of Malaysia
93E, Jalan Birch
Kuala Lumpur 08-02

Founded: 1933
FIFA: 1956
AFC: 1954

Affiliated clubs: *315;* registered players: *7,839;* national stadium: *Merdeka Stadium, Kuala Lumpur (29,000);* largest stadium: *Sultan Mohamed IV, Kelantan (30,000);* colors: *white jerseys with black and gold sleeves, black shorts;* season: *February to September;* honors: *none.*

Malaysia is one of the most active soccer nations in Southeast Asia and the Malaysian city of Ipoh is the site of Asian Football Confederation headquarters. During the postwar era, Malayans played an important role in organizing Asian soccer, even after the separation of Malaya and Singapore in 1965.

After its introduction in Singapore by British colonists, soccer was first played on the Malay peninsula in Perak and Selangor states. The old Football Association of Malaya was founded in 1933, and became affiliated with the English governing body in London shortly thereafter. Its headquarters for many years was divided between Kuala Lumpur and Singapore. In 1956, the F.A. of Malaya was granted separate membership in FIFA, and one year later it introduced the ambitious Merdeka Anniversary Football Tournament to celebrate Malayan independence and the opening of a grand national stadium. (The Merdeka Tournament, held annually since its inception, is open to invited national teams of Asia and is the largest and most respected competition of its kind on the continent.) By the 1950s, a system of regional governing bodies and various national league and cup competitions had been established. When the Asian Champions' Cup was introduced in 1967, Malaysia was one of only five countries to send a representative, Selangor, which lost in the final to Hapoel Tel-Aviv.

Malaysia has continued to be one of the busiest Asian countries in international competition. Its champion teams competed in all editions of the Asian Champions' Cup, and the national team has been active in World Cup and Olympic qualification tournaments. It has won its own Merdeka Tournament a record seven times, the King's Cup of Thailand once, and the Djakarta Anniversary Tournament once. Though a regular entrant in the Asian Cup, it has advanced to the final rounds only once (1976), when it lost to Kuwait and drew with China PR, bowing out in the first round.

The political separation of Singapore from the rest of Malaysia was unquestionably a blow to Malaysian soccer, because Singapore's Chinese population had been instrumental in organizing the game in Malaya and Asia as a whole, but it did not dampen the Malays' enthusiasm. Perak and Selangor continue to be the chief soccer strongholds, while Sarawak and Sabah, located in distant Borneo, lag far behind in organization and number of skilled players.

Mali

Fédération Malienne de Football	Founded: 1960
Stade Ouezzin Coulibaly	FIFA: 1962
B.P. 1020	CAF: 1963
Bamako	

Affiliated clubs: *123;* registered players: *4,600;* national stadium: *Stade Omnisport, Bamako (30,000);* largest stadium: *Stade Omnisport;* colors: *green jerseys, yellow shorts;* season: *October to June;* honors: *African Nations' Cup runner-up (1972).*

Among the numerous strong soccer nations of West Africa, Mali ranks just below the established continental powers, Ghana, Nigeria, Ivory Coast, and Guinea. Its reputation as one of Africa's "sleepers" is derived from its 1972 showing in the African Nations' Cup, in which it reached the final before losing to an excellent Congolese team, and from the 1966 African Champions' Cup, in which Stade Bamako was the losing finalist. The exceptional quality of Mali's best players has become widely known both in Africa and Western Europe.

The game arrived in French Sudan via Bamako from Dakar when French traders settled in the commercial centers along the Niger River. As an Islamic religious capital, however, Timbuktu was less exposed to the recreational activities of the commercial world. As a result, the ancient city's impact on the Mali game is minimal compared with Bamako, Segou, Kayes, Gao, and Sikasso.

In 1972, Mali reached the final rounds of the African Nations' Cup for the first and only time. On five goals by the tournament's leading scorer, Fantamady Keita, it qualified for the semi-finals by drawing with each of its first round group opponents, Togo, Kenya, and Cameroon, and upset Zaire, 4-3, in the penultimate round. The Congo, led by the skillful M'Pelé and M'Bono, scored three goals in the second half of the final and defeated Mali's greatest national team, 3-2. Salif Keita, Mali's famous striker with St. Étienne and later Olympique Marseille in France, was the driving force behind its great success. Mali's international debut occurred in 1961, only one year after the Fédération Malienne de Football was founded, when a national selection visited Eastern Europe. Return matches were played by Lokomotive Moscow that same year.

While a national league has not yet been formed, the regional leagues are very active, and a national cup competition is held annually. Two clubs from Bamako—Stade and Djoliba Athletic—have dominated domestic play and represented Mali in the African Champions' Cup almost every year. In 1966, Stade Bamako advanced to the final of the African Champions' Cup and lost to Stade d'Abidjan of Ivory Coast. Since 1966, Malian clubs have not advanced beyond the quarter final round. There were no Malian entries in either of the first two editions of the African Cup Winners' Cup in 1975 and 1976. The important first division of the Bamako region consists of eight clubs.

Malta

Malta Football Association	Founded: 1900
84, Old Mint Street	FIFA: 1959
Valetta	UEFA: 1960

Affiliated clubs: *238;* **registered players:** *8,164 (416 professional, 53 non-amateur);* **national stadium:** *The Stadium, Gzira (15,000);* **largest stadium:** *The Stadium, Gzira;* **colors:** *red jerseys, white shorts;* **season:** *September to May;* **honors:** *none.*

There was never any doubt that tiny Malta would become a soccer hotbed. A British possession since the early nineteenth century, Malta and the Maltese were exposed to the game from the beginning, mainly through British naval personnel stationed at the Royal Navy's Mediterranean base. The Royal Navy officially sponsored many of the first competitions, and eventually games between military teams and local citizens were encouraged. The problem was that the first soccer field was not constructed until the 1890s, and all previous contests were played in the streets and makeshift grounds. Nevertheless, dense population conditions and a Mediterranean climate contributed significantly to the growth of the Maltese game.

The Malta Football Association was established in 1900, and remained affiliated with The Football Association in London until 1959, two years before Malta's independence. Membership in FIFA and UEFA followed almost immediately. Malta, the colony, first engaged in international competition in 1953 with a visit to The Stadium by an Austrian selection, and was defeated, 3-2. Since then Malta has remained in the European soccer community and resisted the temptation to align itself with African countries, against whom Maltese teams would doubtlessly fare better on the field.

Discouraging playing conditions (the national stadium is still a predominantly dirt pitch) and meager finances, as well as the small population, have kept Malta at the bottom of the European heap along with Cyprus. Despite winning its first full international in 1960 against Tunisia (1-0), Malta's first win against a European opponent was recorded as late as 1975 with a 2-0 shutout over Greece at The Stadium. These two results remain its only victories in full international competition, and in its total number of 25 full

internationals played to date, it has managed to draw only once (against Norway in 1961).

Part-time professionalism was introduced in the immediate postwar years, and for this reason Malta's first official international contests—against Tunisia and Morocco in the 1960 Olympic Games qualification rounds—are not part of Malta's A-team record. The amateur Maltese team in that series drew both home legs and lost in Tunis and Casablanca, and created a furor with FIFA by using a professional player. FIFA was lenient in that squabble and absolved the Malta F.A. from intentional wrongdoing. Since the early 1960s, Malta has been a regular participant in the European Football Championship and World Cup qualifying rounds. One of its finest achievements occurred in 1971, when The Stadium filled to capacity for the only time in its history to watch England, playing its first full international in Malta, defeat the national team by a mere 1-0. Maltese fans were jubilant when world champion West Germany was held to the same result in 1974 and East Germany in 1977, but there have been precious few successes such as these. More typical results are reflected in Malta's overall goal difference in the 25 full internationals played between 1960-78: 7-85.

The first Maltese club and the pioneer of Maltese soccer was St. George's F.C., founded at Valeta in 1890. Floriana F.C., located in Valeta, was founded in 1900, and through the decades has won the lion's share of honors in league and cup competition along with its archrival Sliema Wanderers, which hails from the Valeta suburb of Sliema. In the 1930s, Valeta F.C. emerged as a third leading club, but has failed to challenge Floriana's 24 league championships and 14 cup wins, and Sliema's 21 championships and 15 cup wins. The league, which began operation in 1910, is composed of two divisions. All first division club matches are played at The Stadium in

Gzira on Saturdays and Sundays, since the other pitches on Malta and Gozo have rock-like playing surfaces. The single existing grass pitch was vacated only in 1970 by the British military. There is currently an effort underway to plan a new national stadium (with grass) that would have a capacity of 30,000. Maltese clubs, meanwhile, have participated in the European Cup and the European Cup Winners' Cup since 1961-62, and the Fairs/UEFA Cup since 1968-69. Sliema Wanderers is the only Maltese club to advance beyond the opening round (European Cup 1971-72 and European Cup Winners' Cup 1968-69), but strong foreign opposition has been neutralized more than once at Gzira.

Champions

1910	Floriana	1933	Sliema Wanderers	1956	Floriana
1911	no competition	1934	Sliema Wanderers	1957	Sliema Wanderers
1912	Floriana	1935	Floriana	1958	Floriana
1913	Floriana	1936	Sliema Wanderers	1959	Valletta
1914	Hamrun Spartans	1937	Floriana	1960	Valetta
1915	Valetta United	1938	Sliema Wanderers	1961	Hibernians
1916	no competition	1939	Sliema Wanderers	1962	Floriana
1917	St. George's	1940	Sliema Wanderers	1963	Valetta
1918	Hamrun Spartans	1941	no competition	1964	Sliema Wanderers
1919	K.O.M.R. Milizia	1942	no competition	1965	Sliema Wanderers
1920	Sliema Wanderers	1943	no competition	1966	Sliema Wanderers
1921	Floriana	1944	no competition	1967	Hibernians
1922	Floriana	1945	Valetta	1968	Floriana
1923	Sliema Wanderers	1946	Valetta	1969	Hibernians
1924	Sliema Wanderers	1947	Hamrun Spartans	1970	Floriana
1925	Floriana	1948	Valetta	1971	Sliema Wanderers
1926	Sliema Wanderers	1949	Sliema Wanderers	1972	Sliema Wanderers
1927	Floriana	1950	Floriana	1973	Floriana
1928	Floriana	1951	Floriana	1974	Valetta
1929	Floriana	1952	Floriana	1975	Floriana
1930	Sliema Wanderers	1953	Floriana	1976	Sliema Wanderers
1931	Floriana	1954	Sliema Wanderers	1977	Floriana
1932	Valetta	1955	Floriana	1978	Valetta

Cup Winners

1935	Sliema Wanderers	1947	Floriana	1959	Sliema Wanderers
1936	Sliema Wanderers	1948	Sliema Wanderers	1960	Valetta
1937	Sliema Wanderers	1949	Floriana	1961	Floriana
1938	Floriana	1950	Floriana	1962	Hibernians
1939	Melita	1951	Sliema Wanderers	1963	Sliema Wanderers
1940	Sliema Wanderers	1952	Sliema Wanderers	1964	Valetta
1941	no competition	1953	Floriana	1965	Sliema Wanderers
1942	no competition	1954	Floriana	1966	Floriana
1943	no competition	1955	Floriana	1967	Floriana
1944	no competition	1956	Sliema Wanderers	1968	Sliema Wanderers
1945	Floriana	1957	Floriana	1969	Sliema Wanderers
1946	Sliema Wanderers	1958	Floriana	1970	Hibernians

1971	Hibernians	1974	Sliema Wanderers	1977	Valetta
1972	Floriana	1975	Valetta	1978	Valetta
1973	Gzira United	1976	Floriana		

Manchester United Football Club

Location: *Manchester, England;* stadium: *Old Trafford (60,500);* colors: *red jerseys with white trim, white shorts:* honors: *European Cup (1968), English champion (1908, 1911, 1952, 1956, 1957, 1965, 1967), English cup winner (1909, 1948, 1963, 1977),*

Founded ca. 1878 as Newton Heath F.C. in the eastern Manchester suburb of that name by workers employed with the Lancashire and Yorkshire Railway Co. Newton Heath turned professional in 1885, and in 1892 it was elected to the first division. Relegated two years later, it spent 12 seasons in the second division, and in 1902 went bankrupt. The club was reformed as Manchester United and entered the first division again in 1906 to embark on a highly successful period that included league championships in 1908 and 1911, and a F.A. Cup win in 1909. In 1910, the club moved to the busy dockside sector next to the ship canal at Trafford, where it has remained ever since.

Manchester United has been the most popular club in England since World War II, surpassing even the mighty Arsenal of the 1930s for the passion it evokes. United's fame has not only outdistanced that of Arsenal by virtue of its great success, but the mention of its name also recalls the tragic event when, at the peak of its greatness in 1958, most of the team was decimated by the Munich air disaster. Its rapid return to the front ranks of English soccer under Matt Busby, one of the game's great managers, is as moving a saga as one is likely to find in sports annals. Despite the greater success of Liverpool over the past two decades, United's fame on a world scale is perhaps rivaled only by that of Pelé's great club Santos. In England, United became synonymous with open, attacking soccer, and since the beginning it has been the home of great stars.

The first legend at United was outside right Billy Meredith, the Welsh genius who was lured to the club in 1906 from Manchester City, helping United win its first two championships and its first F.A. Cup. This was also the era of Charlie Roberts, the pioneer attacking center half who steered the club

through its first great period, and was ultimately the inspiration for Vittorio Pozzo's winning *metodo* in Italy during the 1930s. After relegation in 1922, United moved up and down between the first and second divisions until 1938, when it gained promotion once again and stayed there until its one-year slide in 1974-75.

In 1945, Matt Busby took over the helm, and quickly became popular as one of the first "track suit" managers. Aided by his chief scout, Louis Rocca, Busby had a knack for locating gifted players. During his first three years he took the club from the rubbles of the bombed-out Trafford grounds to three second-place finishes in the league and an F.A. Cup victory at Wembley. After a fourth second-place finish in five years, United won its third league championship in 1952, led by the Irish wing half John Carey. In the mid-1950s, Busby built one of the finest assemblages of players ever seen in the Football League. Back-to-back championships were won in 1956 and 1957, and there were serious hopes of unseating Real Madrid in the 1957-58 European Cup. On February 6, 1958, returning home from a quarter-final away leg at Red Star Belgrade, the chartered team plane failed on take-off from Munich Airport, and crashed in the snow. Eight players were killed in the crash (Roger Byrne, Geoff Bent, Eddie Colman, Mark Jones, David Pegg, Tommy Taylor, and Liam Whelan) and one, Duncan Edwards, died later from injuries. Busby himself barely escaped with his life after a long recuperation. There were several internationals among this list, including Edwards, who was widely thought to be the finest right half England had ever produced. The nation went into mourning, and Busby set out to rebuild another collection of "Busby's Babes."

Weeks later, spearheaded by a Munich survivor, Bobby Charlton, the "Babes" appeared in its second successive F.A. Cup final, losing gallantly to Bolton. Busby rebuilt the team with alarming speed. A third F.A. Cup win followed in 1963, and two years later Manchester United was back on top of the league with its sixth championship, advancing also to the semi-finals of the European Cup in 1965-66. The next year United won another league championship with a stunning array of crowd-pleasing stars, three of whom were to win the European Footballer of the Year award (Charlton, Denis Law, and George Best). The "Red Devils" remain the only club in Europe to have had so many recipients of this award on one team at the same time. Appropriately, it was Manchester United that became the first English club to win the European Cup in 1968—on three extra time goals against Benfica at Wembley. Busby was knighted for his amazing comeback, and in 1969 he retired from active management to become a club director.

The team declined soon thereafter. Sir Matt himself was called upon briefly to save it from slumping further, but to no avail, and in 1974 United spent one depressing year in the second division, bouncing back immediately and moving on to another F.A. Cup win in 1977. But its winning ways of old remain inconsistent at best as the 1980s approach. In addition, its legions of youthful supporters gained a fearful reputation during the 1970s for violent behavior at away games, both in England and on the continent, and the near-mythical name of Manchester United became severely tarnished, even though club officials and players hastened to disassociate themselves from this growing national scandal.

Maracanã; Estádio Mário Filho, o

The Maracanã, located in the Aldeia Campista section of Rio de Janeiro, is the world's largest stadium (capacity: 220,000; 178,000 seated, 42,000 standing). This architectural marvel— a testament to Brazilian soccer, the *religião Brasileira*—was begun in 1948 and finally completed in 1965. Though it was adopted immediately as Brazil's national stadium, its original purpose was to take the place of Vasco da Gama's grand Estádio, São Januário. Thus, it was built (and is still owned) by the city and its original name was the Estádio Municipal, o Maracanã. Mário Filho, whose name has now replaced "Municipal," was the founder of Rio's daily sports newspaper *Jornal dos Sports* and a great promoter of the game in his city. "Maracanã" refers to the small river that flows next to the stadium.

It was officially opened June 10, 1950 with a game between junior representative teams of Rio and São Paulo (won by the *paulistas* 3-1), and the first goal was scored by a youngster named Didi. The first great event to be staged there was the 1950 World Cup. On July 16, 1950 it was the scene of the world championship final between Brazil and Uruguay, when a world record attendance of 199,850 was set. This record has yet to be broken, even by subsequent Maracanã crowds. In August 1963, 177,656 watched a Rio league derby between archrivals Flamengo and Fluminense, setting a world club attendance record.

Other internationals have subsequently drawn over 180,000 spectators, and crowds of over 130,000 are reached several times a year during the spring or fall season, when Flamengo, Fluminense, Vasco da Gama, or Botafogo are appearing. Though each of the big Rio clubs has its own small home ground, the major derbies are staged at the Maracanã. Meanwhile, the Brazilian national team has not lost there since 1965.

The stadium is oval in shape, and is distinguished by an uninterrupted cantilevered roof of breathtaking proportions. A moat three meters deep and three meters wide separates the spectators from the pitch. In the years after its construction, several smaller versions of the Maracanã design were built in São Paulo, Belo Horizonte, and other cities, each with a capacity of over 100,000, but the Maracanã remains the crown jewel in Brazil's stunning array of *futebol* venues. The stadium includes extensive medical facilities for spectators and players (for the latter a virtual hospital is on the premises), players' lounges, a cordoned-off area in the stands for children only, numerous massage salons, and two dozen restaurants. An average of 100 matches are played there annually, and it attracts thousands of tourists every month. Approximately five million people have entered its gates since the opening in 1950. In 1966, it provided shelter for 471 families over a period of eight weeks after tragic floods devastated parts of the city; two dozen matches were rescheduled as a result.

An efficiently-run operation in all respects, the stadium employs eight ball boys for each match, each of whom is schooled by the sta-

dium management and is required to participate in rigorous physical education classes. Next to the stadium is the Maracananzinho, "the small Maracanã," which is an indoor arena for boxing, tennis, festivals, indoor soccer, and other events.

---

mark   Also known as "track."

To guard an opposing player; to defend closely against him.

See also: **jockey**

Martinique

The Union des Sociétés Martiniquaises de Sports Athlétiques established an office for soccer in the mid-1930s, and became affiliated with the French governing body in 1938 with 38 clubs and 4071 players registered. It maintains this link to the present day, and many leading Martinique players find their way onto French club rosters. Martinique's

most important internationals have been played against France (Amateur). In 1957, the national selection lost to France (Amateur) twice in Fort de France (1-0 and 3-0), but in 1969, after losing 1-0, it defeated the French amateurs, 2-1. Other international competition is mainly confined to Guadeloupe and the British Caribbean colonies.

Matthews, Sir Stanley C.B.E.   (1915-   )

An international legend eclipsed only by that of Pelé in the history of the game, and the greatest name in English soccer. As with the others in his pantheonic ranking, Matthews' greatness was multifaceted rather than limited to a single attribute. Before the age of 20, he was already regarded as the finest dribbler ever produced in England, a reputation he carried with him until he was well into his forties. Though he was more valuable in feeding halfbacks or other forwards, he himself scored 71 goals in 698 official league appearances and converted for 11 goals in 54 appearances for England; had it not been for the interruption of World War II and the presence of Tom Finney during the immediate postwar years, he would certainly have been England's choice at outside right for 20 years or more. A measure of his esteem in the national life of his country is the knighthood bestowed upon him in 1965—when he was still playing in the first division 34 years after his league debut—an honor not accorded to

any other player in British soccer.

Matthews was signed as an amateur with second division Stoke City at age 15, playing on its Central League team until his first team debut in 1932, and he made his international debut against Wales in 1935. His move to Blackpool in 1947—after helping Stoke to stay in the first division throughout his stay there—was a severe blow to Stoke fans. In 1953, he scored Blackpool's winning goal with only moments left in the F.A. Cup final against Bolton, a legendary match in English annals known affectionately as the "Matthews Final." This proved to be the only cup medal of his career. He became the first European Footballer of the Year in 1956 and was awarded the C.B.E. in 1957, his twenty-fourth year in professional soccer and the year of his last international appearance (at age 42). In 1961, he returned to Stoke City, setting his home town on fire once again and guiding them to promotion in 1963. When he retired two years later, he had already turned 50 years old and had been knighted. He became general manager of Port Vale, Stoke's smaller club, from 1965-1968, and then went to live in Malta, managing Hibernian Valetta in 1970 and ultimately retiring from soccer to pursue his business interests.

Mauritania

Fédération de Foot-Ball de la République Islamique de Mauritanie	Founded: 1961
Service des Sports	FIFA: 1966
B.P. 274	CAF: 1968
Nouakchott	

Affiliated clubs: *59;* **registered players:** *1,930;* **national stadium:** *Stade National, Nouakchott (6,000);* **largest stadium:** *Stade National;* **colors:** *green jerseys, yellow shorts;* **season:** *November to July;* **honors:** *none.*

Sand-swept Mauritania, three-fourths of which is uninhabitable, is a country held together by one major highway and a handful of cultural activities, such as soccer. There is no lack of interest in the game by the Moorish residents who make up 80 percent of the population. Though all indications point to a vigorous domestic game, Mauritania rarely entered international competition until the mid-1970s. After attaining full membership in the African Football Confederation (CAF) in 1976, the national team entered World Cup qualification rounds for the first time (resulting in elimination by Upper Volta), and the Mauritanian federation announced that its champion club intended to participate in the African Champions' Cup of 1977. Mauritanian clubs had not previously entered either of the African club tournaments.

As an Overseas Territory of French West Africa, mauritania first saw the game being played by French colonists and soldiers of the French Foreign Legion. The Islamic cultural restrictions common to most Moslem states until recent years hindered native participation for at least a generation. The Ligue de l'Afrique Occidentale Française, founded immediately after World War II in Dakar, was the only governing body in French West Africa prior to the 1960s, and exerted some influence in colonial Mauritania. The Mauritanian federation was founded in 1961, one year after independence, and affiliation with FIFA followed five years later. The federation made provisional ties with the CAF in 1968.

Fourty-four clubs participate in senior-level competition with roughly 1,000 players registered as senior amateurs. There are national and regional championships, as well as national and regional cup competitions, but a system of promotion and relegation has been left for the future. Aside from Nouakchott, the capital city, the major centers of soccer are the port town of Nouadhibou (formerly Port Étienne), and Rosso, a trading center on the lower Senegal River.

Mauritius

Mauritius Sports Association	Founded: 1952
8, Felicien Mallefille St.	FIFA: 1962
Port Louis	CAF: 1963

Affiliated clubs: *40;* **registered players:** *8,500;* **national stadium:** *King George V Stadium, Curepipe (39,000);* **largest stadium:** *King George V Stadium;* **colors:** *red jerseys, white shorts;* **season:** *September to June;* **honors:** *none.*

Though the British had been established in Mauritius since the early nineteenth century, soccer did not become fully organized there until after World War II. An umbrella governing body for all sports on the island was founded in 1952, and soccer has remained under its aegis ever since. In 1962, six years before independence, Mauritius was given permission to join FIFA, and membership in the African Football Confederation came along one year later.

The Mauritius national team—known as the "Islanders"—eventually surfaced in African Nations' Cup competitions, and in 1974 gained the final round for the first and only time thus far. Its record in the final was poor—opening round losses to Congo, Guinea, and Zaire—but each of its opponents was a major African power and its very presence was the most important sporting accomplishment in Mauritius history. In 1976, Mauritius lost a match to Kenya, 4-3, at a tournament in the Seychelles.

While a national league and a national cup competition have been active for many years, financial difficulties have prevented any clubs from participating in the African Champions' or Cup Winners' Cups. There are 33 senior-level clubs, mostly in the capital of Port Louis, and 12 of these play in the first division. The national stadium is located in Curepipe, the second major city, at the center of the island.

Mazzola, Alessandro   (1942-   )

One of Europe's most talented strikers during the 1960s, Mazzola provided the goalscoring punch for Inter Milan during its great period of domination in Europe, and later achieved further acclaim as the midfield leader in Italy's return to form in 1968 and 1970. He was, by all accounts, the equal of his extraordinary father, Valentino, who died in the Torino air disaster in 1949. Their touching father-and-son story, combining the careers of two immensely popular public figures, is quite unique in Italian sports. Sandro was six years old and already interested in the game when the Torino tragedy occurred, and while still a boy he was brought into the Inter youth program with his younger brother, Ferruccio. In 1961, he graduated to the senior team—his brother eventually moving elsewhere to a fine career with other clubs—and in 1962 he gained a regular place at center forward in the first team, scoring 10 goals in 23 games. He made his international debut in Italy's 1963 defeat of Brazil, scoring once from a penalty kick, and in 1964 he became Italy's first Footballer of the Year. His dazzling footwork and close ball control spearheaded Inter's three Italian championships and two European Cup triumphs between 1963-66.

In the final of the 1968 European Nations' Cup, he emerged as an attacking midfielder, replacing the injured Rivera, and turned the tide for Italy in its win over Yugoslavia. His new role was to cause much controversy over the next two years, as he and Rivera, two of Italy's greatest stars and the opposing captains in Milan's bitter archrivalry, competed for Italy's attacking midfield role. The matter was finally settled by the president of the Italian Football Federation before the 1970 World Cup; Mazzola was to play the first half and Rivera in the second half of each game. This plan was carried out until the final against Brazil, when Mazzola's superb work in the first half precluded any possibility of substitution. Rivera later came on as the replacement center forward. In 1971, Mazzola led Inter to another league championship, and three years later he was the only one of Italy's many aging stars who performed with distinction in the World Cup. He bowed out of international competition immediately afterwards, having accumulated 70 caps and 22 goals, and in 1977 he retired from Inter after 405 appearances and 115 goals, most of them scored before 1968. He is now in charge of Inter's youth program.

Mazzola, Valentino   (1919-1949)

The captain and chief goalscorer of the Torino side that won five Italian championships in a row during the 1940s, and the captain of postwar Italy. He was quite possibly the most gifted inside left ever produced by his country, though his son Sandor's archrival, Gianni

Rivera, would have to be rated his equal. Strong and possessing great stamina, he was a brilliant tactician in his deep-lying post in the W-M formation. Tragically, Mazzola died at the peak of his career in the Torino air disaster of 1949 that decimated his club and national team for years to come. Many believe he would have gone on to greater international glory and lead his club to further championships. As it was, he was already at the pinnacle when he died, and it was only the confusion of war-torn Europe that prevented him from becoming an international idol during his lifetime.

While in his teens, Mazzola joined Tresoldi in his native Cassano d'Adda. After playing for the Alfa Romeo company team in Milan, he was signed by Venezia in 1939, and formed an effective partnership with his inside right, Ezio Loik. He made his international debut in 1942 against Croatia, and with Loik nearly always at his side, appeared in Italy's next 12 consecutive internationals, taking over as captain in his eighth appearance in 1947. Nine of these 12 internationals resulted in victories. In 1942, he and Loik were lured to Torino, and in 1943 he won his first league championship medal. Three more followed in 1946, 1947, and 1948, and in 1947 Mazzola was the league's leading scorer. In 1948-49, he was leading his club to another sure championship, when, five weeks away from the end of the season, the Superga disaster ended the lives of the entire team. All were accorded a state funeral, but Mazzola's loss to Italian soccer was uniquely penetrating. He had scored four goals for Italy, and in little more than 220 club appearances, converted 109 times.

Sandro Mazzola (right), playing for the first time with his lesser known brother, Ferruccio (left), celebrates after scoring the game-winning goal for Inter Milan in a league match against Lanerossi; San Siro Stadium, Milan, 1967. Sandro was by this time the equal of his legendary father, Valentino, who had been killed in the 1949 Superga air disaster.

Meazza, Giuseppe   (1910-   )

The premier goalscorer during much of Italy's golden era in the 1930s. His 355 goals in senior-level competition was an Italian record until it was broken by Silvio Piola, and he placed among the top four scorers in each of the first seven seasons of the national league (1930-36), finishing at the head of the list on three occasions. He was one of only two players to participate in both of Italy's World Cup winning endeavors—1934 and 1938—and he was captain of the team in the latter. His 33 goals in 53 appearances for Italy was also a record only recently broken by Gigi Riva. Meazza was a center forward-turned-inside right, whose skills included nearly every trick at a player's disposal. He was a master dribbler, and had such a feel for the ball that he was equally dangerous on a fast run, or with a delicate flick and pivot.

"Peppino" first appeared in 1927 for Inter Milan (renamed Ambrosiana-Inter in 1928) at age 17, and in his first season scored 12 goals. In 1928-29, the final year of the old regional league system, he scored a career-high 33 goals, and the following season, at age 20, he led the league for the first time. It was also in 1930 that he made his international debut against Switzerland, scoring two goals, and for the next nine years was rarely left out of the national team. In 1933, Italian manager Vittorio Pozzo moved Meazza to inside right, and, with Schiavio and later Piola at center forward, Italy's was the most gifted forward line in prewar Europe. Though Meazza occasionally played at center forward again, both the 1934 and 1938 World Cups were won with him at inside right. An injury shortly after his second World Cup put him out for most of the 1938-39 season, and at year's end he was transferred to AC Milan, the cross-town rivals, where he played intermittently until 1942. He made wartime appearances for Juventus and Varese, and in 1954 signed with Atlanta for one season. In 1946-47, he was Inter's player-manager, scoring two more goals, and some years later he became a coach of Inter's junior team.

Mediterranean Cup

This defunct international competition was played among some nations adjacent to the Mediterranean Sea from 1950-57.

Its precursor, held in Athens in May 1949, was the Friendship Cup, in which Italy, Turkey, Egypt, and Greece participated. While the full international teams of the latter three took part, Italy sent its 'B' team, which had been dormant for ten years, because much of Italy's 'A' team had been decimated two weeks before in the Torino-Superga air disaster.

The first Mediterranean Cup (1950-53) took longer than expected to complete, but it was played without any serious organizational problems. The second Mediterranean Cup (1953-57), on the other hand, was completed after four troublesome years, in which two Spanish legs were not played until after the tournament was over, and Greece and Turkey declined to play each other at all. In addition, the three major powers of the competition (Spain, Italy, and France) sent their 'B' teams.

With the lingering memory of such difficulties, and because of schedule demands placed on national teams by the introduction of the European Nations' Cup in 1958, the Mediterranean Cup was discontinued.

Winners

1949   Italy B
1953   Italy
1957   Spain B

Results

1949 Friendship Cup (in Athens)

Turkey—Egypt   3-2

Turkey—Greece							2-1
Egypt—Greece							3-1
Italy B—Turkey							3-2
Italy B—Egypt							2-1
Italy B—Greece							3-2

	P	W	D	L	F	A	P
Italy B	3	3	0	0	8	5	6
Turkey	3	2	0	1	7	6	4
Egypt	3	1	0	2	6	6	2
Greece	3	0	0	3	4	8	0

1950-53

*Egypt—Greece	2-0, 0-1
Egypt—*Turkey	1-3, 3-0
Greece—*Italy	0-3, 0-0
*Turkey—Italy	0-0, 0-1
Italy—*Egypt	0-3, 6-1
*Greece—Turkey	3-1, 1-0

	P	W	D	L	F	A	P
Italy	6	3	2	1	10	4	8
Greece	6	3	1	2	5	6	7
Egypt	6	3	0	3	10	10	6
Turkey	6	1	1	4	4	9	3

1953-57

*Greece—France B	0-0, 0-1
France B—*Egypt	0-0, 7-1
Italy B—*Turkey	1-0, 1-1
*Italy B—France B	0-0, 1-2
Spain B—*France B	2-0, 3-1
*Greece—Egypt	1-1, 1-1
*Spain B—Greece	7-1, 0-2
*Turkey—France B	0-0, 1-3
Italy B—*Greece	0-0, 7-1
Egypt—*Spain B	1-5, 0-1
Italy B—*Egypt	1-0, 0-1
*Italy B—Spain B	0-1
Turkey—*Egypt	4-0, 1-0
Spain B—*Turkey	0-0

*home team in first leg

	P	W	D	L	F	A	P
Spain B	8	6	1	1	19	5	13
France B	10	4	4	2	14	8	12
Italy B	9	3	3	3	11	6	9
Turkey	7	2	3	2	7	5	7
Greece	8	1	4	3	6	17	6
Egypt	10	1	3	6	5	21	5

Mediterranean Games, Football Tournament of the

The quadrennial Mediterranean Games have been held on a regular basis since 1951, and are open to amateur athletes from all countries adjacent to the Mediterranean Sea. The following countries have participated in the soccer competition: Algeria, Egypt, France, Greece, Italy, Lebanon, Libya, Morocco, Spain, Syria, Tunisia, Turkey, and Yugoslavia. Of these, only Libya and Morocco have failed to finish in the top three.

The first edition in 1951 had only three entrants (Greece, Egypt, and Syria), and by 1963 the field had grown to nine. Italy won three successive titles between 1959-67, and Tunisia must be singled out for placing second and third in 1971 and 1975, respectively.

Algeria's victory in 1975 is the first intercontinental honor in that country's soccer history. The national amateur teams of southern Europe, despite their lowly status at home, have maintained a clear superiority over the full international teams that represent North African states and the Middle East, and this question has become the central interest of the Mediterranean Games series. Syria's early entrance in the competition and Libya's participation in 1975 are also noteworthy features. Lebanon was the host country and took third place in 1959, but there were only three entrants that year.

All editions are held in a city that is located on the shores of the Mediterranean Sea.

Winners

1951	(in Alexandria)	Greece
1955	(in Barcelona)	Egypt
1959	(in Beirut)	Italy
1963	(in Naples)	Italy
1967	(in Tunis)	Italy
1971	(in Izmir)	Yugoslavia
1975	(in Algiers)	Algeria

Merdeka Anniversary Football Tournament

Played in connection with the annual Pestabola Merdeka in Kuala Lumpur, Malaysia, this is the oldest and largest of the regional soccer competitions in the Far East. It was introduced in 1957 to commemorate the opening of the Merdeka Stadium, and over the years has included the following countries: Australia, Burma, China National, Hong Kong, India, Indonesia, Japan, Korea Republic, Kuwait, Malaysia, Pakistan, Singapore, Thailand, and Vietnam Republic. In 1974, the tournament was held in the city of Ipoh, but all other editions have been held at the Merdeka Stadium near the center of the capital. The home country has accumulated the highest number of first and second place finishes, with Korea Republic, Burma, and Indonesia following closely.

The first three editions were organized on a league basis. The rest have been knockout competitions, which have produced three shared titles over the years, each involving South Korea.

Winners

1957	Hong Kong	1967	Korea Republic and	
1958	Malaya		Burma	
1959	Malaya	1968	Malaysia	
1060	Malaya and Korea Republic	1969	Indonesia	
1961	Indonesia	1970	Korea Republic	
1962	Indonesia	1971	Burma	
1963	China National	1972	Korea Republic	
1964	Burma	1973	Malaysia	
1965	China National and Korea Republic	1974	Malaysia	
		1975	Korea Republic	
1966	Vietnam Republic	1976	Malaysia	

Meredith, William (1874-1958)

The first and greatest of all Welsh soccer idols and perhaps the most important European right wing of all time. Billy Meredith was a pioneer of great intelligence who perfected

Britain's two greatest stars after the turn of the century, Billy Meredith of Wales (left) and Steve Bloomer of England (right).

the winger's art by working endlessly on timing and ball control, and he ultimately became the master of crosses on-the-run and other wing skills that are now taken for granted. His career, nearly all of which was played in the first division, was phenomenally long, encompassing 30 years from 1894-24, and his 51 international appearances set a record for Wales that was not broken for many decades. Though he scored over 300 goals, his main function was to assist others in scoring, and it is estimated that he made over 1,000 appearances at club level.

Meredith came from Chirk, a village in the middle of the North Wales coal mining region that was a virtual production center for many Welsh players of the nineteenth century. During the first half of his career, he continued to work in the mines to make ends meet. Manchester City signed him in 1894, and he remained there for 12 seasons, leading his club to its first big success in 1894, only to find himself suspended in 1905-06—with most of the rest of the team—for allegedly receiving illegal bonus payments (totaling five to 10 shillings). City transferred him to Manchester United in 1906 after City had nearly folded as a result of his absence, and there he enjoyed a second and even greater career, helping United's famous pre-World War I team win many league and cup honors. In the early 1920s, he returned to City for three seasons, where he closed out his playing career at age 49. He always felt more warmly toward United, however, and he subsequently served them in a coaching capacity during the 1930s before turning to the hotel business.

Mexico

Federación Mexicana de Fútbol Asociación
Abraham Gonzalez, 74, Colonia Juárez
Mexico, D.F., Z.P.6

Founded: 1927
FIFA: 1929
CONCACAF: 1961

Affiliated clubs: *56;* registered players: *1,331,850 (1,500 professional);* national stadium: *none;* largest stadium: *Estadio Azteca, Mexico City (108,499);* colors: *green jerseys, white shorts;* season: *July to October;* honors: *Championship of CONCACAF (1965), North American Championship (1949), Central American and Caribbean Championship (1935, 1938), Guadalajara, Championship of CONCACAF Club Champions (1963, 1964, 1965), Cruz Azul, Championship of CONCACAF Club Champions (1969, 1970 shared, 1971), Toluca, Championship of CONCACAF Club Champions (1968), Atlético Español, Championship of CONCACAF Club Champions (1975), América, Championship of CONCACAF Club Champions (1977).*

Mexico is far and away the dominant soccer power in the North-Central American and Caribbean region. Its predominance has been so continuous that only three countries in the world have qualified more often than Mexico for the World Cup finals: Brazil, Germany, and Italy. Mexico has participated in the World Championship eight times. In addition, its prestige has been enhanced by some excellent showings in that and other competitions—most notably its 3-1 win over Czechoslovakia in the 1962 World Cup—and by its successful staging of the 1970 edition of the World Cup. It is also the home of Estadio Azteca, the national stadium in Mexico City, which is thought by many to be the finest facility in the Americas. Yet Mexico's isolation from the mainstream of top flight soccer in Europe and South America has held it back from having a real impact on the world game. With almost one million senior level players registered—the fourth highest total in the world—and advanced organizational ability, it remains a potential force and a respected competitor.

Soccer was introduced to Mexico during the last decades of the nineteenth century by British, Spanish, and French technicians who were brought in to modernize technology and commerce in the cities. The first important clubs were established in Mexico City and other towns of the central region. From the beginning, Mexico City, Toluca, Orizaba, Guadalajara, Veracruz, and Pachuca dominated the game. Clubs from the capital—Reforma, España, and América—were almost invincible for 40 years after the founding of

the national league in 1903 (one of the oldest in the Western Hemisphere), but others in the central region waited in the wings until their chance came during World War II. The first league champion was Orizaba Atlético Club, but between 1903-46, only one other provincial name appeared on the list of winners: Pachuca AC España, founded in 1912, became the most famous club in the country, and won a record 15 titles in 40 years. España was finally relegated in 1950, and other Mexico City clubs came to the fore. In the postwar years, Club Social y Deportivo León (founded 1943), and Club Deportivo Guadalajara (founded 1908), won four and nine championships, respectively, effectively removing the power base out of the capital city. Since Guadalajara's golden era during the 1960s, Cruz Azul of Mexico City and Toluca have achieved great success. A Mexican cup competition was introduced in 1944-45, but it has not captured the close attention of the public. The first winner was Puebla.

In international competition, Mexico has a winning record over every country in the CONCACAF region, but, significantly, its first full international was played in 1928 against a European opponent—Spain—at the Amsterdam Olympics; Spain won 7-1. A few days later, the Mexicans played against Chile, also eliminated from the Olympics, in a friendly at Arnhem, and lost 3-1. These teams were sponsored by the new Federación Mexicana de Fútbol Asociación (FMFA), which had been founded the year before as an independent governing body. In 1931, however, trouble began to brew over the issue of professionalism, and the FMFA folded. The rise of professionalism in Mexican soccer coincided with a similar rise in major South American countries, indicating the influence of Latin American sports on the USA's neighbor south of the border. It was also in 1931 that FIFA recognized the newly formed Federación Mexicana del Centro, which was to sanction professionalism almost immediately. In 1935, the federation changed its name to the Federación Nacional de Football Asociación, and the present name was adopted in 1948.

In 1930, Mexico entered the first World Cup in Montevideo, and lost all three of its matches to France, Chile, and Argentina. Unfortunately, this was to set the tone for its poor record in subsequent editions. In 24 World Cup final round matches between 1930-78, it has won only three and scored only 21 goals. These lopsided statistics, however, obscure Mexico's achievements in dominating the CONCACAF region. Mexico has been eliminated from the World Cup in qualification rounds only twice (1934 and 1974), and in 1938 it did not enter.

Its first tournament successes were gained in the Central American and Caribbean Games, which amounted to a regional championship during the 1930s, with outright wins in 1935 and 1938 over five other participants. Mexico was undefeated in both these tournaments, and undoubtedly would have won others, but, in fact, entered only these two. It relinquished possible wins in the Championship of the Confederación Cen-

troamericano y del Caribe de Fútbol during the 1940s and '50s for the same reason. With the introduction of the CONCACAF championship in 1963, it partly reasserted its authority over the area with wins in 1965 and 1977, but its overall record in the various regional competitions that came and went over the years does not accurately reflect its true strength in this arena. Huge wins over regional opponents on a consistent basis from the 1930s on, and occasional successes against major powers are more indicative.

The Mexican game at club level is every bit as well established as the more famous leagues of South America. After World War II, there was a strong Argentine influence, as many players from the big Buenos Aires clubs came north. This gave way to large numbers of Brazilian players in the 1960s, and today some Mexican clubs compete financially with Spanish and Brazilian clubs for South American players. The multidivisional national league includes a first division of 20 clubs and over 1500 professionals, and Mexico City boasts the two largest soccer stadiums north of the Amazon. Great impetus was given to Mexican soccer by the FMFA's successful staging of the 1970 World Cup and the fine showing of its national team in drawing with the Soviet Union and defeating Belgium. Players and spectators everywhere remember the ninth World Championship as the happiest and most festive in the history of the competition.

Champions

1903	Orizaba	1919	España	1935	Necaxa
1904	Mexico Country Club	1920	España	1936	España
1905	Pachuca	1921	España	1937	Necaxa
1906	Reforma	1922	España	1938	Necaxa
1907	Reforma	1923	Asturias	1939	Asturias
1908	Reforma	1924	España	1940	España
1909	Reforma	1925	América	1941	Atlante
1910	Reforma	1926	América	1942	España
1911	Reforma	1927	América	1943	Marte
1912	Reforma	1928	América	1944	Asturias
1913	Mexico Country Club	1929	Marte	1945	España
1914	España	1930	no competition	1946	Veracruz
1915	España	1931	España	1947	Atlante
1916	España	1932	Atlante	1948	León
1917	España	1933	Necaxa	1949	León
1918	Pachuca	1934	España	1950	Veracruz

1951	Atlas/Guadalajara (draw)	1960	Guadalajara	1970	Cruz Azul
1952	León	1961	Guadalajara	1971	América
1953	Tampico	1962	Guadalajara	1972	Cruz Azul
1954	Marte	1963	Oro Jalisco	1973	Cruz Azul
1955	Zacatepec	1964	Guadalajara	1974	Cruz Azul
1956	León	1965	Guadalajara	1975	Toluca
1957	Guadalajara	1966	América	1976	UNAM
1958	Zacatepec	1967	Toluca	1977	Universidad de Guadalajara
1959	Guadalajara	1968	Toluca		
		1969	Guadalajara		

midfielder   Also known as "linkman."

In modern tactical formations, such as the 4-4-2, 4-3-3, 4-2-4, and their variations, the positions that link the defense and attack. Their function is sometimes equivalent to that of the traditional halfback, but with fewer players on the modern forward line they are an increasingly important part of the attack. Elsewhere, the term "midfielder" is interchangeable with "halfback," the latter having fallen out of general use in recent years.

Milan Associazione Calcio

Location: *Milan, Italy;* stadium: *Stadio di San Siro (83,141);* colors: *red and black striped jerseys, white shorts;* honors: *Intercontinental Cup (1969), European Cup (1963, 1969) European Cup Winners' Cup (1968, 1973), Latin Cup (1951, 1956), Italian champion (1901, 1906, 1907, 1951, 1955, 1957, 1959, 1962, 1968), Italian cup winner (1967, 1972, 1973, 1977).*

Founded 1899 as Milan Cricket and Football Club in central Milan by English sportsman Alfred Edwards. The original members were six Britons and fiver upper-crust Italians, including tire manufacturer Piero Pirelli, who frequented the American Bar. AC Milan is the oldest club in Italy's largest city, and the fifth oldest Italian club still in existence. It made its debut in the Italian championship—then a knockout competition restricted to the northwest of Italy—in 1900, and the following year won it with a 1-0 defeat of invincible Genoa in the final. Milan's win broke up Genoa's streak of six titles during the first seven years of the Italian championship. With its immediate source of wealth very much in evidence—Pirelli was to be the club president for many decades—it was not surprising that Milan became the first really successful club after Genoa. It won championships again in 1906 and 1907, the former decided when Juventus refused to meet Milan on the grounds

of US Milanese in the playoff of the final.

In 1908, disgruntled members of AC Milan broke away to form Inter Milan, and the club was seriously weakened for several years, despite the presence of Renzo ("the Son of God") DeVecchi, the first Italian soccer idol. This defection was the birth of one of Europe's greatest rivalries, and it was Internazionale that gained a head start—not merely for a few short seasons, but for an agonizing 43 years. In addition to its frustrating domination by Inter and other clubs between the world wars, Milan was forced by the Fascist government to change its name during World War II to the Italian "Milano," and when the national league was introduced in 1929-30, the *diavoli rossi* ("Red Devils") started off by placing eleventh in the standings. Milan barely rose above eighth place until a vast improvement was seen in the late 1940s.

After the Olympic Games of 1948, Milan signed Sweden's remarkable inside forward trio, Gunnar Gren, Gunnar Nordahl, and Nils Liedholm, known collectively as "Grenoli," and the club became one of the most feared in Europe. Milan placed second in the league in 1950, won the title in 1951, placed second again in 1952, third in 1953 and '54, won again in 1955, placed second in 1956, and won yet again in 1957. Nordahl was the Italian scoring leader five times during this period. Unlike its more defensively oriented crosstown rival Inter, Milan's emphasis was on attack, though it too was capable of an entrenched defense, and in 1955, Gren having departed, additional striking power was added with the Urguayan inside-left Juan Schiaffino. The 1957 title was won by a gaping six-point margin with Liedholm the only remaining member of the Grenoli machine. Milan's strength was further demonstrated by its stunning performances in two Latin Cup victories, the first in 1951 achieved with a 5-0 win over OSC Lille and the second in 1956 after a fine 2-1 defeat of Athletic Bilbao. In 1953, Milan advanced to the final of the Latin Cup, and, expecting to win, lost an historic 3-0 upset to the up-and-coming Stade de Reims of later European Cup fame.

With Liedholm and Schiaffino still working their magic in the attack, Milan won another league title in 1959 with its new Brazilian star José Altafini at center forward. In 1961-62, when it won another championship, it had the sensational 18-year-old inside forward and schemer Gianni Rivera. There was so much goalscoring talent on this team that Milan accumulated 83 goals in the season—22 more than the next highest team—and the highest scorer in the lineup was Altafini with 22. Rivera and Altafini combined in the 1962-63 European Cup to win the final over Benfica 2-

1, and Milan's superlative winning record in European competition began in earnest.

Rivera's team did not win another league title again until 1968, when Nereo Rocco, the stern manager and early exponent of the defensively oriented *catenaccio* system who had left four years earlier, returned, and the defense was bolstered by the resourceful German international Karl-Heinz Schnellinger. In 1967, meanwhile, Milan had won its first Italian cup—traditionally a minor competition in Italian soccer—and it supplemented its 1968 league title by winning the European Cup Winners' Cup. Milan thus became the first Italian club to win both of Europe's major club championships. In 1969, it won the European Cup again with a convincing 4-1 win ovar Ajax Amsterdam in the final, and went on to defeat Argentina's Estudiantes in the Intercontinental Cup. Milan's strength during the 1970s was as a cup fighter. It won three more Italian cups from 1972-77, and in 1973 won a second European Cup Winners' Cup with a series of low-scoring wins in early rounds and in the final against Leeds United.

Gianni Rivera, the name so closely linked with AC Milan for over 15 years, finally announced his retirement effective 1979, after which he is expected to become the club president. AC Milan is the only club in Europe that ranks among the 20 most successful clubs in all three European championships—the European Cup, European Cup Winners' Cup, and Fairs/UEFA Cup—perhaps the most awesome record in European club soccer next to Real Madrid's six European Cup victories. At home, it shares the Stadio di San Siro with Internazionale, whose feats in international competition are nearly equal to Milan's.

Mitropa Cup

Also known as the "Europe Cup," "Zentropa Cup," and "Danube Cup."

Mitteleuropäischer-Cup—Coppa Europa Centrale.

The world's first multi-national club competition, the Mitropa Cup, along with its companion competition at full international level, the Dr. Gëro Cup, was launched in 1927, largely at the instigation of Hugo Meisl, the prime mover of Austrian soccer. In the earliest editions, the participating nations were Austria, Hungary, Czechoslovakia, and Yugoslavia. By the early 1930s, Italy had

become an annual participant. Some editions were held without the inclusion of either Italy or Yugoslavia. Its original purpose was to bring together the champion clubs of each country and, as such, it was a precursor of the European Champions' Cup. Its prestige during the prewar period was without question.

After World War II, however, not enough interest was shown in the old cup to overcome the serious financial difficulties of international competition in war-ravaged Central

Europe. With the inception of the European Champions' Cup and Fairs Cup in 1955, the Mitropa Cup was relegated to minor importance. Although some attempt has been made by national associations to send leading clubs, the field since the mid-1950s has included primarily those first division teams that have finished in their leagues somewhat below UEFA/Fairs Cup level. The tournament is generally played on a home and away basis.

	Winner	**Runner-Up**
1927	Sparta (Czech)	Rapid Vienna (Aus)
1928	Ferencváros (Hung)	Rapid Vienna (Aus)
1929	Újpest (Hung)	Slavia (Czech)
1930	Rapid Vienna (Aus)	Sparta (Czech)
1931	First Vienna (Aus)	Wiener AC (Aus)
1932	Bologna won its semi-final; Slavia-Juventus semi-final suspended; trophy awarded to Bologna.	
1933	FK Austria (Aus)	Ambrosiana (It)
1934	Bologna (It)	Admira (Aus)
1935	Sparta (Czech)	Ferencváros (Hung)
1936	FK Austria (Aus)	Sparta (Czech)
1937	Ferencváros (Hung)	Lazio (It)
1938	Slavia (Czech)	Ferencváros (Hung)
1939	Újpest (Hung)	Ferencváros (Hung)
1940-54	competition suspended during World War II; no postwar tournament until 1951 when unofficial substitute competition was won by Rapid Vienna.	
1955	Vörös Lobogo (Hung)	
1956	Vasas (Hung)	
1957	Vasas (Hung)	
1958	suspended; reinstituted in 1959 with two representatives each from Austria, Czechoslovakia, Hungary, and Yugoslavia.	
1959	Honvéd (Hung)	
1960	suspended; the new European Nations' Cup finals caused severe scheduling problems which could not be remedied by mutual agreement among participating countries of the Mitropa Cup.	
1961	Bologna (It)	
1962	Vasas (Hung)	
1963	MTK Budapest (Hung)	
1964	Spartak Prague (Czech)	
1965	Vasas (Hung)	
1966	Fiorentina (It)	
1967	Spartak Trnava (Czech)	
1968	Red Star Belgrade (Yug)	
1969	Inter Bratislava (Czech)	
1970	Vasas (Hung)	
1971	Celik Zenica (Yug)	
1972	Celik Zenica (Yug)	
1973	Banyasz Tatabanya (Hung)	
1974	Banyasz Tatabanya (Hung)	
1975	Tirol-Svarowski Innsbruck (Aus)	
1976	Tirol-Svarowski Innsbruck (Aus)	

1977   Vojvodina Novi Sad (Yug)
1978   Partizan Belgrade (Yug)

Monaco

The Principality of Monaco supports AS Monaco, one of the leading members of the French league. AS Monaco won the French championship in 1961, 1963, and 1978, and the French Cup in 1960 and 1963. Its relegation to the second division in 1975 ended the most successful period in its history, but it bounced back to the first division in 1977, and won the championship one year later. The Prince of Monaco underwrites and actively encourages the club, but the Principality has no national association and is not separately affiliated with either UEFA or FIFA.

Moore, Robert O.B.E.   (1941-   )

A world class defender whose 10-year captaincy of England drew universal respect and led to an unflinching reputation for consistency and natural leadership abilities. He joined the cockney-based West Ham United in his native East London as a youth, turning professional in 1958, and immediately became an England youth international. Selected for England "Under-23" before he had even reached his club's first team, he went on to make a record 18 "Under-23" appearances. His full international debut was made in 1962 against Peru, and one year later he became England's youngest captain at age 22. As a brilliant reader of the game, he led England to its World Cup victory in 1966, and was voted the outstanding player in the tournament by the journalists present. His O.B.E. was awarded in 1967.

At the World Cup in 1970—his third—he topped his performance of four years earlier, and was named the best defender in the world by many of his opponents, Pelé among them.

In the 1970s, he continued to be unsurpassed in his ability to out-position opponents, a skill he acquired early in his career to make up for his moderate speed off the mark. He remained at West Ham, a previously undistinguished club and one that Moore himself was accused of neglecting, until 1975, guiding it to an unexpected F.A. Cup win in 1964, and an even more surprising European Cup Winners' Cup triumph the following year. In 1974, Sir Alf Ramsey, Moore's mentor during his years as England's captain, finally put him on the substitute's bench, and he retired from the national team with 108 appearances, a world record that stood until 1978. After two seasons with second division Fulham, another London club, two summers in South Africa, and one summer on loan to the San Antonio Thunder, he retired in 1977 to pursue a variety of successful business interests, though he reappeared briefly in 1978 to play in Denmark.

Moreno, José Manuel   (1916-78)

Regarded by some as the most accomplished Argentine player of all time, though Alfredo Di Stefano and Adolfo Pedernera have received this accolade more often than Moreno. His popularity was due not only to his exhilarating artistry as an inside forward, but also to his penchant for getting along well with teammates and the press. Moreno grew up on the junior teams of Ríver Plate in Buenos Aires, and became a regular on the first team in 1934. He was part of the famous River Plate forward line known as *la maquina* that also included Pedernera and Angel Labruna, and the three of them led their club to Argentine championships in 1936, 1937, 1941, and 1942. He made 33 international appearances for Argentina, scoring 20 goals, and was universally touted as the most gifted inside forward in South America in the late 1930s and early '40s.

He joined España of Mexico City from 1944-46, and was the primary reason for this famous Mexican club winning the league title in 1945. Mexican fans, who delighted in his outgoing personality as much as the Argentines, nicknamed him *el charro* ("the horseman"). He returned to Ríver Plate for a spell alongside the young Alfredo Di Stefano, and in 1949 went to Chile and led Universidad Católica to its first-ever national championship. In 1950, he played for one injury-prone season with Boca Júniors, returned to Universidad Católica in 1951, transferred to Defensor Montevideo in 1952, and from 1954-60 was player-manager of Independiente

Medellin in Colombia, where he guided his team to three league championships. He finally retired from active play at age 44, and returned to coach briefly in Argentina before bowing out of the game altogether and spending his final years in Mexico. No other Argentine player had so captured the imagination of his fans, both on and off the field, and the memory of him as a ball control artist and superb header have not been forgotten: months before he died, he was voted onto an all-time World XI by a poll of Argentine players, managers, and journalists.

Morocco

Fédération Royale Marocaine de Football
24 rue Quad Fas
B.P. 51
Rabat

Founded: 1955
FIFA: 1956
CAF: 1966

Affiliated clubs: *285;* **registered players:** *10,300;* **national stadium:** *Stade d'Honneur, Casablanca (40,000);* **largest stadium:** *Stade d'Honneur;* **colors:** *red jerseys with green sleeves and trim, white shorts;* **season:** *September to June:* **honors:** *African Nations' Cup winner (1976).*

Morocco emerged in the late 1960s as the early front-runner of the post-independence era in North African soccer, and became the first new African country to participate in final rounds of the World Cup. Historically, French North Africa has been the strongest bloc of soccer-playing nations in the Arab world. Algeria and Tunisia were more advanced than their neighbor to the west, but this changed in the 1960s, as the stability of Morocco's government served to bolster the Moroccan game. The rise of Tunisia since 1974 has evened the balance of power in the area, but Morocco is still a major force in African soccer.

It is possible that Spanish colonists played soccer at Cueta and Ifni before the turn of the century; soccer was surely played by the French in Tangier, Casablanca, and Fez immediately after 1900, and the French influence ultimately had the greater impact. Soldiers of the French army and Foreign Legion did much to spread the game, especially after the 1910 uprising and during World War I. At about this time, leagues were introduced all across French North Africa, and the Moroccan championship, which encompassed Tangier as well as Morocco, was the first to be established (1916). A governing body, the Ligue du Maroc, was founded in

1923, and became affiliated with the French federation in Paris. Three geographical districts were established—North, Casablanca, and Rabat—and headquarters were located in Casablanca. In 1925, a cup competition, the Cup Steeg, was introduced. The first league champion was Club Athlétique de Casablanca, but the early years were dominated primarily by Union Sportive Marocaine (U.S.M.) and Olympique Marocain (O.M.). The latter won five championships between 1920-30 before it was knocked off its perch by U.S.M., the winner of 10 championships during the 1930s and early 1940s. This small elite of Moroccan club soccer was expanded after World War II to include Wydad Athletic Club (W.A.C.), and eventually, Mohammedia (S.C.C.M.), after independence was achieved in 1956. In the cup competition, many editions during the colonial era were won by clubs from Algeria—all the cup competitions in French North Africa were open to other jurisdictions—until the late 1940s, when W.A.C. began to dominate the Moroccan game completely. Other important clubs of the current 16-member first division are Forces Armées Royale (F.A.R.), Raja Casablanca, and F.U.S. Rabat.

Morocco's first internationals were inter-association matches with other representative teams of French North Africa. A and B selections were put on the field as early as 1927, when a draw was achieved with Oran, and Algiers fell to defeat. In 1930 and 1931, Moroccan selections played host to France B and lost 3-1 and 4-0, respectively, and there were further losses to France B in 1934, 1937, 1942, and 1948, though none of these are officially recognized by France. In 1955, the colonial association was reconstituted as the Fédération Royale Marocaine de Football (FRMF), and separate membership with FIFA was obtained one year later. The international schedule was increased substantially, and in 1962 the FRMF invited Switzerland, Poland, and Hungary B to Casablanca for a mini-series. The Swiss were the only victims, but the tournament helped to establish ties with Central and Eastern Europe. Since the early 1960s, Morocco has defeated Rumania, drawn with the USSR, Bulgaria, and Poland, and lost several times to Yugoslavia, West Germany, and Spain.

Though achieved by a toss of the coin, Morocco's finest hour was in qualifying for the 1970 World Cup in Mexico. Not only was Morocco the first modern African nation to be represented in the competition, but its performance was widely praised. Led by the great Mohammedia striker Ahmed Faras, the Moroccan amateurs nearly upset West Germany, eventually losing 2-1, and drew 1-1 with Bulgaria. Faras led the national team to its first qualification for the final rounds of the African Nations' Cup and the Olympic tournament in 1972, and finally in 1976 he was the driving force behind Morocco's winning of the Nations' Cup in Ethiopia. Undefeated in six matches, it drew the stiffest opposition in the competition, finishing ahead of Nigeria, Sudan, and Zaire in the first round, and Guinea, Nigeria, and Egypt in the final pool.

Morocco's most famous player is the legendary Larbi Ben Barek, a dazzling inside left whose juggling and dribbling impressed French crowds during the late 1930s and '40s. Ben Barek played for several Moroccan clubs before signing with Marseille and Stade Français in France, and in 1938 he made his first of 17 appearances for the French national team.

Morton, Alan   (1896-1971)

Perhaps the most respected and best-loved player in Scottish soccer, the "Wee Blue Devil" compared favorably to his English counterpart on the wing, Stanley Matthews, in his ability to set up attacks, keep the flow of the game going, and in his goalscoring prowess. Aside from his model behavior both on and off the field, he endeared himself to Scotland for all time by playing his entire career with Scottish clubs.

A mining engineer by profession, he made his debut in 1913 at age 17 with Queen's Park of his native Glasgow, and scored in his very first game. In 1920, he turned professional and joined Rangers to embark on an illustrious 13-year career that brought him nine league championship medals and immortality as the greatest Scottish winger of all time. He first played for Scotland in 1920 while still registered with Queen's Park, and for 12 years it was Morton who was the standard-bearer for Scotland's most glorious era in international competition. As one of the legendary "Wembley Wizards" who defeated England 5-1 in 1928, he provided three crosses from the left wing that were tallied for goals. Morton was proficient in all ball control and passing skills, but he was most famous for his hanging lobs into the center, which were invariably taken after outrunning his defender into the corner, and his uncanny dribbling, which is remembered today as being the equal of any player in history. When he retired from Rangers in 1933 with 115 league goals in 490 appearances and five goals in 31 appearances for Scotland, he was immediately elected to the Rangers' board of directors, and in the decades ahead continued to pursue his career in mine engineering, remaining an active Rangers director until 1968.

Mozambique, New People's Republic of

While not yet a member of FIFA or the African Football Confederation, soccer in Mozambique has been organized for over 50 years. Portuguese colonists introduced the game after World War I, and the Associação de Futebol de Lourenço Marques was founded in the capital in 1923 under the name Associação de Football da Provincia de Moçambique; it supported a league whose base of operation was Mavalane Province, and became affiliated with the Portuguese F.A. in 1924. In the north, the Associação de Futebol de Nampula was founded in 1936, and was affiliated to Portugal the following year. Down the coast, near the mouth of the Zambeze River, the Associação de Futebol de Quelimane was founded and affiliated in 1950.

Since attaining independence in 1975, Mozambiquan soccer has been in the throes of reorganization. A national association was in the planning stages in 1978. Mozambique's

best players, like those of other Portuguese colonies, were often poached by clubs from Portugal. The greatest of them all was Benfica star Eusebio, who put his country—and to some extent Portugal—on the soccer map. Gradually, Mozambiquan teams have begun to enter the international arena. Early in 1975, Tanzania was defeated by a Mozambique selection, 2-1, before 19,000 fans in Lourenço Marques, (now renamed Maputo). Later in the year, a Mozambique selection traveled to Tanzania where it lost to the Dar Es Salaam club Taifa Stars by 2-1, and defeated Zanzibar champions Afro Shirazi 4-0. Atlético Clube de Lourenço Marques, the leading club in the country, has also toured Tanzania.

MTK-VM (Magyar Testgyakorlók Köre-Vörös Meteor)

Location: *Budapest, Hungary;* stadium: *MTK-Stadion (27,000);* colors: *white jerseys with multicolored hoops, white shorts;* honors: *Hungarian champion (1904, 1908, 1914, 1920, 1921, 1922, 1923, 1924, 1925, 1929, 1936, 1937, 1951, 1953, 1958), Hungarian cup winner (1910, 1911, 1912, 1914, 1923, 1925, 1932, 1952, 1968).*

Founded 1888 as Magyar Testgyakorlók Köre (Hungarian Gymnastics Club) in Budapest by members of the British-based Budapest Gymnastic and Athletic Club, but it was known as MTK from the beginning. It is Hungary's second oldest club. MTK has gone through several name changes, which reflect a relatively unstable history when compared to its great rival, Ferencváros, and the other big Budapest clubs. During the professional era in the 1930s, it was called Hungária. The new government after World War II named it Textilesek (Textiles) and then Bastya, and in 1952 it became known as Vörös Lobogo (Red Banner). Its name was reverted to MTK in 1956, and in 1975 it merged with the small Budapest club Vörös Meteor (Red Meteor) to arrive at its present name. MTK has spent 71 seasons in the first division.

It has traditionally been the second most popular and successful club in Budapest after Ferencváros, but its golden era occurred long ago. Sadly, it has been able to achieve little since the revamping of Hungarian soccer after the Second World War. MTK entered the league in 1903, and won its first title the following year. After Budapesti Torna Club (BTC) faded from prominence in 1902, MTK and Ferencváros (then FTC) took over control

of the league and dominated the Hungarian game until the rise of Újpest in the 1930s. MTK won a second title in 1908, and in 1914 English coach Jimmy Hogan came to the club from Vienna and taught the short ground passing game to its eager players, laying the groundwork for a revolution in Hungarian soccer. MTK took to Hogan's ideas, and became the club that introduced them to other teams throughout the league. Hogan also discovered a local player named György Orth, who quickly became MTK's star—in practically all positions—and the club proceeded to win 12 consecutive league championships from 1914-25, five of these (1915-19) in the unofficial military league during World War I. Until the early 1920s, Orth was joined by two other famous MTK stars, halfback Kalman Konrad, who eventually left to play for FK Austria, and Alfred Schaeffer, the dynamic center forward who became equally popular at FC Nürnberg during its golden era. There was one more championship to be won in 1929 (as Hungaria) with the remnants of the old team, and in 1936 and 1937, Hungária won back-to-back professional titles.

With the immortal center forward Nandor Hidegkuti and right winger Karoly Sandor leading the attack, it won two noteworthy championships in 1951 (as Bastya) and 1953 (as Vörös Lobogo)—made all the more significant because these two titles were the only interruptions in Honvéd's domination of the Hungarian league during the era of Puskás and Kocsis. Unfortunately, they were to be MTK's last hurrah until it entered the

European Cup Winners' Cup in 1963-64 and advanced to the final in Brussels—after a stunning upset of Glasgow Celtic in the semi-finals—only to lose to Sporting Lisbon. MTK won another Hungarian cup in 1968, but failed in the Cup Winners' Cup the following year.

Müller, Gerdhardt (1945-)

Der Bomber, Müller's nickname, speaks well of his attributes. The extraordinary goalscoring center forward for Bayern München and West Germany holds more records than any other player in history—other than Pelé. Among other unprecedented feats, he became his country's authentic national hero in 1974, when he scored the goal that won the World Cup. He was European Footballer of the Year in 1970; top scorer in the West German league in 1967, 1969, 1970, 1972, 1973, and 1975; leading scorer in three successive European Cups (1973-75) and one European Cup Winners' Cup (1967); top scorer in the 1970 World Cup; the only player in history to score two hat tricks in the final rounds of the World Cup (1970); West German Footballer of the Year in 1967 and 1969; and the sixth highest scorer in the history of the game.

He started his career as a youth player with the small Bavarian club TSV Nördlingen, and in 1964 was signed by Bayern (after training as a weaver) starting for the first team in 1965-66. He made one youth appearance for West Germany, and entered full international

competition in 1966 against Turkey. By the early 1970s, he has surpassed Uwe Seeler's West German scoring record, and when he retired from the national team after the 1974 World Cup after 63 appearances, he had amassed a total of 68 goals. As of 1977-78, he had scored almost 600 times, including 339 in league competition (in less than 380 appearances), 36 in the European Cup, and 75 in the West German cup. Müller's success is due to his explosive shot and his uncanny sense of positioning and anticipation. A competent if unspectacular dribbler and tackler, he specializes in preying on the ball as if lying in wait, and from then on his deadly accuracy and cannonlike power take over, a technique entirely appropriate for his short, muscular form and massive legs. After the departure of Franz Beckenbauer in 1977, Müller adopted a new role as captain of Bayern, a post to which is gentlemanly personality was well suited, but he failed to get along with Bayern's new manager, Gyula Lorant, and accepted a transfer to the Ft. Lauderdale Strikers in 1979.

Gerd Müller, Europe's premier goalscorer of the 1970s, fires his 50th goal for West Germany in the 1972 European Football Championship final, beating Russian goalkeeper Rudakov.

N

Nacional de Fútbol, Club

Location: *Montevideo, Uruguay;* stadium: *Estadio Centenario (75,000);* colors: *white jerseys with red and blue trim, blue shorts;* honors: *Intercontinental Cup (1971), Copa Interamericana (1971), Copa Libertadores (1971), Uruguayan champion (1902, 1903, 1912, 1915, 1916, 1917, 1919, 1920, 1922, 1923, 1924, 1933, 1934, 1939, 1940, 1941, 1942, 1943, 1946, 1947, 1950, 1952, 1955, 1956, 1957, 1963, 1966, 1969, 1970, 1971, 1972, 1977).*

Founded 1899 with the merger of Montevideo F.C. and Defensor F.C. by Uruguayan nationals, the first club in the country not formed by foreigners. Its name was taken from another *porteño* institution, the Club Nacional de Regatas, a sailing club, and its colors—red, white, and blue—were adopted from those of General José Artigo, hero of Uruguayan independence. Nacional entered the Uruguayan league in 1901, its second season in existence, and won its first title the following year. Since then, Nacional and its thoroughly despised crosstown rival Peñarol have swept more than 90 percent of all Uruguayan championships (Peñarol has the slight edge with 35 to Nacional's 32). The club nickname is *los tricolores,* after the official colors.

Nacional's back-to-back championships in 1902 and 1903 were mastered to a great extent by center half and club president Abdon Porte, whose allegiance to Nacional was so great that when he eventually ceased to be an effective administrator he committed suicide on the grounds of the club stadium, Parque Central. His legacy has not been forgotten. In the late 1910s and all through the 1920s, Nacional dominated the Uruguayan league with eight titles in 10 years. During the latter part of this period, Nacional's first internationally famous stars emerged. Hector Scarone, a deceptive inside right, José Nasazzi, fullback and captian, center forward Pedro Petrone, forward Hector Castro, and inside left Pedro Cea helped to lead Uruguay into its golden era during the 1920s, when its extraordinary national team won two Olympic gold medals and the first World Cup in 1930. In 1925, Nacional embarked on an astounding five-month tour of Europe, in which it captured the attention of an entire continent with its dazzling skills. Preceded by Uruguay's fame from the 1924 Olympics in Paris, this Nacional team played 38 games in Austria, Belgium, Czechoslovakia, France, Holland, Italy, Portugal, Spain, and Switzerland, win-ning 26, losing only five, and amassing a 130-30 goal difference.

A second extraordinary team, known widely by the nickname *la máquina,* emerged in the early 1930s, winning consecutive championships in 1933 and 1934, the first two seasons of the new professional league. But an even greater team came along in the late 1930s. Spearheaded by its record-breaking goalscorer Atilio Garcia, an Argentine, Nacional won five titles in succession from 1939-43. Garcia was the leading scorer in the league for seven consecutive years from 1938-44, averaging over 20 goals per season with only 18 games on the schedule. In the 1950s, Nacional again won five championships, led this time by center half José Santamaría of later Real Madrid fame, and in 1953 it won the unofficial Copa Montevideo (of the International Cup) by defeating five leading European and South American clubs.

Nacional continued to win several Uruguayan championships during the 1960s and '70s, and made its Copa Libertadores debut in 1962, losing in the semi-finals to Peñarol. Its first final in the Libertadores was a loss to Independiente in 1964 (by 1-0 after a scoreless draw), and the second occurred in 1967, when it played Rácing Club of Buenos Aires to two scoreless draws before losing the second replay by 2-1. In the 1969 final, Nacional lost both legs to Argentina's Estudiantes, but, in 1971, it finally vindicated its international reputation by winning the trophy for itself. In the first round of this edition, Nacional topped its group with an undefeated record and a gaping four-point margin over Peñarol, and remained undefeated after the semi-final round. In the final, it split home and away legs with Estudiantes, and won the play-off 2-0 to take its first South American club championship.

This triumph led to its participation in the 1971 Copa Interamericana, where it won narrowly over Mexico's Cruz Azul, and the Intercontinental Cup, an anticlimactic affair with the European Cup runner-up Panathinaïkos Athens, in which it had to struggle for a 3-2 win on aggregate. Despite its three close victories, Nacional was now firmly situated at the pinnacle of international soccer at the club level. The hero of this team was Argentine scoring genius Luis Artime, who led the Uruguayan league in goals throughout his three-year stay at Nacional from 1969-71. After this, its best players having been lured away to wealthier clubs abroad, Nacional declined with the rest of Uruguayan soccer, and by the late-1970s it still had not reemerged as a major force on the international circuit.

Nacional's home ground is still the Parque Central, where training sessions are held, but official matches are played at the Estadio Centenario, the national stadium shared with Peñarol.

narrow the angle

A defender's advance on a threatening attacker in order to visibly block as much of the goal as possible, thereby lessening the portion of the goal into which the attacker may shoot. The term is usually made in reference to a goalkeeper's "narrowing the angle" of a potential goalscorer.

National Amateur Challenge Cup

An elimination tournament introduced in 1922 by the United States Football Association when it became apparent that the schedule of the National Challenge Cup was becoming too unwieldly. Challenge Cup fixtures had become so entangled that some effort was needed to lighten the financial burden placed on its participants, and since concern had already been expressed over the preservation of amateur soccer, a tournament was set aside to rededicate the amateur ideal. From the beginning, the National Amateur Cup was closed to professional and semi-professional clubs, sponsored or otherwise. Though it maintains a subordinate position to the Challenge Cup, many clubs have participated in both competitions. The title is decided on a knockout basis with winners of an Eastern and Western final meeting in a national final. It is played under the sponsorship of the United States Soccer Federation.

Poor weather conditions prevented the first edition from being completed. The semi-finalists that first year were Fleisher Yarn Football Club, Philadelphia, and Roxbury Football Club in the East; and Jeannette Football Club, Pennsylvania, and Swedish-American Athetic Association, Detroit, in the West.

Winners and Final Results

(venues in parentheses)

1923 not awarded
1924 Fleisher Yarn Football Club, Philadelphia
(Chicago, Ill.) Fleisher Yarn—Swedish-Americans 3-0
1925 Toledo Football Club
(Cleveland, O.) Toledo—McLeod Council 3-1
1926 Defenders Football Club, New Bedford
(Cleveland, O.) Defenders Heidelberg F.C. 1-0
1927 Heidelberg Football Club, Pittsburgh
(results uncertain)
1928 not awarded*
(finalists: Swedish-Americans and Powers Hudson Essex)
1929 Heidelberg Football Club, Pittsburgh

(Newark, N.J.) Heidelberg—First German S.C. 9-0

1930 Raffies Football Club, Fall River**
(Pittsburgh, Pa.) Raffies—Gallatin S.C. 3-3

1931 Goodyear Football Club, Akron
(New Bedford, Mass.) Black Cats—Goodyear 1-1
(Akron, O.) Goodyear—Black Cats 2-0

1932 Shamrock Football Club, Cleveland
(Cleveland, O.) Shamrock—Stanto Christo 2-1

1933 German-Americans Soccer Club, Philadelphia
(Philadelphia, Pa.) German-Americans—McKnight Beverage 5-1

1934 German-Americans Soccer Club, Philadelphia
(Philadelphia, Pa.) German-Americans—Heidelberg F.C. 1-1

1935 W.W. Riehl Soccer Club, Castle Shannon
(Pittsburgh, Pa.) W.W. Riehl—All-American Cafe 3-0

1936 First German Soccer Club, Brooklyn
(Brooklyn, N.Y.) First German—Castle Shannon 2-1

1937 Highlander Football Club, Trenton
(Pittsburgh, Pa.) Highlander—Castle Shannon 1-0

1938 Ponta Delgada Football Club, Fall River
(Fall River, Mass.) Ponta—Heidelberg F.C. 2-0

1939 St. Michael's Athletic Club, Fall River
(Fall River, Mass.) St. Michael's—Gallatin S.C. 3-1

1940 Morgan-Strasser Soccer Club, Pittsburgh
(No. Tiverton, Mass.) Morgan-Strasser—Firestone 1-0

1941 Fall River Football Club
(Fall River, Mass.) Fall River—Chrysler 2-1

1942 Fall River Football Club (Fall River, Mass.)
Fall River—Morgan U.S.C.O. 4-3

1943 Morgan-Strasser Soccer Club, Pittsburgh
(Baltimore, Md.) Morgan-Strasser—Santa Maria 4-1

1944 Eintracht Soccer Club, Astoria
(New York, N.Y.) Eintracht—Morgan-Strasser S.C. 5-2

1945 Eintracht Soccer Club, Astoria
(New York, N.Y.) Eintracht—Rafertys 1-0

1946 Ponta Delgada Football Club, Fall River
(Fall River, Mass.) Ponta Delgada—Castle Shannon 5-0

1947 Ponta Delgada Football Club, Fall River
(Fall River, Mass.) Ponta Delgada—Curry, Vets 4-1

1948 Ponta Delgada Football Club, Fall River
(Fall River, Mass.) Ponta Delgada—Curry, Vets 4-1

1949 Elizabeth Sports Club
(Astoria, Queens, N.Y.) Elizabeth—Zenthoefer 6-1

1950 Ponta Delgada Football Club, Fall River
(Tiverton, R.I.) Ponta Delgada—Harmarville S.C. 0-1
(Pittsburgh, Pa.) Harmarville S.C.—Ponta Delgada 1-4

1951 German-Hungarian Soccer Club, Brooklyn
(Brooklyn, N.Y.) German-Hungarian—Harmarville S.C. 4-3

1952 St. Louis Raiders
(Ludlow, Mass.) St. Louis Raiders—Lusitano 3-1

1953 Ponta Delgada Football Club, Fall River
(Tiverton, R.I.) Ponta Delgada—Chicago Slovaks 2-0

1954 Beadling Soccer Club, Pittsburgh
(St. Louis, Mo.) Joe Simpkins F.C.—Beadling 5-2
(Pittsburgh, Pa.) Beadling—Joe Simpkins F.C. 5-1

1955 Heidelberg Tornadoes, Pittsburgh
(Chicago, Ill.) Chicago Eagles—Heidelberg Tornadoes 2-2
(Heildelberg, Pa.) Heidelberg Tornadoes—Chicago Eagles 5-0

1956 Kutis Soccer Club, St. Louis
(St. Louis, Mo.) Kutis—Philadelphia Ukrainians 1-0

1957 Kutis Soccer Club, St. Louis (St.

Louis) Kutis—Rochester Ukrainians 1-1

1958 Kutis Soccer Club, St. Louis
(Pittsburgh, Pa.) Kutis—Beadling
S.C. 2-1

1959 Kutis Soccer Club, St. Louis
(St. Louis, Mo.) Kutis—St. Andrew
Scots 5-0
(Detroit, Mich.) St. Andrew Scots—
Kutis 2-2

1960 Kutis Soccer Club, St. Louis
(St. Loius, Mo.) Kutis—Patchogue,
New York 4-0

1961 Kutis Soccer Club, St. Louis
(St. Louis, Mo.) Kutis—Italian-
American Stars 1-0
(Hartford, Conn.) Italian-American
Stars—Kutis 3-3

1962 Carpathia Kickers, Detroit
(Detroit, Mich.) Carpathia
Kickers—American Hungarian 4-0

1963 Italian-Americans, Rochester
(Rochester, N.Y.) Italian-Americans—St. Ambrose 1-0

1964 Schwaben, Chicago
(Chicago, Ill.) Schwaben—German-
Hungarians 4-0

1965 German-Hungarians, Philadelphia
(Philadelphia, Pa.) German-Hungarians—St. Ambrose 6-0

1966 Kickers, Chicago
(Chicago, Ill.) Kickers—Italian
Americans 5-2

1967 Italian-Americans, Hartford
*final not played

(St. Louis, Mo.) Italian-Americans—Kutis S.C. 2-0

1968 Kickers, Chicago
(Detroit, Mich.) Kickers—Carpathia Kickers 2-1

1969 British Lions, Washington, D.C.
(Washington, D.C.) British Lions—
Kutis S.C. 4-1

1970 Kickers, Chicago
(Chicago, Ill.) Kickers—German-
Hungarians 6-5

1971 Kutis Soccer Club, St. Louis
(Cleveland, O.) Kutis—Cleveland In-
ter-Italian 4-1

1972 Busch Soccer Club, St. Louis (St.
Louis, Mo.)
Busch—New Bedford Portuguese 1-
0

1973 Inter, Philadelphia
(Philadelphia, Pa.) Inter—San Jose
Grenadiers 3-2

1974 Inter, Philadelphia
(St. Louis, Mo.) Inter—Big 4 Chev-
rolet 4-3

1975 Kickers, Chicago
(Kearny, N.J.) Kickers—Scotland
S.C. 1-0

1976 Bavarian Blue Ribbon, Milwaukee
(Milwaukee, Wisc.) Bavarian Blue
Ribbon—Trenton Extension 3-2

1977 Denver Kickers Sports Club
(Philadelphia, Pa.) Denver Kick-
ers—United German-Hungarian
S.C. 3-1

**Gallatin forfeited replay

National Day Tournament of the Republic of Vietnam

One of the numerous regional competitions for national teams of Southeast Asia, introduced in 1970 to bolster the social and cultural life of South Vietnam during the war there. Many important soccer powers of the Far East, however, declined to enter, and it remained one of the minor competitions in the region before it came to an end with the fall of the Saigon regime. It was played on a knockout basis. The participants were: Indonesia, Malaysia, Thailand, Vietnam Republic, and occasionally Khmer Republic.

Winners

1970 Vietnam Republic
1971 Vietnam Republic
and Malaysia
1972 Khmer Republic
1973 Indonesia

National Open Challenge Cup

An elimination tournament open to all senior-level clubs, amateur or professional, throughout the United States. The competition was organized during the 1912-13 season just prior to the founding of the United States Soccer Football Association, and was originally offered to amateur teams only. Despite the advance of professional leagues during the 1960s, the winner is still regarded by some as the United States national champion, and has occasionally participated in the CONCACAF Champions' Cup. Clubs of the North American Soccer League, however, have not shown an inclination to enter.

The trophy was donated to the American Amateur Football Association (AAFA) by Sir Thomas R. Dewar, the British sportsman and philanthropist, on the occasion of the AAFA's visit to London around the time of the 1912 Olympic Games. Purchased by Dewar for the equivalent of $500, it was given in the hope of promoting soccer in the United States and in the name of Anglo-American friendship.

The Dewar Cup was first won in 1912 by Yonkers Football Club, which defeated its crosstown rival, Hollywood Inn Football Club, by 3-0 at Lennox Oval, New York City. In 1913, the trophy was officially adopted as the prize of the new National Challenge Cup, and the first winner was Brooklyn Field Club in 1914. The trophy is now held by the winner for one year under a $2000 bond. The competition is decided on a knockout basis with winners of an Eastern and Western final meeting in a national final. With certain exceptions, the national final was a two-leg home and away series between 1929-68. It is played under the sponsorship of the United States Soccer Federation.

Winners and Final Results

(venues in parentheses)

1914   Brooklyn Field Club
(Pawtucket, R.I.) Brooklyn Field Club—Brooklyn Celtic 2-1

1915   Bethlehem Steel Co. Football Club
(So. Bethlehem, Pa.) Bethlehem Steel—Brooklyn Celtic 3-1

1916   Bethlehem Steel Co. Football Club
(Pawtucket, R.I.) Bethlehem Steel—Fall River Rovers 1-0

1917   Fall River Rovers
(Pawtucket, R.I) Fall River Rovers—Bethlehem Steel 1-0

1918   Bethlehem Steel Co. Football Club
(Pawtucket, R.I.) Fall River Rovers—Bethlehem Steel 2-2
(Harrison, N.J.) Bethlehem Steel—Fall River Rovers 3-0

1919   Bethlehem Steel Co. Football Club
(Fall River, Mass.) Bethlehem Steel—Paterson F.C. 2-0

1920   Benn Miller Football Club, St. Louis
(St. Louis, Mo.) Benn Miller—Fore River 2-1

1921   Robins Dry Dock Football Club, Brooklyn
(Fall River, Mass.) Robins Dry Dock—Scullin Steel F.C. 4-2

1922   Scullin Steel Football Club, St. Louis
(St. Louis, Mo.) Scullin Steel—Todd Shipyard 3-2

1923   Paterson Football Club, New Jersey*
(St. Louis, Mo.) Paterson—Scullin Steel 2-2

1924   Fall River Football Club
(Harrison, N.J.) Fall River—Vesper Buick 4-2

1925   Shawsheen Soccer Club, Andover
(Tiverton, R.I.) Shawsheen—Canadian Club 3-0

1926   Bethlehem Steel Co. Football Club
(Brooklyn, N.Y.) Bethlehem Steel—Benn Miller 7-2

1927   Fall River Football Club
(Detroit, Mich.) Fall River—Holley Carburetor 7-0

1928   New York Nationals Soccer Club
(New York, N.Y.) New York Nationals—Bricklayers 2-2

*Scullin Steel forefeited replay

(Chicago, Ill.) Bricklayers—New York Nationals 0-3

1929 Hakoah All-Stars, New York City
(St. Louis, Mo.) Madison Kennels—Hakoah All-Stars 0-2
(Brooklyn, N.Y.) Hakoah All-Stars—Madison Kennels 3-0

1930 Fall River Football Club
(New York, N.Y.) Fall River—Bruell Insurance 7-2
(Cleveland, O.) Bruell Insurance—Fall River 7-2

1931 Fall River Football Club
(New York, N.Y.) Fall River—Bricklawyers 6-2
(Chicago, Ill.) Bricklayers—Fall River, 1-1

1932 New Bedford Football Club
(St. Louis, Mo.) Stix, Baer and Fuller F.C.—New Bedford 3-3
(St. Louis, Mo.) New Bedford—Stix, Baer and Fuller F.C. 5-2

1933 Stix, Baer and Fuller Football Club, St. Louis
(St. Louis, Mo.) Stix, Baer and Fuller—New York Americans 1-0
(New York, N.Y.) New York Americans—Stix, Baer and Fuller 1-2

1934 Stix, Baer and Fuller Football Club, St. Louis
(St. Louis, Mo.) Stix, Baer and Fuller—Pawtucket Rangers 4-2
(Pawtucket, R.I.) Pawtucket Rangers—Stix, Baer and Fuller 3-2
(St. Louis, Mo.) Stix, Baer and Fuller—Pawtucket Rangers 5-0

1935 Central Breweries Soccer Club, St. Louis
(St. Louis, Mo.) Central Breweries—Pawtucket Rangers 5-0
(Pawtucket, R.I.) Pawtucket Rangers—Central Breweries 1-1
(Newark, N.J.) Central Breweries—Pawtucket Rangers 1-3

1936 First German-American Soccer Club, Philadelphia
(St. Louis, Mo.) St. Louis Shamrocks—First German-

American 2-2
(Philadelphia, Pa.) First German-American—St. Louis Shamrocks 3-1

1937 New York Americans Soccer Club
(St. Louis, Mo.) St. Louis Shamrocks—New York Americans 2-0
(New York, N.Y.) New York Americans—St. Louis Shamrocks 4-2

1938 Sparta A.B.A., Chicago
(Chicago, Ill.) Sparta—St. Mary's Celtic 4-0
(New York, N.Y.) St. Mary's Celtic S.C.—Sparta 2-4

1939 St. Mary's Celtic Soccer Club, Brooklyn
(Chicago, Ill.) Manhattan Beer—St. Mary's Celtic 0-1
(New York, N.Y.) St. Mary's Celtic—Manhattan Beer 4-1

1940 not awarded
(Baltimore, Md.) Baltimore Soccer Club—Sparta A.B.A. 0-0
(Chicago, Ill.) Sparta A.B.A.—Baltimore Soccer Club 2-2

1941 Pawtucket Football Club
(Pawtucket, R.I.) Pawtucket—Chrysler 4-2
(Detroit, Mich.) Chrysler—Pawtucket 3-4

1942 Gallatin Soccer Club, Pittsburgh
(Pittsburgh, Pa.) Gallatin—Pawtucket 2-1
(Pawtucket, R.I.) Pawtucket—Gallatin 2-4

1943 Brooklyn Hispano Soccer Club
(New York, N.Y.) Brooklyn Hispano—Morgan Strasser S.C. 2-2
(New York, N.Y.) Morgan-Strasser S.C.—Brooklyn Hispano 2-4

1944 Brooklyn Hispano Soccer Club
(New York, N.Y.) Brooklyn Hispano—Morgan-Strasser S.C. 4-0

1945 Brookhattan Soccer Club, New York City
(New York, N.Y.) Brookhattan—Cleveland Americans 4-1
(Cleveland, O.) Cleveland

Americans—Brookhatten 1-2

1946 Vikings, Chicago
(Fall River, Mass.) Ponta Delgada
F.C.—Vikings 1-1
(Chicago, Ill.) Vikings—Ponta
Delgada F.C. 2-1

1947 Ponta Delgada Football Club, Fall
River
(Chicago, Ill.) Sparta A.B.A.—Ponta
Delgada 2-6
(St. Louis, Mo.) Ponta Delgada—
Sparta A.B.A. 3-2

1948 Joe Simpkins Football Club, St.
Louis
(Philadelphia, Pa.) Joe Simpkins—
Brookhattan 3-1

1949 Morgan Soccer Club, Pittsburgh
(Pittsburgh, Pa.) Morgan—
Philadelphia Nats 0-2
(St. Louis, Mo.) Morgan—
Philadelphia Nats 4-0

1950 Joe Simpkins Football Club, St.
Louis
(Tiverton, R.I.) Ponta Delgada—Joe
Simpkins 1-2
(Bridgeville, Pa.) Joe Simpkins—
Ponta Delgada 1-4

1951 German-Hungarian Soccer Club,
Brooklyn
(Brooklyn, N.Y.) German-
Hungarian—Heidelberg 2-2
(Pittsburgh, Pa.) Heidelberg—
German-Hungarian 2-6

1952 Harmarville Soccer Club, Penn-
sylvania
(Philadelphia, Pa.) Philadelphia
Nats—Harmarville 1-3
(Chicago, Ill.) Harmarville—
Philadelphia Nats 4-1

1953 Chicago Falcons
(Harmarville, Pa.) Harmarville—
Chicago Falcons 0-2
(St. Louis, Mo.) Chicago Falcons—
Harmarville 1-1

1954 New York Americans
(New York, N.Y.) New York
Americans—Kutis S.C. 1-0
(New York, N.Y.) New York

Americans—Kutis S.C. 2-0

1955 Eintracht Soccer Club, Astoria
(Los Angeles, Calif.) Eintracht§h
Americans 2-1

1956 Harmarville Soccer Club, Penn-
sylvania
(Chicago, Ill.) Chicago Schwaben—
Harmarville 1-0
(Harmarville, Pa.) Harmarville—
Chicago Schwaben 3-1

1957 Kutis Soccer Club, St. Louis
(St. Louis, Mo.) Kutis—Hakoah
New York 3-0
(New York, N.Y.) Hakoah New
York—Kutis 1-3

1958 Los Angeles Kickers
(Baltimore, Md.) Los Angeles
Kickers—Pompei Baltimore 2-1

1959 San Pedro Canvasbacks
(Fall River, Mass.) San Pedro
Canvasbacks—Fall River 4-3

1960 Ukrainian Nationals, Philadelphia
(Philadelphia, Pa.) Ukrainian
Nationals—Los Angeles Kickers 5-3

1961 Ukrainian Nationals, Philadelphia
(Philadelphia, Pa.) Ukrainian
Nationals—Los Angeles Scots 2-2
(Philadelphia, Pa.) Ukrainian
Nationals—Los Angeles Scots 5-2

1962 New York Hungarians
(New York, N.Y.) New York
Hungarians—San Francisco Scots 3-2

1963 Philadelphia Ukrainians
(Philadelphia, Pa.) Philadelphia
Ukrainians—Los Angeles
Armenians 1-0

1964 Los Angeles Kickers
(Philadelphia, Pa.) Philadelphia
Ukrainians—Los Angeles Kickers 2-2
(Los Angeles, Calif.) Los Angeles
Kickers—Philadelphia Ukrainians 2-0

1965 New York Ukrainians
(New York, N.Y.) New York
Ukrainains—Hansa Chicago 1-1
(Chicago, Ill.) Hansa Chicago—New

York Ukrainians 0-3

1966 Philadelphia Ukrainians
(Los Angeles, Calif.) Orange
County—Philadelphia Ukrainians 0-1
(Philadelphia, Pa.) Philadelphia
Ukrainians—Orange County 3-0

1967 New York Greek-Americans
(New York, N.Y.) New York
Greek-Americans—Orange County
4-2

1968 New York Greek-Americans
(Chicago, Ill.) Chicago Olympic—
New York Greek-Americans 1-1
(New York, N.Y.) New York
Greek-Americans—Chicago Olympic 1-0

1969 New York Greek-Americans
(Los Angeles, Calif.) New York
Greek-Americans—Montebello
Armenians 1-0

1970 Elizabeth Soccer Club
(New York, N.Y.) Elizabeth—Los
Angeles Croatia 2-1

1971 New York Hota
(Los Angeles, Calif.) New York
Hota—San Pedro Yugoslavs 6-4

1972 Elizabeth Soccer Club
(Elizabeth, N.J.) Elizabeth—San
Pedro Yugoslavs 1-0

1973 Maccabee Athletic Club, Los Angeles
(Los Angeles, Calif.) Maccabee—
Cleveland Inter 5-3

1974 New York Greek-Americans
(New York, N.Y.) New York
Greek-Americans—Chicago
Croatians 2-0

1975 Maccabee Athletic Club, Los Angeles
(Los Angeles, Calif.) Maccabee—
Inter-Giuliana New York 1-0

1976 San Francisco Athletic Club
(New York, N.Y.) San Francisco
Athletic Club—Inter-Giuliana New
York 1-0

1977 Maccabee Athletic Club, Los Angeles
(Los Angeles, Calif.) Maccabee—
United German-Hungarian S.C.,
Phila. 5-0

National Professional Soccer League
See: **North American Soccer League**

---

near post

The area adjacent to the goalpost that is closer
to the ball at a given time, especially when an
attack on goal is being made. On a corner kick,
for example, the near post is on the same side
of the goalmouth as the active corner.

Nepal

All-Nepal Football Association
G.P.P. Box 50
21/500 Thamel
Katmandu

Founded: 1951
FIFA: 1970
AFC: 1971

Affiliated clubs: *33;* registered players: *700;* national stadium: *Dasarath Rangashala,
Katmandu (25,000);* largest stadium: *Dasarath Rangashala;* colors: *red jerseys, white
shorts;* season: *April to November;* honors: *none.*

There was little soccer in Nepal until the immediate postwar years. By 1951, when the Shah King abolished the old autocracy and adopted some forms of modern government, a gradual influx of English-speaking teachers and businessmen, especially from India, occurred, and the All-Nepal Football Association was founded. Though not yet a member of FIFA, Nepal was granted permission in the 1960s to play in preliminary rounds of the soccer tournament of the Asian Games, but it did not advance to the final rounds in several attempts. Nepalese teams have not yet reached any final rounds of the Asian Nations' Cup either, and they have not yet attempted to qualify for the World Cup. There is a national league, centered in Katmandu, and annual national cup competition, as well as lower division regional leagues. The first division is comprised of 17 clubs, but Nepalese champion clubs did not enter any editions of the now defunct Asian Champions' Cup. Four stadiums in Katmandu have a capacity of 5,000 or more.

Netherlands

Koninklijke Nederlandsche Voetbalbond
Woudenbergseweg 56-58
Zeist

Founded: 1889
FIFA: 1904
UEFA: 1954

Affiliated clubs: *6,665;* **registered players:** *882,835 (925 professional);* **national stadium:** *Olympisch Stadion, Amsterdam (67,000);* **largest stadium:** *Olympisch Stadion;* **colors:** *orange jerseys, white shorts;* **season:** *August to June:* **honors:** *World Cup runner-up (1974, 1978), Olympic Games third place (1908, 1912, 1920), Ajax, Intercontinental Cup (1972), Super Cup (1973), European Cup (1971, 1972, 1973), Feyenoord, Intercontinental Cup (1970), European Cup (1970), UEFA Cup (1974), PSV Eindhoven, UEFA Cup (1978).*

The rise of Dutch soccer since the 1960s is Europe's greatest success story of the postwar era. The Netherlands, whose early jump on the rest of Europe (along with Denmark) led to prominence after the turn of the century, floundered in amateurism for decades, as larger—and professional—competitors moved steadily up the European ladder. The advent of professionalism in the 1950s changed the course of the Dutch game, and with the miraculous appearance of gifted players in the 1960s, and an infusion of enlightened tactical innovations, Holland rose to the pinnacle of world soccer.

The association game was imported to Holland about 1865 by English textile workers, and in 1870 it was played by schoolboys at "Pim" Mulier's school in Noordwijk. The first club was Haarlem Football Club, founded in 1879; UD Deventer was founded in 1875, but it played rugby exclusively until many years later. Hercules Utrecht and Robur et Velocitas Apeldoorn were formed in 1882, and several clubs were started in Dordrecht, The Hague, and Leeuwarden the following year. Sparta, the first club in Rotterdam, came along in 1888, and Amsterdam Football Club, the first in Amsterdam, was founded in 1895. The wide geographical dispersion of the early clubs is significant and indicates the pervasive influence of British commerce and culture at the time. In 1889, the Nederlandsche Voetbalbond, the second oldest national association outside the British Isles, was founded at The Hague. (the Danish federation had been established earlier in the year. Governing bodies in Australia, South Africa, and the United States were also established earlier, but these three did not become direct ancestors of modern associations.) The title of "Royal" was added to the name in 1929, resulting in the present Koninklijke Nederlandsche Voetbalbond (KNVB).

Holland became one of Europe's first soccer powers, displaying strength and speed in the northern European tradition, but unlike Denmark, France, and Belgium, it did not participate in the first unofficial Olympic soccer competitions of 1900 and 1904. Its first official international was against Belgium in 1905 at Antwerp—a 4-1 loss—and in Rotterdam one month later, Belgium won again in Holland's home debut. The week after Belgium's crushing victory in Rotterdam (4-0), the NVB became one of the seven founder-members of FIFA, and thus helped to chart the course for the game's world governing body.

Every major town in the country had by now spawned one or more clubs. In 1897-98, a national championship was introduced, and the following season a national cup competition got under way, producing the continent's first complete schedule of league and cup fixtures. The first champion was RAP Amsterdam, and RAP won the first double in 1899. Clubs from The Hague—HVV, HBS, and Quick—dominated the first decade of the new century.

The momentum of Holland's early start resulted in three consecutive Olympic bronze medals in 1908, 1912, and 1920 (the last achieved after Czechoslovakia defaulted), and a fourth place finish in 1924 as well. This record put the Dutch high among the early European elite behind the British and Denmark. Sweden, Austria, Germany, and France were all regular victims of Dutch national teams during this period, but an indication of Europe's relative weakness compared to Great Britain is seen in Holland's results against English *amateur* teams between 1907-13. In nine games Holland failed to gain a single win and scored only seven goal to England's 45.

Between the world wars, Holland continued to participate actively in international competition, but the growth of soccer in more populous —and more professionally oriented countries—left Dutch soccer in its wake. Holland qualified for the World Cups of 1934 and 1938, but it was eliminated in the first round by Switzerland and Czechoslovakia, respectively. Its strength of will and determination to do well was demonstrated by fine results during the 1930s against Germany (one win, two draws, and one loss), Hungary (one win and two losses), England (a 1-0 loss), and Scotland (a 3-1 loss), but this was clearly a departure from its former success as an Olympic medalist.

The outstanding personality of this period was Puck van Heel, the orthodox left halfback who led Feyenoord to multiple championships and cup victories between 1928-40. He also carried the national team through a potentially disastrous period of change. Van Heel was a linkman who distributed with precision and anticipated the needs of his wingers in an era

when the W-M formation—with its emphasis on wing attacks—revolutionized Dutch soccer. More than anyone, van Heel helped to bring Holland out of the old-fashioned days of power soccer and set the stage for the postwar era.

In the years before and immediately after World War II, league and cup titles were spread widely among the major clubs of The Hague, Rotterdam, Amsterdam, Deventer, Eindhoven, Groningen, and other cities, but in the early 1950s, a movement was brewing to end the stagnation of amateur competition—led, among others, by Fortuna Geleen. Semiprofessionalism was adopted in 1954, and full professionalism was finally sanctioned by the KNVD in 1956. This led directly to the rise of Ajax and Feyenoord as the preeminent clubs of the Dutch game. By the mid-1960s, their hold on the league and cup was almost complete, and it was not to be broken until the emergence 10 years later of PSV Eindhoven (the club of the giant Philips consortium). The effect of professionalism on the development of Dutch soccer was slow and steady, but eventually it reaped the highest rewards. An all-time low in Holland's international fortunes was reached with its elimination from the European Nations' Cup by tiny Luxembourg in 1963, but in that same year a Dutch club—Feyenoord—achieved its first success in the European Cup, advancing to the semi-finals. The turning point was just around the corner.

In 1965, Ajax signed a new manager, Rinus Michels, and Johan Cruyff, a forward of unparalleled ability, and the club was instantly transformed. It won three Dutch championships in a row, and in 1968-69 advanced to the European Cup final after eliminating mighty Benfica in the semi-finals. In 1970, Ajax gained the semi-finals of the Fairs Cup, and the depth of a revitalized Dutch soccer was demonstrated unquestionably when Feyenoord won the European Cup that same year with a convincing victory over Celtic. The benefits of a highly competitive rivalry in domestic competition between two strong clubs helped to speed up the growing Dutch onslought in Europe, and in 1971, after winning the double, Ajax brought the European Cup to Holland for the second year in succession.

Ajax's win over Panathinaïkos was even more convincing than Feyenoord's over Celtic, but Ajax's best days were still to come. Michels moved to Barcelona, and Steaua Bucharest manager Sefan Kovacs was brought in to take his place. Kovacs instituted a more fluid *catenaccio*-based system in which players improvised with freedom, and an attacking sweeper provided a constant threat. With an astonishingly high caliber of talent at its disposal—Suurbier, Krol, Haan, Neeskens, Muhren, Cruyff, and Keizer—Ajax's mature and elegant style flourished. Second and third European Cups were won in 1972 and 1973, and the era of Ajax and "total football' took Europe by storm.

Cruyff's departure for Barcelona in 1973 signaled the decline of Ajax. Although Feyenoord grabbed one more European title in 1974—the UEFA Cup—the era of Dutch preeminence in European club competitions was virtually over. It remained only for this success to be translated into international prizes at the national level. Yugoslavia and East Germany had proved to be too difficult in the 1970-72 European Football Championship, and in qualifying for the 1974 World Cup, Belgium held the Dutch to two scoreless draws. In the 1974 finals themselves, however, the magical Cruyff and his supporting cast of improvisators captured the imagination of everyone. Uruguay, Bulgaria, Argentina, East Germany, and Brazil fell to defeat decisively, and Holland became the sentimental favorite to win the World Championship. In the final, however, complacency in the first half and a stalwart West German defense in the second half defeated the Dutch masters, and the ultimate prize was lost.

Though many stars were lured to more lucrative pastures in other countries, Holland had by now produced so many world-class players that the future of the national team looked bright. After a worrisome slump in 1975, Holland rapidly regained its form and qualified for the 1978 World Cup as a cofavorite to win, despite Cruyff's retirement from the team. The dispersion of its great players and the KNVG's curious lack of confidence in Dutch coaches was seen as a likely cause for decline, but the Dutch once again advanced to the final of the World Cup in 1978, and mounted as bold a challenge to Argentina as one could have hoped for. After a disappointing first round, Holland defeated Austria and Italy decisively in the semi-finals, and in the final tenaciously held on before Argentina won in extra time, 3-1, in front of a delirious Buenos Aires crowd. Holland became only the third country in history to gain back-to-back finals in the World Cup, and, unfortunately, the first to lose twice in a row.

The impact of Holland's "total football' on every aspect of the game assured the Dutch of a lasting place in the history of soccer. West Germany came to reign over international competition in the 1970s by adapting it to their needs, and, in the last analysis, it was so influential that the era of *catenaccio* was finally brought to an end.

Champions

1898 RAP	1915 Sparta Rotterdam	1932 Ajax
1899 RAP	1916 Willem II Tilburg	1933 Go Ahead Deventer
1900 HVV Den Haag	1917 Go Ahead Deventer	1934 Ajax
1901 HVV Den Haag	1918 Ajax	1935 PSV Eindhoven
1902 HVV Den Haag	1919 Ajax	1936 Feyenoord
1903 HVV Den Haag	1920 Be Quick Groningen	1937 Ajax
1904 HBS Den Haag	1921 NAC Breda	1938 Feyenoord
1905 HVV Den Haag	1922 Go Ahead Deventer	1939 Ajax
1906 HBS Den Haag	1923 RCH Haarlem	1940 Feyenoord
1907 HVV Den Haag	1924 Feyenoord	1941 Heracles
1908 Quick Den Haag	1925 HBS Den Haag	1942 ADO Den Haag
1909 Sparta Rotterdam	1926 Enschede	1943 ADO Den Haag
1910 HVV Den Haag	1927 Heracles	1944 Volewijckers Amsterdam
1911 Sparta Rotterdam	1928 Feyenoord	1945 no competition
1912 Sparta Rotterdam	1929 PSV Eindhoven	1946 Haarlem
1913 Sparta Rotterdam	1930 Go Ahead Deventer	1947 Ajax
1914 HVV Den Haag	1931 Ajax	

1948	BVV Scheidam	1959	Sparta Rotterdam	1970	Ajax
1949	SVV Scheidam	1960	Ajax	1971	Feyenoord
1950	Limburgia	1961	Feyenoord	1972	Ajax
1951	PSV Eindhoven	1962	Feyenoord	1973	Ajax
1952	Willem II Tilburg	1963	PSV Eindhoven	1974	Feyenoord
1953	RCH Haarlem	1964	DWS Amsterdam	1975	PSV Eindhoven
1954	Eindhoven	1965	Feyenoord	1976	PSV Eindhoven
1955	Willem II Tilburg	1966	Ajax	1977	Ajax
1956	Rapid JC Haarlem	1967	Ajax	1978	PSV Eindhoven
1957	Ajax	1968	Ajax		
1958	DOS Utrecht	1969	Feyenoord		

Cup Winners

1899	RAP	1926	Longa	1953	no competition
1900	Velocitas Breda	1927	VUC	1954	no competition
1901	HBS Den Haag	1928	RCH	1955	no competition
1902	Haarlem	1929	no competition	1956	no competition
1903	HVV Den Haag	1930	Feyenoord	1957	Fortuna Geleen
1904	HFC	1931	no competition	1958	Sparta Rotterdam
1905	VOC	1932	DFC	1959	VVV
1906	Concordia Rotterdam	1933	no competition	1960	no competition
1907	VOC	1934	Velocitas Groningen	1961	Ajax
1908	HBS Den Haag	1935	Feyenoord	1962	Sparta Rotterdam
1909	Quick Den Haag	1936	Roermond	1963	Willem II Tilburg
1910	Quick Den Haag	1937	Eindhoven	1964	Fortuna Geleen
1911	Quick Den Haag	1938	VSV	1965	Feyenoord
1912	Haarlem	1939	Wageningen	1966	Sparta Rotterdam
1913	HFC	1940	no competition	1967	Ajax
1914	DFC	1941	no competition	1968	ADO Den Haag
1915	HFC	1942	no competition	1969	Feyenoord
1916	Quick Den Haag	1943	Ajax	1970	Ajax
1917	Ajax	1944	Willem II Tilburg	1971	Ajax
1918	RCH	1945	no competition	1972	Ajax
1919	no competition	1946	no competition	1973	NAC Breda
1920	CVV	1947	no competition	1974	PSV Eindhoven
1921	Schoten	1948	Wageningen	1975	FC Den Haag
1922	no competition	1949	Quick Nijmegen	1976	PSV Eindhoven
1923	no competition	1950	PSV Eindhoven	1977	Twente Enschede
1924	no competition	1951	no competition	1978	AZ 67 Alkmaar
1925	ZFC	1952	no competition		

Netherlands Antilles

Nederlands Antilliaanse Voetbal Unie
P.O. Box 341
Curaçao, N.A.

Founded: 1921
FIFA: 1932
CONCACAF: 1961

Affiliated clubs: *103;* registered players: *4,300;* national stadium: *Rif Stadium, Willemstad (6,000);* largest stadium: *Rif Stadium;* colors: *white jerseys with red and blue stripes, white shorts;* season: *August to February;* honors: *none.*

The Netherlands Antilles—three tiny islands in the upper Leeward group and three larger islands off the coast of Venezuela—has a long and venerable tradition in Caribbean soccer, as does the region's other former Dutch colony Surinam. It was characteristic of Dutch colonies that they develop their game earlier than many of their British counterparts; and the Netherlands Antilles, under the name Dutch West Indies, was a participant in the 1952 Olympic Games, and Curaçao, the most important of the Netherlands Antilles, and Surinam maintained the busiest international schedule of any colonies in the Caribbean region between 1934-61. Today, both former Dutch colonies are forces to be reckoned with in CONCACAF competition and are recognized as capable of advancing to the front rank at any given time.

The Netherlands Antilles' game began on the island of Curaçao. A Curaçao championship was introduced in Willemstad in 1920. It was dominated for six years by Sparta, one of the first important clubs in the capital, and for many more years by Jong Holland, Asiento, and S.U.B.T. (Sport Unie Brion Trappers). A governing body, De Curaçaosche Voetbalbond, was founded in 1921 with two dozen clubs and over 1,000 players registered. The Aruba Voetbalbond was formed during the 1930s on the colony's second largest island, and became affiliated directly with Curaçao. In both the Curaçao and Aruba leagues, clubs were divided into an A Division, a reserve A Division, and a reserve B Division. The remaining four islands—Bonaire, St. Eustatius, Saba, and St. Martin—lagged far behind with their smaller populations. The Curaçaosche Voetbalbond became a member of FIFA in 1932.

Throughout the 1930s, Curaçao's primary international opposition was Surinam. They played each other nine times between 1934 and the war years, Curaçao winning six and losing two. The biggest wins by either team during this series was 4-1. In 1939, Curaçao became a charter member of the Central American and Caribbean Confederation, and three years later in San José, Costa Rica, it was the only non-Central American participant in the fourth championship of the region. Only Cuba and Jamaica had previously represented the Caribbean in the regional championship. In a field of five teams, Curaçao placed third, drawing with Panama and El Salvador, thrashing Nicaragua, and losing decisively to Costa Rica, the major power in Central America throughout the 1940s.

Curaçao also participated in the 1946 and 1948 editions of the regional championship. In 1946, it achieved some excellent results, including a 4-2 win over Costa Rica and a 14-0 punishment of Puerto Rico (Costa Rica and Panama had beaten Puerto Rico by only 12-0), and placed third in a field of six. The same middle-of-the-table standing prevailed as late as the 1969 Championship of CONCACAF, the successor to the old regional championship, in which Netherlands Antilles defeated Jamaica and Trinidad, drew with Mexico (one of its best showings to date), and lost to Costa Rica and Guatemala.

Outside the official regional championships, Curaçao has often faced Haiti in friendlies, but has not been successful. In a four game series at Port-au-Price in 1947, Haiti won all games played by an aggregate score of 18-1. This disparity has lessened in recent years. In a tour of Europe in 1952, the Curaçao national team lost to France "amateur" 6-1 in Boulogne-sur-Mer, and drew with the Netherlands "amateur" 3-3 in Amsterdam. The islands' major achievement remains its participation in the Olympic tournament of 1952 in Finland, even though its only game was a 2-1 first round loss to Turkey.

Meanwhile, Netherlands Antilles champion clubs have been active in the CONCACAF Champions' Cup, but they have not yet won any honors. In addition to the established clubs of earlier decades, Jong Colombia, previously in the Second Division, has broken through to the top in recent years. Curaçao clubs—Jong Colombia and the rest—continue to maintain their hegemony over Netherlands Antilles soccer, but the strength of the former colony's game rests with the depth of domestic competition on both Curaçao and Aruba.

New Caledonia

One of the most active territories of the South Pacific, New Caledonia has gained a foothold in regional international competition during recent years. The Ligue Calédonienne de Football was founded after World War II and became affiliated with the French Football Federation in 1947. Its offices are still located in Nouméa. New Caledonia's first major international encounter was a series of four matches at home with New Zealand in 1951. The Caledonians won the first of these 2-0 and lost the remaining three by an aggregate score of 7-15.

New Caledonia's participation in the Soccer Tournament of the South Pacific Games has met with considerable success. In 1956, it played host to the second games, in which there were 16 participants, and in 1969 it finished in the middle of the standings after conceding 19 goals and scoring only four. At the fifth games on Guam in 1975, New Caledonia narrowly missed winning the trophy, losing the final to Tahiti after extra time by 2-1. Earlier it had finished at the top of its group, which included Tahiti, New Hebrides and Papua-New Guinea, without a draw or defeat, and in the semi-finals it had crushed the British Solomons.

In 1971, New Caledonia defeated New Zealand twice in a pair of friendlies at the Stade de Magenta in Nouméa. At the First Oceania Cup (1973), the region's most important competition, the Caledonians placed third in a field of five. Close defeats to New Zealand and Tahiti were offset by strong wins over New Hebrides and Fiji, and New Caledonia emerged from the first regional championship with some satisfaction. Since 1971, it has been a provisional member of the Oceania Football Confederation. Under the rules of the French Football Federation, New Caledonia is entitled to send one team to the annual Coupe de France.

New Hebrides

The New Hebrides, a joint French-British condominium in the Southwestern Pacific, has been active in regional Oceania competitions since the early 1960s. The first international forays were made shortly after World War II. In 1951, New Zealand achieved its biggest win to date by crushing New Hebrides 9-0 at a tournament in Nouméa, New Caledonia. In 1963, New Hebrides entered the first South Pacific Games Soccer Tournament, and it has participated in each of the five editions since, generally finishing in the lower half of the table. At the fifth games in Guam (1975), New Hebrides finished third in its group behind New Caledonia and Tahiti but ahead of Papua-New Guinea. It was also one of the five participants in the first Oceania Cup at Auckland in 1973, placing fourth in the table ahead of Fiji. New Hebrides lost all its matches with New Zealand, Tahiti, and New Caledonia, but emerged victorious over hapless Fiji. Its most frequent opponents in the past 30 years have been New Zealand and New Caledonia.

Newton Cup

Copa Richard Newton.

The second competition introduced to accommodate the oldest international rivalry outside the United Kingdom: Argentina vs. Uruguay. It was launched in 1906, two years after the historic Lipton Cup was started, and continued almost unabated until 1930, when professionalism and crowded international schedules proved to be stumbling blocks. It was revived occasionally between 1937-57, but there was a long hiatus between 1957-75. Though Argentina and Uruguay continued to play each other on a regular basis during this suspended period, the Newton and Lipton Cups were seldom awarded. As with the Lipton Cup, the series is played on a one-game basis with the participants taking turns as host country.

The trophy is named for Richard Newton, one of the important English settlers during the mid-nineteenth century who brought European technology to Argentina. This competition has been a nemesis for Uruguay, whose record in this series does not reflect the relative parity of Argentine and Uruguayan soccer.

Winners

1906	Argentina	1917	Uruguay	1929	Uruguay
1907	Argentina	1918	Argentina	1930	shared
1908	Argentina	1919	Uruguay	1937	Argentina
1909	shared	1920	Uruguay	1942	Argentina
1911	Argentina	1922	shared	1945	Argentina
1912	shared	1923	Uruguay	1957	shared
1913	Uruguay	1924	Argentina	1975	Argentina
1915	Uruguay	1927	Argentina	1976	Argentina
1916	Argentina	1928	Argentina		

New York Cosmos   See: **Cosmos**

New Zealand

New Zealand Football Association, Inc.
21, Palmer Street
P.O. Box 1771
Wellington

Founded: 1891
FIFA: 1948
OFC: 1966

Affiliated clubs: *312;* registered players: *10,485 (76 professional, 7,974 non-amateur);* national stadium: *none;* largest stadium: *Newmarket Park, Auckland (18,000);* colors: *white with black trim jerseys, black shorts;* season: *March to October;* honors: *Oceania Cup winner (1973).*

Soccer was introduced to New Zealand during the 1880s, but it immediately took a distant back seat to rugby, whose rough-and-ready image was more conducive to the colonial spirit. While some improvements were made between the world wars, only after World War II did New Zealanders really begin to accept the game. In the 1950s, there was some importing of players from abroad—mainly from Great Britain, Australia, and the Netherlands—and finally in 1970 a watershed was reached with the formation of the first national league. In the past decade, New Zealand has assumed a leadership role in Oceanian soccer as a result of Australia's withdrawal from the region, but at home, rugby is still the favorite.

The association game was played in Dunedin as early as 1880 and in Auckland, Wellington, and Christchurch shortly thereafter. The oldest extant club is North Shore, founded in 1886 at Auckland, and the first governing body, the Auckland Football Association, was formed the same year. The Otago (Dunedin) and Canterbury (Christchurch) associations were formed in 1889, and the Wellington association in 1891. It was also in 1891 that an umbrella body, the New Zealand Football Assocation, was established and sought affiliation with The Football Association in London. The oldest existing clubs other than North Shore are: Northern (1888), Mornington (1889), and Roslyn Wakari (an amalgamation of Roslyn and Wakari, both founded in 1894) in Dunedin and Diamond (1893)—now Wellington Diamond United—in Wellington.

The first representative match between cities was played in 1890 at Christchurch when Canterbury defeated Wellington 2-0, and one year later a similar match was held at Wellington, resulting in a home win by 1-0. This instigated a regularly scheduled competition between provincial teams, and in 1892 the first official tournament, the Brown Shield, was introduced on this basis. The new series heightened spectacular interest, and was played until 1923. The first winner in 1892 was Wellington; Otago and Canterbury were the other participants in the first edition. Auckland entered for the first time in 1893, Ruahine in 1897, Taranaki (New Plymouth) in 1906, and Hawke's Bay, Wanganui, Manawatu, Buller, and Poverty Bay entered subsequently.

As the regional leagues continued to produce annual champions, the first nationwide tournament for clubs was introduced in 1923—the Chatham Cup. Now called the Lion Chatham Cup, this was and still is the premier knockout series in New Zealand soccer. Its first winner in 1923 was Seacliff (Otago). In 1925, a new competition for provincial representative teams, The Football Association Trophy, was launched with Auckland, Canterbury, Otago, and Wellington (the first winner was Auckland). This trophy was named in honor of its donor, The Football Association in London, and the competition has long since fallen by the wayside. Representative games between regions have declined in importance since the formation of the national league and the introduction of more schedules. They are now played irregularly. The Football Association trophy itself is now awarded to the national league champion.

The first unofficial internationals were played in 1904 at home by regional and national representative teams against New South Wales. In a series of nine games, the Australian team defeated New Zealand 1-0, and seven days later played to a 3-3 draw. Regional New Zealand selections won twice, drew once, and lost four times. One year later the visit was returned by a national representative team playing various Australian clubs and a New South Wales selection, and New Zealand won six, drew two, and lost three, including one each against New South Wales. The other opponents on the Australian tour were clubs from New South Wales. New

Zealand did not participate in international competition again until similar tours were set up in 1922 (in New Zealand), and 1923 (in Australia). The results were again mixed, but curiously New Zealand fared better away than at home. In 1924, there was an extensive 22-game tour of New Zealand by a Chinese university selection, dominated by regional New Zealand teams. A Canadian representative team descended on New Zealand in 1927 and won 20 out of 23 games, and, after two further series with various Australian teams in 1933 and 1936, England "Amateur" paid a visit in 1937 and won all nine contests against a representative New Zealand team and assorted regional selections. New Zealand's goal difference against England "Amateur" was 6 for and 84 against, a startling indicator of the relative level of play in New Zealand soccer.

World War II provided increased exposure to the game as New Zealand troops fought their way across North Africa and Europe. As a result, a surge of interest occurred after the war, and in 1948 the New Zealand Football Association, Inc., joined FIFA. In subsequent weeks, New Zealand played its first official internationals against Australia—a series of four games at home—all of which were lost with an aggregate score of 1-25.

In 1951, a national team made its first tour of Oceania, defeating New Caledonia three times and Suva, New Hebrides, and Fiji once each; New Caledonia also won once. This was the beginning of a long and steady association with the islands of the South Pacific, many of which have been among New Zealand's friendliest opponents. A variety of competitions have been held since the 1950s with teams from the Far East and famous clubs from Europe, such as FK Austria, FC Basel, Manchester United, Cardiff City, and Rangers, and the rivalry with Australia continues. The New Zealand F.A. became a charter member of the Oceania Football Confederation (OFC), in 1966 and immediately became an active participant in regional competition. In 1973, it was the first winner of the Oceania Cup for national teams of the region, a unique distinction because this was the first official competition sponsored by the confederation. National teams have also entered the World Cup qualifying rounds three times; they were eliminated by Israel in 1970 and Australia in 1974 and 1978.

The Rothmans National League—sponsored by the tobacco company of the same name—was finally introduced in 1970 with eight clubs. The number has since increased to 12, and is supported by a second division of three provincial leagues: Northern, Central, and Southern. Winners of the three sections are promoted annually to the national league. Clubs from Auckland, Christchurch, and Wellington dominate national league standings. Christchurch United has the most consistent record thus far, but Blockhouse Bay, Eastern Suburbs, and Mount Wellington have

also achieved fine reputations. Stagnant or falling attendances have put the league in constant jeopardy; it was especially disappointing when this trend was not reversed after New Zealand's highly successful tour of Asia in 1975, which was followed by two wins over China PR and an 8-0 thrasing of Indonesia in Christchurch. It seems that the New Zealand national rugby team, the legendary "All Blacks," still hold sway over the hearts and minds of New Zealand fans.

Nicaragua

Federacion Nácional de Fútbol
Estadio Cranshaw
Apartado Postal 976
Managua, D.N.

Founded: 1931
FIFA: 1950
CONCACAF: 1968

Affiliated clubs: *31;* **registered players:** *5,160;* **national stadium:** *Estadio Nacional, Managua (30,000);* **largest stadium:** *Estadio Nacional;* **colors:** *blue and white striped jerseys, blue shorts;* **season:** *June to September;* **honors:** *none.*

Nicaragua is the only Central American country other than the infant Belize that has failed to win a single international tournament. As a national sport, soccer is seriously challenged by the much loved baseball following the lengthy and pervasive presence of the United States Marines in the 1920s, but Nicaraguan soccer now seems to have come into its own.

The first governing body was a section of the Comisión Nacional de Deportes called 'Asesoria de Fútbol," established in 1931 and affiliated with FIFA in 1950—almsot 20 years later. The present association—Federación Nacional de Fútbol—was founded in 1968; its first task was to join CONCACAF. Regional leagues were organized during the 1930s, and after World War II continued to exist, having added multiple divisions. It was not until 1971 that a national league was introduced with regional second divisions and a system of promotion and relegation. In addition, other tournaments for first division clubs are held each January.

Nicaragua entered international competition with its participation in the 1941

Championship of the Confederación Centroamericano y del Caribe de Fútbol (forerunner of the Champsionship of CONCACAF). El Salvador, Panama, Curaçao, and Costa Rica each defeated newcomer Nicaragua by substantial margins in 1941, and this trend continued throughout the 1940s. During its first decade of international competition, Nicaragua compiled a record to improve upon: 9-0-0-9-10-64-0.

Nicaragua has not attempted to qualify for the World Cup, and only rarely for the Olympics, but it has entered some editions of the Championship of CONCACAF, achieving little more than the occasional draw. Nicaraguan clubs have participated in the CONCACAF Champion's Cup, but Diriangen Managua appears to be one of the few clubs with the finances available to enter the competition with any consistency. In 1972, the national stadium was destroyed by earthquake and is still scheduled to be reconstructed in the near future. The smaller Estadio Cranshaw (capacity: 5,000) has since been taken over as the center for Nicaraguan soccer activity.

Niger

Fédération Nigérienne de Foot-Ball
c/o M. Abdoulaye G. Maiga
Secrétaire Général de la FNF
B.P. 2289
Niamey-Balafon

Founded: 1967
FIFA: 1967
CAF: 1967

Affiliated clubs: *45;* registered players: *?;* national stadium: *Stade National, Niamey (7,082);* largest stadium: *Stade National;* colors: *white jerseys, white shorts;* season: *January to June, September to December;* honors: *none.*

Niger, home of the world's largest sand dunes and unspoiled natural game reserve, is understandably among the least advanced soccer nations of Africa. Though French soldiers sometimes played the game in their garrisons at Niamey or Agades during the first decades of this century, the growth of soccer in this part of the Sahara has come about only since independence in 1960. Little connection was made between soccer interests in Niamey and the French West African governing body at Dakar during the colonial era, and a Nigerien (not to be confused with Nigerian) association was not founded until 1967.

Men in the cities of the savanna region in the south—Niamey, the capital, Zinder, and Maradi—constitute the soccer population of Niger. Their clubs make up the nine-member first division while the nomadic caucasians of the north participate very little in organized sports. A national league was introduced in the 1960s, and Nigerien champion clubs entered the African Champions' Cup as early as 1970. A national cup competition is also held, and its winners have been participants in the new African Cup Winners' Cup. The leading clubs are Forces Armées Nigériennes, Liberté, Olimpique Niamey, and Sahel. In addition to these, Secteur VI and Secteur VII of Niamey have also participated in African club competition, but Nigerien clubs have not advanced past the first round. Niger has also attempted to qualify for the last several African Nations' Cups without success. The national stadium at Niamey is exceedingly large by Nigerien standards: the next three largest stadiums (at Zinder, Maradi, and another at Niamey) have capacities for only 1,000 spectators.

Nigeria

Nigeria Football Association
Nigeria National Stadium
P.O. Box 466
Lagos

Founded: 1945
FIFA: 1959
CAF: 1959

Affiliated clubs: *326;* registered players: *80,190;* national stadium: *Nigeria National Stadium, Lagos (50,000);* largest stadium: *Nigeria National Stadium;* colors: *green jerseys with white trim, white shorts;* season: *January to December;* honors: *Shooting Stars, African Cup Winners Cup (1976), Rangers Enugu, African Cup Winners Cup (1977).*

Shortly after independence in 1960, Nigeria emerged as a major soccer power in Africa by virtue of its size if nothing else—it is the most populous country on the continent—but its exceedingly fragmented population has resulted in a certain lack of cohesion at the national level. In consequence, Nigeria has been more successful in African club competitions than World Cup qualifying rounds and the African Nations' Cup. The big

Nigerian cities of Lagos, Ibadan, and Enugu spawn some of Africa's leading clubs and contain teeming populations of rowdy fans. Like the USSR in Europe, Nigeria's national team, the "Green Eagles," can always be counted on to place well in international competition, though others may win more honors.

British missionaries were more influential in importing soccer to Nigeria than commercial or military colonists, but the greatest exposure to the game was seen during World War II when the country was inundated by British troops. The Nigeria Football Association was set up in 1945 as a result, and became affiliated with The Football Association in London. Its first unofficial international was played in 1950 against archrival Gold Coast (now Ghana) at Accra, and was won by the Gold Coast, 1-0. After learning basic elements of the game, the level of play among Nigerians remained fairly static until the early 1960s. European coaches were hired in ever increasing numbers, and a great surge of public interest in soccer—identified strongly with the new spirit of independence—swept through Nigerian cities.

The "Green Eagles" entered World Cup qualification rounds for 1962, and qualified for the final rounds of the 1963 African Nations' Cup, ultimately facing elimination by the vastly more experienced Egypt and Sudan. Shortly, thereafter a turning point in Nigerian soccer occurred with "Green Eagles" tours in the north of England (Blackpool and Sheffield Wednesday), USSR (Dinamo Moscow), and Egypt, but it was not until 1968, after further poor showings in World Cup and African Nations' Cup qualification rounds, that Nigeria appeared on the world scene at the Olympic Games in Mexico City. In the first round, the "Green Eagles" lost decisively to Japan and the Spanish amateurs, but went home with some satisfaction in holding the Brazilian amateurs to a 3-3 draw.

In 1969, Nigeria narrowly missed qualification for the 1970 World Cup when Morocco grabbed the first African berth in modern times by a toss of the coin. Meanwhile, the African Nations' Cup continued to elude the Nigerians, and they bowed out of the 1974 World Cup to Ghana in the third qualifying round. Nigeria finally gained its rightful place among African powers with a third place finish in the Nations' Cup of 1976 by defeating Zaire and Sudan in the first round, and Egypt in the final pool, and it also won the less important African Games of 1973 (held in Lagos). The old rivalry with Ghana, in the meantime, was exacerbated regularly by meetings in the Jalco Cup.

On the club level, Rangers Enugu reached the final of the African Champions' Cup in 1975, losing to Guinea's powerful Hafia, and Shooting Stars won the second edition of the African Cup Winners' Cup in 1976 after escaping from the semi-final round with Egypt's Zamalek on penalty kicks. In the final, Cameroon's Tonnerre proved to be less an obstacle than some had predicted, and succumbed to Shooting Stars 4-1 and 1-0. In 1977, Rangers Enugu to the Cup Winners Cup back to Nigeria for the second year.

In domestic competition, the most coveted trophy in Nigeria is the Challenge Cup, which is contested annually by over 130 clubs. A national league as such does not exist, because the government is still reluctant to bring together hostile ethnic groups from different parts of the country. The leading clubs of Lagos, Ibadan, Enugu, and Kaduna make up the de facto elite of Nigerian soccer. Numerous regional leagues and cup competitions supply a partial outlet for a soccer-playing population that potentially runs into the millions. A curiosity of the Nigerian game is its ability to produce wingers of very high quality. In recent years, for example, Baba Otu Mohammed and Kunle Awesu, right and left wingers respectively, have been widely regarded as the best in Africa.

nomenclature

The term "soccer" came into use in England during the 1880s by university men from Oxford and Cambridge. The use of "association football," as distinct from "rugby football," was already in practice, and "soccer" became a colloquialism formed by extending the second syllable of "association." Today it remains a primarily journalistic or conversational term in Britain and throughout most of the Commonwealth, but in the United States, Canada, and Australia its use is the rule.

Soccer terms the world over reflect the modern game's British origins. English, Scottish, Welsh, and Irish emigrants pervasively influenced the sporting vocabulary of their adopted locales. Where the game developed only by indirect contact with British travelers, as in many parts of Asia and native America, there were few if any English terms. The continuing use of English terms grows more tenuous as the decades pass, but some have been embedded permanently among the world's 45 families of languages.

The word "football" itself is widespread. There are few exceptions to its adaptation into the four main Western language families. The most important aberrations are in Italian and Greek. In Italian, the indigenous football game *calcio*, dating from the fifteenth century, has given rise to the modern term *gioco del calcio*, or, *calcio*. And in Greek we find *podosphairo*, or, *podosfairo*, whose derivation from classical Greek is *pous-sphaira* (foot-ball). Examples of "football's" direct adaptations into other languages follow:

football (French)
fotbal (Rumanian)
fútbol (Spanish)
futebol (Portuguese)
phutabola (Bengali)
fodbold (Danish)

fotball (Norwegian)
fotboll (Swedish)
Fussball (German)
voetbal (Dutch)
fotbal (Czech)
futbol (Bulgarian)

futbol (Russian)
fudbal (Serbo-Croatian)
futball (Hungarian)
futbol (Turkish)
football (Amharic)

Other English terms, such as "derby," "system," "cup," and "club," are also found in several languages. In German, "hands," "hat trick," stopper," and "tackle" are still widely used. In Spanish and Portuguese, one frequently finds "goal average," "goal difference," and tactical terms, such as "one back." As non-British cultures contribute more and more to the development of the modern game, their terms also come into international use. From the Italian, for example, English has adopted "libero" and "catenaccio."

Common soccer terms in the leading Western languages are:

English	French	Spanish	Italian	Portuguese	German
goalkeeper	gardien de bût	golero	portiere	goleiro	Torhüter
right back	arrière droit	zaguero derecho	terzino destro	zagueiro direito	Rechter Verteidiger
left back	arrière gauche	zaguero izquierdo	terzino sinistro	zagueiro esquerdo	Linker Verteidiger
right halfback	demi-droit	medio derecho	mediano destro	medio direito	Rechter Mittel-feldspieler
center halfback	demi-centre	centro-medio	medio-centro	centro-medio	Mittelläufer
left halfback	demi-gauche	medio izquierdo	mediano sinistro	medio esquerdo	Linker Mittel-feldspieler
right wing	ailier droit	puntero derecho	ala destra	extrema direita	Rechtsaussen
inside right	intérieur droit	interior derecho	interno destro	meia direita	Rechtsinnen
center forward	avant-centre	centro-delantero	centro-attaco	centro-atacante	Mittelstürmer
inside left	intérieur gauche	interior izquierdo	interno sinistro	meia esquerda	Linksinnen

English	French	Spanish	Italian	Portuguese	German
left wing	ailier gauche	puntero izquierdo	ala sinistra	extrema esquerda	Linksaussen
field of play	terrain de jeu	campo del juego	campo di giuoco	campo de jogo	Spielfeld
marking	marquage	modo de marcado	segnatura	marcação do campo	abgrenzung
goals	buts	marcos	porte	métas	Tore
goal area	surface de but	area de meta	area della porta	area de meta	Torräume
penalty area	surface de réparation	area de penal	area di rigore	area penal	Strafräume
ball	ballon	balón	palla	bola	Ball
players	joueurs	jugadores	giuocatori	jogadores	Spieler
referee	arbitre	árbitro	arbitro	árbitro	Schiedsrichter
linesmen	jugès de touch	jueces de línea	guarda linne	juizes de linha	Linienrichter
game	partie	partido	partita	partida	Spiel
offside	hors-jeu	fuera de juego	fuori giuoco	impedimento	abseits
fouls	fautes	faltas	falli	infrações	verbotenes Spiel
free kicks	coups francs	tiro libre	calci liberi	tiro livre	Freistoss
penalty kick	coup de réparation	tiro penal	calcio de rigore	penal	Strafstoss
corner kick	coup de coin	saque de esquina	calcio d'angolo	tiro de canto	Eckstoss
throw-in	rentrée de touche	saque de banda	rimessa dalla linea laterale	arremesso lateral	Einwurf

non-amateur

A player classification recognized by FIFA, which is meant to account for a level of professionalism less than full time or fully compensatory. A non-amateur may not qualify for amateur competitions that are sponsored by FIFA, affiliated confederations and associations, or the International Olympic Committee.

Thirty-three countries have registered non-amateur players: Central Africa, Malawi, Rhodesia, Somalia, Canada, Costa Rica, Guatemala, Honduras, El Salvador, Argentina, Bolivia, Chile, Colombia, Ecuador, Paraguay, Uruguay, Hong Kong, Austria, Belgium, France, West Germany, Greece, Iceland, Republic of Ireland, Italy, Malta, Portugal, Sweden, Switzerland, Turkey, Yugoslavia, Australia, and New Zealand.

See also: **professional**

North African Championship

Championnat de Nord-Afrique.

The earliest club competition in Africa between teams from different leagues. This series was introduced in 1919, and was played by leading clubs of the five leagues (i.e., colonial associations) of French North Africa:

Ligue d'Alger, Ligue Constantinoise de Football Association, Ligue du Maroc, Ligue Oranaise de Football Association, and Ligue de Tunisie de Football. The Algiers, Oran, and Constantine leagues were located in present-day Algeria. It continued to be held throughout the colonial period until 1950, interrupted only by the war years. It was supplemented by a similar series beginning in 1930, the North African Cup. (See: *North African Cup)*

Winners

1919	Racing Club Tunis
1920	ASMO Oran
1921	S-C Bel Abbès Oran
1922	FC Blidéen Algiers
1923	S-C Bel Abbès Oran
1924	S-C Bel Abbès Oran
1925	S-C Bel Abbès Oran
1926	S-C Bel Abbès Oran
1927	Gallic Sports Algérois
1928	FC Blidéen Algiers
1929	AS St. Eugène Algiers
1930	Club des Joyeusetés Oran
1931	US Marocaine
1932	US Marocaine
1933	US Marocaine
1934	Racing Universitaire Algérois
1935	Gallia Club Oranais
1936	Gallic Sports Algérois
1937	Jeunesse Bône AC
1938	Racing Universitaire Constantine
1941	US Marocaine
1946	Gallic Sports Algérois
1947	Wydad AC Casablanca
1948	Wydad AC Casablanca
1949	Wydad AC Casablanca

North African Cup

Coupe de Nord-Afrique.

The second important competition between leading clubs of French North Africa. The leagues of Algiers, Oran, Constantine, Tunis, and Morocco were represented. (See: *North African Championship).*

Winners

1930	Club des Joyeusetés Oran
1931	Racing Universitaire Algérois
1932	Club des Joyeusetés Oran
1933	Club des Joyeusetés Oran
1934	Club des Joyeusetés Oran
1935	Italia de Tunis
1936	Racing Universitaire Algérois
1937	Olympique Marocaine
1938	SAM Casablanca
1946	US Marocaine
1947	US Athlétique Casablanca
1948	Wydad AC Casablanca
1949	AS St. Eugène Algiers

North America

See: **Confederación Norte-Centroamericana y del Caribe de Fútbol (CONCACAF)**

North American Football Confederation

See: **Confederación Norte-Centroamericana y del Caribe de Fútbol (CONCACAF)**

North American Football Confederation, Championship of the

A short-lived championship of the now defunct North American Football Confederation (NAFC) contested only twice during the late 1940s and won on both occasions by Mexico. The NAFC was founded in 1939 by Cuba, Mexico, and the USA, and acquired no new members before its quick demise in the mid-1950s. World War II delayed its first championship until 1947. With the formation of CONCACAF in 1961, the already dormant NAFC Championship was officially superseded.

In the first edition at Havana in 1947, all participants played each other once, and the tournament was over within a week. Both Mexico and Cuba easily outclassed the USA, whose team consisted entirely of the Ponta Delgada Football Club, one of the leading semiprofessional industrial teams from Fall River, Massachusetts. In the second edition at Mexico City in 1949, each opponent was played twice, doubling the number of matches to six and increasing the duration of the tournament to three weeks. Again Mexico went without a defeat, but Cuba and the USA confounded speculators by splitting their two legs with equally lopsided scores.

The NAFC Championship has been the only full international self-contained tournament in the history of North American soccer.

Winners

1947 Mexico
1949 Mexico

Results

1947 (in Havana)

Mexico—USA	5-0
Mexico—Cuba	3-1
USA—Cuba	2-5

	P	W	D	L	F	A	P
Mexico	2	2	0	0	8	1	4
Cuba	2	1	0	1	6	5	2
USA	2	0	0	2	2	10	0

1949 (in Mexico City)

Mexico—USA	6-0
Mexico—Cuba	2-0
USA—Mexico	1-1
USA—Cuba	2-6
Cuba—USA	2-5
Cuba—Mexico	0-3

	P	W	D	L	F	A	P
Mexico	4	3	1	0	12	1	7
USA	4	1	1	2	8	15	3
Cuba	4	1	0	3	8	12	2

North American Soccer League

The leading professional soccer league in the United States and Canada, which was formed in 1968 by a merger of the United Soccer Association and the National Professional Soccer League.

The NASL is the flagship of big-time soccer in North America, and more closely resembles a true national league than either the American Soccer League or the various ethnic leagues. Unfortunately, it is regarded abroad with considerable disdain, largely due to its clubs' tendency to poach foreign players on a loan basis, and it suffers from a perilous relationship with FIFA (via the United States Soccer Federation) for its alterations of the time-honored world code. From the point of view of the average American or Canadian fan, however, the NASL is responsible for the emergence of comparatively high quality, senior level soccer on this side of the Atlantic and the Rio Grande. The financial power of its wealthiest clubs, most notably Cosmos of New York, has drawn instant worldwide attention since the signing of Pelé in 1975. The league is now seeking to establish a framework for slowly "Americanizing" its club rosters—in 1978, only 20 percent of its players were born in the United States and Canada—and to urge its members to purchase foreign contracts outright and enter the world transfer market.

The NASL season runs from April to August and is one of the shortest in the world. It culminates in the final weeks with an elimination tournament of the top clubs, and ends in a championship final, the Soccer Bowl. Some variation of this format has been in effect since the formation of the league (except in 1969 when there were only five clubs), but each year there has been a variety of structural changes to accommodate the fluctuating number of league members. No NASL champion has ever won the title under exactly the same conditions as did the previous year's winner. The only club to win more than one championship has been Cosmos. The now defunct Atlanta Chiefs were distinctive in winning one championship (1968) and placing second twice (1969 and 1971), but between 1968-78 the title was won four times by new franchises (1970, 1973, 1974, and 1975). The only charter member of the NASL still in existence under its original name is the Dallas Tornado. A second charter member, the St. Louis Stars, has remained extant but in 1978 the club relocated to Anaheim, California, and became the California Surf.

The history of the NASL resembles that of its counterparts in American football, ice hockey, and basketball. It was the televising of the 1966 World Cup final from England (on a 15-minute delay) that proved to be the impetus for a national professional league. The American Soccer League (ASL) had been in operation since the early 1930s, but, in fact, it was widely perceived as another ethnic league in disguise, and its following was severely limited to a few urban areas in the East. Bill Cox's International Soccer League (ISL), which had imported entire clubs from abroad during the early and mid-1960s, had faded from sight. The high television ratings of the 1966 World Cup final, however, caught the imagination of a host of speculators.

Only months after England's world championship triumph, business interests coalesced into no less than two dozen camps, each seeking a franchise in whatever league structure could be worked out. One of the first assumptions to be made was that certain Canadian cities would be welcomed—especially Toronto and Vancouver—as commercially viable prospects because of their large ethnic populations. The sleepy United States Soccer Football Association (USSFA) and Canadian Soccer Football Association (CSFA) were taken by surprise. Finding themselves in the midst of a "soccer boom," the national bodies meted out franchises for a pittance. So many clubs were formed over the span of a few months that clusters of owners grouped into two separate leagues. FIFA reminded the USSFA and CSFA that under FIFA regulations they could recognize only one national league per country. The national bodies met and urged the two prospective leagues to merge, or they would be forced to recognize one over the other. The leagues refused, and the USSFA and CSFA gave their blessing to the United Soccer Association (USA) for the 1967 season. The second league, the National Professional Soccer League (NPSL), ignoring FIFA's warnings from Zurich, continued to set up its operation and vowed to bury the USA in the competitive marketplace. The USSFA explained the vagaries of American entrepreneurship to FIFA, and asked the world body to refrain from taking action against the United States and Canada and allow a period of grace until matters could be settled. FIFA reluctantly acquiesced.

The USA's plan for success was to borrow Bill Cox's idea of importing clubs wholesale from abroad and assigning them to American franchises. Thus the membership of the United Soccer Association 1967 was comprised entirely of foreign clubs: Boston (alias Shamrock Rovers F.C., Dublin, Ireland); Chicago (Cagliari Calcio, Cagliari, Italy); Cleveland (Stoke City F.C., Stoke-on-Trent, England); Dallas (Dundee United F.C., Dundee, Scotland); Detroit (Glentoran F.C., Belfast, Northern Ireland); Houston (Bangu AC, Rio de Janeiro, Brazil); Los Angeles (Wolverhampton Wanderers F.C., Wolverhampton, England); New York (CA Cerro, Montevideo, Uruguay); San Francisco (ADO, The Hague, Netherlands); Toronto (Hibernian F.C., Edinburgh, Scotland); Vancouver (Sunderland F.C., Sunderland, England); and Washington (Aberdeen F.C., Aberdeen, Scotland).

The USA was divided into eastern and western divisions, and the two divisional winners, the Los Angeles Wolves and the Washington Whips, met in a championship play-off. Los Angeles finally won by 6-5 in an overtime goalscoring bonanza. Although each of the United Soccer Association teams were members of their respective first divisions in their native countries, there were odd differences in style and noticeable gulfs between their levels of play, as befits, for instance, The Football League of England vs. The League of Ireland. Yet, the results in the final standings were remarkably consistent. In addition, some temperamental rivalries surfaced to add a "foreign" zest to the competition, e.g., New York (Cerro) vs. Chicago (Cagliari).

The NPSL, on the other hand, took a different route. Burdened by its renegade status, the NPSL owners were hastily forced to gather what players they could from lowly American ranks and entice either very young or aging veteran players from abroad. This state of affairs resulted not only in a lower standard of play than the USA, but the players themselves risked suspension by FIFA and their respective national associations. (In one remarkable, if unheralded, instance, the St. Louis Stars managed to obtain the incomparable Yugoslav inside forward Dragoslav Sekularac on loan from Karlsruher SC of West Germany.) Ironically, the CBS television network salvaged the league's precarious status by agreeing to broadcast NPSL matches throughout the season. To add to an already self-destructive situation, four NPSL owners in cities where USA franchises also existed (New York, Chicago, Los Angeles, and Toronto) refused to pull out.

In the fall of 1967, when the season was finally over, most of the clubs in both leagues had lost vast sums of money—as much as one million dollars apiece. While the NPSL initiated a lawsuit against FIFA, the leagues commiserated over their collective failure, and in December 1967 they agreed to merge as the North American Soccer League (NASL). The lawsuit was dropped, and the USSFA and CSFA immediately recognized the new league.

The NASL, in its first season, included nine franchises from the United Soccer Association (Boston Beacons, Chicago Mustangs, Cleveland Stokers, Dallas Tornado, Detroit Cougars, Houston Stars, Los Angeles Wolves, Vancouver Royals, and Washington Whips) and eight from the National Professional Soccer League (Atlanta Chiefs, Baltimore Bays, Kansas City Spurs, New York Generals, Oakland Clippers, St. Louis Stars, San Diego Toros, and Toronto Falcons).

The former USA clubs returned without their foreign teams from the previous year, and had to start from scratch. Of the former NPSL clubs, two were relocated from other cities to avoid duplication (San Diego from Los Angeles and Kansas City from Chicago). The USA and NPSL franchises that were not included in the new league but found themselves in NASL "markets" received financial compensation.

The 17 clubs of the NASL modeled their building programs on the work of the NPSL, and scoured all five continents to fill their rosters. Barely one percent of the NASL player membership in 1968 was American or Canadian. The teams were divided into two conferences (eastern and western) with two divisions in each conference. The play-off structure featured two conference championships followed by a league championship, each played on a home and away basis. In the championship of that first season, the eastern title holder, Atlanta, defeated the West's San Diego after a 3-0 romp in the Georgia capital.

But the grand experiment failed once again at the box office, and when the league opened for business in 1969, only five clubs remained: Atlanta, Baltimore, Dallas, Kansas City, and St. Louis. It was the NASL's lowest ebb. To the rescue came former Welsh international Phil Woosnam, player-manager of the Atlanta

Chiefs in 1967-68, to take over as executive director of the crippled league. Woosnam and the league's new director of administration, Clive Toye, (former *London Daily Express* football correspondent and general manager of the Baltimore Bays in 1967-68), set out to learn the ways of American big business, and traveled extensively to attract new speculators from across the nation. Dividends were slow in coming, but the doldrums of 1969 were eventually put behind, and there was a gradual increase in the number of league clubs in 1970 and 1971.

In 1970, the Baltimore Bays gave up its NASL effort after some strong pressure from the Baltimore Orioles baseball club, but the two American Soccer League powerhouses of that year, Rochester and Washington, joined the league and membership was increased to six. The unpredictability of NASL competition was affirmed when the divisional titles were won by none other than Rochester and Washington, the former emerging as league champion. Modest increases in attendance figures helped to maintain optimism in league offices.

The following year brought three changes in the league structure. Kansas City bowed out, but important new franchises were found in New York (the Cosmos under new head Clive Toye), Toronto (the return of a major ethnic center), and Montreal. In addition, there were two major innovations in 1971. The first involved an extension of the regular league schedule in which three foreign clubs (Portuguesa of Sao Paulo, Brazil, Lanerossi-Vicenza of Italy, and Apollo of Greece) were brought in to compete against members of the league in an official cup competition whose results were included in the season standings. In addition, the play-off schedule was increased to bring in greater box office revenues: first and second place clubs from either division engaged in a best-of-three series to determine the participants in a best-of-three final. Lamar Hunt's Dallas Tornado, the NASL's first Cinderella team, defeated Atlanta for the championship.

In 1972, for the first and only time, the number of league members did not change, but a lack of interest in Washington, D.C., prompted the Darts to relocate in Miami. Mounting concern over the absence of American players in the league resulted in the first college draft, and the eight clubs selected 35 collegiate players, of which two eventually made starting lineups. The season was shorter (each club played the others twice on a home and away basis), and the play-off format of the previous year was retained with one-leg semifinals and a one-leg championship. The New York Cosmos, playing before its home crowds in both the semi-final and the final, won the league title over St. Louis, the latter attempting to vindicate St. Louis's long reputation as the bastion of American soccer.

Philadelphia was the only new club to enter the NASL in 1973, leaving the western part of the United States without a franchise for the fifth year in a row. With the makeup of team rosters changing so dramatically each year, it was not surprising that Philadelphia, the only expansion club of the season, won the championship after winning a one-leg semifinal and final against Toronto and Dallas, respectively. In the regular season, the clubs were divided into three divisions of three clubs each, and for the first time a "wild card" team (the idea borrowed from the National Football League) was placed in the play-offs. The major story of the season with the rise to prominence for the first time of two Americans, the Philadelphia Atoms coach Al Miller, and the first American-born scoring leader and Rookie of the Year, Dallas' Kyle Rote, Jr. Optimists proclaimed a new day for American soccer, but the fact remained that the number of top American or Canadian players in the NASL could be counted on one hand.

The first dramatic breakthrough for Commissioner Woosnam and his struggling league occurred in 1974. Membership jumped from nine to 15 clubs. In the East, the cities of Baltimore and Boston returned to the ranks with new owners, and an entire western division was created on the Pacific coast, which included two new cities, Seattle and San Jose, as well as Los Angeles and Vancouver. Atlanta and Montreal, meanwhile, dropped out, but their places were taken by Denver, a new city, and a new Washington club, the Diplomats.

The league's iconoclastic point system—which until now had awarded six points for a win, three for a draw, none for a loss, and one for every goal scored up to and including three per game—was altered, and draws were eliminated entirely. Matches now ending in drawn scores would be decided by a penalty kick contest (as per FIFA regulations) and called a "draw-win"; the winner would be awarded three points and the loser none. Outright wins and losses would still be awarded six and zero points, respectively.

FIFA had strongly disapproved of the old system to begin with, but the new regulations prompted an even stronger reaction. Yet the world body took no action, and the new point system was instituted. Moreover, the NASL was by now developing a reputation for tampering with the venerable Laws of the Game. In 1973, the league had abolished FIFA's offside rule (written in 1866 and painstakingly revised in 1925) and changed the demarcation from the halfway line to an arbitrary line 35 yards from the opponent's goal, i.e., a player could not be offside until he had crossed the 35-yard line in his opponent's half of the field.

In 1975, the "draw-win" was eliminated, and all matches were either won or lost, if necessary by a penalty kick contest. Six points were awarded for a win and none for a loss. Meanwhile, the league was expanded to 20 clubs. New franchises were awarded to Tampa, Hartford, Chicago, San Antonio, and Portland. There were no dropouts, but the Toronto Metros merged with a local ethnic power, Croatia, in an attempt to draw some additional support from the stronger semi-professional leagues of the Toronto area. The four divisions of the 1974 season were retained in their basic configuration, as was the play-off structure of 1974, which included a quarter-final round.

All these years, the established policy of the NASL—and the ASL, ISL, and NPSL before it—was to build a commercially viable American game by importing foreign players. Little serious thought had ever been given to the slow, admittedly frustrating policy of developing a native American game from the grass roots, as other countries had done over the decades. This dependence on foreign players reached a feverish peak during the mid-1970s. When it became apparent around 1974 that the NASL was lifting itself up by the bootstraps and professional soccer on a major scale was here to stay, the possibility of attracting major foreign stars appeared more and more realistic. Hundreds of players were mentioned, and soon the press was dropping a litany of names that read like an international who's who of soccer. The prospect of a grass roots American game, the public was told, would depend not on many years of laborious planning and hard work, but on one or perhaps two star players from abroad; native American acceptance of the game would follow in turn. In June 1975, Clive Toye of the New York Cosmos, backed by its high rolling parent company Warner Communications, succeeded in signing Pelé—the world's most celebrated player and recently retired from his famous club Santos. Pelé's arrival in the NASL was, indeed, a watershed.

Worldwide attention immediately focused on America's upstart league. Pelé's multimillion dollar contract reached the front page of the *New York Times*, as well as newspapers from Boise to Savannah that had not previously been aware of soccer's advance to American shores. Attendances soared (where the Cosmos played), and Pelé himself, at once gracious and ingratiating, promised to deliver the world game to the free world's promised land. Other international idols whose stars were on the wane—George Best, Jimmy Johnstone, Eusebio, Antonio Simoes, Bobby Moore—soon graced American playing fields, but the league and the press had been searching for someone of Pelé's stature and all others were destined to relative obscurity.

Single-handedly, Pelé could not bring the Cosmos a league championship nor even a divisional title, but his club achieved international fame, and Florida's expansion team, the Tampa Bay Rowdies, walked away with the 1975 crown. The championship game was renamed the Soccer Bowl—hearkening once again to the National Football League—and CBS again broadcasted a handful of games (Pelé's Cosmos vs. whomever).

In 1976, Pelé's first full season, the Baltimore Comets moved to San Diego, and Denver relocated to Minneapolis-St. Paul (as the Minnesota Kicks), to give the north country its first NASL franchise. The number of American or Canadian players each club was required to carry was raised to six, and at least one American or Canadian had to be on the field for each team at all times. The four divisions were divided into two conferences, as in 1968, the Atlantic and Pacific, and the play-off schedule was expanded to include the top three finishers from each division. Eusebio was transferred from Boston to Toronto, and no one noticed. In the end, the season proved to be a disappointing anticlimax for most of the NASL's new following, as Toronto, one of the least supported clubs in the league, won the league championship from Minnesota, the best supported club in the league but one that lacked superstars and broad appeal. The New York Cosmos were runner-up to Tampa Bay in their division, and bowed out of the play-offs to the same Tampa Bay in the divisional championship. The major news items of the season were the recordbreaking attendance figures (e.g., 49,572 in Bloomington, Minnesota, for a single game).

By 1977, Pelé and Cosmos had taken a

number of worldwide tours, and had become, in a sense, the superstars of the NASL without winning a title. Extensive pressure was exerted on the New York club to win the 1977 championship, as befitting the club of Pelé and inasmuchas this would be his final year as an active player. To this end, Clive Toye made one last master stroke before leaving Cosmos for greener pastures in Chicago. At the end of the European season, he signed Franz Beckenbauer, captain of Bayern München and the world champion West Germans, and widely regarded as the world's most complete player. Beckenbauer, still at the peak of his career, transformed Cosmos from a mere oddity into a relatively sophisticated team, introducing contemporary tactical methods that had previously been unattainable with available talent. Although Cosmos lost its divisional title to Gordon Banks' Ft. Lauderdale Strikers, it plunged through the play-offs and won the league crown in a much heralded Soccer Bowl '77. Pelé declared that all he had ever wished for was now achieved, and observers were struck by the relative ease with which Cosmos dominated the play-offs after its ups and downs during the regular season.

Cosmos' championship season had seen four changes in the league alignment. San Diego relocated to Las Vegas; Miami moved up the coast to Ft. Lauderdale; Hartford moved downstate to New Haven and took the name of its state; and, San Antonio relocated right off the continent and out of everybody's memories to Honolulu. The major rule change of the year was the adoption of a new tie-breaking procedure called the "shoot-out," which brought renewed warnings of suspension from FIFA and derisive wonderment from players and seasoned fans. But the league declared that American spectators needed the added excitement of a Matt Dillon-type showdown in front of the nets. Attendance records fell in quick succession, and in August the all-time high was reached when 77,691 fans at Giants Stadium saw Cosmos bury Ft. Lauderdale by 8-3 in the divisional championship play-offs, outdrawing professional baseball games in New York on the same day.

In 1978, new franchises were awarded to Boston, Denver, Detroit, Philadelphia, Houston and Memphis, to bring the number of NASL members to 24.

Champions

1967	Los Angeles Wolves (USA)	1973	Philadelphia Atoms
	Oakland Clippers (NPSL)	1974	Los Angeles Aztecs
1968	Atlanta Chiefs	1975	Tampa Bay Rowdies
1969	Kansas City Spurs	1976	Toronto Metros-Croatia
1970	Rochester Lancers	1977	Cosmos
1971	Dallas Tornado	1978	Cosmos
1972	New York Cosmos		

NASL Clubs No Longer Active

(active seasons in parentheses)

New York Generals (1967-68)	Los Angeles Wolves (1968)
Oakland Clippers (1967-68)	San Diego Toros (1968)
Toronto Falcons (1967-68)	Vancouver Royals (1968)
Baltimore Bays (1967-69)	Washington Whips (1968)
Boston Beacons (1968)	Kansas City Spurs (1968-70)
Chicago Mustangs (1968)	Olympique de Montreal (1971-73)
Cleveland Stokers (1968)	Atlanta Apollos (1973)
Detroit Cougars (1968)	Philadelphia Atoms (1973-76)
Houston Stars (1968)	Boston Minutemen (1974-76)

NASL Clubs: Name or Location Changes

(seasons active under given name in parentheses)

California Clippers (1967)—became Oakland Clippers during 1967 season
Chicago Spurs (1967)—relocated to Kansas City in 1968

Los Angeles Toros (1967)—relocated to San Diego in 1968

Washington Darts (1970-71)—relocated to Miami in 1972 as Miami Gatos

Miami Gatos (1972)—became Miami Toros in 1973

Toronto Metros (1971-74)—merged with Croatia in 1975 as Toronto Metros-Croatia

Baltimore Comets (1974-75)—relocated to San Diego in 1976 as San Diego Jaws

Denver Dynamos (1974-75)—relocated to Minneapolis-St. Paul in 1976 as Minnesota Kicks

San Diego Jaws (1976)—relocated to Las Vegas in 1977 as Las Vegas Quicksilver

Miami Toros (1973-76)—relocated to Ft. Lauderdale in 1977 as Ft. Lauderdale Strikers

San Antonio Thunder (1975-76)—relocated to Honolulu in 1977 as Team Hawaii

Hartford Bicentennials (1975-76)—relocated to New Haven in 1977 as Connecticut Bicenntennials

Toronto Metros-Croatia (1975-76)—became Toronto Metros in 1977

New York Cosmos (1971-76)—became Cosmos in 1977

St. Louis Stars (1967-77)—relocated to Anaheim (Orange Co.), California, in 1978 as California Surf

Connecticut Bicentennials (1976)—relocated to Oakland in 1978 as Oakland Stompers

Team Hawaii (1977)—relocated to Tulsa in 1978 as Tulsa Roughnecks

Las Vegas Quicksilver (1977)—relocated (back) to San Diego in 1978 as San Diego Sockers

Colorado Caribou (1978)—relocated to Atlanta in 1979 as Atlanta Chiefs

Oakland Stompers (1978)—relocated to Edmonton in 1979 as Edmonton Drillers

Toronto Metros (1977-78)—became Toronto Blizzard in 1979

Citizenship of NASL Players (1977)

United Kingdom	217	Poland	3
England	172	Ghana	2
Scotland	37	Jamaica	2
N. Ireland	4	Peru	2
Wales	4	Australia	1
United States	103	Austria	1
naturalized	57	Bolivia	1
Yugoslavia	33	Chile	1
Canada	23	Cyprus	1
Portugal	16	Guatemala	1
Mexico	15	Haiti	1
Germany FR	9	Hungary	1
South Africa	8	Israel	1
Brazil	7	Italy	1
Ireland Rep.	7	Netherlands	1
Trinidad	5	Sweden	1
Argentina	3	Turkey	1
Bermuda	3	Uruguay	1

Most Valuable Player (polling by *The Sporting News*)

1967   NPSL—Ruben Navarro (Philadelphia Spartans)

1968   John Kowalik (Chicago Mustangs)
1969   Cirilio Fernandez (Kansas City Spurs)
1970   Carlos Metidieri (Rochester Lancers)
1971   Carlos Metidieri (Rochester Lancers)
1972   Randy Horton (New York Cosmos)
1973   Warren Archibald (Miami Toros)
1974   Peter Silvester (Baltimore Comets)
1975   Steven David (Miami Toros)
1976   Pelé (New York Cosmos)
1977   Franz Beckenbauer (Cosmos)
1978   Mike Flanagan (New England Tea Men)

Leading Scorers

		Games	Goals	Assists	Points
1967	USA Roberto Boninsegna (Chi. Mustangs)	—	10	1	21
	NPSL Yanko Daucik (Tor. Falcons)	17	20	8	48
1968	John Kowalik (Chi. Mustangs)	28	30	9	69
1969	Kaiser Motaung (Atl. Chiefs)	15	16	4	36
1970	Kirk Apostolidis (Dal. Tornado)	19	16	3	35
	Carlos Metidieri (Roch. Lancers)	22	14	7	35
1971	Carlos Metidieri (Roch. Lancers)	24	19	8	46
1972	Randy Horton (N.Y. Cosmos)	13	9	4	22
1973	Kyle Rote, Jr. (Dallas Tornado)	18	10	10	30
1974	Paul Child (San Jose Earthquakes)	20	15	6	36
1975	Steven David (Miami Toros)	21	23	6	52
1976	Giorgio Chinaglia (N.Y. Cosmos)	19	19	11	49
1977	Steven David (L.A. Aztecs)	24	26	6	58
1978	Giorgio Chinaglia (Cosmos)	30	34	11	79

Rookie of the Year

1967   NPSL—Willie Roy (Chicago Spurs)
1968   Kaiser Motaung (Atlanta Chiefs)
1969   Siggy Stritzl (Baltimore Bays)
1970   Jim Leeker (St. Louis Stars)
1971   Randy Horton (New York Cosmos)
1972   Mike Winter (St. Louis Stars)
1973   Kyle Rote, Jr. (Dallas Tornado)
1974   Douglas MacMillan (Los Angeles Aztecs)
1975   Chris Bahr (Philadelphia Atoms)
1976   Steve Pecher (Dallas Tornado)
1977   Jim McAlister (Seattle Sounders)
1978   Gary Etherington (Cosmos)

Leading Goalkeepers

		Games-Min	Saves	Goals	Shut-outs	Avg
1967	NPSL Mirko Stojanovic (Oak. Clippers)	29	-	29	10	1.00
1968	Ataulfo Sanchez (San Diego Toros)	22	130	19	-	0.93
1969	Manfred Kammerer (Atl. Chiefs)	14	56	15	4	1.07
1970	Lincoln Phillips (Wash. Darts)	22	96	21	12	0.95
1971	Mirko Stojanovic (Dallas Tornado)	1359	91	11	8	0.79
1972	Ken Cooper (Dallas Tornado)	1260	107	12	6	0.86
1973	Bob Rigby (Phil. Atoms)	1157	78	8	6	0.62
1974	Barry Watling (Seattle Sounders)	1800	132	16	8	0.80
1975	Shep Messing (Boston Minutemen)	1639	140	17	6	0.93
1976	Tony Chursky (Seattle Sounders)	1981	135	20	9	0.91
1977	Ken Cooper (Dallas Tornado)	2100	120	21	8	0.90
1978	Phil Parkes (Vancouver)	2650	133	28	10	0.95

Major NASL Records (1967-78)

Highest winning percentage in a season: 80 percent, by Cosmos (1978) and Vancouver (1978).

Most games won in a season: 24, by Cosmos (1978) and Vancouver (1978).

Lowest winning percentage in a season: six percent, by Dallas (1968).

Fewest games won in a season: two, by Dallas (1968) and Baltimore (1969).

Most games lost in a season: 26, by Dallas (1968).

Most consecutive games won in a season: 13, by Vancouver (1978).

Largest margin of victory: 10, by Detroit vs. San Jose, 10-0 (12 July 1978).

Highest aggregate score in a single game: twelve, by Toronto vs. Chicago, 8-4 (27 August 1968).

Most goals in a game: 10, by Detroit vs. San Jose, 10-0 (12 July 1978).

Most goals in a season: 88, by Cosmos (1978).

Highest goal scoring average in a season: 3.3 goals/game, by Kansas City (1969).

Fewest goals in a season: 15, by Dallas (1972).

Lowest goal scoring average in a season: .88 goals/game, by Dallas (1968).

Most goals allowed in a season: 109, by Dallas (1968).

Highest goals allowed average in a season: 3.4 goals/game, by Dallas (1968).

Fewest goals allowed in a season: 14, by Philadelphia (1973).

Lowest goals allowed average in a season: .74 goals/game, by Philadelphia (1973).

Most individual goals in a season: 34, by Giorgio Chinaglia for Cosmos (1978).

Most individual goals in a game: five, by Steve David for Miami vs. Washington (20 June 1975), Giorgio Chinaglia for New York vs. Miami (10 August 1976), Ron Moore for Chicago vs. Vancouver (24 June 1977), Mike Flanagan for New England vs. California (9 July 1978), and Trevor Francis for Detroit vs. San Jose (12 July 1978).

Most individual total points in a season: 79, by Giorgio Chinaglia for Cosmos in 1978 (34 goals, 11 assists).

Most individual total points in a game: 12, by Giorgio Chinaglia for New York vs. Miami (10 August 1976).

Most individual assists in a season: 30, by Alan Hinton (Vancouver) in 1978.

Most individual assists in a game: four, by Miguel Perrichon for Toronto vs. Miami (6 May 1972), Roberto Aguirre for Miami vs. New York (14 June 1974), Vito Dimitrijevic for Cosmos vs. Toronto (5 June 1977), Vladislav Bogicevic for Cosmos vs. Ft. Lauderdale (2 Apr 1978), and Bob Bolitho for Vancouver vs. Dallas (12 July 1978).

Best goals against average in a season by a goalkeeper: .62, by Mirko Stojanovic for Dallas in 1971, and Bob Rigby for Philadelphia in 1973.

Fewest goals allowed in a season by a goalkeeper: eight, by Bob Rigby for Philadelphia in 1973.

Largest NASL attendance (also United States

record): 77,691 (Giants Stadium, Cosmos vs. Fort Lauderdale, 14 August 1977).

Largest regular season attendance: 71,219 (Giants Stadium, Cosmos vs. Seattle, 21 May 1978).

Largest attendance for a friendly: 75,641 (Giants Stadium, Cosmos vs. Santos F.C., 1 October 1977).

Largest total attendance for a season: 717,856 (Cosmos, 1978).

Largest attendance average for a season: 47,856 (Cosmos, 1978).

Largest total NASL attendance for a season (including play-offs): 5,351,499 (1978).

Largest NASL attendance average for a season (including play-offs): 14,640 (1977).

USA Standings (1967)

	P	W	D	L	F	A	P
Eastern Division							
Washington	12	5	5	2	19	11	15
Cleveland	12	5	4	3	19	13	14
Toronto	12	4	5	3	23	17	13
Detroit	12	3	6	3	11	18	12
New York	12	2	6	4	15	17	10
Boston	12	2	3	7	12	26	7
Western Division							
Los Angeles	12	5	5	2	21	14	15
San Francisco	12	5	3	4	25	19	13
Chicago	12	3	7	2	20	14	13
Houston	12	4	4	4	19	18	12
Vancouver	12	3	5	4	20	28	11
Dallas	12	3	6	3	14	23	9

Championship

Los Angeles—Washington   6-5
(after extra time)

NPSL Standings* (1967)

	P	W	D	L	F	A	P
Eastern Division							
Baltimore	32	14	9	9	53	47	161
Philadelphia	32	14	9	9	53	43	157
New York	32	11	8	13	60	58	143
Atlanta	31	10	9	12	51	46	135
Pittsburgh	31	10	7	14	59	73	132
Western Division							
Oakland	33	19	6	8	64	34	185
St. Louis	32	14	7	11	54	57	156
Chicago	32	10	11	11	50	55	142
Toronto	32	10	5	17	59	69	127
Los Angeles	32	7	10	15	42	61	114

*point procedure: win, six pts; draw, three pts; loss, zero pts; bonus points, one pt awarded for each goal scored.

Championship
Baltimore—Oakland   1-0, 1-4

NASL Standings and Play-off Results*

1968

EASTERN CONFERENCE

	W	L	D	Pts	Bonus Pts	F	A
Atlantic Division							
Atlanta	18	7	6	48	174	50	32
Washington	15	10	7	56	167	63	53
New York	12	8	12	36	164	62	54
Baltimore	13	16	3	41	128	42	43
Boston	9	17	6	49	121	51	69
Lakes Division							
Cleveland	14	7	11	58	175	62	44
Chicago	13	10	9	59	164	68	68
Toronto	13	13	6	48	144	55	69
Detroit	6	21	4	40	88	48	65

WESTERN CONFERENCE

	W	L	D	Pts	Bonus Pts	F	A
Gulf Division							
Kansas City	16	11	5	47	158	61	43
Houston	14	12	6	48	150	58	41
St. Louis	12	14	6	40	130	47	59
Dallas	2	26	4	28	52	28	109
Pacific Division							
San Diego	18	8	6	60	186	65	38
Oakland	18	8	6	59	185	71	38
Los Angeles	11	13	8	49	139	55	52
Vancouver	12	15	5	49	136	51	60

Play-offs
(Eastern Conference)
Cleveland—Atlanta   1-1, 1-2
(second leg after extra time)

(Western Conference)
Kansas City—San Diego   1-1, 0-1
second leg after extra time)

Championship
San Diego—Atlanta   0-0, 0-3

*note NASL custom of listing wins-losses-draws in that order; in play-off results, home team in first leg listed first.

1969

	P	W	L	D	F	A	Bonus Pts	Pts
Kansas City	16	10	2	4	53	28	38	110
Atlanta	16	11	2	3	46	20	34	109
Dallas	16	8	6	2	32	31	28	86
St. Louis	16	3	11	2	24	47	23	47
Baltimore	16	2	13	1	27	56	27	42

1970

	P	W	L	D	F	A	Bonus Pts	Pts
Northern Division								
Rochester	24	9	9	6	41	45	39	111
Kansas City	24	8	10	6	42	44	34	100
St. Louis	24	5	17	2	26	71	24	60
Southern Division								
Washington	24	14	6	4	52	29	41	137
Atlanta	24	11	8	5	53	33	42	123
Dallas	24	8	12	4	39	39	32	92

Championship
Rochester—Washington   3-0, 1-3

1971

	P	W	L	D	F	A	Bonus Pts	Pts
Northern Division								
Rochester	24	13	5	6	48	31	45	141
New York	24	9	10	5	51	55	48	117
Toronto	24	5	10	9	32	47	32	89
Montreal	24	4	15	5	29	58	26	65
Southern Division								
Atlanta	24	12	7	5	35	29	33	120
Dallas	24	10	6	8	38	24	35	119
Washington	24	8	6	10	36	34	33	111
St. Louis	24	6	13	5	37	47	35	86

Semi-Finals (best-of-three series)
Rochester—Dallas   2-1, 0-3, 1-2
(first & third legs after extra time; third leg in Rochester)

Atlanta—New York   1-0, 2-0
(first leg after extra time)

Championship (best-of-three series)
Atlanta—Dallas   2-1, 1-4, 0-2
(first leg after extra time; third leg in Atlanta)

1972

	P	W	L	D	F	A	Bonus Pts	Pts
Northern Division								
New York	14	7	3	4	28	16	23	77
Rochester	14	6	5	3	20	22	19	64
Montreal	14	4	5	5	19	20	18	57
Toronto	14	4	6	4	18	22	17	53
Southern Division								
St. Louis	14	7	4	3	20	14	18	69
Dallas	14	6	5	3	15	12	15	60
Atlanta	14	5	6	3	19	18	17	56
Miami	14	3	8	3	17	32	17	44

Semi-Finals (in St. Louis and New York)
St. Louis—Rochester   2-0
New York—Dallas   1-0

Championship (in New York)
New York—St. Louis   2-1

*1973

	P	W	L	D	F	A	Bonus Pts	Pts
Eastern Division								
Philadelphia	19	9	2	8	29	14	26	104
New York	19	7	5	7	31	23	28	91
Miami	19	8	5	6	26	21	22	88
Northern Division								
Toronto	19	6	4	9	32	18	26	89
Montreal	19	5	10	4	25	32	22	64
Rochester	19	4	9	6	17	27	17	59
Southern Division								
Dallas	19	11	4	4	36	25	33	111
St. Louis	19	7	7	5	27	27	25	82
Atlanta	19	3	9	7	23	40	23	62

(New York qualifies for semi-finals as "wild card" team)

*point procedure: win, six pts; draw, three pts; loss, zero pts; bonus points, one pt awarded for every
goal scored up to and including three per game.

Semi-Finals (in Dallas and Philadelphia)
Dallas—New York	1-0
Philadelphia—Toronto	3-0

Championship (in Dallas)
Dallas—Philadelphia	0-2

1974

	P	W	L	D-W*	F	A	Bonus Pts	Pts
Northern Division								
Boston	20	10	9	1	36	23	31	94
Toronto	20	9	10	1	30	31	30	87
Rochester	20	8	10	2	23	30	23	77
New York	20	4	14	2	28	40	28	58
Eastern Division								
Miami	20	9	5	6	38	24	35	107
Baltimore	20	10	8	2	42	46	39	105
Philadelphia	20	8	11	1	25	25	23	74
Washington	20	7	12	1	29	36	25	70
Central Division								
Dallas	20	9	8	3	39	27	37	100
St. Louis	20	4	15	1	27	42	27	54
Denver	20	5	15	0	21	42	19	49
Western Division								
Los Angeles	20	11	7	2	41	36	38	110
San Jose	20	9	8	3	43	38	40	103
Seattle	20	10	7	3	37	17	32	101
Vancouver	20	5	11	4	29	30	28	70

(Baltimore & San Jose qualify for quarter-finals as "wild card" teams)

Quarter-Finals
Dallas—San Jose	3-0
Boston—Baltimore	1-0

Semi-Finals
Los Angeles—Boston	2-0
Miami—Dallas	3-1

Championship (in Miami)
Miami—Los Angeles	3-3

(Los Angeles won on penalty kicks)

*point procedure: win, six pts; draw-win (win on penalty kicks after draw in extra time), three pts; loss, zero pts; bonus points, one pt awarded for every goal scored up to and including three per game.

*1975

	P	W	L	F	A	Bonus Pts	Pts
Northern Division							
Boston	22	13	9	41	29	38	116
Toronto	22	13	9	39	28	36	114
New York	22	10	12	39	38	31	91
Rochester	22	6	16	29	49	28	64
Hartford	22	6	16	27	51	25	61
Eastern Division							
Tampa Bay	22	16	6	46	27	39	135
Miami	22	14	8	47	30	39	123
Washington	22	12	10	42	47	40	112
Philadelphia	22	10	12	33	42	30	90
Baltimore	22	9	13	34	52	33	87
Central Division							
St. Louis	22	13	9	38	34	37	115
Chicago	22	12	10	39	33	34	106
Denver	22	9	13	37	42	31	85
Dallas	22	9	13	33	38	29	83
San Antonio	22	6	16	24	46	23	59
Western Division							
Portland	22	16	6	43	27	42	138
Seattle	22	15	7	42	28	39	129
Los Angeles	22	12	10	42	33	35	107
Vancouver	22	11	11	38	28	33	99
San Jose	22	8	14	37	48	35	83

Quarter-Finals

St. Louis—Los Angeles	2-1
Boston—Miami	1-2
(after extra time)	
Tampa Bay—Toronto	1-0
Portland—Seattle	2-1
(after extra time)	

Semi-Finals

Portland—St. Louis	1-0
Tampa Bay—Miami	3-0

Soccer Bowl '75 (in San Jose)

Tampa Bay—Portland	2-0

*point procedure: win, six pts; loss, zero pts; bonus points, one pt awarded for every goal scored up to and including three per game.

ATLANTIC CONFERENCE

*1976

	P	W	L	F	A	Bonus Pts	Pts
Northern Division							
Chicago	24	15	9	52	32	42	132
Toronto	24	15	9	38	30	33	123
Rochester	24	13	11	36	32	36	114
Hartford	24	12	12	37	56	35	107
Boston	24	7	17	35	64	32	74
Eastern Division							
Tampa Bay	24	18	6	58	30	46	154
New York	24	16	8	65	34	52	148
Washington	24	14	10	46	38	42	126
Philadelphia	24	8	16	32	49	32	80
Miami	24	6	18	29	58	27	63

PACIFIC CONFERENCE

	P	W	L	F	A	Bonus Pts	Pts
Western Division							
Minnesota	24	15	9	54	33	48	138
Seattle	24	14	10	40	31	39	123
Vancouver	24	14	10	38	30	36	120
Portland	24	9	16	23	40	23	71
St. Louis	24	5	19	28	57	28	58
Southern Division							
San Jose	24	14	10	47	30	39	123
Dallas	24	13	11	44	45	39	117
Los Angeles	24	12	12	43	44	36	108
San Antonio	24	12	12	38	32	35	107
San Diego	24	9	15	29	47	28	82

Play-offs—First Round
Toronto—Rochester	2-1
Dallas—Los Angeles	2-0
Seattle—Vancouver	1-0
New York—Washington	2-0

Division Championships
Minnesota—Seattle	3-0
San Jose—Dallas	2-0
Chicago—Toronto	2-3
Tampa Bay—New York	3-1

*point procedure: win, six pts; loss, zero pts; bonus points, one pt awarded for every goal scored up to and including three per game.

Conference Championships
Minnesota—San Jose   3-1
Tampa Bay—Toronto   0-2

Soccer Bowl '76 (in Seattle)
Toronto—Minnesota   3-0

*1977

ATLANTIC CONFERENCE

	P	W	L	F	A	Bonus Pts	Pts
Northern Division							
Toronto	26	13	13	42	38	37	115
St. Louis	26	12	14	33	35	32	104
Rochester	26	11	15	34	41	33	99
Chicago	26	10	16	31	43	28	88
Connecticut	26	7	19	34	65	30	72
Eastern Division							
Ft. Lauderdale	26	19	7	49	29	47	161
Cosmos	26	15	11	60	39	50	140
Tampa Bay	26	14	12	55	45	47	131
Washington	26	10	16	32	49	32	92

PACIFIC CONFERENCE

	P	W	L	F	A	Bonus Pts	Pts
Western Division							
Minnesota	26	16	10	44	36	41	137
Vancouver	26	14	12	43	46	40	124
Seattle	26	14	12	43	34	39	123
Portland	26	10	16	39	42	38	98
Southern Division							
Dallas	26	18	8	56	37	53	161
Los Angeles	26	15	11	65	54	57	147
San Jose	26	14	12	37	44	35	119
Hawaii	26	11	15	45	59	40	106
Las Vegas	26	11	15	38	44	37	103

*point procedure: win, six pts; loss, zero pts; bonus points, one pt awarded for every goal scored up to and including three per game.

PLAY-OFFS

First Round
Cosmos—Tampa Bay	3-0
St. Louis—Rochester	0-1
(won by "shoot out")	
Vancouver—Seattle	0-2
Los Angeles—San Jose	2-1
(after extra time)	

Division Championships
Cosmos—Ft. Lauderdale	8-3, 3-2
(second leg won by "shoot-out")	
Rochester—Toronto	1-0, 1-0
(first leg won by "shoot-out")	
Minnesota—Seattle	1-2, 0-1
(first leg after extra time)	
Los Angeles—Dallas	3-1, 5-1

Conference Championships
Rochester—Cosmos	1-2, 1-4
Los Angeles—Seattle	1-3, 0-1

Soccer Bowl '77 (in Portland)
Cosmos—Seattle	2-1

*1978

NATIONAL CONFERENCE

	P	W	L	F	A	Bonus Pts	Pts
Eastern Division							
Cosmos	30	24	6	88	39	68	212
Washington	30	16	14	55	47	49	145
Toronto	30	16	14	58	47	48	144
Rochester	30	14	16	47	52	47	131
Central Division							
Minnesota	30	17	13	58	43	54	156
Tulsa	30	15	15	49	46	42	132
Dallas	30	14	16	51	53	47	131
Colorado	30	8	22	34	66	33	81

*point procedure: win, six pts; loss, zero pts; bonus points, one pt awarded for every goal scored up to
and including three per game.

Western Division

Vancouver	30	24	6	68	29	55	199
Portland	30	20	10	50	36	47	167
Seattle	30	15	15	50	45	48	138
Los Angeles	30	9	21	36	69	34	88

AMERICAN CONFERENCE

Eastern Division

New England	30	19	11	62	39	51	165
Tampa Bay	30	18	12	63	48	57	165
Ft. Lauderdale	30	16	14	50	59	47	143
Philadelphia	30	12	18	40	58	39	111

Central Division

Detroit	30	20	10	68	36	56	176
Chicago	30	12	18	57	64	51	123
Memphis	30	10	20	43	58	41	101
Houston	30	10	20	37	61	36	96

Western Division

San Diego	30	18	12	63	56	56	164
California	30	13	17	43	49	37	115
Oakland	30	12	18	34	59	31	103
San Jose	30	8	22	36	81	35	83

PLAY-OFFS

First Round

San Diego—California	2-1
Tampa Bay—Chicago	3-1
Detroit—Philadelphia	1-0
Vancouver—Toronto	4-0
Cosmos—Seattle	5-2
Portland—Washington	2-1
(after extra time)	
New England—Ft. Lauderdale	1-3
Minnesota—Tulsa	3-1

Conference Semi-Finals

Portland—Vancouver	1-0, 2-1
Ft. Lauderdale—Detroit	4-3, 0-1, 1-0
(1st leg won by "shoot-out"; 3rd leg after extra time)	
San Diego—Tampa Bay	0-1, 2-1, 0-1
(3rd leg won after extra time)	
Minnesota—Cosmos	9-2, 0-4, 0-1
(3rd leg won by "shoot-out")	

Conference Finals
Portland—Cosmos   0-1, 0-5
Ft. Lauderdale—Tampa Bay   3-2, 1-3, 0-1
(3rd leg won by "shoot-out")

Soccer Bowl '78 (in East Rutherford)
Cosmos—Tampa Bay   3-1

Northern Ireland   See: Ireland, Northern

North Yemen   See: Yemen, Arab Republic

Norway

Norges Fotballforbund   Founded: 1902
Ullevål Stadion, Sognsvn. 75,   FIFA: 1908
Postboks 42, Täsen,   UEFA: 1954
Oslo 8

Affiliated clubs: *2,850;* **registered players:** *84,000;* **national stadium:** *Ullevål Stadion, Oslo (24,500);* **largest stadium:** *Lerkendal Stadion, Trondheim (30,000);* **colors:** *red jerseys, white shorts;* **season:** *April to November;* **honors:** *Olympic Games third place (1936), Scandinavian Championship (1932).*

Though Norway has made less of an impact on international soccer than either Sweden or Denmark, it is to be commended for providing an organizational model for thinly populated countries with geographical obstacles. In a nation that is buried under ice and snow, bounded by the world's rockiest coastline, and measuring in length the distance from London to Belgrade, the Norwegian F.A. has successfully included all parts of the country in a sophisticated network of leagues and cup competitions. *Fotball* is the major summertime sport in Norway, as it is in the rest of Scandinavia, and Norwegians are second to none in their love for the game. Indeed, when their own leagues and cup are dormant for the winter, thousands of fans follow the English and Scottish game with equal interest.

Soccer was introduced in Norway by students in Oslo during the 1880s, and it caught on rapidly, especially in the coastal cities between Oslo and Bergen. The oldest of Norway's leading clubs is Odds BK, founded in Skien in 1894, but other important clubs were formed before or around the turn of the century in Oslo, Sarpsborg, Arendal, Larvik, Horten, Drammen, Fredrikstad, Stavanger, and Bergen. The Norges Fotballforbund (NFF) was founded in 1902, and in its first year launched the Norgesmesterskapet (Norwegian Cup) that in many respects is still the most important competition in the country. In 1908, three years after Norway's independence from Sweden, the NFF became one of the early members of FIFA.

The Norweigian Cup was initially won by the Arendal club IK Grane, which was founded only weeks before the competition started. But the first decade was dominated in the main by Odds Skien, victorious four times and the losing finalist four times during the first nine years. The first Oslo club to win the title was Mercantile Ski og F.K. (Mercantile Ski and Football Club) in 1907. Two other big Oslo clubs, Lyn Ski og F.K. and Frigg, helped to keep the cup in Oslo for much of the pre-World War I era. The capital's domination of the cup, however, was temporary, and it was not until the post-World War II period that it once again found a leadership role. Between the wars, the leading clubs of Norway's smaller coastal cities were dominant, and FK Örn Horten, SK Brann Bergen, Sarpsborg FK, Mjöndalen IF, and Fredrikstad FK rose in stature. Brann and Fredrikstad stayed near the top of Norwegian soccer until at least the 1970s.

Norway's first full internationals were played against Sweden between 1908 and 1912, and it lost all four games by an aggregate of 5-21. Most of the national team members at this time were from Lyn and Mercantile. The first non-Scandinavian opponent was Hungary, which stopped off in Oslo before the start of the 1912 Olympic Games in Stockholm and defeated the home team by 6-0. At Stockholm, the Norwegians were eliminated decisively by Denmark, and lost 1-0 in an unofficial consolation match with Austria. Between 1912-18, Norway became very active and played in 20 full internationals—without a win—including 1-1 draws against Czarist Russia and the USA in Oslo. Its first international victories finally occurred in 1918, back-to-back against Denmark and Sweden in Oslo. By the early 1920s, Norway was losing only half its matches. Its first significant win came in 1923, a 2-0 shutout of France in Paris, but most of Norway's victories in the 1920s were at the hands of lowly Finland, which has remained over the decades its most consistently inferior opponent. Since they first played Norway in 1921, the Finns have accounted for more than one-third of Norway's international victories.

In 1924, the quadrennial Scandinavian Championship (Nordic Cup) was introduced by Norway, Sweden, Denmark, and Finland, and for the next 40 years much of Norway's international exposure was through this competition. In 1929-32, it won the cup for the first and only time, marking the beginning of a decade that was to be Norway's most successful. Numerous wins over its Scandinavian opponents were highlighted in 1930 and 1931 by two draws with Germany and victories over Holland and Switzerland. Norway proved to be a nemesis for Germany throughout the 1930s. It drew again with Germany in 1933 and 1935, and at the 1936 Olympic Games in Berlin achieved the biggest upset in its history by knocking Germany out of the competition before a huge crowd that included Hitler himself; the score was 2-0. In the semifinals at Berlin, it lost as expected to Italy, but not until it had taken the Italian amateurs into overtime. A few days later Norway defeated Poland to win a much deserved bronze medal and its greatest honor to date.

The following year, Norway attempted to qualify for the World Cup for the first time, eliminating the Republic of Ireland in the process, and at the games in France in 1938 met the full Italian international team and forced the world champions to an identical overtime result (a 2-1 loss) that had shocked the Italian amateurs in 1936. Though eliminated in the first round, the Norwegians went home heroes once again. During the Nazi occupation, in a particularly evil act of revenge, coach Halvorsen of the 1936 Olympic team was tortured to death by the Gestapo for refusing to allow the national team to play under German sponsorship. Halvorsen had played organized soccer in Hamburg as a student.

In the postwar years, Norway resumed its former rate of success, which included irregular wins over Denmark and Sweden, frequent wins over Finland, and poor results against leading teams on the continent. The late 1940s were punctuated by a 12-0 thrashing of Finland in 1946, and an equally decisive 11-0 shutout of the USA at Oslo in 1948. From 1952, Norway began to participate regularly in World Cup and Olympic qualification tournaments, but to date it has yet to qualify for any final rounds. Norway has also been a consistent participant in the European Football Championship, but in five editions it has managed only to win two games (against Sweden and Northern Ireland).

Domestic competition grew considerably more complex in 1938 when the NFF introduced a national league to run concurrently with the cup, but even the new league did not abandon certain elements of the cup format until 1961. The league is now divided into three divisions. The first division of 12 clubs is national in scope, though, in fact, clubs north of Trondheim have rarely gained entry to it, while the second division is made up of three regional sections (two in the south and one in the north), and the third division is composed of six regional sections. There are also fourth, fifth, sixth and seventh divisions. Fredrikstad and Vikings Stavanger have won first division titles more than any other club. Larvik Turn won a series of championships in the 1950s, and Rosenborg Trondheim emerged as an important club in the 1960s. In cup competition, Bodö-Glimt became the first club from the north to win a major title in 1975. Norwegian clubs have been active participants in the European Cup and European Cup Winners' Cup since the early 1960s, and the Fairs/UEFA cup since 1966-67. Norwegian participants in the Champions' Cup have not advanced beyond the first round. In the Cup Winners' Cup, Rosenborg and Brann have both gained that distinction once, and in 1968-69 Lyn moved to the quarter-finals where it was narrowly eliminated by Barcelona. Rosenborg and Vikings have seen second round play in the UEFA Cup.

Champions

1938 Fredrikstad	1952 Fredrikstad	1966 Skeid Oslo
1939 Fredrikstad	1953 Larvik TIF	1967 Rosenborg Trondheim
1940 no competition	1954 Fredrikstad	1968 Lyn Oslo
1941 no competition	1955 Larvik TIF	1969 Rosenborg Trondheim
1942 no competition	1956 Larvik TIF	1970 Strömsgodset Drammen
1943 no competition	1957 Fredrikstad	1971 Rosenborg Trondheim
1944 no competition	1958 Vikings Stavanger	1972 Vikings Stavanger
1945 no competition	1959 Lilleström	1973 Vikings Stavanger
1946 no competition	1960 Fredrikstad	1974 Vikings Stavanger
1947 no competition	1961 Fredrikstad	1975 Vikings Stavanger
1948 SK Freidig	1962 Brann Bergen	1976 Lillestrom
1949 Fredrikstad	1963 Brann Bergen	1977 Lillestrom
1950 IF Fram	1964 Lyn Oslo	1978 Start Kristiansand
1951 Fredrikstad	1965 Valerengens Oslo	

Cup Winners

1902 Grane Arendal	1922 Odds Skien	1942 no competition
1903 Odds Skien	1923 Brann Bergen	1943 no competition
1904 Odds Skien	1924 Odds Skien	1944 no competition
1905 Odds Skien	1925 Brann Bergen	1945 Lyn Oslo
1906 Odds Skien	1926 Odds Skien	1946 Lyn Oslo
1907 Mercantile Oslo	1927 Örn Horten	1947 Skeid Oslo
1908 Lyn Oslo	1928 Örn Horten	1948 Sarpsborg
1909 Lyn Oslo	1929 Sarpsborg	1949 Sarpsborg
1910 Lyn Oslo	1930 Örn Horten	1950 Fredrikstad
1911 Lyn Oslo	1931 Odds Skien	1951 Sarpsborg
1912 Mercantile Oslo	1932 Fredrikstad	1952 Sparta Sarpsborg
1913 Lyn Skien	1933 Mjöndalen IF	1953 Vikings Stavanger
1914 Frigg Oslo	1934 Mjöndalen IF	1954 Skeid Oslo
1915 Odds Skien	1935 Fredrikstad	1955 Skeid Oslo
1916 Frigg Oslo	1936 Fredrikstad	1956 Skeid Oslo
1917 Sarpsborg	1937 Mjöndalen IF	1957 Fredrikstad
1918 Kvik Halden	1938 Fredrikstad	1958 Skeid Oslo
1919 Odds Skien	1939 Sarpsborg	1959 Vikings Stavanger
1920 Örn Horten	1940 Fredrikstad	1960 Rosenborg Trondheim
1921 Frigg Oslo	1941 no competition	1961 Fredrikstad

1962	Gjövik-Lyn	1968	Lyn Oslo	1974	Skeid Oslo
1963	Skeid Oslo	1969	Strömsgodset Drammen	1975	Bodö-Glimt
1964	Rosenborg Trondheim	1970	Strömsgodset Drammen	1976	Brann Bergen
1965	Skeid Oslo	1971	Rosenborg Trondheim	1977	Lilleström
1966	Fredrikstad	1972	Brann Bergen	1978	Lilleström
1967	Lyn Oslo	1973	Strömsgodset Drammen		

numbered players

Numbered players were introduced in the English F.A. Cup Final of 1933 and made compulsory by The Football League in 1939. The 1939 numbering system, based on the 2-3-5 formation, became tradional world-wide, though recently it has fallen out of use. It is as follows:

1. Goalkeeper	5. Center Halfback	9. Center Forward
2. Right Back	6. Left Halfback	10. Inside Left
3. Left Back	7. Outside Right	11. Outside Left
4. Right Halfback	8. Inside Right	

Nürnberg, 1. Fussball-Club

Location: *Nuremberg, West Germany;* **stadium:** *Städtisches Stadion, Nuremburg (60,000);* **colors:** *red jerseys with white trim, black shorts;* **honors:** *German champion (1920, 1921, 1924, 1925, 1927, 1936, 1948, 1961, 1968), German cup (1935, 1939, 1962)*

Founded 1900. The greatest club name in German soccer, FC Nürnberg is known throughout the country as "der Club." It has won the Deutscher Meisterschaft a record nine times, and despite its drop into the second division in the late 1960s, the club retains nationwide popularity second to none.

Nürnberg's greatest period of success occurred during the 1920s, when it won five national championships without conceding a single goal in any of the finals. In 1922 it narrowly missed out on a sixth after battling to three drawn matches with Hamburger SV and the trophy was withheld. Nürnberg's intelligent and low-key style became so influential that clubs throughout Germany and Central Europe used it as a model (In 1925, the entire German national team was composed of Nürnberg players.) It was finally coopted during the 1930s by Schalke's adoption of Arsenal's revolutonary W-M formation, but FCN still managed to win another championship in 1936, advancing to the final in 1934 and 1937, and winning the first German cup competition in 1935 and the fifth in 1939. In 1940, it advanced to the final of the cup, but dropped an overtime thriller to Dresdner SC. For 20 years, FC Nürnberg was the touchstone by which the German game was measured.

Nürnberg reached the summit again in the early 1960s, just before the formation of the national league, winning the championship in 1961 and the cup half of a double in 1962. Meanwhile, it won the South German championship 13 times, and in 1968, under Austrian manager Max Merkl, it grabbed a Bundesliga title after hovering near the middle of the table during the first four years of the new national league. A startling collapse the following season ended in relegation to the southern section of the second division. Some highly touted managers during the early 1970s—Zlatko Cajkovski and Hans Tilkowski—failed to return the club to its natural place among the nation's elite, and in 1975-76 it missed promotion by one place in the standings. Manager Horst Buhtz finally guided FCN back to the first division in 1978.

obstruction

An infringement in which a player intentionally places his body between an opponent and the ball or otherwise impedes an opponent's movement. The opposing team is awarded an indirect free kick. Goalkeepers are exempt from the obstruction rule in most situations. Although a similar rule was included in the Harrow Rules (1830s), it was not incorporated into the Laws of 1863. By the end of the nineteenth century, however, it was widely accepted. In Latin America, it was not entirely respected until more frequent international exposure during the 1950s resulted in uniform adherence to the FIFA law.

Oceania Cup

Although the Oceania Football Confederation (OFC) was founded as early as 1966, many obstacles stood in the way of introducing a regional tournament for national teams. The question of who should participate was the first problem, since membership in the OFC was sparse from the beginning, and many potential members were still affiliated with England or France, thus precluding their separate membership in the OFC. The second major problem concerned the large sums of money involved in long distance travel. The distance between Tahiti and Australia, or Papua-New Guinea, for example, is 4,000 miles; New Zealand and Papua-New Guinea are 2,500 miles apart; even Fiji and New Caledonia are separated by 900 miles of ocean. The third factor was the "Australia question." Australia, which had always fielded the strongest and most attractive teams in the OFC, was reluctantly participating in OFC affairs to begin with. It wanted, understandably, to be linked with stronger competition in the Asian Football Confederation, but OFC organizers predicted that without Australia it would be impossible to stage a financially successful tournament.

Finally, in 1971 the first Oceania Cup for regional national teams was scheduled at Nouméa, capital of New Caledonia, a relatively central location. At the last moment, however, Australia pulled out when its air fares could not be guaranteed. The Ligue Calédonienne cancelled its sponsorship, fearing financial disaster, and the competition was called off. Shortly thereafter, Australia withdrew from the OFC. In 1973, New Zealand offered to host the first Oceania Cup with or without Australia, and the first edition of the new tournament was played over the course of one week at Newmarket Park, Auckland. With only five teams participating, there was no need for a qualification round. Since 1973, the OFC has fallen into further disarray, and the future of the cup has been left in doubt. A second tournament was tentatively scheduled for 1977 in Fiji.

Winner

1973   New Zealand

Results

1973
(in Auckland)

Tahiti—New Caledonia	2-1	New Hebrides—Tahiti	0-1
New Zealand—Fiji	5-1	New Hebrides—Fiji	2-1
New Hebrides—New Caledonia	1-4	New Zealand—New Caledonia	2-1
Tahiti—New Zealand	1-1	Fiji—Tahiti	0-4
Fiji—New Caledonia	0-2	New Zealand—New Hebrides	3-1

	P	W	D	L	F	A	P
New Zealand	4	3	1	0	11	4	7
Tahiti	4	3	1	0	8	2	7
New Caledonia	4	2	0	2	8	5	4
New Hebrides	4	1	0	3	4	9	2
Fiji	4	0	0	4	2	13	0

Third Place Match
New Caledonia—New Hebrides   2-1

Play-off for First Place
New Zealand—Tahiti   2-0

Oceania Football Confederation (OFC)

Address: *89 Apirana Avenue, P.O. Box 18029, Glen Innes, Auckland, New Zealand;* **Members:** *Fiji, New Zealand, Papua-New Guinea;* **Affiliated clubs:** *650;* **registered players:** *31,185.*

Founded in 1965 when FIFA sanctioned a regional governing body for the Pacific. Australia was the prime instigator of the OFC with New Zealand a strong supporter, but Fiji and Papua-New Guinea were also involved from the beginning. The stability of the OFC has been rocked repeatedly over the years by the changing role of Australia in the organization. With 1100 affiliated clubs and 165,000 registered players, the Australian Soccer Federation was the necessary ingredient for a solvent regional governing body, but Australia soon became frustrated with its Oceania affiliation as it sought to increase its position in international competition. In 1973, it pulled out of the OFC to seek greener pastures in Asia, and put the very existence of the organization in jeopardy. The matter was further complicated by the expulsion of China National from the Asian Football Confederation in 1975, and various plans to instate the Chinese in the OFC were advanced; one of the proposals was linked to the Israeli question in Asia. Meanwhile, Australia was left dangling without any regional affiliation.

New Caledonia and French Polynesia, which are affiliated with the Fédération Française de Football, became provisional members of the OFC in 1971. New Hebrides has also been actively involved in OFC matters. Despite its setbacks, the OFC has administered the soccer competition of the South Pacific Games, the First Oceania Youth Tournament in 1974 (held in Pepeete), and the long-delayed Oceania Cup.

Ocwirk, Ernst   (1926-　)

The last and perhaps greatest of the old-fashioned attacking center halfbacks, who was both the inspiration and backbone of Austria's superb national team during the early 1950s. His classic midfield role was played flawlessly as he guided his team, whether Austria or his club, through their deliberate motions. He passed the ball impeccably and possessed excellent ball control skills, especially for a man of his height (over six feet). He was picked as captain of FIFA World XIs twice during his career, a distinct honor, and he led Austria to many great victories up to and including the 1954 World Cup. By this time, however, Austria's outmoded short passing game was discarded and he switched to an orthodox wing half. While the tactical machinery no longer revolved around him as the hub, his commanding presence naturally preserved his long standing-function as the team dynamo.

His career started with Stadlau and Floridsdorfer AC during World War II, but in 1947 he moved to the venerable FK Austria, where he remained for nine years and established his reputation. He also made his international debut in 1947, and in 62 international appearances he managed to score six goals. In 1956, by now a deep-lying inside forward, he was released to play as a professional at Sampdoria in Genoa, where he remained until 1961. He returned to play for FK Austria for one year, and went back to Sampdoria as manager in 1962. Three years later, he accepted the managership of FK Austria, and remained in that post for five years during which time his old club won two league titles and an Austrian Cup. This was followed by managerial stints with FC Köln in West Germany and Admira/Energie in Vienna.

Ocwirk was quite possibly the most perfectly blended halfback-orchestrator the game has ever known. Perhaps there was an advantage in his playing this role as late as he did, because he seemed to be an ideal composite of all that was best about it.

offside

The offside rule, which on the surface appears to be elusive and confusing, is actually based on a simple concept: it is unfair for an attacking player to gain an undue advantage over his defenders. If this precept is kept in mind, the details of the law follow logically and in good order.

The rule is basically designed for offside infringements that result from a forward pass—by far the most common situation in which the foul is committed. The Laws of the Game stipulate that a player is "offside," that is, "out of play," if he is nearer his opponent's goal line than the ball *at the moment the ball is played to him*, unless any of the following apply: 1) he is in his own half of the field, or, in the North American Soccer League, behind his opponent's "35-yard line"; 2) there are *two* of his opponents nearer their own goal line than he is; 3) the ball was last touched by an opponent or by him; or, 4) he receives the ball direct from a goal kick, corner kick, throw-in, or drop ball. A player who is not in an offside position when the pass is initiated but moves forward into what appears to be an offside position to receive the ball (i.e., advances during the flight of the ball) is *not* offside. In further applying the concept of "unfair advantage," however, the Laws add that a player may be judged offside if he is merely located in an offside position, and, though not actually receiving the ball, is interfering with the play or with an an opponent, or affects the play by advancing toward the ball or an opponent. This sort of offside infringement is less specific and is rarely called.

An offside infringement is penalized by the awarding of an indirect free kick to the opposing team from the spot where the infringement took place.

The roots of the offside law are found in the various football games of the English public schools in the late eighteenth and early nineteenth centuries. By the time Harrow's rules were written during the 1810s or '20s, the offside rule had been given the shape it was to keep until 1866. The Harrow rule stipulated that to receive the ball from any forward pass whatsoever was unlawful. A Harrow player was offside simply by being "nearer the line of the opponent's base [goal line] than the kicker"—an unfair advantage. This stringent regulation, which bears a closer resemblance to rugby than soccer, meant that for many decades the only way to advance the ball up the field (in games using a round ball) was to dribble. Thus a vertical or diagonal line of players, rather than a horizontal forward line as in modern soccer, became the chief tactical formation of the era, and the ball was passed backwards along the line from dribbler to dribbler, like a pass in rugby or lateral in American football.

The earliest break with the original offside concept as laid down at Harrow was made in the Cambridge University Rules of 1848, the first rules to resemble modern soccer, which permitted a player to receive a forward pass if *more than three* opponents were between him and the goal line. Cambridge players were still reminded not to "loiter between the ball and the adversaries' goal." This progressive change was not adopted in the Sheffield Rules of 1857, the second important set of rules that anticipated modern soccer, nor in The Football Association Laws of the Game in

1863, soccer's first official code. Accordingly, the "dribbling (vertical) game" continued to prosper until well into the 1860s.

In 1866, however, The Football Association in London adopted a three-opponent offside rule, in which *at least three* opponents were required between a player and his opponent's goal line. Adjustment to the revolutionary three-opponent concept was not fully realized until the mid-1870s, when the golden era of sophisticated dribbling finally gave way to the "passing game," as promoted by Queen's Park Glasgow and other Scottish teams. In 1873, the Laws first spelled out that the offside rule applied only at "the moment of kicking" (i.e., the moment the ball is played). Goal kicks, meanwhile, had been exempted from the offside rule from the beginning. The clause specifying "last played by an opponent" was added in 1880. Corner kicks were exempted in 1881-82. Offside was limited to the op-

ponent's half of the field in 1907, and throw-ins were exempted in 1921.

Despite these alterations, the three-opponent rule remained basically unchanged until 1925, a watershed year in which the International Football Association Board accepted a proposal of the Scottish Football Association that reduced the required number of opponents to two. The 1925 rule is still in force, except that it was remodeled with the rest of the Laws in 1938. But the change in one word—from "three" to "two"—was so far-reaching that it brought about a second tactical revolution, beginning with the introduction of Arsenal's famous W-M system. All tactical innovations since 1925 have revolved around the two-opponent offside rule. Indeed, the whole history of the game would have been vastly different if the concept of offside were not at its core.

See also: **tactics, offside trap, thirty-five yard line.**

offside trap

A defensive tactic, in which a defender purposely moves forward to put an attacking player offside.

Although the offside trap is still seen on occasion, the offside rule change of 1925 nearly spelled its doom. During the 60-year period from 1866-1925 when the three-opponent offside rule was in effect, its use in England had gradually increased to a point where it had become a menace to the game. In the years immediately before and after World War I, an alarming number of offside infringements were called, which caused the delay of countless games and much protest from the press and public. The "no-back

game," a tactic in which fullbacks moved forward to blend with halfbacks, was at its height. Newcastle United F.C., and in particular its skillful fullback Billy McCracken, was the first important club to exploit the trap as a matter of strategy, and other clubs soon followed. By 1925, its unpopularity became so acute that the International Football Association Board, the body responsible for changes in the Laws of the Game, was compelled to adopt the two-opponent offside rule. Although the change forced radical innovations in team tactics, the heyday of the offside trap was effectively put to an end. Today it remains a ploy that is regarded with some derision.

off the ball

Not having possession of the ball.

"Running off the ball" is attempting to play usefully while not in possession, or, to move into an advantageous position on the field while not in possession; for example, to receive a pass.

Olympic Games, Association Football Tournament of the

In a sport so dominated by professionalism, Olympic soccer competition has lost most of its worldwide significance. Since World War II, it has served primarily as a showcase for the "non-professional" state sponsored teams of Eastern Europe, which have swept gold medals consecutively since 1952, and it has offered a chance for the world's remaining amateur countries of Scandinavia, Africa, and Asia to gain a measure of world prestige. Not since 1928, however, when Uruguay's extraordinary Olympic team was regarded by many as the world's best in any category, have the leading soccer nations of Europe and South America taken Olympic competition seriously.

In the early years, Olympic soccer tournaments were the preeminent events on the international schedule. At the first games in Athens in 1896, a Danish representative team played an unofficial exhibition match against a Greek team and won by an unknown score; all details of this contest have been lost. In 1900 at Paris, three countries entered unofficial teams in another exhibition tournament, and Great Britain, represented by Upton Park F.C., defeated a French representative team sponsored by the Union des Sociétés Françaises des Sports Athlétiques (the score was 4-0). France then defeated a Belgian team, 6-2, but no medals were awarded.

At the third games in St. Louis in 1904, five teams from the United States and Canada were scheduled to hold an unofficial tournament, but only three actually played. Ontario's Galt F.C., representing Canada, was declared the winner after defeating Christian Brothers College of St. Louis (USA I) by 7-0, and St. Rose of St. Louis (USA II) by 4-0. Christian Brothers subsequently defeated St. Rose, 2-0, after two goalless draws to complete the exhibition. There was also an exhibition series played at the Intermediate Olympics at Athens in 1906, in which Denmark defeated teams from Izmir (5-2) and Athens (9-0). Izmir and Athens also played a Salonika team, winning by 3-0 and 5-0, respectively.

The first official soccer tournament of the Olympic Games was held in 1908 at London. Despite the professional status of most high-calibre British players, Great Britain won its first of two successive gold medals, and Denmark, which had received the benefits of British coaching earlier than most countries in Europe, won its first of two successive silver medals. According to Olympic regulations, the British countries, which had already or were about to acquire four separate memberships in FIFA, were required to put one representative British team on the field. Since England was the only British country that had joined FIFA before the Olympic Games of 1908, the winning team at Shepherd's Bush, London, has often been referred to as "England." France, meanwhile, conscious of its role as a leader in organized international soccer, eased scheduling problems at the London games by sending two representative teams, France A and France B; after the latter was defeated 9-0 by Denmark in the first round, the former lost to Denmark in the semi-finals by 17-1, which remains to this day a world co-record for a full international.

A second British-Danish double was completed in 1912 at Stockholm, resulting in some very interesting scores that revealed the relative growth of soccer in participating countries. Aside from the official tournament, an unofficial consolation tournament of six matches was played and won by Hungary. The results were as follows: Germany-Czarist Russia, 16-0; Hungary-Germany, 3-1; Hungary-Austria, 3-0; Austria-Norway, 1-0; Austria-Italy, 5-1; Italy-Sweden, 1-0. Germany's trouncing of Russia equaled the international scoring record set four years earlier by Denmark. The number of participating countries increased modestly from six to 11 in 1912, but France and Belgium withdrew before the games got under way.

The 1920 games at Antwerp were marred by a violent final, in which Czechoslovakia, playing in its very first international competition, walked off the field after a disputed goal, and gave up its chance for a gold medal to Belgium, its opponent and host country. Fourteen nations were entered, and for the first time a non-European state—Egypt, a British protectorate—participated. Czechoslovakia's forfeit necessitated an awkward play-off for a second and third place game, in which the Netherlands once again figured prominently and Spain introduced its flashy style to European soccer for the first time. Egypt and Yugoslavia forfeited their places in the play-off. Great Britain, showing its increasing hostility to alleged professionalism in the tournament, bowed out to lowly Norway in the first round.

In 1924 at Paris, the competition took on a genuinely international flavor: Egypt returned; the USA entered for the first of 11 consecutive attempts; Estonia, Latvia, and Lithuania asserted their fledgling independence by entering separate national teams, as did the Irish Free State; and, Turkey brought Asians into the foray for the first time. The major development, however, was the presence of distant Uruguay, whose players dazzled European crowds with their quickness and agility. Great Britain refused to participate over the issue of compensatory expenses that were paid to players by some national associations. When FIFA ignored the British protest and urged the authorization of such "broken time" payments to the International Olympic Committee (IOC), the IOC accepted, and the British pulled out of FIFA. In the 1924 final, Uruguay delighted its new Parisian audiences by defeating Switzerland with an overwhelming display of ball control and goal scoring intuition. The gold medal left Europe for the first time, and Uruguay entered the next Olympic tournament as the sound favorite.

At Amsterdam in 1928, Argentina, Chile, and Mexico expanded Western Hemisphere participation, and for the first and only time in Olympic history, the final was an all-South American affair. Egypt advanced all the way to the semi-finals after defeating Turkey and Portugal, and the USA received a prophetic drubbing from Argentina (11-2). Uruguay's confrontation with Argentina in the final was one of the most heralded soccer events in many years, such was Argentina's fine reputation as the equal of its gifted neighbors across the Rio de la Plata. The game ended in a draw, and the replay, which Uruguay won, was icing on the cake for European spectators. By now it was apparent that certain South American countries had arrived in the upper ranks of the world game. In the space of two Olympiads, Uruguay had beaten Germany, Italy, France, Yugoslavia, Switzerland, and the Netherlands (twice), all on European soil, and this record, in addition to the key issue of professionalism, was an important factor in the introduction of the World Cup in 1930.

The new World Cup (open to professional as well as amateur players), the complete absence of a soccer tournament in the 1932 games at Los Angeles, and the oppressive conditions of the 1936 games in Berlin combined to weaken forever the prestige of Olympic soccer. Only 16 countries entered the Berlin tournament—won by Italy—including Great Britain, Axis power Japan, China, Peru, and Egypt. There was seldom much gaiety during the competition, and the low point was achieved by Peru, whose small but vocal following rioted during the second overtime period against Austria, causing two quick Peruvian goals in the mayhem. Austria protested, and a replay was ordered by the IOC. Peru failed to show up for the replay, and Austria advanced to the next round and eventually the final.

When the Olympic Games reemerged in 1948, the soccer tournament took on a different appearance. South America and Europe had become almost entirely professional, and Eastern Europe laid claim to the concept of "amateur" state sponsored players. When the world soccer powers of Western Europe and South America were not able to put their top players on the Olympic field, the era of Russian, Hungarian, Yugoslav, Czech, East German, Polish, and Bulgarian domination began, though Yugoslavia later turned professional. Great Britain made its last Olympic hurrah in 1948 with a fourth place finish; Sweden actually won the tournament in 1948 with its world famous forward line; and Denmark placed third in 1948 and second in 1960. There were occasional breakthroughs by India (1956), Egypt (1964), and Japan (1974); but of the 25 medals awarded between 1948-76, 19 went to Eastern European countries, while Sweden and Denmark, legitimate bastions of amateur soccer, won two medals each.

Yet, participation has increased dramatically during the postwar era. Qualification rounds were introduced in 1952 when 25 countries sought a place in the final rounds. There were 27 entrants in 1956, 52 in 1960, 59 in 1964, 64 in 1968, 80 in 1972, and 91 in 1976. Nevertheless, many observers argue that soccer no longer has a place in Olympic competition in its present form, and some have urged its deletion from the schedule altogether. Others, such as FIFA President João Havelange, have suggested it be limited to Under-23 national teams. The FIFA Amateur Committee, which is primarily responsible for setting Olympic soccer regulations, and the IOC will one day be forced to confront this volatile issue. Meanwhile, it continues to be a primary source of box office revenue for smaller countries and host nations.

Medal Winners

	Gold	Silver	Bronze
1908	Great Britain	Denmark	Netherlands
1912	Great Britain	Denmark	Netherlands
1920	Belgium	Spain	Netherlands
1924	Uruguay	Switzerland	Sweden
1928	Uruguay	Argentina	Italy
1936	Italy	Austria	Norway
1948	Sweden	Yugoslavia	Denmark
1952	Hungary	Yugoslavia	Sweden
1956	USSR	Yugoslavia	Bulgaria
1960	Yugoslavia	Denmark	Italy
1964	Hungary	Czechoslovakia	German DR
1968	Hungary	Bulgaria	Japan
1972	Poland	Hungary	USSR, German DR
1976	German DR	Poland	USSR

Classification of Medals (1908-76)

		Gold	Silver	Bronze	Total
1.	Hungary	3	1	0	4
2.	Great Britain	2	0	0	2
3.	Uruguay	2	0	0	2
4.	Yugoslavia	1	3	0	4
5.	Sweden	1	0	2	3
6.	USSR	1	0	2	3
7.	Poland	1	1	0	2
8.	Germany DR	1	0	2	3
9.	Italy	1	0	2	3
10.	Belgium	1	0	0	1
11.	Denmark	0	3	1	4
12.	Bulgaria	0	1	1	2
13.	Spain	0	1	0	1
14.	Switzerland	0	1	0	1
15.	Argentina	0	1	0	1
16.	Austria	0	1	0	1
17.	Czechoslovakia	0	1	0	1
18.	Netherlands	0	0	3	3
19.	Norway	0	0	1	1
20.	Japan	0	0	1	1

Scoring Leaders

1908	S. Nielsen (Denmark), 11		1920	H. Karlsson (Sweden), 7
1912	Fuchs (Germany), 10		1924	Petrone (Uruguay), 8
	(includes unofficial games)		1928	Tarasconi (Argentina), 7

1936	Frossi (Italy), 7	1960	Galic and Kostic (Yugoslavia), 7
1948	Nordahl (Sweden) and Nansen (Denmark), 7	1964	Bene (Hungary), 12
1952	Zebec and Mitic (Yugoslavia), 7	1968	Kamamoto (Japan), 7
1956	Milanov (Bulgaria) and d'Souza (India), 4	1972	Deyna (Poland), 9
		1976	Szarmach (Poland), 6

Other Records: most qualification bids—Great Britain and Netherlands, 12; most consecutive qualification bids—USA, 11 (1924-76); most final rounds participated in—France, nine; aggregate scoring leader—S. Nielsen (Denmark, 1908-12) and A. Dunai II (Hungary, 1968-72), 13; biggest win—Denmark—France A, 17-1 (1908).

Results

1908 (in London)

First Round

Great Britain—Sweden	12-1
Denmark—France B	9-0

Semi-Finals

Great Britain—Netherlands	4-0
Denmark—France A	17-1

Third Place Game

Netherlands—Sweden	2-1

Final

Great Britain (Chapman, Woodward)	2	Denmark	0

1912 (in Stockholm)

First Round

Finland—Italy	3-2
Netherlands—Sweden (after extra time)	4-3
Austria—Germany	5-1

Second Round

Great Britain—Hungary	7-0
Finland—Russia	2-1
Netherlands—Austria	3-1
Denmark—Norway	7-0

Semi-Final

Great Britain—Finland	4-0
Denmark—Netherlands	4-1

Third Place Game
  Netherlands—Finland   9-0

Final
  Great Britain   4   Denmark   2
  (Berry, Walden, Hoare 2)   (Olsen 2)

1920 (in Antwerp)

First Round
  Spain—Denmark   1-0
  Netherlands—Luxembourg   3-0
  Sweden—Greece   9-0
  Italy—Egypt   2-1
  Norway—Great Britain   3-1
  Czechoslovakia—Yugoslavia   7-0

Second Round
  Belgium—Spain   3-1
  Netherlands—Sweden   5-4
  (after extra time)
  France—Italy   3-1
  Czechoslovakia—Norway   4-0

Semi-Finals
  Belgium—Netherlands   3-0
  Czechoslovakia—France   4-1

Play-Off for Second and Third Place Game
  Italy—Norway   2-1
  Spain—Sweden   2-1
  Spain—Italy   2-0

Second and Third Place Game
  Spain—Netherlands   3-1

Final
  Belgium   2   Czechoslovakia   0
  (Swardenbrocks, Copée)
  (Czechoslovakia walked off the field and was disqualified; Belgium was leading, 2-0)

1924 (in Paris)

Preliminary Round
  Uruguay—Yugoslavia   7-0
  USA—Estonia   1-0
  Hungary—Poland   5-0
  Italy—Spain   1-0

Czechoslovakia—Turkey	5-2
Switzerland—Lithuania	9-0

First Round

Uruguay—USA	3-0
France—Latvia	7-0
Netherlands—Rumania	6-0
Irish Free State—Bulgaria	1-0
Sweden—Belgium	8-1
Egypt—Hungary	3-0
Italy—Luxembourg	2-0
Switzerland—Czechoslovakia	1-1, 1-0

Second Round

Uruguay—France	5-1
Netherlands—Irish Free State	2-1
(after extra time)	
Sweden—Egypt	5-0
Switzerland—Italy	2-1

Semi-Finals

Uruguay—Netherlands	2-1
Switzerland—Sweden	2-1

Third Place Game

Sweden—Netherlands	1-1, 3-1

Final

Uruguay	3	Switzerland	0
(Petrone, Cea, Romano)			

1928 (in Amsterdam)

Preliminary Round

Portugal—Chile	4-2

First Round

Uruguay—Netherlands	2-0
Germany—Switzerland	4-0
Italy—France	4-3
Spain—Mexico	7-1
Egypt—Turkey	7-1
Portugal—Yugoslavia	2-1
Belgium—Luxembourg	5-3
Argentina—USA	11-2

Second Round

Uruguay—Germany	4-1

Italy—Spain	1-1, 7-1
Egypt—Portugal	2-1
Argentina—Belgium	6-3

Semi-Finals

Uruguay—Italy	3-2
Argentina—Egypt	6-0

Third Place Game

Italy—Egypt	11-3

Final

Uruguay	1	Argentina	1

Uruguay	2	Argentina	1
(Figueroa, Scarone)		(Monti)	

1936 (in Berlin)

First Round

Italy—USA	1-0
Japan—Sweden	3-2
Norway—Turkey	4-0
Germany—Luxembourg	9-0
Poland—Hungary	3-0
Great Britain—China	2-0
Peru—Finland	7-3
Austria—Egypt	3-1

Second Round

Italy—Japan	8-0
Norway—Germany	2-0
Poland—Great Britain	5-4
Austria—Peru	2-4

(game disallowed: Austria won by default when Peru refused replay)

Semi-Finals

Italy—Norway	2-1
(after extra time)	
Austria—Poland	3-1

Final

Italy	2	Austria	1
(Frossi 2)		(K Kainberger)	
	(after extra time)		

1948 (in London)

Preliminary Round
Netherlands—Ireland Rep	3-1
Luxembourg—Afghanistan	6-0

First Round
Sweden—Austria	3-0
Korea—Mexico	5-3
Denmark—Egypt	3-1
(after extra time)	
Italy—USA	9-0
Great Britain—Netherlands	4-3
(after extra time)	
France—India	2-1
Turkey—China	4-0
Yugoslavia—Luxembourg	6-1

Second Round
Sweden—Korea	12-0
Denmark—Italy	5-3
Great Britain—France	1-0
Yugoslavia—Turkey	3-1

Semi-Finals
Sweden—Denmark	4-2
Yugoslavia—Great Britain	3-1

Third Place Game
Denmark—Great Britain	5-3

Final
Sweden	3	Yugoslavia	1
(Gren 2, G Nordahl)		(Bobek)	

1952 (in Helsinki)

Preliminary Round
Hungary—Rumania	2-1
Italy—USA	8-0
Egypt—Chile	5-4
Brazil—Netherlands	5-1
Luxembourg—Great Britain	5-3
(after extra time)	
Denmark—Greece	2-1
Poland—France	2-1
USSR—Bulgaria	2-1
(after extra time)	
Yugoslavia—India	10-1

First Round
Hungary—Italy	3-0
Turkey—Dutch West Indies	2-1
Sweden—Norway	4-1
Austria—Finland	4-3
Germany FR—Egypt	3-1
Brazil—Luxembourg	2-1
Denmark—Poland	2-1
Yugoslavia—USSR	5-5, 3-1
(after extra time)	

Second Round
Hungary—Turkey	7-1
Sweden—Austria	3-1
Germany FR—Brazil	4-2
(after extra time)	
Yugoslavia—Denmark	5-3

Semi-Finals
Hungary—Sweden	6-0
Yugoslavia—Germany FR	3-1

Third Place Game
Sweden—Germany FR	2-0

Final
Hungary	2	Yugoslavia	0
(Puskás, Czibor)			

1956 (in Melbourne)

First Round
USSR—Germany FR	2-1
Great Britain—Thailand	9-0
Australia—Japan	2-0

Second Round
USSR—Indonesia	0-0, 4-0
(after extra time)	
Bulgaria—Great Britain	6-1
India—Australia	4-2
Yugoslavia—USA	9-1

Semi-Finals
USSR—Bulgaria	2-1
(after extra time)	
Yugoslavia—India	4-1

Third Place Game
Bulgaria—India	3-0

Final

| USSR | 1 | Yugoslavia | 0 |

(Ilyin)

1960 (in Rome)

Group 1

Yugoslavia—UAR	6-1
Bulgaria—Turkey	3-0
Bulgaria—UAR	2-0
Yugoslavia—Turkey	4-0
Yugoslavia—Bulgaria	3-3
UAR—Turkey	3-3

	P	W	D	L	F	A	P
Yugoslavia	3	2	1	0	13	4	5
Bulgaria	3	2	1	0	8	3	5
UAR	3	0	1	2	4	11	1
Turkey	3	0	1	2	3	10	1

Group 2

Brazil—Great Britain	4-3
Italy—China	4-1
Brazil—China	5-0
Italy—Great Britain	2-2
Italy—Brazil	3-1
Great Britain—China	3-2

	P	W	D	L	F	A	P
Italy	3	2	1	0	9	4	5
Brazil	3	2	0	1	10	6	4
Great Britain	3	1	1	1	8	8	3
China	3	0	0	3	3	12	0

Group 3

Poland—Tunisia	6-1
Denmark—Argentina	3-2
Argentina—Tunisia	2-1
Denmark—Poland	2-1
Denmark—Tunisia	3-1
Argentina—Poland	2-1

	P	W	D	L	F	A	P
Denmark	3	3	0	0	8	4	6
Argentina	3	2	0	1	6	4	4
Poland	3	1	0	2	7	5	2
Tunisia	3	0	0	3	3	11	0

Group 4

| Hungary—India | 2-1 |
| France—Peru | 2-1 |

Hungary—Peru							6-2
France—India							1-1
Hungary—France							7-0
Peru—India							3-1

	P	W	D	L	F	A	P
Hungary	3	3	0	0	15	3	6
France	3	1	1	1	3	9	3
Peru	3	1	0	2	6	9	2
India	3	0	1	2	3	6	1

Semi-Finals

Yugoslavia—Italy	1-1
(Yugoslavia won on toss of the coin)	
Denmark—Hungary	2-0

Third Place Game

Italy—Hungary	2-0

Final

Yugoslavia	3	Denmark	1
(Galic, Matus, Kostic)		(Nielsen)	

1964 (in Tokyo)

Group 1

German DR—Iran	4-0
German DR—Mexico	2-0
German DR—Rumania	1-1
Mexico—Iran	1-1
Rumania—Iran	1-0
Rumania—Mexico	3-1

	P	W	D	L	F	A	P
German DR	3	2	1	0	7	1	5
Rumania	3	2	1	0	5	2	5
Mexico	3	0	1	2	2	6	1
Iran	3	0	1	2	1	6	1

Group 2

Hungary—Yugoslavia	6-5
Yugoslavia—Morocco	3-1
Hungary—Morocco	6-0

	P	W	D	L	F	A	P
Hungary	2	2	0	0	12	5	4
Yugoslavia	2	1	0	1	8	2	2
Morocco	2	0	0	2	1	9	0
Korea DPR			withdrew				

Group 3

Brazil—Korea Rep	4-0
UAR—Brazil	1-1

Czechoslovakia—Brazil	1-0
UAR—Korea Rep	10-0
Czechoslovakia—Korea Rep	6-1
Czechoslovakia—UAR	5-1

	P	W	D	L	F	A	P
Czechoslovakia	3	3	0	0	12	2	6
UAR	3	1	1	1	12	6	3
Brazil	3	1	1	1	5	2	3
Korea Rep	3	0	0	3	1	20	0

Group 4

Japan—Argentina	3-2
Ghana—Japan	3-2
Ghana—Argentina	1-1

	P	W	D	L	F	A	P
Ghana	2	1	1	0	4	3	3
Japan	2	1	0	1	5	5	2
Argentina	2	0	1	1	3	4	1
Italy	withdrew						

Quarter-Finals

UAR—Ghana	5-1
German DR—Yugoslavia	1-0
Czechoslovakia—Japan	4-0
Hungary—Rumania	2-0

Semi-Finals

| Czechoslovakia—German DR | 2-1 |
| Hungary—UAR | 6-0 |

Third Place Game

| German DR—UAR | 3-1 |

Final

| Hungary | 2 | Czechoslovakia | 1 |
| (Vojta og, Bene) | | (Brumovsky) | |

1968 (in Mexico City)

Group 1

Mexico—Colombia	1-0
France—Mexico	4-1
Mexico—Guinea	4-0
Colombia—Guinea	2-3
France—Colombia	1-2
France—Guinea	3-1

	P	W	D	L	F	A	P
France	3	2	0	1	8	4	4
Mexico	3	2	0	1	6	4	4
Colombia	3	1	0	2	4	5	2
Guinea	3	1	0	2	4	9	2

Group 2

Spain—Brazil	1-0
Spain—Nigeria	3-0
Spain—Japan	0-0
Brazil—Nigeria	3-3
Japan—Brazil	1-1
Japan—Nigeria	3-1

	P	W	D	L	F	A	P
Spain	3	2	1	0	4	0	5
Japan	3	1	2	0	4	2	4
Brazil	3	0	2	1	4	5	2
Nigeria	3	0	1	2	4	9	1

Group 3

Israel—Ghana	5-4
Hungary—Ghana	2-2
Ghana—El Salvador	1-1
Israel—El Salvador	3-1
Hungary—Israel	2-0
Hungary—El Salvador	4-0

	P	W	D	L	F	A	P
Hungary	3	2	1	0	8	3	5
Israel	3	2	0	1	8	6	4
Ghana	3	0	2	1	7	8	2
El Salvador	3	0	1	2	2	8	1

Group 4

Bulgaria—Thailand	7-1
Bulgaria—Czechoslovakia	2-2
Bulgaria—Guatemala	2-1
Guatemala—Thailand	4-1
Czechoslovakia—Thailand	8-0
Guatemala—Czechoslovakia	1-1

	P	W	D	L	F	A	P
Bulgaria	3	2	1	0	11	3	5
Guatemala	3	2	0	1	6	3	4
Czechoslovakia	3	1	1	1	10	3	3
Thailand	3	0	0	3	1	19	0

Quarter-Finals

Japan—France	3-1
Mexico—Spain	2-1

Hungary—Guatemala	1-0
Bulgaria—Israel	1-1
(Bulgaria won by toss of the coin)	

Semi-Finals

Hungary—Japan	5-0
Bulgaria—Mexico	3-2

Third Place Game

Japan—Mexico	2-0

Final

Hungary	4	Bulgaria	1
(Menczel, Juhasz, Antal Dunai 2)		(Dimitrov)	

1972 (in Munich)

Group A

Malaysia—Germany FR	0-3
Morocco—USA	0-0
Germany FR—Morocco	3-0
USA—Malaysia	0-3
USA—Germany FR	0-7
Morocco—Malaysia	6-0

	P	W	D	L	F	A	P
Germany FR	3	3	0	0	13	0	6
Morocco	3	1	1	1	6	3	3
Malaysia	3	1	0	2	3	9	2
USA	3	0	1	2	0	10	1

Group B

Burma—USSR	0-1
Sudan—Mexico	0-1
USSR—Sudan	2-1
Mexico—Burma	1-0
Mexico—USSR	1-4
Sudan—Burma	0-2

	P	W	D	L	F	A	P
USSR	3	3	0	0	7	2	6
Mexico	3	2	0	1	3	4	4
Burma	3	1	0	2	2	2	2
Sudan	3	0	0	3	1	5	0

Group C

Iran—Hungary	0-5
Brazil—Denmark	2-3

Hungary—Brazil	2-2
Denmark—Iran	4-0
Denmark—Hungary	0-2
Brazil—Iran	0-1

	P	W	D	L	F	A	P
Hungary	3	2	1	0	9	2	5
Denmark	3	2	0	1	7	4	4
Iran	3	1	0	2	1	9	2
Brazil	3	0	1	2	4	6	1

Group D

Ghana—German DR	0-4
Colombia—Poland	1-5
German DR—Colombia	6-1
Poland—Ghana	4-0
Colombia—Ghana	3-1
Poland—German DR	2-1

	P	W	D	L	F	A	P
Poland	3	3	0	0	11	2	6
German DR	3	2	0	1	11	3	4
Colombia	3	1	0	2	4	12	2
Ghana	3	0	0	3	1	11	0

Semi-Finals

Group 1

Germany FR—Mexico	1-1
Hungary—German DR	2-0
German DR—Mexico	7-0
Germany FR—Hungary	1-4
German DR—Germany FR	3-2
Hungary—Mexico	2-0

	P	W	D	L	F	A	P
Hungary	3	3	0	0	8	1	6
German DR	3	2	0	1	10	4	4
Germany FR	3	0	1	2	4	8	1
Mexico	3	0	0	3	1	10	0

Group 2

Morocco—USSR	0-3
Denmark—Poland	1-1
Morocco—Denmark	1-3
Poland—USSR	2-1

Poland—Morocco						5-0
Denmark—USSR						0-4

	P	W	D	L	F	A	P
Poland	3	2	1	0	8	2	5
USSR	3	2	0	1	6	2	4
Denmark	3	0	1	2	4	6	1
Morocco	3	0	0	3	1	11	0

Third Place Game
USSR—German DR   2-2
(shared Bronze Medal)

Final

Poland	2	**Hungary**	1
(Deyna 2)		(Varadi)	

1976 (in Montreal)

Group A

Brazil—German DR	0-0
Brazil—Spain	2-1
Spain—German DR	0-1

	P	W	D	L	F	A	P
Brazil	2	1	1	0	2	1	3
German DR	2	1	1	0	1	0	3
Spain	2	0	0	2	1	3	0
Zambia		withdrew					

(Brazil won draw on lots to advance)

Group B

France—Mexico	4-1
Israel—Guatemala	0-0
Mexico—Israel	2-2
France—Guatemala	4-1
Mexico—Guatemala	1-1
France—Israel	1-1

	P	W	D	L	F	A	P
France	3	2	1	0	9	3	5
Israel	3	0	3	0	3	1	3
Mexico	3	0	2	1	4	7	2
Guatemala	3	0	2	1	2	5	2

Group C

Poland—Cuba	0-0
Iran—Cuba	1-0
Poland—Iran	3-2

	P	W	D	L	F	A	P
Poland	2	1	1	0	3	2	3
Iran	2	1	0	1	3	3	2
Cuba	2	0	1	1	0	1	1
Nigeria			withdrew				

Group D

USSR—Canada	2-1
Korea DPR—Canada	3-1
USSR—Korea DPR	3-0

	P	W	D	L	F	A	P
USSR	2	2	0	0	5	1	4
Korea DPR	2	1	0	1	3	4	2
Canada	2	0	0	2	2	5	0
Ghana			withdrew				

Quarter-Finals

Poland—Korea DPR	5-0
Brazil—Israel	4-1
USSR—Iran	2-1
German DR—France	4-0

Semi-Finals

| German DR—USSR | 2-1 |
| Poland—Brazil | 2-0 |

Final

| German DR | 3 | Poland | 1 |
| (Schade, Hoffman, Hafner) | | (Lato) | |

Oman

This sandy sultanate on the Arabian peninsula is not affiliated with either FIFA or the Asian Football Confederation, but soccer is beginning to be organized there. In 1976, Oman participated in the fourth Arabian Gulf Football Cup, and placed sixth among seven entrants, compiling the following record: 6-1-1-4-4-20-3. Aside from North Yemen, Oman had been the last remaining country on the peninsula to enter international competition.

origins of the game

The lineage of modern soccer from the Middle Ages to the present is easily discernible, but its earlier ties are more difficult to identify. The various forms of English football and other ball games played in the British Isles between 1066-1863 are the direct ancestors of all modern football games: soccer, rugby, American football, Canadian football, Gaelic football, Australian Rules, etc. The stumbling block has been to establish the relationship between the British ball games and the Greco-Roman games that preceded them. There is precious little evidence, for example, that the conquered Britons of the first-fifth centuries A.D. learned Roman ball games from Caesar's legions, yet this theory remains likely and very attractive. The matter is further complicated by the knowledge of indigenous ball games among the Celts that predate the Roman invasions. As a general statement, however, it is certain that the mainstream of football history flows through British culture. Meanwhile, it is not surprising to find similar ball games in other parts of the world that developed their own distinct and unrelated histories, and these must be treated separately.

Several ancient cultures spawned games that have some relation to soccer in appearance only, but no evidence of their relationship to the British games exists. The earliest of these is thought to be the Chinese game *tsu chu*, whose beginnings have been traced to 2500 B.C. In Japan, a football game known as *kemari* was played as early as 600 B.C. *Kemari* bears a closer resemblance to soccer than most ancient ball games, because kicking a ball into a "goal" appears to have been its central feature. (After 300 B.C., the goal depicted in descriptions of *kemari* consisted of five-yard high bamboo stakes.) Like *tsu chu*, *kemari* had a religious and political significance; it was played in some form until the third century A.D., and possibly as late as the Mongol invasions.

Pacific islanders—especially tribes of the Philippine archipelago, the Maoris, and certain Polynesians—were among the first to play ball games using their hands and feet; they used pig bladders, coconuts, and oranges for balls. The pre-Columbian ball games of Mexico and Central America (ca. 600-1600) were an essential element in the religious life of Aztec and Toltec communities and are well documented in their art. Among the Indian tribes of South America, there are two games of special interest, both dating from the Middle Ages: *pilimatun*, played by the Araucanians of present-day Chile, and *tchoekah* of the Tehuelche tribes in Patagonia. The old eskimo game *aqsaqtuk* might today be

Kemari, the ancient Japanese football game, which coincidentally resembled modern soccer, from a woodcut.

mistaken for soccer on the ice, so closely does it resemble the modern game. And North African tribes played a form of football with leather balls.

Other ball games of historical interest are sometimes linked to the prehistory of modern football, but in fact they bear it little resemblance. *Koura*, for example, was a game played by certain Semitic tribes in the Middle East, but its appearance is closer to that of lacrosse than football. Some historians have inconclusively linked fertility rites in ancient Egypt and other religious ceremonies of the ancient Near East with the beginnings of Western football.

The seeds of a true football genealogy may be found in the ancient art of ball juggling, an exercise that was regarded as a legitimate sport, or game, by the Romans and quite possibly by Egyptians and Greeks as well. All three cultures practiced juggling extensively. The earliest known reference to it is a painting on an Egyptian tomb dating from 2000 B.C. An Athenian gravestone relief depicts a man juggling a ball approximately six inches in diameter on his thigh. There is no reason to believe that juggling was in any way part of a team effort, but the idea of developing "ball juggling skills" was of great importance.

The concept of a team moving a ball up and down a field is clearly represented in the ball games of Greece (both Athens and Sparta) and Rome, though classical writers did not mention the use of feet in their descriptions of the rules. The Greco-Roman ball games, while employing two organized teams, were restricted to catching, passing, and throwing with the hands—a more natural movement than the use of feet—but other characteristics of modern soccer were unquestionably present. A Greek ball game of this kind, *episkyros*, was played as early as the sixth century B.C. Two teams of equal size lined up on either half of a field, and they were separated by a line of small stones (the *skyros*) on which a ball was placed. Parallel lines were marked behind both teams, and the field of play thus resembled a kind of soccer pitch with a halfway line and two goal lines. Players attempted to gain possession of the ball and throw it over the heads of their opponents—passing and intercepting were key elements—and the first team to push all of its opponents over the line behind them achieved the desired result: whether this was recorded as a score or an outright win remains unknown. The appearance of *episkyros* must have ap-

proximated that of modern team handball, a game developed by the Athenian-conscious Germans in the early twentieth century, and a close relative of soccer and rugby.

The related Roman ball game, *harpastum*, is less well defined; some classicists have interpreted an element of dodge ball in it. The key player was the "middle runner." His position on the field was located somewhere between two groups of players who in turn threw a small hard ball between them. The middle runner attempted to intercept or snatch the ball in the line of flight or, possibly, to seize it from a player in possession. Whether the ball was eventually deposited or thrown over a "goal line" is unclear. Some popular historians in recent years have attempted to describe this game as Roman football, but its use of kicking skills was minimal.

None of the Greek or Roman ball games enjoyed the popularity of track and field or wrestling, and there is no record of their having been played in arenas before large crowds. Their interest to football historians—especially that of *episkyros*—is in the invention of advancing the ball up the field to pass over a "goal line." With the knowledge that ball juggling skills using feet and thighs were also known to the Romans, it is only a short step to conceptualize a fusing of the two ideas, though no evidence of such a combination exists in Roman art and writing. *Harpastum*, or similar ball games, were certainly exported to other parts of the Roman Empire. There are records of such in Dalmatia dating from the second century A.D., and in Nimes and Lyons from the fifth century. Finally, in the historical annals of Derby there is the mythical legend of a ball game played between local residents and Roman troops in 217 A.D. (won by the Britons) that resulted in the expulsion of the military oppressors. The veracity of the story is unimportant, but it illustrates the possible importation of a Roman ancestor of soccer to the land that eventually gave birth to the modern game.

It must be remembered that there is no conclusive evidence of Romano-Britain learning to play handball-football from its conquerors; it is merely a probability. In the period following the departure of the Romans from Britain—the fifth-eleventh centuries—the picture becomes so confused that historians have yet to agree on a pattern. It is almost certain that variations of mass football games developed in different parts of the

British Isles during this time—though there is no contemporary record of them—and the games varied from region to region. There are three formidable hypotheses in connection with the origins of these games, each of which is linked to the sweeping changes that took place in medieval Britain as successive waves of Angles, Saxons, Danes, Norse, and Normans swept over the islands.

The first is that football grew out of the game called camp-ball (field ball) in the eastern counties settled by Angles and Saxons. Although the eventual cultural influence of the eastern counties on the rest of Britain was certainly important, the Anglo-Saxon theory of origin is weak because there is no indication that ball games were ever played in the Anglo-Saxons' native Denmark and Germany. Eastern county settlers may have learned a ball game from someone else—perhaps the Celts.

A stronger hypothesis is that of a Celtic origin. It is thought that the Irish played a ball game as early as the first century B.C. A precursor to hurling—the Irish national sport—was played in Ireland by the seventh century A.D. Hurling was also played by the Celts in Cornwall, and the Welsh (also Celtic) played an indigenous game called knappan; both of these date back to at least the early post-Roman period. Neither of them was an actual football game—the ball was not kicked—but both contained the basic football concept of projecting a ball into a "goal." In addition, it is known that the early medieval ball game of Brittany (la soule) bore a close resemblance to these Celtic games, and, in fact, was imported when the Celts of Britain settled on the Breton coast. The early abundance of ball games throughout the Celtic regions (Ireland, western Scotland, Wales, Cornwall, and northwestern France) is a plausible indication that the Anglo-Saxons who drove the Celts westward when they conquered England might have incorporated ball games into their own culture.

The third and best supported hypothesis on the basis of established evidence is that English football developed primarily from a ball game imported by the Normans in 1066. The strength of this theory is that virtually all known accounts of football in England postdate the Norman conquest. The first literary reference to football dates from 1175 (William Fitzstephen). The Norman game might have originated in Scandinavia, the ancestral home of Norman aristocracy, or in the Latin culture that the Normans

enthusiastically adopted, but more likely it was an adaptation of Brittany's *la soule*. The Normans, who had conquered Brittany, called their game *la choule*.

For centuries after the Norman invasion, mass football was played in England and Scotland on a wide scale. It was most notably linked with the festivities of Shrove Tuesday, the pre-Lenten celebration, or "carnival," of Western Christendom. By the twelfth century, it had already become a sprawling and violent contest, usually played over great distances and sometimes between towns and villages. "Goals" were generally designated by landmarks located many miles apart. Throwing, kicking, and everything else was employed, because there were no rules, and in due course its reputation as a worthy cultural pastime suffered in the eyes of the authorities. Many myths grew up around these rituals, particularly regarding their origins. Some legends referred to ancient military exploits against the Romans, others to heroic feats involving Danish or Norse invaders. The legends varied

The direct ancestors of soccer and rugby were the sprawling medieval football games of Britain and France. This print recreates a village match in 17th-century England, showing rowdy players, barking dogs, and startled spectators. The ball is at lower left.

according to geographical location and historical legacy, but since few were set down on paper before the seventeenth century, their inspiration may generally be regarded as wishful thinking.

In the fourteenth century, there were growing signs of football becoming a common recreation for the lower classes. As the game surfaced in city streets and villages squares, a succession of royal bans was issued—the first by Edward II in 1314—but the undeniable pleasure of kicking or throwing a ball through bleak medieval thoroughfares could not be suppressed. The popularity of football grew. In the sixteenth century, there was a burgeoning of interest. A group of students at Cambridge University organized contests ca. 1620, and in 1681 Charles II sanctioned football for his servants. The game that was evolving looked more like rugby than soccer—hands as well as feet were used—but there is no doubt that it was "foote ball." It was also played widely in Scotland, partly as a result of French influences after the twelfth-century Scottish alliance with France, and its existence in Ireland was officially recognized by the Statutes of Galway in 1527. A Welsh football contest was described by a self-confessed fan named Anna Beynon in 1720.

In the eighteenth century, mass football games in England nearly died out, the few exceptions being an occasional Shrovetide ritual, and lower-class interest in the sport became almost dormant. During the reign of George III, however, upper-class school boys and university students began to give it attention. Football had been played by a small minority at Cambridge and Trinity College,

Dublin, for almost two centuries, but after 1800 the rising prominence of English public schools provided the impetus for gentlemanly pursuits on the playing field. Football was adopted as a trendy recreation in which unwritten codes of upper-class conduct could be displayed. In 1814, contests were organized at Harrow, and in the course of the next 45 years, dozens of other institutions did the same. This period, during which the sprawling English football games of past centuries were codified and given shape, marks the birth of the modern game.

Each school developed its own variation of the rules, which were dependent on the layout of available playing areas. The disorganized ball game that was inherited by these gentleman players must surely have emphasized the use of feet rather than hands, because in 1823, when a certain pupil at Rugby School picked up the ball and ran with it—marking the unofficial beginning of rugby football—it caused a sensation and drew the lines that would eventually lead to the split between soccer and rugby enthusiasts. Harrow, Charterhouse, Westminster, Aldenham, Shrewsbury, and Uppingham schools became most closely associated with the "dribbling game," though there were others of lesser note, and the graduates (old boys) of these schools eventually went on to draw up the influential rules for the dribbling game at Cambridge in 1848 and subsequently for the first governing body of soccer. The formation of The Football Association by old boys in 1863 heralded the modern era and the official beginning of soccer as a sport.

See also: **England, history of the game, aqsaqtuk, pre-Columbian ball games,** and **tsu chu.**

Orth, György (1901-1962)

Perhaps Hungary's greatest player of all time, certainly its most complete. Orth played in five different positions for Hungary during the early and mid-1920s, and as many as six for his club MTK, which he led to nine consecutive championships between 1917-25. As a 15-year-old prodigy, he was already a spectacular goalscorer for MTK, and at the age of 16 he made his international debut for Hungary. Discovered by the legendary Scottish manager Jimmy Hogan—then of MTK—he was an idol in every sense of the word, drawing huge crowds to club and international matches, though fans were often uncertain which position he would play on a given day. On one occasion, he was even Hungary's goalkeeper. He made 30 international appearances for Hungary and scored 13 goals, many of them among the most famous and breathtaking in Hungary's distinguished soccer history. A crushing injury in a club match against FK Austria ended his career in 1927, and he took up coaching, first in a variety of countries in Western Europe and then in South America, most notably as manager of the Peruvian national team in the late 1950s.

Oswaldo Cruz Cup

Copa Oswaldo Cruz—Taça Oswaldo Cruz.

An occasional trophy awarded since 1950 to the winner of designated matches between Brazil and Paraguay.

Winners

1950	Brazil	1961	Brazil
1955	Brazil	1962	Brazil
1956	Brazil	1968	Brazil
1958	Brazil	1976	Brazil

out of play

A ball is "out of play" when it crosses entirely over the goal line or the touch line, or when the referee stops play for any reason.

outside   Also known as "winger," "wing," "flank," "No. 7," and "No. 11."

The positions at either extremity of a five-player forward line, the outside right on the right side of the line and the outside left on the left side. The two outer positions on a four-player forward line may also be known as outsides, or wings, depending on whether or not they fulfill the traditonal functions of an outside. With the advance in recent years of 4-3-3, 4-4-2, and 4-2-4 formations, their historical place in team strategies has diminished, though the increasingly rare talents of a natural outsides such as Deyna, Jairzinho, and Džajić, are generally exploited by coaches whenever they are discovered.

outswinger

A pass or shot which curves away from the goal, usually in reference to a corner kick.

See also: **inswinger**

overhead kick

A kick in which the ball is propelled over the kicker's own head.

See also: **bicycle kick**

overlap

The action of a fullback, center halfback, or other defender in coming forward to aid in an attack, though the player's primary function is defensive.

over-the-ball tackle

An often unlawful tackle in which the defending player jumps over the ball and plays the legs of the dribbler. It is referred to in the Laws as "jumping at the opponent," and draws a direct free kick by the offended side.

own goal   Also known as "self goal."

A goal scored by a player against his own team.

An own goal has decided the outcome of important international competitions on four occasions. Hungary won the 1964 Olympic gold medal after an own goal by Czechoslovakia's Vojta. In 1961, Benfica won the European Cup when Barcelona's goalkeeper Ramallets nudged a poor clearance by a teammate into his own goal. Two editions of the European Cup Winners' Cup have been decided by own goals. In 1964, MTK's Dansky scored an own goal that allowed Sporting Lisbon to equalize and force a replay; Sporting eventually won the replay and the trophy. In 1966, Borussia Dortmund won the cup on an own goal by Liverpool's Yeats.

An own goal figured prominently in the 1975 edition of the South American Championship. In the final, Columbia won the first leg, and in the second leg was losing by one when Zarate scored an own goal to give Peru a 2-0 win, forcing a play-off, which was won by Peru. Ultimately it was to be Zarate's own goal that put Colombia's first major international honor out of reach.

P

Pakistan

Pakistan Football Federation	Founded: 1948
Major Malik Mohammad Haussain	FIFA: 1948
HQ Log Area	AFC: ?
Rawalpindi	

Affiliated clubs: *576;* registered players: *13,000;* national stadium:*Karachi Stadium, Karachi (35,000);* largest stadium: *Karachi Stadium;* colors: *green jerseys, white shorts;* season: *March to October;* honors: *none.*

The growth of soccer in Pakistan occurred while the country was still a province of British India. At the time of its independence in 1947, Pakistan showed promise as a future power in Asian soccer, having jumped to a head start over its non-British rivals by several years. Though it has continued to prosper as the sport of the masses and in numerical terms has equaled the traditional national sports of field hockey and cricket, Pakistani soccer has in many ways remained static since the 1940s, and in international competition Pakistan has very little to show for itself.

When the Pakistan Football Federation was founded in 1948, it already had 500 affiliated clubs and 10,000 registered players. These figures have changed very little in 30 years. A national championship was introduced in 1950, but this has been a knockout tournament for representative teams of the various provincial and regional associations rather than a club competition. The first winner was Baluchistan state. The series has been dominated, however, by the Punjab, which includes Lahore, Pakistan's largest city. During the early 1950s, the Pakistan F.F. attempted to modernize the game by extending the length of individual matches from 70 minutes, which was common in South Asia, to the standard 90 minutes, and to prohibit playing in bare feet in official competitions. It is quite possible that these radical alterations, required by FIFA statutes, were important factors in the slowdown of soccer's growth in this vast and arid country.

In 1950, Pakistan won its first international,

a 5-1 defeat of Iran in Tehran. In 1952 and 1953, Pakistan participated in two editions of the International Quadrangular Tournament with India, Ceylon, and Burma. At Colombo in the 1952 edition, it shut out Ceylon and Burma and drew with India, and one year later in Rangoon gained second place by roundly defeating Ceylon (6-0), drawing with Burma, and losing to India. These results leave little doubt that Pakistan held its own in regional international competition during the fledgling years, and this was also hown by its 1-0 defeat of India in a 1953 friendly at Rangoon.

Pakistan's lack of progress in international competition since the 1950s has also been caused by the rapid growth of the game in other parts of Asia, and by consistent political and economic turbulence at home. As a result of these disorders, Pakistan has rarely been seen in important Asian tournaments such as the Asian Games, the Asian Cup, and qualifying rounds for the Olympic Games and World Cup. In 1968, it attempted to qualify for the Asian Games, but its efforts were thwarted by losses to Cambodia and Burma, though it did manage to gain a draw with India. In 1970, Pakistan placed third in a three-way tournament with Iran and Turkey, called the R.C.D. Pact Tournament, but the instability of Pakistani life during the 1970s has undermined any possibility of regular participation in international competition. Pakistan also failed to enter the short-lived Asian Champions' Cup. Today, the upper divisions of the numerous regional championships in Pakistan include 160.

Palestine

A Palestinian Arab representative team is invited regularly to participate in the biennial Palestine Football Cup, an all-Arab tourna-

ment for national teams introduced in 1971 and named in honor of an Arab Palestine. Its known results are a draw (0-0) and a loss (0-1) to Sudan in the 1975 edition at Tunis. Nearly all soccer activity in pre-1948 Palestine was carried on by Jewish residents.

See also: **Israel**

Palestine Football Cup

One of two regional competitions open to the national teams of Arab countries (the second being the Arab Cup held in conjunction with the Pan Arab Games). Approximately ten countries have entered in each biennial edition. Among the invited participants is a representative team of Palestinians, in whose honor the cup is named.

Winners

1971   (in Iraq) Egypt
1973   (in Libya) Tunisia
1975   (in Tunisia) Egypt

Palmeiras, Sociedade Esportiva

Location: *São Paulo, Brazil;* **stadium:** *Parque Antártica;* **colors:** *green jerseys with white trim, white shorts;* **honors:** *Rio-São Paulo Tournament winner (1933 unofficial, 1951, 1965), National Championship (1967, 1969, 1972, 1973), São Paulo champion (1920, 1926 APEA, 1927 APEA, 1932, 1933, 1934, 1936 LPF, 1940, 1942, 1944, 1947, 1950, 1959, 1963, 1966, 1972, 1974, 1976).*

Founded 1914 as Palestra Itália by Luigi Cervo and other Italian immigrant workers of the Industrias Reunidas Matarazzo, São Paulo, after exhibition matches were played at Parque Antártica and Velódromo between Torino and Pro Vercelli, two of Italy's leading clubs. An advertisement was placed in the Italian language magazine *Fanfulla* complaining that the British, Germans, and Portuguese in São Paulo had their own clubs, so why not the Italians. Two weeks later Palestra Itália was officially established. It had to wait for two years, however, to be admitted to the breakaway league in São Paulo, the Associação Paulista de Esportes Atléticos, and its first championship was won in 1920 in the fourth year of the São Paulo league merger. The Parque Antártica—the first great stadium in São Paulo—was acquired in 1919, and remodeled in 1933. The name of the club was changed to Palmeiras in 1942, when all public references to the "Axis" powers were forbidden by the government.

Though Palmeiras is not quite as well supported as its archrival Corinthians, it is by all measures the most successful São Paulo club of all time. Palmeiras has won a record 18 *paulista* championships, three Rio-São Paulo Tournaments (one unofficial), and a record four national championships. During the 1920s and '30s, as Palestra Itália, it shared most of the *paulista* honors with Corinthians in both the APEA and the reunited professional league. It won seven championships during this period, including three in succession between 1932-34, and some difficult obstacles were overcome in losing several key players to big clubs in Italy. Juventus, Genoa, and Lazio each poached the Italian-based Palestra almost dry by the late

1920s, but fortunately its greatest star, Romeu, remained until 1935, when he moved to Rio de Janeiro's Fluminense.

In 1951, Palmeiras won the first International Cup—the Taça Rio—for invited champion clubs of Europe and South America, defeating Juventus in the final by a 3-2 aggregate. This was its first foray into organized international competition, occurring at the same time as its great back-to-back wins of the *paulista* championship and the Rio-São Paulo Tournament. These successes coincided with the Palmeiras career of the legendary inside left Jair, as well as right wing Lima, left back Juvenal, and right back Salvador, less internationally known stars than Jair but players of great talent.

When Corinthians and then Santos began to dominate *paulista* competition in the 1950s, Palmeiras receded slightly, but it remained consistently near the top and even managed to appear from time to time in the *paulista* honors list. Santos would have won 12 consecutive championships were it not for

Palmeiras's three in 1959, 1963, and 1966. It won another Rio-São Paulo Tournament in 1965, and when that series became the transitory forerunner of the Campeonato Nacional, Palmeiras again stole the limelight from Santos and won the Brazilian championship in 1967 and 1969. With its two consecutive national championships in the early 1970s, it became Brazil's most successful postwar club after Santos. In keeping with the pattern of other Brazilian clubs in the Copa Libertadores, Palmeiras has achieved little in the way of international honors, but it does have the highest point accumulation of any Brazilian club in that competition, and it advanced to the final round twice—in 1961 and 1968. Palmeiras's greatest stars of the modern era have been Mazzola (Jose Altafini), who went on to AC Milan after the 1958 World Cup, and Djalma Santos, who startled fans by playing his last years with Palmeiras after a long career with crosstown rival Portuguêsa.

Panama

Federación Nacional de Fútbol de Panamá
Apartado Postal 1867
Panamá 1

Founded: 1937
FIFA: 1938
CONCACAF: ?

Colors: *red, blue, and white jerseys, blue shorts;* honors: *Central American and Caribbean Championship (1951). (Further information unavailable.)*

The strong American presence in Panama since the turn of the century dampened the possibility that soccer would find an early home there, but the game eventually seeped into the country by social osmosis from neighboring states. Panama has traditionally been the second weakest Central American country on the soccer field after Nicaragua (discounting Belize), and the organization of soccer domestically appears to be less than efficient. Baseball is still prominent, and soccer is virtually unknown in the culturally influential American Canal Zone.

In the 1930s, however, there was a small boom in soccer activities, and the Federación Nacional de Fútbol was founded in 1937. (The longer name now in use was adopted in 1972.) The new federation wasted little time in affiliating with FIFA, and it immediately set out to participate in regional soccer activities. The Central American and Caribbean Games,

held in Panama in 1938, provided its first opportunity, and Panama made its international debut in the soccer tournament of that competition. In its first match it defeated baseball-mad Venezuela 2-1, but went on to lose to lowly Colombia, 4-0, and Costa Rica, 11-0 before surprising Mexico with a 2-2 draw, placing fifth in a field of six. It entered the Championship of the Central American and Caribbean Confederation in 1941 and 1946 (this series replaced the soccer tournament of the Central American and Caribbean Games as the regional championship), but placed second from the bottom on both occasions. This trend was continued in 1946 and 1948, and finally in 1951 it broke through and won the top prize, its only major trophy to date. Panama's participation in subsequent editions of this series, as well as its successor, the Championship of CONCACAF, has been sporadic. Olympic qualification has been consistently out of reach, and Panama made its first attempt to qualify for the World Cup with the 1978 edition, resulting in a last place finish in the Central American group. Panama has also entered the soccer tournaments of the Bolivarian Games and the Panamerican Games, the latter yielding very poor results. Meanwhile, Panamanian clubs have rarely been seen in the CONCACAF Champions' Cup.

Pan American Football Confederation

See: **Confederación Panamericana de Football**

Pan American Games, Football Tournament of the

Torneo Fútbol de los Juegos Desportivos Panamericanos.

The all-amateur Pan American Games were established by a congress of 16 national Olympic committees from South, Central, and North America in 1940 at Buenos Aires. The first official games were scheduled to be held in 1942, but were called off because of the war. They were finally introduced in 1951 in the Argentine capital, and soccer was on the program from the start. Professionalism in South America and a few countries in Central America has precluded the Pan American Games competition from becoming a true test of power in the hemisphere, and most of the major soccer countries have paid little attention to its outcome. Indeed, the 1975 result was attained by a forfeit. It remains, however, the only hemisphere-wide soccer tournament in the world, though it has been dominated completely by two countries, Argentina and Mexico. Unofficial, preliminary Pan American Games were held in Dallas, Texas, in 1937.

Winners

1937 (in Dallas) Argentina [unofficial]	1963 (in São Paulo) Brazil
1951 (in Buenos Aires) Argentina	1967 (in Winnipeg) Mexico
1955 (in Mexico City) Argentina	1971 (in Cali) Argentina
1959 (in Chicago) Argentina	1975 (in Mexico City) Mexico

Papua-New Guinea

Papua-New Guinea Football Association
P.O. Box 2606
Konedobu P.N.G.

Founded: 1962
FIFA: 1963
OFC: 1966

Affiliated clubs: *320;* **registered players:** *5,700;* **national stadium:** *Port Moresby Stadium, Port Moresby (22,000);* **largest stadium:** *Port Moresby Stadium;* **colors:** *green jerseys with white trim, white shorts;* **season:** *February to November;* **honors:** *none.*

Soccer was played by British soldiers and technicians at Port Moresby before the turn of the century, and in Rabaul and other settlements by the British and Australians during World War II, but Papuans themselves received little exposure to the game until the 1950s. Australians were mainly responsible for teaching it to townspeople during the mandate, and helped local administrators to set up a governing body with permission from FIFA. Papua-New Guinea, largely through its strong Australian connection, was active in the formation of the Oceania Football Confederation in 1966. It has participated regularly in the soccer tournament of the South Pacific Games, and, in fact, placed second to Fiji in the 1969 edition. Unfortunately, it was not able to organize a national team for the first Oceania Cup in 1973. In the most recent edition of the South Pacific Games (1975), Papua-New Guinea and Guam compiled the worst records in the competition.

Papua-New Guinea remains one of only three full-fledged members of the Oceania Football Confederation. Over 60 clubs compete in domestic competitions, and these include a national championship, a national cup competition, and regional championships centered in Port Moresby, Rabaul, Madang, Lae, Bulolo, and Goroka. The Papua-New Guinea Football Association, which was founded in 1962 and affiliated with FIFA one year later, even sponsors a youth program for upwards of 50 youth teams. Stadiums with capacities from 3,000 to 9,000 have been built in each major city.

Paraguay

Liga Paraguaya de Fútbol
Estadio de Sajonia
Calles Mayor Martínez y Alejo García
Asunción

Founded: 1906
FIFA: 1921
CONMEBOL: 1921

Affiliated clubs: *742;* registered players: *110,000 (100,000 non-amateur);* national stadium: *Estadio de la Liga Paraguaya de Fútbol, Asunción (50,000);* largest stadium: *Estadio de la Liga Paraguaya;* colors: *red and white striped jerseys, blue shorts;* season: *May to December;* honors: *South American Championship winner (1953), runner-up (1929, 1949, 1963).*

Paraguayan soccer has a long and venerable history, and the Paraguayan style of play is traditionally gallant rather than subtle. Its wide experience has yielded a fair share of successes in international competition, especially when one considers its small population. Soccer is at the center of Paraguayan cultural life, and every town and village supports at least one highly prominent club. The capital, Asunción, boasts over 30 clubs at the senior level. In overall South American Championship standings, Paraguay ranks fourth in total points, only a few short of mighty Brazil.

The national league, centered in Asunción, was founded in 1906, and is one of the oldest in Latin America. The usual separation of league and national association did not take place when Paraguayan soccer was first organized and thus, the founding date of the governing body and the league are the same. The early years of league competition were dominated by some of the same clubs which still figure prominently in the first division: Guarani, Cerro Porteño, Olímpia, and Libertad. Argentine influence on Paraguayan soccer was considerable. Paraguay's first official internationals were played in 1919 against Argentina at Asunción. Four matches in quick succession were played over a period of ten days, and the visitors won all four by an aggregate score of 12-3.

In 1921, the Liga Paraguaya de Fútbol (LPF) joined FIFA and CONMEBOL, and the national team participated in the South American Championship for the first time, placing fourth in a field of four. Its first international victory was won in this competition with a 2-1 result over Uruguay. In the 1922 edition of the South American Championship, Paraguay finished in first place but level on points with Brazil, and lost the playoff, 3-1. (Uruguay also finished with the same number of points, but it withdrew after its equalizer was disallowed in the final game against Paraguay.) Throughout the interwar years, Paraguay continued to place third or fourth in the South American Championship behind Argentina and Uruguay, with Brazil and Chile as its chief rivals. In the 1929 edition, it showed real strength for the first time, crushing both Uruguay and Peru and achieving a second place finish. In the first World Cup a year later, a discouraging loss to the burly Americans was offset by a 1-0 win over Belgium, Paraguay's first European opponent.

The upward momentum of Paraguayan

soccer was thwarted inopportunely by the war with Bolivia between 1929-35, and by the confusion that resulted from the adoption of professionalism in 1931. The league suspended competition for three years, and the national team missed the thirteenth edition of the South American Championship (1935) after being one of that series' most consistent participants. Olímpia and Cerro Porteño, Paraguay's most popular and successful clubs, had by now come to dominate the league— Cerro from 1913-19 and Olímpia during the late 1920s—and after the adoption of professionalism, their leadership continued. Paraguay produced its greatest player during this period, Arsenio Erico, who unfortunately never played for a major club in his native country. He was, instead, the hero of Independiente in Argentina, and led his adopted club to successive honors in the late 1930s. The expansion of professionalism in South America during the 1930s helped to raise the standard of play in Paraguay, but it also marked the beginning of a player exodus to wealthier leagues in Argentina, Brazil, Spain, and Italy. Erico was one of many Paraguayans in the 1930s and subsequent decades to take this route.

The immediate postwar years were an age of growth and enthusiasm in Paraguayan soccer. Several clubs emerged as champions of the first division, holding Olímpia and Cerro to a pair of titles each, and the LPF built a grand new stadium in Asunción during the early 1950s. Fleitas Solich was hired to manage the national team, which had already achieved an unprecedented pair of back-to-back second place results in the 1947 and 1949 South American Championship, and under him Paraguay raced undefeated to the 1953 title in Lima. A noteworthy triumph in many respects, this win was charged with historical import and controversy. Paraguay appeared to win the competition outright with a two-point margin over World Cup runners-up Brazil, but its 3-0 win over Chile was rescinded because of a substitution violation. This put Paraguay and Brazil level on points, and a play-off was organized in Lima by the Liga Paraguaya de Fútbol, which the Paraguayans won, 3-2. The result, however, is still not officially acknowledged by Brazil. Meanwhile, Solich had introduced a new tactical concept to an unwary opposition, which was eventually recognized as a 4-2-4 formation. This went almost unnoticed at the time, and five years later, when Brazil made the new system

famous in the World Cup, the importance of its earlier introduction by Paraguay was not properly acknowledged.

Paraguay's performance in the 1950 World Cup, meanwhile, had done little to capture world attention, as Sweden easily coasted to a 2-2 draw, and the weakest Italian team in decades assured Paraguay's elimination with a 2-0 shutout. Paraguay qualified for the World Cup again in 1958, after stunning Uruguay in the qualification round by a 7-0 aggregate score, but it was no match for the seven goals scored by France in the first round at Norköpping. It did, however, manage to hold the strong Yugoslavian team to a draw, and Scotland went down to an expected 3-2 defeat. These generally favorable results punctuated Paraguay's most successful decade in international competition. Paraguay has not qualified for the World Cup since 1958, and the newly found strength of Chile and Peru, in addition to the traditional power of Brazil, Argentina, and Uruguay, has kept Paraguay in relative obscurity in recent years.

Olímpia, the league champion five years in a row in the late 1950s, reached the final of the first Copa Libertadores in 1960 after burying Colombia's Millionarios in the semi-finals, but in the final, Uruguay's Peñarol squeaked by with a 1-0 second-leg win. This remains the only appearance by a Paraguayan club in the final of the South American club championship. Olímpia, Cerro Porteño, and Guarani, however, are all ranked among the top ten Libertadores clubs in total points. This reflects not only the consistency of these clubs at home, but their overall ability to maintain superiority over the clubs of weaker South American countries as well. Olímpia again reached the semi-finals in 1961, as did Guarani in 1966 and Cerro Porteño in 1973.

The Liga Paraguaya de Fútbol consists of a first division with ten members, lower divisions, and over 40 regional leagues. The national champion is the winner of the first division. After the first division championship ends, the top six finishers in the first division play against the major provincial champions in a second competiton. The winner of this series plays the runner-up of the already completed first division for the second berth in next year's Copa Libertadores. The first berth is automatically taken by the first division winner. Olímpia has now won a total of 24 national championships, five more than its archrival Cerro Porteño.

Champions

1906	Guarani	1930	Libertad	1954	Cerro Porteño
1907	Guarani	1931	Olímpia	1955	Libertad
1908	no competition	1932	no competition	1956	Olímpia
1909	Nacional	1933	no competition	1957	Olímpia
1910	Libertad	1934	no competition	1958	Olímpia
1911	Nacional	1935	Cerro Porteño	1959	Olímpia
1912	Olímpia	1936	Olímpia	1960	Olímpia
1913	Cerro Porteño	1937	Olímpia	1961	Cerro Porteño
1914	Olímpia	1938	Olímpia	1962	Olímpia
1915	Cerro Porteño	1939	Cerro Porteño	1963	Cerro Porteño
1916	Olímpia	1940	Cerro Porteño	1964	Guarani
1917	Libertad	1941	Cerro Porteño	1965	Olímpia
1918	Cerro Porteño	1942	Nacional	1966	Cerro Porteño
1919	Cerro Porteño	1943	Libertad	1967	Guarani
1920	Libertad	1944	Cerro Porteño	1968	Olímpia
1921	Guarani	1945	Libertad	1969	Olímpia
1922	no competition	1946	Nacional	1970	Cerro Porteño
1923	Guarani	1947	Olímpia	1971	Olímpia
1924	Nacional	1948	Olímpia	1972	Cerro Porteño
1925	Olímpia	1949	Guarani	1973	Cerro Porteño
1926	Nacional	1950	Cerro Porteño	1974	Cerro Porteño
1927	Olímpia	1951	Sportivo Luqueño	1975	Olímpia
1928	Olímpia	1952	Presidente Hayes	1976	Libertad
1929	Olímpia	1953	Sportivo Luqueño	1977	Cerro Porteño

pass

The lawful movement of the ball from one player to another, as distinct from a shot on goal.

See also: **back pass, cross, square ball, through ball, throw-in, wall pass**

Pedernera, Adolfo (1918-)

Pedernera, *el maestro*, was quite possibly the greatest Argentine forward of all time, though he is challenged by several others for this honor in a country that has produced many great stars. He was, nevertheless, a true genius in his favorite position of center forward, though he was so versatile that Argentina used him in all five forward positions. He was the leader of the most famous Argentine forward line in history, *la maquina*, which took Ríver Plate to great heights in the early 1940s. Flanked by two other Argentine immortals, José Moreno and Angel Labruna, he was a supreme strategist and precision shooter, and left a legacy for the Argentine game in perfecting the role of deep-lying center forward.

He made his debut for Ríver's first team in 1936 at age 18, contributing mightily to that club's five championships over the next few years, and went on to play for the national team 21 times. In 1947, he was replaced by Alfredo Di Stefano, and in 1949, after brief stints with Atlanta and Huracán, he led the mass migration of players to Colombia's Millonarios, where he played until 1953 in the company of Di Stefano and other Argentine compatriots. He remained there after the rest had left, however, to take over as player-coach of Millonarios and eventually Colombia's national team. He later returned to Argentina to coach for several years, and accepted an offer to manage Colombia again in its surprisingly successful 1962 World Cup showing—actually a tribute to Pedernera's tactical know-how. Immediately thereafter, he became manager of Argentina's Gimnasia y Esgrima, Boca Júniors, Huracán, Independiente, and finally, the Argentine national team. In 1978, he accepted yet another post with San Lorenzo of Buenos Aires.

Pelé (1940-)

(Full name: Edson Arantes do Nascimento.) The most celebrated player of all time and probably the best, though some Brazilians still believe Artur Friedenreich has never been surpassed, and some Europeans would rank Alfredo Di Stefano as his equal. Pelé's statistical record is staggering, but anyone who has ever seen him play will think first of his genius as a stylist on the field. It is probably true, as Brazilian observers have often pointed out, that Pelé would have become the world's most accomplished player at any position, but it was at inside left that he received all the accolades a player could possibly muster. The perfection of his physical attributes, moreover, has been miraculously paralleled by a gracious and engaging personality, as well as a strong desire to teach and lead, which have given him universal recognition as a genuine world idol.

Memories focus on flashes of movement: body feints, dribbles in which his feet are an unnecessary luxury, dummies sold, headers taken over towering defenders, and widely arched shots around walls of players. In his first goal against Sweden in 1958, he pushed the ball over his shoulder with his thigh, pivoted, and fired a shot past the hapless goalkeeper. In 1961, against Fluminense at the Maracanã, he dribbled from his own penalty area past six oncoming defenders and the goalkeeper—into the opponent's net. (This famous goal became immortalized as the *Gol de Placa*, or, Commemorative Plate Goal.) Among his haunting, yet prophetic, near-misses was that quick shot in his World Cup debut against the USSR that hit the post and left the great Yashin beaten. Some have tried to explain Pelé's magical qualities in physiological terms: his well-placed center of gravity for the particular skills needed in the game, or his uncommon peripheral vision, or even some form of advanced neurological development. Pelé himself, however, simply points to God-given gifts for which he is very thankful.

Born in the small village of Três Coraçóes in the state of Minas Gerais, he was the son of Dondinho, a lowly paid professional center forward with second division Bauru, the local club. While playing on the "barefoot team" Sete de Sétembro in 1952, he acquired the name Pelé, the meaning of which is unknown even to him. He appeared briefly with Ameriquinha, the youth team whose inspiration was the big Rio club América FC, and at age 13 he was discovered by former World Cup star Waldemar de Brito, manager of Bauru. After 2 1/2 years on the Bauru junior team, Baquinho, Waldemar de Brito brought him to Santos FC in the port city of the same name, and there he played on its junior team for the summer. In 1956, Pelé made his first team debut for Santos against AIK Stockholm in an international friendly. At age 16, he became a regular first team member, and before he turned 17 made his international debut for Brazil against Argentina. Coming on as a substitute, he scored Brazil's lone goal, and three days later he started for Brazil against the same Argentine team.

In the 1958 World Cup, he appeared in Brazil's third game against the USSR, and played in each game thereafter, scoring six goals, including a hat trick against France and two against Sweden in the final that won Brazil's first world championship. These performances in Sweden captured the imagination of the soccer world, and elevated him immediately to the heights of international acclaim. Every wealthy club in Europe offered record transfer fees for his services, but the Congress of Brazil declared him an official national treasure and forbade his sale or trade. In 1960, he signed a second contract with Santos.

Pelé's Santos became the dominant force in Brazilian soccer. It won four São Paulo championships between 1958-62, two more in 1964 and 1965, and three in a row between 1967-69. Throughout this period, Pelé achieved feats that became legends in their own time: 127 goals in 1959, 110 goals in 1961, 101 goals in 1965, and in the intervening years an average of over 70 goals per season. In 1962 and 1963, he led Santos to win both the Copa Libertadores and the Intercontinental Cup, the latter before appreciative crowds in Lisbon and Milan. Santos' tours of Europe became the talk of the continent.

An injury in Brazil's opening game of the 1962 World Cup prevented Pelé from participating in his country's second world championship win, and in the years that followed additional injuries became a serious problem. Invariably, less talented opponents resorted to triple-teaming and brutal hacking. After Brazil was knocked out of the 1966

World Cup in England, Pelé complained bitterly of permissive referees, and vowed not to play in a World Cup again. But four years later he shone more brightly than ever before in helping Brazil to win an unprecedented third world championship. His stunning header against Italy's Albertosi in the final put Brazil ahead, and he assisted on each of Brazil's additional goals in an unforgettable display of the technical lexicon. In 1969, he became the third player in history to score 1,000 goals, though his were undoubtedly achieved with stiffer opposition than those of Friedenreich and Franz Binder before him. In 1971, before 130,000 impassioned fans at the Maracanã, he retired from the national team, and in 1974 played his last game with Santos. In that sad farewell appearance with his club of 18 years, he trotted around the stadium before leaving the field at half time, and with tears running down his face, listened to the sounds of chanting throngs pleading with him to: "Stay! Stay!" His retirement was thought to be permanent.

In 1975, he stunned the soccer world by signing a $3.5 million contract with Warner

Pelé, world idol and the King of Soccer, dribbling through a maze of defenders. Untold millions have witnessed this magic moment. Santos vs. Schalke 04 in Essen, 1963.

Communications, owners of the New York Cosmos. The contract called for him not only to play for Cosmos, but also to promote the game throughout the United States with an eye to turning it into a major commercial sport. After 2 1/2 seasons, he made a second farewell appearance at Giants Stadium in 1977, and turned his attention to a host of business obligations and touring the world in highly selective efforts to promote the skills and sportsmanship in soccer that he himself faithfully practiced. In 1976, he was the assistant coach of a Rio selection in a friendly against the USSR, and he has also worked

Pelé celebrates his magnificent goal against Italy in the 1970 World Cup final. Jairzinho's embrace represented the affection of viewers everywhere.

intermittently in sports broadcasting for Brazilian television.

Biographies of Pelé have been written in or translated into over 100 languages, and the giant stadium at Maceió, Estádio Rei Pelé, is named for him. He is thought to hold the world record for number of appearances in any category (1,362), though his total number of goals scored (1,280) remains second in ranking behind that of Friedenreich. He holds the world record for number of career hat tricks (92), number of goals scored at full international level (97), including a record seven international hat tricks), and he was the scoring leader in São Paulo league competition from 1957-65, 1969, and in 1973. He was also the scoring leader in the South American Championship in 1959 and the Copa Libertadores in 1965, and was selected Latin American Footballer of the Year in 1973. Nickname: *pérola negra*, or "Black Pearl."

Bauru Atlético Clube (1953-56); Santos FC (1956-74), 1,114 appearances, 1,088 goals; Cosmos (1975-77), 105 appearances, 55 goals. Brazil (1957-71), 93 appearances, 97 goals; Brazilian Army team (1959), ten appearances, 14 goals; São Paulo selections, Santos/Vasco da Gama selections, and Professional Footballers Association selections, 19 appearances, 18 goals.

penalty decision

In 1970, the International Football Association Board accepted a proposal that provided for a penalty kick contest to replace the practice of choosing lots to decide the result of a drawn game. The penalty kick contest is put into effect only if extra time has not produced a winner, and it is restricted exclusively to knockout competitions, such as national cups and international championships. The rules and conditions of the procedure, whose official name is "taking of kicks from the penalty mark," are as follows:

1. The goal at which all the kicks are taken is chosen by the referee.
2. A coin toss by the referee determines which team kicks first.
3. Each team is entitled to at least five kicks, which are taken alternately, first by one team then the other.
4. If, before five kicks are completed, one player fails to score and his opposite number scores, the taking of kicks is ended by the referee.
5. If, after five kicks are completed, both teams have scored the same number of goals, the procedure continues until one team has scored more than the other after both have taken an equal number of kicks.
6. The team that scores the greater number of goals is declared the winner of the contest, but the game is recorded as a draw with an additional notation that the winner was decided on penalty kicks.
7. If the goalkeeper is injured during the contest, he may be replaced by a teammate who is already on the field or by a substitute, the latter provided his team has not already made use of the maximum number of substitutes permitted by the rules.
8. Only players who are on the field at the end of the match may qualify to take kicks.
9. No player may take a second kick until all eligible teammates have had their turn.
10. Other than the kicker and goalkeeper, all players must remain within the center circle while the kick is in progress.
11. The goalkeeper who is waiting for his turn to defend must remain in the field of play but outside the penalty area at least 10 yards from the penalty spot and further than 18 yards from the goal line.
12. Unless superseded expressly by the rules above, all Laws of the Game apply throughout the contest.

The final results of important international competitions that have been decided on penalty kicks are:

Copa Interamericana

1974:
Independiente (Arg)—Dep. Municipal (Guat)   1-0, 0-1
(Independiente won on penalty kicks)

1976:
Independiente—Atlético Español (Mex)   2-2, 0-0
(Independiente won on penalty kicks)

European Football Championship

1976:
Czechoslovakia—Germany FR   2-2
(Czechoslovakia won on penalty kicks)

African Champion's Cup

1976:
Hafia Conakry (Guinea)—Mouloudia (Algeria)   3-0, 0-3
(Mouloudia won on penalty kicks)

---

penalty kick   Also known as "spot kick."

A direct free kick from the penalty spot, which is awarded to an offended team for any serious foul committed in the opponent's penalty area. It consists of an unimpeded shot on goal and the attempt to save it by the opposing goalkeeper.

There are numerous regulations governing the penalty kick: 1) the goalkeeper must stand on the goal line without moving until the ball is kicked; 2) all players other than the two principals must be within the field of play but outside the penalty area and ten yards from the penalty spot, i.e., outside the penalty arc; 3) the kick itself must be made in the direction of the goal; 4) the kicker may not play the ball a second time until it has been touched by another player; and 5) the referee must always ensure that a penalty kick is taken even if time has run out. If any regulation is broken by one of the defending team, the penalty kick must be retaken if a score did not result. If any regulation is broken by the team taking the penalty kick, the goal, if scored, is disallowed, and the kick must be taken over. If the penalty kicker commits a foul after the kick is taken, the opposing side is awarded an indirect free kick.

The penalty kick was introduced by the Irish Football Association during the 1890-91 season. The first goal from a penalty kick was made by an American named Jeffrey of the Pawtucket club of Rhode Island during a match between Linfield F. C. and a combined USA-Canada team at Belfast in 1891. England adopted the penalty kick for the 1891-92 season.

Peñarol, Club Atlético

Location: *Montevideo, Uruguay;* stadium:*Estadio Centenario (75,000);* colors: *black and yellow striped jerseys, black shorts;* honors: *Intercontinental Cup (1961, 1966), Copa Libertadores (1960, 1961, 1966), Uruguayan champion (1900, 1901, 1905, 1907,*

1911, 1918, 1921, 1926, 1928, 1929, 1930, 1932, 1935, 1936, 1937, 1938, 1944, 1945, 1949, 1951, 1953, 1954, 1958, 1959, 1960, 1961, 1962, 1964, 1965, 1967, 1968, 1973, 1974, 1975, 1978).

Founded 1891 as Central Uruguay Railway Cricket Club by four British employees of the Ferrocarril Central (Central Railroad), a British-owned company. The founding members were Arthur Davenport, Frank Henderson, Frank Hudson, and Roland Moor. By 1892, there were enough members to organize a team, and the first game was played against the British School of Montevideo, the Cricket Club winning 2-0. Its opposition throughout the 1890s was made up of other British clubs and scratch teams, including Albion, and the new German club, Deutscher Fussballklub. In 1900, a member of the Cricket Club founded the Uruguayan Football Association and the Uruguayan league, and the club was joined by Albion, Deutscher FK, and Uruguay F.C. in launching the first season. The Cricket Club went undefeated and won the first Uruguayan championship, followed by a second title in 1901. A third championship was won in 1905 without conceding a loss or a single goal.

In 1909, a Scotsman named John Harley introduced the Scottish short-passing game to the Cricket Club, but, despite its growing tactical sophistication, its position in the league was challenged successfully for several years by Wanderers and the Buenos Aires club, Ríver Plate. Harley, meanwhile, remained associated with Peñarol until his death in the 1960s. In 1914, when the Ferrocarril Central was passed on to Uruguayan ownership, the name of the club was changed to Club Atlético Peñarol, after the district in Montevideo where the company was located. After its title-winning season of 1914, Peñarol steadily became less British in composition, and the domination of Uruguayan soccer by Peñarol and Nacional, the two Montevideo giants, began in earnest. The *oro y negro* (Peñarol's nickname and colors) and Nacional went on to win over 90 per cent of all Uruguayan championships in subsequent decades, and by 1978, Peñarol had a small lead with a total of 35 wins to Nacional's 32. From an international perspective, Peñarol has been the most successful club in South American soccer and, next to Santos, the most famous.

Peñarol's first great star was José Piendibene, a goalscoring artist who joined in 1908 as a right wing but spent most of his 22 years with the club as a deep-lying center forward.

He was the driving force behind Peñarol's many tournament wins outside the league championship, such as the Copa Honor (1909, 1918), Copa Competencia (1910, 1916), and Copa Rio de la Plata (1919, 1928). But Peñarol was dominated throughout much of the 1910s and '20s by Nacional in league competition. The bulk of Uruguay's astounding national team that won two Olympic gold medals and the first World Cup between 1924-30 was made up of Nacional stars, and it was not until the ten-year period from 1928-38 that Peñarol achieved its first dynastic hold on the league. Though it won eight championships during this period, it failed to achieve the international fame that had come to Nacional in the 1920s, because Uruguay did not participate in the 1934 and 1938 World Cups.

Peñarol's fortunes were rising again, however, as the 1950 World Cup approached, and this edition of the cup brought to Peñarol the national glory that had earlier come to Nacional. Peñarol won the first division title in 1949 without losing a game, and when the 1950 World Cup team was selected there were seven Peñarol players in the starting lineup. Uruguay won its second world championship, and Peñarol's wing half Rodriguez Andrade, right wing Chico Ghiggia, inside left Juan Schiaffino, left wing Ernesto Vidal, goalkeeper Roque Maspoli, and especially Obdulio Varela, captain and center half, became international heroes.

The club's greatest era started in 1958 with the first of five successive league titles. Led by the Ecuardorean goalscoring sensation Alberto Spencer, Peñarol at this time was the major threat to the fame and success of Pelé's Santos. In 1960, Peñarol became the first important South American club to take the new Copa Libertadores seriously, and won the first edition without a defeat. In the first Intercontinental Cup, Real Madrid, now at its peak, proved too great a match, but Peñarol won the second Copa Libertadores the following year, defeating Brazil's Palmeiras in the final, and the second Intercontinental Cup over Portugal's Benfica. This brilliant Peñarol team, now beyond a doubt the world's best, featured many superb players other than Spencer, among them center half and captain Nestor Gonçalvez, the ball juggling inside right José Sasia, and right winger Luis Cubilla. In the

Montevideo leg of the 1961 Intercontinental Cup with Benfica, Peñarol converted five unanswered goals.

In 1962, Peñarol reached the final of the Copa Libertadores for the third straight year, but succumbed to Santos, and the following year bowed out in the semi-finals to Argentina's Ríver Plate. Peñarol's fortunes at home continued. There were four more championships from 1964-68, and in 1965 it reached the Copa Libertadores final once again, losing a hard fought three-game series to Argentina's Independiente. Then in 1966, it won the South American club championship for the third time, eliminating the frustrated Nacional and showing superior individual skills against Ríver Plate in another three-game final. Peñarol reached the final again in 1970, but for the most part Nacional was the more successful club in both domestic and international competition during the late 1960s and early '70s. Peñarol's new stars, goalkeeper Ladislao Mazurkiewicz and schemer Pedro Rocha, joined the long list of Uruguayan players sold to wealthy foreign clubs to make ends meet, and, despite the sometime presence of center forward Fernando Morena, Uruguay's finest talent of the 1970s, the club declined in form with Nacional and the rest of Uruguayan soccer by the mid-1970s.

Peñarol's home ground and training field is the "Pocitos," formerly Las Acacias, (taken over way back in 1916), but all matches are played in the huge Estadio Centenario on a shared basis with Nacional.

Peñarol at the height of its brilliance in 1965. World domination on the club level was achieved under the leadership of manager Roque Maspoli (standing, far right), Uruguay's goalkeeper in the 1950 World Cup. Its great stars were Ecuadorean goalscoring genius Alberto Spencer (seated, far right), schemer Pedro Rocha (seated, second from left), and goalkeeper Ladislao Mazurkiewicz (standing, fourth from left).

Peru

Federación Peruana de Fútbol
Estadio Nacional—Puerta No. 4
Cale José Diaz
Lima

Founded: 1922
FIFA: 1924
CONMEBOL: 1926

Affiliated clubs: *6,158;* registered players: *139,360 (400 professional);* national stadium: *Estadio Nacional, Lima (45,000);* largest stadium: *Estadio Universidad de San Marcos, Lima (60,000);* colors: *white jerseys with red diagonal stripe, white shorts;* season: *April to December;* honors: *South American Championship winner (1939, 1975).*

Peru is comfortably situated with Chile as a secondary power in South American soccer, and it is the spawning ground of several dazzling players of world caliber, including the incomparable Teofilo Cubillas, perhaps the most gifted non-Brazilian ball artist to have come from South America in the last 30 years. The Peruvian style of play in the upper ranks is fluid and pleasing to the eye. When good Peruvian teams are in top form, they can challenge the best of both Europe and South America, as shown by their performances in the 1970 World Cup. The national team has suffered greatly in recent years by the exodus of top players to Europe and Mexico, and the concern now is that there are few to take the place of its great stars of the 1970s. Peru is also the home of CONMEBOL, the South American Football Confederation, a throwback to Lima's having been the political and cultural capital of Spanish South America for many centuries.

Soccer was introduced to Peru according to the familiar pattern in Latin America. British advisors, engineers, and other technicians played the game among themselves in Callao and other commercial centers during the last decades of the nineteenth century, and the game eventually found its way to the local population. A league was established in Lima as early as 1912, with Peruvian-based clubs among its membership, but this was not a direct ancestor of the present national federation.

In the early 1920s (a period of tremendous growth in South American soccer), efforts were made to organize Peruvian soccer fully. The Federación Peruana de Fútbol (FPF) was founded in 1922—the first of five national associations founded in the northern part of South America around this time—and, while it gained membership in FIFA two years later, administrative difficulties caused a reorganization in 1925. This led to the introduction of the Liga Nacional de Football in 1926, with clubs from Lima and Callao. The first champion was Club Sport Progreso, but Club Alianza Lima, which became strongly identified with black and poor mestizo neighborhoods in the capital, and Club Uni-

versitario de Deportes, founded by Spanish students in 1924, eventually took control of the league. (Alianza Lima has now won a record 16 championships to Universitario's 15.) Alianza won six titles between 1927-34, and several in the 1950s and '60s. Universitario's success has been spread evenly over the decades since its first title in 1929. Sport Boys and Deportivo Municipal were multiple winners in the league between 1935-50, and Sporting Cristal emerged as a leading club during the 1960s. A national championship for regional selections representing the various leagues was introduced in 1928, and held every three or four years until 1946.

Peru's international debut was made in 1927 as host of the eleventh South American Championship. Argentina and Uruguay, both major world powers during the 1920s, defeated the fledgling home team decisively (5-1 and 4-0), but Bolivia, the fourth participant, lost 3-2, and Peru took third place. In the next three editions of the competition, Peru took last or next to last place each time, but in 1939, when the championship was staged again in Lima, the home side advantage helped Peru win its first South American Championship and international victory. Peru was undefeated in four games against Uruguay, Paraguay, Chile, and Ecuador, but, without either Argentina or Brazil participating, some of the significance of this win was surely compromised.

The Peruvian federation's early interest in international tournaments was further reflected by its entrance in the first World Cup in 1930 at Montevideo, but this proved to be the beginning of a stormy decade in global competition. A brutal 3-1 loss to Rumania, in which the Peruvian captain was sent off and another Peruvian's leg was broken, was followed by a bitter 1-0 loss to the eventual world champion, Uruguay, and both games suffered from poor refereeing. Peru was duly eliminated in the first round.

Though professionalism was adopted in 1931, the FPF was still able to send many of its best players to take part in the Nazi Olympics of 1936 at Berlin. Since this was Peru's first major sporting effort in Europe, a small but volatile group of Peruvian fans gathered in Berlin to lend support. In the first round, the Finnish amateurs were easy prey for Peru's skilled forwards, but against Austria in the second round extra time was required. Peruvian supporters rioted in the second overtime period, and after Peru scored two goals in all the confusion, Austria protested. The game was disallowed and a replay was ordered. Peru refused to show up for the replay, Austria was awarded the two points, and Peru went home in disgust. This incident erased the good will and respect achieved in 1933 by Universitario's 30-game tour of Europe, which lasted six months and in some respects marked a turning point in the advancement of Peruvian soccer.

Throughout the 1940s and '50s, Peru continued to participate in most editions of the South American Championship, usually finishing in the middle of the standings. It narrowly lost to Brazil in 1958 World Cup qualifications rounds, and in 1959 (under Hungarian manager and former great György Orth) it defeated England, 4-1, in Lima. In 1970, it finally qualified again for the World Cup. Managed by the Brazilian star Didi, Peru was the surprise of the 1970 competition, showing flair and a high level of skill. Its 20-year-old inside forward Teofilo Cubillas became the most highly touted South American player since Pelé. After winning elegantly over Bulgaria and Morocco, the same good form was shown in losing to West Germany (on a hat trick by Gerd Müller) and, in the quarter-finals, to Brazil. By now, Peru was clearly producing players of international caliber, and it was fitting that a Brazilian was chosen to bring them together and create an atmosphere in which they could fully display their great skills.

Peru's depth of talent was demonstrated in 1975, when it played the same brand of fluid, improvisational soccer, and, with more than its fair share of luck, managed to win its second South American Championship. Having eliminated Chile and Bolivia in the first round, Peru was fortunate to play a provincial Brazilian selection in the semi-finals and then advance to the final on choice of cards after the two countries played to an even goal aggregate. In the final, Peru faced traditionally weak Colombia, and on the basis of the tournament's point system was forced to a third and deciding match in neutral Caracas before finally winning the title. Meanwhile, the decline of Uruguay, and Argentina's and Brazil's fielding of provincial teams, had removed much of Peru's real opposition. Peru went on to qualify for the 1978 World Cup in Argentina with nagging managerial disputes threatening it potential effectiveness. In the first round, however, it landed on top of its group after a 3-1 upset of Scotland and a scoreless draw with Holland. Sadly, this talented team of World Cup veterans failed to score in losses to Brazil, Poland, and Argentina in the semi-finals, and went home in disgrace.

In the Copa Libertadores, the South American club championship, Universitario (known as "U") has participated 11 times and accumulated the third highest point total of any club in South America. Only Uruguay's Peñarol and Nacional rank higher. Universitario also became the first and only Peruvian club to advance to the final of this series in 1972, when it lost by one goal to the hard-hitting Independiente of Argentina. Sporting Cristal and Alianza Lima, which have played in six and five editions respectively, have overall losing records in the Copa Libertadores, disappointing their huge followings at home.

Peru's first division is now composed of 22 clubs, more than any other first division in the world except England, and represents all parts of the country. Unfortunately, the success of Peru's 1970 World Cup team resulted in financial setbacks for the national league, as Cubillas, Sotil, Rojas, Mifflin, Carbonell, Muñante, Salinas, and Reyes went abroad to play, and fans failed to support their now depleted favorite clubs.

In 1964, the worst disaster in the history of soccer occurred in Lima, when 318 people were killed and over 500 injured in a tragic riot at the Estadio Nacional. Indignation over this event threatened the stability of the Peruvian government for almost a week.

See also: **disasters and tragedies**

Champions

1926	C.S. Progreso	1928	Alianza Lima	1930	Atlético Chalaco
1927	Alianza Lima	1929	Universitario	1931	Alianza Lima

1932 Alianza Lima	1948 Alianza Lima	1965 Alianza Lima
1933 Alianza Lima	1949 Deportivo Municipal	1966 Universitario
1934 Alianza Lima	1951 Sport Boys	1967 Universitario
1935 Sport Boys	1952 Alianza Lima	1968 Sporting Cristal
1936 no competition	1953 Mariscal Sucre	1969 Universitario
1937 Sport Boys	1954 Alianza Lima	1970 Sporting Cristal
1938 Deportivo Municipal	1955 Alianza Lima	1971 Universitario
1939 Universitario	1956 Sporting Cristal	1972 Sporting Cristal
1940 Deportivo Municipal	1957 Alianza Lima	1973 Sporting Cristal
1941 Universitario	1958 Sport Boys	1974 Defensor Lima
1942 Sport Boys	1959 Universitario	1975 Universitario
1943 Deportivo Municipal	1960 Universitario	1976 Unión Huaral
1944 Mariscal Sucre	1961 Sporting Cristal	1977 Alianza Lima
1945 Universitario	1962 Galianza Lima	1978 Alianza Lima
1946 Universitario	1963 Alianza Lima	
1947 Atlético Chalaco	1964 Universitario	

Pesta Sukan Football Tournament

One of the minor international competitions for national teams of South and East Asia, d: continued after two years. The Pesta Sukan .ries was held in Singapore in connection with the famous annual festival of the same name. The second title was won by one Indonesian team over another.

Winners

1971 India and Vietnam Republic
1972 Indonesia "A"

Petrone, Pedro (1903-1964)

Unlike the other great goalscoring forwards of Uruguay during the 1920s, Petrone was an opportunist rather than a polished technician. He became world-famous for being in the right place at the right time, and somehow he always knew how best to get the ball where he wanted it. He starred for Uruguay in its three South American Championship victories during the mid-1920s, its two Olympic gold medal triumphs of 1924 and 1928, and for Nacional during that fabulous era when it supplied most of Uruguay's starting lineup. His teammates—Piendibene for Nacional and Andrade, Cea, and Scarone for Uruguay— would typically spot him lying in wait, and quickly feed him the ball. Year after year, Petrone scored astounding goals in this manner. In 1930, he was dropped from the national team after the first game of the World Cup, and was replaced by Pelegrin Anselmo, but in 1931-32, he was lured to Italy's Fiorentina for one season and co-led the

Italian league in scoring with 25 goals. Uncomfortable in the highly charged atmosphere of Fascist Italy, he returned to Nacional after one season, and helped his old club win two more championships before retiring.

Philippines

Philippine Football Association
P.O. Box 602
Makati, Rizal

Founded: 1907
FIFA: 1928
AFC: 1954

Affiliated clubs: *350;* **registered players:** *7,000;* **national stadium:** *Rizal Memorial Football Stadium, Manila (30,000);* **largest stadium:** *Rizal Memorial Football Stadium;* **colors;** *blue and red jerseys, blue shorts;* **season:** *July to April;* **honors:** *none.*

The Republic of the Philippines (then the American territory of the Philippines) was the principal instigator and organizer of soccer and other sports in the Far East region immediately after the turn of the century. Its importance in this regard is unchallenged. After the 1920s, however, it failed to make any impact at all in international soccer, and disappeared entirely from the mainstream of the Asian game due to the rising influence of American sports such as baseball and basketball after World War I. In the postwar era, the Philippines have rarely been seen in major international soccer competitions, and in recent years have not even entered World Cup qualifying rounds.

Soccer was first played in the Philippines by students at missionary schools and Filipino students who had studied in Spain. It was given its first real impetus by the growing interest in Olympic events and the formation of the Philippine Amateur Athletic Federation (PAAF) in 1907, the first governing body for sports in the Far East. The PAAF included a soccer section, and the date of its founding is therefore regarded as that of the Philippine Football Association (made independent in the 1950s). The first national championship in Asia was introduced in Manila in 1911 with several members from the various sports clubs of the city. All-Manila Sports Club was the first winner, but the next 15 years were dominated by Bohemian Club, which won ten championships before 1928. The national championship was sometimes determined by a league format (when few clubs were

competing) or a knockout system (when there were many clubs). In the 1930s, the championship was dominated by San Beda Athletic Club. Other winners before the championship was discontinued in 1936 were Nomads Sport Club, Cantabria, International, Ateneo de Manila, San Beda College, Peña Iberica, Sto. Tomas University, and in the last season before the competition's demise, a team from Singapore called Malaya Command.

The PAAF, impressed by the Olympic Games of 1912 at Stockholm, organized and staged the first biennial Far East Games in 1913, and saw to it that soccer was included in the schedule. For the next 21 years, the soccer tournament of the Far East Games was the only consistent international forum available for players of the region. The Philippines' first and only great rival was China. Making its international debut at the first edition of the games, the Philippines defeated China, 2-1. Sadly, this was to be its first and last international trophy, as China won the next nine tournaments in succession (1915-34), though the Philippines won another game over China in 1919. Only two other countries participated in this series, and the Philippines had better luck against them. It defeated Japan in 1917 (15-2) and in each edition from 1919-25, and narrowly defeated the Dutch East Indies in 1934.

After World War II, the PAAF organized all-Manila teams to play a series of three international friendlies with Hong Kong (1948-50), and the Filipinos lost all three by an aggregate score of 3-14. In 1953, Indonesia defeated the Philippines, 5-0, at Manila. Other internationals since World War II have been confined to qualifying rounds of the Asian Games, Asian Cup, or Olympic Games. A measure of the Philippines' decline since the 1920s is reflected in its results from the 1967 Asian Games Eastern Region qualifying round, in which it lost to Taiwan, 9-0, Indonesia, 6-0, Japan, 2-0, and South Korea, 7-0. It is also one of the few countries never to have won any of the Southeast Asian regional tournaments for national teams.

Pinto Durán Cup

Copa Juan L. Pinto Durán.

An occasional trophy awarded to the winner of certain series played between Chile and Uruguay. The first edition was played on a home and away basis. It is named for the past general secretary of the Federación de Football de Chile.

Winners

1967   shared
1975   Uruguay

Piola, Silvio   (1913-   )

A strong tall center forward, perhaps the greatest Italy has ever produced and possibly the best in Europe during the 1940s. Piola was aggressive rather than delicate, and he was especially good in the air. Whenever he got the ball, there was sure to be movement toward the goalmouth. Early in his international career, he was the star of Italy's World Cup triumph of 1938, providing a marked contrast to the more subtle Meazza. Eventually, Piola broke Meazza's Italian record of 355 league goals, and in 34 international appearances he scored 30 times. Though his number of international appearances was cut short by the war, his career was nonetheless very long and transcended at least two generations of Italian players. He broke the Italian league appearance record with 566, and led the league in scoring in 1937 and 1943.

Piola's senior-level career started in 1929 with Pro Vercelli, the venerable old Piemontese club, and in 1934 he began a nine-year stay at Lazio of Rome, where he scored 143 goals. In 1935, Vittorio Pozzo brought him into the national team after six appearances with Italy "B," and he soon succeeded Meazza as the premier Italian goalscorer. He was the spearhead of Italy's superb attack in the 1938 World Cup, scoring five goals and helping Meazza and others with most of their goals. In 1943-44, he played for one year with Torino in the wartime league, scoring 27 goals, and the following year he joined Juventus, remaining there for two seasons before going to unfashionable Novara to round out his career. His association with Novara, however, lasted until 1954, and when it finally ended, he had played in the first or second division for 25 years. He became manager of Lazio for a brief spell, and then took over Italy's first Under-23 squad. After sporadic coaching assignments, he was hired as a technical advisor for the Italian federation in 1960, a post he held until 1976. A public outcry resulted in 1976, when the Italian press discovered him living in a Roman slum barely sustaining himself on a small pension.

pivot kick

A kick in which the player swerves, or pivots, at the moment of impact, projecting the ball in the direction of his turn.

place kick

Any kick taken with the ball in a stationary position; for example, a goal kick or kickoff.

Plánička, František (1915-   )

Plánička rivaled Spain's Ricardo Zamora as the greatest goalkeeper in Europe between the world wars. Discovered as a boy by lowly SK Bubanec, he was brought through the youth teams of SK Slavia, and remained with this great Prague club for the rest of his career. From 1925-38, he made 74 international appearances for Czechoslovakia, a record since broken by Ladislav Novak, and held down the keeper position with utmost consistency. As national team captain, he was a driving force behind Czechoslovakia's rise to the front ranks of European soccer, and starred in the 1934 and 1938 World Cups. With Slavia he made over 700 appearances.

Among his most memorable internationals were two World Cup matches against Brazil in 1938, the first of these remembered as the infamous "Battle of Bordeaux." Flamengo's legendary Leônidas squared off with Plánička in both games, and the great Czech goalkeeper astounded French crowds with his ability to stop the Brazilian's every move. It was not learned until later that he had been playing with a broken arm. Plánička was not tall for a goalkeeper, but he was exceptionally fast and was a model for other keepers in his ability to position himself with uncanny anticipation. He continued to play for veteran teams while still in his sixties, though he had retired from Slavia in 1939, perhaps the greatest Czech player of all time.

point system

The universal point system, which is employed in nearly every league in the world and in all international competitions where a league system is followed, awards two points per game: two for a win, one to both teams for a draw, and none for a defeat.

The French point system, used in favor of the universal system in France and some French territories until 1976, awards a bonus point to a team that wins by two or more goals. In French-speaking North Africa and a handful of small countries elsewhere, three points are awarded for a win, two for a draw, and one for a loss (i.e., completing a game).

The North American Soccer League, in which drawn games are not allowed, has developed a unique system whereby six points are awarded for a win, none for a loss, and one additional point for every goal scored up to and including three per game. In the American Soccer League, five points are awarded for a win, two for a draw, none for a loss, and one bonus point for every goal scored up to and including three per game.

Poland

Polski Zwiazek Pilki Noznej
(Polish Football Association)
Al Ujazdowskie 22
Warszawa

Founded: 1919
FIFA: 1923
UEFA: 1955

Affiliated clubs: *4,702;* registered players: *188,585;* national stadium: *10th Anniversary Stadium, Warsaw (87,000);* largest stadium: *Slaski Stadium, Chorzów (93,000);* colors: *white jerseys, red shorts;* season: *August to November, March to June;* honors: *World Cup third place (1974), Olympic Games winner (1972), runner-up (1976).*

For 80 years Polish soccer suffered the consequences of political division, a long search for identity, and what seemed to be an incurable inferiority complex. Surrounded geographically by traditional soccer powers, it faced a rare challenge. In 1970, Polish soccer came of age, and the national team gained and maintained a place among the top half dozen countries in Europe. Now that Poland is near the top of the European ladder, it is about to face the test of consistency, as its first generation of international stars fades from the scene.

From the beginning, each turning point in Polish soccer has coincided closely with political changes in the country as a whole. The game was first played in Poland by British engineers in Lodz around 1890, but Czarist administrators in central Poland—then part of Russia—suppressed the formation of clubs and leagues, because they were thought to represent the threat of revolutionary activity. On the other hand, the game flourished in those areas of the modern Polish state that were part of Germany or Austria. In German Poland, several clubs were founded before the turn of the century: Alter Turn-Verein (ATV) Liegnitz, now Legnica, in 1896; Verein für Rasensport (VfR) Breslau, now Wroclaw, in 1897; and Ball und Eislauf-Verein (BEV) Danzig, now Gdansk, around 1898. ATV Liegnitz and VfR Breslau were among the pioneer clubs in Silesia, a region in the southwest that eventually became a center of soccer activity in the Polish republic. These and other clubs played in the Pomeranian-West Prussian league (Balten-verband) and Silesian league (Südostdeutschland) after 1900.

In Austrian Poland (Galicia), the university city of Kraków spawned the first club in the southeastern region—Cracovia Football Club—founded in 1906. (Cracovia is now the oldest Polish club still in existence.) Other Galician clubs followed, and in 1911, as befitting Cracovia's cosmopolitan reputation, organizers in Kraków introduced international competition in Poland by inviting Aberdeen F.C. for a two-game series against a local representative team. The Scots won, 11-1 and 8-1, but before World War I, this was to be expected when any British team visited the continent. Efforts to start regional governing bodies in Prussia, Pomerania, Silesia, and Galicia met with some success between 1900-14, but Czarist bureaucrats thwarted a prewar attempt to launch a Polish soccer federation that included Russian Poland. Thus, when FIFA received an application for membership from Polish soccer administrators, it was turned down. In Czarist Poland, meanwhile, there were barely any clubs to be found.

Poland's self-proclaimed independence in 1918 opened a Pandora's box. In 1919, only six months after the ratification of Polish independence at the Treaty of Versailles, the Polski Zwiazek Pilki Noznej (PZPN) was formed, and all aspects of Polish soccer grew by leaps and bounds. Clubs sprang up everywhere, especially in the industrial regions of Silesia and Galicia. When the PZPN gained membership in FIFA in 1923, there were hundreds of clubs and over 15,000 players registered, though Warsaw and other former Russian-held regions were slower to develop. Two leagues—one in the north and one in the south—were introduced in 1920, and the first Polish champion (Cracovia) was crowned after a play-off between the two league leaders. In 1927, this burgeoning activity led to the formation of a national league. The first club to dominate the league in the 1920s was Pogon Lwow, which is now in the Silesian part of the Ukraine. All but six of Poland's champion clubs have since come from Silesia and Galicia.

Having just missed in its attempt to enter the 1920 Olympics in Antwerp, Poland made its international debut one year later with a friendly against Hungary in Budapest (lost 1-0), and in 1922 won its first international matches—both away—against Sweden and Yugoslavia. The rise of professionalism in Central Europe, however, soon advanced the level of play in Austria, Hungary, and Czechoslovakia beyond the capabilities of late-blooming Poland. Balkan, Scandinavian, and Baltic opponents were the only consistently weaker teams during the 1920s and '30s. A 5-0 loss to Hungary at the 1924 Olympics, Poland's first official international competition, set the tone for many results that were to follow against the rising Magyar tide.

In its first attempt to qualify for the World Cup in 1933, the Poles indicated a marked improvement by holding Czechoslovakia to a 2-1 win in Warsaw. In 1935, they defeated Austria in a friendly, and despite a discouraging loss to Norway at the 1936 Olympic Games, Poland's first crop of truly excellent players came to the fore. Led by inside forward Ernest Wilimowski, Poland qualified for the 1938 World Cup by eliminating Yugoslavia, and had the misfortune of drawing Brazil in the first round of the final stages. This match became one of the great scoring bonanzas in World Cup history with Wilimowski and Leônidas scoring four goals each in a 6-5 Brazilian win, and for the first time the world took notice of Polish soccer. It was a short-lived day in the sun, however, and after several more losses in 1938 and 1939, the Nazi devastation ended Poland's rise as a budding soccer power.

During the Stalinist years from 1945-56, Poland became easy prey for all Eastern Europe. Its record during this period was: 47-10-13-24-67-111-33. The only Western countries to play Poland until the late 1950s were Norway, Sweden, Denmark, and Finland, the last of which accounted for four of Poland's ten wins during the postwar years. Hungary and Yugoslavia buried Polish teams repeatedly. In the Polish league, traditional powers Ruch Chorzów and Wisla Kraków were knocked off their perches in the mid-1950s by CWKS (Centralny Wojskowy Klub Sportowy), the Central Army Sports Club of Warsaw, whose name was changed to Legia Warsaw in 1958.

This represented a major change in the Polish league, because the first club from Warsaw that had won a championship was Polonia as late as 1948. Legia was only the third (and last) club from the capital to break the hegemony of the industrial south. In 1950-51, the PZPN introduced a national cup competition, an idea that had not interested Poles in the past, and it attracted little attention until the appearance of the European Cup Winners' Cup in the early 1960s.

Another turning point in Polish soccer was reached with the changes in the Polish government that came about in 1956. The end of the Stalinist era signaled the reentry of Poland into European and worldwide competition. Poland attempted to qualify for the 1958 World Cup, but the Soviets were emerging as an international power at the time and won Poland's qualification round group. And it met with successive failures in Olympic and World Cup qualification rounds and European Nations' Cups throughout the 1960s.

The seeds of a renaissance, however, were sown with the rise of Poland's greatest club, Klub Sportowy Górnik, in the late 1950s. Górnik Zabrze won its first championship in 1957, and behind deep-lying forward Ernest Pol it began to dominate league and cup competition in the early 1960s. With the appearance of inside forward Wlodzimierz Lubanski in 1963, Górnik began an amazing run of titles that included five championships in a row from 1963-67, and five successive cup victories from 1968-72. In 1970, when the political climate in Poland was relaxed again with a change in regimes, Górnik reached the final of the European Cup Winners' Cup, and Kazimierz Gorski became manager of the national team. The impetus provided by Górnik's success and the combined genius of Lubanski, Gorski, and Legia's extraordinary midfielder Kazimierz Deyna transformed the Polish national team.

Poland captured the gold medal at the 1972 Olympic Games, with Deyna winning the scoring title, and, based on Górnik and Legia players, qualified handily for the 1974 World Cup by eliminating England and Wales. When Lubanski was seriously injured in 1973, putting his international career into a five-year hiatus, Górnik center forward Andrzej Szarmach was brought in by Gorski, and the Polish manager also picked Stal Mielec forward Grzegorz Lato to play on the right wing, Legia left wing Robert Gadocha, and

Stal Mielec midfielder Henryk Kasperczak. This lineup became the basis for what many believed to be the finest team in the 1974 World Cup. They disposed of Argentina, Italy, and Haiti in the first round, and Sweden and Yugoslavia in the second before losing to the home team and eventual world champions West Germany by a mere 1-0. In the third place game, they outplayed Brazil, and Lato, high scorer in the tournament, drove home the winning goal. Playing fluid, crisp soccer on the order of Holland's and West Germany's "total football," Poland had come from nowhere in the space of five years to win the Olympic gold medal and third place in the World Cup.

After a slump in 1975, Poland returned to form and took the silver medal at the 1976 Olympics, and went on to qualify for the 1978 World Cup with many of its 1974 stars intact. The attractive Polish style remained, though doubts arose that it could be translated into winning goals in the harsh atmosphere of

Argentina. But in Buenos Aires and Rosario, Poland won its first round group from the world champion West Germans, and despite lackluster performances in the semi-finals against Argentina and Brazil—Deyna's decline in form was especially noticeable—it bowed out of the World Cup with its international reputation only slightly tarnished.

The first division of the Polish league was increased from 14 to 16 clubs in 1973 as a result of interest generated at home by the Olympic success, and it is now supported by a 32-club second division with two sections, a similar third division, and district leagues. The extraordinary domination of the league and cup by Silesian clubs, mainly from the coal centers of Katowice, Chorzów, Zabrze, Sosnowiec, Mielec, and Bytom continues, and, while Polish clubs have been seen increasingly in the final rounds of European club championships, they have yet to win a European title.

Champions

1921	Cracovia	1941	no competition	1961	Górnik Zabrze
1922	Pogon Lwow	1942	no competition	1962	Polonia Bytom
1923	Pogon Lwow	1943	no competition	1963	Górnik Zabrze
1924	no competition	1944	no competition	1964	Górnik Zabrze
1925	Pogon Lwow	1945	no competition	1965	Górnik Zabrze
1926	Pogon Lwow	1946	Polonia Warsaw	1966	Górnik Zabrze
1927	Wisla Kraków	1947	Warta	1967	Górnik Zabrze
1928	Wisla Kraków	1948	Cracovia	1968	Ruch Chorzów
1929	Warta	1949	Wisla Kraków	1969	Legia Warsaw
1930	Cracovia	1950	Wisla Kraków	1970	Legia Warsaw
1931	Garbarnia Kraków	1951	Wisla Kraków	1971	Gornik Zabrze
1932	Cracovia	1952	Ruch Chorzów	1972	Gornik Zabrze
1933	Ruch Chorzów	1953	Ruch Chorzów	1973	Stal Mielec
1934	Ruch Chorzów	1954	Polonia Bytom	1974	Ruch Chorzów
1935	Ruch Chorzów	1955	CWKS Warsaw	1975	Ruch Chorzów
1936	Ruch Chorzów	1956	CWKS Warsaw	1976	Stal Mielec
1937	Cracovia	1957	Gornik Zabrze	1977	Slask Wroclaw
1938	Ruch Chorzów	1958	LKS Lódź	1978	Wisla Kraków
1939	not completed	1959	Gornik Zabrze		
1940	no competition	1960	Ruch Chorzów		

Cup Winners

1951	Ruch Chorzów	1954	Gwardia Warsaw	1957	LKS Lódź
1952	Polonia Warsaw	1955	CWKS Warsaw	1958	no competition
1953	no competition	1956	CWKS Warsaw	1959	no competition

1960	no competition	1967	Wisla Kraków	1974	Ruch Chorzów
1961	no competition	1968	Górnik Zabrze	1975	Stal Rzeszów
1962	Zaglebie Sosnowiec	1969	Górnik Zabrze	1976	Slask Wroclaw
1963	Zaglebie Sosnowiec	1970	Górnik Zabrze	1977	Zaglebie Sosnowiec
1964	Legia Warsaw	1971	Górnik Zabrze	1978	Zaglebie Sosnowiec
1965	Gornik Zabrze	1972	Górnik Zabrze		
1966	Legia Warsaw	1973	Legia Warsaw		

Portugal

Federação Portuguêsa de Futebol   Founded: 1914
Praça de Alegria No. 25   FIFA: 1926
Lisboa   UEFA: 1954

Affiliated clubs: *880;* **registered players:** *45,947 (824 professional; 19,257 non-amateur);* **national stadium:** *Estádio Nacional, Lisbon (51,000);* **largest stadium:** *Estádio da Luz, Lisbon (70,000);* **colors:** *red jerseys, blue shorts;* **season:** *September to July;* **honors:** *World Cup third place (1966), Benfica, European Cup (1961, 1962), Latin Cup (1950), Sporting Lisbon, European Cup Winners' Cup (1964).*

Portugal's game has progressed consistently over the decades after a later start than much of the rest of Europe. Its political isolation became an advantage during World War II, because it was able to play against other neutral countries, such as Spain and Switzerland, and improve its level of play substantially. Behind the incomparable brilliance of Mozambiquan striker Eusebio, Portugal and its leading club Benfica came of age during the 1960s and played some of the best soccer seen anywhere. Benfica shared dominance over Europe with the defensive-minded Italian clubs, and, indeed, it would have been fitting if the Portuguese national team had emerged victorious in the 1966 World Cup. Portugal's international standing has declined following the departure of Eusebio and his teammates, while the threatened political instability of the mid-1970s and Portugal's loss of its African reservoir of good players has caused an uncertain future for Portuguese soccer.

Soccer was first played in Portugal in 1866 by British university students in Lisbon. During the 1870s it was still played by Britons only, but Lisbon Football Club, probably the first club in Portugal, was established in 1875. The first public game took place in the Campo da Parada, Cascais, in 1888. By this time a number of Portuguese clubs had been formed: Real Gínasio Clube Portuguêsa (football

section), Clube Lisbonense, Carcavelos Club, FC Esperança, FC Estrêla, and in Porto the Oporto Cricket Club started a football section in 1893. The 1890s saw widespread acceptance of the game by the Portuguese themselves, as Portuguese boys returned from school in England. Most of the major clubs that were to distinguish themselves in later years were formed around the turn of the century: Clube Internacional de Futebol (1903), Sport Lisboa e Benfica (1904), and Sporting Clube de Portugal (1906). The Liga de Futebol was founded in 1909 in Lisbon by Carcavelos, Benfica, Lisbon Cricket Club, and Internacional. In 1910, the Associação de Futebol de Lisboa (Lisbon) was founded. Four years later the Lisbon association merged with the União Portuguêsa de Futebol (Porto and Portalegre) to form the Federação Portuguêsa de Futebol, and 26 district associations were set up.

World War I delayed Portugal's international debut until 1921. Its first four internationals were played against Spain between 1921-25 without a win, but in 1925 it managed to slip by Italy 1-0 in Lisbon. Its first significant victory took place in Porto in 1928, and again it was Italy that fell. In 1928, Portugal entered the Olympic Games at Amsterdam, where it defeated the tired Chileans and a disorganized Yugoslavia before losing to Egypt. Spain continued to be the focus of its international activity, though friendlies were arranged with France, Belgium, Yugoslavia, Czechoslovakia, and Hungary during the early 1930s. Portugal's long-standing reputation for losing away games stems from this period. Indeed, a number of European opponents were not defeated on their home grounds by Portugal until the 1960s or '70s. Portugal did not defeat Spain on Spanish soil until 1947. Its first away win, other than the Olympic Games of 1924, was against the Republic of Ireland in 1947 (2-0).

Portugal has entered each World Cup since 1934, and all editions of the European Football Championship, the latter unsuccessfully. It was eliminated from the 1934 World Cup in the qualifying round by Spain, and was knocked out by Switzerland in the qualifying round of 1938. Spain once again eliminated Portugal in 1950, and four years later the fine postwar Austrian national team led by Ernst Ocwirk mounted a 9-1 thrashing in Vienna that knocked Portugal out of the 1954 edition. Northern Ireland proved to be the surprise winner of Portugal's 1958 qualifying group, but Italy split its results in that group with the rising Portuguese team in 3-0 and 0-3 home and away legs. In its 1962 qualifying group Portugal lost its away leg to Luxembourg (4-2) in one of the great upsets of the postwar era. But this was to be Portugal's finest testament to having the worst away record of any European nation.

With elimination from the 1970, 1974, and 1978 World Cups, Portugal's participation in the 1966 edition in England remains its only World Cup venture in ten attempts. In the end, it was a remarkable debut. Portugal wore down the fine Hungarian team led by Bene and Albert and easily overwhelmed Bulgaria, and, as if that were not enough, effectively ended Brazil's dominance over the world game by winning 3-1. True, Pelé was injured and the Brazilian team as a whole had not been performing well in previous games, but the depth of Brazil's bench—much used in this game—was itself thought to be capable of neutralizing Portugal. As it turned out, the Brazilian manager's rejection of Garrincha, Gilmar, and Jairzinho, and the heavily bandaged knee of Pelé, mattered after all, and Brazil could not regroup after giving up two goals early in the first half. (There is a famous photograph from this game of Pelé lying on the field, his face contorted with pain and the trainers tending to his leg, while the man cushioning Pelé's head with his hands is Eusebio—an extraordinary image of two great stars.)

In the quarter-finals, Eusebio single-handedly saved Portugal from the upset of the decade by scoring four goals against the Cinderella team from North Korea after losing 3-0 early in the game. The final score was 5-3 in Portugal's favor. Two of Eusebio's goals were from the penalty spot after some hard tackles by determined Korean defenders.

The sting of North Korea's surprise must have been felt in the semi-final match against England, and the stalwart backfield of Cohen, Moore, and Jackie Charlton won the game for the soon-to-be world champions. It was a noteworthy match for the sportsmanlike conduct of all players involved, but ultimately it was won by two skillful goals by Bobby Charlton. Portugal's 2-1 third place win over the USSR was not decided until the last two minutes with a goal by Torres, yet Portugal had played more skillfully than the defense-minded Russians all along. Having nearly reached the pinnacle of world soccer, the tired Portuguese team returned home, drained by the Koreans and numbed by the English, with the knowledge that this was Portugal's finest hour.

The rise of Portuguese clubs to the forefront of European soccer corresponded with the successes of the national team, and was made possible by the same personnel: Eusebio, Coluña, et. al. The first Portuguese national championship, centered at the time in Lisbon and Oporto, had been launched in 1922. Its first winner was FC Porto, but it was played on a knockout basis, and is now considered to be the forerunner of the Portuguese cup rather than the league. The national league was introduced in 1934-35, again with FC Porto the first winner, and a second division was added in 1938-39, followed by a third division in 1947-48. In modern times, the second division has consisted of North, Central, and South sections, and the third division includes six sections, A-F. In league competition, the great Lisbon clubs Benfica and Sporting have won 36 championships and 32 cups between them. There has never been a period when one or the other has not dominated either league or cup competition. (Benfica has 23 league titles and 18 cup wins; Sporting has 14 league titles and cup wins apiece.) Benfica's greatest era, however, stands out for the quality of its team and for the 11 championships it won between 1960-1973. In addition, Benfica won the European Cup in 1961 and 1962, the latter by defeating mighty Real Madrid in the final, and it was a finalist in 1963, 1965, and 1968, the best record of any European club during the 1960s. Sporting Lisbon, meanwhile, won the European Cup Winners' Cup in 1964.

The explanation for Portugal's success since the late 1950s rests with the influx of many good coaches from abroad, several of them from England and especially that of the Hungarian, Bela Guttmann, who took over Benfica in 1959, and the importation of African players from the vast reservoir in the former colonies. Now, a new political reality in Portugal has demanded a regrouping of great proportions.

Champions

1935	FC Porto	1950	Benfica	1965	Benfica
1936	Benfica	1951	Sporting	1966	Sporting
1937	Benfica	1952	Sporting	1967	Benfica
1938	Benfica	1953	Sporting	1968	Benfica
1939	FC Porto	1954	Sporting	1969	Benfica
1940	FC Porto	1955	Benfica	1970	Sporting
1941	Sporting	1956	FC Porto	1971	Benfica
1942	Benfica	1957	Benfica	1972	Benfica
1943	Benfica	1958	Sporting	1973	Benfica
1944	Sporting	1959	FC Porto	1974	Sporting
1945	Benfica	1960	Benfica	1975	Benfica
1946	Belenenses	1961	Benfica	1976	Benfica
1947	Sporting	1962	Sporting	1977	Benfica
1948	Sporting	1963	Benfica	1978	FC Porto
1949	Sporting	1964	Benfica		

Cup Winners

1922	FC Porto	1941	Sporting	1960	Belenenses
1923	Sporting	1942	Belenenses	1961	Leixoes
1924	Olhanense	1943	Benfica	1962	Benfica
1925	FC Porto	1944	Benfica	1963	Sporting
1926	Maritimo	1945	Sporting	1964	Benfica
1927	Belenenses	1946	Sporting	1965	Vitoria Setubal
1928	Carcavelinhos	1947	no competition	1966	Sporting Braga
1929	Belenenses	1948	Sporting	1967	Vitoria Setubal
1930	Benfica	1949	Benfica	1968	FC Porto
1931	Benfica	1950	no competition	1969	Benfica
1932	FC Porto	1951	Benfica	1970	Benfica
1933	Belenenses	1952	Benfica	1971	Sporting
1934	Sporting	1953	Benfica	1972	Benfica
1935	Benfica	1954	Sporting	1973	Sporting
1936	Sporting	1955	Benfica	1974	Sporting
1937	FC Porto	1956	FC Porto	1975	Boavista
1938	Sporting	1957	Benfica	1976	Boavista
1939	Academica Coimbra	1958	FC Porto	1977	FC Porto
1940	Benfica	1959	Benfica	1978	Sporting

post   See: **far post** and **near post**

pre-Columbian ball games

The pre-Columbian ball games of Mexico and Central America were among the most advanced football-oriented games outside the direct lineage of modern soccer. Variations were played by the Aztecs (*tlachtli*), Maya (*pokyah*), Zapotecs (*táladzi*), and possibly others, from roughly 600 A.D. to the destruction of the last pre-Columbian civilization in the sixteenth century (though some evidence exists of a similar ball game as early as 500 B.C.). Archaeological digs from Arizona to Honduras reveal wide geographical dispersion of the games, and their depiction in all forms of pre-Columbian art—particularly ceramics and sculpture—has given us a marvelously clear picture of their characteristics and cultural significance.

In their most common form, the games were played in a recessed court 40 to 50 feet long and shaped like the letter "I". The vertical walls surrounding the playing area were many feet high, and in the middle of either wall along the stem of the "I" a stone or wooden ring was mounted vertically (i.e., at right angles to a basketball hoop). The object was to project a hard rubber ball through one of the rings; only the feet, legs, hips, and elbows could be used. A player's most important tool was his skill in juggling the ball without the use of hands. Aztec players wore loincloths attached to leather belts, and leather protection for their hips, groin, thighs, and elbows. The Mayan garb was similar, but it was embellished by colorful costumes and tall headdresses. In *táladzi*, the "goals" were not vertical rings but two rectangular niches carved out of the wall, one each at the northeastern and southeastern corners of the "I".

These games were not only the most popular sporting activities of the day but also lay at the center of the religious life of the pre-Columbian culture. Players' activities before and after each game were ritualistically supervised by religious leaders or perhaps the king himself, and ball courts were usually built adjacent to the temple. In *tlachtli*, losing players humbly submitted to sacrifice at the altar. Though the games probably reached their peak under the Aztecs at Tenochtitlan (the site of Mexico City), the greatest ball court was that at Chichén Itzá, the Mayan ceremonial center in Yucatán. Perhaps the most important legacy of these games is the invention of rubber balls, which were developed by unknown ancestors of the Aztecs and introduced to Europeans via the Spanish conquistadors.

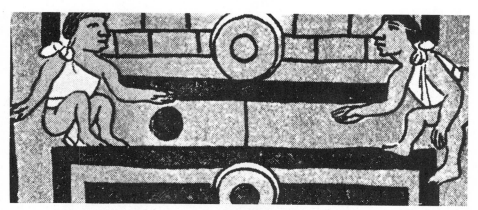

The pre-Columbian ball games were widely depicted in Aztec, Toltec, and Mayan art. This Aztec vase painting shows the game's I-shaped court, two goals, (in the form of rings), a round ball, and two players dressed unceremoniously.

President's Cup

A knockout competition for invited national teams of the Far East and, after 1975, representative teams and clubs from other continents as well. It is held annually in Seoul, Pusan, and Taegu, and is named in honor of the president of the Republic of Korea.

Winners

1971	Burma and Korea Republic
1972	Burma
1973	Burma and Khmer Republic
1974	Korea Republic
1975	Korea Republic

professional

The checkered history of professionalism in soccer has yielded the following definition of the term according to "FIFA Statutes, Regulations, and Standing Orders":

> Players who receive regular wages, payments for playing, bonuses, salaries, deferred payments, or any other allowances, other than [actual expenses for travel, necessary maintenance and hotel charges or expenses for equipment, physical preparation and insurance against accidents during play and whilst travelling], or who have only an apparent, fictitious or sham employment or profession, are considered to be professionals or non-amateurs.

This definition is expressly for the use of FIFA in determining the eligibility of players for international competitions under its administration. FIFA points out, however, that in domestic competition this may be superseded by another definition authorized by the relevant national association.

The countries in which professionalism is officially recognized are: Malawi, Somalia, South Africa, Zambia, Canada, El Salvador, Mexico, USA, Argentina, Brazil, Chile, Colombia, Ecuador, Peru, Uruguay, Venezuela, Hong Kong, Austria, Belgium, Denmark, England, France, Germany FR, Ireland Northern, Ireland Republic, Italy, Malta, Netherlands, Portugal, Scotland, Spain, Turkey, Wales, Yugoslavia, and New Zealand. Czechoslovakia and Hungary sanctioned professionalism during the 1920s and '30s, and Cuba did so from 1949-59.

There are certain regulations governing the activities of professionals and non-amateurs, as stipulated by FIFA: 1) all professionals and non-amateurs must be registered as such by the national association concerned; 2) they may not participate in any international tournaments that are officially designated as amateur; and 3) they may, if they wish, be reinstated as amateurs by their respective national associations, but cannot, under any circumstances, again participate in officially designated amateur international tournaments.

Professionalism in soccer was introduced in England between 1876-85, and was one of the major features of the growth of the game among working-class people in the northern and Midlands counties. Until the mid-1880s, payments to players were made secretly. The impetus for professionalism was the desire of struggling clubs to attract good players from other parts of the country by offering a wage, a job, and perhaps new lodgings in an unfamiliar town. Many English clubs sought to attract Scottish players during the 1870s and '80s, because it was generally accepted that Scottish tactics and techniques were more advanced. The Football Association, which was still dominated at this time by well-heeled upper- and middle-class sportsmen with university backgrounds, fought hard against the adoption of professionalism throughout the early 1880s, citing the practice as disreputable, corrupt, and ultimately evil.

In 1885, professionalism was finally legalized after Preston North End F.C. openly admitted to paying its players, but only clubs in the north and Midlands indulged in it for many years to come. The first London club to accept professionalism, Arsenal in 1891, was at first dropped from the schedules of other southern clubs as a protest, but by the turn of the century the disgruntled London clubs had also begun to sign some professionals. The adoption of professionalism in England, as elsewhere in subsequent decades, led to greater participation in top flight competition, more advanced coaching, a rise in the standard of play, and the birth of league competition.

See also: **amateur** and **non-amateur**.

---

promotion and relegation

The system of advancing or demoting teams between upper and lower divisions (major and minor leagues) after the end of each season.

The USA and Canada are among the only soccer-playing countries in the world that have not adopted this procedure. In most countries, a "league" is made up of a number of "divisions," the "first division" being the most advanced. At season's end, a prescribed number of teams at the top of each division is promoted to the next highest division, and a prescribed number of teams at the bottom of each division is relegated to the next lowest division. Those teams that finish at the bottom of the lowest division in a league are usually required to seek reelection to the league for the following year, or to undergo some other kind of test, such as a play-off, to retain their place. Some countries, e.g., Argentina and Brazil, hold an additional competition after the close of the regular league season to determine the national champion. In most cases, however, the winner of the first division is regarded as the national champion.

The concept of promotion and relegation arose from the sporting traditions of England during the nineteenth century, and was introduced in The Football League at the end of the 1892-93 season, the first year of the new English second division. Until 1895-96, test matches, or play-offs, were held to determine promotions and relegations. The first clubs to gain promotion from the second to the first division in 1893 were Small Heath (now Birmingham City) and Darwen (now playing in the non-professional Lancashire Football Combination). Relegated to take their places in the second division were Notts Co. and Accrington Stanley.

Automatic promotion and relegation based on standings in the division tables was introduced at the end of the 1898-99 season, when Manchester City and Glossop were promoted at the expense of Sheffield Wednesday and Bolton Wanderers. Although a Division II was formed in the Scottish League as far back as 1893, automatic promotion and relegation in Scotland was not adopted until after the 1921-22 season. In subsequent years, countries in Europe, Latin America, Africa, and Asia borrowed the promotion and relegation system, as the growth of the game demanded the formation of multi-divisional leagues. Other than the USA and Canada, only those countries too small to support more than one division have not yet adopted some variation of the promotion and relegation idea.

Puerto Rico

Federación Puertorriqueña de Fútbol
Dr. Roberto A. Monroig
Apartado 989
Guayama, Puerto Rico 00654

Founded: 1940
FIFA: 1960
CONCACAF: 1962

Affiliated clubs: *21;* registered players: *6,818;* national stadium: *Country Club, Urbanización Country Club (8,000);* largest stadium: *Country Club;* colors: *red and white striped jerseys, blue shorts;* season: *March to June;* honors: *none.*

The Commonwealth of Puerto Rico, which has maintained a confusing state of political semi-autonomy from the United States since 1952, presents an unusual story among soccer nations. The game was introduced to the island during the 1890s by Spanish colonists, probably before the American takeover in 1898. The first important clubs were España Foot-Ball Club and Real San Juan Foot-Ball Club, and a strong rivalry between the two developed that eventually became the backbone of Puerto Rican soccer. Its heyday occurred during the 1930s, and resulted in the founding of the Asociación de Football de Aficionados (AFA) in 1940.

Though Puerto Rico did not join the new Central American and Caribbean Confederation when it was formed in 1938, the AFA boldly entered the 1946 edition of the soccer tournament of the Central American and Caribbean Games at Baranquilla. It was by far the weakest team in the field, and lost all six matches: to Costa Rica, 12-0; Panama, 12-0; Curaçao 14-0; Colombia, 4-1; Guatemala, 4-1; and Venezuela, 6-0.

During the 1940s and '50s, España and Real San Juan declined in stature, and their demise brought on a public falling out and a general decline of the Puerto Rican game. As a result, many of the best Puerto Rican players since World War II have left the island to play elsewhere in the Caribbean. The 1946 results at Baranquilla reflect that migration. A Puerto Rican selection participated in the Central American and Caribbean Games in 1959 at Caracas and the 1966 edition, held in San Juan itself. Puerto Rico also entered the 1974 World Cup qualifying round and was eliminated immediately by Haiti (7-0 and 5-0). No attempt was made for the 1978 World Cup.

In 1960, the national association joined FIFA, and it became an early member of CONCACAF in 1962. Unfortunately, Puerto Rican clubs have rarely been seen in regional club championships, but there is a reasonably active league structure in spite of formidable opposition from baseball, the island's leading sport. Sixteen clubs participate in upper-level competition, and a national championship as well as an annual cup competition, are supported by regional leagues and knockout tournaments. The primary centers of soccer activity outside San Juan are the cities of Mayaguez and Guayama. The present name of the national association was adopted in the early 1970s. In 1975, the largest crowd ever to see a game in Puerto Rico—11,000—was recorded in San Juan when the New York Cosmos defeated the Puerto Rican national team by 12-1.

punt

A British term referring to any kick that is not a long "boom" down the field.

Puskás, Ferenc (1926-   )

The stocky "Galloping Major of Hungary" is one of the leading figures in postwar European soccer. As an inside left with Honvéd and the legendary Hungarian national team of the early 1950s, he possessed one of the most powerful left-foot shots ever seen, and his abilities were little diminished when he began a second career with Real Madrid after the 1956 Hungarian uprising. He scored 83 goals in 84 appearances for Hungary, and made a habit of leading the league in scoring both in Hungary and his adopted Spain. Puskás defied all the commonly accepted traits of a great player. He was short, squat, paunchy, and seldom used his right foot or his head, but in the end all he needed was his exceptional knowledge of the game and that left foot.

His playing career began in 1943 with Kispest in the Budapest suburb of that name, and in 1945, at age 18, he made his international debut against Austria in his country's first postwar international match. In 1948, his club was incorporated into the new army club, Honvéd, and with his long-time friend and teammate Jószef Bozsik, he became the nucleus of Honvéd's great success. He was the Hungarian scoring leader in 1948 (50 goals), 1949-50 (31), 1950 (25), and 1953 (27), and with the title of major in the Hungarian army, he was captain of the national team that became a legend in its own time. Led by

Puskás's scoring prowess, Hungary was undefeated from 1950-54, won the Olympic gold medal in 1952, and advanced to the final of the 1954 World Cup.

While he was deep in South America on a tour with Honvéd in 1956, the Hungarian uprising took place, and Puskás decided not to return home. Shortly thereafter the European press reported his apocryphal death, but, in fact, he had fled to Italy, where he spent the next year and a half playing in various friendlies. In 1958 he was signed by Real Madrid, home of the legendary Alfredo Di Stefano and a string of European Cup medals, and his career was reborn. Puskás resumed his role at inside left, snugly positioned between center forward Di Stefano and the flying outside left Francisco Gento, resulting in one of the greatest forward lines in history. Real was elevated to new heights, including a fifth consecutive European Cup triumph, and a sixth several years down the road. Puskás was the Spanish scoring leader in 1960 (26), 1961 (27), 1963 (26), and 1964 (10), and he eventually made four international appearances for Spain. When he finally retired from Real in 1966 at age 39, he had amassed 324 goals in 372 games. Perhaps his two most memorable feats were the four goals he scored against Eintracht Frankfurt in the 1960 European Cup final and his hat trick at the hands of Benfica in the 1962 final, both for Real Madrid.

Since 1967, Puskás has drifted across five continents from one coaching job to another. He started with the San Francisco Gales and Vancouver Royals in 1968, and led Panathinaïkos Athens to the final of the European Cup in 1971. By 1975, he was trying to mold a national team for Saudi Arabia, and the following year he embarked on a two-year stint with Colo Colo in Chile. In 1978, Puskás returned to Greece, and took over AEK Athens.

Q

Qatar

Qatar Football Association
Khaleej Street
P.O. Box 2511
Doha

Founded: 1960
FIFA: 1970
AFC: 1972

Affiliated clubs: *11;* registered players: *1,200;* national stadium: *Doha Athletic Stadium, Doha (8,000);* largest stadium: *Doha Athletic Stadium;* colors: *maroon and white jerseys, white shorts;* season: *October to May;* honors: *none.*

The Sheikdom of Qatar was introduced to the game by British soldiers who were stationed on the peninsula durings its period as a military protectorate from 1916-71, but the local population did not become active participants until well after World War II. The organizing of domestic competition preceded Qatar's international debut by more than 10 years with the founding of the Qatar Football Association (QFA) in 1960. The standard of play in Qatar ranks roughly level with that of Bahrain among Persian (Arabian) Gulf states but substantially below Saudi Arabia and the regional leader Kuwait. Qatar did not attempt to qualify for the 1974 World Cup, but in 1976 was grouped with Afghanistan, Bangladesh, India, Jordan, Nepal, Saudi Arabia, and the eventual qualifier Iraq in its bid for a place in the sixth Asian Nations' Cup. In qualification rounds for the 1978 World Cup, Qatar was defeated twice by Kuwait and split home and away legs with Bahrain, finishing at the bottom of its group of three. It has also entered each edition of the Arabian Gulf Football Tournament.

The national league is composed of a Super Division with six clubs and a First Division with five clubs, each club supporting a youth team. The championship season is divided into two parts, and the Qatar F.A. Cup is contested simultaneously. Though each club has its own grounds, most league and cup matches are played at Doha Athletic Stadium, the only grounds with a grass field and lights. Sand pitches are predominant all over the Arabian Pennisula. Of the 1,200 players registered with the QFA, 975 are in the youth or veteran category.

R

Rácing Club

Location: *Avellaneda, Argentina;* stadium: *Estadio Rácing Club (70,100);* colors: *sky blue and white striped jerseys, black shorts;* honors: *Intercontinental Cup (1967), Copa Libertadores (1967), Argentine league champion (1913 shared, 1914 shared, 1915, 1916, 1917, 1918, 1919 AAAF, 1921 AAAF, 1925 AAAF, 1949, 1950, 1951, 1958, 1961, 1966).*

Founded 1905 as Club Colorados Unidos del Sur in Avellaneda, the large industrial suburb of Buenos Aires, by dissident members of the *porteño*-based Club Barracas al Sur. Only weeks after its formation, there was an influx of French immigrants into the club, and they succeeded in changing the name to Rácing Club after the famous Racing Club de Paris, for whom some of the Frenchmen were alleged to have played. The famous sky blue of Racing Club de Paris is still worn. Racing represented another important break from British domination of Argentine soccer around the turn of the century, and during the 1910s became the first non-British club to dominate the Argentine league. Its historical importance in this regard and the influence it wielded are unique, and for this reason it became known by the nickname "The Academy." After it joined the first division in 1911, seven consecutive championships were won between 1913-19, followed by two more in 1921 and 1925, the last three of these in the "outlaw" league.

In 1931, Rácing adopted professionalism and joined the breakaway Liga Argentina de Football along with many of the other leading clubs of the day, but failed to win any honors until the late 1940s. Having relinquished its mass popularity to Boca Júniors and Ríver Plate in the preceding 20 years, Rácing was revived after World War II by the patronage of Ramon Cereijo, a leading Peronist deputy who was an avid fan of "The Academy." Careijo arranged for government money to be lent to Rácing, and helped to steer favors in its direction, including revenues to build a new stadium, the Estadio Presidente Peron (now Estadio Rácing Club). With vast reserves of cash available, Rácing was able to purchase many fine players, and eventually won three championships in a row between 1949-51.

While the new Rácing was at least talented enough to challenge Ríver Plate's hegemony over the postwar Argentine game—this team inlcuded the fine center forward Ruben Bravo—the public was well-aware of its Peronist backing, and mockingly nicknamed the club *Deportivo Careijo* ("Careijo Sports Club"). Well after the departure of Bravo to Botafogo, Nice, and Monaco, Rácing continued to be a strong force in the first division, winning further championships in 1958 and 1961.

In 1966, it surged to the top again, playing 25 league games in a row without a defeat (an Argentine record), and in 1967 entered the Copa Libertadores for the second time. After narrowly eliminating Peru's Universitario in a Copa Libertadores semi-final play-off, it played to two scoreless draws with Uruguay's Nacional in the final, and won the third and deciding match to take its first South American club championship. This earned Racing the right to play Celtic in the Intercontinental Cup, and it was here that it displayed a tendency toward the violent tactics that opened Europe's eyes to this coming trend among Argentine clubs. After split legs in Glasgow and Buenos Aires, both of which were reduced to rugby-like melees, a play-off was held in Montevideo, and six players were sent off (two Argentines) before Racing finally won.

In the following years, the fortunes of Rácing declined measurably, due in no small part to its growing financial crisis, and in the mid-1970s it was relegated briefly to the *Primera B*. Despite its important place in Argentine soccer history, Rácing has come to be remembered elsewhere for its savage tactics when it rose to the zenith of international club competition.

Racing Club de Paris

Location: *Paris, France;* stadium: *Stade de Colombes (63,000);* colors: *sky blue and white hooped jerseys, black shorts;* honors: *French champion (1936), French cup winner (1936, 1939, 1940, 1945, 1949).*

Founded 1896 as the soccer section of Racing Club de France, the famous omni-sport club formed in 1882. The soccer team became autonomous in 1932 and adopted the name Racing Club de Paris. In 1966, it merged with Union Athlétique Sedan-Torcy under the name Racing Club de Paris-US Sedan, and one year later it disappeared altogether, the newly merged organization continuing to play as Club Sportive Sedan-Ardennes in the second and third divisions.

Racing was known simply as "le club de France." Its worldwide fame outshone its accomplishments on the field by a wide margin, but there were several compensating factors. As an outgrowth of the most established sporting institution in Paris, cultural capital of the world during the late nineteenth and early twentieth centuries, it became the focal point of the game's *haut monde* for many decades in what is now a mixed bag of legend and fact.

On the factual side, Rácing Club of Buenos Aires adopted its name in tribute in 1905, and the Parisian club itself enjoyed considerable success in French soccer from 1930-60. Racing Club de Paris was an original member of the French league in 1932-33, placing third in "Group A" at the end of the first season. It placed third in 1934-35, and the following year won the league-cup double with Austrian *Wunderteam* goalkeeper Rudi Hiden minding

the nets. Its 1936 league title was achieved by a gaping 13-point margin, and the cup was won that year after eliminating Lille OSC and Sochaux—two of the leading French clubs of the day—in early rounds. The losing finalist was Charleville. Aside from Hiden, the best-known player on this team was French international and left half Edmond Delfour.

Racing won four more French cups before 1949 with the majestic center-half Gusti Jordan, a naturalized Austrian and French international. In the 1950s, Racing featured center forward Thadée Cisowski, a goalscoring French international, and after 1953 the extraordinary Roger Marché, left back and captain of France during its golden era of the late 1950s.

As to the legend, Racing became a home for players of all nationalities and especially naturalized Europeans who sought a lifestyle that only Racing Club de Paris, and the city of Paris, could offer. Racing spent a year in Division II in 1953-54, but Marché guided the team back to several moderately successful years in the upper ranks, culminating in two second place finishes in the early 1960s. In 1964, Racing was relegated again, and it never reemerged. Its absorption into US Sedan-Torcy in 1966 finally spelled its doom, and the name "Racing Club" was dissolved. In 1978, rumors of a rebirth were widely circulated in Parisian soccer circles.

Rangers Football Club

Location: *Glasgow, Scotland;* stadium: *Ibrox Park (75,000);* colors: *royal blue jerseys, white shorts;* honors: *European Cup Winners' Cup (1972), Scottish champion (1891 shared, 1899, 1900, 1901, 1902, 1911, 1912, 1913, 1918, 1920, 1921, 1923, 1924, 1925, 1927, 1928, 1929, 1930, 1931, 1933, 1934, 1935, 1937, 1939, 1947, 1949, 1950, 1953, 1956, 1957, 1959, 1961, 1963, 1964, 1975, 1976, 1978), Scottish cup winner (1894, 1897, 1898, 1903, 1928, 1930, 1932, 1934, 1935, 1936, 1948, 1949, 1950, 1953, 1960,*

1962, 1963, 1964, 1966, 1973, 1976, 1978), Scottish league cup winner (1947, 1949, 1961, 1962, 1964, 1965, 1971, 1976).

Founded 1873 (fourth oldest Scottish club in existence) by various sports-minded members of three Protestant families (Campbell, Vallance, and McNeill), playing first at Glasgow Green in the East End and moving subsequently to the Paisley Road section on the South Bank of the Clyde. Between 1885-87, it defected from the Scottish F.A. to The Football Association in London, but upon returning in 1887, it moved a few blocks westward to its present location at Ibrox. By the late 1870s, Rangers had become the second most important club in Glasgow (after Queen's Park) having already gained two cup finals in 1877 and 1879. But the power base in Scottish soccer until the 1890s was in the Vale of Leven and above all at Queen's Park, and it was only with the formation of the Scottish Football League in 1890 that Rangers really began to make its mark. Its strong Protestant base of support existed from the beginning, and it has not yet relinquished its policy of allowing only Protestant players to wear the famous blue jersey.

The phenomenal success of Celtic since the 1960s has tended to obscure the other half of the "Auld Firm," as the Celtic-Rangers archrivalry is called, but in fact Rangers has had long periods of complete domination over the Roman Catholic Celtic club, and it holds the Scottish record for most league championships (37). In the Scottish F.A. Cup, however, Rangers' 22 victories are three less than Celtic's total.

Rangers F.C. was one of the founding members of the Scottish league in 1890, but despite its 15-year seniority over Celtic, it had not won any honors up to that time. In the very first year of the league, it shared the championship with Dumbarton, and after three more second place results won its first championship outright in 1899 (without a single loss) to begin its first era of league prominence. Rangers had a second run of league successes before World War I, and in 1920, Willy Struth, the greatest name in Rangers' history, became the "Blues'" manager. Struth remained in his post for 34 years, and built the club's greatest teams. Rangers dominated Scottish soccer decisively from 1920 to the outbreak of World War II, winning 15 championships and six cups during that period.

The greatest players under Struth's command were Alan (the "wee Blue Devil") Morton, a five foot four inch right winger and idol of millions, and David Meiklejohn, the Rangers' captain and center half turned right half during the 1920s and '30s. After World War II, Struth's highly disciplined—some would say Victorian—approach produced another golden era of unqualified successes, including the first Scottish treble in 1949 and, before his retirement in 1954, a total of four more championships and four cup victories. Another Ibrox idol appeared during this period, Scotland captain George Young, who had a long career at center and left half. Struth's retirement did not spell the end of Rangers' success, and it went on to gain many more honors before the great Celtic era began in 1965.

Among its plentiful appearances in European competition, it was a losing finalist twice in the European Cup Winners' Cup (1961 and 1967) before finally winning that competition in 1972, unfortunately under ignominious circumstances. After eliminating three formidable opponents, Sporting Lisbon, Torino, and Bayern München, Rangers met Dinamo Moscow in Barcelona for the final, and scraped by with a 3-2 win. Rangers' supporters, however, battled with the police in ugly scenes both in and outside the stadium, causing one death and a one-year ban from competition. Coming at a time when the club was trying desperately to challenge Celtic's domination over the Scottish game, the ban was a cruel blow. Sixteen months later, disaster had struck the club when 66 people were killed by the collapse of a steel barrier during an "Auld Firm" match at Ibrox. This was the second such calamity at Rangers' home ground, prompting an embarrassing outcry. (The first had occurred in 1902 when 25 spectators fell to their deaths in a collapse of the West Stand during an international between Scotland and England.)

In the mid-1970s, Rangers once again surfaced at the top of Scottish competitions, promising another period of domestic and international glory, but its less-than-consistent ability to put up attractive teams and a lack of finishing power in Euorpean competition left some doubt as to the club's eventual success.

Rapid Wienerberger, Sport-Klub

Location: *Vienna, Austria;* **stadium:** *Hutteldorfstadion;* **colors:** *green and white striped jerseys, black shorts;* **honors:** *Mitropa Cup (1930), Austrian champion (1912, 1913, 1916, 1917, 1919, 1920, 1921, 1923, 1929, 1930, 1935, 1938, 1940, 1941, 1946, 1948, 1951, 1952, 1954, 1956, 1957, 1960, 1964, 1967, 1968), German champion (1941), Austrian cup winner (1919, 1920, 1927, 1946, 1961, 1968, 1969, 1972, 1976), German cup winner (1938).*

Founded 1898 as 1. Arbeiter-Fussballklub (First Vienna Workers' F.C.); it adopted its present name one year later when there was an influx of British players. Rapid Vienna is the greatest and most popular club in Austrian soccer, having won a record 25 national championships and nine cups. An internationally famous name since the pre-World War I era, Rapid dominated the Austrian game during the 1910s and '20s, and in the early 1950s it was arguably the best club in Europe. After Jimmy Hogan introduced the Scottish short passing game to Austrian soccer in 1912 via Amateure, Rapid became its greatest exponent and was widely known as the bastion of the *Wienerschule.*

Led by the robust center forward Josef Braunstädter, Rapid won eight Austrian championships from 1912-23, supplemented by a pair of cup victories in 1919-20, and advanced to the final of the first two Mitropa Cups in 1927 and 1928. It won two more league titles in 1929-30, helping to generate the momentum that created Austria's stunnign *Wunderteam* of the 1930s, and still managed to win a championship in 1935 when Admira and First Vienna were the dominant clubs in the Austrian capital. At the end of manager Karl Rappan's tour of duty in 1930, Rapid appeared in the final of the Mitropa Cup for the third time in four years after burying Genoa and Ferencváros in early rounds, and defeated Sparta Prague in the final, 2-0 and 3-2. The backbone of Rapid's attack at this time was center half Pepe Smistik, an all-around player with complete technical mastery. In the mid-1930s, Franz "Bimbo" Binder joined Rapid from St. Polten, and his goalscoring genius at center forward sparked another highly successful era. He led Rapid to a Germany cup victory in 1938 (major Austrian clubs played in German competitions after the 1938 *Anschluss*), Austrian titles in 1938, 1940, and 1941, and a German championship in 1941 as well. Playing for Rapid until 1950, Binder became the first and only European to score over 1,000 goals in senior-level competition (his total was 1,006).

After World War II, Rapid emerged with its greatest team ever, which was eventually led by wing half Gerhardt Hanappi, one of the game's most successful creators of scoring chances and Austrian player of the year eight times. Rapid's stopper-center half at this time was the redoubtable Ernst Happel, later an important coach in Western Europe. The club won seven Austrian championships from 1946-57, a period that coincided with Austria's second golden era at the national level. Its claim as the world's best club resulted when Rapid was on the winning end of Honvéd's first defeat in four years and MTK's first in three years, and in the 1956-57 European Cup, when it nearly eliminated Real Madrid in the first round.

As Austrian soccer began its decline in the late 1950s and early '60s, Rapid continued to win several championships. But the tragic downfall of the Austrian game was made apparent by the great club's lack of success in European competition. To this day, its furthest advance in Europe has been to the semi-finals of the 1960-61 European Cup, when it lost to Benfica by a 4-1 goal aggregate. A quarter-final finish in the 1968-69 European Cup did little to bolster its tarnished image, and its plight, along with that of Austrian soccer in general, has since gone from bad to worse.

R.C.D. Pact Football Tournament

An occasional competition for the national teams of Iran, Turkey, and Pakistan, named in honor of the Regional Corporation for Development, a cultural and economic agreement between the three countries. Its first winner in 1970 was Iran, with Turkey and Pakistan finishing in that order.

Real Madrid Club de Fútbol

Location: *Madrid, Spain;* stadium: *Estadio Santiago Bernabéu (101,663);* colors: *white jerseys, white shorts;* honors: *Intercontinental Cup (1960), European Cup (1956, 1957, 1958, 1959, 1960, 1966), Latin Cup (1955, 1957), Spanish champion (1932, 1933, 1954, 1955, 1957, 1958, 1961, 1962, 1963, 1964, 1965, 1967, 1968, 1969, 1972, 1975, 1976), Spanish cup winner (1905, 1906, 1907, 1917, 1934, 1936, 1946, 1947, 1962, 1970, 1974, 1975).*

Founded 1898 as Madrid Foot-ball Club by students who played in, among other locations, the adjacent fields of the Plaza de Toros in Guindalera. (Its date of incorporation, 1902, is also regarded as a founding date.) Madrid F.C. subsequently adopted the Velodrome grounds in Ciudad Lineal, and in 1948 moved to the Estadio Chamartin, later renamed for its legendary club president, Santiago Bernabéu. Madrid F.C. was an important club from the start, perhaps the second most successful in Spain after Athletic Bilbao prior to World War I. It was one of four clubs to participate in the first Spanish cup in

Real Madrid's Raymond Kopa (left), Ferenc Puskás (center), and Alfredo Di Stefano (right). For a brief spell in 1958-59, this trio of Real Madrid immortals formed part of the greatest forward line ever seen. Puskás wears the uniform of his former Budapest club, Honvéd.

1902, and shared most of the earliest cup honors with Bilbao. In 1920, its title, *Real* ("Royal"), was bestowed by Alfonso XIII. One of the earliest Spanish clubs to turn professional (1929), it became an original member of the Spanish league in 1928, and has never been relegated.

Between 1955-69, Real Madrid reached such dizzying heights of success that the general perspective one has of greatness and achievement in soccer was altered in its wake. Real created a new standard by which the game would subsequently be measured. There can be no higher accolade. Madrid became the new sporting capital of Europe, indeed of the world, and the myriad *madrileños* who shared in the glory were touched uncannily by the aura of this Spanish institution that was, and is, so uniquely beloved. Real during this period produced the best and most exciting club-level teams ever seen in the game. Their overall record—six European championships (five of them in succession), 12 Spanish championships in 16 years (including eight during the 1960s), and the first Intercontinental Cup, is all the more phenomenal, because it was achieved at a time when at least six other European clubs (Manchester United, Stade de Reims, Barcelona, AC Milan, Inter Milan, and Benfica) were themselves among the greatest teams ever seen, and during a period when four other Spanish clubs (Barcelona, Valencia, Real Zaragoza, and Atlético Madrid) were also good enough to win European honors.

After its pre-World War I cup successes under the leadership of Don Juan Padros Rubio, Real's founding father, first captain, and president, the club continued to prosper in the regional Campeonato del Centro, whose champions in turn played in the Copa del Rey. Real won the regional title from 1904-08, 1913, 1922-24, 1926-27, and 1929. In 1930, it secured the services of goalkeeper Ricardo Zamora, the idol of Spanish soccer, and with an excellent defensive team won two championships and two cups before Zamora retired in 1936. A turning point came in 1943 with the appearance of a new club president and owner, Don Santiago Bernabéu (1895-1978), former center forward with Madrid F.C. in the 1910s. In 1947-48, Real placed eleventh in the league standings, narrowly escaping relegation, and Don Santiago resolved then to build a unique club of winning teams that at the same time might assume a family-like atmosphere and contribute to the community that supported it.

His first important signing in 1948 was Miguel Muñoz, the "motor" of the rebuilt team at right half (and ultimately the manager from 1959-74). In 1953 Bernabéu secured the transfer of Alfredo Di Stefano from Millonarios of Colombia, Francisco Gento from Santander, and Héctor Rial from Nacional in Uruguay. The list of triumphs began to mount almost immediately: In 1954 Real took its first league championship in 20 years, a second came in 1955, as did a Latin Cup victory over Reims in the same year, followed by its first European Cup title in 1956. The great Reims international, Raymond Kopa, was lured to Real in 1956, and in 1957 and 1958, it won a second set of back-to-back Spanish championships and defended its European Cup successfully both times. As the list of superlatives grew, Real's invincibility became legendary.

In 1958, Ferenc Puskás, the "Galloping Major" of Hungary's immortal team in the early 1950s, was also signed, and though he was unable to find a comfortable place in this star-studded lineup until the 1959-60 season, Real won a fourth consecutive European Cup in 1959 with Kopa, Di Stefano, and Gento. Kopa returned to Reims, and Puskás settled into the forward line next to Di Stefano. The expected clash of egos did not materialize, as it had between Di Stefano and others, and Real reached its peak of excitement and virtuosity with its fifth consecutive European Cup win in 1960—the now classic 7-3 defeat of Eintracht Frankfurt in Glasgow. Real's forward line had differed only marginally in five European Cup triumphs. Individually or collectively, it ranks among the best ever seen in the history of the game. For the record, they were: Joseíto, Marchal, Di Stefano, Rial, Gento (1956); Kopa, Mateos, Di Stefano, Rial, Gento (1957); Kopa, Mateos, Di Stefano, Rial, Gento (1958); Kopa, Mateos, Di Stefano, Rial, Gento (1959); and Canario, Del Sol, Di Stefano, Puskás, Gento (1960).

Di Stefano became captain when Muñoz took over as manager in 1959, and in 1962 Real reached the European Cup final again, losing to Benfica. In the league Real continued to win championship after championship, with Di Stefano leading the league in scoring five times and Puskás four. Finally, in 1964, Di Stefano left and Gento became captain, followed by Puskás' retirement after yet another European Cup triumph in 1966. Gento continued to be a gifted and experienced leader, and it was he who guided the club to more honors until the end of the decade. After a short slump in the early 1970s, Muñoz and Bernabéu defied growing public criticism and built another young team (around the veteran forward Amancio) that was affectionately called the "Baby Show," and started once again to achieve successive honors in both league and cup competitions.

Red Star Belgrade   See: Crvena Zvezda, Fudbal Klub

referees and linesmen

A referee is the official in charge of a match with respect to all aspects of the Laws and facts of the game. His decisions are final. He is supported in his effort by two linesmen, whose task is to assist in administering the Laws.

Referees have nine basic duties to perform, as specified by the Laws:

1. Enforce the Laws.
2. Administer the advantage rule.
3. Keep score and act as timekeeper.
4. Suspend or terminate the game if necessary, submitting a detailed report of the decision to the proper authority.
5. Caution, and if necessary, send off players guilty of fouls or misconducts, submitting a detailed report of the decision to the proper authority.
6. Prevent all persons other than authorized players and linesmen from entering the field of play without permission.
7. Stop the game to allow a seriously injured player to be attended.
8. Restart the game after a stoppage.
9. Decide that the game ball meets all specified requirements.

A referee's authority begins as soon as he enters the field and extends to offenses committed during a stoppage or when the ball is out of play. He may choose to reverse a decision of his own if he wishes, provided he has not already restarted play. Application of the advantage rule is irreversible, even if the expected advantage does not materialize. He should take care that his stoppages are wholly necessary and do not unduly impede the progress of the game: the Laws are written to penalize deliberate fouls or misconducts. Although the referee is empowered to terminate a game in the event of "grave disorder," he may not determine the results of the game; this is left to proper authorities upon receipt of the referee's detailed report. When a player commits two separate offenses at the same time, the referee should address the more serious offense.

Although the linesmen are merely his assistants on the field, the referee is obliged to accept their information regarding an action that he was not in a position to see clearly. On the other hand, if the referee determines that he was, in fact, well positioned to see a given action, such contrary opinions as may be expressed by a linesman should be ignored. If a linesman is guilty of improper conduct, the linesman should be relieved of his duties by the referee and replaced with a suitable substitute.

As the name indicates, linesmen are positioned on the sidelines, one on each side of the field. Each is supplied a brightly colored flag by the host team, preferably one of red or yellow. A linesman's specific duties are to indicate when the ball is out of play, and to assist in determining which team is entitled to a corner kick, goal kick, or throw-in. In addition, when it is apparent that the referee did not see an offense being committed, the linesman must signal the referee immediately, but he may not determine and administer penalties for fouls or misconducts. If, however, in the opinion of the referee, a foul or misconduct was observed clearly by the referee, the linesman should refrain from assisting him unless called upon by him to do so.

All international matches, other than those in the amateur or youth categories, must be officiated by referees and linesmen from the official list of International Referees, as supplied by FIFA. International referees and linesmen must be selected from a neutral country or countries, unless otherwise agreed upon by both teams. They are required to wear the authorized FIFA badge on their shirt or blazer, and should take care that the color of their uniform is distinct from the colors of players' uniforms. Black is recommended.

Domestic matches must be officiated by properly authorized referees and linesmen if the results are to be officially recognized by FIFA, the relevant continental confederation, or the the national association under whose jurisdiction the match is played.

As of 1974, there were 292,025 referees registered by member associations of FIFA around the world: Africa (10,674), Asia (10,272), CONCACAF (6,709), Europe (248,-999), Oceania (2,415), and South America (12,983). The USSR has the largest number (94,000). The smallest number is found in Bahamas (eight), although the number of registered referees in some member-states of FIFA is uncertain: Afghanistan, Burundi, Liberia, Panama, and United Arab Emirates. The USA has 1,100 licensed referees, and Canada has 391, as of 1974. Approximately 750 referees are licensed by FIFA to officiate at international matches.

During the first half of the nineteenth century, the presence of referees in the various football games of English public schools and universities was irregular. At unusually important matches, each team supplied an umpire, but none of the playing codes or lists of rules during this period required that an official be present. Indeed, it was thought that the wider code of gentlemanly conduct would prevail. The Cheltenham College rules of 1867, however, called specifically for two umpires, one chosen by each team, and a referee appointed by the umpires, whose opinion was consulted if the umpires disagreed. But Cheltenham played the rugby game, and it was not until 1871, in the rules of the new F.A. Cup, that the first mention of a referee appears in any association football rules. The cup regulations specified two umpires and a referee. In 1874, the use of umpires was first codified in the official Laws of the Game and in 1880 referees were introduced in the Laws:

> By mutual consent of the competing clubs in matches, a referee shall be appointed whose duty shall be to decide in all cases of dispute between umpires. He shall also keep a record of the game and act as timekeeper, and in the event of ungentlemanly behaviour on the part of any of the contestants, the offender or offenders shall, in the presence of the umpires, be cautioned, and in the case of violent conduct, the referee shall have power to rule the offending player or players out of play, and order him or them off the ground, transmitting name or names to the committee of the Association under whose rules the game was played, and in whom shall be solely vested the right of accepting an apology.

It remained, however, that the final authority *de jure* rested in the hands of the governing association, rather than the referee, and a reluctance to depart from traditional public school manners was still very much evident. Finally, in 1891, umpires were replaced by linesmen, and by 1894 the referee had moved onto the field of play from the sidelines and had gained ultimate authority over the game. Referees and linesmen, as we know them today, had become fully sanctioned.

Numerous attempts have been made over the decades to increase the number of referees to two, but the International Football Association Board has consistently rejected such a proposal. The decision that referees at international matches should come from neutral countries was made by the International Board in 1950.

Réunion

A national selection from Réunion, a French Overseas Department, surfaced in 1976 to participate in the Tournoi Inter-Ocean in Victoria, Seychelles, to commemorate the independence of its Indian Ocean neighbor. Réunion defeated the hosts, 4-1. The Fédération Sportive Réunionnaise was founded at the end of World War II, and became affiliated with the French Football Federation in 1945, with 20 clubs and 1,000 players registered.

Rhodesia

Football Association of Rhodesia
P. O. Box M98
Mabelreign
Salisbury

Founded: 1965
FIFA: 1965

Affiliated clubs: *605;* registered players: *11,684 (704 non-amateur);* national stadium: *Rufaro Stadium, Salisbury (54,000);* largest stadium: *Rufaro Stadium;* colors: *white jerseys, black shorts;* season: *February to October;* honors: *none.*

Rhodesia's racial policies and unilateral declaration of independence (UDI) from the United Kingdom in 1965 have caused unending problems for the development of soccer. The game was brought to the area during the 1890s by British settlers arriving in Fort Salisbury, and for many decades it was played exclusively by white colonists. The small number of whites in what became Southern Rhodesia in 1923 limited the widespread growth of domestic competition, and eventually, strong links were made with the game in nearby Transvaal province of the Union of South Africa.

After World War II, sports administrators in the colonial government formed a national team, and in 1948 it was entered in South Africa's Currie Cup (amateur), in which provincial representative teams competed for South Africa's national championship. Rhodesia continued to participate annually in the Currie Cup until the 1960s, winning the competition only once (1959). Attempts were made to join the African Football Confederation (CAF) during the early 1970s, but the CAF was distrustful of Southern Rhodesia's promises of an integrated sports program. Immediately after UDI in 1965, the Football Association of Rhodesia was reconstituted, and it joined FIFA the same year. It was admitted to the CAF for a few short months, but the declared racial policies of the new regime resulted in a quick expulsion.

In 1968, Rhodesia tried to participate in qualifying rounds for the 1970 World Cup, but the black African states refused to play Rhodesia. Instead, FIFA grouped Rhodesia with Australia (in the Oceania sector), Japan, and Korea Republic (both in the Asia sector), but Rhodesia got no further than Australia. The first two games with Australia were drawn, but Australia won the third and deciding contest for the right to meet Israel. Rhodesia's team in this series was racially mixed (five blacks and six whites), but this was its last venture to date in official international competition.

In 1970, the FIFA Congress voted to suspend Rhodesia from the world body. The official reasoning for this action, which was supported by England and the other British associations, was that Rhodesia's alleged political autonomy (resulting from UDI) was unlawful, thereby rendering its separate affiliation with FIFA unlawful under FIFA statutes. The Football Association in London, with which the colonial Southern Rhodesian association had been affiliated, had never given permission to the reconstituted Rhodesian F.A. to break away and seek separate membership. Behind the technical charge, however, was the desire of many members to see Rhodesia suspended for violating the world body's statutes regarding human rights, and it was this issue that gained such widespread support for the suspension measure. (South Africa had been suspended from FIFA on the racial issue in 1964 and eventually expelled.)

Rhodesia was thus excluded from participating in any sanctioned international tournaments. Internally, the state of the game remained strong until the civil war, though always in steep competition with rugby, traditionally the white man's sport in Southern Africa. Rhodesian soccer has achieved a greater degree of racial integration than that of South Africa, but the National Football Association, which administers soccer among Rhodesia's "African" population, has continued to exist. The racial ratio of registered players in the country is roughly the same as the general population (95 percent black). Most of the leading clubs, in fact, are black, the most famous being Zimbabwe Saints. In 1977, a racially mixed national team took the field against South Africa's first racially mixed national team in Johannesburg and lost by 7-0.

Rhodesia is one of only a handful of African states to employ non-amateur players, and in proportion to its total population has one of the highest numbers of registered players and clubs on the continent. Twelve clubs participate in the first division, and much activity is centered on the national championship and annual cup competition. There are also several regional leagues and knockout tournaments. Bulawayo, Umtali, and Wankie are the major soccer centers other than the capital.

Rio Branco Cup

Copa Río Branco—Taça Rio Branco.

An occasional trophy awarded to the winner of certain matches played between Brazil and Uruguay, though overall it represents a small portion of these meetings. It is decided on a one-game basis with the participants taking turns as host country. In 1976, it doubled as one leg of the revived Atlantic Cup. The series is named for the small Uruguayan town that is situated on the Brazilian border along the main road between the two countries.

Winners

1931	Brazil	1947	Brazil	1967	shared
1932	Brazil	1948	Uruguay	1968	Brazil
1940	Uruguay	1950	Brazil	1976	Brazil
1946	Uruguay				

rivalries

The great rivalries of Europe and South America are the foundation of modern soccer. Their intensity is unsurpassed in all the rest of sport, and are likely the source for more discussion, or argument, than any other single topic on earth, romance and politics included. The greatest rivalries are seen on the club level, rather than in international competition, because club-level teams have a chance to meet more frequently, and they are generally enlivened by supporters who live relatively close to each other. The major exception to this general rule is in Great Britain, where the oldest international rivalry in the world, England (the *auld* enemy) vs. Scotland, still creates the most passionate atmosphere imaginable, particularly on the part of the Scots and most especially when the venue is Hampden Park, Glasgow.

Aside from the other British rivalries involving Wales and Northern Ireland, all of which date back to 1884 or before, the most intensely felt international rivalries are found either between nations that are linked culturally or historically, or between traditional political enemies. The former category includes Austria vs. Hungary, Belgium vs. Holland, Belgium vs. France, Czechoslovakia vs. Hungary, Germany FR vs. Austria, Spain vs. Portugal, and in South America, Argentina vs. Uruguay, and Argentina vs. Paraguay. In the latter category must be included France vs. Germany FR, USSR vs. Germany FR, and Greece vs. Turkey. Many other great international rivalries have resulted from two countries having competed for top honors over a long period of time: Italy vs. Austria, Italy vs. Germany FR, England vs. Italy, Germany FR vs. England, and in South America, Brazil vs. Argentina, and Brazil vs. Uruguay. The greatest of all these non-British rivalries, however, are undoubtedly Austria vs.

Hungary, whose debut in 1902 launched international competition on the continent of Europe, and Argentina vs. Uruguay, whose debut in 1905 did the same in South America.

Club rivalries exist in all countries where league competitions have had a chance to build up a tradition, and for one reason or another, pressure is brought to bear on one opponent above all others. The most common involve major clubs from the big cities—either the same city or different cities that clash in a sociopolitical context. Many in this category, however, are of interest only to those directly involved, and there are dozens of examples: in Africa, Stade Bamako vs. Djoliba in Mali, T.P. Mazembe vs. Vita Club in Zaire, Al Ahly vs. Al Zamalek in Egypt, A.S.E.C. Abidjan vs. Stade d'Abidjan in Ivory Coast, and Canon vs. Tonnerre in Cameroon; in South America, Alianza vs. Universitario in Peru, Nacional vs. Liga Deportiva Universitaria and Emelec vs. Barcelona in Ecuador, Cerro Porteño vs. Olímpia in Paraguay, The Strongest vs. Bolivar in Bolivia, Colo Colo vs. Union Española in Chile, and Atlético Mineiro vs. Cruzeiro and Internacional vs. Grêmio in Brazil.

In Europe, there is KB vs. BK 93 in Denmark, Lyn vs. Skeid in Norway, Ajax vs. Feyenoord in Holland, RSC Anderlecht vs. Standard Liège in Belgium, Red Star vs. Paris F.C. in France, Benfica vs. Sporting in Portugal, Atlético Madrid vs. Real Madrid in Spain, Roma vs. Lazio in Italy, Red Star Belgrade vs. Partizan Belgrade in Yugoslavia, Partizan vs. Dinamo in Albania, Olympiakos vs. Panathinaïkos and Aris vs. PAOK in Greece, CSKA vs. Levski-Spartak in Bulgaria, Rapid vs. Venus in Rumania, Sparta vs. Slavia in Czechoslovakia, Ferencváros vs. MTK in Hungary, Cracovia vs. Wisla Kraków in Poland, the Dinamo-Spartak-Torpedo derbies of Moscow in the USSR, Rapid vs. FK Austria in Austria, Linfield vs. Glentoran in Northern Ireland, Shamrock Rovers vs. Shelbourne in Eire, Heart of Midlothian vs. Hibernian and Dundee vs. Dundee United in Scotland, and Newcastle United vs. Sunderland and the Aston Villa-Birmingham City-West Bromwich Albion derbies of England. Some of these, such as the French, Polish, Czech, Danish, and Rumanian rivalries listed above, are relics of the distant past, but they all have a special significance in domestic competition.

There are certain archrivalries, however, which are rooted deeply in emotional conflicts—perhaps idiosyncratic to the clubs involved—and for one reason or another have captured the imagination of an international audience. The greatest and oldest of these is the Scottish "auld firm"—Celtic vs. Rangers—the twin titans of Glasgow, whose bitter rivalry dates from 1888 and stems quite simply from religious antagonism. Celtic was founded and is supported by Roman Catholics, most of whom came from Ireland, and Rangers is the most Protestant of all Scottish secular establishments, refusing even to this day to allow non-Protestants on its payroll. The fact that they have shared domination of Scottish soccer decisively since the 1890s and that one (Celtic) hails from the east side of the city while the other (Rangers) hails from the west side, adds considerably to the intensity of the situation.

In England, there are three great archrivalries. The biggest is that of Liverpool vs. Everton, two of England's most successful clubs, which started on that day in 1892 when a small group of Everton players defected to form a a new club, Liverpool. The bitterness on Merseyside is augmented by the geographical proximity of the two home grounds, which are located on either side of a common city park. In Manchester, the passionate feelings aroused between supporters of Manchester United and Manchester City have for years been inflamed by the extraordinary success of United, while the frustrations of City build with each passing season. In London, the most passionate rivalry is between the two North London giants, Arsenal and Tottenham Hotspur. Negative feelings in this sector were first aroused in 1913 when Arsenal moved to its present location from South London, prompting bitter resentment on the part of Spurs, who charged that Arsenal infringed on its territory and stole its fans. This was heightened in 1919 when Arsenal gained promotion to the first division of The Football League through the personal intercession of its director, a prominent Member of Parliament.

In Spain, the heated archrivalry between Real Madrid and Barcelona is primarily a result of the Spanish Civil War, when Barcelona, the Catalan capital, remained one of the strongholds of Republican resistance to Franco's forces. Real Madrid, the national capital's most famous cultural establishment and a bastion of Castilian pride, ranks at the top of the list as a symbol to Catalans of all that was lost in that bloody war. The major archrivalry in Italy is between the two Milan giants, Internazionale and AC Milan, the former an outgrowth of the latter and both at one time or another in control of European club championships. In the Italian tradition, the two clubs play in the same stadium (Stadio San Siro), and feelings were never higher than during the period of 1963-65, when the European Cup was won first by one, then the other. The great Turin archrivalry between Juventus and Torino is less intense than that of Milan's, but still ranks as one of the most bitter in Europe. The Fiat auto works, which owns Juventus, also employs many of Torino's supporters (as well as Juve's), and paradoxically, though Juventus is the most popular club in Italy, Torino is the more popular in Turin itself.

In South America, there are three archrivalries that have proved the equal of those in Spain and Italy. The most famous is Brazil's *Fla-Flu*, Flamengo vs. Fluminense, the most popular clubs of Rio de Janeiro. Their derbies have set numerous world attendance records in the mammoth Maracanã Stadium (177,656 in 1963 was the highest), and regularly draw 130,000 spectators in Rio league or Campeonato Nacional matches. Peñarol and Nacional of Montevideo, Uruguay, have so dominated soccer in that country and have shared so many international honors that the general population is substantially divided into their two camps. They share the huge Estadio Centenario, site of the first World Cup in 1930. The vitriolic archrivalry between Boca Júniors and River Plate in Buenos Aires has been plagued by more violence than other South American rivalries, and traces its roots to the opposing ethnic backgrounds of the clubs, Boca being the first great Italian club of Argentine soccer, and River getting its inspiration from British residents and Spanish-speaking *porteños*.

Rivera, Gianni (1943-   )

Perhaps the cleverest inside forward in Italian soccer history, Rivera's bumpy career was crowned in 1969 when he was chosen European Footballer of the Year and became the only one of Italy's half dozen major international stars of the period to be so honored. A prodigy in his teens, he gained a first team place with his second division hometown club, Alessandria, at age 15, and he made eight appearances with Italy's youth team before having his option purchased by AC Milan in 1960 for $182,000. At the time, he was still 16 years old. He immediately won a first team place with Milan, and in 1962 he made his full international debut against Belgium. One year later, at age 19, he was the runner-up to Lev Yashin in European Footballer of the Year balloting, based largely on his extraordinary contribution to Milan's European Cup triumph.

Though most of the Italian team was to blame for the *azzurri's* lamentable showing in the 1966 World Cup, Rivera received more blame than most, and his career fluctuated from then on. Through his magical footwork and inventive playmaking, he continued to excel for his club, and as captain in 1968 he led Milan to another league championship by a gaping nine-point margin, followed the next year by a second European Cup win and the European Footballer of the Year Award. Between 1968-70, he was embroiled in a sharp controversy with Sandro Mazzola, his opposite number and captain at Inter Milan, over who should adopt which role on the national team. When it was decided by the president of the Italian Football Federation that in the 1970 World Cup both would play in their newly found attacking midfield roles—with Rivera substituting for Mazzola at half time— it was Rivera who appeared to get the short end of the bargain. But in the 1970s, he regained his composure after his troubles with the national team, and resumed his scheming inside forward role to lead Milan to a European Cup Winners' Cup title in 1973. He bowed out of international competition after the 1974 World Cup with 60 caps and 14 goals, and in subsequent years he became involved in a power struggle with club owners for control of the AC Milan purse strings. After announcing his retirement from active play in 1978 with 127 club-level goals in 514 appearances—joining Giacinto Facchetti in breaking the one-club appearance record for Italy—he prepared to take over as president of AC Milan after at least one more season in uniform.

Ríver Plate, Club Atlético

Location: *Buenos Aires, Argentina;* stadium: *Estadio Monumental (77,000);* colors: *white jerseys with broad red diagonal stripe, black shorts;* honors: *National Championship winner (1975), Argentine league champion (1920 AAF, 1932 LAF, 1936, 1937, 1941, 1942, 1945, 1947, 1952, 1955, 1956, 1957, 1976, 1977), Uruguayan champion (1908, 1910, 1913, 1914).*

Founded 1901 in the central Buenos Aires barrio of Boca by British players from Santa Rosa F.C. and Rosales F.C. When one faction of players wanted to name the new club "Forwards" and another faction "Ríver Plate," a game was played to settle the dispute. For many years, the new club played in the Uruguayan league under Peñarol coach John Harley, winning that competition four times between 1908-14. In 1935, it moved out of the congested Boca barrio, and built the Estadio Monumental on the banks of the Río de la Plata at Nuñez. The Monumental was the greatest stadium in South America from the time of its opening until the appearance of the Maracanã in 1950, and in the mid-1970s it was enlarged for the 1978 World Cup.

Ríver Plate is Argentina's second most popular club (after Boca Júniors), and for many years it has been the wealthiest. It ranks second to Boca Júniors in the number of honors received—14 first division championships and one national championship—but in its production of gifted players it is the undisputed leader; few clubs in the world have turned out more. Ríver dominated Argentine soccer decisively during the 1940s and '50s, winning eight championships in 17 years. Knowledgeable Argentine observers believe the greatest team ever seen in Argentina was the Ríver Plate of 1941-47; the forward line of that team (nicknamed the *maquina*, or "machine") was composed of Muñoz, Moreno, Pedernera, Labruna, and Loustau (or Deambrosi), often ranked with Real Madrid's all-conquering line of the late 1950s. Adolfo Pedernera was perhaps the finest Argentine center forward of all time after Alfredo Di Stefano, and in the 1960s he managed Boca Júniors and many other clubs; Angel Labruna, the "Stanley Matthews" of South America, scored over 500 career goals, and was still playing for Argentina in the 1958 World Cup;

and José Moreno was a deft ball artist at inside right. In 1946, Pedernera was replaced by Di Stefano, whom Ríver had discovered in 1942, and it was in the championship winning team of 1947 that "the Blond Arrow" was nurtured and became perhaps the most complete player in the history of the game.

The amateur years (pre-1931) were not especially fruitful for Ríver—it won a single "regular" league title in 1920—but in 1932, it entered the front ranks. Its first successful period during the 1930s might well have started sooner had Ríver held on to its great star of the 1920s, the incomparable left winger Raimondo Orsi, who was poached by Juventus immediately after the 1928 Olympic Games in Amsterdam. In 1932, however, River signed Bernabé (*Dinamitero*) Ferreyra from Tigre, and he became the first true Argentine idol, drawing great crowds to Ríver's matches and enabling the club to embark on its famous spending spree. River became known as *Los Millonarios* ("The Millionaires") as a result of this, and professionalism in Argentina, still in its infancy, was given its final shot in the arm. Ríver won three championships during this period, and established itself firmly at the top of Argentine soccer.

After Di Stefano departed for Colombia in 1949, Ríver entered its third golden era in the early 1950s with a new generation of players (and Labruna), and made another sensational discovery in inside right Omar Sivori, a world-class ball juggler who helped both Ríver and Argentina to many honors before transferring to Juventus in 1957. After Sivori's world record transfer, the club began a frustrating 20-year period in which it became fossilized, or so it seemed, as the runner-up in the first division. It reached the final of the Copa Libertadores once (1966), losing to Peñarol in three games. In 1975, Ríver finally broke its long drought, causing much celebration in

Buenos Aires, and won the national championship-first division double. The following year, a defensive-minded Ríver narrowly lost the final of the Copa Liber- tadores to the more talented Cruzeiro of Brazil, and again the club of so many legends of the past failed to gain international club honors.

Roca Cup

Copa Julio Roca—Taça Julio Roca.

An occasional trophy contested by Brazil and Argentina. Brazil's first full international match ever was the 1914 edition of this series, from which Brazil emerged the winner, 1-0. The 1939 match in Rio was especially memorable, as two Brazilian goals were disallowed, and when a penalty was converted by the home team, Argentina left the field in protest over its legality. The police were called in to restore order, and Argentina went on to crush Brazil by 5-1. The first four editions were played on a one-game basis in alternating countries, but in 1940 home and away legs were introduced (with 1971 an exception). In 1976, the results counted double as part of the revived Atlantic Cup.

The trophy was given by General Julio Roca, who as a colonel in the late nineteenth century unified the Indian tribes of Argentina under the control of the central government.

Winners

1914	Brazil	1940	Argentina	1963	Brazil
1922	Brazil	1945	Brazil	1971	shared
1923	Argentina	1957	Brazil	1976	Brazil
1939	Argentina	1960	Brazil		

Romeu (1911-   )

(Full name: Romeu Pellicciari.) A scintillating center forward with Brazil during the 1930s and the star of São Paulo's Palestra Itália during its heyday. Later he became an equally effective midfield general. Romeu was signed at age 15 by Barranco FC in São Paulo, and moved quickly to São João, at that time one of the leading clubs in the city, taking over the first string center forward position immediately. In 1930, he was signed by Palestra Itália, the famous Italian-based club that later became Palmeiras, and together they went from one triumph to another. He won three league championship medals in succession from 1932-34, and the first Torneo Rio-São Paulo in 1933, but in 1935 he suddenly tranferred to Rio's Fluminense at the start of the professional era, and became the most recognizable player in Brazil with his famous tricolored skull cap. By this time, he had switched to inside right, and at Fluminense he combined with the extraordinary Tim at inside left and Carreiro at outside left to form one of Brazil's great prewar forward lines. He starred for Brazil in the 1938 World Cup and went on to make 13 international appearances, mainly in a scheming midfield role, scoring three goals. In 1942, he returned to Palestra Itália and scored his club's last goal under its old name. After remaining with Palmeiras for one more year, his playing career was rounded out with Commercial, and following a brief stint as a coach, he opened a cafe in his native São Paulo.

Rosa Chevallier Boutell Cup

Copa Rosa Chevallier Boutell.

The first of two series played between national teams of Argentina and Paraguay (the second is the recently introduced Bogado Cup). It has been contested under a variety of conditions, usually on a one-game basis, but has never been won outright by Paraguay. The Boutell and Bogado cups together account for less than one-quarter of the meetings between these two old rivals.

Winners

1923	shared	1939	Argentina	1950	Argentina
1924	shared	1940	Argentina	1956	Argentina
1925	shared	1943	shared	1963	Argentina
1926	Argentina	1945	Argentina	1964	Argentina
1931	Argentina	1946	shared	1971	Argentina

Rumania

Federatia Româna de Fotbal
16, rue Vasile Conta
Bucuresti

Founded: 1908
FIFA: 1930
UEFA: 1955

Affiliated clubs: *5,214;* **registered players:** *102,727;* **national stadium:** *23 August Stadium, Bucharest (95,000);* **largest stadium:** *23 August Stadium;* **colors:** *yellow jerseys, blue shorts:* **season:** *August to July;* **honors:** *Balkan Cup winner (1931, 1933, 1936).*

For decades Rumania has showed great promise of becoming a major soccer power, but it has not yet accomplished anything that would point to its arrival. Other than the ostracized Albanians, Rumania has been the least successful Eastern European country in international competition, though vast enthusiasm and support for the game exists within its borders. Crowds of 90,000 are not uncommon for important matches held at the national stadium. But there is neither the overall winning record of Hungary, Yugoslavia, Czechoslovakia, or the USSR, nor the persistent threat of a winning era that is characteristic of Bulgaria, nor the rapidly rising standard of play of Poland and East Germany. Rumania has consistently managed to stay just outside the mainstream of European soccer. This may also be said of Rumanian clubs, which have yet to make an impact on international competition.

The early history of Rumania's game engendered considerable hope. British engineers in the oilfields near Ploiesti introduced soccer during the late 1890s, and in 1899 the first competitions were started in Bucharest and Arad. The game's adoption by the Rumanian populace received its first real impetus from Prince Carol, an inveterate fan, and largely through his aggressive support the Associata Cluburilor Române de Football, the first national association, was founded in 1908. Two years later, Carol himself formed the Federation Societatilor de Sport din România, an umbrella body for all Rumanian sports, and became its first general secretary. The soccer association beame a section within the federation. Olimpia Bucharest won the first two national championships, organized in 1909. In 1930, when Carol returned to Rumania as king, the sports federation was renamed the Uniunea Federatilor Sportive din România, and control of soccer was transferred to the reconstituted Federatia Romăna de Fotbal Asociatie, precursor of the present-day FRF.

In 1922, Rumania made its international debut in Belgrade against Yugoslavia, a new country still disorganized after a mere three years in existence, and won, 2-1. A great majority of Rumania's prewar contests were played against other Balkan states, mostly in connection with the Balkan Cup. Rumania won three editions of the Balkan Cup before World War II, the first edition played on a home and away basis (1929-31), the third in Bucharest (1933), and the sixth in Sofia (1936). Opposition in the first two consisted of Yugoslavia, Bulgaria, and Greece, but only Bulgaria and Greece faced Rumania in the third. In the 1933 edition, Rumania won all three matches by an aggregate score of 13-0, its best showing ever in international competition. The early 1930s, indeed, was Rumania's strongest period, and it was during this time that it achieved its biggest wins, an 8-1 trouncing of Greece in 1930 and a 7-0 shutout of Bulgaria in 1933, both at home. None of the Balkan states at this time, however, was a major force in Europe, and Rumania's most convincing losses in friendlies before World War II were to Sweden, Czechoslovakia, and Germany. More important, however, were the severe disappointments of World Cup competition.

At the personal instigation of King Carol, Rumania became one of the small handful of European nations to make the long journey to Montevideo for the first World Cup in 1930. The team was picked by the king himself. Its first round match against Peru was compromised by unfortunate circumstances: The competence of the referee was questionable, Rumania's right back broke his leg in a melee of hard tackling, and Peru's captain was sent off, leaving Peru severely weakened. Nevertheless, Rumania emerged victorious by 3-1. Against the great Uruguayan team (winner of the 1924 and 1928 Olympic tournaments and eventual winner in this first World Cup), Rumania met with its first world-class opposition and was lucky to lose by only 4-0.

In the 1934 World Cup, Rumania was eliminated in the first round by Czechoslovakia, one of Europe's leading teams at the time. In 1938, defeat came at the hands of unknown Cuba, which had qualified only after Mexico withdrew. The first match with Cuba, a 3-3 draw after extra time, was one of the best contests in the 1938 competition. Equalizers were scored moments before the end of regulation time and extra time. In the replay, however, despite the benching of Cuba's impressive goalkeeper, Carvajales, the Cubans dominated the veteran Rumanian team and won 2-1 on goals scored in the second half, including one that was thought by many to be from an offside position. Rumania was out of the World Cup until 1970, having participated in all three prewar competitions.

The national team maintained a record of above 50 percent success before World War II, primarily through its lack of meetings with the stronger nations of Western Europe. In the postwar years, however, nearly the same rate of success has been maintained, despite the more rapid advance of many Warsaw Pact countries. Rumanian teams have not yet defeated Hungary in 13 outings, and their record against Czechoslovakia stands today at five won, five drawn, and 13 lost. Meanwhile, the scars of World War II left Rumania unprepared for the 1950 World Cup, and Rumania was eliminated from the 1954 World Cup by Czechoslovakia and from the 1958 World Cup by Yugoslavia. At Guadalajara in 1970, Rumania was shut out in the opening round by England. The following day, Dumitrache and Dembrovski were able to score against the Brazilians' traditionally mediocre defense, but, with two goals by Pelé and one by Jairzinho, Rumania showed that it could not match the world-class talent of the best teams, and once again the quarter-finals were put out of reach.

In its only Olympic match of the prewar era in 1924, the losing finalist of that year, Holland, crushed the fledgling Rumanian team, 6-0. In 1952, at Turku, Rumania was eliminated in the first round by eventual gold medalist Hungary, and did not try to qualify again until 1960, when Bulgaria won the qualification round. Having gone through to the final rounds in 1964, it was again eliminated by Hungary in the quarter-finals after an excellent showing against East Germany, Mexico, and Iran in the first round. Rumania has not qualified for any Olympic tournament since 1964. By this failing, Rumania has become the least successful Eastern European country in Olympic competition, a fact that has caused it great frustration in the face of enormous competitive pressure from Warsaw Pact neighbors that dominate Olympic soccer.

Rumania's best showings in the European Football Championship have been to reach the quarter-finals in 1958-60 and 1970-72. Its eventual defeat by Czechoslovakia in 1960 was decisive, but in 1970-72 Rumania was impressive in eliminating Czechoslovakia, Wales, and Finland in the first round, and in the quarter-finals it forced a rematch against Hungary in neutral Yugoslavia after drawing twice. The waning Hungarians, however, won the third game and an eagerly awaited semi-final confrontation with the USSR did not materialize.

Rumania's most difficult opposition from Western Europe over the years has been West Germany (including prewar Germany) and Sweden, against which it has yet to win. Its overall record against other Warsaw Pact states is mixed. Rumania's best record in this group is against Poland: 19-8-10-1-31-8-26.

Its occasional periods of extreme weakness were demonstrated in 1966 when it lost three consecutive matches in Africa, to Ethiopia (2-1), Congo-Brazzaville (1-0), and Congo-Kinshasa (3-2).

In domestic competition, the league was dominated before World War II by two clubs from Timisoara—Chinezul in the 1920s and Ripensia, which shared most honors in the 1930s with Venus Bucharest. Rapid Bucharest became a specialist as a cup winner in the immediate prewar years. By far the most successful postwar clubs have been Steaua Bucharest (formerly CCA Bucharest), the Central Army club, and Dinamo Bucharest, the electrical workers team. Before World War II, the national league was divided into a Division A of 14 clubs and a Division B with

two sections of 14 clubs each. After the war, Division A was reduced to 12 clubs and the sections of Division B were increased to 16 clubs each. A structural reorganization in 1957 raised the number of Division A clubs to 18. Several regional championships exist below Division B level. A national cup competition, the Cupei României, was introduced in 1934, and has been won a record 12 times by Steaua. Since the cup's inception, it has been won by clubs from 12 different cities.

The first Rumanian club to enter European competition was Dinamo Bucharest, which in 1957-58 narrowly defeated Galatasaray Istanbul before losing in the first round to CDNA Sofia. Rumanian clubs have not yet reached the semi-final round of any of the three European club competitions.

Champions

1910 Olimpia Bucharest	1933 Ripensia Timisoara	1956 CCA Bucharest
1911 Olimpia Bucharest	1934 Venus Bucharest	1957 no competition
1912 United Ploiesti	1935 Ripensia Timisoara	1958 Petrolul Ploiesti
1913 Colentina Bucharest	1936 Ripensia Timisoara	1959 Petrolul Ploiesti
1914 Colentina Bucharest	1937 Venus Bucharest	1960 CCA Bucharest
1915 Soc. RA Bucharest	1938 Ripensia Timisoara	1961 Steaua Bucharest
1916 Prahova Ploiesti	1939 Venus Bucharest	1962 Dinamo Bucharest
1917 no competition	1940 Venus Bucharest	1963 Dinamo Bucharest
1918 no competition	1941 Tricolor	1964 Dinamo Bucharest
1919 no competition	1942 Rapid Bucharest	1965 Dinamo Bucharest
1920 Venus Bucharest	1943 Craiova Bucharest	1966 Petrolul Ploiesti
1921 Venus Bucharest	1944 no competition	1967 Rapid Bucharest
1922 Chinezul Timisoara	1945 no competition	1968 Steaua Bucharest
1923 Chinezul Timisoara	1946 no competition	1969 UT Arad
1924 Chinezul Timisoara	1947 Flacara Rosie Arad	1970 UT Arad
1925 Chinezul Timisoara	1948 Flacara Rosie Arad	1971 Dinamo Bucharest
1926 Chinezul Timisoara	1949 IC Oradea	1972 FC Arges
1927 Chinezul Timisoara	1950 Flacara Rosie Arad	1973 Dinamo Bucharest
1928 Coltea Brasov	1951 CCA Bucharest	1974 Uni. Craiova
1929 Venus Bucharest	1952 CCA Bucharest	1975 Dinamo Bucharest
1930 Juventus Bucharest	1953 CCA Bucharest	1976 Steaua Bucharest
1931 SUD Resita	1954 Flacara Rosie Arad	1977 Dinamo Bucharest
1932 Venus Bucharest	1955 Dinamo Bucharest	1978 Steaua Bucharest

Cup Winners

1934 Ripensia Timisoara	1938 Rapid Bucharest	1942 Rapid Bucharest
1935 CFR Bucharest	1939 Rapid Bucharest	1943 CFR Turnu Severin
1936 Ripensia Timisoara	1940 Rapid Bucharest	1944 no competition
1937 Rapid Bucharest	1941 Rapid Bucharest	1945 no competition

1946	no competition	1957	no competition	1968	Dinamo Bucharest
1947	no competition	1958	Stiinta Timisoara	1969	Steaua Bucharest
1948	UT Arad	1959	Dinamo Bucharest	1970	Steaua Bucharest
1949	CCA Bucharest	1960	Progresul Bucharest	1971	Steaua Bucharest
1950	CCA Bucharest	1961	Ariesul Turda	1972	Rapid Bucharest
1951	CCA Bucharest	1962	Steaua Bucharest	1973	Chimia Vilcea
1952	CCA Bucharest	1963	Petrolul Ploiesti	1974	Jiul Petroseni
1953	Flacara Rosie Arad	1964	Dinamo Bucharest	1975	Rapid Bucharest
1954	Metalul Resita	1965	Stiinta Cluj	1976	Steaua Bucharest
1955	CCA Bucharest	1966	Steaua Bucharest	1977	Uni. Craiova
1956	Progresul Oradea	1967	Steaua Bucharest	1978	Uni. Craiova

Russia   See: **USSR**

Rwanda

Although Rwanda is not yet a member of FIFA or the African Football Confederation, soccer is a passion among Rwandan sports fans. International competition is rare, but in 1975 the Rwandan national team (called the "Amavubi") visited neighboring Uganda and drew with Kampala's oldest and most established club, Nsambya F.C., 2-2. Rwanda ranks with neighboring Burundi as one of the poorest countries in the world, but unlike its neighbor to the south it has not yet found a way to finance continuous international competition and affiliation with external governing bodies.

S

Saar

During the brief period after World War II when the Saar enjoyed political semi-autonomy, this small and densely populated region entered international competition on its own and supported an independent league. Prior to this, the Saar had been affiliated with Germany and some of its clubs played in the Südwestdeutschland section of the German league. In 1948, the Saarländischer Fussball-bund was founded in Saarbrucken, and it joined FIFA as a full member in 1950. There were 270 clubs and 8,000 adult players registered—all amateur. The top two or three clubs continued to play in the German Südwest Oberliga, and the others joined the four-division Saarland league. The Saarland Cup, a knockout competition, was played until 1953.

The Saar made its international debut in 1950 against Switzerland "B," winning 5-2 in Saarbrucken, and in 1951 defeated both Austria "B" and Switzerland "B" again, the latter in Berne. Its first loss was in 1951 to Austria "B" in Vienna (4-1). The Saar split home and away friendlies with France "B" in 1952, and in 1953 made its full international debut against Norway (at Oslo) in a World Cup qualifying round, losing 3-2. In all, the Saar played in eight full internationals from 1953-56, losing six and drawing two. In 1953 it drew with Norway in Saarbrucken (0-0), and lost to the other member of its World Cup qualifying round, West Germany, in Stuttgart (3-0). The second match with West Germany was lost 3-1 at Saarbrucken in 1954, and the Saar finished at the bottom of its group. Later on in 1954, Yugoslavia visited Saarbrucken, and won a friendly, 5-1. In 1955, the Netherlands won a friendly in Saarbrucken, 2-1, and the following year won the return, 3-2. The Saar's last full international was played in Saarbrucken against Switzerland in May 1956, and it ended in a 1-1 draw. In 1957, the Saar voted to rejoin Germany in a plebiscite, and the Saarländischer Fussballbund withdrew from FIFA.

An important industrial and mining center, the Saar today supports a regional league and many clubs that play in the West German league. The biggest and most successful of them are FC Saarbrücken (1903), FC Homburg-Saar (1908), Borussia Neunkirchen (1905), and Röchling Völkingen (1906). Saarbrücken and Neunkirchen have both played in the Bundesliga at various times.

San Marino

The Principality of San Marino does not support a national association, and is not separately affiliated with FIFA or UEFA. The local club, FC San Marino, is a member of the Italian Football Federation, but, as an amateur team, it does not compete in any division of the national league.

Santos, Djalma   (1929-   )

Perhaps the greatest right back in the history of the game, Djalma Santos's longevity became a Brazilian legend. He played in four World Cups (1954-66), having made his international debut in 1952, and retired in 1968 at age 39 after he had made his 100th international appearance in a Copa Rio Branco match against Uruguay. But longevity was far from his only attribute. He was a master tackler who remained cool and unperturbed no matter what the opposition. His style was to jockey rather than charge, and when the moment was ripe he moved in lithely for the kill, rarely if ever overcommitting himself. The success of his strategy was seen throughout his entire career. In addition, he was Brazil's deadly accurate penalty taker, and, in consort with his frequent partner in the backfield, Nilton Santos (no relation), he never hesitated to overlap and go on the attack.

Djalma Santos spent his lengthy career entirely in his home town of São Paulo. He entered senior-level competition 1948 with Portuguêsa de Desportos, and stayed there until 1959, when he was transferred to the much larger Palmeiras. His coolness and leadership led directly to Palmeiras's splendid run to the final of the Copa Libertadores in 1961, and, to Portuguêsa's dismay, the 34-year-old Djalma

Santos was selected for the 1962 World Cup-winning team in Chile after his former club had decided he was finished. He also played in the 1963 commemorative game in London between England and FIFA's World XI, demonstrating his wide-ranging talents once again before an appreciative European audience. In his waning years, he moved to the little *paulisto* club Atletico Paranaense, and retired after almost 25 years of exceptional service to the Brazilian game.

Brazil's legendary Djalma Santos, veteran of four World Cup campaigns and the most accomplished right back in South American soccer.

Santos, Nilton   (1926-   )

(Full name: Nilton dos Santos.) With Djalma Santos (no relation), he was one-half of the greatest attacking fullback combination in

history. Nilton played on the left side for both his club, Botafogo, and Brazil. In international competition he and Djalma Santos perfected a tandem that was based on good communication and an understanding of each other's abilities. When one would attack, the other would stay behind, and vice versa. Though they never played together at the club level, they starred together for Brazil over 70 times, Nilton accumulating a total of 83 caps.

Nilton's career was extraordinarily long, and almost all of its was spent with Botafogo. He started as a goalscoring forward with Flecheiras, located on the Ilha do Governador in Rio, but in 1948 Botafogo took him on as a center half. He made his first team debut, however, as a left half, and never abandoned that position throughout his career. His first appearance for Brazil was in 1949 at the South American Championship, but he did not participate in the 1950 World Cup. Nilton's low point, unfortunately, was the infamous "Battle of Berne" against Hungary in the 1954 World Cup, when he was sent off amid all the scuffling, but he went on to serve the Brazilian national team with distinction in its World cup triumphs of 1958 and 1962, the latter at age 37. In 1964, having won practically every trophy available to a Brazilian player, he retired.

Santos Dumont Cup

Copa Santos Dumont—Taça Santos Dumont.
A rarely played series between Brazil and Peru, confined to the post-World War II era.

Santos Futebol Clube

Location: *Santos, Brazil;* stadium: *Estádio Urbano Caldeira, Vila Belmiro (20,000);* colors: *white jerseys, white shorts;* honors: *Intercontinental Cup (1962, 1963), Copa Libertadores (1962, 1963), Rio-São Paulo Tournament (1959, 1963, 1964 shared, 1966 shared), National Championship (1968), São Paulo champion (1935 LPF, 1955, 1956, 1958, 1960, 1961, 1962, 1964, 1965, 1967, 1968, 1969, 1973 shared).*

Founded 1912 as Santos Football Club by three student members of Americano, who elected to remain in the port city of Santos when their club relocated 30 miles up the road to São Paulo. The three pioneers, Raimundo Marques, Mário Ferras de Campos, and Argemiro de Sousa, Jr., sent out circulars, convened meetings, and in the borrowed quarters of Club Concórdia formally established the new club. Before the end of 1912, they rented a field in the barrio of Macuco, and began to play pick-up games against Thereza Team, a group of former members of a club called Santos that had folded in 1910.

In 1913, Santos adopted a black-and-white striped uniform (its present away colors), joined the local Santos league and won the title in its first attempt. The big São Paulo state league invited the club to join in 1914, but after playing the entire season away from home because its own grounds were too small, it returned to the Santos league in 1915. After winning the Santos league again, it found a larger facility at Vila Belmiro, rejoined the São Paulo league in 1916, and has remained there since. In 1933, it was one of the first two Brazilian clubs to adopt professionalism. For nearly 40 years, it was a moderate force in the league, breaking through once in 1935 to win a Liga Paulista de Futebol title. Most of its big matches are played a the Estádio Municipal do Pacaembu in São Paulo.

The rebirth of Santos began in 1952 with the signing of wing half—then multipurpose player—Zito, who led Santos to much-heralded *paulista* championships in 1955 and 1956. In September 1956, Pelé, aged 16, gained a place on the first team in a friendly against AIK Stockholm, and with one stroke, the fortunes of Santos, and world soccer at large, changed dramatically. With Pelé reaching over 100 goals per season by 1959, Santos became the first Brazilian club since Paulistano in the 1910s to dominate a league so decisively. Between 1955-69, Santos' run on *paulista* championships was interrupted only four times for a total of 11 league titles—an unpresedented feat in the upper reaches of South American soccer. During this same period, it collected five national titles, two South American club championships, and two "world" club championships, all achieved with record-breaking goal differences and the utmost panache. In 1961, the club acquired an already established star player for the first time in Santos-born Gilmar, the best goalkeeper Brazil has ever produced, and the heights of its success appeared boundless.

Initially, its international fame was achieved largely through the knowledge that Pelé, hero of the 1958 World Cup, was a member of the team. But with the winning of the Copa Libertadores in 1962 and 1963, the club traveled to Europe to face Benfica and AC Milan in the Intercontinental Cup, and it was then, in addition to its ceaseless international tours, that the imagination of the world was captured and Santos became an international household word much as Arsenal and Manchester United had been in the past, yet to a greater degree. European clubs guaranteed upwards of $50,000 for one appearance, and the club became wealthy. Eight more *paulista* titles were won during the 1960s—convincingly—and the other giant clubs of São Paulo simply had to ride out the storm.

The 1962 season was Santos' peak. It breezed through the 1962 Copa Libertadores on 29 goals in nine games, defeating Benfica in the Intercontinental Cup, by 3-2 in Rio and a stunning 5-2 in Lisbon. Another peak was reached in 1965 with a perfectly blended 6-4 win over the Czech national team.

Historians recalled that in 1920, Corinthians Paulista had buried the fledgling Santos by 11-0 in a league match, but by 1958 it was Santos on top, first by a 10-0 win over Uruguayan super-power Nacional, then Ponta Preta by 12-1 in 1959, Juventus São Paulo by 10-0 in 1960, and Botafogo São Paulo by 11-0 in 1966. By the early 1970s, Santos had accumulated the second best record in the history of *paulista* competition, largely through its post-1954 results. With Pelé aging, Santos finally ceased to be the invincible force it once was, though it shared yet another league title in 1973. In 1974 Pelé retired from the club in a tearful departure that was beamed around the world.

Still among the leaders of the São Paulo league, Santos has since lost its wealth and is struggling through a difficult emotional period when world adoration is not longer a guarantee. Its standing in the world soccer community, however, will not soon diminish with so many millions of people harboring memories of the thrills and continually entertaining soccer Santos exported to every corner of the earth.

São Paulo Futebol Clube

Location: *São Paulo, Brazil;* **stadium:** *Estádio Morumbi (150,000);* **colors:** *white jerseys with single red and black horizontal bands separated by white, white shorts;* **honors:** *National Championship (1977), São Paulo champion (1931, 1943, 1945, 1946, 1948, 1949, 1953, 1957, 1970, 1971, 1975).*

Founded 1930 when members of CA Paulistano, whose soccer section had folded in 1929, invited AA das Palmeiras—then in dire financial straits—to join with them in forming a new club. São Paulo FC was blessed from the beginning by the presence of Brazil's greatest idol, Artur Friedenreich, who had been Paulistano's center forward, and under his guidance finished its first season in the São Paulo league (1930) with a second place medal. One year later, it won its first *paulista* championship, followed by three consecutive second place finishes.

In 1933, São Paulo became the first Brazilian club to officially adopt professionalism, and almost immediately it won the patronage of wealthy São Paulo supporters. High-level financial intrigues, however, soon ravaged the club's bank account, and in 1935 the directors announced its dissolution. The membership rose up in protest, and in the space of a few months collected enough guarantees to assure the club's reformation. In December 1935, São Paulo FC was reborn, and it joined the Liga Paulista de Futebol in time for the 1936 season. Much of the emotion behind São

Paulo's rebirth lay in its name, which not only bears the name of the city but also harkens to the fondly-remembered São Paulo Athletic Club of the pre-1914 era.

In 1942, the club purchased the immortal Leônidas of 1938 World Cup fame—then the most famous sports figure in the country—for a record fee, and won five championships before Leônidas' retirement in 1950. Known as *O Mais Querido* ("The Best Loved"), São Paulo was the main attraction of *paulista* soccer during the 1940s, with Leônidas the drawing card. Under its youth program, many excellent players were developed, such as the wing half Bauer, who joined São Paulo's first team in 1946 and in later years discovered

Eusebio in his travels as a manager. The successes of the 1940s brought great wealth which was generally invested in facilities and programs rather than players, and in the 1950s the club won only two championships, one of them—in 1957—largely through its extraordinary good luck in obtaining Hungarian national team manager Bela Guttmann, who in turn lured the great Zizinho to São Paulo for one season. After a sparse decade and a half, São Paulo won back-to-back *paulista* titles in 1970 and 1971, sparked by the revived Brazilian midfield hero Gerson, and in the mid-1970s a new team lacking superstars captured a league championship and its first national championship.

Saudi Arabia

Saudi Arabian Football Federation
P.O. Box 5844
Riyadh

Founded: 1959
FIFA: 1959
AFC: 1972

Affiliated clubs: *104;* **registered players:** *8,200;* **national stadium:** *Malaz Ground, Riyadh (25,000);* **largest stadium:** *Jiddah Stadium, Jiddah (35,000);* **colors:** *green jerseys with white trim, white shorts;* **season:** *September to May;* **honors:** *none.*

The game was slow to establish itself among the Saudis, whose religious and cultural beliefs prohibited the adoption of Western games until the recent postwar years. Lacking much exposure to European colonists, Saudi adoption of the game was left to a process of slow infiltration from the growing number of western engineers and workers who came to develop the oil industry after World War II. Currently, Saudi Arabia takes second place on the Arabian peninsula to the powerful Kuwaitis, but it has not yet made an impact on the Asian game as a continental power. Like other oil-producing nations of the area, Saudi Arabia attracts European coaches by offering vast sums of money and inviting as many leading teams of Europe as possible to play exhibition games with native players. None other than Ferenc Puskás was hired to coordinate a national soccer program and coach the national team for a one-year stint in 1975-76.

Although its national association was founded in 1959 and membership in FIFA was granted the same year, Saudi Arabia's regular participation in international competition did not start until the early to mid-1970s. It was

one of four original participants in the first biannual Arabian Gulf Tournament in 1970 with Bahrain, Qatar, and the winner, Kuwait. Saudi Arabia placed third. In the next Arabian Gulf Tournament in 1972, it placed second, losing on goal difference to Kuwait after compiling an undefeated record against Bahrain, Qatar, and United Arab Emirates. In 1976, among a field of seven countries, Saudi Arabia won two and lost four in placing fourth alongside little Bahrain, an exceedingly disappointing result after the arrival of Puskás. In its first attempt to qualify for the World Cup in 1976-77, Saudi Arabia split home and away legs with Syria (2-0 and 1-2), but lost to Iran (0-3 and 0-2) and was eliminated. It has never qualifed for the final rounds of the Asian Nations' Cup, nor were its clubs seen in the final stages of the Asian Champions' Cup before that competition's demise in 1971.

The national league of Saudi Arabia consists of 18 clubs from the major commercial cities: Riyadh, Jiddah, Dhahran, Dammam, and other ports. About 36 additional clubs participate in the lower divisions. The national cup, His Majesty's Cup, is contested vigorously each year. There is little soccer in the holy cities of Mecca and Medina. Scheduled for completion in 1982 is the ornate new international stadium on the outskirts of Riyadh. Located in a desert setting, the $350 million complex will hold 80,000 spectators and feature a royal pavilion, gold leaf engravings, armor-plate glass at entrances, and a restaurant high in the sky overlooking the Najd.

save

The gathering, deflecting, or punching of a shot to prevent it from scoring. This is the chief function of a goalkeeper.

Scandinavian Championship

Also known as the "Nordic Cup."

Europe's first international competition between nations outside the United Kingdom. It was launched in 1924 by Denmark, Norway, Sweden, and Finland, and in the relatively tranquil political climate of the north, has been held regularly ever since. Even the fourth championship, which was interrupted by war, was completed.

Results are determined on a league basis. Each country faces its three opponents annually, reversing venues the following year. After four years with two games at home and two away against each opponent, the standings are tallied up and the championship is decided on points. Each country thus meets the other three participants a total of four times. A grand total of 24 games are played in each tournament. Since the 1930s the championship has been dominated by Sweden, the perennial power of the region, but this was not always the case. From 1890-1920, Denmark was the prime mover in Scandinavian soccer, and the results of the first championship reflect this. Since the Swedish takeover, Denmark has more often than not held onto second place. Norway and Finland have each broken through to the top once, but they have usually finished third or fourth.

Winners

1924-29	Denmark	1952-55	Sweden
1929-32	Norway	1956-59	Sweden
1933-36	Sweden	1960-63	Finland
1937-47	Sweden	1964-67	Sweden
1948-51	Sweden	1968-71	Sweden

Scarone, Hector   (1898-1968)

Of all the great Uruguayan stars of the 1924-30 period, Scarone stands out as a prototype of the traditional Uruguayan forward. His mastery of all the skills associated with a classic inside right was developed to its limit. Scarone was an exceptionally hard worker and very tough competitor, but the genius of old-fashioned Uruguayan scoring artists was that they could switch instantly from their role as effective team player to that of individual ball artist. No one was more successful at this than Hector Scarone. He scored regularly for both club and country, schemed with great sophistication when he was off the ball, and shot with pinpoint accuracy.

His career began in 1912 when, at age 14, he joined the third division Montevideo club Sportsman, and he was quickly snapped up by Nacional the following year. Nicknamed *el Magico* ("The Magician"), he made his international debut in 1919 in the South American Championship. He played an important role in the winning of Uruguay's gold medal at the 1924 Olympics, and two years later he accepted an offer to play for Barcelona in Spain. He returned after only six months and was high scorer in the South American Championship of 1927. At the 1928 Olympics, he scored the winning goal for Uruguay in the final, elevating his status as a national hero still further, and he was one of only two players in Uruguay's 1930 World Cup-winning team that had played in both the 1924 and 1928 Olympics finals. In all, he appeared 64 times for Uruguay, an exceptionally high total in the golden era of amateur soccer in South America.

Scarone's incredible career continued. After 1930, he returned to Europe briefly to play for Ambrosiana-Inter in Italy, and after World War II he was a coach at Real Madrid. At the age of 55, he returned to Nacional not as a coach but as a player for a short spell, and broke all age records for playing in the Uruguayan first division.

Schalke 04, Fussball-Club Gelsenkirchen-

Location: *Gelsenkirchen, West Germany;* stadium: *Parkstadion (70,600);* colors: *blue jerseys with white trim, white shorts;* honors: *German champion (1934, 1935, 1937, 1940, 1942), West German champion (1958), German cup winner (1937), West German cup winner (1972).*

Founded 1904 in the central Gelsenkirchen neighborhood of Schalke. Gelsenkirchen is a mining center in the Ruhr, hence the club's nickname, *knappen* ("miners"). Schalke was a prime instigator of the game in its native Westphalia, and came to prominence in the Westdeutschland league in the late 1920s, winning four regional championships from 1929-33; however, it failed to win a national championship under the old format that required regional winners to meet in a knockout tournament to determine that honor. Scandal hit the club in 1930, when it was found guilty of making illegal payments to its players. Despite a pardon the following year, Schalke players were banned from the national team until the late 1930s.

Spurred by its world class stopper-center half Fritz Szepan, and to a lesser extent by Szepan's brother-in-law, Ernst Kuzorra, Schalke developed a home version of the W-M formation in the early 1930s, described by many as "stingy" but highly successful nonetheless, and before long the *Schalker Kreisel* (Schalke spinning-top) replaced FC Nürnberg's less intense approach, which had been the most popular and successful style in the country for over 10 years. Szepan led Schalke to six German championships in nine years, beginning in 1934, and Schalke's home grounds, then called the Glückauf Kampf-bahn, became the best-known stadium in the Third Reich. From 1937-42, Schalke advanced to the final of every national championship, and in 1940 created a unbeatable record by defeating Kasseler SC 16-0 during the final rounds of the competition.

Schalke won further regional titles in 1951 and 1958, and won the Westdeutschland cup in 1954. In 1963-64, it was made a charter-member of the Bundesliga, West Germany's national league, and placed in the middle of the standings at the end of its first season. Schalke has managed to win only one West German national title since World War II, a cup victory in 1972, and it bowed out of the European Cup Winners' Cup the following year to Sparta Prague in the quarter-finals. Schalke's winning of this West Germany cup was, in fact, a considerable feat, because the year before the club had been demoralized by another scandal in which it was convicted of purposely losing a league match to Arminia Bielefeld to help that club escape relegation. Schalke players, including Erwin Kremers and Reinhard Libuda, were banned from the national team. By the late 1970s, Schalke had returned to top form once again behind the goalscoring prowess of center forward Klaus Fischer. Today it remains one of West Germany's three most popular clubs and the rallying point for West Germany's mining industry.

Schiaffino, Juan (1925-   )

The extraordinary inside forward of Peñarol and Uruguay, whose opportunistic instincts and fighting spirit carried on the great tradition of Uruguayan players in that position. Not large in size, he defied predictions that he could not last in international class competition against bruising defenders, and he proved to be one of the great players of the 1950s. In 1943, at age 17, he was brought into Peñarol's youth team, and one year later he started on the first team at inside left. The following year, he was selected for Uruguay in the South American Championship, and eventually became the star of two World Cups and two of the most famous games in World Cup history. In the final match of the 1950 World Cup against Brazil, Schiaffino scored Uruguay's first goal and set up the second by Ghiggia, creating the 2-1 win that gave his country its second world championship. In the 1954 World Cup, having increased his usefulness by becoming a wing half with scheming responsibilities, he became a world star. In the famous semi-final against Hungary, some-times called the greatest game ever played, Uruguay held on until well into overtime and it was only after Schiaffino's injury that Hungary was able to win 4-2. In all he made 22 appearances for his native country.

After the 1954 World Cup, he was signed by AC Milan for a world record transfer fee of $200,000, and he immediately spurred the giant Italian club to a league title. He led Milan to two more championships, and only six months after the 1954 World Cup played the first of four internationals for Italy, his parents having been Italian-born. In 1958, he took Milan to the European Cup final, but two years later he was released to AS Roma. Having slowed down considerably, he played in a variety of positions for two years and retired in 1962. He left the game for 15 years, returned to coach Peñarol for six months in 1976 and Uruguay for a brief two games, but, aside from coaching at the amateur level for pleasure, his life since 1962 has been devoted primarily to business interests.

Schlosser, Imre (1888-1968)

Hungary's first idol and goalscoring legend, who made 68 international appearances between 1906-27, a runaway world record until it was broken by Czechoslovakia's František Plánička and Switzerland's Severino Minelli in the late 1930s. His record of 59 goals for Hungary was not broken until Puskás and Kocsis surpassed it in the early 1950s, and in Hungarian league competition he was the leading scorer for seven consecutive seasons from 1909. In 1911, he scored six goals against Switzerland and five against Czarist Russia in 1912, but his most famous international goals were the two he made in Hungary's 6-1 romp over Italy in 1910. His league goalscoring high mark was 42 in 1910-11 and 1912-13.

A bow-legged inside left, he was most closely associated with the great Budapest club Ferencváros, and when he was transferred to archrival MTK in the late 1910s, fans were incredulous. He led both clubs to many successive league championships, and in the 1920s returned to his first love, Ferencváros, to finish his career. He later became a leading referee, and in 1955, wearing his old international jersey, he ceremoniously kicked off the ball in Hungary's one-hundredth meeting with Austria, a unique honor accorded by the Hungarian F.A.

scissors kick

A kick taken in the air by meeting the ball with one foot while the other foot moves rapidly in the opposite direction to provide leverage, as in the snapping motion of scissors.

See also: **bicycle kick**

Scotland

Scottish Football Association Ltd.
6 Park Gardens
Glasgow, G3 7YE

Founded: 1873
FIFA: 1910-20
1924-28
1946
UEFA: 1954

Affiliated clubs: *3,874;* **registered players:** *117,000 (4,000 professional);* **national stadium:** *Hampden Park, Glasgow (134,580);* **largest stadium:** *Hampden Park;* **colors:** *dark blue jerseys with white trim, white shorts;* **season:** *August to June;* **honors:** *Home International Championship (1884, 1885, 1886 shared, 1887, 1889, 1890 shared, 1894, 1896, 1897, 1900, 1902, 1903 shared, 1910, 1912 shared, 1921, 1922, 1923, 1925, 1926, 1927 shared, 1929, 1931 shared, 1935 shared, 1936, 1939 shared, 1949, 1951, 1953 shared, 1956 shared, 1960 shared, 1962, 1963, 1964 shared, 1967, 1970 shared, 1972 shared, 1974 shared, 1976, 1977), Celtic, European Cup (1967), Rangers, European Cup Winners' Cup (1972).*

The former Kingdom of Scotland has been politically united with England since 1707, but an unbroken tradition of independence still exists on such cultural matters as organized sport. The separation of the four British soccer associations—England, Scotland, Wales, and Northern Ireland—has continued because of this historical precedent and in respect for the game itself having been developed and codified in Great Britain in the first place. Thus, the first meeting of representative English and Scottish teams in 1870 is regarded as the genesis of international soccer, and from the start the Scottish game took on some unique characteristics.

Though England was the birthplace of soccer as we know it, Scotland was involved from the beginning, and, in fact, may be called the world's first great international power, since it dominated England decisively during the 1870s and '80s. Scottish teams made the game's first tactical advances during those years, and for many decades remained the strongest influence on changing styles and techniques. Scotland's insularity, however, hindered its exposure to advances that were made in other parts of Europe after the turn of the century, and it was not until 1929 that Scotland faced a non-British national team for

the first time. The sophisticated styles that had developed in Central Europe were a shock to the uninitiated Scots, and, as further evidence of Scotland's provinciality, the Scottish F.A. did not even appoint a regular national team manager until 1954. To this day Scotland has not fully emerged as a major international power.

On the other hand, the two great Glasgow clubs, Celtic and Rangers, are world famous. Celtic has won the European Champions' Cup and Rangers has won the European Cup Winners' Cup, and both are perennial contenders in international club championships. These titanic crosstown rivals have dominated Scottish league and cup competition since 1891, and between them over 75 percent of league championships and 50 percent of Scottish cups. During the quarter of a century before the "auld firm" (Celtic-Rangers) took the spotlight, the prime forces in Scottish soccer were Queen's Park Glasgow (the venerable pioneer of all Scottish clubs), and a coterie of three famous little clubs from the Vale of Leven, a valley in Dunbartonshire between Loch Lomond and the Clyde. The three were Dumbarton, Renton, and Vale of Leven, only the first of which is still in existence. In 1888, Scottish Cup winner

Renton became "champion of the world" when it defeated English cup winner West Bromwich Albion in an unofficial playoff.

Scotland was uniquely qualified as England's competitor in the early history of the game. The newly codified "association football" originated on English playing fields and spread to Scotland during the 1860s, but, in fact, the Scots, like the English, had already logged over a thousand years of football experience. The sprawling medieval versions of football that were played in various parts of the British Isles enjoyed their greatest popularity in Scotland. The rough and ready personality of rural border and southern counties lent itself to this notoriously violent game more easily than that of the more sedate English, while the Irish and Welsh had their hurling and knappan.

The precise origin of football in Scotland is lost in the confused muddle of medieval ball games. One improbable theory is that it grew from early football games imported by Scandinavians who settled in the Orkneys during the Norse invasions. This is maintained by Orkney legend, but it is viewed elsewhere merely as evidence to substantiate the Scandinavian origin of Orkney residents. Rather than football infiltrating the mainland from the Orkneys, it is more likely that the reverse took place. A second improbable theory is that of a Celtic origin to Scottish football, but, while there is much evidence that football games originated with the Celts in the first place, it is known that medieval football in Scotland was not played among the Celtic peoples who settled in the highlands. More important is the certainty that medieval football was played by large numbers of people in the low-lying border counties whose links were stronger with the English than with Celtic highlanders.

The likeliest source of Scottish football was a gradual infiltration from the Anglo-Saxon south—indicated by its early popularity in the border counties—with a strong impetus provided by Scotland's exposure to French football during the twelfth-century political alliance with France. The popularity of the game was so great that the first of several royal bans was issued as early as 1424 by the Scottish king, James I. Like its counterpart in England, this game was not exactly football, because players handled the ball over long distances and there was little chance to dribble on the bumpy and undulating fields on which it was played. But it was enjoyed widely from Ayrshire to Fifeshire, and it was even played as early as 1584 in Elgin, Morayshire.

Though football was more popular in Scotland than in England, its suppression by Scottish Protestant authorities after the Reformation was more severe than in England, especially over the issue of playing on Sundays. The movement to stamp out Sunday football became the hottest sports issue of the sixteenth and seventeenth centuries, but fortunately (or unfortunately) it coincided with the game's biggest rise in popularity. A measure of Scottish interest in football was the game's continued growth in spite of bans, edicts, sermons, and special legislation. James IV, who had dutifully prohibited the game in 1491, started to play himself in 1497. The seventh Earl of Argyll (1576?-1638) became the first Scottish peer to embrace the game, and in 1573 a record was made of regular Shrovetide matches in Glasgow that were financed by the municipal government! The church stood little chance against such odds. Highly publicized Shrovetide games were a regular feature of seventeenth and eighteenth century life in Roxburghshire, Berwickshire, Selkirkshire, Peeblesshire, Lothian, Lanarkshire, Ayrshire, and Fifeshire.

In the late sixteenth century, football was sometimes a prelude to military skirmishes along the border between English and Scottish militia—soldiers being avid football players even then—and it was occasionally used as bait to attract enemy regiments. In 1601, the Privy Council itself had to hear a case in Berwickshire in which shots were fired as a result of a football dispute. Incidents such as these contributed to the game's reputation as a recreation for the heartier elements of society.

Yet, some schools in Scotland adopted football surprisingly early. Enterprising teachers at the Aberdeen Grammar School in 1633 wrote Latin grammar exercises using common football language in an effort to attract the interest of their pupils. Its slow but steady adoption by respected segments of Scottish society was amply demonstrated in 1815, when the famous Carterhaugh (Selkirk) match was played between Selkirk and Yarrow players, the former backed by Sir Walter Scott, a well-known fan, and the latter by the Earl of Home. Of the 2,000 spectators at the Carterhaugh match, several dozen were from titled families. This and other matches prompted Scott to write some of the finest verse ever composed on football games, and the Carterhaugh match took its place in Scottish folklore.

In the eighteenth and early nineteenth centuries, football declined in popularity throughout Scotland, as it did in England, and did not regain its former status until it reappeared as association football and rugby football after 1863. Well-to-do students at public schools and universities in England were the first Scots to be exposed to nineteenth-century football codes (soccer and rugby). Those who did not remain in England brought the new soccer rules north to Glasgow (and rugby rules to Edinburgh), where, after continued interest showed by other gentlemanly players, it was eventually picked up by urban working people. The first Scottish club, Queen's Park Football Club, was formed on the south side of Glasgow in 1867 by members of the Y.M.C.A. who had gathered regularly in Queen's Park to play pickup games. At the beginning, its rules allowed some use of hands, touchdowns, and 15-20 players per side, but the club tried diligently to conform to new association rules and soon other "association" clubs began to appear.

Several clubs were founded in Glasgow and its suburbs, and in 1869, the first outlying club, Kilmarnock F.C., was founded in Ayrshire. After Glasgow and the coalfields of Lanarkshire, the second major spawning ground for clubs during the early years was the Vale of Leven (Renton, Dumbarton, and Vale of Leven), and in 1870, Stranraer F.C. was founded in the small port of that name in the extreme south (only 40 miles from the Irish port city of Belfast). In 1873 Rangers F.C. was formed by three outspoken Protestand families in Glasgow who were members of The Football Association (London). Queen's Park, in the meantime, was invited to participate in the first two editions of the F.A. Cup in England (1871-72 and 1872-73). Travel and expenses, however, made scheduling impossible, and all its matches were forfeited.

The new cup competition in London planted the idea for a similar series in Scotland, and in 1873 Queen's Park organized a meeting in a Glasgow hotel to plan the tournament. Seven clubs playing under association rules were represented at the meeting—Queen's Park, Clydesdale, Dumbreck, Eastern, Granville, Third Lanark (Third Lanark Rifle Volunteers), and Vale of Leven. Kilmarnock could not attend but sent a message of support. These eight clubs set up an annual cup competition and, at the same time, founded the Scottish Football Association (SFA), the world's second oldest governing body. Queen's Park and Dunbartonshire clubs proceeded to dominate the Scottish Cup for over 15 years, establishing a pattern that was not broken until the rise of Celtic and Rangers around 1890.

Edinburgh, the intellectual and political capital of Scotland, had strongly favored the rugby game since the formation a of local football association in 1863, because the city had such a small working class population. (Soccer was poorly regarded by both the educated establishment and the influential upper class students who came from England to attend school.) In 1873, two teams representing Glasgow were sent to Edinburgh by the SFA to promote the association game. Although three Edinburgh clubs—Thistle, Blue Bonnets, and Southern—had already been playing under compromise rules, the first genuine soccer club did not emerge in the capital until 1873, when Thistle switched entirely over to soccer rules. In 1874, a few months after the Glaswegian exhibition match, Third Edinburgh Rifles Volunteer Corps also adopted the soccer code, and the first Edinburgh derbies were played. Later in 1874, one of the capital's two great clubs of the future, Heart of Midlothian, (originally known as White Star F.C.), was founded at The Meadows, near the city's center. Hearts played association rules exclusively, and eventually rose to the forefront of Scottish soccer.

In 1875, Edinburgh Hibernians (later Hibernian) was founded by Irishmen, and, after first having its applications for membership in both the Edinburgh and Scottish associations rejected because of its reputation for rough play, finally entered official competitions and developed into Hearts' archrival. For several more years, rugby remained the important game in Edinburgh, with loyalties split clearly along class lines. It was not until 1878, with the formation of a soccer team at Edinburgh University, that middle- and upper-class residents started to play soccer in large numbers. Edinburgh (rugby playing and a middle upper-class bastion) contrasted sharply with Glasgow (Scotland's working-class metropolis and a soccer stronghold), and the famous rivalry between the two cities began.

The number of Scottish clubs, meanwhile, increased dramatically during the 1870s and

'80s. The big names during this period—Queen's Park, Third Lanark, Rangers, Renton, Vale of Leven, and Dumbarton—compared favorably with their counterparts in England, and the first internationals between England and Scotland demonstrated the Scots' greater sophistication. Between 1870-72, representative teams of England and Scotland met in five unofficial internationals, each played in London, with England winning three and the other two drawn. But nearly all players on these Scottish teams were London residents and members of London teams. Beginning with the first official international in 1872 (a goalless draw played at Partick, Glasgow), Scottish teams consisted entirely of players living in Scotland, the very first being an all-Queen's Park team. The trend in England's favor reversed completely. Of the 16 meetings between England and Scotland from 1872-87, Scotland won 10 and lost two. Such consistent domination demanded the attention of English clubs and officials.

Two things became clear as the English gazed enviously northward. First, Scottish teams were making tactical advances that rendered the English out of date. England, which favored the dribbling method of advancing the ball upfield, stood little chance against the more sophisticated short passing techniques of Queen's Park, whose players made up the bulk of Scotland's national team. Second, the passing skills of Scottish players were obviously more advanced, and after Scotland's great run of victories, the English sought to emulate them. In the 1880s, some Scottish players were signed by English clubs, enticed by money and a job, and this ultimately led to the rise of professionalism in soccer. By the 1890s, the big English clubs of Lancashire and the northeast were well stocked with Scottish players who were dubbed "Anglo-Scots" by their kinfolk back home and ostracized from the national team. In Scotland, professionalism was not adopted until 1893, and even then with great reluctance.

During the 1870s and '80s, Scottish players were great exporters of the game to other countries, ranking second only to England in this respect, and many Scottish coaches went abroad as well. Scots were responsible for introducing soccer to Ireland in 1878, with an exhibition match in Belfast between Queen's Park and Caledonian. Many of Belfast's important early clubs were manned with Scottish players. Scots were influential in introducing soccer to Canada, and they had an important hand in spreading the game in the United States and Australia. A visit by a Canadian team to Scotland in 1888 was the first transatlantic tour in soccer history, and the first visit to Britain of any team from a non-British country. After the turn of the century, Scottish coaches helped central European teams become the most advanced on the continent.

In 1890-91, the Scottish Football League was introduced. The charter members were: Celtic, Rangers, Heart of Midlothian, Dumbarton, St. Mirren, Third Lanark, Abercorn, Cowlairs, Cambuslang, Renton, and Vale of Leven—the last five no longer in existence. Amateur status was a prerequisite for membership, and a few weeks into the first season Renton was expelled for playing a suspected professional club, St. Bernard's Edinburgh. Queen's Park, conscious of its great tradition and fearful of rubbing shoulders with professionals, declined to join. The first championship was shared by Rangers and Dumbarton, and one year later, the league had 12 clubs. The second division was added in 1893. Promotion and relegation was determined by "test matches" until automatic promotion and relegation was instituted in 1921. A third division was formed in 1923, broken into two sections in 1950, and dissolved in 1955. Three divisions reappeared in 1975 with the creation of a Premier Division of 10 top clubs.

Celtic F.C., founded in Glasgow in 1888 by Irish Catholics, rose immediately to the top of Scottish soccer, and became the first Scottish club run as an efficient business concern. Its staunch Catholicism (Protestant players were not allowed on its teams) led to the great archrivalry with Rangers (where only Protestant players were allowed.) Celtic and Rangers dominated the league almost from the beginning, though Hearts won several championships and Scottish cups during the 1890s.

One of the SFA's major interests at this time was in finding a stadium to accommodate the huge crowds at international matches—especially against England. The popularity of internationals was now greater in Scotland than elsewhere in Britain, and, furthermore, these matches were now providing the SFA with most of its income. When Queen's Park F.C. completed the second Hampden Park in 1884, it was widely thought to be the most modern facility ever built, but the SFA was disappointed by its limited size, and England-Scotland matches were ultimately entrusted to

Rangers and Celtic. In 1894, the new Celtic Park opened with a capacity of 50,000 (then the largest in the world), and in 1900 it was increased to 60,000. This, in addition to Celtic's sophisticated security arrangements, appeared to solidify the club's role as the host of Scottish internationals. Queen's Park, openly jealous of Celtic's exalted position, built a third Hampden Park in 1903 with a capacity equal to that of Celtic Park, and, with the sentimental edge already in its favor, became the home of all major internationals and Scottish Cup finals after 1904. In 1920, Queen's Park's famous stadium was enlarged to accommodate more than 120,000 and in subsequent years became the frequent site of world record attendance figures. Its status as the world's largest stadium was finally surpassed in 1950 with the opening of the Maracanã in Rio de Janeiro.

In the Home International Championship, Scotland's domination of the pre-1890 era was finally halted after England learned to play the Scottish passing game, and by the outbreak of World War I, England had surpassed Scotland in total number of British championships. Wales and Ireland were considerably weaker than Scotland from the beginning, and the net result in British competition after the first 50 years was that England and Scotland stood relatively even on their records—a standing that has remained to this day (taking into consideration only the Home Internationals).

In the 1920s, Scotland passed through its greatest era in international competition, and perhaps in production of great players as well. It won seven Home International Championships between 1920-29 (Wales won the other three), and in 1928, ironically one of the years Wales won the title, the Scots buried hapless England (at Wembley) 5-1 in the most memorable British game in history. The "Wembley Wizards," as this famous 1928 Scottish team was called, included an illustrious forward line: Jackson, Dunn, Gallacher, James, and Morton. Scotland's great victory prompted an ever increasing list of invitations to play in Europe, and finally in the summer of 1929, Scotland traveled outside the United Kingdom for its first non-British internationals. After two wins over Norway (their official status is in dispute), the first full-level match on this tour, against Germany in Berlin, ended in a 1-1 draw, and the second, against the Netherlands in Amsterdam, was won, 2-0. After these encouraging results, Scotland defeated France in Paris the next year, but in 1931 got its first taste of top flight European soccer with a 5-0 loss to Austria (without the benefit of many of its top players), and a 3-0 loss to Italy. Partial revenge was gained in 1933 with a draw against Austria in Glasgow (the first visit to Scotland by a non-British country), and before the decade was finished further wins were recorded over Germany, Czechoslovakia, and Hungary, all in Glasgow. Defeats of these major international powers spoke well of Scotland's potential in post-World War II competition.

In fact, Scotland's prewar potential never materialized, though its international schedule increased substantially. The Scots qualified for the 1954 and 1958 editions of the World Cup, after declining their rightful berth in 1950, but failed to win a single one of their five matches in the final rounds. The low point was reached with a 7-0 loss to Uruguay in 1954, and an equally embarrassing loss to Paraguay in 1958. Though the score of the latter was only 3-2, it helped to expose Scotland's lack of international experience. The blissful days of the 1920s with Hughie Gallacher, Alex James, and Alan ("the wee Blue Devil") Morton receded into the distant past. After 10 straight Home International wins by England between 1952-61, two finally came Scotland's way in the early 1960s, but these occasional victories could not offset poor showings in the World Cup finals and failure to qualify for the finals in 1962, 1966, and 1970. Scottish teams were not to be underestimated on a given day, no matter what the opposition, but sophistication and consistency deferred to simple determination and hard play, and these attributes were seldom good enough to match the more subtle tactics of the postwar international powers.

A partial revival was thought to be in the making in the 1970s, as Scotland qualified for the 1974 World Cup and remained undefeated in the final rounds (one win and two draws), and qualified for the 1978 World Cup in Argentina. But a return to poor form in 1977 was a familiar omen, and an overconfident Scottish team crashed resoundingly in the final rounds to Peru and an outsider, Iran, bringing national disgrace to the proud Scottish fans.

Scotland's overall record in international competition remains very good. It has won over 150 games against 65 losses, but two-thirds of its total number of games have been played against British opposition. Less than one-third of its defeats have been at British hands, most of them to England, underscoring Scotland's difficulties with European and South American opposition. Despite its lack of success in tournament play since World War II, Scotland has produced several world class players during this period, most notably striker Denis Law of Manchester United and Torino fame, the Leeds United midfielder Billy Bremner, Celtic's tiny winger Jimmy ("the flea") Johnstone, and Celtic's magnificent back Danny McGrain.

Scottish clubs have occasionally done well in European club championships—Dunfermline Athletic, a small and impoverished club from Fifeshire, had phenomenal success in the European Cup Winners' Cup and the Fairs Cup during the 1960s—and Celtic and Rangers are always feared by continental opponents. Celtic became the first British club to win the European Champions' Cup in 1967 with a much-heralded win over Inter Milan in the final. Celtic gained the final again in 1970, and Rangers, Dundee F.C., and Hibernian have all been semi-finalists. Rangers won the European Cup Winners' Cup in 1972 and advanced to the final in 1961 and 1967; meanwhile, Rangers' bid to emulate its archrival's feat in the elite champions' cup continues. Kilmarnock, Dundee F.C., and Rangers have been semi-finalists in the Fairs/UEFA Cup.

Such excellent results in European club championships are surprising when one considers the size and meager financial resources of Scottish clubs. Some Premier Division clubs are still semi-professional, and the vast majority of Scotland's good players migrate to England for higher wages and greater fame. In addition, the runaway wealth and success of Celtic and Rangers has made it difficult for smaller clubs to compete in the Scottish transfer market, and attendances in the second division sometimes dip below 1,000. The big matches, however, regularly draw over 100,000 spectators (over 300,000 applications for tickets are received for most home England-Scotland matches), and the SFA, as well as the "auld firm" itself, attempts to make all ends meet. When the venerable Queen's Park (the last remaining club in the league to hold out against professionalism), was in dire financial straits in 1971, it was Celtic that came through with a £10,000 gift.

Champions

1891	Dumbarton/Rangers (draw)	1912	Rangers	1933	Rangers
1892	Dumbarton	1913	Rangers	1934	Rangers
1893	Celtic	1914	Celtic	1935	Rangers
1894	Celtic	1915	Celtic	1936	Celtic
1895	Heart of Midlothian	1916	Celtic	1937	Rangers
1896	Celtic	1917	Celtic	1938	Celtic
1897	Heart of Midlothian	1918	Rangers	1939	Rangers
1898	Celtic	1919	Celtic	1940	no competition
1899	Rangers	1920	Rangers	1941	no competition
1900	Rangers	1921	Rangers	1942	no competition
1901	Rangers	1922	Celtic	1943	no competition
1902	Rangers	1923	Rangers	1944	no competition
1903	Hibernian	1924	Rangers	1945	no competition
1904	Third Lanark	1925	Rangers	1946	no competition
1905	Celtic	1926	Celtic	1947	Rangers
1906	Celtic	1927	Rangers	1948	Hibernian
1907	Celtic	1928	Rangers	1949	Rangers
1908	Celtic	1929	Rangers	1950	Rangers
1909	Celtic	1930	Rangers	1951	Hibernian
1910	Celtic	1931	Rangers	1952	Hibernian
1911	Rangers	1932	Motherwell	1953	Rangers

1954	Celtic	1963	Rangers	1972	Celtic
1955	Aberdeen	1964	Rangers	1973	Celtic
1956	Rangers	1965	Kilmarnock	1974	Celtic
1957	Rangers	1966	Celtic	1975	Rangers
1958	Heart of Midlothian	1967	Celtic	1976	Rangers
1959	Rangers	1968	Celtic	1977	Celtic
1960	Heart of Midlothian	1969	Celtic	1978	Rangers
1961	Rangers	1970	Celtic		
1962	Dundee	1971	Celtic		

Cup Winners

1874	Queen's Park	1909	not awarded	1944	no competition
1875	Queen's Park	1910	Dundee	1945	no competition
1876	Queen's Park	1911	Celtic	1946	no competition
1877	Vale of Leven	1912	Celtic	1947	Aberdeen
1878	Vale of Leven	1913	Falkirk	1948	Rangers
1879	Vale of Leven	1914	Celtic	1949	Rangers
1880	Queen's Park	1915	no competition	1950	Rangers
1881	Queen's Park	1916	no competition	1951	Celtic
1882	Queen's Park	1917	no competition	1952	Motherwell
1883	Dumbarton	1918	no competition	1953	Rangers
1884	Queen's Park	1919	no competition	1954	Celtic
1885	Renton	1920	Kilmarnock	1955	Clyde
1886	Queen's Park	1921	Partick Thistle	1956	Heart of Midlothian
1887	Hibernian	1922	Morton	1957	Falkirk
1888	Renton	1923	Celtic	1958	Clyde
1889	Third Lanark	1924	Airdrieonians	1959	St. Mirren
1890	Queen's Park	1925	Celtic	1960	Rangers
1891	Heart of Midlothian	1926	St. Mirren	1961	Dunfermline Athletic
1892	Celtic	1927	Celtic	1962	Rangers
1893	Queen's Park	1928	Rangers	1963	Rangers
1894	Rangers	1929	Kilmarnock	1964	Rangers
1895	St. Bernard's	1930	Rangers	1965	Celtic
1896	Heart of Midlothian	1931	Celtic	1966	Rangers
1897	Rangers	1932	Rangers	1967	Celtic
1898	Rangers	1933	Celtic	1968	Dunfermline Athletic
1899	Celtic	1934	Rangers	1969	Celtic
1900	Celtic	1935	Rangers	1970	Aberdeen
1901	Heart of Midlothian	1936	Rangers	1971	Celtic
1902	Hibernian	1937	Celtic	1972	Celtic
1903	Rangers	1938	East Fife	1973	Rangers
1904	Celtic	1939	Clyde	1974	Celtic
1905	Third Lanark	1940	no competition	1975	Celtic
1906	Heart of Midlothian	1941	no competition	1976	Rangers
1907	Celtic	1942	no competition	1977	Celtic
1908	Celtic	1943	no competition	1978	Rangers

screen

Protecting the ball from a defender with the body, usually during the act of dribbling.

SEAP Games

See: **Southeast Asian Peninsular Games, Football Tournament of the**

Seeler, Uwe   (1936-   )

The most popular player in German soccer and a symbol of German gallantry on the field, Seeler was greeted with chants of "Uwe! Uwe!" by German crowds throughout his entire career. He was an acrobatic and thoroughly courageous center forward, whose physical prowess belied his short and stocky frame, best exemplified, perhaps, by his famous flying headers and bicycle kicks. He played in four World Cups for West Germany (1958-70), and to his lasting credit spent his entire career with one club, Hamburger SV. Indeed, his father had been a player with HSV, and Uwe himself signed on at age 10. As a youth player, he scored approximately 600 goals for HSV teams, and in 1954, at age 17, he made his full international debut for West Germany against France. In 72 appearances for his country, he scored 43 goals, a record since broken by Gerd Müller. His career with HSV's first team lasted from 1954-72, during which time he scored 551 senior-level goals, another record broken by Müller, and made upwards of 700 appearances. He was the leading goalscorer in West Germany in 1956

(32), 1959 (29), 1960 (36), 1961 (30), and 1964 (30), and was West German Footballer of the Year three times.

He made his first real impact on the national team in the 1958 World Cup, and probably reached his peak at the 1962 World Cup in Chile. He captained the West German squad in the 1966 and 1970 editions, and, having successfully adopted a new role as attacking midfielder, finally retired from the national team after a friendly against Hungary in 1970. He led HSV to three championship play-offs in 1957, 1958, and 1960, gaining the title itself in the last of these, and in 1968 he scored eight goals in HSV's highly successful European Cup Winners' Cup campaign. His career almost ended with an Achilles tendon injury in 1965, but it was saved by a miraculous tendon transplant operation, and he only missed six months of active play. In 1972, he retired altogether after his injuries finally slowed him down, but there is little doubt that the likes of "Uwe! Uwe!" will never be heard again.

Sekularac, Dragoslav   (1939-   )

An inside forward whose ball juggling skills were a main feature of international soccer for several years. Perhaps the most talented Yugoslav player of all time, his dribbling and body feints bordered on the sublime. He was the most gifted of many great stars with his club, Red Star Belgrade, during the late 1950s and early '60s, and with Yugoslavia during its strong runs for the World Cup in 1958 and 1962, but injuries and an outspokenly

rebellious personality eventually cut short his career in the top echelons of the game. "Sekki," as he was called, the grandson of a gypsy, signed with Red Star Belgrade at age nine and first came to international attention in the European Cup before he was 18. He excelled as an inside left for Yugoslavia in the 1958 World Cup, and in 1960 he was suspended for 18 months by Red Star when he struck a referee in one of his many outbursts.

Switching to inside right, he was responsible more than anyone for his country's fourth place finish at the 1962 World Cup, and in 1964 he suffered his first serious injury, causing a decline in form.

Already the highest paid player in Yugoslavia, he went on strike in 1966 after Red Star refused to transfer him to Karlsruher in West Germany, but when it was apparent that his international career was over—he made the last of his 39 appearances for Yugoslavia in 1966—permission was finally granted. His two-year stint at Karlsruher was less than successful. He was lent to the St. Louis Stars in the United States during the 1967 off-season, but his form remained well below par, and his former greatness was not acknowledged. In 1968, he returned home to play for OFK Belgrade, finding some of his original form, but two years later, dissatisfied and cantankerous, he left for Colombia, leading Independiente Santa Fe and Millonarios to successive championships in 1971 and 1972. He remained in Colombia for most of the 1970s as a player-coach and ultimately as a manager, but numerous brushes with soccer and police authorities assured him of a lasting controversial image. In 1979, he returned to the United States as coach of the American Soccer League's New York Eagles.

selection

A national, regional, or otherwise specially chosen representative team, which usually indicates unofficial or less than "full international" status. The Spanish language term *seleccion*, however, is a standard reference to any national or representative team.

self goal   See: own goal

sell a dummy

Any number of body feints, fake moves, or outmaneuverings by a dribbler that lead a defender to believe that the movement of the ball will be in one direction, whereas it is actually moved in another. In its strictest meaning, it is the act of showing the ball to one player but passing it to a second or playing it oneself. "Dummy" refers to the imaginary placement of the ball that nonpluses a defender.

The idea of "selling a dummy" is as old as the ball games of ancient Greece and Rome. Historians have described a position in both *episkyros* and *harpastum*, known as the "in-between man" on the field, whose duties remain unclear, but among them was the act of showing the ball to one player and passing it elsewhere. He appears to be one of the central figures on the field, and his "hoodwink" was undoubtedly a common tactic. H.A. Harris describes Pollux's definition of the widely-used term *phaininda* in the context of *episkyros*. This is used when a player shows the ball to one man and throws it to another.

Dummies in soccer may also be sold to goal-keepers, as when Pelé almost scored against Mazurkiewicz of Uruguay in Brazil's semi-final win during the 1970 World Cup.

send off

The ejection of a player from the field of play by the referee. A player who is sent off may not be replaced. To administer a send off the referee must stop play and signify the action by showing the offending player a red card. The player is then ordered off the field verbally. All send offs must be reported by the referee to the committee under whose aegis the match is being played. By the rules of most governing bodies, a player who is sent off may also be suspended from playing for a specified number of games in the future. In international competition, ejected players are automatically suspended by FIFA for succeeding international matches.

The Laws of the Game require that a player be sent off for the following:

1. Violent conduct or serious foul play.
2. Foul or abusive language.
3. Persistent misconduct after receiving a caution.

The red card policy was officially introduced by FIFA at the Olympic Games of 1968.

Senegal

Fédération Sénégalaise de Football
Avenue El-Hadji Malick Sy
B.P. 7021
Dakar

Founded: 1960
FIFA: 1964
CAF: 1963

Affiliated clubs: *65;* registered players: *3,168;* national stadium: *Dempa Diop, Dakar (13,000);* largest stadium: *Dempa Diop;* colors: *green jerseys, yellow shorts;* season: *October to July;* honors: *none.*

It was appropriate that Senegal should become one of the first countries from the former French West Africa to qualify for the final rounds of the African Nations' Cup in 1965. French colonists established the French West African League (Ligue de l'Afrique Occidentale Française) in Dakar immediately after World War II, with 45 clubs and 3,000 players registered, and this remained the only governing body of its kind in the entire region until the independence movement surfaced 15 years later. Dakar was thus given a head start on the other French West African colonies, and as early as 1956 France (Amateur) visited Dakar and defeated a Senegalese representative team 9-2, a substantial loss but a gain of valuable experience.

In 1960, two years after independence, Senegal's own Fédération Sénégalaise de Football was founded, and for a few brief months its jurisdiction included Mali as well as Senegal, as the two countries attempted a political merger. Affiliation with FIFA and the African Football Confederation followed in that order. In 1963, Dakar was host to an international tournament called the Jeux de l'Amitiée, in which a team representing the French football federation played against national teams of Senegal, Gambia, Upper Volta, Gabon, and Madagascar. In the course of Senegal's march to the final of this tournament, it defeated the French team 2-0 in the semi-finals.

In Senegal's first African Nations' Cup in 1965, it drew with Tunisia in the first round and crushed Ethiopia, a waning continental power, 5-1, to find itself in the third place game with Ivory Coast. Though it lost this match, 1-0, Senegal's fourth place finish remains its highest accomplishment in major international competition. Senegal qualified again in 1968, but failed to advance to the semi-finals as it had the previous edition. It's qualification for these two early editions of the Nations' Cup indicates that soccer in Dakar was relatively advanced as a result of the postwar French West African League, but its strength in relation to other African countries declined gradually as they too gained international experience.

Domestic soccer in Senegal, which features both national and regional competitions, is centered on Dakar, but there is much activity in Thies, Kaolack, Saint-Louis, Louga, and in the remote and isolated Casamance region to the south, Ziguinchor. Dakar, however, has three major stadiums. The leading Senegalese club is Jaraaf de Dakar, which has participated several times in the African Champions' Cup, reaching the quarter-finals in 1976. Jeanne d'Arc and Forces Armées are the other top Dakar clubs.

Seychelles

The game in this tropical Indian Ocean playland was becoming organized at the time of its independence in 1976. To celebrate its new nationhood, the Seychelles Football Association played host to an international tournament at Victoria, in which the home selection lost to neighboring Réunion, 4-3, and Kenya defeated regional rival Mauritius, 4-3. Efforts were also being made during the late 1970s to affiliate with FIFA.

Sheffield Rules

The rules adopted by the world's first football club, Sheffield F.C., in 1857. The game, as laid down in these rules, may not yet be called "association football," or "soccer," but after the Harrow School Rules and the Cambridge University Rules, the Sheffield Rules were one of the last crucial sets of laws drawn up in anticipation of The Football Association's Laws of the Game in 1863. Their major significance is the introduction of organized football to the north of England, a part of the country that had the most profound effect on the development of modern soccer.

The Sheffield Rules are linked with soccer rather than rugby, because their primary characteristic was the dribbling rather than the handling game, though it is clear that limited handling of the ball was permitted. Comparative studies of the Sheffield Rules and those of Harrow and Cambridge reveal many common elements between them. Hacking, for example, was forbidden by all three codes, and Sheffield's fair catch rule (no.3) bears a strong resemblance to the Cambridge (1854-58) fair catch rule (no. 8) and Harrow's three-yard rule (Harrow no. 6). Handling of the ball is limited to the fair catch and a quick free kick with the ball in the player's hands, and to changing the direction of the ball with one's hands without actually catching the ball. In Sheffield rule no. 11 the earliest mention of differing team colors was made.

The Sheffield Rules wielded much influence in northern counties, especially in West Riding and Nottinghamshire. They were immediately adopted by Hallam Football Club, also founded in 1857 and Sheffield's first rival, and in 1862 by Notts County Football Club, the oldest club still in senior competition today. As the influence of the new London-based Football Association of 1863 spread, the competition for recognition by those who supported The Football Association Laws of the Game and those playing by the Sheffield Rules caused England to be divided roughly into two camps. Allegiance was based primarily on geographical location as a matter of convenience. But in 1877 the Sheffield Football Association (founded 1867) and The Football Association agreed on common rules. The Sheffield Rules' existence as a separate code vanished with that agreement.

The text of the Rules is as follows:

1. The kick off from the middle must be a place kick.
2. Kick Out must not be from more than 25 yards out of goal.
3. Fair Catch is a catch from any player provided the ball has not touched the ground or has not been thrown from touch and is entitled to a free kick.
4. Charging is fair in case of a place kick (with the exception of a kick off as soon as the player offers to kick) but he may always draw back unless he has actually touched the ball with his foot.
5. Pushing with hands is allowed but no hacking or tripping up is fair under any circumstances whatever.
6. No player may be held or pulled over.
7. It is not lawful to take the ball off the ground (except in touch) for any purpose whatever.
8. The ball may be pushed on or hit with the hand, but holding the ball except in the case of a free kick is altogether disallowed.
9. A goal must be kicked but not from touch nor by a free kick from a catch.
10. A ball in touch is dead, consequently the side that touches it down must bring it to the edge of the touch and throw it straight out from touch.
11. Each player must provide himself with

a red and dark blue flannel cap, one colour to be worn by each side.

See also: **Cambridge University Rules; Harrow Games, Rules of the**

shinguard

A protective pad worn between a player's sock and the lower front half of his leg. Shinguards help thwart bruises, sprains, and fractures that may result from a hard tackle or kick.

They were invented and patented in 1874 by Samuel W. Widdowson, a lace manufacturer who was an agile center forward with Nottingham Forest from 1866 to the mid-1880s. (Widdowson also played once for England in 1880, and was known to be one of the great hurdlers and sprinters of his day, as well as a cricketer. He later became chairman of Nottingham Forest and a member of The Football Association Committee.)

Shinguards were worn by some players from the date of their invention, but they were not mentioned in the Laws until 1880. From that date, their use has been expressly permitted, but the current Laws make no specific reference to them.

shoot-out

The tie breaking procedure of the North American Soccer League (NASL), in which players from both teams challenge the opposing goalkeeper, one-on-one, and attempt to score against him.

The rules and conditions of the procedure are as follows:

1. The visiting (away) team kicks first.
2. Each team is entitled to at least five kicks, which are taken alternately, first by one team then the other.
3. If, before five kicks are completed, one team has accumulated an insurmountable number of goals (e.g., one team scores its first three while the other team misses its first three, the shoot-out is ended by the referee.
4. If the number of goals scored by both teams is equal after five attempts, the procedure continues until one team has scored more than the other after both have taken an equal number of kicks.
5. Each kicker starts with the ball on his opponent's 35-yard line, and must take his shot within five seconds after the referee's signal is given.
6. The kicker and goalkeeper are not restricted in their movement during the five-second period.
7. Only players who are on the field at the end of the match may qualify to take kicks.
8. No player may take a second kick until all eligible teammates have had their turn.
9. The order of a team's rotation may vary in each round of kicks.

Initiated in 1977, the shoot-out is essentially a modification of the penalty decision, but, unlike the penalty decision, must be implemented in any NASL game in which a win has not resulted from extra time, including league games as well as knockout competitions. All games in the NASL must be won and lost; draws have not been allowed since 1975. As a result of this regulation, the league felt motivated to devise a tie breaking procedure that would provide a high level of excitement for the North American fan. The experiment has thus far been confined to North America, and, with respect to professional soccer, appears destined to remain that way.

shoulder charge

A lawful body contact between two players when only the shoulders touch and the arms remain motionless. The ball must be within "playing distance," as determined by the referee. In most countries, the goalkeeper may not be shoulder charged.

See also: **charge**

show the ball

The commitment of a player in possession to dribble or otherwise move the ball in a given direction, whether actually intended or in order to sell a dummy.

See also: **sell a dummy**

sideline

The touchline.

Sierra Leone

Sierra Leone Amateur Football Association
c/o The National Sports Council
P.O. Box 1181, Tower Hill
Freetown

Founded: 1967
FIFA: 1967
CAF: 1967

Affiliated clubs: *? (104 clubs compete in leagues);* registered players: *8,120;* national stadium: *Brookfields Stadium, Freetown (15,000);* largest stadium: *Brookfields Stadium;* colors: *green, white, and blue jerseys, white shorts;* season: *May to December;* honors: *none.*

Among the former British colonies in West Africa, Sierra Leone is culturally more British in character than all the others, yet on the soccer field it has built a meager existence at best. In international competition, it ranks near the bottom of the African list. At home, the game is sustained by a large population, though widely dispersed, and the possibility that its diamond and iron ore industries might offer a financial boost. In 1975, the government launched its first serious campaign to promote the game throughout the country. An organizational overhaul received official encouragement, and for the first time it was publicly announced that Sierra Leone intended to enter the mainstream of African soccer. Given the poor state of the game at the present time, it is surprising to learn that a colonial governing body was founded in Freetown more than 30 years ago and that it was affiliated directly with The Football Association in London.

Sierra Leone's handful of attempts to qualify for the all-amateur African Games, the Olympics, and the World Cup have met with instant failure. It has yet to enter qualification rounds for the African Nations' Cup. Mighty Black Pool and Port Authority F.C. have each entered the African Champions' Cup once, and that has been the limit of Sierra Leone's participation in official international competition. There are domestic league and cup competitions, and seven stadiums in the country with capacities of 1,000 or more—in Freetown, Bo (two), Kenema, Makeni, Yengema, and Bunumbu.

signing-on fee

The portion of a transfer fee that is earmarked for the player himself rather than his club. Until recently, the accepted procedure was to put aside five percent of the transfer fee for this purpose, but percentages now fluctuate more widely, and are always higher when top stars are involved. Signing-on fees stem from the transfer system employed in most countries of Western Europe. This differs slightly from the system of bonuses that is common to the United States and Canada, in which there is no direct connection between the amount of the bonus and the amount of money that passes between clubs.

See also: **transfer**

Sindelar, Matthias   (1903-1939)

Generally regarded as the finest player Austria has ever produced. He was an extraordinary center forward with skills so subtle that he became famous for dribbling the ball into the net rather than shooting. His nickname was *der Papierene* ("the Man of Paper"), because he was extremely thin and his agile movements often gave the appearance of a piece of paper floating through the air. His inventiveness was truly amazing, and defenders never knew what he would pull out of his bag of tricks next. Sindelar, or "Motzl," as his friends called him, first played for Hertha Vienna in his late teens, and in 1923 he was signed by Amateure (later renamed FK Austria). His international debut for Austria was made in 1926 against Czechoslovakia, in which he scored a goal, and his rise to fame corresponded exactly with that of the famous *Wunderteam* that came to dominate European soccer during the early 1930s.

Sindelar was not a prolific goalscorer, but he sometimes converted several times in one game, as in Austria's famous 2-1 defeat of Italy in 1932, and its still more memorable 8-2 burial of Hungary later that same year. In the game against Hungary, Sindelar scored three goals and created the other five with selfless cunning. His last international for Austria—against Switzerland in 1937—was marked by another goal, his 27th in 43 appearances. His movements, even at this time, defied description, and were sorely missed when he finally retired to realize his dream of operating a coffee house in Vienna, named Cafe Annahof, for his wife. Sindelar was a Jew, and in 1939, having been harassed by Nazi authorities, he grew depressed and disappeared from sight—some have said he committed suicide. After his disappearance, the small street in which his cafe was located was renamed Sindelar-gasse.

Singapore

Football Association of Singapore
Jalan Besar Stadium
Tyrwhitt Road, P.O. Box 1094
Singapore 8

Founded: 1892
FIFA: 1952
AFC: 1954

Affiliated clubs: *79;* registered players: *1,710;* national stadium: *Jalan Besar Stadium, Singapore 8 (20,000);* largest stadium: *Jalan Besar Stadium;* colors: *sky blue jerseys, sky blue shorts;* season: *March to December;* honors: *none.*

Singapore is a middle-level Asian soccer power where the game has had little difficulty in capturing the attention of a predominantly Chinese population. With an immensely strong British presence there since the early nineteenth century, it is little wonder that the Singapore Amateur Football Association, founded in 1892, was the first governing body for soccer in the Far East, predating its Malaysian counterpart by 40 years. The British were the only players around for some time, but gradually local residents—especially the Chinese—took up the game. It was not until after World War II that Singapore teams became actively involved in international competition. This delay was caused in part by the island's political connections with Malaya to the north, and was ended when the enormous influx of British soldiers during World War II revitalized Singapore's game.

In 1951, Indonesia defeated Singapore 4-1 in Singapore—the first officially recorded international—and in 1952, the Singapore Amateur Football Association became affiliated with FIFA. In 1953, South Korea visited Singapore on a Far Eastern tour to play nine matches against various teams, and managed to win four of them; Singapore teams won three and drew two. These two series launched international soccer in Asia's busiest port city, and in 1966, one year after independence, the governing body renamed itself the Football Association of Singapore, and reaffiliated with FIFA. Singapore has never advanced to the final rounds of the Asian Cup or Asian Games, but recorded wins in the qualifying round for the 1978 World Cup over Thailand and Malaysia in its unsuccessful bid for regional glory. At home, local matches are invariably well attended.

Sivori, Enrique Omar   (1935-   )

The enfant terrible of Argentina, Sivori was a gifted inside left with subtle and complete ball control skills, who first made his mark in his native Argentina and later took Italy by storm. While he was a ball artist supreme, Sivori was also hot-tempered and was cautioned by referees constantly. This caused him much notoriety, and he was thrown out of at least 20 senior-level games during his career. Yet, he was elected European Footballer of the Year in 1961, and every wealthy club in Europe sought his services.

Sivori was raised in the ranks of Ríver Plate, the great Buenos Aires club, and made 12 appearances for Argentina, including its 1957 South American Championship victory, all before the age of 22. In 1957, Italy's Juventus paid Ríver Plate a world record 190 million lire for him, and placed him next to the Welsh center forward John Charles. Sivori and Charles led Juventus to Italian championships in 1958, 1960, and 1961, and in 1960, Sivori led the Italian league in scoring with 27 goals. He went on to play for Italy nine times, scoring eight goals, and became proficient at several positions in the midfield as well as on the forward line. He scored 135 goals for Juventus before he was transferred to Napoli in 1965, and four years later he retired after a slow and steady decline. He returned to Argentina a millionaire, and was eventually asked to coach Rosario and Estudiantes before taking over Argentina's junior team in 1972 and Ríver Plate in 1974. After another brief stint with the Argentine F.A. in 1976, he returned to coach in Naples, and in 1978 he became coach of Velez Sarsfield in Buenos Aires.

sixth forward

A midfielder or back, usually a center halfback, who supports the forward line in an attacking position. The term is applicable only with regard to variations of the traditional 2-3-5 formation. The so-called "Central European system," for example, employs a "pivot" who lies just behind the five forwards, and serves both as a supporting attacker and a link between the front line and the defense (two halfbacks and two backs).

See also: **tactics**

Slavia, Sportovního Klubu

Location: *Prague, Czechoslovakia;* stadium: *Slavia Stadion (43,000);* colors: *red and white halved jerseys, white shorts;* honors: *Mitropa Cup (1938), Czech champion (1913, 1924, 1929, 1930, 1931, 1933, 1934, 1935, 1937, 1940, 1941, 1942, 1943, 1944, 1947).*

Founded 1892 as the soccer section of the Sport Klub Slavia, a famous Bohemian cyclist and gymnastic club formed 10 years earlier; it is now the oldest soccer club in Czechoslovakia. After Sparta was founded one year later, the rivalry between these two clubs became the most intense in Central Europe for decades. The five-point star imprinted on the white half of Slavia's jerseys soon became a much-respected insignia, and during the first decade of this century this famous club became quite possibly the strongest in all of Europe. Between 1903-08, Slavia vanquished many leading clubs of Austria, Hungary, and Germany by astonishing margins: First Vienna, 8-2 and 11-0; Sturm Graz, 14-0; Budapest Torna Club, 12-0; Union Berlin, 10-1; FC Nürnberg, 12-2; and Bayern München, 13-0. It also defeated the Dutch national team 8-0 during this period. In 1906, Slavia drew with Glasgow Celtic 3-3 and defeated Southampton 4-0. Its unrivaled star player at this time was Jan Košek, the famous inside left who had Olympic speed and a blinding shot on goal.

Slavia was a leading participant in the first Czech (actually Bohemian) national championship in 1912, and won the title itself in 1913. During the professional era between the world wars, Slavia and its archrival Sparta won every Czech championship except one. Slavia's golden era occured from 1929-37, when it won seven titles and appeared in the Mitropa Cup final twice: in 1929, losing to Újpest of Hungary, and 1938, defeating Hungary's Ferencváros to win the trophy. In the quarter-finals of 1938, Slavia defeated Inter Milan 9-0. Two of its many stars at the time were Josef Bican, the goalscoring wonder of both the Czech and Austrian national teams, and František Plánička, one of the greatest European goalkeepers of all time. Plánička minded the nets for Slavia over 700 times from 1923-37. At left half was Vlasta Kopecky, another Czech international, and Antonin Puc on the left wing, hero of Czechoslovakia's 1934 World Cup team. The mainstay of these Slavia teams, however, was coach Harry Madden, a Scot who guided the club both on and off the field from 1905-38, and introduced the short passing game to Czech soccer, much as Jimmy Hogan did in Austria and Hungary.

In the aftermath of the Plánička-Bican era, Slavia won four more championships from 1940-43 and an unofficial league title in 1944. With the change in political regimes in 1948, the beloved name of Slavia was changed to Dynamo Slavia, and five years later "Slavia" was dropped altogether. In 1961, having finished in last place in the league for the first time in its history, Dynamo slid into the second division for one season and it did so again from 1963-65. At this point, the club took the name Slavia again, and it has remained in the first division ever since. Despite its total absence of league or cup honors since 1948, it remains, with Sparta, one of Czechoslovakia's two most popular clubs, and since 1970 has amassed the fourth best record in the Czech league.

sliding tackle   Also known as "split tackle."

A tackle in which the defender skims across the ground to take the ball from a player, sometimes appearing to jump at the ball from some distance. When the tackler is able to combine this with a front-block tackle, his action is known as a sliding-block tackle.

Slovakia   See: Czechoslovakia

Smith, Gilbert Oswald   (1872-1943)

The outstanding center forward of the Victorian era, G. O. Smith first gained recognition in 1891 at Oxford University, then one of England's leading teams, but he achieved his greatest prominence with the legendary Corinthians F.C. between 1892-1903. He played 20 times for the full England team (a pre-World War I record), causing havoc wherever he appeared. Though slight in build, his deftness at distributing the ball to his wings became famous throughout Britain; indeed, his lasting contribution to the history of the game was his development of passing skills on the forward line at a time when Corinthians were a great proponent of the passing game, which had only recently come into general use. As a dribbler, he was second to none, and his shot was regarded as one of the most dangerous in England. A gentleman amateur until his retirement in 1903, he also played top flight cricket, and eventually turned all his attention to his profession of teaching, ultimately as a headmaster in his later years.

snap shot

A quick, impulsive shot on goal that is taken from a deflection, usually in the form of a volley or half-volley at or near the goalmouth.

Solomon Islands

This former British protectorate, which gained independence in 1977, has not enjoyed the same success in South Pacific competition that Fiji and Tahiti have experienced, nor has it become a provisional member of the Oceania Football Confederation as have its French-speaking neighbors New Hebrides and New Caledonia. The Solomon Islands Football Association (SIFA), however, has been very active in regional tournaments, beginning with the first edition of the South Pacific Games in 1963. Its regular participation in this triannual series finally yielded success in the fifth edition in 1975, when the Solomons won third place in a field of seven countries. In the first round, the Solomons drew with archrival Fiji, 1-1, and defeated little Guam, 5-1, gaining a berth in the semi-finals. New Caledonia defeated the Solomons 5-0 in the semi-finals, but in the third place game the Solomons bounced back and upset Fiji, 3-2. This was a far cry from the results of the 1969 games, when the Solomons placed last and failed to win a game, scoring two goals to their opponents' 17. Unfortunately the Solomons were not able to participate in the first Oceania Cup in 1973.

A league was introduced in 1947 at Honiara, Guadalcanal, the capital, with only eight clubs registered. SIFA has made considerable progress since then, and the islands are now divided into 20 regional leagues. In Honiara there are three divisions, and the most important clubs are Kakamora, K.G. Old Boys, Rangers, and Sunrise. Like all island nations of the South Pacific, the Solomons' great problem in organizing the game are the logistical and financial difficulties of traveling.

Somalia

Federazione Somala Gioco Calcio
Stadio C.O.N.I.
C.P. 523
Mogadiscio

Founded: 1951
FIFA: 1961
CAF: 1968

Affiliated clubs: *16;* registered players: *816 (132 professional, 44 non-amateur);* national stadium: *C.O.N.I. Stadium, Mogadiscio (15,000);* largest stadium: *C.O.N.I. Stadium;* colors: *sky blue jerseys, white shorts;* season: *September to February;* honors: *none.*

The Somalis, an Islamic and basically nomadic people, had little to do with soccer in the former British Somaliland and Italian Protectorate of Somalia until after World War II. The British had played the game among themselves in Hargeisa before World War I, and the more numerous Italians introduced it in Mogadiscio and Chisimaio after the war. It was not until the Federazione Somala Gioco Calcio (FSGC) was founded under Italian guidance in 1951 that Somalis themselves took an active role in soccer.

Islamic cultural restrictions continued to hold back development of the game throughout the 1950s and '60s, but in the port cities, where exposure to foreign ways were a part of daily life, interest grew steadily. In 1961, a year after the birth of the Somali Republic, the FSGC joined FIFA and seven years later became affiliated with the African Football Confederation (CAF). Somalia's late affiliation date with the CAF automatically relegated it to the lower depths of African soccer where it has remained. This is not likely to last much longer, however, because Somalia is one of only four countries in Africa that has sanctioned open professionalism for its eight first division clubs. While the national team has been relatively inactive in World Cup qualification rounds and unsuccessful in the African Nations' Cup, Somali clubs have participated regularly in the African Champions' Cup since joining the CAF. The only year in which the Somali champion did not enter was 1976, the year after Somalia's devastating drought. Mogadiscio's Horsed FC, the leading club, has played in the Champions' Cup four times, and Livori Publici Club, the team of the public works company, has participated twice. Neither have advanced beyond the first round. The winter season in Somalia is short due to the harsh desert climate.

South Africa

Soccer in South Africa has inevitably been dominated by the issue of racial separation. The sport has a long history in this part of Africa, and, aside from emotional and moral aspects, the practice and policy of racial division has seriously hindered the advance of South African soccer from a pragmatic standpoint. If the 80 percent of the population that is "non-white" had been allowed to participate fully in South Africa's long association with soccer, there is little doubt that South Africa would be the dominant power on African playing fields today. But as soccer emerged as the most popular sport in black Africa in the wake of Pan-Africanism, South Africa found itself ostracized from the boom. It was never allowed to join the African Football Confederation, and finally in 1976 South Africa was expelled from FIFA, ending any possibility of significant growth through international exposure, at least for the time being.

With the possible exception of Morocco, Tunisia, and Egypt, the level of play of the best non-white South African players is probably the highest on the continent. Whites, although active in soccer from the beginning, have preferred rugby. Blacks and "coloreds," however, have enthusiastically embraced soccer as their game, and non-white clubs are more fervently supported than white clubs. Whites invariably play soccer in their youth, but above grade school level their allegiance to rugby has traditionally been automatic and a matter of social conformity.

Soccer was first played on the continent of Africa in Port Elizabeth, Cape Province, in the 1860s by British settlers. Whether association or rugby rules predominated at this early date is unclear, but the association game was certainly played, and it was quickly introduced in other British settlements in Cape Province and Natal. The Dutch republics of Transvaal and Orange Free State were exposed to the game several years later. The first South African club, Pietermaritzburg County, was founded in the Natal city of that name in 1879. Despite the more obvious popularity of rugby, there was enough interest for a Natal Football Association to be founded in 1882 with five charter-member clubs. The Natal association and the New South Wales F.A. that was founded in Australia at the same time were the first governing bodies for soccer outside the United Kingdom. A Cape Province association followed, and the first league was established in Cape Town in 1891.

In 1892, the Natal, Cape Province, and other governing bodies formed the South African Football Association (SAFA), forerunner of the present association, and the SAFA soon became affiliated with The Football Association in London. Organized soccer in Transvaal and the Orange Free State were not under the jurisdiction of the SAFA until after the Union of South Africa was created in 1910. The first official competition, the Currie Cup, was introduced in 1892, and the O'Reilly Cup was introduced in Cape Town the following year. In 1897, the famous Corinthians F.C. of England was the first foreign team to play a South African selection on African soil, winning three matches by an aggregate of nine goals to two. These results compared favorably with those of other teams in Europe and elsewhere that played against the mighty Corinthians about the same time.

With the influx of British military personnel during and after the Boer War (1899-1902), soccer gained in stature, and the Boer cities of Johannesburg and Pretoria began to make an impact on the national game. Three important clubs from the Transvaal date from this period or before: Rangers of Johannesburg (1889), Arcadia Shepherds of Pretoria (1903), and Callies of Germiston (1906). A South African selection made up entirely of players from Natal and Cape Province toured South America in 1906—the first journey abroad by a South African team—and played 12 matches in Argentina, Uruguay, and Brazil, losing only once (4-1 to Argentina). In São Paulo, a representative team of *paulistas* lost 6-0 in the first Brazilian international. The relatively advanced skills of these South African players were demonstrated by their accumulating an overwhelming 60-7 goal difference in only a dozen games.

South Africa's international record since then has been sparse and decidedly unsuccessful. Only two full international teams have ever visited South Africa to play in officially recognized matches. In 1950, Australia played a series of four games in Johannesburg and Cape Town, winning once and losing once, and Israel won a single match by 3-1 in 1954. Fifty-five other internationals have been played by South Africa at home against representative teams or clubs, most of them British, but all but 12 of these have been lost. Away from home, South African selections or full international teams played in 28 games after 1906, the last in Portugal in 1958, losing all but nine times. The vast majority of these away matches were not full internationals, and the status of some remain questionable. South Africa did not engage in any full internationals after 1958. In 1975, South Africa played against Rhodesia four times, winning one and losing two. Tours of South Africa by English representative teams took place in 1910, 1920, 1929, 1939, and 1956, and South African national teams visited England (Amateur) in 1924, 1953, and 1958.

All these international contests involved white South African players only.

Blacks in South Africa began playing the game around 1900, and after World War II embraced it wholeheartedly. By 1960, their adherence to FIFA Laws was fairly uniform, especially among the Bantu. The 1950s saw great changes in South African soccer. The SAFA became a member of FIFA in 1952, but it was during this period that apartheid developed as an official policy in all areas of South African life, including sports. In 1956, South Africa attempted to join Egypt, Sudan, and Ethiopia in founding the African Football Confederation, but when it became clear that the SAFA intended to field an all-white and "colored" team in the first African Nations' Cup, the other three participants blocked South Africa's membership.

In 1959, professionalism was adopted with the formation of the all-white National Professional Football League, now known as the National Football League (NFL), by eleven clubs from Pretoria and Johannesburg. (In more recent years it consisted of 13 clubs.) The prominence of Transvaal clubs in the NFL stems from the faster growth of soccer in former Dutch areas than in former British areas such as Cape Town, where interest in rugby is high. Highlands Park F.C. of Johannesburg has been the most successful club in the NFL, having won seven championships and six cups, including three doubles. Durban City and Cape Town City have also been very successful. The non-white league in South Africa is called the National Professional Soccer League (NPSL), founded in 1972, and it consists of 16 clubs. Orlando Chiefs of Johannesburg has been the most successful NPSL club, having won the double in 1973 and 1975, and Kaizer Chiefs of Johannesburg has also had considerable success.

A complex series of events has taken place in recent years in a modest effort to integrate the South African game. The Football Association of South Africa (FASA), as the SAFA was called in the 1960s, was suspended from FIFA in 1964 for violating antidiscrimination codes in the FIFA charter (specifically Article 2, paragraph 4.5). In 1970, South Africa was expelled from the International Olympic Committee, and pressure on South African authorities to change their policies intensified. With the birth of the NPSL came the formation of a separate governing body for non-whites, the South African Soccer Federa-

tion (SASF), whose officers included some non-whites. This was seen clearly as a way to accommodate growing non-white interests in the game without having to include them directly in white policy-making bodies.

Citing Article 2, paragraph 4.5 once again, FIFA expelled South Africa in 1976 by a vote of 78-9, with 13 abstentions. A few weeks later, the South African Sports Council decided to allow three players of "another race" on each white and non-white club. Eleven white clubs in the NFL agreed to participate. This concept of so-called "multinational sport" was extended in September 1976 to allow white and non-white teams to play each other for the first time. The first such game was played in April 1977 at Rand Stadium, Johannesburg, in which Cape Town City of the NFL defeated Vaal Professionals, a leading black club, 3-0. A new interracial league was introduced on a temporary basis under the sponsorship of a large liquor corporation named Mainstay, for whom the league was named. Later, Vaal Professionals defeated the white-based East London United 2-0 with three white players in its lineup in a match that marked the first foray of a white team into a black stadium.

Meanwhile, a rift occurred among non-white soccer administrators. The NPSL, which enjoys widespread support among the black population, has resisted integration efforts because its fears loss of public interest for soccer in the black community. In an effort to expedite the integration effort, the white NFL merged with the non-white supervisory body, although its real desire was to merge with the NPSL to form an integrated national league. The NPSL, however, has not only refused to merge with the NFL, but has also disassociated itself from the SASF as well. The SASF, for its part, would like the NPSL and NFL to merge under its aegis. The role of the Football Association of South Africa in all this remains aloof.

A further restructuring of the South African game took place in 1978. Two leagues, one along the coast and one inland, were formed. The top six clubs from either league were to form a "super league," the winner of which was to be the South African champion. Since these new leagues were to be played under the auspices of the SASF, however, the NPSL was unlikely to join in the experiment, leaving the NFL and a few non-NPSL black clubs to play among themselves. If the NPSL does join, then nine clubs from either league will form two "super leagues," and two clubs from both of these will participate in a play-off to determine the champion.

Ceaseless international pressure has also resulted in another change. In May 1977, the first racially mixed South African national team took the field against Rhodesia (already integrated) before 30,000 spectators at Rand Stadium. The South African team included eight whites and seven non-whites, and won handily 7-0; four goals were scored by whites and three by non-whites.

South America   See: **Confederación Sudamericana de Fútbol (CONMEBOL)**

Southeast Asian Peninsula Games, Football Tournament of the

The soccer competition is the major attraction in these amateur games (known popularly as the SEAP Games), which are held biannually in a designated city. The participants are (or have been): Burma, Malaysia, Singapore, Thailand, and Vietnam Republic. The series has continued since the unification of Vietnam, but none of the socialist states of the region are invited. The third edition (1963) was canceled. Burma won five titles in a row between 1965-73.

Winners

1959 (in Bangkok) Vietnam Republic
1961 (in Rangoon) Malaysia
1965 (in Kuala Lumpur) Burma and Thailand
1967 (in Bangkok) Burma

1969 (in Rangoon) Burma
1971 (in Kuala Lumpur) Burma
1973 (in Singapore) Burma
1975 (in Bangkok) Thailand

South Pacific Games, Football Tournament of the

This regional sports festival based on the Olympic model includes a soccer competition that has been played by representative or national teams from the following countries and dependencies: American Samoa, Solomon Islands, Cook Islands, Fiji, Gilbert and Ellice Islands, Guam, Nauru, Niue, New Caledonia, New Hebrides, Papua-New Guinea, French Polynesia (as well as Tahiti separately), Tokelau, Tonga, Wallis and Horn Islands, and Western Samoa. Of these, only Fiji and Papua-New Guinea are members of FIFA and the Oceania Football Confederation (OFC), but many have governing bodies that are affiliated with the national associations of England or France, and some are provisional members of the OFC.

The games have been held five times: 1963, 1966, 1969, 1972, and 1975. The two known winners are Fiji (1969) and Tahiti (1975). Each edition is played in a host country or territory. Participants are divided into two groups under a league system. Group winners and runners-up advance to a knockout series ending with a third place game and a final. The four major powers of the South Pacific—excluding Australia and New Zealand—are Fiji, Tahiti, New Caledonia, and New Hebrides. Despite the introduction of the Oceania Cup in 1973, this tournament remains the only all-encompassing competition for representative teams in the region.

Spain

Real Federación Española de Fútbol
Calle Alberto Bosch, 13
Apartado postal 347
Madrid 14

Founded: 1905
FIFA: 1913
UEFA: 1954

Affiliated clubs: *5,344;* **registered players:** *164,588 (2,264 professional);* **national stadium:** *none;* **largest stadium:** *Estadio Santiago Bernabéu, Madrid (101,663);* **colors:** *red jerseys, blue shorts;* **season:** *September to June;* **honors:** *Olympic Games runner-up, (1920) European Nations' Cup winner (1964), Real Madrid, Intercontinental Cup (1960, 1974), European Cup (1956, 1957, 1958, 1959, 1960, 1966), Latin Cup (1949, 1953, 1955, 1957), Atlético Madrid, Intercontinental Cup (1974), European Cup Winners' Cup (1962), Barcelona, Fairs Cup (1958, 1960, 1953), Valencia, Fairs Cup (1962, 1963), Real Zaragoza, Fairs Cup (1964).*

Spanish soccer has found unparalleled success in club competitions at the international level. Its most famous club, Real Madrid, is virtually a bench mark in this respect, and four other Spanish clubs have won major European championships. Yet, many of these accomplishments have been generated by the presence of foreign players who have come to wealthy Spanish clubs from almost every country in Europe and South America. Wealthy Spanish clubs rank with their big Italian counterparts as the richest in all of Europe. Spanish national teams, on the other hand, have little to match the clubs in the way of trophies, and have failed to live up to expectations, at least in the postwar era. There have been several Spanish-born players of genuine world class caliber—Zamora, Suarez, Gento, and Amancio—but most good ones have been overshadowed by foreign talent that has come to Spain since the early 1950s. Kubala, Di Stefano, Kocsis, Kopa, Czibor, Didi, Vavá, Puskás, Cruyff, Netzer, and Kempes have all sought to make their fortunes in Spain.

Like Italy, Spain did not evolve into an important soccer-playing country until after World War I. Soccer was brought to Spain via the Basque provinces by British mining engineers during the 1890s, a relatively late date by European standards, though it had been played elsewhere on the Iberian peninsula (Gibralter and Portugal) many years earlier. British military personnel and residents also introduced the game before the turn of the century in Madrid, Barcelona, and Valencia, and these four locations spawned the

first important clubs. The oldest club is the flagship of Basque nationalism, Athletic Club de Bilbao, founded in the Basque capital in 1898 as Athletic Club. In the same year Madrid Football Club, later Real ("Royal") Madrid, was formed in the national capital by students. A now defunct club called Sociedad de Football Sky was also formed in Madrid at this time. Hans Gamper, a naturalized Swiss, introduced soccer in the Catalan capital of Barcelona, and founded Foot-ball Club Barcelona in 1899.

The first recorded match in Spain took place in 1894 at Bilbao between a team of British residents and Basques, the British winning 5-0, but matches were probably played as early as 1894 in Madrid as well. To celebrate the coronation of Alfonso XIII in 1902, a knockout tournament was organized in Madrid with four participants: Biscaya (a joint team of Athletic Club and the new Bilbao F.C.), Madrid F.C., Barcelona, and Español (a second Barcelona club). Biscaya defeated all three opponents, and the competiton was turned into an annual event that eventually became the Spanish national cup competition. The Spanish cup determined the national champion until as late as 1928-29 when a national league was finally introduced.

A governing body, the Asociación Madrileña de Clubs de Foot-Ball, was founded in Madrid in 1900, but it included only Madrid clubs, and in 1905 it was superceded by the new Federación Española de Fútbol, which soon received its royal designation *Real.* No attempts were made to form a properly authorized national team, but the Real

Federación Española de Fútbol (FEF) joined FIFA in 1913 with the obvious intent of entering international competition. But World War I intervened, and Spain's debut was delayed until 1920. The burgeoning Spanish Cup, meanwhile, was dominated by Athletic Bilbao, though Madrid F.C. won a sizable share of trophies too, and before 1920, four other Basque clubs—Ciclista Sebastian, Rácing de Irún, Real Unión de Irún, and Arenas Bilbao—won the cup to assure the Basque provinces of near total domination of Spanish soccer. Between 1910-13, ethnic and regional rifts shook the FEF, and Catalan clubs broke away to stage their own competition on two occasions, Barcelona winning both times.

Spain finally made its first appearance in international competition at the Olympic Games of 1920 in Antwerp, and it was a great success. Spain's debut was actually staged in Brussels—a 1-0 win over Denmark—but in the second round it lost to Belgium and faced elimination from the tournament. When Czechoslovakia walked off the field in the middle of the final and the gold medal was awarded to Belgium, a play-off series was quickly organized to determine second and third place. Spain was given a second chance, and proceeded to defeat Sweden and Italy in successive games for the right to meet Holland in the "second and third place game." The Spaniards won, and in their very first international competition went home with silver medals. Ricardo Zamora, one of Europe's greatest goalkeepers between the world wars, made his first appearance for Spain during this competition. Zamora went on to play in 46 of Spain's 57 full internationals between 1920-36.

Following the Olympics of 1920 Spain won five friendlies in a row against Belgium, Portugal (twice), and France (twice), and its overall record during the 1920s was one of the best in Europe. Led by Zamora, Spain won more than once over Austria, Hungary, and Switzerland, as well as its more frequent opponents France and Portugal, and several of these were away matches. One of its few losses, unfortunately, was to Italy in the preliminary round of the 1924 Olympics in Paris. At the 1928 games in Amsterdam, Mexico was easily brushed aside, but in the second round a 1-1 draw with Italy forced a replay that the budding Italians won by a huge 7-1 margin. This has remained Spain's worst defeat in history, matched only by another 7-1 loss to England in 1931 at Wembley. In 1930,

Spain partly avenged its Olympic defeat by topping Italy in Bologna, 3-2, and Zamora's team continued its wining ways right through to the 1934 World Cup. Spain had prepared for its first World Cup by demolishing Bulgaria 13-0 in Madrid the year before and eliminating Portugal 9-0 and 2-1 to qualify. In the first round, the confident Spaniards held talented but disorganized Brazil in check, winning 3-1, and Zamora, now one of the great stars of Europe, emerged as perhaps the most popular player in the competition. Spain's opponent in the second round was the home team Italy, which Zamora held to a 1-1 draw, forcing a replay. Only four players from the first match against Italy returned for the replay—the injured Zamora was not one of them—and Meazza's goal was all the Italians needed to win the game.

This was another rare and untimely loss, but other major victories followed in 1935; it was not until the bleak civil war of 1936 that Spain lost as many as three games in succession. Its cumulative international record (1920-36) was exceptional: 57-36-9-12-134-56-81. Twenty-one of these 36 wins were shutouts, and 17 were played on foreign soil. Its percentage of success during this period was roughly equal to that of West Germany from 1954-74, when that country won two World Cups. Sadly, Spain was not able to reap such rewards during an era when international soccer was less structured. Spain was never to see anything like this level of success with its national team again.

International competition ceased during the civil war of 1936-39. The new national league that had started in 1928-29 and the Spanish Cup were also suspended. The league, which introduced professionalism and a new competitiveness to the Spanish game, began with 10 clubs in the first division—Barcelona, Real Madrid, Athletic Bilbao, Real Sociedad, Arenas de Guecho, Atlético Madrid, Español, Europa, Real Unión de Irún, and Real Santander—finishing the first season in that order. In 1934-35, the number of participants was increased to 12. It was hardly surprising that when the league was resumed in 1939-40, the winner for two years running was Atlético Avación, the new air force club that had just been created by the new government with a merger of Atlético Madrid and the lowly Club Aviación. The manager was Ricardo Zamora. (Atlético Madrid was reborn in 1947.)

International competiton was resumed briefly in 1941 with matches against neutral

Portugal and Switzerland, and in 1945 a pair of games with Portugal opened the postwar era. Among the dozen friendlies played during the late 1940s were four against the Republic of Ireland, two of which were won and two lost, and five more games with Portugal, which by now had become Spain's most frequent opponent. In the 19 full internationals played between Spain and Portugal from 1921-50, Spain won 12 and lost one. Since 1950, these Iberian neighbors have met only four times, splitting the results. It was Portugal that Spain eliminated to gain entry in the 1950 World Cup in Brazil. In this highly successful venture, Spain defeated the USA, Chile, and, for the second time in its history, England to win its first round group. In the final pool, the Spaniards managed to hold the eventual winner Uruguay to a draw, but crashed to the home team Brazil by a 6-1 margin. The determined Swedes dealt them another defeat to close out the pool, and Spain settled for fourth place. This 1950 team featured the excellent Basque center forward Zarra from Athletic Bilbao making his international debut, and Barcelona's outstanding goalkeeper Antonio Ramallets, who was nevertheless replaced after the Brazilian debacle. Spain had entered the competition as a non-contender and finished with its highest placing ever in the World Cup.

Spain did not qualify for either the 1954 or 1958 World Championships, but the story of Spanish soccer from 1953-66 had little to do with the national team in any case. At Real Madrid, Santiago Bernabéu took over as president in 1943, and troubled by losing repeated trophies to Barcelona, the ancient enemy, he began to build an extraordinary team based on attentive worldwide scouting. In 1953, he signed Alfredo Di Stefano, Francisco Gento, and Hector Rial all in one year, and Real Madrid was instantly transformed. Two Spanish championships were won immediately, and in 1955 Real won the coveted Latin Cup with a stunning 2-0 win over Stade de Reims. Real's Spanish championship of 1955 put Bernabéu's team in the inaugural edition of the European Cup, and in 1956 Real won its first of five European Cup titles in succession, the greatest feat in the history of international club competition. Barcelona, in the meantime, had won several Spanish championships and cups, as well as two Latin Cups, and was now poised to enter another decade of bitter rivalry with Real over the leadership of Spanish soccer.

The bloodless war between Real and Barcelona, one club representing the Castilian establishment in Madrid, the other a personification of Catalan nationalism, was waged on all fronts. In the international transfer market, Real and Barcelona vied with the big Italian clubs for world class stars, and each alternated in outspending the other. Hungary's Sandor Kocsis and Zoltan Czibor went to Barcelona, joining the Spanish idol Luis Suárez. Raymond Kopa and Ferenc Puskas joined Di Stefano and another Spanish idol, Francisco Gento, at Real. As Real busied itself with its five European Cups victories, Barcelona won two successive Fairs Cups (1958 and 1960). The hatred and bitterness peaked in 1960. Real and Barcelona met head-to-head in the semi-finals of the 1959-60 European Cup, and Real won both legs by an identical 3-1 score; in the first round of the 1960-61 edition, however, Barcelona eliminated Real from the competition it had dominated for five years by an aggregate score of 4-3. Real's long-running superiority in the rivalry had finally been ended, at least temporarily.

But Madrid and Barcelona were not the only Spanish cities to produce European championship clubs. In the 1961-62 Fairs Cup, Valencia defeated none other than Barcelona in an all-Spanish final—winning the Valencia leg by 6-2—and won the 1962-63 Fairs Cup as well with wins over Dinamo Zagreb in the final. Spain's incredible domination over European club competitions continued the next year when Real Zaragoza, the popular standard-bearer of soccer in Aragon, advanced to the final of the Fairs Cup, there confronting two-time winner Valencia in another all-Spanish affair, winning its first and only European title. In 1965-66, a third all-Spanish Fairs Cup final took place with Barcelona defeating Zaragoza in extra time.

In the European Cup, meanwhile, Real reached the final again in 1961-62 and 1963-64, losing both times, and in 1965-66 won the cup for the sixth time with a new generation of players. Atlético Madrid, not to be left out of the European picture, won the European Cup Winners' Cup in 1961-62 with its own roster of foreign imports, and reached the final again the following year, losing to Tottenham Hotspur. All told, Spanish clubs won a total of 13 European club championships from 1955-66, a record unequaled, with trophies spread around the board rooms of five different Spanish clubs.

These successes managed to spill over into the national team's endeavors briefly in the early 1960s. After reaching the final rounds of the 1962 World Cup and quickly bowing out with mediocre performances, Spain was partly compensated with a distinguished win in the 1962-64 European Football Chamionship. While its opposition in early rounds was not the most difficult—Rumania, Northern Ireland, Repubic of Ireland, and Hungary—its opponent in the final was the defensive-minded USSR with Lev Yashin in goal, and it took the genius of Suárez to guide Spain to a 2-1 win. The winning goal was scored by Zaragoza's center forward Marcelino. This team also included Real's star right winger Amancio and early international appearances of the Basque goalkeeper from Athletic Bilbao, Iribar, who was to keep goal for Spain until 1977.

Spain qualified for the World Cup again in 1966 with a narrow play-off victory over its frequent if unlikely opponent, the Republic of Ireland. In the final rounds, Argentina hacked the Spanish stars Suárez and Amancio into submission, and won 2-1, while Switzerland proved a surprisingly worthy opponent in losing by the same score. In its third match of the group, Spain and West Germany fought a close contest, but a goal by Uwe Seeler gave the game to the Germans, and as expected, Spain left the tournament after the first round. After failing to qualify for the World Cup in 1970 and 1974, a tactically sophisticated team led by Real's captain Pirri staggered into the 1978 World Cup finals after a bruising qualification series with Rumania, but its chances for advancing beyond the first round were dashed by Austria and Brazil. Spain's European Football Championship results since the 1964 victory have been mixed. It reached the quarter-finals in 1966-68, but world champion England ended Spain's hopes in two closely fought matches.

Since the European Cup winning era of Real Madrid, the Spanish league has continued to be dominated by the famous *Madrileño* club with occasional interruptions by crosstown rivals Atlético, but Real has failed to make any serious headway in European competition. Spanish clubs, indeed, have not won a European tournament since 1966, though Atlético Madrid replaced Ajax Amsterdam in the 1974 Intercontinental Cup and defeated Argentina's Independiente for that title. Real, Atlético, Barcelona, and Bilbao are seldom taken lightly in international competition, but the glory days of the 1950s and '60s have yet to return. At home, Athletic Bilbao has continued to vindicate its reputation as Spain's greatest cup fighter, but the other big five of Spanish clubs—Real, Atlético, Barcelona, Valencia, and Zaragoza—have each had their successful years.

The Spanish league is divided into four divisions. The premier and second divisions are national in composition. The Second Division B is roughly divided into two groups along an imaginary line across the country from northeast to southwest, and the Third Division is made up of six geographically divided sections (northwest, north, northeast, central, east and south). Real has now amassed 18 championships, a record, and 13 cup wins. Athletic Bilbao has won the league title six times and the cup an astonishing 23 times, also a record. Barcelona's nine championships and 18 cup win rates a high ranking, as do Atlético Madrid's eight league titles and five cup victories. Valencia has won four of each. Imported players from Spanish-speaking countries have figured prominently in Spanish soccer since World War II, but their importation is governed by two-per-club rule that applies to all foreign players.

Champions

1929	Barcelona	1937	no competition	1945	Barcelona
1930	Athletic Bilbao	1938	no competition	1946	Seville
1931	Athletic Bilbao	1939	no competition	1947	Valencia
1932	Real Madrid	1940	Aviación	1948	Barcelona
1933	Real Madrid	1941	Aviación	1949	Barcelona
1934	Athletic Bilbao	1942	Valencia	1950	Atlético Madrid
1935	Betis	1943	Athletic Bilbao	1951	Atlético Madrid
1936	Athletic Bilbao	1944	Valencia	1952	Barcelona

1953	Barcelona	1962	Real Madrid	1971	Valencia
1954	Real Madrid	1963	Real Madrid	1972	Real Madrid
1955	Real Madrid	1964	Real Madrid	1973	Atlético Madrid
1956	Athletic Bilbao	1965	Real Madrid	1974	Barcelona
1957	Real Madrid	1966	Atlético Madrid	1975	Real Madrid
1958	Real Madrid	1967	Real Madrid	1976	Real Madrid
1959	Barcelona	1968	Real Madrid	1977	Atlético Madrid
1960	Barçelona	1969	Real Madrid	1978	Real Madrid
1961	Real Madrid	1970	Atlético Madrid		

Cup Winners

1902	Bizcaya Bilbao	1937	no competition
1903	Athletic Bilbao	1938	no competition
1904	Athletic Bilbao	1939	Seville
1905	Madrid F.C.	1940	Español
1906	Madrid F.C.	1941	Valencia
1907	Madrid F.C.	1942	Barcelona
1908	Madrid F.C.	1943	Athletic Bilbao
1909	Ciclista Sebastian	1944	Athletic Bilbao
1910	Athletic Bilbao/Barcelona	1945	Athletic Bilbao
1911	Athletic Bilbao	1946	Real Madrid
1912	Barcelona	1947	Real Madrid
1913	Rácing de Irún/Barcelona	1948	Seville
1914	Athletic Bilbao	1949	Valencia
1915	Athletic Bilbao	1950	Athletic Bilbao
1916	Athletic Bilbao	1951	Barcelona
1917	Madrid F.C.	1952	Barcelona
1918	Real Unión de Irún	1953	Barcelona
1919	Arenas Bilbao	1954	Valencia
1920	Barcelona	1955	Athletic Bilbao
1921	Athletic Bilbao	1956	Athletic Bilbao
1922	Barcelona	1957	Barcelona
1923	Athletic Bilbao	1958	Athletic Bilbao
1924	Real Unión de Irún	1959	Barcelona
1925	Barcelona	1960	Atlético Madrid
1926	Barcelona	1961	Atlético Madrid
1927	Real Unión de Irún	1962	Real Madrid
1928	Barcelona	1963	Barcelona
1929	Español	1964	Real Zaragoza
1930	Athletic Bilbao	1965	Atlético Madrid
1931	Athletic Bilbao	1966	Real Zaragoza
1932	Athletic Bilbao	1967	Valencia
1933	Athletic Bilbao	1968	Barcelona
1934	Real Madrid	1969	Athletic Bilbao
1935	Seville	1970	Real Madrid
1936	Real Madrid	1971	Barcelona

1972	Atlético Madrid	1976	Atlético Madrid
1973	Athletic Bilbao	1977	Real Betis
1974	Real Madrid	1978	Barcelona
1975	Real Madrid		

Sparta, Československý Klubu

Location: *Prague, Czechoslovakia;* stadium: *Sparta Stadion (38,000);* colors: *cherry jerseys, white shorts;* honors: *Mitropa Cup (1927, 1935), Czech champion (1912, 1919, 1920, 1921, 1922, 1923, 1925, 1926, 1927, 1932, 1936, 1938, 1939, 1946, 1948, 1952, 1954, 1965, 1967), Czech cup winner (1964, 1972, 1976).*

Founded 1893 as Athletic Club Královske Vonobrady (King's Vineyard) and renamed Atheltic Club Sparta the following year. Its archrivalry with SK Slavia has been the mainstay of Czech soccer since the 1890s. Despite Slavia's greater international fame immediately after the turn of the century, Sparta was roughly its equal, and in 1912 it was Sparta rather than Slavia that won the first Czech national championship.

As Slavia was to dominate the 1930s, so Sparta ruled over the 1920s with eight league titles in nine years. At the tail end of this glorious era, Sparta won the first edition of the important Mitropa Cup in 1927, having disposed of Rapid Vienna in the final By the mid-1930s, when Slavia's hegemony was on the wane, Sparta emerged as Czechoslovakia's better international competitor. In 1935, it won the Mitropa Cup again, defeating Ferencváros in the final by an aggregate score of 4-2, and it was a finalist again in 1936. By this time, Sparta had seven Czech internationals in its lineup, including inside left Oldrich Nejedly, who formed one of Europe's best left wing pairs with Slavia's Antonin Puc on the Czech national team.

Unlike Slavia, Sparta has been able to win several league and cup honors since the 1948 change in political regimes. It did not, however, escape the inevitable name changes. In 1948-49, it was known as Bratsvi Sparta, then as Sparta Sokolovo and Spartak Prague Sokolovo, and finally, in 1965, the name was changed to the present CK Sparta. The club has not been particularly successful in European competitions, though it won the now unimportant Mitropa Cup in 1964. It was relegated briefly in the mid-1970s, but it retains the Czech record for most league titles with 19.

square ball

A cross-field or lateral pass.

Sri Lanka

Football Federation of Sri Lanka
Ramakrishna Terrace No. 1
Colombo 6

Founded: 1939
FIFA: 1950
AFC: 1958

Affiliated clubs: *575;* registered players: *17,375;* national stadium: *Sugathadasa Stadium (25,000);* largest stadium: *Sugathadasa Stadium;* colors: *maroon and gold jerseys, white shorts;* season: *September to March;* honors: *none.*

Throughout the years, the resources of the Football Federation of Sri Lanka have been weighted heavily in favor of the domestic game at the expense of international competition. Soccer in the former British colony of Ceylon has had an active and diverse internal structure since the immediate prewar years, and it has successfully withstood strong competition from field hockey, the traditional team sport of South Asia.

The Ceylon Football Association was founded in 1939. During the war years it became defunct, but it was revived in 1946. The first major competition was a national cup competition, the Sir Stanley Rous Cup, which got under way in 1951 and is still contested among the various regional cup winners. (The first winner was Sunrise Sports Club.) Sri Lanka is divided into 38 associations, each with its own league. There is a Premier Cup League with two divisions (the trophy for which was donated by The Football Association in London), the National Championship Tournament, and the Football Federation of Sri Lanka Challenge Cup Tournament, as well as the Rous Cup. All 575 clubs participate in the leagues of the 38 regional associations, and each league is allowed up to three tournaments per season. Of Sri Lanka's 17,375 registered

players, more than 15,000 are in the adult category, indicating a high level of participation in senior competition.

By the early 1950s, Ceylon was beginning to feel its way into international competition. In 1952, it played host to India and Pakistan in friendlies at Colombo, losing both games by 3-0 and 2-0, respectively. One year later, in Rangoon, Ceylon participated in the International Quadrangular Tournament with its three closest neighbors, but it proved to be the weakest team in the field. It was defeated by Burma (3-2), India (2-0), and Pakistan (6-0), with India emerging the winner. Though Sri Lanka's international experience has been limited, a national coach has been retained for many years to train a team of 45 players from league ranks. Nevertheless, Sri Lanka has not attempted to qualify for the World Cup and has not been seen in any final edition of the Asian Nations' Cup. Most recently, Sri Lanka expressed its intention to enter the 1976 Nations' Cup, but at the last moment withdrew. The present name of the national association was adopted in 1972.

Stade de Reims

Location: *Reims, France;* stadium: *Stade Auguste-Delaune (18,000);* colors: *red jerseys with white sleeves, white shorts;* honors: *Latin Cup (1953). French champion (1949, 1953, 1955, 1958, 1960, 1962), French cup winner (1950, 1958).*

Founded 1931 with the merger of Sporting Club Rémois and Société Sportive du Parc Pommery. Reims's highly successful period during the 1950s under Albert Batteux earned it the distinction of becoming the greatest team ever seen in France, and, despite the record-breaking feats of St. Étienne since the 1960s, remains the standard by which the French game is measured.

In 1953, after winning the French title a second time, Reims shocked an unsuspecting Europe by defeating AC Milan in the final of the Latin Cup. This 3-0 upset of a club that was regarded as the best in Europe—and by a team from a country that had previously failed to win any international competitions—initiated an unbroken era of high honors. French championships followed in 1955, 1958, 1960, and 1962, in addition to a second French Cup in 1958, the year of Reims' only double. Batteux brought Reims to the summit of European club competition in 1956 and 1959

with appearances in the final of the European Cup, but its opposition on both occasions was the mighty Real Madrid. In its 4-3 loss in 1956, Real came back to win after Reims had opened up a 2-0 lead early in the game, but equally frustrating for Reims was the resulting departure of its legendary center forward, Raymond Kopa, to Real. By 1959, Real was practically unbeatable, and Reims' 2-0 loss in the final was kept respectably by the laudable defensive effort of Robert Jonquet.

As Stade Rémois, it won the French Amateur Championship in 1935, its last season before turning professional, and in 1942 it won the northern division of the wartime championship. A second division club until the national league was restructured after World War II, it was given a place in the new Division I in 1946. In 1949, it won the national championship for the first time with the seeds of its future greatness already in the lineup: Roger Marché at left back, Jonquet at center half, and Batteux at inside-right. Winning the French Cup followed in 1950, and Batteux was signed as manager, a post he kept until 1963.

Reims's true reign as the standard bearer of French soccer began in 1951 with Batteux's acquisition of Kopa from Angers. The best French player in history, Kopa flourished during his first period with Reims (1951-56) and led the club to two championships. After four highly successful years with Real Madrid, during which he was elected European Footballer of the Year, he returned to Reims in 1960 and played for four more years before retiring. The backbone of Batteux's teams, however, was the captain Jonquet, who was also the perennial captain of France and his country's finest center half ever. Jonquet was with Reims from 1942-60, providing the consistent element around which Batteux could rebuild the team as other important players (like Marché, Kopa, and Fontaine) came and left. Marché achieved immortality with Reims during the early years of success and was an inspirational captain of France during the same period, but he left for Racing Club de Paris in 1953. Center forward Just Fontaine replaced Kopa only weeks after the latter's move to Real Madrid, and functioned more as a pure goalscorer than did his predecessor. Shortly before Fontaine's career was tragically ended by a car accident in 1960, Kopa had returned to his old club, and the two stars of the 1958 World Cup were reunited briefly. Though Reims scored 86 goals in 34 matches during the great 1952-53 season, its best team in generally thought to be that of

1955-56 when it fielded seven French internationals.

Batteux's teams were characterized by a technical perfection that emphasized dribbling and passing skills and shunned hard, physical play. These qualities resulted in great popularity among international and domestic fans and were an important factor in Reims' rapid rise to the top. In its first three seasons in the first division during the 1940s, it finished fourth, second, and third, respectively, and won the title itself in its fourth attempt. Indeed, the only years prior to 1964 in which Reims was not in contention for the championship were 1953 (the year of Reims' Latin Cup run) 1956, and 1959. Its league wins in 1958 and 1960 were achieved by gaping seven-point margins.

The decline came equally fast. It finished third in the league in 1961, a distant seven points behind the winner, Monaco, and in 1962 won the championship from Racing Club on goal average (1.383 to 1.365). In 1963, its second place finish and quarter-final elimination by Feyenoord in the European Cup were thought by the owners to be a slump, and Batteux was fired. Reims immediately slid into the second division, and Kopa retired the same year. In recent years, Reims has regained its place in the first division, but there has been no evidence of a serious challenge to bring back the glory of old to the Champagne district of the northeast.

Reims' women's team has dominated the Championnat de France Féminin since the league's formation in 1974.

stadiums

Excluding the Indianapolis Motor Speedway, all of the world's largest sports facilities have been built primarily or exclusively for soccer. There are two basic stadium designs. The first, known commonly as the "English" style, is rectangular in shape and is characterized by stands or terraces that hug the field closely on all four sides. "English"-styled grounds are known for their intimate atmosphere as a result of the crowd's proximity to action on the field, and, with less than a half-dozen exceptions, are found throughout the British Isles. There are also some examples in the Benelux countries, France, Spain, Italy, Switzerland, and West Germany. The second

design is the more common oval shape, which generally allows for a diversification of activities, such as track and field and non-sporting events. Most of the world's largest stadiums fall into this category. Of the 23 grounds with a capacity of 100,000 spectators or more, only one resembles the "English" style: Bernabéu.

Seven of the world's 10 largest stadiums are located in Brazil. All are variations of the oval design, and almost all have been built since 1960. The instigation for this surge of great stadium construction was the extraordinary Maracanã in Rio, which was built for the 1950 World Cup finals and remains the largest

Great stadiums of the past and present. (Top) the Crystal Palace grounds, South London, the world's first stadium to hold 100,000 persons. In progress is the F.A. Cup final of 1911, Newcastle United vs. Bradford City. (Bottom) Estádio Maracanã, Rio de Janeiro, the world's largest stadium (capacity: 220,000), on Fla-Flu derby day, 1977.

stadium in the world. Its perfectly oval shape and futuristic design has provided the basic concept for many of Brazil's giant *futebol* facilities.

Nine stadiums with a capacity of 100,000 or more are located in South America; six are in Europe, four in Asia, and two each in Africa and North America. The first stadium to have a 100,000 capacity was the old Crystal Palace ground in South London (demolished in 1915), which was the site for the F.A. Cup final from 1895-1914. The first recording of a soccer crowd reaching over 100,000 was at Crystal Palace for the cup final of 1901, when 110,820 fans watched Tottenham Hotspur draw the Sheffield United, 2-2. The oldest home site for any league club in the world is the Recreation Ground of England's Chesterfield F.C. This location has been in continual use by the Derbyshire club since its founding in 1866. It was originally named the New Recreation Ground, and presently holds 28,500 spectators.

The following is a list of those stadiums whose official capacities are said to be 100,000 or more. Figures in parentheses indicate actual highest recorded attendances if official capacity is exceeded.

1.	Mário Filho (Maracanã), Rio de Janeiro, Brazil	220,000
2.	Pinheirão, Curtiba, Brazil	180,000
3.	Morumbi, São Paulo, Brazil *	150,000
4.	Hampden Park, Glasgow, Scotland (149,547) **	134,580
5.	Alacid Nunes, Belém, Brazil	120,000
6.	Plácido Castelo, Fortaleza, Brazil	120,000
7.	Beira Rio, Pôrto Alegre, Brazil	110,000
8.	Magalhaes Pinto-Mineirão, Belo Horizonte, Brazil	110,000
9.	Senajan Stadium, Djakarta, Indonesia	110,000
10.	Estadio Azteca, Mexico City, Mexico (110,000)	108,499
11.	Lenin Stadium, Moscow, USSR	104,000
12.	Estádio Santiago Bernabéu, Madrid, Spain (134,000)	101,663
13.	Stade Ahmadou-Ahidjo, Yaoundé, Cameroon	100,000
14.	Aria Mehre, Karadj Auto Band, Iran	100,000
15.	Estádio de la Ciudad Universitaria, Mexico City, Mexico	100,000
16.	Corporation Stadium, Calicut, India	100,000
17.	Eden Garden Stadium, Calcutta, India	100,000
18.	Empire Stadium, Wembley, England (126,047)+	100,000
19.	Kirov Stadium, Leningrad, USSR	100,000
20.	Nasser Stadium, Cairo, Egypt	100,000
21.	Otavio Mangabeira, Salvador, Brazil	100,000
22.	Rei Pelé, Maceió, Brazil	100,000
23.	Zentralstadion, Leipzig, German DR	100,000

*Cambodian officials list the capacity of the Complexe Sportif National in Phnom-Penh at 170,000, but this is thought to be the combined figure for all the facilities at this location rather than a single stadium.

** Hampden Park is limited to a capacity of 134,000, but it was actually measured to accommodate 183,570.

+Turnstiles recorded this record figure on opening day in 1923, but it was estimated that as many as 200,000 may have entered the stadium.

See also: **Maracanã; Estádio Mário Filho, o** and **Wembley; the Empire Stadium,**

stoppage

The temporary or permanent cessation of play by the referee. The referee's discretionary power to stop a game extends from his normal duties of citing a foul to include the termination of a game for bad weather, spectator interference, or any other reason he deems necessary. In most countries, a whistle is blown to stop play on the field but is not used to restart the game, especially after a foul.

stopper

A deep back whose duties are exclusively defensive. In the third-back game, it is usually the center halfback, and with four-back systems, the stopper is likely to be one of the center backs. His function is primarily to plug the area in front of the goalkeeper but is seldom as free in his movement as the modern sweeper.

striker

Any forward whose function is primarily to score goals. The number on a given team may vary from one to four. The term has come about only since the demise of the traditional five-player forward line.

Suárez Miramonte, Luis (1935-   )

Spain's legendary inside left, whose lengthy career spanned over 20 years and brought him many honors both in Spain and Italy. He was a player of many skills, being equally accomplished in passing, shooting, and scheming, and ranks as perhaps the finest talent ever produced in his native country. He was signed at age 18 (1953) by one of his hometown clubs, RCD La Coruña, and after a showstopping debut against Barcelona in a first division match, he was secured by the same Barcelona as quickly as possible. In 1955-56, while still a second-team member, he scored 10 goals in 21 appearances, and made his international debut for Spain in 1957 before he had even secured a first-string place on the star-studded Barcelona team. In the late 1950s, he was an important member of the extraordinary Spanish forward line that included Kubala, Di Stefano, and Gento, and at Barcelona his combinations with Kubala and Kocsis made theirs the only forward line in Europe that could challenge the fame and success of Real Madrid's front five. He was chosen European Footballer of the Year in 1960, and after 216 appearances and 112 goals, was brought to Inter Milan in 1961 by his former Barcelona manager, Helenio Herrera, for a world record fee of 263 million lire ($420,000).

Under Herrera's *catenaccio* system, Suárez became a deep-lying inside forward who actually served as the midfield schemer, and he carried out his role with the utmost success. He was the major factor behind Inter's domination of European club competitions in the mid-1960s, and his leadership and all-around abilities led Spain to its European Nations' Cup triumph of 1964. In 1970, he was suddenly transferred to Sampdoria, and in 1972, after 30 international appearances and 13 goals, his old teammate and now Spain's national boss, Ladislav Kubala, called on the aging master to make another appearance for his country against Greece, resulting in his most memorable performance. After retiring, he became a coach with Genoa, an unsuccessful manager of Inter and Cagliari, and in the late 1970s was in charge of the Italian second Division club, S.P.A.L. Ferrara. A measure of his greatness is the common Spanish practice of referring to the 10-centavo coin as a "Luisito," in honor of the number he usually wore.

substitution

Substitutions in soccer have traditionally been a highly restrictive undertaking. One of the early axioms of football games in the nineteenth century was that if a team suffered the loss of an injured player, it was just bad luck and had to be endured. The notion of substituting one player for another as a tactical maneuver was thought to be unfair.

The present rule, as delineated by a decision of the International Football Association Board and governing all levels of competition throughout the world, allows five substitutions per game, providing the names of prospective substitutes are made known to the referee before the kickoff. The actual Laws of the Game, however, restrict the number of substitutions per game to two. The five-substitution decision is meant to give local authorities a perameter within which to formulate their own policies regarding substitutions. The two-substitute rule is enforced in all competitions that come under the direct supervision of FIFA. Most of the world's leading soccer nations have retained the two-substitution rule, and it is this rule which is most commonly observed in first-class competition. In the North American Soccer League, four substitutes per game are allowed. American collegiate rules allow five substitutes and unlimited resubstitution, which is in violation of the Laws.

Unauthorized substitutions, however, are not new. The first substitution in international competition was that of Welsh goalkeeper A. Pugh, who came on for the injured S. G. Gillam against Scotland in 1889.

Laws permitting substitution are a recent development. A decision of the International Board in 1932 first mentioned it by allowing limited substitution in international matches if mutually agreed upon by both teams. In 1956, the International Board authorized incapacitated goalkeepers to be replaced at any time during the game and one other incapacitated player at any time before the end of the first half, but this rule was restricted exclusively to youth tournaments under FIFA auspicies. Two years later, the 1956 rule was extended to include all levels of competition and thus for the first time substitution was not specifically forbidden in the upper reaches of the game. The total number of substitutions, however, was restricted to two, and the names of two nominated substitutes were required to be given to the referee in advance of the game.

In 1965, the number of nominated players was increased to five, but actual substitutions remained at two. A major change occurred in 1967, when FIFA authorized two substitutes per game for any reason, injury or otherwise, but the ruling was restricted to friendlies and qualification rounds for the 1968 Olympic Games and the 1970 World Cup. When the rule was eventually adopted for the final rounds of these competitions, the two-substitution rule came into common use as an integral part of the Laws. The five-substitution decision of the International Board was adopted in 1971, and remains restricted to those competitions or leagues whose governing authorities have themselves sanctioned the rule. Indeed, national associations have the legal authority to restrict substitutions as they see fit, providing the perameters of the Laws and decisions are not exceeded.

There are additional rules that govern the substitution of players: 1) a player who is sent off may not be replaced; and 2) a substitute may not enter the field of play except at stoppages and after the referee has beckoned him to do so, nor may he enter the field of play until the player he is replacing has left the field of play.

Sudamericana, Copa

Campeonato Sud-Americano.

The South American Championship for national teams. The Copa Sudamericana has been played irregularly since 1916, and is open to all members of CONMEBOL, the South American confederation. While 30 tournaments have taken place, the actual trophy of the championship, the Copa América, has been awarded only 23 times—the first in 1917. The competition has been dominated decisively by Argentina and Uruguay, which have won 23 titles between them.

An aborted attempt to establish a South American championship was made by Argentina in 1910 at Buenos Aires to commemorate the centenary of Argentine independence, but without an organizing body to oversee the tournament's continuation, the idea was not followed up. The participants in 1910 were Argentina, Chile, and Uruguay, and four matches were played: Argentina defeated Uruguay 4-1, Uruguay blanked Chile 3-0, and Argentina beat Chile twice, 3-1 and 5-1.

In 1916, the national associations of Argentina, Brazil, Chile, and Uruguay met in Buenos Aires to stage a new South American championship. The games were played over a period of two weeks, and halfway through the competition the four participants officially announced the formation of the Confederación Sudamericana de Football (CONMEBOL), whose first priority would be an annual championship for national teams. According to the adopted format, each edition would be held in a host city under a league system. In case of a tie for first place, there would be a play-off. This structure was not changed until the thirtieth edition in 1975.

Initially, the competition was held almost annually, but a long hiatus occurred during the early 1930s when most South American countries were in the throes of turning professional. Paraguay first entered in 1921, Bolivia in 1926, and Peru in 1927. The first edition in which all seven early participants competed together was 1936-37. Ecuador entered in 1939 and Colombia in 1945.

Venezuela, which did not form a national league until the mid-1950s, did not enter until 1967.

Plagued from the beginning by violence and wavering interest, the series appeared to be slowly grinding to a halt in the postwar years. The introduction of the Copa Libertadores (South American club championship) in 1960 nearly spelled its doom, and during the 1960s only two editions were held. Preoccupied with World Cup qualification rounds, international club competition, and domestic championships, many national associations refused to take the financial risk involved in a protracted stay in a foreign city. Finally in 1975, CONMEBOL instituted a home and away policy for all rounds of the competition, and the belated thirtieth edition attracted all ten members of the confederation for the first time. Public interest was greater than at any time since the 1920s.

Countries other than Argentina, Uruguay, and Brazil have won the championship only four times: Peru twice and Bolivia and Paraguay once each. Two the these four wins involved home field advantage. Brazil's poor showing relative to its overall standing in world competition (three wins and nine times runners-up) reflect a lack of interest, fear of financial loss, and preoccupation with other competitions. As late as 1975, Brazil was represented by a Minas Gerais state selection.

Winners

1916	Uruguay	1927	Argentina	1949	Brazil
1917	Uruguay	1929	Argentina	1953	Paraguay
1919	Brazil	1935	Uruguay	1955	Argentina
1920	Uruguay	1936-37	Argentina	1956	Uruguay
1921	Argentina	1939	Peru	1957	Argentina
1922	Brazil	1941	Argentina	1959	Argentina
1923	Uruguay	1942	Uruguay	1959	Uruguay
1924	Uruguay	1945	Argentina	1963	Bolivia
1925	Argentina	1946	Argentina	1967	Uruguay
1926	Uruguay	1947	Argentina	1975	Peru

Cumulative Ranking (1916-75)
(number of editions in parentheses)

	P	W	D	L	F	A	P
1 Argentina (27)	144	83	15	19	321	113	181
2 Uruguay (28)	122	76	10	36	299	144	162
3 Brazil (20)	99	56	14	29	256	134	126

4	Paraguay (21)	102	44	13	44	181	202	101
5	Chile (23)	107	33	17	57	170	227	83
6	Peru (16)	85	33	14	38	136	146	80
7	Bolivia (11)	59	11	8	40	63	196	30
8	Colombia (6)	41	9	6	26	44	116	24
9	Ecuador (12)	65	3	11	51	62	220	17
10	Venezuela (2)	9	1	0	8	8	42	2

Scoring Leaders

1916	Oradin (Uru), 3
1917	Romano (Uru), 4
1919	Neco (Bra), 4
1920	Perez (Uru), 4
1921	—
1922	Francia (Arg), 4
1923	Aguirre (Arg) and Petrone (Uru), 4
1924	Petrone (Uru), 4
1925	M. Seoane (Arg), 6
1926	Scarone (Uru) and Castro (Uru), 6
1927	Carricaberry-Luna (Arg), Petrone (Uru), Scarone (Uru), and Figueroa (Uru), 3
1929	Gonzalez (Par), 5
1935	Massantonio (Arg), 4
1937	Roro (Chi), 7
1939	Fernandez (Per), 7
1941	Marvezzi (Arg), 5
1942	Moreno (Arg), 5
1945	Menendez (Arg), 7
1946	Medina (Uru), 7
1947	Menendez (Arg) and Fallero (Uru), 6
1949	Pinto (Bra), 6
1953	Molina (Chi), 7
1955	Micheli (Arg), 7
1956	Hormazabel (Chi), 4
1957	Maschio (Arg) and Ambrosis (Uru), 9
1959	Pelé (Bra), 8
1963	Sanfilippo (Arg), 6
1967	Rodriguez (Arg), Zárate (Par), and Raffo (Ecu), 5
1975	Artime (Arg), 5

Standings

1916 (in Buenos Aires)

	P	W	D	L	F	A	P
Uruguay	3	2	1	0	6	1	5
Argentina	3	1	2	0	7	2	4
Brazil	3	0	2	1	3	4	2
Chile	3	0	1	2	2	11	1

1917 (in Montevideo)

	P	W	D	L	F	A	P
Uruguay	3	3	0	0	9	0	6
Argentina	3	2	0	1	5	3	4
Brazil	3	1	0	2	7	8	2
Chile	3	0	0	3	0	10	0

1919 (in Rio de Janeiro)

	P	W	D	L	F	A	P
Brazil	3	2	1	0	11	3	5
Uruguay	3	2	1	0	7	4	5
Argentina	3	1	0	2	7	7	2
Chile	3	0	0	3	1	12	0

Play-off:
Brazil—Uruguay   1-0

1920 (in Valparaiso)

	P	W	D	L	F	A	P
Uruguay	3	2	1	0	9	2	5
Argentina	3	1	2	0	4	2	4
Brazil	3	1	0	2	1	8	2
Chile	3	0	1	2	2	4	1

1921 (in Buenos Aires)

	P	W	D	L	F	A	P
Uruguay	3	3	0	0	5	0	6
Brazil	3	1	0	2	4	3	2
Uruguay	3	1	0	2	3	4	2
Paraguay	3	1	0	2	2	7	2

1922 (in Rio de Janeiro)

	P	W	D	L	F	A	P
Brazil	4	1	3	0	4	2	5
Paraguay	4	2	1	1	5	3	5
Uruguay*	4	2	1	1	3	1	5
Argentina	4	2	0	2	6	3	4
Chile	4	0	1	3	1	10	1

Play-off:
Brazil—Paraguay   3-2

*Uruguay withdrew after its last game against Paraguay, in which two
Uruguayan goals were disallowed.

1923 (in Montevideo)

	P	W	D	L	F	A	P
Uruguay	3	3	0	0	6	1	6
Argentina	3	2	0	1	6	6	4
Paraguay	3	1	0	2	4	6	2
Brazil	3	0	0	3	2	5	0

1924 (in Montevideo)

	P	W	D	L	F	A	P
Uruguay	3	2	1	0	8	1	5
Argentina	3	1	2	0	2	0	4
Paraguay	3	1	1	1	4	4	3
Chile	3	0	0	3	1	10	0

1925 (home and away basis)

	P	W	D	L	F	A	P
Argentina	4	3	1	0	11	4	7
Brazil	4	2	1	1	11	9	5
Paraguay	4	0	0	4	4	13	0

1926 (in Santiago)

	P	W	D	L	F	A	P
Uruguay	4	4	0	0	17	2	8
Argentina	4	2	1	1	14	3	5
Chile	4	2	1	1	14	6	5
Paraguay	4	1	0	3	8	20	2
Bolivia	4	0	0	4	2	24	0

1927 (in Lima)

	P	W	D	L	F	A	P
Argentina	3	3	0	0	15	4	6
Uruguay	3	2	0	1	15	3	4
Peru	3	1	0	2	4	11	2
Bolivia	3	0	0	3	3	19	0

1929 (in Buenos Aires)

	P	W	D	L	F	A	P
Argentina	3	3	0	0	9	1	6
Paraguay	3	2	0	1	9	4	4
Uruguay	3	1	0	2	4	6	2
Peru	3	0	0	3	1	12	0

1935 (in Lima)

	P	W	D	L	F	A	P
Uruguay	3	3	0	0	6	1	6
Argentina	3	2	0	1	8	5	4
Peru	3	1	0	2	2	5	2
Chile	3	0	0	3	2	7	0

1936-37 (in Buenos Aires)

	P	W	D	L	F	A	P
Argentina	5	4	0	1	12	7	8
Brazil	5	4	0	1	17	9	8
Paraguay	5	2	0	3	10	16	4
Uruguay	5	2	0	3	11	14	4
Chile	5	1	1	3	12	13	3
Peru	5	1	1	3	7	10	3

Play-off:
Argentina—Brazil 2-0

1939 (in Lima)

	P	W	D	L	F	A	P
Peru	4	4	0	0	13	4	8
Uruguay	4	3	0	1	13	5	6
Paraguay	4	2	0	2	9	8	4
Chile	4	1	0	3	8	12	2
Ecuador	4	0	0	4	4	18	0

1941 (in Santiago)

	P	W	D	L	F	A	P
Argentina	4	4	0	0	10	2	8
Uruguay	4	3	0	1	10	1	6
Chile	4	2	0	2	6	3	4
Peru	4	1	0	3	5	5	2
Ecuador	4	0	0	4	1	21	0

1942 (in Montevideo)

	P	W	D	L	F	A	P
Uruguay	6	6	0	0	21	2	12
Argentina	6	4	1	1	11	6	9
Brazil	6	3	1	2	15	7	7
Paraguay	6	3	1	2	12	10	7
Chile*	6	1	2	3	4	15	4
Peru	6	1	1	4	5	11	3
Ecuador	6	0	0	6	4	21	0

1945 (in Santiago)

	P	W	D	L	F	A	P
Argentina	6	5	1	0	22	5	11
Brazil	6	5	0	1	19	5	10
Chile	6	4	1	1	15	4	9
Uruguay	6	3	0	3	14	6	6
Colombia	6	1	1	4	7	25	3
Bolivia	6	0	2	4	3	16	2
Ecuador	6	0	1	5	8	27	1

1946 (in Buenos Aires)

	P	W	D	L	F	A	P
Argentina	5	5	0	0	17	3	10
Brazil	5	3	1	1	13	7	7
Paraguay	5	2	1	2	8	8	5
Uruguay	5	2	0	3	11	9	4
Chile	5	2	0	3	8	11	4
Bolivia	5	0	0	5	4	23	0

1947 (in Guayaquil)

	P	W	D	L	F	A	P
Argentina	7	6	1	0	28	4	13
Paraguay	7	5	1	1	16	11	11
Uruguay	7	5	0	2	21	8	10
Chile	7	4	1	2	14	13	9
Peru	7	2	2	3	12	9	6
Ecuador	7	0	3	4	3	17	3
Bolivia	7	0	2	5	6	21	2
Colombia	7	0	2	5	2	19	2

*Chile withdrew from its last game and defaulted

1949 (in Brazil)

	P	W	D	L	F	A	P
Brazil	7	6	0	1	39	7	12
Paraguay	7	6	0	1	21	6	12
Peru	7	5	0	2	20	13	10
Bolivia	7	4	0	3	13	24	8
Uruguay	7	2	1	4	14	20	5
Chile	7	2	1	4	10	14	5
Ecuador	7	1	0	6	7	21	2
Colombia	7	0	2	5	4	23	2

Play-off:
Brazil—Paraguay   7-0

1953 (in Lima)

	P	W	D	L	F	A	P
Paraguay*	6	4	2	0	10	4	8
Brazil	6	4	0	2	15	6	8
Uruguay	6	3	0	3	13	5	6
Chile	6	3	1	2	10	10	7
Peru	6	2	2	2	4	6	6
Bolivia	6	1	1	4	6	15	3
Ecuador	6	0	2	4	1	13	2

Play-off:
Paraguay—Brazil   3-2

1955 (in Santiago)

	P	W	D	L	F	A	P
Argentina	5	4	1	0	18	6	9
Chile	5	3	1	1	19	8	7
Peru	5	2	2	1	13	11	6
Uruguay	5	2	1	2	12	12	5
Paraguay	5	1	1	3	7	14	3
Ecuador	5	0	0	5	4	22	0

*Two points for Paraguay's win over Chile were rescinded because of a substitution violation; play-off organized by Parguayan Football League

1956 (in Montevideo)

	P	W	D	L	F	A	P
Uruguay	5	4	1	0	9	3	9
Brazil	5	3	2	0	7	2	8
Argentina	5	3	0	2	5	3	6
Chile	5	2	0	3	8	11	4
Paraguay	5	0	2	3	3	8	2
Peru	5	0	1	4	6	11	1

1957 (in Lima)

	P	W	D	L	F	A	P
Argentina	6	5	0	1	25	6	10
Brazil	6	4	0	2	23	9	8
Uruguay	6	4	0	2	15	12	8
Peru	6	4	0	2	12	9	8
Colombia	6	2	0	4	10	25	4
Chile	6	1	1	4	9	17	3
Ecuador	6	0	1	5	7	23	1

1959 (in Buenos Aires)

	P	W	D	L	F	A	P
Argentina	6	5	1	0	19	5	1
Brazil	6	4	2	0	17	7	10
Paraguay	6	3	0	3	12	12	6
Chile	6	2	1	3	9	14	5
Peru	6	1	3	2	10	11	5
Uruguay	6	2	0	4	15	14	4
Bolivia	6	0	1	5	4	23	1

1959 (in Guayaquil)

	P	W	D	L	F	A	P
Uruguay	4	3	1	0	13	1	7
Argentina	4	2	1	1	9	9	5
Brazil	4	2	0	2	7	10	4
Ecuador	4	1	1	2	5	9	3
Paraguay	4	0	1	3	6	11	1

1963 (in La Paz)

	P	W	D	L	F	A	P
Bolivia	6	5	1	0	19	13	11
Paraguay	6	4	1	1	13	7	9
Argentina	6	3	1	2	15	10	7
Brazil	6	2	1	3	12	13	5
Peru	6	2	1	3	8	11	5
Ecuador	6	1	2	3	14	18	4
Colombia	6	0	1	5	10	19	1

1967 (in Montevideo)

	P	W	D	L	F	A	P
Uruguay	5	4	1	0	13	2	9
Argentina	5	4	0	1	12	3	8
Chile	5	2	2	1	8	6	6
Paraguay	5	2	0	3	9	13	4
Venezuela	5	1	0	4	7	16	2
Bolivia	5	0	1	4	0	9	1

1975
Group 1

	P	W	D	L	F	A	P
Brazil	4	4	0	0	13	1	8
Argentina	4	2	0	2	17	4	4
Venezuela	4	0	0	4	1	26	0

Group 2

	P	W	D	L	F	A	P
Peru	4	3	1	0	8	3	7
Chile	4	1	1	2	7	6	3
Bolivia	4	1	0	3	3	9	2

Group 3

	P	W	D	L	F	A	P
Colombia	4	4	0	0	7	1	8
Paraguay	4	1	1	2	5	5	3
Ecuador	4	0	1	3	4	10	1

Semi-Finals
*Colombia—Uruguay   3-0, 0-1
*Brazil—Peru   1-3, 2-0
(Peru won on choice of card)

*home team in first leg

Finals

Colombia (Castro)	1	Peru	0
Peru (Zarate og, Ramirez)	2	Colombia	0
Play-off (in Caracas): Peru (Sotil)	1	Colombia	0

Sudan

Sudan Football Association
P. O. Box 437
Khartoum

Founded: 1936
FIFA: 1948
CAF: 1956

Affiliated clubs: *750;* **registered players:** *36,840;* **national stadium:** *Khartoum Stadium, Khartoum (30,000);* **largest stadium:** *Mereikh Stadium, Omdurman (60,000);* **colors:** *white jerseys, white shorts;* **season:** *July to June;* **honors:** *African Nations' Cup winner (1970), runner-up (1957, 1959, 1963).*

Sudan, a pioneer in African soccer, shared domination over the continent with Egypt during the late 1950s and early 1960s, and in one last ditch effort in 1970 finally won Africa's most coveted prize. Sudanese independence in 1956 was the catalyst for the formation of the African Football Confederation, of which Sudan was a founding-member, and for many years Sudanese officials played a leading role in its administration. Sudanese clubs have not had the success of their national team in African competition, but soccer has a great following in the major population centers. The Sudanese game is at its most active in four provinces—Khartoum, Blue Nile, Kordofan, and Kassala—where the country's predominantly Islamic population has historically received the greatest exposure to British and other foreign elements. In the rest of this vast microcosm of African culture, the tribal bushmen and desert nomads have been slow to adopt the national sport.

The Sudanese watched British soldiers play soccer in the streets of Khartoum during the years after Lord Kitchener's famous military takeover in 1898. After World War I, small numbers of Sudanese began to get involved with the game in Khartoum, Omdurman (the sprawling residential city across the Nile from Khartoum), Khartoum North (the commer-

cial and industrial center across the Nile from Khartoum in the other direction), Port Sudan (the country's only port), and Wad Medani (the cotton production center up the Blue Nile). In 1936, the British helped the Sudanese set up the Sudan Football Association (SFA), and after World War II interest in the game increased substantially. The SFA joined FIFA in 1948. In 1950-51, the Sudan Cup Competition was introduced with 16 clubs playing under a knockout format. By this time, there were over 200 clubs and 5,500 registered players, all but a few being Sudanese nationals, and seven stadiums with a capacity of 5000 or more. The first recorded international involving Sudan was an unofficial 8-0 loss to France (Amateur) in 1956 at a multinational invitational tournament in Bamako, Mali.

In 1956, when Sudan was still one of only three countries in the region affiliated with FIFA, the Egyptian F.A. seized upon the new political climate created by Sudan's recently enacted independence, and invited Sudan and Ethiopia to join with it in forming the African Football Confederation (CAF). To celebrate Sudan's independence, Khartoum was selected as the site for the first CAF congress and the first African Nations' Cup competition in 1957. Sudan's 2-1 loss to Egypt in this two-day tournament represents its official debut in international competition. On the basis of this narrow score, Sudan was declared the runner-up, because Ethiopia lost to Egypt, 4-0. Sudan and Ethiopia did not play one another.

Sudan took second place again in 1959, when it defeated Ethiopia and lost to Egypt. Political instabilities at home kept Sudan out of the 1962 edition, but in 1963 Sudan entered once again and gained second place for the third time in a row. The Sudanese won their first round group with a 4-0 defeat of Nigeria and a 2-2 draw with Egypt. In the final, the mighty Ghanaians, trailblazers of black African soccer, defeated them 3-0 on a pair of goals by the redoubtable Wilberforce Mfum. Sudan failed to qualify in 1965 and 1968, but in 1970, with political calm restored at home, Sudan played host to the tournament and qualified automatically. Its aging and unexciting team was bouyed greatly by the fanaticism of its fans, and in the first round it managed to defeat Ethiopia and Cameroon, providing passage to the semi-finals. In the semi-final, Sudan defeated its archrival, Egypt, by 2-1, and entered the final against Ghana in Khartoum. The Sudanese fans were now demanding a Nations' Cup victory after so many second place finishes, and when Sudan's second goal was disallowed by the referee with the score 1-0, they rioted. Ghanaian players were attacked on the field, a melee broke out, and the police were called in. At the final whistle, the score stood at 1-0 in Sudan's favor, and the disgusted Ghanaians left the stadium without accepting the runner-up trophy. Government leader Col. Ga'afer Mohamed Nimeri, acting on behalf of his people's sentiments at the time, ordered the Ghanaian team out of the country that night.

Sudanese clubs participated in the African Champions' Cup from its inception in 1964, depending on the political climate at home, but they have achieved little. The two most successful Sudanese clubs are Mareikh and Hilal, both of Omdurman, perennial champions since the late 1960s. Their home stadiums are the largest facilities in the country—bigger even than the national stadium across the river in Khartoum—with capacities of 60,000 and 45,000, respectively.

In 1972, Sudan attained a second great international plateau by qualifying for the Olympic Games in Munich. Its opposition in the first round was formidable. It lost successive matches to Mexico's amateurs (1-0), the USSR full international team (2-1), and Burma's full international team (2-0), placing last in its group. Its low scoring result against the Russians, however, was considered tantamount to an upset.

Bleak days were ahead for Sudanese soccer. In 1972, Sudan played poorly in the final rounds of the African Nations' Cup, and in 1974 did not even qualify. In the 1976 final rounds, it failed to win a single game because of a sweeping reordering of political priorities at home. Early in 1976, the SFA was put under the auspices of the new General Association for Popular Sports, and was ordered to align itself more closely with the ideals of the Sudanese Socialist Union. Interaction with foreign governing bodies was severely limited, and all existing clubs were dissolved. All sports competitions were confined to the local level, ruling out international matches, at least for the time being. Mareikh withdrew from the 1976 African Champions' Cup before the first round, and the national team, once one of Africa's most feared powers, forfeited the first round of the 1978 World Cup qualification tournament to Kenya.

summer tournaments

The summer off-season in Europe has customarily been a period for friendly club competition of all kinds, often involving visits abroad or at least across the nearest border. In Spain, the European capital of summer tournaments, leading clubs from all over the world are invited to compete in small competitions lasting two weeks or less, maintaining a Spanish tradition that was begun in the early 1950s. Dozens of cities on the Iberian peninsula play host to these tournaments, and the pleasing summer climate of the region provides a suitable backdrop. The tournaments give clubs a chance to regroup after the previous season, test new players, meet famous clubs from other countries, and, above all, gain additional revenue. Many of the greatest clubs of Europe and South America take part on a regular basis.

The following is a list of extant Spanish summer competitions (as of 1977): Trofeo

Carranza (Cádiz), Ciudad de Barcelona, Ciudad de Cordoba, Ciudad de Granada, Ciudad de La Linea, Ciudad de León, Ciudad de Palma de Mallorca, Ciudad de Santa Cruz de Tenerife, Ciudad de Sevilla, Ciudad de Tarrasa, Ciudad de Valladolid, Ciudad de Vigo, Ciudad de Zaragoza, Trofeo Colombina (Huelva), Trofeo Conde de Fenosa (La Coruña), Costa del Sol (Malaga), Trofeo Costa Verde (Gijon), Trofeo Festa d'Elig (Elche), Trofeo Iberica (Badajoz), Trofeo Juan Gamper (Barcelona), Trofeo Naranja (Valencia), Principe de España (Santander), Trofeo Tiede (Tenerife), Teresa Herrera (La Coruña), Villa de Bilbao, and Villa de Madrid.

To cite just one example of the breadth and scope of the Spanish summer tournaments, the participants in the Trofeo Carranza in Cádiz, since its introduction in 1955, have included the following giants of international competition: Peñarol, Nacional, Benfica, Torino, Inter, AC Milan, Racing Club de Paris, Stade de Reims, Ajax, Flamengo, Botafogo, Corinthians Paulista, Vasco de Gama, Palmeiras, Bayern München, Eintracht Frankfurt, Boca Júniors, Independiente, Estudiantes, Standard Liège, Atlético Madrid, Barcelona, and Real Madrid.

"Sunday shot"

A colloquial term to indicate a very long or otherwise almost impossible shot on goal, which in fact results in a goal. It is that kind of shot a player might try hundreds of times during practice sessions without success, and the one time it is attempted during a league match on Sunday the ball goes in.

Super Cup [i]

An unofficial competition between the winners of the European Champions' Cup and the European Cup Winners' Cup. It is usually held in the first half of the following season, and is played on a home and away basis, with the winner determined by goal aggregate.

The series was instigated by the Dutch newspaper *De Telegraaf* in 1972 after Ajax Amsterdam won its second European Champions' Cup in succession. It was not sanctioned by UEFA until the second edition, and the European governing body has consistently refused to become its official sponsor. A cup, as such, is not awarded, rather a commemorative plaque is given to each winner. Its continued existence hangs in balance from year to year, depending on the response of its participants.

Results

1972 (played in 1973)   Ajax

| Rangers | 1 | Ajax | 3 |
| (MacDonald) | | (Rep, Cruyff, Haan) | |

| Ajax | 3 | Rangers | 2 |
| (Haan, Muhren, Cruyff) | | (Young, MacDonald) | |

1973 (played in 1974)   Ajax

| AC Milan | 1 | Ajax | 0 |
| (Chiarugi) | | | |

Ajax (Mulder, Keizer, Neeskens, Rep, Haan, Muhren pen)	6	AC Milan	0

1974   (no competition; the scheduled participants, Bayern München and FC Magdeburg, were drawn by chance to meet in the second round of the European Champions' Cup—1974-75 edition—which Bayern won, 3-2 and 2-1, and it was decided that the results of these matches would determine the Super Cup winner for 1974)

1975   Dinamo Kiev

Bayern München	0	Dinamo Kiev (Blokhin)	1
Dinamo Kiev (Blokhin 2)	2	Bayern München	0

1976   RSC Anderlecht

Bayern München (Müller)	2	RSC Anderlecht (Haan)	1
RSC Anderlecht (Rensenbrink 2, van der Elst, Haan)	4	Bayern München (Müller)	1

1977   Liverpool

Hamburger SV (Keller)	1	Liverpool (Fairclough)	1
Liverpool (McDermott 3, Thompson, Fairclough, Dalglish)	6	Hamburger SV	0

1978   RSC Anderlecht

RSC Anderlecht (Vercauteren, van der Elst, Rensenbrink)	3	Liverpool (Case)	1
Liverpool (Hughes, Fairclough)	2	RSC Anderlecht (Van der Elst)	1

Super Cup [ii]

An international club competition that was not completed in either of its two editions. It sought to bring together the European and South American clubs that had previously won the European Champions' Cup or Copa Libertadores more than once: Real Madrid, Benfica, and Internazionale from Europe and Santos, Penarol, and Independiente from South America. The aborted 1968-69 edition, in which some of the eligible clubs did not participate, ended after one leg of a final between Santos and Internazionale, won by the former, 1-0. In 1969-70, the European legs were not completed, and Penarol, having won the South American legs, was awarded the trophy.

Surinam

Surinaamse Voetbal Bond
Cultuurtuinlaan 7
P.O. Box 1223
Paramaribo

Founded: 1920
FIFA: 1929
CONCACAF: ?

Affiliated clubs: *174;* registered players: *3,810;* national stadium: *Suriname Stadion, Paramaribo (20,000);* largest stadium: *Suriname Stadion;* colors: *green & white jerseys, white shorts;* season: *March to December;* honors: *Transvaal, Championship of CONCACAF Club Champions (1973), co-winner (1970).*

The story of soccer in former Dutch Guiana closely parallels that of the Netherlands Antilles, the other former Dutch colony in the Caribbean region, except that Surinam has been considerably less adventurous in international competition. Yet Surinam is by far the most advanced of the three Guianas in all aspects of the game, despite the head start received by Guyana (former British Guiana). Dutch colonists laid a strong foundation for a Surinamese game, and passed the baton to an enthusiastic soccer-playing population. In a country of curious racial diversity, the creoles (Surinamese-born blacks) took the lead when it came to soccer—nearly all the leading players have come from this group—while some "hindustanis" (Asian Indians), Indonesians, and Chinese are active at the lower levels.

The Surinaamse Voetbal Bond (Surinam Football Association) was founded in 1920, one year before the Curaçao association in the Netherlands Antilles, and a championship was introduced in 1923-24. The first winner was Olympia, and the second was Transvaal, still a leading club in Paramaribo today. The pre-World War II era was dominated by Cicerone, but championships were also won by Ajax and Excelsior. Three cup competitions were also launched before World War II. The Dragten Cup (1929) was first won by Ajax and subsequently by Vorwaarts, Cicerone and Transvaal. The Emancipatie Cup (1929), whose first winner was Ajax, was dominated by the same clubs, as, indeed, was the short-lived Bueno Cup (1933-35). In 1934, a championship for representative teams of the four sub-associations was launched for Moengo, Nickerie, Coronie, and Commewyne.

The Surinaamse Voetbal Bond (SVB) joined FIFA in 1929, having secured permission from the Netherlands, and Surinam made its international debut in 1934 against Curaçao met nine times before World War II. Surinam won two of these and lost six. In 1934, the Surinam selection visited Port of Spain and held Trinidad to a 3-3 draw. Unlike Curaçao, however, Surinam did not participate in either the Central American and Caribbean Games or the Championship of the Central American and Caribbean Confederation that was introduced in 1941. Surinam did not become a member of the confederation until the early 1950s, and it was only then that it began to participate in the regional championship. Its interest in regional competition continued when the Championship of CONCACAF was introduced in 1963. Surinam has entered the last several World Cup qualifying rounds, and saw its first measure of success in 1976-77 when it advanced to the final group of six. The national team's most stunning victory, however, has been a 2-1 upset of Denmark on a recent European tour.

The domestic picture in Surinam became confused as early as 1924, when a rival national association was set up called the Nederlands Guyanese Voetbal Bond (NGVB). Its league ran in competition with the SVB's, and there was little interaction between members of one association and the other. The matter was finally brought under control in 1952 by SVB president Emile de la Fuente, who incorporated the NGVB into the SVB and turned it into a governing body for youth soccer called the Geformeerde Voetbal Bond

(NIEUW). The last vestige of the old NGVB is in the name of its stadium—NGVB Stadion—which is still situated in northern Paramaribo.

In the present national league, nine clubs make up the Surinamese first division, and each year the top clubs compete in the coveted Sterrentoernooi (Tournament of Stars). The leading clubs in recent years have been Transvaal, Robin Hood, and Vorwaarts, from which the national team is normally selected. Transvaal has been one of the Caribbean region's most successful clubs, having shared the CONCACAF club championship in 1970 and won it outright in 1973.

Sweden

Svenska Fotbollförbundet
Box 1216
S-171 23 Solna 1

Founded: 1904
FIFA: 1904
UEFA: 1954

Affiliated clubs: *3,016;* **registered players:** *127,655 (95,115 non-amateur);* **national stadium:** *Fotbollstadion, Solna (52,000);* **stadium of equal size:** *Ullevi, Göteborg (52,000);* **colors:** *yellow jerseys, blue shorts;* **season:** *April to October;* **honors:** *World Cup runner-up (1958), third place (1950), Olympic Games winner (1948), third place (1924, 1952), Scandinavian Championship (1936, 1947, 1951, 1955, 1959, 1967, 1971).*

Sweden ranks as one of the world's most successful soccer-playing countries in proportion to its size. It has won a host of important trophies, and in playing an unusually full schedule within a short season, Sweden has produced several outstanding players of world-class caliber. Between the world wars, Sweden took over the lead in Scandinavian soccer from Denmark, and in the postwar era has defeated every world power in its schedule at least once, including Brazil, England, West Germany, Hungary, and Uruguay. This has been accomplished without the benefit of full-time professionalism and in spite of the ceaseless poaching of its best players by wealthy clubs in Europe. Its ability to rejuvenate its international strength with each new generation of players has been little short of awesome. The exodus of players to the continent, however, has thwarted Swedish clubs in their quest for European honors, and its lack of success in this regard is its only weakness. Sweden's most successful club in international competition, Malmö FF, ranks

about 85th in overall European standings.

The details of the birth of Swedish soccer are hazy, but it is certain that the game was played in Gothenburg (Göteborg) and Stockholm as early as the 1870s. British embassy personnel in Stockholm and Scottish textile workers in Gothenburg are credited with introducing both soccer and rugby, but until 1891 it is difficult to separate the development of the two games. The first soccer club was probably Örgryte IS from Gothenburg, founded by Scots, and the city of Gothenburg has continued to be Sweden's most important soccer hotbed. In 1891, the Velocipede (Cyclists') Ball Club in Malmö translated and circulated a set of soccer rules from England, and from there the game grew into the most popular of summer sports. Rugby faded into the background, and for the first time a uniform playing code was followed.

In 1895-96, the Svenska Sport- och Idrottsförening (Swedish Sports and Athletic Association), based in Gothenburg, introduced an annual championship that was open to local clubs only. Örgryte won the first four editions, and when a small number of Stockholm clubs were brought into the fold in 1899-1900, the big Stockholm club of the day, Allmänna Idrottsklubben (AIK), or General Sports Club, won a pair of titles in succession. Örgryte returned to the top in 1902 with six championships in eight years, punctuated with two wins by the second major Gothenburg club, Idrottsföreningen Kamraterna (IFK). Örgryte went on to accumulate 13 championships before 1928, which still stands as a Swedish record. The league introduced by the Gothenburg association has remained the national league of Sweden, but until 1924-25 it was played on a knockout basis. AIK and another important Stockholm club, Djurgårdens FF, dominated the league before and during World War I, but this was the last time Sweden's capital and largest city held such power.

The unofficial Svenska Fotbollförbundet (Swedish Football Association) was founded in 1902 to break the control of Gothenburg's sports association, but the present SFF was actually formed in 1904, prompted by the founding of FIFA earlier in the year. The unofficial SFF was a charter-member of FIFA. It took four years to mount a national team for international competition; the spark that caused this move was the official inclusion of soccer in the 1908 Olympics—soccer's first foray into official international competition. To prepare for the Olympics Sweden met Norway in Gothenburg, where the only decent playing fields in the region were located. The result was a resounding 11-3 victory in Sweden's favor. At the 1908 Olympics, however, Sweden had the misfortune of facing Great Britain's amateur team in the first round, and lost 12-1. In the third place game, the Swedes lost to Holland by a respectable 2-1, and placed fourth overall in a field of six.

Between the London games in 1908 and the next Olympics in 1912 (which took place in Stockholm), Sweden played as busy an international schedule as other developing powers of the time—10 matches in all—and of these won six. It split home and away friendlies with Germany, drew with Hungary, defeated Norway and Finland several times, and lost to Belgium and Holland. The Dutch put Sweden out of the Olympic tournament in 1912 before a disappointed home crowd, and in the consolation series Italy defeated Sweden, 1-0, behind the wondrous display of Renzo ("the son of God") De Vecchi. Like

Denmark and Norway, Sweden continued its international activity throughout World War I, which included at least one uncommon non-European opponent, the United States, in a 3-2 loss at Stockholm in 1916. Its rivalry with Denmark began in 1913 with the first of five successive losses. These five internationals produced a negative goal difference of 0-24, indicating the Danes' decisive head start during those early years. Sweden's biannual contests with Norway, on the other hand, resulted more often than not in substantial victories.

At the 1920 Olympics in Antwerp, the fledgling Greeks were an easy obstacle to overcome, but once again Holland won after extra time in the second round, and in the special play-off for second and third place the rapidly improving Spanish team held on for a narrow victory. Central European opponents entered Sweden's schedule in 1921 with generally unsuccessful results from Sweden's point of view, and England's full international team arrived in Stockholm for the first time in 1923 to win back-to-back games. The relatively close margins of its losses to England and its subsequent wins over Austria and Germany paved the way for Sweden's first international honors at the 1924 Olympic Games in Paris. Huge wins over Belgium and Egypt in the first and second round were followed by a narrow loss to Switzerland in the semi-finals. In the third place game, the Swedes finally overcame the Dutch nemesis and defeated Holland in the replay of an earlier draw to take the bronze medal.

In 1924, having already played in 25 internationals with Norway, 16 with Denmark, and 10 with Finland, Sweden and its three neighbors introduced the Scandinavian Championship, the results of which are determined on a league basis over a period of three years. The first two editions (1924-29 and 1929-32) were won by Denmark and, surprisingly, Norway. While the first outcome was entirely expected, the second was attributed as much to Denmark's weakness during that period as to Norway's newly found (and temporary) strength. Sweden lost three of its four contests with Norway during that series while splitting results evenly with Denmark. Its growing power, however, was proven by winning the third edition in 1933-36, and in seven subsequent editions of this competition the Swedes have won all but one, the exception being Finland's surprise of 1960-63.

With only Estonia and Lithuania to overcome in the qualification rounds, Sweden entered its first World Cup in 1934. Little was expected of Sweden, but Argentina, now depleted of its great players from the 1930 championship, was not able to unravel the Swedes' effective teamwork, and Sweden's left wing Knut Kroon scored the winning goal late in the second half. In the second round, Sweden lost one of its players through injury, but the result had already been decided as Germany bludgeoned its way to a 2-1 win. Sweden left Italy with its first taste of World Cup success, and began its work on the development of more skillful players to add to its natural inclination for solid teamwork. This, however, was to come several years in the future. Sweden's first jolting disappointment in world competition came in the 1936 Olympics in Berlin with a 3-2 loss to Japan, a previously unknown force from the far reaches of Asian soccer.

In the 1938 World Cup, which Sweden reached after eliminating Finland and Estonia in qualifying rounds, more predictable losses were suffered at the hands of Hungary and Brazil, both budding world powers, but not before Norrköping's Gustav Wetterström had scored four goals (a World Cup co-record) in a colossal 8-0 win over Cuba in early rounds. This drew international attention to Sweden and the possibility that Sweden was indeed able to turn out excellent individual players. The win over Cuba put Sweden in the semi-finals against Hungary. But according to a popular tale, Zsengeller, Dr. Sarosi, and other Hungarian forwards so dominated this match that a large bird landed in the Hungarian part of the field and was left undisturbed for most of the second half. The final score was 5-1 in Hungary's favor, but it might well have been higher. In the third place game, Sweden performed admirably against Brazil, but the incomparable Leônidas and the other Brazilian ball artists were more than Sweden could contain. In losing 4-2, Sweden, dubbed "the team of steel" by the press, settled willfully for a fourth place finish in the World Championship. It was a remarkable feat, undiminished by Sweden's losses to Hungary and Brazil. Sweden's last non-Scandinavian opponent before the outbreak of war was little Lithuania, which journeyed to Karlståd only to be trounced 7-0 in its final international as an independent nation.

Finland and Switzerland provided some opposition during World War II and allowed a degree of continuity in Swedish soccer when the game in other countries came to a grinding halt. In 1941, the first national cup competition, His Majesty's Cup (now the Svenska Cupen), was introduced and was won by IF Hälsingborg, the dominant power in the league during the 1930s. The league continued to flourish during the war, and so did the growth of highly skilled players. The Scandinavian Championship edition that had started in 1937 was resumed in 1945 only days after the liberation of Denmark, and when this was finally completed in 1947, Sweden's second successive title was won by a huge margin. Between the resumption of play in 1945 and the Olympic Games of 1948, Sweden won 16 games and lost four, non-Scandinavian opponents providing three of these losses.

In 1948, Sweden's national team was taken over by the Englishman George Raynor, who instituted coaching clinics and coalesced Swedish soccer interests in support of his team. At the 1948 Olympics, Sweden not only entered with the best team in the competition, but looked the equal of any professionally based team in Europe. Sweden's success in this tournament was achieved at a time when the state-paid "amateur" countries of Eastern Europe had yet to initiate their domination of postwar Olympiads. The best players in England, Italy and other big power countries had long since turned professional, but no one doubted Sweden's ability to hold its own with the best of them, Hungary being the lone exception. In London, Austria, Korea, and Denmark went down in quick succession by an aggregate score of 19-2, and in the final Sweden defeated the superlative "A" team of Yugoslavia, 3-1, to win the gold medal.

Never before or since has Sweden produced such a fine collection of players. The team included three brothers, center forward Gunnar, center half Bertil, and right back Knut Nordahl, (all of whom played for IFK Norrköping), and featured inside right Gunnar Gren and left wing Nils Liedholm. The Gren-Nordahl-Liedholm combination on the forward line eventually became known fondly as "Grenoli," and dazzled crowds, as well as Italian and Spanish scouts, in the postwar era's first outstanding series of international performances. Their skills were so highly touted that all three Nordahls, Gren, Liedholm, and right wing Kjell Rosen were immediately snapped up by wealthy Italian clubs. AC Milan, in fact, secured the entire "Grenoli" trio, and Gunnar Nordahl went on to shatter Italian league goalscoring records. Liedholm is still in Italy today working as a manager. Inside left Garvis Carlsson, meanwhile, went to Atlético Madrid.

Only Knut Nordahl and left back Erik Nilsson of the 1948 team were able to join the Swedish squad that qualified for the 1950 World Cup in Brazil. George Raynor, however, disciplined and popular as ever with his players, had discovered inside right Kalle Palmer and a counterpart on the left side, "Nacka" Skoglund. In Brazil, Sweden defeated Italy 3-2 (eight members of this Swedish team were eventually signed by Italian clubs), and drew with Paraguay before entering the final pool of four teams. But Brazil's extraordinary talents were too strong and skillful for what was virtually a "B" Swedish team, and Brazil routed the Swedes, 7-1. This was followed by Sweden's 3-2 loss to Uruguay, eventual winner of the competition, and the series was closed with Sweden's fine 3-1 win over Spain, which captured third place in the World Championship for a country that was, after all, depleted of its best players—an extraordinary accomplishment. Raynor's next task was to retain Sweden's Olympic gold medal in the 1952 games at Helsinki. This proved to be a more competitive Olympic tournament than the last, and no team in the world could have stopped Hungary from winning a deserved first place. Had it not been for an unlucky draw of opponents in the semi-finals, however, Sweden would likely have won the silver. As it happened, Sweden met Hungary in the semi-finals instead of West Germany or Yugoslavia, and crashed by six unanswered goals. Sweden settled instead for a respectable third place and a bronze medal after brushing aside West Germany in the third place game. In the space of five years, Sweden won Olympic gold and bronze medals and took third place in the World Championship with virtually two separate teams. The price they paid for victory was high, however, as Swedish clubs were now stripped of all their major stars as a result of their exposure to the outside world.

The 1950 and 1952 teams played without the stars of 1948 because the SFF refused to allow professionals of any kind on the national team. This rule was rescinded before the 1958 World Cup—held in Sweden—and paved the way for Sweden's greatest triumph of all and the homecoming of Nils Liedholm, now an inside left. It also marked the return to international competition of Gunnar Gren, now playing once again for a Swedish club.

They were joined by right wing Kurt Hamrin, from Padova in Italy, and the entire country was delighted by a nostalgic return to the glory days of 1948. Even George Raynor was at the helm after coaching in Italy and England.

It is unlikely that Swedish nationalism has ever surfaced quite so fervently as it did in the 1958 World Cup. In the first round, Sweden disposed of Mexico 3-0, and defeated the Hungarians on two deft goals by Hamrin. Though Wales held Sweden to a goalless draw, Sweden won its group without a defeat in three matches. In the quarter-finals, Hamrin led Sweden to a 2-0 shutout over the Russians, and Swedish fans shifted proudly into overdrive. The semi-final against West Germany took place in Sweden's soccer capital, Gothenburg, accounting, no doubt, for the noisiness of the crowd, but the game's intensity also rose because it was uncharacteristically violent. In a rare display of Swedish virulence, one German player was sent off and West Germany's star player, Fritz Walter, was injured and had to hobble through the rest of the game. Nonetheless, late in the second half Gren scored Sweden's third and clinching goal in a 3-1 win. Skeptical Swedes could hardly believe it, but Raynor's veterans had advanced to the final of the World Cup.

Unfortunately, Sweden's opponent in Stockholm had everything the Swedes lacked—speed, a host of sublime ball artists, and youth—these in addition to soccer's new sensation, Pelé. Brazil had been turning international soccer upside down with its brilliant displays in earlier rounds, unleashing not only Pelé but "the Little Bird," Garrincha, perhaps the greatest dribbler anyone had ever seen. There was no reason for Brazil to break this momentum, even for the much-respected Swedes. In the final, Hamrin and Skoglund were neutralized by Djalma Santos and Nilton Santos, yet Liedholm scored after only four minutes. It was an elusive early goal. Vavá scored twice in the first half, and with Pelé's first goal in the second half the game was virtually over. Mario Zagalo scored a fourth Brazilian goal, and Pelé scored his second to make it five, and though center forward Agne Simonsson gave Sweden its second goal, the final score of 5-2 was only partially indicative of just how much this scintillating Brazilian team deserved to win the World Cup.

Fine Swedish teams were seen in the years ahead—rarely have they been poor—but the era of 1948-58 was never again duplicated. Gren, G. Nordahl, Nils Liedholm, and Kurt

Hamrin remain the greatest Swedish forwards of all time, and during their heyday they were among the finest in the world. In 1962, Raynor barely missed taking Sweden to the World Cup again when a replay in Berlin was lost to the team of another veteran national manager, Karl Rappan's Switzerland. Success was not forthcoming in other competitions either. Sweden has not done well in the European Football Championship, and its ability to field "A" teams for the Olympic Games was diffused by the exodus of players during the 1950s.

In the Swedish league, which changed from a winter to a summer schedule in 1958-59, the postwar era has brought about numerous shifts of power. IFK Norrköping, the club of the Nordahls and Nils Liedholm, dominated the 1940s and '50s, but Malmö FF emerged after World War II and is now one championship short of tying Örgryte's ancient record for most league titles. Malmö, having gained the first division in 1936 and never been relegated, also holds the runaway record for most cup victories, and it has been the major Swedish club in both league and cup competition since the mid-1960s. The traditional powers—IFK Göteborg, AIK Stockholm, and Örgryte—have fallen out of their leadership roles, but they still play in the first division more often than not. IFK Göteborg, in fact, is still the best supported club in Sweden. Aside from these four clubs, GAIS Göteborg and IF Elfsborg (from the city of Boras) have spent the most seasons in the first division. Practically all the first division clubs down through the years have hailed from southern Sweden. The only club north of Stockholm that has ever won the league title was IF Brynäs from the coastal town of Gävle (1925).

Sweden made an inauspicious return to the World Cup in 1970 when a 1-1 draw with Israel ruined its chances for advancing to the second round. This was a good national team, but it lacked finishing power even with the presence of Feyenoord's European Cup hero Ove Kindvall. In 1974, Sweden returned to the World Championship again with a slow and unspectacular team that nevertheless held mighty Holland to a scoreless draw in the first round and advanced to the second round without a defeat. West Germany and Poland were vastly superior in second round wins, but Sweden did manage to defeat bewildered Yugoslavia. In Ronnie Hellström, Sweden had the finest goalkeeper in its history, and he has now become one of the three or four best in the world. With Hellström in the nets, Sweden qualified for the 1978 World Cup, its seventh in 10 attempts, but in Argentina it failed to score in losses to Spain and Austria, and finished last in its first round group. Once again, however, Sweden had to gather a team of players from all over Western Europe, and despite this handicap, showed that it can still play in the upper reaches of international competition—a testament to its high productivity and unifying spirit.

Meanwhile, Sweden's long-time captain and stopper, Björn Nordqvist, broke Bobby Moore's all-time world record for most international appearances with 115 by the end of 1978.

Champions

1896	Örgryte	1909	Örgryte
1897	Örgryte	1910	IFK Göteborg
1898	Örgryte	1911	AIK Stockholm
1899	Örgryte	1912	Djurgården
1900	AIK Stockholm	1913	Örgryte
1901	AIK Stockholm	1914	AIK Stockholm
1902	Örgryte	1915	Djurgården
1903	IFK Göteborg	1916	AIK Stockholm
1904	Örgryte	1917	Djurgården
1905	Örgryte	1918	IFK Göteborg
1906	Örgryte	1919	GAIS Göteborg
1907	Örgryte	1920	Djurgården
1908	IFK Göteborg	1921	IFK Eskilstuna

1922	GAIS Göteborg	1951	Malmö FF
1923	AIK Stockholm	1952	IFK Norrköping
1924	IF Göteborg Fässberg	1953	Malmö FF
1925	IF Brynäs Gävle/GAIS Göteborg	1954	GAIS Göteborg
1926	Örgryte	1955	Djurgården
1927	GAIS Göteborg	1956	IFK Norrköping
1928	Örgryte	1957	IFK Norrköping
1929	IF Hälsingborg	1958	IFK Göteborg
1930	IF Hälsingborg	1959	Djurgården
1931	GAIS Göteborg	1960	IFK Norrköping
1932	AIK Stockholm	1961	IF Elfsborg
1933	IF Hälsingborg	1962	IFK Norrköping
1934	IF Hälsingborg	1963	IFK Norrköping
1935	IFK Göteborg	1964	Djurgården
1936	IF Elfsborg	1965	Malmö FF
1937	AIK Stockholm	1966	Djurgården
1938	IF Sleipner	1967	Malmö FF
1939	IF Elfsborg	1968	Öster Växjö
1940	IF Elfsborg	1969	IFK Göteborg
1941	IF Hälsingborg	1970	Malmö FF
1942	IFK Göteborg	1971	Malmö FF
1943	IFK Norrköping	1972	Åtvidaberg
1944	Malmö FF	1973	Åtvidaberg
1945	IFK Norrköping	1974	Malmö FF
1946	IFK Norrköping	1975	Malmö FF
1947	IFK Norrköping	1976	Halmstads BK
1948	IFK Norrköping	1977	Malmö FF
1949	Malmö FF	1978	Öster Växjö
1950	Malmö FF		

Cup Winners

1941	IF Hälsingborg	1954	no competition	1967	Malmö FF
1942	GAIS Göteborg	1955	no competition	1968	no competition
1943	IFK Norrköping	1956	no competition	1969	IFK Norrköping
1944	Malmö FF	1957	no competition	1970	Åtvidaberg
1945	IFK Norrköping	1958	no competition	1971	Åtvidaberg
1946	Malmö FF	1959	no competition	1972	Landskrona BOIS
1947	Malmö FF	1960	no competition	1973	Malmö FF
1948	Råå	1961	no competition	1974	Malmö FF
1949	AIK Stockholm	1962	no competition	1975	Malmö FF
1950	AIK Stockholm	1963	no competition	1976	AIK Stockholm
1951	Malmö FF	1964	no competition	1977	Öster Växjö
1952	no competition	1965	no competition	1978	Malmö FF
1953	Malmö FF	1966	no competition		

sweeper

A deep-lying defender who marks oncoming attackers by roaming over the entire width of the defensive area, either behind or in front of the defensive line and sometimes both. The most sophisticated sweepers have capitalized on their freedom to move where they please by bringing the ball forward and initiating the attack themselves.

The concept of sweeper, or *libero* in Italian, was brought to the world's attention by the great Inter Milan team of the early to mid-1960s under tactical innovator Helenio Herrera, whose rigid interpretation of the *catenaccio* system placed an unprecedented emphasis on defense. In the early years of *catenaccio*, sweepers did not overlap to the extent that they do now, but the sweeper's importance as a "defensive general" existed from the beginning. The position was first exemplified by Inter's Armando Picchi, a former right back whose outlook on his adopted role of *libero* was decidedly negative. The enormous success of Inter during this period prompted other clubs and many national teams to adopt variations of the *catenaccio* idea, and eventually an attacking function was added to Picchi's original model. None has been more successful in perfecting the double threat of an attacking sweeper than Franz Beckenbauer, captain of Bayern München and West Germany. Thus, while *catenaccio* appeared to be on the wane by the mid-1970s, its driving force and mainstay, the sweeper, has thrived in a more advanced conception.

Switzerland

Schweizerischer Fussball-Verband/
   Association Suisse de Football
Laubeggstrasse 70
B.P. 24
3000 Bern 32

Founded: 1895
FIFA: 1904
UEFA: 1954

Affiliated clubs: *1,313;* **registered players:** *131,500 (400 non-amateur);* **national stadium:** *Wankdorfstadion, Berne (60,000);* **stadium of equal size:** *St. Jakobs-Stadion, Basle (60,000);* **colors:** *red jerseys, white shorts;* **season:** *August to June;* **honors:** *Olympic Games runner-up (1924).*

Switzerland's importance in world soccer is derived from its historical role as the home of FIFA and its significant contribution to the founding and growth of that body. Switzerland is also the home of UEFA, and has participated actively in the organization of European soccer. In addition, the Swiss were among the early pioneers of the game. From the beginning, Switzerland has been a fulcrum of stability on which Central and Western European soccer could depend, and its reputation for fairness and sportsmanship over the years has augmented this role. On the playing field, however, Switzerland is another matter. Surrounded by several major world powers, and having aligned itself in competition with four giants of European soccer since the 1920s—Austria, Hungary, Czechoslovakia, and Italy—Switzerland's international record is both poor and understandable. Bright spots have been rare and brief, except on its home grounds where the best teams in the world are liable to go under at any given time.

English football in its various forms was probably first played on the European continent by English exchange students in Switzerland around 1855. The earliest documented date is 1869, when English students at La Châtelaine College in Geneva, near the present site of Servette FC, played under "association" rules. A handful of small clubs sprang up over the next decade in academic towns around the country, and in 1879 Fussball-Club St. Gallen, the oldest club in existence today, was founded in the German-speaking northeast. Grasshopper-

Club, the most successful club in Swiss soccer, was formed in Zurich by English students in 1886, and Servette Football-Club, the second most successful club, was founded in Geneva in 1890. Many important Swiss clubs in both German and French parts of the country appeared during the 1890s: Fussball-Club Basel (1893); Football Club La Chaux-de-Fonds (1894); Fussball-Club Biel, Fussball-Club Zürich, Lausanne-Sports, and Fussball-Club Winterthur (all in 1896); and Berner Sportclub Young Boys (1898).

The strong British influence on Swiss soccer is evident by many club names, but the Swiss themselves were very active by the 1880s and '90s. In 1895, the Schweizerische Football Association (SFA) was founded at Olten, in the German-speaking north, by seven charter clubs. (The present German-French name of the federation was adopted later.) A league was introduced in 1897, and the first champion in 1898 was Grasshoppers, whose team by this time comprised mostly Swiss nationals. The second champion was the Anglo-American Football Club of Zurich, whose players were mostly from Great Britain. In 1898, Switzerland played in its first unofficial international, a match in Basle between representative teams from the country at large and South Germany. The Swiss won, 3-1, but among its players were several Britons from British-based clubs in Zurich. A return of this match was held in 1899 at Zurich, but this time the Germans came out on top by 3-0. Later in the year, a similar Swiss team defeated an Italian representative team in Turin, 2-0. Three unofficial internationals involving Swiss representative teams were played in 1900 and 1901, and then the practice was suspended until the 1920s. In 1900, meanwhile, Surrey Wanderers became the first English team to tour Switzerland.

In 1904, the SFA was one of the first governing bodies to be approached by France and Belgium to help with the founding of FIFA, and Switzerland duly became one of seven charter members at the inaugural meeting in Paris. FIFA headquarters was located in Zurich where it has remained ever since. The following year, Switzerland played in its first full international against France in Paris, France winning 1-0, but three years lapsed before the next full international took place in Geneva, again versus France. A few weeks later, the Swiss won their first international by 5-3 over Germany, and

Hungary and Italy were added to the schedule in 1911. Switzerland played 22 full internationals between 1905 and the First World War, winning five and losing 14. Hungary, France, and Italy were each defeated once and Germany twice.

Grasshoppers and Young Boys Berne each won four league titles before World War I, giving German-speaking Switzerland early dominance over the French, but other titles during this period were widely spread among both German and French clubs. The important Italian clubs (Lugano, Bellinzona, and Chiasso), all of which are located in the canton of Ticino, were not even formed until after the turn of the century and have never figured prominently in Swiss soccer. After World War I, Servette came to the fore and challenged Grasshoppers' and Young Boys' supremacy, and by the end of the 1930s Servette had become Switzerland's most successful French-based club. Lausanne hit its stride during the 1930s with three championships and assured a French-dominated decade. In 1938, Lugano became the first Italian club to win a league title. In the Swiss Cup, which started in 1925-26, Grasshoppers jumped to an early lead in trophies won, capturing not only the first two editions, but six out of seven from 1937-43.

In international competition, Switzerland benefited considerably from its neutrality in World War I, and emerged with a unified team when it resumed its schedule in 1920. There were successive wins over Italy, Holland, Sweden, and Germany in that year, and in 1921-22 successive draws with Austria, Italy, and Germany, though most of these seven matches were played in Switzerland. Switzerland's first official competition was the 1924 Olympic Games in Paris, and in the wake of its postwar momentum this turned out to be Switzerland's finest hour. The Swiss buried Lithuania, 9-0, in the preliminary round, escaped from a reply with Czechoslovakia in the first round, upset Italy in the second round, and gained the Olympic final with a win over Sweden in the semi-finals. In the final, Switzerland's first encounter with a non-European team, the mighty Uruguayans were far too skilled and sophisticated and had little trouble in shutting out the Swiss, 3-0. Still, Switzerland's silver medal from the Paris Olympics remains to this day its highest achievement.

Switzerland's busy schedule continued, but the growing power and experience of Central and Western European countries began to show in the results. After 1924, victories became scarce, and in the first edition of the International Cup (1927-29), Switzerland placed last after losing all eight matches to Italy, Austria, Czechoslovakia, and Hungary. Finishing last, indeed, was to be its ultimate fate in each edition of the International (Dr. Gëro) Cup that followed, and on all but one occasion its losing margin was five points or more. The six editions of the International Cup (1927-60) accounted for 50 of Switzerland's 256 full internationals before 1960. The Swiss won only four games in this series, and this fact has contributed significantly to their poor overall record. Outside the International Cup, Switzerland has had slightly better results.

The Swiss were eliminated from the 1928 Olympics by Germany in the first round, and narrowly qualified for the 1934 World Cup at the expense of Yugoslavia and Rumania. Their luck continued in 1934 with a first round upset win over Holland on a fluke goal, but in the second round Czechoslovakia won on superior skill and conditioning. Switzerland entered the 1938 World Cup after eliminating lowly Portugal, and here the Swiss made a memorable showing.

Two events that occurred before the 1938 World Cup gave Switzerland a big boost: the defeat of all-powerful England by a score of 2-1 in Zurich, and the hiring of Austrian Karl Rappan as manager of the national team the year before. Switzerland's victory over England two weeks before the start of the competition was its greatest win of the pre-World War II era, and Rappan, the sometime manager of the Grasshoppers and Servette, became one of the most respected strategists in European soccer. In four different stints as national team manager between 1937-62, he brought prestige and some degree of success to his adopted country. Rappan developed the innovative *verrou*, or "Swiss Bolt," system, in which his entire team, including a fourth (deep center) back, retreated to the opponent's half of the field to defend against an attack. This fluid—and effective—defense system was a scourge to the many attacking teams of the 1930s and '50s, and proved to be a sensible answer to the consistent superiority of Europe's great powers. Rappan's *verrou* anticipated Italy's *catenaccio* of the postwar era, and given *catenaccio's* later importance, must be regarded as a strong influence in the tactical evolution of the game, even though Switzerland remained a middle-level power.

In the 1938 World Cup, Rappan's Switzerland held a German team swelled with Austrians and others from conquered lands to a 1-1 draw in the first round, and in the replay defeated Germany 4-2 after losing 2-0. The Swiss goalscoring hero was Trello Abegglen, but it was the system itself and Rappan's leadership that paved the way. In the second round, Hungary's goalscoring ace Zsengeller scored two unanswered goals, and Switzerland bowed out of the competition. Rappan's team was able to notch further wins over major powers such as Italy and Hungary before the outbreak of World War II, and during the war itself it played several games against politically neutral Sweden and Portugal.

Under Rappan, Switzerland again qualified for the World Cup in 1950, but the great master did not join his team in the final rounds in Brazil. After losing as expected to Yugoslavia, the Swiss met Brazil in São Paulo—a weakened Brazil to be sure—and once again the bolt closed doors to even the most skilled forwards. The Swiss counterattack was potent enough to equalize near the end of the game, and little Switzerland walked away with a 2-2 draw. After a win over Mexico, Switzerland still lacked the necessary points to advance to the next round, but it left Brazil muttering in its wake.

Rappan again took over the national team in 1953 to prepare for the next World Cup—to be held in Switzerland. With the *verrou* squarely in place, the Swiss reached the quarter-finals of the World Championship before home crowds and for the first and only time in their history. In the first round, they defeated Italy, 2-1, a major accomplishment even if it was a low period for Italian soccer, and lost to England 2-0. A replay with Italy was forced to determine which team would join England in the next round, and this was won convincingly by the Swiss, 4-1. This game was one of Switzerland's proudest accomplishments, equaled only by its qualification for the 1962 World Cup eight years later. Swiss euphoria came to a horrifying end in the second round, however, when Austria, led by the magnificient Ernst Ocwirk, scored five goals in a record seven minutes to win, 7-5. The complete breakdown of Rappan's *verrou*, as it happened, was not the result of tactical errors but of a chink in the armor. Swiss captain and center half Roger Bocquet was at the time suffering from a serious tumor, and against Rappan's suggestion insisted on starting the game. On the field, he was mesmerized by the heat, and was ultimately responsible for letting in several goals. Bocquet was the most popular player in Switzerland, and the agonizing question of whether to remove him from the field or switch him to another position was partly decided by Bocquet himself—he refused to leave the field—and partly by the game's strict stoppage laws. At any rate, Switzerland lost the game at its potentially finest hour. (Bocquet's subsequent operation to remove his tumor was successful.)

Spain and Scotland prevented the Swiss from entering the 1958 World Cup in qualifying rounds, but in 1962 Switzerland gained the finals by eliminating Belgium and Sweden in a remarkable series of victories (including a play-off with Sweden in neutral Berlin). This was regarded as a startling triumph, and once again Karl Rappan, who had taken over the team for a fourth time in 1960, was at the helm. In Chile, however, West Germany, Italy, and Chile each won first round games over a Swiss team lacking some of the skills it had displayed in 1938 and 1954. Rappan again stepped down from his post, but he retired as a national sports hero.

Swiss fortunes in international competition have further declined since the early 1960s. Switzerland qualified again for the World Cup in 1966, but was virtually knocked out of the running by West Germany in the first game. It has not advanced beyond the first round in the European Football Championship in four attempts, and has not qualified for the World Cup final rounds since 1966.

At home, the domination of Grasshoppers and Servette has been broken in the past 30 years by the rebirth of Young Boys Berne and especially by the rise of FC Zurich and FC Basel. Zurich and Basel have won 11 of the last 13 championships as well as several Swiss Cups. While their record in European club championships is not good, Zurich and Basel are not to be taken lightly on home soil. As in Austria, Swiss players in the top echelons are paid part-timers but (they do not have to hold down other jobs), all other players are amateur. There is widespread agreement that full professionalism would give Swiss soccer its first real impetus to improve in many decades. As it is now, an inferiority complex has settled on Swiss clubs and players in their quest for international honors. The last streamlining of the federation occurred in 1958, when the Swiss Athletic Association, which had been united with the soccer federation since the early part of the century, broke away to form an independent body.

The Swiss league, one of the most complex in Europe, is divided into three levels. The national league (28 teams in all) comprises Divisions A and B, or first and second divisions. Since 1976-77, the revised national league format has required the 12 clubs of Division A to play in two mini-seasons (like Albania and many South American countries.) In the first mini-season, each club plays all but one of the other clubs on a home and away basis. The top six from this series form a new series, the winner of which is the Swiss champion. The bottom six finishers form their own series to determine relegation. The second level is called the First League, and is comprised of 26 teams operating on a standard league basis. The third level is made up of the 13 local leagues around the country, and is referred to as the ZUS (Zusammenschluss unterer Serien). The Östschweiz league of the ZUS includes many Lichtensteiner clubs.

Champions

1898	Grasshoppers	1909	Young Boys Berne	1920	Young Boys Berne
1899	Anglo-American FC	1910	Young Boys Berne	1921	Grasshoppers
1900	Grasshoppers	1911	Young Boys Berne	1922	Servette
1901	Grasshoppers	1912	Aarau	1923	no competition
1902	FC Zurich	1913	Lausanne	1924	FC Zurich
1903	Young Boys Berne	1914	Aarau	1925	Servette
1904	FC St. Gallen	1915	SC Brühl St. Gallen	1926	Servette
1905	Grasshoppers	1916	Cantonal-Neuchatel	1927	Grasshoppers
1906	Winterthur	1917	Winterthur	1928	Grasshoppers
1907	Servette	1918	Servette	1929	Young Boys Berne
1908	Winterthur	1919	La Chaux de Fonds	1930	Servette

1931	Grasshoppers	1947	FC Biel	1963	FC Zurich
1932	Lausanne	1948	AC Bellinzona	1964	La Chaux de Fonds
1933	Servette	1949	Lugano	1965	Lausanne
1934	Servette	1950	Servette	1966	FC Zurich
1935	Lausanne	1951	Lausanne	1967	FC Basel
1936	Lausanne	1952	Grasshoppers	1968	FC Zurich
1937	Grasshoppers	1953	FC Basel	1969	FC Basel
1938	Lugano	1954	La Chaux de Fonds	1970	FC Basel
1939	Grasshoppers	1955	La Chaux de Fonds	1971	Grasshoppers
1940	Servette	1956	Grasshoppers	1972	FC Basel
1941	Lugano	1957	Young Boys Berne	1973	FC Basel
1942	Grasshoppers	1958	Young Boys Berne	1974	FC Zurich
1943	Grasshoppers	1959	Young Boys Berne	1975	FC Zurich
1944	Lausanne	1960	Young Boys Berne	1976	FC Zurich
1945	Grasshoppers	1961	Servette	1977	FC Basel
1946	Servette	1962	Servette	1978	Grasshoppers

Cup Winners

1926	Grasshoppers	1944	Lausanne	1962	Lausanne
1927	Grasshoppers	1945	Young Boys Berne	1963	FC Basel
1928	Servette	1946	Grasshoppers	1964	Lausanne
1929	Urania Geneva	1947	FC Basel	1965	FC Sion
1930	Young Boys Berne	1948	La Chaux de Fonds	1966	FC Zurich
1931	Lugano	1949	Servette	1967	FC Basel
1932	Grasshoppers	1950	Lausanne	1968	Lugano
1933	FC Basel	1951	La Chaux de Fonds	1969	FC St. Gallen
1934	Grasshoppers	1952	Grasshoppers	1970	FC Zurich
1935	Lausanne	1953	Young Boys Berne	1971	Servette
1936	Young Fellows Zurich	1954	La Chaux de Fonds	1972	FC Zurich
1937	Grasshoppers	1955	La Chaux de Fonds	1973	FC Zurich
1938	Grasshoppers	1956	Grasshoppers	1974	FC Sion
1939	Lausanne	1957	La Chaux de Fonds	1975	FC Basel
1940	Grasshoppers	1958	Young Boys Berne	1976	FC Zurich
1941	Grasshoppers	1959	FC Grenchen	1977	Young Boys Berne
1942	Grasshoppers	1960	FC Luzern	1978	Servette
1943	Grasshoppers	1961	La Chaux de Fonds		

Syria

Fédération Arabe Syrienne de Football
Nouri Pacha-Djisr
B.P. 241
Damascus

Founded: 1936
FIFA: 1937
AFC: 1970

Affiliated clubs: *105;* **registered players:** *16,660;* **national stadium:** *Stade Al-Abbassiyne, Damascus (45,000);* **largest stadium:** *Stade Al-Abbassiyne;* **colors:** *white jerseys, white shorts;* **season:** *September to June;* **honors:** *none.*

With the exception of Jordan, North Yemen, and Oman, Syria is the least conspicuous of Arab countries on the soccer field. Under the French mandate, the game was not promoted as aggressively in Syria as it was in British mandated countries of the Middle East, and in later years, without the benefit of extensive oil reserves, Syria was less exposed to the hordes of Western European workers and technicians who ultimately helped to establish the game in other Arab states. After Syria gained independence in 1941, Islamic mores and religious beliefs hindered the growth of soccer still further.

Nevertheless, the Fédération Syrienne de Football was founded in 1936 and became affiliated with FIFA in 1937. ("Arabe" was added to the name in the early 1970s.) A system of regional committees was developed after World War II to administer local competitions in Damascus, Aleppo, Homs, Hama, Deir ez Zor, and Latakia. A championship of Syria, contested by the leading clubs of each region, was introduced at the same time.

Syria's first full international was played in 1949 in a World Cup qualification match against Turkey at Ankara. The Turks won, 7-0. Five days later the same team traveled to Athens and lost a friendly to Greece, this time by a mere 2-0. In 1951, Syria entered the sparsely attended football tournament of the first Mediterranean Games at Alexandria, in which only three countries participated.

Though its presence there was surprising and encouraging for the future of Syrian soccer, the team suffered two lopsided defeats, 4-0 against Greece and 8-0 against Egypt.

From there, Syria's participation in international competition virtually ceased until the qualification rounds of the 1974 World Cup. Syria's reemergence coincided with the rise of soccer in the Middle East generally, and appeared to indicate a turning point in Syria's desire to enter the mainstream of the Asian game. Grouped with Syria in the 1974 World Cup qualification rounds were Iran, Korea DPR, and Kuwait. The Syrians managed to win over Kuwait twice and Iran once, surely the best results in their history, but were not able to compete with Iran before the latter's home crowds in Tehran. Syria's second place finish, however, was encouraging, especially given such formidable opposition. In the qualification rounds for the 1978 World Cup, Syria again achieved good results by splitting home and away matches with the determined Saudis, but a spirited Syrian team lost to Iran in Tehran and forfeited the return leg, ending all hope of further success in its third World Cup attempt.

Meanwhile Syrian teams have not attempted to qualify for any major Asian competitions, but they have participated in the politically inspired Palestine Football Cup, contested biannually since 1971 by Arab states and a Palestinian representative team.

T

tackle

To lawfully take the ball away from a player in possession by using one's feet.

See also: **front-block tackle, over-the- ball tackle, sliding tackle.**

tactics

Soccer is primarily an intuitive exercise; this has been one of it great appeals to potential ball jugglers in all parts of the world. To confine it to "patterns," such as those of American football and basketball, would undermine its attraction to viewers and practitioners alike. The Laws themselves are indicators of this characteristic, since they leave an inordinate amount of discretion to the referee, more so than in almost any other ball game. The desire to carry on these traditions

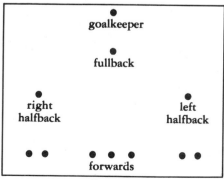

English coach Jimmy Hogan, a major influence on the tactics of twentieth-century soccer, demonstrating the art of passing to Brentford F.C. players in 1945.

and to refrain from the adoption of quasi-military maneuvers has been reaffirmed in recent years by the game's sharp reaction to the entrenched atmosphere of *catenaccio*, a product of Italy, in favor of the free and fluid "total football" of Holland and Germany in the 1970s.

The biggest conflict in the tactical evolution of the game has been that of orientation: attack vs. defense. Weaker teams at all levels

of every game are prone to resort to defense-oriented approaches; highly skilled teams tend to have the confidence to attack. If there is an identifiable historical trend it is probably the general transformation of soccer from a purely attacking strategy to a more defensive one. The gentlemen players of Victorian England were hardly inclined to let the game come to them. Indeed, goalkeepers of the mid-nineteenth century took turns in that role, because it was duly regarded as the least honorable position to play. Sam Hardy, Américo Tesoriero, and other pioneer goal-keepers changed all that, and, conversely, in the twentieth century many of the world's leading offensive players have been fullbacks, center halfbacks, and sweepers. In the end, nostalgic worries over the loss of attacking soccer in the modern game are easy to come by but of little use; all these trends are cyclical.

Alcock's Dribbling Game (figure 1): The earliest soccer "formation" emerged in the 1860s when football teams were gradually splitting into two camps—association football and rugby football. Until the 1860s, most codes prohibited forward passing altogether, necessitating forward movement of the ball by dribbling only. C. W. Alcock and his club, Wanderers F.C., the chief proponents of the

goalkeeper

fullback

right
halfback

left
halfback

forwards

figure 1

dribbling game, argued that it represented pure soccer, as distinct from rugby where passing the ball (albeit by hand) was a distinctive trait. In the dribbling game, there were seven (or eight) forwards, each a dribbling expert, one or two halfbacks in support of the attack, and one fullback to challenge the opposing dribbler.

Scottish Passing Game (figure 2): Queen's Park Glasgow, the Scottish national team, and the London club Royal Engineers created the first tactical revolution during the 1870s when they introduced the concept of passing among their players. The soccer-rugby split had occurred by this time, and the passing game was the first sign that soccer was maturing. To accommodate the increased goalscoring potential, another fullback was added on defense, thus reducing the forward line to six players. The Scottish method was eventually perfected by the English amateur club Corinthians during the 1880s, and became commonplace. Ultimately, it signaled the birth of modern soccer.

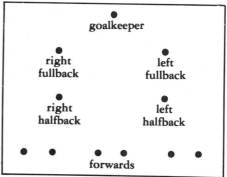

figure 2

The Classic Formation, 2-3-5 (figure 3): The development of passing techniques spelled the need for tighter, more sophisticated defenses, and in the late 1870s a third halfback was seen on some teams (Cambridge University, 1877, and Wrexham F.C., 1878). England's national team first employed three halfbacks in 1884, followed by Scotland in 1887, by which time the practice was widely adopted. Preston North End was the first really successful club to use the 2-3-5, winning the first two English championships in 1889 and 1890. The 2-3-5 remained the standard formation in soccer for 40 years, and was used in Central Europe until the post-World War II era, modified by a lower intensity and a more fluid expression, yielding the so-called "Danubian" style.

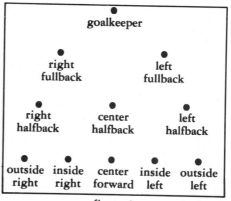

figure 3

Charlie Buchan's Third Back Game (figure 4): After the offside law change of 1925, goalscoring in English soccer increased immediately by 33 percent. Arsenal's inside forward Charlie Buchan, an exceptionally bright player with excellent goalscoring skills in his own right, suggested to his manager Herbert Chapman that the center half be pulled back to a purely defensive position to mark the opposing center forward (hence his designation as stopper). In addition, an inside forward who was more adept at distribution than goalscoring was pulled back to a deeply-lying forward position. Chapman's Arsenal adopted this with great success in the late 1920s.

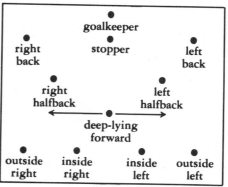

figure 4

W-M Formation (figure 5): This became an immediate extension of Buchan's third back plan, in which both inside forwards, rather than just one, were drawn back, creating the geometric appearance of a W-shaped defense and M-shaped offense. Herbert Chapman's Arsenal of the 1930s, which dominated English soccer for a decade, made it world famous, and it remained the standard formation in England and assorted anglophile strongholds until the 1950s.

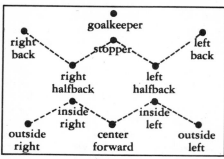

figure 5

Metodo, or "Method" (figure 6): Vittorio Pozzo, manager of Italy's national team during its decade of world domination in the 1930s, adapted the highly successful attacking center half concept of Manchester United's 1907-11 team—which he had observed closely while living in England—and combined it with the attacking M of Arsenal's W-M formation. In the 1940s, Pozzo reluctantly transformed his attacking center half into a stopper, a revised plan he called *sistema* ("system").

figure 6

Verrou, or Swiss Bolt (figures 7 & 8): Developed by Karl Rappan, Austrian manager of Servette Geneva and Grasshoppers Zurich during the 1930s, the "Swiss Bolt" called for separate attack and defensive formations. In the attack (figure 8), a 3-3-4 pattern emerged in which the center back and two wing backs advanced all the way to the midfield line; the three halfbacks supported the forward line of two wings and two insides, the center half serving as a virtual deep-lying center forward. In the defense (figure 7), all 11 players retreated deep into their own half; the center half became a center back, and the center back became a deep center back who roved from one side to the other (hence the "bolt" designation), much as the *libero*, or sweeper did in later years. The purpose of the plan was to create the illusion that an opposing attack or defense was in turn, outmanned, but it required great stamina from its players. *Verrou* was important in anticipating the more garrisoned Italian bolt system, *catenaccio*.

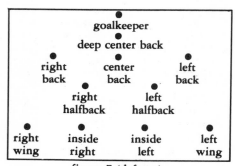

figure 7 (defense)

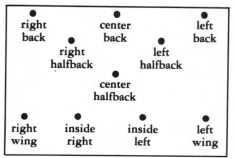

figure 8 (attack)

Hungarian W Attack (figure 9): Hungary lost one match in six years between 1950-56 (the World Cup final in 1954) playing its own 4-2-4, a system unknown in Europe up to that time, and more accurately called the Hungarian W attack. It called for three center forwards, one deep-lying (Hidegkuti) and two well-advanced (Kocsis on the right and Puskás on the left), flanked by two slightly receding wings. The two midfielders were staggered, Bozsik on the right supporting the attack, Zakarias on the left acting as the first line of defense. Three backs brought up the rear, but they too advanced to the opponent's half of the field on attacks.

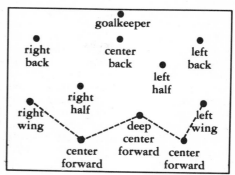

figure 9

The 4-2-4 System (figure 10): This was introduced by the Paraguayan national team under coach Fleitas Solich in the 1953 South American Championship, but it was made famous by the scintillating Brazilian World Cup-winning team of 1958. Brazil's two center backs in the middle of the defense were flanked by two wing backs who were expected to initiate attacks along the touch lines (resulting in an astonishing 2-4-4). The two midfield players were offense-minded as well, and the forward line consisted of two central strikers (Vavá and Pelé), and two wings (Garrincha and Zagalo), the former an attacking right side winger, the latter a supportive winger who dropped back on the left side.

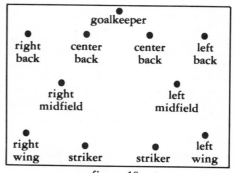

figure 10

The 4-3-3 System (figure 11): This system, still widely used, was seen in its most entertaining form when Brazil employed two central strikers and a wing on the forward line. The former left wing of the 4-2-4 (Zagalo) had by now dropped back to an authentic left midfield role. Right and left backs were free to advance at will as they had in the 4-2-4. A modified form of the 4-3-3 has one center forward and two wings evenly displaced.

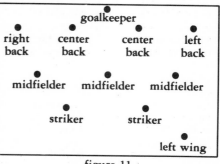

figure 11

Wing-less 4-4-2 (figure 12): England won the World Cup of 1966 with this formation, but eventually entered a long period of mediocrity with it as well. There were four backs at the rear; a roving "defensive screen" (Stiles) in the sweeper tradition (but in front of his other defenders); three midfielders, the central one of these (Charlton) a virtual deep-lying center forward; and two central strikers. The wing positions were in effect erased from the field. This was one of the weakest attacking systems yet devised, but it provided an effective defense.

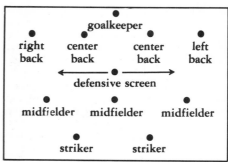

figure 12

Catenaccio (figures 13 & 14): The roots of this pervasive defense plan go back to the northeast of Italy in the late 1930s, probably as a result of exposure to the *verrou*. In 1948, Triestina employed it successfully against the big clubs of the Italian league that had recently been inundated with high-scoring foreign players. Other small clubs adopted some form of *catenaccio*, and by the early 1950s even the giant Milan and Turin clubs had adopted it.

Catenaccio ("great bolt or chain") involved three or four defenders who were supported in the rear by a *libero* (sweeper) who roamed from side-to-side plugging up the slightest hole left by a defender. In front of the defense, three midfielders more often defended than attacked, and there were two or three strikers on the forward line. In *catenaccio*, the offensive thrust usually took the form of a counterattack rather than a slow build-up. Its most garrisoned form involved a back line of four plus the sweeper, and a forward line of only two (figure 13). A second form included three backs and three forwards (figure 14). *Catenaccio* eventually engulfed Italy, and helped its well-rehearsed practitioners to dominate European club tournaments during the 1960s. The Italian national team however, was unsuccessful with this system, and it was eventually unable to disassociate the system itself from the defensive attitude it created.

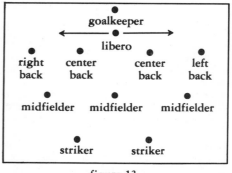

figure 13

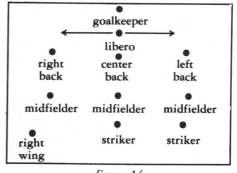

figure 14

Beckenbauer's All-Purpose Sweeper Plan: The various systems were so interlocked by the late 1960s that diagrammatic patterns began to lose their significance altogether. In West Germany, the ex-midfielder Franz Beckenbauer, one of the most complete players in the history of the game, transformed the sweeper position into an attacking as well as defensive role. Beckenbauer roamed from side to side both in front of and behind the defensive line, and occasionally launched an attack, sometimes advancing into the opponent's penalty area to score goals. Though Beckenbauer's sweeper role could be adapted to almost any existing system, it has most often been incoporated into a 4-3-3. The genius of Beckenbauer's concept, however, was that it virtually obviated all traditional systems, and anticipated the less restrictive marking that gave rise to "total football."

Total Football: "Total football," as practiced first by the superbly gifted Dutch club Ajax

and eventually by Holland and West Germany, is less a system than an attitude, in which intuitive playmaking and individual initiative allow all players to adopt attacking or defensive postures as the situation warrants. It combines very high levels of skill with thoughtful, deliberate passing, yet without rigid patterns. It is a constant movement and refocusing of pivotal points on the field, wholly dependent on the action that has immediately preceded it. Players of enormous-ly wide-ranging talent, such as Franz Becken-bauer and Johan Cruyff, are particularly well suited to it.

Tahiti   See: **French Polynesia**

Tanzania

Football Association of Tanzania
P.O. Box 1574
Dar es Salaam

Founded: 1930
FIFA: 1964
CAF: 1960

Affiliated clubs: *? (51 clubs compete in leagues);* **registered players:** *?;* **national stadium:** *National Stadium, Dar es Salaam (3,000);* **largest stadium:** *National Stadium;* **colors:** *green jerseys with yellow sleeves, black shorts;* **season:** *September to August;* **honors:** *none.*

Soccer in Tanzania has been slower to develop than in other major countries of Africa. The population of Tanganyika, the bulky mainland portion of the United Republic of Tanzania, is so sparsely and widely distributed that the use of recreational time is difficult to organize. Zanzibar, more compact and orderly, has too small a population to make a large difference in the state of the national game, and its semiautonomous politics is not helpful in unifying Tanzania's soccer interests. The change from German to British colonization also damaged the game's growth. In addition, the major sporting activities of most East Africans center on track and field. (East Africa is the only part of the continent in which soccer is not the undisputed leading sport.) Tanzania also lacks the major industrialized urban centers that have historically bred soccer powers in Africa and elsewhere.

The Football Association of Tanganyika was founded in 1930 and soon became affiliated with The Football Association in London, yet by this time, the smaller but older

Sports Association of Zanzibar was already affiliated. A merger of the two associations resulted from the unification of the two countries in 1964, but their special relationship calls for a certain degree of autonomy. In the African Nations' Cup, as well as World Cup and Olympic qualification rounds, the Tanzanian national team represents both Tanganyika and Zanzibar. While not a separate member of the African Football Confederation, Zanzibar retains separate membership in the East and Central African Football Federation along with Tanzania (here representing Tanganyika), and Zanzibar regularly fields its own selection in internation friendlies, and the East and Central African Challenge Cup. During the mid-1970s, Tanzania became the first country to begin regular competition with teams from Mozambique, the new independent neighbor to the south.

Tanzania has not yet qualified for any final rounds of the African Nations' Cup. Its lack of success in international competition has also extended to club tournaments. In the African Champions' Cup, the only year in which a Tanzanian entry has advanced beyond the first round was in 1974 when Simba S.C. of Dar es Salaam succumbed in the semi-finals to Mehalla of Egypt (on penalty kicks) after eliminating Linare (Lesotho), Sahbia Army (Zambia), and Heart of Oaks (Ghana). Tanzania's champion club in 1971, 1972, 1973, and 1975 was Young Africans F.C. of Dar es Salaam, the country's most popular and successful club. Tanzania's first representative in the African Cup Winners' Cup (1976) was Youth League F.C., which lost in the first round to Metchal of Ethiopia.

The other leading clubs in Tanzania are: Mseto Sports, Tanga Old Stars F.C., Coastal Union S.C., and African Sports Club, all of Tanga; Taifa Stars of the Eastern Province (Dar es Salaam region); and Afro-Shirazi F.C.

of Zanzibar. Afro-Shirazi is believed to be the world's first major club founded and sponsored by a political party, in this case Zanzibar's ruling Afro-Shirazi Party. The three most important regional leagues are located in Dar es Salaam, Tanga, and Zanzibar.

Tanzanian soccer is also known in Africa for its absence of adequately sized stadiums. The National Stadium in Dar es Salaam is no larger than most small club grounds in the major soccer nations of Africa, and Zanzibar's most important stadium, Mao Tse-Tung Stadium, is even smaller. The domestic structure of the Tanzanian game has not yet advanced to the point of establishing a national league, but the annual cup competition is held nationwide. Though a major political and moral force in Africa, Tanzania barely qualifies as one of the top two dozen soccer powers on the continent.

Tesoriero, Américo Miguel (1899-1977)

Argentina's greatest goalkeeper of all time. Intuitive, daring, and tenacious, he played during the "romantic era" of South American soccer and was known for his keen sense of positioning around the goalmouth. Tactically, Tesoriero was ahead of his time in that he regularly came out to intercept attacking forwards. His career (1916-27) was spent almost entirely at Boca Júniors—he played briefly for Deportivo del Norte in 1922—and

he made 41 international appearances for Argentina, an exceptionally high figure in view of the fewer number of internationals played in those early years. His international debut for Argentina was made in 1919 against Paraguay. Always the most magnetic player on the field, Tesoriero was instantly recognizable by his slender physique and his ever-present grey woolen sweater.

Thailand

Football Association of Thailand
c/o National Stadium
Rama 1 Road
Bangkok

Founded: 1916
FIFA: 1925
AFC: 1957

Affiliated clubs: *115;* registered players: *5,000;* national stadium: *Suphachalasai Stadium, Bangkok (39,924);* largest stadium: *Suphachalasai Stadium;* colors: *crimson red jerseys, white shorts;* season: *November to April;* honors: *none.*

Thailand, the only country in Southeast Asia that was not colonized by a European power, was nevertheless introduced to soccer by British tradesmen and technicians around the turn of the century or before, and in 1916 foreigners established the Football Association of Siam to regulate local competitions. As

an independent country, Siam was able to join FIFA early by Asian standards—in 1925—but little was seen of any Siamese teams in international competition until well after World War II.

Among East and Southeast Asian countries, Thailand ranks below the middle level on the basis of official results, but it has been very active on several levels of international competition and it is a respected organizer of tournaments. The Asian Games have been held twice in Bangkok, and in 1968 the Football Association of Thailand introduced the King's Cup Football Tournament, one of the region's major competitions for national teams. Burma, Indonesia, South Korea, Malaysia, and Singapore are invited regularly. Unfortunately, Thailand itself has never won the King's Cup, nor has it won any other regional tournaments. Its first European foray was a visit to Bergen, Norway, in 1965, when it lost to Norway's full national team, 7-0.

In the Asian Cup, Thailand had its first success with a third place finish in 1972, when the final rounds were played in Bangkok. In the first round, it drew with Iraq, 1-1, and lost narrowly to Iran, 3-2. South Korea defeated this fine Thai team on penalty kicks in the semi-finals, and in the third place game Thailand was forced to a penalty decision again, this time coming out on top after a 2-2 draw in extra time. Thailand's most important accomplishment has been reaching the final rounds of the 1972 Olympics in Munich, where it lost its first round games to Bulgaria (7-1), Guatemala (4-1), and Czechoslovakia (8-0). Observers thought the Thai players less skilled than their Japanese, Chinese, or Korean counterparts, but at home they continued to press on in the qualifying rounds of the 1974 and 1978 World Cups. The leading Thai clubs—Bangkok Bank and Police Football Club—were regular participants in the Asian Champion Teams' Cup, but failed to advance beyond the first round in any edition of that now defunct competition.

third back

A nominal halfback, usually the center half, who adopts a defensive position in conjunction with the backs, forming in effect a three-back line, e.g., the W-M system.

See also: **tactics**

thirty-five yard line

In the North American Soccer League, two lateral lines on the field of play that run from side line to side line and are 35 yards from each goal line.

In 1973, the NASL introduced the 35-yard line concept in order to modify clause "a" of the offside rule in the Laws of the Game. The official offside rule states that a player cannot be offside if he is in his own half of the field.

Under the 35-yard line rule, an attacking player cannot be offside until he is within 35 yards of his opponent's goal. The intent of the new rule is to effectively pull back a given defense, and allow for a more uninhibited attack.

The 35-yard line concept has not spread beyond the North American Soccer League, and FIFA has refused to sanction it.

through ball

A pass that is played forward and penetrates the opponent's defense, especially to a waiting attacker or to one who then runs onto the ball.

throw-in

The action taken in returning the ball to play when it has crossed a touchline. The rules and conditions of a throw-in are as follows:

1. The throw is taken from the point where the ball crossed the touchline.
2. Both feet of the thrower must either be on the touchline or on the ground inside the touchline.
3. The throw is delivered with both hands from behind and over the head.
4. The thrower may not play the ball again until it has been touched by another player.
5. A goal cannot be scored from a throw-in.
6. Defending players may not intentionally distract or impede the thrower.
7. In taking a throw-in, some part of the player's body must face the field of play.
8. A player who receives the ball direct from a throw-in cannot be offside.

Throw-ins have been part of the game since the first modern rules were established in the early nineteenth century. The Harrow Rules of ca. 1835 required a throw-in when the ball passed over either the touchline or the goal line, and could be delivered in any direction the player chose. Beginning with the Cambridge University Rules of 1848, however, throw-ins were restricted to balls that crossed the touchline only. This innovation extended to all subsequent codes. The Cambridge Rules, as well as the Sheffield Rules of 1857, specified that the throw-in must be delivered in a perpendicular direction from the touchline. The freedom to throw in any direction a player chooses was reintroduced in The Football Association Laws of the Game in 1863. The one-handed throw was lawful under all these early codes. Scottish teams, however, developed a two-handed throw-in and adopted it into their rules, but in England, the two-hand throw-in was resisted until the mid-1870s. Finally, in 1882, The Football Association agreed to adopt the two-hand rule in an effort to lessen tension that had built up between the English and Scottish associations. Since then, the throw-in as we now know it has remained largely unchanged.

Togo

Fédération Togolaise de Football
C.P. 5
Lomé

Founded: 1960
FIFA: 1962
CAF: 1963

Affiliated clubs: *144;* **registered players:** *4,340;* **national stadium:** *Stade Général Étienne Eyadema, Lomé (20,000);* **largest stadium:** *Stade Général Étienne Eyadema;* **colors:** *red jerseys with yellow and green stripes, white shorts;* **season:** *October to July;* **honors:** *none.*

Togo, like many small nations on the international soccer horizon, has shown that it cannot promote a successful national team and a vital league at the same time. In 1971-72, the Togo Football Federation made the decision to support the national team's effort in the African Nations' Cup to such an extent that the clubs at home were nearly abandoned in the process. For the first and only time in the Nations' Cup history, Togo went through to the final rounds. In the final rounds, Togo managed to draw with the eventual finalist, Mali, as well as with Kenya before losing to powerful Cameroon by 2-0. Togo's success was the surprise of the tournament. Between 1972-74, however, Togo's national team did not engage in international play, as the strain of the Nations' Cup run had seriously jeopardized the state of domestic competition. All resources now had to be redirected to save the league from irretrievable harm.

Meanwhile, Togolese clubs have managed

to participate regularly in international club competitions. Togo's champion club has entered the African Champions' Cup each of the last several years. Ironically, neither of Togo's leading clubs—Dynamic and Modele Lomé—have done as well in the tournament as Lomé I, which reached the semi-finals in 1975. Lomé's march through the first two rounds in 1975 was characterized by a certain degree of luck (its preliminary round opponent was the impoverished Liberian champion Bama, and its first round opponent, Djoliba of Mali, forfeited), but in the quarter-finals it met mighty ASEC Abidjan of the Ivory Coast and achieved a 3-2 win on aggregate to earn the right to meet Hafia de Conakry of Guinea, the best club in Africa during the early 1970s. Hafia finally eliminated Lomé I, but only by 1-0 and 1-1. In other years of African Champions' Cup competition, Togolese clubs have not advanced beyond the first round, with the exception of Dynamic's strong run in 1971, when quarter-final adversary Canon of Cameroon—African champions for that

year—stood in the way. In the new African Cup Winners' Cup, Omnisport Lomé advanced to the quarter-finals before losing to the Ivory Coast's Stella Club in 1975, and Lama-Kara bowed out to powerful Tonnerre of Cameroon in the first round in 1976.

It is not certain whether soccer was introduced to present-day Togo during the pre-World War I era of German colonization or after World War I when Britain and France divided the area between them, but the French legacy eventually predominated, and some influence was felt from the Ligue de l'Afrique Occidentale Française (French West Africa League) in Dakar, Senegal, which alone administered the game in colonial French West Africa.

The Fédération Togolaise de Football was founded immediately after Togo achieved independence in 1960. The association supports a national championship and an annual national cup competition, but the country is too small in size to organize any regional competitions.

Torino Calcio

Location: *Turin, Italy;* stadium: *Stadio Comunale (71,180);* colors: *dark red jerseys, white shorts;* honors: *Italian champion: (1928, 1943, 1946, 1947, 1948, 1949, 1976), Italian cup winner (1936, 1943, 1968, 1971).*

Founded 1906 with the merger of two Turin clubs, FC Internazionale (not to be confused with Inter Milan) and FC Torinese, themselves formed in 1890 and 1894, respectively. Among its founders was Vittorio Pozzo, who maintained an affiliation with the club until 1929. Several of Torino's first players were defectors from Juventus, its bitter crosstown rival, and Torino's first stadium, the Umberto I Velodrome, was appropriated from Juventus through the latter's disgruntled former president. Juventus' new grounds eventually became the Stadio Comunale, which the two clubs now share in an amicable partnership (via a municipal committee).

FC Internazionale and Torinese had participated in the first Italian championship in 1898. In 1907, its first year in the championship, Torino placed second in the standings. The following year it did not enter, but did so continuously from 1909, failing to win a league title until 1927, when its trophy

was revoked by the Italian federation because it had tampered illegally with a game against Juventus. The strength of this team was proven when it bounced back to win the championship again in 1928.

The name of Torino, however, is synonymous with the 1940s, because during this decade its exceptional team of gifted players won five championships in seven years and a wartime Italian cup to boot. In 1947, Torino won by an eye-popping 10-point margin, and in 1948 by an even greater 16-point margin. The spearhead of this great side was the inside forward duo of Ezio Loik on the right and Valentino Mazzola on the left, whom the club had purchased as a pair from Venezia in 1942. Mazzola was the most gifted Italian player of the 1940s, with the possible exception of Silvio Piola, but the war years and their aftermath prevented the rest of Europe from seeing much of him. Guglielmo Gabetto at center forward, Aldo Ballarin at right back, and Valerio Bacigalupo in the goal were also outstanding, and these five provided the nucleus of Italy's postwar national team.

On May 4, 1949, Torino having gained another healthy lead in the league standings with six games left to play, the plane that was bringing the team back from a friendly in Lisbon crashed into the basilica on Superga hill just west of Turin, and the entire team was killed. Among the dead were one French, one Czech, and ten Italian full internationals. The deceased players were: Valerio Bacigalupo, Aldo Ballarin, Dino Ballarin (brother of Aldo), Emilio Bongiorni (the Frenchman), Eusebio Castigliano, Rubens Fadini, Guglielmo Gabetto, Ruggero Grava, Giuseppe Grezar, Ezio Loik, Virgilio Maroso, Danilo Martelli, Valentino Mazzola, Romeo Menti, Pietro Operto, Franco Ossola, Mario Rigamonti, and Giulio Schubert (a Hungarian-born Czech). They were given a state funeral, and the crowds attending were said to be the largest in modern Italian history. In fact, the entire country closed down for a week. Still stunned by the tragedy, the league eventually opened once again to complete the season, and the Italian federation gave the club permission to play out the rest of its schedule with its youth team, which met the youth teams of its opponents and won all the remaining games. The 1948-49 championship was awarded to Torino on this basis.

This disaster destroyed not only Torino's future but also the hopes of the Italian national team. The club never recovered from its suffering, and after several years of poor showings in the league, it was finally relegated after the 1958-59 season, its name having been temporarily changed to Talmone-Torino (after a baking company that underwrote financial losses for two years). The public outcry to its name change was so intense, however, that it reverted to Torino once again, and after one season in *Serie B* it gained promotion to *Serie A*, where it has remained ever since. Torino's first sign of a reemergence into the mainstream of Italian soccer did not occur until it won a league title in 1976 with several outstanding internationals bringing glory back to *la granata*. Old timers, however, remember the Torino of Valentino Mazzola as the most gifted team ever to play in Italian soccer.

Tostão (1947-)

(Full name: Eduardo Gonçalves de Andrade.) The selfless center forward and decoy of Brazil's 1970 World Cup team, who himself penetrated defenses mercilessly. He was that rare center forward who was as useful with his back to the goal as he was facing it. Tostão's strength was his exceptional intelligence and knowledge of the game, though his skills were highly refined as well, especially those involving his left foot. His function as a decoy for Pelé and others was a natural outgrowth of his keen awareness of all that occurred around the penalty area. Penetrating with the ball or taking a through pass, he would often attract the attention of his defenders and in an instant pass with perfect accuracy to an oncoming teammate who himself would score the goal. Just as often, he would have his back to the goal, and pivot on a dime to score. His rare blend of skills and selflessness was a key element in the astounding performance of Brazil in the 1970 World Cup.

Tostão was also a hero in domestic competition. As a boy he was signed by América of Belo Horizonte in the Minas Gerais state league, and in 1963, his extraordinary potential having already been recognized, he was lured to Cruzeiro by its dynamic new president, Félicio Brândi. His signing turned Cruzeiro into the undisputed leader of *mineirão* soccer. The first of five successive league titles came in 1965, and, largely due to Tostão's abilities, Cruzeiro defeated mighty Santos in 1966 to win the Taça Brasil. At age 19, he made his international debut for Brazil against Chile, and a few short weeks later began scoring goals for his national team, in particular against Hungary in the 1966 World Cup.

By 1969, many thought Tostão's career as a world-class player had ended when he was hit in the left eye by a ball in a league match against Corinthians Paulista. The medical diagnosis pointed to a detached retina, and with the World Cup just around the corner, he decided to have surgery performed at an eye hospital in Houston, Texas. The operation was successful, but the press and fans worried about his every move. In the World Cup itself, he directed vital passes to Pelé, Jairzinho, and

Rivelino, playing in every game and setting up numerous goals. He became a national hero, and received worldwide fame. The following year, he was elected the first Latin American Footballer of the Year. In 1972, he was transferred to Vasco da Gama for a record $520,000, but one year later the eye injury became aggravated again, and he was forced to retire.

Now a widely respected public figure in Brazil, he went on to pursue various business interests, including service stations and sports magazines, and in 1975 he entered medical school.

Tottenham Hotspur Football Club

Location: *London, England;* stadium: *White Hart Lane (52,000);* colors: *white jerseys, blue shorts;* honors: *European Cup Winners' Cup (1963), UEFA Cup (1972), English champion (1951, 1961), English cup winner (1901, 1921, 1961, 1962, 1967), English league cup winner (1971, 1973).*

Founded 1882 by young members of the Hotspur Cricket Club in the North London suburb of Tottenham. In 1885, they added Tottenham to their name to avoid confusion with another North London club, London Hotspur. The name "Hotspur" was taken from a well-known fifteenth-century personality, Harry Percy, the legendary hotspur, whose titled family, the Northumberlands, owned much of Tottenham during the late Middle Ages. Based in the same neighborhood from the beginning, Tottenham moved to its present location in 1898 from grounds only a few blocks away.

Spurs became one of the most popular English clubs of the postwar era, sharing domination of the league with Manchester United and Wolverhampton Wanderers throughout the 1950s (a period fondly remembered as a golden era in English soccer), and coming to even greater prominence in the 1960s. There were actually two great postwar teams at Tottenham, one built by manager Arthur Rowe in the late 1940s and '50s, and another by the outstanding manager Bill Nicholson in the late 1950s and early 1960s. Rowe's team became famous for its simple and attractive "push-and-run" technique, and in 1950 and '51 won back-to-back second and first division titles. The Spurs' legacy continued to grow, as the legendary Irish wing half Danny Blanchflower came to White Hart Lane in 1954 and set the tone for the transition to Bill Nicholson in 1958. This highly respected team was known for its thoughtful yet marvelously entertaining style.

Blanchflower was joined on the right side by Welsh winger Cliff Jones and Scottish inside forward John White, and on the left side by the wing half Dave Mackay, who became the second most influential personality on the Nicholson team. It reached its zenith with the winning of a league-cup double in 1961, attractively mounted and richly deserved, and became the first English club to achieve this feat since the Aston Villa of 1897, when the league and cup were younger and much smaller in scope. Tottenham's 31 victories in 1961 were a first division record, and its 115 goals one of the highest totals in first division history. The incomparable Jimmy Greaves was signed from AC Milan, and with him another cup followed in 1962. In 1962-63, Spurs forged its way through the European Cup Winners' Cup with style and grace, winning the final with a 5-1 romp over Atlético Madrid. This was the first honor won by an English club in European competition.

In subsequent years, Nicholson brought together a galaxy of excellent players with the club's newly found wealth, but Blanchflower retired in 1964, Jones went into decline, and Dave Mackay was left to lead the team to another cup victory in 1967. Its standing in the league remained very high until the early 1970s, and a UEFA Cup victory (won over England's own Wolverhampton) and two League Cup victories were added to the list of honors between 1971-73. This was followed by a general downward trend, and after the awkward firing of Bill Nicholson, Tottenham was relegated in 1977, though its stay in the second division lasted only one year.

The early history of this famous London club is less glorious than that of the Rowe-Nicholson eras, but no less filled with great tales. A member of the Southern League until its much-delayed election to Division 2 in

1908, Tottenham became the first and only non-league club to win the F.A. Cup (1901) since the league was introduced. The first leg of this historic cup final against Sheffield United was played at Crystal Palace before 110,820 spectators (the earliest known crowd of over 100,000 in history), but it ended in a draw, and in the replay at Bolton, Spurs won by 3-1. Its election into The Football League in 1908 was only the fifth for a southern England club, and helped to launch London's biggest rivalry, Spurs vs. Arsenal. This confrontation became substantially more serious after Arsenal's move from South to North London in 1913—viewed by Tottenham as an encroachment of territory—and much bitterness ensued. The rivalry is now on more healthy terms, though perhaps not in the eyes of North London fans, and the two managements have recently come together to consider the possibility of building a new joint stadium at Alexandria Park.

touch

The area of the playing field that is outside the two touchlines. Hence, a ball "in touch" has crossed over a sideline and is out-of-bounds.

The term has survived from the eighteenth and early nineteenth centuries when in most types of football, the ball was touched down out-of-bounds to register a score. As early as the Harrow Rules of ca. 1835, English rulemakers differentiated between a ball "in touch" and one "behind." A throw-in was required for a "touch" ball or one that crossed over the opponent's goal line, and a kickout was specified when the ball went "behind" one's own goal line. In the Cambridge University Rules of 1848, all balls "in touch" were thrown in, and all balls "behind" were kicked out. The Cambridge rule, which distinguishes between the two out-of-bound areas, remains in modern Laws XV and XVI.

transfer

The movement of a player from one club to another.

Transfers in Europe and South America have traditionally involved straight cash transactions. The trading of one player for another, or trades combined with a sum of cash, is uncommon and confined mainly to North America. The transfer system, which was developed in England near the end of the last century, is currently undergoing a major upheaval, because the amounts of players' signing-on fees, i.e., the percentage of a transfer fee to which a player is entitled, are increasing rapidly, sometimes reaching vast six-figure sums. While historically limited to 5 percent, signing-on fees have recently taken on the appearance of bonuses, as practiced in major American sports.

In Western Europe, where the rights of players are generally more respected than elsewhere, the transfer system is based on a traditional procedure. When, for strategic or personal reasons, a club decides to dispense with a player's services, it notifies the player of its intention, and puts him on a *transfer list*. A value price, or proposed *transfer fee*, is established, and other clubs are invited to meet that price. In some cases, a player is offered as a *free transfer*, in which case his market value is zero. After an agreement has been reached by two clubs, the fee is paid by the purchasing club, usually in installments over a period of time.

An agreement cannot be completed unless the player consents to move to the new club. Certain countries in which player associations have little power do not require a player's consent. Uruguay, in particular, has suffered a number of player strikes in recent years over this issue. In some cases, a player may request to be transferred to a specific club, but he will probably waive his right to a percentage of the transfer fee if he does so. A transfer may involve other kinds of reciprocation, especially in the case of international transfers. If the purchasing club is especially popular or successful, a friendly may be arranged with the selling club in order to gain box-office revenues. In Eastern Europe, except for Yugoslavia, money and gifts sometimes change hands, as in the West, but many transfers are determined by sports officials, who, for one reason or another, wish to elevate the stature of a given club, or to punish a given player.

Various national associations have, for specified periods of time, prohibited their players from being transferred abroad, or vice versa. Such restrictions are usually made in an effort to minimize the impact of transfers on gate receipts, the quality of play at home, or a national team manager's ability to organize and prepare his squad properly. Spain allows two foreign players per club. Austria prohibits the transfer abroad of any player under 26 years of age. In preparation for the 1978 World Cup, both Argentina and Uruguay blocked all transfers abroad of selected internationals. Eastern European countries, with the exception of Yugoslavia, have stringent international transfer regulations, although Poland made some exceptions after its high placement in the 1974 World Cup. There are no restrictions on transfers between any two British countries or between them and the Republic of Ireland.

Transfers existed in England even before the legalization of professionalism in 1885, although all transactions were made under the table. Aston Villa was the first big spender in the marketplace. As early as 1892, Villa paid £ 100 to West Bromwich Albion for Scottish star Willie Groves, and an additional £ 40 for John Reynolds, the great right halfback. Any fees or bonuses given to players during this period were informally decided. One of the earliest records of a signing-on fee has been traced to an unknown forward, formerly of Celtic, who in 1892 asked "£8 down; £ 3 a week and 25s. during the close season" to sign with the little Liverpool club Bootle F.C. But to trade athletes in a commodities market like so many pounds of beef was reprehensible to the opponents of professionalism. Indeed, the subject of transfer fees became the most rankling issue within the larger debate over professionalism in both soccer and rugby. A

Captain Philip Trevor, writing in *Badminton Magazine* (April 1897), had this to say for misguided ideals:

... transfer papers have been prepared with all the detailed care and accuracy of the title deeds of a property and his leasehold services have been acquired in accordance with the fluctuating conditions of the market and the then value of the article bartered. The old gladiator system lacked the completeness of the recognized procedure under which prominent football players are now bought, sold and manipulated, but the balance of sportsmanship probably lies with the Romans.

Nevertheless, the practice of transferring players to help a club improve the quality of its team became increasingly common. In 1899, an attempt was made to place a ceiling on the amount that could be requested in a transfer fee, but in 1908 the last effort to set ceilings was abandoned as impracticable. Finally, in 1912, the legality of the transfer system was upheld in the English courts in the famous test case, "L.J. Kingaby vs. Aston Villa." Kingaby, a Villa player whose desire to be transferred had been thwarted by the excessive transfer fee his club was asking, lost his suit to be released from the club, but, in so doing, established the legality of the existence of Villa's transfer fee in the first place.

Transfer systems adopted by other countries in subsequent decades were modeled on the English idea, whether inadvertently or by design, and remain unchanged to this day, with the exception of appropriate legal variations. Some countries have now formulated free agent clauses, whereby a player cannot be retained against his will after his contract has expired. England was one of the first countries to enact such a rule in 1963.

Record Transfers (*Although no transfer fee was paid as part of Pelé's signing with the Cosmos in 1975, the overall sum of $3.5 million, which was the total value of the multifaceted contract, is a world record for any soccer transaction.*)

1893	John Southworth. Blackburn Rovers to Everton	£ 400
1905	Alfred Common. Sunderland to Middlesbrough	£ 1000
1922	Sydney Puddefoot. West Ham United to Falkirk	£ 5000
1928	David Jack. Bolton Wanderers to Arsenal	£ 10,890

1947	Tommy Lawton. Chelsea to Notts Co.	£ 20,000
1951	John Sewell. Notts. Co. to Sheffield Wednesday	£ 4,500
1954	Juan Schiaffino. Peñarol to AC Milan	L. 111,000,000 ($200,000)
1961	Luis Suárez. Barcelona to Inter	£ 262,500,000 ($420,000)
1968	Pietro Anastasi. Varese to Juventus	£ 666,000,000 ($1.2 million)
1973	Johann Cruyff. Ajax to Barcelona	90 million-ptas. ($1.53 million)
1975	Giuseppi Savoldi. Bologna to Napoli	£ 2 billion ($2.8 million)

See also: **signing-on fee**

trap

To interrupt the line of flight of a ball, and gain possession by any lawful use of the body. There are numerous ways to trap a ball, among them the inside-of-the-foot trap, outside-of-the-foot trap, chest trap, thigh trap, stomach trap, and sole trap (with the bottom of the foot), as well as those that use the head or lower part of the leg.

Trinidad and Tobago

Trinidad and Tobago Football Association
110 Abercromby Street
P.O. Box 400
Port of Spain

Founded: 1906
FIFA: 1963
CONCACAF: 1964

Affiliated clubs: 132; registered players: 3,590; national stadium: Queen's Park Oval, Port of Spain (20,000); largest stadium: Queen's Park Oval; colors: red jerseys, black shorts; season: June to December; honors: none.

The Trinidad Amateur Football Association is the second oldest British-instituted association in the Caribbean region, and was the first to become directly affiliated with The Football Association in London, in 1906. The population of Trinidad, however, was so small and the distance from many potential Caribbean opponents so great that Port of Prince was never included on the main soccer-playing routes. The earliest record of a Trinidad international, though it was less than a full international, is a 3-3 draw with Surinam in 1934 at Port of Spain.

In 1963, one year after independence, the new Trinidad Football Association joined FIFA as a full member, and proceeded to enter as many competitions as it could. The major clubs, Malvern, Maple Club, and Palo Seco, were seen in the CONCACAF club championship, and Trinidad became a regular participant in the Championship of CONCACAF. Its highest achievement to date has been a second place finish in the CONCACAF qualifying rounds for the 1974 World Cup, after defeating Surinam, Guatemala, Mexico, and Netherlands Antilles—major forces in the Caribbean region. In 1969, Trinidad heralded its arrival in the mainstream of Caribbean soccer by holding Mexico to a scoreless draw in the CONCACAF Championship. In 1972-73, this small cricket-playing island came within two points of going to West Germany and meeting Italy, Argentina, and Poland in the first round of the 1974 World Cup. Honduras and the eventual qualifier, Haiti, thwarted Trinidad's momentous opportunity.

Trinidad and its smaller sister island of Tobago have 74 clubs competing in the national league or national cup competition, but there are 122 senior-level clubs overall. Most soccer activity is on the island of Trinidad, but Tobago was added to the name of the national association in 1975.

trip

To intentionally throw an opponent with the feet or legs, causing him to stumble or lose balance; or to intentionally stoop in front of or behind an opponent, causing him to be thrown. The offended side is awarded a direct free kick. An attempt to trip is also penalized by a direct free kick. Tripping has been prohibited by all football codes since the first rules were drawn up in the early nineteenth century, i.e., Harrow Rules, Cambridge Rules, Sheffield Rules, and Football Association Laws of the Game.

See also: **hack**

tsu chu

The ancient Chinese game of football, *tsu chu*, was first played during the reign of Emperor Huang-Ti (ca. 2500 B.C.). Historians believe this is the earliest date ever associated with a football game of any kind. During the Ts'in Dynasty (255-206 B.C.), and possibly as early as the period of the contending states in the fourth century B.C., some form of the game is known to have been used in training soldiers. Records also show that it was played extensively during the Han Dynasty (206 B.C.-220 A.D.).

"Tsu" translates as "kicking a ball with one's feet"; "chu" refers to "a stuffed ball made of animal skin." *Tsu chu*, as well as the Japanese game *kemari*, is in some ways more closely related to modern soccer than the more famous Greek game *episkyros* and Roman *harpastum*. It appears to have been played in front of the emperor's palace in celebration of his birthday. Two elements of play have been reconstructed from Han sources by Chinese scholars. A net, or mesh, was stretched between two 30-foot high bamboo poles, and the players attempted to kick a ball through a gap in the net. Players dribbled the ball and were allowed to use their chests, backs, and shoulders to keep the ball from the opposing team. Historians have emphasized the importance of the players' ability to dribble.

No evidence of a historical link between *tsu chu* and the modern game has been found, though one or two Italian historians have suggested that medieval Italian explorers brought back a forerunner of *calcio* from China around the time of Marco Polo.

Tunisia

Fédération Tunisienne de Football
28 rue Lénine
P.O. Box 297
Tunis

Founded: ca. 1956
FIFA: 1960
CAF: 1960

Affiliated clubs: *145;* registered players: *14,500;* national stadium: *Stade Olympique, Tunis (50,000);* largest stadium: *Stade Olympique;* colors: *red jerseys, white shorts;* season: *September to June;* honors: *African Nations' Cup runner-up (1965).*

Tunisia ranks with Morocco as the major soccer-playing country in former French North Africa. It was the first African nation other than Egypt to gain the final rounds of the Olympic Games, and it was an early participant in the African Nations' Cup. Like their counterparts in Morocco and Algeria, Tunisian clubs have been reluctant to travel the length and breadth of Africa to compete in African club championships, but they are nevertheless among the strongest on the continent, having benefited from almost 60 years of continuous competition at home. In the late 1970s, Tunisia's national team was among the most powerful in Africa, and became the strongest of all in qualifying for the 1978 World Cup final rounds.

Although French colonists began playing soccer in Tunis around the turn of the century, the rapid growth of Tunisian soccer began, as it did in France itself, immediately after World War I. The Ligue de Tunisie de Football was founded in 1921 and became affiliated with the French Football Federation. Two club competitions were started immediately—a league called the Division d'Honneur in 1921 and a cup competition, the Coupe de Tunis, in 1922. Prior to this, however, Tunisian clubs competed in the annual North African Championship with Algerian and Moroccan clubs beginning in 1919, and it was a Tunisian team, Racing Club de Tunis, that won the very first edition.

In the Division d'Honneur, the first winner was again Racing Club, and, while Racing won again in 1924, other important clubs such as Stade Gaulois, Sporting Club, Avant-Garde, Union Sportive Tunisienne, Italia, Savoia de La Goulette, and Club Sportif Gabesien, all of Tunis, won the remaining league titles before World War II. Sfax Railway Sports in 1933 was the only provincial winner. In the Coupe de Tunis, whose first winner was Avant-Garde, the same clubs held sway, and in 1938 Espérance Sportive Tunis, still a major force in Tunisian soccer in the 1970s, won its first trophy. Tunis selections began to compete with their opposite numbers from Algiers, Oran, and Constantine on an annual basis in the 1930s and with Morocco in 1948. They accumulated an overall winning record against Constantine, but were less successful against Algiers, Oran, and Morocco. The North African Cup, launched in 1930 along similar lines to the North African Championship, was won only once by a Tunisian club before World War II—Italia in 1935. In 1928, Tunisia made its unofficial international debut with a 3-2 loss to France "B" in Tunis. Tunisian selections played over a half dozen games against France "B" from 1928-56, losing each one.

Tunisian soccer expanded again after World War II, and in the mid-1950s the Tunisian league finally broke ties with France to form the Fédération Tunisienne de Football. In 1960, Tunisia blazed an African trail into the final rounds of the Olympic Games, but was thwarted in its first bid for world honors by three first round losses to Denmark and Poland, full international teams, and Argentina. In 1962, Tunisia became the first French-speaking North African country to enter the African Nations' Cup, but in a field of four it had to settle for third place behind experienced Egypt and Ethiopia. Tunisia entered again in 1963, failing to emerge from its first round group with a win, and in 1965 it qualified automatically as host of the competition. Tunisia won its first round group—on goal average over Senegal—and moved into the final against Ghana, losing 3-2. The outstanding player in this game was Tunisia's captain and playmaker, Majid Chetali, who in 1978 coached the national team in its successful run for the final rounds of the World Cup. This was Tunisia's last serious African Nations' Cup bid until 1978.

Tunisia's interest in the World Cup, like that of its archrival Morocco, has always been keen. The French-speaking North African countries are closer to the mainstream of European soccer than the rest of Africa, and Europe's World Cup fever spills easily across the Mediterranean. Morocco having been the first African country in 36 years to qualify for the World Cup final rounds in 1970, Tunisia put together an impressive effort for the 1978 edition to avenge its rival's accomplishment, defeating four big African powers in qualifying rounds—Morocco, Guinea, Nigeria, and Egypt—a tough list of opponents. Under Chetali's German-trained guidance, this team was widely hailed as the finest ever to have come out of Africa. Of its many famous stars, two stood out—1978 African Footballer of the Year Dhiab Tarak at left midfield (from Espérance), and the long-time captain Sadok Sassi Attouga in the goal (from Club Africain). In the first round of the World Cup finals in Argentina, the Tunisian team surpassed even optimistic expectations, defeating Mexico 3-1, losing to mighty Poland by a mere 1-0, and, best of all, holding West Germany to a goalless draw. Though it failed to advance beyond the first round, Tunisia emerged as the Cinderella team of 1978, and following the competition virtually the whole team received lucrative contracts from wealthy Saudi Arabian clubs.

The first division of the Tunisian league now consists of 14 clubs, most of which come from Tunis. The venerable Club Africain, Espérance, and Stade Tunisien are among the leading clubs in the capital. Of late, Club Sportive Sfax, from Tunisia's second city down the coast, has also become a production center for many top players. Other cities where soccer is firmly implanted include Sousse, Bizerte, and Gabes to the south.

Turkey

Türkiye Futbol Federasyonu
Ulus Is Hani A Blok Kat: 4
Ankara

Founded: 1923
FIFA: 1923
UEFA: 1962

Affiliated clubs: *1,432;* **registered players:** *43,229 (2,101 professional, 268 non-amateur);* **national stadium:** *19 Mayis Stadi, Ankara (35,000);* **largest stadium:** *Atatürk Stadi, Izmir (70,000);* **colors:** *white jerseys, white shorts;* **season:** *September to June;* **honors:** *none.*

The history of Turkish soccer is an unusually accurate reflection of the modernization Turkey has experienced in its overall cultural life. Growth of the sport falls squarely into two distinct periods: during the Ottoman Empire, and since the birth of the republic. Turkey has been surprisingly active in international competition, especially after World War II, and since its official induction into the European soccer community in the early 1960s, it has been every bit as active as the other minor soccer-playing countries of Europe. Turkish teams have occasionally broken through in major international competitions, only to be beaten down again, and in recent years a hefty domestic schedule has helped to spread the power in Turkish soccer to population centers other than Istanbul.

The game was first played in Turkey by British residents and Greek students in Smyrna (Izmir), the Aegean port city, in 1895 or 1896. From the beginning, Ottoman authorities were fearful that soccer was linked with insurrectional instincts, and in the volatile atmosphere of the Ottoman Empire in its last years, the game alone was cause enough to warrant swift retaliatory measures. To make matters worse, the game immediately became associated in the minds of the police with Armenians, Greeks, Bulgarians and other potential "enemies" of the state. When a group of Galatasaray High School students in Constantinople attempted to form a team around 1899, the effort was suppressed.

In 1905, another brave band of Galatasaray students formed a team, and this was to be the proud forerunner of the present Galatasaray club, the oldest in the country. At about this time, an Istanbul Sunday Amateur League was introduced, and in 1907, Fenerbahçe Spor Kulubu, the most successful of all Turkish clubs, was founded in the Beyoglu section of Constantinople, not far from the Galatasary High School. There is some evidence that young Turkish players learned the game quickly after the turn of the century, because in 1911 Galatasaray defeated a Hungarian club at home by 4-2, and buried Olimpia Bucharest by 11-1 in Bucharest. Between 1908-12, more clubs were founded in Constantinople and Smyrna, but they were usually formed along ethnic lines, and there was little uniformity of rules. The Balkan War of 1912 aggravated Ottoman repression, and the "ethnic" games nearly disappeared altogether.

The turning point was the fall of the Turkish Empire after World War I. The Türk Spor Kurumu (Turkish Sports Committee) was established in 1920, and Turks began playing in ever-increasing numbers. In 1923, the founding date of the republic, the Türkiye Futbol Federasyonu (TFF) was established in the new capital city of Ankara, and plans were made to introduce a national championship for the 1923-24 season. From that date until 1951, Turkish champions were determined by a knockout competition between the winners of each district league. The first winner in 1924 was Harbuje, another Beyoglu district club in Istanbul. During the next seven years, the championship was completed only once, and between 1922-35 it reappeared, with three Istanbul clubs taking away the honors. The league was nearly dormant throughout the late 1930s, but was revived with some regularity from 1940-50. Istanbul clubs continued to predominate until 1949.

Turkey made its international debut only months after the founding of the Turkish F.A. in 1923 against Rumania in Istanbul, resulting in a 2-2 draw. One year later, the TFF ambitiously entered the Olympic Games in Paris, but was unfortunate to be drawn against Czechoslovakia (at that time one of Europe's finest teams), and the result was a predictable 5-2 loss. This was followed by a tour of the Baltic states, against which Turkey won all three matches, and Poland. In the next four years Turkey played 11 full internationals, all of them friendlies and restricted to the Balkans, the USSR, and Poland. The latter two were Turkey's most difficult opponents during this period, but Bulgaria and Rumania were both defeated at least once. Only a half dozen internationals were played between 1928 and World War II, two of them severe losses in Olympic competition: 1-7 against precocious Egypt in 1928, and 0-4 vs. Norway at the Nazi Olympics in 1936. Between 1923 and its last prewar international against Yugoslavia in 1937, Turkey emerged from the Ottoman legacy and managed to win seven and draw three of its 24 games.

After 1950, modernization progressed still further, and the outmoded national championship was halted in 1951 with the introduction of professionalism. The controversies that inevitably resulted were primarily caused by the fear that professionalism would widen the gap between large and small clubs. Regional league championships were continued throughout the 1950s, but Istanbul's position as the hotbed of soccer competition prospered under professionalism. Beşiktaş and Fenerbahçe, two of Istanbul's wealthiest clubs, won the first two professional championships in 1952 and 1953, but the popular Galatasaray did not participate in league competition until some years later. A national champion was not crowned again until the first genuine national league was established in 1958, to conform to European Cup regulations.

The rise of professionalism spawned Turkey's finest era in international competition. Between 1948-55, the national team won 13 games and lost only 11, including a 2-1 win over Germany FR in West Berlin and the surprising elimination of Spain in qualification rounds for the 1954 World Cup. Turkey reached its first World Cup, and promptly defeated hapless Korea Republic. Not having to play against Hungary in its opening round group, Turkey succumbed twice (the second was a replay under old World Cup rules) to the eventual world champion, West Germany, by an aggregate of 11-3, and was eliminated, though the replay was played without its great goalkeeper and captain, Turgay. Turkey's winning form continued, however, and nine months before the Soviet invasion of Budapest it defeated Hungary, 3-1, in Istanbul to register the Magyar's second defeat in six years and the biggest win in Turkish soccer history. The hero of this era was goalscoring ace

Küçükandonyadis Lefter, the Fenerbahçe forward who played briefly for Fiorentina and OGC Nice.

There were to be no more World Cup qualifications for Turkey, and since 1956, it has returned almost exactly to its pre-World War I level of success, winning about a dozen of its 45 full internationals. Turkey played in the first European Nations' Cup in 1958-60, bowing out to Rumania, and was roundly defeated by Italy in 1962-64. In subsequent editions, Turkey has failed to advance to the second round. Its best result in this series has been a 1-1 draw away to Germany FR in 1970-72. The Turkish national amateur team, meanwhile, failed to qualify for any editions of the postwar Olympic Games. Historical mistrust and Turkey's efforts to Europeanize have limited contacts on the playing field with Middle East neighbors, but with the introduction of the R.C.D. Pact Tournament in 1970, a link has been established with Iran and Pakistan. Recently, Turkey has played Algeria, Saudi Arabia, Syria, and Tunisia, losing only to Algeria.

Turkish clubs have been eager participants in all three European club competitions. In the European Cup, Galatasaray was fortunate to play in the 1956-57 edition on the basis of its Istanbul league championship, and from 1958-59 Turkish champions have regularly taken part in the competition. Turkey's furthest advance has been Galatasaray's elimination in the 1969-70 quarter-finals by Legia Warsaw. In the European Cup Winners' Cup, three clubs have advanced to the quarter-finals: Fenerbahçe in 1963-64, Göztepe Izmir in 1969-70, and Bursapor in 1974-75. Göztepe, meanwhile, did better than expected in the Fairs Cups of the mid- to late-1960s, gaining the third round twice, and in 1969-70 moving all the way to the semi-finals on a string of good luck results, including a walkover against Hamburger SV in the quarter-finals.

The Turkish first division now comprises 16 clubs. A welcome break from Istanbul's hegemony in the league occurred in the mid-1970s, when Trabzonspor, from the eastern Black Sea city of Trabzon, won two championships in a row. Since the introduction of the national league in 1958, however, the big Istanbul clubs, Fenerbahçe, Galatasaray, and Beşiktaş, have generally swept league honors. Lesser clubs have been able to advance more often in the Turkish Cup, but the credibility of this relatively new competition (it is Europe's newest cup) is not yet established.

Champions

1924	Harbuje	1943	no competition	1962	Galatasaray
1925	no competition	1944	Gençlerbirligi	1963	Galatasaray
1926	no competition	1945	Harb Okulu Gücü	1964	Fenerbahçe
1927	Muhafiz Gücü	1946	Gençlerbirligi	1965	Fenerbahçe
1928	no competition	1947	Demirspor	1966	Beşiktaş
1929	no competition	1948	no competition	1967	Beşiktaş
1930	no competition	1949	Ankara Gücü	1968	Fenerbahçe
1931	no competition	1950	Göztepe Izmir	1969	Fenerbahçe
1932	Istanbulspor	1951	no national champion	1970	Fenerbahçe
1933	Fenerbahçe	1952	no national champion	1971	Galatasaray
1934	Beşiktaş	1953	no national champion	1972	Galatasaray
1935	Fenerbahçe	1954	no national champion	1973	Galatasaray
1936	no competition	1955	no national champion	1974	Fenerbahçe
1937	no competition	1956	no national champion	1975	Fenerbahçe
1938	no competition	1957	no national champion	1976	Trabzonspor
1939	no competition	1958	no national champion	1977	Trabzonspor
1940	Demirspor	1959	Fenerbahçe	1978	Fenerbahçe
1941	Gençlerbirligi	1960	Beşiktaş		
1942	Harb Okulu Gücü	1961	Fenerbahçe		

Cup Winners

1963	Galatasaray	1968	Fenerbahçe	1974	Fenerbahçe
1963	Galatasaray	1969	Göztepe Izmir	1975	Beşiktaş
1964	Galatasaray	1970	Göztepe Izmir	1976	Galatasaray
1965	Galatasaray	1971	Eskisehirspor	1977	Trabzonspor
1966	Galatasaray	1972	Ankara Gücü	1978	Trabzonspor
1967	Altay Izmir	1973	Galatasaray		

U

UEFA Cup

Coupe UEFA—UEFA-Pokal.

Played under a variety of names over the years, this is the third-ranking European championship for clubs, and in some ways the most revealing. By its sheer number of participants, the UEFA Cup holds a unique place in international competition as a vast showcase for teams from every corner of Europe.

Introduced in 1955 as the International Industries Fairs Inter-Cities Cup, known commonly as the Fairs Cup, it was established as a tournament for the cities of Europe that sponsored international industrial fairs, and was originally intended to be contested by representative teams from those cities. Its prime mover was Ernst Thommen, a Swiss vice president of the Union of European Football Associations (UEFA). In April 1955, less than one year after the formation of UEFA, Thommen organized a conference in Basel and invited representatives of 12 cities from ten countries to establish plans for the competition. The first edition began in the fall of that year, and was to be played over a period of two seasons to minimize conflicts with domestic schedules.

As it turned out, the first competition took three years to complete, and some of the participating teams (Barcelona, Milan, and Birmingham, for example) were actually major clubs representing their cities. The teams representing Vienna and Cologne withdrew before the competition started, but the other ten cities at the charter meeting carried through with their commitments. The second edition (1958-60) was played almost exclusively by major clubs rather than city-wide selections. In 1960-61, the series was established as an annual event, and became widely regarded as the third major European club championship, dropping its pretense as a friendly gathering of trade fair cities.

By the early 1960s, the organizing committee decided that the competition should be opened to the leading clubs of each country that were not eligible for either the European Champions' Cup or the European Cup Winners' Cup (a policy still in effect). In 1966-67, the competition became known as the European Fairs Cup, and though it had been sanctioned by UEFA from the beginning, its organization and administration were performed by a special committee wholly outside the structure of UEFA. In 1971, it was announced that the European governing body would assume official responsibility for the cup beginning with the 1971-72 edition. Its name was changed to the UEFA Cup, and a special play-off was held between the first winner (Barcelona) and the current winner (Leeds United) to decide which should retain permanent possession of the trophy. Barcelona won, and a new trophy was donated by UEFA.

The present UEFA Cup is played along the same lines as the champions' and cup winners' cups (except for the two-leg final): home and away knockout basis with the winner decided by goal aggregate. The away goals rule applies in case of a draw, to be followed by penalty kicks if so needed after the second leg. Each country is designated a specific number of berths in each competition depending on UEFA's estimation of the relative strength of each national league. The present number of berths allotted to each country is as follows: four (England, Germany FR, and Italy); three (Spain); two (Austria, Belgium Bulgaria, Czechoslovakia, Denmark, France, German DR, Greece, Hungary, Netherlands, Norway, Poland, Portugal, Rumania, Scotland, Sweden, Switzerland, Turkey, USSR, and Yugoslavia); one (Albania, Cyprus, Finland, Iceland Northern Ireland, Republic of Ireland, Luxembourg, and Malta). These numbers have fluctuated very little over the years. (The major Welsh clubs are members of the English league, and Liechtenstein has not yet formed a national league.)

The outstanding feature of the Fairs and UEFA Cups has been their domination by English clubs, indicating the overall depth and strength of The Football League in England. English clubs have won the competition a record seven times, appearing in the final in 12 of the 20 editions through 1978. In addition, as many as seven different English clubs have appeared in these 12 finals. Six of

England's victories were in succession between 1968-73. Spanish clubs have won six titles, including five of the first six, but three of these victories were achieved by one club and two by another—pointing to the strength of these clubs, but not necessarily to the overall strength of the Spanish league. Italian clubs have won twice, and the other winners have been spread evenly among Hungary, Yugoslavia, and the Netherlands. Barcelona is the only club to have won the competition three times, and the double has been achieved by Valencia, Leeds United, and Liverpool. Four clubs, Ferencváros, Juventus, Dinamo Zagreb, and Borussia Mönchengladbach, have each won once and lost in the final once.

The history of the Fairs/UEFA Cup has fallen roughly into four periods: 1) the initial period (1955-61), when the original concept of the competition was followed or being phased out; 2) the early years of the annual competition (1961-66), which were dominated by Spanish clubs; 3) the English period (1966-74); and 4) the current period (1974-present).

1955-61. The first Fairs Cup (1955-58) was not played on a knockout basis until the semifinal round. In the first round, the 12 entrants were separated into four groups of three teams each, and they played on a league basis. After Vienna and Cologne withdrew, the remaining teams were selections from Copenhagen, Zagreb, Lausanne, Leipzig, London, Frankfurt, and Basel, as well as CF Barcelona representing the Catalan capital, Inter Milan representing Milan, and Birmingham City F.C. representing Birmingham. The competition stretched into a three-year marathon, which made it extremely difficult for selectors to return a cohesive team to each match. The result was a smashing victory for the experienced club side of CF Barcelona. The handwriting was already on the wall regarding the subject of city selections vs. established clubs.

When the second edition (1958-60) started, nearly all the participants were clubs, and the best among them won the cup for the second time in a row. The knockout format of the European Champions' Cup was adopted for all rounds, and the competition was completed within the prescribed two years. Barcelona's second win, however, spelled doom for the original concept of the series. As long as individual countries were at liberty to send the team of their choice, some entrants would inevitably be strong club teams such as Barcelona. It was apparent that such a circumstance rendered the tournament a foregone conclusion, so for the third edition (1960-61), the series became an annual event for leading clubs in Europe that were not eligible for either of the big two continental championships. Birmingham City, as experienced as any English club in European competition, reached the final again, but Italy found its first winner in AS Roma with the last leg left incomplete until the fall of 1961.

1961-66. Although Barcelona had won two of the first three Fairs Cups, its opposition was, if anything, eclectic. Between 1961-62 and 1965-66, however, Spanish clubs not only won the trophy four times, but both finalists were Spanish in three of these. In addition, only three Spanish clubs were involved. In the 1962 final, Valencia defeated Barcelona; in 1964, Real Zaragoza defeated Valencia; and in 1966, Barcelona defeated Real Zaragoza. This was accomplished with 32 or more European clubs seeking the same trophy. Not even the English in their upcoming halcyon days could claim such a feat.

1966-74. Between 1966-67 and 1973-74, English clubs appeared in every final without exception, and of these they won all but the first and last, a total of six successive championships. Five different clubs, Leeds United, Newcastle United, Arsenal, Tottenham Hotspur, and Liverpool shared these victories, with Leeds repeating once. Leeds, in addition, was losing finalist in 1967, and Tottenham lost the final in 1974. It was also during this period that the number of participants jumped dramatically from 32 clubs in 1966-67, to 64 in 1969-70, where it remains today.

1974-present. The great English clubs declined, and their place was taken by a variety of leading clubs from West Germany, Italy, Spain, Belgium, and the Netherlands, although England's Liverpool won the cup a second time and became the fourth English club to do so.

Winners

1955-58	CF Barcelona	1961-62	Valencia
1958-60	CF Barcelona	1962-63	Valencia
1960-61	AS Roma	1963-64	Real Zaragoza

1964-65	Ferencváros	1971-72	Tottenham Hotspur
1965-66	CF Barcelona	1972-73	Liverpool
1966-67	Dinamo Zagreb	1973-74	Feyenoord
1967-68	Leeds United	1974-75	Borussia Mönchengladbach
1968-69	Newcastle United	1975-76	Liverpool
1969-70	Arsenal	1976-77	Juventus
1970-71	Leeds United	1977-78	PSV Eindhoven

Cumulative Ranking of the Top 20 Clubs (1955-78)

(number of editions in parentheses)

			P	W	D	L	F	A	P
1.	Barcelona (16)	(Spa)	102	51	23	28	209	127	125
2.	Juventus (9)	(Ita)	76	45	14	17	134	59	104
3.	FC Köln (13)	(GFR)	76	40	9	27	156	105	89
4.	Leeds United (7)	(Eng)	61	31	20	10	103	49	82
5.	Valencia (10)	(Spa)	56	30	11	15	117	74	71
6.	Liverpool (6)	(Eng)	46	28	9	9	90	30	65
7.	Ferencváros (8)	(Hun)	55	28	8	19	98	61	64
8.	Dinamo Zagreb (11)	(Yug)	57	23	15	19	97	68	61
9.	Hibernian (11)	(Sco)	51	24	9	28	90	80	57
10.	Athletic Bilbao (8)	(Spa)	50	23	10	17	67	56	56
11.	Vitoria Setubal (8)	(Rum)	48	24	5	19	77	55	53
12.	AS Roma (8)	(Ita)	44	22	9	13	76	50	53
13.	Inter Milan (10)	(Ita)	47	23	8	16	90	55	53
14.	Tottenham Hotspur (3)	(Eng)	34	22	7	5	83	27	51
15.	Real Zaragoza (7)	(Spa)	44	23	5	16	88	69	51
16.	Twente Enschede (5)	(Net)	38	19	6	13	75	46	44
17.	Borussia M'bach (2)	(GFR)	24	20	2	2	68	21	42
18.	AC Milan (6)	(Ita)	37	17	8	12	52	38	42
19.	Hamburger SV (5)	(GFR)	30	17	6	7	60	32	40
20.	Napoli (7)	(Ita)	30	15	7	8	39	35	37

Miscellaneous Records and Statistics

Most editions participated in: 16, by FC Barcelona.
Most games played: 102, by FC Barcelona.
Most wins: 51, by FC Barcelona.
Most losses: 28, by FC Barcelona.
Most goals for: 209, by FC Barcelona.
Most goals against: 127, by FC Barcelona.
Record home victory: FC Köln 13, US Luxembourg 0, 1965-66.
Record away victory: US Rumelange 0, Feyenoord 12, 1972-73.
Best goal aggregate in a final: 8-2 (CF Barcelona drew with London 2-2 and defeated them by 6-0, 1955-58).
Record victory in a final leg: CF Barcelona 6, London 0, 1955-58.

Highest aggregate score in a match: 13 (FC Köln 13, US Luxembourg 0, 1965-66).

Best goal aggregate in a round: 21-0 (Feyenoord defeated US Rumelange by 9-0 and 12-0, 1972-73).

Record attendance: 80,000 (AC Milan vs. Athlone, Stadio San Siro, Milan, 1975-76; Barcelona vs. Liverpool, Estadir Nou Camp, Barcelona, 1975-76).

Record attendance for a final: 76,000 (Ferencváros vs. Leeds United, Népstadion, Budapest, 1967-68).

Results

FAIRS CUP

1955-58

Group 1

*Barcelona—Copenhagen   6-2, 1-1

	P	W	D	L	F	A	P
Barcelona	2	1	1	0	7	3	3
Copenhagen	2	0	1	1	3	7	1
Vienna			withdrew				

Group 2

Birmingham City—*Internazionale   0-0, 2-1
Birmingham City—*Zagreb   1-0, 3-0
Internazionale—*Zagreb   1-0, 4-0

	P	W	D	L	F	A	P
Birmingham City	4	3	1	0	6	1	7
Internazionale	4	2	1	1	6	2	5
Zagreb	4	0	0	4	0	9	0

Group 3

Lausanne—*Leipzig   3-6, 7-3

	P	W	D	L	F	A	P
Lausanne	2	1	0	1	10	9	2
Leipzig	2	1	0	1	9	10	2
Cologne			withdrew				

Group 4

London—*Basel   5-0, 1-0
*London—Frankfurt   3-2, 0-1
*Frankfurt—Basel   5-1, 2-6

	P	W	D	L	F	A	P
London	4	3	0	1	9	3	6
Frankfurt	4	2	0	2	10	10	4
Basel	4	1	0	3	7	13	2

Semi-Finals

Barcelona—*Birmingham City	3-4, 1-0, 2-1
(play-off in Basel)	
London—*Lausanne	1-2, 2-0

Final

(first leg in London; att. 45,466)

Barcelona	2	London	2
(Tejada, Martinez)		(Greaves, Langley pen)	

(second leg in Barcelona; att.: 62,000)

Barcelona	6	London	0

(Suárez 2, Martinez, Evaristo 2, Verges)

*home team in first leg

1958-60

First Round

Barcelona—*Basel	2-1, 5-2
*Internazionale—Olympique Lyon	7-0, 1-1
*Belgrade—Lausanne	6-1, 5-3
Chelsea—*Frem Copenhagen	3-1, 4-1
*Union St. Gilloise—Leipzig	6-0, 0-1
AS Roma—*Hannover 96	3-1, 1-1
*Zagreb—Ujpest Dozsa	4-2, 0-1
Birmingham City—*FC Köln	2-2, 2-0

Quarter-Finals

*Barcelona—Internazionale	4-0, 4-2
Belgrade—*Chelsea	0-1, 4-1
*Union St. Gilloise—AS Roma	2-0, 1-1
*Birmingham City—Zagreb	1-0, 3-3

Semi-Finals

Barcelona—*Belgrade	1-1, 3-1
Birmingham City—*Union St. Gilloise	4-2, 4-2

Final

(first leg in Birmingham; att. 40,500)

Barcelona	0	Birmingham City	0

(second leg in Barcelona; att. 70,000)

Barcelona	4	Birmingham City	1
(Czibor 2, Martinez, Coll)		(Hooper)	

*home team in first leg

1960-61

First Round

AS Roma—*Union St. Gilloise	0-0, 4-1
FC Köln—*Olympique Lyon	3-1, 1-2
Hibernian—*Lausanne	2-0, —
(Lausanne withdrew)	
Barcelona—*Zagreb	1-1, 4-3
Belgrade—*Leipzig	2-5, 4-1, 2-0
(play-off in Budapest)	
*Internazionale—Hannover 96	8-2, 6-1
*KB Copenhagen—FC Basel	8-1, 3-3
*Birmingham City—Újpest Dózsa	3-2, 2-1

Quarter-Finals

AS Roma—*FC Köln	2-0, 0-2, 4-1
(play-off in Rome)	
Hibernian—*Barcelona	4-4, 3-2
*Internazionale—Belgrade	5-0, 0-1
Birmingham City—*KB Copenhagen	4-4, 5-0

Semi-Finals

AS Roma—*Hibernian	2-2, 3-3, 6-0
(play-off in Rome)	
Birmingham City—*Internazionale	2-1, 2-1

Final

(first leg in Birmingham; att. 21,000)

AS Roma	2	Birmingham City	2
(Manfredini 2)		(Hellawell, Orritt)	

(second leg in Rome; att. 60,000)

AS Roma	2	Birmingham City	0
(Farmer og, Pestrin)			

*home team in first leg

1961-62

First Round

*Valencia—Nottingham Forest	2-0, 5-1
Internazionale—FC Köln	2-4, 2-0, 5-3
(play-off in Milan)	
Heart of Midlothian—*Union St. Gilloise	3-1, 2-0
Leipzig—*Spartak Brno	2-2, 4-1
MTK Budapest—*Racing Club Strasbourg	3-1, 10-2
Vojvodina Novi Sad—*AC Milan	0-0, 2-0
Red Star Belgrade—*FC Basel	1-1, 4-1
*Hibernian—Belenenses	3-3, 3-1
Español—*Hannover 96	1-0, 2-0
Sheffield Wednesday—*Olympique Lyon	2-4, 5-2
Dinamo Zagreb—*KB Copenhagen	7-2, 2-2
Barcelona—*West Berlin	0-1, 3-0

Second Round

Valencia—*Lausanne	4-3, —
(Second leg not played)	
Internazionale—*Heart of Midlothian	1-0, 4-0
*MTK Budapest—Leipzig	3-0, 0-3, 2-0
(play-off in Bratislava)	
Vjovodina Novi Sad—*Iraklis Solonika	1-2, 9-1
Red Star Belgrade—Hibernian	4-0, 1-0
*Español—Birmingham City	5-2, 0-1
*Sheffield Wednesday—AS Roma	4-0, 0-1
*Barcelona—Dinamo Zagreb	5-1, 2-2

Quarter-Finals

*Valencia—Internazionale	2-0, 3-3
MTK Budapest—*Novi Sad	4-1, 2-1
Red Star Belgrade—*Español	1-2, 5-0
Barcelona—*Sheffield Wednesday	2-3, 2-0

Semi-Finals

*Valencia—MTK Budapest	3-0, 7-3
Barcelona—*Red Star Belgrade	2-0, 4-1

Final

(first leg in Valencia; att. 65,000)

Valencia	6	Barcelona	2
(Yosu 2, Guillot 3, H Nuñez)		(Kocsis 2)	

(second leg in Barcelona; att. 60,000)

Valencia	1	Barcelona	1
(Guillot)		(Kocsis)	

*home team in first leg

1962-63

First Round

*Valencia—Celtic	4-2, 2-2
Dunfermline—*Everton	0-1, 2-0
*Hibernian—KB Copenhagen	4-0, 3-2
*DOS Utrecht—Tasmania Berlin	3-2, 2-1
AS Roma—*Altay Izmir	3-2, 10-1
(second leg in Istanbul)	
Real Zaragoza—*Glentoran	2-0, 6-2
Red Star Belgrade—*Rapid Vienna	1-1, 1-0
Barcelona—Belenenses	1-1, 1-1, 3-2
(all legs in Barcelona)	
Ferencváros—*Viktoria Cologne	3-4, 4-1
*Sampdoria—Aris Luxembourg	1-0, 2-0
*Petrolul Ploesti—Spartak Brno	4-2, 0-1
Leipzig—*Vojvodina Novi Sad	0-1, 2-0
Bayern München—*FC Basel	3-0, —
(second leg not played)	
*Drumcondra—BK 09 Odense	4-1, 2-4
Union St. Gilloise—*Olympique Marseille	0-1, 4-2
Dinamo Zagreb—*FC Porto	2-1, 0-0

Second Round

*Valencia—Dunfermline	4-0, 2-6, 1-0
(play-off in Lisbon)	
Hibernian—*DOS Utrecht	1-0, 2-1
AS Roma—*Real Zaragoza	4-2, 2-1
*Red Star Belgrade—Barcelona	3-2, 0-1, 1-0
(play-off in Nice)	
Ferencváros—*Sampdoria	0-1, 6-0
*Petrolul Ploesti—Leipzig	1-0, 0-1, 1-0
(play-off in Budapest)	
*Bayern München—Drumcondra	6-0, 0-1
*Dinamo Zagreb—Union St. Gilloise	2-1, 0-1, 3-2
(play-off in Linz)	

Quarter-Finals

*Valencia—Hibernian	5-0, 1-2
*AS Roma—Red Star Belgrade	3-0, 0-2
*Ferencváros—Petrolul Ploesti	2-0, 0-1
Dinamo Zagreb—*Bayern München	4-1, 0-0

Semi-Finals

*Valencia—AS Roma	3-0, 0-1
Dinamo Zagreb—*Ferencváros	1-0, 2-1

Final
(first leg in Zagreb; att. 40,000)

| Valencia | 2 | Dinamo Zagreb | 1 |
| (Waldo, Urtiago) | | (Zambata) | |

(second leg in Valencia; att. 55,000)

| Valencia | 2 | Dinamo Zagreb | 0 |
| (Mano, Nuñez) | | | |

*home team in first leg

1963-64

First Round

*Real Zaragoza—Iraklis Salonika	6-1, 3-0
*Lausanne—Heart of Midlothian	2-2, 2-2, 3-2
(play-off in Lausanne)	
*Atlético Madrid—FC Porto	2-1, 0-0
*Juventus—OFK Belgrade	2-1, 1-2, 1-0
(play-off in Trieste)	
FC Liège—*Aris Luxembourg	2-0, 0-0
Arsenal—*Staevnet Copenhagen	7-1, 2-3
Partick Thistle—*Glentoran	4-1, 3-0
*Spartak Brno—Servette	5-0, 2-1
*FC Köln—AA Gent	3-1, 1-1
Sheffield Wednesday—*DOS Utrecht	4-1, 4-1
AS Roma—*Hertha Berlin	3-1, 2-0
Belenenses—*Tresnjevka Zagreb	2-0, 2-1
*Újpest Dózsa—Lokomotiv Leipzig	0-0, 3-2
Lokomotiv Plovdiv—*Red Flag Brasov	3-1, 2-1
*Rapid Vienna—Racing Club Paris	1-0, 3-2
Valencia—*Shamrock Rovers	1-0, 2-2

Second Round

Real Zaragoza—*Lausanne	2-1, 3-0
*Juventus—Atlético Madrid	1-0, 2-1
FC Liège—*Arsenal	1-1, 3-1
Spartak Brno—*Partick Thistle	2-3, 4-0
*FC Köln—Sheffield Wednesday	3-2, 2-1
*AS Roma—Belenenses	2-1, 1-0
*Újpest Dózsa—Lokomotiv Plovdiv	0-0, 3-1
Valencia—*Rapid Vienna	0-0, 3-2

Quarter-Finals

*Real Zaragoza—Juventus	3-2, 0-0
*FC Liège—Spartak Brno	2-0, 0-2, 1-0
(play-off in Liège)	

FC Köln—*AS Roma	1-3, 4-0
*Valencia—Újpest Dózsa	5-2, 1-3

Semi-Finals

Real Zaragoza—*FC Liège	0-1, 2-1, 2-0
(play-off in Zaragoza)	
*Valencia—FC Köln	4-1, 0-2

Final (in Barcelona; att. 50,000)

Real Zaragoza	2	Valencia	1
(Villa, Marcelino)		(Urtiaga)	

*home team in first leg

1964-65

First Round

Juventus—*Union St. Gilloise	1-0, 1-0
Stade Français—*Betis	1-1, 2-0
Petrolul Ploesti—*Goeztepe Izmir	2-1, 1-0
Lokomotiv Plovdiv—*Vojvodina Novi Sad	1-1, 1-1, 2-0
(play-off in Sofia)	
DOS Utrecht—*KB Copenhagen	4-3, 2-1
FC Liège—*Valencia	1-1, 3-1
Shelbourne—*Belenenses	1-1, 0-0, 2-1
(play-off in Dublin)	
Atlético Madrid—*Servette	2-2, 6-1
*FC Basel—Spora Luxembourg	2-0, 0-1
*Racing Club Strasbourg—AC Milan	2-0, 0-1
*Barcelona—Fiorentina	0-1, 2-0
Celtic—*Leixoes Oporto	1-1, 3-0
*Borussia Dortmund—Girondins	4-1, 0-2
*Manchester United—Djurgaarden	1-1, 6-1
Kilmarnock—*Eintracht Frankfurt	0-3, 5-1
Everton—*Valerengen	5-2, 4-2
*Athletic Bilbao—OFK Belgrade	2-2, 2-0
Antwerp—*Hertha Berlin	1-2, 2-0
VfB Stuttgart—*Odense BK 13	3-1, 1-0
*Dunfermline Athletic—Örgryte	4-2, 0-0
*Dinamo Zagreb—Grazer AK	3-2, 6-0
AS Roma—*Aris Salonika	0-0, 3-0
*Wiener SK—Lokomotiv Leipzig	2-1, 1-0
*Ferencváros—Spartak Brno	2-0, 0-1

Second Round

Juventus—*Stade Français	0-0, 1-0
Lokomotiv Plovdiv—*Petrolul Ploesti	0-1, 2-0

FC Liège—*DOS Utrecht	2-0, 2-0
Atlético Madrid—*Shelbourne	1-0, 1-0
Racing Club Strasbourg—*FC Basel	1-0, 5-2
*Barcelona—Celtic	3-1, 0-0
Manchester United—*Borussia Dortmund	6-1, 4-0
Everton—*Kilmarnock	2-0, 4-1
*Athletic Bilbao—Antwerp	2-0, 1-0
*Dunfermline Athletic—VfB Stuttgart	1-0, 0-0
AS Roma—*Dinamo Zagreb	1-1, 1-0
*Ferencváros—Wiener SK	0-1, 2-1, 2-0
(play-off in Budapest)	

Third Round
*Juventus—Lokomotiv Plovdiv	1-1, 1-1, 2-1
(play-off in Turin)	
Atlético Madrid—*FC Liège	0-1, 2-0
*Racing Club Strasbourg—Barcelona	0-0, 2-2, 0-0
(play-off in Barcelona; Strasbourg won by toss of the coin)	
*Manchester United—Everton	1-1, 2-1
*Athletic Bilbao—Dunfermline	1-0, 0-1, 2-1
(play-off in Bilbao)	
Ferencváros—*AS Roma	2-1, 1-0

Quarter-Finals
Manchester United—*Racing Club Strasbourg	5-0, 0-0
*Ferencváros—Athletic Bilbao	1-0, 0-1, 3-0
(play-off in Budapest)	
Juventus	bye
Atlético Madrid	bye

Semi-Finals
Juventus—*Atlético Madrid	1-3, 3-1, 3-1
(play-off in Turin)	
Ferencváros—*Manchester United	2-3, 1-0, 2-1
(play-off in Budapest)	

Final (in Turin; att. 25,000)

Ferencváros	1	Juventus	0
(Fenyvesi)			

*home team in first leg

1965-66
(16 byes)

First Round
Barcelona—*DOS Utrecht	0-0, 7-1
*Antwerp—Glentoran	1-0, 3-3

FC Pórto—*Stade Français	0-0, 1-0
Sporting Lisbon—*Girondins	4-0, 6-1
Dinamo Zagreb—*FC Liège	0-1, 2-0
*TSV München 1860—Malmö FF	4-0, 3-0
*AIK Stockholm—Daring Brussels	3-1, 0-0
*AC Milan—Racing Club Strasbourg	1-0, 1-2, 1-1
(play-off in Milan; Milan won by toss of the coin)	
*Wiener SK—PAOK Salonika	6-0, 1-2
*Chelsea—AS Roma	4-1, 0-0
*Leeds United—Torino	2-1, 0-0
Valencia—*Hibernian	0-2, 2-0, 3-0
(play-off in Valencia)	
FC Köln—*US Luxembourg	4-0, 13-0
Everton—*FC Nürnberg	1-1, 1-0
Fiorentina—*Red Star Belgrade	4-0, 3-1
*Spartak Brno—Lokomotiv Plovdiv	2-0, 0-1

Second Round

Barcelona—*Antwerp	1-2, 2-0
*Hannover 96—FC Porto	5-0, 1-2
Español—*Sporting Lisbon	1-2, 4-3, 2-1
(play-off in Barcelona)	
Red Flag Brasov—*Dinamo Zagreb	2-2, 1-0
TSV München 1860—*Goeztepe Izmir	1-2, 9-1
Servette—*AIK Stockholm	1-2, 4-1
AC Milan—*Vitoria Setubal	0-2, 2-0, 1-0
(play-off in Milan)	
Chelsea—*Wiener SK	0-1, 2-0
Leeds United—*Lokomotiv Leipzig	2-1, 0-0
Valencia—*FC Basel	3-1, 5-1
FC Köln—*Aris Salonika	1-2, 2-0
*Újpest Dózsa—Everton	3-0, 1-2
*Dunfermline—KB Copenhagen	5-0, 4-2
Spartak Brno—*Fiorentina	0-2, 4-0
*Heart of Midlothian—Valerengen	1-0, 3-1
Real Zaragoza—*Shamrock Rovers	1-1, 2-1

Third Round

Barcelona—*Hannover 96	1-2, 1-0, 1-1
(replay in Hannover; Barcelona won by toss of the coin)	
*Español—Red Flag Brasov	3-1, 2-4, 1-0
(play-off in Barcelona)	
TSV München 1860—*Servette	1-1, 4-1
Chelsea—*AC Milan	1-2, 2-1, 1-1
(replay in Milan; Chelsea won by toss of the coin)	
*Leeds United—Valencia	1-1, 1-0
Újpest Dózsa—*FC Köln	2-3, 4-0
*Dunfermline—Spartak Brno	2-0, 0-0

Real Zaragoza—*Heart of Midlothian (replay in Zaragoza)	3-3, 2-2, 1-0

Quarter-Finals

Barcelona—Espãnol	1-0, 1-0
Chelsea—*TSV München 1860	2-2, 1-0
*Leeds United—Újpest Dózsa	4-1, 1-1
Real Zaragoza—*Dunfermline	0-1, 4-2

Semi-Finals

*Barcelona—Chelsea (replay in Barcelona)	2-0, 0-2, 5-0
*Real Zaragoza—Leeds United (replay in Leeds)	1-0, 1-2, 3-1

Final

(first leg in Barcelona; att. 70,000)

Barcelona	0	Real Zaragoza (Canario)	1

(second leg in Zaragoza; att. 70,000)

Barcelona (Pujol 3, Zaballa)	4	Real Zaragoza (Marcelino 2)	2

-after extra time; 3-2 at regulation time-

*home team in first leg

1966-67

First Round

Valencia—*FC Nürnberg	2-1, 2-0
*Red Star Belgrade—Athletic Bilbao	5-0, 2-0
*DOS Utrecht—FC Basel	2-1, 2-2
*Bologna—Goeztepe Izmir	3-3, 2-1
Lokomotiv Leipzig—*Djurgaarden	3-1, 2-1
Antwerp—*US Luxembourg	1-0, 1-0
Girondins—*FC Porto	1-2, 2-1
(Girondins won by toss of the coin)	
Eintracht Frankfurt—*Drumcondra	2-0, 5-1
Örgryte—*OGC Nice	2-2, 2-1
Ferencváros—*Olympija Ljubljana	3-3, 3-0
Burnley—*VfB Stuttgart	1-1, 2-0
Napoli—*Wiener SK	2-1, 3-1
*Juventus—Aris Salonika	5-0, 2-0
*Dinamo Pitesti—Seville	2-0, 2-2
Dunfermline—*Frigg Oslo	3-1, 3-1
Dinamo Zagreb—*Spartak Brno	0-2, 2-0
(Dinamo won by toss of the coin)	

Second Round

Leeds United—*DWS Amsterdam	3-1, 5-1
*Valencia—Red Star Belgrade	1-0, 2-1
*West Bromwich Albion—DOS Utrecht	5-2, 1-1
Bologna—*Sparta Prague	2-2, 2-1
Lokomotiv Leipzig—*FC Liège	0-0, 2-1
Benfica—*Spartak Plovdiv	1-1, 3-0
Kilmarnock—*Antwerp	1-0, 7-2
*AA Gent—Girondins	1-0, 0-0
*Eintracht Frankfurt—Hvidovre	5-1, 2-2
Ferencváros—*Örgryte	0-0, 7-1
Burnley—*Lausanne	3-1, 5-0
Napoli—*BK 09 Odense	4-1, 2-1
*Juventus—Vitoria Setubal	3-1, 2-0
Dundee United—*Barcelona	2-1, 2-0
Dinamo Pitesti—*Toulouse	0-3, 5-1
Dinamo Zagreb—*Dunfermline	2-4, 2-0
(Dinamo won on away-goals rule)	

Third Round

*Leeds United—Valencia	1-1, 2-0
*Bologna—West Bromwich Albion	3-0, 3-1
*Lokomotiv Leipzig—Benfica	3-1, 1-2
*Kilmarnock—AA Gent	1-0, 2-1
*Eintracht Frankfurt—Ferencváros	4-1, 1-2
*Burnley—Napoli	3-0, 0-0
*Juventus—Dundee United	3-0, 0-1
Dinamo Zagreb—*Dinamo Pitesti	1-0, 0-0

Quarter-Finals

Leeds United—*Bologna	0-1, 1-0
(Leeds won by toss of the coin)	
Kilmarnock—*Lokomotiv Leipzig	0-1, 2-0
*Eintracht Frankfurt—Burnley	1-1, 2-1
Dinamo Zagreb—*Juventus	2-2, 3-0

Semi-Finals

*Leeds United—Kilmarnock	4-2, 0-0
Dinamo Zagreb—*Eintracht Frankfurt	0-3, 4-0

Final

(first leg in Zagreb; att. 40,000)

Dinamo Zagreb	2	Leeds United	0
(Cercer 2)			

(second leg in Leeds; att. 35,604)

Dinamo Zagreb	0	Leeds United	0

*home team in first leg

1967-68

First Round

Leeds United—*Spora Luxembourg	9-0, 7-0
FC Liège—*PAOK Salonika	2-0, 3-2
Atlético Madrid—*Wiener SK	5-0, 2-1
Girondins—*St. Patrick's Athletic	3-1, 6-3
Real Zaragoza—*DOS Utrecht	2-3, 3-1
*Napoli—Hannover 96	4-0, 1-1
*Bologna—Lyn Oslo	2-0, 0-0
Fiorentina—*OGC Nice	1-0, 4-0
Rangers—*Dynamo Dresden	1-1, 2-1
TSV München 1860—*Servette	2-2, 4-0
Ferencváros—*Argesul Pitesti	1-3, 4-0
Liverpool—*Malmö FF	2-0, 2-1
*Hibernian—FC Porto	3-0, 1-3
Nottingham Forest—*Eintracht Frankfurt	1-0, 4-0
*Dinamo Zagreb—Petrolul Ploesti	5-0, 0-2
Sporting Lisbon—*FC Brugge	0-0, 2-1
Athletic Bilbao—*Frem Copenhagen	1-0, 3-2
*FC Zürich—Barcelona	3-1, 0-1
*Lokomotiv Leipzig—Linfield	5-1, 0-1
Dundee—*DWS Amsterdam	1-2, 3-0
*Partizan Belgrade—Lokomotiv Plovdiv	5-1, 1-1
*Vojvodina Novi Sad—Vitoria Setubal	1-0, 3-1
*FC Köln—Slavia Prague	2-0, 2-2
Goeztepe Izmir—*Antwerp	2-1, 0-0

Second Round

FC Zürich—*Nottingham Forest	1-2, 1-0
(Zürich won on away-goals rule)	
Athletic Bilbao—*Girondins	3-1, 1-0
*Dundee—FC Liège	3-1, 4-1
*Vojvodina Novi Sad—Lokomotiv Leipzig	0-0, 2-0
Ferencváros—*Real Zaragoza	1-2, 3-0
*Liverpool—TSV München 1860	8-0, 1-2
*Rangers—FC Köln	3-0, 1-3
*Bologna—Dinamo Zagreb	0-0, 2-1
Hibernian—*Napoli	1-4, 5-0
Leeds United—*Partizan Belgrade	2-1, 1-1
Sporting Lisbon—*Fiorentina	1-1, 2-1
Goeztepe Izmir—*Atlético Madrid	0-2, 3-0

Third Round

*Ferencváros—Liverpool	1-0, 1-0
*Leeds United—Hibernian	1-0, 1-1
*Vojvodina Novi Sad—Goeztepe Izmir	1-0, 1-0
*FC Zürich—Sporting Lisbon	3-0, 0-1

Athletic Bilbao	bye
Bologna	bye
Dundee	bye
Rangers	bye

Quarter-Finals

*Ferencváros—Athletic Bilbao	2-1, 2-1
Leeds United—*Rangers	0-0, 2-0
*Dundee—FC Zürich	1-0, 1-0
*Bologna—Vojvodina Novi Sad	0-0, 2-0

Semi-Finals

Leeds United—*Dundee	1-1, 1-0
*Ferencváros—Bologna	3-2, 2-2

Final

(first leg in Leeds; att. 25,268)

Leeds United	1	Ferencváros	0
(Jones)			

(second leg in Budapest; att. 76,000)

Leeds United	0	Ferencváros	0

*home team in first leg

1968-69

First Round

*Chelsea—Morton	5-0, 4-3
*Newcastle United—Feyenoord	4-0, 0-2
Aberdeen—*Slavia Sofia	0-0, 2-0
*Athletic Bilbao—Liverpool	2-1, 1-2
(Bilbao won by toss of the coin)	
*Rangers—Vojvodina Novi Sad	2-0, 0-1
Hibernian—*Ljubljana	3-0, 2-1
OFK Belgrade—*Rapid Bucharest	1-3, 6-1
Slavia Prague—*Wiener SK	0-1, 5-0
AIK Stockholm—*Skeid Oslo	1-1, 2-1
Real Zaragoza—*Trakia Plovdiv	1-3, 2-0
(Zaragoza won on away-goals rule)	
Fiorentina—*Dinamo Zagreb	1-1, 2-1
Legia Warsaw—TSV München 1860	6-0, 3-2
Panathinaïkos—*Daring Brussels	1-2, 2-0
Eintracht Frankfurt—*Wacker Innsbruck	2-2, 3-0
*Sporting Lisbon—Valencia	4-0, 1-4
*Bologna—FC Basel	4-1, 2-1
*Aris Salonika—Hibernians Valetta	1-0, 6-0

Dundalk—*DOS Utrecht	1-1, 2-1
SV Waregem—*Atlético Madrid	1-2, 1-0
(Waregem won by toss of the coin)	
*Hansa Rostock—OGC Nice	3-0, 1-2
*Goeztepe Izmir—Olympique Marseille	2-0, 0-2
(Goeztepe Izmir won by toss of the coin)	
Hamburger SV—*Metz	4-1, 3-2
*Olympique Lyon—Coimbra Academica	1-0, 0-1
(Lyon won by the toss of the coin)	
Juventus—*Lausanne	2-0, 2-0
DWS Amsterdam—*Beerschot	1-1, 2-1
*Hannover 96—BK 09 Odense	3-2, 1-0
*Vitoria Setubal—Linfield	3-0, 3-1
Leeds United—*Standard Liège	0-0, 3-2
*Napoli—Grasshoppers	3-1, 0-1

Second Round

*Hibernian—Lokomotiv Leipzig	3-1, 1-0
*Leeds United—Napoli	2-0, 0-2
(Leeds won by toss of the coin)	
*Rangers—Dundalk	6-1, 3-0
Real Zaragoza—*Aberdeen	1-2, 3-0
DWS Amsterdam—*Chelsea	0-0, 0-0
(DWS Amsterdam won by toss of the coin)	
Newcastle United—*Sporting Lisbon	1-1, 1-0
*Vitoria Setubal—Olympique Lyon	5-0, 2-1
*Goeztepe Izmir—Argesul Pitesti	3-0, 0-2
Fiorentina—*Hansa Rostock	2-3, 2-1
(Fiorentina won on away-goals rule)	
*Hamburger SV—Slavia Prague	4-1, 1-3
Athletic Bilbao—*Panathinaïkos	0-0, 1-0
Legia Warsaw—*SV Waregem	0-1, 2-0
Eintracht Frankfurt—*Juventus	0-0, 1-0
*OFK Belgrade—Bologna	1-0, 1-1
Újpest Dózsa—*Aris Salonika	2-1, 9-1
Hannover 96—*AIK Stockholm	2-4, 5-2

Third Round

*Leeds United—Hannover 96	5-1, 2-1
*Hamburger SV—Hibernian	1-0, 1-2
(Hamburger SV won on away-goals rule)	
Újpest Dózsa—*Legia Warsaw	1-0, 2-2
Newcastle United—*Real Zaragoza	2-3, 2-1
(Newcastle won on away-goals rule)	
Goeztepe Izmir—*OFK Belgrade	1-3, 2-0
(Goeztepe won on away-goals rule)	
Athletic Bilbao—Eintracht Frankfurt	1-0, 1-1

| Rangers—*DWS Amsterdam | 2-0, 2-1 |
| *Vitoria Setubal—Fiorentina | 3-0, 1-2 |

Quarter-Finals

*Newcastle United—Vitoria Setubal	5-1, 1-3
*Rangers—Athletic Bilbao	4-1, 0-2
Újpest Dózsa—*Leeds United	1-0, 2-0

(Goeztepe Izmir won by default; Hamburger SV withdrew)

Semi-Finals

| Újpest Dózsa—*Goeztepe Izmir | 4-1, 4-0 |
| Newcastle United—*Rangers | 0-0, 2-0 |

Final

(first leg in Newcastle; att. 60,000)

| Newcastle United | 3 | Újpest Dózsa | 0 |

(Moncur 2, Scott)

(second leg in Budapest; att. 37,000)

| Newcastle United | 3 | Újpest Dózsa | 2 |

(Moncur, Arentoft, Foggen)   (Bene, Gorocs)

*home team in first leg

1969-70

First Round

*Arsenal—Glentoran	3-0, 0-1
Newcastle United—*Dundee United	2-1, 1-0
*Liverpool—Dundalk	10-0, 4-0
Újpest Dózsa—*Partizan Belgrade	1-2, 2-0
FC Brugge—*Sabadel	0-2, 5-1
Hertha Berlin—*Las Palmas	0-0, 1-0
Ruch Chorzów—*Wiener SK	2-4, 4-1
*Rouen—Twente Enschede	2-0, 0-1
*Vitoria Guimaraes—Banik Ostrava	1-0, 1-1
*Sporting Lisbon—ASK Linz	4-0, 2-2
*Carl Zeiss Jena—Altay Izmir	1-0, 0-0
Vasas Györ—*Lausanne	2-1, 2-1
Southampton—*Rosenborg Trondheim	0-1, 2-0
*Hansa Rostock—Panionios Athens	3-0, 0-2
*Dinamo Bacau—Floriana Valetta	6-0, 1-0
*Slavia Sofia—Valencia	2-0, 1-1
*Internazionale—Sparta Prague	3-0, 1-0
*Juventus—Lokomotiv Plovdiv	3-1, 2-1
*VfB Stuttgart—Malmö FF	3-0, 1-1

Ajax—*Hannover 96	1-2, 3-0
Cagliari—*Aris Salonika	1-1, 3-0
Napoli—*Metz	1-1, 2-1
*Barcelona—BK 09 Odense	4-0, 2-0
*Gwardia Warsaw—Vojvodina Novi Sad	1-0, 1-1
*Dunfermline—Girondins	4-0, 0-2
Kilmarnock—*FC Zürich	2-3, 3-1
Skeid Oslo—*TSV München 1860	2-2, 2-1
RSC Anderlecht—*Valur Reykjavik	6-0, 2-0
*SC Charleroi—FNK Zagreb	2-1, 3-1
FC Porto—*Hvidovre	2-1, 2-0
Coleraine—*Jeunesse Esch	2-3, 4-0
*Vitoria Setubal—Rapid Bucharest	3-1, 4-1

Second Round

Arsenal—*Sporting Lisbon	0-0, 3-0
*RSC Anderlecht—Coleraine	6-1, 7-3
*Vitoria Setubal—Liverpool	1-0, 2-3
(Vitoria won on away-goals rule)	
Newcastle United—*FC Porto	0-0, 1-0
*Ajax—Ruch Chorzów	7-0, 2-1
Internazionale—*Hansa Rostock	1-2, 3-0
*Carl Zeiss Jena—Cagliari	2-0, 1-0
*Hertha Berlin—Juventus	3-1, 0-0
Barcelona—*Vasas Györ	3-2, 2-0
Napoli—*VfB Stuttgart	0-0, 1-0
*Kilmarnock—Slavia Sofia	4-1, 0-2
Újpest Dózsa—*FC Brugge	2-5, 3-0
(Újpest Dózsa won on away-goals rule)	
Dinamo Bacau—*Skein Oslo	0-0, 2-0
Rouen—*SC Charleroi	1-3, 2-0
(Rouen won on away-goals rule)	
Southampton—*Vitoria Guimaraes	3-3, 5-1
*Dunfermline—Gwardia Warsaw	2-1, 1-0

Third Round

*Newcastle United—Southampton	0-0, 1-1
(Newcastle won on away-goals rule)	
*RSC Anderlecht—Dunfermline	1-0, 2-3
(Anderlecht won on away-goals rule)	
Arsenal—*Rouen	0-0, 1-0
Dinamo Bacau—*Kilmarnock	1-1, 2-0
*Carl Zeiss Jena—Újpest Dózsa	1-0, 3-0
Internazionale—*Barcelona	2-1, 1-1
Hertha Berlin—*Vitoria Setubal	1-1, 1-0
Ajax—Napoli	0-1, 4-0

Quarter-Finals

Ajax—*Carl Zeiss Jena	1-3, 5-1
Internazionale—*Hertha Berlin	0-1, 2-0
*RSC Anderlecht—Newcastle United	2-0, 1-3
(Anderlecht won on away-goals rule)	
Arsenal—*Dinamo Bacau	2-0, 7-1

Semi-Finals

*RSC Anderlecht—Internazionale	0-1, 2-0
*Arsenal—Ajax	3-0, 0-1

Final

(first leg in Brussels; att. 30,000)

Arsenal	1	RSC Anderlecht	3
(Kennedy)		(Devrindt, Mulder 2)	

(second leg in London; att. 51, 612)

Arsenal	3	RSC Anderlecht	0
(Kelly, Radford, Sammels)			

*home team in first leg

1970-71

First Round

Twente Enschede—*AEK Athens	1-0, 3-0
RSC Anderlecht—*Zeleznicar	4-3, 5-4
Hamburger SV—*AA Gent	1-0, 7-1
*Liverpool—Ferencváros	1-0, 1-1
Leeds United—*Sarpsborg	1-0, 5-0
*Coleraine—Kilmarnock	1-1, 3-2
*Dundee United—Grasshoppers	3-2, 0-0
Arsenal—*Lazio	2-2, 2-0
Barcelona—*Katowice	1-0, 3-2
Beveren-Waas—*Wiener SK	2-0, 3-0
Sturm Graz—*Ilves-Kissat	2-4, 3-0
*Juventus—US Rumelange	7-0, 4-0
Eskisehir—*Seville	0-1, 3-1
*Vitoria Guimaraes—Angouleme	3-0, 1-3
*Hajduk Split—Slavia Sofia	3-0, 0-1
Hertha Berlin—*Nyköping	4-2, 4-1
Dynamo Dresden—*Partizan Belgrade	0-0, 6-0
Dinamo Zagreb—*Barreirense	0-2, 6-1
Fiorentina—*Ruch Chorzów	1-1, 2-0
*Sparta Prague—Athletic Bilbao	2-0, 1-1
*Akademisk—Sliema Wanderers	7-0, 3-2
*Dinamo Bucharest—PAOK Salonika	5-0, 0-1

Vitoria Setubal—*Lausanne	2-0, 2-1
*FC Köln—Sedan-Torcy	5-1, 0-1
Newcastle United—*Internazionale	1-1, 2-0
*Spartak Trnava—Olympique Marseille	2-0, 0-2
(Spartak won on penalty kicks)	
*Bayern München—Rangers	1-0, 1-1
Valencia—*Cork Hibernian	3-0, 3-1
*Hibernian—Malmö FF	6-0, 3-2
Pecsi Dozsa—*Universitatea Craiova	1-2, 3-0
Coventry City—*Trakia Plovdiv	4-1, 2-0
*Sparta Rotterdam—*IA Akranes	6-0, 9-0

Second Round

Arsenal—*Sturm Graz	0-1, 2-0
*Sparta Rotterdam—Coleraine	2-0, 2-1
*Leeds United—Dynamo Dresden	1-0, 1-2
(Leeds won on away-goals rule)	
*Liverpool—Dinamo Bucharest	3-0, 1-1
Pecsi Dózsa—*Newcastle United	0-2, 2-0
(Pecsi Dózsa won on penalty kicks)	
*Bayern München—Coventry City	6-1, 1-2
*Sparta Prague—Dundee United	3-1, 0-1
*Hibernian—Vitoria Guimaraes	2-0, 1-2
Twente Enschede—*Eskisehir	2-3, 6-1
RSC Anderlecht—*Akademisk	3-1, 4-0
Beveren-Waas—*Valencia	1-0, 1-1
Spartak Trnava—*Hertha Berlin	0-1, 3-1
Juventus—*Barcelona	2-1, 2-1
*Dinamo Zagreb—Hamburger SV	4-0, 0-1
*Vitoria Setubal—Hajduk Split	2-0, 1-2
FC Köln—*Fiorentina	2-1, 1-0

Third Round

*Arsenal—Beveren-Waas	4-0, 0-0
*Leeds United—Sparta Prague	6-0, 3-2
FC Köln—*Spartak Trnava	1-0, 3-0
*Bayern München—Sparta Rotterdam	2-1, 3-1
Twente Enschede—*Dinamo Zagreb	2-2, 1-0
*Liverpool—Hibernian	1-0, 2-0
Vitoria Setubal—*RSC Anderlecht	1-2, 3-1
Juventus—*Pecsi Dózsa	1-0, 2-0

Quarter-Finals

*Juventus—Twente Enschede	2-0, 2-2
*FC Köln—Arsenal	1-2, 1-0
(FC Köln won on away-goals rule)	
*Liverpool—Bayern München	3-0, 1-1
*Leeds United—Vitoria Setubal	2-1, 1-1

Semi-Finals
  Leeds United—*Liverpool   1-0, 0-0
  Juventus—*FC Köln   1-1, 2-0

Final
  (first leg in Turin; att. 40,000)

                -abandoned after 50 minutes: water-logged field-

  (first leg replay in Turin; att. 42,000)

| Juventus | 2 | Leeds United | 2 |
| (Bettega, Capello) | | (Madeley, Bates) | |

  (second leg in Leeds; att. 42, 483)

| Leeds United | 1 | Juventus | 1 |
| (Clarke) | | (Anastasi) | |

                -Leeds won on away-goals rule-

*home team in first leg

GAME TO DECIDE PERMANENT POSSESSION

(in Barcelona; att. 35,000)

| Barcelona | 2 | Leeds United | 1 |
| (Duenas 2) | | (Jordan) | |

UEFA CUP

1971-72

First Round

*Hertha Berlin—Elfsborg Boras	3-1, 4-1
*Dundee—Akademisk	4-2, 1-0
*Rosenborg Trondheim—IFK Helsinki	3-0, 1-0
*Vasas Budapest—Shelbourne	1-0, 1-1
Eintracht Braunschweig—*Glentoran	1-0, 6-1
Tottenham Hotspur—*IB Keflavik	6-1, 9-0
Aberdeen—*Celta Vigo	2-0, 1-0
*FC Den Haag—Aris Luxembourg	5-0, 1-1
*Wolverhampton Wanderers—Academica Coimbra	3-0, 4-1
FC Köln—*St. Étienne	1-1, 2-1
Legia Warsaw—*FC Lugano	3-1, 0-0
FC Nantes—*FC Porto	2-0, 1-1
*St Johnstone—Hamburger SV	1-2, 3-0
Athletic Bilbao—*Southampton	1-0, 2-0
*Bologna—RSC Anderlecht	1-1, 2-0
Rapid Bucharest—*Napoli	0-1, 2-0
*Vitoria Setubal—Nîmes	1-0, 1-2
(Vitoria Setubal won on away-goals rule)	

Panionios Athens—*Atlético Madrid	1-2, 1-0
(Panionios won on away-goals rule)	
*Carl Zeiss Jena—Lokomotiv Plovdiv	3-0, 1-3
Real Madrid—*FC Basel	2-1, 2-1
Juventus—*Marsa	6-0, 5-0
*Dinamo Zagreb—Botev Vratza	6-1, 2-1
*UT Arad—Austria Salzburg	4-1, 1-3
Ferencváros—*Fenerbahçe	1-1, 3-1
*AC Milan—Dighenis Morphou	4-0, 3-0
*Spartak Moscow—VSS Kosice	2-0, 1-2
*OFK Belgrade—Djurgaarden	4-1, 2-2
*Zeleznicar—FC Brugge	3-0, 1-3
*Zaglebie Walbryzch—Union Teplice	1-0, 3-2
*Lierse SK—Leeds United	0-2, 4-0
PSV Eindhoven—*Chemie Halle	0-0, —
(Chemie Halle withdrew from second leg)	
Rapid Vienna won by default: Vlanznija withdrew	

Second Round

Lierse SK—*Rosenborg Trondheim	1-4, 3-0
(Lierse SK won on away-goals rule)	
*Rapid Bucharest—Legia Warsaw	4-0, 0-2
Dundee—*FC Köln	1-2, 4-2
Wolverhampton Wanderers—*FC Den Haag	3-1, 4-0
*Zeleznicar—Bologna	1-1, 2-2
(Zeleznicar won on away-goals rule)	
Tottenham Hotspur—*FC Nantes	0-0, 1-0
*Eintracht Braunschweig—Athletic Bilbao	2-1, 2-2
*St. Johnstone—Vasas Budapest	2-0, 0-1
Victoria Setubal—*Spartak Moscow	0-0, 4-0
*AC Milan—Hertha Berlin	4-2, 1-2
Carl Zeiss Jena—*OFK Belgrade	1-1, 4-0
UT Arad—*Zaglebie Walbryzch	1-1, 2-1
Rapid Vienna—*Dinamo Zagreb	2-2, 0-0
(Rapid won on away-goals rule)	
PSV Eindhoven—*Real Madrid	1-3, 2-0
(PSV Eindhoven won on away-goals rule)	
*Juventus—Aberdeen	2-0, 1-1
*Ferencváros—Panionios Athens	6-0, —
(Panionios disqualified)	

Third Round

*AC Milan—Dundee	3-0, 0-2
Wolverhampton Wanderers—*Carl Zeiss Jena	1-0, 3-0
Ferencváros—*Eintracht Braunschweig	1-1, 5-2
Lierse SK—*PSV Eindhoven	0-1, 4-0
Juventus—*Rapid Vienna	1-0, 4-1
Zeleznicar—*St. Johnstone	0-1, 5-0

| *Tottenham Hotspur—Rapid Bucharest | 3-0, 2-0 |
| *UT Arad—Vitoria Setubal | 3-0, 0-1 |

Quarter-Finals

*AC Milan—Lierse SK	2-0, 1-1
Tottenham Hotspur—*UT Arad	2-0, 1-1
Wolverhampton Wanderers—*Juventus	1-1, 2-1
*Ferencváros—Zeleznicar	1-2, 2-1
(Ferencváros won on penalty kicks)	

Semi-Finals

| Wolverhampton Wanderers—*Ferencváros | 2-2, 2-1 |
| *Tottenham Hotspur—AC Milan | 2-1, 1-1 |

Final

(first leg in Wolverhampton; att. 45,000)

| Tottenham Hotspur | 2 | Wolverhampton Wanderers | 0 |
| (Chivers 2) | | | |

(second leg in London; att. 54,303)

| Tottenham Hotspur | 1 | Wolverhampton Wanderers | 1 |
| (Mullery) | | (Wagstaffe) | |

*home team in first leg

1972-73

First Round

*Liverpool—Eintracht Frankfurt	2-0, 0-0
*AEK Athens—Salgotarjan	3-1, 1-1
Dynamo Berlin—*Angers	1-1, 2-1
Levski Sofia—*Universitatea Cluj	1-4, 5-1
*Dynamo Dresden—VOEST Linz	2-0, 2-2
*Ruch Chorzów—Fenerbahçe	3-0, 0-1
*FC Porto—Barcelona	3-1, 1-0
FC Brugge—*Atvidaberg	5-3, 1-2
Tottenham Hotspur—*Lyn Oslo	6-3, 6-0
*Olympiakos Piraeus—Cagliari	2-1, 1-0
*Red Star Belgrade—Lausanne	5-1, 2-3
Valencia—*Manchester City	2-2, 2-1
*Vitoria Setubal—Zaglebie Sosnowiec	6-1, 0-1
Fiorentina—*Eskisehirspor	2-1, 3-0
*Internazionale—FC Valetta	6-1, 0-1
Norrköping—UT Arad	2-1, 2-0
*Honvéd—Partick Thistle	1-0, 3-0
*Beroe Stara Zagora—FK Austria	7-0, 3-1
*Feyenoord—US Rumelange	9-0, 12-0
OFK Belgrade—*Dukla Prague	2-2, 3-1
*Slovan Bratislava—Vojvodina Novi Sad	6-0, 2-1

Las Palmas—*Torino	0-2, 4-0
Frem Copenhagen—*Sochaux	3-1, 2-1
Twente Enschede—*Dinamo Tbilisi	2-3, 2-0
*Grasshoppers—Nîmes	2-1, 2-1
Ararat Erevan—*EPA Larnaca	1-0, 1-0
CUF Barreirense—*Racing White	1-0, 2-0
Kaiserslautern—*Stoke City	1-3, 4-0
*Viking Stavanger—IB Vestmannaey	1-0, 0-0
*FC Köln—Bohemians	2-1, 3-0
Hvidovre	bye
(IFK Helsinki withdrew)	
Borussia Mönchengladbach—*Aberdeen	3-2, 6-3
(second leg played in Nuremburg)	

Second Round

*Liverpool—AEK Athens	3-0, 3-1
*Dynamo Berlin—Levski Sofia	3-0, 0-2
Dynamo Dresden—*Ruch Chorzów	1-0, 3-0
*FC Porto—FC Brugge	3-0, 2-3
*Tottenham Hotspur—Olympiakos Piraeus	4-0, 0-1
*Red Star Belgrade—Valencia	3-1, 1-0
*Vitoria Setubal—Fiorentina	1-0, 1-2
(Vitoria Setubal won on away-goals rule)	
*Internazionale—Norrköping	2-2, 2-0
*Beroe St. Zagora—Honvéd	3-0, 0-1
OFK Belgrade—*Feyenoord	3-4, 2-1
(OFK Belgrade won on away-goals rule)	
*Las Palmas—Slovan Bratislava	2-2, 1-0
Twente Enschede—*Frem Copenhagen	5-0, 4-0
Ararat Erevan—*Grasshoppers	3-1, 4-2
Kaiserslautern—*CUF Barreirense	3-1, 0-1
FC Köln—*Viking Stavanger	0-1, 9-1
*Borussia Mönchengladbach—Hvidovre	3-0, 3-1
(first leg played in Nuremburg)	

Third Round

Liverpool—*Dynamo Berlin	0-0, 3-1
Dynamo Dresden—*FC Porto	2-1, 1-0
*Tottenham Hotspur—Red Star Belgrade	2-0, 0-1
*Vitoria Setubal—Internazionale	2-0, 0-1
*OFK Belgrade—Beroe St. Zagora	0-0, 3-1
*Twente Enschede—Las Palmas	3-0, 1-2
Kaiserslautern—*Ararat Erevan	0-2, 2-0
(Kaiserslautern won on penalty kicks)	
Borussia Mönchengladbach—*FC Köln	0-0, 5-0

Quarter-Finals

*Liverpool—Dynamo Dresden	2-0, 1-0

*Tottenham Hotspur—Vitoria Setubal	1-0, 1-2
(Tottenham won on away-goals rule)	
Twente Enschede—*OFK Belgrade	2-3, 2-0
Borussia Mönchengladbach—*Kaiserslautern	2-1, 7-1

Semi-Finals

*Liverpool—Tottenham Hotspur	1-0, 1-2
(Liverpool won on away-goals rule)	
*Borussia Mönchengladbach—Twente Enschede	3-0, 2-1

Final

(first leg in Liverpool; att. 44,967)

       -abandoned after 27 minutes: water-logged field-

(first leg replay in Liverpool; att. 41,169)

Liverpool	3	Borussia Mönchengladbach	0
(Keegan 2, Lloyd)			

(second leg in Mönchengladbach; att. 35,000)

Borussia Mönchengladbach	2	Liverpool	0
(Heynckes 2)			

*home team in first leg

1973-74

First Round

*Grasshoppers—Tottenham Hotspur	1-5, 1-4
*Östers Växjö—Feyenoord	1-3, 1-2
*VfB Stuttgart—Olympiakos Nicosia	9-0, 4-0
*Fredrikstad—Dinamo Kiev	0-1, 0-4
*Fenerbahçe—Arges Pitesti	5-1, 1-1
*Panathinaïkos—OFK Belgrade	1-2, 1-0
*Fortuna Düsseldorf—Naestved IF	1-0, 2-2
*Eskisehirspor—FC Köln	0-0, 0-2
*Dinamo Tiflis—Slavia Sofia	4-1, 0-2
*Ferencváros—Gwardia Warsaw	0-1, 1-2
*Fiorentina—Universitatea Craiova	0-0, 0-1
*Ruch Chorzów—Wuppertaler SV	4-1, 4-5
*Torino—Lokomotiv Leipzig	1-2, 1-2
*Sliema Wanderers—Lokomotiv Plovdiv	0-2, 0-1
*BK 03 Copenhagen—AIK Stockholm	2-1, 1-1
*Strömsgodset—Leeds United	1-1, 1-6
*Ipswich Town—Real Madrid	1-0, 0-0
*Carl Zeiss Jena—Mikkelin	3-0, 3-0
*Belenenses—Wolverhampton Wanderers	0-2, 1-2
*Hibernian—IB Keflavik	2-0, 1-1

*Admira Wacker—Internazionale	1-0, 1-2
(Admira Wacker won on away-goals rule)	
*Panachaiki Patras—GAK Graz	2-1, 1-0
*Lazio—FC Sion	3-0, 1-3
*US Luxembourg—Olympique Marseille	0-5, 1-7
*Östers Växjö—Feyenoord	1-3, 1-2
*Dundee—Twente Enschede	1-3, 2-4
*Ards—Standard Liège	3-2, 1-6
*Español—RWD Molenbeek	0-3, 2-1
*Tatran Presov—Velez Mostar	4-2, 1-1
*VSS Kosice—Honvéd	1-0, 2-5
*OGC Nice—Barcelona	3-0, 0-2
*Vitoria Setubal—Beerschot	2-0, 2-0
*Aberdeen—Finn Harps	4-1, 3-1

Second Round

*Aberdeen—Tottenham Hotspur	1-1, 1-4
*Feyenoord—Gwardia Warsaw	3-1, 0-1
*Olympique Marseille—FC Köln	2-0, 0-6
*OGC Nice—Fenerbahçe	4-0, 0-2
*Dinamo Tblisi—OFK Belgrade	3-0, 5-1
*VfB Stuttgart—Tatran Presov	3-1, 5-3
*Admira Wacker—Fortuna Düsseldorf	2-1, 0-3
*Vitoria Setubal—RWD Molenbeek	1-0, 1-2
*Ipswich Town—Lazio	4-0, 2-4
*Dinamo Kiev—BK 03 Copenhagen	1-0, 2-1
*Lokomotiv Plovdiv—Honvéd	3-4, 2-3
*Ruch Chorzow—Carl Zeiss Jena	3-0, 0-1
*Leeds United—Hibernian	0-0, 0-0
(Leeds won on penalty kicks)	
*Standard Liège—Universitatea Craiova	2-0, 1-1
*Lokomotiv Leipzig—Wolverhampton Wanderers	3-0, 1-4
*Panachaiki Patros—Twente Enschede	1-1, 0-7

Third Round

*Dinamo Tblisi—Tottenham Hotspur	1-1, 1-5
*Standard Liège—Feyenoord	3-1, 0-2
(Feyenoord won on away-goals rule)	
*Dinamo Kiev—VfB Stuttgart	2-0, 0-3
*Fortuna Düsseldorf—Lokomotiv Leipzig	2-1, 0-3
*OGC Nice—FC Köln	1-0, 0-4
*Ipswich Town—Twente Enschede	1-0, 2-1
*Honvéd—Ruch Chorzów	2-0, 0-5
*Leeds United—Vitoria Setubal	1-0, 1-3

Quarter-Finals

*FC Köln—Tottenham Hotspur	1-2, 0-3
*Ruch Chorzów—Feyenoord	1-1, 1-3

*VfB Stuttgart—Vitoria Setubal   1-0, 2-2
*Ipswich Town— Lokomotiv Leipzig   1-0, 0-1
  (Lokomotiv won on penalty kicks)

Semi-Finals
*Lokomotiv Leipzig—Tottenham Hotspur   1-2, 0-2
*Feyenoord—VfB Stuttgart   2-1, 2-2

Final
  (first leg in London; att. 46,281)
  Tottenham Hotspur   2   Feyenoord   2
  (England, van Daele o.g.)   (van Hanegem, De Jong)

  (second leg in Rotterdam; att. 59,317)
  Feyenoord   2   Tottenham Hotspur   0
  (Rijsbergen, Ressel)

*home team in first leg

1974-75

First Round
*Swarovski Innsbruck—Borussia Mönchengladbach   2-1, 0-3
*Vitoria Setubal—Real Zaragoza   1-1, 0-4
*Valur Reykjavik—Portadown   0-0, 1-2
*Olympique Lyon—Red Boys Differdange   7-0, 4-1
*FC Nantes—Legia Warsaw   2-2, 1-0
*FC Köln—Kokkolan PV   5-1, 4-1
*Östers Växjö—Dinamo Moscow   3-2, 1-2
  (Dinamo won on away-goals rule)
*Randers Freja—Dynamo Dresden   1-1, 0-0
  (Dynamo won on away-goals rule)
*RWD Molenbeek—Dundee   1-0, 4-2
*Ipswich Town—Twente Enschede   2-2, 1-1
  (Twente won on away-goals rule)
*Start Kristiansand—Djurgaarden   1-2, 1-5
*Hamburger SV—Bohemians   3-0, 1-0
*Derby County—Servette   4-1, 2-1
*Rosenborg Trondheim—Hibernian   2-3, 1-9
*Stoke City—Ajax   1-1, 0-0
  (Ajax won on away-goals rule)
*Sturm Graz—Antwerp   2-1, 0-1
  (Antwerp won on away-goals rule)
*FC Porto—Wolverhampton Wanderers   4-1, 1-3
*Etar Tirnovo—Internazionale   0-0, 0-3
*FC Amsterdam—Hibernians Valetta   5-0, 7-0
*Real Sociedad—Banik Ostrava   0-1, 0-4

*Lokomotive Plovdiv—Vasas Györ	3-1, 1-3
(Györ won on penalty kicks)	
*Torino—Fortuna Düsseldorf	1-1, 1-3
*Gornik Zabrze—Partizan Belgrade	2-2, 0-3
*Vorwärts Frankfurt—Juventus	2-1, 0-3
*Besiktas—Steagul Rosu Brasov	2-0, 0-3
*Spartak Moscow—Velez Mostar	3-1, 0-2
*Rapid Vienna—Aris Salonika	3-1, 0-1
*Napoli—Videoton	2-0, 1-1
*Grasshoppers—Panathinaïkos	2-0, 1-2
*Boluspor—Dinamo Bucharest	0-1, 0-3
*KB Copenhagen—Atlético Madrid	3-2, 0-4
Dukla Prague won by default: Peoporikos Larnaca withdrew	

Second Round

*Borussia Mönchengladbach—Olympique Lyon	1-0, 5-2
*Internazionale—FC Amsterdam	1-2, 0-0
*FC Nantes—Banik Ostrava	1-0, 0-2
*Djurgaarden—Dukla Prague	0-2, 1-3
*Partizan Belgrade—Portadown	5-0, 1-1
*Hamburger SV—Steagul Rosu Brasov	8-0, 2-1
*Twente Enschede—RWD Molenbeek	2-1, 1-0
*Dinamo Bucharest—FC Köln	1-1, 2-3
*Rapid Vienna—Velez Mostar	1-1, 0-1
*Derby County—Atlético Madrid	2-2, 2-2
(Derby won on penalty kicks)	
*Vasas Györ—Fortuna Düsseldorf	2-0, 0-3
*Hibernian—Juventus	2-4, 0-4
*Napoli—FC Porto	1-0, 1-0
*Dynamo Dresden—Dinamo Moscow	1-0, 0-1
(Dynamo Dresden won on penalty kicks)	
*Grasshoppers—Real Sociedad	2-1, 0-5
*Ajax—Antwerp	1-0, 1-2
(Ajax won on away-goals rule)	

Third Round

*Borussia Mönchengladbach—Real Sociedad	5-0, 4-2
*Partizan Belgrade—FC Köln	1-0, 1-5
*Dukla Prague—Twente Enschede	3-1, 0-5
*Hamburger SV—Dynamo Dresden	4-1, 2-2
*Napoli—Banik Ostrava	0-2, 1-1
*Derby County—Velez Mostar	3-1, 1-4
*Juventus—Ajax	1-0, 1-2
*FC Amsterdam—Fortuna Düsseldorf	3-0, 2-1

Quarter-Finals

*Banik Ostrava—Borussia Mönchengladbach	0-1, 1-3
*Velez Mostar—Twente Enschede	1-0, 0-2

*FC Köln—FC Amsterdam	5-1, 3-2
*Juventus—Hamburger SV	2-0, 0-0

Semi-Finals

*FC Köln—Borussia Mönchengladbach	1-3, 0-1
*Twente Enschede—Juventus	3-1, 1-0

Final

(first leg in Düsseldorf; att. 42,368)

Borussia Mönchengladbach	0	Twente Enschede	0

(second leg in Enschede; att. 21,767)

Twente Enschede	1	Borussia Mönchengladbach	5
(Drost)		(Simonsen 2, 1 pen, Heynckes 3)	

*home team in first leg

1975-76

First Round

*Hibernian—Liverpool	1-0, 1-3
*Glentoran—Ajax	1-6, 0-8
*MSV Duisburg—Paralimni	7-1, 3-2
*Grasshoppers—Real Sociedad	3-3, 1-1
(Real Sociedad won on away-goals rule)	
*PAOK Salonika—Barcelona	1-0, 1-6
*Tirgu Mures—Dynamo Dresden	2-2, 1-4
*Molde SK—Östers Växjö	1-0, 0-6
*Universitatea Craiova—Red Star Belgrade	1-3, 1-1
*Bohemians Prague—Honvéd	1-2, 1-1
*Chernomonretz Odessa—Lazio	1-0, 0-3
*Torpedo Moscow—Napoli	4-1, 1-1
*Vojvodina Novi Sad—AEK Athens	0-0, 1-3
*Hertha Berlin—HJK Helsinki	4-1, 2-1
*FC Köln—BK 03 Copenhagen	2-0, 3-2
*AIK Stockholm—Spartak Moscow	1-1, 0-1
*Young Boys Berne—Hamburger SV	0-0, 2-4
*GAIS Göteborg—Slask Wroclaw	2-1, 2-4
*VÖEST Linz—Vasas Budapest	2-0, 0-4
*Holbaek IF—Stal Mielec	0-1, 1-2
*Rapid Vienna—Galatasaray	1-0, 1-3
*Everton—AC Milan	0-0, 0-1
*Antwerp—Aston Villa	4-1, 1-0
*Carl Zeiss Jena—Olympique Marseille	3-0, 1-0
*AS Roma—Dounav Russe	2-0, 0-1
*Olympique Lyon—FC Brugge	4-3, 0-3
*FC Porto—Avenir	7-0, 3-0
*Feyenoord—Ipswich Town	1-2, 0-2

*Levski Spartak—Eskisehirspor	3-0, 4-1
*Athlone Town—Valerengen	3-1, 1-1
*Inter Bratislava—Real Zaragoza	5-0, 3-2
*IB Keflavik—Dundee United	0-2, 0-4
*Sliema Wanderers—Sporting Lisbon	1-2, 1-3

Second Round

*Real Sociedad—Liverpool	1-3, 0-6
*Athlone Town—AC Milan	0-0, 0-3
*Inter Bratislava—AEK Athens	2-0, 1-3
(Inter won on away-goals rule)	
*Red Star Belgrade—Hamburger SV	1-1, 0-4
*Slask Wroclaw—Antwerp	1-1, 2-1
*MSV Duisburg—Levski Spartak	3-2, 1-2
(Levski Spartak won on away-goals rule)	
*Östers Växjö—AS Roma	1-0, 0-2
*Vasas Budapest—Sporting Lisbon	3-2, 1-2
*Galatasaray—Torpedo Moscow	2-4, 0-3
*Hertha Berlin—Ajax	1-0, 1-4
*Spartak Moscow—FC Köln	2-0, 1-0
*Ipswich Town—FC Brugge	3-0, 0-4
*Dundee United—FC Porto	1-2, 1-1
*Lazio—Barcelona	0-4, —
(first leg awarded to Barcelona, 3-0, when Lazio refused to play, fearing public demonstrations against Spanish government)	
*Carl Zeiss Jena—Stal Mielec	1-0, 0-1
(Stal won on penalty kicks)	
*Honvéd—Dynamo Dresden	2-2, 0-1

Third Round

*Slask Wroclaw—Liverpool	1-2, 0-3
*Inter Bratislava—Stal Mielec	1-0, 0-2
*Hamburger SV—FC Porto	2-0, 1-2
*Dynamo Dresden—Torpedo Moscow	3-0, 1-3
*AC Milan—Spartak Moscow	4-0, 0-2
*Barcelona—Vasas Budapest	3-1, 1-0
*FC Brugge—AS Roma	1-0, 1-0
*Ajax—Levski Spartak	2-1, 1-2
(Levski Spartak won on penalty kicks)	

Quarter-Finals

*Dynamo Dresden—Liverpool	0-0, 1-2
*FC Brugge—AC Milan	2-0, 1-2
*Hamburger SV—Stal Mielec	1-1, 1-0
*Barcelona—Levski Spartak	4-0, 4-5

Semi-Finals
*Barcelona—Liverpool   0-1, 1-1
*Hamburger SV—FC Brugge   1-1, 0-1

Final
(first leg in Liverpool; att. 56,000)
Liverpool   3   FC Brugge   2
(Kennedy, Case, Keegan pen)   (Lambert, Cools)

(second leg in Brugge; att. 32,000)
FC Brugge   1   Liverpool   1
(Lambert pen)   (Keegan)

*home team in first leg

1976-77

First Round
*Manchester City—Juventus   1-0, 0-2
*Glentoran—FC Basel   3-2, 0-3
*Fram Reykjavik—Slovan Bratislava   0-3, 0-5
*Queen's Park Rangers—SK Brann   4-0, 7-0
*Naestved IF—RWD Molenbeek   0-3, 0-4
*Porto—Schalke 04   2-2, 2-3
*PS Kuopio—Östers Växjö   3-2, 0-2
*Feyenoord—Djurgaarden   3-0, 1-2
*FC Köln—GKS Tychy   2-0, 1-1
*Celtic—Wisla Kraków   2-2, 0-2
*Paralimni—Kaiserslautern   1-3, 0-8
*Derby County—Finn Harps   12-0, 4-1
*Swarovski Innsbruck—Start Kristiansand   2-1, 5-0
*Ajax—Manchester United   1-0, 0-2
*Belenenses—Barcelona   2-2, 2-3
*Eintracht Braunschweig—Holbaek IF   7-0, 0-1
*Hibernian—Sochaux   1-0, 0-0
*Red Boys Differdange—SC Lokeren   0-3, 1-3
*Español—OGC Nice   3-1, 1-2
*Grasshoppers—Hibernians Valetta   7-0, 2-0
*Schachtjor Donetzk—Dynamo Berlin   3-0, 1-1
*Újpest Dózsa—Athletic Bilbao   1-0, 0-5
*Dinamo Bucharest—AC Milan   0-0, 1-2
*Slavia Prague—Akademik Sofia   2-0, 0-3
*FC Magdeburg—Cesena   3-0, 1-3
*AEK Athens—Dinamo Moscow   2-0, 1-2
*Fenerbahçe—Videoton   2-1, 0-4
*ASA Tirgu Mures—Dinamo Zagreb   0-1, 0-3
*Internazionale—Honvéd   0-1, 1-1

*Austria Salzburg—Adanaspor	5-0, 0-2
*Sportul Studentes—Olympiakos Piraeus	3-0, 1-2
*Lokomotiv Plovdiv—Red Star Belgrade	2-1, 1-4

Second Round

*Manchester United—Juventus	1-0, 0-3
*Schachtjor Donetzk—Honvéd	3-0, 3-2
*Wisla Krakow—RWD Molenbeek	1-1, 1-1
(Molenbeek won on penalty kicks)	
*Hibernian—Östers Växjö	2-0, 1-4
*FC Köln—Grasshoppers	2-0, 3-2
*Kaiserslautern—Feyenoord	2-2, 0-5
*Akademik Sofia—AC Milan	4-3, 0-2
*Slovan Bratislava—Queen's Park Rangers	3-3, 2-5
*Eintracht Braunschweig—Español	2-1, 0-2
*FC Basel—Athletic Bilbao	1-1, 1-3
*AEK Athens—Derby County	2-0, 3-2
*FC Magdeburg—Dinamo Zagreb	2-0, 2-2
*Swarovski Innsbruck—Videoton	1-1, 0-1
*Austria Salzburg—Red Star Belgrade	2-1, 0-1
*Barcelona—SC Lokeren	2-0, 1-2
*Sportul Studentes—Schalke 04	0-1, 0-4

Third Round

*Juventus—Schachtjor Donetzk	3-0, 0-1
*RWD Molenbeek—Schalke 04	1-0, 1-1
*AEK Athens—Red Star Belgrade	2-0, 1-3
*Östers Växjö—Barcelona	0-3, 1-5
*Queen's Park Rangers—FC Köln	3-0, 1-4
(QPR won on away-goals rule)	
*Español—Feyenoord	0-1, 0-2
*Athletic Bilbao—AC Milan	4-1, 1-3
*FC Magdeburg—Videoton	5-0, 0-1

Quarter-Finals

*FC Magdeburg—Juventus	1-3, 0-1
*Feyenoord—RWD Molenbeek	0-0, 1-2
*Athletic Bilbao—Barcelona	2-1, 2-2
*Queen's Park Rangers—AEK Athens	3-0, 0-3
(AEK won on penalty kicks)	

Semi-Finals

*Juventus—AEK Athens	4-1, 1-0
*RWD Molenbeek—Athletic Bilbao	1-1, 0-0
(Bilbao won on away-goals rule)	

Final

(first leg in Turin; att. 75,000)

Juventus	1	Athletic Bilbao	0
(Tardelli)			

(second leg in Bilbao; att. 43,000)

Athletic Bilbao	2	Juventus	1
(Irureta, Carlos)		(Bettega)	

-Juventus won on away-goals rule-

*home team in first leg

1977-78

First Round

*Glenavon—PSV Eindhoven	2-6, 0-5
*Torino—Apoel Nicosia	3-0, 1-1
*Fiorentina—Schalke 04	0-0, 1-2
(first leg awarded to Schalke, 3-0: Fiorentina used ineligible player)	
*Odra Opole—FC Magdeburg	1-2, 1-1
*Servette—Athletic Bilbao	1-0, 0-2
*Bohemians—Newcastle United	0-0, 0-4
*Boavista—Lazio	1-0, 0-5
*Gornik Zabrze—Valkeakosken Haka	5-3, 0-0
*Landskrona BOIS—Ipswich Town	0-1, 0-5
*Standard Liège—Slavia Prague	1-0, 2-3
(Standard won on away-goals rule)	
*Eintracht Frankfurt—Sliema Wanderers	5-0, 0-0
*Carl Zeiss Jena—Altay Izmir	5-1, 1-4
*Frem Copenhagen—Grasshoppers	0-2, 1-6
*AZ 67 Alkmaar—Red Boys Differdange	11-1, 5-0
*Las Palmas—Sloboda Tuzla	5-0, 3-4
*RC Lens—Malmö FF	4-1, 0-2
*Start Kristiansand—Fram Reykjavik	6-0, 2-0
*Internazionale—Dinamo Tbilisi	0-1, 0-0
*Rapid Vienna—Inter Bratislava	1-0, 0-3
*Marek Stanke Dimitrov—Ferencváros	3-0, 0-2
*Manchester City—Widzew Łódź	2-2, 0-0
(Widzew won on away-goals rule)	
*Bayern München—Mjøndalen JF	8-0, 4-0
*Aston Villa—Fenerbahçe	4-0, 2-0
*Olympiakos Piraeus—Dinamo Zagreb	3-1, 1-5
*Dinamo Kiev—Eintracht Braunschweig	1-1, 0-0
(Eintracht won on away-goals rule)	
*Linzer ASK—Újpest Dózsa	3-2, 0-7
*FC Zurich—CSKA Sofia	5-1, 3-1
*Barcelona—Steaua Bucharest	5-1, 3-1
*Dundee United—KB Copenhagen	1-0, 0-3

*RWD Molenbeek—Aberdeen	0-0, 2-1
*ASA Tirgu Mures—AEK Athens	1-0, 0-3
*Bastia—Sporting Lisbon	3-2, 2-1

Second Round

*Widzew Lódź—PSV Eindhoven	3-5, 0-1
*Torino—Dinamo Zagreb	3-1, 0-1
*FC Magdeburg—Schalke 04	4-2, 3-1
*Újpest Dózsa—Athletic Bilbao	2-0, 0-3
*FC Zürich—Eintracht Frankfurt	0-3, 3-4
*Lazio—RC Lens	2-0, 0-6
*Aston Villa—Gornik Zabrze	2-0, 1-1
*Ipswich Town—Las Palmas	1-0, 3-3
*AEK Athens—Standard Liège	2-2, 1-4
*RWD Molenbeek—Carl Zeiss Jena	1-1, 1-1
(Jena won on penalty kicks)	
*Inter Bratislava—Grasshoppers	1-0, 1-5
*AZ 67 Alkmaar—Barcelona	1-1, 1-1
(Barcelona won on penalty kicks)	
*Start Kristiansand—Eintracht Braunschweig	1-0, 0-4
*KB Copenhagen—Dinamo Tbilisi	1-4, 1-2
*Bayern München—Marek Stanke Dimitrov	3-0, 0-2
*Bastia—Newcastle United	2-1, 3-1

Third Round

*PSV Eindhoven—Eintracht Braunschweig	2-0, 2-1
*FC Magdeburg—RC Lens	4-0, 0-2
*Aston Villa—Athletic Bilbao	2-0, 1-1
*Eintracht Frankfurt—Bayern München	4-0, 2-1
*Ipswich Town—Barcelona	1-1, 1-1
(Barcelona won on penalty kicks)	
*Carl Zeiss Jena—Standard Liège	2-0, 2-1
*Dinamo Tbilisi—Grasshoppers	1-0, 0-4
*Bastia—Torino	2-1, 3-2

Quarter-Finals

*FC Magdeburg—PSV Eindhoven	1-0, 2-4
*Aston Villa—Barcelona	2-2, 1-2
*Eintracht Frankfurt—Grasshoppers	3-2, 0-1
(Grasshoppers won on away-goals rule)	
*Bastia—Carl Zeiss Jena	7-2, 2-4

Semi-Finals

*PSV Eindhoven—Barcelona	3-0, 1-3
*Grasshoppers—Bastia	3-2, 0-1
(Bastia won on away-goals rule)	

Final

(first leg in Bastia; att. 15,000)

| Bastia | 0 | PSV Eindhoven | 0 |

(second leg in Eindhoven; att. 27,000)

| PSV Eindhoven | 3 | Bastia | 0 |

(W van der Kerkhof, Deykers,
van der Kuylen)

*home team in first leg

Uganda

Federation of Uganda Football Associations
P.O. Box 20077
Kampala

Founded: 1924
FIFA: 1959
CAF: 1959

Affiliated clubs: *400;* **registered players:** *1,582;* **national stadium:** *Nakivubo Stadium, Kampala (50,000);* **largest stadium:** *Nakivubo Stadium;* **colors:** *yellow jerseys, black shorts;* **season:** *January to November;* **honors:** *none.*

Uganda is a middle-level soccer power in Africa with a misleading international record that makes its real strength difficult to pin down. Only three other black African states have qualified more times than Uganda for the final rounds of the African Nations' Cup, each of them major African powers. But Uganda's overall record in the final rounds is so poor that it ranks at the bottom of the list of 20 participants. Still, there is little doubt that Ugandan soccer is the strongest in East Africa, though this region is by far the least developed on the continent, and soccer has become the most popular sport there despite the country's international reputation for boxing and track and field.

British colonists and workers played soccer in Kampala before the turn of the century, and in 1915 the first club was founded—Nsambya F.C. The mini-boom in African soccer after World War I produced the first Ugandan governing body in 1921, and this became affiliated with The Football Association in London shortly thereafter. Clubs and local leagues, especially in Kampala, were founded in large numbers between the world wars, and with greater intensity after World War II. In 1959, the Federation of Uganda Football Associations (FUFA) joined FIFA, with England's permission, and the first modern-day competition, the Aspro Cup, was in-

troduced for representative teams of each province. The name of this trophy was changed in the 1960s to the Madhvani Cup, and the competition continues today under the name Uganda Challenge Cup. Uganda became one of the first black African states to join the African Football Confederation in 1959.

In 1962, Uganda was the first sub-Saharan country to participate in the African Nations' Cup. Though its results in this tournament were discouraging, Uganda paved the way for a transformation of African soccer and the eventual removal of its power base from the north to the center and west. As for its losses to Egypt and Tunisia in 1962, it was recalled that Ugandan players had begun to wear shoes on the field only five years before, and their techniques and skills were still, according to Ethiopian accounts, rather primitive. "The Cranes," as Uganda's national team is known, qualified again in 1968, 1974, and 1976, but in four editions it has failed to win a single game.

For decades, Ugandan soccer was played under a regional league system with the Kampala League far and away the most important. In 1967, the Kampala League was disbanded, and one year later the Uganda National League was introduced, but of late the National League has merely administered the first and second divisions of regional leagues—third divisions are organized by the

Provincial and District Football Associations—in a return to the regional system. The winner of the Central Province League (Kampala and environs) is considered the national champion. The Uganda Cup, a knockout competition, was instituted in the late 1960s, but it was discontinued in 1971. When the African Cup Winners' Cup was introduced in 1975, the Uganda Cup was reestablished.

Kampala is the home of all the leading clubs. The most popular is Express F.C., which was founded in 1959 by the newspaper *Uganda Express* and has miraculously survived the closing of that paper. The most successful club is Simba F.C., the team of the Ugandan Army, which reached the final of the African Champions' Cup in 1972, losing to Guinea's Hafia de Conakry. Simba has even made a moderately successful tour of Europe. The third major Kampala club, and the one best known for its sophisticated techniques and tactics, is Kampala City Council F.C., which is underwritten by its namesake, the capital's legislative body. Police Football Club and Prisons Football Club round out the top five of Ugandan soccer. Uganda's leading player in recent years has been Polly Ouma, a goalscoring center forward and player-coach with Simba F.C., who was reportedly arrested by the police in 1975 and promptly disappeared from sight.

Újpesti Dózsa Sport Club

Location: *Budapest, Hungary;* stadium: *Újpesti Dózsa-Stadion (30,000);* colors: *lilac jerseys with white sleeves, white shorts;* honors: *Mitropa Cup (1929, 1939), Hungarian champion (1930, 1931, 1933, 1935, 1939, 1945, 1946, 1947, 1960, 1969, 1970, 1971, 1972, 1973, 1974, 1975, 1978), Hungarian cup winner (1969, 1970, 1971 1975).*

Founded 1885 as Újpesti Torna Egylet in the northeastern Budapest suburb of Újpest, it is the oldest club in Hungary. Known as UTE during the first 25 years of this century, it became Újpest Football Club during the professional era (1926-35), and adopted its present name after World War II. (Dózsa is the name of a Hungarian national hero.) In the late 1940s, the club became officially associated with the Ministry of the Interior (police, et al.).

Újpest first achieved success after it turned professional in 1926, when the captain of the team was fullback Karoly Fogl, a man as much feared for his painful handshake as his effective tackling. Championships came in rapid succession during the early 1930s. Újpest's first great goalscoring star was inside forward Gyula Zsengeller, who joined the club at the end of this period and spearheaded the Hungarian attack in the 1938 World Cup. Újpest's biggest achievements were in winning the coveted Mitropa Cups of 1929 and 1939 with fine wins in these finals over Slavia Prague and Ferencváros. In the new postwar league, Újpest was an immediate success, winning three consecutive league titles from 1945-47. Its 13-year hiatus during Honvéd's golden era ended with another title in 1960, and in subsequent years the club was led by the forward duo of Ferenc Bene, the gifted right-side striker, and center forward Antal Dunai, both highly successful Hungarian internationals. Újpest has dominated the Hungarian game ever since it won league-cup doubles in 1969, 1970, and 1971. Another double was won in 1975, but throughout this entire period Újpest failed to win any of the three European club championships. Its highest achievements have been to reach the quarter-finals of the European Cup in both 1972 and 1973, and the semi-finals of the 1969 Fairs Cup.

Union of European Football Associations (UEFA)

Address: *Case Postale 16, CH-3000 Berne 15, Switzerland.* Members: *Albania, Austria, Belgium, Bulgaria, Cyprus, Czechoslovakia, Denmark, England, Finland,*

France, German DR, Germany FR, Greece, Hungary, Iceland, Ireland Northern, Ireland Republic, Italy, Liechtenstein, Luxembourg, Malta, the Netherlands, Norway, Poland, Portugal, Rumania, Scotland, Spain, Sweden, Switzerland, Turkey, USSR, Wales, Yugoslavia. **Affiliated clubs:** *210,481;* **registered players:** *14,392,796.*

Founded in 1954 by the representative governing bodies of 30 European countries. They were joined subsequently by Turkey (1955), Malta (1960), Cyprus (1964), and Liechtenstein (1974). The idea for a European governing body was canvassed as early as 1952. UEFA represents two-thirds of organized soccer in the world, and is the most active of all continental confederations. It administers the European Football Championship, European Champion Clubs' Cup, European Cup Winners' Cup, since 1971 the UEFA Cup (formerly the Fairs Cup), European Under-21 Championship, European Amateur Championship, and the UEFA Youth Tournament. UEFA is also responsible for disciplining clubs and players whose behavior is unacceptable in UEFA-sponsored competitions, a function that the confederation has been exercising more and more frequently in recent years. The overall policy of UEFA, however, is not to interfere with the local problems of member-associations.

Aside from membership dues, UEFA is funded by the following: 4 percent of gross gate receipts from all internationals played under its aegis; 10 percent of all television fees paid out by broadcasters to parties involved in internationals played under its aegis; royalties from film and television showings; and revenue from advertising space sold at European stadiums. In addition to organizational expenses, UEFA's expenditures include: underwriting deficits incurred by the Youth Tournament; financial compensation for losses accrued by clubs during the first round of UEFA-sponsored competitions; assistance given to the less developed member-associations; and instructional services provided to administrative and technical personnel of member-associations.

Union of Arab Football Associations

Founded in 1963 as the Arab Football Confederation, the Union of Arab Football Associations is an independent regional organization not affiliated with FIFA. Its primary function is to oversee the Arab Cup (Football Tournament of the Union of Arab Football Associations), a competition held in conjunction with the Pan Arab Games. The Union also serves to promote soccer in an area that has experienced a great surge of interest in the game during recent years.

Its membership includes Algeria, Bahrain, Egypt, Iraq, Jordan, Kuwait, Lebanon, Libya, Morocco, Qatar, Sudan, and United Arab Emirates, all members of FIFA, and Yemen Arab Republic, which is not a member of FIFA. Arab Palestine is also a full member of the Union. All but the Arabian Gulf states were charter-members.

Union of Arab Football Associations, Football Tournament of the

Known commonly as the Arab Cup, this is the soccer competition held in association with the Pan Arab Games, and is open to all members of the Union of Arab Football Associations. It has been played every three years since 1963. The most recent winner was Morocco in the 1975 games at Damascus.

United Arab Emirates

United Arab Emirates Football Association
P.O. Box 5458
Dubai

Founded: ?
FIFA: 1972
AFC: ?

Colors: *red jerseys, red shorts (Further information unavailable.)*

The United Arab Emirates is a confederation of six emirates on the Persian Gulf, and consists of the area formerly known as Trucial Oman (later the Trucial States). Its interest in soccer now appears to be as enthusiastic as that of its neighbors, Qatar and Bahrain. It is, however, the weakest of the Persian Gulf states on the soccer field, due in no small part to its exceptionally late start in organizing the game.

There are 32 clubs in the U.A.E., which are divided among the emirates as follows: Dubai (10), Abu Dhabi (9), Sharja (8), Ajman (2), Fujaira (2), and Umm Al Quwaim (1). Of the 25 playing fields located throughout the federation, more than half are in Dubai and Abu Dhabi. Clubs are generally divided into "first class" and "second class" teams, and both classes have their own tournaments in each emirate. The national cup competition is called the Cup of High Highness the Head of State of the U.A.E., and is contested among all first and second class teams.

International competition with its Arabian peninsula rivals increased markedly after affiliation with FIFA in 1972, but the U.A.E. had previously played host to national teams or selections from Bahrain, Qatar, Kuwait, Ceylon, and Arab Palestine. U.A.E. clubs and national selections have also played against Ismaili Cairo and other clubs from the Middle East. The U.A.E.'s only forays into official international tournaments have been its participation in the regional Arabian Gulf Tournament in 1972, 1974, and 1976. On each occasion the emirates placed last in the standings, failing to win any of their matches in the 1972 and 1976 editions. U.A.E. teams have not attempted to qualify for the Asian Nations' Cup, the Olympic Games, or the World Cup. In 1977, the U.A.E. Football Association took its biggest step yet by signing England's former national team manager Don Revie to a multiyear contract to supervise the development of the game and steer the U.A.E. national team to regional success.

United Kingdom   See: **England; Scotland; Wales;** and **Ireland, Northern**

United Soccer Association   See: **North American Soccer League**

United States Soccer Federation

This is the controlling body of soccer in the United States, and, as such, represents American soccer interests in FIFA, the world governing body, and CONCACAF, the North-Central American and Caribbean confederation.

Under its original name, the United States Football Association, it was founded in 1913 after considerable feuding and strong competition from other organizations. The competing powers were the old American Football Association (AFA), the organizers of the American Cup, whose influence was felt primarily in New England, New Jersey, and Philadelphia, and the newer American Amateur Football Association (AAFA), whose control was centered in New York State.

In 1912, representatives of both associations clashed at the FIFA Congress in Stockholm to argue their case for international recognition. The AFA, which was affiliated with The Football Association in London, was represented by Sir Frederick Wall, secretary of The F.A., who pointed out that the AAFA did not represent professional players, thereby diminishing its potential authority. Wall also admonished that the feud should be settled back in the United States rather than brought before the FIFA Congress to seek arbitration. The AAFA, for its part, was represented by Thomas W. Cahill, secretary of the association and the official representative of the AAFA at the Stockholm Olympic Games then in progress. FIFA agreed with Wall's admonition, and recommended to Cahill that he return to New York and try to organize a mutually acceptable national association that could be brought to FIFA for recognition.

After Cahill returned to New York, the two associations appointed committees to find a solution to their difficulties. The AFA committee was made up of Joseph Hughes of Paterson, N.J.; John Gundy of Bayonne, N.J.; A.N. Beveridge of Kearny, N.J.; A. Albert Frost, of Philadelphia; and Andrew M. Brown, of New York City. The AAFA committee was composed of Dr. G. Randolph Manning, William A. Campbell, and Nathan Agar, all of New York. A series of conferences between the two committees began on October 12, 1912, at the Astor House in New York City, but on December 8, when an agreement appeared imminent, the AFA voted to discontinue negotiations and dismiss its committee. This unpopular action gained the AAFA much support among local and regional associations. In March 1913, the Allied American F.A. of Philadelphia and the F.A. of Philadelphia switched their allegiance to the AAFA, and it was this newly found strength from two important Philadelphia associations that gave the AAFA the necessary stimulus to prevail.

On April 5, 1913, representatives from associations across the nation met at the Astor House to formally establish the United States Football Association (USFA), and a com-

mittee was appointed to draft a constitution and bylaws. A second convention was held on June 21, 1913, at the Broadway Central Hotel, and the first election of officers was held: Dr. G. Randolph Manning, president; Oliver Hemingway of the F.A. of Philadelphia, vice-president; Thomas H. McKnight of Chicago, second vice-president; William D. Love of Pawtucket, R.I., third vice-president; Archibald Birse of the Peel Challenge Cup Commission, Chicago, treasurer; and Thomas Cahill, secretary.

The AAFA application to FIFA was withdrawn, and a USFA application submitted. At the FIFA Congress of 1913 in Copenhagen, the pending AFA application was ignored, and the USFA was officially recognized. The AFA, upon hearing the news, voted to join the newly formed national governing body.

The USFA's name was changed in 1945 to the United States Soccer Football Association, and the present name was adopted in 1974.

The USSF, a nonprofit corporation registered in New York State, consists of 37 regional associations, the North American Soccer League, the American Soccer League, the Intercollegiate Soccer Association of America, National Soccer Coaches Association of America, and United States Youth Soccer Association. Via its affiliation with the United States Olympic Committee, it also sponsors the United States Olympic soccer team, and it organizes the National Open Challenge Cup and the National Amateur Cup. The American Youth Soccer Organization and the National Intercollegiate Soccer Officials Association are not members of the USSF, and it is estimated that about 30 percent of all players connected with organized competition in the United States are not registered. In addition to its apparent inability to coalesce soccer interests across the country, whether on the youth, amateur, or professional levels, the USSF has come into very strong criticism from FIFA in recent years for organizational ineptitude, especially for sanctioning rule changes in collegiate soccer and the North American Soccer League. (This is primarily in reference to the NASL's elimination of drawn games, the "shoot-out," and the 35-yard line.) In 1978, FIFA warned the USSF that if these matters were not conformed to world standards, the United States risked expulsion from the world body.

Upper Volta

Fédération Voltaïque de Foot-ball   Founded: 1960
B.P. 57   FIFA: 1964
Ouagadougou   CAF: 1964

Affiliated clubs: *55;* registered players: *3,510;* national stadium: *Stade Municipal de Ouagadougou, Ouagadougou (4,000);* largest stadium: *Stade Municipal de Ouagadougou;* colors: *black jerseys, white shorts;* season: *October to June;* honors: *none.*

One of the poorest countries of West Africa, Upper Volta is an underdeveloped soccer nation as well. It ranks well down in the bottom quarter of African members of FIFA when considered on the basis of international success at both national and club levels, but this is caused by financial and organizational woes rather than the inferiority of its players. The national team, known as "the Stallions," has not yet advanced to the final rounds of the African Nations' Cup, but it attempted to qualify for the World Cup in 1974 and 1978, and in the former defeated Mauritania by a 3-1 aggregate in the preliminary round. Ivory Coast, one of West Africa's major powers, eventually stopped the Stallions' advancement by the same goal difference, and did so again in 1978.

Most of Upper Volta's major clubs have had some international exposure, but only one has traveled out of West Africa: Silures' first round meeting with C.A.R.A. of the Congo in the 1975 African Champions' Cup. None of Upper Volta's entrants in either the Champions' Cup or the African Cup Winners' Cup has advanced beyond the first round. Upper Volta's league champions participated in the Champions' Cup in 1972, 1973, 1975, and 1976, but Silures' first round endeavors in 1975 remain the highest achievement to date. Asfav went out in the preliminary round in 1972 to Djoliba of Mali, while the promising Jeanne d'Arc withdrew from the first round in 1973 after defeating powerful Mighty Jet of Nigeria in preliminaries. Silures had to withdraw from the preliminary round in 1976 without a single game being played. Upper Volta's lone entry in the Cup Winners' Cup has been Kadiogo in 1976, which did well to eliminate Gambia Port Authority before losing to Kaleum Star of Guinea in the first round.

Soccer was brought to the capital, Ouagadougou, by French colonists around 1896, but as was the case in all countries of the Sahel, it got off to a slow start even after the French partition of 1932. During the colonial period, soccer in Upper Volta was under the aegis of the Ligue de l'Afrique Occidentale Française in Dakar, which administered the game in all of French West Africa, but little evidence of its activities existed. Enthusiasm increased considerably after World War II, however, and the Fédération Voltaïque de Foot-ball (FVF) was founded immediately after independence in 1960, followed closely by affiliation with FIFA and the African Football Confederation.

The FVF supports a national championship with 20 upper-level clubs and a national cup competition, as well as regional leagues and knockout tournaments. A total of 60 clubs compete in senior-level competition. Most of Upper Volta's domestic soccer activity is centered in Ouagadougou and Bobo-Dioulasso, the second largest city and former economic and political hub during the colonial era.

Uruguay

Asociación Uruguaya de Fútbol   Founded: 1900
Av. 18 de Julio 1520/28   FIFA: 1923
Montevideo   CONMEBOL: 1916

Affiliated clubs: *970;* **registered players:** *101,550 (550 professional, 12,000 non-amateur);* **national stadium:** *Estadio Centenario, Montevideo (75,000);* **largest stadium:** *Estadio Centenario;* **colors:** *sky blue jerseys with white trim, black shorts;* **season:** *March to December;* **honors:** *World Cup winner (1930, 1950), Olympic Games winner (1924, 1928), South American Championship winner (1916, 1917, 1920, 1923, 1924, 1926, 1935, 1942, 1956, 1959, 1967), runner-up (1919, 1927, 1939, 1941), Peñarol, Intercontinental Cup (1961, 1966), Copa Libertadores (1960, 1961, 1966), Nacional, Intercontinental Cup (1971), Copa Libertadores (1971).*

With a population of only three million, Uruguay may justly claim to be the world's most disproportionately successful soccer country. It is certainly high on anyone's list of the world's top ten, and a strong case can be made for its being the world's leading exporter of good players too. Uruguay dominated world soccer decisively between 1924-30 with two Olympic gold medals and a World Cup victory, and in 1950 it won the World Cup a second time. In 1954 and 1970, Uruguay advanced to the semi-finals of the World Cup, and in the South American Championship, its record over the years is second only to that of Argentina, its fierce rival across the Rio de la Plata.

The legendary Uruguayan clubs, Peñarol and Nacional, have been dominant forces in South America ever since international club competitions were organized and have at times beaten Europe's best clubs to achieve world honors. Indeed, it is possible that more players of world stature have donned the uniforms of Peñarol and Nacional than any other clubs in the world. Sadly, they have not been continental powers since 1971, and the national team has declined even more dramatically. The famed sky blues played poorly at the 1974 World Cup and were eliminated altogether from the finals of the 1978 World Cup, a bitter disappointment to Uruguayan fans who were prepared to attend the tournament *en masse* in neighboring Argentina.

Soccer was introduced in Uruguay during the 1870s by British residents and workers. In 1882, an English professor at the University of Montevideo formed the first club, composed entirely of British students, and other clubs were soon established. The first regularly scheduled series of games was played in 1886 at Punta Carretas, Montevideo, the site of the present Estadio Luis Franzini, home of CA Defensor. In 1891, the Central Uruguay Railway Cricket Club was founded by British employees of the Ferrocarril Central in Montevideo, and a soccer section was es-tablished the following a year. Its first match was against the British School in 1892. In 1899, the first native Uruguayan club, Nacional, was founded, and one year later the Uruguayan Football Association was established by Central Uruguay Railway, Albion, another all-British club, and the Deutscher Fussballklub, a German-based club, all of Montevideo. The first season of the new Uruguayan league was played in 1900 by these three clubs and Uruguay F.C., another British team, and was won by Peñarol, the informal name already given to the railway company team and adopted officially in 1914 after it won five championships in 13 years. In 1901, Nacional joined the league, and from the outset Peñarol and Nacional dominated the competition.

The founding of the Uruguayan F.A. anticipated the formation of a national team, and on August 15, 1905, the first international in South America was played between Uruguay and Argentina in Buenos Aires, ending in a scoreless draw. This match also inaugurated the Lipton Cup, which along with the Newton Cup (1906) became the basis for the great Uruguay-Argentina rivalry, one of the oldest in the world. Until 1916, all of Uruguay's international matches were played against Argentina, except on one occasion in 1910 when it met Chile in Buenos Aires in an aborted attempt to establish a three-way South American Championship. Between 1905-16, Uruguay won 13 of 43 matches with Argentina, drawing eight and scoring 59 goals to Argentina's 75. In 1916, Uruguay met Brazil for the first time in the first edition of the South American Championship in Buenos Aires; Uruguay won 2-1, and a second great South American rivalry was born. These were formative years for Uruguay in international competition, foreshadowing the great period to come.

Uruguay's other primary South American opponents came along during the 1920s: Paraguay (1921), Bolivia (1926), and Peru (1927). In subsequent years, Uruguay would dominate each of these middle-level continental powers with Paraguay proving to be the most difficult. Indeed, Argentina would not gain momentum over Uruguay until the 1930s and Brazil not until the 1940s. Uruguay began to make its mark on international competition in the South American Championship before 1920. In the first ten editions (1916-26), Uruguay won the title six times and finished runner-up once. Of the other three, one was lost in a special play-off after accumulating an equal number of points with Brazil (1919), one was played without Uruguay's participation (1925), and in the other Uruguay withdrew in protest after accumulating an equal number of points with Brazil and Paraguay (1922). Uruguay won or shared each Lipton Cup between 1919-29, all Newton Cups (except one) between 1917-24, and lost only one encounter with Brazil between 1916 and 1930.

At the 1924 Olympic Games in Paris, Uruguay launched its golden era of world predominance, and introduced the famous midfield line known widely as *la costilla metallica* ("the iron curtain"), which was made up of world-class right half José Andrade, attacking center half Lorenzo Fernandez, and left half Alvaro Gestido. On the forward line were the legendary inside right Hector Scarone, inside left Pedro Cea, and center forward Pedro Petrone, each a prolific goalscorer who excelled in the various South American Championships of the 1920s. At Paris in 1924, Uruguay became the first non-European country to win the Olympic soccer tournament with defeats of Yugoslavia (7-0), USA (3-0), France (5-1), the Netherlands (2-1), and Switzerland in the final (3-0). The victory made world stars of many Uruguayan players, and at the 1928 Olympic Games in Amsterdam, Uruguay entered as the odds-on favorite.

In Amsterdam, Uruguay prevailed over strong opposition, defeating the Netherlands (2-0), Germany (4-1), Italy (3-2), and mighty Argentina in the final (2-1 in a replay after drawing 1-1). Uruguay's successes in the Olympic Games of 1924 and 1928, achieved before South America and most of Europe had turned professional, carried further significance in establishing South America as a coequal center of the world game; Uruguay had won its Olympic honors in distant Europe and the seriousness with which it took the game made a deep impression on European observers.

It was appropriate, therefore, that the staging of the first World Cup (1930) was awarded to little Uruguay. The Asociación Uruguaya de Football (AUF), as the national association was now called, promised FIFA that it would build a great new stadium in Montevideo as a worthy location for the first world championship. But a protest by European associations over the staging of the tournament in so remote a place as Uruguay was loud and at times offensive, and Uruguayan administrators were piqued by the outcry. Sadly, most of the leading soccer nations of Europe stayed away. France, Belgium, and Yugoslavia grudgingly agreed to participate, while Rumania entered willingly at the behest of King Carol himself, an avid fan. In the end, the most formidable opposition to Uruguay was its bitter rival Argentina.

Though the grand Estadio Centenario was not completed in time for the first matches, it was eventually opened ceremoniously before Uruguay's encounter with Peru, won sluggishly by the home side 1-0. Uruguay played only four matches to win this first world championship, but with two Olympic wins to its credit, few ventured to say it was undeserved. There were easy victories over Rumania (4-0) and Yugoslavia (6-1), and in the final the Olympic champions defeated star-studded Argentina 4-2 on goals from Dorado, Cea, Iriarte, and Castro. England and the powerful Central European teams were sorely missed, and the satisfaction of Uruguay's victory was tarnished by the impact of Europe's snub. When the time came to register for the 1934 World Cup in Italy, the hurt had not lessened and Uruguay declined to participate, the only time in the history of the World Cup a holder has failed to return.

Professionalism was adopted in Uruguay in 1933 by the leading clubs, Peñarol and Nacional, about the same time as other important South American powers did likewise. Peñarol and Nacional had won 24 of the 32 nonprofessional league titles since 1900, and by the 1930s the country had begun to accept domination of its domestic game by the two Montevideo giants, a pattern the AUF has done little to alter over the decades. The first of many international club competitions between the champions of Uruguay and Argentina was introduced in 1909, perhaps the world's first such competition. The Cup Honor (1909-20) was won all but one year by Uruguayan participants: Nacional (4), Peñarol (2), Wanderers (1), and Universal

(1). A second competiton, the Cup Competencia (1902-20), was also dominated by Uruguayan clubs: Nacional (4), Peñarol (2), and Wanderers (2). Peñarol and Nacional also dominated the Cup Rio de la Plata (1916-28). Although the national league was composed of Montevideo clubs only (a characteristic that existed until 1978), the great Argentine club River Plate of Buenos Aires also participated during the years before World War I by special arrangement, and broke the hegemony of Peñarol and Nacional by winning Uruguayan titles four times. After professionalism was introduced, Peñarol and Nacional won every league title without exception until 1976 when the small Montevideo club CA Defensor broke through to the top. Even greater international glories awaited Peñarol and Nacional in the 1960s and '70s.

Uruguay's international experience since 1930 has been fraught with anomalies and uncertainties. The AUF again declined to enter the 1938 World Cup, due in part to a residue of hurt pride from 1930 but also resulting from confusion at home over the question of professionalism. In 1950, however, in only its second attempt, Uruguay won the world championship again, this time upsetting the home favorite, Brazil. The Uruguayan team of 1950, seven of whom played with Peñarol, included a second generation of world-famous names—left half Rodriguez Andrade (the nephew of 1930 star José Andrade), right wing Chico Ghiggia, and the extraordinary inside left Juan Schiaffino, to name just three—but the genius of the earlier 1924-30 squad was not evident. In addition, Hungary, whose golden era of Puskás & Co. had already begun, was not in the tournament, nor was Argentina, and England entered without any tactical cohesion or competitive experience after decades of self-exile from world competition. Uruguay advanced to the final pool after only one match—an 8-0 trouncing of Bolivia on four goals by Schiaffino—and faced the decisive match with Brazil after drawing with Spain, 2-2, and slipping past the strong Swedish team by a single goal (3-2). Uruguay's 2-1 win over Brazil in what amounted to a "final" was an upset, and will be further remembered as the game that set the world record attendance figure (199,850) that still stands today. Uruguay was once again at the apex of world soccer, and eight Uruguayans reportedly died of heart attacks in the celebrations.

In its fourth place finish in the 1954 World Cup in Switzerland, Uruguay met virtually all the world's leading national teams, and the results on this basis alone are noteworthy: Czechoslovakia (2-0), Scotland (7-0), England (4-2), Hungary (2-4), and Austria (1-3). Seldom has a World Cup participant had to take on such formidable opposition. Having failed to qualify for the 1958 World Cup, Uruguay fared poorly in 1962 in Chile, placing third in its first round group after the USSR and Yugoslavia. In 1966, a skillful Uruguayan squad entered the final rounds in England, but its recently adopted defensive posture was no match for the highly motivated English and West Germans, and Uruguay was lucky to advance to the quarter-finals from its first round group with England, Mexico, and France.

In 1970, Uruguay qualified once again. Grouped with Italy, Sweden, and Israel, it finished second in its first round group on goal difference after a win over Israel, a scoreless draw with Italy, and a loss to Sweden. Though not among the favorites to win the 1970 Cup, Uruguay advanced to the quarter-final round where it was fortunate not to play against Italy, West Germany, or Brazil. Instead, Uruguay faced the floundering USSR, and squeaked through by 1-0 after extra time and a disallowed, questionable goal. In the semi-finals Brazil played at the peak of its form against Uruguay, with Pelé selling dummies and wingers Jairzinho and Rivelino skillfully taking advantage of all opportunities. Uruguay became defensive and rough in its tackling, eventually losing 3-1, and took a surprisingly high fourth place in the competition after dropping the third place game to West Germany. Uruguayan goalkeeper Mazurkiewicz drew much praise from observers and was touted as one of the world's best custodians. By 1974, Uruguay had slipped into its current decline, and at the World Cup in West Germany, its performance was the worst anyone could remember. Decisive losses to the Netherlands and Sweden were followed by a 1-1 draw with Bulgaria, and Uruguay finished last in its group of four with only one goal to its credit.

Uruguay has not participated in any final rounds of the Olympic Games since its legendary achievements of 1924 and 1928. By the time soccer was reintroduced to the Olympic program in 1936, the best Uruguayan players had turned professional. After the golden era of 1924-30, Uruguay's success in the South American Championship was not as frequent as that of Argentina, whose prestige rose after 1928, but its record still exceeds that of Brazil, the third-ranking country in the competition. After 1930, Uruguay won the South American title five times and placed second twice, compared to Argentina's winning of the championship eight times during the same period with three second-place finishes. Uruguay has participated in all but two of the 30 editions of the South American Championship since 1916, more than any other country. Its overall record in the competition (1916-75) is: 122-76-10-36-299-144-162.

In the first division, Peñarol had already won 23 national titles and Nacional had won 25 by 1959. A new international challenge opened up in 1960 with the introduction of the Copa Libertadores, the South American club championship. Both Peñarol and Nacional were well experienced in international competition. Since the 1920s, they had made extensive and frequent tours abroad to help defray the high cost of monopolizing Uruguayan soccer, and could often be seen paying visits to Europe and even Africa, as well as the rest of Latin America. The most famous of these international tours was made by Nacional in 1925 when it spent five months in Europe and played 38 games in nine countries. Led by the goalscoring artistry of Hector Scarone, Nacional won 26 of these matches, scoring 130 goals and allowing only 30 goals.

Thus the two clubs were at home in 1960 when the new continental championship was launched, and Uruguayan clubs completed the first decade with more honors than any others in South America. Peñarol was the first of the Montevideo giants to excel in this series. It won the title in 1960, 1961, and 1966, and placed second in 1962, 1965, and 1970. Nacional won the championship in 1971, and finished runner-up in 1964, 1967, and 1969. In the early 1970s, Uruguayan soccer entered a period of financial crisis that seriously affected its international results, and Peñarol and Nacional had to sell many of their leading players to pay off mounting debts. By 1973, the Montevideo clubs ceased to make an impact on the Copa Libertadores, though they still have the two best overall records in the competition.

In the Intercontinental Cup (the unofficial transatlantic competition played between the winners of the Copa Libertadores and the European Champions' Cup), both Peñarol and Nacional have extended their fame worldwide. In 1961, Peñarol buried Portugal's Benfica by winning its home leg 5-0, and in 1966 a reorganized Real Madrid suffered 2-0 defeats to Peñarol both home and away. Alberto Spencer, Peñarol's Ecuadorean center forward, and Pedro Rocha, the elegant inside forward, led Peñarol's attack in these great international victories, and helped to establish Peñarol as one of the world's two or three leading clubs of the decade. Nacional's Intercontinental Cup win in 1971, on the other hand, was marred by Ajax's refusal to participate for fear of its physical safety in Montevideo, and Nacional had to settle for European Cup runner-up Panathinaïkos of Athens, which succumbed to the Uruguayans by an aggregate score of 3-2. This was Uruguay's last hurrah to date in major international club competition, though Peñarol and Nacional continue to dominate the league at home.

The first division, or Liga Mayor, is composed of 12 clubs. The championship and its trophy, the Copa Uruguaya, is won after many stages of competition. All 12 members of the first division play each other once and accumulate points. Then, the top eight from this round play each other again, still accumulating points, and any necessary tie-breaking play-offs follow. The top two finishers automatically enter the following year's Copa Libertadores. Uruguay also has a First "B" Division and an Intermediate Division, both with 12 clubs, and a lower division of regional sections. The trophies of defunct international competitions between Uruguayan and Argentine champion clubs are now awarded for post-season tournaments that include clubs already eliminated from the Liga Mayor.

The financial crisis in the domestic game in recent years has carried over into the activities of the AUF. Uruguay's poor showing in the 1974 World Cup was a direct outgrowth of this financial crisis, as leading Uruguayan players continued their mass exodus to Brazil, Argentina, and Western Europe, leaving the national selectors with third and fourth choice players to fill the national roster. Despite Uruguay's present disappointing position in the South American game, its legacy is extraordinary enough to be indelible. The little republic on the Rio de la Plata continues to produce more excellent players than any other nation of comparable size, and the legendary names of its past greatness—Porte,

Nasazzi, Scarone, Petrone, Andrade, Piendibene, Maspoli, Cea, Varela, Sosa, Schiaffino,
Rocha, and Mazurkiewicz—assure Uruguay's
high position in the pantheon of world soccer.

Champions

1900	Peñarol	1926	Peñarol	1952	Nacional
1901	Peñarol	1927	Rampla Juniors	1953	Peñarol
1902	Nacional	1928	Peñarol	1954	Peñarol
1903	Nacional	1929	Peñarol	1955	Nacional
1904	no competition	1930	Peñarol	1956	Nacional
1905	Peñarol	1931	Wanderers Montevideo	1957	Nacional
1906	Wanderers Montevideo	1932	Peñarol	1958	Peñarol
1907	Peñarol	1933	Nacional	1959	Peñarol
1908	Ríver Plate	1934	Nacional	1960	Peñarol
1909	Wanderers Montevideo	1935	Peñarol	1961	Peñarol
1910	Ríver Plate	1936	Peñarol	1962	Peñarol
1911	Peñarol	1937	Peñarol	1963	Nacional
1912	Nacional	1938	Peñarol	1964	Peñarol
1913	Ríver Plate	1939	Nacional	1965	Peñarol
1914	Ríver Plate	1940	Nacional	1966	Nacional
1915	Nacional	1941	Nacional	1967	Peñarol
1916	Nacional	1942	Nacional	1968	Peñarol
1917	Nacional	1943	Nacional	1969	Nacional
1918	Peñarol	1944	Peñarol	1970	Nacional
1919	Nacional	1945	Peñarol	1971	Nacional
1920	Nacional	1946	Nacional	1972	Nacional
1921	Peñarol	1947	Nacional	1973	Peñarol
1922	Nacional	1948	no competition	1974	Peñarol
1923	Nacional	1949	Peñarol	1975	Peñarol
1924	Nacional	1950	Nacional	1976	Defensor
1925	no competition	1951	Peñarol	1977	Nacional
				1978	Peñarol

USA

United States Soccer Federation
Empire State Building
350 Fifth Ave.
Room 4010
New York, New York 10001

Founded: 1913
FIFA: 1913
CONCACAF: 1961

Affiliated clubs, *1,202;* **registered players:** *42,685;* **national stadium:** *none;* **largest stadium:** *Giants Stadium, East Rutherford, New Jersey (76,891);* **colors;** *red jerseys with white trim, red shorts;* **season:** *April to August;* **honors:** *none.*

The history of soccer in the United States is certainly unique. There are few parallels to be found anywhere, nor is there a country that has failed so consistently to live up to its early potential. Indeed, its impact on the world game until very recently was almost nonexistent. American soccer has been characterized by disorganization domestically, isolation from the international mainstream, the triumph of speculators over planners, and an unfortunate vote of no confidence in its native players at the highest levels of the game. By the 1970s, however, it appeared that the United States had its first chance to nurse genuine development of its vast reserves. In America's youth, potential for moderate, regional international success by the 1980s became evident, and public acceptance of soccer as a spectator sport began to rise, threatened only by the possibility that entrepreneurs would impatiently destroy its natural rate of growth.

In the seventeenth century, the American colonies were the first overseas territory of the British Empire to play football-like games, and two centuries later the United States was the first sovereign country outside Great Britain to establish a soccer club and one of the first to form a national governing body. However, the USA national team, as late as 1948, lost to lowly Norway by the score of 11-0, and as late as 1975 lost to Italy by 10-0, not to mention a 2-1 defeat at the same time by the reserve squad of the Italian second division club Pescara. Such embarrassments were eased by two high spots in American soccer annals: the USA's advance to the semi-finals of the first World Cup in 1930, and its shock upset of England in the 1950 World Cup. Towering achievements though these were, they are remembered elsewhere as aberrations that resulted from extraordinary circumstances.

Some form of football, a forerunner of modern soccer and rugby, was played, though to what extent we do not know, in the Virginia settlement as early as 1609. The rules of the Jamestown game are unknown, but they must have resembled the sprawling Shrovetide games of the home country. In any event, foootball was soon forbidden by ordinance, and for the next two centuries it resurfaced only among the least puritanical segments of the English colonies. Its adoption by French, German, Dutch, and Scandinavian settlements is less certain.

The first descriptions of the game in the United States were written by the students and alumni of the great colleges of the Northeast. Freshman and sophomore classes at Harvard initiated an annual football contest in 1827. It was played on the first Monday of the new school year, and entailed such rough play that the annual date became known as "Bloody Monday." The Harvard faculty banned this event in 1860, but similar games continued to be played less formally. Princeton students played "ballown," in which the ball was hit with the fist, as well as other parts of the body, and by 1840 their form of the game was organized into intramural tournaments. At Yale, "roughhouse football" was played as early as 1840, and became ritualized as the "annual rush" between freshmen and sophomores in 1851. Various forms of football were also being played during this period at Amherst and Brown. The round, rubber ball was introduced in the 1850s, at which time dribbling and passing skills associated with modern soccer were learned; games resembling soccer, rather than rugby, continued to predominate until the mid-1870s. During the Civil War, the prep schools of the Northeast, especially in New England, kept the game alive.

Meanwhile, British immigrants in the large cities were beginning to introduce soccer to the general public. In 1862, three years after the formation of the first "dribbling" club in England, the Oneida Football Club was founded in Boston by Gerritt Smith Miller. Oneida F.C. was not only the first "dribbling" club in the United States but also the first known club established anywhere outside England. It preceded the first Scottish club by five years, the first Welsh club by 11 years, and the first Irish club by 17 years. Oneida F.C. played on the Boston Common against scratch teams from 1862-65 without conceding a game or a single goal. These were the first public games played with a round ball in the United States. All 17 members of the club are thought to have been English by birth or heritage.*

Immediately after the Civil War, collegiate play was resumed. In 1866, Beadle & Co. of New York published the new rules of both association football (soccer) and the "handling" game (rugby), the latter having been virtually unknown in the United States. In 1867, Princeton and Rutgers drew up their own sets of rules that adhered to the soccer code. At Princeton, where the rules called for 25 players on each side, an intramural game under the new association rules was played that same year against Princeton Theological Seminary. The first intercollegiate game

*A plaque to Oneida F.C. was dedicated in 1925 at the Boston Common.

under rules approximating soccer was played on November 6, 1869, at New Brunswick, New Jersey, between Princeton and Rutgers. After Rutgers won, 6-4, a return match was played at Princeton a week later and was won by Princeton, 8-0. A third match was canceled by faculty members worried about roughhousing. These historic games were played under the rules of the home team, both of which were based on the London Football Association "Laws of the Game" (1863), the official soccer code. Common to both games were the following rules: a maximum of 25 players allowed on either team; a field measuring 110 meters (360 feet) by 70 meters (225 feet) wide; a goal measuring seven meters (24 feet) wide; six points to win; a round ball made of inflated rubber; movement of the ball with all parts of the body, including hands (the ball could not be carried or thrown while the player was in motion); and restrictions against tripping and holding.

The dribbling game with a round ball was adopted at Yale, Columbia, and Cornell, and at Harvard it was taken up again in 1871 in a hybrid form known as the Boston Game, in which the soccer code was combined with the rugby characteristic of picking the ball up and running with it (carrying). In 1873, Princeton, Yale, Columbia, and Rutgers met in New York to draw up a uniform set of rules that were based on the London Football Association laws of 1863. They settled on the following: 20 players to a team; a field measuring 400 feet by 250 feet; a goal measuring 25 feet wide; six goals to win; and, a point scored by passing the ball between the goal posts. Carrying the ball was prohibited. In the fall of 1873, Yale defeated Princeton, 3-0, under soccer rules, and initiated the longest continuous rivalry in collegiate sports, though it was soon to become a gridiron football rather than soccer rivalry. Within weeks, a team of Englishmen calling itself Eton Players (its captain and other members were Old Etonians) traveled to New Haven to play against Yale in the first Anglo-American international match. For this occasion, Yale was persuaded to adopt the English custom of 11 players to a team, and the idea was so well-received that it was permanently incorporated into the Yale game. The English method of scoring (one-point goals) was also adopted, and Yale won the match by 2-1. In subsequent years, Yale argued for universal adoption of the 11-player rule among its collegiate opponents. The principle was accepted generally in 1880, and was

eventually incorporated into American gridiron football.

Harvard, meanwhile, became more interested in the rugby code, and sought competition with like-minded teams. McGill University of Montreal had also adopted rugby, and in 1874, three years after the formation of the Rugby Football Union in England, a two-game series between the two rugby adherents was played in Cambridge. The second of these matches was played with an oval ball under Rugby Union rules and marks the beginning of American gridiron football. It also spelled doom for the future of soccer in the United States. In November 1875, Harvard played Yale in a game held under "concessionary rules," which included many rugby characteristics, such as scoring by tries (touchdowns), as well as one-point goals, and a 15-player team instead of the 11-player team preferred by Yale. Harvard won by four goals and four tries to none, and Yale, after becoming one of the earliest advocates of the soccer code, reassessed its position and took to the rugby rules as played at Harvard. The Princeton observers present at the Harvard-Yale match were also favorably impressed by the rugby rules and returned to New Jersey to report their change of mind.

In 1876, Harvard, Princeton, and Columbia met to form the Intercollegiate Football Association and adopt a code of Rugby Union rules. With this agreement, the soccer code was delivered a death blow that changed forever the acceptance of the dribbling game in the United States. Stevens, Wesleyan, and Pennsylvania Colleges, all of which were playing soccer-like games, were also won over by the rugby code. At Lexington, Virginia, the Virginia Military Institute and Washington and Lee, both of which played soccer from 1873, switched to rugby in 1876, and the transformation spread to all geographical areas. Colleges and universities that introduced football programs after this period adopted the rugby game to the exclusion of soccer, anticipating the future of the two games in the United States for the next century.

After the demise of collegiate soccer in 1876, the game was kept alive by its adherents away from the college campus. The rise of the "ethnic game" during this period signified a second important transformation in early American soccer and one that put its mark permanently on the American game. In the British Isles, as elsewhere in Europe, the working classes were rapidly taking to soccer as their chosen pastime, rugby increasingly being adopted as the sport of the upper classes. Simultaneously in the United States, as millions of immigrants flooded the major urban centers of the East and Midwest, they brought with them fragments of their culture. Soccer, ever more distinct from the rugby code in Europe, became a major recreational bridge between the old country and the new. As assimilation into American society took on greater importance, however, immigrants turned increasingly to baseball and American gridiron football. Thus, the number of soccer adherents arriving in the United States was canceled out by the growing number of those who sought "Americanization." The un-written social code of the day stipulated that Americans played gridiron football and baseball; foreigners played soccer. This pattern was predominant until the great era of mass immigration came to a close after World War II.

The first regions to become ethnic soccer hotbeds were the West Hudson section of New Jersey, New York City, and Philadelphia. The industrial towns of New England soon followed, and by the end of the 1870s factory towns such as Fall River, Massachusetts were primarily soccer-playing communities. At first, the game was played in pick-up fashion or by loosely organized groups of teams, but in time the corporations that employed largely immigrant workers began to sponsor factory clubs and lend financial assistance to local and regional leagues. Similar developments were seen in the industrial centers of the Midwest.

Many British immigrants who were not necessarily employed by factories also sought to organize the game, and in 1884, a group of British-born soccer enthusiasts met in Newark, New Jersey to discuss their future. The eventual outgrowth of this meeting was the founding of the American Football Association (AFA), the first governing body of soccer in the United States and the third to be formed outside the British Isles. (The Natal F.A. and the New South Wales F.A. were founded in 1882.)

On November 28, 1885, the United States made its unofficial international debut against Canada in Newark. Canada won, 1-0, over an American team selected by the AFA from clubs of the West Hudson region. This important game predates the first continental

European international by 17 years and the first South American international by 20 years, though its status with FIFA remains unrecognized. In 1886, a second Canadian-American international was played in Newark, and the USA won, 3-2, with two goals scored near the end of the game.* Once again, however, the growth of American soccer lost its momentum. The inability of administrators to hold together a represen-tative national association precluded the USA from engaging in any further international competition for a period of 30 years, which coincided with the phenomenal development of the game in Europe and Latin America.

Nevertheless, clubs and regional associations were beginning to form in many parts of the country. The Pullman Railroad Car Co. of Chicago supported an active team with its own grounds from 1883. The St. Louis Football Association was founded in 1886, and the Bristol County Soccer League was es-tablished the same year, reflecting the strength of the game in and around Fall River. In 1887, the New England Association Football League was established, and the New England Football Association was founded as a regulatory body. British immigrants dominated most of these governing bodies and competitions, but in 1890, the St. Louis championship was won by Kensington, a club composed entirely of American citizens. Upstate New York and Eastern Pennsylvania also became important soccer centers. Churchville Thistles was founded in Rochester around 1890. At the same time, the Pennsylvania Football Union was formed, and in 1892 the Denver Association Football Club was founded, the first known soccer organiza-tion in the Far West. In Cincinnati, where German immigrants had dominated the sports scene since the mid-nineteenth century, the Irish-based Shamrock Association Foot-ball Club was established in 1898. By 1902, the California Association Football Union had been formed in San Francisco, and in 1906 the Cleveland Soccer Football League was founded in Ohio.

As the game grew at a moderate pace, the American Football Association was soon burdened by dissent, anticipating the dishar-mony that was to weaken American soccer consistently over the decades. Corporate sponsorship had made possible the advance of semiprofessionalism in some areas, and New

---

*Some accounts exist of a three-game series played in Canada in 1886 and a three-game return series played in Newark in 1887 that resulted in two won, two drawn, and two lost, but these series remain unverified.

York clubs, having generally been organized on a cultural basis rather than by factories, remained amateur. But the schedules drawn up by the AFA favored the semiprofessional clubs. In 1890, the New York clubs withdrew from the AFA in protest, and founded the American Amateur Football Association (AAFA). For the next 23 years, the AFA drew its support from New England, New Jersey, and Pennsylvania, while the AAFA represented New York City and upstate New York.

The quality of the American game relative to other countries before the turn of the century is difficult to measure. In 1891, there was a tour of the British Isles by a combined USA-Canada team, which included a match in Belfast against Linfield F.C. The Linfield game became significant in historical annals, because Pawtucket F.C.'s Jeffrey scored from the first penalty kick ever taken under a new rule adopted by the Irish Football Association. The first significant visit by a foreign club to the United States occurred in 1904 when Pilgrims F.C., a selection of leading amateur players from England, played a series of 23 matches, winning 21 and losing two. Pilgrims toured the United States again in 1909, this time winning 16 and drawing four in a series of 22 matches. England's legendary amateur club, Corinthians F.C., toured the country in 1906 and 1911 and won 31 of 36 matches. These tours were the major international highlights of early American soccer.

The formation of FIFA in 1904 and the official inclusion of soccer in the schedule of the 1908 Olympic Games caused renewed interest in international competition among American players and administrators. But membership in the new world body and subsequent participation in official international tournaments were not possible without a governing body that represented United States soccer interests collectively. A bitter struggle was waged between the American Football Association, which by this time had become affiliated with The Football Association in London, and the American Amateur Football Association. FIFA refused to recognize either one at its Congress of 1912 in Stockholm. Urged by FIFA to solve their problems at home before applying for membership again, the AFA and the AAFA strained for nearly ten months to settle their differences. Tactical errors by the AFA offended a growing body of onlookers and eventually nudged some key regional associations into the AAFA camp, and on April 5, 1913, the United States Football Association (USFA) was founded in New York by the swelling membership of the AAFA. The 1913 FIFA Congress accepted the USFA application and the AFA threw its lot in with the new national association soon after hearing the news from Copenhagen. [For details of the USFA's formation, see *United States Soccer Federation*.]

Now that the USA could enter international competition on an official basis, the national team ventured to Scandinavia in 1916 and gained a 3-2 win over the fledgling Swedes and a 1-1 draw with Norway. This was the USA's official debut in full international competition. The American team held its own against European opponents for the first time, and showed cause for an optimistic future. Once again, however, the gathering momentum was halted at an inopportune moment as the nations of Europe floundered in a long world war. For the third time in 40 years, the advancement of American soccer was interrupted. American officials felt ill at ease with South America as an alternate opponent because it was culturally distant, and the rest of Latin America and the Caribbean had yet to enter international competition. The Olympic Games of 1924 in Paris would prove to be the next test.

At home, a broadly based cup competition, the National Challenge Cup, was introduced during the 1912-13 season. Its trophy, the Dewar Cup, had been awarded unofficially the previous year, but it was now adopted by the USFA as the official trophy of the new challenge cup. The first winner of the National Challenge Cup in 1914 was Brooklyn Field Club. For over 20 years the cup remained in the hands of clubs from the Northeast and St. Louis. Open to all clubs that wished to enter, it has been dominated since its introduction by semiprofessional and sponsored teams from industrial areas, and until the formation of professional leagues during the late 1960s, it was considered the premier soccer competition in the country. [See *National Open Challenge Cup*.] In 1922-23, the USFA introduced the National Amateur Cup to accommodate unwieldy schedule conflicts created by the growing number of clubs participating in the National Challenge Cup, though many amateur clubs continued to participate in both. The first winner of the National Amateur Cup in 1923-24 was Fleisher Yarn F.C. of Philadelphia. [See *National Amateur Cup*.]

In 1924, the USA embarked on a relatively successful ten-year period in international competition. At the Olympic Games of 1924 in Paris, it defeated little Estonia, 1-0, and managed to hold mighty Uruguay, the eventual gold medalist, to a 3-0 win. After the Olympic Games, the same USA team visited Warsaw and Dublin before returning home.

The American amateurs defeated Poland, 3-2 (on an own goal), but their luck ran out six days later with a 3-1 loss to the Irish Free State. After two wins and a loss against Canada in the mid-1920s, the USA again made its way to the Olympic Games in 1928 at Amsterdam and received an 11-2 first round drubbing from Argentina, then ranked with Uruguay as

Passon (in white jerseys) vs. German-Americans on a factory field in Philadelphia, 1939. Semi-professional immigrant and factory teams represented the highest level of soccer in the United States from the 1880s to the 1960s.

one of the world's leading teams. This was followed by a friendly in Warsaw that resulted in a 3-3 draw.

The first real high point in American soccer was the USA's participation in the first World Cup in 1930, though the event went virtually unnoticed in the United States. For the first time the American game was thrust into the international limelight. The refusal by most of Europe to make the long journey to Montevideo severely weakened the opposition, leaving only 13 countries to participate, and four pools were set up in the absence of the number required to organize a knockout competition. The American team was managed by the Brooklyn Wanderers' Jack Croll, and was made up of five former Scottish professionals and one Englishman. Nicknamed the "shot-putters" by the French, the American players were large in size and strong on defense and running attacks. Performing well up to expectations, they defeated both Belgium and Paraguay, 3-0, and emerged winners of their group. Center forward Bert Patenaude of Fall River F.C. scored three of the American goals, and the Scottish-born left wing Bart McGhee scored two. These were the USA's first major victories in international competition.

Misfortune struck in the semi-finals against powerful Argentina, whose stars Monti and Stabile were world class in stature yet anything but gentlemanly. American center half Raphael Tracy of Ben Millers S.C. had his leg broken at ten minutes, reducing the team to ten players, and goalkeeper Jim Douglas of the New York Nationals was virtually crippled by the end of the first half (not to mention left half Andy Auld of Providence, who played most of the game with his mouth stuffed full of gauze after a kick in the face). Argentina scored five goals in the second half and went on to win, 6-1. On its way home the American team stopped off to play Brazil in Rio and lost by 4-3 after two goals from Patenaude. Brazil, with inside left Preguinho perhaps the only world-class player on its team at the time, had yet to surface as a world power.

It is difficult to determine what would have happened if the USFA had been able to maintain the positive momentum that resulted from the USA's respectable showing in 1930, because, once again, the United States did not seriously attempt to enter the mainstream of world soccer in the years that followed. Other than its 1-0 loss to the Italian amateurs at the 1936 Olympic Games in Berlin, the USA's only official foray into international competition during the 1930s was at the 1934 World Cup in Italy. After winning an awkward qualification match against Mexico in Rome, an Italian team inflated with talent and the political climate of Mussolini's capital city buried the American contingent in the opening round, 7-1. Soundly beaten, the USA opted out of international competition until 1947.

On the domestic front, the formation of the German-American Football Association (GAFA) in 1923 and the American Soccer League (ASL) in 1933 further fragmented the game. The GAFA not only became the bastion of ethnic soccer in the New York area but also a model for all other ethnic leagues across the country. Its annual custom of inviting a leading German club to play a friendly against the GAFA All-Stars was the major event of each season. On May 1, 1926, an American attendance record of 35,000 was set in New York for such a contest against Hakoah Vienna, then the leading Jewish-based club in Austria. The visitors won by 3-0, but the attendance record stood until the mid-1970s.

While the GAFA was primarily semi-professional in the ethnic league tradition, the ASL sought to become the nation's first fully professional league. Its ultimate success, however, was compromised for decades by the all-too-familiar ethnic look of its membership, thus precluding its widespread appeal, and some ASL clubs retained their ethnic names until the 1970s. The ASL championship dates from 1933-34, when the first winner was New Jersey's Kearney Irish. Both these leagues have continued to operate without interruption to the present time (the GAFA changed its name to the Cosmopolitan Soccer League in 1977), but neither has attracted national attention, with their severely limited geographical base, and the ASL's repeated attempts to become the focal point of soccer in the United States have merely divided American soccer interests further.

Sponsored and semiprofessional soccer outside the ASL, much of it linked with ethnic groups, retained its place at the highest levels of the American game during the 1920s and '30s. The leading clubs were: Fall River F.C., Bethlehem Steel Co. F.C., Stix Baer and Fuller F.C. (St. Louis), Heidelberg F.C. (Philadelphia), German-American S.C. (Philadelphia), First German-American S.C. (Philadelphia), and others from Fall River, St. Louis, New York, Philadelphia, and New

Jersey. Other important clubs were: Robins Dry Dock F.C. (Brooklyn), Central Breweries S.C. (St. Louis), Scullin Steel F.C (St. Louis), Hakoah All-Stars (New York), Fleisher Yarn F.C. (Philadelphia), St. Michael's Athletic Club (Fall River), and Goodyear F.C. (Akron), to name a few. After World War II, other ethnic clubs emerged: Kutis S.C. (St: Louis), Ponta Delgada F.C. (Fall River), Ukrainian Nationals (Philadelphia), Joe Simpkins F.C. (St. Louis), and later, New York Greek-Americans, Los Angeles Kickers, and Maccabi Los Angeles.

In 1945, the USFA changed its name to the United States Soccer Football Association (USSFA). (The "Football" was dropped in 1974.) After joining the new North American Confederation in 1939, the USA participated in two championships of the region against Cuba and Mexico in 1947 (at Havana) and 1949 (at Mexico City), and was disappointed to finish third and second respectively. The 1947 team was composed entirely of players from the semiprofessional Ponta Delgada of Fall River.

With two berths allocated to the North-Central American and Caribbean region at the 1950 World Cup in Brazil, the USA qualified for the final rounds by virtue of its second-place finish in the North American Confederation championship in 1949. The team was managed by Bill Jeffrey of Penn State (a Scot whose record over a period of 30 years was unparalleled in collegiate soccer), and included only three foreign-born Americans: captain Eddie McIlvenny, who later played for Manchester United and coached the Irish club Waterford; Larry Gaetjens, the Haitian center forward who was to end his career as a professional with Racing Club de Paris and Alès in Southern France and eventually disappeared mysteriously in Haiti around 1970; and Joe Maca, the left back from Belgium.

In the first round, the USA was grouped with Spain, England, and Chile at Curtiba. Against Spain, the Americans maintained a 1-0 lead until ten minutes from time, and impressed the opposition with their durable play. But the stalwart American defense, led by Maca and spurred by J. Souza's goal in the 17th minute, finally collapsed and allowed three

The outstanding event in American soccer history. Brazilian fans in Belo Horizonte pay tribute to Larry Gaetjens, scorer of the USA's only goal in its 1-0 upset of England in the 1950 World Cup.

quick goals. The final score was 3-1 in Spain's favor. Four days later, however, at Belo Horizonte, the United States cast itself as David to England's Goliath and perpetrated the greatest upset in the history of modern soccer: USA 1, England 0. The lineups for the match were as follows:

England: Williams; Ramsey, Aston; Wright, Hughes, Dickinson; Finney, Mannion, Bentley, Mortensen, Mullen.

USA: Borghi; Keough, Maca; McIlvenny, Colombo, Bahr; Wallace, Pariani, Gaetjens, J. Souza, E. Souza.

Many English apologists over the years have demeaned the accomplishments of the USA on this day, but, by the same token, too many American observers have claimed that world soccer was turned upside down in a single stroke. Neither of these biases is accurate: England suffered from missed opportunities which were caused by a lack of competitive edge after decades of self-exile from organized world competition, and its inability to adjust to tactical and personnel conflicts arising from the recent appointment of England's first permanent manager-selector, Walter Winterbottom. The USA, on the other hand, played well above its accepted standard. Tragically, the American public never heard of its team's achievement, and once again American soccer lost a chance to emerge from obscurity. Inevitably, the USA wandered through the remainder of the 1950s with 11 losses in 13 full internationals.

The American goal against England was not convincing: in the 37th minute, left half Walter Bahr crossed the ball to the goalmouth. English goalkeeper Bert Williams failed to gather it cleanly, and oncoming center forward Gaetjens deflected the ball into the net with his head, some would say unwittingly. England, having thus far failed to convert with every conceivable type of shot, did not rise to the occasion, and the American defense was opportunistic in its clearing and distributing. After the final whistle, thousands of supportive Brazilian fans rushed onto the field and carried the giant-killers around the stadium on their shoulders. The USA, riding a crest of stunned euphoria, fell decisively to Chile, 5-2, in its third first round match, and Spain advanced from its group. Jeffrey's team, perhaps the greatest spoilers in World Cup history, returned home to muted adulation in some ethnic quarters and then oblivion.

The United States national team has had some further success in international competition during the postwar era, but little has been noteworthy. The majority of American victories have come at the hands of Haiti, Bermuda, and Canada, while Cuba, Honduras, Mexico, and El Salvador have each succumbed once. Only a 1-0 upset of Poland in 1973 stands out. Mammoth full international defeats at the hands of Norway (11-0), Scotland (6-0), Mexico (6-0), England (8-1 and 10-0), Poland (7-0), Italy (10-0), and France (6-0) served to put the postwar American game into perspective.[*] The USA has not reached the final rounds of the World Cup since 1950.

While the United States has failed thus far to make an impact on international soccer, the domestic game has drawn world attention because of its unprecedented outlay of money. By the late 1970s, this aspect of American soccer was still on the increase and causing great controversy. Though the passage of time has worked cruelly against the rise of an indigenous American game, the country's wealth creates an appearance of respectability that might eventually translate into legitimate international stature.

As the number of important foreign clubs visiting the United States increased during the postwar years, it became apparent to observant entrepreneurs that importing players from abroad might prove to be the panacea needed to launch the game into the front ranks of American sports. The first important thrust away from the stagnant ethnic game occurred in 1960 when Bill Cox, the banished former owner of the Philadelphia Phillies baseball club, organized the International Soccer League (ISL). With his base in New York, Cox persuaded 11 foreign clubs, all from European and South American first divisions, to spend the summer in the United States competing for a new league trophy. To the list of 11, he added a selection of Americans known as "American All-Stars" to lend an air of domestic legitimacy. All ISL matches that first year were played at the Polo Grounds in New York, and they attracted regular crowds of

---

[*]Similar results have been characteristic of postwar American participation in the Olympic Games. The USA was eliminated in 1949 by Italy (9-0), in 1952 by Italy (8-0), and in 1956 by Yugoslavia (9-1). In 1972, the American Olympic team placed last in its first round group after losing to West Germany (7-0) and Malaysia (3-0).

over 10,000 to watch a level of play considerably superior to the ethnic leagues. Eventually the league expanded to Chicago and a handful of other cities.

Though it was modestly successful, the ISL perpetuated the image of soccer as a foreign sport. Clubs and businessmen earned money to put in the bank, but American soccer and American players were not enriched as a result. In addition, the ISL's appeal was limited primarily to an ethnic public in a few cities.

In 1966, a turning point occurred when the final of the World Cup between England and West Germany was broadcast on national television with surprisingly high Nielsen ratings. This caused speculators to take notice, and potential investors coalesced into three groups, each seeking to form a national league. FIFA regulations stipulated, however, that national governing bodies could recognize only one national league. After much wrangling, two of the groups merged. The two remaining groups sought affiliation with the USSFA and the right to be the official national league. The matter was further confused by the continued presence of the ASL, which was eventually ruled a regional league and therefore ineligible. Finally, the USSFA decided to recognize the United Soccer Association (USA) under the leadership of Californian Jack Kent Cooke, but the second group, the National Professional Soccer League, resolved to go ahead and establish a pirate league anyway, demonstrating its disdain for FIFA regulations.

In 1967, the two leagues were launched in head-to-head competition for the marketplace, much to the chagrin of the USSFA and its ally, the Canadian Soccer Football Association, which had tried in vain to stave off such a catastrophe. The United Soccer Association was made up of ten clubs, each imported intact from abroad and assigned an American name to correspond with its franchise location. The 1967 United Soccer Association championship was won by the Los Angeles Wolves (alias Wolverhampton Wanderers, which had just been promoted to the English first division). The runners-up were the Washington Whips (alias Aberdeen of the Scottish first division). The other members of the United Soccer Association were: Bangu (Brazil), Cagliari (Italy), Cerro (Uruguay), Glentoran (Northern Ireland), Hibernian (Scotland), Shamrock Rovers (Eire), Stoke City (England), and Sunderland (England). The National Professional Soccer League,

meanwhile, hurriedly sent scouts throughout Europe and South America to buy or borrow as many players as they could find. Its task was exceedingly difficult, because under FIFA regulations, clubs or players caught dealing with an outlaw league such as the NPSL are suspended from all official domestic and international competition. Nevertheless, the NPSL managed to put together a league made

Clippers won the 1967 title with the Baltimore Bays the runner-up.

In 1968, the following year, the two leagues merged as the North American Soccer League, the original name of the United Soccer Association, and the idea of wholesale importation of foreign clubs was dropped. Membership in the new league fluctuated wildly over the next few years, dropping to as low as five in 1969 and rising to 24 in 1978. [for details of the NASL, USA, and NPSL, see *North American Soccer League*.] The ASL saw a mild revival during the same period as it absorbed managerial and player personnel spun off by the NASL. In the mid-1970s, the ASL expanded to the Midwest and California. Marginal growth, enthusiastic promises, and hordes of imported players sustained the ASL through the late 1970s.

In 1975, the NASL turned the corner and announced that the New York Cosmos, the league's wealthiest club, had signed Pelé, the world's most celebrated player, to a 2 1/2-year contract. An important facet of the contract was that Pelé would attempt to establish soccer as a major sport throughout the country by making appearances and actively promoting the game wherever possible. For all intents and purposes, the Cosmos' gamble worked. Among other reasons for its success was the opening of the floodgates to other international stars, enabling inexperienced American players to rub shoulders with such soccer greats as Franz Beckenbauer, George Best, Eusebio, Bobby Moore, Gordon Banks, and many, many others. Of these, Beckenbauer would prove to be the most important, because he was the first world-class player to cross the Atlantic not long after the peak of his career rather than at the end, an action that would serve as an example to other stars abroad. The corresponding rise in the level of play challenged the American teammates of big foreign stars, and by 1978 a noticeable improvement in the skills of American players was seen. Meanwhile, the old ethnic clubs began to absorb a growing number of nonethnic players, anticipating the possibility that they might eventually serve as stepping stones to the major league, much the same as lower-ranked amateur clubs in Europe.

American soccer features a host of cosmetic and legal aberrations that are not found elsewhere and in some cases have drawn raised eyebrows abroad. The NASL, for example, has in recent years adopted certain rule changes in an effort to attract television contracts and a demanding public whose tastes respond to spectacle and action. NASL matches must be won or lost, because drawn games are considered unacceptable to the average spectator, according to league administrators. And the penalty decision as a method of tie-breaking has been supplanted by the "shoot-out," a variation on the penalty theme that officials say captures the imagination of the American psyche. The offside rule

has a uniquely American feature in the presence of two "35-yard lines" (a term taken from American gridiron football), behind which a player may not be offside. In the NASL, three substitutions are allowed by either team rather than the usual two. Most important to players, however, is the prevalence of artificial surfaces on playing fields, a controversial innnovation in other American sports as well, and one that is regarded with much fear by the uninitiated. League matches in the United States are seen by their promoters as an entertainment package that includes narration over the public address system by an announcer, and a variety of entertainments unrelated to the game of soccer to fill in "empty" moments. Attempts to compromise further the traditions of soccer, such as the effort to enlarge the size of the goal, continue to take place.

See also: **Cosmos, National Amateur Cup, National Open Challenge Cup, North American Soccer League, shoot-out, thirty-five yard line, United States Soccer Federation.**

USA Full International Results (1916-1979)

1916	20 Aug	Sweden	3-2	W	Stockholm
	3 Sep	Norway	1-1	D	Oslo
1924	10 Jun	Poland	3-2	W	Warsaw
	16 Jun	Irish Free State	1-3	L	Dublin
1925	27 Jun	Canada	0-1	L	Montreal
	8 Nov	Canada	6-1	W	Brooklyn
1926	6 Nov	Canada	6-2	W	Brooklyn
1928	10 Jun	Poland	3-3	D	Warsaw
1930	13 Jul	Belgium (WC)*	3-0	W	Montevideo
	17 Jul	Paraguay (WC)	3-0	W	Montevideo
	26 Jul	Argentina (WC)	1-6	L	Montevideo
	17 Aug	Brazil	3-4	L	Rio de Janeiro
1934	24 May	Mexico	4-2	W	Rome
	27 May	Italy (WC)	1-7	L	Rome
1947	13 Jul	Mexico (NAC)	0-5	L	Havana
	20 Jul	Cuba (NAC)	2-5	L	Havana
1948	6 Aug	Norway	0-11	L	Oslo
	11 Aug	Northern Ireland	0-5	L	Belfast
1949	4 Sep	Mexico (NAC)	0-6	L	Mexico City
	14 Sep	Cuba (NAC)	1-1	D	Mexico City

	18 Sep	Mexico (NAC)	2-6	L	Mexico City
	21 Sep	Cuba (NAC)	5-2	W	Mexico City
1950	25 Jun	Spain (WC)	1-3	L	Curtiba
	29 Jun	England (WC)	1-0	W	Belo Horizonte
	2 Jul	Chile (WC)	2-5	L	Recife
1952	30 Apr	Scotland	0-6	L	Glasgow
1953	8 Jun	England	3-6	L	New York
1954	10 Jan	Mexico	0-4	L	Mexico City
	14 Jan	Mexico	1-3	L	Mexico City
	3 Apri	Haiti	3-2	W	Port-au-Prince
	4 Apr	Haiti	3-0	W	Port-au-Prince
1955	25 Aug	Iceland	2-3	L	Reykjavik
1957	7 Apr	Mexico	0-6	L	Mexico City
	28 Apr	Mexico	2-7	L	Long Beach
	22 Jun	Canada	1-5	L	Toronto
	6 Jul	Canada	2-3	L	St. Louis
1959	28 May	England	1-8	L	Los Angeles
1960	6 Nov	Mexico	3-3	D	Los Angeles
	13 Nov	Mexico	0-3	L	Mexico City
1964	27 May	England	0-10	L	New York
1965	7 Mar	Mexico	2-2	D	Los Angeles
	12 Mar	Mexico	0-2	L	Mexico City
	17 Mar	Honduras	1-0	W	San Pedro Sula
	21 Mar	Honduras	1-1	D	Tegucigalpa
1968	15 Sep	Israel	3-3	D	New York
	25 Sep	Israel	0-4	L	Philadelphia
	17 Oct	Canada	2-4	L	Toronto
	20 Oct	Haiti	6-3	W	Port-au-Prince
	21 Oct	Haiti	2-5	L	Port-au-Prince
	23 Oct	Haiti	1-0	W	Port-au-Prince
	27 Oct	Canada	1-0	W	Atlanta
	2 Nov	Bermuda	6-2	W	Kansas City
	10 Nov	Bermuda	2-0	W	Hamilton
1969	20 Apr	Haiti	0-2	L	Port-au-Prince
	11 May	Haiti	0-1	L	San Diego
1972	20 Aug	Canada	2-3	L	St. John's
	29 Aug	Canada	2-2	D	Baltimore
	3 Sep	Mexico	1-3	L	Mexico City
	10 Sep	Mexico	1-2	L	Los Angeles
1973	17 Mar	Bermuda	0-4	L	Hamilton
	20 Mar	Poland	0-4	L	Lodz
	3 Aug	Poland	0-1	L	Chicago
	5 Aug	Canada	2-0	W	Windsor
	10 Aug	Poland	0-4	L	San Francisco
	12 Aug	Poland	1-0	W	New Britain
	9 Sep	Bermuda	1-0	W	Hartford
	16 Oct	Mexico	0-2	L	Puebla
	3 Nov	Haiti	0-1	L	Port-au-Prince

	5 Nov	Haiti	0-1	L	Port-au-Prince
	13 Nov	Israel	1-3	L	Tel-Aviv
	15 Nov	Israel	0-2	L	Beersheba
1974	5 Sep	Mexico	1-3	L	Monterrey
	8 Sep	Mexico	0-1	L	Dallas
1975	26 Mar	Poland	0-7	L	Poznan
	4 Apr	Italy	0-10	L	Rome
	24 Jun	Poland	0-4	L	Seattle
1976	24 Sep	Canada	1-1	D	Vancouver
	3 Oct	Mexico	0-0	D	Los Angeles
	15 Oct	Mexico	0-3	L	Puebla
	20 Oct	Canada	2-0	W	Seattle
	10 Nov	Haiti	0-0	D	Port-au-Prince
	12 Nov	Haiti	0-0	D	Port-au-Prince
	14 Nov	Haiti	0-0	D	Port-au-Prince
	22 Dec	Canada	0-3	L	Port-au-Prince
1977	15 Sep	El Salvador	2-1	W	San Salvador
	25 Sep	Guatemala	0-2	L	Guatemala City
	27 Sep	Mexico	0-3	L	Monterrey
	30 Sep	El Salvador	0-0	D	Los Angeles
1978	3 Sep	Iceland	0-0	D	Reykjavik
	6 Sep	Switzerland	0-2	L	Lucerne
1979	2 May	France	0-6	L	East Rutherford

*WC (World Cup final rounds)
NAC (North American Championship)

USA Full International Record (1916-1979)

	P	W	D	L	F	A	P
Argentina	2	0	0	2	1	12	0
Belgium	1	1	0	0	3	0	2
Bermuda	4	3	0	1	9	6	6
Brazil	1	0	0	1	3	4	0
Canada	13	5	2	6	27	28	12
Chile	1	0	0	1	2	5	0
Costa Rica	1	0	0	1	1	3	0
Cuba	3	1	1	1	8	8	3
El Salvador	2	1	1	0	2	1	3
England	4	1	0	3	5	24	2
France	1	0	0	1	0	6	0
Guatemala	1	0	0	1	0	2	0
Haiti	12	4	3	5	15	15	11
Honduras	2	1	1	0	2	1	3
Iceland	2	0	1	1	2	3	1

Ireland, Northern	1	0	0	1	0	5	0
Irish Free State	1	0	0	1	1	3	0
Israel	4	0	1	3	4	12	1
Italy	2	0	0	2	1	17	0
Mexico	21	1	3	17	17	68	5
Norway	2	0	1	1	1	12	1
Paraguay	1	1	0	0	3	0	2
Poland	8	2	1	5	7	25	5
Scotland	1	0	0	1	0	6	0
Spain	1	0	0	1	1	3	0
Sweden	1	1	0	0	3	2	2
Switzerland	1	0	0	1	0	2	0
Totals	**94**	**22**	**15**	**57**	**118**	**270**	**59**

USSR

USSR Football Federation
Skatertnyi pereulok 4
Moscow 69

Founded: 1912
FIFA: 1946
UEFA: 1954

Affiliated clubs: *50,163;* registered players: *4,300,000;* national stadium: *Lenin Stadium, Moscow (104,000);* largest stadium: *Lenin Stadium;* colors: *red jerseys, white shorts;* season: *February to November;* honors: *Olympic Games winner (1956), third place (1976), shared third place (1972), European Football Championship winner (1960), runner-up (1964, 1972), Dinamo Kiev, Super Cup (1975), European Cup Winners' Cup (1975).*

The Soviet Union is a potential giant in world soccer. It is blessed with great organizational capabilities, high motivation, a vast reservoir of players, and since the 1950s has produced several stars of world-class caliber. After a late arrival on the international scene, the USSR moved with astounding speed to the front ranks of European soccer, though its only really significant international honor to date has been a second place finish in the 1972 European Football Championship. None of its other big trophies have been won against a representative sampling of major international powers.

At the same time, Soviet soccer has been held back by two natural obstacles. The first is the long and ferocious winter that most of the country endures, causing ceaseless disorders in schedules and training programs. Second is its distant location from the major soccer centers of Europe. These factors are often combined, as was the case in the famous 8,000-mile trip that Cardiff City made in the 1967-68 European Cup Winners's Cup after Torpedo Moscow's home leg was transferred to Tashkent because of icy conditions in Moscow. The extraordinary potential of Soviet soccer may also have been held back by political considerations. Its long isolation from official international competition (1925-52) was the result of Stalinist policies, and since the USSR's emergence in the postwar years, a great many international meetings have been with Warsaw Pact states or other politically compatible nations, rather than the strongest opposition that could be found. This accounts for the Soviets' superlative overall record in international competition, which in

1977 stood as follows: 216-117-57-42-399-208-291.

Despite all one hears about Soviet gymnastics, track and field, ice hockey, skating in pairs, and the rest, the national passion is soccer. Even the personal preferences of the Soviet leadership have leaked out of the Kremlin. Nikita Khrushchev, a soccer player in his youth, was a Dinamo Kiev fan; Leonid Brezhnev is a supporter of CSKA Moscow, the Red Army club; Alexei Kosygin follows Dinamo Moscow; and Nikolai Podgorny is a keen Spartak Moscow fan. It is a matter of policy that the first nonessential structure planned for each new industrial city is the local soccer stadium—capacity never less than 50,000. The USSR Football Federation has more registered players in senior competition than any country in the world. The strongest soccer-playing region is the Ukraine, which combines a high population density, comparatively moderate weather, great industrial centers, and proximity to the rest of Europe. There are 26 senior-level Ukrainian clubs, and all play in the three upper divisions of the Soviet league. No less than 838 stadiums dot the Ukrainian landscape.

Soccer was introduced in Czarist Russia in 1887 by Britons Clement and Harry Charnock, whose family managed the Morozov Cotton Mills in Orekhovo Zuyevo, an industrial town in Moscow Province about 50 miles east of the city of Moscow. Clement Charnock gathered together a dozen clerks at the mill, and formed a team. He supplied the soccer balls, and had uniforms made up in the colors of his favorite club, Blackburn Rovers (blue and white), and paid all the expenses for one year. The Clements' uncle took over the team for a spell, and around 1890 Harry Charnock developed the club further, and even recruited soccer-playing textile mill workers in the British press.

Despite the influence of the Morozov club and the eventual formation of other Muscovite clubs, the game caught on more rapidly in St. Petersburg. In 1897, the Amateur Sports Club of St. Petersburg formed a team, and others in the capital quickly sprang up in workers' settlements and the industrial suburbs. Clubs were also formed, however, by middle- and upper-middle class students at military and secondary schools, and when a St. Petersburg Football League was started before the turn of the century, the entrance fees were set so high that working-class clubs and players were not able to join. This was a pattern that had

already been established in Moscow. The first recorded game in the city of Moscow took place in 1901 on the site of the present Spartak stadium. A Moscow league was founded shortly after the turn of the century, and the winner for five consecutive seasons was the popular Morozovtsi (as the popular Morozov club came to be called). The Moscow league, composed mainly of factory teams, attracted 10,000-15,000 fans per game. In 1906, Morozovtsi was renamed Orekhovo Klub Sport (OKS), and in later years was relocated to Moscow. (It was adopted by the Soviet Electrical Trades Union in 1923 and became the famous Dinamo Moscow.) With leagues already established in St. Petersburg and Moscow, regional leagues were also started in Kiev, Odessa, Kharkov, Rostov, Kazan, Baku, Tiflis, Omsk, Irkutsk, and even Vladivostok. In the Baltic region, the Germans founded SV Prussia at Königsberg in 1904, and established a regional governing body, the Baltenverband, at about the same time.

The game found little opposition among Czarist officials. Indeed, it was given tacit support, as a way to mitigate revolutionary fervor, the opposite view taken by Ottoman rulers in Turkey. In keeping with the government's effort to Europeanize the cultural life of the empire, Russian sports federations were soon established, and in 1912 the Vserossyski Futbollnnyi Sojuz (All-Russian Football Union) was founded to regulate Russian soccer. A national championship for teams representing their respective cities was introduced in that same year, and the Football Union joined FIFA in time to send a national team to the 1912 Olympic Games in Stockholm. Russia's debut in the Swedish capital resulted in a 2-1 loss to Finland. Two days later in the unofficial consolation tournament for losing teams, Russia was decimated by Germany, 16-0, a score that established a co-record for the biggest international win in soccer history. Before World War I, Russia played in six more unofficial internationals. In 1912, Hungary defeated the Russians twice in Moscow by an aggregate of 21-0. Losing to Sweden 4-1 and drawing with Norway at Moscow in 1913, the Russian team returned these visits in 1914 by drawing games in both Stockholm and Oslo.

The war and the revolution caused a ten-year hiatus in international competition, but in 1924 the newly formed Committee of Physical Culture and Sport invited the inexperienced Turks to Moscow, where the national team won for the first time by a comfortable 3-0 margin. In 1925, the Soviets traveled to Ankara and won again. Aside from one obscure match with Estonia, these two wins represented the Soviet Union's complete official international record before Stalin came to power and withdrew his country·from all official international competition.

Though a Soviet team was not to surface in the West until 1945, and a Soviet national team was not to engage in an official competiton until 1952, a small number of unofficial international contacts were made between 1925-39, always undertaken with the utmost political scrutiny. On the national level, Soviet and Turkish "A" teams met on several occasions and a selection representing the Committee of Physical Culture and Sport made an extensive tour of Finland, Sweden, and Norway. Switzerland's nonalignment was acknowledged in the 1930s with a match involving the Swiss F.A. and a Moscow selection, but the contest was held in neutral France. On the club level, teams from Central Asia and the Caucasus region played in Iran, and several of the big Moscow and Ukrainian clubs visited Turkey, Finland, Sweden, Czechoslovakia, and even France. During the Spanish Civil War, at least one Soviet club bolstered the spirits of sympathetic supporters behind Republican-held lines.

The domestic side of soccer in Czarist Russia was not able to develop fully before the outbreak of World War I. With the October Revolution came a total restructuring of sports programs and their administrative bodies. The great Soviet clubs of the future unfolded one by one: Dinamo Moscow; Dinamo Kiev (the Ukrainian Electrical Workers' club, founded 1927); Spartak Moscow (the Soviet Producers' Cooperative club, founded 1922); CSKA Moscow (the Central Army club, founded 1923); and Torpedo Moscow (the Stalin—later Likhatchev—Automobile Works club, founded 1930). The coaches of the prerevolution era, some of whom had been influenced by their exposure to the game in Western Europe, disappeared, and a new generation of inexperienced Soviet officials came to the fore. Playing skills and coaching techniques were ignored, and paramilitary discipline became the byword of the day. The Soviet game stagnated.

This policy was gradually replaced in the 1930s by an effort to adopt some elements of modern soccer and increase the standard of play. In 1936, a small national league and a national cup competition were finally introduced. The first league season was divided into two parts, spring and fall, won respectively by Dinamo Moscow and Spartak Moscow. The first cup was won by the railroad workers' club, Lokomotive Moscow. Dinamo and Spartak dominated both league and cup until the outbreak of World War II. Perhaps the outstanding player of the prewar era was Dinamo's goalscoring forward Mikhail Yakushin, later to become the most influential of Soviet coaches. It was Yakushin who managed the Dinamo team that traveled to Sweden and Great Britain in 1945 as a Soviet gesture of gratitude to its anti-Fascist allies.

The famous Dinamo Moscow tour of 1945 was a startling and bewildering experience for all concerned. After brushing aside the Swedish champions IFK Norrköping, 5-0, Dinamo descended on Britain amid unparalleled publicity, and gained draws at Chelsea and Glasgow Rangers before defeating Cardiff City, 10-1, and Arsenal, 4-3 (in dense fog). Local attendance records were set, and before anyone knew it, Dinamo was on its way home. Aside from the phantomlike quality of Dinamo's appearance (a Soviet team was not to play again in Western Europe until 1952), British players and fans were stunned by the seriousness of Dinamo's effort. Training sessions were conducted with match-day intensity, and in the games themselves Dinamo's fluid teamwork and *en bloc* defensive retreats demonstrated an overbearing will to win. Despite a tendency toward harsh and physical play, Dinamo's success was due largely to a surprisingly high level of individual skills and great speed. From an international perspective, Dinamo's tour was the turning point for Soviet soccer.

The All-Russian Football Union having ceased to exist in 1917, the reconstituted Soviet governing body became separately affiliated with FIFA in 1946. Its name was the Football Section of the Committee of Physical Culture and Sport under the Council of Ministers of the USSR, later to be renamed the USSR Football Federation. Domestic competition in the immediate postwar years was dominated by CSKA Moscow, many of whose players had continued to play throughout the war years. The postwar CSKA team is still thought by some to have been the greatest Soviet team of all time, and when a Soviet national side surfaced to participate in the 1952 Olympic Games at Helsinki, all but one of its members were Central Army Club players. Throughout the 1950s, the league and cup continued to be dominated by the big Moscow clubs, especially Dinamo and Spartak, the latter reaching its peak during the last years of the decade when it supplied the bulk of the national team.

The Soviet reentry into official international competition at the 1952 Olympic Games was ended in the first round by the talented Yugoslavs, but in 1956 at the Melbourne games, after three unconvincing rounds against marginal oppostion, it won the gold medal with a narrow defeat of Yugoslavia in the final. Its goalkeeper at Melbourne was the youthful Lev Yashin, who in the 1958 World Cup was to become the USSR's first international idol and ultimately the most respected goalkeeper in the history of the game. Some of the Soviet Union's results before 1956, however, were more significant than its Olympic triumph. It defeated world champion West Germany twice, at home in 1955 and in Hanover one year later, and after defeating Sweden twice by an aggregate of 13-0, it played Hungary in Budapest and held the "Magnificent Magyars" to a 1-1 draw. After the Melbourne Olympics, there were several wins over weaker Eastern European teams, and in 1957 it squeaked by Poland to qualify for its first World Cup.

It was a marvelously gifted team that prepared for the 1958 World Cup in Sweden by holding England to a 1-1 draw in Moscow. The Spartak-dominated World Cup squad included Yashin in goal, captain Igor Netto at left half, and the Armenian center forward Nikita Simonian, and after the heartening results of the past three years much was expected from them. Grouped with England, Brazil, and Austria in the opening round, the first matches were difficult for the USSR. Against Brazil, Vavá's two goals and Pelé's World Cup debut dealt the USSR its only loss of the round, but another draw with England forced a play-off (its third match in one month against the English), which it barely managed to win on a goal by Ilyin. Exhausted by the high quality of the first round opposition, the Soviets finally succumbed in the quarter-finals to Sweden.

Having tasted the exalted heights of World Cup competition, Soviet soccer authorities began to deemphasize Olympic competition in favor of the more elite World Championship and the newly inaugurated European Nations' Cup. Though the latter was not to gain its present stature until 1966-68, the USSR led a large Eastern European contingent into the first edition in 1958-60. As it turned out, all of its opponents in the series were part of that contingent. It defeated Hungary in the first round, and after Spain refused to play the Soviet team in the quarter-finals for political reasons, it eased past Czechoslovakia in the semi-finals, and won the championship with a narrow victory over Yugoslavia in the final. Doubts remained, however, over the Soviets' ability to compete consistently well against the world's top teams.

The doubts remained two years later, when the Soviet team stumbled repeatedly at the 1962 World Cup in Chile. In the first round, it defeated Yugoslavia in a brutal grudge match, and defeated Uruguay. Unknown and weak Colombia, however, pulled back from a 3-1 deficit at the half to force a 4-4 draw, and handed the USSR its biggest upset ever. After a poorly played loss to Chile in the quarter-finals, the Soviet team was eliminated and dejected, and critics pointed to all the mistakes Yashin had made between the sticks. The results were all the more disappointing, because the team had made a very successful tour of South America just before the competition.

At the 1966 World Cup in England, the USSR won its first round group against Italy, Korea DPR, and Chile without a defeat, and in the quarter-finals upset one of the favorites, Hungary, with superior physical strength. The semi-finals, however, produced a bruising loss to West Germany, and the Soviets' reputation for hard play was clearly manifested. In the third place match, the deft skills of Portugal proved superior to the Soviets' more combative skills, and the USSR took fourth place in the tournament. Nevertheless, it was its highest finish yet in World Cup competition, and while the team had not been as impressive as it was in 1958, the result was in keeping with its newly found place among the top echelons of world soccer.

The USSR's growing list of successes was also lengthened by a commendable second place finish in the 1962-64 European Nations' Cup, in which it lost the final to Spain, and neutralized Italy's durable *catenaccio*. Four years later, in the semi-finals of the 1966-68 Nations' Cup, these two teams met once again and battled to a scoreless draw, but Italy gained a vengeance of sorts by winning the toss. Still led by Yashin in goal, the Soviets lost the third place match to world champion England.

In 1970, the USSR qualified for its fourth consecutive World Cup, and was undefeated in its first round group against Mexico, Belgium, and El Salvador. Lacking Yashin in goal, this was a less spirited Soviet team, and it was rumored to be demoralized by broken promises over bonus payments. Whatever the frustrations may have been, its morale was not lifted when it lost the quarter-final to Uruguay by 1-0 on a highly suspect goal. In the 1970-72 Eurpean Football Championship, however, the Soviet team disposed of Spain, Yugoslavia, and Hungary—all stalwart opponents—and gained its third final in four editions of Europe's most elite tournament. In the final against West Germany, the Soviets acquitted themselves as well as could be expected, but the flowing, skillful West German game, now reaching its peak, would have defeated any team on earth, and a 3-0 loss was somehow appropriate.

It was not until the mid-1970s that the Soviets' extraordinary series of runs for the World Cup and the European Football Championship lost its momentum. In 1973, it refused to play Chile on the grounds of the National Stadium in Santiago (citing the stadium's earlier use as a detention center for political prisoners), and FIFA ruled the Soviet Union out of the 1974 World Cup. The USSR failed to qualify in 1978 after losses to Greece and Hungary, and it was eliminated in the quarter-finals of the 1974-76 European Football Championship by a resurgent Czechoslovakia. In less than 20 years, however, the USSR had amassed the best international record of any country in Europe; it advanced beyond the first round in four consecutive World Championships, and it appeared in three Nations' Cup finals. Its teams were technically proficient, as were so many of its individual players, but ultimately the style it came to be associated with relied on a uniquely Russian combination of skill and hard physical play.

The first Soviet club to do well in European competition was Dinamo Moscow, which reached the final of the 1971-72 European Cup Winners' Cup against Glasgow Rangers. The most important development at the club level, however, has been the rise of Dinamo Kiev to the front ranks. Always a first division club (an honor shared only with Spartak and Dinamo Moscow), Kiev did not achieve consistent championship results until the late 1960s. Turning its back on the bearlike qualities of postwar Soviet soccer, it sought to adopt elements of the Dutch-German approach (flowing teamwork with a license to opt for highly skilled individual performances), and in 1974-75, it won the European Cup Winners' Cup after Oleg Blokhin, probably the most gifted forward the Soviets have ever produced, won the European Footballer of the Year award. In keeping with administrative tradition, the USSR national team during the mid-1970s was based entirely on the Kiev team, but unlike the CSKA-Dinamo Moscow-Spartak eras of the past, the heightened international schedule of the 1970s drained the players of their stamina, and results on the national level were disappointing.

The growing power of non-Moscow clubs was further in evidence with the rising prominence of the Armenian club Ararat Erevan, Dinamo Tbilisi of Georgia, and two other Ukrainian clubs, Karpaty Lvov and Saria Voroschilovgrad. In recent years much effort has been given to adapting domestic schedules to fit the European fall-spring season. In 1976, two short league seasons were instituted: A spring competition from April to July was held to determine entrants for the 1976-77 UEFA Cup, and a fall competition was held from August to September to determine a national champion. The same clubs participated in both series. In October 1976, a new fall-spring championship was introduced, but in 1977-78, the old format was revived after a chaotic winter the year before. Below the 20-member second division (called the First League), the regional divisions operate on a staggered schedule depending on their climate: the South from March to December, central regions from April to October, and the North from May to September.

Champions

1936	Dinamo Moscow (spring)	1938	Spartak Moscow
	Spartak Moscow (fall)	1939	Spartak Moscow
1937	Dinamo Moscow	1940	Dinamo Moscow

1941	no competition	1961	Dinamo Kiev
1942	no competition	1962	Spartak Moscow
1943	no competition	1963	Dinamo Moscow
1944	no competition	1964	Dinamo Tbilisi
1945	Dinamo Moscow	1965	Torpedo Moscow
1946	CSKA Moscow	1966	Dinamo Kiev
1947	CSKA Moscow	1967	Dinamo Kiev
1948	CSKA Moscow	1968	Dinamo Kiev
1949	Dinamo Moscow	1969	Spartak Moscow
1950	CSKA Moscow	1970	CSKA Moscow
1951	CSKA Moscow	1971	Dinamo Kiev
1952	Spartak Moscow (short season)	1972	Saria Voroschilovgrad
1953	Spartak Moscow	1973	Ararat Erevan
1954	Dinamo Moscow	1974	Dinamo Kiev
1955	Dinamo Moscow	1975	Dinamo Kiev
1956	Spartak Moscow	1976	Dinamo Moscow (spring)
1957	Dinamo Moscow		Torpedo Moscow (fall)
1958	Spartak Moscow	1977	Dinamo Kiev
1959	Dinamo Moscow	1978	Dinamo Tbilisi
1960	Torpedo Moscow		

Cup Winners

1936	Lokomotive Moscow	1958	Spartak Moscow
1937	Dinamo Moscow	1959	no competition
1938	Spartak Moscow	1960	Torpedo Moscow
1939	Spartak Moscow	1961	Donets Shaktyor
1940	no competition	1962	Donets Shaktyor
1941	no competition	1963	Spartak Moscow
1942	no competition	1964	Dinamo Kiev
1943	no competition	1965	Spartak Moscow
1944	Zenit Leningrad	1966	Dinamo Kiev
1945	CSKA Moscow	1967	Dinamo Moscow
1946	Spartak Moscow	1968	Torpedo Moscow
1947	Spartak Moscow	1969	Karpaty Lvov
1948	CSKA Moscow	1970	Dinamo Moscow
1949	Torpedo Moscow	1971	Spartak Moscow
1950	Spartak Moscow	1972	Torpedo Moscow
1951	CSKA Moscow	1973	Ararat Erevan
1952	Torpedo Moscow	1974	Dinamo Kiev
1953	Dinamo Moscow	1975	Ararat Erevan
1954	Dinamo Moscow	1976	Dinamo Tbilisi
1955	CSKA Moscow	1977	Dinamo Moscow
1956	no competition	1978	Dinamo Kiev
1957	Lokomotive Moscow		

V

Vasco da Gama, Clube de Regatas

Location: *Rio de Janeiro, Brazil;* stadium: *Estádio de São Januário (50,000);* colors: *black jerseys with white diagonal stripe, white shorts;* honors: *Rio-São Paulo Tournament (1958, 1966 shared),. National Championship (1974), Rio de Janeiro champion (1923, 1924 LMDT, 1929, 1934 LCF, 1936 FMD, 1945, 1947, 1949, 1950, 1952, 1956, 1958, 1970, 1977).*

Founded 1898 as the sailing club of Lusitânia Esporte Clube, one of the major Portuguese-based sports clubs in Rio de Janeiro. Vasco was a late bloomer compared to the other major clubs of Rio—Flamengo, Fluminense, and Botafogo. In 1914, Lusitânia lost its affiliation with the Liga Metropolitana, because of Vasco's closed membership policies, and the following year Vasco was reorganized as an independent club. It entered the third division of the Rio league in 1916, gaining promotion after its first season, and won promotion to the first division in 1923. In its first season among the great clubs of Rio, Vasco lost only one match—to Flamengo in a game played at Fluminense's stadium—and won the championship. Aside from its astounding first division debut, this championship team became equally famous for its unusual racial content—it contained at least five players of nonwhite origin—a significant reversal of its image ten years earlier, and ultimately one of the most important breakthroughs in the history of Brazilian soccer. Vasco's popularity skyrocketed, and it won another title in 1929 with the brilliant center half Fausto, outside right Benedito, and center forward Carvalho Leite, all of whom played for Brazil in the 1930 World Cup. In 1926, Vasco built the glorious new Estádio de São Januário, a colonial-style structure that was to remain one of South America's finest stadiums until the appearance of Maracanã in 1950. São Januário was Rio's principal venue for internationals and tournament finals for over 20 years.

Other championships followed in 1934 and 1936, but the club achieved its greatest reputation in the postwar years. It won four league titles from 1945-50 and another in 1952. In 1948, it triumphed in the Campeonato Sudamericano de Campeones, a one-time forerunner of the Copa Libertadores, which included champion clubs from all over South America. Vasco supplied no less than eight players to Brazil's World Cup team of 1950, including the incomparable Ademir and the goalkeeper Barbosa. Spearheaded by center forward Vavá and Brazil's captain, Belini, Vasco won two more championships in the late 1950s and its first Rio-São Paulo Tournament in 1958. Because of its policy of purchasing players from other clubs rather than concentrating on youth and B teams, Vasco slid into a long decline in the 1960s when box office revenues were sparse. A four-way tie for the Torneo Rio-São Paulo in 1966 was little compensation, and it was not until its 1970 league championship that Vasco's prestige and wealth rose again. With a highly popular National Championship win in 1974, Vasco again became one of Brazil's top clubs, and a Rio title in 1977 helped to insure large gates for the immediate future. Vasco's great star in the 1970s has been the tall, elegant striker Roberto.

Venezuela

Federación Venezolana de Fútbol
Av. Este Estadio Nacional
Quinta Claret, 28. El Paráiso
Apado. Postal 14160. Candelaria
Caracas

Founded: 1926
FIFA: 1952
CONMEBOL: 1952

Affiliated clubs: *600;* registered players: *21,670 (170 professional);* national stadium: *none;* largest stadium: *Estadio Olímpico Ciudad Universitaria, Caracas (25,000);* colors: *dark red jerseys, black shorts;* season: *March to December;* honors: *none.*

Venezuela is the least successful of all South American countries in international competition, and is widely accepted as having the poorest standard of play as well. This has been due largely to the great popularity of baseball, the national sport, from the early years of this century—a phenomenon whose roots are in the economic ties Venezuela has enjoyed with the United States. In the 1970s, soccer finally began to develop into Venezuela's second major sport, as shown by the signing in 1977 of Brazil's great winger Jairzinho to Portuguesa Acarigua, the leading club from the interior. Jairzinho was also hired to promote the game nationwide as did Pelé in the United States. Portuguesa's bright showing in the 1977 Copa Libertadores, the South American club championship, was the first fruit of this new direction. Nevertheless, Venezuelan soccer has little to show for itself, and still remains a virtual outsider in South America as a whole.

The early history of Venezuelan soccer is more properly regarded in the context of Central America and the Caribbean rather than South America. Soccer got a late start along the old Spanish Main, and the founding dates are more reminiscent of organized soccer in the Caribbean than in South America. From the beginning there was difficulty in establishing a unified national association. The Federación Venezolana de Fútbol (FVF) was founded in 1926, but in 1929 a second group of clubs established the Asociación Venezolana (AV) and organized a rival league. A merger was achieved in 1930, and two years later a true national league, the Liga Venezolana, was introduced by the reconstituted federation, now given the name Asociación Nacional de Football. The original name of the association, Federación Venezolana de Fútbol, was reinstated in the mid-1950s. The first champion club of the original FVF in 1926 was Centro Atlético, which also won the inaugural title of the merged league in 1930. The first AV champion in 1929 was Deportivo Venezuela. The first years of the new national league of 1932 were dominated by Union SC and Deportivo Venezuela.

The major characteristic of Venezuelan soccer, indeed one of the many facets that resemble the game in the United States, has been the importance of ethnic groups in forming clubs. Spanish, Portuguese, and Italian immigrants to Venezuela stuck closely together as they attempted to advance the game in a nation devoted to baseball. The names of Venezuelan clubs down through the decades reflect the state of soccer in Venezuela as an ethnic game: Deportivo Portugues (Caracas), Portuguesa (Acarigua), Deportivo Italia (Caracas), Deportivo Galicia (Caracas), and Union Deportivo Canarias (Caracas).

A member of the now defunct Central American and Caribbean Confederation since the 1930s, Venezuela's first international competition was in the Central American and Caribbean championship of 1938 in Panama. Venezuela placed last in a field of six (the other participants were Mexico, Colombia, Costa Rica, El Salvador, and Panama), and managed to win only one game in five (2-1, over Colombia). Venezuela's first foray into South American soccer also occurred in 1938 when it participated in the unofficial Juegos Boliviaranos in Barranquilla against Bolivia, Colombia, Ecuador, and Peru. Again Venezuela finished last, though there was a convincing win over Ecuador (5-2). Eventually, with the demise of the old Central American and Caribbean confederations in the 1950s, Venezuela joined the South American confederation (CONMEBOL), but did not participate in the South American Championship, the principal international competition of CONMEBOL, until 1967. Ecuador, previously the last of South America's nations to enter the competition, had been participating since 1939. Of the two editions of the South American Championship in which it has participated, Venezuela has placed second from the bottom once (1967) and last in its first round group of three (1975). Only in recent years has Venezuela entered qualifying rounds for the World Cup.

The first Venezuelan club to enter the Copa Libertadores was Deportivo Italia in 1964; it placed last in its first round group with Colo

Colo of Chile and Barcelona of Ecuador. Portuguesa was the first Venezuelan club to advance beyond the first round of the Copa Libertadores in 1977. The present national league, which is mostly professional, dates from 1956, and has only eight members. Galicia, Italia, and Deportivo Portugues were the most successful participants until the 1970s, when Portuguesa Acarigua emerged as the strongest team in the renewed effort to establish soccer as a major sport. The most popular club in Venezuela is Galicia. A cup competition, that rarity in Latin American soccer, was introduced in 1963 for the leading clubs, but the first division remains the primary focus of attention. Among the numerous amateur competitions, the Torneo Iberico, which was started in 1949 as a tournament for Spanish and Portuguese immigrant clubs only, remains high on the list for Venezuelan fans and claims to be the oldest exclusively amateur competition in Latin America.

Champions

1956	Lasalle	1967	Deportivo Portugues
1957	Tiguire Aragua	1968	Union Dep. Canarias
1958	Deportivo Italia	1969	Deportivo Galicia
1959	Celta Deportivo	1970	Deportivo Galicia
1960	Deportivo Portugues	1971	Valencia
1961	Deportivo Italia	1972	Deportivo Italia
1962	Deportivo Portugues	1973	Portuguesa Acarigua
1963	Deportivo Italia	1974	Deportivo Galicia
1964	Deportivo Galicia	1975	Portuguesa Acarigua
1965	Lara Barquisimeto	1976	Portuguesa Acarigua
1966	Deportivo Italia	1977	Portuguesa Acarigua

Vietnam, Democratic Republic

Association de Football de
  la République Democratique du Viêt-nam
36, rue Tran-Phu
Hanoi

Founded: 1962
FIFA: 1964

Affiliated clubs: *55;* registered players: *16,000;* national stadium: *Stade Hang Day, Hanoi (40,000);* largest stadium: *Stade Hang Day;* colors: *red jerseys, white shorts;* season: *November to May;* honors: *none.* [See also: Vietnam, Republic]

Northern Vietnam has traditionally been less developed in soccer than the South, where French cultural and commercial influences were stronger. Northern representative teams competed in Vietnamese cup competitions before the partition in 1954, but seldom won any trophies. The Football Association of the Democratic Republic of Vietnam was not founded until 1962, and though it became affiliated with FIFA two years later it did not join the Asian Football Confederation because of the AFC's prior acceptance of South Vietnam. With political unification in 1975, the path cleared for affiliation with the AFC, but Vietnamese soccer has much catching up to do. North Vietnam had been the least active soccer-playing country in all of Asia. As a result of its non-affiliated status, the North never participated in an authorized international tournament of any kind, including the historic 1976 Asian Cup, in which the People's Republic of China, Korea DPR, and Yemen DPR joined the Asian fold. Since 1975, the Vietnamese national team has played against a selection representing the People's Republic of China, Korea DPR, and an East German "B" team, but the state of Vietnam's domestic game is uncertain.

Vietnam, Republic

Soccer was established in Vietnam earlier than in the rest of Indochina, and before the creation of two Vietnams in 1954, Vietnam as a whole was as active as any colony in Southeast Asia. South Vietnam was a major participant in Southeast Asian soccer from 1956-74, winning several minor tournaments and appearing early in official Asian competitions. After the fall of Saigon in 1975, the Tong-Cuoc Bong Tron (Vietnam Football Federation) ceased to function as a national governing body, but its official status in relation to FIFA was uncertain. In all probability, its direct affiliation with FIFA has ended.

The game was introduced in Indochina via Saigon before World War I, and the great influx of French military personnel and engineers during and after the war permanently established the game. The Fédération Cochinchinoise de Football, the first governing body on the Indochina peninsula, was founded in Saigon in 1923 and became affiliated with the French federation in 1934. Much of Vietnam's pre-World War II soccer activity was centered around French colonists and was fairly restricted to southern Vietnam (Cochinchina) and Hanoi. Activity heightened considerably under the Vichy administration during the war, and by 1948 the Cochinchinese federation had assumed direct control of soccer throughout the colony. In 1949, France traveled to Saigon and defeated a Cochinchina selection, 4-1, and a Vietnam selection, 2-1. In 1950, a Vietnam selection lost, 5-2, to France "B" in Nice. The federation's name was changed to Tong-Cuoc Bong Tron, after 1948, and in 1952 it became affiliated directly with FIFA despite Vietnam's colonial status at the time. The unified Vietnam of the post-World War II era was divided into three regional leagues—Southern, Central, and Northern—and by 1952 there were six major competitions being played: a first division ("Honorary Division"), second division ("First Division"), two cup competitions for clubs (Coupe Veuve Cliquot and Coupe de Sud-Viêt-nam), and two cup competitions for regional selections (Coupe Union and Coupe de President Tran Van Huu). The leading club in the early 1950s was Association de Jeunesse Sportive (A.J.S.) of Saigon, and the dominant regional team was that of the South.

The jurisdiction of the Tong-Cuoc Bong Tron reverted to South Vietnam after the partition in 1954. (North Vietnam founded its own association in 1962.) In 1956, with the lion's share of Vietnam's experienced players and coaches still inside its borders, the South was prepared to enter international competition and it became one of four participants in the first Asian Cup. Unfortunately, it placed last, losing to South Korea 5-3, in its official international debut, to Israel 2-1, and drawing with Hong Kong, 2-2. It suffered a similar fate in the second edition of the Asian Cup in 1960, when it lost to South Korea, Israel, and Taiwan. These were South Vietnam's last appearances in the Asian Cup.

South Vietnam won the soccer tournament of the first Southeast Asian Peninsula Games in 1959 at Bangkok, the 1966 edition of the Merdeka Anniversary Tournament in Malaysia, and was co-winner of the 1971 Pesta Sukan Tournament in Singapore. It was also active in Olympic qualifying rounds and the Asian games. The clubs of Vietnam Customs and Vietnam Police participated in the 1967 and 1968 editions, respectively, of the Asian Champion Teams' Cup. The only win achieved by either of these teams was Police's 7-0 thrashing of the Philippines' Manila Lions. In 1972-73, South Vietnam lost its World Cup qualifying round matches to Hong Kong (1-0) and Japan (4-0). The full national team's last officially recorded match was a 4-1 loss to France "Amateur Under-23" in Saigon in the summer of 1974.

volley

A kick that is taken before the ball touches the ground. Volleys are usually made with either the side or instep of the foot. An overhead volley is any kick taken before the ball touches the ground and is directed over the kicker's own head, whether or not the player has both feet off the ground.

See also: **half-volley** and **bicycle kick**

Wales

Football Association of Wales, Ltd.
3 Fairy Road
Wrexham,
Denbighshire
LL13 7PS

Founded: 1876
FIFA: 1910-20
1924-28
1946
UEFA: 1954

Affiliated clubs: *1,424;* **registered players:** *46,500 (500 professional);* **national stadium:** *Ninian Park, Cardiff (58,000);* **largest stadium:** *Ninian Park;* **colors:** *red jerseys, white shorts;* **season:** *August to May;* **honors:** *Home International Championship (1907, 1920, 1924, 1928, 1933, 1934, 1937, 1939 shared, 1952 shared, 1956 shared, 1960 shared, 1970 shared).*

The Principality of Wales, while making little impact on the world game in modern times, was a pioneer in the development of association football, and by virtue of its permanent place on the International Football Association Board, has wielded considerable influence on the administration of the game off the playing field. On the playing field, less than one-fifth of its international opponents have been countries outside the British Isles. Though it has occasionally dominated the home countries, Wales' international record outside Britain is only fair. Nevertheless, Welsh teams command respect whenever they are met, and Wales' ability to produce high quality players is disproportionate to its small population: Billy Meredith, Ivor Allchurch, Trevor Ford, and John Charles were indisputably world-class players. Wales' accomplishments have been achieved in spite of enormous competition at home from rugby, the principality's favorite sport, and the pervasive drain of Wales' best players to The Football League in England.

Like Scotland and Northern Ireland, Wales' administrative privileges (and absence of privileges) in international competition are peculiar to the United Kingdom. These aberrations arise from its unique place in the early history of the modern game. Wales, Scotland, and Northern Ireland have separate memberships in FIFA from that of England. All four have permanent places on the International Football Association Board, which governs the world Laws of the Game. On the other hand, though the winner of the Welsh Cup is allotted a berth in the European Cup Winners' Cup, the champion club of the Welsh League is excluded from participating in the European Champions' Cup, because

Wales' four leading clubs, Cardiff City, Wrexham, Swansea City, and Newport County, are members of The Football League in England. This ruling by the Union of European Football Associations also precludes Welsh clubs from participating in the UEFA Cup, Europe's third major club competition. Thus, to a greater degree than either Scotland or Northern Ireland, Wales remains an anomaly in European soccer.

The football games of the Roman legions were rarely seen in the distant mountains of present-day Wales, though some exposure to them was likely. And there is the possibility that Celtic tribes of the Welsh highlands developed their own games of football, as appears to be the case in Ireland. Football does not seem to have followed the migration of the Celts into Wales following the Anglo-Saxon invasions. If any forms of medieval football were played in Wales, they were probably indigenous, with a separate growth from that of the Roman or Anglo-Saxon tradition. At the same time, there is virtually no record to indicate that football was even played in Wales during the medieval period.

Descriptions of a local game in Pembrokeshire, however, surfaced during the reign of Elizabeth I. This was the famous *knappan*, which was known to have been played in South Wales since Roman times, and whose direct links with medieval football are unclear. *Knappan* is related to *hurling*, the ancient game of Ireland and Cornwall, and to *la soule*, the Breton football game. These were all games involving masses of players, and in the case of *knappan* the ball was thrown rather than kicked. The game in South Wales, as described by George Owen in 1603, was important because it brought social prestige and honor to its players. Unlike many early games in England and Scotland, the Welsh game *knappan* continued to thrive well into the eighteenth century. Eventually, as Welsh culture was absorbed into English life during the nineteenth century and the influence of English public schools and universities came to be felt in all British sports, the Welsh game, as such, lost its identity. The next stage in the growth of Welsh football was linked with the advance of the industrial revolution in Great Britain as a whole.

The hardiness of Welsh culture, particularly in the lifestyle of the huge mining population, and the rugged, damp terrain of the Welsh counties, led to the rapid growth of rugby at the expense of soccer in the late nineteenth century. This was especially true in the southern counties; in the North, the economic and social links with industrial Cheshire and Lancashire in England gave rise to a more rapid growth of soccer and it is here that the roots of modern Welsh soccer are found.

In 1876, the Football Association of Wales was founded at Wrexham, in the North, by a group of Welshmen trying to organize an international match with Scotland. This match, the first international ever played after the start of the England-Scotland rivalry four years earlier, took place in March of that year at Glasgow, resulting in a 4-0 win for the Scots. But a controversy arose when players from South Wales protested that the Welsh team did not include any representatives from the southern counties. In fact, the charge was true, and many years passed before either the Welsh F.A. or the national team included representatives from South Wales. In addition, most Welsh internationals before World War I continued to be played at Wrexham, rather than Cardiff or Swansea in the South. The leading Welsh clubs came from the North as well. The first, Druids F.C., was formed at Ruabon, near Wrexham. Wrexham F.C., the oldest Welsh club still in senior competition, was formed in 1873, followed closely by Oswestry and Chirk, the other great pioneer clubs of Wales. South Wales did not become active in the Welsh F.A. until the late 1880s, and the first southern league was not formed until 1890.

Throughout this period, the most important personality in the growth of Welsh soccer was L. Ll. Kenrick, a Welsh international from Ruabon, who also played for Shropshire Wanderers F.C. in England. Kenrick was instrumental in getting the Welsh F.A. off the

ground during an era when the game had not yet been firmly established in Wales. After the formation of the South Wales F.A. and the Monmouthshire F.A. in 1893, soccer was finally accepted as a serious rival to the popular rugby, but the game's ultimate acceptance was not seen until after the turn of the century, especially under the aegis of Welsh F.A. president E. Robbins, who assumed his post in 1910.

The Welsh Cup, the world's third oldest cup competition, was introduced in 1877. For more than 30 years, until the rise of Cardiff City, the cup was dominated by the leading clubs of the North: Wrexham (winner of the first cup), Druids, Oswestry, and Chirk. The Welsh Cup is open to all Welsh clubs regardless of league affiliation and to clubs from nearby English counties. The Welsh Football League, on the other hand, was introduced in 1902, and experienced difficulties from the beginning, as the important Welsh clubs sought to play in higher levels of competition in England. Wrexham, for example, was a member of the North Wales Alliance for many years and joined the Birmingham League in the English Midlands during the period before World War I. The four leading Welsh clubs, Wrexham, Cardiff City, Swansea City (formerly Town), and Newport County have been members of The Football League in England since the early 1920s. This has lessened the importance of the Welsh League over the years, and has relegated it to a rank alongside the lower-level regional leagues of England. Today, the Welsh League has 47 members divided into three divisions: the Premier, Division 1, and North Division 1, the last indicating the historical predominance of North Wales.

Wales' only international competitors until 1933 were England, Scotland, and Ireland (later Northern Ireland). In the Home International Championship, begun as a fourway competition in 1884, Wales has won the title outright seven times, including three in the 1920s and three in the 1930s, and it has shared the title five times. England and Scotland have otherwise maintained clear dominance over Wales throughout the 100 years of international competition in the British Isles, Ireland remaining a poor fourth. Wales lost each of its first seven internationals between 1876-81—to Scotland five times and England twice. Its first international victory was a 1-0 win over England in 1881 at Blackburn, and the subsequent meeting with

England in 1882 at Wrexham resulted in a second win for Wales, this time by 5-3. The strength of Scottish soccer during the 1870s and '80s, however, was such that Wales' record against Scotland until 1890 was 1 drawn, 14 lost, 7 goals for, and 65 against. Wales did not defeat Scotland until 1905-07, when it won three in succession.

Wales first met Ireland in 1882, and dominated Britain's fourth home country consistently until the turn of the century, after which the Irish began to win occasionally. Wales' biggest win during the pre-1900 era was an 11-0 trouncing of Ireland in 1888 at Wrexham. Its worst loss was by 9-0 to Scotland in 1878 at Glasgow. Wales' losses to England were on the whole less severe than those to Scotland, but after 1882 Wales did not manage to defeat England again until 1920 (a noteworthy 2-1 victory at Highbury, London). Meanwhile, the first international held in the southern counties was at Swansea in 1894 against Ireland. Wales' first international at Cardiff was a 9-1 thrashing by England in 1896.

A major factor in the growth of Welsh soccer in the early days was the presence of Billy Meredith, the legendary right wing from the town of Chirk (in the North) whose skills and goalscoring genius spanned some 38 years between 1893-1924. His importance to Welsh soccer is analogous to that of Artur Friedenreich of Brazil as a result of the level of expertise he brought to his country's game. Meredith made over 1,100 appearances in top-level competition and appeared in approximately 50 Welsh internationals, most of them while playing for Manchester City and Manchester United in England. His influence on Welsh soccer resulted from the emphasis he placed on developing new ball control skills which he ceaselessly promoted during an era when a preoccupation with tactical innovations was on the rise. Meredith also anticipated the difficulties that Wales was to experience in securing the release of Welsh players from English clubs for Welsh internationals. Seldom has one player had such a significant impact on the development of the game on a national basis.

Wales' first non-British international was against France in 1933 at Paris, a 1-1 draw, but Wales ventured away from the home countries only once again before World War II—to Paris in 1939—resulting in a 2-1 loss. While the period between the wars included Wales' most successful results in British competition, the post-World War II era saw a concerted effort to participate in European and world competition, particularly in connection with the World Cup and the European Football Championship.

The Welsh F.A., like the other British associations, had withdrawn from FIFA between 1920-24 and 1928-46, and so the World Cup of 1950 provided Wales its first opportunity to qualify for the world championship. This effort was thwarted by England and Scotland, whose wins in the Home International Championship of 1949 doubled as World Cup elimination contests. The same situation occurred in 1953 when England and Scotland prevented Wales from entering the final rounds of the 1954 World Cup. In 1958, however, all four British countries advanced to the final rounds of the World Cup in Sweden, although Wales' route was one of the most indirect ever taken. In its 1958 qualifying round, Wales placed second to Czechoslovakia. In the Africa-Asia-Oceania qualifying rounds, however, the African states, as well as Indonesia and Turkey, refused to play Israel for political reasons, causing one forfeit after another. Israel thus advanced to the World Cup final rounds without having to play a single match. FIFA, astonished at the thought of such a development, invited Wales to play Israel in a home and away series to determine that World Cup berth, and the Israelis succumbed in both games by 2-0.

To the surprise of everyone but loyal Welsh fans, FIFA's gift resulted in Wales' greatest international achievement to date. In its first round group, it drew 1-1 with Hungary, 1-1 with Mexico, and 0-0 with Sweden. In the playoff with Hungary, Wales emerged victorious by 2-1 on goals by Allchurch and Medwin, advancing to the quarter-final round to play against Brazil. Wales' most memorable achievement in that World Cup, perhaps in all Welsh soccer history, was in holding the legendary Brazilians to a scoreless draw for much of that game. Brazil's game-winning and only goal, on an opportunistic rebound shot by the 17-year-old Pelé, was a miraculous individual effort, and Wales was given due credit for successfully challenging Brazil's superiority. Leading the attack for Wales in the 1958 World Cup was center forward John Charles, the greatest Welsh player since Billy Meredith, who was released by his Italian club Juventus after Italy itself failed to qualify for the World Cup.

Wales has not qualified for any world

championship since 1958. Aside from World Cup qualifying rounds, Wales' activity outside the United Kingdom has mainly been in connection with the European Football Championship (formerly the European Nations' Cup). Wales' overall record in this competition (as of 1976) is: 22-8-5-9-29-30-21. Among the 33 countries that have participated in the European Football Championship, Wales ranks number 20 overall, an enviable showing for one of the small nations of Europe. Wales was eliminated in the Nations' Cup by Hungary in 1962-64, and in 1966-68 it placed third in its first round group, which consisted of the four home countries. In 1970-72, Wales was dominated by Czechoslovakia and Rumania for its first round group and placed third ahead of Finland. Its best showing in the European Championship was in 1974-76 when it won its first round group over Hungary and Austria after losing only one match in six (to Austria), though it lost to Yugoslavia in the quarter-finals. These 1974-76 results marked the beginning of another successful period in Welsh soccer, in which the national team's spirit and optimism was clearly on the rise. Some excellent results in the qualifying round for the 1978 World Cup pointed further to a bright future.

Other than England and Scotland, Wales' most difficult opponents in the postwar period have been Austria, Italy, Czechoslovakia, and Brazil. Wales' only winning records, other than against Eire and Northern Ireland, are against Finland, Israel, Luxembourg, and surprisingly, Hungary. All Welsh wins and draws against Hungary occurred after the breakup of Hungary's great postwar team in 1956. Wales' biggest wins since World War II have been 5-0 defeats of Northern Ireland and Luxembourg. Its worst defeats have been 4-0 trouncings by England and Switzerland. Wales has thus held its own as a small, active soccer nation, and the maturity and consistency of its game is reflected in the absence of devastating defeats by the world giants.

On the club level, Welsh Cup winners have fared rather well in the European Cup Winners' Cup. Cardiff City, Wales' leading club since it became the first and only English league member from Wales to win the English F.A. Cup in 1927, advanced to the semi-finals of the Cup Winners' Cup in 1967-68. Wrexham, the early kingpin of Welsh soccer, remains an important second division club in the English league, and retains the distinction of having supplied more players to Welsh national teams than any other Welsh club. Swansea City and Newport County continue to struggle in the third and fourth divisions of the English league.

While the overall record against England and Scotland is poor (vs. England: 88-11-19-59-82-232-41; vs. Scotland: 89-15-20-54-42-228-50), the Welsh F.A. has been encouraged by the recent ruling that British players whose fathers were born in Wales, Scotland, or Northern Ireland may now choose to play for those national teams, even though the players themselves were born in England. Meanwhile, Wales' record against Northern Ireland (and Ireland before World War I) remains favorable: 83-38-18-26-173-122-94. The most significant aspect of Welsh soccer, however, has continued to be the contentious rivalry between rugby, a game for which the Welsh are world famous, and soccer, whose preeminence in the rugged terrains of little Wales could well have been doomed from the start.

Cup Winners

1878	Wrexham	1888	Chirk	1898	Druids
1879	Newtown	1889	Bangor	1899	Druids
1880	Druids	1890	Chirk	1900	Aberystwyth
1881	Druids	1891	Shrewsbury Town	1901	Oswestry
1882	Druids	1892	Chirk	1902	Wellington
1883	Wrexham	1893	Wrexham	1903	Wrexham
1884	Oswestry	1894	Chirk	1904	Druids
1885	Druids	1895	Newtown	1905	Wrexham
1886	Druids	1896	Bangor	1906	Wellington
1887	Chirk	1897	Wrexham	1907	Oswestry

1908	Chester	1932	Swansea Town	1956	Cardiff City
1909	Wrexham	1933	Chester	1957	Wrexham
1910	Wrexham	1934	Bristol City	1958	Wrexham
1911	Wrexham	1935	Tranmere Rovers	1959	Cardiff City
1912	Cardiff City	1936	Crewe Alexandra	1960	Wrexham
1913	Swansea Town	1937	Crewe Alexandra	1961	Swansea Town
1914	Wrexham	1938	Shrewsbury Town	1962	Bangor City
1915	Wrexham	1939	South Liverpool	1963	Borough United
1916	no competition	1940	Welling Town	1964	Cardiff City
1917	no competition	1941	no competition	1965	Cardiff City
1918	no competition	1942	no competition	1966	Swansea Town
1919	no competition	1943	no competition	1967	Cardiff City
1920	Cardiff City	1944	no competition	1968	Cardiff City
1921	Wrexham	1945	no competition	1969	Cardiff City
1922	Cardiff City	1946	no competition	1970	Cardiff City
1923	Cardiff City	1947	Chester	1971	Cardiff City
1924	Wrexham	1948	Lovells Athletic	1972	Wrexham
1925	Wrexham	1949	Merthyr Tydfil	1973	Cardiff City
1926	Ebbw Vale	1950	Swansea Town	1974	Cardiff City
1927	Cardiff City	1951	Merthyr Tydfil	1975	Wrexham
1928	Cardiff City	1952	Rhyl	1976	Cardiff City
1929	Connah's Quay	1953	Rhyl	1977	Shrewsbury Town
1930	Cardiff City	1954	Flint Town United	1978	Wrexham
1931	Wrexham	1955	Barry Town		

wall

A closely knit line of defenders, which is usually positioned between the ball and the goal to prevent a direct free kick from scoring. The wall must be at least ten yards from the ball.

wall pass

The give-and-go: a player passes to a nearby teammate, and immediately runs to a third position in order to receive his teammate's deflection of the original pass. The teammate is used, in effect, as a rebounding wall.

Walter, Fritz (1920-   )

This energetic inside forward was the first great figure in postwar German soccer, and did more than any player to elevate West Germany to the front ranks of world competition. He was primarily an inside left, but throughout much of his career he fell back into the midfield, pushing his other forwards toward the goal and distributing accurate through balls, many of which eventually found their way into the net. He was first and foremost the on-field emissary of German national team manager Sepp Herberger, with whom he developed an extraordinary 18-year relationship, and, as captain, he led the West German team that won the 1954 World Cup. A tactical wizard and inspirational leader, Walter led that surprising team to one of the greatest upsets in the history of the game, the 3-2 victory over Hungary in the final, and paved the way for the eras of Seeler and Beckenbauer.

Already a goalscoring inside left for FC Kaiserslautern, the only club he ever played for, he was selected by Herberger for the national team in 1940 against Rumania, and scored twice in that debut. Hat tricks followed in the next two matches, but the war intervened, and

Walter was drafted as a paratrooper. His experiences in the war were so painful that for the rest of his career he never flew to away games no matter what inconvenience it caused him. After the war, he was reunited with Herberger, and led West Germany back into international competition after its reinstatement with FIFA in 1950. Walter and his brother Otmar led Kaiserslautern to national championships in 1951 and 1953, and in the 1954 World Cup in Switzerland he finally achieved the international recognition he deserved. His skills and leadership were among the highlights of the competition. After a year away from the national team, Herberger brought him back for the 1958 World Cup, and once again he was an inspiration. After a total of 61 international appearances (scoring 33 goals) and over 20 years with Kaiserslautern, he retired to go into business, and rejected the inevitable coaching offers that came his way.

Wanderers Football Club

Location: *London, England;* stadium: *Kennington Oval, various grounds in London;* colors: *orange, violet, and black;* honors: *English cup winner (1872, 1873, 1876, 1877, 1878).*

Founded in 1864 by members of the recently disbanded Forest F.C., which was the first football club in the south of England (founded 1859) and the first club anywhere to devote itself exclusively to the "dribbling game," as distinct from the "handling game." Forest was formed in the northeast suburbs of London by C.W. and J.F. Alcock and other Harrow graduates, and for four years played against other new clubs in the London area, gradually acquiring some non-Harrovian players. In 1864, when C.W. Alcock decided to move the club from its Epping Forest grounds in the northeast to play in a variety of locations near central London, some of the players objected to "wandering from place to place," and the name Wanderers was adopted.

Wanderers was linked directly with the first "dribbling" club in the game's history, and under its own name became the first great soccer power. It was invincible during the 1860s and early 1870s, and when the world's first organized competition, The Football Association Cup, was introduced in 1871-72, Wanderers became the first winner. It went on to win a total of five cups during the 1870s,

building the first soccer dynasty, and influencing the early years of the game immeasurably. In 1878, it was awarded the cup outright to commemorate its fifth victory in seven years, though the trophy was actually returned for future use.

The central figure in the Wanderers' success was C.W. Alcock, the outstanding personality in the early years of soccer. Alcock became honorary secretary of The Football Association in 1870, and in the following year he was the driving force behind the introduction of the F.A. Cup. In addition to being the most prolific and authoritative historian of those first years, he had a pervasive impact on the game. As the cofounder and sometime captain of Wanderers, he became the chief promoter of dribbling tactics during that chaotic period when soccer was without direction or form.

In opposition to those clubs that advanced the art of teamwork and passing skills (chief among them were Royal Engineers and Queen's Park Glasgow), the Wanderers' approach was to emphasize individual dribbling skills, as this was said to be a purer expression of association football. Its success during the 1870s seemed to support this claim, but by the end of the decade the tide began to turn, as Scottish teams won match after match against English teams by employing the passing style of Queen's Park. Though the dribbling style eventually fell out of favor, the Wanderers' contribution to the early history of soccer was incalculable. It was at that very time—the 1860s and '70s—that association football was separating from rugby football, whose rules were necessarily identified with passing skills (albeit by hand) and teamwork. Once association football was able to develop a sense of self-identification (by the late 1870s), other more sophisticated tactics became welcome. Hence, the rise of the passing game, association style.

There were many famous names in the Wanderers' lineup other than the Alcocks: C.H.R. Wollaston, a banker by profession who played on the inside of a very long forward line; R.W.S. Vidal, the first "Prince of Dribblers"; M.P. Betts, the all-purpose player who scored the only goal in the first F.A. Cup; and G.H. Heron, a clever winger, who was often accused—even on this club—of being selfish with the ball. Each of them played for England during the 1870s. But above all there was A.F. Kinnaird, later Lord Kinnaird, who eventually became the president of The Football Association from 1890 until his death in 1923. After C.W. Alcock, Lord Kinnaird became the most influential figure in the development of the early game.

After its F.A. Cup win in 1878, the Wanderers participated in two more cup competitions without success, and in 1880, after most of its members had drifted into various "Old Boys" clubs, it was disbanded.

wasted ball

A pass or shot on goal that is seriously off its mark, usually one that crosses the touchline or goal line; a very bad kick.

Wembley; The Empire Stadium,

In 1921, the Prince of Wales urged that the showpiece for the newest (and last) British Empire Exhibition (1924) should be "a great national sports ground" that would be the mecca for world soccer and an escape that would "appeal to all Britishers" on grand sporting occasions. Wembley Stadium became just that, and 55 years after its completion it remains the most famous and hallowed soccer venue in the world. In the late 1970s, its official capacity of 100,000 was reduced slightly for safety reasons, thus ending the era when an automatic 100,000 spectators were expected for F.A. Cup finals and important international matches. But the significance of Wembley is in its mystique—the apparent need for the world's most popular sport to have at least one location that serves as a kind of unofficial headquarters or focal point. It is no longer the world's largest stadium—it now ranks about twentieth—but there is seldom a player, whether he has traveled from as far away as Rio de Janeiro or as nearby as the northwest London suburb of Wembley itself, who has not commented on the thrill he experiences when emerging from the tunnel to the deafening chants of a Wembley crowd.

Ground was broken at Wembley by the Duke of York, later George VI, in January 1922, and within one year the stadium was completed, an astounding rate of construction that has yet to be equaled for a facility of this size. Though its official opening had already taken place, its real inauguration was the first Wembley F.A. Cup final on April 28, 1923, between Bolton Wanderers and West Ham United, the famous "White Horse Final." Turnstile operators officially let in 126,047 spectators on that day, but at least 150,000 and probably 200,000 people got into the stadium, and another 100,000 hovered just outside. There were so many people that the crowd filled the playing area itself—solidly from goal to goal. Incredibly, this sea of humanity remained calm, and the occasion was characterized by a total absence of misbehavior or trouble of any kind. Officials met to plan a way to disperse the crowd so that the game could get underway, but they decided instead to call the match off. Before the announcement could be made, Police Constable George Storey—soon to become a legend in English folklore—appeared on the field mounted atop his shining white stallion Billie, and single-handedly nudged and coaxed until everyone was pushed back to the edge of the playing area. The players were called out of the locker rooms, and the game commenced before an undetermined number of people. Spectators were so tightly packed around the field that one goal was disputed because it was thought that a fan sitting on the goal line had kept the ball in play with his foot. The game ended with a 2-0 win for Bolton, and the next day photographs of Billie and the crowd he gently brought under control were on the front page of every newspaper in the country.

The Empire Stadium is owned by a private corporation and is the regular site for England's home games, the F.A. Cup final, the Football League Cup final, the F.A. Charity Shield, the F.A. Amateur Cup, the F.A. Challenge Vase, the annual University Match (Oxford vs. Cambridge), as well as Rugby League, boxing, track and field meets (it was the principal stadium for the 1948 Olympic Games), hockey, show-jumping, and assorted festivals. Nearby is the Empire Pool, London's major indoor sports arena. In 1962, the roof at Wembley was extended around the entire seating (and standing) area, and it was built of fiberglass, rather than concrete or metal, to allow in sunlight.

West African Football Union

The West African Football Union/L'Union Ouest-Africaine de Football was founded in Abidjan, Ivory Coast, in 1975 to organize mutual soccer interests among the states of West Africa. For administrative purposes, the WAFU region is divided into the following four zones: 1) Cape Verde Islands, Mali, Mauritania, and Senegal; 2) Gambia, Guinea, Guinea-Bissau, and Sierra Leone; 3) Ivory Coast, Ghana, Upper Volta, and Liberia; and, 4) Benin, Niger, Nigeria, and Togo. Competition among national and youth teams is being organized and funds are being raised to defray the cost of West African teams in their bids for international honors.

West Germany   See: **Germany, Federal Republic of**

whistles

It is generally accepted that a whistle was used for the first time by a referee at Nottingham, England in 1878 during a match between Sheffield Norfolk and Nottingham Forest.

wins and defeats

The longest undefeated run in international competition was achieved by Hungary—a stretch of 29 matches between May 14, 1950 (3-5 vs. Austria) and the World Cup final, July 4, 1954 (2-3 vs. Germany FR). This run included only four draws.

Excluding war years, Hungary was un-defeated at home for 17 consecutive years between June 8, 1939 (1-3 vs. Italy) and May 20, 1956 (2-4 vs. Czechoslovakia). If unofficial wartime internationals are included, this run extends only from 1943 (2-7 vs. Sweden) to 1956. Both are records.

Brazil has been undefeated in its national

stadium, the Maracana, for 22 consecutive years: from July 7, 1957 (1-2 vs. Argentina) to the present.

Real Madrid was undefeated at home for eight consecutive years between February 1957 (2-3 vs. Atlético Madrid) and March 1965 (0-1 vs. Atlético Madrid). This run included 114 wins and 8 draws.

Fiorentina was undefeated for 33 consecutive Italian first division matches in 1955-56, and compiled the following record: 34-20-13-1-59-20-53.

Longest undefeated run in the World Cup: 13 matches by Brazil between 1954 (2-4 vs. Hungary) and 1966 (1-3 vs. Hungary).

Most wins in the World Cup: 33 (Brazil)

Most defeats in the World Cup: 17 (Mexico)

Most wins in the European Football Championship (to 1974-76): 24 (USSR)

Most defeats in the European Football Championship (to 1974-76): 18 (Denmark)

Most wins in the South American Championship (to 1975): 83 (Argentina)

Most defeats in the South American Championship (to 1975): 57 (Chile)

Most wins in the European Cup (to 1977-78): 68 (Real Madrid)

Most defeats in the European Cup (to 1977-78): 30 (Real Madrid)

Most wins in the European Cup Winners' Cup (to 1977-78): 23 (Atlético Madrid)

Most defeats in the European Cup Winners' Cup (to 1977-78): 13 (Cardiff City)

Most wins in the Fairs/UEFA Cup (to 1977-78): 46 (Barcelona)

Most defeats in the Fairs/UEFA Cup (to 1977-78): 27 (FC Köln)

Most wins in the Copa Libertadores (to 1976): 70 (Peñarol)

Most defeats in the Copa Libertadores (to 1976): 38 (Peñarol)

---

witchcraft

Witchcraft shrouds the sport in some parts of Africa, especially in the East African nations of Kenya, Uganda, and Tanzania. It is reported that in Kenya, 90 percent of all clubs in the upper divisions of the league employ witch doctors. Although African sports officials have sought to stamp out such occult elements, the practitioners of the ancient science have apparently gained a strong foothold in at least these three countries. The Report of the XIIth General Assembly of the African Football Confederation (1976) specifically mentions the witchcraft problem: "We would like to seize this opportunity to launch an appeal to all African member associations asking them to strive in order to free the African sport from all the evils which obstruct the realization of the noble objectives which we have chosen. These evils take the form of tribalism, ju-ju and other primitive magics which have always been encouraged in our countries and among our people by colonialism in the hope of obliterating the African personality and controlling our people." In addition, the Kenya Football Association has attempted to impound paraphernalia used by witch doctors, but this effort seems to have been unsuccessful.

The function of the witch doctor is to cast spells on his client's opponent. In return for this, the modern football witch doctor is paid between £5 and £175 per match, depending on the wealth of his club, the importance of a given match, and the stature of the witch doctor. Payment is always made in advance. To prepare for his wizardry, the witch doctor fasts, concentrates on his mission for a period of time, and eventually performs a variety of chants. Many witch doctors now employ Islamic as well as pagan prayers. The most intense prayer periods occur just before the game in question. Mirrors may be used by the witch doctor to cast a reflection of the opponent so that easier contact can be made. Some spells may be cast on the ball itself. Several players have described how their game ball has suddenly turned into a snake as they were about to make contact with it on the field. Other spells are said to result in goalkeepers seeing two balls at once when a shot is made. Opposing players of a team known to employ witch doctors often avoid certain areas of the stadium in fear of cast spells. Potions are also an essential ingredient. They are eaten, worn, or placed around the field prior to a game, and usually consist of herbs, powdered animal and snake skins, roots, or a variety of murky liquids.

Witchcraft in East Africa is the last remaining pagan rite connected with organized soccer, but unlike the deeply seeded ritual of pre-Columbian games, its motivation is primarily monetary rather than spiritual. Though it is likely to linger for years to come, witchcraft in soccer inevitably faces a slow but eventual decline.

women's soccer

Women are known to have played some form of football as early as the sixteenth century in England, and in the late eighteenth century there was a locally famous match played every year between married and unmarried women in Iveresk, near Edinburgh, Scotland. Between the Restoration and the modern era, women were rarely involved in the game except in the north of England and Scotland, and then only as part of established rituals or celebrations such as the Shrovetide games. In the early 1890s, however, women's clubs began to form in England, attracting as many as 10,000 spectators to such grounds as Crouch End in North London. Preston, in industrial Lancashire, was a center for women's soccer during this period. In 1894, a Preston club called Dick Kerr's XI was organized, and became widely known for its charity work. One women's club from Preston toured the United States in 1892.

Unwilling to draw up a special set of rules for women, The Football Association in London ruled in 1902 that women's clubs were ineligible to join its ranks, because the F.A. could not be responsible for the many injuries expected. Practically all the European governing bodies followed this pattern in subsequent years. Nevertheless, the growth of women's soccer gained some momentum in the wake of the suffragette movement in Western Europe, especially in the early 1920s, and a women's international between France and England in 1920 was seen by 10,000 spectators. The rate of growth considerably abated by 1925. After World War II, efforts to revive the movement failed repeatedly in most countries, though some women's teams continued to exist.

In 1957, two years after the Deutscher Fussball-Bund officially declared that women's soccer would remain outside its protective jurisdiction in West Germany, an unofficial European Women's Football Championship was held in West Berlin. The participants were national selections from Austria, England, West Germany, and the Netherlands. In the final, England defeated West Germany, 4-0. A great surge in women's soccer began during the 1960s, launched primarily by those countries in Eastern Europe whose state-sponsored sports programs included women's teams for factory workers, office leisure groups, and schools. Czechoslovakia was a pioneer in this growth. In Western Europe, a sporadic movement took shape in the last years of the decade, spurred in some cases by the success of women's basketball and team handball.

Women's teams also sprang up in other parts of the world before 1970, though FIFA refused to lend a helping hand and a coordinated international effort of any kind was virtually nonexistent. There was some form of organized competition at this time in Scotland, England, Wales, France, Belgium, the Netherlands, West Germany, Switzerland, Italy, Denmark, Sweden, Austria, Czechoslovakia, Rumania, Argentina, Brazil, Venezuela, Guatemala, Jamaica, Mexico, the United States, New Zealand, Taiwan, Hong Kong, Singapore, Malaysia, Thailand, South Vietnam, Japan, Algeria, Kenya, Uganda, Upper Volta, and South Africa. At the same time, women's soccer was officially recognized by the governing bodies of England, Wales, France, West Germany, Sweden, Guatemala, Jamaica, Taiwan, Singapore, Thailand, Algeria, Upper Volta, and South Africa. Official leagues existed in Sweden, Guatemala, Taiwan, and Singapore, and official cup competitions were held in France, Guatemala, Jamaica, Taiwan, and Singapore.

In Western Europe, women's teams have generally fallen into two categories: those sponsored by business concerns or industry, and those affiliated with established men's clubs. One of the countries to assume a leadership role in the development of women's soccer has been France. A French cup competition for women was launched in 1968, and in that year perhaps the most famous women's team in Europe was founded. This was the Football Club Féminin Reims. FCF Reims, under the guidance of its founder Pierre Geofroy, became an important promoter of women's soccer both in France and on the international scene. In 1970, it became affiliated with the famous men's club Stade de Reims, and toured Canada and the

Early years of the current movement to organize women's soccer. England's Mary Bee (l) and Margaret Hilton (r) charge past the West German goalkeeper in the final of the 1957 European Women's Football Championship in West Berlin. England won the unofficial title, 4-0.

United States with the women's team of Lazio (Rome). FCF Reims visited Indonesia and Spain (1972), Ireland (1973), the Antilles and Haiti (1974), and Hungary and Czechoslovakia (1975). On each occasion crowds numbered in the tens of thousands. In 1975 and 1976, FCF Reims won the first two editions of the new official Championnat de France Féminin. There are now over 400 affiliated women's teams in France, with some 7,000 registered players.

In England, The Football Association reversed its 1902 decision and recognized women's soccer in 1969. Women's clubs became affiliated with county associations, and the Women's Football Assocation was founded in 1971. In England alone there are now over 300 teams affiliated with 20 leagues. In Scotland, the Women's Football League was started in 1972, and is divided into Eastern and Wester Sections made up of seven clubs each. There are also a host of national and regional cup competitions, but the Scottish F.A. did not recognize women's soccer until 1975. The dominant team throughout the 1970s has been Edinburgh Dynamo. The Northern Irish

Women's Football Association is an honorary member of The Football Association in London, while women's organizations in Wales are affiliated directly with the Welsh F.A.

In West Germany, women's soccer was officially recognized in the late 1960s, and the Deutscher Damen-Meisterschaft was introduced in 1974. This is a knockout tournament for the leading teams of each region, and has been won by TuS Wörrstadt, Bonner SC, and the women's team of Bayern München. There is also a national championship for representative teams of the 16 provincial associations. Over 2,000 women are registered with the Deutscher Fussball-Bund.

Italy is the only Latin country in Europe that has introduced women's soccer on a major scale. Many teams are heavily subsidized by consortiums, and professionalism is widespread. Because Italy's 1964 ban on imported players did not extend to women's organizations, players from as far away as Scotland have come to play. Many Italian teams regularly draw 10-20,000 spectators. In Belgium, women's soccer was recognized in

1971. Fifty clubs became affiliated with the Belgian association, and women's leagues were introduced. The same pattern has been followed in the Netherlands, Sweden, Denmark, and Switzerland. The Iceland F.A. recognized women's soccer in 1971, and inaugurated a women's competition in conjunction with the Icelandic Championship Tournament of Indoor Football, which is held annually during the Easter holiday. Poland's first unofficial Women's Football Championship was held in 1975 with 99 teams participating. In the Eastern European tradition, all teams in Poland are organized by *ognisko* (factory or office groups), rather than by existing men's clubs. The most successful Polish team has been TKKF Checz of Danzig. Less is known about women's competitions in other Eastern European states, but all have become well organized. Other than Czechoslovakia, women's soccer in Eastern Europe appears to have developed most completely in Yugoslavia, where teams such as Zenskog Nogometnog Kluba Union, ZNK Zagreb, and ZNK Ljubljana have been dominant forces in 1970s.

In Latin America, there is continued resistance to the growth of women's soccer. Paraguay has specifically banned women from playing at all, declaring that it is "against their natural femininity." Women players, however, have bravely coalesced their interests in Argentina, Brazil, and Venezuela. Guatemalan women have broken through traditional social barriers, and have introduced full-fledged league and cup competitions. Mexico became the first Latin American country to allow women's teams to affiliate with local associations. In 1971, a commercially sponsored unofficial World Championship for Women was held in Mexico City for representative teams from England, West Germany, France, Italy, Czechoslovakia, Denmark, and various Latin American states. The final, which drew 100,000 spectators to the Aztec Stadium, was won by Denmark.

In the Far East, interest in women's soccer has grown rapidly since the 1960s. Singapore, Taiwan, and Thailand were the first to give it official recognition, and Singapore, a hotbed of soccer activity in Asia, and Taiwan introduced league and cup competitions in the late 1960s. In South Vietnam, company teams were common until 1975, and in the same year, the Asian Football Confederation sanctioned the first Asian Women's Football Tournament in Hong Kong—the first of its kind anywhere—

for national teams of Asia and Australasia. The participants were Singapore, Malaysia, Thailand, Hong Kong, New Zealand, and Australia, with New Zealand emerging the winner. A second edition was held in 1977 in Bangkok, where the number of entrants was considerably larger and included Burma, Thailand, Malaysia, Indonesia, Hong Kong, Japan, South Korea, New Zealand, and Australia. New Zealand won the title again, and the runner-up was Thailand.

In New Zealand, a strong Northern Women's Football Association has been in operation on North Island since the early 1970s with two league divisions and a cup competition. The National Women's Soccer Association was founded in 1975, and has established numerous multi-divisional leagues on both North and South Island. The principal clubs are located in Christchurch, Auckland, Wellington, Taupo, Hamilton, Gisborne, Masterton, Palmerston, and Dunedin. A thriving Australian association has also been formed, and, despite New Zealand's successes in the Asian championship, its leading clubs, St. George, Blacktown Spurs, and Ingleburn RSL, have dominated New Zealand teams in international competition.

Women's soccer in the United States and Canada has not begun to reach the level of sponsorship or the standard of play found in Europe and Australasia. The highest level of women's soccer in the United States involves a handful of women's teams that are affiliated with semiprofessional men's clubs in leagues such as the Cosmopolitan Soccer League (formerly the German-American F.A.), located in the New York City area. The burgeoning youth soccer movement in North America has brought about the rapid growth of weekend leagues in most parts of the country, especially in the suburbs. Teams in this category are affiliated with the various local associations and not directly with the United States Soccer Federation. Two recently introduced organizations might prove to be the foundation for a nationally based women's association. The American Ladies' Soccer Organization was formed in 1974 in Los Angeles, and has grown to a membership of 13 teams with about 25 players each, but its scope appears to be confined to weekend teams in the Los Angeles area in spite of its name. A National Women's Soccer Association, based in Belleville, New Jersey, has also been organized, but its national aspirations have yet to be realized.

After several years of continuous growth, women's soccer has still not received the official blessing of FIFA. Efforts by the Italians and others to establish official international competitions have been thwarted, because, FIFA asserts, special rules for women have not been agreed upon by the International Board. Some special regulations have been adopted in Europe, however, and UEFA is in the process of organizing a continental-wide tournament. In most European countries, a full-sized ball is used (France has accepted youth-sized balls), and some women wear a stiff padding for protection under their jerseys. One change in the FIFA rules allows women to protect their chests with the forearm but only when lined up in a wall or to block a hard kick. In addition, women's games are usually divided into 35-minute halves. The Netherlands and Switzerland have an abundance of women referees, but this is a rarity elsewhere. The strongest national teams are generally thought to be England, Scotland, Denmark, and Sweden, though Italy, West Germany, France, Eire, Switzerland, the Netherlands, Belgium, Austria, Czechoslovakia, Yugoslavia, and others have also gained wide experience. Without a regularly scheduled international competition, however, the relative stature of women's soccer between countries will remain largely unknown.

World Championship—FIFA World Cup

Championnat du Monde-Coupe du Monde de la FIFA, Campeonato Mundial-Copa Mundial de la FIFA, Fussball-Weltmeisterschaft-FIFA-Weltpokal, Campeonato do Mundo-Copa do Mundo da FIFA, Campionato del Mondo-Coppa del Mondo della FIFA.

The World Cup, officially called the World Championship, is the premier showcase of world soccer, and during the postwar era it has eclipsed even the Olympic Games as the world's most captivating sporting event. Open to all FIFA members in good standing, the cup is held every four years midway between Olympiads. Its social significance beyond the sport itself cannot be underestimated, particularly in Europe, Latin America, and parts of Africa and Asia; in 1974 and 1978, a billion people around the world watched it on television via the most complex broadcasting networks ever devised.

Ten to 12 years in advance, the final rounds of each World Cup are assigned by FIFA to a single member-nation, which in turn selects five or six suitable venues in major population centers within its borders. Two years prior to the final rounds, a worldwide elimination procedure begins in which more than 100 nations give way to the final 16 qualifiers. The host country and defending champion automatically qualify. In recent years, so much pressure was put on FIFA by African, Asian, and Oceanian members to expand the final group to 24, thereby allowing a larger representation from the developing soccer nations, that such a rule was finally adopted for the 1982 edition.

The changes in FIFA's geographical allocation of openings for the final rounds are reflected in the following tables (number of finalists in parentheses):

1930 (13)	1934 (16)		1938 (15)	
All applicants qualified automatically, regardless of geographical origin.	Europe	12	Europe	11
	South America	2	(1 withdrawal)	
	North and		Europe-Africa	1
	Central America	1	Europe-Asia	1
	Africa and		South America	1
	Asia	1	North America	1
			(withdrew)	
			Central America	1
			Asia	1

1950 (13)		1954 (16)		1958 (16)	
Europe	6	Europe	10	Europe	11
(1 withdrawal)		Europe-Africa	1	Europe-Asia	1
Europe-Asia	2	Europe-Asia	1	South America	3
(1 withdrawal)		South America	2	North and	
South America	5	North and		Central America	1
North America	2	Central America	1		
Asia	1	Asia	1		
(withdrew)					

1962 (16)		1966 (16)		1970 (16)	
Europe	9	Europe	8	Europe	9
Europe-Asia	1	Europe-Asia	2	South America	3
South America	5	South America	4	CONCACAF	2
North and		CONCACAF	1	Africa	1
Central America	1	Asia-Oceania	1	Asia-Oceania	1

1974 (16)		1978 (16)	
Europe	9	Europe	9
Europe-		Europe-	
South America	1	South America	1
South America	3	South America	3
CONCACAF	1	CONCACAF	1
Africa	1	Africa	1
Asia-Oceania	1	Asia-Oceania	1

Recent allocations as reflected in the tables, especially from 1966 to the present, mirror the growth of modern regional confederations, the last of which (Oceania Football Confederation) was founded in 1966.

The concept of a world championship was first mentioned at the first FIFA Congress in Paris in 1904. It was proposed again at the 1920 Congress in Antwerp, and in 1924 FIFA delegates in Paris debated the proposal in some detail, as Uruguay was about to become the first non-European country to win the football tournament of the Olympic Games. Four years later, Uruguay repeated its victory, and the challenge to Europe could not be ignored. In addition, professionalism in Europe was by now widespread, and European nations could no longer send their best players to the Olympics. A competition was needed to allow the full international teams of each country to meet.

The Congress of 1928 in Amsterdam adopted a resolution to organize a world championship, by a vote of 25-5, and agreed the following year to begin the quadrennial series in 1930. Uruguay was chosen as the first host country in honor of its centenary and in recognition of its recent Olympic triumph. The primary instigators of the World Cup were Jules Rimet, president of FIFA from 1921-54 and president of the Fédération Française de Football, and Henri Delaunay, general secretary of the French federation. Their lobbying efforts and determination had been instrumental in World Cup debates throughout the 1920s.

FIFA regulations stipulated that FIFA was to provide a trophy, called the World Cup, for presentation to each winner of the World Championship. The national association of each winning country would retain the trophy under bond until the next winner became known, and the name of each winner would be engraved on the trophy—designed by the French sculptor Abel Lafleur. In 1946, FIFA officially named the trophy the Jules Rimet Cup. According to FIFA regulations, any country that won the World Championship three times was entitled to retain permanent possession of the cup. When Brazil reached this extraordinary plateau in 1970, the nine-pound, solid gold trophy was presented to the Confederação Brasileira de Desportos and put on public display at its headquarters in Rio de Janeiro. After 1970, a new trophy was designed in Italy, also of solid gold and standing 32 centimeters high, and was named the FIFA World Cup. Unlike its predecessor, the new World Cup remains the permanent possession of FIFA. Winners of the World Championship each receive a smaller replica of the trophy for their own use on a permanent basis. The replicas may be given, on their own, commemorative names in honor of individuals for services rendered to the game.

1930. The tempo and personality of the World Cup was firmly established at Montevideo in 1930. Security arrangements provided by the Uruguayan government were lavish: Cavalry regiments guarded the rapidly completed Centenary Stadium (planned capacity 100,000 but later reduced to 75,000). Soldiers with fixed bayonets were assigned to protect visiting teams, especially Argentina, and for two weeks a small nation of two million people became the center of world attention. Uruguay had been awarded the first World Championship over the vehement protest of nearly everyone, on the basis of two very convincing Olympic victories in 1924 and 1928—and by promising to underwrite all the travel and hotel expenses of its European guests. One by one, however, the major soccer powers of Europe dropped out, refusing to make the tedious, two-week voyage. The only participants were France, which was obliged to attend by Rimet and Delaunay, Belgium, Rumania, and Yugoslavia. The Uruguayans were outraged and insulted. Meanwhile, the four British countries had withdrawn from FIFA in 1928 over the issue of part-time payments to amateurs at the Amsterdam Olympic Games. Thus, none of Europe's strongest teams were present. South America, on the other hand, was represented by seven countries: Uruguay (the cup favorite), Brazil,

Chile, Bolivia, Paraguay, Peru, and mighty Argentina. North America was represented by a weak Mexico and a hulking group of naturalized Americans from England and Scotland.

Bizarre events filled the schedule, aggravated by disputes over refereeing. France was in hot pursuit of a goal against Argentina in the opening round, and would surely have equalized when the Brazilian referee, Almeida Rego, blew his whistle five minutes before the end of regulation time. Under vigorous protest, Rego remorsefully conceded his mistake and reassembled the players. Argentine inside left Cierro fainted at the thought of restarting. The tragically demoralized French team never regained its momentum, and lost the game. Four days later, five of Argentina's six goals against Mexico were scored by penalty kicks that were awarded, to everyone's embarrassment, by the Bolivian referee, Ulysses Saucedo.

Argentine players brutalized the opposition in their merciless defeat of Chile, and a full-scale melee broke out that was finally brought under control by the police. In the Argentina vs. USA semi-final, the famous Belgian referee, John Langenus—wearing his characteristic tie, knickers, and cap—cited an American for a foul, enraging the American trainer. In a fit of anger, the trainer ran onto the field in protest and hurled his medicine case onto the pitch, breaking a bottle of chloroform. The fumes consumed the unwary doctor, and he was helped from the field by sympathetic bystanders.

In the semi-finals, the clear superiority of Uruguay and Argentina was evident, though Yugoslavia and the USA had exceeded expectations in the opening round. The mammoth Centenary Stadium, which had opened only a few days before, provided a magnificent setting for the final, but it was under virtual siege by mounted police, ecstatic Uruguayan supporters, and the thousands of Argentines who had made their way across the Rio de la Plata in a variety of shipping vessels. At the half, Uruguay was losing by 2-1, but early in the second half its inside left Cea equalized, and left wing Iriarte put his team ahead ten minutes later. Uruguay's fourth goal was scored in the final seconds by replacement center forward Castro. The Uruguayans' extraordinary spirit and dazzling ball artistry had won the first World Championship. Nasazzi, Andrade, Scarone, Castro, and Cea became world heroes, and sealed Uruguay's claim to world domination and a memorable golden era. A national holiday was declared, and in Buenos Aires the Uruguayan consulate was assaulted and stoned by angry mobs.

1934. The second World Championship saw the rise of politics for the first time in both its staging and outcome. Italy, firmly under the bootstraps of Mussolini's myth of *machismo* and Fascist adventurism, lobbied vigorously to host the tournament, and won the honor by virtue of its widespread, first-class facilities. Indeed, all eight first round games were held in different cities. The dominant figure of Mussolini, who attended some of the matches, dictated the tone of the competition. This was to be a distinct advantage for the Italian team, whose members were filled with patriotic zeal. The mood was also dictated by the towering figures of the European game during the 1930s: Vittorio Pozzo, *Commissario Unico* of the Italian team, and Hugo Meisl, the guiding force of Austria's *Wunderteam*, now on the decline. Both men were authoritarian personalities whose national teams had reigned over Europe and were expected to meet in the final.

For the first time, there was a qualification round to determine the final 16 teams, but Latin American contenders felt left out and unfairly treated and the knockout format that FIFA had devised resulted in the departure of South America's two entrants—Argentina and Brazil—after playing only one match. Mexico, which failed to make the final 16 when it was eliminated by the USA in Rome one day before the opening ceremonies, returned home without competing. And few could forget that Uruguay, the holder, had refused to participate at all, piqued by its snub from the European dropouts in 1930. On the other hand, Egypt, which had eliminated Palestine in the qualification round, became Africa's first representative, adding further international flavor.

In the all-European quarter-finals, Italy was shocked by Spain and forced into a replay, eventually winning by a fluke goal. It was a tournament of three legendary goalkeepers: Spain's Zamora, Czechoslovakia's Plánička, and Italy's Combi—vying to undo the others' great reputations. In the end, the Spanish and Czech idols would retain their equal standing as the world's best, and Giampiero Combi would receive the World Cup as captain of the winning team.

In the semi-finals, Italy won a spirited contest over Austria, whose short-passing game was still a delight to watch, and Czechoslovakia defeated a strong German team. The Italian victory over Austria was noteworthy for the stamina Italy displayed after so short a rest from the Spanish replay, but it was also significant because the winning goal was scored by Guaita, one of Pozzo's three Argentine players of Italian parentage and dubious eligibility. Two of these players, Monti and Orsi, were undeniably world class in stature; Orsi's three goals during the competition and Guaita's goal against Austria collectively won the World Cup for Italy. In the final, Czechoslovakia, whose style was similar to the delicate movements of the Viennese game, was no match for the robust technique of Italy, whose players were not only stronger but possessed great skills of their own. Italy's 2-1 victory was achieved in overtime on a goal by center forward Schiavio, and Pozzo's desire to win the World Championship, as the political order had demanded, was fulfilled.

1938. Italy emerged as the major power of the 1930s in the third World Championship, while the number of qualifiers decreased from 29 to 22 countries, and Brazil surfaced at the front ranks of international competition. For the first time, the host country and holder received byes to the final rounds. The tournament was staged in France with matches in nine cities: Paris, Strasbourg, Le Havre, Toulouse, Marseilles, Reims, Lille, Bordeaux, and Antibes. The four British countries were invited to participate, despite their ineligibility as nonmembers of FIFA, but they declined. In addition, three important withdrawals occurred before the qualification rounds began: Argentina resented that it was rejected to host the competition, Austria had been overrun by Germany (though some of its players donned German uniforms), and Spain was in the throes of civil war. Asia was represented for the first time— by the Dutch East Indies, which had founded a separate national association with Holland's permission in 1930. Unfortunately, the East Indians were sent home after only one game because FIFA decided to retain its knockout format.

Italy returned with only two starters from 1934, but in Silvio Piola, greatest Italian center forward of all time, and the inside duo of Ferrari and the great Meazza, Vittorio Pozzo's team rendered a punishing forward line. Czechoslovakia, still experiencing one of its finest periods, put another magnificent side on the field, but lost its two biggest assets to injury in its 1-1 bloodbath with Brazil: Plánička, goalkeeper and captain, and Nejedly, the star of Sparta Prague and the goalscorer who had equalized in that game. Czechoslovakia fell out of the competition after suffering such important losses.

More than any other team, however, Brazil created the most dazzling spectacle of all. Its unforgettable 6-5 win over Poland after extra time was one of the great World Cup matches in history: The breathtaking center forward Leônidas played in his bare feet and scored four goals, only to be matched by Poland's Ernest Willimowski, who also scored four times. Sadly, Brazil's first match with Czechoslovakia in Bordeaux, the 1-1 draw, developed into a horrifying contest of brutality, which resulted in three ejections and numerous hospitalizations. Leônidas was left out of the semi-final match against Italy, and other mistakes lost the game for South America's only representative in the tournament.

The skillful Hungarian team, then practitioners of a less delicate Central European style than Austria or Czechoslovakia, was no match for the combined fortitude and skill of the Italians, who won the final, 4-2. Pozzo's superbly trained team was repeatedly challenged, but won its second World Championship in succession with two goals each from Piola and Colaussi. This was to be the best Italian team of all; few skeptics now questioned Italian superiority in international competition. Meanwhile, 84 goals in 18 games had produced the first genuinely exciting World Cup.

1950. In the fourth World Championship (the first Jules Rimet Cup), Brazil had the trophy in hand, but the cup slipped through its fingers. As the host country, it was justifiably proud of its incredible new stadium in Rio de Janeiro, the Maracanã, whose 200,000 seating capacity was the largest in the world. FIFA decided with some concern to award the games once again to South America, a worry that was borne out of the relatively few European countries to enter qualification rounds. Virtually all of Eastern and Central Europe, as well as Belgium, Holland, Denmark, Norway, and West Germany declined to participate. The four British countries, whose Home International Championship doubled as a qualification tournament, entered the competition for the first time. Argentina was again passed over by FIFA and refused to enter, but South America was still overly

represented by five countries. In Asia, India qualified after Burma forfeited, but withdrew suddenly for financial reasons. The lopsided list of participants was completed with two entrants from North America, Mexico, and the USA, which had qualified easily at the expense of Cuba.

FIFA at last decided to set up league competitions in the first round, but the plan was compromised by the elimination of knockout semi-finals and a final. Instead, a final pool (league) would include the four first round group winners, and the world champion would be decided on points. In the first round, the greatest upset in the history of international competition took place in Belo Horizonte, when the burly squad from the USA defeated hallowed England by 1-0. The goalscorer was a naturalized Haitian immigrant from New York named Larry Gaetjens, who was carried from the field on the shoulders of jubilant Brazilian fans. England, whose lack of preparation and experience in topflight international competition sealed its fate, never recovered from the shock and lost to Spain three days later, ending its first World Cup adventure.

The stars of the 1950 World Cup were Brazil's astounding front three, Ademir, Jair, and Zizinho. Between them they scored 11 of their team's 22 goals, and dazzled the crowds both on and off the field. The Brazilians battled their way to the final pool with fine wins over Mexico and Yugoslavia, but they stumbled along the way over a gallant Swiss team which held them to a 2-2 draw. Uruguay, meanwhile, had only to bury hapless Bolivia by 8-0 to reach the last stage. In the final pool, Sweden and Spain were swept away by Brazil, 7-1 and 6-1, respectively, but Uruguay gained only one point from Spain and had to struggle past a weakened Sweden.

On the final day of the competition, Brazil and Uruguay squared off before a world record crowd of 199,850 (the record stands to this day) at the giant Maracanã to determine whether Uruguay could stop Brazil's massive goalscoring power. Shortly after the start, it was apparent that Uruguay was prepared to accept the challenge, as the score remained 0-0 at the half after repeated Brazilian attacks. In the second half, frustration settled into the Brazilian squad, and Uruguay counterattacked with a goal apiece from Schiaffino and Ghiggia. Brazil's only goal, scored just after the half by right wing Friaca, stood alone at the end of 90 minutes, and little Uruguay, heroic in its response to an insurmountable situation, had won its second World Championship in as many tries. In Montevideo, eight deaths by heart attack were attributed to the extraordinary news.

1954. Though Switzerland was unprepared to take on the enormous burden of a World Cup, it seemed only fair that the home of FIFA should be given a chance, at least as a gesture in honor of its service to the game. The tournament produced a confusing mixture of attractive teams (at least a half dozen in all) and some of the ugliest international contests ever seen. For the second time in a row, the hands-down favorite was denied the championship in the final. A sensible format evolved that survives to the present time: four first round groups under a league system with quarter-final and semi-final rounds following on a knockout basis.

Hungary, led by Puskás, Hidegkuti, Kocsis, and the brightest array of world class stars ever assembled, went into the competition undefeated in four years and duly won its first round group with a 9-0 thrashing of South Korea and an astounding 8-3 win over West Germany. But the German manager, Sepp Herberger, with the cunning reminiscent of German folklore, had fielded mainly his reserves in that loss, hoping that Germany's true strength would not be revealed until later rounds. The outside favorites, Brazil, Uruguay, Austria, and England, also advanced to the quarter-finals, as did the host country, Switzerland, which had upset Italy in a bruising match that featured a Brazilian referee being chased off the field by Italian players.

The quarter-finals provided a plethora of goals and battered bodies. In Hungary vs. Brazil, the Hungarian captain Bozsik was sent off, as well as Brazil's Nilton Santos and Tozzi, and the ceaseless stoppages on the field punctuated a series of fights and hard kicks that came to be known as the "Battle of Berne." The rivalry between Austria and Switzerland took a bizarre turn during this round when Switzerland's famous tactical system, the "Swiss Bolt," cracked, and a total of 12 goals were scored by the two teams. The final tally, 7-5 in favor of Austria, achieved the all-time record for an aggregate score in World Cup final round competition.

In the semi-finals, Hungary and Uruguay met in one of the most memorable contests on record. Both teams displayed their contrasting styles in no uncertain terms, though Puskás remained injured after his first round confrontation with West Germany. Ultimately, Sandor (the "Golden Head") Kocsis headed in the two winning goals for Hungary, and Uruguay lost a World Cup game for the first time in its illustrious history. In the other semi-final, West Germany warmed up for its confrontation with Hungary by routing an Austrian team in poor form.

As the rain that had soaked much of the tournament swept through the stadium of Young Boys Berne, an over-confident Hungary took the field for the final against West Germany in anticipation of a well-deserved world championship. Ninety minutes later Hungary walked off in defeat, the winning goal being scored by German right winger Helmut Rahn, who had also put in the equalizer. Herberger's legendary gamble of fielding reserves in earlier rounds had paid off. No other manager in history has been given so much credit for winning a major international competition. An extraordinary tournament of highs and lows ended in a devastating anticlimax.

1958. By this time, the World Championship had achieved a stature of mammoth proportions. International television coverage had begun in 1954 (in Europe only), and the number of aspiring international powers continued to grow. South America had again been passed by, and Sweden, which had won the Olympic competition ten years before and proved itself a worthy opponent on any occasion, was chosen to host the games. For the first and only time, all four British countries qualified for the final rounds, Wales by eliminating Israel after East Germany withdrew, and the others by winning their qualification rounds. The Northern Irish had even knocked out mighty Italy to gain entry. Ironically, Wales and Northern Ireland advanced to the quarter-finals while England and Scotland faced early elimination.

The sixth World Championship also featured the USSR's maiden appearance, the return of Argentina, a resourceful comeback by Swedish veterans, and a display of French talent that became one of the hallmarks of the competition. Above all, 1958 was the year of Pelé, Garrincha, and Brazil. For years it had been apparent that Brazil was a veritable factory of great players. In Sweden the team came up with a tactical approach to match its artistry (the 4-2-4). In the first round, Brazil disposed of Austria and the USSR, but ran into trouble with the English defense and settled for a scoreless draw.

West Germany, France, and Sweden won

the other first round groups. The Swedish lineup gave home supporters a nostalgic look back to the Olympic gold medal team of 1948 with the appearance of aging forwards Gren and Liedholm, two-thirds of the famous Swedish front line that had also included the incomparable Gunnar Nordahl. Sweden's passage to the quarter-finals was rocky but demonstrative of a spirit that would carry it through to the final.

Meanwhile, Brazil, with at least eight players of world class stature, dazzled the Swedish crowds. Their incredible skills came to light in the first round game against the USSR. Immediately after the kickoff a shot from Garrincha hit the post, and, in the third minute, the gifted center forward Vavá scored. Though the scoring ended at a mere 2-0, Brazil continued to demonstrate its remarkable gifts throughout the match.

In the semi-final against France, it appeared that Brazil was firmly fixed on winning the cup. France was unfortunate to lose center half Jonquet to injury early in the game. His presence had been essential in thwarting the omnipresent Brazilian attack, and after his departure (with the score tied at 1-1), Pelé, Vavá, and Didi were relatively unimpeded in mounting their acrobatic attacks. Indeed, Pelé's hat trick firmly established him as the new wonder of modern soccer. Despite its 5-2 thrashing by Brazil, France characteristically went on to regain its form and bury West Germany in the third place game by 6-3.

Sweden, whose determination and skill took it through the quarter- and semi-finals, now faced an unstoppable Brazil in the final and its presence there was in itself a surprising achievement. On the field, Swedish forwards were effectively put out of service by Djalma Santos and Nilton Santos, while at the other end of the field, Pelé, Garrincha, Didi, and Vavá worked their miracles. Brazil's great 5-2 win in this game was an important event in postwar soccer annals, because it served to counterpoint the growing tendency in Europe toward defensive tactics and systems. Brazil's marvelously free-spirited attack kept alive the memory of attractive soccer for the next 12 years.

1962. Brazil's fame now preceded it. Pelé, the 17-year-old boy in Sweden who had wept for joy before all the world in 1958, was now a household word from Timbuktu to Omsk. The most impressive aspect of Brazil's rise to international preeminence was the depth of its talent. Were it not for the presence of Pelé, two or three other Brazilians would surely have occupied the limelight. It was a period of unrivaled productivity for Brazilian soccer.

Chile, which had recently been devastated by earthquakes, was chosen to host the seventh World Championship, simply because, as Chilean F.A. President Carlos Dittborn put it, "we have nothing else." The Chilean team, which had long been a middle-level soccer power in South America, responded by achieving its highest honor to date in taking third place in the competition. Brazil, Uruguay, Argentina, and Colombia rounded out the large South American contingent. With Western Europe entering an era of defensive tactics, it was up to Czechoslovakia and Yugoslavia (the latter making its fifth run for the World Cup), to carry the European banner to the semi-finals. Asia and Africa were unrepresented, as few of the emerging soccer nations could consider the long trip to the Pacific Coast of South America. The northern reaches of the Western Hemisphere were again represented by Mexico, still posing little threat in international competition.

Brazil suffered a tragic loss in its second game of the tournament against Czechoslovakia when Pelé pulled a muscle and had to drop out from the rest of the competition. Meanwhile, Colombia raced back from a 4-1 deficit with the overconfident Soviets to tie the match at 4-4 in the second half after some rare mistakes by the great goalkeeper Yashin. Colombia's goalscoring drive was formidable and had it not been for Yashin's recovery from complacency it might have won the game. In Group 2, the spirited Chileans fought with Italy in one of the uglier games of the competition (Chile's star outside left Leonel Sánchez broke Humberto Maschio's nose), but the home team, backed by frenetic crowds in the stands, upset *catenaccio*-laden Italy by 2-0.

Garrincha, Vavá, and others continued to maintain Brazil's momentum in the quarter- and semi-final rounds without the benefit of Pelé, but overall play was less inspired than in 1958. Indeed, by Brazil's standards, there had been some lackluster performances. Czechoslovakia exceeded its own expectations after finishing runner-up to Brazil in the first round, and found itself in the final with Brazil after eliminating stronger teams from Hungary and Yugoslavia. Brazil's 3-1 win over Czechoslovakia in the final was less than memorable—the winners played competently at best and the losers let the match get away by making too many defensive mistakes. While the superior team had won the World Championship for the second time in a row, there was an ominous joylessness that seemed to emerge from the Chilean tournament. It was difficult to determine whether Brazil's declining form was caused by the depressing atmosphere of Chile in mid-winter or, perhaps, the other way around.

1966. England was the host country, and the World Cup finally "came home." The mother country of modern soccer, which had barely provided one inspired performance in four championship series, discovered its role in this international spectacle for the first time. Excellent venues were plentiful and relatively close together; accommodations were adequate, and the tournament was organized with aplomb. The sport itself, on the other hand, was in a state of flux and uncertainty. While innovative tactical methods continued to suppress individual skills, the popularity of the game received new impetus from the growing number of countries participating in international competition. In 1966, global television coverage added to this growth immeasurably. Still, there were fewer attractive teams than ever before, and Brazil's aging veterans could not be counted on to repeat their 1958 performance.

The revitalized Hungarians and a flowing, skillful team from Portugal based on the great Lisbon club Benfica were the main attractions for students of attacking soccer. Italy was strong and talented, but its counterattacking style dominated action on the field, and it was more feared than enjoyed. Argentina, which had qualified for the final rounds again, was simply feared. West Germany, on the other hand, had begun to find a new style of play, distant from its traditional use of skilled confrontation, and entered the competition with the seeds of its great teams of the future. And England, with perhaps three players of rare ability, Bobby Charlton, Gordon Banks, and Bobby Moore, had been molded into a seasoned team by its new manager, Alf Ramsey; yet, its fate against the likes of Portugal and Brazil was the cause of great concern.

North Korea emerged from the first round as a genuine Cinderella team, having pushed Australia aside to qualify. After holding Chile to a 1-1 draw, North Korea startled Italy (entrenched in its customary defensive posture) by scoring off the foot of Pak Doo Ik in the first half. But when Italy attempted a comeback it discovered that the frenetic North Korean defense could not be penetrated. Italy returned home in defeat, subjected to highly publicized scenes of scorn and ridicule. In the quarter-finals against Portugal, North Korea led in the first half by an astounding 3-0, but Eusebio, perhaps the most gifted player in the tournament, led his team back to a 5-3 win by scoring four goals, two from the penalty spot.

Portugal defeated Hungary, and Hungary impressively swept by Brazil, which was now a shade of its former self. In Portugal vs. Brazil, Pelé was tackled harshly time after time, and eventually limped off the field and out of the tournament, deploring permissive refereeing and declaring that he would never play in a World Championship again. Eusebio's two goals won the game, and Brazil was eliminated. West Germany and England won their groups, and proceeded through the quarter- and semi-finals to the final.

England's morale was solid going into its confrontation with West Germany. Its semi-final win over Portugal proved to be one of the best matches of the competition, and both teams played their vastly differing styles without resorting to personal clashes. England's Charlton, Banks, and Moore were stable and instructive leaders who epitomized the cohesive spirit of Alf Ramsey's team. The Germans, with an equal but not superior array of talent, featured veterans Seeler and Schnellenger and a youthful Franz Beckenbauer, whose genius was already evident.

The final itself became the most controversial game in the history of international competition. In the first half, Haller scored for West Germany and England's Hurst equalized. In the second half, Peters put England ahead, and the championship appeared to be sewn up, but Weber equalized from the penalty spot after a questionable foul, and an agonizing overtime was forced. Ramsey called a meeting in the middle of the field, the whistle blew, and play was restarted. Hurst took a cross from Alan Ball and thumped a shot against the crossbar, sending the ball downward. England claimed the ball crossed the line; West Germany claimed it did not. The referee was unable to decide and appealed to the Russian linesman, who awarded the goal. The German players were devastated and demoralized, and a few moments later Hurst easily penetrated West Germany's exhausted defense to complete a hat trick, the first and only one to date in a World Cup final. Bobby Moore was handed the Jules Rimet Cup by the Queen, and years of endless debate over Hurst's second goal commenced. In England, Ramsey was knighted, and apologists pointed to that fourth English goal whenever nagging doubts were raised about the victory.

1970. Mexico was FIFA's enlightened choice to host the ninth World Championship, and it turned out to be a happy and festive affair, despite the high altitudes. The astonishingly beautiful Aztec Stadium in Mexico City, which had been built for the 1968 Olympic Games, held 110,000 spectators and served as the site of the final. Other matches were played in Toluca, Leon, Guadalajara, and Puebla.

Africa was represented (for the first time since 1934) by Morocco, which surprised the West Germans by its resourcefulness, and Asia was represented by Israel, a semi-Europeanized soccer nation that had long been a dominant force in Asian soccer. The favorites were Brazil, West Germany, England, and Italy. Of these, only England failed to reach the semi-finals. Peru, coached by Brazilian immortal Didi, featured an elegant style built around inside forward Cubillas, and emerged as the sensation of the tournament. El Salvador's tragic saga in reaching the final rounds was punctuated by no less than a full-scale military war with neighboring Honduras, known somewhat misleadingly as the "Fútbol War," which had been sparked by World Cup qualification matches between the two countries. Mexico, even as host, was not seriously in the running.

In the first round, England faced Brazil in a fine contest reminiscent of England vs. Portugal in 1966, with opposing styles producing a good game. Brazil won by 1-0, but both teams advanced to the quarter-finals. Italy, whose chances for success were placed squarely on the shoulders of striker Gigi Riva, much to his discontent, won Group 2 from Uruguay and Sweden by scoring only one goal. West Germany's prospects were maintained by winning Group 4. Included in West Germany's squad were the awesome Uwe Seeler and Gerd "der Bomber" Müller, the latter probably the most instinctive goalscoring artist of his generation. Brazil, however, entered the quarter-finals as the team to beat.

The major quarter-final confrontation occurred between West Germany and England. As in 1954, German coaching prowess was once again a decisive factor. With FIFA's new two-substitute rule in effect for the first time in the World Cup, Helmut Schön, the German manager, waited until England's defense became tired and brought on his superb winger, Jürgen Grabowski, who

was instrumental in bringing his team back from a 2-0 deficit to a 3-2 win. In the titanic struggle of the semi-final round, Italy and West Germany remained drawn at 1-1 at the end of regulation time, but in overtime five goals were scored, Müller trading off with Burgnich and Riva until Rivera finally put Italy into the final against Brazil.

Brazil's impressive victories over Czechoslovakia, England, Peru, and Uruguay showed it had regained a masterful touch since the debacle of 1966. Pelé, fortunately, had not retired after all, and, in fact, was at his peak. Jairzinho, Tostão, and Rivelino completed one of the greatest forward lines ever seen. Italy, led by the towering Giacinto Facchetti in the backfield, would have to rely on its man-to-man marking to contain what was virtually an all-attacking Brazilian team. The task was too great. Jairzinho pulled Italian defenders in all directions, and Tostão and Pelé threatened the goal repeatedly. All four Brazilian goals electrified the crowded stadium, and there was not a dry eye in the place. It was a never-to-be-forgotten performance, rendered all the more satisfying by Italy's admirable showing in the losing role.

The Jules Rimet Cup was made the permanent possession of the Brazilian Sports Confederation, and Brazil was immortalized as the apotheosis of modern soccer.

1974. The spectre of the Olympic tragedy in Munich in 1972 hung like a cloud over the tenth World Championship in West Germany. Security was extraordinary, but it was widely accepted as justifiable, given the current climate caused by international terrorism. An unusually large number of great soccer powers from the past were eliminated in qualification rounds, among them England, Austria, Hungary, Portugal, Spain, USSR, and Czechoslovakia, but two new international success stories were in the making: those of Poland and the Netherlands. Brazil without Pelé was an unknown quantity, as were aging Italy and unpredictable Yugoslavia, but some combination of these three would surely place high in the list of results. West Germany's European Football Championship win of 1972, a breathtaking performance of precision and intelligence, coupled with the homeside advantage, made it a slight favorite, but Holland was given a good chance with its sensational forward Johan Cruyff and a sophisticated style similar to that of West Germany. Chile participated in the tournament only because the USSR refused to play a qualification match in Santiago for political reasons.

The saddest disappointment of the competition was Brazil's decline. Despite its eventual fourth place finish, Brazil's rough, defensive tactics precipitated a serious backlash of sentiment in the wake of its glorious 1970 triumph. Indeed, Brazil did not play a single outstanding game in the tournament. Elsewhere, the first round featured narrow eliminations of Italy and Scotland on goal difference, a 9-0 thrashing of Zaire by Yugoslavia (tying Hungary's record against South Korea in 1954), and the politically significant first full international meeting of the two Germanys, producing West Germany's only loss in the competition. Holland, meanwhile, was in glowing form, and a German-Dutch final appeared likely.

Yugoslavia faltered in the semi-finals (which were restructured in 1974 as two groups of four teams, each playing under a point system), and lost all three matches to West Germany, Poland, and Sweden. Poland, however, advanced to a well-deserved berth in the third place game against Brazil. The Dutch, meanwhile, looked the best team in the competition after three consecutive shutouts over Brazil, East Germany, and Argentina. Holland played fluid, attacking soccer, and Cruyff, at once the orchestrator and spearhead, solidified his reputation as the most talented striker-midfielder in Europe. Poland, blessed with the largest array of first-class players in its history, seemed instinctive in its attack and played with a fluidity that closely resembled that of West Germany and Holland.

The final, drawing the largest television audience in history, was played by the two finest teams in the competition, West Germany and Holland, under the guidance of the two most complete players of the post-Pelé era, Beckenbauer and Cruyff. West Germany was as prepared as any team could be, its rumored differences before the start of the tournament well under wraps. The Dutch, backed by the public support of Queen Juliana and a unified country of supporters, had the crowds and most of the world's press behind them. Neeskens scored for Holland from the penalty spot only one minute into the game and before a German had even touched the ball. Twenty-four minutes later, Breitner converted a penalty for West Germany, and the Germans regained their balance. The Dutch relaxed, and two minutes before the half, Gerd Müller received a not-too-accurate cross from winger Grabowski on the run, pivoted with the ball, and inevitably, blasted it into the back of the net. In the second half, Holland regrouped to pressure the German defense for most of the duration, but its ceaseless playmaking was challenged by equal determination. With Cruyff neutralized, the score remained 2-1 at the final whistle.

For the second time in World Cup competition, West Germany had won the final over a more popular team. On the other hand, its combined European Championship win of 1972 and World Cup win of 1974 opened a new era of West German-dominated international competition. The great success of West German clubs in Europe during the same period added to its adopted role of leading soccer away from the dark days of *catenaccio*.

1978. Argentina successfuly staged the eleventh World Championship, an event viewed with fear and skepticism in European quarters, though the Argentine Football Association had been promised the games as early as 1966. The FIFA leadership, plagued by its guilt over rejecting Argentina's bid for so long, remained undaunted in its support of successive Argentine governments, as, one-by-one, each regime guaranteed a trouble-free competition. The unique position of Argentina as the birthplace of soccer in South America and its extraordinary record in South American competition, moreover, could not be overlooked. The unprecedented concern over the tournament's well-being reached a peak in 1976 when the president of the Argentine World Cup Organizing Committee, Retired General Omar Actis, was assassinated by guerrillas. The Argentines themselves, meanwhile, were nursing deeply felt regional jealousies after the five World Cup triumphs of neighboring Brazil and Uruguay. All of these factors helped to create an explosive yet dour atmosphere throughout the entire proceedings.

The competition was further dampened by the absence of the top stars of five participating countries, all of whom were established leaders of their respective teams: West Germany's Franz Beckenbauer (unreleased by his club), the Netherlands' Johan Cruyff (voluntary withdrawal), Italy's Giacinto Facchetti (voluntary withdrawal), Scotland's Danny McGrain (injury), and Brazil,'s Roberto Rivelino (injury), though Rivelino appeared briefly and stunningly in two games. Argentina, by virtue of its home support, joined Brazil, the Netherlands, and West

Germany in the list of favorites. Italy could not be discounted, and the fluid and engaging French were highly regarded and immensely popular. Scotland, whose qualifications at the expense of Wales was the gift of a referee's mistake, and Poland were given an outside chance of reaching the final.

In the first round, attention was focused on Group 1, the toughest first round clustering since Group 4 in 1958. Under manager César Luis Menotti, Argentina defied its detractors, and settled into a less physical style than opponents had experienced for many years. Opting instead for breakneck speed and an aggressive attack, Argentina seemed the team to beat after its exciting defeat of France, and, in spite of a loss to Italy, the home team raced inexorably into the semi-finals. The Italians also advanced and won many new friends by playing a more attacking and open style than they had played since the 1940s. In Group 2, West Germany was barely recognizable without Beckenbauer, and Poland escaped as the leader of a weak group after three lackluster games. Tunisia became the surprise of the competition by rolling over hapless Mexico and holding the world champion West Germans to a scoreless draw. This was surely the finest team ever to have come out of Africa, and it finished deservedly with the best record in the bottom eight.

In Group 3, Austria gained some surprising results, but Brazil looked depressed by its internal squabbling, the loss of Rivelino, and uncomfortable conditions in a hostile country. In Group 4, Peru was another first round sensation, eliminating not only the pathetic Scots but outplaying the up-and-down Dutch as well. The Netherlands, whose team without Cruyff, Geels, and van Hanegem still looked capable of defeating any opposition in the tournament, was enigmatic at best. Scotland was rocked by a major international scandal when left winger Willie Johnston was permanently banned from international competition for taking an illegal medicine. After weak performances against Peru and Iran, Scotland went home in disgrace, though it had demonstrated its real strength by defeating the Dutch after it was too late.

The semi-finals saw the decline and collapse of first round upstarts Austria and Peru, further mediocre showings by West Germany and Brazil, and Italy's return to defensive tactics and a familiar loss of finishing power. Above all, however, Argentina established an inviolability in the semi-finals that few thought possible—other than the Argentines themselves. Attacking left midfielder Mario Kempes emerged as the most exciting player of the competition, and the team as a whole showed strength on all parts of the field. Its 6-0 thrashing of Peru, which put undefeated Brazil out of the final on goal difference, was a model of precision and, in a larger sense, the climax of Argentina's seething frustration after years of poor treatment in the world press. It was, indeed, the most significant game ever played by an Argentine team, and, regardless of the outcome in the final, it reinstated Argentina among the upper ranks of world powers. In the other semi-final group, the Dutch rediscovered their lost genius in a 5-1 defeat of Austria, and outclassed the West Germans in a replay of the 1974 final, though the stalwart German defense held them to a draw. A convincing win over Italy put Holland in the World Cup final against a home country for the second time in a row.

Fifty years after it had lost the replay of the Olympic final to archrival Uruguay—in distant Amsterdam—Argentina won its first World Cup in a blaze of glory. The Estadio Monumental (the site of a tragic riot exactly ten years earlier in which 74 spectators lost their lives) provided the setting for a blinding maelstrom of confetti and the unleashing of a nation's collective pride. The purpose of this ritualistic gathering was made abundantly clear from the beginning: to set right an aging injustice. The potential violence of the exercise surfaced even before the opening kickoff, and, indeed, the game evolved into one of the stormiest World Cup finals on record.

The Netherlands fielded what appeared to be a 3-4-3 formation, though elements of the systemless "total football" were also evident. The premier Dutch striker, Robby Rensenbrink, missed several sure goals in the first and second halves—simply by shooting off target—and these ultimately became the Netherlands' only real opportunities to win the match. Argentina won the championship with stellar performances by goalkeeper Fillol, defender Galvan, right wing Bertoni, and the heroic Mario Kempes. Seldom has a whole nation owed so much joy and celebration to one individual as Argentina owed to Kempes. He scored Argentina's first goal before the half with aggressive footwork in a goalmouth tussle for the ball, and, in extra time, after the Dutch substitute Nanninga had headed the equalizer late in the second half, he created and scored the winning goal by cleverly piercing the Dutch defense. In the second extra time period, he seemed set for a third goal but after breaking through the defense yet again, he pushed the ball to Bertoni, who scored the clincher. The Netherlands, which appeared more determined in this effort than in the 1974 final, became the first country ever to lose back-to-back World Cup finals—sad compensation for a small nation that in the previous decade had contributed so much to the game.

The 1982 World Championship will be held in Spain and the 1986 edition is scheduled for Colombia, although much doubt remains over that country's ability to organize it alone. Among the 1990 applicants are the Soviet Union and the United States.

		First	Second	Third	Fourth
Winners	1930	Uruguay	Argentina	--	--
	1934	Italy	Czechoslovakia	Germany	Austria
	1938	Italy	Hungary	Brazil	Sweden
	1950	Uruguay	Brazil	Sweden	Spain
	1954	Germany FR	Hungary	Austria	Uruguay
	1958	Brazil	Sweden	France	Germany FR
	1962	Brazil	Czechoslovakia	Chile	Yugoslavia
	1966	England	Germany FR	Portugal	USSR
	1970	Brazil	Italy	Germany FR	Uruguay
	1974	Germany FR	Netherlands	Poland	Brazil
	1978	Argentina	Netherlands	Brazil	Italy

Cumulative Ranking (1930-78)
(number of editions in parentheses)

		P	W	D	L	F	A	P
1	Brazil (11)	52	33	10	9	115	58	76
2	Germany FR (9)*	47	28	9	10	110	68	65
3	Italy (9)	36	20	6	10	62	40	46
4	Uruguay (7)	29	14	5	10	57	39	33
5	Argentina (6)	29	14	5	10	55	43	33
6	Hungary (7)	26	13	2	11	73	42	28
7	Sweden (6)	28	11	6	11	48	46	28
8	England (6)	24	10	6	8	34	28	26
9	Yugoslavia (6)	25	10	5	10	45	34	25
10	USSR (4)	19	10	3	6	30	21	23
11	Poland (3)	14	9	1	4	27	17	19
12	Netherlands (4)	16	8	3	5	32	19	19
13	Austria (4)	18	9	1	8	33	36	19
14	Czecho-slovakia (6)	22	8	3	11	32	36	19
15	Chile (5)	18	7	3	8	23	24	17
16	Spain (5)	18	7	3	8	22	25	17
17	France (7)	20	8	1	11	43	38	17
18	Switzerland (6)	18	5	2	11	28	44	12
19	Portugal (1)	6	5	0	1	17	8	10
20	Mexico (8)	24	3	4	17	21	62	10

21	Peru (3)	12	4	1	7	17	25	9
22	Scotland (4)	11	2	4	5	12	21	8
23	German DR (1)	6	2	2	2	5	5	6
24	Paraguay (3)	7	2	2	3	12	19	6
25	USA (3)	7	3	0	4	12	21	6
26	Wales (1)	5	1	3	1	4	4	5
27	Northern Ireland (1)	5	2	1	2	6	10	5
28	Rumania (4)	8	2	1	5	12	17	5
29	Bulgaria (4)	12	0	4	8	9	29	4
30	Tunisia (1)	3	1	1	1	3	2	3
31	Cuba (1)	3	1	1	1	5	12	3
32	Korea DPR (1)	4	1	1	2	5	9	3
33	Belgium (5)	9	1	1	7	12	25	3
34	Turkey (1)	3	1	0	2	10	11	2
35	Israel (1)	3	0	2	1	1	3	2
36	Morocco (1)	3	0	1	2	2	6	1
37	Australia (1)	3	0	1	2	0	5	1
38	Colombia (1)	3	0	1	2	5	11	1
39	Iran (1)	3	0	1	2	2	8	1
40	Norway (1)	1	0	0	1	1	2	0
41	Egypt (1	1	0	0	1	2	4	0
42	Dutch East Indies (1)	1	0	0	1	0	6	0
43	Korea Republic (1)	2	0	0	2	0	16	0
44	El Salvador (1)	3	0	0	3	0	9	0
45	Haiti (1)	3	0	0	3	2	14	0
46	Zaire (1)	3	0	0	3	0	14	0
47	Bolivia (2)	3	0	0	3	0	16	0

*includes prewar Germany

Scoring Leaders

1930 Stabile (Argentina) 8, Cea (Uruguay) 5, Subiabre (Chile) 4

1934 Nejedly (Czechoslovakia) 5, Conen (Germany) and Schiavio (Italy) 4

1938 Leônidas (Brazil) 7, Sarosi (Hungary) Piola (Italy) and Willimowski (Poland) 5

1950 Ademir (Brazil) 9, Schiaffino (Uruguay) 5

1954 Kocsis (Hungary) 11, Morlock (Germany FR) Hügi (Switzerland) and Probst (Austria) 6

1958 Fontaine (France) 13, Rahn (Germany FR) and Pelé (Brazil) 6

1962 Albert (Hungary) Garrincha (Brazil) Ivanov (USSR) Jerkovic (Yugoslavia) Sánchez (Chile) and Vavá (Brazil) 4

1966 Eusebio (Portugal) 9, Haller (Germany FR) 6

1970 Müller (Germany FR) 10, Jairzinho (Brazil) 7, Cubillas (Peru) 6

1974 Lato (Poland) 7, Szarmach (Poland) and Neeskens (Netherlands) 5

1978 Kempes (Argentina) 6, Rensenbrink (Netherlands) and Cubillas (Peru) 5

Miscellaneous Records and Statistics

Brazil is the only country to appear in all 11 final rounds (1930-78).

Most consecutive undefeated games in the final rounds: 13, by Brazil, in 1958 (6), 1962

(6), and 1966 (1), ending with a 3-1 defeat by Hungary. Two of the 13 games were drawn.

Biggest win in a World Cup match (including qualification rounds): Germany FR 12, Cyprus 0, 1969.

Biggest win in final rounds: Hungary 9, Korea Republic 0, 1954; Yugoslavia 9, Zaire 0, 1974.

Highest aggregate score in a final round match: 12; Austria 7, Switzerland 5, 1954.

Highest number of goals by a single country in one edition of the final rounds: 27 by Hungary in 1954.

Most final rounds appeared in by an individual: 5, by Mexico's Antonio Carbajal (1950, 1954, 1958, 1962, 1966).

Goalscoring record by an individual in one edition of the final rounds: 13, by Fontaine (France) in 1958.

Highest individual score in a final: 3, by Hurst (England) in 1966.

Eight players have scored a record four goals in a single game during the final rounds: Leônidas for Brazil vs. Poland in 1938, Willimowski for Poland in the same game, Wetterstroem for Sweden vs. Cuba in 1938, Schiaffino for Uruguay vs. Bolivia in 1950, Ademir for Brazil vs. Sweden in 1950, Kocsis for Hungary vs. Germany FR in 1954, Fontaine for France vs. Germany FR in 1958, and Eusebio for Portugal vs. Korea DPR in 1966.

Twenty players have scored hat tricks in a single game during the final rounds: Stabile for Argentina vs. Mexico in 1930, Cea for Uruguay vs. Yugoslavia in 1930, Schiavio for Italy vs. USA in 1934, Conen for Germany vs. Belgium in 1934, Schiavio for Italy vs. USA in 1934, Conen for Germany vs. Belgium in 1934, Szengeller for Hungary vs. Sweden in 1938, Cremaschi for Chile vs. USA in 1950, Kocsis for Hungary vs. Korea Republic in 1954, Burhan for Turkey vs. Korea Republic in 1954, Morlock for Germany FR vs. Turkey in 1954, Probst for Austria vs. Czechoslovakia in 1954, Borges for Uruguay vs. Scotland in 1954, Wagner for Austria vs. Switzerland in 1954, Fontaine for France vs. Paraguay in 1958, Pelé for Brazil vs. France in 1958, Jerkovic for Yugoslavia vs. Colombia in 1962, Albert for Hungary vs. Bulgaria in 1962, Hurst for England vs. Germany FR in 1966, Müller (twice) for Germany FR vs. Bulgaria and Peru in 1970, Bajevic for Yugoslavia vs. Zaire in 1974, Szarmach for Poland vs. Haiti in 1974, Rensenbrink for Netherlands vs. Iran in 1978, and Cubillas for Peru vs. Iran in 1978.

In eight of 11 finals, the eventual winner has been behind at some point during the game. The exceptions were 1938, and 1970, and 1978.

In the confrontation for world supremacy between Europe and Latin America, the following records have been compiled by European and Latin American countries in playing against each other in World Cup competition (final rounds only):

	P	W	D	L	F	A	P
Europe	118	50	22	46	206	185	122
Latin America	118	46	22	50	185	206	114

Goal Totals and Averages

	Games	Goals	Average		Games	Goals	Average
1930	18	70	3.88	1962	32	89	2.78
1934	17	70	4.12	1966	32	89	2.78
1938	18	84	4.67	1970	32	95	2.97
1950	22	88	4.00	1974	38	97	2.55
1954	26	140	5.38	1978	38	102	2.68
1958	35	126	3.60		308	1050	3.58

Results

1930 (in Uruguay)

Group 1

France	4	Mexico	1
(Laurent, Langiller, Maschinot 2)		(Carreno)	
Argentina	1	France	0
(Monti)			
Chile	3	Mexico	0
(Vidal, Subiabre 2)			
Chile	1	France	0
(Subiabre)			
Argentina	6	Mexico	3
(Stabile 3 pen,		(Lopez, Rosas F, Rosas M)	
Varallo 2 pen, Zumelzu)			
Argentina	3	Chile	1
(Stabile 2, Evaristo M)		(Subiabre)	

	P	W	D	L	F	A	P
Argentina	3	3	0	0	10	4	6
Chile	3	2	0	1	5	3	4
France	3	1	0	2	4	3	2
Mexico	3	0	0	3	4	13	0

Group 2

Yugoslavia	2	Brazil	1
(Tirnanic, Beck)		(Neto)	
Yugoslavia	4	Bolivia	0
(Beck 2, Marianovic,			
Vujadinovic)			
Brazil	4	Bolivia	0
(Visintainer 2, Neto 2)			

	P	W	D	L	F	A	P
Yugoslavia	2	2	0	0	6	1	4
Brazil	2	1	0	1	5	2	2
Bolivia	2	0	0	2	0	8	0

Group 3

Rumania	3	Peru	1
(Staucin 2, Barbu)		(Souza)	
Uruguay	1	Peru	0
(Castro)			
Uruguay	4	Rumania	0
(Dorado, Scarone,			
Anselmo, Cea)			

	P	W	D	L	F	A	P
Uruguay	2	2	0	0	5	0	4
Rumania	2	1	0	1	3	5	2
Peru	2	0	0	2	1	4	0

Group 4

USA	3	Belgium	0
(McGhee 2, Patenaude)			
USA	3	Paraguay	0
(Patenaude 2, Florie)			
Paraguay	1	Belgium	0
(Pena)			

	P	W	D	L	F	A	P
USA	2	2	0	0	6	0	4
Paraguay	2	1	0	1	1	3	2
Belgium	2	0	0	2	0	4	0

Semi-Finals

Argentina	6	USA	1
(Monti, Scopelli,		(Brown)	
Stabile 2, Peucelle 2)			
Uruguay	6	Yugoslavia	1
(Cea 3, Anselmo 2, Iriarte)		(Seculic)	

Final (in Montevideo; att. 90,000)

Uruguay	4	Argentina	2
(Dorado, Cea, Iriarte, Castro)		(Peucelle, Stabile)	

Uruguay: Ballesteros; Nasazzi, Mascheroni; Andrade, Fernandez, Gestido; Dorado, Scarone, Castro, Cea, Iriarte
Argentina: Botosso; Della Torre, Paternoster; Evaristo J, Monti, Suárez; Peucelle, Varallo, Stabile, Ferreira, Evaristo M

1934 (In Italy)

First Round

Italy	7	USA	1
(Schiavio 3, Orsi 2,		(Donelli)	
Meazza, Ferrari)			
Czechoslovakia	2	Rumania	1
(Puc, Nejedly)		(Dobai)	
Germany	5	Belgium	2
(Conen 3, Kobierski 2)		(Voorhoof 2)	
Austria	3	France	2
(Sindelar, Schall, Bican)		(Nicolas, Verriest pen)	

-after extra time-

Spain	3	Brazil	1
(Iraragorri pen, Langara 2)		(Silva)	
Switzerland	3	Netherlands	2
(Kielholz 2, Abegglen)		(Smit, Vente)	
Sweden	3	Argentina	2
(Jonasson 2, Kroon)		(Belis, Galateo)	
Hungary	4	Egypt	2
(Teleky, Toldi 2, Vincze)		(Gawzi 2)	

Second Round

Germany	2	Sweden	1
(Hohmann 2)		(Dunker)	
Austria	2	Hungary	1
(Horwath, Zischek)		(Sarosi pen)	
Italy	1	Spain	1
(Ferrari)		(Regueiro)	

-after extra time-

Replay:

Italy	1	Spain	0
(Meazza)			
Czechoslovakia	3	Switzerland	2
(Svobada, Sobotka, Nejedly)		(Kieholz, Abegglen)	

Semi-Finals

Czechoslovakia	3	Germany	1
(Nejedly 2, Krcil)		(Noack)	
Italy	1	Austria	0
(Guaita)			

Third Place Game

Germany	3	Austria	2
(Lehner 2, Conen)		(Horwath, Seszta)	

Final (in Rome; att. 55,000)

Italy	2	Czechoslovakia	1
(Orsi, Schiavio)		(Puc)	

-after extra time-

Italy: Combi; Monzeglio, Allemandi; Ferraris, Monti, Bertolini; Guaita, Meazza, Schiavio, Ferrari, Orsi
Czechoslovakia: Plánička; Zenišek, Ctyroky; Kostalek, Cambal, Krcil; Junek, Svoboda, Sobotka, Nejedly, Puc

1938 (In France)

First Round

Switzerland	1	Germany	1
(Abegglen)		(Gauchel)	

-after extra time-

Replay:

Switzerland	4	Germany	2
(Wallaschek, Bickel, Abegglen 2)		(Hahnemann, Loertscher o.g.)	
Cuba	3	Rumania	3
(Tunas, Maquina, Sosa)		(Covaci, Baratki, Dobai)	

-after extra time-

Replay:

Cuba	2	Rumania	1
(Socorro, Maquina)		(Dobai)	
Hungary	6	Dutch East Indies	0
(Kohut, Toldi, Sarosi 2, Zsengeller 2)			
France	3	Belgium	1
(Veinante, Nicolas 2)		(Isemborghs)	
Czechoslovakia	3	Netherlands	0
(Kostalek, Boucek, Nejedly)			

-after extra time-

Brazil	6	Poland	5
(Leônidas 4, Peracio, Romeu)		(Willimowski 4, Piontek)	
Italy	2	Norway	1
(Ferrari, Piola)		(Brustad)	

-after extra time-

Second Round

Sweden	8	Cuba	0
(Andersson, Jonasson, Wetterström 4, Nyberg, Keller)			
Hungary	2	Switzerland	0
(Zsengeller 2)			
Italy	3	France	1
(Colaussi, Piola 2)		(Heisserer)	
Brazil	1	Czechoslovakia	1
(Leônidas)		(Nejedly pen)	

-after extra time-

Replay:

Brazil	2	Czechoslovakia	1
(Leônidas, Roberto)		(Kopecky)	

Semi-Finals

Italy	2	Brazil	1
(Colaussi, Meazza pen)		(Romeu)	
Hungary	5	Sweden	1
(Zsengeller 3, Titkos, Sarosi)		(Nyberg)	

Third Place Game

Brazil	4	Sweden	2
(Romeu, Leônidas 2, Peracio)		(Jonasson, Nyberg)	

Final (in Paris; att. 65,000)

Italy	4	Hungary	2
(Colaussi 2, Piola 2)		(Titkos, Sarosi)	

Italy: Olivieri; Foni, Rava; Serantoni, Andreolo, Locatelli; Biavati, Meazza, Piola, Ferrari, Colaussi

Hungary: Szabo; Polger, Biro, Szalay, Szucs, Lazar; Sas, Vincze, Sarosi, Zsengeller, Titkos

1950 (in Brazil)

Group 1

Brazil	4	Mexico	0
(Ademir 2, Jair, Baltazar)			
Yugoslavia	3	Switzerland	0
(Tomasevic 2, Ognanov)			
Yugoslavia	4	Mexico	1
(Bobek, Cajkowski 2, Tomasevic)		(Casarin)	
Brazil	2	Switzerland	2
(Alfredo, Baltazar)		(Fatton, Tamini)	
Brazil	2	Yugoslavia	0
(Ademir, Zizinho)			
Switzerland	2	Mexico	1
(Bader, Fatton)		(Velasquez)	

	P	W	D	L	F	A	P
Brazil	3	2	1	0	8	2	5
Yugoslavia	3	2	0	1	7	3	4
Switzerland	3	1	1	1	4	6	3
Mexico	3	0	0	3	2	10	0

Group 2

Spain	3	USA	1
(Basora 2, Zarra)		(Souza J)	
England	2	Chile	0
(Mortensen, Mannion)			
USA	1	England	0
(Gaetjens)			
Spain	2	Chile	0
(Basora, Zarra)			
Spain	1	England	0
(Zarra)			
Chile	5	USA	2
(Robledo, Cremaschi 3, Prieto)		(Pariani, Souza J)	

	P	W	D	L	F	A	P
Spain	3	3	0	0	6	1	6
England	3	1	0	2	2	2	2
Chile	3	1	0	2	5	6	2
USA	3	1	0	2	4	8	2

Group 3

Sweden	3	Italy	2
(Jeppson 2, Andersson)		(Carapellese, Muccinelli)	
Sweden	2	Paraguay	2

(Sundqvist, Palmer)   (Lopez A, Lopez F)
Italy   2   Paraquay   0
(Carapellese, Pandolfini)

	P	W	D	L	F	A	P
Sweden	2	1	1	0	5	4	3
Italy	2	1	0	1	4	3	2
Parguay	2	0	1	1	2	4	1

Group 4
Uruguay   8   Bolivia   0
(Schiaffino 4, Miquez 2,
Vidal, Ghiggia)

	P	W	D	L	F	A	P
Uruguay	1	1	0	0	8	0	2
Bolivia	1	0	0	1	0	8	0

Final Pool

Uruguay   2   Spain   2
(Ghiggia, Varela)   (Basora 2)
Brazil   7   Sweden   1
(Ademir 4, Chico 2, Maneca)   (Andersson pen)
Uruguay   3   Sweden   2
(Ghiggia, Miguez 2)   (Palmer, Sundqvist)
Brazil   6   Spain   1
(Jair 2, Chico 2, Zizinho, Parra o.g.)   (Igoa)
Sweden   3   Spain   1
(Johnsson, Mellberg, Palmer)   (Zarra)
Uruguay)   2   Brazil   1
(Schiaffino, Ghiggia)   (Friaca)

	P	W	D	L	F	A	P
Uruguay	3	2	1	0	7	5	5
Brazil	3	2	0	1	14	4	4
Sweden	3	1	0	2	6	11	2
Spain	3	0	1	2	4	11	1

Uruguay: Maspoli; Gonzales, Tejera; Gambretta, Varela, Andrade; Ghiggia, Perez, Miguez, Schiaffino, Moran
Brazil: Barbosa; Augusto, Juvenal; Bauer, Banilo, Bigode; Friaca, Zizinho, Ademir, Jair, Chico

1954 (in Switzerland)

Group 1
Yugoslavia   1   France   0
(Milutinovic)
Brazil   5   Mexico   0

(Baltazar, Didi, Pinga 2, Julinho)

France					3	Mexico	2
(Vincent, Cardenas o.g., Kopa pen)						(Naranjo, Balcazar)	
Brazil					1	Yugoslavia	1
(Didi)						(Zebec)	

	P	W	D	L	F	A	P
Brazil	2	1	1	0	6	1	3
Yugoslavia	2	1	1	0	2	1	3
France	2	1	0	1	3	3	2
Mexico	2	0	0	2	2	8	0

Group 2

Hungary					9	Korea Rep	0
(Czibor, Kocsis 3,							
Puskás 2, Lantos, Palotas 2)							
Germany FR					4	Turkey	1
(Klodt, Morlock, Schaefer, Walter 0)						(Suat)	
Hungary					8	Germany FR	3
(Hidegkuti 2, Kocsis 4, Puskás, Toth)						(Pfaff, Hermann, Rahn)	
Turkey					7	Korea Rep	0
(Burhan 3, Erol, Lefter, Suat 2)							

	P	W	D	L	F	A	P
Hungary	2	2	0	0	17	3	4
Germany FR	2	1	0	1	7	9	2
Turkey	2	1	0	1	8	4	2
Korea Rep	2	0	0	2	0	16	0

Play-off:

Germany FR					7	Turkey	2
Morlock 3, Walter 0,						(Mustafa, Lefter)	
Walter F, Schaefer 2)							

Group 3

Austria					1	Scotland	0
(Probst)							
Uruguay					2	Czechoslovakia	0
(Miguez, Schiaffino)							
Austria					5	Czechoslovakia	0
(Stojaspal 2, Probst 3)							
Uruguay					7	Scotland	0
(Borges 3, Miquez 2, Abbadie 2)							

	P	W	D	L	F	A	P
Uruguay	2	2	0	0	9	0	4
Austria	2	2	0	0	6	0	4
Czechoslovakia	2	0	0	2	0	7	0
Scotland	2	0	0	2	0	8	0

Group 4

England	4	Belgium	4
(Broadis 2, Lofthouse 2)		(Anoul 2, Coppens, Dickinson o.g.)	

-after extra time-

Switzerland	2	Italy	1
(Ballaman, Hügi)		(Boniperti)	
England	2	Switzerland	0
(Mullen, Wilshaw)			
Italy	4	Belgium	1
(Pandolfini pen, Galli, Frignani, Lorenzi)		(Anoul)	

	P	W	D	L	F	A	P
England	2	1	1	0	6	4	3
Switzerland	2	1	0	1	2	3	2
Italy	2	1	0	1	5	3	2
Belgium	2	0	1	1	5	8	1

Play-off:

Switzerland	4	Italy	1
(Hügi 2, Ballaman, Fatton)		(Nesti)	

Quarter-Finals

Germany FR	2	Yugoslavia	0
(Horvat o.g., Rahn)			
Hungary	4	Brazil	2
(Hidegkuti, Kocsis 2, Lantos pen)		(Santos D pen, Julinho)	
Austria	7	Switzerland	5
(Koerner A 2, Ocwirk, Wagner 3, Probst)		(Ballaman 2, Hügi 2, Hanappi o.g.)	
Uruguay	4	England	2
(Borges, Varela, Schiaffino, Ambrois)		(Lofthouse, Finney)	

Semi-Finals

Germany FR	6	Austria	1
(Schaefer, Morlock, Walter F 2 pens, Walter 0 2)		(Probst)	
Hungary	4	Uruguay	2
(Czibor, Hidegkuti, Kocsis 2)		(Hohberg 2)	

-after extra time-

Third Place Game

Austria	3	Uruguay	1
(Stojaspal pen, Cruz o.g., Ocwirk)		(Hohberg)	

Final (in Berne, att. 55,000)

Germany FR	3	Hungary	2
(Morlock, Rahn 2)		(Puskás, Czibor)	

Germany FR: Turek; Posipal, Kohlmeyer; Eckel, Liebrich, Mai; Rahn, Morlock, Walter O, Walter F, Schaefer

Hungary: Grosics; Buzanszky, Lantos; Bozsik, Lorant, Zakarias; Czibor, Kocsis, Hidegkuti, Puskás, Toth

1958 (in Sweden)

Group 1

Germany FR (Rahn 2, Schmidt)	3	Argentina (Corbatta)	1
Northern Ireland (Cush)	1	Czechoslovakia	0
Germany FR (Schaefer, Rahn)	2	Czechoslovakia (Dvorak pen, Zikan)	2
Argentina (Corbatta 2 (1 pen), Menendez)	3	Northern Ireland (McParland)	1
Germany FR (Rahn, Seeler)	2	Northern Ireland (McParland 2)	2
Czechoslovakia (Dvorak, Zikan 2, Feureisl, Hovorka 2)	6	Argentina (Corbatta)	1

	P	W	D	L	F	A	P
Germany FR	3	1	2	0	7	5	4
Czechoslovakia	3	1	1	1	8	4	3
Northern Ireland	3	1	1	1	4	5	3
Argentina	3	1	0	2	5	10	2

Play-off

Northern Ireland (McParland 2)	2	Czechoslovakia (Zikan)	1

-after extra time-

Group 2

France (Fontaine 3, Piantoni, Kopa, Wisnieski, Vincent)	7	Paraguay (Amarilla 2 (1 pen) Romero)	3
Yugoslavia (Petakovic)	1	Scotland (Murray)	1
Yugoslavia (Petakovic, Veselinovic 2)	3	France (Fontaine 2)	2
Paraguay (Aguero, Re, Parodi)	3	Scotland (Mudie, Collins)	2
France (Kopa, Fontaine)	2	Scotland (Baird)	1
Yugoslavia (Ognjanovic, Rajkov, Veselinovic)	3	Paraguay (Parodi, Aguero, Romero	3

	P	W	D	L	F	A	P
France	3	2	0	1	11	7	4
Yugoslavia	3	1	2	0	7	6	4
Paraguay	3	1	1	1	9	12	3
Scotland	3	0	1	2	4	6	1

Group 3

Sweden	3	Mexico	0

(Simonsson 2, Liedholm pen)

Hungary	1	Wales	1

(Bozsik)   (Charles J)

Wales	1	Mexico	1

(Allchurch)   (Belmonte)

Sweden	2	Hungary	1

(Hamrin 2)   (Tichy)

Hungary	4	Mexico	0

(Tichy 2, Sandor, Bencsics)

Sweden	0	Wales	0

	P	W	D	L	F	A	P
Sweden	3	2	1	0	5	1	5
Wales	3	0	3	0	2	2	3
Hungary	3	1	1	1	6	3	3
Mexico	3	0	1	2	1	8	1

Play-off:

Wales	2	Hungary	1

(Allchurch, Medwin)   (Tichy)

Group 4

England	2	USSR	2

(Kevan, Finney pen)   (Simonian, Ivanov A)

Brazil	3	Austria	0

(Mazzola 2, Santos N)

England	0	Brazil	0
USSR	2	Austria	0

(Ilyin, Ivanov V)

Brazil	2	USSR	0

(Vavá 2)

England	2	Austria	2

(Haynes, Kevan)   (Killer, Koener)

	P	W	D	L	F	A	P
Brazil	3	2	1	0	5	0	5
USSR	3	1	1	1	4	4	3
England	3	0	3	0	4	4	3
Austria	3	0	1	2	2	7	1

Play-off :

USSR	1	England	0
(Ilyin)			

Quarter Finals

France	4	Northern Ireland	0
(Wisnieski, Fontaine 2, Piantoni)			
Germany FR	1	Yugoslavia	0
(Rahn)			
Sweden	2	USSR	0
(Hamrin, Simonsson)			
Brazil	1	Wales	0
(Pelé)			

Semi-Finals

Brazil	5	France	2
(Vavá, Didi, Pelé 3)		(Fontaine, Piantoni)	
Sweden	3	West Germany	1
(Skoglund, Gren, Hamrin)		(Schaefer)	

Third Place Game

France	6	Germany FR	3
(Fontaine 4, Kopa pen, Douis)		(Cieslarczyk, Rahn, Schaefer	

Final (in Stockholm; att. 49,737)

Brazil		Sweden	2
(Vavá 2, Pelé 2, Zagalo)		(Liedholm, Simonsson)	

Brazil: Gilmar; Santos D, Santos N; Zito, Bellini, Orlando; Garrincha, Didi, Vavá, Pelé, Zagalo
Sweden: Svensson; Bergmark, Axbom; Boerjesson, Gustavsson, Parling; Hamrin, Gren, Simonsson, Liedholm, Skoglund

1962 (in Chile)

Group 1

Uruguay	2	Colombia	1
(Cubilla, Sasia)		(Zaluaga)	
USSR	2	Yugoslavia	0
(Ovanov, Ponedelnik)			
Yugoslavia	3	Uruguay	1
(Skoblar, Galic, Jerkovic)		(Cabrera)	
USSR	4	Colombia	4
(Ivanov 2, Chislenko, Ponedelnik)		(Aceros, Coll, Rada, Klinger)	
USSR	2	Uruguay	1
(Mamikin, Ivanov)		(Sasia)	
Yugoslavia	5	Colombia	0
(Galic, Jerkovic 3, Melic)			

	P	W	D	L	F	A	P
USSR	3	2	1	0	8	5	5
Yugoslavia	3	2	0	1	8	3	4
Uruguay	3	1	0	2	4	6	2
Colombia	3	0	1	2	5	11	1

Group 2

Chile	3	Switzerland	1
(Sánchez L 2, Ramirez)		(Wuthrich)	
Germany FR	0	Italy	0
Chile	2	Italy	0
(Ramirez, Toro)			
Germany FR	2	Switzerland	1
(Brülls, Seeler)		(Schneiter)	
Germany FR	2	Chile	0
(Szymaniak pen, Seeler)			
Italy	3	Switzerland	0
(Mora, Bulgarelli 2)			

	P	W	D	L	F	A	P
Germany FR	3	2	1	0	4	1	5
Chile	3	2	0	1	5	3	4
Italy	3	1	1	1	3	2	3
Switzerland	3	0	0	3	2	8	0

Group 3

Brazil	2	Mexico	0
(Zagalo, Pelé)			
Czechoslovakia	1	Spain	0
(Stibranyi)			
Brazil	0	Czechoslovakia	0
Spain	1	Mexico	0
(Peiró)			
Brazil	2	Spain	1
(Amarildo 2)		(Adelardo)	
Mexico	3	Czechoslovakia	1
(Diaz, Del Aguila, Hernandez H pen)		(Masek)	

	P	W	D	L	F	A	P
Brazil	3	2	1	0	4	1	5
Czechoslovakia	3	1	1	1	2	3	3
Mexico	3	1	0	2	3	4	2
Spain	3	1	0	2	2	3	2

Group 4

Argentina	1	Bulgaria	0
(Facundo)			
Hungary	2	England	1
(Tichy, Albert)		(Flowers pen)	

England	3	Argentina	1
(Flowers pen, Charlton R, Greaves)		(Sanfilippo)	
Hungary	6	Bulgaria	1
(Albert 3, Tichy 2, Solymosi)		(Sokolov)	
Argentina	0	Hungary	0
England	0	Bulgaria	0

	P	W	D	L	F	A	P
Hungary	3	2	1	0	8	2	5
England	3	1	1	1	4	3	3
Argentina	3	1	1	1	2	3	3
Bulgaria	3	0	1	2	1	7	1

Quarter-Finals

Yugoslavia	1	Germany FR	0
(Radakovic)			
Brazil	3	England	1
(Garrincha 2, Vavá)		(Hitchens)	
Chile	2	USSR	1
(Sánchez L. Rojas)		(Chislenko)	
Czechoslovakia	1	Hungary	0
(Scherer)			

Semi-Finals

Brazil	4	Chile	2
(Garrincha 2, Vavá 2)		(Toro, Sánchez L pen)	
Czechoslovakia	3	Yugoslavia	1
(Kadraba, Scherer 2 (1 pen))		(Jerkovic)	

Third Place Game

Chile	1	Yugoslavia	0
(Rojas)			

Final (in Santiago, att. 69,068)

Brazil	3	Czechoslovakia	1
(Amarildo, Zito, Vavá)		(Masopust)	

Brazil: Gilmar; Santos D, Santos N; Zito, Mauro, Zozimo; Garrincha, Didi, Vavá, Amarildo, Zagalo
Czechoslovakia: Schroiff; Titchy, Novak; Pluskal, Popluhár, Masopust; Pospichal, Scherer, Kvasnak, Kadraba, Jelinek

1966 (In England)

Group 1

England	0	Uruguay	0
France	1	Mexico	1
(Hausser)		(Borja)	

Uruguay	2		France	1			
(Rocha, Cortes)			(De Bourgoing pen)				
England	2		Mexico	0			
(Charlton R; Hunt)							
Uruguay	0		Mexico	0			
England	2		France	0			
(Hunt 2)							

	P	W	D	L	F	A	P
England	3	2	1	0	4	0	5
Uruguay	3	1	2	0	2	1	4
Mexico	3	0	2	1	1	3	2
France	3	0	1	2	2	5	1

Group 2

Germany FR	5	Switzerland	0
(Held, Haller 2 (1 pen) Beckenbauer 2)			
Argentina	2	Spain	1
(Artime 2)		(Pirri)	
Spain	2	Switzerland	1
(Sanchis, Amancio)		(Quentin)	
Argentina	0	Germany FR	0
Argentina	2	Switzerland	0
(Artime, Onega)			
Germany FR	2	Spain	1
(Emmerich, Seeler)		(Fuste)	

	P	W	D	L	F	A	P
Germany FR	3	2	1	0	7	1	5
Argentina	3	2	1	0	4	1	5
Spain	3	1	0	2	4	5	2
Switzerland	3	0	0	3	1	9	0

Group 3

Brazil	2	Bulgaria	0
(Pelé, Garrincha)			
Portugal	3	Hungary	1
(Augusto 2, Torres)		(Bene)	
Hungary	3	Brazil	1
(Bene, Farkas, Meszöly pen)		(Tostão)	
Portugal	3	Bulgaria	0
(Vutzov o.g., Eusebio, Torres)			
Portugal	3	Brazil	1
(Simoes, Eusebio 2)		(Rildo)	
Hungary	3	Bulgaria	1
(Davidov o.g., Meszöly, Bene)		(Asparoukhov)	

	P	W	D	L	F	A	P
Portugal	3	3	0	0	9	2	6
Hungary	3	2	0	1	7	5	4
Brazil	3	1	0	2	4	6	2
Bulgaria	3	0	0	3	1	8	0

Group 4

USSR (Malafeev 2, Banishevsky)	3	Korea DPR	0
Italy (Mazzola, Barison)	2	Chile	0
Chile (Marcos pen)	1	Korea DPR (Pak Seung Jin)	1
USSR (Chislenko)	1	Italy	0
Korea DPR (Pak Doo Ik)	1	Italy	0
USSR (Porkujan 2)	2	Chile (Marcos)	1

	P	W	D	L	F	A	P
USSR	3	3	0	0	6	1	6
Korea DPR	3	1	1	1	2	4	3
Italy	3	1	0	2	2	2	2
Chile	3	0	1	2	2	5	1

Quarter-Finals

England (Hurst)	1	Argentina	0
Germany FR (Held, Beckenbauer, Seeler, Haller)	4	Uruguay	0
Portugal (Eusebio 4 (2 pens), Augusto)	5	Korea DPR (Pak Seung Jin, Yang Sung Kook, Li Dong Woon)	3
USSR (Chislenko, Porkujan)	2	Hungary (Bene)	1

Semi-Finals

Germany FR (Haller, Beckenbauer)	2	USSR (Porkujan)	1
England (Charlton R 2)	2	Portugal (Eusebio pen)	1

Third Place Game

Portugal (Eusebio pen, Torres)	2	USSR (Malafeev)	1

Final (in London; att. 93,000)

England	4	Germany FR	2
(Hurst 3, Peters)		(Haller, Weber)	

-after extra time-

England: Banks; Cohen, Wilson; Stiles, Charlton J, Moore; Ball, Hurst, Hunt, Charlton R, Peters

Germany FR: Tilkowski; Höttges, Schnellinger; Beckenbauer, Schulz, Weber; Held, Haller, Seeler, Overath, Emmerich

1970 (in Mexico)

Group 1

Mexico	0	USSR	0
Belgium	3	El Salvador	0
(Van Moer 2, Lambert pen)			
USSR	4	Belgium	1
(Byshovets 2, Asatiani, Khmelnitsky)		(Lambert)	
Mexico	4	El Salvador	0
(Valdivia 2, Fragoso, Basaguren)			
USSR	2	El Salvador	0
(Byshovets 2)			
Mexico	1	Belgium	0
(Pena pen)			

	P	W	D	L	F	A	P
USSR	3	2	1	0	6	1	5
Mexico	3	2	1	0	5	0	5
Belgium	3	1	0	2	4	5	2
El Salvador	3	0	0	3	0	9	0

Group 2

Uruguay	2	Israel	0
(Maneiro, Mujica)			
Italy	1	Sweden	0
(Domenghini)			
Uruguay	0	Italy	0
Sweden	1	Israel	1
(Turesson)		(Spiegler)	
Sweden	1	Uruguay	0
(Grahn)			
Italy	0	Israel	0

	P	W	D	L	F	A	P
Italy	3	1	2	0	1	0	4
Uruguay	3	1	1	1	2	1	3
Sweden	3	1	1	1	2	2	3
Israel	3	0	2	1	1	3	2

Group 3

England	1	Rumania	0
(Hurst)			
Brazil	4	Czechoslovakia	1
(Rivelino, Pelé, Jairzinho 2)		(Petras)	
Rumania	2	Czechoslovakia	1
(Neagu, Dumitrache pen)		(Petras)	
Brazil	1	England	0
(Jairzinho)			
Brazil	3	Rumania	2
(Pelé 2, Jairzinho)		(Dumitrache, Dembrovski)	
England	1	Czechoslovakia	0
(Clarke pen)			

	P	W	D	L	F	A	P
Brazil	3	3	0	0	8	3	6
England	3	2	0	1	2	1	4
Rumania	3	1	0	2	4	5	2
Czechoslovakia	3	0	0	3	2	7	0

Group 4

Peru	3	Bulgaria	2
(Gallardo, Chumpitaz, Cubillas)		(Dermendjiev, Bonev)	
Germany FR	2	Morocco	1
(Seeler, Müller)		(Houmane)	
Peru	3	Morocco	0
(Cubillas 2, Challe)			
Germany FR	5	Bulgaria	2
(Libuda, Müller 3 (1 pen), Seeler)		(Nikodimov, Kolev)	
Germany FR	3	Peru	1
(Müller 3)		(Cubillas)	
Bulgaria	1	Morocco	1
(Jetchev)		(Ghazouani)	

	P	W	D	L	F	A	P
Germany FR	3	3	0	0	10	4	6
Peru	3	2	0	1	7	5	4
Bulgaria	3	0	1	2	5	9	1
Morocco	3	0	1	2	2	6	1

Quarter-Finals

Uruguay	1	USSR	0
(Esparrago)			
Italy	4	Mexico	1
(Domenghini, Riva 2, Rivera)		(Gonzales)	
Brazil	4	Peru	2
(Rivelino, Tostão 2, Jairzinho)		(Gallardo, Cubillas)	
Germany FR	3	England	2
(Beckenbauer, Seeler, Müller)		(Mullery, Peters)	

-after extra time-

Semi-Finals

Italy	4	Germany FR	3
(Boninsegna, Burgnich, Riva, Rivera)		(Schnellinger, Müller 2)	

-after extra time-

Brazil	3	Uruguay	1
(Clodoaldo, Jairzinho, Rivelino)		(Cubilla)	

Third Place Game

Germany FR	1	Uruguay	0
(Overath)			

Final (in Mexico City, att. 110,000)

Brazil	4	Italy	1
(Pelé, Gerson, Jairzinho, Carlos Alberto)		(Boninsegna)	

Brazil: Felix; Carlos Alberto, Brito, Wilson Piazza, Everaldo; Clodoaldo, Gerson; Jairsinho, Tostão, Pelé, Rivelino
Italy: Albertosi; Burgnich, Cera, Rosato, Facchetti; Bertini (s. Juliano), Mazzola, De Sisti; Domenghini, Boninsegna (s. Rivera), Riva

1974 (In West Germany

Group 1

Germany FR	1	Chile	0
(Breitner)			
German DR	2	Australia	0
(Curran o.g., Streich)			
Germany FR	3	Australia	0
(Overath, Cullman, Müller)			
Chile	1	German DR	1
(Ahumada)		(Hoffmann)	
Australia	0	Chile	0
German DR	1	Germany FR	0
(Sparwasser)			

	P	W	D	L	F	A	P
German DR	3	2	1	0	4	1	5
Germany FR	3	2	0	1	4	1	4
Chile	3	0	2	1	1	2	2
Australia	3	0	1	2	0	5	1

Group 2

Brazil	0	Yugoslavia	0
Scotland	2	Zaire	0
(Lorimer, Jordan)			
Yugoslavia	9	Zaire	0
(Bajevic 3, Džajić, Surjak,			
Katalinski, Bogicevic, Oblak,			

Petkovic)

Scotland		0	Brazil				0
Brazil		3	Zaire				0

(Jairzinho, Rivelino,
Valdomiro)

Scotland		1	Yugoslavia	1
(Jordan)			(Karasi)	

	P	W	D	L	F	A	P
Yugoslavia	3	1	2	0	10	1	4
Brazil	3	1	2	0	3	0	4
Scotland	3	1	2	0	3	1	4
Zaire	3	0	0	3	0	14	0

Group 3

Sweden		0	Bulgaria	0
Netherlands		2	Uruguay	0

(Rep 2)

Netherlands		0	Sweden	0
Bulgaria		1	Uruguay	1
(Bonev)			(Pavoni)	
Sweden		3	Uruguay	0

(Edström 2, Sandberg)

Netherlands		4	Bulgaria	1

(Neeskens 2 pen, Rep, de Jong)   (Krol o.g.)

	P	W	D	L	F	A	P
Netherlands	3	2	1	0	6	1	5
Sweden	3	1	2	0	3	0	4
Bulgaria	3	0	2	1	2	5	2
Uruguay	3	0	1	2	1	6	1

Group 4

Italy		3	Haiti	1
(Rivera, Benetti, Anastasi)			(Sannon)	
Poland		3	Argentina	2
(Lato 2, Szarmach)			(Heredia, Babington)	

Poland		7	Haiti	0

(Lato 2, Deyna, Szarmach 3,
Gorgon)

Argentina		1	Italy	1
(Houseman)			(Perfumo o.g.)	
Argentina		4	Haiti	1
(Yazalde 2, Houseman, Ayala)			(Sannon)	
Poland		2	Italy	1
(Szarmach, Deyna)			(Capello)	

	P	W	D	L	F	A	P
Poland	3	3	0	0	12	3	6
Argentina	3	1	1	1	7	5	3
Italy	3	1	1	1	5	4	3
Haiti	3	0	0	3	2	14	0

Semi-Finals

Group A:

Netherlands (Cruyff 2, Rep, Krol)	4	Argentina	0
Brazil (Rivelino)	1	German DR	0
Netherlands (Neeskens, Rensenbrink)	2	German DR	0
Brazil (Rivelino, Jairzinho)	2	Argentina (Brindisi)	1
Netherlands (Neeskens, Cruyff)	2	Brazil	0
Argentina (Houseman)	1	German DR (Streich)	1

	P	W	D	L	F	A	P
Netherlands	3	3	0	0	8	0	6
Brazil	3	2	0	1	3	3	4
German DR	3	0	1	2	1	4	1
Argentina	3	0	1	2	2	7	1

Group B:

Germany FR (Breitner, Müller)	2	Yugoslavia	0
Poland (Lato)	1	Sweden	0
Poland (Deyna pen, Lato)	2	Yugoslavia (Karasi)	1
Germany FR (Overath, Bonhof, Grabowski, Hoeness pen)	4	Sweden (Edström, Sandberg)	2
Germany FR (Müller)	1	Poland	0
Sweden (Edström, Torstensson)	2	Yugoslavia (Surjak)	1

	P	W	D	L	F	A	P
Germany FR	3	3	0	0	7	2	6
Poland	3	2	0	1	3	2	4
Sweden	3	1	0	2	4	6	2
Yugoslavia	3	0	0	3	2	6	0

Third Place Game

Poland	1	Brazil	0
(Lato)			

Final (in Munich; att. 80,000)

Germany FR	2	Netherlands	1
(Breitner pen, Müller)		(Neeskens pen)	

Germany FR: Maier; Vogts, Beckenbauer, Schwarzenbeck, Breitner; Hoeness, Bonhof, Overath; Grabowski, Müller, Hölzenbein
Netherlands: Jongbloed, Suurbier, Rijsbergen (s. de Jong), Haan, Krol; Jansen, Neeskens, van Hanegem; Rep, Cruyff, Rensenbrink (s. R van der Kerkhof)

1978 (in Argentina)

Group 1

France	1	Italy	2
(Lacombe)		(Rossi, Zaccarelli)	
Hungary	1	Argentina	2
(Csapo)		(Luque, Bertoni)	
Italy	3	Hungary	1
(Rossi, Bettega, Benetti)		(A Toth pen)	
Argentina	2	France	1
(Passarella pen, Luque)		(Platini)	
France	3	Hungary	1
(Lopez, Berdoll, Rocheteau)		(Zombori)	
Italy	1	Argentina	0
(Bettega)			

	P	W	D	L	F	A	P
Italy	3	3	0	0	6	2	6
Argentina	3	2	0	1	4	3	4
France	3	1	0	2	5	5	2
Hungary	3	0	0	3	3	8	0

Group 2

Germany FR	0	Poland	0
Tunisia	3	Mexico	1
(Kaabi, Ghommidh, Dhouib)		(Vásquez Ayala)	
Mexico	0	Germany FR	6
		(D Müller, H Müller, Rummenigge 2, Flohe 2)	
Poland	1	Tunisia	0
(Lato)			

Mexico	1	Poland	3
(Rangel)		(Boniek 2, Deyna)	
Tunisia	0	Germany FR	0

	P	W	D	L	F	A	P
Poland	3	2	1	0	4	1	5
Germany FR	3	1	2	0	6	0	4
Tunisia	3	1	1	1	3	2	3
Mexico	3	0	0	3	2	12	0

Group 3

Spain	1	Austria	2
(Dani)		(Schachner, Krankl)	
Sweden	1	Brazil	1
(Sjöberg)		(Reinaldo)	
Brazil	0	Spain	0
Austria	1	Sweden	0
(Krankl pen)			
Sweden	0	Spain	1
		(Asensi)	
Brazil	1	Austria	0
(Roberto)			

	P	W	D	L	F	A	P
Austria	3	2	0	1	3	2	4
Brazil	3	1	2	0	2	1	4
Spain	3	1	1	1	2	2	3
Sweden	3	0	1	2	1	3	1

Group 4

Peru	3	Scotland	1
(Cueto, Cubillas 2)		(Jordan)	
Iran	0	Netherlands	3
		(Rensenbrink 3 (2 pen))	
Scotland	1	Iran	1
(Eskandarian o.g.)		(Danaiifar)	
Netherlands	0	Peru	0
Peru	4	Iran	1
(Velasquez, Cubillas 3 (2 pen))		(Rowshan)	
Scotland	3	Netherlands	2
(Dalglish, Gemmill 2 (1 pen))		(Rensenbrink pen, Rep)	

	P	W	D	L	F	A	P
Peru	3	2	1	0	7	2	5
Netherlands	3	1	1	1	5	3	3
Scotland	3	1	1	1	5	6	3
Iran	3	0	1	2	2	8	1

Semi-Finals
Group A:

Germany FR	0	Italy	0
Austria (Obermayer)	1	Netherlands (Brandts, Rensenbrink pen, Rep 2, W van der Kerkhof)	5
Italy (Rossi)	1	Austria	0
Netherlands (Haan, R van der Kerkhof)	2	Germany FR (Abramczik, D Müller)	2
Netherlands (Brandts, Haan)	2	Italy (Brandts o.g.)	1
Austria (Vogts o.g., Krankl 2)	3	Germany FR (Rummenigge, Hölzenbein)	2

	P	W	D	L	F	A	P
Netherlands	3	2	1	0	9	4	5
Italy	3	1	1	1	2	2	3
Germany FR	3	0	2	1	4	5	2
Austria	3	1	0	2	4	8	2

Group B:

Poland	0	Argentina (Kempes 2)	2
Brazil (Dirceu 2, Zico pen)	3	Peru	0
Argentina	0	Brazil	0
Peru	0	Poland (Szarmach)	1
Brazil (Nelinho, Roberto 2)	3	Poland (Lato)	1
Peru	0	Argentina (Kempes 2, Tarantini, Luque 2, Houseman)	6

	P	W	D	L	F	A	P
Argentina	3	2	1	0	8	0	5
Brazil	3	2	1	0	6	1	5
Poland	3	1	0	2	2	5	2
Peru	3	0	0	3	0	10	0

Third Place Game

Italy	1	Brazil	2
(Causio)		(Nelinho, Dirceu)	

Final (in Buenos Aires; att. 77,000)

Argentina	3	Netherlands	1
(Kempes 2, Bertoni)		(Nanninga)	

-after extra time-

Argentina: Fillol; Olguín, Galván, Passarella, Tarantini; Ardiles (s. Larrosa), Gallego, Kempes; Bertoni, Luque, Ortiz (s. Houseman)
Netherlands: Jongbloed; Jansen (s. Suurbier), Krol, Brandts, Poortvliet; Neeskens, Haan, W van der Kerkhof; R van der Kerkhof, Rep (s. Nanninga), Rensenbrink

---

World Cup   See: **World Championship—FIFA World Cup**

Wright, William, C.B.E.   (1924-   )

A world class halfback whose skills in the middle part of the field were overshadowed by his staggering statistics as an English international. After his debut against Belgium in 1947, he played in all but three of England's next 107 games, including 70 in a row after October 1951, a world record. During this time, he captained England 90 times, another world record, finally bowing out of international competition in 1959 with 105 appearances, yet another world record that has since been broken. His first 51 internationals were played at right half, but he later switched to center half, where he appeared 46 consecutive times. Though his teams fared poorly in three World Cups, he himself was always exempt from criticism, and in 1954 he came close to turning the tide for England when he

made his famous change from wing half to the pivot. His leadership both on and off the field was unquestioned, and he even suffered at times from the public's skepticism of his "perfect" image.

His club-level career, spent entirely at Wolverhampton, was equally impressive. He began in 1938 on the Wolves' grounds crew, and signed as a professional in 1941, remaining faithfully with the Midlands team until his abrupt retirement in 1959, only a few months after his last game for England. He started as an outside right, moved soon thereafter to inside right, and finally made his mark at wing half after his success in that position for England in the late 1940s caught the attention of his manager, Stan Cullis. In the Cullis tradition, Billy Wright was the mainstay in

Wovles' speedy long ball style, distributing and tackling precisely and directing traffic with flawless accuracy. As captain of Wolves, he led his club to three league championships and an F.A. Cup victory within a span of 11 years, a period fondly remembered by Wolves' fans as the golden era. In 1962, he began a four-year tenure as manager of Arsenal, but he was unsuccessful and turned instead to television sports production, where he has remained as a well-established producer. He was awarded a C.B.E. in 1959.

Yashin, Lev (1929-   )

The greatest and most famous Russian player of all time, he was also the most admired goalkeeper of his or any other era. His acrobatics and reliability were obvious to all, but a further measure of his greatness was his ability to instill confidence in his entire team and spread his good sportsmanship over the whole field. Yashin controlled not only his goalmouth during a game but the entire penalty area—to a greater extent than most keepers dare contemplate. Always dressed in his black jersey or sweater, he led his club, Dinamo Moscow, and especially the USSR, to fame and success during the 1950s and '60s.

After playing for a factory team called Tushino near his native Moscow in 1945, he joined Dinamo as an ice hockey player, but the great Dinamo goalkeeper Alexei Khomich discovered him in 1950 and trained him to be his successor. Yashin made his debut for Dinamo in 1953, and his international debut against Bulgaria in 1954, achieving instant international recognition with the Soviet national team at the 1956 Olympic Games. He was the guiding light of the Soviet teams that reached the quarter-finals of three World Cups (1958-66) and won the first European Nations' Cup in 1960. For his services he was awarded his government's Red Banner of Labor and Order of Lenin medals as early as 1957 and 1960, respectively. Soviet sports have never known another hero like him. He made a record 600 appearances for Dinamo, including 291 in league competition, another record, and finally bowed out of international competition with 78 caps. In 1971, a com-

Lev Yashin, Soviet sports hero and the most admired goalkeeper in history, warms up for his farewell game in Moscow, 1971 (Dinamo Moscow vs. FIFA XI).

memorative game was played in his honor in Moscow between Dinamo and a FIFA World XI before 100,000 spectators, and the next day he became general manager of the only club he had ever played for.

Yemen, Arab Republic

The former Yemen (or North Yemen), an independent republic since 1918, has started to play the game in recent years, but it has not joined FIFA or been nearly as active as Yemen PDR to the south. Yemen's link with organized soccer is its membership in the Union of Arab Football Associations, the group of national associations of Arab League member-nations that organizes the Football Tournament of the Pan Arab Games.

Yemen, People's Democratic Republic

P.D.R. Yemen Football Union
P.O. Box 4238
Crater-Aden

Founded: 1940
FIFA: 1967
AFC: ?

Affiliated clubs: *?;* registered players: *1,700;* national stadium: *Stadium of the Martyr Al-Habashie, Crater-Aden (4,500);* largest stadium: *Al-Habashie Stadium;* colors: *light blue jerseys, white shorts;* season: *September to May;* honors: *none.*

Soccer has been a well-known game in Yemen PDR for many decades. As the former Aden Protectorate, under British rule since 1839, its port city of Aden was the commercial hub of the main route between Europe and the East. British sailors, workers, and businessmen played the game there since the late nineteenth century, and it is little surprise that the Aden Football Association was founded as early as 1940 as an adjunct of the Aden Sports Association. This was the first governing body formed on the Arabian peninsula; it did not, however, become affiliated with The Football Association in London. Today, as in years past, the Yemen PDR game is almost exclusively restricted to the city of Aden where a league and annual cup competition are contested by 14 senior clubs.

The Aden Sports Association became affiliated with FIFA in 1967 at the time of Aden's independence from Britain. For the next three years, the new South Arabian Federation continued to be known by FIFA as Aden. The present name, P.D.R. Yemen Football Union, was adopted in 1970. Though a member of the Asian Football Confederation, Yemen PDR is not affiliated with the Union of Arab Football Associations. The longevity of the Asian Champion Teams' Cup (1967-71) did not coincide with Yemen PDR's membership in the Asian confederation, but in 1976 Yemen PDR advanced to the final rounds of the Asian Cup in Tehran. Compiling the poorest record in the tournament, it was eliminated after a 1-0 defeat by Iraq and an 8-0 thrashing by Iran, Asia's perennial power. Its inclusion in the tournament was due more to withdrawals over the China question than to Yemen's legitimate advancement through qualification rounds, yet the event was its most significant international appearance to date. After ten years of disruptive political instability, Yemen PDR approached the late 1970s ready to take advantage of the new left-leaning climate of the Asian Football Confederation and to stake a claim on its corner of Asian soccer.

Yugoslavia

Fudbalski Savez Jugoslavije
(Yugoslav Football Association)
P.O. Box 262
Terazije 35—11000
Beograd

Founded: 1919
FIFA: 1919
UEFA: 1955

Affiliated clubs: *7,455;* registered players: *122,372 (570 professional, 1,237 non-amateur);* national stadium: *none;* largest stadium: *Crvena Zvezda Stadium, Belgrade (95,000);* colors: *blue jerseys, white shorts;* season: *September to June;* honors: *Olympic Games winner (1960), runner-up (1948, 1952, 1956), European Nations' Cup runner-up (1960), European Football Championship runner-up (1968), Balkan Cup (1935, 1976), Dinamo Zagreb, Fairs Cup (1967).*

While it has always had a reputation for producing an unusually high number of excellent players, Yugoslavia presents a unique set of circumstances among Eastern European countries. In international competition, Yugoslavia has excelled both in Europe and worldwide, but its record is fraught with peculiarities. Like Denmark and Uruguay, Yugoslavia has suffered the loss of many players to other countries as a result of liberal transfer policies; yet, new players of great skill and natural ability appear from a seemingly endless reservoir. In the postwar years, Yugoslavia has had one of the half-dozen best international records in Europe, though if its frequent opponents had been the stronger nations of Central Europe rather than the weaker Balkan states, this ranking would surely dip several notches. In addition, Yugoslav teams are often criticized for their inconsistency in not performing up to their potential, particularly away from home, and for their characteristic lack of finishing power. These same athletes, however, have high levels of skill and instinctive soccer ability, and this contradiction is a Yugoslav trademark.

Yugoslav archaeologists in recent years have sought to establish that a form of football was played on the Adriatic coast in Croatia in the second century A.D. A sculpture that is said to depict such a game was discovered at Senj in 1950. Various names have been given to the Dalmatian football games of this period, including *kèndi, kida,* and *chola,* but their existence is in little doubt, given the known penchant for Roman legions to spread their various football games to all parts of their empire. Unfortunately, little is known of indigenous football games between the Roman period and the modern era in what is now Yugoslavia.

Soccer was introduced in present-day Yugoslavia via Belgrade in the early 1890s by British residents and workers, though whether or not any local citizens became involved at that time is less certain. In the succeeding 20 years, the game spread to other major industrial centers of the area, and in 1911, the oldest Yugoslav club still in senior competition, Hajduk, was formed in Split on the Dalmatian coast. Hajduk Split remains one of Yugoslavia's four leading clubs today. Further growth appeared imminent, but the outbreak of the Balkan civil wars and the start of World War I in 1914 put a stop to any advancement.

A national association, the Jugoslavenski Nogometni Savez, was founded immediately after the formation of a South Slavic state in 1919. (It acquired its present name in 1948.) Yugoslavia's first international was played against another new state, Czechoslovakia, at the 1920 Olympic Games in Antwerp, and ended in triumph for the vastly more experienced Czechs; the score was 7-0. In 1921, Yugoslavia ventured to Prague for a friendly, and again lost decisively (6-1). Yugoslavia's record against Central European competition during the 1920s reflects the inferior state of the game on the Balkan peninsula at that time. Its further losses to Czechoslovakia during this period included scores of 7-0, 6-2, and 7-1. At Zagreb in 1924,

Austria defeated Yugoslavia, 4-1, and in 1927 Hungary won in Budapest, 3-0. Yugoslavia's worst defeat, other than by Czechoslovakia, was a 7-0 loss to Uruguay, the eventual gold medalist and world champion, in the 1924 Olympic Games at Paris. Most of Yugoslavia's early wins were against Rumania and other Balkan opposition such as Bulgaria and Turkey.

Competition with other Balkan states increased rapidly with the introduction of the Balkan Cup in 1929, one of Europe's first regional competitions for national teams. Yugoslavia did not win a Balkan Cup until the fourth edition in 1934-35, but it managed to achieve second place in each of the three previous editions, Bulgaria and Rumania emerging the winners.

Yugoslavia's first significant international success was its defeat of Brazil and Bolivia in the first World Cup in 1930 at Montevideo. While Brazil was not yet an international power, Yugoslavia's 2-1 victory reflected well on the growing skill of Yugoslav players. Olympic champion and host team Uruguay, however, leveled Yugoslavia's optimism with a 6-1 victory, and in 1934 and 1938 Yugoslavia failed to qualify altogether.

At home, the national league was introduced in 1922, and its first champion was Gradjanska of Zagreb. The dominant club of the period between the world wars was Beograd SK, but Hajduk Split, Gradjanska, and Concordia Zagreb also achieved a major share of honors. Beograd SK won five championships during the 1930s. With the reorganization of the Yugoslav game at the end of World War II, Beograd was absorbed into the new army club, Partizan. Many other clubs were not so lucky, and the postwar era saw the birth of numerous reconstituted clubs whose names were compatible with socialist society. As well as Partizan, two other great Yugoslav clubs, Dinamo Zagreb, the electrical workers' club, and Red Star Belgrade, the Belgrade University club, were founded in 1945.

From the outset in 1947, Yugoslavia's big four clubs dominated domestic competition. Between 1947-51, Partizan, Dinamo Zagreb, Hajduk Split, and Red Star Belgrade each won a championship, and when the new national cup competition got under way in 1947, the first winners were Partizan and Red Star, the latter three times in succession by 1950. The Yugoslav Cup has also been dominated by the big four. In the 30 years since the new league was formed and the great postwar clubs were founded, none of the big four has been relegated from the first division. Red Star has the best record, followed by Partizan, Dinamo Zagreb, and Hajduk, in that order. Support for the major clubs in Yugoslavia is among the best in Europe. The most important derby, Red Star vs. Partizan, regularly draws 95,000 spectators to Red Star Stadium in Belgrade.

The administration of soccer in Yugoslavia reflects the nation's independence of character in Eastern Europe. It is, for example, the only country in the region that has officially adopted professionalism. Both Divisions I and II are fully professional, and are supported by large regional leagues divided according to historic ethnic boundaries: Serbia, Bosnia, Croatia, Slovenia, etc. Transfers that involve the exchange of money are regulated by the national association, but they *are* permitted, and foreign transfers are sanctioned after a minimum age. Yugoslavia's permissive transfer policies have resulted in an enormous drain of leading players to Western Europe, causing a permanent state of anguish for national team selectors. Literally hundreds of Yugoslavs have made the trip to the West since the 1960s, though a surprisingly large number have returned either to finish their careers or to take up coaching positions. Moreover, the FSJ has accepted with mixed emotions the large number of Yugoslav coaches who are sought abroad, often at the expense of coaching needs at home.

Since World War II, Yugoslavia has amassed one of the finest international records in the world. Though its highest placing in the World Cup has been fourth (1962), Yugoslavia's Olympic and European Championship records rank close to the top. In 1950, it was left out of the final pool of the World Cup by a 2-0 loss to Brazil after defeating Switzerland and Mexico, and in 1954 and 1958, it was eliminated from the final rounds altogether. In 1962, however, a 3-1 win over Uruguay enabled Yugoslavia to advance from its first round group along with the USSR. In the quarter-finals, against defensive-minded West Germany, the more skillful Yugoslavs prevailed. Its 4-2-4 system, however, was not suitable to penetrating the strong Czech defense in the semi-finals. In the third place match, Yugoslavia was defeated by the home team, Chile, and narrowly missed its first World Cup medal.

With characteristic unpredictability, Yugoslavia failed to qualify in 1966 and 1970. At the 1974 World Cup in West Germany, it entered as a possible contender, led by the indomitable left winger Dragan Džajić. Though Yugoslavia's performances were sometimes disappointing, especially to the fans at home, it finished on top of its first round group after drawing with the fallen idol of Brazil, drawing a second time with the physically tough Scots, and burying hapless Zaire, 9-0. In the second round, it lost three straight matches to West Germany, Poland, and Sweden.

Yugoslavia's Olympic experience, on the other hand, has been very successful. In 1948, only the great Swedish team led by Gren, Nordahl, and Liedholm prevented Yugoslavia from winning the gold medal, and in 1952 and 1956, it won the silver once again, the former after losing to mighty Hungary in the final. In 1960, it finally won the gold with a 3-1 win over Denmark in the final. East Germany blocked its way in 1964 at Tokyo, and in 1968 it failed to qualify for the Mexico City games. Yugoslavia also fell out during qualification rounds for 1972 and 1976, but it was clear that by the late 1960s, the FSJ had set its sights on the European Football Championship as a higher prize than the Olympics. In this regard, Yugoslavia was probably the first soccer power in Eastern Europe to recognize the lost qualities of Olympic soccer in a world of professionalism.

Two of Yugoslavia's highest achievements have been to place second in the European Football Championships of 1960 and 1968. In the 1958-60 edition, when the series was still called the European Nations' Cup, Yugoslavia eliminated Bulgaria, Portugal, and finally France, then one of Europe's leading teams, before facing the USSR in the final. An own goal by Russia's Igor Netto accounted for Yugoslavia's only goal in a 2-1 loss after extra time. The high placings for both Yugoslavia and the USSR, however, were tempered by the widespread absence of Western European participants.

Yugoslavia's best results in the European Football Championship to date were seen in 1966-68. In its small first round group with West Germany and Albania, Yugoslavia emerged on top after the Germans were surprisingly held to a 0-0 draw at Tirana. In the quarter-finals, the superbly skilled Yugoslavs, led by Džajić, buried France by 5-1 after a 1-1 draw. Its brawling semi-final win over England was seriously marred by rough play on both sides, but it was noteworthy that the world champion had been eliminated. The final against Italy ended in a 1-1 draw, after an equalizer by Džajić, and in the replay careful realignments in Italy's *catenaccio* formation put more scoring potential on Italy's forward line. Yugoslavia could not match the individual skills of Gigi Riva, and it lost before a Roman audience by a respectable 2-0. Since by now the European Football Championship had become a competition of great prestige, Yugoslavia's second-place finish was hailed as a significant accomplishment.

In UEFA, only the USSR, West Germany, Hungary, Italy, and England have a better overall record than Yugoslavia since World War II. In European club competitions, Yugoslav clubs have also broken through to the top. In 1966-67, Dinamo Zagreb won the Fairs Cup on a 2-0 win over Leeds United in the Zagreb leg. Among Dinamo's opponents en route to that final were Juventus and Eintracht Frankfurt. Dinamo had previously figured prominently in the first edition of the Fairs Cup in 1955-58, when its players were the mainstay of the team that represented the city of Zagreb under the old format. Previously in the Fairs Cup, Red Star Belgrade had reached the semi-finals in 1962, and Dinamo Zagreb the finals in 1963.

In the European Champions' Cup, Yugoslavia's highest achievement has been Partizan's splendid run to the final in 1966, eliminating Sparta Prague and Manchester United before losing in the end to Real Madrid at the tail end of the Di Stefano-Puskás era. In the European Cup Winners' Cup, Dinamo Zagreb reached the semi-finals in 1961, OFK Belgrade in 1963, Hajduk Split in 1973, and Red Star Belgrade in 1975.

Yugoslavia's overall international record since 1919 indicates a winning record against all Balkan opponents except Rumania. Curiously, Rumania has dominated competition with Yugoslavia since World War II, the era of Yugoslavia's emergence as the regional power. Yugoslavia's other significant losing records are against Czechoslovakia, Hungary, West Germany (and Germany), and the USSR. Its most frequent wins have been against Bulgaria, Greece, Indonesia, Turkey, Norway, and—a second curiosity—England. In 12 outings with England, Yugoslavia has won five, including a 2-0 shut-out at Belgrade in 1939 and a 5-0 trouncing at Belgrade in 1958. Nevertheless, the record shows that Yugoslavia has been unsuccessful against Europe's leading soccer nations, an important qualification that tempers its high rank among UEFA members.

Champions

1923	Gradjanska Zagreb	1942	no competition	1961	Partizan Belgrade
1924	Jugoslavija Belgrade	1943	no competition	1962	Partizan Belgrade
1925	Jugoslavija Belgrade	1944	no competition	1963	Partizan Belgrade
1926	Gradjanska Zagreb	1945	no competition	1964	Red Star Belgrade
1927	Hajduk Split	1946	no competition	1965	Partizan Belgrade
1928	Gradjanska Zagreb	1947	Partizan Belgrade	1966	Vojvodina Novi Sad
1929	Hajduk Split	1948	Dinamo Zagreb	1967	FC Sarajevo
1930	Concordia Zagreb	1949	Partizan Belgrade	1968	Red Star Belgrade
1931	Beograd SK	1950	Hajduk Split	1969	Red Star Belgrade
1932	Concordia Zagreb	1951	Red Star Belgrade	1970	Red Star Belgrade
1933	Beograd SK	1952	Hajduk Split	1971	Hajduk Split
1934	no competition	1953	Red Star Belgrade	1972	Zeljezrucar Sarajevo
1935	Beograd SK	1954	Dinamo Zagreb	1973	Red Star Belgrade
1936	Beograd SK	1955	Hajduk Split	1974	Hajduk Split
1937	Gradjanska Zagreb	1956	Red Star Belgrade	1975	Hajduk Split
1938	H.A.S.K. Zagreb	1957	Red Star Belgrade	1976	Partizan Belgrade
1939	Beograd SK	1958	Dinamo Zagreb	1977	Red Star Belgrade
1940	Gradjanska Zagreb	1959	Red Star Belgrade	1978	Partizan Belgrade
1941	no competition	1960	Red Star Belgrade		

Cup Winners

1947	Partizan Belgrade	1958	Red Star Belgrade	1969	Dinamo Zagreb
1948	Red Star Belgrade	1959	Red Star Belgrade	1970	Red Star Belgrade
1949	Red Star Belgrade	1960	Dinamo Zagreb	1971	Red Star Belgrade
1950	Red Star Belgrade	1961	Vardar Skopje	1972	Hajduk Split
1951	Dinamo Zagreb	1962	OFK Belgrade	1973	Hajduk Split
1952	Partizan Belgrade	1963	Dinamo Zagreb	1974	Hajduk Split
1953	BSK Belgrade	1964	Red Star Belgrade	1975	Hajduk Split
1954	Partizan Belgrade	1965	Partizan Belgrade	1976	Hajduk Split
1955	BSK Belgrade	1966	OFK Belgrade	1977	Hajduk Split
1956	no competition	1967	Hajduk Split	1978	Nogometni Rijeka
1957	Partizan Belgrade	1968	Red Star Belgrade		

Z

Zaire

Fédération Zaïroise de Football-Association
P.O Box 1284
Avenue de l'Enseignement, 14
Kinshasa 1

Founded: 1919
FIFA: 1964
CAF: 1963

Affiliated clubs: *2,011;* **registered players:** *49,170;* **national stadium:** *Stade Tata Raphael, Kinshasa (60,000);* **largest stadium:** *Stade Tata Raphael;* **colors:** *green jerseys, yellow shorts:* **season:** *June to March;* **honors:** *African Nations' Cup winner (1968, 1974), Englebert Lumbumbashi, African Cup of Champion Clubs (1967, 1968), Vita Club, African Cup of Champion Clubs (1973).*

Zaire, formerly Congo-Kinshasa, has been one of the leading soccer powers in Africa since the mid-1960s. In the international arena, Zaire has won the biannual African Cup of Nations twice, and its champion clubs have won the African Champions' Cup three times. In 1974, Zaire captured the attention of a politically embattled continent and became the first black African nation to enter the World Cup. Though the Zaire government spared no effort to help "The Leopards" make a worthy showing, the strength of Brazil, Yugoslavia, and Scotland was no match for Congolese inexperience, and Africa's hope in the world championship suffered three successive shut-outs, one, a 9-0 loss to Yugoslavia that tied the record for the most lopsided defeat in World Cup history. Zaire's humiliating setback in West Germany appeared to be an unfortunate turning point, as its dismal results in the 1976 African Nations' Cup and early withdrawal from 1978 World Cup qualification rounds indicated. The depth and quality of Zairian domestic competition, however, is widely acknowledged and precludes the possibility that Zaire will be out of the mainstream for very long.

Belgian missionaries introduced soccer in the Belgian Congo via Matadi and Boma near the mouth of the Congo River in 1912. In 1919, the Association Royale Sportive Congolaise (ARSC) was founded in Léopoldville, and a soccer section was established to regulate the league championship that was formed in 1918. The first champion was Coastman F.C., but most of the first clubs were made up entirely of colonists. Among the numerous divisions set up in subsequent years was a "Bare-footed Section" for native Congolese, comprising 13 clubs. The geographical focus of the ARSC was Léopoldville, but eventually clubs from Kasai, Kivu, Katanga, Equateur, and Orientale became affiliated. From the beginning, however, the dominant clubs in the association were from Léopoldville: Union, Cercle, and Vita Club. By the 1950s, 75 clubs were under the aegis of the ARSC.

In 1923, the Ligue de Football da Katanga was founded, and the problem of overlapping jurisdiction so common in the colonial period in Africa became an issue, even though a full-fledged championship was not introduced in Katanga until 1936. At its height during the 1950s, 11 clubs were members of the Katanga league. Then in 1924, the Fédération de Football Association du Pool was formed at Léopoldville, as an adjunct of the Union Sportive de Kinshasa, to administer the game around the Stanley Pool, the lake that separates the capital of the Belgian Congo, Léopoldville, from the capital of the French Congo, Brazzaville. The federation became affiliated with the Belgian F.A. in 1928. The first champion of the Pool league was Cercle Olympique. The other leading Pool league clubs over the years were Cercle Sportif Belge, Amical Sportiva Portuguêsa, and Cercle Athlétique Brazzavillois. The Pool federation was unique in its inclusion of clubs from French Brazzaville as well as the Belgian side of the lake, and emerged in later years as the most important league in the Belgian colony. In 1928, the Cup of Léopoldville was introduced, and its first winner was Etoile Sportive Congolaise.

By the mid-1930s, an umbrella sports organization, the Fédération Royale des Associations Sportives Indigènes (Royal Federation of Native Sports Associations) was regulating league competition among Congolese-based clubs in the various regions, especially Léopoldville and Elizabethville

(Katanga), where a higher proportion of Congolese played the game. The three governing bodies, ARSC, the Pool federation in Léopoldville, and the Katanga league in Elizabethville, administered their own competitions until the end of the colonial era.

The reorganization of Congolese soccer was postponed from the year of independence (1960) to the end of the Congolese civil war in 1963. The first problem was to give a name to the national association that would distinguish it from that of the French Congo across the river, so the reconstituted national association was named the Fédération Congolaise de Football Association. The present name was adopted in 1972 when the country became known as Zaire. A national championship was introduced in 1964, and for the first time the major clubs were able to rise above regional competitions. The Zaire Cup was also inaugurated in 1964, and with the completion of its domestic organization, Zaire began its rise to a place among the soccer elite of sub-Saharan Africa. This development, so inevitable as a result of the country's population and large number of competent players, had been cruelly delayed by domestic strife following independence.

Congo-Léopoldville's first foray into the African Nations' Cup in 1965 was unsuccessful, as Ghana and the Ivory Coast, two of West Africa's perennial powers, both defeated the Congolese with ease in the first round. In only its second attempt, however, in 1968, Congo-Kinshasa won the Nations' Cup, though its path to the top was strewn with ironies and near-misses. In its first round group, Congo-Kinshasa placed second to Ghana, and in the semi-finals, it needed extra time to push by historically strong Ethiopia. In the final, its opponent was none other than Ghana, and in the semi-finals, it beat the Leopards by 1-0.

In 1970, Congo-Kinshasa placed last in its first round group with Egypt, Ghana, and Guinea. Two years later, as "Zaire" for the first time, a reversal of 1968 took place and Congo (Brazzaville), which in the first round had placed second to Zaire, won the cup while Zaire placed fourth. In 1974, Zaire achieved its second African Nations' Cup victory. The final with Zambia, however, had to replayed after the first attempt ended in a 2-2 draw. Zaire won the replay 2-0. All four Zairian goals were scored by central striker Ndaye Mulamba, or "Mutumbula" as he is known, the star of Vita Club and the new holder of the Nations' Cup

scoring record. It was Mulamba of whom so much was expected in Zaire's ill-fated World Cup venture of 1974. Goalkeeper Kazadi Muamba made a record 55 international appearances for Zaire during this period; he was finally replaced in 1975. Sadly, the minister of sport abruptly withdrew the national team from 1978 World Cup Qualification rounds, citing the poor form of many players and a general lack of discipline throughout the ranks.

Zairian clubs have been among Africa's most successful in international competition, especially in the late 1960s. Englebert Lumbumbashi has won the African Champions' Cup twice and placed second twice, while some years later Vita Club also won the Champions' Cup. Englebert is one of Africa's greatest clubs. Founded in 1936 at Elizabethville (Lumbumbashi), Katanga, its original name was Saint George F.C., and the founders were missionaries whose lives were dedicated primarily to the development of the Boy Scout movement. In 1944, the name was changed to Saint Paul F.C. When the club again changed its name to Englebert F.C. in 1947, it won the local "native" championship and in the off-season assumed the name Tout-Puissant (All-Powerful) Englebert F.C. Its rise to the top of Katangan soccer was rocky, but by 1967 it had reached the national championship. Englebert triumphed in the African Champions' Cup in 1967 and 1968, and in 1969 and 1970, it placed second in the cup to Ismaili of Egypt and Kotoko Kumasi of Ghana, respectively, thus establishing a real dominance in African club competition. Englebert has now relocated to Kinshasa—safe from Katangan civil wars—as T-P Mazembé.

Vita Club of Kinshasa, meanwhile, had grown up in the 1930s and '40s as one of the established clubs of the Pool league, having won the Pool championship in 1942, 1946, 1947, and 1950. In 1973, Vita Club defeated Kotoko Kumasi for the African championship after struggling past Cameroon's champion club, Léopard. Vita Club also advanced to the semi-finals of the African Cup Winners' Cup in 1976. These achievements by Englebert and Vita were important in helping to establish Zaire as a true continental power after the international accomplishments of the national team, and it comes as no surprise that the major derby in Zaire is the annual meeting of these two clubs at Kinshasa's Stade Tata Raphael.

Zambia

Football Association of Zambia
P.O. Box 3474
Lusaka

Founded: 1929
FIFA: 1964
CAF: 1964

Affiliated clubs: 20; *registered players:* 4,100 (330 *professional*); national stadium: *Independence Stadium, Lusaka (30,000);* largest stadium: *Independence Stadium;* colors: *green and copper jerseys, white, green, black, and red shorts;* season: *March to November;* honors: *African Nations' Cup runner-up (1974).*

In the mid-1970s, Zambia emerged as an important soccer power in Africa, largely as a result of becoming one of only four countries on the continent to adopt open professionalism. Zambia is the most advanced of all black African states in this respect, a trump card that will surely serve it well in the near future. In 1974, its watershed year, it just missed out on representing Africa in the World Cup, losing in that bid to neighboring Zaire, and in the 1974 African Nations' Cup it qualified for the final rounds for the first time, advancing all the way to the final, where it lost to Zaire again.

Zambians (or Northern Rhodesians) learned the game from British railroad and mining engineers who flooded the country after the turn of the century and possibly from South African whites who trekked northward during the era of the South Africa Company's rule over the area (1889-1924). A Northern Rhodesia Football Association was founded in Lusaka in 1929, and was affiliated with the Nyasaland Football Association until the postwar era. (Nyasaland's association in turn was linked directly with The Football Association in London.) After World War II, British, South African, and Rhodesian whites spread the game widely in both Lusaka and the copperbelt region just north of the capital. In 1964, the year of Zambia's independence, the Northern Rhodesian association became the Football Association of Zambia, and quickly joined FIFA and the African Football Confederation. By 1972, Zambian clubs were participating regularly in the African Champions' Cup, and Zambia was coming closer to gaining entry to the Nations' Cup final rounds.

In the 1970s, Zambia became a prime mover in the formation of the East and Central African Football Federation, whose championship it has won often. In 1974, Zambia's superb assault on the African Nations' Cup ended with an exciting final in which a replay was forced for the first time in the series' history. Zambia had earlier defeated two big continental powers, Ivory Coast and Congo, to reach the final, and now met its feared rival Zaire. The first game resulted in a 2-2 draw after extra time, but in the replay Zambia lost by a disappointing 2-0.

Zambia's top club is Green Buffaloes F.C. of Lusaka, the army club, whose attacking style is highly regarded throughout Africa. Green Buffaloes has advanced to the quarter-finals of the African Champions' Cup twice. Another big club is Kabwe Warriors F.C. from the copperbelt city of Kabwe, and it too has reached the quarter-finals of the Champions' Cup twice. A second army club, Sahbia Army, has also won league titles. Other leading clubs are Mufulira and Rokana United. A constant source of friction in Zambian soccer is the ceaseless poaching of players from civilian clubs by Green Buffaloes, Sahbia, and the air force team, which the little clubs have asserted is unfair and exploitative. The Zambian league is composed of the First Division League and the Second Division League. Clubs vie for the Challenge Cup and the Champion of Champions, a kind of "Super Cup," as well as league titles. The leading clubs have also organized "B" teams and youth teams, the latter made up of the sons of "A" team members.

Zamora Martinez, Ricardo (1901-1978)

The greatest of all Spanish idols, Zamora was Europe's most spectacular goalkeeper during the 1920s and '30s, and, unlike his equally great Czech counterpart and contemporary,

František Plánička, the object of an unprecedented cult in his native country. Zamora was an acrobatic and flashy keeper in the Latin style, and in a record 47 international appearances spanning 16 years, he conceded only 40 goals, seven of them at the hands of England in one match in 1931. In that famous international at Arsenal Stadium, played while he was at the height of his powers, he was reduced to tears at the whistle in one of the most memorable scenes in international soccer annals.

At age 15 he signed with the lesser of Barcelona's two big clubs, Español, but in 1919 he moved across town to CF Barcelona. After three seasons, he returned to his beloved Español, and remained there until 1930. He made his international debut in the 1920 Olympic Games, leading Spain to a silver medal, and starred for his country 14 years later against Italy in the second World Cup. In 1930, Real Madrid paid Español a world record transfer fee for a goalkeeper of 150,000 pesetas, and Zamora finally retired from active play in 1936 after making a total of 473 club appearances. He was the manager of the newly reconstituted Atlético Aviación de Madrid (Atlético Madrid) in 1939, and after World War II managed several clubs, including Español, before taking over the national team briefly in 1952. In 1967, he was honored with a FIFA testimonial match, Spain vs. Rest of the World, and in retirement remained the most popular sports figure in Spanish history.

Zanzibar   See: **Tanzania**

Bibliography

Several thousand books about soccer have appeared since the first publication of the Laws of the Game in 1863. Most have been instructional guides for players and coaches, biographies and tributes to famous players, or juvenile books. There are so many titles in these three categories that it is virtually impossible to keep an accurate account of them. It seemed appropriate, therefore, that this list deal exclusively with the history and lore of the game. Certain nineteenth-century technical books and a handful of important biographies have general historical value, and they too are included. The wealth of significant material in English and the unavailability of many foreign language books in the United States and Canada justified the inclusion of English language titles only.

Using these criteria the following subjects have been omitted: technical and tactical manuals, coaching and training, biographies, club histories and tributes, fiction, juvenile literature, medicine and hygiene, humor and satire, bookmaking, legal and legislative studies, and official reports and registers of national governing bodies. All titles on this list—and many more in other languages—were consulted in compiling this encyclopedia.

GENERAL REFERENCE

Avis, Frederick C. *Soccer Dictionary*, 3rd ed. London, 1970. (1st ed. published in 1954 as *Soccer Reference Dictionary*)
Barrett, Norman (ed.). *Purnell's Encyclopedia of Association Football*, 3rd ed. London, 1974.
_____. *World Soccer from A to Z*. London, 1973.
Handbook, 1932-33. Zurich, 1933 (Fédération Internationale de Football Association, pub.)
_____. *Handbook, 1950*. Zurich, 1950.
_____. *Supplement 1954 to the 1950 Handbook*. Zurich, 1954.
Golesworthy, Maurice. *The Encyclopedia of Association Football*, 12th ed. London, 1976.
_____, and MacDonald, Roger. *The AB-Z of World Football*. London, 1966.
Johnston, F. (ed.) *Football Encyclopedia*. London, 1934.

ANNUALS AND YEARBOOKS

Alcock, C. W. (ed.). *The Football Annual*. London, 1869-1909.
Association Football Handbook, 1894-95. London, 1894.
Cahill, Thomas W. *Spalding's Official "Soccer" Football Guide*. New York, 1907-1913, 1923. (title varies)
Football Annual. London, 1946-? (*The Daily Worker*, pub.)
Football Annual. London, 1946-47. (*Sunday Chronicle*, pub.)
Football Directory. London, 1909-?
Football Handbook. London, 1900-14.
Football Who's Who and Guide to Association Clubs and Players. London, 1900-07.
Gamage's Association Football Annual, 1911-12. England.
Glanville, Brian (comp.). *World Football Handbook*. London, 1966-pres.
Hollander, Zander (ed.). *The Complete Handbook of Soccer*. Bergenfield, 1976-pres.
Northern Ireland Soccer Yearbook. Belfast, ? (Howard, pub.)
Playfair Football Annual. London, 1948/49-? (Playfair Books, pub.)
Post Football Guide. Nottingham, 1903/04-pres. (T. Bailey Forman, pub.)
Scottish Football League Handbook. Glasgow, 1889-?
Spalding's Association Football Annual. New York, 1907-12. (Spalding, pub.)
Sport Association Football Year Book. London, 1949-?
Vernon, Leslie, and Rollin, Jack (comp.). *Rothman's Football Yearbook*. London, 1970/71-pres.

ORIGINS AND EARLY HISTORY OF FOOTBALL GAMES

Brailsford, D. *Sport and Society, Elizabeth to Anne*. London, 1969.
Culin, Stewart. *Korean Games with Notes on the Corresponding Games of China and Japan*. Philadelphia, 1895.
Gardiner, E. Norman. *Athletics of the Ancient World*. Oxford, 1930.

Magoun, Francis P., Jr. *History of Football from the Beginnings to 1871*. Bochum, 1938, in English. (reprinted in New York, 1966)

Malcolmson, R. W. *Popular Recreations in English Society, 1700-1850*. Cambridge (Eng.), 1973.

Monckton, O. P. *Pastimes in Times Past*. London, 1913.

Strutt, J. *The Sports and Pastimes of the People of England*, 1st ed. London, 1801; 2nd ed., 1876; 3rd ed., 1903.

GENERAL

Alcock, C. W. (ed.). *The Book of Football*. London, 1906.

——. *The Book of Rules of the Game of Football, as Adopted and Played by the English Football Associations*. New York, 1871.

——. "Football," *Encyclopedia Britannica*, 11th ed. Cambridge (Eng.) and New York, 1910.

——. *Football: Our Winter Game*. London, 1874.

——. *Football: The Association Game*. London, 1890. (revised 1897, 1902, 1906, and 1919)

——, and Hill, Rowland (eds.). *Famous Footballers, 1895-96*. London, 1896.

All-India Football. Calcutta, ? (S. L. Ghosh, ed.)

Alsner, I., and Frenkel, I. *All About Football in Brief*. Palestine, 1947.

Anderson, Chalmers. *Association Football: Scotland v. England, 1872-1946*. Edinburgh, 1947.

Archer, Ian, and Royle, Trevor (eds.). *We'll Support You Evermore: The Impertinent Saga of Scottish "Fitba."* London, 1976.

Arnold, Peter, and Davis, Christopher. *The Hamlyn Book of World Soccer*, 2nd ed. London, 1975.

Bailey, L. N. (ed.). *European Soccer*. London, 1970.

Bebbington, James. *Football in Colour*. Poole, 1976.

Bettesworth, W. A. "Football, Association," *Encyclopedia Britannica*, 14th ed. London, etc., 1939.

Budd, A., Fry, C. B., *et al. Football*. England, 1897.

Butler, Francis J. *The Picture Story of Football*. London, 1963.

Cascio, Chuck. *Soccer U.S.A.* Washington, 1975.

Catton, J. A. H. *The Real Football: A Sketch of the Development of the Association Game*. London, 1899.

Chadwick, Henry (ed.). *Beadle's Dime Book of Cricket and Football, Being a Complete Guide to Players, and Containing All the Rules and Laws of the Ground and Games*. New York, 1866.

Churchill, Reginald. *English League Football*. London, 1961. (originally pub. as *Sixty Seasons of League Football* in 1958)

Corbett, B. O. *Football*. London, 1901

Cottrell, John. *A Century of Great Soccer Drama*. London, 1970.

Delaney, Terence. *A Century of Soccer*. London, 1963.

Dougan, Derek. *On the Spot: Football as a Profession*. London, 1974.

Douglas, Peter. *The Football Industry*. London, 1973.

Evers, B. S., and Davies, C. E. H. *The Complete Association Football*. London, 1912.

Farror, Morley, and Lamming, Douglas. *A Century of English International Football, 1872-1972*. London, 1972.

Flannery, Jerome (ed.). *Association Football Guide*. New York, 1905.

Football: A Popular Handbook of the Game. London, 1887. (Religious Tract Society, pub.)

Football in New China. Peking, 1953. (All-China Athletic Federation, pub.)

Gardner, Paul. *The Simplest Game: The Intelligent American's Guide to the World of Soccer*. Boston, 1976.

Gee, Harry. *Wembley: Fifty Great Years*. London, 1972.

Glanville, Brian. *Know About Football*. London, 1963.

——. *Soccer: A History of the Game, Its Players, and Its Strategy*. London, 1968.

——. *Soccer: A Panorama*. London, 1969.

——. *Soccer Nemesis*. London, 1955.

Goodall, John. *Association Football*. London, 1898.

Granger, Vivian. *The World Game Comes to South Africa*. South Africa, 1961.

Grant, Sid (comp.). *Jack Pollard's Soccer Records*. North Sydney, 1974.

Graves, John. *Herbert Chapman on Football*. London, 1933.

Green, Geoffrey. *Great Moments in Sport: Soccer*. London, 1953.

——. *History of the Football Association*. London, 1953.

——. *The Official History of the F. A. Cup*, rev. ed. London, 1960.

——. *Soccer in the Fifties*. London, 1974.

_____. *Soccer—The World Game*. London, 1953.

_____, and Fabian, A.H. (eds.). *Association Football*, 4 vols. London, 1960.

Greenland, Walter E. *The History of the Amateur Football Alliance*. London, 1966.

Hart, Hugh S. *Official Guide to Gaelic and Association Football*. New York, 1893.

Hill, Barrington J. W. *Football*. Oxford, 1961.

Hoh, Gunsun. *Physical Education in China*. Shanghai, 1926.

Hopcraft, Arthur. *The Football Man*, 2nd ed. London, 1971.

Hopley, Edward. *Football: Complete Rules for Playing the Association Game; Containing Full Instructions for Refereeing and Umpiring the Game*. Brooklyn, 1890.

Hough, George. *Bedside Book of Soccer*. London, 1972.

Houston, John. *Association Football in New Zealand: Jubilee Yearbook*. Wellington, 1952.

Jackson, N. L. *Association Football*. London, 1899. (2nd ed., 1900)

James, Brian. *England v. Scotland*. London, 1969.

Jeffrey, Gordon. *European International Football*. London, 1963.

_____. *Soccer, The International Way*. New York, 1968.

Jones, J. L. *Association Football*. London, 1904.

Kane, Basil G. *Soccer for American Spectators; A Fundamental Guide to Modern Soccer*. South Brunswick, 1970.

Keeton, George. *The Football Revolution: A Study of the Changing Pattern of Association Football*. Newton Abbot, 1972.

King, George J. *A Popular History of Association Football*. London, 1949.

Lerry, G. G. *The Football Association of Wales: 75th Anniversary Book*. Wrexham, 1951.

Levin, Zevi (ed.). *Soccer Goodwill Tour to U.S.A., Fall 1948*. Tel-Aviv, 1948.

Lewell, S. H. D. *Book on Football*. London, 1911.

Litchfield, Eric. *Book of Soccer*. Johannesburg, 1965.

_____. *Goals in the Sun*. Johannesburg, 1963.

Lowndes, W. *The Story of Football*. London, 1952.

McDonald, Roger. *Britain Versus Europe*. London, 1968.

Mallory, Jim (ed.). *Football League Tables: 1889 to the Present*. Glasgow and London, 1977.

Marples, Morris. *A History of Football*. London, 1954.

Mason, Nicholas. *Football: The Story of All the World's Football Games*. London, 1974.

Meisl, Willy. *Soccer Revolution*. London, 1955.

Motson, John. *Second to None: Great Teams of Post-War Soccer*. London, 1972.

Moynihan, John. *Football Fever*. London, 1974.

Needham, E. *Association Football*. London, 1900.

Orlov, Zvy. *Football*. Jerusalem, 1913.

Pawson, Tony. *The Football Managers*. London, 1973.

_____. *100 Years of the F. A. Cup: The Official Centenary History*. London, 1972.

Perel', A. *Football in the U.S.S.R.*, trans. by Vic Shneerson. Moscow, 1958.

Pickford, William, and Gibson, Alfred. *Association Football and the Men Who Made It*, 4 vols. London, 1906.

Poe, Edgar Allan. *Poe's Football: How to Play the Most Popular Amateur Game; Containing the Latest American Intercollegiate Association and Rugby Rules*. New York, 1891.

Price, C. C. (ed.). *Men Famous in Football—Footballers Almanac*. London, 1903. (rev. ed., 1904, 1905)

Prole, David R. *Cup Final Story, 1946-65*. London, 1966.

Punchard, Frank N. *Survivals of Folk Football*. Birmingham, 1928.

Rafferty, John. *100 Years of Scottish Football*. London, 1973.

Rollin, Jack. *Soccer: A Picture Survey*, rev. ed. London, 1973 (originally pub. as *A Source Book of Football* in 1971)

Rous, Sir Stanley. *Football Worlds: A Lifetime in Sport*. London, 1978.

_____, and Ford, Donald. *A History of the Laws of Association Football*. Zurich, 1974.

The Scottish Football Book. London, ? (St. Paul, pub.)

The Scots Book of Football. London, 1968. (Wolfe, pub.)

Scudder, Winthrop S. *An Historical Sketch of the Oneida Football Club of Boston, 1862-65*. Boston, 1926-?

Sewell, Albert. *The Observer's Book of Association Football*. London, 1972.

Sewell, E. H. D. *The Book of Football*. London, 1911.

Sharpe, Ivan (comp.). *The Football League's Jubilee Book*. London, 1963.

Shearman, Montague. *Athletics and Football*. London, 1887. (2nd ed., 1888) The Badminton Library.

———. *Football.* London, 1899. (rev. ed., 1908) The Badminton Library.

———, and Vincent J. *Football: Its History for Five Centuries.* London, 1885.

Signy, Dennis. *Pictorial History of Soccer*, 4th ed. London, 1971.

Smith, Stratton (ed.). *The Brazil Book of Football.* London, 1963.

Spalding's Official "Soccer" Football Guide. New York, 1907. (American Sports Publishing Co., pub.; rev. ed., 1911)

Squires, John. *Soccer Story.* London, 1973.

Starostin, Andrei P. *Football in the U.S.S.R.* London, 1958.

Stuart, Colin. *Wembley: 50 Glorious Years in Pictures.* London, 1971.

Sutcliffe, C. E., and Hargreaves, F. *History of the Lancashire F. A., 1878-1928.* Blackburn, 1928.

———, Brierley, J. A., and Howarth, F. *The Story of the Football League, 1888-1938.* Preston, 1938.

Tagholm, John. *Football: How Much Do You Really Know?* London, 1975.

Tyler, Martin. *Soccer Club Colours.* London, 1976.

———. *The Story of Football.* London, 1967.

Vukadinović, Ljubomir. *Yugoslav Football.* Belgrade, 1950.

Walker, P. *How to Play Association Football.* London, 1906.

Wall, Sir Frederick. *Fifty Years of Football.* London, 1935.

Walvin, James. *The People's Game: A Social History of British Football.* London, 1975.

Whiddon, Harold. *One Hundred Years of Playing the Game, 1874-1974.* London, 1974.

Williams, A. J. *Association Football: The Science of Combination.* London, 1911.

Wolstenholme, Kenneth. *Kenneth Wolstenholme's Book of World Soccer.* Manchester, 1971.

Young, Percy M. *The Appreciation of Football.* London, 1951.

———. *Football, Facts and Figures.* London, 1950.

———. *Football in Sheffield.* London, 1962.

———. *Football on Merseyside.* London, 1963.

———. *The Football Year.* London, 1956.

———. *A History of British Football.* London, 1968.

WORLD CUP

Finn, Ralph L. *England: World Champions, 1966.* London, 1966.

———. *World Cup 1970.* London, 1970.

Glanville, Brian. *The Sunday Times History of the World Cup.* London, 1973.

———, and Weinstein, Jerry. *World Cup.* London, 1958.

Greene, Patrick. *Dramas of the World Cup.* London, 1966.

Jeffrey, Gordon, et al. (eds.). *World Cup '62: The Report from Chile.* London, 1962.

McIlvanney, Hugh. *World Cup '66.* London, 1966.

———. *World Cup '70.* London, 1970.

Mayes, Harold. *World Cup Report, 1966.* London, 1967.

Miller David. *World Cup 1970.* London, 1970.

Rollin, Jack. *England's World Cup Triumph.* London, 1966.

World Cup, 74: Offizielle Dokumentarwerk. Munich, 1974. (Wilfried Gerhardt, supv.) (in English)

A 14   87   4